THE HANDBOOK OF
CRIME & PUNISHMENT

THE HANDBOOK OF

CRIME & PUNISHMENT

EDITED BY
MICHAEL TONRY

New York • Oxford

Oxford University Press

1998

Oxford University Press

Oxford   New York
Athens   Auckland   Bangkok   Bogota   Bombay
Buenos Aires   Calcutta   Cape Town   Dar es Salaam
Delhi   Florence   Hong Kong   Istanbul   Karachi
Kuala Lumpur   Madras   Madrid   Melbourne
Mixico City   Nairobi   Paris   Singapore
Taipei   Tokyo   Toronto   Warsaw

and associated companies in
Berlin   Ibadan

Copyright © 1998 by Oxford University Press, Inc.

Published by Oxford University Press, Inc.
198 Madison Avenue, New York, New York 10016

Oxford is a registered trademark of Oxford University Press

Library of Congress Cataloging-in-Publication Data
The handbook of crime and punishment / edited by Michael Tonry.
p.   cm.
Includes bibliographical refrences and index.
ISBN 0-19-511066-8
1. Crime—United States.   2. Crime—Government policy—United States.
3. Criminal justice, Administration of—United States.   4. Punishment—United
States.   I. Tonry, Michael H.
HV6789.H25   1998
364.973—dc21   98-15633

9 8 7 6 5 4 3 2 1

Printed in the United States of America
on acid-free paper

Preface

Crime and punishment have been at the center of American political and public policy agendas for a quarter century. The debates have changed little over time. To many on the right, crime is the product primarily of bad character, irresponsibility, and morally bad choices. Punishment is the answer, and it remains the answer despite a fivefold increase since 1972 in the number of people confined in prisons and jails.

To many on the left, crime is the product primarily of disadvantage, deteriorated cities, and disappointed dreams. Improved social policies aimed at improving the life chances of the worst-off and equalizing the life chances of all are the answer, and they remain the answer despite a quarter century of failed social programs and policies.

In the United States in the 1990s, the conservative view of crime and punishment is ascendant, and swollen prisons and underfunded social programs are the consequence; but it has not always been that way and will not always be. During much of this century, American crime and punishment policies were no harsher than those of other Western countries, and less harsh than some. Today those policies are vastly harsher than in any other country to which the United States would normally be compared.

In a sensible world, no matter what the prevailing political mood, people would want to form their opinions and public officials to base their decisions on the most reliable current knowledge. This book attempts—in a single volume—to distill current knowledge on most important subjects relating to crime and punishment in modern America.

Some day a book like this one will draw on writers from around the globe, but this is not yet that day. However, when the subject matter of an essay or the multinational character of the relevant literature allowed, articles for this book were solicited from scholars in other English-speaking countries and in Europe. The writers are among the most knowledgeable on their subjects in the English-speaking world. Although treatment of some subjects, such as sentencing or public prosecution, requires focus on one country's institutions and policies—necessarily for this book those in the United States—treatment of other subjects was not so confined. Writers were asked, when the relevant literature crossed national boundaries, to write about the current state-of-the-art of knowledge obtainable from English-language sources.

More than a third of the writers are based outside the United States. Some, such as David Farrington, Per-Olof Wikström, Kathleen Daley, Vernon Quinsey, Andrew von Hirsch, and Julian Roberts, write on subjects in which American researchers have been active but on which the relevant research community transcends the Atlantic and Pacific oceans, so it would be more difficult (and less comprehensive) to restrict coverage to American research than to cast a wider net. Others, such as John Braithwaite and Trevor Bennett, write on subjects that are on the American agenda but concerning which both the preponderance of research and the bulk of policy innovation have occurred elsewhere. Still others, such as Roy King, Roger Hood, and Richard Harding, have as great a knowledge of American research on their subjects as do American scholars but also bring research from elsewhere to bear.

We have tried to provide a comprehensive set of articles on crime and punishment that are topical, readable, and up to date, and that an interested citizen or an honest politician could consult to advantage. Whether or not we have succeeded, readers will decide for themselves.

Castine, Maine   M.T.
1998

Acknowledgments

Any book as large and diverse as this one owes its existence and such quality as it has achieved to many people. The idea was Helen McInnis's, and the inspiration was *The Oxford Handbook of Criminology* first published in England in 1994 and edited by Mike Maguire, Rod Morgan, and Robert Reiner. Thomas LeBien, Oxford's law editor, patiently oversaw the book's development, and MaryBeth Branigan painstakingly oversaw its production. The writers, whose work is the book, worked to tighter deadlines than scholars ordinarily experience and to tighter specifications than scholars ordinarily tolerate, and with uniformly good humor. Kate Blake of Castine Research Corporation made her limitless knowledge of graphics, editing, and book production available as and when we needed it. Most important of all, however, were the efforts of Leena Kurki and Barbara Damchik-Dykes of the University of Minnesota Law School, who devoted hundreds of hours to editing, proofreading, checking references, communicating with writers, and doing all of the other thankless tasks of coordination without which a book like this could never be published. To all of these people, but especially to Leena, Barbara, and Kate, I am enormously grateful.

Contents

Contributors

Trevor Bennett is lecturer in criminology, Institute of Criminology, University of Cambridge.

John Braithwaite is professor of law, Australian National University.

Kathleen Daly is associate professor, School of Justice Administration, Griffith University, Queensland, Australia.

David P. Farrington is professor of psychological criminology, Cambridge University.

Barry C. Feld is Centennial Professor of Law, University of Minnesota.

Richard S. Frase is Benjamin N. Berger Professor of Law, University of Minnesota.

Gerald G. Gaes is director of research for the Federal Bureau of Prisons.

Richard J. Gelles is professor of sociology and psychology and director of the Family Violence Research Program, University of Rhode Island.

Richard W. Harding is professor of criminology and director of the Crime Research Centre, University of Western Australia.

Roger Hood is professor of criminology, director of the Centre for Criminological Research, and fellow of All Souls College, University of Oxford.

James B. Jacobs is professor of law and director of the Center for Research in Crime and Justice, New York University.

Roy D. King is professor of criminology and criminal justice and director of the Centre for Comparative Criminology and Criminal Justice, University of Wales, Bangor.

Malcolm W. Klein is professor of sociology, University of Southern California.

Janet L. Lauritsen is associate professor of criminology and criminal justice, University of Missouri at St. Louis.

Robert MacCoun is associate professor of public policy, Goldman School of Public Policy, University of California, Berkeley.

Candace McCoy is associate professor of criminal justice, School of Criminal Justice, Rutgers University.

Daniel S. Nagin is professor of management, School of Public Policy and Management, Carnegie-Mellon University.

Christopher Panarella is a practicing attorney in New York, New York.

Joan Petersilia is professor of criminology, law, and society, School of Social Ecology, University of California at Irvine.

Anne Morrison Piehl is assistant professor of public policy, John F. Kennedy School of Government, Harvard University, and Robert Wood Johnson Foundation scholar in health policy research, University of California, Berkeley.

Vernon L. Quinsey is professor of psychology and psychiatry, Department of Psychology, Queen's University in Kingston, Canada.

Kevin R. Reitz is professor of law, University of Colorado.

Peter Reuter is professor and director of social policy programs, University of Maryland at College Park.

Julian V. Roberts is professor of criminology, University of Ottawa.

Robert J. Sampson is professor of sociology, University of Chicago.

Lawrence W. Sherman is professor of criminology and chair of the School of Criminal Justice and Criminology, University of Maryland at College Park.

Neal Shover is professor of sociology, University of Tennessee.

Loretta J. Stalans is associate professor of criminal justice, Loyola University, Chicago.

Andrew von Hirsch is Honorary Professor of Penal Theory and Penal Law, Cambridge University.

Per-Olof Wikström is university lecturer in sociology of crime, Institute of Criminology, University of Cambridge, and fellow of Girton College.

THE HANDBOOK OF
CRIME & PUNISHMENT

Crime and Punishment in America

MICHAEL TONRY

Contemporary policies concerning crime and punishment are the harshest in American history and of any Western country. No other Western country still uses the death penalty except the United States: 3300 prisoners were on death row in 1997 and more people were executed—76—than in any year since 1955. No other Western country routinely sentences offenders to prison terms longer than two years except the United States: 39 percent of state prisoners in 1991 had been sentenced to ten years or longer. No other Western country on an average day holds more than 125 per 100,000 of its residents in jail or prison except the United States: in 1998 nearly 700 per 100,000 Americans were behind bars on a typical day. And, most importantly, in no other Western country except the United States are crime and punishment central issues in partisan politics.

American punitiveness is not the result of higher crime rates or of a steeper increase in crime in recent years. For most serious crimes, America's rates are not the highest among Western countries (Mayhew and van Dijk 1997), and other countries experienced equally sharp increases in crime rates during the 1970s and 1980s (Tonry and Hatlestad 1997, part 4). The difference is attributable to crime and punishment's entanglement in American politics.

Crime and punishment have been high on American political agendas since the late 1960s, and policies and institutions have been transformed as a result. Before Republican presidential candidate Barry Goldwater raised "crime in the streets" as a partisan issue in his unsuccessful 1964 campaign against Lyndon Johnson, public safety was generally seen as one among several important but unglamourous core functions of government, like public health, public transit, and public education. Public officials were expected to do their work conscientiously and effectively, and systematic knowledge was widely seen as relevant to the formulation of policies and the improvement of institutions and practices. This is evident in the 1967 report of the President's Commission on Law Enforcement and Administration of Justice, which observed that "the greatest need is the need to know" (p. 273) and that "we need to know much

3

more about crime. A national strategy against crime must be in large part a strategy of search" (p. 279). The primary subject of criminal justice law-reform efforts in the 1950s and 1960s was the movement to develop the *Model Penal Code* (American Law Institute 1962) and then to encourage states to adopt new criminal codes based on it. Many jurisdictions overhauled their codes, but others, including the federal government, tried and failed. Reasonable people differed over the need for the overhauls and specific proposed changes, but the debates were seldom partisan or ideological. Criminal justice policy was a subject for practitioners and technocrats, and sentencing was the specialized, case-by-case business of judges and corrections officials.

In recent decades, however, crime control has been at the center of partisan politics, and policies have been shaped as much (or more) by symbols and rhetoric as by substance and knowledge. Political scientists and journalists tell a story of how that happened, which is largely uncontroversial. Until the 1960s, in most of the South, the Democratic Party had dominated electoral politics since the end of Reconstruction. Although many southern voters held conservative views on social and racial issues, policy differences were fought out within a state's Democratic Party rather than between parties. The civil rights movement, however, created a fissure within the Democratic Party between racial and social policy liberals and economic and social policy conservatives, initially in the South but eventually nationally (e.g., Edsall and Edsall 1991; Applebome 1996). Republican strategists seized the opportunity to appeal to "Nixon [later Reagan] Democrats" by defining sharp differences between the parties on three "wedge issues": crime control, welfare, and affirmative action. On crime control, conservatives blamed rising crime rates on lenient judges and soft punishments and demanded "toughness." On welfare, conservatives blamed rising welfare rolls on "welfare cheats" and laziness and demanded budget cuts. On affirmative action, conservatives blamed white un- and underemployment on "quotas" and urged elimination of affirmative action.

Few people would disagree that Republicans and conservatives for the past thirty years have used crime, welfare, and affirmative action to distinguish themselves from Democrats and liberals. There are, however, deep disagreements about motives. Critics claim that political use of the wedge issues was a cynical effort to appeal to racist attitudes of white voters without doing so explicitly. Presidential candidate George Bush's 1988 use of pictures of Willie Horton, a black murderer of a white man and rapist of a white woman, is usually cited as an extreme instance: Willie Horton reminded white voters that blacks are disproportionately involved in violent crime and conjured up the inflammatory image of a black man raping a white woman. Apologists disagree and argue that crime control is a matter of high importance to voters and that Willie Horton's race was irrelevant: campaign planners stumbled upon the dramatic story of a convicted murderer on furlough from prison who then committed a rape; it was coincidental that he was black. Whatever the truth of the Willie Horton story, it illustrates how the three wedge issues simultaneously raised policy subjects and evoked racial stereotypes (Anderson 1995).

A second deep disagreement about partisan use of the wedge issues is whether it reflected or precipitated public concern about crime and public support for harsh policies. Critics claim that Republicans and other conservatives cynically heightened public anxieties about crime by stressing it relentlessly in campaigns and legislative chambers and then promised to assuage those anxieties by promoting harsh policies. There is considerable evidence to support this claim. Heightened political and media attention to crime and drug issues nearly always precedes increases in the percentages of Americans who name crime or drug abuse as "America's most pressing problem" (Tonry 1995, chap. 1; Beckett 1997). Critics also point to a mass of research from the United States and other countries that shows that ordinary people's knowledge of the justice system comes mostly from sensational cases covered in the mass media and so, not surprisingly, when asked simple questions out of context—"Are the sentences judges impose too harsh, too lenient, or just about right?"—they give simple answers based on stereotypes ("too lenient"). However, when asked about individual cases of which they have personal knowledge, or when given enough information to dispel stereotypes, representative samples of ordinary citizens have complicated and ambivalent beliefs about crime and criminals, wanting offenders to be punished but also wanting them to be rehabilitated (Roberts and Stalans 1997).

Apologists, however, disagree and argue three things (Bennett, DiIulio, and Walters 1996). First, public anxiety about crime is real, even if sometimes latent, and conservative politicians are doing no more than responding to it, legitimately and appropriately. Second, even if public anxiety is in part a product of politicians' concentration on crime issues, they are important issues and the public benefits both from being alerted to them and from the adoption of new policies aimed at reducing crime. Third, whatever the sources of their opinions and concerns, voters in recent decades have elected politicians who ran on "tough-on-crime" platforms, and in a democracy there is no better evidence of what citizens want.

Crime's role as a wedge issue has had important consequences. Issues that are debated on television and examined in 15- and 30-second commercials necessarily are presented in simplistic and emotional terms. Matters about which judges and prosecutors agonize in individual cases are addressed in slogans and symbols, which often leads later to adoption of ham-fisted and poorly considered policies. Notable recent examples include widespread adoption of broadly defined "three-strikes-and-you're-out laws," mandatory minimum sentence laws, and "sexual psychopath" laws. Few judges or informed scholars support such laws in the forms in which they are typically adopted, principally for practical reasons: (1) they are too rigid and often result in unjustly harsh penalties; (2) they result in circumvention by judges and lawyers who believe their application inappropriate in individual cases; and (3) they are often redundant because serious cases nearly always result in severe penalties anyway. Many judges and scholars would support such laws if they were narrowly drawn and carefully crafted to encompass only genuinely serious crimes and threatening offenders. However, in a "sound-bite politics" era, few politicians are prepared to act as voices of moderation and parsimony and, as a result, new sentencing laws often lack those qualities.

When crime control became one of the focal issues in the liberal-to-conservative transformation of American politics that has occurred over the past thirty years, it ceased being a specialized policy subject and became instead a symbol or metaphor for, broadly, concepts like "personal responsibility" and vindication of victims' interests, and, more narrowly, ideas about criminals' immorality and irresponsibility. A broadly defined sexual psychopath law, a three-strikes law, or a mandatory minimum sentence law may be ineffective, cruel, or unduly costly, but none of that may matter. If the law's proponents and voters view it as a symbol of revulsion with crime and outrage toward criminals, whether it will work or achieve just results in individual cases is often politically irrelevant. When issues are defined in polar terms of morality and immorality, or responsibility and irresponsibility, few elected officials are prepared to be on the wrong pole.

As a result, systematic knowledge also becomes irrelevant and elected officials sometimes wind up proposing or supporting policies they know to be unwise or unjust. The political values underlying proposed anti-crime policies are often so powerful or emotional that elected officials believe they risk their jobs by opposing the policies: opposition to ill-considered legislation may be interpreted as lack of sympathy for victims, lack of outrage about heinous crimes, or support for immoral conduct. A vivid example in the 1990s is a federal policy that punishes sellers of crack cocaine as if they had sold 100 times as much powder cocaine (Tonry 1995, pp. 188–90). It is well established that the two forms of cocaine are pharmacologically indistinguishable and comparably addictive. Most people arrested for selling crack are inner-city minority young people. The law thus results in much harsher punishment of black crack dealers than of white powder dealers. Very few people regard that difference as ethically justifiable but, despite serious proposals to repeal the 100-to-1 law, Congress always refuses because members fear an opponent will later accuse them of weakening drug-law sentences and being "soft on drugs" (Bertram et al. 1996).

In a gentler decade, comedians offered "Are you still beating your wife?" as the prototypical unfair question. "Yes" acknowledged that the respondent beat his wife. "No" acknowledged that he once did. The modern political equivalents are "Are you for victims or for criminals?" or "Are you for or against tough policies?" Few politicians who aspire to elected office are willing to risk being labeled as "for criminals" or against tough policies.

As a result, systematic knowledge and research had comparatively little influence on formulation of crime policy in the 1980s and 1990s (Moore 1995). If crime policy is mostly about affirmations of partisan advantage and political symbolism, research has little relevance. If officials, for reasons of personal ideology, believe that putting more people in prison or making penalties harsher will reduce crime rates or drug abuse, they are not likely to seek out or be influenced by research findings that suggest or demonstrate the contrary. And, if few politicians dare risk being called soft on crime, proposed new harsh policies will seldom be vigorously resisted even when there are knowledge-based reasons to question or oppose them.

An important line, however, should be drawn between high-visibility and politically contentious issues and other, lower-visibility issues. Concerning politically popular programs or the severity of punishments, research findings have little influence. For example, American policymakers have been conspicuously uninterested in evaluation research showing that politically popular programs are ineffective. Examples include research literatures showing that Project DARE (Drug Abuse Resistance Education) does not reduce drug abuse (Botvin 1990), that boot camps do not reduce recidivism rates (Parent 1995), that Neighborhood Watch programs do not reduce crime rates (Hope 1995), and that intensive street-level drug law enforcement and mandatory minimum prison sentences for drug dealers do not reduce drug abuse or availability (Wilson 1990). Nor have legislators been interested in the findings of a series of expert National Academy of Sciences panels that concluded that increases in sanction severity have few significant deterrent or incapacitative effects on crime rates (Blumstein, Cohen, and Nagin 1978; Blumstein, Cohen, Roth, and Visher 1986; Reiss and Roth 1993). Whether because of ideological conviction, partisan politics, political symbolism, or distrust of researchers, policy-makers in many jurisdictions happily disregard inconvenient research findings on issues they care greatly about.

However, research on crime and punishment remains vital and has become voluminous, as the articles in this handbook show. Work proceeds in many disciplines on many topics and some of it, including diverse evaluation literatures and much basic work on causes and correlates of crime and delinquency, continues to influence policy making on other than the most contentious issues.

Because the politics of crime and punishment have changed greatly since the 1960s, the institutions, policies, and practices of the criminal justice system have also changed greatly. Within the agencies of the criminal justice system, the most drastic changes have involved the sentencing and corrections systems. Patterns of both crime and punishment have changed drastically in thirty years. Overall, crime and crime victimization rates have fallen sharply since at least 1980 (albeit with fluctuations) but, within that decline, crime by women and young people has proportionately increased. Importantly, however, the proportionate involvement by blacks in serious, violent crime has not increased for a quarter century. By contrast, incarceration rates have increased continuously since 1973 with the increases being somewhat larger for women than for men and vastly larger for blacks than for whites.

The rest of this introduction provides an overview of crime and punishment in America at the end of the twentieth century. The first section describes the major changes in the final third of this century to the institutions that make up the criminal justice system. The following section describes changes in crime and victimization rates and in the use of jail, prison, probation, and parole sentences. The final section discusses relations between crime patterns and punishment policies.

Criminal Justice Institutions

Changes in criminal justice agencies and operations over the past thirty years have mirrored those in other American institutions. Staff are better trained and educated and are increasingly diverse. Female and minority judges, prosecutors, police chiefs, and prison commissioners are no longer uncommon. Computers, electronic communication, and modern management techniques have proliferated, and day-to-day operations have changed with them. Within the criminal justice system, however, the most drastic changes have affected sentencing and corrections (Tonry 1996, chap. 1).

As recently as 1975, every American state, the federal system, and the District of Columbia had what was called an "indeterminate sentencing system." Although systems varied in their details, the outline everywhere was the same and had not changed in important respects since 1930 (Rothman 1980). Legislatures passed laws that defined crimes and set maximum and sometimes minimum sentences for each type of crime. Prosecutors had nearly unlimited discretion to decide what if any charges to file and whether to offer defendants the opportunity to plead guilty in exchange for dismissal of some charges or for a reduced sentence.

Judges, corrections officials, and parole boards had broad, unreviewable discretion to determine the nature and severity of punishments. Unless a minimum mandatory sentence applied, and that was not common except for murder, the judge could decide whether a convicted offender would be sentenced to a fine, probation, or confinement. If the sentence was confinement, the judge could choose between a short sentence, usually a year or less in a local jail, or a longer sentence to state (or in federal courts, federal) prison. If an offender was sentenced to prison, the judge set a maximum and often a minimum sentence. Prison authorities could affect prison terms by awarding or withdrawing "good" and "gain time" (time off for good behavior or for participation in work or treatment programs). Depending on the jurisdiction, prisoners became eligible for parole release after serving at least one year, the minimum sentence, or one third of the maximum, and a parole board decided when the prisoner would be released. Except in rare circumstances, none of these decisions could be appealed to a court.

Most of that had changed by the 1990s. Many jurisdictions had replaced "indeterminate" with "determinate" sentencing. Many judges no longer had broad discretion. Every state had adopted laws requiring mandatory minimum sentences for drug and violent crimes, including in many states three-strikes laws that required life or very long sentences following a third conviction. In addition, a third of the states and the federal government had adopted some form of sentencing guidelines. Some jurisdictions developed systems of appellate review of sentencing.

The discretion of corrections and parole officials was also reduced. Nearly a dozen states and the federal system abolished discretionary parole release, and two-thirds established truth-in-sentencing laws under which people convicted of selected violent crimes must serve at least 85 percent of the announced prison sentence. To satisfy the 85 percent test (in order to qualify for federal funds for prison construction), states limited the powers of parole boards to set release dates, or of prison managers to award good and gain time, or both.

The operations and organization of pre-adjudication agencies experienced less change. Probation offices continued to supervise most offenders in caseloads of 100 to 300 probationers per officer and to be responsible for preparation of presentence investigation reports (Petersilia 1997). Jails continued to house alleged offenders before trial and those sentenced to short terms of confinement. Both probation offices and jails developed new "intermediate sanctions" like intensive supervision, house arrest, electronic monitoring, day-reporting centers, and community service, but these affected only a small percentage of offenders and typically neither diverted offenders from prison or jail nor reduced recidivism rates (Tonry 1996, chap. 4).

The legal framework and organization of prosecution offices changed least of all. Prosecutors retained all the discretion they had possessed thirty years earlier and, although management practices and computer technologies changed day-to-day operations, few prosecutors from the 1960s would be surprised by what they would see in the 1990s. The prosecuting attorney in most places remained a powerful local elected official, often with ambitions for higher office, and most of the assistants stayed only for a few years to gain trial experience before entering private practice.

Police departments likewise underwent few major structural changes. Most police agencies in the 1960s were and are now organized at municipal and county levels, are managed as uniformed paramilitary organizations, and are headed by chiefs chosen by local elected officials. Police officers in the 1990s, however, are more diverse in gender and ethnicity, are better educated, and are more likely to belong to a union. As with prosecutors, new management techniques and computer technologies have changed day-to-day practices, but in ways that are linear extensions of earlier practices. Although many urban police departments have shifted from a "professional model" of police work that stressed centralized management and motorized patrol to "community-based" and "problem-solving" models that celebrated decentralized operations and foot patrol (Moore 1992), it is not clear as yet how much of that shift is substantive and enduring and how much is cosmetic and transient (Bayley 1994).

The contrast between the revolutionary changes affecting the powers and operations of judges, corrections officials, and parole boards and the evolutionary changes that have affected police and prosecutors is striking and requires explanation. One reason may be structural but coincidental: the outcomes of sentencing and release decisions are much more visible than the outcomes of police and prosecution decisions, and if someone is to be blamed for rising crime rates or sensational crimes by ex-prisoners, judges and corrections officials are an easy, available, and not very politically powerful target. Another is that legislators, especially conservative legislators, have more confidence in police and prosecutors than in judges and corrections officials (Boerner 1995). Prosecutors are elected officials. They have professional and political reasons to be aggressive advocates and are as likely as legislators to adopt "tough-on-crime" policies. This may be why "lenient" judges and "light" sentences were often criticized by conservatives, although prosecutors—who have greater power over criminal cases than judges do—seldom faced such criticisms and were virtually never the objects of statutory efforts to reduce their powers or discretion.

Crime and Punishment Patterns

The final quarter of the twentieth century has been characterized by fluctuating crime rates and a historically unprecedented increase in the number of people in prisons and jails. Between 1971 and 1996, the official rates for serious violent and property crime at times rose significantly and the incarceration rate (people held in state and federal prisons) more than quadrupled. Among people arrested for serious violent crimes, the percentage of blacks declined throughout that period and the percentage of females increased by half. Among prison inmates, the proportion of blacks grew sharply from around 40 percent in 1971 to more than 50 percent in the early 1990s and the percentage of females doubled.

There is widespread agreement about what these data show, but little agreement about what they mean. The most vigorous disagreements are over the answers to two questions: (1) Has the enormous increase in the use of incarceration reduced crime rates or otherwise made America a safer place? and (2) Why has the proportion of blacks in prison increased so dramatically when the proportion of blacks among those arrested for serious violence has not only not increased but fallen?

Figure I.1 shows the rate per 100,000 inhabitants of serious ("Index")[1] property and violent crimes known to the police and the rate per 100,000 of convicted offenders confined in state and federal prisons for the years between 1971 and 1996. Three things stand out. First, the incarceration rate increased every year after 1972, quadrupling from 93 per 100,000 in 1972 to 427 per 100,000 in 1996. By June 30, 1997, that rate had increased to 436 per 100,000 (Bureau of Justice Statistics 1998).

Second, crime rates fluctuated. The violent crime rate rose from 1971 to 1981, fell until 1985, rose again until 1991, and fell again until 1996. Overall, however, the 1996 rate (634 per 100,000) was 60 percent higher than the 1971 rate (396 per 100,000). Property crime rates (divided by 10 in Figure I.1) fluctuated in much the same pattern and were 18 percent higher in 1996 than in 1971.

Third, these patterns can support almost any hypothesis about the relationship between the incarceration rate and crime rates, depending on the period examined. Over the entire period, for example, crime rates rose while the incarceration rate quadrupled, suggesting either, radically, that increased imprisonment caused crime rates to rise or, more modestly, had no discernible effect on crime rates. These inferences could also be drawn for the periods 1971–1981 and 1986–1991 when incarceration and crime rates both rose sharply. During the periods 1981–1986 and 1991–1996, when incarceration rates rose but crime rates fell, the opposite inference might be drawn: that increased use of punishment caused

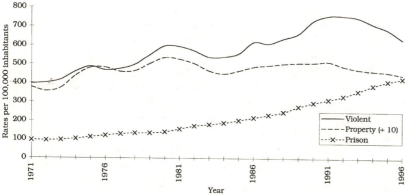

Figure I.1 Violent crime, property crime, and prison incarceration rates per 100,000 inhabitants, 1971–1996. *Sources:* Bureau of Justice Statistics (1997c); Federal Bureau of Investigation (1997); Maguire and Pastore (1997). *Note:* Property crime rates are divided by ten for purposes of presentation.

crime rates to fall. The soundest conclusion, however, is that there is no simple relationship between incarceration and crime rates.

Ideologues on both the right and left misuse these data, by disingenuously focusing on particular time periods in the ways shown above to "prove" that more incarceration does or does not reduce crime rates. Former U.S. Attorney General William Barr, for example, in a notorious tract called "The Case for More Incarceration" (e.g., Barr 1992), focused on the period in the 1980s when crime rates fell while incarceration rates rose to support his claim that prison "works."

The analysis presented in the preceding paragraphs is oversimplified in at least two important respects. First, it is naive or unrealistic to attempt to learn anything important from simple comparisons of crime and incarceration rates. Crime rates are influenced by changes in demographics, labor markets, and other economic, social, cultural, and normative factors. Incarceration rates are more influenced by deliberate policy changes than by crime rates. Thus, incarceration rates easily can increase (and in the 1990s have) while crime rates fall because policymakers have decided they want more people to be locked up. Similarly, crime rates can rise sharply (and in the 1970s did) because of important social-structural changes in the world even when incarceration rates also are rising sharply.

Second, changes in how crime rates are measured can distort the patterns they appear to show. We know, for example, that crime rates for some kinds of crimes, notably rape and aggravated assault, were increased by changes in reporting; victims of non-stranger rapes and domestic (and other) assaults were considerably more likely to report the incidents to the police in 1996 than in 1971, and the police were more likely to record them as crimes. Similarly, increased coverage of property losses by homeowners, renters, and automobile insurance provided victims with greater incentives to report losses covered by insurance to the police. We also know that professionalization of the police beginning in the 1970s and increased use of computerized records systems led police to record more of the incidents known to them as crimes.

Such measurement considerations, however, do not undermine agnostic conclusions about the effects of increased incarceration rates on crime rates. While more complete reporting and recording must raise crime rates, they can't explain why rates for the affected crimes fell at various times. Moreover, as Figure I.2 shows, the general pattern of fluctuation applied not only to rape, aggravated assault, and various property crimes, but also to murder and robbery, for which there is no reason to suppose that there were major, systematic reporting and recording changes between 1971 and 1996.

Figure I.2 shows rates of police-recorded crime from 1971 to 1996 for the seven major index felonies of murder, rape, robbery, aggravated assault, burglary, theft, and motor vehicle theft. The murder rate is multiplied by ten and the burglary, theft, and motor vehicle rates are divided

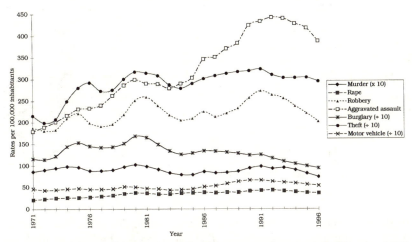

Figure I.2 Offenses known to police rates per 100,000 inhabitants, 1971–1996. *Sources:* Federal Bureau of Investigation (1997); Maguire and Pastore (1997). *Note:* Murder rates are multiplied by 10, and burglary, theft, and motor vehicle theft rates are divided by ten for purposes of presentation.

by ten so that trends can be compared in one figure. Most rates peaked at some point in the 1980s and were at lower levels in 1996. Murder and burglary rates were lower in 1996 than in 1971 and robbery and motor vehicle theft rates were only slightly higher in 1996 than in 1971, and were well below their peaks in the 1980s. Only rape, aggravated assault, and theft were significantly higher in 1996 than in 1971, and for those crimes there are good reasons to believe that changes in reporting and recording are an important part of the explanation. Table I.1, showing crime rates in 1971, 1981, 1991, and 1996, makes the same point numerically.

The general public is largely unaware of changes in crime rates. Every year from 1968 to 1990 and irregularly since the Gallup Organization has asked representative samples of Americans, "Is there more crime in the U.S. than there was a year ago, or less?" Each time the question was asked through 1992, large majorities of respondents answered "more," irrespective of whether crime rates were rising or falling. Only in 1996 (71 percent) and 1997 (64 percent) did the answers finally begin to reflect changes in crime rates (Maguire and Pastore 1997, table 2.27).

That crime rates *have* been falling can be confirmed by consulting data from the National Crime Victimization Survey (NCVS) conducted since 1973 by the U.S. Bureau of the Census for the U.S. Bureau of Justice Statistics. The NCVS data are obtained from interviews conducted at six-month intervals from 45,000 to 60,000 households selected so as to be representative of the U.S. population. The data are a better overall indica-

Table I.1. Index Crime Rates per 100,000 Inhabitants, 1971, 1981, 1991, 1996

	Murder	Rape	Robbery	Aggravated Assault	Burglary	Theft	Motor Vehicle Theft
1971	8.6	20.5	188.0	178.8	1,163.5	2,145.5	459.8
1981	9.8	36.0	258.7	289.7	1,649.5	3,139.7	474.7
1991	9.8	42.3	272.7	433.3	1,252.0	3,228.8	659.0
1996	7.4	36.1	202.4	388.2	943.0	2,939.5	525.9
Percent change 1971–1996	-14.0	+76.1	+7.7	+117.0	-19.0	+37.0	+14.4

Source: Maguire and Pastore (1997, table 3.106).

tor of crime patterns than are police data, which are in some respects a measure of both police behavior and crime, because they come unfiltered from victims and include information on many attempted and completed crimes that are never reported to the police.

Figures I.3 and I.4 summarize data on violent and property crime victimization rates from 1973 to 1996. They are not directly comparable to the official crime data shown in Figures I.1 and I.2. The official data, for example, are reported as rates per 100,000 U.S. inhabitants while the NCVS violent crime data are reported per 1000 persons aged 12 or over and the NCVS property crime data are reported per 1000 households. The NCVS is a broader measure because it collects data on crimes that

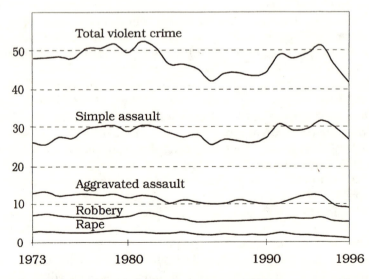

Figure I.3 Violent crime victimization rates per 1,000 persons age 12 or older, 1973–1996. *Source:* Bureau of Justice Statistics (1997b).

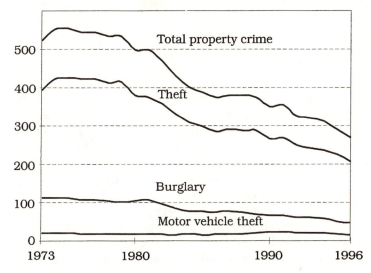

Figure I.4 Property crime victimization rates per 1,000 households, 1973–1996. *Source:* Bureau of Justice Statistics (1997b).

were not reported to the police (as well as data on when and why crimes are not reported). The NCVS thus yields considerably higher national estimates of the total number of crimes. Finally, the NCVS is a representative national household survey, which means that it does not include interviews of people in jails, prisons, reformatories, and mental institutions and, like all representative national surveys (including the U.S. Census), it undercounts young, mobile people (and others) without permanent residences. All of these groups have high victimization rates, so to the extent of their exclusion, the NCVS provides an underestimation of crime levels. Because young men have the highest murder and victimization rates of any group (Cook and Laub 1998), excluding criminally active young men who are in jail or prison may result in a significant undercount of the most serious assaultive crimes.

Those considerations do not, however, deprive the NCVS data of credibility. Insofar as NCVS data collection methods have remained constant over time, biases of the type described should be relatively consistent from year to year, which means that they undermine claims that the NCVS data accurately indicate absolute crime volumes but do not undermine NCVS data as indicators of trends. What this means is that the NCVS data provide a reasonable picture of crime victimization affecting the 90–95 percent of the population that is adequately captured by representative national surveys.

The trends on property crime victimization shown in Figure I.4 are broadly similar to those shown in the official crime data. Both exhibit increased rates in the 1970s that peak around 1980, drop sharply in the early 1980s, fluctuate during the late 1980s, and drop substantially in the 1990s. According to the NCVS data, victimization rates for all three offenses shown fell substantially from their starting levels in 1973—theft (down 48 percent), burglary (down 48 percent), and motor vehicle theft (down 30 percent) (Bureau of Justice Statistics 1997b).

The NCVS trends shown in Figure I.3 for the serious violent crimes (rape, robbery, and aggravated assault) reveal a similar pattern: a generally downward pattern with peaks around 1980 and sharp drops in the early 1990s. On balance, then, the official record and NCVS crime data are in agreement about crime trends in America. Modern crime rates peaked for most crimes around 1980, fell sharply in the early eighties, rose again for a few years, and then fell even more sharply in the nineties.

Within that pattern of generally declining crime rates, however, a number of patterns of involvement in crime warrant mention. Arrests measure criminal suspects rather than crimes, and there are grounds for believing arrests to be reasonable indicators of group differences in criminality (Blumstein 1993b; Tonry 1995, chap. 2; Sampson and Lauritsen 1997). The arrest data show two important trends.

First, as Figure I.5 shows, female involvement in serious crimes has slowly but steadily been increasing for a quarter century. Women were 10.2 percent of persons arrested for index violent crimes in 1973 compared with 15.1 percent in 1996. In 1973, 21.1 percent of those arrested for index property crimes were women, compared with 27.9 percent in 1996. Although the absolute percentages of women remain low, the female percentages have grown by a few tenths of a point nearly every year and show no sign of stopping. There is no generally accepted causal explanation for that trend (Daly and Tonry 1997). However, as Figure I.6

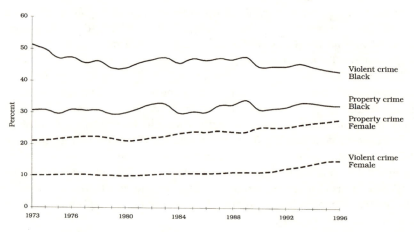

Figure I.5 Black and female percentages among arrestees, index violent and property crimes, 1973–1996. *Source:* Federal Bureau of Investigation, various years.

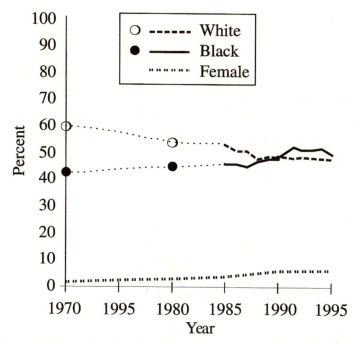

Figure I.6 Prisoners in state and federal prisons on census date, by race and sex, 1970–1995. *Sources:* Bureau of Justice Statistics (1997a); Maguire and Pastore (1997); Tonry (1995). *Note:* Prisoners sentenced to more than one year, census date December 31.

shows, the arrest trend is paralleled by a rising fraction of women prison inmates.

Second, as Figure I.5 shows, black involvement in serious violent crimes, as measured by arrest percentages, has been declining since 1973, and involvement in property crime has increased only slightly. Of those arrested in 1973 for the four violent index crimes (murder, rape, robbery, and aggravated assault), 51.3 percent were black. The trend since then, though fluctuating, has been generally downward, falling to 43.2 percent in 1996. Among index property crime arrestees in 1973, 30.6 percent were black, rising to a peak of 34 percent in 1989 and falling back to 32.4 percent in 1996. These trends are striking because, unlike the male–female arrest trends, they are not paralleled by prison population trends. The percentage of prison inmates who are black has not declined as the violent crime arrest pattern would suggest it should. As Figures I.6 and I.7 show, it has increased continuously and substantially since 1973.

Figure I.6 shows the percentages of black, white, and female prisoners in year-end state and federal prison populations from 1970 to 1995. The female percentage doubled from 2.9 percent in 1970 to 6.1 percent in

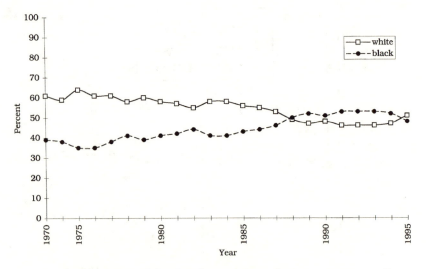

Figure I.7 Admissions to federal and state prisons, by race, 1970–1995. *Source:* Bureau of Justice Statistics (1997a); Tonry (1995).

1996, which in relative terms exceeds the 50-percent increase noted earlier in the proportion of women among people arrested for violent index crimes. Another way to assess the increase in imprisonment of women is to look at changes in women's incarceration rates compared with men's. The women's rate increased from 5 per 100,000 in 1970 to 48 in 1975, an increase of 860 percent. During the same period, the men's rate increased by 311 percent (Maguire and Pastore 1997, table 6.21).

The percentage of black prisoners, however, grew from 41 percent in 1970 to more than 50 percent in 1992–1994, and then fell to 49.9 percent in 1995. The mystery, accordingly, is why the proportion of blacks in prison went up by more than a quarter during a period when the black proportion among violent crime arrestees fell by nearly 20 percent.

The black disproportion among confined populations is much larger than it may at first appear. Because 12 to 13 percent of the U.S. population is black, it is natural to compare that figure with the approximately 50 percent of the prison population who are black and to conclude that blacks are overrepresented in prison by a factor of four. That would be wrong, however, as Table I.2 shows, because it fails to take into account the underrepresentation of whites.

Table I.2 shows the combined federal and state jail and prison populations for the years 1985–1995, broken down by race and sex. In 1995, blacks were slightly less than half of the population of inmates. Yet white men were confined at a rate of 919 per 100,000 and black men at a rate of 6,926 per 100,000; the black men's rate was thus 7.5 times higher than the white men's. Even more strikingly, however, the white men's rate

Table I.2. Number and Rate (per 100,000 Adult Residents in Each Group) of Adults Held in State or Federal Prisons or Local Jails

	Number[a]				Rate[b]			
	White		Black		White		Black	
	Male	Female	Male	Female	Male	Female	Male	Female
1985	382,800	21,400	309,800	19,100	528	27	3,544	183
1986	417,600	23,000	342,400	19,900	570	29	3,850	189
1987	439,000	27,700	356,300	23,200	594	35	3,943	216
1988	469,200	32,600	407,400	28,000	629	41	4,441	257
1989	516,000	38,500	472,800	35,500	685	47	5,066	321
1990	545,900	39,300	508,800	38,000	718	48	5,365	338
1991	566,800	42,200	551,000	40,600	740	51	5,717	356
1992	598,000	44,100	590,300	42,400	774	53	6,015	365
1993	627,100	46,500	624,100	47,500	805	58	6,259	403
1994	674,400	51,800	676,000	52,300	851	61	6,682	435
1995	726,500	57,800	711,600	55,300	919	68	6,926	456

Source: Maguire and Pastore (1997, table 6.12).

[a]Populations are estimated and rounded to the nearest 100.
[b]Data are based on the resident population for each group on July 1 of each year.

increased from 528 to 919 per 100,000 in ten years, an increase of 391 per 100,000. The black men's rate increased from 3,544 to 6,926 per 100,000, an increase of 3,482 per 100,000, or nearly ten times the white men's increase. The trends for women, broken down by race, are similar.

There are two primary reasons why black imprisonment rates have been increasing. First, as Figure I.7 shows, the percentage of blacks among people committed to federal and state prisons has increased from the 30-percent range in the 1970s to the 40-percent range in the 1980s to the low 50-percent range in the 1990s, peaking at 53 percent in 1993. The cause of that increase is not, as Figure I.5 showed, that blacks are committing increasing proportions of the violent crimes that traditionally resulted in prison sentences. The cause, instead, is the "War on Drugs" declared in the 1980s and carried on fitfully throughout the 1990s, which emphasized mass arrests, prosecutions, and imprisonment of street-level drug dealers. In disorganized inner-city areas where such arrests are most commonly made, most dealers are poor and black or Hispanic. The arrest rates per 100,000 for drug offenses are six times higher for blacks than for whites (Blumstein 1993a,b; Tonry 1995, chap. 3). Thus a large part of the increased incarceration of blacks is the deliberate product of the strategies employed in the drug wars.

Second, the law-and-order crime control policies of the 1980s and 1990s have substantially increased sentence lengths for people convicted of violent crimes. In the federal system and in many states, this has taken the form of the passage of three-strikes laws, mandatory minimum sentence laws, and truth-in-sentencing laws that abolish parole release and require inmates to serve 85 percent of their announced sentences. All of these laws increase sentences for violent crimes. Because blacks constitute a large percentage among people arrested for violent crimes (43.1 percent in 1996), black prisoners disproportionately bear the burden of the longer sentences for violent crimes.

Direct bias and invidious discrimination against blacks are not major causes of prison disparities. Though bias no doubt exists and though some police, prosecutors, and judges no doubt treat minority suspects and defendants unfairly, every major recent review of the literatures on racial disparities in the justice system has concluded that bias is not a primary cause of punishment disparities (e.g., Wilbanks 1987; Tonry 1996; Sampson and Lauritsen 1997). The principal problem is not biased decision-making by criminal justice officials but adoption of policies that are known to affect minority offenders disproportionately harshly.

The major trends affecting prison populations that have been discussed in detail in the preceding paragraphs also affect the probation, jail, and parole populations, as Table I.3 shows. The numbers of adults in prison and jail, or on probation or parole, grew enormously between 1985 and 1995. The total number of people under correctional control grew by 78.5 percent, and the number in prison grew by 121.2 percent. And as shown by Table I.4, which breaks down the 1995 data by race and sex, all those populations are disproportionately black.

Table I.3. Number of Adults on Probation, in Jail or Prison, or on Parole, 1985–1995

Year	Total	Probation	Jail	Prison	Parole
1985	3,011,500	1,968,712	254,986	487,593	300,203
1986	3,239,400	2,114,621	272,735	526,436	325,638
1987	3,459,600	2,247,158	294,092	562,814	355,505
1988	3,714,100	2,356,483	341,893	607,766	407,977
1989	4,055,600	2,522,125	393,303	683,367	456,803
1990	4,348,000	2,670,234	403,019	743,382	531,407
1991	4,535,600	2,728,472	424,129	792,535	590,442
1992	4,762,600	2,811,611	441,781	850,566	658,601
1993	4,944,000	2,903,061	455,500	909,381	676,100
1994	5,141,300	2,981,022	479,800	990,147	690,371
1995	5,374,500	3,096,529	499,300	1,078,545	700,174
Percent change 1985–1995	78.5%	57.3%	95.8%	121.2%	133.2%

Source: Bureau of Justice Statistics (1997a, table 1.1).

Note: Counts for probation, prison, and parole populations are for December 31 of each year and have been revised based on the most recently reported counts. Jail population counts are for June 30 of each year. Prisoner counts are for inmates in custody only.

Table I.4. Estimated Number of Adults on Probation, in Jail or Prison, or on Parole and Their Percent of Adult Population, by Sex and Race, in 1995

	Total	Sex		Race		
		Male	Female	White	Black	Other
Total	5,374,500	4,546,400	828,100	3,210,200	2,090,900	73,300
Probation	3,096,500	2,454,000	642,500	2,057,600	999,200	39,600
Jail	499,300	448,000	51,300	262,200	228,500	8,600
Prison	1,078,500	1,014,500	64,000	522,100	538,500	17,900
Parole	700,200	629,900	70,300	368,300	324,700	7,200

Source: Bureau of Justice Statistics (1997a, table 1.2).

Note: Detail may not add to total because of rounding. In cases where sex or race was unknown or not reported, percentages were applied based on known cases.

Relations Between Crime and Punishment

The relationships between crime and punishment are much less well understood than members of the general public might expect. This can be shown by considering two equally plausible, but inconsistent, assumptions about the relationship between crime and imprisonment. It is reasonable to assume that incarceration rates will rise when crime rates rise; assuming the chances of getting caught remain the same, more criminals will be caught and sent to prison. However, it is also reasonable to assume that crime rates will fall when incarceration rates rise; more criminals will be incapacitated from committing new crimes and others should be deterred. Added together, the two assumptions paint a tidy picture: rising crime rates in one period cause incarceration rates to increase which, in turn, cause crime rates in the ensuing period to decline. Life, unfortunately, is more complicated. That cyclical pattern has never occurred.

Crime rates rise and fall over long periods, and it is unclear how much and in what ways changes in law enforcement and punishment affect them. While it is natural to assume that rational people weigh the costs and benefits of their actions, and that increasing the costs of crime by raising penalties should reduce its incidence, the most authoritative examinations of the evidence conclude that penalty increases sometimes have some, but generally modest, deterrent effects (Blumstein, Cohen, and Nagin 1978; Cook 1980; Nagin 1998).

Crime has never been distributed evenly, as Robert Barr and Ken Pease (1990) showed in an influential essay in which they pointed out that governments could, if they wished, more nearly equalize peoples' risks of victimization by doing such things as permitting red light districts to be placed in middle-class neighborhoods and shifting land uses typically characterized by high crime rates from poor and inner-city areas to more affluent neighborhoods. The epidemiological insight was not original.

Since early in the nineteenth century, statisticians and others have shown that crime rates are higher in urban than in rural places, in poor than in affluent neighborhoods, and in commercial than in residential areas.

What was provocative in the Barr and Pease essay was the idea that governments, in the name of equality, might want to provide equal vulnerabilities to all citizens to experience the bad things of life just as idealists have long argued that governments should attempt to provide equal opportunities to all to experience the good. Few candidates could, of course, hope to win elections on a crime-risk equalization platform. Voters in the large majority of districts with low crime rates would vigorously and effectively resist, and their representatives would see to it that crime risks remained unevenly distributed. What is important about these ideas is their recognition that crime rates and patterns are influenced more by economic, social, and other contextual conditions than by the activities of criminal justice agencies and that those conditions tend to change slowly, and crime rates and patterns with them.

Historians have long known that crime rates rise and fall over extended periods for reasons that have little to do with crime control policies. The three most influential scholars on the subject—historian Roger Lane (1992) and political scientists Ted Robert Gurr (1981) and James Q. Wilson (e.g., Wilson and Herrnstein 1985)—concur that crime rates in the United States, England, and other Western countries have followed a "U-curve," falling from the second quarter of the nineteenth century through the middle of the twentieth century and rising until late in the twentieth century. They disagree as to why that happened. Gurr and Lane argue that the century-long decline is associated with the emergence of the industrial economy and the development of bureaucratic institutions like schools, factories, and the military that socialized people into patterns of behavioral conformity, rule observance, and deference to authority. Wilson argues that religious revivalism in the nineteenth century and a related moral awakening enhanced character-building processes and law-abidingness. However, none of them attributes the decline to changes in criminal justice system agencies or policies. Many of the major institutions of modern criminal justice systems—the penitentiary, the reformatory, probation and parole, and the juvenile court—were first established during the period when rates were falling but neither then nor now has the fall been attributed to them.

More recently, there is evidence that crime rates in Western countries may have begun another long-term decline. In the United States, for example, NCVS data show that rates for many crimes fell steadily from 1973 to the 1980s, after which they increased or stabilized for a few years and then resumed a downward path. Data from the FBI's *Uniform Crime Reports* show a somewhat different (but reconcilable) pattern of crime rates that rose through 1981, fell through 1986, rose again through 1991, and have plummeted since to levels not seen for some crimes since the 1960s and 1970s. English and Dutch victimization survey data likewise show significant victimization rate declines in the 1990s as do data from many countries that participate in the International Crime Victimization Survey (Mayhew and van Dijk 1997).

Drug use and policies also exhibit long-term trends with periods of prohibitionism in the 1850s, 1890–1920, and 1980 to the present, alternating with periods of greater tolerance. Historian David Musto (1987) has shown that anti-drug policies interact in predictable ways with patterns of drug use. In a seemingly perverse but understandable twist, the harshest policies are adopted and the most vigorous prosecutions are carried out after drug use has begun to decline. In our era, for example, self-reported use of marijuana, heroin, and amphetamines peaked for every age group in 1979–1980 (for cocaine in 1984–1985) and fell steadily thereafter, but the harshest federal anti-drug laws were not enacted until 1988, and the first federal "drug czar" was not named until 1989 (Tonry 1995, chaps. 1, 3). If reduced drug use was its aim, the war had been won a decade before it was declared.

The reason this is understandable is that recreational drug use during prohibitionistic periods is widely seen as immoral and socially destructive. Such attitudes explain why increasing numbers of people stop using and experimenting with drugs and why, after drug use begins falling, comparatively few voices are raised in opposition to harsh policies. Few people, especially elected public officials, are comfortable speaking out on behalf of "immorality." In more tolerant periods, by contrast, many more people celebrate traditional Enlightenment ideals of moral autonomy and individuals' rights to make choices about their own lives and comfortably oppose harsh laws and policies on those grounds.

I mention the well-documented and recurrent interaction between drug use patterns and drug-abuse policy because similar patterns may characterize interactions between contemporary crime patterns and crime-control policies. Three similarities stand out. First, the harshest crime control policies—three-strikes laws, lengthy mandatory minimum sentences, widespread parole abolition, truth-in-sentencing laws, sexual psychopath laws, increased use of the death penalty—were adopted in the early and mid-1990s, long after crime rates began their steep decline in the 1970s or 1980s (depending on whether victimization or FBI reported crime data are consulted).

Second, few elected officials have been prepared to oppose proposals for harsher laws. Earlier I discussed the unwillingness of politicians to risk being labeled "soft on crime" or "for criminals" rather than victims.

Third, because harsh laws are enacted when crime rates are already falling, people who want to make year-to-year comparisons can easily show that crime rates have fallen in the years immediately after the change compared with the year immediately before. This has happened in relation to New York City's adoption in the early 1990s of "zero-tolerance policing," California's adoption in 1994 of a broadly defined three-strikes law, and the fivefold increase since 1972 in America's prison and jail populations. These may be plausible claims on the part of people who are unaware of long-term crime trends, but for people who are, they are disingenuous. The year-to-year crime rate declines are at least as likely to be merely the continuation of long-term trends as they are to be effects of policy changes. Nonetheless, such patterns bedevil efforts to devise rational and humane public policies for crime (and for drugs) because they seem to provide plausible short-term data that support ideological and partisan claims that harsh policies "work."

In recent years scholars have been trying to make sense of the seeming anomaly that public support for harsh crime policies remained high in the late 1990s even in the face of a substantial and long-term drop in crime rates. A cynical explanation mentioned earlier, for which there is some evidence (e.g., Beckett 1997), is that conservative politicians have found it in their interest to keep voters' attention focused on an issue about which liberals are reluctant to disagree, and the public attitudes are simply a predictable response in an era of declining crime rates and moralized policies.

A related explanation is that the mass media have learned that crime pays in terms of a mass public fascination with the darker sides of life and that the fears vicariously enjoyed in front of the television or the movie screen are generalized to life outside the home. There is evidence that people's opinions about crime and punishment often are based on the unusual, dramatic, and unrepresentative cases that they learn about from the mass media (Roberts and Stalans 1997).

A third explanation, consistent with Musto's account of drug policy history and its extension to crime, is that in the 1990s people don't really care about the effectiveness of crime and drug-abuse policies but instead support harsh policies for "expressive" reasons (Doob and Marinos 1995; Doob 1997; Tyler and Boeckmann 1997). The argument, for which there is considerable public opinion survey evidence, is that people value the denunciatory qualities of harsh laws.

Unfortunately, it is always easier to see clearly with hindsight to other times or, from afar, to other places. The sight lines are impaired and the images much less distinct in our own time and place. Only time will tell whether American crime policies can be made more effective and more humane in coming years—more like those of America in other times or those of other Western countries today—or whether the United States will long remain trapped in Musto's paradigm. Until fundamental policy changes are made, the seemingly inexorable increases in incarceration and the grossly disproportionate presence of blacks in prisons and jails will continue.

Note to Introduction

1. Index violent offenses are murder, rape, robbery, and aggrivated assault; index property offenses are burglary, theft, and motor vehicle theft.

References

American Law Institute. 1962. *Model Penal Code (Proposed Official Draft)*. Philadelphia: American Law Institute.

Anderson, David. 1995. *Crime and the Politics of Hysteria: How the Willie Horton Story Changed American Justice*. New York: Time Books.

Applebome, Peter. 1996. *Dixie Rising: How the South Is Shaping American Values, Politics, and Culture*. New York: Time Books/Random House.

Barr, Robert, and Ken Pease. 1990. "Crime Placement, Displacement, and Deflection." In *Crime and Justice: A Review of Research*, vol. 12, edited by Michael Tonry and Norval Morris. Chicago: University of Chicago Press.

Barr, William P. 1992. *The Case for More Incarceration*. Washington, D.C.: U.S. Department of Justice, Office of Policy Development.

Bayley, David H. 1994. *Police for the Future*. New York: Oxford University Press.

Beckett, Katherine. 1997. *Making Crime Pay: Law and Order in Contemporary American Politics*. New York: Oxford University Press.

Bennett, William J., John J. DiIulio, and John P. Walters. 1996. *Body Count: Moral Poverty and How to Win America's War Against Crime and Drugs*. New York: Simon and Schuster.

Bertram, Eva, Morris Blackman, Kenneth Sharpe, and Peter Andreas. 1996. *Drug War Politics: The Price of Denial*. Berkeley and Los Angeles: University of California Press.

Blumstein, Alfred. 1993a. "Making Rationality Relevant: The American Society of Criminology 1992 Presidential Address." *Criminology* 31:1–16.

———. 1993b. "Racial Disproportionality of U.S. Prison Populations Revisited." *University of Colorado Law Review* 64:743–60.

Blumstein, Alfred, Jacqueline Cohen, and Daniel Nagin. 1978. *Deterrence and Incapacitation*. Report of the National Academy of Sciences Panel on Research on Deterrent and Incapacitative Effects. Washington, D.C.: National Academy Press.

Blumstein, Alfred, Jacqueline Cohen, Jeffrey Roth, and Christy Visher. 1986. *Criminal Careers and "Career Criminals."* Report of the National Academies of Sciences Panel on Criminal Careers. Washington, D.C.: National Academy Press.

Boerner, David. 1995. "Sentencing Guidelines and Prosecutorial Discretion." *Judicature* 78(4):196–200.

Botvin, Gilbert. 1990. "Substance Abuse Prevention: Theory, Practice, and Effectiveness." In *Drugs and Crime*, edited by Michael Tonry and James Q. Wilson. Chicago: University of Chicago Press.

Bureau of Justice Statistics. 1997a. *Correctional Populations in the United States, 1995*. Washington, D.C.: U.S. Department of Justice, Bureau of Justice Statistics.

———. 1997b. *Criminal Victimization, 1973–95*. Washington, D.C.: U.S. Department of Justice, Bureau of Justice Statistics.

———. 1997c. *Prisoners in 1996*. Washington, D.C.: U.S. Department of Justice, Bureau of Justice Statistics.

———. Bureau of Justice Statistics. 1998. *Prison and Jail Inmates at Midyear 1997*. Washington, D.C.: U.S. Department of Justice, Bureau of Justice Statistics.

Cook, Philip J. 1980. "Research in Criminal Deterrence: Laying the Groundwork for the Second Decade." In *Crime and Justice: An Annual Review of Research*, vol. 2, edited by Norval Morris and Michael Tonry. Chicago: University of Chicago Press.

Cook, Philip J., and John Laub. 1998. "The Unprecedented Epidemic in Youth Violence." In *Youth Violence in America*, edited by Michael Tonry and Mark H. Moore. Chicago: University of Chicago Press.

Daly, Kathleen, and Michael Tonry. 1997. "Gender, Race, and Sentencing." In *Crime and Justice: A Review of Research*, vol. 22, edited by Michael Tonry. Chicago: University of Chicago Press.

Doob, Anthony. 1997. "Fear, Victimization, and Attitudes to Sentencing, the Courts, and the Police." *Canadian Journal of Criminology* 39:275–91.

Doob, Anthony, and Voula Marinos. 1995. "Reconceptualizing Punishment: Understanding the Limitations on the Use of Intermediate Punishments." *University of Chicago Law School Roundtable* 2:413–433.

Edsall, Thomas, and Mary Edsall. 1991. *Chain Reaction: The Impact of Race, Rights, and Taxes on American Politics*. New York: Norton.

Federal Bureau of Investigation. 1997. *Crime in the United States—1996*. Washington, D.C.: U.S. Government Printing Office.

Gurr, Ted Robert. 1981. "Historical Trends in Violent Crimes: A Critical Review of the Evidence." In *Crime and Justice: An Annual Review of the Research*, vol. 3, edited by Michael Tonry and Norval Morris. Chicago: University of Chicago Press.

Hope, Tim. 1995. "Community Crime Prevention." In *Building a Safer Society: Strategic Approaches to Crime Prevention*, edited by Michael Tonry and David P. Farrington. Chicago: University of Chicago Press.

Lane, Roger. 1992. "Urban Police and Crime in Nineteenth-Century America." In *Modern Policing*, edited by Michael Tonry and Norval Morris. Chicago: University of Chicago Press.

Maguire, Kathleen, and Ann L. Pastore. 1997. *Sourcebook of Criminal Justice Statistics—1996*. Washington, D.C.: U.S. Government Printing Office.

Mayhew, Pat, and Jan J. M. van Dijk. 1997. *Criminal Victimisation in Eleven Industrialised Countries*. The Hague: Dutch Ministry of Justice.

Moore, Mark H. 1992. "Problem-solving and Community Policing." In *Modern Policing*, edited by Michael Tonry and Norval Morris. Chicago: University of Chicago Press.

———. 1995. "Learning While Doing: Linking Knowledge to Policy in the Development of Community Policing and Violence Prevention in the United States." In *Propensity and Opportunity*, edited by P.-O. H. Wikström, Ronald V. Clarke, and Joan McCord. Stockholm: Fritzes Kundtjänst.

Musto, David. 1987. *The American Disease: Origins of Narcotic Control*. New York: Oxford University Press.

Nagin, Daniel. 1998. "Criminal Deterrence Research at the Outset of the Twenty-first Century." In *Crime and Justice: A Review of Research*, vol. 23, edited by Michael Tonry. Chicago: University of Chicago Press.

Parent, Dale. 1995. "Boot Camps Failing to Achieve Goals." In *Intermediate Sanctions in Overcrowded Times*, edited by Michael Tonry and Kate Hamilton. Boston: Northeastern University Press.

Petersilia, Joan. 1997. "Probation in the United States." In *Crime and Justice:*

A Review of Research, vol. 22, edited by Michael Tonry. Chicago: University of Chicago Press.

President's Commission on Law Enforcement and Administration of Justice. 1967. *The Challenge of Crime in a Free Society*. Washington, D.C.: U.S. Government Printing Office.

Reiss, Albert J. Jr., and Jeffrey Roth. 1993. *Understanding and Controlling Violence*. Report of the National Academy of Sciences Panel on the Understanding and Control of Violence. Washington, D.C.: National Academy Press.

Roberts, Julian, and Loretta Stalans. 1997. *Public Opinion, Crime, and Criminal Justice*. Boulder, Colo.: Westview Press.

Rothman, David. 1980. *Conscience and Convenience*. Boston: Little, Brown.

Sampson, Robert, and Janet Lauritsen. 1997. "Racial and Ethnic Disparities in Crime and Criminal Justice in the United States." In *Ethnicity, Crime, and Immigration—Comparative and Cross-National Perspectives*, edited by Michael Tonry. Chicago: University of Chicago Press.

Tonry, Michael. 1995. *Malign Neglect—Race, Crime, and Punishment in America*. New York: Oxford University Press.

————. 1996. *Sentencing Matters*. New York: Oxford University Press.

Tonry, Michael, and Kathleen Hatlestad, eds. 1997. *Sentencing Reform in Overcrowded Times—A Comparative Perspective*. New York: Oxford University Press.

Tyler, Tom R., and Robert J. Boeckmann. 1997. "Three Strikes and You Are Out, but Why? The Psychology of Public Support for Punishing Rule Breakers." *Law and Society Review* 31(2):237–65.

Wilbanks, William. 1987. *The Myth of a Racist Criminal Justice System*. Monterey, Calif.: Brooks/Cole.

Wilson, James Q. 1990. "Drugs and Crime." In *Drugs and Crime*, edited by Michael Tonry and James Q. Wilson. Chicago: University of Chicago Press.

Wilson, James Q., and Richard Herrnstein. 1985. *Crime and Human Nature*. New York: Simon and Schuster.

Part I

THE CONTEXT

1

Crime, Criminal Justice, and Public Opinion

JULIAN V. ROBERTS & LORETTA J. STALANS

Public opinion plays a vital, at times determinant, role in the evolution of criminal justice policy and practice. This is true for most Western nations, but particularly for the United States. Politicians frequently cite (not always accurately) the views of the public in support of various policies. This has been true in the areas of gun control, parole, drugs, and above all sentencing reform. Sentencing commissions at the state and federal levels acknowledge the importance of developing guidelines consistent with community sentiment. Sometimes this is acknowledged by commission staff; occasionally it is explicitly stated within a formal commission publication. Specific sentencing laws such as the "three-strikes" laws mandating long periods of imprisonment for offenders convicted of a felony for the third time were passed in large measure in the name of growing public concern about recidivist, violent offenders.

Judges and politicians often appeal to the public demand for more rigorous criminal justice policies in the hope of enhancing their own electoral prospects. In this belief they are probably not mistaken. Four out of five Americans acknowledge that they would be more likely to vote for a political candidate who advocated harsher sentencing (Hindelang 1975). Indeed, the politics of law and order can sometimes shift the balance of power in an election year. The aggressive exploitation of the Willie Horton case inflicted irreparable harm on the presidential campaign of Michael Dukakis in 1988. The same is true for many political campaigns in other countries. American judges who have to face reelection are probably more responsive to the public mood (or what they perceive as the public mood) than are judges in other countries such as Canada or the United Kingdom, who are appointed for the duration of their professional lives. The U.S. Supreme Court, too, appears to pay a great deal of attention to community sentiment as it grapples with the constitutionality of issues such as the death penalty, abortion, and pornography. Regrettably, the Court has not always been as thorough as it might have been with regard to determining the true nature of public attitudes toward these controversial issues.

There is a crucial intermediary between politicians and the public: the news media. Crime and criminal justice have always attracted widespread attention from the news media in the United States and in other countries. Usually this involves coverage of sensational cases. Media attention to crime reached its apotheosis in 1995 with the live coverage of, and commentary about, the O. J. Simpson trial. The blanket coverage of that case exceeded the amount of attention paid to all previous trials. In fact, the Simpson case became the number one news story of the year, not just the most frequently cited crime story. Well over 100 million people in America tuned in to watch live television coverage of the verdict being announced. That case focused attention on criminal justice issues beyond the guilt or innocence of a single defendant. These issues included racism in the criminal justice system, domestic violence, and the differential treatment of wealthy defendants. Polls conducted after the verdict was announced indicated that the Simpson trial had had an important and possibly lasting impact on the way Americans perceive their system of criminal justice.

Media attention to crime and justice ensures that the link between criminal justice and the public is closer in the United States than in other nations. A primary reason for this difference is the presence of television cameras in court. Americans are able to follow every televised trial as if they were jurors. For those viewers who do not have the time to watch live coverage, several prime-time programs summarize recent developments in high-profile cases. In other countries (such as Canada), cameras are not permitted inside courtrooms. This deprives the public of the immediacy associated with live coverage and may explain in part why public interest in crime is more muted in countries without such intense television coverage of criminal cases.

Despite all this media attention, when placed in the context of other social problems, to date crime has not assumed a very high profile in public surveys. Throughout the 1980s, no more than 5 percent of the American public ever identified crime as the most important problem facing the country. However, a significant shift in public priorities appears to have occurred in the early 1990s. In August 1994, over one-half of the public identified crime as the number one problem (Maguire and Pastore 1995, Table 2.1). Similarly, a poll conducted as the federal crime bill passed in 1994 found that four out of five Americans believed crime was the most serious threat to individual rights and freedoms (Maguire and Pastore 1995, Table 2.7). Another index of community concern is public willingness to allocate additional funds to criminal justice. Three-quarters of Americans polled in 1994 believed that insufficient funds were being spent to combat crime (Maguire and Pastore 1995, Table 2.27). It is ironic (and worthy of research attention) that public concern should have peaked at a time when crime rates had for a number of years been stable or falling across the nation. These trends attest to the influence of the news media (and perhaps politicians) in setting the nation's public policy agenda.

Widespread concern over crime is accompanied by a highly negative view of the criminal justice response. Although there is considerable bedrock support for institutions such as the Supreme Court and for certain criminal justice professionals such as the police, the overall evaluation of the administration of criminal justice is both critical and cynical. Most Americans view the justice system as excessively lenient and overly concerned with ensuring due process protections for suspects and defendants. In 1989, Americans were asked to state whether they were more worried about criminals "being let off too easily" or whether "the constitutional rights of accuseds" were being ignored. Fully four-fifths of respondents were more concerned about offenders escaping due punishment than about accuseds receiving less-than-sufficient due process (Flanagan and Maguire 1990, Table 2.37).

When Americans were asked in a 1995 poll to identify the cause of increased crime rates, the most popular option was leniency on the part of the courts and the correctional system (Maguire and Pastore 1995, Table 2.2). The latest war on drugs has also met with a great deal of skepticism: two-thirds of the respondents to the National Crime and Justice Survey in 1995 believed that the war on drugs had had no effect on drug use (Cintron and Johnson 1996). This concern about the crime problem and negative view of the official response form the backdrop to our review of research on public knowledge and opinion.

In this chapter we summarize the vast literature on public knowledge of, and attitudes toward, crime and justice in America (see Roberts 1992 for an earlier review). Pollsters have paid particular attention to criminal justice over the past few decades. In addition, public opinion research has become a major subject of criminological inquiry. For many years, the annual publication *Sourcebook of Criminal Justice Statistics* (e.g., Maguire and Pastore 1995) has devoted an entire chapter to presenting the results of public opinion polls. The 1995 National Crime and Justice Survey provides the most comprehensive examination of Americans' attitudes toward crime and justice in over a decade (see Flanagan and Longmire 1996). Accordingly, we know a great deal about the nature of public opinion in this area. Since a number of key questions have been posed repeatedly, we also have a good historical record upon which to draw. Our focus is on Americans' perceptions of crime and justice, although where strong parallels exist with public opinion trends in other countries, this is noted. Before describing the substantive findings, we review current methods used by researchers in the field. We then proceed to the question of public knowledge, for only an understanding of what people know about crime and criminal justice will permit a reasoned evaluation of public attitudes toward these issues. This discussion includes material on the public's sources of information about crime and criminal justice. The following sections review, in turn, public perceptions of crime seriousness and attitudes toward the police, the courts, parole boards, juvenile justice, and gun control. Finally, we draw some conclusions about the nature of public opinion, and the research priorities that remain to be explored.

Research Methods

There are three principal approaches to researching public opinion: representative surveys, focus groups, and experiments using purposive, nonrandom samples of the public. Surveys of representative samples of the public account for most contemporary research. These polls are typically conducted by major polling companies (e.g., Gallup) either as an independent survey for a specific client or as part of a monthly or annual sweep. More recently there has been an increase in the number of polls conducted by university-based polling centers. Representative polls use a probability sampling procedure to ensure a final sample that conforms to the characteristics of the population from which the sample was drawn. This entails oversampling respondents in certain categories that would be underrepresented by a simple "sweep" survey in which interviews are conducted with whomever happens to be at home when the interviewer calls. The principal utility of the representative poll is to place public opinion toward some issue within known statistical boundaries and to provide information about national trends. The disadvantage of such polls is the limited respondent time available, with the result that the questions posed tend to be simple and to allow for little elaboration.

This limitation is in part overcome by an innovation known as computer-assisted telephone interviewing (CATI). This is a computerized opinion poll that has several advantages in terms of cost-saving and efficiency but also permits greater flexibility in the nature of the questions posed. Specifically, CATI permits the researcher to manipulate variables such as the wording of the question or the nature of the information that precedes the question. For example, in a survey about capital punishment, half the respondents would be given a minimal amount of information about the case, while the other half would be given a more complete account. Both groups would then be asked to respond to the same question (e.g., "Is the death penalty appropriate in this case?"). Thus a randomized experiment is possible, using a representative survey of respondents. Of course, the technique can also go much further than this. The computer can easily provide additional information to respondents, the exact nature of the information being contingent on their responses to the preliminary question. Innovations of this kind will have considerable application in criminal justice, where, to date, polls have typically employed more traditional techniques.

Focus groups constitute the principal qualitative approach to public opinion research. They generate an environment in which respondents have the opportunity to reflect on the question posed and then discuss their reflections with other participants. These groups are designed to go beyond the reflexive (but far from reflective) responses elicited by large-sample surveys posing simplistic questions. Generally speaking, focus group studies consist of small groups (usually ten to fifteen participants) selected to represent major demographic categories (to the extent that this is possible with so small a number). In short, focus groups are a kind of public opinion jury, in which the task is not to render a verdict (in this case a single unanimous opinion) but to generate qualitative material that is recorded and later summarized for publication.

Unlike juries, there is usually a moderator present who directs the discussion and, in some cases, is responsible for introducing material to which group discussants are asked to respond. Focus groups also provide researchers with an opportunity to test the strength of attitudes by providing discussants with relevant information, counterarguments, and so on. This function of a focus group was explored with considerable success in several analyses of public attitudes toward punishing offenders (e.g., Doble and Klein 1989). Focus group participants were asked to sentence several offenders described in vignettes. At a later point, the moderators provided information about alternative dispositions and asked discussants to resentence the offenders. The sentencing preferences of the group shifted significantly once participants were made aware of the alternative sanctions. This technique is less feasible in a large-scale survey.

Between focus groups and large-scale, representative surveys lies a new, hybrid approach to exploring public opinion known as a *deliberative poll*. This concept is founded in large measure on the distinction, advanced by Daniel Yankelovich (1991), between public opinion and public judgment. The latter refers to opinion that originates in deliberation, rather than a reflexive responding. A deliberative poll allows people the chance to reflect on the issues, discuss their ideas, and even to pose questions to experts in the field. The first (and to date only) deliberative poll on crime was conducted in England in 1994 (see Fishkin 1995). A random sample of the public was contacted and asked to participate. Of this sample, a subset of 300 people spent a weekend together discussing issues related to crime and justice. In addition, they were able to hear experts (and politicians) debate the issues. After the so-called deliberative weekend, respondents completed (for the second time) a questionnaire on criminal justice. Significant shifts of opinion occurred for some issues. For example, before the weekend sessions, one-third of the group was opposed to sending first-time burglars to prison; this rose to half the sample at the second administration. Significant shifts emerged for other issues such as the right of suspects to remain silent under questioning from the police. Attitudes toward capital punishment did not change.

It is still too early to conclude that deliberative polling is the wave of the future. One obvious impediment to its widespread application is the cost of assembling the respondents in a country as large as the United States. Furthermore, there is as yet no scholarly literature on the topic. A number of methodological considerations remain: the nature of shifts of opinion will be highly dependent on the kinds of information provided to participants, and the identity of the expert panelists, as well as their "performance" during the sessions. Without scrupulous attention to balancing the material on controversial, bipolar issues such as the use of imprisonment and the rights of the accused, the outcome of the deliberative poll may not reflect real shifts of opinion or informed public judgment so much as the agenda of the organizers.

Finally, a great deal of public opinion research is conducted using small, purposive samples of respondents. This category of research includes all experimental, quasi-experimental, and correlational research, usually conducted on a university campus, but sometimes using more heterogeneous samples of subjects than university students. While not generalizable to national, state, provincial, or county populations, these studies have permitted researchers to examine the effects of various experimental manipulations, the length of which precludes their use on representative surveys.

A comprehensive and accurate portrait of public opinion in this area can be obtained only by a multimethod approach to research. Representative, national polls are necessary to set the approximate bounds on attitudes, while focus groups and research with purposive samples are needed to evaluate the depth of a particular opinion. The research reviewed here draws on all these methodologies.

Public Knowledge of Crime and Criminal Justice

The vast majority of polls have ignored public knowledge and have focused exclusively on public opinion. For example, people are repeatedly asked whether they favor or oppose the death penalty or three-strikes legislation but are almost never asked how much they *know* about the effects of the former or the costs of the latter. Nevertheless, the limited literature on public knowledge in this area does permit some conclusions about public awareness of crime and justice.

It would be trite to say that people know little about the nature of crime and the functioning of the criminal justice system. Criminal justice is one of many social issues that crowd the pages of newspapers and attract public attention. However, the nature of crime in the media—the unfolding of conflicting versions of events, the drama of violence—appeals to the public in a way not matched by the economy, health care, or other important social issues. Ironically, the issues that attract the greatest interest—sentencing and capital punishment—are the ones that generate the most distorted perceptions. The death penalty is a good example. Debate over the deterrent efficacy and morality of executing offenders has raged for decades; execution stories have always been in the news, going back to the Loeb and Leopold case in the 1920s. Despite this level of interest, most people know little about the administration of the death penalty, and less about the effects of capital punishment on murder rates.

Crime Rates, the Distribution of Crime, and Characteristics of Offenders

Surveys conducted across the country have consistently demonstrated the existence of several misperceptions relating to crime and offenders. One of these—which holds at the state and the national level—is that crime rates are constantly rising. To cite one example, 80 percent of the public in Ohio believed that the crime rate had increased over the previous three years, when in fact it had not (Knowles 1987). In the early to mid-1990s, official crime statistics showed a decline. For example the rate of index crimes reported by the FBI dropped 4 percent from 1991 to 1992, 3 percent from 1992 to 1993, and 2 percent from 1993 to 1994 (Federal Bureau of Investigation 1995). Violent crime rates also declined over the same period. By 1995, the U.S. crime rate had fallen to its lowest level in a decade. The American public, however, continued to believe that crime rates were rising inexorably.

Although no recent poll has been conducted on the topic, it is likely that most Americans are unaware that the murder rate also declined significantly across the country in the early 1990s. Canadian homicide data demonstrate a steady decline since capital punishment was abolished in 1976. The homicide rate in 1995 (the most recent year for which data are currently available) was the lowest since 1969. Nevertheless, most Canadians responding to surveys believe that the homicide rate has in fact been increasing (Roberts 1994).

A significant body of research in America and elsewhere has demonstrated that the public accepts a specific stereotype of offenders. To the public, offenders are physically unattractive, unemployed individuals who are frequently gang members. The negative characteristics of this stereotype may explain why many people admit to feeling uneasy in the presence of someone known to have spent time in prison. The public also overestimates the proportion of recorded crime that involves violence. For many members of the public, crime is committed by a small, identifiable group. There is little public awareness of the broad range of criminal behavior, or the significant numbers of people who are involved in criminal behavior at some point in their lives. Americans would probably be surprised to learn that many millions of their fellow citizens carry criminal records. The attribution of criminality is also accompanied by the expectation of future offending, as can be demonstrated by examining public estimates of recidivism rates. People over-estimate the percentage of offenders who will reoffend. Many people appear to subscribe to the misperception "once an offender, always an offender." As well, they assume a high degree of specialization, believing that when recidivism occurs, it is always within the same category as the previous offending (Roberts and White 1986). Recidivism data on crime specialization fail to support this stereotype.

It is important to understand public stereotypes of offenders, for they undoubtedly have an impact on support for various crime control policies, as well as the administration of justice. The public focus on an identifiable number of offenders has important consequences for popular support for crime control policies. Research in Canada has shown that almost half the population believes there is a link between race and crime. A nationwide 1993 Gallup Poll found that more than one-third of the public believed that African Americans were "more likely" than other groups to commit crimes (Gallup Monthly Poll 1993, p. 37). Research on smaller samples of U.S. residents has shown that they attribute certain crimes to African Americans. These perceptions appear to influence jurors' decision making in cases involving ethnic minorities. Stereotypes about race and crime may mean that some jurors are predisposed to believe that an African-American defendant is guilty, particularly when charged with a crime that the public associates with this racial minority. This may be particularly disadvantageous if the African-American defendant admits, on taking the stand in his or her own defense, to having previous convictions similar to the current charge. In addition, a wealth of research suggests that judicial instruction—the legal remedy to correct such public biases—is generally ineffective. These stereotypes affect other social attitudes as well: almost half the Americans surveyed recently believed that store owners should be able to refuse to let young African Americans enter their stores at night.

Knowledge of the Legal System

Knowledge of the legal system tends to be poor among members of the public, and awareness of legal rights is far from widespread. A national survey conducted in 1978 found that almost half the respondents incorrectly believed that the onus is upon a defendant to prove his or her innocence (Yankelovich, Skelley, and White, Inc. 1978). Most disturbingly, low-income groups are the least knowledgeable. Specific laws also escape the attention of many people, as is apparent from several examples. In 1990, Ohio passed a significant piece of legislation relating to drug crimes. Surveys showed that nine out of ten Ohio residents (including, presumably, many illegal drug users) had not heard anything about the new law (Schroot 1990).

Perhaps the most egregious example of public misperception documented in the research literature concerns the insanity defense. Surveys of attitudes show that most Americans disapprove of the defense. Yet how much do they actually know? The insanity defense received widespread media coverage in the wake of the acquittal of John Hinckley Jr., who had been charged with attempting to assassinate President Ronald Reagan. Fully 90 percent of the public disapproved of the verdict in that case, yet when asked to provide an approximate definition of the defense, fewer than 1 percent came anywhere close to the correct legal definition of insanity. As well, there is a perception among the public that the insanity defense is frequently invoked. The public estimates that over one-third of defendants use the insanity plea, when in reality the figure is less than 1 percent.

Knowledge of Trends in Criminal Justice Statistics

Misperceptions of the criminal justice system abound, forming a constellation of attitudes that reflect a theme of leniency. Surveys conducted in California and Arizona found that the public has little awareness of the magnitude of statutory maximum penalties (California Assembly Committee on Criminal Procedure 1975). This finding is consistent with research conducted in Canada and Great Britain. People also know little about alternatives to incarceration, or intermediate punishments. The public tends to underestimate the severity of sentences imposed and to overestimate the proportion of inmates who are released in parole. For example, research in Ohio found that three-quarters of the public were unaware that the parole board had become tougher in its releasing decisions. In fact, over half the sample believed that parole had become easier to obtain (Knowles 1987). Prison life itself is seen as insufficiently harsh, although few of those who hold this view have ever visited a correctional facility.

The news media appear to be the source of these misperceptions. Although there are many potential sources of information about criminal justice, the vast majority of the public cites the news media as their primary or exclusive source. News media coverage of criminal justice is highly selective, episodic, and focused on a limited number of offenses. Public overestimates of the proportion of crime involving violence can be directly traced to the overrepresentation of violent crime, particularly homicide, in news stories. By emphasizing violent crime and lenient sentences, the news media also encourage the public to subscribe to a false syllogism involving crime and punishment. In the public mind, crime rates are constantly rising, and the system is always too lenient. The solution to rising crime rates must therefore be to pass more punitive crime control policies. Finally, public confusion with regard to the criminal justice system cannot be entirely explained by idiosyncratic media coverage. The complexity of the system is also responsible, as has been documented by systematic surveys.

Perceptions of Crime Seriousness

Public perception of the seriousness of criminal acts is central to the criminal law. Crime seriousness determines when police are allowed to use deadly force, the priority prosecutors assign to cases, and the severity of sentences judges impose on convicted offenders. The public's perception of crime seriousness shapes its satisfaction with prosecutorial and judicial decisions. Judges and prosecutors alike attempt to make decisions that are in accord with public views of crime seriousness. Moreover, in order to secure compliance with criminal law, the public must believe that the laws are legitimate and the punishment for a violation is fair (Robinson and Darley 1995). Finally, punishments whose severity exceeds community sentiment regarding crime seriousness may be perceived as violating the Eighth Amendment of the U.S. Constitution, which prohibits cruel and unusual punishment.

Methodological Issues

Most studies on crime seriousness provide respondents with clear definitions of crimes and examples of specific incidents. This design partially resolves (but does not completely eliminate) the unrealistic perceptions of the consequences of different crimes that people may use in forming judgments of seriousness. Because public perceptions of crime seriousness still reflect stereotypical conceptions of crimes, however, comparisons between the public and criminal justice professionals may reveal differences in knowledge about the true nature of crimes rather than disagreements about seriousness. Two types of crime seriousness have been explored by researchers. *Relative seriousness* refers to public perceptions about the ranking of crimes in terms of their seriousness relative to all other crimes. The concept of *absolute seriousness* raises the question of whether two groups (e.g., laypersons and professionals) assign similar ratings of seriousness to a specific crime regardless of how they rank-order a series of crimes. Thus, different populations can demonstrate consensus about the relative seriousness of crimes but lack consensus about the absolute seriousness of specific offenses.

What Determines the Seriousness of a Particular Crime?

Most researchers ask respondents to rate the seriousness of crime descriptions that lack information about the offenders' and victims' characteristics, and the degree of intentionality and culpability. This approach assumes that people have a simple definition of seriousness that corresponds to the amount of harm inflicted. Research shows that for members of the public, seriousness has multiple meanings. Both the harmfulness and the wrongfulness of the act affect judgments of crime seriousness. The degree of physical harm or the value of the property stolen contributes to perceived seriousness (Sellin and Wolfgang 1964). In addition, members of the public adjudge intentional criminal acts to be more serious than crimes of recklessness or negligence. The prior record of an offender also shapes perceived seriousness ratings through perceptions of intent or of the likelihood of recidivism.

Historical Variation in Seriousness Judgments

If public views about crime seriousness reflect some basic understanding about the degree of harm, seriousness ratings should be quite stable over time. And, in fact, comparisons over time periods have revealed considerable stability in the relative seriousness of different crimes. Since Sellin and Wolfgang's classic study in 1964, research has repeatedly found that violent crimes are perceived as more serious than property crimes, which in turn are judged to be more serious than white-collar, public order, and victimless crimes. At the same time, some interesting changes have emerged from these historical comparisons. Whereas rape was viewed as the most serious crime in the 1920s, by the 1960s murder was viewed as more serious than rape. Since this time, studies generally find that murder is considered the most serious crime. In the United States (and other countries) the public has become more aware of the true nature of white-collar crimes, leading to changed perceptions of the seriousness of these offenses. Drug crimes also have been judged as more serious in recent years.

Comparison of Seriousness Judgments by the Public and Criminal Justice Professionals

Do police officers and citizens hold similar views about the seriousness of different crimes? Research suggests that officers and citizens agree on the seriousness of some crimes but disagree about the seriousness of other crimes. Sellin and Wolfgang (1964) found that police officers, judges, and citizens generally had similar views regarding the relative seriousness of different crimes. Subsequent research has found that the public and police in England agreed that violent crimes such as aggravated battery and robbery and burglary of business were the most serious crimes. Police officers, however, ranked residential burglary much higher in relative seriousness than did citizens, whereas citizens ranked reckless driving and selling of marijuana much higher than did officers. The public viewed white-collar crimes, fraud, and statutory rape as more serious than did police officers. Thus officers placed priority on street crimes of battery, robbery, and burglary, whereas the public also viewed other crimes such as reckless driving, selling marijuana, and white-collar crimes as deserving attention from the justice system. Further clarifying this research, Skogan (1996) reviewed national and regional surveys conducted in England in the 1990s and found that the public placed importance on sexual assault and burglary, followed by drunk driving, vandalism, and robbery, as problems deserving police attention.

Cross-Cultural Perceptions of
Crime Seriousness

Is the concept of harm, which underlies perceptions of crime serious-ness, culturally relative, or are there certain basic human values (such as a prohibition against the taking of human life) which people from all cul-tures agree should not be violated? Durkheim and other supporters of the consensus model proposed that criminal laws reflect the "collective con-sciousness of society," and criminal laws are made to protect consensual community values through enforcement and punishment. Neo-Marxist and other "radical" criminologists have challenged this view of criminal law and have proposed the alternative conflict model. This model asserts that people from different social classes and ethnicities disagree about which acts should be criminalized and subject to punishment. It further posits that criminal laws serve to protect the interest of the powerful members who create the laws and then enforce them against the less powerful members of society such as the poor, women, and ethnic mi-norities. Cross-cultural comparisons of crime seriousness judgments thus address the question of whether criminal laws reflect basic human values or are culturally relative and reflect the view of the more powerful mem-bers of a given society.

Because cultures define crimes in different ways, it is difficult to make adequate comparisons between societies. Researchers try to minimize dif-ferences due to cultural knowledge by providing respondents with fairly general descriptions of crimes that do not reflect any particular statutory definition. The limited research on this issue suggests that there is a sig-nificant degree of agreement across countries in terms of the relative seri-ousness of different crimes. Many studies have replicated the relative ranking of crimes across a number of countries, including Canada, Den-mark, Finland, Great Britain, Holland, Kuwait, Norway, Puerto Rico, and the United States. There are exceptions, however, as the following exam-ples illustrate. Kuwaitis and Americans perceive rape to be more serious than the violent crimes of robbery or aggravated assault, whereas respon-dents from Scandinavia and Great Britain perceive these offenses as having the same seriousness level. Kuwaitis considered selling heroin or marijuana to be more serious than any other offense except murder, whereas respondents from other countries do not consider drug offenses as serious as other violent crimes (Scott and Al-Thakeb 1977).

People from dissimilar backgrounds in the same country such as the United States or Canada also agree about the relative seriousness of dif-ferent crimes. Ethnicity, social class, and prior victimization do not ap-pear to affect views of the relative seriousness of different crimes. Gen-der, however, affects perceptions of the relative seriousness of rape and murder. Compared with women, men in England, China, and Canada perceived murder as more serious. In these same studies, seriousness ratings of rape derived from female respondents were higher than those de-rived from male respondents. Recent research in the United States has found that both men and women agree that murder is more serious than rape (Rauma 1991). Some research also suggests that different perspectives about crime and attitudes toward government may result in diminishing consensus about the ranking of crimes.

Evaluating the Police and the Courts

Public evaluations of the police and courts have two distinct dimensions: evaluations of performance and evaluations of fairness and equality. While performance is important to the public, it is fairness and equality that determine levels of public support for various institutions and peoples' willingness to obey decisions made by legal officials. Public evaluations also determine willingness to seek help from officials, for example, when people are victims of crime.

Quality of Performance

Americans generally hold the Supreme Court in high regard and have more confidence in the Supreme Court than in local courts. Americans, however, have more confidence in the police than in other criminal justice institutions, including the Supreme Court. This finding is consistent with the results from surveys of the public in other countries. Most respondents believe that the police are doing a good job; however, evaluations of performance vary widely from city to city, and ethnic disagreement about police performance also varies from city to city. Over half of the individuals from different ethnic backgrounds believe the police are doing a good job at preventing crime. African Americans, however, are less satisfied with police efforts at solving crimes than are Hispanic Americans and Caucasian Americans. A paradox seems to emerge from this literature. Despite the fact that the public perceives crime rates to be constantly rising, people still have a very positive view of police performance. Other findings help resolve the paradox, however. The public holds the courts rather than the police responsible for the crime problem. This result reflects a widespread but erroneous perception that crime rates can be brought down if the courts impose harsher sentences on convicted felons.

In addition to dissatisfaction with the courts' response to crime, the public expresses discontent with several aspects of court administration. In a nationwide survey of U.S. residents in 1995, the majority of respondents indicated that allowing six months to pass from arrest to trial, expensive lawyers, and expensive courts were current problems in the court system (Myers 1996). These findings replicate findings from two decades earlier. Further, the public is strongly opposed to the practice of plea bargaining. To members of the public, negotiated pleas are simply a means by which offenders escape deserved punishment.

Ethicality and Treatment

Studies over the past few decades have found that the majority of the public has a positive impression of the ethical standards of the police and the courts. Nationwide polls show that over half of the respondents in all ethnic groups express a great deal of respect for the police, believe that the police are helpful and friendly, and feel that the police respond quickly to calls for assistance. Individuals from different ethnic backgrounds, however, disagree about two issues. First, less than one-third of Hispanic Americans and African Americans (compared with almost half of the Caucasian Americans) believed that the police are very honest and maintain ethical standards. Second, only about a third of African Americans believe that the police treat people fairly, whereas over half of Hispanic Americans and Caucasian Americans hold this view.

One of the most widely publicized acts of official misconduct is the use of excessive force by police officers. A poll conducted in 1991 found that a greater number of Americans believed that police brutality occurred more frequently then than it had three decades earlier. In 1965, 9 percent of respondents believed that police brutality was a problem in their area, whereas 35 percent responded this way in 1991. A nationwide survey of U.S. residents conducted in 1995 found that many Americans believed the use of excessive force by the police was a problem. Race was the most important predictor: fewer Caucasian Americans than African Americans and Hispanic Americans believed that the police often use excessive force. Consistent with prior surveys, two-thirds of African Americans and over half of the Hispanic Americans in the 1995 survey thought that excessive use of force by the police was a problem. Under half of the Caucasian Americans held this view (Huang and Vaughn 1996). Younger respondents, urban dwellers, and liberal respondents also were more likely to perceive excessive force as a problem. Most Caucasians and African Americans, however, support the use of deadly force when persons suspected of rape or robbery are attempting to escape police custody. However, fewer African Americans than Caucasians support the use of deadly force to stop persons suspected of burglary (Cullen et al. 1996).

Fairness of Decision Making and Decisions

Most respondents hold a very positive view of the procedures local and U.S. Supreme Court justices follow when making a decision. For example, the majority of respondents in a nationwide survey of U.S. residents believed that local courts and the U.S. Supreme Court made decisions in a fair way, made decisions only after reviewing all the relevant information, gave interested citizens an opportunity to express their views, and considered all sides before making decisions (Gibson 1989). A 1995 nationwide survey of U.S. residents also found that few respondents believed that disregarding defendants' rights was a problem in the courts (Myers 1996). This finding is consistent with several prior surveys, which indicate the majority of the populace thinks the court places too much emphasis on defendants' rights and should be more concerned about crime prevention and the effective prosecution of cases. However, once again people from different ethnic backgrounds disagree: the majority of African Americans indicated that disregarding defendants' rights was a problem, whereas less than one-third of Caucasians perceived this to be a problem (Myers 1996).

For several decades, the public's dissatisfaction with the police and the courts has centered around perceptions they are biased in favor of wealthy, Caucasian defendants. In a review of research conducted in the 1960s and 1970s, Sarat (1977) noted that the perception of unequal justice is one of the most pervasive in the United States. Similar results emerge from national surveys in Canada, Great Britain, France, and Germany (see Roberts 1992). Perceptions of an advantage for the wealthy occur presumably because Americans conclude that the wealthy can hire better attorneys. This view may have been reinforced by the coverage of the Simpson trial, in which the defendant was represented by several famous defense attorneys. The high-profile media cases such as the Rodney King case and direct experience of being subjected to unjustified stops by the police may contribute to perceptions of ethnic discrimination.

Substantial disagreement among ethnic groups also exists about whether low-income individuals and ethnic minorities receive less equitable outcomes. For example, consistent with prior surveys, a 1995 nationwide survey found that most Americans believed that differential treatment of the poor by the courts was a problem, and African Americans and Hispanic Americans were more likely to indicate this was a problem (Myers 1996). Moreover, this same survey found that most African Americans and Hispanic Americans, but only one-third of Caucasians, believed that differential treatment of minorities was a problem in the courts. In a number of polls conducted in the early 1990s, a substantial majority of African Americans (more than two-thirds) also have indicated that the police were tougher on African Americans, whereas less than half of Caucasian Americans and Hispanic Americans held this belief.

Demographic Variation in Evaluations of
Police and Court

The two most consistent and strongest predictors of attitudes toward the police are ethnicity and age. Ethnic minorities and younger respondents hold less favorable views of the police. Age and ethnicity, however, are less consistently related to attitudes toward local courts and the Supreme

Court. Age is unrelated to beliefs about whether local courts or the Supreme Court uses fair decision-making procedures. Studies have found mixed results for the relationship between race and attitudes toward the Supreme Court. However, race is not related to views about fair procedures of local courts or honesty of local judges. Race does substantially affect perceptions of whether courts give equal treatment to all citizens.

The Role of Experience in Shaping Public Support for Police and Courts

The public has little knowledge of the court system at either the local or the Supreme Court level. Does direct experience with the court raise or lower peoples' evaluations? Several studies in the 1960s and 1970s suggested that the more knowledgeable people were about how the court actually functioned, the less satisfied they were with court performance. A nationwide survey in 1978 (Yankelovich, Skelly, and White, Inc. 1978) indicated that dissatisfaction centers around court administration. The more knowledgeable individuals believed that several problems occurred frequently: they believed that delays of at least six months from arrest to trial were common, that trials were expensive, and that the number of judges was insufficient to handle the caseload of the courts. Individuals with limited knowledge and those with extensive knowledge held similar views about the fairness of the courts' decision making and decisions.

Is satisfaction with the police and the courts grounded entirely in prior beliefs, or does the actual behavior of authorities shape public evaluations? Several longitudinal studies have addressed this question. Research in both the United States and England suggests that prior beliefs shape peoples' views of their treatment, but the actual conduct of authorities also matters. For example, in England, police made an effort to send the message that they were concerned about and valued sexual assault victims, but they exerted less effort to send this message to victims of physical assault. This police action led to positive results: sexual assault victims were more satisfied with the police handling of their case than were physical assault victims, even after removing the effects of victim's gender, victim's familiarity with the offender, and agreement or disagreement between police and victim about how to proceed (Shapland, Willmore, and Duff 1985).

Do direct positive or negative encounters with the police or courts influence the public's diffuse support for these institutions? Diffuse support refers to the amount of goodwill and respect toward the institution (Easton 1965). Prior research found that the fairness of procedures in specific experiences had more influence on diffuse support than did the fairness or favorability of the outcome (Tyler 1990). Prior studies have consistently found that direct experiences involving procedural unfairness lowered support for the police and courts. Research, however, has produced mixed results on whether positive direct experiences raise support for the police and courts.

Support for the Jury as a Decision-Making Body

Trial by jury is a cornerstone of the criminal justice systems in the United States, Canada, the United Kingdom, and many other countries. Indeed, in the United States, trial by jury is guaranteed by the Sixth Amendment of the Constitution. Surveys of the general public as well as jurors reveal the deep public attachment to the concept of trial by jury. Almost nine out of ten respondents supported the continued presence of juries in the criminal justice system. Surveys have shown that most Americans would prefer a jury trial if they were a victim of a crime or were accused of a crime. Almost all respondents preferred a jury trial over a bench trial for murder cases, but less than half preferred a jury trial for shoplifting cases (MacCoun and Tyler 1988). The majority of respondents believed that compared with trial by judge, trial by jury was more accurate, more thorough, more likely to minimize bias, and more likely to represent minorities. Although the public expresses disagreement and discontent with jury verdicts in certain high-profile cases such as the acquittals of the officers charged with using excessive force against Rodney King, the public continues to support the jury system based on the perceived fairness of the process. The widespread dismay over the verdict in the Simpson trial may have dampened some of this public enthusiasm for juries.

The strong degree of public support for the jury system is consistent with a public preference for adversarial versus inquisitorial justice. An important line of research has addressed the domain of procedural justice (see Thibault and Walker 1975). Respondents in several countries have been asked to choose between an adversarial system, in which theoretically equal adversaries represent the two sides of a dispute, and an inquisitorial system, in which court-appointed attorneys assist the investigating magistrates. People from the United States, France, Great Britain, and Germany prefer adversarial over inquisitorial procedures for handling their disputes.

Sentencing

Sentencing attracts more public interest (and criticism) than any other criminal justice issue. For this reason, pollsters have repeatedly posed questions about attitudes toward sentencing in general, and the death penalty in particular. Surveys of public attitudes toward capital punishment have been conducted for over sixty years. In addition, there is a wealth of academic research on attitudes toward punishment; accordingly, we know more about public opinion regarding punishment than about any other issue.

Purposes of Sentencing

Many surveys have asked the American public to identify the purposes of sentencing offenders. As is the case with judges, the public does not favor one purpose to the exclusion of all others. When asked to rate the importance of different objectives, respondents give high ratings to most objectives. For example, in 1989, 79 percent of Americans rated deterrence as very important, but almost as many (72 percent) endorsed rehabilitation to the same degree. However, two sentencing purposes appear to lie at the heart of public attitudes: deterrence and desert. The public expects the sentencing system to deter offenders, and a principal source of disappointment is that the sentencing process has not had the effect of lowering crime rates. Equally if not more important to public views is the notion of desert. Central to the just deserts philosophy of sentencing is the principle of proportionality between crime seriousness and sentence severity. Research shows that the severity of sentences derived from the public correlates significantly with the seriousness of the crimes for which they are imposed. When the two purposes (deterrence and desert) are placed in opposition, it would appear that the public is more influenced by retributivism than utilitarianism. In contrast to many previous polls, the most recent national survey on this issue, conducted in 1995, showed clear differentiation between the sentencing purposes. Over half the respondents identified retribution as the most important sentencing purpose. There was far less support for the utilitarian goals. Rehabilitation was supported by 21 percent, while deterrence and incapacitation each attracted 13 percent of the sample (Gerber and Engelhardt-Greer 1996). This may reflect a recent shift in the public mood away from crime control considerations and toward retributive sentencing.

After the seriousness of the offense, the offender's criminal record is the most important variable influencing public sentencing preferences. In this respect, the public is consistent with state and federal sentencing guideline systems, many of which assign a great deal of importance to an offender's criminal history. This would suggest that the public is strongly supportive of recidivist statutes such as the "three-strikes" legislation contained in the federal 1994 crime bill. When asked directly whether they support such legislation, three-quarters of Americans respond affirmatively (Maguire and Pastore 1995, Table 2.35). However, more refined research reveals important limits to the public support for recidivist legislation and habitual offender sentencing provisions (see Finkel et al. 1996). In addition, it is clear that people tend to endorse "three-strikes" laws because they have the worst-case offender in mind. They think of an offender who has been convicted of a serious felony for the third time. They are unaware that for many offenders the third, triggering offense is not always very serious.

Attitudes Toward Sentence Severity

This qualification on public support for "three-strikes" laws echoes throughout the public opinion literature. The one-shot survey can provide only a very imperfect measure of community sentiment. The same is true for other issues such as sentence severity and capital punishment. When responding to a poll, most people state that sentences are too lenient and say that they endorse the death penalty. However, there are clear boundaries to public support for harsher sentencing and the death penalty. This conclusion has been sustained by research in the United States and elsewhere.

When people respond to surveys that ask a single, simple question, they have in mind the worst kind of offender. Questions relating to the death penalty, for example, are more likely to provoke images of a serial killer like Wayne Gacy or Ted Bundy than a more typical case of murder. Researchers have accordingly compared "sentences" derived from a sample of the public with sentences imposed in court. Such comparisons are difficult to make. Nevertheless, a consistent result from most studies is that the public is no more severe than judges (e.g., Diamond and Stalans 1989). This finding is consistent with public opinion research in other countries, including Great Britain, Canada, and Australia (Hough 1996; see Roberts and Stalans 1997 for a review). These results often come as a surprise to criminal justice professionals and policy makers, who tend to overestimate the punitiveness of the public sentiment. This has been demonstrated in several places. To take just one example, a 1985 survey found that fewer than one-quarter of criminal justice decision makers believed that the public would support the use of alternatives to incarceration. In fact, public surveys in the state (Michigan) found that fully two-thirds of respondents approved of the use of such sentencing alternatives.

Capital Punishment

According to polls, approximately three-quarters of the American public support the death penalty (71 percent in 1995). In fact, with the exception of a few polls conducted in the 1960s, support has been at or near this level since the first survey on this topic was conducted in 1936 (see Zeisel and Gallup 1989). However, there are many categories of murder for which the public oppose the imposition of the death penalty. Public support for the death penalty is restricted to certain offenses and certain kinds of offenders. For example, most states have felony murder provisions. However, the public does not favor the execution of individuals

convicted of murders committed during the commission of another offense such as robbery. The public's position on capital punishment and
felony murder cases shows that people can make sophisticated distinctions in terms of the relative culpability of offenders. They reject a law
that favors the imposition of the death penalty on all offenders convicted
of murder. Members of the public appear interested in establishing degrees of culpability—between offenders who set out to kill and others
who set out to commit a crime but end up becoming accessories to a
homicide. Underlying the public's position on this topic may be a sense
of fairness in the allocation of punishments. People see the essential unfairness of punishing accessories and principals with the same degree of
severity. Although the Supreme Court has ruled that it is not unconstitutional to execute juvenile offenders and mentally deficient offenders, the
public is opposed to the execution of both these categories of offender.
This is an area in which community sentiment and criminal justice practice are clearly at odds.

One final research initiative relating to the death penalty has consequences for public attitudes toward many criminal justice issues. A number of studies have measured public support for the death penalty before
and after respondents have been given information about the administration and effects of the death penalty. Research along these lines has
shown that the public is relatively uninformed about the manner in
which the death penalty is administered, and that shifts in attitudes occur when subjects are "informed" rather than naive. A slight majority of
the public still favors the death penalty, but the level of support is significantly attenuated. A 1995 nationwide survey of U.S. residents asked
both proponents and opponents of the death penalty whether certain information would cause them to alter their original position. About half of
the supporters of the death penalty indicated that they were more likely
to oppose the death penalty for mentally retarded offenders and if innocent people are subjected to the death penalty (Longmire 1996). Once
again there are parallels in other areas of criminal justice. When members
of the public read a brief newspaper account of a sentence, they are usually critical, and favor a harsher sentence. However, when provided with
a fuller account of the case, including details about the offense, the judicial reasoning behind the sentence, and so forth, people are more likely
to perceive the sentence as being appropriate (e.g., Roberts and Doob
1990).

The general lesson is clear: if researchers wish to know exactly where
the public stands, respondents must be given sufficient time and information to come to an informed decision. Unfortunately, pollsters have
yet to fully appreciate this obvious point. They continue to conduct simplistic polls that can generate spurious interpretations of community sentiment. As long as this continues, there are clear dangers for criminal justice policy development.

Parole

Parole has not received the same degree of attention from researchers as sentencing. Nevertheless, it is clear where Americans stand on the issue. As with some other criminal justice topics such as sentencing, they appear to strongly support the underlying principle for certain offenders but are opposed to the way they believe the parole system functions. A poll conducted in 1984 found that over four-fifths of the public endorsed the view that parole was useful in both deterring offenders and promoting reintegration (Jamieson and Flanagan 1986). However, most people also feel that parole is granted both to too many inmates and too soon into the sentence. Over 80 percent of Americans favor making parole more difficult to obtain. A comparable percentage is opposed to granting parole a second time to inmates who have previously been granted parole for a serious crime (Flanagan 1996).

An important issue for the public relates to the effect of parole on sentences of imprisonment. The public is aware that in states with parole, terms of imprisonment do not correspond to the sentences imposed in court. The issue of truth in sentencing is of particular concern when people consider life imprisonment. A British survey found that nine out of ten Britons wanted a life sentence to mean that the inmate would never be released from prison, and there is little doubt that Americans feel the same way. There may be more consensus on this issue than on any other in the area of sentencing.

Several parallels exist between attitudes toward parole and attitudes toward sentencing. First, it is clear that, as with questions dealing with sentencing, people have a concrete image of an offender when they respond to the issue of parole. In both areas, people tend to think of violent or recidivist offenders. Second, while Americans strongly support parole for nonviolent offenders, the level of support declines when they are asked for their reactions to parole for violent felons. In other words, they favor a two-track policy. People are supportive of alternatives to incarceration, and parole, for nonviolent offenders, but they favor imprisonment and flat-time sentencing for violent offenders. Finally, it is worth noting that people tend to be far more punitive (favoring the use of incarceration and opposing parole) when asked a general question. When asked to sentence a specific offender, however, or to decide whether a specific inmate should be granted parole, members of the public are more flexible and liberal than the results of simple polls would suggest (Doob and Roberts 1983).

Juvenile Justice

Along with the public in other Western nations, Americans share a concern about juvenile crime. Public attention to juvenile crime has been growing for years, stimulated in part by high-profile incidents such as the murder of five-year-old Jamie Bulger by two ten-year-olds. Although this crime occurred in England, it received widespread international coverage, and there have since been other cases of homicide involving very young persons in North America. In 1990, 47 percent of Americans surveyed endorsed the view that juvenile crime had increased. By 1993, this percentage had risen to 64 percent. As with other criminal justice issues, this perception is an exaggeration of the magnitude of the problem. People know little about juvenile crime trends or juvenile justice statistics. In 1988, four-fifths of the public stated that the juvenile crime rate had increased, although in reality there had been a decline. In a comparable way, research in California found that only 17 percent of the public in that state was aware of the punitive sentencing trends at the juvenile level. As with crime at the adult level, people perceive (in the absence of any supportive evidence) the lenient justice response as being in large part responsible for increases in juvenile crime rates.

Americans are divided in their views regarding the most appropriate way to respond to juvenile crime. The majority of Americans support the concept of rehabilitation as a goal of juvenile justice. Almost three-quarters of Americans polled in 1988 agreed that it is more important to emphasize rehabilitation for juveniles than for adults (Steinhart 1988). The 1995 National Crime and Justice Survey found that while only 21 percent of the public endorsed rehabilitation as the most important sentencing objective for adults, the percentage endorsing rehabilitation rose to 50 percent when the question related to the sentencing of juvenile offenders (Gerber and Engelhardt-Greer 1996). As well, they are opposed to legal provisions that result in the automatic transfer of juvenile defendants to the adult court system. Although many states have created statutes that require adult trials for all juveniles accused of murder or felony one crimes, research has demonstrated that these laws run contrary to community sentiment (Stalans and Henry 1994). At the same time, the public does support transferring juvenile offenders with serious criminal histories to adult court.

Although Americans feel that sentences for juveniles are too lenient, most members of the public share the opinion that penalties for juveniles should be more lenient than for adults convicted of the same crimes. Over 80 percent of the polled public disagreed with the assertion that juveniles convicted of serious property crimes should be sentenced in the same way as adults. Finally, it is worth pointing out an important parallel between sentencing preferences at the juvenile level and the adult level. Earlier we noted that when people state that sentences should be harsher for adults, they have specific individuals in mind: recidivist, violent offenders. The same phenomenon emerges at the level of juvenile justice. Sprott (1996) found that the majority of people who believed that sentences for juveniles were too lenient were also thinking of violent juveniles with a history of prior violent offending. In contrast, respondents who stated that they were thinking of all offenders were far more likely to believe that sentences are appropriate.

Gun Control

Most Western nations are concerned about the proliferation of firearms, particularly handguns. The debate over legislating gun control has been around for years, but it became particularly visible as the Congress debated passage of the so-called Brady Bill. In the United States the problem is particularly acute, in light of the fact that guns are easily accessible. The Bureau of Alcohol, Tobacco and Firearms has estimated that Americans own over 200 million firearms, almost one gun for every adult. The large number of privately owned firearms sets America apart from many other Western nations. This fact has obvious consequences for public attitudes toward gun control legislation: Americans are significantly less enthusiastic than Canadians or Western Europeans about legislating tighter controls on the acquisition of firearms.

The American public does not see gun control legislation as a solution to the problem of violent crime. When asked to identify the most important causes of violent crime, only 8 percent identified the availability of guns. Although most people see the easy availability of guns as a contributing factor, only 9 percent believed that gun control was the most important step that could be taken to reduce the violent crime rate. Gun control appears to rank far below other methods of controlling violent crime, such as crime prevention programs and harsher sentences for convicted felons.

Nevertheless, surveys conducted over the past twenty years have found that the majority of Americans favor stricter laws to regulate the acquisition of firearms. Over this period, an average of 65 percent of respondents have favored stricter controls. The most important piece of federal gun control legislation was passed in 1993. The Brady Handgun Violence Prevention Act receives the overwhelming support of the public: 90 percent of nonowners and almost as many owners endorsed the bill (Moore and Newport 1994). In terms of specific restrictions, the most popular option (supported by four-fifths of those sampled) was a law that would require potential purchasers to obtain a permit from police prior to purchasing a weapon. Almost as many people endorse the idea of a mandatory waiting period to allow authorities sufficient time to check the applicant's criminal antecedents, and the same percentage supports a law requiring the registration of handguns (Moore and Newport 1994). Far fewer people (only one-third of the sample) supported other gun control proposals such as permitting lawsuits against the police when it appears that they conducted an insufficiently thorough check. There is strong support for legislation that would deny certain categories of individuals access to firearms. Almost 90 percent of Americans favor barring juveniles from purchasing a gun, and almost as many support a bar against gun ownership for persons with criminal records.

Conclusions

It is difficult to summarize the research literature on a topic as vast and diverse as public opinion and crime. Nevertheless, some themes emerge repeatedly across a number of subjects. First, the public in America (and elsewhere) is generally quite sophisticated in its reactions to crime and criminal justice. Whether the issue is the sentencing of offenders convicted of murder, the transfer of juveniles to adult court, or the allocation of criminal justice expenditures, the public often makes complex distinctions when responding to researchers' questions. This is true even though the knowledge base on which the public draws is frequently poor.

The fact that public knowledge of criminal justice is sketchy at best should be borne in mind by those who interpret the results of surveys, particularly large-scale polls that pose relatively simple questions. We would argue that no opinion poll should be reported without at least some discussion of what the public knows about the issue in question, as well as information about the limitations of the research methodology. Without such contextual information, pollsters can easily misinterpret the views of the community. The most obvious example concerns the insanity defense. Without the data showing how misinformed people are, it would be tempting to conclude that they favor abolition of the defense. They do not; in this case people are simply reacting to their (mis)perception of the way the defense works.

The public holds several misconceptions about offenders and crime rates. The distorted presentation of crime in the media, which focuses on the most severe and atypical offenses and offenders, creates the public's misconceptions about crime. The public overestimates the proportion of violent crime and the number of offenders who will reoffend. The public also has limited knowledge about the legal system and about specific criminal laws. These misconceptions affect public judgments about crime seriousness, as well as public views about judicial sentencing of adult and juvenile offenders. Thus, polls that ask simple, abstract questions and do not provide details of offenders and offenses may often obtain data that distort the public's true position on an issue.

Much more research is needed on public knowledge about crime, the legal system, and legislative statutes. In addition, we know little about public views of the jury system, and how verdicts from high-profile cases affect support for the jury system as an institution. For example, we have noted that large numbers of Americans were shocked at the jury's speedy acquittal of O. J. Simpson. Did this decision undermine support for the jury among such members of the public? If so, how lasting was this effect? Additional research also needs to examine how direct negative and positive experiences influence support for the police and courts.

In several areas, public sentiment is contrary to the media's portrayal of public desires and to legislators' beliefs about what the public desires. The public is more lenient toward sentencing adult criminal offenders than the mandatory minimum sentences allow. The public also does not support the automatic waiver statutes that require trying all juveniles who are charged with a specific felony as an adult. In other areas, public sentiment is consistent with legislative statutes. The public supports the Brady Bill and other minor restrictions on gun control such as requiring the registration of handguns.

Ethnic background is one of the most consistent predictors of public opinion across several issues. It is strongly related to public attitudes toward the police, perceptions of the equality of treatment, ratings of the absolute seriousness of crimes, and support for the death penalty. However, it is not consistently related to views about the honesty of the court or crime seriousness. African Americans hold less favorable views of the fairness and honesty of the police, and they believe that lower-income individuals and ethnic minorities receive less equitable outcomes from the police and the courts. These findings suggest that ethnic differences may occur through differential experience with authorities and socialization about authorities, and may not be a product of ethnic identity. Thus, individuals from different ethnic backgrounds may hold the same values, which contributes to their agreement about crime seriousness and views of the court's ethicality.

References

California Assembly Committee on Criminal Procedure. 1975. "Public Knowledge of Criminal Penalties." In *Perception in Criminology*, edited by R. Henshel and R. Silverman. Toronto: Methuen.

Cintron, M., and W. Johnson. 1996. "The Modern Plague: Controlling Substance Abuse." In *Americans View Crime and Justice*, edited by T. Flanagan and D. Longmire. Thousand Oaks, Calif.: Sage.

Cullen, F. T., L. Cao, J. Frank, R. H. Langworthy, S. L. Browning, R. Kopache, and T. J. Stevenson. 1996. "Stop or I'll Shoot: Racial Differences in Support for Police Use of Deadly Force." *American Behavioral Scientist* 39:449–60.

Diamond, S. S., and L. J. Stalans. 1989. "The Myth of Judicial Leniency in Sentencing." *Behavioral Science and the Law* 7:73–89.

Doble, J., and J. Klein. 1989. *Punishing Criminals: The Public's View*. New York: Edna McConnell Clark Foundation.

Doob, A. N., and J. V. Roberts. 1983. *Sentencing: An Analysis of the Public's View*. Ottawa: Department of Justice Canada.

Easton, D. 1965. *A Systems Analysis of Political Life*. Chicago: University of Chicago Press.

Federal Bureau of Investigation. 1995. *Crime in the United States—1994*. Washington, D.C.: U.S. Government Printing Office.

Finkel, N. J., S. T. Maloney, M. Z. Valbuena, and J. Groscup. 1996. "Recidivism, Proportionalism, and Individualized Punishment." *American Behavioral Scientist* 39:474–87.

Fishkin, J. 1995. *The Voice of the People*. New Haven, Conn.: Yale University Press.

Flanagan, T. 1996. "Reform or Punish: Americans' Views of the Correctional System." In *Americans View Crime and Justice*, edited by T. Flanagan and D. Longmire. Thousand Oaks, Calif.: Sage.

Flanagan, T., and D. Longmire, eds. 1996. *Americans View Crime and Justice*. Thousand Oaks, Calif.: Sage.

Flanagan, T., and K. Maguire, eds. 1990. *Sourcebook of Criminal Justice Statistics, 1989*. Washington, D.C.: U.S. Department of Justice, Bureau of Justice Statistics.

Gallup Poll Monthly. 1993. Princeton, N.J.: The Gallup Poll.

Gerber, J., and S. Engelhardt-Greer. 1996. "Just and Painful: Attitudes Toward Sentencing Criminals." In *Americans View Crime and Justice*, edited by T. Flanagan and D. Longmire. Thousand Oaks, Calif.: Sage.

Gibson, J. L. 1989. "Understanding of Justice: Institutional Legitimacy, Procedural Justice, and Political Tolerance. *Law and Society Review* 23:467–96.

Hindelang, M. 1975. *Public Opinion Regarding Crime, Criminal Justice and Related Topics*. Washington, D.C.: U.S. Department of Justice.

Hough, M. 1996. "People Talking About Punishment." *Howard Journal* 35:191–214.

Huang, W. S., and M.S. Vaughn. 1996. "Support and Confidence: Public Attitudes Toward the Police." In *Americans View Crime and Justice*, edited by T. Flanagan and D. Longmire. Thousand Oaks, Calif.: Sage.

Jamieson, K., and T. Flanagan, eds. 1986. *Sourcebook of Criminal Justice Statistics, 1985*. Washington, D.C.: U.S. Department of Justice, Bureau of Justice Statistics.

Knowles, J. 1987. *Ohio Citizen Attitudes Concerning Crime and Criminal Justice*. Columbus, Ohio: Governor's Office of Criminal Justice Services.

Longmire, D. R. 1996. "Americans' Attitudes About the Ultimate Weapon: Capital Punishment." In *Americans View Crime and Justice*, edited by T. Flanagan and D. Longmire. Thousand Oaks, Calif.: Sage.

MacCoun, R. J., and T. R. Tyler. 1988. "The Basis of Citizens' Perceptions of the Criminal Jury: Procedural Fairness, Accuracy, and Efficiency." *Law and Human Behavior* 12:333–52.

Maguire, K., and A. Pastore, eds. 1995. *Sourcebook of Criminal Justice Statistics, 1994*. Washington, D.C.: U.S. Department of Justice, Bureau of Justice Statistics.

Moore, D., and F. Newport. 1994. "Public Strongly Favors Stricter Gun Control Laws." *Gallup Poll Monthly* 340:18–22.

Myers, L. B. 1996. "Bringing the Offender to Heel: Views of the Criminal Court." In *Americans View Crime and Justice*, edited by T. Flanagan and D. Longmire. Thousand Oaks, Calif.: Sage.

Rauma, D. 1991. "The Context of Normative Consensus: An Expansion of the Rossi/Berk Consensus Model, with an Application to Crime Seriousness." *Social Science Research* 20:1–28.

Roberts, J. V. 1992. "Public Opinion, Crime, and Criminal Justice." In *Crime and Justice: A Review of Research,* vol. 16, edited by Michael Tonry. Chicago: University of Chicago Press.

————. 1994. *Public Knowledge of Crime and Criminal Justice.* Ottawa: Department of Justice Canada.

Roberts, J. V., and A. N. Doob. 1990. "News Media Influences on Public Views of Sentencing." *Law and Human Behavior* 14:451–68.

Roberts, J. V., and L. J. Stalans. 1997. *Public Opinion, Crime and Criminal Justice.* Boulder, Colo.: Westview Press.

Roberts, J. V., and N. R. White. 1986. "Public Estimates of Recidivism Rates: Consequences of a Criminal Stereotype." *Canadian Journal of Criminology* 28:229–41.

Robinson, P. H., and J. M. Darley. 1995. *Justice, Liability and Blame: Community Views and the Criminal Law.* Boulder, Colo.: Westview Press.

Sarat, A. 1977. "Studying American Legal Culture: An Assessment of Survey Evidence." *Law and Society Review* 11:427–88.

Schroot, D. 1990. *Ohio Citizen's Attitudes Concerning Drug and Alcohol Use and Abuse.* Columbus, Ohio: Governor's Office of Criminal Justice.

Scott, J. E., and F. Al-Thakeb. 1977. "The Public's Perceptions of Crime: A Comparative Analysis of Scandinavia, Western Europe, the Middle East, and the United States." In *Contemporary Corrections: Social Control and Conflict,* edited by C. Ronald Huff. Beverly Hills, Calif.: Sage.

Sellin, T., and M. Wolfgang. 1964. *The Measurement of Delinquency.* New York: Wiley.

Shapland, J., J. Willmore, and P. Duff. 1985. *Victims in the Criminal Justice System.* Brookfield, Vt.: Gower.

Skogan, W. G. 1996. "The Police and Public Opinion in Britain." *American Behavioral Scientist* 39:423–34.

Sprott, J. 1996. "Understanding Public Views of Youth Crime and the Youth Justice System." *Canadian Journal of Criminology* 38:271–91.

Stalans, L. J., and G. T. Henry. 1994. "Societal Views of Justice for Adolescents Accused of Murder: Inconsistency Between Community Sentiment and Automatic Legislative Transfers." *Law and Human Behavior* 18:675–96.

Steinhart, D. 1988. *Public Attitudes on Youth Crime.* San Francisco: National Council on Crime and Delinquency.

Thibault, J., and L. Walker. 1975. *Procedural Justice: A Psychological Analysis.* Hillsdale, N.J.: Erlbaum.

Tyler, T. R. 1990. *Why People Obey the Law: Procedural Justice, Legitimacy, and Compliance.* New Haven, Con.: Yale University Press.

Yankelovich, D. 1991. *Coming to Public Judgment.* Syracuse, N.Y.: Syracuse University Press.

Yankelovich, Skelly, and White, Inc. 1978. *The Public Image of Courts.* Williamsburg, Va.: National Center for State Courts.

Zeisel, H., and G. Gallup. 1989. "Death Penalty Sentiment in the United States." *Journal of Quantitative Criminology* 5:285–96.

2

Minorities, Crime, and Criminal Justice

JANET L. LAURITSEN & ROBERT J. SAMPSON

The study of minority differences in delinquency, crime, victimization, and criminal justice processing has produced a rapidly expanding area of research, including meta-analyses and reviews. In this chapter, we summarize the "big picture"—that is, the one suggested by robust findings that hold up across disparate investigators, forms of data collection, and analytical methods. To organize this vast literature, we present first the empirical findings on minority experiences with crime as victims and offenders. Our focus is on general patterns of involvement in crime, the extent to which they are disparate by race and ethnicity, and the theoretical explanations most important for understanding these patterns. Next we summarize the research on minorities in the criminal justice system, emphasizing the conditions under which differential treatment is most likely to occur and the various theoretical approaches for understanding such differences. Finally, we conclude with our own interpretations of the literature on minorities, crime, and criminal justice, and discuss what we believe are the important implications for future theoretical development and research.[1]

We recognize that the meaning of the term *minority* is socially and historically bound. Currently in the United States, the term is used to refer to racial and ethnic groups that are of non-European ancestry. Americans tend to use the term *race* to refer to skin pigmentation or color, whereas *ethnicity* indicates the countries from which a person's ancestors can be traced. For various historical and social reasons, definitions of race in the United States have included five categories that are assumed to be mutually exclusive: white; black; American Indian, Eskimo, or Aleut; Asian or Pacific Islander; or other. Although *ethnicity* is a term with many more categories, criminological data on ethnicity typically refer to whether or not a person is of "Hispanic" origin.[2] According to the U.S. Census Bureau, Hispanics are self-identified persons of Spanish-speaking origin, who may belong to any one of the above race groups.

Numerous ongoing political and scholarly debates challenge the usefulness and implications of these terms in American society.[3] Space limitations prevent us from discussing these issues in detail here. However, we do sympathize with those who argue that by highlighting minority differences in crime and criminal justice, such work has the potential to exacerbate problems of institutional racism and stereotyping. Nonetheless, profound race and ethnic differences currently exist in the representation of citizens in the criminal justice system. In our view, knowledge about the origins and consequences of these discrepancies is preferable to deliberate neglect and nescience.

In this chapter we focus primarily on "black" and "white" comparisons. The reason stems from a lack of crime data that consistently classify information for Hispanics and non-Hispanics, and for groups such as Asians and Native Americans. Where available and appropriate, data reflecting these latter classifications are presented. However, most analytical work on disparity and discrimination in crime and criminal justice has focused on comparisons between blacks and whites.

Unfortunately, the types of crime covered here are also limited by the availability of data and thus are not fully representative of the landscape of criminal behavior. For many crimes (e.g., white-collar), sound data permitting systematic study of race and ethnic variations simply do not exist. Race and ethnic comparisons are usually possible for violence (i.e., murder, rape, robbery, and assault) and property crime (e.g., larceny and burglary), and hence we focus most of our discussion on these types of incidents. Of these two general crime types, we give more attention to violence. As seen in the following, minority disparities in both criminal victimization and offending tend to be greatest among violent crimes. With homicide mortality rates now at least eight times higher among young black males than young white males (National Center for Health Statistics 1995, Table 6), a sense of public urgency has emerged regarding high levels of violence in the black community. We recognize that by focusing our attention on violence, we are in danger of overemphasizing the importance of race or ethnicity in crime and underemphasizing its influence on criminal justice decision making. We thus compensate for this bias by including relevant information on other crime types—particularly drug offending—and on sanctioning, both of which have received much recent attention in the United States (see Blumstein 1993a; Tonry 1995).

Minority Disparities in Victimization

What are the risks of criminal victimization to persons of different racial and ethnic groups? Are these differences stable over recent time periods? Answers to these questions are primarily obtained through analyses of data from the National Crime Victimization Survey (NCVS), an ongoing survey conducted by the Bureau of Justice Statistics that is designed to measure the extent of personal and household victimization in the United States. The primary advantage of the NCVS is the ability to estimate victimizations that may be incorrectly reflected in official police data (e.g., because of nonreporting of incidents or arrest bias). The NCVS therefore constitutes the best available data source on the risk of victimization for various population subgroups. The exception, of course, is for homicide, where most estimates are based on vital statistics and the FBI's supplemental homicide reports, which provide a racial classification of homicide victims.

Victimization research over the past two decades has consistently shown that the distribution of victimization varies systematically across different subgroups. In terms of race, both the NCVS and national vital statistics confirm that blacks are disproportionately the victims of violent crimes. Differences in homicide risk are the most pronounced; in 1992, blacks were between six and seven times more likely than whites to become victims of homicide (Federal Bureau of Investigation 1993b; National Center for Health Statistics 1995). The differentials in gun-related homicide are particularly striking. In 1990, the peak death rate for young black males was more than ten times greater than the peak death rate for young white males—140 versus 12 per 100,000 (Fingerhut 1993).

Estimates of lifetime homicide risk further underscore minority disparities. By 1990, black women and black men were, respectively, four and six times more likely than white women and white men to be murdered in their lifetime (Reiss and Roth 1993, p. 63). Estimates of lifetime homicide risk for American Indians, blacks, and whites are presented in Reiss and Roth (1993, pp. 62–63).[4] The lifetime risk for black males is 4.16 per 100, followed by American Indian males (1.75), black females (1.02), white males (0.62), American Indian females (0.46), and white females (0.26). Reiss and Roth also note that less than one-fourth of Americans' lifetime risk for homicide is incurred before the twenty-fifth birthday. Consequently, the very high homicide rates among young black males in particular must be considered in conjunction with the higher homicide rates of black males at all ages.

For violent victimization, both rate and trend differences by race are substantial. Beginning about 1990, reported rates of violence among blacks increased to their highest level ever recorded in the NCVS. This trend parallels the trajectory of homicides measured by death records—that is, increases in homicide rates since the mid- to late 1980s in the United States have been racially selective. In particular, while white rates remained relatively stable, the firearms death rate among young black males more than doubled from 1984 to 1988 alone (see Fingerhut et al. 1991).

As with homicide, blacks report greater levels of robbery victimization than do whites (Bureau of Justice Statistics 1994a). Over the past two decades, the risk of robbery for blacks has been between two and three times greater than that for whites. While the risk of robbery among whites has declined slightly in the last twenty years, the risk among blacks fluctuates more from year to year and shows no clear evidence of decline. Unlike homicide and robbery, rates of assault victimization for blacks and whites tend not to differ consistently, although the majority of assaults reported by blacks tend to be incidents of aggravated assault versus simple assaults among whites (Bureau of Justice Statistics 1994a).

Significant race differentials do not exist for personal theft victimizations (larceny with or without contact; Bureau of Justice Statistics 1994b), even though rates of household theft victimization (burglary, larceny, and motor vehicle theft) are somewhat higher for blacks than for whites. While the risk of property victimization has declined over the last two decades for both blacks and whites, race differentials in household crime have remained stable.

In sum, the available race-specific data on victimization suggest the following pattern. Blacks suffer much higher rates of personal violence and homicide victimization than do whites. Racial differences are reduced considerably in magnitude when it comes to household crimes and especially personal theft victimizations. And, while overall victimization trends are similar for blacks and whites, robbery and homicide are the two notable exceptions. Recent trends for these two violent crimes show greater increases for blacks than whites.

The NCVS reports only limited information on ethnic differences in victimization risk, restricted mainly to Hispanic versus non-Hispanic comparisons. According to the NCVS, Hispanics experience higher rates of violent and household victimization than do non-Hispanics (39.6 vs. 35.3, and 265.6 vs. 204.5, respectively). Conversely, non-Hispanics report somewhat higher rates of personal theft (80.3) than do Hispanics (74.9; Bureau of Justice Statistics 1990). Government vital statistics on mortality provide another source of information, reporting that the leading cause of death among Hispanics aged fifteen to twenty-four is homicide (National Center for Health Statistics 1995).

Caution is warranted in interpreting the Hispanic versus non-Hispanic comparisons. Recall that available data sources do not treat race and ethnicity as mutually exclusive categories. Because Hispanics may be designated as either black or white (or "other"), compositional effects may account for the higher NCVS victimization rates of Hispanics. Since NCVS summary reports do not present differences between non-Hispanic whites, non-Hispanic blacks, and Hispanics, it is difficult to know precisely to what degree these subgroups differ in their risks of victimization. Similarly, while vital statistics data permit within-group rankings of cause of death information, they do not allow between-group comparisons (e.g., Hispanics vs. blacks) because the population estimates necessary to determine the denominator for such rate calculations are uncertain.

Minority Disparities in Offending

Estimating minority differences in criminal offending also requires careful consideration of methodological issues. Because this topic has received extensive consideration elsewhere (e.g., Hindelang, Hirschi, and

Weis 1979; Elliott and Ageton 1980), we mention only a few of these qualifications here. A primary concern is whether the findings are based on official, self-report, or victimization data. Findings based on official data such as arrest statistics published in the FBI's *Uniform Crime Reports* (*UCR*) are limited to the extent that apprehended offenders differ in some way from nonapprehended offenders (e.g., because of racial bias). Findings based on self-report surveys may be limited either by the respondents' intentional or unintentional errors in reporting or by sampling restrictions (e.g., an almost exclusive focus on juveniles or males, or on minor offenses). Although NCVS victimization data provide information on the *perceived* race of offenders, government tabulations are available only for those incidents involving a single or lone offender, and face-to-face contact between the offender and victim. It is also known that victims of personal crimes underreport certain types of incidents, especially those involving victimization by family members and acquaintances (Hindelang 1978). These sources of error are all relevant to inferences about minorities and crime. Consequently, we emphasize convergent findings across various data sources.

Because nationwide arrest reports are available by race but not by ethnicity, we begin by describing the most recent race-specific arrest data by offense type (see Maguire and Pastore 1995, Table 4.11). Although whites are arrested for the majority of all crimes (approximately 67 percent), blacks and American Indians are most likely to be overrepresented in arrest statistics reported in the *UCR*. For example, in 1993, blacks accounted for 31 percent of total arrests yet constituted 12 percent of the population, and American Indians accounted for 1.1 percent of total arrests while constituting 0.8 percent of the population. Asians appear to be underrepresented in arrest statistics; they account for 1.0 percent of all arrests yet make up 2.9 percent of the population.

The relationship between race and offending is not the same for all crime types—there are certain offenses for which each subgroup is overrepresented. For instance, whites are disproportionately arrested for driving while intoxicated, and Asians are overrepresented in arrests for illegal gambling. Blacks are consistently more likely to be arrested for crimes of violence (Federal Bureau of Investigation 1993a). In 1993, blacks accounted for 45 percent and 50 percent of adult and youth arrestees, respectively, for murder, rape, robbery, and aggravated assault (Maguire and Pastore 1995, pp. 389–90). The crime in which blacks are most overrepresented is robbery, accounting for 62 percent of arrestees in 1993. In general, relative to population numbers, blacks are approximately six times more likely to be arrested for violent crimes than are whites (Federal Bureau of Investigation 1993a).

Overall trends in index-crime arrest rates for the last twenty-five years show a fluctuating pattern, peaking in the early 1990s for adults and in the mid-1970s and early 1990s for juveniles (Federal Bureau of Investigation 1993a). When race-specific trends in these crimes are compared, black and white differentials in arrest rates have *decreased* somewhat over time. For instance, in 1965, arrest rates for black juveniles and adults were 3.1 and 5.7 times those of white juveniles and adults. By 1992, black-white differences in index-crime arrest rates had dropped to 2.3 and 4.9 (Federal Bureau of Investigation 1993a). Such comparisons are problematic, however, because Hispanics have increased their proportionate representation in the population and tend to report "white" as their race status. Because Hispanics on average have higher arrest rates than whites, part of the convergence of white-black patterns may be artifactual.

An important exception to these time trends appears for drug-related arrests. From 1965 through the early 1980s, blacks were approximately twice as likely as whites to be arrested for a drug-related offense (Blumstein 1993a; Tonry 1995). Following the federal government's initiation of the "war on drugs," black arrest rates skyrocketed, while white arrest rates increased only slightly. By the end of the 1980s, blacks were more than five times more likely than whites to be arrested for drug-related offenses. It is highly unlikely that these race differences are a simple reflection of substance use patterns, since drug arrests grew at a time when national self-report data showed that drug use was declining among both blacks and whites. Rather, these differences reflect the government's targeting and enforcement of specific types of drug use and trafficking (Blumstein 1993a; Tonry 1995).

The obvious critique of official arrest statistics is that police decisions to arrest may be racially biased. In an important investigation of this issue, Hindelang (1978) examined whether black overrepresentation in official violent crime arrest data was explained by differential involvement or by differential selection into the criminal justice system via police arrests. He compared the distribution of arrestees by race from the 1974 *UCR* to the distribution of perceived race of offenders derived from the 1974 NCVS and found that most of the race difference in arrest rates for violence is explained by greater black involvement in personal crimes. Data for violent crime as reported in the 1992 NCVS and the 1992 *UCR* arrest data show much the same pattern. However, there is a slightly larger discrepancy between the two estimates of racial involvement. The 1992 NCVS estimate of black involvement in robbery is 56 percent, whereas the *UCR* data report that 61 percent of robbery arrestees were black (see Maguire and Pastore 1995, Table 4.11; Bureau of Justice Statistics 1994b, Table 45). However, these differences between *UCR* and NCVS data do not necessarily indicate increasing selection bias in robbery arrests over time. If race-specific robbery incidents are more or less likely to involve two or more offenders now than they were twenty years ago, such changes would influence the estimates of the percent black involvement in *UCR* and NCVS data.

The limitations of using NCVS victim reports to validate *UCR* arrest data have been discussed elsewhere (e.g., Hindelang 1981; Reiss and

Roth 1993), including the concern that race estimates are based solely on NCVS victim reports of lone-offender crimes and that the NCVS data produce incidence rates instead of prevalence rates. The problem of relying on NCVS incidence rates is significant if each racial subgroup contains different proportions of repeat offenders. The *UCR* data share a similar limitation in that they use arrest incidents (and not offenders) as the unit of analysis. The potential inaccuracy of victims' reports of an offender's race in the NCVS data is also a concern, but is not considered a serious limitation (Hindelang 1981).

The majority of violent crimes are also known to be *intra*racial. In other words, whites tend to victimize other whites and blacks tend to victimize other blacks more so than would be expected based on chance (Sampson 1984; O'Brien 1987). Racial crossover is especially rare in nonfelony homicides—that is, killings that occur without an accompanying felony such as a robbery or rape (Cook 1987). Because nonfelony homicides tend to be nonstranger homicides, and the routine activities and residences of blacks and whites are in large part segregated, these findings are perhaps not surprising. By contrast, felony homicides (e.g., robbery-murders) are more likely to be interracial than are nonfelony homicides because they typically involve strangers (Block 1985; Cook 1987). In felony homicides, as in robberies, black offenders are more likely to victimize whites than white offenders are to victimize blacks (Wilbanks 1985). Yet this is to be expected, since blacks are the smaller subgroup and have more chances to interact with whites. Variations in the relative sizes of the black and white populations thus explain the patterning of interracial violence (Sampson 1984).

Attempting to overcome the limitations of both official statistics and victimization surveys, self-reported delinquency data have been brought to bear on the race question. Many studies, especially those in the 1960s and 1970s, found little or no differences in self-reported offending among juveniles of different racial and ethnic groups (see Hindelang, Hirschi, and Weis 1979, 1981). One reaction to these findings was to attribute racial bias to official statistics. Others posited methodological explanations. In particular, Hindelang, Hirschi, and Weis (1979) argued that self-report studies typically measure less serious forms of common delinquency, whereas official arrest statistics showing race differentials refer primarily to serious index crimes. Nationally representative self-report data on serious offense involvement for adults are rare, and cross-method validation has not been completed (Elliott 1994). Consequently, the evidence to date suggests that the domains of behavior are not isomorphic across data sources.

Another critique, in many ways more powerful, is that the self-report method itself is differentially valid by race, with blacks underreporting certain offenses at higher rates than whites. In a reverse record check analysis, Hindelang, Hirschi, and Weis found that black males were least likely to self-report offenses recorded by the police (e.g., 33 percent of total offenses known and 57 percent of serious offenses known to police were not self-reported by black males; 1981, p. 172). Hence the issue of differential validity according to race is of concern when the behavior elicited by the self-report method is a serious offense such as burglary, robbery, or weapons violation.

Advances in self-report methodology have resolved some of these issues. For example, Elliott and Ageton (1980) have shown that police and self-report differences in the relationship, between race and offense involvement are to a large extent a function of delinquency instrument construction, especially item content and response set range. Race (and class) differences in delinquency are most likely to be found at the high end of the frequency continuum and for serious offenses like robbery where police contacts are more likely (see also Elliott 1994). Thus, the magnitude of the race-crime correlation is higher in official statistics than in self-reported data. Although limitations exist for both official and self-report data, it appears that race differences in offending as recorded in arrest reports and victimization surveys "reflect real differences in the frequency and seriousness of delinquent acts" (Elliott and Ageton 1980, p. 107). Precise estimates of the magnitude of these differences are unavailable.

Explaining Minority Disparities in Victimization and Offending

Few criminological theories have been designed a priori to explain minority differences in victimization or offense involvement. Rather, most theories have been applied post hoc to race-related differences. To explain minority differences in victimization, lifestyle and routine activities perspectives offer similarity of personal associations and proximity to offender groups as the leading hypotheses, while subcultural explanations emphasize the role of shared norms conducive to the use of violence for resolving disputes. However, neither perspective has been empirically validated as an explanatory hypothesis of race differentials; lifestyle-routine activities research has not been able to account for race differences by controlling for individual-level factors (such as lifestyle or choice of associates), and key methodological difficulties must to be resolved before it can be said whether differences in normative contexts account for racial differences in violent victimization (for more discussion see Sampson and Lauritsen 1997).

Most theories of minority-related differences in offending have also been applied in a post hoc manner. Some of the more common hypotheses used to explain racial differences in offending are based on constitutional, family socialization, subculture of violence, and economic inequality/deprivation theories (Wilson and Herrnstein 1985). Yet each of these traditional theories is unsatisfactory. Constitutional explanations are problematic on empirical grounds—the variations within any minority group are much greater than variations between them. Although there is good evidence that family socialization influences children's delinquency and aggressive behavior patterns, there is no consistent evidence that factors such as lack of supervision and erratic/harsh discipline account for race differences in crime when socioeconomic conditions are taken into account. Subcultural explanations of group variation in offending have yet to show that black and white Americans differ significantly in their attitudes and values regarding crime, or that these differences in values have an independent influence on offending disparities. Finally, research emphasizing access to the legitimate economic system typically finds that race differences persist even after controlling for socioeconomic status (Kornhauser 1978). Relatedly, other minority groups, such as Chinese, Japanese, and Hispanic, have also experienced economic exclusion but exhibit much lower offending rates than those of blacks. It is unknown to what extent structural or cultural differences account for lower offending rates among other ethnic groups, but clearly socioeconomic status and deprivation alone are inadequate explanations.

An alternative is to focus on the macro- and community-level underpinnings of the race-crime connection. Unlike the dominant tradition in criminology that seeks to distinguish offenders from nonoffenders, the macrosocial or community-level explanation asks what it is about community structures and cultures that produces differential rates of crime. As such, the goal of macrolevel research is not to explain individual involvement in criminal behavior but to isolate characteristics of communities, cities, or even societies that lead to high rates of criminality.

In their classic work, *Juvenile Delinquency and Urban Areas*, originally published in 1942, Shaw and McKay (1969) argued that three structural factors—low economic status, racial/ethnic heterogeneity, and residential mobility—led to the disruption of local community social organization, which in turn accounted for variations in crime and delinquency rates. Subsequent research has generally supported these findings, although most research on violence has examined racial composition—usually percentage black—rather than racial heterogeneity per se. Also, while descriptive data show that percentage black is positively and strongly correlated with rates of violence, multivariate research has yielded conflicting findings; some studies report a sharply attenuated effect of race once other factors are controlled, whereas others report that the percentage black effect remains strong (Sampson and Lauritsen 1994, pp. 53–54).

Whether or not race has a direct effect on crime rates, Sampson and Wilson (1995) argue that a key to solving the race-crime conundrum is traceable to Shaw and McKay (1969). Arguably the most significant aspect of Shaw and McKay's research was their demonstration that high rates of delinquency persisted in certain areas over many years, regardless of population turnover (but see Bursik and Webb 1982). More than any other, this finding led them to reject individual-level explanations of delinquency and to focus instead on the processes by which delinquent patterns of behavior were transmitted in areas of social disorganization and weak social controls (Shaw and McKay 1969, p. 320). This community-level orientation led Shaw and McKay to an explicit contextual interpretation of correlations between race/ethnicity and rates of delinquency. Their logic was set forth in a rejoinder to a 1949 critique by Jonassen, who had argued that ethnicity had direct effects on delinquency. Shaw and McKay countered:

> The important fact about rates of delinquents for Negro boys is that they too, vary by type of area. They are higher than the rates for white boys, but it cannot be said that they are higher than rates for white boys in comparable areas, since it is impossible to reproduce in white communities the circumstances under which Negro children live. Even if it were possible to parallel the low economic status and the inadequacy of institutions in the white community, it would not be possible to reproduce the effects of segregation and the barriers to upward mobility. (1949, p. 614)

Shaw and McKay's insight raises interesting questions that are still relevant today. First, to what extent do rates of black crime vary by type of ecological area? Second, how do the community conditions of blacks and whites compare? The first question is crucial, for it signals that blacks are not a homogeneous group any more than are whites. It is racial stereotyping that assigns to blacks a distinct or homogeneous character, allowing simplistic comparisons of black-white group differences in crime. As Shaw and McKay thus recognized, the key point is that there is heterogeneity among black neighborhoods that corresponds to variations in crime rates. To the extent that the structural sources of variation in black crime are not unique, rates of crime by blacks should also vary with social-ecological conditions in a manner similar to whites.

To disentangle the contextual basis for race and crime requires racial disaggregation of both the crime rate and the explanatory variables of theoretical interest. This approach was used in research that examined racially disaggregated rates of homicide and robbery by juveniles and adults in over 150 U.S. cities in 1980 (Sampson 1987). These results showed that the scarcity of employed black males relative to black women was directly related to the prevalence of families headed by females in black communities (see also Wilson 1987). Black family disruption, in turn, was significantly related to rates of black murder and robbery—especially by juveniles—independently of income, region, density, city size, and welfare benefits. The finding that family disruption had a stronger relationship with juvenile violence than adult violence, in conjunction with the inconsistent findings of previous research on individual-level delinquency and broken homes, supports the idea that family structure is related to macrolevel patterns of social control and guardianship, especially regarding youth and their peers (Sampson and

Groves 1989). Moreover, the results offer a clue as to why unemployment and economic deprivation have had weak or inconsistent direct effects on violence rates in past research—joblessness and poverty appear to exert much of their influence indirectly through family disruption.

Despite a large difference in mean levels of family disruption between black and white communities, the percentage of white families headed by a female also had a significant positive effect on white juvenile and white adult violence. In fact, the relationships for white robbery were in large part identical in sign and magnitude to those for blacks. As a result, the influence of black family disruption on black crime was independent of alternative explanations (e.g., region, income, population density, age composition) and could not be attributed to unique factors within the black community because of the similar effect of white family disruption on white crime.[5]

Black communities are thus not homogeneous in either their crime rates or their levels of social organization. Moreover, the fact that the considerable variations in black violence are explained by generic features of urban social structure goes some way toward dispelling the idea of a unique "black" subculture. The sources of violent crime appear to be remarkably similar across race and to be rooted instead in the structural differences among communities, cities, and regions in economic and family organization. It is important to note, however, that a structural perspective need not dismiss wholesale the relevance of culture. Rather, cultural influences may be triggered by structural features of the urban environment (for further elaboration, see Sampson and Wilson 1995).

Bearing in mind the general similarity of black-white variations in crime by social-ecological context, consider the next logical question. To what extent are blacks as a group differentially exposed to criminogenic structural conditions (Sampson and Wilson 1995)? More than forty years after Shaw and McKay's assessment of race and urban ecology, we still cannot say that blacks and whites share a similar environment—especially with regard to concentrated urban poverty. Moreover, broader changes over the last three decades have produced increases in urbanization, inequality, and class segregation that have had a disproportionate impact on blacks (see, e.g., Massey 1996). In 1970, approximately one of every five poor blacks lived in high-poverty areas. By 1980, this proportion had nearly doubled to two of five (Wilson et al. 1988), and by 1990 the percentage of blacks living in such poor areas had increased to slightly more than two of five (Kasarda 1993). Comparably, in 1990 about one in ten poor whites lived in very poor neighborhoods (Kasarda 1993).

These patterns illustrate the degree to which poverty and race are concentrated, and thus confounded, in U.S. cities (Wilson 1987; Land, McCall, and Cohen 1990). Analogous to research on urban poverty, simple comparisons between poor whites and poor blacks are confounded with the fact that poor whites reside in areas that are ecologically and economically very different from those of poor blacks. Hence, observed relationships involving race and crime are likely to reflect unmeasured advantages in the ecological niches that poor whites occupy (Wilson 1987, pp. 58–60).

Partial evidence supporting this interpretation is found in Peeples and Loeber's (1994) contextual analysis of ethnic difference in delinquency using data from a longitudinal study of male juveniles in Pittsburgh. Consistent with past research, African-American youth exhibited much higher rates of delinquency, especially serious crime, than did whites. However, when the "underclass" status of the subject's residential neighborhood was controlled, racial and ethnic differences in delinquency disappeared. Perhaps most striking, the delinquency rates of African-American youth living in non-underclass neighborhoods were largely equivalent to those of whites living in non-underclass areas. Although Peeples and Loeber were unable to study whites in disadvantaged areas, their findings support the idea that community context helps us interpret the race-crime association.

Sampson and Wilson (1995) and others have argued that the increasing concentration of poverty in urban neighborhoods produces a wide range of negative consequences for the members of those communities. These concentration effects, reflected in a range of outcomes from degree of labor-force attachment to social dispositions, are created by the constraints and opportunities that the residents of inner-city neighborhoods face in terms of access to jobs and job networks, involvement in quality schools, availability of marriageable partners, and exposure to conventional role models.

While the concentration of poverty has been fueled by macrostructural economic changes related to deindustrialization, political factors have operated to increase the concentration of poor blacks in urban areas. Bickford and Massey (1991, p. 1035) have argued that public housing represents a federally funded, physically permanent institution for the isolation of black families by class, and therefore must be considered an important structural constraint on ecological area of residence (see also Massey and Denton 1993). When segregation and concentrated poverty represent structural constraints embodied in public policy and historical patterns of racial subjugation, concerns that individual differences (or self-selection) explain community-level effects on violence are considerably diminished (see also Tienda 1991; Sampson and Lauritsen 1994).

Boiled down to its essentials, then, linking theories of community social organization with research on political economy and urban poverty suggests that both historic and contemporary macrosocial forces (e.g., segregation, migration, housing discrimination, structural transformation of the economy) interact with local community-level factors (e.g., residential turnover, concentrated poverty, family disruption) to impede the social organization of inner cities (Sampson and Wilson 1995). This viewpoint focuses attention on the proximate structural characteristics and mediating processes of community social organization that help to explain crime and its connection to race in contemporary American cities, while at the same time recognizing the larger historical, social, and political forces shaping local communities.

The logic of this theoretical perspective suggests that the profound changes in the structure of urban minority communities in the 1970s and early 1980s may hold a key to understanding recent increases in violence. Research has consistently demonstrated the early onset of delinquency and its relative long-term stability (Sampson and Laub 1992). These differences among individuals that are highly stable over time imply that to understand the present high crime rates among adolescents and young adults we must come to grips with their earlier life experiences.

Considered from this perspective, the roots of urban violence among today's fifteen- to twenty-one-year-old cohorts may be attributable in part to childhood socialization that took place in the late 1970s. Indeed, large increases in crime among youth—but not adults—in the late 1980s and early 1990s may be a harbinger of things to come as the massive secular changes that transformed the context of childhood socialization in the 1970s and 1980s are now beginning to exert their influence on those entering the peak years of offending. In short, massive social change in American inner cities during the 1970s and continuing into the 1980s may be a partial clue to unraveling recent race-related patterns of urban violence.

Minorities in the Criminal Justice System

Criminologists have produced a voluminous body of research on racial differences in criminal justice processing. This research, conducted over the course of several decades, has addressed the major decision points in the justice systems of the United States. Rather than trying to make sense of every study, we consult state-of-the-art reviews of extant research to provide an overview of major findings. In some cases we consider seminal or recent studies in detail, but for the most part we highlight general patterns and trends established in multiple works.[6]

We begin with the institution that suspects are likely to first encounter—the police. Earlier we noted that, for the most part, racial differences in arrests for index crimes are attributable to differential involvement of blacks in criminal offending (Hindelang 1978, 1981). However, two other dimensions to policing influence race disparities: police-citizen encounters when offenses are minor, and police shootings of civilians.

The literature in the area of police discretion to arrest originated with research on juvenile encounters. Such analyses have shown that when offenses are minor, officers often rely on the juvenile's demeanor or attitude to determine how to handle the case (e.g., Black and Reiss 1970). The suspect's race is relevant insofar as it serves as a proxy for police perceptions of disrespectful attitudes, which increase the likelihood of an official write-up or arrest.

Extending the scope of analysis to adults, Smith (1986) found that neighborhood context influenced the willingness of police to arrest and to use coercive authority. Smith reports that the police are more likely to arrest and to use or threaten force against suspects in racially mixed or minority neighborhoods. Within these areas, however, a suspect's race did not serve as an additional predictor of police behavior. Smith (1986) found that black suspects in white neighborhoods are treated less coercively than black suspects in minority neighborhoods, and that white suspects are treated similarly regardless of neighborhood. In other words, neighborhood characteristics such as racial composition and socioeconomic status interact with suspect characteristics to predict arrest and use of coercive authority.

Another line of inquiry into police-citizen encounters involves the overrepresentation of blacks in police shootings of criminal suspects. In analyses of data from New York City, Fyfe (1982) reports that blacks were more likely than whites to be shot by police because they were disproportionately involved in armed incidents at the time of the encounter. By contrast, a similar analysis based on data from Memphis showed that blacks were no more likely than whites to be involved in armed incidents but were more likely to be shot by police while retreating. Similar to the interaction effects noted earlier, the importance of a suspect's race for predicting police use of deadly force appears to vary across social context (e.g., neighborhoods, cities).

Following arrest, the next major decision point in the criminal justice system is whether an accused will be held in detention pending case disposition or instead will be released on bond. Prior studies of bail decision making tend to show that the direct influence of race on pretrial release is insignificant once a defendant's dangerousness to the community (e.g., offense charged, prior record, weapons use) and prior history of failing to appear at trial are controlled. Nonetheless, contrary findings exist. Albonetti et al. (1989) show that race is related to bail decision making in complex, interactive ways. In a study of male defendants across ten federal court districts, they report that defendants with lower levels of education and income receive significantly more serious pretrial release decisions, controlling for community ties and dangerousness. Moreover, they report that white defendants benefited more from the nonlegal effects of education and income than did black defendants with equal resources. Prior record also had a stronger negative effect on pretrial release decisions among blacks than it did for whites. On the other hand, dangerousness and offense severity had stronger influences on bail decisions for whites. While these results reveal that under certain conditions whites are treated more severely at pretrial release, they also suggest that white defendants "receive better returns on their resources" (Albonetti et al. 1989, p. 80).

The consensus of prior research on conviction likelihood goes against a simplistic discrimination thesis—in the aggregate, blacks tend to be convicted less often than whites (e.g., Wilbanks 1987; Petersilia 1983). In studies that control for type of crime, there also is no consistent evidence that minorities are disadvantaged at the stage of criminal conviction. As Burke and Turk conclude, "race has no independent effect upon case dispositions" (1975, pp. 328–29; see also Petersilia 1983, p. 19; Langan 1994).

Research on the sentencing of criminal defendants has generated the greatest interest among those studying racial disparities. The earliest research on this topic suggested that bias against minority defendants was significant. These studies included the research of Sellin, in particular his well-known conclusion that "equality before the law is a social fiction" (1935, p. 217). However, these early studies were rather crude methodologically, and almost none controlled for legally relevant variables in assessing race effects. Reviews of subsequent, more sophisticated research converge in their conclusion that the effect of race in prior studies was in large part a proxy for the legally relevant factor of prior criminal record (see Hagan 1974; Kleck 1981; Hagan and Bumiller 1983). Once the latter was controlled, the direct effect of race on sentencing was for the most part eliminated. That is, the racial disparities in sentencing (e.g., to prison) arose from the greater proportional involvement of minorities in criminal behavior, which in turn was reflected in longer and/or more serious prior records.

Hagan's and Kleck's exhaustive reviews, covering dozens of empirical studies, were largely responsible for creating what has been labeled by Wilbanks (1987) as the "no discrimination thesis" (NDT). However, as Zatz (1987, p. 73) argues, many criminologists quoting the NDT glossed over two of the caveats that these reviews emphasized. One caveat was that race might have a cumulative effect on sentencing outcomes by operating indirectly through other variables that disadvantage minority group members. The second was that race may interact with other factors to influence decision making. We shall return to these arguments later, but here it is important to clarify that the NDT refers specifically to the insignificant *direct* effects of race on sentencing.

Discrimination research of the late 1970s and 1980s was more methodologically refined, including corrections for selection bias (the nonrandom selection of defendants into the system) and specification error (the omission of explanatory variables; see Zatz 1987, p. 75). Researchers also investigated historical changes in sentencing practices and expanded the focus to types of crimes not previously emphasized (e.g., drug processing). For example, Peterson and Hagan (1984) found that the sentencing of black drug offenders in New York depended on shifting symbolic contexts—minor black dealers were treated more leniently than white counterparts, but major black dealers ("kingpins") were treated more harshly than white dealers because they were perceived as inflicting further harm on an already victimized nonwhite population (1984, p. 67). Other research began to examine racial bias in terms of the victim's status rather than the offender's. This line of inquiry suggests that defendants are more harshly sentenced by the criminal justice system when the victim is white rather than black (Myers 1979).

Findings from this period of research are not easily summarized, for many studies uncovered contradictory findings or began to explore hypotheses tangential to the NDT. For example, some researchers found expected patterns of discrimination, while others did not, and a fair number of studies showed that whites received harsher sentences than blacks in certain cases (Zatz 1987, pp. 74–78). Overall, though, the thrust of research during this era seemed to shift away from the NDT to the idea that there is *some* discrimination, *some* of the time, in *some* places. These contingencies undermine the broad reach of the NDT, but the damage is not fatal to the basic argument that race discrimination is not pervasive or systemic in criminal justice processing.

In our view, the most promising contemporary research on sentencing investigates the salience of macrosocial contexts. Primed by earlier studies suggesting interaction and contextual effects, scholars began to design research that could disentangle the role of macrolevel contexts (e.g., country poverty, urbanism) on sentencing. One of the best studies to date of race and sentencing—Myers and Talarico's *Social Contexts of Criminal Sentencing* (1987)—emerges from this concern. Analyzing more than 26,000 felons convicted between 1976 and 1985 in the forty-five judicial courts of Georgia, the authors employ state-of-the-art statistical methods to counter the limitations of previous research. The findings are complex, and, as the title would indicate, Myers and Talarico report that sentencing outcomes vary significantly as a function of social context (e.g., urbanization of the county). This pattern supports the contingency model of criminal sentencing and rejects the idea that invariant laws or modes of behavior characterize the criminal justice system as a whole.

In terms of race, however, the data analyzed by Myers and Talarico (1987) clearly failed to support the thesis of systemic race discrimination, even in a contingent manner. As they summarize the book's key findings:

> The analyses reported in previous chapters indicate that there is little system-wide discrimination against blacks in criminal sentencing. This is an important finding, because general charges of discrimination are common not only in some interpretations of conflict theory, but also in some sectors of the popular and academic press. To be sure, the absence of evidence of system-wide discrimination does not mean that all courts and judges are color blind in the administration of criminal law. Interactive analysis revealed context-specific patterns of discrimination. Importantly, however, there were many instances in which blacks received disproportionately lenient punishment. (Myers and Talarico 1987, pp. 170–71).

National summaries of felony cases in the seventy-five most populous urban areas come to a similar conclusion (Langan 1994). Following a felony charge, blacks were prosecuted at a slightly lower rate than were whites (66 percent vs. 69 percent) and were slightly less likely to be convicted than were whites (75 percent vs. 78 percent). However, of those convicted, blacks were more likely to be sentenced to prison (51 percent vs. 38 percent), although there were no significant differences in length of sentence. Langan reports that the observed race differences in imprisonment were the result of type of crime, prior record, and aggregation effects. Black defendants were more likely to be charged with robbery or another violent offense and were more likely to have had prior felony convictions. Examination of aggregation effects revealed that black defendants were also more likely to be adjudicated in jurisdictions that were more likely to hand out prison sentences. Yet, within these harsher jurisdictions, blacks were treated no differently than whites. Based on these findings, Langan concludes that the "Justice Department survey provides no evidence that, in the places where blacks in the United States have most of their contacts with the justice system, the system treats them more harshly than whites" (1994, p. 51). However, the potential contextual relationship between race and the decision to imprison was not further explored.

A recent review of thirty-eight studies on race and sentencing by Chiricos and Crawford (1995) also concludes that blacks are more likely than whites to be sentenced to prison but experience no differences in sentence length. These authors also investigated the contextual characteristics of the samples used in each of the studies and found that, controlling for crime type and prior record, black defendants were more likely to receive imprisonment in high unemployment areas, in places where blacks constitute a larger percentage of the population, and in the South. This meta-analysis strongly suggests the plausibility of contextual influences on the decision to imprison. As they argue, "[T]hese specific structural contexts lend support to the premise that criminal punishment not only responds to crime, but responds as well to specific community conditions" (1995, p. 301). Thus, unlike Langan's dismissal of race differences in the decision to imprison, Chiricos and Crawford focus explicitly on the context in which these decisions are most likely to occur. The implication of such research is that multiple-jurisdiction or comparative studies are essential to disentangling racial disproportionality.

National-level data also have been used to account for the racial disproportionality of U.S. prison populations (e.g., Blumstein 1982, 1993b; Crutchfield, Bridges, and Pritchford 1994). Generating considerable attention, the seminal article in this area was published by Blumstein in 1982. Using state prison and arrest statistics from 1974 and 1979, Blumstein reported that while blacks represented 43 percent of arrestees, they constituted approximately 49 percent of the prison population. Consequently, he concluded that racial disproportionality in offending explained 80 percent of the racial disproportionality in prison populations.

In an update of this research, Blumstein (1993b) reexamined race disproportionality in light of the enormous growth in U.S. imprisonment since the early 1980s. Following decades of relative stability, the 1990 U.S. incarceration rate was nearly triple that of 1975, and the total number of drug offenders in prison increased nearly tenfold. Despite this unprecedented growth, the 1991 level of racial disproportionality in incarceration rates remained similar to what it had been in 1979 (seven to one), and overall differences in arrests explained slightly less of the disproportionality in the 1991 prison rates (76 percent). However, the importance of the war on drugs becomes particularly pronounced for race differences in incarceration by 1991. For drug offending, differences in drug arrests accounted for only 50 percent of the race disproportionality in drug incarceration. As the distribution of offense types changes in prison populations, it becomes crucial to examine the issue of imprisonment disparity by disaggregating data by crime type as well.

Finally, the ultimate criminal sanction—death—has been the subject of much empirical research and philosophical debate. Research covering the period since the 1976 *Gregg* decision shows that, controlling for type of homicide, it is the race of the victim that appears to significantly influence prosecutors' willingness to seek the death penalty, and judges' and juries' willingness to impose a sentence of death. Black offenders found guilty of murdering white victims are at the highest risk for receiving the death penalty. Offenders (of either race) found guilty of murdering black victims are least likely to receive the death penalty. These differential patterns of risk for the death penalty were found to persist despite stringent controls for the seriousness of the incident (e.g., defendant's deliberation, heinousness of the murder) and other legally relevant factors (see, e.g., Keil and Vito 1989).

Although research on criminal justice processing in the United States is complex and fraught with methodological problems, the weight of the evidence suggests the following. When restricted to index crimes, most individual-level studies have shown that a simple *direct* influence of race on pretrial release, plea bargaining, conviction, sentence length, and the death penalty is small to nonexistent once legally relevant variables (e.g., prior record) are controlled. Racial differentials at these stages of the criminal justice system appear to broadly match the large racial differences in criminal offending. On the other hand, research on the decision to imprison suggests that race does matter in certain contexts. When one controls for crime type and prior record, black defendants in some jurisdictions are more likely to receive a prison sentence than are white defendants. As many have argued (Hagan 1987; Myers and Talarico 1987; Sampson and Laub 1993; Chiricos and Crawford 1995), the key to resolving racial differences in processing may turn in large part on contextual or macrolevel differences. This parallels the arguments made in favor of a community-level interpretation of racial differences in criminal offending.

An important caveat should be emphasized here regarding race or ethnic comparisons for groups other than blacks or whites. While a few studies certainly do exist, we have no extensive empirical basis from which to draw conclusions about other ethnic minorities' experiences with crime or the criminal justice system. It is clear that research is needed on the full array of minority groups that make up an increasingly diverse society.

Explaining Minority Disparities in Criminal Justice

Most criminal justice research has drawn on conflict perspectives to interpret substantive findings (Hagan 1989). A key proposition from conflict theory is that groups that threaten the hegemony of middle- and upper-class rule are more likely to be subjected to intensified social control—more criminalization, more formal processing by the criminal justice system, and increased incarceration—than are groups that are perceived as less threatening to the status quo (see also Brown and Warner 1992). Furthermore, conflict theorists have argued that minorities (especially blacks), the unemployed, and the poor represent such threatening groups (see, e.g., Brown and Warner 1995).

The criticisms of conflict theory are well known. Elites do not form a unitary whole, monopolize decision making, or in fact appear particularly vulnerable to the objective threats of subordinates (Liska 1987; Tittle 1994). Perhaps more damaging, the evidence on personal and property crimes points to legal variables as the prime determinants of criminal justice processing.

Attempting to transcend the limitations of traditional conflict theory, recent work is forging a more contextually nuanced appreciation of minority group threat. While there may indeed be a general consensus in society on core values, it is not the objective level of threat but the symbolic aspect of social conflict that may be the salient feature driving crime control (Myers 1989). For instance, Tittle and Curran (1988) emphasize perceptions of threat that "provoke jealousy, envy, or personal fear among elites" rather than the actual threat these groups represent to reigning political positions. They found differential sanctioning of juveniles in Florida counties depending on the size of the nonwhite population, with the largest discriminatory effects found in juvenile justice dispositions for drug and sexual offenses, which, they argue, "represent overt behavioral manifestations of the very qualities [that] frighten white adults or generate resentment and envy" (1988, p. 52).

These findings are also consistent with a study in Washington State in which nonwhites were sentenced to imprisonment at higher rates in counties with large minority populations (Bridges, Crutchfield, and Simpson 1987). Follow-up interviews with justice officials and community leaders revealed a consistent public concern with minority threat and "dangerousness." With crime conceptualized as a minority problem, leaders openly admitted using race as a code for certain patterns of dress and lifestyles thought to signify criminality. It was decision makers' perceptions of minority problems as ecologically concentrated that seemed to reinforce the use of race as a screen for criminal attribution (p. 356).

In short, recent theory has turned to a macrosociological orientation by focusing on the symbolic and contextual aspects of minority group threat. In this view, "the poor," "the underclass," and "the rabble" (i.e., poor minorities) are perceived as threatening not only to political elites but also to "mainstream America"—middle- and working-class citizens who represent the dominant majority in American society.

The symbolic nature of "underclass" threat seems to be particularly relevant for understanding the "war on drugs" in the United States. Data on arrest rate trends by race show that in 1980 the rate of drug law violations was nearly equal for whites and blacks; however, during the 1980s, white rates declined while black rates increased markedly (Snyder 1992). Juvenile court data show that the number of white youth referred to court for drug law violations declined by 6 percent between 1985 and 1986; the number of referrals for black youth increased 42 percent (Snyder 1990). More generally, Blumstein (1993a) has shown that the dramatic growth in state prison populations during the 1980s was driven in large part by increasing admissions of blacks on drug convictions.

These trends suggest an increasing punitiveness toward drug offenders—especially those perceived to be gang members from a growing underclass population (Jackson 1992). Drawing on a revised conflict theory, Sampson and Laub (1993) argue that the rising concentration of socioeconomic disadvantage corresponds precisely with that population perceived as threatening, and the population at which the war on drugs has been aimed. They found that counties with greater concentrations of underclass poverty and racial income inequality had higher levels of juvenile confinement, especially for drug offenses, and that these effects tended to be larger for black juveniles than for white juveniles. The dual image of "underclass" offenders and the evils of "crack" cocaine thus appears to have triggered a "moral panic" (Goode and Ben-Yehuda 1994; Chiricos and Crawford 1995), further reinforcing a drug war by law enforcement. In sum, while overt racial discrimination at the individual level appears to be weak, a body of recent contextual evidence suggests that a different scenario may be at work for macrolevel variations in juvenile and adult court processing.

Implications for the Future

Our review of the literature on minorities and criminal justice suggests that racial discrimination emerges some of the time at some stages of the system in some locations, but there is little evidence that racial disparities reflect systemic, overt bias on the part of criminal justice decision makers. Rather, the most compelling evidence concerning racial discrimination in the administration of justice involves community and national constructions of "moral panics" and political responses to those contexts. Tonry (1995) points out that the war on drugs was initiated at a time when national drug use patterns had already exhibited a considerable decline. Tonry further argues that the politically charged war on drugs, with its legislative and budgetary emphasis on the type of drug most likely to be used and detected in black disadvantaged urban areas (i.e., "crack" cocaine), could be viewed as racially discriminatory in intent and consequences.

Although overt race discrimination in criminal justice processing appears to be a problem restricted to specific spatial and temporal contexts, the fact remains that racial disparities in serious crimes have reached a critical stage in the United States. Homicide currently is the leading cause of death among young black males and females, and the majority of persons in state and federal prisons are black (Bureau of Justice Statistics 1995). With such enormous disproportionality in sanctioning, it should be of little comfort that most of the disparity is a result of differential involvement in nondrug criminal offending.

We believe that to more fully understand minority disparities in crime and justice, at least four areas are in need of further research. First, it is clear that racial differences in criminal victimization and offending, especially for violence, must be studied from a more complex, multilevel perspective. Prior theory on criminal offending has usually been couched at the level of analysis least likely to yield an understanding of racial differences—the individual. Posing the problem in a contextual framework, on the other hand, suggests that the relationship between race and criminal offending varies substantially across ecological contexts. With few exceptions, criminologists have only recently realized the extent to which correlations between community contexts and crime are confounded with associations between race and crime. Macrolevel analysis thus offers an alternative mode of inquiry into the social bases of race and crime.

Second, the role that formal sanctioning plays in producing cumulative disadvantage across the life course of individuals requires a new agenda of research. The voluminous research on the direct effects of race on conviction, sentencing, and other later stages of adult processing (e.g., imprisonment) appears to have reached a dead end. We know that by the time adults penetrate the justice system to the later stages of sentencing and imprisonment, decision makers rely primarily on prior record and seriousness to dispose of cases. Rather than more studies of adults in the legal versus extralegal mold, research is needed to track offenders backward and forward in time to understand the dynamics of criminal careers and the consequences of criminal justice sanctioning for both individuals and their communities. In particular, attention to the consequences of disproportionate detention and imprisonment must be a priority.

Third, the extent to which crime wars are waged disproportionately against minorities needs to be examined from a contextual, social constructionist perspective (Best 1990; Goode and Ben-Yehuda 1994; Hawkins 1995). As discussed earlier, the recent drug war in the United States has had its greatest effect on the lives of minorities. While drug arrests have declined among whites, they have skyrocketed among blacks. And while "crack" cocaine has generated an intense law enforcement campaign in our nation's black ghettos, "powder" cocaine use among whites is quietly neglected (perhaps even portrayed as fashionable). These differences cannot be attributed solely to objective levels of criminal danger, but rather to the way in which minority behaviors are symbolically constructed and subjected to official social control (Tonry 1995; Chambliss 1995). As conflict theorists argue, the study of race discrimination in sentencing, controlling for crime type, is irrelevant insofar as "moral panics," legislation, and enforcement activities are designed to target the kinds of lifestyles or areas associated with racial minorities. Close attention to how crime is defined and the social construction of social "problems" is necessary to the study of racial disparity in criminal justice (Goode and Ben-Yehuda 1994).

Finally, we encourage the development of theoretical models designed to understand the links between crime, criminal justice, and minority group status. It seems reasonable to argue that perceptions of the fairness of law and criminal justice are related to individuals' stakes in conventional society. Yet more needs to be known about how such perceptions are formed and maintained across various racial and ethnic subgroups, and how experiences with crime and the criminal justice system shape behaviors and community cultures. To be sure, these are only a sampling of the questions that can be asked, but addressing them is a necessary first step toward eliminating racial disparities at all levels of the criminal process.

Notes

1. Our review of the empirical evidence on racial differences in victimization, offending, and criminal justice processing, and our theoretical arguments regarding communities, race, and crime, are largely drawn from three previous papers—Sampson and Lauritsen (1994, 1997) and Sampson and Wilson (1995).

2. This is the current definition of race and ethnicity used by the U.S. Census Bureau. The bureau is likely to change how it measures "race" and "ethnicity" before implementation of the next decennial census.

3. Biological research reminds us that there is no single set of traits that satisfactorily distinguish one group from another.

4. As discussed later, similar estimates based on vital statistics data are unavailable for Hispanics versus non-Hispanics because population estimates by race and ethnicity remain uncertain.

5. There is some recent evidence that black crime rates are related to some

structural features differently than white crime rates (see especially LaFree et al. 1992; Harer and Steffensmeier 1992). However, these studies have been based either on national trends over time or on large macrolevel units (Standard Metropolitan Statistical Areas). More important, the point is not whether all the predictors of white and black crime rates match exactly, but the systematic variation in rates of black violence according to basic features of structural context.

6. Because of space limitations, the role of minority status in juvenile justice processing is not reviewed here.

References

Albonetti, Celesta, Robert Hauser, John Hagan, and Ilene Nagel. 1989. "Criminal Justice Decision Making as a Stratification Process: The Role of Race and Stratification Resources in Pretrial Release." *Journal of Quantitative Criminology* 5:57–82.

Best, Joel. 1990. *Threatened Children*. Chicago: University of Chicago Press.

Bickford, Adam, and Douglas Massey. 1991. "Segregation in the Second Ghetto: Racial and Ethnic Segregation in American Public Housing, 1977." *Social Forces* 69:1011–36.

Black, Donald, and Albert J. Reiss Jr. 1970. "Police Control of Juveniles." *American Sociological Review* 35:63–77.

Block, Carolyn R. 1985. "Race/Ethnicity and Patterns of Chicago Homicide, 1965 to 1981." *Crime and Delinquency* 31:104–16.

Blumstein, Alfred. 1982. "On the Racial Disproportionality of the U.S. States' Prison Population." *Journal of Criminal Law and Criminology* 73:1259–81.

———. 1993a. "Making Rationality Relevant." *Criminology* 31:1–16.

———. 1993b. "Racial Disproportionality of U.S. Prison Populations Revisited." *Colorado Law Review* 64:743–60.

Bridges, George, Robert Crutchfield, and Edith Simpson. 1987. "Crime, Social Structure and Criminal Punishment: White and Nonwhite Rates of Imprisonment." *Social Problems* 34:345–61.

Brown, M. Craig, and Barbara D. Warner. 1992. "Immigrants, Urban Politics, and Policing in 1900." *American Sociological Review* 57:293–305.

———. 1995. "The Political Threat of Immigrant Groups and Police Aggressiveness in 1900." In *Ethnicity, Race, and Crime: Perspectives Across Time and Place*, edited by Darnell Hawkins. Albany: State University of New York Press.

Bureau of Justice Statistics. 1990. *Hispanic Victims, Special Report*. Washington, D.C: U.S. Department of Justice, Bureau of Justice Statistics.

———. 1994a. *Criminal Victimization in the United States, 1973–1992 Trends*. Washington, D.C.: U.S. Department of Justice, Bureau of Justice Statistics.

———. 1994b. *Criminal Victimization in the United States, 1992*. Washington, D.C.: U.S. Department of Justice, Bureau of Justice Statistics.

———. 1995. *Correctional Populations in the United States, 1993*. Washington, D.C.: U.S. Department of Justice, Bureau of Justice Statistics.

Burke, Peter, and Austin Turk. 1975. "Factors Affecting Post-Arrest Decisions: A Model for Analysis." *Social Problems* 22:313–32.

Bursik, Robert J., Jr., and Jim Webb. 1982. "Community Change and Patterns of Delinquency." *American Journal of Sociology* 88:24–42.

Chambliss, William J. 1995. "Crime Control and Ethnic Minorities: Legitimizing Racial Oppression by Creating Moral Panics." In *Ethnicity, Race, and Crime: Perspectives Across Time and Place*, edited by Darnell Hawkins. Albany: State University of New York Press.

Chiricos, Theodore G., and Charles Crawford. 1995. "Race and Imprisonment: A Contextual Assessment of the Evidence." In *Ethnicity, Race, and Crime: Perspectives Across Time and Place*, edited by Darnell Hawkins. Albany: State University of New York Press.

Cook, Philip. 1987. "Robbery Violence." *Journal of Criminal Law and Criminology* 78:357–76.

Crutchfield, Robert, George Bridges, and Susan Pritchford. 1994. "Analytical and Aggregation Biases in Analyses of Imprisonment: Reconciling Discrepancies in Studies of Racial Disparity." *Journal of Research in Crime and Delinquency* 31:166–82.

Elliott, Delbert. 1994. "Serious Violent Offenders: Onset, Developmental Course, and Termination—The American Society of Criminology 1993 Presidential Address." *Criminology* 32:1–21.

Elliott, Delbert, and Suzanne Ageton. 1980. "Reconciling Race and Class Differences in Self-Reported and Official Estimates of Delinquency." *American Sociological Review* 45:95–110.

Federal Bureau of Investigation. 1993a. *Age-Specific Arrest Rates and Race-Specific Arrest Rates for Selected Offenses, 1965–1992.* Washington, D.C.: U.S. Government Printing Office.

———. 1993b. *Uniform Crime Reports for the United States, 1992.* Washington, D.C.: U.S. Government Printing Office.

Fingerhut, Lois. 1993. "The Impact of Homicide on Life Chances: International, Intranational and Demographic Comparison." In *Proceedings of the Second Annual Workshop of the Homicide Research Working Group.* Washington, D.C.: U.S. Department of Justice.

Fingerhut, Lois, J. Kleinman, E. Godfrey, and H. Rosenberg. 1991. "Firearms Mortality Among Children, Youth, and Young Adults 1–34 Years of Age, Trends and Current Status: United States, 1979–88." *Monthly Vital Statistics Report* 39(11):1–16.

Fyfe, James. 1982. "Blind Justice: Police Shootings in Memphis." *Journal of Criminal Law and Criminology* 73:707–22.

Goode, Erich, and Nachman Ben-Yehuda. 1994. "Moral Panics: Culture, Politics, and Social Construction." *Annual Review of Sociology* 20:149–71.

Hagan, John. 1974. "Extra-Legal Attributes and Criminal Sentencing: An Assessment of a Sociological Viewpoint." *Law and Society Review* 8:357–84.

———. 1987. "Review Essay: A Great Truth in the Study of Crime." *Criminology* 25:421–28.

———. 1989. "Why Is There So Little Criminal Justice Theory? Neglected Macro- and Micro-Level Links Between Organization and Power." *Journal of Research in Crime and Delinquency* 26:116–35.

Hagan, John, and Kristen Bumiller. 1983. "Making Sense of Sentencing: A Review and Critique of Sentencing Research." In *Research on Sentencing: The Search for Reform*, edited by Alfred Blumstein, Jacqueline Cohen,

Susan Martin, and Michael Tonry. Washington, D.C.: National Academy Press.

Harer, Miles, and Darrel Steffensmeier. 1992. "The Differing Effects of Economic Inequality on Black and White Rates of Violence." *Social Forces* 70:1035–54.

Hawkins, Darnell. 1995. "Ethnicity, Race, and Crime: A Review of Selected Studies." In *Ethnicity, Race, and Crime*, edited by Darnell Hawkins. Albany: State University of New York Press.

Hindelang, Michael. 1978. "Race and Involvement in Common-Law Personal Crimes." *American Sociological Review* 43:93–109.

———. 1981. "Variations in Sex-Race-Age-Specific Incidence Rates of Offending." *American Sociological Review* 46:461–74.

Hindelang, Michael, Travis Hirschi, and Joseph Weis. 1979. "Correlates of Delinquency: The Illusion of Discrepancy Between Self-Report and Official Measures." *American Sociological Review* 44:995–1014.

———. 1981. *Measuring Delinquency*. Beverly Hills, Calif.: Sage.

Jackson, Pamela Irving. 1992. "Minority Group Threat, Social Context, and Policing." In *Social Threat and Social Control*, edited by Allen E. Liska. Albany: State University of New York Press.

Jonassen, Christen. 1949. "A Reevaluation and Critique of the Logic and Some Methods of Shaw and McKay." *American Sociological Review* 14:608–14.

Kasarda, J. 1993. "Inner-City Concentrated Poverty and Neighborhood Distress: 1970–1990." *Housing Policy Debate* 4:253–302.

Keil, Thomas, and Gennaro Vito. 1989. "Race, Homicide Severity, and Application of the Death Penalty." *Criminology* 27:511–31.

Kleck, Gary. 1981. "Racial Discrimination in Criminal Sentencing: A Critical Evaluation of the Evidence with Additional Evidence on the Death Penalty." *American Sociological Review* 46:783–805.

Kornhauser, Ruth. 1978. *Social Sources of Delinquency: An Appraisal of Analytic Models*. Chicago: University of Chicago Press.

LaFree, Gary, Kriss Day, and Patrick O'Day. 1992. "Race and Crime in Post-War America: Determinants of African-American and White Rates." *Criminology* 30:157–88.

Land, Kenneth, Patricia McCall, and Lawrence Cohen. 1990. "Structural Covariates of Homicide Rates: Are There Any Invariances Across Time and Space?" *American Journal of Sociology* 95:922–63.

Langan, Patrick. 1994. "No Racism in the Justice System." *Public Interest* 117:48–51.

Liska, Allen E. 1987. "A Critical Examination of Macro Perspectives on Crime Control." *Annual Review of Sociology* 13:67–88.

Maguire, Kathleen, and Ann Pastore, eds. 1995. *Sourcebook of Criminal Justice Statistics, 1994*. Washington, D.C.: U.S. Department of Justice, Bureau of Justice Statistics.

Massey, Douglas S. 1996. "The Age of Extremes: Concentrated Affluence and Poverty in the Twenty-First Century." *Demography* 33:395–412.

Massey, Douglas S., and Nancy Denton. 1993. *American Apartheid: Segregation and the Making of the Underclass*. Cambridge, Mass.: Harvard University Press.

Myers, Martha. 1979. "Offended Parties and Official Reactions: Victims and the Sentencing of Criminal Defendants." *Sociological Quarterly* 20:529–40.

———. 1989. "Symbolic Policy and the Sentencing of Drug Offenders." *Law and Society Review* 23:295–315.

Myers, Martha, and Susette Talarico. 1987. *The Social Contexts of Criminal Sentencing.* New York: Springer-Verlag.

National Center for Health Statistics. 1995. "Advance Report of Final Mortality Statistics, 1992." *Monthly Vital Statistics Report,* vol. 43, no. 6, Supplement. Washington, D.C.: U.S. Department of Health and Human Services.

O'Brien, Robert. 1987. "The Interracial Nature of Violent Crimes: A Re-Examination." *American Journal of Sociology* 92:817–35.

Peeples, Faith, and Rolf Loeber. 1994. "Do Individual Factors and Neighborhood Context Explain Ethnic Differences in Juvenile Delinquency?" *Journal of Quantitative Criminology* 10:141—58.

Petersilia, Joan. 1983. *Racial Disparities in the Criminal Justice System.* Santa Monica, Calif.: RAND.

Peterson, Ruth D., and John Hagan. 1984. "Changing Conceptions of Race: Towards an Account of Anomalous Findings of Sentencing Research." *American Sociological Review* 49:56–70.

Reiss, Albert J. Jr., and Jeffrey Roth, eds. 1993. *Understanding and Preventing Violence: Panel of the Understanding and Control of Violent Behavior.* Vol. 1. Washington D.C.: National Academy Press.

Sampson, Robert J. 1984. "Group Size, Heterogeneity, and Intergroup Conflict: A Test of Blau's Inequality and Heterogeneity." *Social Forces* 62:618–39.

———. 1987. "Urban Black Violence: The Effect of Male Joblessness and Family Disruption." American Journal of Sociology 93:348–82.

Sampson, Robert J., and W. Byron Groves. 1989. "Community Structure and Crime: Testing Social Disorganization Theory." *American Journal of Sociology* 94:774–802.

Sampson, Robert J., and John H. Laub. 1992. "Crime and Deviance in the Life Course." *Annual Review of Sociology* 18:63–84.

———. 1993. "Structural Variations in Juvenile Court Processing: Inequality, the Underclass, and Social Control." *Law and Society Review* 27:285–311.

Sampson, Robert J., and Janet L. Lauritsen. 1994. "Violent Victimization and Offending: Individual, Situational, and Community-Level Risk Factors." In *Understanding and Preventing Violence: Social Influences,* vol. 3, edited by Albert J. Reiss Jr. and Jeffrey Roth. Washington, D.C.: National Academy Press.

———. 1997. "Racial and Ethnic Disparities in Crime and Criminal Justice in the United States." In *Ethnicity, Crime, and Immigration: Comparative and Cross-National Perspectives,* edited by Michael Tonry. Chicago: University of Chicago Press.

Sampson, Robert J., and William Julius Wilson. 1995. "Toward a Theory of Race, Crime, and Urban Inequality." In *Crime and Inequality,* edited by John Hagan and Ruth Peterson. Stanford, Calif.: Stanford University Press.

Sellin, Thorsten. 1935. "Race Prejudice in the Administration of Justice." *American Journal of Sociology* 41:212–17.

Shaw, Clifford, and Henry McKay. 1949. "Rejoinder." *American Sociological Review* 14:614–17.

———. 1969. *Juvenile Delinquency and Urban Areas*. Rev. ed. Chicago: University of Chicago Press.

Smith, Douglas A. 1986. "The Neighborhood Context of Police Behavior." In *Communities and Crime*, edited by Albert J. Reiss Jr. and Michael Tonry. Chicago: University of Chicago Press.

Snyder, Howard. 1990. *Growth in Minority Detentions Attributed to Drug Law Violators*. Washington, D.C.: Office of Juvenile Justice and Delinquency Prevention.

———. 1992. *Arrests of Youth, 1990*. Washington, D.C.: Office of Juvenile Justice and Delinquency Prevention.

Tienda, Marta. 1991. "Poor People and Poor Places: Deciphering Neighborhood Effects on Poverty Outcomes." In *Macro-Micro Linkages in Sociology*, edited by Joan Huber. Newbury, Calif.: Sage.

Tittle, Charles R. 1994. "The Theoretical Bases for Inequality in Formal Social Control." In *Inequality, Crime, and Social Control*, edited by George Bridges and Martha Myers. Boulder, Colo.: Westview Press.

Tittle, Charles R., and Debra A. Curran. 1988. "Contingencies for Dispositional Disparities in Juvenile Justice." *Social Forces* 67:23–58.

Tonry, Michael. 1995. *Malign Neglect: Race, Crime, and Punishment in America*. New York: Oxford University Press.

Wilbanks, William. 1985. "Is Violent Crime Intraracial?" *Crime and Delinquency* 31:117–28.

———. 1987. *The Myth of a Racist Criminal Justice System*. Monterey, Calif.: Brooks/Cole.

Wilson, James Q., and Richard Herrnstein. 1985. *Crime and Human Nature*. New York: Simon and Schuster.

Wilson, William Julius. 1987. *The Truly Disadvantaged: The Inner City, the Underclass, and Public Policy*. Chicago: University of Chicago Press.

Wilson, William Julius, R. Aponte, J. Kirschenman, and Loic Wacquant. 1988. "The Ghetto Underclass and the Changing Structure of American Poverty." In *Quiet Riots: Race and Poverty in the United States*, edited by F. Harris and R. W. Wilkins. New York: Pantheon.

Zatz, Marjorie. 1987. "The Changing Forms of Racial/Ethnic Biases in Sentencing." *Journal of Research in Crime and Delinquency* 24:69–92.

3

Gender, Crime, and Criminology

KATHLEEN DALY

I t is not possible to distill in one essay all that has been written, just in the last decade, on women, gender, and crime. The
area continues to challenge criminology and related disciplines, to provoke the public's anxieties about crime, and to inspire activism for legal
change. In the second edition of *Women and Crime*, Frances Heidensohn
(1996, pp. xiii–xv) identified the following developments in the academic
arena: recognition, expansion, engendering the agenda, and deconstructing the categories. In the first of four sections in this chapter, I discuss
these developments to highlight debates in the field. In the second section,
I review research on girls' and women's lawbreaking (or gender differences in lawbreaking), and in the third, I analyze the ways it has been
explained. In the final section, I consider future directions in light of two
observations. First, women's lawbreaking (or gender differences in lawbreaking) is informed by different kinds of knowledge, and researchers are
taking different approaches toward what is to be explained and thus are
producing diverse, and often incompatible, knowledges and theories. Second, feminist explanations for lawbreaking have become more complex
and interesting than they were a decade ago. Female lawbreakers may be
constructing themselves differently than before, and a recent generation of
feminist scholars is more inclined to interpret women's behavior through
a lens of agency, action, and pleasure, even as that "agency" may serve to
reproduce structures of gender inequality and male domination.

My review will not describe patterns of gender and victimization, except as these relate to lawbreaking. Nor shall I consider recent work in
gender and criminal law, policing, courts, prisons, or criminal justice occupations (see Belknap 1996; Daly and Tonry 1997; Heidensohn 1992,
1994b; Martin and Jurik 1996; Pollock-Byrne 1990; Schulhofer 1995).[1]
Developments in U.S. theory and research are the main, though not the
exclusive, focus of my review.

Recent Developments

Heidensohn (1996, pp. xiii–xiv) notes that "women and crime" is now
recognized as an important topic in mainstream criminological readers

85

and theory texts. A cursory review of the literature supports her claim. Many criminology textbooks not only have sections devoted to feminist perspectives in criminology, but the authors also attempt to differentiate feminist and nonfeminist analyses. Textbook treatments by male authors of "feminist perspectives" vary in quality, accuracy, and depth (see, e.g., Akers 1997; Beirne and Messerschmidt 1995; Einstadter and Henry 1995). Although I wince when reading some authors' caricatures of feminist analyses, I am glad they are trying to address the deep-seated androcentrism (or male-centeredness) in the field. Only several years ago, a discussion of feminist perspectives was absent in criminology or criminal justice texts (Wonders and Caulfield 1993).

That the field has expanded is an understatement. It has become so large that one cannot keep up with it, especially if one reads across disciplinary boundaries, particularly in law, women's studies, and sociology; across national boundaries; or in areas such as media and cultural studies that work the edges of social science and literary forms. In addition to this growth in scholarly production, U.S. government reports on crime, victimization, courts, and prisons now gather and present statistics with both men and women in mind.

Field expansion comes from two major sources. One source is research by nonfeminist scholars in criminology (and related social science areas) who are interested in studies of "women and crime" or "race and gender differences in. . . ." A second source is research by feminist scholars from a range of disciplines, coupled with activists and policy makers with varied political stances. Whereas the first source has an understanding of debates in the criminological literature, its members may not have a grasp of feminist theories and research on gender. The second has a theoretical and political analysis of women's (and men's) situations, but its members may not grasp the limits of criminalization or be familiar with theories of crime and punishment. These distinctive sources of field expansion have created a somewhat incoherent theoretical field. To simplify: whereas one source produces criminological knowledge with little feminist content, another produces feminist knowledge that is unaware of or reluctant to engage with criminological content. Some feminist scholars in criminology straddle both sources of knowledge, and others may work from the second source to challenge criminological thought and to build from feminist theories.

Shifts in engendering the agenda and in deconstructing the categories are less dramatic than field expansion. Their presence is felt when feminist theories of sex/gender are applied to victimization, lawbreaking, and its response. Most criminologists do not use feminist theories in their work on lawbreaking; far more do so in studies of victimization. The primary reason is a division of intellectual labor in criminology: there are greater concentrations of feminist scholars in victimization than in lawbreaking. This situation appears to be changing, however, as a new cohort of scholars is entering the field, having conducted research on girls, women, and crime with feminist questions in mind (e.g., Maher 1995a; Miller 1996).

An important contribution in engendering the agenda has been to render the familiar male subject of lawbreaking strange. A focus on masculinities and masculine identities helps us to see how the street, the workplace, and the home are gendered sites (see, e.g., Canaan 1991; Jefferson 1996; Messerschmidt 1993; Ptacek 1988). There is, however, a problem with a masculinities focus: it may all too easily act as a theoretical bully, crowding out or ignoring the life worlds and identities of girls and women.[2] Let me clarify. Offending and victimization should be studied with an eye to their gendered (and sexed) character, which would include a focus on masculine identities and lines of social action. Yet it would be ironic should this recent development in criminology again foreground men and their activities, placing women in the periphery as cheerleaders and supporters of men.

Rendering the familiar terms and assumptions of criminology strange is what is entailed in deconstructing the categories.[3] Which terms and assumptions should be challenged is, however, a matter of debate. One axis of variability is the continuum of knowledge claims or varied "ways of knowing," which was originally identified by Sandra Harding (1986). The continuum ranges from traditional forms of positivist inquiry, where scholars assume a knowable and measurable world separate from themselves; to standpoint knowledges, where scholars assume a power relationship in the production of knowledge and problematize their own particular site in producing knowledge; to postmodern knowledges, where scholars assume that no one privileged (or authoritative) site or practice of knowledge exists (whether scientific-objective or standpoint). There can be spaces in between these positions, and scholars may move between them (as is my preference).[4] Thus, I would argue that it is possible to "deconstruct the categories" as a positivist or a poststructuralist, even as poststructuralists may wish to claim ownership of the term.

Women and Gender Differences in Lawbreaking

The research literature on women and gender differences in lawbreaking can be divided into two categories. The first is concerned with aggregate patterns and trends from a variety of data sources, and the second addresses the qualities of offenses committed and the life worlds of lawbreakers.

Patterns and Trends

Recent reviews of the delinquency and crime literatures in the United States that draw from self-report, arrest, and victimization data have been produced by Belknap (1996), Chesney-Lind and Shelden (1992), Daly and Tonry (1997), Denno (1994), Hill and Crawford (1990), Kruttschnitt

(1994, 1996), Laub and McDermott (1985), Simpson (1991), Sommers and Baskin (1992), Steffensmeier (1993), Steffensmeier and Allan (1996), and Tripplet and Myers (1995). From this body of work, the following patterns and trends are evident.

First, self-report studies of lawbreaking show higher rates of prevalence (committing an offense) and incidence (number of times) for boys than girls. From the Denver Youth Survey (1976–1980), boys' prevalence rates were higher than girls' for eighteen of twenty offenses. Girls' prevalence rates were slightly higher for "running away from home" and "hitting a parent" (Chesney-Lind and Shelden 1992; Tripplet and Myers 1995). In general, as offense seriousness increases, the gender gap widens in measures of prevalence and incidence. A 1988–1991 survey of self-reported crime by Denver youths in "high-risk" neighborhoods (Esbensen and Huizinga 1993, p. 574) found higher prevalence rates for nongang boys than nongang girls for street crime, drug sales, and "serious offenses" but not for minor offenses or alcohol or drug use. (Incidence rates were also higher for the boys than the girls for street crime, drug sales, and alcohol use.) Not surprisingly, for both groups, prevalence rates were greater for those boys and girls who were involved in gangs, and especially so for the girls. This "gang effect" in enhancing crime involvement was stronger, however, for the boys than for the girls in reported incidence rates.

Second, arrest data show larger gender ratios of lawbreaking than self-report studies, although a similar structure of offending is apparent. Specifically, gender gaps in lawbreaking are largest for the more serious offenses (such as violent offenses) and smaller for minor forms of property offenses. The structure of offenses for which men and women are arrested is similar: the most typical are substance abuse offenses (alcohol or drug-related) and larceny-theft (Steffensmeier and Allan 1996, p. 461).

Third, trend data for arrests from 1960 to 1990 show that the female share of all arrests rose from 10 to 20 percent; these shifts are evident for younger (under eighteen) and older women.[5] For both age-groups, increases were greatest for larceny-theft; for older women, increases were also apparent for fraud and forgery (Steffensmeier 1993, pp. 415–21). For the thirty-year period, Darrell Steffensmeier (1993, p. 419) sees a shift in the offenses for which both men and women are arrested: today a larger share are arrested for driving under the influence, larceny-theft, and drug law violations, with a comparatively smaller share arrested for public drunkenness and disorderly conduct. Trends from the National Crime Victimization Survey (1975–1990) for the perceived sex of offenders in robbery, simple and aggravated assault, burglary, and motor vehicle theft show that the female share has remained the same over time (Steffensmeier and Allan 1996, p. 463).

Fourth, arrest data suggest that in societies and groups where there are high male arrest rates, there are high female arrest rates; where there are low male rates, there are low female rates. Over time, male and female arrest rates will rise and fall in parallel fashion, suggesting roughly similar responses to broader socioeconoimc and legal forces (Steffensmeier and Allan 1996, p. 465). With such a pattern, we would expect that the profile of men and women accused, prosecuted, and imprisoned for crime would have a similar class- and race-based structure. And indeed the profile is similar: compared with their proportions in the general population, criminalized men and women are more likely to be economically marginalized and to be members of racial/ethnic minority groups; they are less likely to have completed high school.

Fifth, gender differences in arrest rates cannot be understood apart from race, ethnicity, and class. Analyses of victimization, self-report, and arrest data show major racial differences in the likelihood of involvement in crime, especially in violent offenses (Laub and McDermott 1985; Simpson 1991; Hill and Crawford 1990). For example, arrest rates for black, white, and Hispanic women for three violent offenses in New York City during 1987–1990 show significant differences: 1,670 per 100,000 for black women compared with 503 and 126, respectively, for Hispanic and white women (Sommers and Baskin 1992, p. 194). These racial/ethnic differences may be explained, in part, by where the women lived: those who lived in high-poverty neighborhoods had the highest arrest rates for violent crime compared with those who lived in low- or moderate-poverty areas. Substantially higher proportions of arrested black women lived in high-poverty neighborhoods (69 percent) than did arrested Hispanic or white women (20 and 11 percent, respectively; Sommers and Baskin 1992, p. 199). It should be noted that studies of female arrest rates, which are linked to measures of race and class, are quite rare (see review by Simpson 1991).

Sixth, although violent crime represents a low to moderate share of female and male arrests,[6] it has commanded a good deal of recent attention from researchers. Deborah Denno's (1994, p. 94) review of research on "violent male and female career criminals" finds that over the life course, women are involved in less violent behavior than men, their violent offending "begins and peaks earlier" than men's, and they are less likely to repeat and more likely to desist from future violence than are men.

Qualities of Offenses and Life Worlds of Offenders

Other U.S. studies have been conducted on gender differences in the qualities, contexts, and roles in specific offenses, or participation in gangs. This body of work has been reviewed or produced by Alarid et al. (1996), Campbell (1990, 1991), Daly (1989, 1994), Decker et al. (1993), Esbensen and Huizinga (1993), Joe and Chesney-Lind (1995), Miller (1996), Moore (1991), and Sommers and Baskin (1993). There are, in addition, interview and ethnographic studies of girls and women who are incarcerated, use or sell drugs, work in the sex industry, or are defined as being at "high risk" (e.g., Bottcher 1995; Cain 1989; Daly 1992; Gilfus 1992; Maher 1997; Maher and Curtis 1992; Maher and Daly 1996; Miller 1986; Miller 1995; Rosenbaum 1981; Sanchez 1996). Five patterns are evident from the literature.

First, female involvement in gangs is more varied than earlier research (from the 1940s to the 1960s) had revealed. It is impossible to know whether girls are more involved in gangs than before or whether they are involved in more serious criminal activity. In gang research prior to the early 1980s, researchers either did not bother to ask or they excluded girls from study (Campbell 1990). Today, problems are evident at both ends of the spectrum: some claim a "new" female gang criminal unlike any seen before (Taylor 1993), whereas others neglect to report, even in a footnote, what they learned from the female gang members in their sample (Hagedorn 1994). In surveys of gangs, estimates of female involvement range from 10 to 38 percent (Miller 1996). Esbensen and Huizinga (1993, p. 581) say that their survey-based estimate—that girls or women constitute 25 percent of gang members—is consistent with the gender composition of gangs in other research on urban areas in the late 1980s. But saying that you are "in" a gang and that you participate in criminal activities may not mean the same thing for male and female gang members. Esbensen and Huizinga (1993, pp. 572, 574) found that offending rates were twice as high for gang boys as for gang girls across a range of delinquent acts; the differences were greatest for serious forms of delinquency. It should be emphasized that even in "high-risk" areas in Denver, recent surveys suggest that the percentage of youths reporting gang membership is small, ranging from 3 to 7 percent (Esbensen and Huizinga 1993, p. 572).

Second, little is known about women's involvement or gender differences in white-collar crime. Beginning with Edwin Sutherland ([1949] 1983), researchers have assumed that *the* white-collar offender is male (e.g., Mann, Wheeler, and Sarat 1980),[7] a not unreasonable assumption when one examines the profile of those convicted of white-collar crime (Daly 1989). For those offenses considered to be "real" forms of white-collar lawbreaking (i.e., committed by those in occupational positions of power, such as antitrust violations and securities fraud), an analysis of federal court convictions in the late 1970s shows the female share of convictions to be very low (0.5 to 2 percent; Daly 1989, p. 776). The female share of convictions for bank embezzlement was higher (45 percent); but when the specific job that convicted embezzlers held was examined, few women were bank officers or managers (7 percent), whereas just over half of the men were (Daly 1989, p. 782).

An obvious explanation for gender differences in white-collar crime is to say that there are fewer workplace opportunities for women to engage in such crime. Less obvious but better explanations focus on the gendered structure of opportunities. Such explanations draw linkages between men's sexism toward women in the "upperworld" and "underworld" that may serve to exclude women from men's crime groups (Messerschmidt 1993; Steffensmeier 1983). They may also include attention to gender-based variability in motive, the size of the crime group, and offense roles that would defy a simple "workplace opportunities" argument (Daly 1989). Analyses of drug markets suggest that "opportunities" are circumscribed by particular masculine qualities thought necessary for selling and distributing drugs (Maher and Daly 1996). Gang research reveals that women themselves ratify gender hierarchies and female devaluation, even as they claim to be the equals of men (Miller 1996). Elucidating the gendered structures of illegitimate and workplace opportunities for crime will prove a more fruitful strategy than one which makes the glib assumption that "men and women will behave in like manner when occupying similar positions in the social structure" (Simon and Landis 1991, p. 14). Indeed, this assumption cannot be sustained in explaining the lawbreaking of poor or marginalized men and women, as we have already seen. Why would we ever assume that gender divisions are less salient for more affluent men and women or those in the paid labor force?

Third, women's roles in offenses are varied. In their review of the literature, Leanne Alarid and colleagues (1996) found that in eleven of nineteen studies, women played minor or secondary roles. Alarid et al. also interviewed 104 young women (average age, twenty years) in boot camp, asking them what part they played in the crime for which they were incarcerated. They found that 15 percent of the women said they acted alone, whereas identical proportions of about 42 percent each said they had primary (or equal) and secondary roles. When the women acted with others, two sources of variability in their offense roles were noted: the woman's race-ethnicity and the offense she committed. A somewhat higher proportion of African-American (48 percent) and Hispanic women (45 percent) played primary or equal offense roles, compared with Anglo women (36 percent).[8] Women were more likely to play primary or equal roles (56 percent) for drug offenses than for property (36 percent) or violent (31 percent) offenses.[9] The women were asked who influenced them to become involved in crime during the past year. While just over half of the Anglo and Hispanic women said they were "influenced by men," only 20 percent of the African-American women said they were influenced by men. But when the women were asked whether they acted as a "leader or a follower when with [their] friends," a similar proportion of both Anglo (38 percent) and African-American (33 percent) women said they were followers. My interpretation of these data is that a larger portion of African-American women are influenced by other African-American women to become involved in crime than are Anglo women, whose deviant pathways appear to be related more to men's influences. Such Anglo and African-American differences were also found in Lisa Maher's (1995b) research on New York City women's initiation into drug use.

It can be difficult to determine whether women (or particular minority groups of women) are more likely to take primary or equal offense roles today than they were in previous decades. Differences in the source and composition of samples, the offenses analyzed,[10] how women talk about themselves, the context of researchers' questions and what researchers are prepared to hear, and whether the findings are based on a onetime interview or longer-term ethnographic study—these ways of gathering and interpreting data all make a difference in what we "find." Compared with the characterizations of women's lawbreaking by Gilfus (1992), Joe and Chesney-Lind (1995), and Miller (1986), what struck me was how Alarid et al. described the women who considered themselves leaders (57 percent of the sample). For this group, the authors noted "their assertiveness and their stronger self-concept. [They] were sure of themselves and made their own decisions" (1996, p. 449). One wonders whether, for young women in recent U.S. samples, explaining one's actions as a lawbreaker may be easier today than it was in the recent past. Alternatively (or in combination), researchers may be interpreting women's accounts of themselves differently. It may not be possible to separate the question of change in women's lawbreaking (or their roles) from how researchers orient themselves to the women they study and to their understandings of women's lives and lawbreaking.

Fourth, research on gender, offense contexts, and motives is most developed for homicide (see reviews by Ogle, Maier-Katkin, and Bernard 1995; Wilson and Daly 1992).[11] From this research we find that women represent a small share (about 10–12 percent) of homicide arrests. They are more likely to kill intimates (spouses or partners) than are men, who are more likely to kill acquaintances or strangers. The victims of women's homicides are more likely to have initiated the violence than are the victims of men's homicides. Women's homicides generally occur in their own or the victim's residence, while men's homicides occur more frequently outside residential settings. The situational and relational differences in men's and women's homicides can be explained, in part, by the fact that fewer women's homicides occur in the course of robberies, burglaries, or rapes. Ogle, Maier-Katkin, and Bernard report that the "consistency of the pattern of homicides by women, as well as the differences from the patterns of homicides by men, suggests the need for a separate theoretical explanation of female homicide" (1995, p. 174). I am not persuaded that homicide requires a separate theory from, say, aggravated or simple assault. More important, it is not clear that homicide patterns for women are "consistent" when one considers data from other countries. Margo Wilson and Martin Daly (1992, p. 191) show that U.S. women (especially black women) are far more likely to kill male spouses or cohabitants than are women in Canada, England and Wales, Scotland, Australia, or other countries. They argue against a simple "underclass" or "black" explanation for this pattern and instead suggest a focus on structured and situational sources of marital conflict: the social and economic devaluation of minority group men, which affects the men's desire to co-erce female partners; residential and kin patterns, which may empower some women to retaliate; and the incidence of step-relationships, which may increase the frequency with which women need to defend their children.

Fifth, girls' and women's pathways to lawbreaking are many and var-ied. Drawing from U.S. and non-U.S. studies, I identified what I termed the "leading feminist scenario" of women's lawbreaking, that of street women (Daly 1994). These women may have run from abusive house-holds to the street, or they may have been attracted to the "fast money" of a deviant lifestyle. Once on the street, young women engage in petty hus-tles or prostitution. Life on the street may lead to drug use and addiction, which may lead to more frequent lawbreaking to support a drug habit.

Interview studies by Arnold (1990), Chesney-Lind and Shelden (1992, chap. 9), and Gilfus (1992) have centered attention on girls' sexual and physical victimization while growing up, their efforts to escape abuse and violence, and the consequent "criminalizing of girls' survival" (Chesney-Lind 1989) on the streets. Eleanor Miller (1986) identified sev-eral routes for Milwaukee street women: those running away from home to the streets, and those whose households were connected to the streets via "domestic networks." In my analysis of the biographies of forty women prosecuted in the New Haven felony court, I found that street women characterized about a third of my sample. As frequent was a second group I termed "harmed and harming women." These women had chaotic and difficult experiences growing up, with violent or "out of control" behavior evinced in childhood or adolescence. Other groups of New Haven women had associates who used or sold drugs (drug-con-nected women, about 15 percent) or were fending off and fighting abu-sive partners (battered women, about 10 percent; Daly 1994).[12]

While my analysis focused on women accused of violent, property, and drug offenses, Baskin and Sommers (1993) examined the life histo-ries of women arrested for violent felonies in New York City (excluding domestic-related assaults). They identified two groups: an "early onset group," 60 percent of their sample, who were frequently involved in fights and possessing weapons at an early age (eleven years); and a "later onset group," 40 percent of their sample, who had no early history of fighting or weapons possession. Baskin and Sommers found no differ-ences in the two groups' experiences with physical and sexual abuse by family members or guardians. Indeed, the only family-related measure for which they found differences is whether a family member had been in a psychiatric hospital. In general, the later onset group's pattern of vio-lent crime was related to their initiation into drug use, whereas the early onset group's violence was linked to growing up in very poor neighbor-hoods and having delinquent peers.[13] There are, of course, inevitable problems associated with theorizing about crime and conformity from samples of those who have been caught up in the criminal justice system.

Gendered pathways highlight the varied trajectories toward, as well as in and out of, lawbreaking (primarily as retrospective accounts). They can also be used in prospective studies of income generation, drug use, and movement between street and straight worlds.

Explaining Patterns of Lawbreaking

A decade ago, Meda Chesney-Lind and I identified two related, though distinct, theoretical problems for criminology in the study of women, gender, and crime. They are the gender ratio problem (why are men more likely involved in or arrested for crime than women?) and the generalizability problem (do theories of crime based on boys' or men's lives apply to girls or women?; Daly and Chesney-Lind 1988). For most nonfeminist scholars, interest remains in addressing the gender ratio problem, with the working assumption that a "gender-neutral" theory is preferable. Here we see a clash in theoretical objectives.

On the one hand, Darrell Steffensmeier and Emilie Allan suggest that "the traditional gender-neutral theories [derived from male samples] provide reasonable explanations of less serious forms of [crime]" for men and women (1996, p. 473). Such thinking is common in nonfeminist and liberal feminist[14] analyses of gender and crime (e.g., Smith and Paternoster 1987; Simon and Landis 1991). On the other hand, feminist scholars, including myself, find it illogical to say that traditional theories derived from male samples are gender-neutral. Traditional theories are more appropriately labeled *male-specific*, not gender-neutral. Such theories may, of course, be relevant to girls and women: we would expect that elements of social control, learning, labeling, and opportunity would be applicable in a general sense. However, even if particular elements are applicable, they may not be applicable in the same ways or to the same degree. Likewise, elements from theories developed from all-female samples may be applicable to boys and men, but not necessarily in the same ways or to the same degree.

We should abandon the concept of, and the quest for, gender-neutral criminological theories. Instead, we should use terms that better describe the theoretical enterprise: to identify variables, factors, or conceptual elements that have similar and different influences on lawbreaking for boys/men and girls/women. This is just one potential focus of theoretical work; there are others, as follows.

Gender ratio of crime. What is the nature of, and what explains the "gender gap" in, lawbreaking and arrests for crime? What is the nature of, and what explains variation in, the kinds of offenses that girls/women and boys/men get involved with (or arrested for), in terms of both prevalence and incidence? What is the nature of, and what explains gender-based variation in, arrest rates across nations, including developed and developing countries?

Gendered crime. What are the contexts and qualities of boys'/men's and girls'/women's illegal acts? What is the social organization of specific offenses (e.g., drug dealing, prostitution, and credit frauds)?

Gendered pathways to lawbreaking. What is the nature of, and what explains the character of, girls'/women's and boys'/men's pathways to lawbreaking? What brings people to the street, to use illegal drugs, to become involved in workplace crime, or to be arrested and prosecuted for crime? How do boys/men and girls/women move in and out of foster homes, conventional work, jails and prisons, hospitals, and halfway houses?

Gendered lives. How does gender organize the ways in which men and women survive, take care of themselves and their children, and find shelter and food? How does gender structure thinkable courses of action and identities?

Researchers may address these thematics with a focus on class, racial-ethnic, age, regional, or other sources of variability. Or they may decide to analyze one particular group, such as black women. Using Don Gibbons's (1994) categories, the gender ratio of crime and gendered crime address "the rates question," gendered crime and gendered pathways attend to questions of "why they did it," and gendered lives examines general life course trajectories that may or may not include lawbreaking. These thematics can also be linked to the sources of field expansion discussed earlier. Nonfeminist inquiries on gender and crime are principally focused on the gender ratio and gendered crime problems; they attempt to measure rates of involvement in crime/delinquency and to explain "gaps" in such involvement. Scholars in this tradition may draw from a nascent understanding of feminist theories, but their guiding metaphors and concepts come largely from criminology. By comparison, feminist inquiries on gender and crime are principally focused on demonstrating the ways in which the social organization of gender shapes women's and men's lives on the streets and in neighborhoods, workplaces, and households. Research tends to focus on gendered crime, gendered pathways, and gendered lives, although not exclusively.

All four thematics are relevant to research on boys and men. Specifically, boys' and men's lawbreaking, pathways to crime, and lives are no less gendered than girls' or women's. Yet with the exception of emergent research on masculinities and crime, gendered and racialized analyses of boys and men have largely been unexplored by mainstream criminology.

Gender Ratio of Crime

For two reasons, this is the largest and most heavily populated research area: it accords with a sociological preference to examine patterns and variability across aggregates, and the requisite large data sets (self-report, victimization, arrests) are available for descriptive and predictive numerical analyses, which have been the preferred data source for developing theory in mainstream criminology. Scholars focus on gender differences in rates of crime involvement or variable rates of involvement for particular crime categories, such as violent, property, or public order offenses. The most popular explanations for the gender ratio of crime have been versions of control, opportunity, and social learning theories (e.g., Adler 1975; Hagan, Gillis, and Simpson 1987, 1990; Heidensohn 1985; Morris 1987; Simon 1975). Recent contributions by Broidy and Agnew (1997), Heimer (1995), and Jensen (1996) identify variables that reduce gender gaps in lawbreaking. They include measures of machismo, risk taking, self-esteem, and respect for the law.

One problem that can emerge in statistical analyses of the gender ratio of crime is that scholars may assume (wrongly) that women's arrest rates should always be lower than men's. For example, Sommers and Baskin, based on their analysis of arrest rates for men and women, disaggregated by race and ethnicity, conclude that "the claim of a clear and consistent gender-ratio relationship is spurious" (1992, p. 197). One wonders why the authors thought it necessary to set up this "straw-man" sort of argument. To posit an invariant relationship would necessitate an assumption of some essential gender difference that stands outside history and culture, an untenable assumption in light of the past three decades of feminist scholarship. Gender-ratio claims can be made, but they must be keyed to roughly similar groups, and they must take social, economic, and cultural organization seriously.

Gendered Crime

Gendered crime may be used in conjunction with the gender ratio of crime, as scholars aim to interweave gender ratios with analyses of the gendered social organization of crime. For example, Steffensmeier and Allan present a "gendered model of female offending and gender differences in crime" (1996, p. 475) that centers largely, although not exclusively, on the gender ratio of crime and gendered crime.[15] I use the term *gendered crime* to refer to (1) the ways in which street life, drug and sex markets, informal economies, crime opportunities, and crime groups are ordered by gender and other social relations; and (2) variation in the sequencing and contexts of men's and women's lawbreaking, including their offense roles, accounts of themselves, and how their acts are translated into official crime categories. Ethnographic research and some interview studies may capture both of these aspects of gendered crime.

There are several ways to conduct research on gendered crime. One can count the frequency of offense elements, such as the size of the crime group, the role played (e.g., Alarid et al. 1996; Daly 1989; Decker et al. 1993), even as we know that these elements may not be sufficiently nuanced to reveal the gestalt of crime (Daly 1994, pp. 165–67). Another approach is to link gender (and race, class, age) identities to crime as a gendered line of action and as situationally accomplished (Messerschmidt 1993). Recent research on boys and men reveals the ways in which mas-

culine identities and privileges enable certain types of risk-taking behavior in boys (Canaan 1991) more so than in girls (Bottcher 1995), encourage certain forms of violence (Polk 1994), and solidify male group
identities in the workplace (Messerschmidt 1993). In fact, the more one
becomes familiar with the literature on gendered crime, the more one
sees the limits of "gender gap" explanations. The latter lack a sense of
place (e.g., neighborhood, workplace, the street); group contexts (e.g.,
peer groups, families, sports, schools, gangs, clubs, detention centers);
and the performance and consolidation of gender identities and reproduction of gender hierarchies.

Gendered Pathways

The idea of gendered pathways emphasizes biographical elements, life-
course trajectories, and developmental sequences. There are nonfeminist
and feminist versions of the pathways idea. The former draws on the notion of "career" to chart deepening commitments to deviant identities
and activities, as well as pathways to desistance (e.g., Rosenbaum 1981;
the life-course analyses of Sampson and Laub 1993; the criminal career
orientation of Blumstein, Cohen, and Farrington 1988). Feminist versions
may draw on the concept of "blurred boundaries" of victimization-
criminalization to describe linkages between girls' experiences of victimization and their subsequent involvement in crime (e.g., Arnold 1990;
Chesney-Lind 1989; Gilfus 1992; Joe and Chesney-Lind 1995). Gendered
pathways can be linked to gendered crime in charting sequences of girls'
routes to the street, likely forms of income generation, and relationships
with other women, men, and children (Carlen 1988; Maher 1997; Miller
1986). These feminist versions of the pathways idea are compatible with
the longitudinal tradition in criminology, although that tradition has not,
until recently, been mindful of sex/gender divisions.

Here I briefly consider feminist work on the blurred boundaries of victimization and criminalization. During the 1980s, it became apparent to
some feminist activists and academics that a portion of imprisoned
women, especially those convicted of homicide-related offenses, were
confined because they were fighting back against abusive mates. Although activists gave the impression that *most* imprisoned women were
sexually or physically abused while growing up (see Daly 1992, p. 49),
surveys of convicted and imprisoned women put the figure at about 30
percent (Bureau of Justice Statistics 1992, p. 10; Daly 1994, p. 293).
Something of a causal nexus began to emerge in explaining a portion of
women's crime as arising from their having been victimized, whether in
the immediate or distance past. Moreover, there was evidence from Cathy
Widom's (1989) research that children who were adjudicated abused or
neglected were more likely than a control group to be arrested for crime
as adults.[16] This kind of explanation, which focused on women's experiences of victimization as one precipitant of their lawbreaking, contrasted

sharply with 1970s explanations, which centered on women's freedom from constraints and new opportunities for crime (Adler 1975; Simon 1975).

Prior victimization (and socioeconomic marginality, more generally) can render male and female lawbreakers less blameworthy for their acts (Daly 1994). At the same time, such explanations may obscure actors' agency and responsibility for crime (Allen 1987). Recent feminist analyses are now challenging both 1970s and 1980s explanations of women's crime. Whereas a major 1970s explanation (focusing on women's liberation from constraints) accorded "too much" volition and freedom in depicting girls' and women's lawbreaking, a major 1980s explanation (focusing on women's victimization as a precipitant of crime) accorded too little (Maher 1997). Pat Carlen suggests a way out of this conceptual problem: "[W]omen's own vivid accounts [show us] how they set about making their lives within conditions . . . not . . . of their own choosing." Acting or "choosing" to act is constrained within "certain [material] conditions, political discourses, and gender ideologies" (1988, pp. 14, 108). Working with gendered pathways and gendered lives, feminist scholars are now showing the ways in which female lawbreakers move within overlapping spheres of volition and constraint. We are depicting women's behavior and actions in context, along with women's understandings of themselves and others, which have long featured in studies of men.

Gendered Lives

Martha Fineman (1990), a feminist legal scholar, coined the term *women's gendered lives* to refer to significant differences in the ways that "women experience society" compared with men. "The concept of a gendered life," Fineman (1995, p. 45) suggests,[17] begins with the observation that women's existences are constituted by a variety of experiences—material, psychological, physical, social, and cultural—some of which may be described as biologically based, while others seem more rooted in culture and custom. For some time, Fineman has been challenging gender-neutral legal theories, especially in family law and policy, for their "neutering" of gender difference and effacement of women's life worlds, experiences, and contributions. Her critique of gender-neutral legal theory is applicable to gender-neutral criminological theory.

There are several ways to develop the idea of women's (or men's) gendered lives in criminological research. One is to show how the "gender-related conditions of life" (Bottcher 1995) structure delinquent (and nondelinquent) actions and identities. Jean Bottcher's interviews of "high-risk" adolescents (those whose brothers had been incarcerated) suggest that the social organization of gender acts as social control: compared with the boys, girls were "insulated . . . from delinquent interest and activity" (p. 37). This approach reverses the dependent and independent variables in traditional criminological theories: rather than analyze gender as a correlate of crime, one would analyze crime as a correlate of gender. In taking such an approach, one needs to draw from research on "how gender actually plays out in personal lives, especially among adolescents" (p. 35). Unfortunately, research on "personal lives" is typically absent in theories of gender and crime (see, e.g., Hagan, Gillis, and Simpson 1987, 1990; Heimer 1995), leading to the predictable consequence of generating critiques of terms and assumptions used (e.g., Morash and Chesney-Lind's 1991 critique of power-control theory). We may do better by starting with concrete studies of boys'/men's and girls'/women's lives, rather than with ungrounded, commonsensical assumptions in the professional rush to devise grand theory.[18]

Another approach to gendered lives, which can be used with gendered pathways, is to document how varied methods of income generation over time relate to turning points in women's lives (such as pregnancy and care of children) and to state supports for housing or welfare. Regina Austin (1992, pp. 1801–11) shows what can be learned by studying "hustling" as women (and men) move between "street and straight" worlds, and Maher (1997) documents the connections between neighborhood conditions, drug markets, and the declining value of sex work for women in New York City neighborhoods. It is rare to find criminologists using "gender-related conditions of life" as a starting point in describing and explaining girls' or women's lawbreaking. Such an approach is more common in anthropological research on lawbreaking (e.g., Sullivan 1989; Valentine 1978) and feminist research on victimization (e.g., Hester, Kelly, and Radford 1996; Kelly 1988; Stanko 1990).

Future Directions

Different sources of field expansion, one beginning with theories of crime and the other beginning with theories of gender, have created several types of knowledge about women, gender, and crime. The field of criminology is more complex than my dichotomy would suggest, but this scheme helps to clarify the directions the field is taking today.

The first source of field expansion, which begins with theories of crime, is following in the footsteps of traditional criminology by aiming to develop a grand or "comprehensive" theory of gender and crime (or gender and delinquency) that explains gender gaps in lawbreaking. A sense that nearly all the important variables have been discovered can be gleaned from statements such as "The model completely accounts for the gender gap in school deviance, theft, drug use, and violence. There is no significant gender difference in *any* form of delinquency once differences in means and slopes of predictor variables are taken into account" (Heimer 1995, p. 164).

To translate, this means that several key variables in the model, risk taking and self-esteem, had different influences on male and female delinquency. Heimer's (1995) study is astonishing in that she argues for developing an "interactionist" model of delinquency that attends to how "the *meaning* of behavior . . . varies across gender" (p. 167), but her empirical referent is derived solely from multivariate analyses of survey data. She cites no research on the life worlds of adolescents or on how meanings are constructed in interaction.

The second source of field expansion comes from feminist scholars, who are interested to begin with theories of gender and with studies of women's lives, and to apply this body of knowledge to crime. This group is less interested in devising a grand theory of gender and crime, and more inclined to identify the ways in which gender structures men's and women's life worlds, identities, and thinkable courses of action.

Whereas one source of knowledge seeks to explain away gender gaps, the other seeks to reveal the tenacity of gender (and other social divisions) in social life. Whereas one wishes to identify a gender-neutral theory of crime, the other sees no meaning in devising such a theory in a social world ordered by gender divisions. Steffensmeier and Allan (1996), who attempt to put these disparate sources of knowledge together, say they want to develop a "gendered" approach that is "gender-neutral" (p. 474). They argue that there is "no need for gender-specific theories," but they acknowledge that "qualitative studies reveal major gender differences in the context and nature of offending" (p. 482). They propose taking a "middle road" position, which "acknowledges the utility of traditional theory and . . . the organization of gender" (p. 482).

Although one may appreciate Steffensmeier and Allan's (1996) desire to have it both ways, I would argue that the theoretical road they wish to travel is a muddled one. Taking a cue from Fineman (1994, drawing from Merton), we may do better by developing theories of the middle range, rather than of the middle ground. Middle-range theories of gender and crime would not endeavor to synthesize the gender ratio of crime, gendered crime, gendered pathways, and gendered lives, as Steffensmeier and Allan (1996) aim to do. The approach instead would be to take one, or perhaps several, of these thematics, and to provide a partial window of understanding on gender and crime. And most crucially, rather than explaining away gender gaps, we should aim to bring gender into view by analyzing how it affects the life worlds of men and women (as crime victims, offenders, or criminologists), as well as the production of knowledge about crime.

Intellectual work does not occur in a vacuum. A recent generation of feminist scholars is interpreting women's lawbreaking somewhat differently than a decade ago (see also Campbell 1990). This development reflects a shift in theoretical stance and may also reflect differences in the age cohorts and the circumstances of the women studied. An older cohort of women and those who have been imprisoned may more often give victimization-based accounts of themselves (see, e.g., Daly 1994; Gilfus

1992), although studies by Carlen (1988) and Maher (1997) of women in this cohort depict a more volitional actor. We might expect that research on a younger cohort of women by a younger cohort of scholars would reflect actors invested with "more agency," even as they are constrained by structures of male domination. Studies by Miller (1996) and Ogilvie (1996) are indicative of this tendency. Miller (1996) challenges previous research for depicting gang girls merely as "victims of male gang members' sexism," for using victimization as the primary explanation for girls' involvement in crime, or for characterizing young women as "street feminists." She argues for a more layered understanding of victimization and agency, which recognizes that girls "actively participate in gender oppression," even as they say they are the equals of the boys. Emma Ogilvie (1996) critiques Judith Allen's (1989) emphasis on "the masculinity of criminality," arguing that it forecloses an ability to register female lawbreaking and denies women agency, responsibility, and pleasure in lawbreaking. The theoretical stance of a researcher matters, of course: some studies of younger cohorts of women may continue to focus on girls' experiences with victimization (Joe and Chesney-Lind 1995).

While acknowledging these complexities, my impression is that arguments explaining girls' or women's crime as spawned, in part, from women's victimization are not as popular with a younger cohort of feminist scholars in the 1990s as they were in the 1980s. Nor, as importantly, may such victimization explanations be popular with the female subjects of feminist research. It is not possible to disentangle major themes in academic and pop feminism today (more interested in female "agency"; not wanting to be "victims") from how girls and women construct themselves in interviews with researchers. As Heidensohn suggests, modern feminism may have had an indirect effect on "how deviant women perceive themselves, act on those perceptions, and address their problems" (1994a, p. 32). Perhaps women's deviance in the 1990s is considered less deviant, both to researchers and to women lawbreakers themselves, than it was twenty or thirty years ago. Or perhaps little has changed, but today we pay greater attention to the words, experiences, and life worlds of girls and women, and are interpreting them differently. Theoretical wisdom would suggest the need to contemplate these interpretive problems: they feature in any commentary on gender in a gendered social order.

Acknowledgments My thanks to Tamara Burrows, Martha Fineman, Hennessey Hayes, Lisa Maher, Jody Miller, Emma Ogilvie, and Michael Tonry for comments on an earlier draft.

Notes

1. To do justice to these two other bodies of research would require a substantially longer essay. Of the scholarship on lawbreaking, victimization, and

citizen/justice system responses, that on women and gender differences in lawbreaking has been the least developed theoretically, especially from a feminist perspective.

2. In addition, the arguments can be tautological. For example, when boys/men are committing crime, they are said to be "doing masculinity," and the evidence for the claims is that boys/men are committing crime. Similarly, in explaining variability in masculine expressions, the evidence for "accommodating masculinity" is conformity to adult expectations, whereas the evidence for "oppositional masculinity" is nonconformity. The terms and evidence are circular.

3. Not long ago, I was averse to using the term *deconstruction* because it had a specific technical meaning in literary analyses, one that did not transport well to the social sciences. However, scholars now seem to use the term more loosely. For example, Heidensohn (1996) uses *deconstruction* to refer to "challeng[ing] the categorical assumptions" (p. 204) or "questioning all assumptions and meanings" (p. 205); this seems no different from saying that concepts are socially and historically constructed.

4. I resist defending or opposing "quantitative" and "qualitative" methods in the social sciences. It should be apparent by now that both approaches have strengths and limitations. Further, quantitative analyses should not be viewed as "objective and abstract," and qualitative analyses should not be viewed as "subjective and concrete" (Kruttschnitt and Gartner 1993, p. 325). Contrasts like this inhibit rather than build new methodological approaches that can move us beyond these dualisms. In my contrast of disparate sources of knowledge and theoretical aims, I am not focusing principally on comparing quantitative and qualitative applications. Rather I am more interested in what researchers intend to explain and whether they want to devise a "gender-neutral" or "comprehensive" theory.

5. Women's arrest rates have also increased in absolute terms.

6. Using data for 1991, of the eight *Uniform Crime Reports* index offenses, the four violent offenses account for 13 percent and 28 percent, respectively, of female and male arrests. When all offense categories are considered, the offenses of homicide, rape, aggravated and simple assult, and robbery account for 10 percent and 13 percent, respectively, of female and male arrests (Maguire, Pastore, and Flanagan 1993, p. 432).

7. Sutherland ([1949] 1983, p. 5) argued that criminal behavior could not be explained by poverty because, among other reasons, there was a significantly greater proportion of boys (85 percent) than girls (15 percent) "adjudged delinquent" in juvenile courts. If boys and girls were "equally in poverty," lived in poor housing and without recreational facilities, then poverty could not "explain the difference in the delinquency rates of the two sexes." Unfortunately, Sutherland's comment on the gendered conditions of poverty was not pursued in his theory of differential association.

8. The authors report that a higher proportion of African-American women played primary and equal offense roles than did Anglo and Hispanic women (p. 446), but their data in Table 4 (p. 444) show that five of eleven Hispanic women played equal and primary roles.

9. These percentages are based on my reanalysis of the data reported in Alarid et al. (1996, Table 4, p. 444); they were not reported by the authors.

10. From my analysis of child abuse cases (Daly 1994, pp. 140–45), I

found that the terms *primary* and *secondary roles* did not well characterize women's actions (or inactions) in the abuse. Decker et al. (1993) found that women played primary and secondary roles in burglary; however, they noted that "in no case . . . did a male respondent admit to being subservient to a woman during offenses" (p. 154).

11. By *criminal homicide,* criminologists refer to data gathered by the police for all reported or discovered cases of murder and nonnegligent manslaughter; legal scholars, by contrast, may differentiate among kinds of homicide according to legally meaningful categories of intent (e.g., various degrees of murder and manslaughter).

12. The "battered women" were in the New Haven court on charges related to assaulting or killing partners. A higher proportion of women (29 percent) reported having been in relationships with abusive men.

13. The authors do not discuss whether there is racial-ethnic variation in early and later onset groups.

14. While there are differences between nonfeminist and liberal feminist analyses, I term this group *nonfeminist.* I want to distinguish it from feminist analyses that utilize a more critical, sophisticated approach in describing and explaining women's (and men's) life worlds and circumstances, gender differences, and linkages with other social divisions such as class, race-ethnicity, and age. Nonfeminist analyses use commonsensical understandings of gender, in the same way that members of the general population use commonsensical understandings of class rather than the more sophisticated analyses of class by sociologists.

15. The authors also touch on gendered pathways and the social organization of gender. Ultimately, however, all the arrows in their model point toward an explanation of the gender ratio of crime (Steffensmeier and Allan 1996, p. 475).

16. In Widom's model, with an expected arrest rate of 20 percent, having been abused or neglected as a child increased that rate to 25 to 36 percent. Variable risk factors based on gender, race, and age explain the range, with the highest risk category being those who were older, black, and male.

17. Fineman also addresses differences among women, which I do not discuss here.

18. Howard Becker's (1973, pp. 189–94) critique of sociologists making "common events and experiences mysterious" is applicable to criminology: "Sociologists have generally been reluctant to take a close look at what sits in front of their noses" (p. 194), even though "common sense and science enjoin us to look at things closely before we start theorizing about them" (p. 192). One consequence is that "we may find ourselves theorizing about activities which never occur in the way we imagine" (p. 192).

References

Adler, Freda. 1975. *Sisters in Crime: The Rise of the New Female Criminal.* New York: McGraw-Hill.

Akers, Ronald L. 1997. *Criminological Theories: Introduction and Evaluation.* 2nd ed. Los Angeles: Roxbury.

Alarid, Leanne Fiftal, James W. Marquart, Velmer S. Burston Jr., Francis T.

Cullen, and Steven J. Cuvelier. 1996. "Women's Roles in Serious Offenses: A Study of Adult Felons." *Justice Quarterly* 13:431–54.

Allen, Hilary. 1987. *Justice Unbalanced*. Philadelphia: Open University Press.

Allen, Judith. 1989. "Men, Crime and Criminology: Recasting the Questions." *International Journal of the Sociology of Law* 17:19–39.

Arnold, Regina. 1990. "Processes of Victimization and Criminalization of Black Women." *Social Justice* 17:153–66.

Austin, Regina. 1992. "'The Black Community,' Its Lawbreakers, and a Politics of Identification." *Southern California Law Review* 65:1769–817.

Baskin, Deborah, and Ira Sommers. 1993. "Females' Initiation into Violent Street Crime." *Justice Quarterly* 10:559–83.

Becker, Howard S. 1973. *Outsiders*. New York: Free Press.

Beirne, Piers, and James W. Messerschmidt. 1995. *Criminology*. 2nd ed. San Diego: Harcourt Brace Jovanovich.

Belknap, Joanne. 1996. *Invisible Woman: Gender, Crime, and Justice*. Belmont, Calif.: Wadsworth.

Blumstein, Alfred, Jacqueline Cohen, and David Farrington. 1988. "Criminal Career Research: Its Value for Criminology." *Criminology* 26:1–35.

Bottcher, Jean. 1995. "Gender as Social Control." *Justice Quarterly* 12:33–57.

Broidy, Lisa, and Robert Agnew. 1997. "Gender and Crime: A General Strain Theory Perspective." Unpublished manuscript, Department of Sociology, Washington State University.

Bureau of Justice Statistics. 1992. *Women in Jail, 1989*. Washington, D.C.: U.S. Department of Justice, Bureau of Justice Statistics.

Cain, Maureen, ed. 1989. *Growing Up Good*. Newbury Park, Calif.: Sage.

Campbell, Anne. 1990. "On the Invisibility of the Female Delinquent Peer Group." *Women and Criminal Justice* 2:41–62.

———. 1991. *The Girls in the Gang*. 2nd ed. New York: Basil Blackwell.

Canaan, Joyce E. 1991. "Is 'Doing Nothing' Just Boys Play? Integrating Feminist and Cultural Studies Perspectives on Working-Class Young Men's Masculinity." In *Off-Centre: Feminism and Cultural Studies*, edited by Jackie Stacey, Sarah Franklin, and Celia Lury. New York: HarperCollins Academic.

Carlen, Pat. 1988. *Women, Crime and Poverty*. Philadelphia: Open University Press.

Chesney-Lind, Meda. 1989. "Girls' Crime and Woman's Place: Toward a Feminist Model of Female Delinquency." *Crime and Delinquency* 35:5–29.

Chesney-Lind, Meda, and Randall G. Shelden. 1992. *Girls, Delinquency, and Juvenile Justice*. Pacific Grove, Calif.: Brooks/Cole.

Daly, Kathleen. 1989. "Gender and Varieties of White-Collar Crime." *Criminology* 27:769–94.

———. 1992. "Women's Pathways to Felony Court: Feminist Theories of Lawbreaking and Problems of Representation." *Southern California Review of Law and Women's Studies* 2:11–52.

———. 1994. *Gender, Crime, and Punishment*. New Haven, Conn.: Yale University Press.

Daly, Kathleen, and Meda Chesney-Lind. 1988. "Feminism and Criminology." *Justice Quarterly* 5:497–538.

Daly, Kathleen, and Michael Tonry. 1997. "Race, Gender, and Sentencing." In *Crime and Justice: A Review of Research*, vol. 22, edited by Michael Tonry. Chicago: University of Chicago Press.

Decker, Scott, Richard Wright, Alison Redfern, and Dietrich Smith. 1993. "A Woman's Place Is in the Home: Females and Residential Burglary." *Justice Quarterly* 10:143–62.

Denno, Deborah W. 1994. "Gender, Crime, and the Criminal Law Defenses." *Journal of Criminal Law and Criminology* 85:80–180.

Einstadter, Werner, and Stuart Henry. 1995. *Criminological Theory: An Analysis of Its Underlying Assumptions*. New York: McGraw-Hill.

Esbensen, Finn-Aage, and David Huizinga. 1993. "Gangs, Drugs, and Delinquency in a Survey of Urban Youth." *Criminology* 31:565–87.

Fineman, Martha. 1990. "Challenging Law, Establishing Differences: The Future of Feminist Legal Scholarship." *Florida Law Review* 42:25–43.

———. 1994. "Feminist Legal Scholarship and Women's Gendered Lives." In *Lawyers in a Postmodern World*, edited by Maureen Cain and Christine B. Harrington. Buckingham, England: Open University Press.

———. 1995. *The Neutered Mother, the Sexual Family, and Other Twentieth-Century Tragedies*. New York: Routledge.

Gibbons, Don C. 1994. *Talking About Crime and Criminals: Problems and Issues in Theory Development in Criminology*. Englewood Cliffs, N.J.: Prentice-Hall.

Gilfus, Mary E. 1992. "From Victims to Survivors to Offenders: Women's Routes of Entry and Immersion into Street Crime." *Women and Criminal Justice* 4:63–89.

Hagan, John, A. R. Gillis, and John Simpson. 1987. "Class in the Household: A Power-Control Theory of Gender and Delinquency." *American Journal of Sociology* 90:1151–78.

———. 1990. "Clarifying and Extending Power-Control Theory." *American Journal of Sociology* 95:1024–37.

Hagedorn, John M. 1994. "Homeboys, Dope Fiends, Legits, and New Jacks." *Criminology* 32:197–219.

Harding, Sandra. 1986. *The Science Question in Feminism*. Ithaca, N.Y.: Cornell University Press.

Heidensohn, Frances M. 1985. *Women and Crime*. New York: New York University Press.

———. 1992. *Women in Control? The Role of Women in Law Enforcement*. Oxford: Oxford University Press.

———. 1994a. "From Being to Knowing: Some Issues in the Study of Gender in Contemporary Society." *Women and Criminal Justice* 6:13–37.

———. 1994b. "Gender and Crime." In *The Oxford Handbook of Criminology*, edited by Mike Maquire, Rod Morgan, and Robert Reinder. Oxford: Oxford University Press.

———. 1996. *Women and Crime*. 2nd ed. London: Macmillan.

Heimer, Karen. 1995. "Gender, Race, and the Pathways to Delinquency." In *Crime and Inequality*, edited by John Hagan and Ruth Peterson. Palo Alto, Calif.: Stanford University Press.

Hester, Marianne, Liz Kelly, and Jill Radford, eds. 1996. *Women, Violence and Male Power*. Philadelphia: Open University Press.

Hill, Gary D., and Elizabeth M. Crawford. 1990. "Women, Race and Crime." *Criminology* 28:601–26.

Jefferson, Tony. 1996. "Introduction" to special issue on "Masculinities, Social Relations, and Crime." *British Journal of Criminology* 36:337–47.

Jensen, Gary. 1996. "Gender Variation in Juvenile Crime: New Findings on Persistent Issues." Paper presented at the annual meeting of the American Society of Criminology, Chicago.

Joe, Karen, and Meda Chesney-Lind. 1995. "'Just Every Mother's Angel': An Analysis of Gender and Ethnic Variations in Youth Gang Membership." *Gender and Society* 9:408–30.

Kelly, Liz. 1988. *Surviving Sexual Violence*. Minneapolis: University of Minnesota Press.

Kruttschnitt, Candace. 1994. "Gender and Interpersonal Violence." In *Understanding and Preventing Violence*, vol. 3, *Social Influences*, edited by Albert J. Reiss and Jeffrey Roth. Washington, D.C.: National Academy Press.

———. 1996. "Contributions of Quantitative Methods to the Study of Gender and Crime, or Bootstrapping Our Way into the Theoretical Thicket." *Journal of Quantitative Criminology* 12:135–61.

Kruttschnitt, Candace, and Rosemary Gartner. 1993. "Introduction to the Special Issue on Gender, Crime, and Criminal Justice." *Journal of Quantitative Criminology* 9:323–27.

Laub, John H., and Joan M. McDermott. 1985. "An Analysis of Serious Crime by Young Black Women." *Criminology* 23:81–98.

Maguire, Kathleen, Ann L. Pastore, and Timothy J. Flanagan, eds. 1993. *Sourcebook of Criminal Justice Statistics, 1992*. Washington, D.C.: U.S. Government Printing Office.

Maher, Lisa. 1995a. "Dope Girls: Gender, Race, and Class in the Drug Economy." Ph.D. diss., School of Criminal Justice, Rutgers University.

———. 1995b. "In the Name of Love: Women and Initiation to Illicit Drugs." In *Gender and Crime*, edited by R. Emerson Dobash, Russell P. Dobash, and Lesley Noakes. Cardiff: University of Wales Press.

———. 1997. *Sexed Work: Gender, Race, and Resistance in a Brooklyn Drug Market*. Oxford: Clarendon Press.

Maher, Lisa, and Richard Curtis. 1992. "Women on the Edge of Crime: Crack Cocaine and the Changing Contexts of Street-Level Sex Work in New York City." *Crime, Law, and Social Change* 18:221–58.

Maher, Lisa, and Kathleen Daly. 1996. "Women in the Street-Level Drug Economy: Continuity or Change?" *Criminology* 34:465–91.

Mann, Kenneth, Stanton Wheeler, and Austin Sarat. 1980. "Sentencing the White-Collar Offender." *American Criminal Law Review* 17:479–500.

Martin, Susan E., and Nancy C. Jurik. 1996. *Doing Justice, Doing Gender*. Newbury Park, Calif.: Sage.

Messerschmidt, James W. 1993. *Masculinities and Crime: Critique and Reconceptualization of Theory*. Lanham, Md.: Rowman and Littlefield.

Miller, Eleanor. 1986. *Street Woman*. Philadelphia: Temple University Press.

Miller, Jody. 1995. "Gender and Power on the Streets." *Journal of Contemporary Ethnography* 23:427–52.

———. 1996. "Female Gang Involvement in a Midwestern City: Correlates, Nature, and Meanings." Ph.D. diss., University of Southern California, Department of Sociology.

Moore, Joan. 1991. *Going Down to the Barrio: Homeboys and Homegirls in Change*. Philadelphia: Temple University Press.

Morash, Merry, and Meda Chesney-Lind. 1991. "A Reformulation and Partial Test of the Power-Control Theory of Delinquency." *Justice Quarterly* 8:347–77.

Morris, Allison. 1987. *Women, Crime and Criminal Justice*. New York: Basil Blackwell.

Ogilvie, Emma. 1996. "Masculine Obsessions: An Examination of Criminology, Criminality and Gender." *Australian and New Zealand Journal of Criminology* 29:205–26.

Ogle, Robbin, Daniel Maier-Katkin, and Thomas J. Bernard. 1995. "A Theory of Homicidal Behavior Among Women." *Criminology* 33:173–93.

Polk, Kenneth. 1994. "Masculinity, Honour, and Confrontational Homicide." In *Just Boys Doing Business?* edited by Tim Newburn and Elizabeth A. Stanko. New York: Routledge.

Pollock-Byrne, Jocelyn M. 1990. *Women, Prison, and Crime*. Pacific Grove, Calif.: Brooks/Cole.

Ptacek, James. 1988. "Why Do Men Batter Their Wives?" In *Feminist Perspectives on Wife Abuse*, edited by Kersti Yllo and Michele P. Bogard. Newbury Park, Calif.: Sage.

Rosenbaum, Marsha. 1981. *Women on Heroin*. New Brunswick, N.J.: Rutgers University Press.

Sampson, Robert J., and John Laub. 1993. *Crime in the Making: Pathways and Turning Points Through Life*. Cambridge, Mass.: Harvard University Press.

Sanchez, Lisa. 1996. "Agency and Resistance in a Local Sexual Economy." Unpublished manuscript, Department of Criminology, Law and Society, University of California-Irvine.

Schulhofer, Stephen J. 1995. "The Feminist Challenge in Criminal Law." *University of Pennsylvania Law Review* 143:2151–207.

Simon, Rita. 1975. *Women and Crime*. Lexington, Mass.: Lexington Books.

Simon, Rita, and Jean Landis. 1991. *The Crimes Women Commit, the Punishments They Receive*. Lexington, Mass.: Lexington Books.

Simpson, Sally S. 1991. "Caste, Class, and Violent Crime: Explaining Difference in Female Offending." *Criminology* 29:115–35.

Smith, Douglas A., and Raymond Paternoster. 1987. "The Gender Gap in Theories of Deviance: Issues and Evidence." *Journal of Research in Crime and Delinquency* 24:140–72.

Sommers, Ira, and Deborah Baskin. 1992. "Sex, Race, Age, and Violent Offending." *Violence and Victims* 7:191–201.

———. 1993. "The Situational Context of Violent Female Offending." *Journal of Research in Crime and Delinquency* 30:136–62.

Stanko, Elizabeth A. 1990. *Everyday Violence: How Women and Men Experience Male Violence*. New York: Routledge.

Steffensmeier, Darrell. 1983. "Organization Properties and Sex-Segregation in the Underworld: Building a Sociological Theory of Sex Differences in Crime." *Social Forces* 61:1010–32.

———. 1993. "National Trends in Female Arrests, 1960–1990: Assessment and Recommendations for Research." *Journal of Quantitative Criminology* 9:411–41.

Steffensmeier, Darrell, and Emilie Allan. 1996. "Gender and Crime: Toward a Gendered Theory of Female Offending." *Annual Review of Sociology* 22:459–87.

Sullivan, Mercer L. 1989. *"Getting Paid": Youth Crime and Work in the Inner City*. Ithaca, N.Y.: Cornell University Press.

Sutherland, Edwin H. [1949] 1983. *White Collar Crime: The Uncut Version*. New Haven, Conn.: Yale University Press.

Taylor, Carl S. 1993. *Girls, Gangs, Women and Drugs*. East Lansing: Michigan State University Press.

Tripplet, Ruth, and Laura B. Myers. 1995. "Evaluating Contextual Patterns of Delinquency: Gender-Based Differences." *Justice Quarterly* 12:59–84.

Valentine, Bettylou. 1978. *Hustling and Other Hard Work: Lifestyles in the Ghetto*. New York: Free Press.

Widom, Cathy Spatz. 1989. "Child Abuse, Neglect, and Violent Criminal Behavior." *Criminology* 27:251–71.

Wilson, Margo, and Martin Daly. 1992. "Who Kills Whom in Spouse Killings? On the Exceptional Sex Ratio of Spousal Homicides in the United States." *Criminology* 30:189–215.

Wonders, Nancy A., and Susan L. Caulfield. 1993. "Women's Work? The Contradictory Implications of Courses on Women and the Criminal Justice System." *Journal of Criminal Justice Education* 4:79–100.

Part II

TOPICAL CRIME PROBLEMS

4

Street Gangs

MALCOLM W. KLEIN

G angs are informal social groups. As such, most of them have no membership rosters, no organizational charts, no constitutions and bylaws, no written criteria for membership or for acceptable and unacceptable behavior. Thus it can be difficult to distinguish gangs from other groups, or gang members from nonmembers.

What Are Street Gangs?

Frederick Thrasher, the first major scholar to study urban gangs (1927), defined them as interstitial groups drawn together by conflict. Klein (1971) emphasized the group characteristics of gangs, including self-recognition and community recognition of the groups, along with a heightened level of antisocial behavior. Miller (1980) attempted to define gangs both in relation to other forms of youth groups and by reference to specific characteristics assigned to them by police, social agencies, and the press. Horowitz (1990), considering these and other definitional exercises and the seeming arbitrariness of defining a variable and changing phenomenon, concluded that it might be wiser not to define the term, for fear of limiting the scholarly process of learning about gangs.

The various attempts at definition are in fact laudable—scientists should be in agreement about the nature of what they study. Yet the Horowitz position, too, has merit, in that each of the available definitions is in one way or another too limiting. Recent data, however, suggest that the issue may be one of form more than substance, an idea that derives from trying to specify operational definitions of gangs for the purposes of empirical research. Certain studies, in attempting to distinguish between youths who are and others who are not gang members, have yielded a consistent finding: youths themselves distinguish effectively between the gang and nongang categories in response to direct questions (e.g., "Are you now a member of a local gang?" or "Is this group you belong to a gang?" or "Are there gangs in your neighborhood; are you a member?" and so on). Follow-up questions may ask about the time of joining a gang; whether the gang has a name, initiation rites, special symbols or language; and other such presumed cultural aspects of gang life. But the

111

principal distinguishing factor is the youth's statement that he or she is or is not a gang member.

The differences between the admittees and deniers are often large—that is, the operational definition is "robust." Those who respond differently to the question also differ in a crucial way in their level and type of involvement in delinquency and crime. They also differ on a substantial number of other factors about themselves, their values, and their families. It is a difference that makes a difference—one that would not emerge were it not strong enough to overcome gang-nongang similarities in this research on neighborhoods of residence, schools attended, and so on. Furthermore, this robust definitional approach has emerged despite major methodological differences in the studies, and their locations across the country (Esbensen, Huizinga, and Weiher 1993; Klein 1995; Sanders 1994; Thornberry et al. 1993).

There is, as yet, no similar operational resolution to a related definitional problem: what to include as gang-related crime. The issue is important both to understanding the nature of gang crime and to accounting for it in police and court operations. On one side are those who would count as "gang-related" any offense committed by or against a gang member (leaving aside, perhaps, such irrelevant examples as domestic conflict or accidental victimization as on the Fourth of July). The rationale stems both from the gang member's involvement and from the fact that membership clearly increases the propensity for crime (i.e., the event might well not have occurred without gang membership; Tracy 1979; Esbensen, Huizinga, and Weiher 1993; Thornberry et al. 1993).

The contrary view would count as gang-related only those offenses committed in the furtherance of gang interests, that is, crime motivated by gang values. These would include events related to gang rivalries, retaliations, territoriality, status enhancement, or the sharing of spoils from robberies, drug sales, and the like. The arguments in favor of each definition are too complex to detail here, but they are both conceptual and methodological. But the issue can be important when one attempts to state how much crime is attributable to gangs. Recent research (Maxson and Klein 1996) compared recorded gang homicides in Los Angeles and Chicago, the nation's two heaviest contributors to gang crime. The Los Angeles police department uses the member-based definition, and Chicago's the motive-based decision. The findings of the research were twofold. First, the member-based definition yields roughly twice the number of gang-related homicides. Second, member-defined and motive-defined homicides do not differ substantially in their character, that is, in the kinds of individuals involved and the characteristics of the incidents themselves. Thus, here we have a difference that *does not* make a difference in understanding gang crime, but *does* make one in assessing how much of it there is. When Chicago recently changed its definitional approach, it reported a massive increase in gang-related homicides as a result (Maxson and Klein 1996). Los Angeles now counts it both ways.

Finally, crime attributed to gangs can be defined differently by its seriousness or, quite similarly, by its stereotypical character. The public image of gang-related crime is largely shaped by press and law enforcement reports. As a result of the large increase in gang problems in the 1980s and 1990s, law enforcement has combined with politicians to define gangs and gang crime in order to improve gang prosecutions and to apply heavier punishments specifically to gang members. To accomplish these ends, antigang legislation has increasingly defined gang-related crime in limited terms: homicide, assault, robbery, graffiti-vandalism, witness intimidation, drive-by shootings, and drug sales are among the most commonly listed "gang crimes" (Klein 1995). The result is that police often limit their recording of gang crimes to these offenses (at the expense of all the property, status, and victimless offenses that actually constitute the bulk of illegal acts committed by gang members). If police record only these serious and stereotypical crimes, then these are also the only ones they report, yielding a vastly distorted image for public consumption.

Characterizing Street Gangs

Gang is a broad term. It appears in Chaucer and Shakespeare with little of the meaning now ascribed to it. Since most of the public concern and the police response involve street gangs, scholars have found it useful to separate these from other gang forms. Thus the term *street gang,* the principal subject of this chapter, is meant to exclude such demonstrably different groups as prison gangs, motorcycle gangs, terrorist groups, organized crime families and organizations, and a wide assortment of youth peer groups that on occasion get into legal trouble but do not orient themselves toward illegal behavior. Less clearly distinguished from street gangs, yet often of a distinct character, are supremacist groups such as skinheads and specialty groups that focus on specific crime types—for example, auto theft cliques or drug sales gangs (although these may have evolved and separated out of street gangs).

While, as will be shown, street gangs manifest a wide variety of structures, they can be loosely characterized as follows:

- Street gangs are composed principally of youths, but with age ranges from nine or ten years to the thirties. Average age is generally between late teens and early twenties.
- Street gangs are composed principally of racial and ethnic minorities, with whites constituting less than 10 percent by inclusion of supremacist groups.
- Street gangs are primarily male, but with gender ratios reported from 10-to-1 to 1-to-1. Autonomous female gangs exist but are rare.
- Street gangs are generally located in inner-urban areas, but more recently they have been found in the minority enclaves of many towns that are not generally thought of as "urban."
- The illegal behaviors of street gangs are generally highly versatile;

that is, they participate in a wide variety of crimes rather than specializing in one or a few types (specialty gangs excepted, by definition). Thus most gangs are not violent gangs or drug gangs or conflict gangs. Indeed, given the preponderance of certain nonserious forms of behavior, they might more properly be called alcohol gangs, petty theft gangs, loitering gangs, or graffiti gangs.

- Street gangs often define themselves as oriented to crime, given their own recognition that they are in fact more crime-involved than are most youthful groups. It is suggested that there is an ill-defined "tipping point" in criminal orientation that effectively separates street gangs from many other groups.
- In contrast to the public image, street gangs more often than not are relatively loose structures of only moderate cohesiveness, with distributed or unclear leadership, considerable membership turnover and instability, and codes of honor and loyalty strongly felt but often broken when convenient. The *West Side Story* image of street gangs is mythical and grossly misleading.

Gang Structures

There has been a tendency to typologize gangs in terms of behavior patterns—violent gangs, party gangs, and the like—despite the almost universal finding of their criminal versatility. Understandably, these typologies have not held up well empirically, although they tend to capture the public imagination. Recent research (Klein and Maxson 1996) has taken a different tack, emphasizing a series of structural dimensions such as gang size, duration, internal cliquing, ages, and so on. Using information taken from hundreds of police gang experts, this research has revealed five basic street gang structures, of which three are the most revealing: traditional gangs, compressed gangs, and specialty gangs.

Traditional street gangs are long-lived, regenerating themselves through two or more generations of members over twenty years or more. They are very large, averaging close to 200 members, each broken into a number of subgroups based on different ages or neighborhoods. They are versatile in their crime patterns and strongly territorial. The age range is surprisingly wide, encompassing as much as twenty or even thirty years from oldest to youngest. They are more common, by a 3-to-1 margin, among Hispanic than among black populations.

Compressed gangs manifest a shorter life—generally ten years or less—and are far smaller, averaging somewhat under fifty members. They typically do not have subgroups. Although versatile in their crime patterns, they may or may not develop a strong territorial emphasis. The age range is comparatively narrow—less than ten years between youngest and oldest members—and skewed toward the adolescent ages. Ethnic balance is greater than in traditional gangs, with almost equal numbers of Hispanic and black groups but substantial numbers of Asian, white, and mixed backgrounds as well.

Specialty gangs are also ordinarily under ten years duration and are the smallest of the gang types, the average size being around twenty-five members. They do not develop subgroups but may develop rather distinct crime roles for individual members. They are far less versatile in their crime patterns, specializing instead on a few focused crimes. Thus they may be drug distribution gangs, graffiti gangs, burglary gangs, auto theft gangs, and so on. They are often territorial, but the territory is less likely to be based on residence than on crime target territories (where drug markets can be established, or where there is a ready supply of vulnerable homes or autos). There is no particularly strong ethnic pattern to specialty gangs, other than a predominance of blacks among the drug gangs concentrating on crack cocaine.

Because of differences in size, traditional gangs generate almost twice as many arrests as do compressed and specialty gangs, yet specialty gangs yield almost twice the number of arrests per member as do traditional gangs, with compressed gangs in the middle. Because of their durability, traditional gangs have more often been the focus of research, especially in the 1950s and 1960s, when some of the breakthrough studies of gangs were undertaken (Miller 1958, 1962; Short and Strodtbeck 1965; Spergel 1964; Klein 1971). Yet despite their size, durability, and amenability to research, traditional gangs are not predominant. Compressed gangs are far more common, by a ratio of 3- or 5-to-1, and twice as many cities contain compressed gangs as traditional gangs or specialty gangs.

It is the specialty gangs, constituting fewer than one in five of the total, that most challenge the definitions of street gangs. White supremacist or skinhead groups, for instance, differ radically in their focus (Hamm 1993); "tagger crews," or graffiti gangs, show very low cohesiveness and little serious criminality; drug gangs are much higher than most others in cohesiveness, organization, and criminal orientation (Padilla 1992; Klein 1995). It is characteristics like these, revealed by a structural analysis, that hold promise for developing differentiated gang intervention programs.

Less can be said about female gangs, in part because they are not tracked by law enforcement to the same extent as are male gangs. Field studies, however, generally show two patterns: female groups as "auxiliary" to male gangs, or females integrated into male structures. Fully autonomous female gangs have generally been rare over many decades. Their crime patterns, although similar in kind to those of males, are far lower in actual numbers of offenses per member. With fewer female gang members and lower criminal involvement, research on female gang members is less complete than that on males.

Gang Locations

Street gangs have generally been considered a big-city problem, but in fact they also have been located in smaller urban centers over the years.

Research through 1992 revealed that the number of cities with gangs roughly doubled from prior to 1960 to 1970, doubled again by 1980, and then quadrupled by the early 1990s, with a documented 800 and an estimated 1,100 gang cities by 1992 (Klein 1995). An even more comprehensive survey of 4,200 jurisdictions in the mid-1990s put the number at over 1,400 cities, towns, and counties, with a total of 25,000 gangs and 652,000 gang members, although most of these areas do not have large numbers of gangs or gang members (Institute for Intergovernmental Research 1996).

The northeastern section of the nation, with stereotypical gang cities such as New York, Philadelphia, and Boston, is nonetheless less gang-involved than the western and southwestern sections. California is far more gang-populated than any other state. The Los Angeles and Chicago areas have long been the most active gang locations, where traditional gang structures and confederations of gangs have been most common.

Within any town or city, the location of gangs is signaled by patterns of ethnic and racial settlement. In earlier decades, when European immigration rates were high, ethnic enclaves led to the formation of gangs of Poles, Irish, Germans, Eastern European Jews, and so on. With such groups now absorbed into the American mainstream, urban gang areas today are those featuring segregated black, Hispanic, and Asian populations. Many towns and cities have such areas, so that even towns of fewer than 10,000 citizens can produce street gangs. The more poverty-stricken the area, the likelier yet are gang developments. It seems clear that street gangs reflect social structure, fomented most notably among the unaccepted, the alienated, and the discouraged segments of our population.

Such groups are not a feature of American society alone. Reports of gangs have been common in Asia, Africa, Central and South America, and Europe (Clinard and Abbott 1973; Spergel 1995; Covey, Menard, and Franzese 1992). These reports have often been sketchy and uniformly uncoordinated by way of common definitions and common research methods. Still, the descriptions often sound similar to those of American gangs.

Most recently, two reviews of gangs in Europe (Klein and Gatz 1993; Klein 1996) suggest that cities in England, Sweden, Germany, Holland, Belgium, and Russia are facing a slowly increasing gang problem. Further, the distinction between traditional, compressed, and specialty gangs appears to apply reasonably well to the European situation. As in the United States, traditional and specialty gangs are less common than are compressed gangs. Yet in none of the European nations, nor in any other nation described so far, is gang proliferation anywhere near as great as in the United States.

Characterizing Gang Members

The most important point to make about members of street gangs is that in many respects they are not obviously different from their neighborhood peers. The bulk of their hours, as with their peers, are spent in sleeping, eating, attending school or jobs, being with family and friends, and spending time with girlfriends and boyfriends. It is the quality of these activities that often distinguishes gang from nongang life; despite occasional bursts of excitement from real or recalled exploits, it is a relatively boring, desultory life.

Less connected to school, less able to obtain or hold jobs, more alienated from their families, gang members more often are found "hanging out" in the streets, in alleys, in public parks, on the fringes of school grounds, and generally where they can observe the goings-on of others while not themselves actively engaging in neighborhood life (although evening partying is common). Most of this time is not spent in delinquent or criminal activity, and this is perhaps the second most important point to make about gang members. They do what the rest of us do, more or less, most of the time. Usually they are not marauding, pillaging, assaulting, stealing, using or selling dope, or behaving as something between neighborhood pests and committed criminals.

Still, more than other young people, gang members do engage in antisocial and criminal activities, and it is this facet of their lives that most draws public and official attention. Most commonly, this includes drinking, minor drug use, public order offenses such as loitering and graffiti writing and disturbing the peace, petty theft, minor fighting among themselves, and threatening other peers. These are not desirable behaviors, but they are neither glamorous (as portrayed in some movies) nor dramatic (as portrayed in the press). Thus they do not achieve the visibility of the offenses that receive most official and public attention. Since the 1980s, interpersonal violence and drug sales have dominated public discourse about gangs.

Gang violence—or, more properly, violence committed by gang members—typically exhibits several patterns:

- It is a relatively small portion of all gang offending.
- It is more often committed against other gang members than against the nongang general public.
- It is most often nonlethal, but lethality has been increased by the ready accessibility of handguns.
- In its most severe forms, it is concentrated in a small number of the members of a gang and in a small number of gangs in a multigang jurisdiction: a few gangs and a few gang members contribute disproportionately to gang violence.
- Violence, like all offending, is more common among gang than nongang offenders: gang membership exacerbates most forms of offending, especially serious or violent forms of offending.
- Most gang violence, contrary to many media and law enforcement portrayals, is not committed in the furtherance of drug sales and distribution, nor in the furtherance of any organizational pursuits other than intergang rivalry and revenge.

Drug distribution, the second offense pattern now commonly associated in the public's mind with street gangs, is in fact a recent and only occasional component of gang life. It is correct to say that many gang members engage in the sale of drugs, usually sporadically but occasionally in a stable manner. Most of these sales, however, are for the individual seller's benefits; there is no gang "treasury" to which profits are contributed. Most gang sellers are engaged at the street level, where profits are minimal in any case (Maxson and Klein 1994).

Studies in the southern California area (Maxson 1995) reveal that the majority of street sellers are not gang-affiliated. Surveys of police nationwide reveal that the gang–drug sales connection is weak, although notable exceptions such as Detroit and Washington, D.C., fuel the myth of gang-controlled drug distribution.

It is the confusion of most street gangs—traditional and compressed, as described earlier—with specialty drug gangs that requires clarification. Drug gangs, either street gang cliques that have spun off independently or new groups formed specifically for the drug business, do not resemble traditional and compressed gangs. Drug gangs are more cohesive and structured, smaller, and more tightly led; they use violence for instrumental purposes to protect business interests, consist of older members, and are far more vulnerable to rationally devised law enforcement crackdown procedures. Most important, they constitute but a small fraction of all the gangs in our towns and cities.

With all this emphasis on the proliferation of street gangs and their purported indulgence in violence and drugs, one is apt to think of them as a quintessential American problem. However, some forms of street gangs can be found worldwide. The violence of some gangs in Manila, for example, far surpasses most American descriptions (Francia 1991). Groups in Mexico City are reportedly ubiquitous. Drug gangs in London and Manchester, England, while relatively new, are growing in both numbers and violence. Compressed gangs are now to be found in Holland, Germany, Belgium, Sweden, and Switzerland, while traditional gangs of over ten years' standing have been described both in Berlin and in up to a dozen Russian cities. Although the prevalence of street gangs in these locations is far, far lower than in the United States, their occurrence in the same forms and in similar contexts of segregated areas of ethnic poverty strongly suggests that street gangs are not an American phenomenon; they are an urban, ethnic phenomenon, arising from similar circumstances, perhaps aggravated by similar societal responses, and presumably treatable by similar programs.

How Do We Account for Street Gangs?

There are several ways to phrase the question Whence street gangs? We can ask, Why are there street gangs? Why do youths join street gangs? Why do street gangs proliferate? Most theoretical work has asked the first question, while the second has been asked and answered, with surprising consistency, through qualitative research but almost never through quantitative research. The question about gang proliferation is the newest of the three and is subject more to speculation than to research.

Theories of Gang Existence

The Chicago School of Sociology set the first parameters for gang theory in the 1930s and 1940s, emphasizing urban disorganization and inter-group conflict (Thrasher 1927; Shaw and McKay 1942). The 1950s and 1960s saw an explosion of interest in street gangs among social scientists, primarily in response to the question of why gangs form. Three theoretical perspectives seemed to best capture important aspects of gang etiology.

Albert Cohen (1955) observed that gangs were located principally among disadvantaged groups—lower-class populations in which youth desired middle-class accoutrements but seemed blocked from attaining them. Cohen used the school context to good effect as a case in point. Lower-class youths often came to the school situation with poor academic preparation, as well as aspiration levels that worked against them when they faced schools and teachers that embodied middle-class values. They could not succeed against the "middle-class measuring rod," failed to achieve status, became frustrated, found fellowship among their peers, and struck back in a "reaction formation" against middle-class values. Gangs facilitated this process and expressed this collective frustration. As a result, gang youths as described by Cohen were self-interested, hedonistic, and antagonistic toward mainstream society. Their ganging and delinquency were thus expressive more than instrumental, reflecting a form of social class rebellion.

Richard Cloward and Lloyd Ohlin (1960) combined some of Cohen's thinking with a more calculating, less expressive sense of what produced gangs. These authors, influenced by the sociologist Robert Merton, saw not only that lower-class youths were blocked from middle-class attainment but also that, within their own communities, they might also be blocked from illegitimate and legitimate paths to success. Thus, for instance, blocked opportunities would lead to property crimes designed to yield the material goods that otherwise might not be available, thus creating a "criminal subculture." But if in one's own neighborhood even the criminal opportunities were not sufficient, one could strike back in the form of violent activity and thus the creation of a "conflict subculture." Finally, if community opportunities and controls prevented this conflict solution, youths would fall back protectively and escape into a world of alcohol and drugs, creating a "retreatist subculture." From these three subcultures, it was hypothesized, three behavioral types of gangs would emerge: criminal gangs, conflict gangs, and retreatist gangs. Cloward and Ohlin then described gang youths as more actively striving to work around the barriers to middle-class success and responding differentially depending on what alternate routes were available. Like Cohen's youths, these were unhappy youngsters, displeased with their lot in life, but not as mean-spirited as the Cohen gang members. In both cases, however, gangs emerged as a response to class-based social strains, and therefore both theories are known as "strain theories."

Some contrast is offered by Walter Miller's approach (1958). Miller, an anthropologist who saw the issues more proximally accounted for by class-based culture conflict, analyzed lower-class life for those structural elements that yielded a "lower-class culture as a generating milieu" for gangs. The structural elements included the female-dominated households of gang members and a lifestyle that was natural and normal within the lower class rather than a reaction against the middle class. The female-dominated household forced the young male to turn to the streets and his male peers as a way to reassert his masculinity in a setting that stressed lower-class "focal concerns" of toughness, street smarts, and fatalism. When the behaviors generated naturally in this context were confronted by the carriers of middle-class values—teachers, police, agency workers—the resulting clash of values led to the negative labeling of gangs and the street activities of gang members. Thus, Miller's gang youths were not the status-frustrated, antagonistic, hedonistic boys of Cohen's gangs, nor the opportunity-seeking delinquents posited by Cloward and Ohlin. Rather, they were the overly masculine carriers of a class culture that rewarded such behavior. One gets the sense that Miller's boys were a happier lot.

An anecdotal attempt to test these theories was made by a group of gang researchers who undertook a brief (one-week) set of street observations of the members of four large traditional gangs. The purpose of the exercise was to determine if these gang members most closely resembled Cohen boys, Cloward and Ohlin boys, or Miller boys. The results from four independent sets of field observations were both striking and consistent. Each observer came back saying that there were Cohen boys out there, and Cloward and Ohlin boys, and Miller boys. Further, at different times of the afternoon and evening (when gang observations are most feasible), the same youth could appear to be each type of gang member. In sum, each theorist had observed one aspect of gang life, where all three were available.

A more systematic test of these theoretical perspectives was undertaken in a large, comprehensive study of gangs in Chicago (Short and Strodtbeck 1965) using observations, gang worker reports, and extensive interviews with both gang and nongang youth. These researchers concluded that none of the three theories stood up well under test. They did, however, emphasize yet another factor they thought deserved more attention, namely, "group process," as they called it, or group dynamics more generally.

The import of this emphasis is that what spawns gangs only begins to explain gang behavior, and the group processes within the gang structure need explication as well. This view was readily confirmed among Los Angeles gangs by Klein (1971), who measured gang cohesiveness and found that it played a principal role in the rise and fall of street gangs, especially those being served by various gang intervention programs.

In addition to strain theories and group process theories, a third set of approaches, in some ways similar to Miller's, were expounded by scholars such as Horowitz in Chicago (1983) and Vigil in Los Angeles (1988). Perhaps reflecting the Hispanic culture of the gangs they observed (but Miller's gangs were not Hispanic), these writers viewed gangs as a natural mechanism for lower-class, ethnically marginalized groups to express cultural norms of honor, individual respect, and masculinity. Noting an almost separate "street culture" requiring specific survival techniques, youngsters growing up in inner-city enclaves learned through observation and mimicry a set of "street smarts" for both self-protection and status attainment that was best exemplified in the local male groupings labeled gangs by themselves or others. In this view, gang, culture, and neighborhood become intertwined as the context of public youthful behavior. Comfortable and exciting adaptations to the street are more immediately salient than are strain or culture conflicts.

Theories of Gang Membership

The group process emphasis of Short and Strodtbeck and of Klein, together with the cultural emphases exemplified by Miller, Horowitz, and Vigil, form a bridge to questions of why youths join gangs, in that they help to explain reasons both for "trying on" gang membership and for receiving satisfaction from joining. It is important to understand in this context that most gang-age youths are not drawn to gangs even in heavily gang-involved communities. An estimated 5 to 20 percent of local males join gangs in these settings; nongang status is the norm. Furthermore, of those who do begin to affiliate, or "hang," with gangs, many soon depart, while others remain on the periphery.

Thus, there are important selection factors that separate committed gang members from nongang members. The scholarly and practitioner literatures are remarkably consistent in characterizing what youths derive from gang membership: status, identity, something to belong to in the face of inadequate home and school attachment, a sense of protection from real or imagined threats, excitement and challenge, and, for many, a door to delinquent or criminal gain.

Some clues to which youngsters are most drawn to these advantages come from Klein's early (1971) research that isolated two factors. More-involved gang members differed from those peripherally involved in their individual deficits: they had lower intelligence and school performance and lower impulse control; they were more aggressive, more disturbed, and more criminally involved; and they had fewer alternative skills and interests. Second, more-involved members had a higher social affiliation need, being more involved in spontaneous events, in clique activities, in leadership requirements, and in being more accepted by other members.

We can think of such characteristics as risk factors, individual propensities above and beyond the risk associated with living in segregated, poor, ethnic or racial enclaves. More recent research also implicates having gang members in the family, exposure to violence at home and in the neighborhood, and negative self-images as risk factors for gang membership. How all these factors and others interact, however, is as yet unclear. There exists a paucity of theory to put them together to predict effectively, in a given neighborhood, which youths will and which will not turn to gang membership and in what numbers as a function of neighborhood characteristics. A further glaring lacuna is the absence of good data on the nature of the family contribution. Family structure does not seem to separate gang from nongang youths. If there are contributing family processes (other than family gang member influence), these have yet to be well isolated.

We are left, then, with a theoretical gap, but one that at least is framed by several points:

- Neighborhood characteristics can yield clues to levels of gang emergence but not to the selection of youths who will join gangs.
- Family characteristics contributing to the selection of gang members are more likely to be processual than structural.
- Individual characteristics are likely to consist of both personal deficits and aggressivity on the one hand and social affiliation needs on the other.
- The usual characterization of the gains from gang membership—status, identity, belonging, and the like—may only superficially represent the combination of family, individual, and social needs that yield higher probabilities of gang membership (where gangs are available for joining).

Theories of Gang Proliferation

Gang proliferation across the country—or the recognition of this proliferation—is quite recent. Thus, there is even less accepted theory in this area than is the case for gang existence or gang membership. Three factors have received the greatest attention (Klein 1995), all of them tied temporally to the fact that gang proliferation was a slow and steady process through the early 1980s and then accelerated phenomenally beginning in the mid-1980s.

The Crack and Drug Explosion.   At just about the time that the number of gang cities was dramatically increasing—around the mid-1980s—crack cocaine emerged as a major product in California, and then over several years in many cities stretching to the East Coast. Although gang proliferation largely preceded the crack explosion, many have blamed it on the new drug. Specifically, many law enforcement agencies (federal, state, and local) pronounced that black gangs emanating first from Los Angeles became the principal distributors of crack, setting up franchising in numerous cities and creating new gangs to market their product.

The evidence was weak, but the notion fueled the need of many to explain both proliferations simultaneously. Contrary evidence and logic have proved otherwise, despite specific instances where such franchising did in fact take place. For instance, the crack sales theory did nothing to explain the equally great proliferation of Hispanic gang cities during the same period (nor the lower growth of Asian gang problems). It failed to review the temporal relations closely to note that the new gang cities appeared earlier than or contemporaneous with the spread of crack. It failed to seek alternative reasons for gang member migration (normal residence changes by families, to better job markets, and so on; Maxson 1996), which are cited by police gang experts as more common than drug-franchising purposes. Finally, it failed to be based on information from the police in the presumably affected jurisdictions (Klein 1995), or to recognize how unevenly the two proliferations emerged across the nation.

At best, we can see the gang-city proliferation and the crack explosion as the partial confluence of two social problems within temporal proximity. This probably speaks more to the state of the nation than to direct cause-and-effect relations. It teaches, as well, that jumping to conclusions about massive social change on the basis of a few instances comes closer to creating moral panic than social science.

The Urban Underclass. A more appealing explanation for gang-city proliferation stems from notions popularized by William Julius Wilson (1987) because Wilson's characterization of urban environments is at the same level of explanation as the gang phenomenon; the unit for both is the city or—closer yet—the segregated ethnic enclaves of the city. The urban underclass, being the location of "persistent and pervasive poverty," has taken hold in more and more cities and towns:

- The industrial base has shifted from city to suburb, leaving a dearth of working-class jobs and too-heavy dependence on the service economy, for which many inner city youths are poorly prepared.
- There has been a dramatic reduction in social service resources— welfare, health care, job training—and a worsening of the educational system.
- Middle-class black and Hispanic populations have migrated from city to suburb, taking with them their middle-class institutions (churches, YMCAs, parent groups, etc.) and their penchant for social organization at the neighborhood and community levels.
- Minority segregation in the inner city has increased, yielding a more dense minority population divorced from easy access to white and middle-class opportunities.

- These factors have reduced the viability of stable two-parent households, in part because marriageable employed males are less available.

This depiction has been used by Klein (1995) and others (Jackson 1991) to suggest that in each town and city increasingly manifesting the urban underclass, there is a consequent increase in factors likely to spawn urban gangs. What is needed for these gangs to appear, suggests Klein, is "sufficient numbers of lower-class, minority males, aged ten to thirty, hard-to-employ, in an area featured by high crime, absence of social controls, and absence of alternative activities" (Klein 1995, p. 198). These factors are predictable from urban underclass theory and are predictive of gang emergence in cities heretofore free of gang problems. It is precisely the era initiated by conservative federal and state policies of the Reagan administration that manifests this deterioration of so many of our cities and towns, and, suggests this theory, has created the situations in which gangs have been generated at increasing rates.

Empirical evidence for this approach has been scant to date but is best seen in works by Jackson (1991) and Hagedorn (1988), the first a macro-level analysis and the second an intensive case study of gang development in the rapidly deteriorating center of Milwaukee. Fagan (1996) and Klein (1995) provide preliminary data suggesting that the causal connection may be more typical of black than of Hispanic gang situations. What is needed is a stronger, dynamic correlational study, city by city over many locations, of the underclass development and emergence of street gangs.

Diffusion of Gang Culture. How severe the underclass situation must be to spawn new gang cities is unclear, but it may be difficult to apply the underclass hypothesis to many of the smaller cities and towns in which street gangs have appeared. An alternative or interacting factor, equally applicable to small and large jurisdictions, is the diffusion of "gang culture" throughout the country. Various aspects of this culture—styles of dress, tattooing, linguistic patterns, postures, group values—have been disseminated through movies, television, magazines, and experts' lectures, as well as by the migration of gang members. The baggy pants, cholo walk, and phrases like "homeboys" and "gangbanging" have become so common as to be incorporated into a larger youth culture and thus legitimated.[1] "Gangsta rap" music is perhaps the most controversial component of this culture.

Youths in all parts of the country, in small towns and large cities, have learned to "walk the walk and talk the talk." They can imitate gang styles or incorporate them. Groups that otherwise might remain recreational or minor offending youth groups, from break-dancers to taggers, have been described as coming into competition with each other, developing rivalries and intergroup conflict, and being transformed into street gangs (Hagedorn 1988; Klein 1995).

Adolescents are often "testers" of tolerances and limits. Trying out ganglike behaviors on parents, peers, teachers, and community officials becomes part of the test. Most find the response uncongenial, but some sense the excitement and challenge that accompany ganglike behavior, and both the behavior and the peer and adult responses become reinforcers of the values assumed to accompany the behavior. School rivalries, for instance, can be transformed into territorial imperatives, and neighborhoods become turfs. If most young people who try on the mantle of gang "wannabe" soon abandon it, enough remain who find it rewarding—providing the identity, status, and sense of group affiliation typical of gang membership. Thus the diffused culture provides the opportunity; the selective factors that traditionally provided the fodder for gang formation can then become activated in hundreds or thousands of new locations, the inner-town segregated ethnic and racial enclaves now so abundant in our society. Inadvertently, adult society has taught its youths how to imitate gang attitudes and behaviors; selected youths can take it from there.

What Is in the Future?

Have street gangs become institutionalized in our society? More than one authority believes this to be the case (Fagan 1996; Klein 1994). Evidence of the most obvious sort is this: throughout the nation, where the estimates now range up to 1,400 or more gang-involved jurisdictions, there are almost no ex-gang cities. Once a jurisdiction has formed street gangs, it seems unable to rid itself of them.

Extrapolating from Patterns

Gang activity levels are not stable but instead reveal cycles of greater and lesser activity (Jansyn 1967; Klein 1995). In Los Angeles, gang-related homicides peaked around 1980 and receded through the next few years, only to rise to another peak in the mid-1990s. In Chicago, gang-related homicides peaked in 1970, again in 1981, and again in the early 1990s. Unfortunately, in each city the subsequent peaks and valleys in the homicide numbers were in each instance higher than the previous ones, yielding an uneven but inexorable rise in the overall pattern. Many other cities, although far less impacted than Chicago and Los Angeles, report an overall rise in gang violence levels.

Adding this to the continuing proliferation of gangs in more and more jurisdictions, and to the absence of demonstrably successful antigang programs, the most reasonable expectation is for matters to become increasingly worse.

Forms of Response

Some approaches to gang intervention have become widespread; others have received attention only recently but seem likely to be implemented more widely. Among the latter are special narcotics intervention strategies, omitted from this discussion because they are commonly applied to street gangs by agencies that still confuse street gangs with drug gangs. Other approaches that are most likely to be highly visible as gang problems continue or increase are law enforcement suppression, gang databases, legal programs, gang truces, and community organization approaches.

Law Enforcement Suppression. Where police departments are sufficiently large and the gang problem sufficiently visible or persistent, the most common form of enforcement response is the establishment of special gang units. These may range from one or two officers to several hundred, as in Los Angeles and Chicago. The most common function for police gang units is the gathering of intelligence on gangs—their size, location, crime patterns, and the names and identifiers of individual members. Gang unit officers may also run gang awareness programs for schools and community groups, and engage in suppression efforts that go beyond ordinary police activity. The latter include periodic "gang sweeps" of specific gang territories, selective enforcement (crackdowns, harassment) of known gang gathering spots, and heightened surveillance or targeting of hard-core gang members. Occasionally other enforcement agencies, such as prosecutors or federal agencies, develop their own versions of intensive operations specifically aimed at gangs, but it is the local police agencies that carry out the bulk of gang suppression programs.

A second and increasingly common form of gang suppression has been the crafting of special antigang legislation. These laws, occasionally at the federal and municipal levels but usually at the state level, expand the opportunities for law enforcement and court responses to gangs. Common elements of such laws include achieving constitutionally defensible definitions of street gangs and gang crime; formal notification of gang members that they are at increased risk of apprehension and conviction; spreading the reach of antigang laws (e.g., activity within a given distance of a school, recruitment of new members, special attention to drive-by shootings or witness intimidation); and enhancement (increases) of sentences imposed specifically on conviction for gang-related crimes. The basic intent and effect of these new laws is to make gang crime different from other crime, to provide additional resources for combating it, and to provide more punitive consequences.[2]

Gang Databases. Directly tied to the intelligence function to enhance these suppression activities has been the development in many jurisdictions of special gang member rosters or databases that can, with certain safeguards, be shared across enforcement agencies. A typical entry for a gang member might be his name, age, address, moniker, automobile used, prior police contacts, name of gang, and known gang associates. Police departments have found these databases useful in case investigations and in identifying suspected gang members migrating from other jurisdictions. Legal arguments about rights to privacy have led to implementation of selected safeguards, such as periodic purging of inactive cases and specification of the criteria for labeling a person a gang member.

Originally developed as intelligence systems within single departments, these databases have often expanded to regional territories and have been made available for entry by police investigators nationwide. There is currently in development a plan to institute a nationwide gang roster administered by the federal Bureau of Alcohol, Tobacco, and Firearms. Balancing the expense of such a system, the gains in case investigation and clearance, and the dangers of misuse of the information is the current task of Congress and the federal agencies involved, each of these three elements being ambiguous at best.

Civil Legal Procedures. Two relatively new civil procedures have been applied to gang crime. The first is the use of civil abatements to interfere with gang activity, especially with drug sales. Evidence concerning undersirable gang behavior is gathered and presented to a judge. An injunction is then issued, which allows enforcement of both civil and criminal statutes to harass and charge gang members. Examples include zoning laws and municipal codes for plumbing, electricity, parking of cars on lawns, trash deposits, and the like. A special prosecutor can team up with various city inspectors to roust gang members from their hangouts and crack houses, giving the rest of the community an opportunity to regain control of the area.

A similar approach uses antigang injunctions to prohibit notified members from using specified parks and playgrounds and to enjoin them from specific behavior that might be related to criminal activities. Examples of such enjoined behaviors are late-night appearance, wearing certain clothing; carrying of beepers, "slim-jims" for entering cars, whistles, or implements that could be used to break into cars or houses; appearing on rooftops, and so on.

Understandably, civil rights organizations have attempted to block such injunctions as interfering with individual rights, but so far have had little success. Unfortunately, nothing but anecdotal information gathered by enforcement agencies has been offered to measure the success of these newer applications of civil law. The wide applicability of such procedures clearly calls for more definitive tests of their utility, and possible negative consequences as well.

Gang Truces. For decades, serious intergang rivalries have seen the emergence of attempts at truces or "peace treaties." Sometimes totally in-

effective but at other times associated with reduction of intergang violence for varying periods, truces have had an interesting appeal. They
generally have involved both intervention by professionals or well-mean-
ing lay leaders and active involvement of influential gang leaders. It is
the potential for gang members themselves to be involved in violence reduction efforts that has often caught public attention (along with law enforcement skepticism).

As with other approaches, gang truces are seldom evaluated with anything other than anecdotal evidence and claims of success or failure from
interested parties. Certainly, there is no evidence of permanent cessation
of intergang violence attributable to truce movements. On the other hand,
police-verified temporary reductions in violence have been reported in
some instances, and there is little reason to doubt them. What is at issue,
however, is whether the reductions are caused by the truces or whether
truces emerge at the peak of intergang hostilities; peaks, by definition, are
followed by downturns.

Over time, one interesting pattern may be discernible, involving a
distinction between truces brought about externally (initiated by nongang personnel) and truces brought about internally (initiated by gang
members themselves). My impression, gathered from reports of widely
scattered instances in space and time, is that gang-initiated truces tend
to last longer and yield greater violence reductions. This is not to say
that professionals do not get involved in gang-initiated truces. They often do, as in the selective truce between some Crips and Bloods factions
started just prior to the 1992 Los Angeles riot and continued for many
months thereafter. But gang initiation of truces may yield greater legitimacy and commitment among the participants than initiation by public
or private officials who have to convince feuding gangs of the value of
peace.

In either case, gang truces are interesting but sporadic attempts at intervention. They do not represent widespread, institutional responses
of the magnitude needed to effect major change in the American gang
scene. For this, we must revert to larger intervention modalities such as
the law enforcement and legislative approaches outlined earlier, or the
community-level approaches discussed next.

Community Organization. Ironically, the community organization approach to gang control pioneered in Chicago in the 1930s and 1940s,
never adequately evaluated but widely praised nonetheless, has in altered form reemerged as the best hope as we approach the millennium.
As more and more communities across the nation have confronted their
gang problems and learned the practical limits of law enforcement control, they have turned to their own resources to search for avenues to
gang control. Featuring various combinations of police attention, grassroots services, job training, street work, community activism, and interagency coordination, many cities have concluded that only a comprehen-

sive approach to gang intervention can produce lasting effects. The variation in approach to coordinated models is almost as wide as the dispersion of cities involved, such as Dallas/Fort Worth, Portland (Oregon), Aurora (Colorado), Wichita, Fort Wayne, Columbus (Ohio), Austin, Evanston, and Los Angeles.

Over the coming years, depending on the degree to which these communities undertake careful evaluation of their first efforts, more may be learned about the capacity of a jurisdiction to reduce gang problems through some combination of prevention and direct intervention. Critical questions should include the degree to which the most impacted gang neighborhoods are actually targeted, and the degree to which these local neighborhoods are assisted in developing informal social control of their own problems. It does little good for outside institutions—the police, the mayor's office, the school system, and so forth—to impose formal controls on gang behavior if the root causes of gang existence are not attacked and if community residents themselves cannot play a strong hand. Imposed control will inevitably weaken; only local control can persist.

Aside from these separate programs initiated since the mid-1980s proliferation of gang-involved cities, a newer, centralized model has emerged and been offered for adoption by willing communities. Developed at the University of Chicago (Spergel 1995) with support from the federal Office of Juvenile Justice and Delinquency Prevention (OJJDP),the model derives from a review of prior gang intervention attempts, including police suppression, community organization, provision of resources and opportunities for gang members, social intervention by street workers, and advocacy on behalf of gang members in agencies such as schools, courts, job programs, and the like. The new Chicago model offers modules of intervention by communities, police, schools, courts, prosecution, and social agencies. These modules are to be adopted and coordinated as a holistic package within a given jurisdiction. With special funding from the OJJDP, the comprehensive model is being tested in the late 1990s in five selected areas. An attached independent evaluation program is designed to assess the model's eventual success and applicability to other jurisdictions.

In the long run, gang development will be seriously curtailed only by reducing the economic underclass problems that pervade so many of our minority communities. In the meantime, these community organization approaches, both separately developed and coordinated versions, seem our best hope for reducing the level of gang existence and violence now facing the country. Gangs are spawned and largely active in their own communities. The members belong to families in those communities and attend the community schools. The job opportunities most meaningful to them will be those within their grasp near these same communities. It is not unreasonable, then, to expect control of gangs to derive as well from these communities. The task at hand is to learn how best to enable and empower communities to come to their own defense.

Notes

1. In December 1995, a cable television channel broadcast the annual
fashion model of the year awards. During an articulate acceptance speech,
the male model of the year (early twenties, African American) thanked his
family, friends, agent, and so on, then thanked his homeboys, and concluded
his speech with a Crip gang hand sign over his chest.

2. An example at the federal level is a recent proposal by a western senator to (1) double penalties for federal crimes committed by street gang members, (2) double penalties for crossing state lines to commit a gang-related
crime, and (3) provide prison sentences of up to ten years for gang recruitment.

References

Clinard, M. B., and D. J. Abbott. 1973. *Crime in Developing Countries.* New
    York: Wiley.
Cloward, R. A., and L. E. Ohlin. 1960. *Delinquency and Opportunity.* New
    York: Free Press.
Cohen, A. K. 1955. *Delinquent Boys: The Culture of the Gang.* New York: Free
    Press.
Covey, H. C., S. Menard, and R. J. Franzese. 1992. *Juvenile Gangs.* Spring-
    field, Ill.: Charles C. Thomas.
Esbensen, F-A., D. Huizinga, and A. W. Weiher. 1993. "Gang and Non-Gang
    Youth: Differences in Explanatory Factors." *Journal of Contemporary
    Criminal Justice* 9:94–116.
Fagan, J. 1996. "Gangs, Drugs, and Neighborhood Change." In *Gangs in
    America*, 2nd ed., edited by C. R. Huff. Thousand Oaks, Calif.: Sage.
Francia, L. 1991. "The Dusty Realm of Bagong Barrio." *Icarus* 3:13–30.
Hagedorn, J. M. 1988. *People and Folks: Gangs, Crime and the Underclass in
    a Rustbelt City.* Chicago: Lake View Press.
Hamm, M. S. 1993. *American Skinheads: The Criminology and Control of
    Hate Crime.* Westport, Conn.: Praeger.
Horowitz, R. 1983. *Honor and the American Dream: Culture and Identity in a
    Chicano Community.* New Brunswick, N.J.: Rutgers University Press.
———. 1990. "Sociological Perspectives on Gangs: Conflicting Definitions
    and Concepts." In *Gangs in America,* edited by C. R. Huff. Thousand
    Oaks, Calif.: Sage.
Institute for Intergovernmental Research. 1996. "Results of 1995 National
    Youth Gang Survey." Presentation to the National Youth Gang Sympo-
    sium, Dallas, June 20.
Jackson, P. I. 1991. "Crime, Youth Gangs, and Urban Transitions: The Social
    Dislocations of Postindustrial Economic Development." *Justice Quar-
    terly* 8:379–96.
Jansyn, L. R. 1967. "Solidarity and Delinquency in a Street Corner Group."
    American Sociological Review 31:600–14.
Klein, M. W. 1971. *Street Gangs and Street Workers.* Englewood Cliffs, N.J.:
    Prentice-Hall.

————. 1992. *Street Gangs in American Cities: A Final Report to the Chiefs.* Los Angeles: University of Southern California, Social Science Research Institute.

————. 1994. "Street Gang Cycles." In *Crime,* edited by J. Q. Wilson and J. Petersilia. San Francisco: ICS Press.

————. 1995. *The American Street Gang.* New York: Oxford University Press.

————. 1996. "Street Gangs in the United States and Europe." *European Journal for Criminal Policy and Research* 4:63–80.

Klein, M. W., and M. Gatz. 1993. "Europe's New Gangs Break American Pattern." *Psychology International* 4:1–11.

Klein, M. W., and C. L. Maxson. 1996. *Gang Structures, Crime Patterns, and Police Responses.* Los Angeles: University of Southern California, Social Science Research Institute.

Maxson, C. L. 1995. "Street Gangs and Drug Sales in Two Suburban Cities." National Institute of Justice, *Research in Brief* (September): 1–14.

————. 1996. "Street Gang Migration: How Big a Threat?" *National Institute of Justice Journal,* no. 231 (February): 2631.

Maxson, C. L., and M. Klein. 1994. "Gangs and Cocaine Trafficking." In *Drugs and the Criminal Justice System,* edited by D. MacKenzie and C. Uchida. Newbury Park, Calif.: Sage.

————. 1996. "Defining Homicide: An Updated Look at Member and Motive Approaches." In *Gangs in America,* 2nd ed., edited by C. R. Huff. Thousand Oaks, Calif.: Sage.

Miller, W. B. 1958. "Lower-Class Culture as a Generating Milieu of Gang Delinquency." *Journal of Social Issues* 14:5–19.

————. 1962. "The Impact of a 'Total Community' Delinquency Control Project." *Social Problems* 10:168–91.

————. 1980. "Gangs, Groups, and Serious Youth Crime." In *Critical Issues in Juvenile Delinquency,* edited by D. Shichor and D. H. Kelly. Lexington, Mass.: Lexington.

Padilla, F. M. 1992. *The Gang as an American Enterprise.* New Brunswick, N.J.: Rutgers University Press.

Sanders, W. B. 1994. *Gangbangs and Drive-Bys: Grounded Culture and Juvenile Gang Violence.* New York: Aldine de Gruyter.

Shaw, C. R., and H. D. McKay. 1942. *Juvenile Delinquency and Urban Areas.* Chicago: University of Chicago Press.

Short, J. F., Jr., and F. L. Strodtbeck. 1965. *Group Process and Gang Delinquency.* Chicago: University of Chicago Press.

Spergel, I. 1964. *Racketville, Slumtown, Haulburg: An Exploratory Study of Delinquent Subcultures.* Chicago: University of Chicago Press.

————. 1995. *The Youth Gang Problem: A Community Approach.* New York: Oxford University Press.

Thornberry, T. P., M. D. Krohn, A. J. Lizotte, and D. Chard-Wierschem. 1993. "The Role of Juvenile Gangs in Facilitating Delinquent Behavior." *Journal of Research in Crime and Delinquency* 30:55–87.

Thrasher, F. M. 1927. *The Gang: A Study of 1,133 Gangs in Chicago.* Chicago: University of Chicago Press.

Tracy, P. 1979. *Subcultural Delinquency: A Comparison of the Incidence and Seriousness of Gang and Nongang Member Offensivity.* Philadelphia:

University of Pennsylvania Center for Studies in Criminology and Criminal Law.

Vigil, J. D. 1988. *Barrio Gangs: Street Life and Identity in Southern California.* Austin: University of Texas Press.

Wilson, W. J. 1987. *The Truly Disadvantaged: The Inner City, the Underclass, and Public Policy.* Chicago: University of Chicago Press.

5

White-Collar Crime

NEAL SHOVER

Nearly six decades have passed since Edwin Sutherland
(1940) introduced the concept of *white-collar crime*. In
his 1939 presidential address to the American Sociological Society,
Sutherland outlined the case for its importance, criticized academic social scientists for the class bias in their near-exclusive focus on crimes of
the disadvantaged, and called for more attention to respectable crime. He
was not the first to point a finger at upperworld crime, but his efforts gave
initial direction to investigations of it and its perpetrators. He also be-
queathed a muckraking animus that is shared by many who find their
way to studies of white-collar crime. Despite Sutherland's efforts to move
it into the criminological mainstream and the efforts of his successors,
theoretical and empirical investigations of white-collar crime remain
marginal to and largely unaffected by paradigmatic debates and core developments in criminology. They are the principal focus of research for
proportionately few academics. One possible reason is the fact that few
areas of criminological investigation are plagued with the intractable
controversies that envelop this one. The conceptual ambiguities, distinctions, and taxonomies characteristic of the study of white-collar crime
cause many to look elsewhere for their subject matter.

Conceptual Issues

That the concept white-collar crime has become securely rooted in lay
and scholarly lexicons suggests nonetheless that it is widely understood
and used to denote a type of crime that differs fundamentally from street
crime. One difference involves the backgrounds and characteristics of its
perpetrators; the poor and disreputable fodder routinely encountered in
police stations and in studies of street crime are seldom in evidence here.
White-collar crime also differs in its innocuous appearance. Whereas
street crimes typically are committed by confronting victims or entering
their homes or businesses to steal their valuables, most white-collar
crimes are committed by using guile, deceit, or misrepresentation to create and exploit for illicit advantage the appearance of a routine legitimate

transaction. Others are committed by abusing for illicit purposes the power of organizational position or public office.

Fraud, defined generally as use of deception to secure unfair or unlawful gain, is the core component of many white-collar crimes. Investment brokers commit fraud when they knowingly encourage clients to invest their funds in bogus stock. Doctors commit fraud when they submit for reimbursement charges for procedures that were not performed or services that were not delivered. And university administrators commit fraud when they spend federal research monies improperly while asserting the contrary to regulatory overseers. There is more to white-collar crime than fraudulent economic transactions, however; it includes behaviors abusive of trusted position, whether committed by state officials or by private parties. When judges demand sex from criminal defendants' wives or girlfriends in return for favorable bail decisions, they commit white-collar crime. When employers knowingly or negligently subject their workers to an unsafe work environment, they also commit white-collar crime.

Defining White-Collar Crime

Sutherland defined white-collar crime as "crime committed by a person of respectability and high social status in the course of his occupation" (Sutherland [1949] 1983, p. 7). This definition has proved to be ambiguous and imprecise, which largely explains why it has drawn criticism from all quarters. The challenge of improving on it has attracted many takers, although their efforts on the whole have met with no greater success than Sutherland's formulation. There is little doubt that Sutherland considered their respectable social status to be the most important characteristic distinguishing white-collar criminals from street offenders (Geis 1992).

He is not alone in this belief. Preference for a status-based definition of white-collar crime is shared by all who argue that differentials of power and influence are key to identifying, satisfactorily framing, and unraveling fundamental questions about crime and crime control. Like the death penalty, white-collar crime is a defining issue in criminology, one that can throw into analytic relief dynamics of inequality in wealth, power, and repute (Braithwaite 1991). Investigations of sexual harassment, for example, have shown that offender-victim power differentials are a common feature of contexts where it occurs. With their potential for shedding light on the significance for crime commission of greed and arrogance, the results of research on white-collar crime can be placed beside what has been learned in studies of crime committed out of need and desperation. This may reveal a great deal about the diverse contexts and meanings of criminal behavior generally. As important, status-based definitions of white-collar crime draw on and reaffirm criminological ties to macrolevel analyses of social and political processes.

Others, who counter that offenders' social position and repute are of little value theoretically, suggest the designation white-collar crime be replaced or complemented by a focus on crimes with specific formal characteristics without regard to the status of those who commit them. Instead of collaring the criminal, they advocate collaring the crime(s). The concept of *abuse of trust* is an example of a formal definition of white-collar crime. Abuse of trust, or trust crime, is exploitation of a fiduciary position by an agent responsible for custody, discretion, information, or property rights. It occurs when accounting firms issue optimistic reports for businesses on the brink of insolvency, when bankers make unsecured loans to friends at low interest, or when service station clerks steal and sell customers' credit card numbers. Because trust crimes are committed by citizens who wear blue collars as well as those who wear white ones, this definitional construction lumps together for analytic and policy purposes the pursuits of itinerant door-to-door vinyl siding fraudsters and the crimes of international bankers. This is said to be justified by its potential for speeding development of theoretical understanding and crime control policy. It is time to look beyond "perpetrators' wardrobe and social characteristics" to "the modus operandi of their misdeeds and the ways in which they establish and exploit trust" (Shapiro 1990, p. 363). Whatever the merits of this position, the lesson—and it is easily overlooked—is that white-collar crime does not occur only where offenders are powerful and victims are ordinary citizens. When citizens do fall prey to white-collar crime, odds are high that they will be victimized by offenders closer to home than international banking conspirators. It is not only managers of Fortune 500 corporations who victimize us but also the local attorney and the neighborhood automotive repair shop.

A tactical response to the impasse over how to conceptualize white-collar crime is to distinguish for research and policy purposes elite white-collar crime from its more ordinary varieties. Elite crime, defined broadly as offenses committed by the wealthy, respectable, and powerful, is the research focus for many who call their intellectual home the analysis of white-collar crime. It remains to be seen whether the distinction between elite and ordinary white-collar crime has explanatory and predictive merit. For the present, however, there is no compelling reason to sweep under a rug of definitional formalism status and inequality, their dynamics, or their consequences.

Sutherland's restriction of white-collar crime to acts committed by women and men "in the course of" their occupation excludes extravocational crime—acts, say, of weekend shoplifting by bank presidents or spousal abuse by university administrators. It matters not that these crimes statutorily and behaviorally may be indistinguishable from crimes committed in their occupational role. Nor do the crimes of professional criminals count, since they are not committed in the normal course of a legitimate occupation. Empirically, however, the line between legitimate occupations and organizations and illegal ones is not always as clear as this analytic distinction implies. Critics of restricting white-collar crime to acts committed in offenders' occupational role note that many putatively white-collar offenses do not occur as part of offenders' occupations, particularly if a formal definition of white-collar crime is employed. Research suggests this is the case with many offenders (Weisburd et al. 1991). Providing false information on a loan application, for example, can be committed either apart from or in an occupational role; potential home buyers may commit loan fraud as well as businesses.

Definitional nets vary not only in the status characteristics and occupational status of offenders they ensnare but also in the nature of rule violations that put one at risk of acquiring the designation *criminal*. Should the *crime* in white-collar crime—or in trust crime, for that matter—be defined broadly or narrowly? Assuming crime cannot exist independent of published rules, judgments, or orders, which ones count? Are violations of rules promulgated and enforced by administrative bureaucracies to be included with felonies? Should adverse civil decisions and court-ordered punitive damages be included with criminal convictions as evidence of crime? These have been contentious issues among investigators of white-collar crime. In his own research, Sutherland counted as crime not only violations of criminal law but also adverse civil decisions and penalties imposed administratively (Sutherland [1949] 1983). He justified this by arguing that all are state-imposed sanctions for acts recognized as potentially harmful. Sutherland cast a broad definitional net. Clinard and Yeager used a similar one when they defined white-collar crime as any act "that is punished by the state, regardless of whether it is punished under administrative, civil, or criminal law" (1980, p. 16). A corporate manager's negligent or willful failure properly to post workplace safety regulations would be counted as crime, as would the intentional release of toxic chemicals into the environment.

Others contend it is inappropriate to extend the label *crime* to behaviors where legal strictures of culpability either are not required or cannot be demonstrated. They further question the appropriateness of labeling as crime business practices that may be legal, albeit "sharp" or aggressive behaviors. Noting that moral ambiguity colors and constrains our assessment of many white-collar crimes and their perpetrators, they suggest the designation *illegalities* for acts that violate technical rules for which there is limited moral consensus, negligible harm, and minor penalties. Failure to distinguish violations of administrative rules and crime runs the risk, they contend, of treating as crime these technical violations and those who commit them as criminals. The label *crime* is thereby reserved for acts that violate the criminal code and are punishable in criminal courts.

Although this position is widely accepted, controversy over alternative definitions of white-collar crime unquestionably will continue, if only because the outcome is consequential for the kinds of persons who will bear the opprobrium of *criminal*. If it does nothing else, this disagreement shows there is an unavoidably arbitrary underpinning to the way we think about and study white-collar crime. If it is defined formally, as by specifying that all crimes with designated characteristics will be included, the forms it assumes and the offenders who pursue it will include few wealthy corporate executives or high-ranking state managers. This is apparent from analysis of information included in presentence investigation reports on 1,094 individuals tried for white-collar crimes in seven federal districts during 1976–1978 (Weisburd et al. 1991). Defendants were designated as white-collar offenders based on their conviction of one or more of eight statutory offenses: securities fraud, antitrust violations, bribery, bank embezzlement, postal and wire fraud, false claims and statements, credit and lending institution fraud, and tax fraud. Analysis showed that most of the crimes committed by sample members were not complex, had few victims, and resulted in modest financial losses. This pattern of findings, combined with what was learned about defendants' backgrounds and characteristics, led investigators to dub these offenses "crimes of the middle classes." It is an alternative and richly evocative label for ordinary white-collar crime.

When formal definitions of white-collar crime are used, both crimes and offenders are characterized by white-collar banality (e.g., Croall 1989). A substantial proportion of offenders, perhaps as large as one-third, are unemployed when their crimes are committed (Daly 1989; Weisburd et al. 1991). When a status-based definition of white-collar crime is used, however, the population of offenders is more homogeneous demographically and more advantaged in background and resources. Their crimes can be substantially more complex and costly as well.

Individual and Organizational Offenders

In the industrialized and postindustrialized world, individuals overwhelmingly are employed by and in organizations. In local labor union offices, in state agencies, or in business firms ranging in size from three-employee painting contractors to the General Motors Corporation, they labor on behalf of their organizational employer. Whereas many white-collar crimes are committed by freewheeling predators without attachment to legitimate organizations, others are committed by individuals or groups in their roles as owners, managers, or employees of these organizations. A conceptual distinction generally is drawn between *occupational* white-collar crimes and *organizational* ones.

The former include both crimes committed in their occupational role by organizationally unattached individuals and crimes committed for exclusively personal goals or enrichment by employees, managers, or owners of legitimate organizations. Many times their organizational employers are the victims of their crimes, as when, for example, accountants embezzle company funds. Organizational crime, by contrast, is committed in the context and in pursuit of organizational goals or objectives

(Reiss and Tonry 1993). Whereas employees who use their job for illicit personal advantage are not organizational criminals, those who violate the law in order to increase the chances of organizational success are.

The category of organizational crime excludes crime committed in the context and in pursuit of goals of avowedly illicit organizations. The crimes of La Cosa Nostra and drug smugglers are organized but are not organizational crime. In practice, this conceptual distinction can become blurred, as when a legitimate business is converted gradually into one that is criminal, or when it serves as the organizational context for one that is exclusively criminal (Passas and Nelken 1993). Faced with declining profits and gloomy prospects, small-business owners, for example, may engage in crimes more characteristic of experienced confidence men. They use the appearance of a stable and profitable enterprise to purchase goods before closing the business and reneging on their bills (Levi 1981). Legitimate organizations also may establish and maintain mutually beneficial relationships with criminal organizations (Ruggiero 1996). Overlap empirically between organized and organizational crime is further evidence of the conceptual ambiguity characteristic of research on white-collar crime. Examples of organizational crime include reports of bogus research findings by corporate or university-based scientists and crimes directed, encouraged, or condoned by state managers.

The rationale for distinguishing organizational white-collar crime rests largely on the assumption that organizational and extraorganizational forces are autonomous and potentially important forces in the onset of and responses to crime. Organizational characteristics and practices, including indoctrination and incentive programs, differential authority, specialized expertise, and formalized channels of communication, may play a part in the genesis and persistence of crime. Occupational white-collar crimes, by contrast, are committed by individuals or groups of individuals without ties to legitimate organizations or whose organizational positions do not figure in their crimes. To talk of organizational crime, however, is neither to reify a collectivity nor to endow it with volitional properties (Cressey 1995). This does not exclude organizations in which crime is committed openly, with apparent indifference, if not tacit endorsement, by management. Where there are clear patterns of violation, organizational conditions usually are a major reason. They often have the effect, for example, of diffusing responsibility for misconduct and thereby facilitating individual willingness to participate. Research in police departments has shown that corruption and abuse can be so prevalent in organizations that the organization itself can be considered criminal.

Corporate crime is a form of organizational crime given autonomous analytic status by many investigators (Geis 1993). The principal justification for this status is belief that the pervasiveness and power of corporations and the corporate form are too important to treat as a subtype of white-collar crime. Skeptics contend, however, that there is no reason to single out for special criminological attention any particular organizational form; much can be learned about white-collar crime by examining crime in a variety of organizations. Whether they are philanthropic, voluntary, profit-seeking, or state-sector organizations, moreover, may be unimportant; corporations *are* organizations. There may be payoff in studies of illegal conduct by law enforcement officials for understanding crime by business executives. This in no way denies that large corporations are among the most powerful institutions and political actors in the modern world, or that corporations may be unusually criminogenic settings. Whether the latter is true is an issue to be settled empirically. A convincing case has not been made thus far.

Costs of White-Collar Crime

No one can determine or estimate with confidence the total cost of white-collar crime. There are no authoritative procedures or guidelines for doing so, and results are influenced heavily by initial assumptions. Enormous variation is inevitable. Development of comprehensive, reliable estimates requires systematically collected data on the prevalence of white-collar crime, the numbers of victims, and their losses. At present these data do not exist. In marked contrast to street crime, data on white-collar offenses and offenders are not routinely collected, collated, and disseminated by centralized offices of state or federal government. For white-collar crime investigators there is no counterpart of the Federal Bureau of Investigation's Uniform Crime Reporting program. The absence of standardized crime definitions, moreover, makes it difficult to interpret available data and use them for comparative purposes. Adding to the challenges faced by those who explore white-collar crime, other types of data, including offender self-reports and victimization surveys, are in equally short supply.

Paradoxically, there are many sources of data on white-collar crime. Most, however, are not published or disseminated widely, and they usually are limited to specific forms of rule breaking (Reiss and Biderman 1980). Typically they are generated by government agencies charged with investigating and responding to designated white-collar crimes, exemplified by state consumer protection agencies or county environmental enforcement bureaucracies. Summary data on enforcement activities and penalties generally are included in the annual reports issued by these agencies, which are dispersed sparingly in libraries and official files. It can require painstaking work to put together useful statistical data even for one type of white-collar crime, for one industry, or for one offender. In addition, it is impossible to know whether the results provide a representative picture of any larger population of either theoretical or policy significance.

No one seriously disputes that white-collar crime exacts a heavy aggregate financial toll, one that dwarfs comparable losses to street criminals. For individuals, families, and organizations, the consequences of victimization range in severity from minor to devastating. Garden-variety offenses and offenders probably leave more victims angry and inconvenienced following modest financial losses than emotionally wrecked and financially destroyed. Surprisingly little is known about the numbers of individuals and organizations victimized by white-collar crime, but they clearly are large. The effects of victimization, moreover, can ripple far beyond its immediate victims to harm others. When organizations dispose of hazardous materials in reckless and criminal fashion, the costs may be an increased risk of health problems for innocent parties, as well as the financial costs of cleaning up their poisonous legacies. The environmental damage caused by these crimes can make neighborhoods or communities uninhabitable and force the relocation of dozens of families. There is remarkably little research on the organizational consequences of victimization, but harmful effects are easy to imagine (Levi 1981). Small businesses, which are disproportionately victimized by white-collar crime, may be forced into bankruptcy and their employees onto unemployment rolls. Where public bureaucracies are victimized by white-collar crime, the larger community of taxpaying citizens may be the ultimate victim. Taxpayers must pay the fare, for example, when local school districts are charged artificially high prices for products as a result of price-fixing by ostensibly competitive suppliers.

Whereas tangible costs of crime include victims' loss of money and property and physical injuries or death, its intangible costs include pain, suffering, and reduced quality of life. Estimates of the harm caused by crime are influenced heavily by whether these intangible costs are acknowledged, measured, and priced. The intangible costs of white-collar crime may be singularly wide-reaching and destructive (Meier and Short 1983). Because it violates trust, white-collar crime may breed distrust, lower social morale, and "attack the fundamental principles of American institutions" (Sutherland [1949] 1983, p. 10). When public officials use their office for illicit enrichment, or when police and prosecutors knowingly employ prohibited investigatory techniques, the result may be harm to public trust in government and loss of confidence in political institutions, processes, and leaders. A similar consequence may result from economic white-collar crimes. Trust is "truly the foundation of capitalism." In its absence, "people would not delegate discretionary use of their funds to other entrepreneurs . . . [and] capitalism would break down as funds were stuffed into mattresses, savings accounts, and solo business enterprises rather than invested in the business ventures of American corporations" (Shapiro 1984, p. 2). Citizens victimized by fraudulent use of their credit records or credit cards, for example, may lose faith in the integrity of credit transactions. When public officials and agencies charged with responding to white-collar crime tolerate it, this may complicate the task of convincing citizens that they should be honest. Public morality and commitment to conformity are eroded by the

perception that everyone is behaving selfishly. These potential delegiti-
mation effects are important and frequently sketched consequences of
white-collar crime, but they have been neglected by investigators.

Official and Victim Responses

White-collar crime victimizes large numbers of citizens and organizations, but only the most rapacious, tactically arrogant, or inept of perpetrators ever achieve the level of notoriety or public outrage normally
accorded street offenders. Public opinion surveys show that some white-
collar offenses are judged as serious as violent street crimes, particularly
ones that result in physical harm to innocent parties (Schrager and Short
1980). Many others are regarded as mundane. This may help explain why
white-collar crimes usually do not come to mind first when the subject of
crime is raised in conversation or is featured in the media. Despite the
perception by some academics of a social movement against crime in the
suites, it is unclear whether the public generally shares the level of concern about or moral condemnation of white-collar criminals that is commonplace in academic circles. White-collar crime, in more ways than
one, is invisible crime.

Because a form of conduct is demonstrably and seriously injurious
does not ensure that it will be the focus of private or public controls. Private parties and the state enjoy enormous discretion in these matters. The
latter can turn a blind eye toward harmful behaviors or choose to make
them the focus of attention. It can take the lead in identifying and crafting controls for harmful behaviors, or it can wait until pressed to do so
through action by citizens and organized groups. The outcome of campaigns for new or tougher controls on a form of conduct is never assured,
however. Many harmful practices and behaviors do not win the kind of
popular condemnation and movement strength needed for successful
criminalization, and this may be true particularly of campaigns to impose new or more effective controls on business interests. These efforts
invariably meet with opposition from trade and professional organizations which charge that the proposed rules either are unnecessary and
heavy-handed examples of big government or that they only harm legitimate economic interests. When it does act, the state can fashion responses and remedies from revocation of a professional license to civil
penalties and, ultimately, to criminal prosecution. The bulk of the state's
effort and output, however, is rules that carry minimal civil penalties for
most forms of white-collar rule breaking; the body of statute law that organizations and citizens in their occupational roles are expected to meet
is small when compared with the volume of regulatory rules that confronts them.

Would-be burglars and robbers are neither consulted nor listened to
when officials shape burglary statutes and penalties. It is very different
for behaviors engaged in by more respectable offenders; they and their

representatives play an active part in crafting the laws and regulatory standards that circumscribe their conduct. Through monetary contributions and social contacts, they gain the access to rule makers that is needed to ensure their views are made known and taken seriously. Fronted by a phalanx of attorneys, publicists, and hired technical experts, they press their self-interested notions of what is fair and reasonable control. Unlike reformers, they are in the battle for the long haul, they press the fight on many fronts, and their advance, if largely imperceptible, is relentless. Their efforts are helped by the fact that many reformers eventually relax their guard or abandon the field for other causes. The actions of business interests are moved by the wish to avoid restrictions on their discretionary behaviors and, where loss or concession is unavoidable, to accept the obligation to do only what is "practicable." In this way, statutes that represent weak or merely symbolic threats to their injurious or destructive conduct are followed by rules and practices of administrative bureaucracies unwilling or unable to mount serious efforts against white-collar criminals. Their success at these endeavors is the first step in what many believe is a process of accumulating advantages afforded to white-collar criminals by the state.

A great deal of white-collar crime goes unreported for the simple reason that many of its victims are unaware they have been victimized. Unlike robbery, burglary, and other street crimes, acts of white-collar crime frequently do not stand out in victims' experiences; they characteristically have the look of routine legitimate transactions. Victims who realize or suspect what has happened may have no idea where to report the incident; it is also characteristic of white-collar crimes that the appropriate places or agencies to report to are either unknown or unfamiliar. Many victims do not report. Those who do so are typically motivated by hopes of recovering lost funds and protecting others from a similar experience. Victims who do not report frequently believe that the incident either was not worth the trouble of doing so or that no real harm was done. Others elect to handle the matter privately. This is not appreciably different from what is known about the reporting decisions of street-crime victims. Another reason victims of white-collar crimes do not report is because they often reserve a measure of blame for themselves. Believing they should have been more careful in the first place, victims often feel a sense of embarrassment and shame, and prefer that others not learn what happened to them (Levi 1992; Shover, Fox, and Mills 1994).

The uncertainties and problems of white-collar crime victims give to those who commit these offenses another advantage over their underclass criminal cousins. Victims who eventually find their way to the police, to prosecutors, or to regulatory agencies generally meet with experiences remarkably similar to and no less frustrating than the experiences of street-crime victims. A substantial proportion of those who victimize them avoid prosecution and severe sanctions because investigating and responding to their crimes can be an expensive and resource-depleting enterprise. Local-level officials must use finite budget and personnel resources judiciously. Much less is known about organizational victims of white-collar crime and their reactions to the experience, although it is reasonable to assume that many have an interest in keeping quiet about crimes against them.

When they investigate complaints, officials routinely encounter behaviors that can range from straightforward and easily understood acts to complex behaviors of many individuals that are difficult to comprehend and reconstruct. The organizational veil can obscure and make virtually impossible the task of determining how crimes occurred, who was responsible for them, and who participated. Reactive enforcement frequently must be dispensed with in favor of techniques commonly employed against syndicated crime. These may include undercover investigators, informants, and sting operations. Threats and inducements can be used to elicit information from knowledgeable organizational participants about how crimes occurred and those who participated. This is one of the most important reasons that culpable but key participants in white-collar crimes may avoid harsh penalties; their centrality and the information they can provide give them bargaining power with regulators and prosecutors.

Officials generally have at their disposal an array of administrative, civil, and criminal options for responding to white-collar crime. A study of local prosecutors in the United States examined factors they take into account in screening cases of suspected corporate violations (Benson, Cullen, and Maakestad 1990). Data were collected in a mail survey returned by 419 urban prosecutors and in case studies of four jurisdictions. In their decision making, prosecutors said they paid attention particularly to the number of victims and the extent of physical harm to them, whether there was evidence of multiple offenses, and the extent of economic harm caused by suspected offenders. Their decisions also were heavily influenced by the availability of resources and occasionally by concern for local economic interests. Prosecutors indicated that on occasion they elected not to pursue aggressively crimes committed by local businesses for fear of harming employment and the local economy. When culpable individuals cannot be identified or sufficient evidence cannot be put together, prosecutors may see no course but to decline to charge the organization with criminal conduct. An inability to establish criminal intent also is a major reason that prosecutors frequently pursue civil action instead of criminal charges. Uncertain of their ability to convict culpable individuals and lacking the resources needed to investigate more extensively or thoroughly, they instead opt for civil action and the less onerous standard of proof these responses require. Prosecutors also may pursue corporations rather than individuals because the former can be assessed and pay heavier penalties, and because the odds of winning in contests with organizational defendants are better. And regardless of their other objectives, prosecutors like winning.

What is known about prosecutors' handling of white-collar crime cases and what has been learned from research in regulatory bureaucracies shows that when responding to white-collar crimes and illegalities officials generally opt for conciliatory and restorative interventions rather than criminal penalties; from high-level management to field-level inspectors, use of harsh sanctions is extremely infrequent (Shapiro 1984; Weisburd et al. 1991; Jesilow, Pontell, and Geis 1992). Findings from an analysis of 499 investigations undertaken by the U.S. Securities and Exchange Commission between 1948 and 1972 are typical (Shapiro 1985). Civil, administrative, and diversionary actions were the norm; only 6 percent of the cases resulted in judgment before a criminal court. Owing to the efforts of the U.S. Sentencing Commission, there is some evidence of modest increases in recent years, but penalties imposed on white-collar criminals generally are less severe than the sentences meted out to street offenders.

For defendants whose crimes are disposed of in criminal court, matters frequently are not so bleak as the institutional setting would suggest. Judges commonly use as justification for not imposing prison time defendants' suffering and the damage to reputation caused by arrest and prosecution. When sentencing Medicaid fraudsters, for example,

> [j]udges recognize that damage to a physician's reputation is a form of punishment in itself. As one Medicaid official noted, "You put [a doctor's] name on the front page of the paper as a thief, you've destroyed him." . . . In this peculiar bit of folk wisdom, falls from high places are the stuff of tragedy, but the tumbles of those who had not climbed so high are assumed to be less painful—the latter are supposed to suffer less because they are accustomed to having so little. Nonetheless, judges typically refer to the loss of standing already experienced by a white-collar criminal as a basis for a light sentence. (Jesilow, Pontell, and Geis 1992, p. 99)

Their cultural and financial resources, combined with the advantages that accrue to white-collar offenders at successive stages of the criminal process, produce a capacity to resist, to defeat, or to delay control efforts that is available to few street offenders.

Sentencing research shows that among the strongest determinants of sentencing outcome are the nature and extent of defendants' prior criminal record, whether there is evidence of criminal intent, and the seriousness of the crime. Prosecutors and judges use as indicators of seriousness the financial or social harm caused by defendants, the number and types of their victims, and the legally prescribed range of penalties for their crime. These case characteristics are strong predictors of sentences for street-level offenders as well. Beyond their recognized influence, however, it is difficult to capture or describe the conflicting results from individual-level sentencing research. Not only is it difficult in these studies to determine whether sentencing disparity is caused by sociodemographic characteristics of the offender or by the offense, but there also may be contextual variation in sentencing; statistical relationships may not work the same way in all jurisdictions.

The extent and sources of interclass variation in punishment is one of the most important problems in analysis of white-collar crime, although it has received little attention from investigators. Empirical evidence for the conventional wisdom that white-collar criminals are treated leniently by administrative agencies, prosecutors, and the courts is not strong; most research into sentencing of white-collar criminals has been limited to examination of intraclass variations. Simply put, because the samples used in past sentencing studies do not include appreciable numbers of the very wealthy and powerful, the capacity to examine sentences across the full range of wealth and status variation is weak. It is useful, more-over, to keep in mind that there are several points of the criminal process where defendants can be diverted from the pathway that eventuates in judicial sentencing. Suite criminals' success may be so great at earlier stages that by sentencing time, when official decisions are most visible, evidence of leniency is least visible. Judicial sentencing of white-collar criminals is not representative of the overall treatment afforded white-collar crime and criminals by the state apparatus (Mann 1985).

What is the impact of sanctions and other control measures on white-collar offenders? Deterrence-based notions of crime control suggest it should be substantial, in large measure because these offenders are thought to be more rational than street offenders (Weisburd, Waring, and Chayet 1995). Unlike the latter, they do not routinely make decisions to offend in hedonistic contexts of competition and display where drug consumption clouds both judgment and the ability to calculate beforehand. Coupled with the fact that many live and work in worlds structured to promote, monitor, and reward rational decision making, this suggests that sanctions should have greater deterrent impact on their conduct. Whether or not this assumption is correct, however, is unknown. For one thing, the impact of external controls probably varies with severity; notices of violation for regulatory offenses are one thing; imprisonment or large fines are another. The possibility that some convicted white-collar offenders see crime as a good bet is suggested by their surprisingly high rate of recidivism (Weisburd, Waring, and Chayet 1995). Evidence of this point is extremely limited, however, and recidivism may be concentrated among unemployed and economically marginal offenders.

The social stigma and economic losses sustained by convicted white-collar criminals are not invariant across offense types or categories of offenders. Conviction for rape is one thing; embezzlement of small sums of money is another. Overall, self-employed professionals often recover from the experience rather quickly, whereas public-sector managers sometimes pay a much stiffer toll. Interviews with convicted white-collar offenders show them generally to be an unrepentant lot who are remarkably slow to accept responsibility for their crimes. Whereas convicted street offenders characteristically acknowledge their guilt to all who in-quire once proceedings have ended, white-collar offenders often protest their innocence long past this point, insisting, for example, that what they did caused no harm and hardly merited prosecutors' attention (Benson 1985; Jesilow, Pontell, and Geis 1992).

Variation and Explanation

Regardless of how it is defined, there seems little doubt that the prevalence of white-collar crime varies temporally and spatially. Data limitations make it impossible to measure or interpret this variation with confidence, however. Investigators have made only modest progress in documenting geographic variation, and the picture is only marginally better where temporal variation is concerned (Simpson 1986). It is a long way from current, rather crude, understanding of how it varies to identification and description, say, of hot spots of white-collar crime. Still, variation is apparent, and this is true whether we examine the prevalence of illegalities or felonies (Shover and Bryant 1993). In his pathbreaking research on the seventy largest privately owned corporations and fifteen largest publicly owned utilities in the United States, Sutherland ([1949] 1983) noted both temporal and firm-level variation in white-collar crime and its disproportionate concentration in a few industries. Analysis of federal enforcement actions initiated or completed against America's 582 largest publicly owned manufacturing, wholesale, retail, and service corporations for the years 1975–1976 showed similar variation; both the type and rate of corporate crime varied by firm and by industry. Rates are highest in the petroleum, pharmaceutical, and motor vehicle industries and lowest in the apparel and beverage industries. The study also showed that whereas a small proportion of corporations commit a highly disproportionate share of all violations, a larger proportion had no record of infractions (Clinard and Yeager 1980). With organizations as with individuals, there are model citizens as well as habitual criminals.

When compared with street criminals, individuals convicted of white-collar crimes are older and less often members of minority groups. An analysis of data on 1,342 defendants convicted of white-collar crimes in seven U.S. district courts during 1976–1978 shows, moreover, that few approximate the popular depiction of white-collar criminals as elite or "fat-cat" businesspersons (Daly 1989). Gender differences, if not unexpected, are instructive also. Males are overrepresented, and their crimes range from petty to sophisticated. Nearly all women's crimes, by contrast, were small-time, less organized, and less profitable than crimes committed by males. Whereas more than half of the males were managerial or professional workers, employed female offenders worked disproportionately in clerical positions. Generally, the higher the proportion of women committing an offense, the higher the proportion of nonwhites and less-educated. Women's modest take from white-collar crime reflects both the limited criminal opportunities available to clerical personnel and the absence of women from the top ranks of large organizations.

White-Collar Crime Theory

The theory of crime as *choice* has gained unrivaled dominance as a general explanation for variation in criminal behavior. Although it has been applied principally to street crime and its perpetrators, the notion of crime as choice can be applied to white-collar crime as well. In the logic and language of this theoretical construction, crime is purposeful, chosen behavior. Criminal decisions are products of cognition and calculation in which decision makers pursue utilities, examine options, and weigh risks. Many substantively narrow criminological theories are compatible logically with this theoretical approach (Shover and Bryant 1993).

The theory of crime as choice posits that variation in crime is produced by variation in opportunities and in motivation. Criminal opportunities are arrangements or situations individuals and groups encounter that offer attractive potential for criminal reward with little apparent risk of detection or penalty (Coleman 1987). For street criminals, they are homes filled with electronic equipment that are left unoccupied much of the day; for white-collar criminals the counterpart is impersonal trust relationships. The aggregate rate of white-collar crime varies directly with the supply of criminal opportunities and with the supply of individuals and organizations predisposed or motivated to exploit them. What causes variation in these?

The sources of variations in criminal opportunities are poorly charted but, clearly, diverse and numerous. In the United States, fundamental shifts following World War II in the public welfare functions of the state and in the national economy transformed and substantially increased its size while creating a host of new criminal opportunities as well. Expansion of government largesse for citizens across the income spectrum, mass marketing of insurance, and the expansion of consumer credit all contributed to these developments (Jesilow, Pontell, and Geis 1992). Revolutionary changes in communications, in record-keeping technology, and in the growth of electronic financial transactions mean that funds can be transferred around the world over telephone lines and satellite networks. Presidential decisions and congressional legislation during the 1980s also played a part in transforming and increasing criminal opportunities, most visibly in the U.S. savings and loan industry. We have witnessed the emergence of "finance capitalism," a form of productive enterprise distinguished not by the manufacture of goods or services but instead by the "production" of paper profits through manipulation of financial accounts (Calavita, Pontell, and Tillman 1997). Finance capitalism is production at the computer keyboard, increasingly from the privacy of the home.

Changes in transaction systems, or the ways individuals typically relate to one another and to organizations, also affect the supply of opportunities for white-collar crime. Generally, transaction systems have become more impersonal and difficult to monitor as commercial exchanges based on face-to-face communication yield to complex and impersonal transaction systems within and between organizations (Vaughan 1982). Offenders and their victims may know one another outside of the transaction, but, given the spread of impersonal business practices and financial transactions the world over, increasingly they do not. The process of verifying credentials is no longer the easy matter it is when parties interact personally or within geographically circumscribed and culturally shared worlds. White-collar criminals are quick to exploit the growth of impersonal trust. The very complexity of transaction systems also can be criminogenic, as when they cause individuals or organizations to develop illicit, if successful, shortcuts.

Sources of variation in the supply of motivated white-collar offenders and of variation, therefore, in the rate of white-collar crime are matters of theoretical conjecture but little research. Fluctuations in the business cycle have been linked repeatedly to the rate of white-collar crime, chiefly because of their influence on the supply of offenders (Simpson 1986). Economic downturns stimulate crime by depressing income and pushing increasing numbers of citizens and organizations closer to insolvency and desperation, thus causing an increasing proportion to cross the line into criminal conduct. The record of research on this explanation is thin but generally supportive (Simpson 1986; Baucus and Near 1991).

Temporal and spatial cultural variation also plays a part in determining the supply of motivated offenders. Criminogenic cultures stimulate crime by providing to potential offenders perspectives and rationalizations that either conflict with or call into question ethical and legal norms of behavior. Important also is the relative strength of a culture of competition that elevates and rewards success above all else (Coleman 1987). Individuals in competitive cultures are disproportionately driven to strive for success, usually but not exclusively financial. Still, they worry ceaselessly about conditions that might stand in their way. Pervasive insecurity can be a powerful motivation for crime for poor and rich alike. Competitive cultures stimulate excess and crime during boom times as well, when there is widespread belief that "everyone is getting rich." In these circumstances, many come to believe that to pass up any opportunity is to miss the boat.

Prevailing estimates of the formal risk of crime occupy a prominent place in crime-as-choice theory. The level of commitment to and resources invested in rule enforcement is thought to play an important part in shaping collectively held notions about the legitimacy and efficacy of official controls. When it is widely believed that the law is little more than technical rules devoid of moral content, when the risks of crime are seen as minimal, or when penalties threatened by the law are dismissed as inconsequential, the supply of motivated offenders swells. Crime-as-choice theory posits an inverse relationship between the intensity and severity of rule enforcement and the rate of crime. There is consistent though weak support for this proposition from research on street-level property crime. Besides the web of state organizations and personnel engaged in detecting, investigating, and penalizing white-collar offenders, a variety of private organizations function to do the same. Professional societies, for example, promulgate and enforce codes of ethics and generally accepted practices. Under as yet undetermined conditions, fear of adverse publicity also may restrain the behavior of potential white-collar offenders.

Despite its axiomatic status in crime-as-choice theory, the hypothesized inverse relationship between variation in use of sanctions and the rate of white-collar crime has received little attention from investigators. Thus it offers no basis for confident conclusions about their individual or comparative effectiveness. Structural covariates of white-collar crime generally have been ignored in previous research. The hypothesized causal significance of organizational size is a case in point. Increasing size escalates both the internal complexity of organizations and perhaps the difficulty of establishing and maintaining strong normative controls and effective supervision. As organizations increase in size, their power may increase also, perhaps leading to crime commission from arrogance. Both reasons lead us to expect a positive relationship between size and criminal participation. Research results are inconsistent, although most investigators find support for the existence of the relationship (Clinard and Yeager 1980; Baucus and Near 1991). One possible explanation is that giant corporations are subject to a much larger number and variety of laws than smaller ones. Many regulatory statutes, for example, exempt firms with few employees and limited productive output. Another explanation is methodological: samples used in past studies generally have not been representative of the entire size spectrum. Investigators have focused disproportionately on large organizations while ignoring smaller ones and a wide range of types.

Regardless of whether the rate of white-collar crime is high or low, some individuals and organizations are less likely than others to commit it. Even when surrounded by abundant criminal opportunities and indications that others are exploiting them, not all individuals and organizations do so. Why? When employed to explain individual-level or organization-level variation in criminal participation, crime-as-choice theory suggests that the odds of choosing to exploit criminal opportunities are constrained by estimates of the expected net gains from doing so. Of course, not all are aware of or sensitized to the criminal opportunities around them, or else they lack the knowledge and contacts required to exploit them. Business owners, for example, who lack both legitimate business contacts willing to consign large quantities of merchandise on credit and underworld connections to dispose of them illicitly are unlikely candidates for many kinds of fraud (Levi 1981). Others, including some who are wise to opportunity, simply do not weigh and calculate equally the potential consequences of rule breaking. Whether individuals or organizations see, calculate, and believe the expected rewards of white-collar crime exceed the likelihood and the unpleasantness of being caught is determined by three variables: performance pressure, the estimated certainty and severity of aversive consequences if their crimes are detected, and the ready availability and accepted use of crime-facilitative cultural constructions.

A hypothesized direct relationship between pressure to meet self-defined or externally imposed standards of successful performance is one of the most widely endorsed propositions in white-collar crime research. When medical scientists experience pressure to produce research break-throughs, when athletic coaches have a string of losing seasons, or when business owners see their profits decline, the odds that they will resort to criminal solutions are increased. The reasons may be external, perhaps in organizational policies and practices, or in pressure to produce "success," or they may originate with the individual. Regardless of its source, the line separating lawful and unlawful conduct becomes less important, particularly in highly competitive environments. Illegal lines of action are appealing particularly when circumstances make unlikely goal attainment by legitimate means.

White-collar crime is behavior that puts one at risk of aversive consequences. The theory of crime as choice posits an inverse relationship between estimates of the certainty, severity, and celerity of punishment and the odds of committing white-collar crime. Individuals or groups that see the law and its agents as remote, illegitimate, and improbable actors presumably are more likely to break the law than those who see them as a legitimate, credible, and effective presence. An individual also can be turned from a criminal decision by a wish to avoid a troubled conscience, to maintain a favorable conception of self, or to avoid harming his or her reputation. The record of research on offender perceptions of risk and participation in white-collar crime is too sparse to warrant conclusions.

Local cultural conditions are important for the animus and direction they give to criminal motivation. Two dimensions of variation are critical. One is the extent to which cultural conditions provide rhetorical constructions and authoritative endorsement of normatively unrestrained competition and meritocracy. The second is the extent to which they make available techniques of neutralization that excuse and facilitate crime (Shover and Bryant 1993). These variables indicate the pervasiveness and influence of criminogenic cultures in particular regions or industries.

The Research Legacy

The insoluble conceptual disputes endemic to the study of white-collar crime and the absence of systematically collected data on its frequency and distribution have slowed the pace and distorted the advancement of empirical research. Theoretical developments have far outpaced research that examines their merits. A case in point is empirical neglect of the magnitude and sources of variation in the supply of motivated white-collar offenders. Community-level variables that may determine these have yet to be examined. Economic inequality is one of the strongest predictors of variation in rates of violent and predatory street crime, and the same may be true for white-collar crime. Given the absence of research, however, we do not know. Inequality may stimulate crime by making it easier for street offenders to invoke motives and rationalizations for it rooted in anger, a sense of injustice, or the belief that everyone is "taking what they can get." It is unclear whether the growing disparity between elite and ordinary wealth finds expression in the crimes of respectable citizens as well as ordinary ones.

The same pattern of empirical neglect describes the hypothesized relationship between organizational cultural variation and criminal participation. This explanation has captured support from a range of investigators and is also featured prominently in media accounts of crime. Despite this consensus, however, compelling direct evidence has not appeared; there are no studies of the culture-crime nexus that develop systematic and independent measures of white-collar crime and cultural variables. Overall, the gaps in knowledge of white-collar crime are considerably larger and more numerous than in substantive areas of criminology in which investigators are in well-informed and confident agreement.

In numbers, in methodological sophistication, and in the use of state-of-the-art theoretical or substantive developments, studies of white-collar crime generally lag behind research into street crime, a situation that further slows timely and confident resolution of theoretical issues. Survey methods are used widely to study the incidence, experience, and aftermath of street-crime victimization, but limited use has been made of these procedures to examine white-collar crime. "Career criminals," individuals who commit crime at a high rate, some over a period of many years, have been a concern of elite academicians and policy makers for nearly two decades, but investigators have been slow to apply the criminal career framework and research agenda to white-collar criminals. The results when they do so call into question received notions about white-collar offenders; a substantial proportion have previous criminal convictions, which suggests they are anything but the "technical" or one-time transgressors sketched by business spokespersons and sympathetic politicians. Here, however, as in most areas of white-collar crime research, findings understandably hinge on how concepts are defined. If a status-based definition is used, white-collar criminals almost certainly appear most distinctive and unlike street offenders; if a formal definition is used, these differences are far less pronounced. If check forgery is counted as abuse of trust, together with price-fixing and other crimes committed by the respectable, examination of offenders inevitably will show a much larger proportion of persons with criminal records, some from blue-collar backgrounds. "Vice-presidents in charge of going to jail," by contrast, are required to do so but once.

Ethnographic research techniques are commonplace in research on street offenders. Generally, however, investigators have shown a striking reluctance or inability to get close to white-collar crime. The lives and routines of street robbers and drug dealers have been described repeatedly, but there are few comparable reports on white-collar criminals. We know a great deal about rule breaking by blue-collar shop-level employees but almost nothing comparable about middle- or upper-level management. No one disputes that there is substantial variation in white-collar crime across organizations, but there are few descriptions of the internal worlds associated with high and low rates of violation. Whether the internal organizational structure and culture of business with high violation rates reflect weak or erratic management concern with rule compliance as an organizational priority cannot be said. Personal interviews have been used in many studies of white-collar crime, but systematic observation is conspicuously absent. Archival materials have been employed extensively; more than in other areas of criminological scholarship, investigators have found it necessary to spend countless hours in libraries or in government archives collecting data.

Other than individual-level studies of criminal sentencing, there are remarkably few investigations of white-collar crime that employ large samples and multivariate statistical methods of analysis. Longitudinal studies are few in number (Simpson 1986, 1987) and generally limited to examination of change over short time spans (e.g., Clinard and Yeager 1980; Baucus and Near 1991). The use of experimental designs in white-collar crime research is rare.

There may be no other area of criminological scholarship in which case studies make up such a large proportion of the research tradition. The studies span the topical landscape, from rule making to rule enforcement, although they are concentrated in some areas more than others. There are few investigations of lawmaking, but there are outstanding studies of crime in various professions, industries, and financial markets, including descriptions and post hoc interpretations of unusually egregious or costly crimes. There are excellent studies of the organizational and practical consequences of new statutes and policies (e.g., Tonry and Reiss 1993). Anthologies, some richly dosed with case study analyses, provide the base of textbook knowledge of white-collar crime. Case studies can generate insights and refined hypotheses about white-collar crime, but they are poorly suited for theory testing. It is difficult, if not impossible, with this technique to demonstrate covariation, to control for the possible influence of extraneous variables, and to refute confidently rival explanations. An ability to generalize findings from case studies to populations of significance for improved theoretical understanding and control is unknown as well.

Beyond their limited value in arbitrating theoretical disagreement, however, case studies of white-collar crime may play an important part in shaping students' perspectives on the nature of such crimes and the challenges it poses. True-life accounts of white-collar greed, indifference, and unjust deserts can have an eye-opening and energizing effect on those exposed to them for the first time. This is not without the risk of giving a false picture of white-collar crime and its perpetrators. The fact that the state and the media single out for attention only the most egregious incidents and offenders means that estimates of the nature and seriousness of the problem derived from these reports are distorted. Highly publicized and unusually harmful crimes do not constitute the bulk of either street crime or white-collar crime.

White-collar crime encompasses such a diverse array of harmful behaviors that it is difficult to determine whether knowledge gained from studies of one type applies to or sheds light on others. Development of a generalized understanding of white-collar crime requires attention to cross-offense tests of theoretical explanations. A disproportionate share of the corpus of research thus far is limited to studies of crimes harmful to competition, chiefly price-fixing (e.g., Jamieson 1994). Understandings and explanations gained from this research must be tested in studies, say, of environmental crime and abuse of public trust before we can be confident of their broad application.

Policy Issues and Agenda

Crime prevention has grown to become one of the most important areas of criminological theory and practice (e.g., Tonry and Farrington 1995). Prevention programs, most guided by the theory of crime as choice, have been employed successfully in numerous locales and targeting a variety of crimes. Although, on its face, the heavy toll exacted by white-collar crime would make this a candidate for preventive initiatives, strategies of situational crime prevention have largely bypassed it. Its narrow focus on manipulation of conditions in the immediate environment as a way of controlling crime suggests, moreover, that situational crime prevention may have limited application to crimes committed by remote, impersonal others. The problems of white-collar crime victims provide an opportunity for advocates of situational crime prevention to show their approach has broad, effective application.

The Ambiguities of White-Collar Crime

Neglect of white-collar crime prevention may be part of a larger failure to acknowledge and publicly condemn white-collar crime. Media inattention to and distortion of issues surrounding white-collar crime are well known (Levi and Pithouse 1998). Policy makers and academics are not immune to the same, as indicated by willingness to employ alternative rhetorical constructions for felonious white-collar violations of the criminal code. Eschewal of the label *crime* in favor of *illegalities,* which is common particularly among students of white-collar crime trained at elite universities or located in business schools, makes it easy for elite offenders to define their behavior as illegal but not criminal.

It is doubtful that any aspect of white-collar crime has received less attention than its victims; even the crime victims' movement has ignored them. The U.S. Department of Justice spends heavily to support the National Crime Victimization Survey, but it has been slow to demonstrate the same monetary commitment and methodological creativity where white-collar crime research is concerned. Whatever the reasons, this inattention suggests that many of those victimized by white-collar crime, particularly its economic varieties, are seen by the public as persons who "asked for it." Their experiences and the experiences of rape victims share some characteristics, including the fact that responses by others often turn on the victim's behavior. As with street crime, repeat victimization of individuals and organizations is both an explanatory challenge and a policy problem.

The case study research designs that are commonplace in white-collar crime investigations were put to good advantage, particularly in studies of regulatory bureaucracies and processes. In several countries, a remarkably large number of regulatory bureaucracies and practices were examined, many in comparative studies of multiple agencies or settings. But matters have changed considerably. The effects of national administrations hostile to state regulation, in combination with the growth of the global economy, have weakened the confident optimism of those who advocate use of state-funded and state-implemented crackdowns to reduce violations of law. Restructured national economies and the uncertainty they breed have left political leaders across the ideological spectrum less inclined than they were a decade ago to call or press for vigorous state regulation. Policy makers and state managers understand they are in no position to tell business what to do. Industry is mobile, but regulatory regimes are not. The contemporary emphasis on cooperative regulation and other conditions that foster and maintain compliance has pushed to the background theoretical and research interest in state regulation. The move increasingly is to identify nonstate sources of constraint on organizations and white-collar personnel.

The effectiveness of various methods for controlling white-collar crime is virgin territory for empirical research. Codes of ethics and internal compliance programs have been developed by many organizations in recent years, but the effectiveness of these presumed behavioral constraints is largely unknown. If the content of the former is any indication, there is reason for skepticism. Organizational codes of ethics generally emphasize the importance of treating the organizational employer ethically, but they are conspicuously silent about employees' obligation to obey the law.

Global White-Collar Crime

White-collar crime is ever-changing. It adapts to exploit opportunities and avoid external controls made possible by technological and political-economic change. The emergence of the global economy has fundamentally altered both the face of white-collar crime and the challenges it poses to both those who study it and those who work to control it. The global economy also helps explain why exploration of white-collar crime, which until recent years was dominated by the perspectives and research interests of American investigators, has become an international pursuit. Growth of the world economic system has opened up new opportunities for white-collar crime. Even mundane confidence games and frauds now span national borders. Police and prosecutors in most local jurisdictions and Third World nations do not have the budgets, expertise, and other resources needed to pursue these cases. Increasingly, the challenge of white-collar crime must be met with coordinated interagency responses representing multiple state and national governments.

Trade agreements among nations have created new economic production and trading entities and the increasingly free flow of goods and services. The process of forging these agreements also creates criminal opportunities. Agricultural subsidies in the European Community designed to ensure quality, sufficient production, and stable incomes for farmers exemplify this process. Misrepresentation of the quality, origin, and destination of goods can be a profitable venture. In the simplest of schemes, unscrupulous growers have taken advantage of subsidies paid for withholding surplus wine from the market. This is accomplished by supplementing their supposed local production with clandestine purchases abroad and by collecting payment for cellars full of adulterated liquids (Clarke 1993; Passas and Nelken 1993).

The signatories to international trade agreements typically pledge to adopt and enforce in their home countries elementary regulatory standards for worker and product safety, although not all nations are equally prepared or committed to monitor these conditions. The same exploitation that is common, if largely invisible, in America's internal colonies is reproduced on a grander and more harmful and destructive scale around the world. Transnational corporations are key actors in these trends. The difficulties of controlling white-collar criminals were enormous even in a world of national economies and corporate actors, but the ability of corporations to move funds almost instantaneously and to shield their operations behind the laws of friendly nations complicates substantially the challenge of controlling them.

One of the most urgent problems created by development of the global economy is determining which laws and regulatory rules will be used as standards for individual and organizational behavior (Michalowski and Kramer 1987). Should crime be defined to include violations of international agreements that perhaps do not violate criminal statutes of all states or nations? When firms do business in countries with inconsistent laws and rules, which provide the standard for determining criminal conduct? Should regulations be aimed at producers or importers? More important, corporate owners and managers respond to calls for tighter controls with the threat of relocation and the loss of jobs and tax revenues to countries with less restrictive regulatory regimes. Relocation is an incentive for potential host countries to develop physical and legal infrastructures that are beneficial to corporations. Third World countries may be incapable of resisting or effectively controlling their incursions, their self-interested interpretations of rules, or their socially injurious conduct. The most attractive resources for use in industrial recruitment for many countries are cheap labor and weak regulation. Crops are harvested and goods produced beyond the watch of competent and committed regulatory authorities. In the global economy, transnational corporations are in an increasingly powerful position to craft the statutory and regulatory standards they are expected to meet.

Technological change and the emergence of transnational corporations have produced an unprecedented widening of the population at risk of victimization by white-collar crime. Third World countries, reeling under the burden of enormous indebtedness, routinely produce for distant markets. Across the globe, states' will to confront white-collar crime clearly has flagged substantially under the exigencies of competition as business argues that such efforts are unnecessary and costly. It is clear that states have moved significantly in the direction of strategies of cooperative regulation. The question raised by this move and the growing dominance of large organizations is whether they are now "beyond the law" (Tonry and Reiss 1993). This and other challenges posed by its ever-changing face increase the importance of understanding and controlling white-collar crime.

Acknowledgments   I am grateful to a number of colleagues who read and critiqued a draft of this chapter. I particularly appreciate the thoughtful and helpful comments provided by Kathleen Daly, Gilbert Geis, and Andrew Hochstetler.

References

Baucus, Melissa S., and Janet P. Near. 1991. "Can Illegal Corporate Behavior Be Predicted? An Event History Analysis." *Academy of Management Journal* 34:9–36.

Benson, Michael L. 1985. "Denying the Guilty Mind: Accounting for Involvement in a White-Collar Crime." *Criminology* 23:589–99.

Benson, Michael L., Francis T. Cullen, and William J. Maakestad. 1990. "Local Prosecutors and Corporate Crime." *Crime and Delinquency* 36:356–72.

Braithwaite, John. 1991. "Poverty, Power, and White-Collar Crime: Sutherland and the Paradoxes of Criminological Theory." *Australian–New Zealand Journal of Criminology* 24:40–58.

Calavita, Kitty, Henry N. Pontell, and Robert Tillman. 1997. *Big Money Crime: Fraud and Politics in the Savings and Loan Crisis.* Berkeley: University of California Press.

Clarke, Michael. 1993. "EEC Fraud: A Suitable Case for Treatment." In *Global Crime Connections: Dynamics and Control,* edited by Frank Pearce and Michael Woodiwiss. London: Macmillan.

Clinard, Marshall B., and Peter C. Yeager. 1980. *Corporate Crime.* New York: Free Press.

Coleman, James W. 1987. "Toward an Integrated Theory of White-Collar Crime." *American Journal of Sociology* 93:406–39.

Cressey, Donald R. 1995. "Poverty of Theory in Corporate Crime Research." In *White-Collar Crime: Classic and Contemporary Views,* 3rd ed., edited by Gilbert Geis, Robert F. Meier, and Lawrence M. Salinger. New York: Free Press.

Croall, Hazel. 1989. "Who is the White-Collar Criminal?" *British Journal of Criminology* 29:157–74.

Daly, Kathleen. 1989. "Gender and Varieties of White-Collar Crime." *Criminology* 27:769–93.

Geis, Gilbert. 1992. "White-Collar Crime: What Is It?" In *White-Collar Crime Reconsidered,* edited by Kip Schlegel and David Weisburd. Boston: Northeastern University Press.

———. 1993. "The Evolution of the Study of Corporate Crime." In *Understanding Corporate Criminality,* edited by Michael B. Blankenship. New York: Garland.

Jamieson, Katherine M. 1994. *Organization of Corporate Crime: Dynamics of Antitrust Violation.* Thousand Oaks, Calif.: Sage.

Jesilow, Paul, Henry N. Pontell, and Gilbert Geis. 1992. *Prescriptions for Profit: How Doctors Defraud Medicaid.* Berkeley: University of California Press.

Levi, Michael. 1981. *Phantom Capitalists: The Organization and Control of Long-Firm Fraud.* London: Heinemann.

———. 1992. "White-Collar Crime Victimization." In *White-Collar Crime Reconsidered,* edited by Kip Schlegel and David Weisburd. Boston: Northeastern University Press.

Levi, Michael, and Andrew Pithouse. 1998. *Victims of White-Collar Crime: The Media and Social Construction of Business Fraud.* Oxford: Clarendon.

Mann, Kenneth. 1985. *Defending White-Collar Crime: A Portrait of Attorneys at Work.* New Haven, Conn.: Yale University Press.

Meier, Robert F., and James F. Short, Jr. 1983. "The Consequences of White-Collar Crime." In *White-Collar Crime: An Agenda for Research,* edited by Herbert Edelhertz. Lexington, Mass.: Lexington.

Michalowski, Raymond J., and Ronald C. Kramer. 1987. "The Space Between Laws: The Problem of Corporate Crime in a Transnational Context." *Social Problems* 34:34–53.

Passas, Nikos, and David Nelken. 1993. "The Thin Line Between Legitimate and Criminal Enterprises: Subsidy Frauds in the European Community." *Crime, Law and Social Change* 19:223–43.

Reiss, Albert J., Jr., and Albert D. Biderman. 1980. *Data Sources on White-Collar Law-Breaking.* Washington, D.C.: U.S. Department of Justice, National Institute of Justice.

Reiss, Albert J., Jr., and Michael Tonry. 1993. "Organizational Crime." In *Beyond the Law: Crime in Complex Organizations,* edited by Michael Tonry and Albert J. Reiss, Jr. Chicago: University of Chicago Press.

Ruggiero, Vincenzo. 1996. *Organized and Corporate Crime in Europe: Offers That Can't Be Refused.* London: Dartmouth.

Schrager, Laura Shill, and James F. Short, Jr. 1980. "How Serious a Crime? Perceptions of Organizational and Common Crimes." In *White-Collar Crime: Theory and Research,* edited by Gilbert Geis and Ezra Stotland. Beverly Hills, Calif.: Sage.

Shapiro, Susan P. 1984. *Wayward Capitalists: Targets of the Securities and Exchange Commission.* New Haven, Conn.: Yale University Press.

———. 1985. "The Road Not Taken: The Elusive Path to Criminal Prosecution for White-Collar Offenders." *Law and Society Review* 19:179–217.

———. 1990. "Collaring the Crime, Not the Criminal: Reconsidering 'White-Collar Crime.'" *American Sociological Review* 55:346–65.

Shover, Neal, and Kevin M. Bryant. 1993. "Theoretical Explanations of Corporate Crime." In *Understanding Corporate Criminality,* edited by Michael B. Blankenship. New York: Garland.

Shover, Neal, Greer Litton Fox, and Michael Mills. 1994. "Long-Term Consequences of Victimization by White-Collar Crime." *Justice Quarterly* 11:301–24.

Simpson, Sally S. 1986. "The Decomposition of Antitrust: Testing a Multi-Level, Longitudinal Model of Profit-Squeeze." *American Sociological Review* 51:859–75.

———. 1987. "Cycles of Illegality: Antitrust Violations in Corporate America." *Social Forces* 65:943–63.

Sutherland, Edwin H. 1940. "White-Collar Criminality." *American Sociological Review* 5:1–11.

———. [1949] 1983. *White-Collar Crime: The Uncut Version,* with an introduction by Gilbert Geis and Colin Goff. New Haven, Conn.: Yale University Press.

Tonry, Michael, and David P. Farrington, eds. 1995. *Building a Safer Society: Strategic Approaches to Crime Prevention.* Vol. 19 of *Crime and Justice: A Review of Research.* Chicago: University of Chicago Press.

Tonry, Michael, and Albert J. Reiss, Jr., eds. 1993. *Beyond the Law: Crime in Complex Organizations.* Vol. 18 of *Crime and Justice: A Review of Research.* Chicago: University of Chicago Press.

Vaughan, Diane. 1982. "Transaction Systems and Unlawful Organizational Behavior." *Social Problems* 29:373–79.

Weisburd, David, Elin Waring, and Ellen Chayet. 1995. "Specific Deterrence in a Sample of Offenders Convicted of White-Collar Crimes." *Criminology* 33:587–607.

Weisburd, David, Stanton Wheeler, Elin Waring, and Nancy Bode. 1991. *Crimes of the Middle Classes.* New Haven, Conn.: Yale University Press.

6

Organized Crime

JAMES B. JACOBS & CHRISTOPHER PANARELLA

In the United States, the term *organized crime* is frequently associated with an Italian-American crime syndicate called the Mafia, La Cosa Nostra, or Cosa Nostra. With roots in Sicilian society and culture and in diverse gangs in the United States in the first third of the century, this syndicate emerged in something like its current form in the 1930s and reached the zenith of its power in illicit rackets, legitimate industry, labor unions, and politics in the 1960s and 1970s. Since the late 1970s, Cosa Nostra crime families throughout the country have been the target of a relentless federal law enforcement effort that has sent most of Cosa Nostra's top leaders to prison and has challenged its control of unions and industries. At the same time, and perhaps because of the law enforcement attack, there are many signs of internal disarray and disintegration. While it is premature to declare Cosa Nostra dead or even mortally wounded, its survival into the twenty-first century is not assured. So far no other organized crime group has the strength and sophistication to take the place of Cosa Nostra.

After explaining the reasons for focusing primarily on Cosa Nostra and reviewing the principal sources of reliable information on the subject, this chapter describes the history, structure, and activities of Cosa Nostra and identifies issues that have generated debate and controversy among experts. It also outlines the history and key components of the modern-day law enforcement attack on Cosa Nostra.

The problem of defining organized crime has consumed the attention of criminologists and policy makers for many years (Maltz 1985). The term would seem to refer to criminal conduct that is planned by a group of individuals. However, such a literal definition might encompass all crime that is not individual or spontaneous. A definition covering so much criminal conduct would be of no use because it would not focus attention and analysis on a distinctive type of criminality. Even defining organized crime as crime committed by gangs, professional criminals, white-collar criminals acting in concert, and other formal and informal groups in furtherance of economic goals would sweep in too many types of criminality to be useful. Intuitively and analytically, there are more differences than similarities between Cosa Nostra and street gangs and between Cosa Nostra and a sophisticated burglary ring. Thus we, along with many other writers, adopt a specialized definition of organized crime that refers not to conduct but to a crime syndicate: a type of criminal formation with an organizational structure, rules, history, division of labor, reputation, capacity for ruthless violence, capacity to corrupt law enforcement and the political system, and power to infiltrate labor unions and legitimate business.

Admittedly, even this specialized definition might well include groups other than Cosa Nostra. In the 1920s and 1930s, there were very strong Jewish, Irish, and German organized crime groups in New York City and elsewhere (Fox 1989; Peterson 1983). There have been black organized crime groups throughout the twentieth century active in numbers, prostitution, and other rackets in the black neighborhoods of American cities (e.g., Schatzberg 1993). In the waning years of the twentieth century, we have seen the emergence of Russian organized crime groups (Finckenauer 1994; Handelman 1995), Chinese triads or tongs (Chin 1990, 1994), Colombian drug traffickers, Jamaican posses, and other groups (Kenny and Finckenauer 1995). In New York City, an Irish gang called the "Westies" (English 1990) has attracted a good deal of attention because of its extreme and savage violence, often carried out at the behest of a Cosa Nostra crime family. Crime groups like these clearly have the capacity to mount sophisticated criminal operations and scams and to use deadly violence when necessary to further their goals. None of them, however, has so far shown anything like the sophistication and acumen necessary to fill Cosa Nostra's shoes. More specifically, none of these groups has shown that it can control labor unions, much less play the role of influence peddler, cartel enforcer, and "fixer" for whole industries. None of these groups has shown the ability to become a significant political force through control of grassroots party organization and campaign contributions. In other words, what makes Cosa Nostra distinctive, even unique, is its successful penetration of labor unions, legitimate industry, and politics, and its simultaneous power and influence in both the underworld and the upperworld. These activities, and the resulting power and prestige, justify treating Cosa Nostra as a criminological topic in its own right. Indeed, a comprehensive urban history of the United States in the twentieth century should devote considerable attention to the role of Cosa Nostra.

Sources of Information

It ought not to be difficult to study Cosa Nostra because, by design and necessity, it carries out its activities in the open. Cosa Nostra is in the business of selling its services as a "fixer," "influence peddler," and provider of diverse goods and services that are illegal; to be successful, it has to develop and maintain a presence and a reputation. Cosa Nostra bosses are "fixers" to whom businessmen, politicians, and criminals reach out in order to solve a variety of problems with other criminals, labor organizations, law enforcement, and government regulators. Thus, for example, the presence and influence of Cosa Nostra figures are obvious and well known to all who work in New York City's construction industry, Fulton Fish Market, garment center, waste-hauling industry, and several other industries and economic sectors. For decades Cosa Nostra figures played a visible role in the day-to-day life of these industries. In their neighborhoods, many Cosa Nostra bosses have attained almost mythical stature, with their distinctive manner of dress and bearing. People pay respect and even homage to them on the street and in their clubs. For their part, many Cosa Nostra bosses have carefully cultivated their image and their reputation for reliability and ruthlessness.

Some Cosa Nostra bosses—for example, Albert Anastasia, Frank Costello, Carlo Gambino, Vito Genovese, John Gotti, Thomas Lucchese, and Charles "Lucky" Luciano (New York City); Angelo Bruno and Nicodemo Scarfo (Philadelphia); Raymond Patriarca (Rhode Island); Tony Accardo, Al Capone, and Sam Giancana (Chicago); Nick Civella (Kansas City); and Carlos Marcello (New Orleans)—have attained widespread notoriety, even national prominence. They are the subject of endless newspaper stories, magazine articles, popular books and movies, and even scholarly biographies. It would not be an exaggeration to say that these Cosa Nostra bosses have been part of the power elite in their home cities and, in some cases, nationally.

Cosa Nostra is, however, a secret organization that swears its members to *omerta,* a code of silence. Cosa Nostra does not hold open meetings or issue earnings statements. It does not maintain corporate headquarters or office blocks, nor does it keep meticulous books and records. Thus, until Joseph Valachi defected from the mob and went public in 1963 (Maas 1968), no member of Cosa Nostra had ever admitted to the organization's existence, much less described its history, structure, rules, and activities. With the exception of Ianni and Reuss-Ianni (1972), sociologists and criminologists have not been able to carry out case studies of Cosa Nostra; nor does the subject lend itself to quantitative analysis (Reuter 1994).

Until the 1970s, although Cosa Nostra was a fixture in American popular culture, many academics regarded it as a myth (e.g., Smith 1975). That position was substantially undermined by the release in trial proceedings of the famous "De Cavalcante tapes" in the mid-1960s. The FBI recorded hundreds of conversations in which Sam De Cavalcante, the head of a minor New Jersey Cosa Nostra family, and various colleagues discussed the structure, organization, history, and politics of Cosa Nostra (see Zeiger 1973, 1975). Even though the defections and prosecutions of the 1980s and 1990s have proved the existence of Cosa Nostra beyond any shadow of a doubt, the "Mafia as myth" literature remains on the shelves of libraries and is sometimes perpetuated in the contemporary scholarship of academic writers whose eyes and ears seemingly remain closed to the masses of information on Cosa Nostra that are now available.

There have been dozens of major criminal trials of Cosa Nostra bosses since the late 1970s and well over a thousand prosecutions (Jacobs, Panarella, and Worthington 1994). Practically all of the trials have relied on extensive electronic eavesdropping based on "bugs" that the FBI and various state and local law enforcement agencies have planted in Cosa Nostra members' cars, homes, and social clubs. The overheard conversations, which have been made public through their presentation in civil and criminal cases, provide extremely reliable information about the nature of organized crime and its activities.

Until Valachi, there had been no defectors willing to testify about Cosa Nostra. Beginning in the 1970s, however, Cosa Nostra's much-vaunted code of *omerta* began to disintegrate, and, in a few years, many high-ranking organized crime figures agreed to testify for the government in exchange for leniency and placement in the federal Witness Protection Program, which, for the first time, offered the hope of survival to a Cosa Nostra figure who turned against his comrades.

The defectors have provided a wealth of information about Cosa Nostra's membership, organizational hierarchy, rules, and criminal activities. One of the first Cosa Nostra members to "flip" was Aladema "Jimmy the Weasel" Fratianno, acting boss of the Los Angeles crime family; he testified for the government in the first RICO (Racketeer Influenced and Corrupt Organizations Act) prosecution against a Cosa Nostra boss (*United States v. Tieri*) and later in the "commission case" brought against the leaders of the New York families (citations to court cases discussed are provided in the table of cases on p. 149). In the famous "pizza connection case" (*United States v. Badalamenti*), Tomasso Buscetta provided extensive information about a cooperative drug trafficking relationship between Mafia groupings in Italy and the Bonanno family in New York City. Salvatore "Sammy the Bull" Gravano, a former underboss of the Gambino crime family, provided a rich description of that family's operations in the prosecution of John Gotti and in several other cases. For the government's civil racketeering suit against the International Teamsters Union and its executive board, Angelo Lonardo, former underboss of the Cleveland crime family, provided an extraordinary deposition detailing Cosa Nostra's role in designating the president of the Teamsters Union and in controlling that union. Vincent Cafaro has likewise been extensively debriefed and used in many prosecutions. The defectors' testimony in many cases has passed through a number of screens that ought to assure a high degree of reliability: savvy prosecutors believe the testimony to be truthful, as do grand juries and trial juries (beyond a reasonable doubt), the latter even after such testimony has been exposed to extensive cross-examination by skilled defense lawyers.

The information that emanates from electronic eavesdropping and the live testimony of defectors is confirmed and supplemented by the testimony of other witnesses, including FBI and other law enforcement agents, labor union officials, and private citizens who have done business with or been victimized by the mob. The most famous law enforcement witness is Joe Pistone, the only FBI agent ever to penetrate Cosa Nostra. For six years (1976–1982), Pistone (calling himself Donnie Brasco) hung out with organized crime members and their associates based in New York City, in effect conducting a participant-observation study unparalleled in the history of criminology. Throughout this period, Pistone passed vital information about the mob along to the top echelons of the FBI. Pistone's observations have been thoroughly presented and cross-examined in court and published as a narrative (Pistone and Woodley 1987). In 1997, Pistone's exploits were dramatized for the public in the popular film *Donnie Brasco*.

Much less reliable than the electronically seized conversations and the cross-examined court testimony of former Cosa Nostra members, but still valuable, are a number of autobiographies by Cosa Nostra members. Among these the most prominent are Joseph Bonanno and Sergio Lalli's *A Man of Honor* (1983); Ovid Demaris's *The Last Mafioso: The Treacherous World of Jimmy Frattiano* (1980); Nick Pileggi and Henry Hill's *Wiseguy: Life in a Mafia Family* (1985); Vincent Teresa and Thomas Renner's *My Life in the Mafia* (1973); and Peter Maas's *Underboss: Sammy the Bull Gravano's Story of Life in the Mafia* (1997).

In addition to the primary sources, there are many reports by special commissions, the U.S. General Accounting Office, the U.S. Department of Justice, and congressional committees. Taken together, these reports, based to a significant extent on live testimony, provide a mass of information about the activities of Cosa Nostra and of the law enforcement agencies most significantly involved in investigations and prosecutions. The President's Commission on Law Enforcement and Administration of Justice (1967) published *Task Force Report: Organized Crime* (written by criminologist Donald Cressey in close collaboration with New York City Police Department organized crime specialist Ralph Salerno). While the report, which also formed the basis for Cressey's *Theft of the Nation* (1969), probably exaggerated the formal organizational structure of Cosa Nostra and the authority of its "ruling commission," it constitutes a very useful source. Two decades later, the President's Commission on Organized Crime (1986b) published a series of volumes on various organized crime matters, including important analyses of labor racketeering and the role of organized crime in legitimate industry (1986a).

A great deal of important information about organized crime can be found in congressional hearings beginning with Senator Estes Kefauver's hearings (Special Committee on Organized Crime in Interstate Commerce) in 1950–1951 (see Kefauver 1951; Moore 1974). The committee took testimony from more than 600 witnesses in hearings around the country. The most dramatic moment in the hearings was the committee's grilling of NYC mob boss Frank Costello, whose rambling, evasive, and disingenuous answers spoke volumes. Perhaps the committee's main contribution was exposing the ties between corrupt political machines (like Tammany Hall) and organized crime bosses (like Frank Costello) in many cities (see Peterson 1983).

In 1956, Senator John McClellan began a series of hearings for the Senate Select Committee on Improper Activities in the Labor or Management Field (McClellan 1962). Robert Kennedy served, for a period, as chief counsel to this committee and, before a national television audience, engaged in an angry exchange with Jimmy Hoffa, whose activities in the Teamsters Union the committee was investigating (Kennedy 1960). The McClellan Committee's findings led, in 1959, to passage of the Landrum-Griffin Act, which was an attempt to bolster union members' rights vis-à-vis their own unions. In 1963, with U.S. Attorney General Kennedy's support and assistance, Senator McClellan and his colleagues on the Permanent Subcommittee on Investigations publicly questioned Joseph Valachi about his thirty-three years in the Genovese crime family. Valachi had decided to go public when, while serving a prison term, he determined that he had been marked for execution.

In the 1980s, the U.S. Senate Permanent Subcommittee on Investigations, under Senator Sam Nunn's chairmanship, convened hearings on various organized crime issues and elicited testimony from hundreds of witnesses, including former Sicilian Mafia boss Tomasso Buscetta and Cosa Nostra defectors Vincent Cafaro and Angelo Lonardo (see, e.g., U.S. Senate, Permanent Subcommittee on Investigations 1981, 1983).

Among the state crime commission reports on organized crime, the New York State Organized Crime Task Force's *Corruption and Racketeering in the NYC Construction Industry* (1990) stands out. This report provides an in-depth examination and analysis of Cosa Nostra's involvement in labor unions and construction and supply companies in the New York City metropolitan area. It shows how Cosa Nostra, through its labor power, established and policed employer cartels and how it converted power and influence in a major industry into cash. Another outstanding government report is the Pennsylvania Crime Commission's *Organized Crime in Pennsylvania: A Decade of Change* (1990), which covers Cosa Nostra's extensive operations in traditional rackets and the legitimate economy throughout Pennsylvania, in small cities as well as in Philadelphia and Pittsburgh. Crime commissions in New Jersey and Illinois have also provided many useful reports on organized crime operations in those states.

There is also a rich scholarly literature on organized crime, beginning perhaps with John Landesco's classic *Organized Crime in Chicago* (1968). An excellent introduction to scholarship in the field is Howard Abadinsky's *Organized Crime* (1994; see also Sifakis 1987). Two excellent histories are Virgil Peterson's *The Mob: 200 Years of Organized Crime in New York* (1983) and Stephen Fox's *Blood and Power: Organized Crime in Twentieth Century America* (1989). Peter Reuter has produced a valuable economic analysis, based on empirical study of organized crime's role in establishing and maintaining cartels in legitimate industry (Reuter 1983, 1987; see also Florentini and Peltzman 1995; Kleinknecht 1996). In addition, there are a number of excellent biographies of organized crime figures (e.g., Al Capone, Meyer Lansky, Arnold Rothstein, Frank Costello, Vito Genovese) and law enforcement officials (e.g., Harry J. Anslinger, Thomas Dewey, J. Edgar Hoover).

History

There is a lively debate in the scholarly literature over whether Italian organized crime in the United States was transplanted from Italy or is an essentially American phenomenon. Those who favor the transplant theory point to the strong Mafia tradition in Sicily (Arlacchi 1986; Gambetta 1993; Hess 1973) and to the role of Sicilian immigrants in developing organized crime groups in the United States in the first decades of the twentieth century. Those who favor a nativism theory point to the ways in which the Italian organized crime groupings connect to American society and its economy (Bell 1964). There is no reason to treat these as rival theories. It is entirely plausible to hold that Italian organized crime has its roots in Italian and especially Sicilian society and culture and, over the years, has adapted to American society and taken on a distinctly American cast.

It should be emphasized that the American Cosa Nostra and the Italian Mafia are not now and never have been a single organization or even two branches of a single organization. They operate as separate and distinct organizations, although members of the two groups undertake cooperative ventures, as was demonstrated in *United States v. Badalamenti*.

It is now common to assign to the Castellammarese War of the early 1930s the emergence of the modern-day Cosa Nostra from the various Italian organized crime groups that had existed up to that point. Much of this history was first revealed by Valachi, who recounted a conflict between major Italian-American organized criminal groups. While the reliability of this history has been vigorously questioned (Block 1994), the standard account holds that in early 1930, Joseph Masseria and his cohorts decreed a death sentence for any underworld figure who originated from the locality of Castellammare de Golfo, Sicily. The warfare that followed was known as the Castellammarese War. One faction was led by Masseria, the other by Salvatore Maranzano. Other gangs and underworld leaders linked themselves to one of the two factions. Vito Genovese, Lucky Luciano, Dutch Schultz, and Al Capone supported Masseria. In 1931, Masseria was double-crossed and assassinated when Genovese and Luciano invited him to a restaurant to discuss plans for killing Maranzano. Masseria's death concluded the Castellammarese War. Maranzano held a meeting in New York City with almost 400 members of organized crime groups in order to create a structure and rules for the organized crime groups. The jurisdiction of various organized crime "families" throughout the United States was recognized. This was also the origin of the famous "commission," which has been alleged to govern organized crime affairs throughout the United States. Maranzano himself was assassinated only months after the historic meeting. Lucky Luciano consolidated power and reinforced the structure of Cosa Nostra from that point.

In the 1920s and 1930s, there were a number of ethnically based (e.g., Jewish, Irish, German) organized crime syndicates in the United States (Peterson 1983; Fox 1989). Underworld figures like Arnold Rothstein and Dutch Schultz were among the most powerful overlords of organized crime. With the important exception of Meyer Lansky, the non-Italian organized crime groups did not make the transition into the post-Prohibition world. By the 1950s, Cosa Nostra had achieved virtual hegemony in the underworld of organized crime. Italian organized crime "families" were entrenched in most large American cities and in many smaller ones as well. New York City has long had five crime families—Genovese, Gambino, Lucchese, Bonanno, and Colombo—that engaged in supplying illicit goods and services, such as drugs, prostitution, usurious loans, and pornography, and infiltrated labor unions and industries. In addition, they participated in (usually Democratic Party) politics. In fact, the history of the Cosa Nostra is intertwined with the history of the urban political machines (Peterson 1983).

Organization

Each of the twenty-four Cosa Nostra families (or probably fewer as of 1997, since several have effectively been dismantled) is headed by a *boss*. The second in command is the *underboss*. The third position in the family's ruling triumvirate is known as *consigliere*, or counselor. The boss chooses a limited number of *capos* (*caporegines*), each with authority over crews consisting of *soldiers* ("made members" of Cosa Nostra) and *associates*. All "made members" of Cosa Nostra are Italian, and, needless to say, all are male.

Before Senator McClellan's committee, Joseph Valachi described the secret ceremony whereby members are inducted into Cosa Nostra families and the code of *omerta* to which all members swear fealty. Valachi's description of the initiation ceremony has subsequently been confirmed by other defectors and, in one case, by an eavesdropping device. The ritual involves the prospective member being asked a number of questions that demonstrate his commitment (willingness to kill) and loyalty. Then a picture of a saint is burned in the initiate's hand. The individual must swear fealty to the family and allegiance to the oath of *omerta*, promising never to divulge secrets. Then the initiate's hand is pricked with a pin until blood is drawn.

There has been a good deal of debate about the degree of coordination among the individual organized crime families. The task force report of the President's Commission on Law Enforcement and Administration of Justice (1967), drafted chiefly by the noted criminologist Donald Cressey, claimed that Cosa Nostra was a nationwide syndicate governed by a ruling commission. In his autobiography, Joseph Bonanno also spoke about a nationwide commission. However, other than a mysterious 1956 conclave at Apalachin, New York (see *United States v. Bufalino*), which was attended by Cosa Nostra figures from all over the country, there is little empirical evidence to support that claim. Perhaps a loose commission, with representatives from various crime families, did exist at one time but has subsequently lapsed.

In the "commission case" (*United States v. Salerno*), the U.S. attorney in the Southern District of New York obtained an indictment against the bosses of four of New York City's Cosa Nostra crime families. Each boss was charged with participating in the affairs of an enterprise (the Cosa Nostra Commission) through a pattern of racketeering activity (including operating a concrete cartel in violation of the antitrust laws). The case was built on extensive eavesdropping and electronic surveillance evidence and resulted in convictions and life sentences for the defendants. The government's case, though successful, still left much unclear about the precise jurisdiction and authority of the commission. Clearly, it did not operate as a day-to-day executive board but instead functioned intermittently, more like a court called upon to solve occasional disputes. The fact that all the members of this commission were leaders of New York City crime families throws doubt on the claim that there is, today at least, a commission that represents and has authority over Cosa Nostra affairs throughout the country.

That Cosa Nostra is not a single nation-wide organization with centralized control and command and a single authority structure does not mean that there is not a degree of cooperation among the families. For example, there seems to have been a great deal of communication and cooperation among families in the process of choosing leaders for the Teamsters Union. Interfamily violence has been very rare, even in New York City. The gangland violence that does occur is practically always intrafamily.

At the present time, then, it is best to think of Cosa Nostra as a mélange of locally based crime families, each of which has exclusive jurisdiction in its own geographic area. The five families in New York City are not organized by territory; each operates all over the city and throughout the metropolitan area in various rackets and legitimate industries. The families themselves operate as patrimonial organizations and not as formal bureaucracies. Each of the crews, in effect, has a franchise to engage in diverse criminal ventures, as long as the family's boss approves and is provided the appropriate percentage of the proceeds. Cosa Nostra soldiers must be entrepreneurs in crime, seeking out profitable opportunities in both the underworld and the upperworld.

Activities

Among organized crime groups, Cosa Nostra stands out for the diversity of its criminal activities. In a real sense, Cosa Nostra has an instinct and an aptitude for criminal opportunities ranging from the supply of illicit goods and services, to thefts, hijackings, and frauds, to price-fixing, cartel creation, and enforcement, and to labor racketeering. Unlike such organized crime groups as the Colombian drug cartels, for example, Cosa Nostra does not specialize in a single service or sector. However, running through all of Cosa Nostra's activities is its use of violence or the threat of violence. Cosa Nostra's success has also been built on the organization's willingness and ability to provide goods and services that are not legally available. Cosa Nostra bosses have been extraordinarily successful in functioning as power brokers in both the underworld and the upperworld, and as a bridge between those worlds.

Illicit Goods and Services

Traditionally, Cosa Nostra made money through the provision of goods and services which the legislature had made illegal. Thus, organized crime flourished during national Prohibition and has always profited from gambling, prostitution, and loan-sharking. Cosa Nostra's involvement in illicit drug trafficking is more controversial. Cosa Nostra members and others have often claimed that Cosa Nostra crime families have a strict rule, enforceable by capital punishment, against selling illicit mind-altering drugs—marijuana, heroin, cocaine, amphetamine, and so forth—although there is no agreement on the reason for such a rule. If the rule ever existed, it was often honored in the breach. There have been criminal prosecutions involving Cosa Nostra for drug trafficking all the way back to the early decades of the century (e.g., *United States v. Bruno* [1939]). Vito Genovese, boss of the Luciano/Genovese family and one of the most powerful mob figures of all time, was actively involved in drug trafficking (as was Luciano) from the 1930s and was sent to prison in 1959 for conspiracy to violate the narcotics laws. In the 1980s, the famous "pizza connection case" (*United States v. Badalamenti*) illuminated the involvement of Cosa Nostra in large-scale international drug trafficking. The indictment, filed on February 19, 1985, charged thirty-five defendants with conspiracy to import drugs and to evade banking and money-laundering laws. Twenty of the defendants were members of two groups of Sicilian mafiosi. Salvatore Catalano, a capo in the Bonanno crime family and the highest-ranking Cosa Nostra member, was accused of running the Bonanno organization's drug importation business.

Labor Racketeering

In sharp contrast with the European organized crime experience, labor racketeering has been a key source of Cosa Nostra power and profits from the early twentieth century when companies frequently called upon mobsters to break strikes. The mobsters used the opportunity to infiltrate the unions themselves. Unions became much more important after the Wagner Act mandated collective bargaining. Organized crime could then use its union power to extort payoffs for labor peace or to solicit bribes for sweetheart contracts.

After the election in 1957 of Jimmy Hoffa as president of the International Brotherhood of Teamsters, Cosa Nostra became the dominant force in the United States' largest labor union. No one could attain the position of president of the Teamsters International without a green light from the organized crime bosses. In effect, bosses from different parts of the country promoted their own candidates for the top spot in the Teamsters. This history is effectively told by both Roy Williams and Jackie Presser in their depositions in *United States v. International Brotherhood of Teamsters* and in a number of books about the Teamsters and Jimmy Hoffa (Moldea 1978; Brill 1978). In return for supporting figures like Jimmy Hoffa for the Teamsters presidency, the mob bosses were, in effect, given control of Teamster locals, access to the Teamster pension funds, and influence over diverse matters in which the Teamsters played a role.

For decades, Cosa Nostra exercised influence and control in the International Longshoremen's Association, the Laborers Union, the Hotel Employees and Restaurant Employees Union, and many craft unions (President's Commission on Organized Crime 1986a). The film *On the Waterfront* (1954), starring Marlon Brando, is credited with having stimulated the first congressional hearings on labor racketeering.

As union pension funds became more and more important, Cosa Nostra–dominated unions could place their own members or associates as trustees of these funds and then plunder them at will. Indeed, as prosecutions in the 1960s and 1970s clearly showed, organized crime used the massive Central States Pension Fund as a kind of mob bank (*United States v. Dorfman*). Sweetheart loans from the fund were used to finance Cosa Nostra's huge and hugely successful operations in Las Vegas (Skolnick 1978).

Bugsy Siegel was Cosa Nostra's trailblazer in Las Vegas beginning in the early 1940s. Through control of the wire service in Las Vegas, Siegel dominated all Las Vegas bookmaking operations (Abadinsky 1994). With mob financing, Siegel also built the Flamingo, the first of Las Vegas's huge gambling hotels. Over time, Cosa Nostra bosses obtained interests in many of the largest casinos in Las Vegas and enjoyed a huge return on their investments by skimming money from the gross receipts. In 1986, with the aid of Angelo Lonardo's testimony, a number of midwestern mobsters were sentenced to prison for tax evasion emanating from the Las Vegas operations (e.g., *United States v. Dominic Spinale*).

Business Racketeering

Through its labor racketeering, Cosa Nostra has been able to establish and police employer business cartels in many industries (Gambetta and Peltzman 1995). In New York City, for example, there were for decades cartels in concrete production and pouring, garment industry trucking, and drywall installation. Cosa Nostra controlled the unions, and the unions controlled who could participate in the industry. A company that was not unionized could not work in these industries (see New York State Organized Crime Task Force 1990); at the very least, its operations would be picketed and sabotaged. Even among unionized firms, only those owned by or those that paid off Cosa Nostra could function in the industry. Cosa Nostra maintained cartels that allocated contracts and fixed prices. In the "commission case" (*United States v. Salerno*), the prosecutors proved the existence of a Cosa Nostra cartel over concrete production and pouring. The mob permitted only one (Cosa Nostra–controlled) firm to carry out the largest contracts. Middle-size contracts were allocated to a half dozen firms in which the various Cosa Nostra families held interests. Companies that were permitted to carry out smaller contracts had to kick back a percentage to the mob bosses. Through this cartel, the mob controlled every concrete contract in the city for more than a decade.

Union power has also been convertible into political power (Peterson 1983). Mob bosses have played key roles in grassroots political party organizations. Others have operated as power brokers, anointing political candidates and serving as a source of funds and manpower for political campaigns. Organized crime bosses like Frank Costello and Ralph Scopo kept company with mayors and governors. Harry Davidoff (president of a Teamsters local that operated at Kennedy Airport) and Alan Dorfman (Chicago) are two examples of mob associates who operated as major power brokers in the nation's largest cities.

Cosa Nostra's operations span a large number of industries—for example, New York City's Fulton Fish Market, cargo operations at Kennedy Airport, solid waste hauling and disposal, moving and storage, securities manipulation, linen businesses, and even homeless shelters. The crime families have also been active in food processing, importation, and retail distribution (Kwitny 1979). Several major cases of fraud in the securities industry that involve organized crime have come to light in recent years.

"Traditional Crimes"

Cosa Nostra, of course, has also been extremely active in many traditional crimes. For example, through its influence in cargo operations at Kennedy Airport it has been able to identify valuable shipments and has carried out truck hijackings and a spectacular $5-million heist of the Lufthansa cargo hangar in 1978 (the basis for the movie *Goodfellas*). Cosa Nostra has an extensive record in bankruptcy fraud ("bust-out" schemes), taking over a legitimate company, looting its assets, and leaving its creditors high and dry.

Busting the Mob

Until the massive federal law enforcement organized crime control initiatives of the last quarter of the twentieth century, anti–organized crime initiatives were sporadic and ineffective. To be sure, there have been successes, like Thomas Dewey's famous prosecutions of Lepke Buchalter (murder), the only organized crime figure ever to be executed, and Lucky Luciano (compulsory prostitution), and the government's success in jailing Al Capone (income tax evasion). Such prosecutions, however, made hardly a dent in Cosa Nostra's activities and power. Successors quickly stepped forward, although intrafamily leadership transitions have often posed short-term problems for Cosa Nostra families.

Organized crime was able to flourish because of an absence of any serious federal resistance. Perhaps local police departments and prosecutors did not have the resources or the tools to investigate and prosecute powerful organized crime figures. In addition, it is likely that a symbiotic relationship between organized crime and the urban political machines provided insulation from sustained law enforcement initiatives. Despite the Kefauver, McClellan, and other congressional hearings, the FBI's director J. Edgar Hoover would not devote resources to organized crime investigations; indeed, until well into the 1960s, he refused even to recognize the existence of organized crime. This extraordinary intransigence, even for Hoover, has never been satisfactorily explained: whether it was due to his desire not to divert the FBI's attention from "more important" targets, like the Communist Party, or perhaps to organized crime compromising him in some way (as some have alleged), has never been established. What is certain, however, is that the nation's principal federal law enforcement agency was not involved in anti–organized crime operations until the 1970s.

As the McClellan Committee's chief counsel in the late 1950s, Robert F. Kennedy learned a great deal about labor racketeering. The more he learned, the more incensed he became (Kennedy 1960). His conviction that the corrupt Teamster president Dave Beck had been succeeded by the mob-controlled Jimmy Hoffa sparked a commitment to bring down Hoffa. The commitment reached fruition when Kennedy became U.S. attorney general in 1961. He launched an intensive investigation of Hoffa that resulted in misdemeanor conflict-of-interest charges in 1962. The jury failed to convict. Two years later, however, Hoffa was sent to prison for eight years for jury tampering.

As U.S. attorney general from 1961 to 1964, Kennedy implemented a number of important organized crime control innovations in the U.S. Department of Justice, particularly formation of the organized crime and racketeering section. After Kennedy left the Department of Justice, the organized crime initiatives stalled for a period, but they were reenergized in the late 1960s. In 1967, the Justice Department established Organized Crime Strike Forces, composed of federal prosecutors and federal law enforcement agents, in fourteen cities (Ryan 1994). These strike forces brought together a level of resources and expertise that had never before been assembled in the pursuit of organized crime.

In 1968, following publication of the report of the President's Commission on Law Enforcement and Administration of Justice (1968) Congress passed new legislation authorizing electronic eavesdropping with a warrant and according to other guidelines (Title III of the Omnibus Crime Control and Safe Streets Act of 1968). Since, at the time, Cosa Nostra defectors were unheard of and victims rarely wished to testify against Cosa Nostra, electronically seized conversations were the best source of evidence in developing organized crime cases. In a few years, organized crime bosses were blanketed with eavesdropping devices, to the point that they could never assume, no matter where they were, that law enforcement agents were not listening in.

The new eavesdropping law was accompanied by a fundamental change in the priority the FBI assigned to organized crime. In the post-Hoover period, the FBI became fully committed to putting Cosa Nostra out of business. Perhaps the modern era in the government's anti–organized crime war dates to the FBI's massive UNIRAC investigation of the International Longshoremen's Association in the late 1970s. This labor racketeering investigation, the subject of special Senate hearings in 1981, resulted in the conviction of 130 businessmen, union officials, and Cosa Nostra members, including Anthony Scotto. UNIRAC was followed by dozens of other large-scale investigations of labor unions, industries, and criminal schemes.

In New York and other cities, the FBI organized squads for each Cosa Nostra crime family. These squads set out to document each family's command structure and criminal activities. When that was accomplished, eavesdropping orders were obtained, evidence was gathered, and continuous prosecutions were initiated.

Beginning in the 1970s, joint federal, state, and local task forces began to make significant headway in overcoming agency parochialism. In 1970, the National Council on Organized Crime was established to formulate a strategy to eliminate organized crime. While the council failed to develop a national strategy, it mobilized attention to the problem of interagency relations. In 1976, the National Organized Crime Planning Council was formed to facilitate planning and coordination between the organized crime strike forces and federal law enforcement agencies. In 1980, the Executive Working Group for Federal-State-Local Prosecutorial Relations was initiated. These formal institutional mechanisms of cooperation were supplemented and reinforced by many informal multi-agency working arrangements.

In 1970, Congress passed the most important substantive anti–organized crime statute in history, the Racketeer Influenced and Corrupt Organizations Act (RICO), which, among other things, makes it a crime to acquire an interest in, to participate in the affairs of, or to invest the profits acquired from an enterprise through a pattern of racketeering activity (Lynch 1987). An enterprise can be a legitimate or wholly illegitimate organization or any group of individuals associated in fact. A pattern of racketeering activity was defined as any two of a long list of federal or state crimes.

RICO made it possible to bring to a single trial whole criminal groups and families—all those defendants who participated in the affairs of the same criminal enterprise (e.g., one of the crime families) through a pattern of racketeering activity. RICO's penalties are draconian. In addition to twenty-year maxima for violation of both the substantive and the conspiracy provisions, RICO also provides for massive fines and for mandatory forfeiture of the defendant's property that can be traced to the proceeds of racketeering activity.

Although it took a decade for federal prosecutors to begin using RICO, once they did so, practically every significant organized crime prosecution was brought under RICO (Jacobs, Panarella, and Worthington 1994). Rudolph Giuliani, the U.S. attorney for the Southern District of New York, brought RICO prosecutions against the leaders of each of the New York City crime families (the so-called "family RICO" prosecutions) and then a follow-up suit against the bosses of the families, alleging that they were participating in the affairs of an organized crime commission through a pattern of racketeering activity (the "commission case").

RICO also contains two civil remedial provisions. One that gives private victims the right to sue racketeers for triple their damages has not been used against organized crime, although it has become very popular (and controversial) in commercial litigation. However, a provision allowing the government to sue racketeers for injunctions, restraining orders, and other equitable remedies has been used a great deal and has provided the government with a powerful tool in its effort to purge organized crime from labor unions and industries (Jacobs, Panarella, and Worthington 1994).

In 1982, the Newark Strike Force made history by filing the first civil RICO suit against a labor union, Local 560, the largest Teamster local in the state, and a union that had been dominated by organized crime through the Provenzano brothers and the Genovese crime family since the 1950s. The suit resulted in a court-imposed trusteeship, which gave the trustee extensive powers to run the union until the racketeering element could be purged and fair elections held. Six years later, the U.S. attorney's office in the Southern District of New York filed a RICO suit against the International Brotherhood of Teamsters, its general executive board, and the board's incumbents; under a consent decree that settled the case, the entire general executive board was removed. The Teamsters agreed to a three-person trusteeship whose goals were to purge corruption and racketeering and to supervise a direct election of the president and general executive board. Dozens of Teamster officials were removed from locals around the country. Several years later, after the first general election in which the rank and file could vote, an insurgent reformer, Ron Carey, won the presidency. He, along with the trustees, continued to purge racketeers from various locals around the country.

In New York City, as a result of civil RICO suits, court-appointed trustees and monitors were appointed in more than half a dozen RICO cases involving historically mobbed-up unions. In addition, a court-appointed trustee was appointed to monitor the Fulton Fish Market. As the result of a plea bargain, Thomas Gambino agreed to sell off his entire interest in trucking related to the garment center. When, in 1993, the former U.S. attorney, Rudolph Giuliani, became mayor of New York City, yet another organized crime control strategy was implemented. The city used its regulatory authority to license businesses and individuals in the Fulton Fish Market and in the waste-hauling industry. Once again, this resulted in a purge of numerous Cosa Nostra members and associates.

Conclusion

Cosa Nostra deserves its own chapter in the history of crime in America. It constitutes a criminal grouping or formation that is, by an order of magnitude, larger, more diverse, and more powerful than any other. There have been and still are other organizations that engage in some of the same crimes and schemes as Cosa Nostra, but none that engage in as many. More important, no other criminal organization has achieved so much power, influence, and prestige in the upperworld—in labor, business, and politics.

For the last two decades of the twentieth century, Cosa Nostra has been under relentless law enforcement attack. The bosses of every crime family have been sent to prison for life or very long terms. In many cases, their successors and their successors' successors have also been sent to prison. Court-appointed trustees have entrenched themselves in labor unions and industries that only a few years ago were thought to be irremediably "mobbed up." Moreover, the loyalty and commitment that for most of the century made Cosa Nostra practically untouchable by law enforcement have substantially eroded. Even bosses and underbosses have entered into cooperative agreements with the government. Thus, the glue that for almost a century kept Cosa Nostra together has come unstuck. It is entirely possible, then, that the kind of organized crime threat that Cosa Nostra posed for most of the twentieth century will not carry over into the twenty-first. And, if law enforcement agencies remain attentive, it seems unlikely that any other organized crime grouping will achieve the level of power that Cosa Nostra enjoyed at its height.

References

Abadinsky, Howard. 1994. *Organized Crime*. 4th ed. Chicago: Nelson Hall.
Arlacchi, Pino. 1986. *Mafia Business: The Mafia Ethic and the Spirit of Capitalism*. London: Verso.
Bell, Daniel. 1964. *The End of Ideology*. Glencoe, Ill.: Free Press.
Block, Alan. 1994. "Organized Crime: History and Historiography." In *Handbook of Organized Crime in the United States*, edited by Robert Kelly, Ko-Lin Chin, and Rufus Schatzberg. Westport, Conn.: Greenwood Press.
Bonanno, Joseph, and Sergio Lalli. 1983. *A Man of Honor: The Autobiography of Joseph Bonanno*. New York: Simon and Schuster.
Brill, Steven. 1978. *The Teamsters*. New York: Simon and Schuster.
Chin, Ko-Lin. 1990. *Chinese Subculture and Criminality: Non-Traditional Crime Groups in America*. New York: Greenwood Press.
———. 1994. "Chinese Organized Crime in America." In *Handbook of Organized Crime in the United States*, edited by Robert Kelly, Ko-Lin Chin, and Rufus Schatzberg. Westport, Conn.: Greenwood Press.
Cressey, Donald. 1969. *Theft of the Nation: The Structure and Operations of Organized Crime in America*. New York: Harper and Row.
Demaris, Ovid. 1980. *The Last Mafioso: The Treacherous World of Jimmy Frattiano*. New York: Times Books.
English, T. J. 1990. *The Westies: Inside Hell's Kitchen Irish Mob*. New York: Putnam.
Finckenauer, James. 1994. "Russian Organized Crime in America." In *Handbook of Organized Crime in the United States*, edited by Robert Kelly, Ko-Lin Chin, and Rufus Schatzberg. Westport, Conn.: Greenwood Press.
Florentini, G., and S. Peltzman, eds. 1995. *The Economics of Organized Crime*. New York: Cambridge University Press.
Fox, Stephen. 1989. *Blood and Power: Organized Crime in Twentieth Century America*. New York: William Morrow.
Gambetta, Diego. 1993. *The Sicilian Mafia: The Business of Private Protection*. Cambridge, Mass.: Harvard University Press.
Gambetta, Gianluca, and Sam Peltzman. 1995. "Conspiracy Among Many: The Mafia in Legitimate Industries." In *The Economics of Organized Crime*, edited by G. Florentini and S. Peltzman. New York: Cambridge University Press.
Handelman, Stephen. 1995. *Comrade Criminal: Russia's New Mafia*. New Haven, Conn.: Yale University Press.
Hess, Henner. 1973. *Mafia and Mafiosi: The Structure of Power*. Lexington, Mass.: Lexington.
Ianni, Francis, and Elizabeth Reuss-Ianni. 1972. *A Family Business: Kinship and Social Control in Organized Crime*. New York: Russell Sage.
Jacobs, James B., Christopher Panarella, and Jay Worthington. 1994. *Busting the Mob*. New York: New York University Press.
Kefauver, Estes. 1951. *Crime in America*. New York: Doubleday.
Kennedy, Robert F. 1960. *The Enemy Within*. New York: Popular Library.

Kenny, Dennis J., and James O. Finckenauer. 1995. *Organized Crime in America.* New York: Wadsworth.

Kleinknecht, William G. 1996. *New Ethnic Mobs: Changing Face of Organized Crime in America.* New York: Free Press.

Kwitny, Jonathan. 1979. *Vicious Circles: The Mafia in the Marketplace.* New York: Norton.

Landesco, John. 1968. *Organized Crime in Chicago.* Chicago: University of Chicago Press. (Originally published in 1929.)

Lynch, Gerald E. 1987. "Rico: The Crime of Being a Criminal." *Columbia Law Review* 87:661–764; 920–84.

Maas, Peter. 1968. *The Valachi Papers.* New York: Putnam.

———. 1997. *Underboss: Sammy the Bull Gravano's Story of Life in the Mafia.* New York: HarperCollins.

Maltz, Michael. 1985. "Towards Defining Organized Crime." In *The Politics and Economics of Organized Crime,* edited by H. Alexander and G. Caiden. Lexington, Mass.: Heath.

McClellan, John. 1962. *Crime Without Punishment.* New York: Duell, Sloane and Pearce.

Moldea, Dan E. 1978. *The Hoffa Wars.* New York: Charter Books.

Moore, William H. 1974. *The Kefauver Committee and the Politics of Crime.* Columbia: University of Missouri Press.

New York State Organized Crime Task Force. 1990. *Corruption and Racketeering in the NYC Construction Industry.* New York: New York University Press.

Pennsylvania Crime Commission. 1990. *Organized Crime in Pennsylvania: A Decade of Change.* Conshohucken, Pa.: Pennsylvania Crime Commission.

Peterson, Virgil. 1983. *The Mob: 200 Years of Organized Crime in New York.* Ottawa, Ill.: Green Hill Publishers.

Pileggi, Nick, and Henry Hill. 1985. *Wiseguy: Life in a Mafia Family.* New York: Simon and Schuster.

Pistone, Joseph D., and Richard Woodley. 1987. *Donnie Brasco: My Undercover Life in the Mafia.* New York: New American Library.

President's Commission on Law Enforcement and Administration of Justice. 1967. *Task Force Report: Organized Crime.* Washington, D.C.: U.S. Government Printing Office.

———. 1968. *The Challenge of Crime in a Free Society.* New York: Avon.

President's Commission on Organized Crime. 1986a. *The Edge: Organized Crime, Business, and Labor Unions.* Washington, D.C.: U.S. Government Printing Office.

———. 1986b. *The Impact: Organized Crime Today.* Washington, D.C.: U.S. Government Printing Office.

Reuter, Peter. 1983. *Disorganized Crime.* Cambridge, Mass.: MIT Press.

———. 1987. *Racketeering in Legitimate Industries: A Study in the Economics of Intimidation.* Santa Monica, Calif.: Rand.

———. 1994. "Research on American Organized Crime." In *Handbook of Organized Crime in the United States,* edited by Robert Kelly, Ko-Lin Chin, and Rufus Schatzberg. Westport, Conn.: Greenwood Press.

Ryan, Patrick J. 1994. "A History of Organized Crime Control: Federal Strike Forces." In *Handbook of Organized Crime in the United States,* edited by

Robert Kelly, Ko-Lin Chin, and Rufus Schatzberg. Westport, Conn.: Greenwood Press.

Schatzberg, Rufus. 1993. *Black Organized Crime in Harlem: 1920–1930.* New York: Garland.

Schoenberg, Robert. 1992. *Mr. Capone.* New York: Morrow.

Sifakis, Carl. 1987. *The Mafia Encyclopedia.* New York: Facts on File.

Skolnick, Jerome. 1978. *House of Cards: Legalization and Control of Casino Gambling.* Boston: Little, Brown.

Smith, Dwight. 1975. *The Mafia Mystique.* New York: Basic Books.

Teresa, Vincent, and Thomas Renner. 1973. *My Life in the Mafia.* Garden City, N.Y.: Doubleday.

United States Senate, Permanent Subcommittee on Investigations. 1981. *Waterfront Corruption.* Washington, D.C.: U.S. Government Printing Office.

———. 1983. *Organized Crime in Chicago.* Washington, D.C.: U.S. Government Printing Office.

United States Senate, Permanent Subcommittee on Investigation of the Committee on Governmental Affairs. 1988. *Organized Crime: 25 Years After Valachi.* 100th Cong. 2d sess. Washington, D.C.: U.S. Government Printing Office.

Zeiger, Henry. 1973. *Sam the Plumber.* Bergenfield, N.J.: New American Library.

———. 1975. *The Jersey Mob.* Bergenfield, N.J.: New American Library.

Table of Cases

United States v. Badalamenti [the "pizza connection case"], 84 CR 236 (S.D.N.Y. 1987), convictions aff'd on *United States v. Casamento,* 887 F.2d 1141 (2d Cir. 1989).

United States v. Bruno (1939), 105 F.2d 921, rev'd on other grounds, 308 U.S. 287 (1939).

United States v. Bufalino, 285 F.2d 408 (2nd Cir. 1960).

United States v. Dorfman, 470 F.2d 246 (2d Cir. 1972).

United States v. International Brotherhood of Teamsters, 708 F.Supp. 1388 (S.D.N.Y. 1989).

United States v. Local 560, 581 F.Supp. 279 (D.N.J. 1984), aff'd 780 F.2d 267 (3d Cir. 1985).

United States v. Salerno [the "commission case"], 868 F.2d 524 (2d Cir. 1989).

United States v. Dominic Spinale, No. 86-95, D.Nev. 76/15/86.

United States v. Tieri, No. 80-381 (S.D.N.Y., June 15, 1980).

7

Family Violence

RICHARD J. GELLES

Over the last three decades, family and intimate violence has been transformed from an issue obscured by selective inattention to a problem that receives increasing professional, public, and policy attention. The explosive growth in our knowledge and understanding of the various aspects of family violence has produced a wealth of empirical data, as well as deep and intensive controversies about those data and their meaning. The topic of this chapter is family violence, but there really is no unified field of study or practice that falls neatly under that term. Family violence is only rarely viewed as a holistic problem.

Despite the segmentation, or balkanization, of the field, one consensus may have been reached. There is evidence that virtually every type and form of family and intimate relationship has the potential of being violent. Researchers and clinicians have found violence and abuse in every type of intimate relationship.

The Nature and Scope of Family Violence

Until the early 1960s, violence between family members was thought to be rare and committed only by mentally ill or otherwise disturbed individuals. Only the most sensational and lurid cases received public attention, and there was a general belief that even though family violence was a significant problem, it was not widespread. The question of the extent of family violence has not been easy to answer; in the 1990s, it still leads to contentious debates over the scientific adequacy and rigor of incidence and prevalence estimates (see, e.g., Sommers 1994). The answer to the question How big is the problem? depends on two factors: the definition of family violence and how the incidence and prevalence of family violence are measured.

Defining "Family Violence"

The definitional question has been debated for more than three decades. One definition specifies that family violence is *any* act that is harmful to the victim. This broad definition includes physical attacks, threatened physical attacks, psychological or emotional aggression and abuse, sexual assaults or threatened sexual assaults, and neglectful behavior. A narrower definition is confined only to acts of physical violence.

There is no consensus regarding how broad or narrow the definition should be, or regarding how to characterize the specific components of any definition (e.g., violence, neglect, rape, psychological abuse, or even the term *family*). The discussions about definitions are influenced by a variety of perspectives. First, there is the scientific or research perspective that seeks a clear nominal definition that is grounded in theory and can be reliably and validly operationalized. This perspective tends toward a narrow definition of violence because violence is, at least theoretically, viewed as conceptually distinct from other methods of inflicting harm or pain on another person (Etzioni 1971). A humanistic perspective takes a broader approach and conceptualizes a definition that captures the full range of harm that can be inflicted on individuals—harm being defined as acts of commission or omission that interfere with a human being achieving her or his developmental potential. Finally, a political or advocacy dimension defines the behavior in terms of advocacy or political goals; thus feminists define the problem as one of "violence against women" rather than spouse abuse, domestic violence, or family violence.

Measuring Family Violence

Even if there was a consensus definition, there would be different estimates of the scope of violence between intimates because there have been, and continue to be, various methods for measuring the incidence and prevalence of family violence.

There are three main sources of data on family violence: clinical data, official report data, and social surveys. Clinical studies carried out by psychiatrists, psychologists, and counselors continue to be a frequent source of data, primarily because these investigators have the most direct access to cases of family violence. The clinical or agency setting (including hospital emergency rooms and shelters for battered women) provides access to extensive in-depth information about particular cases of violence. Studies of violence toward women have relied heavily on samples of women who seek help at shelters (Dobash and Dobash 1979; Giles-Sims 1983; Pagelow 1981). Such samples are important because they are often the only way to obtain detailed data on the most severely battered women. Such data are also necessary to study the impact of intervention programs. However, such data, because they are based on small, nonrepresentative samples, cannot be used to estimate the incidence and prevalence of intimate violence.

Official reports constitute a second source of data. While there are an abundance of official report data on child maltreatment (because of mandatory reporting laws), there has not been a tradition of officially re-

porting spouse abuse, with the exception of a handful of states that collect data on spouse abuse. The *Uniform Crime Reports* provide data on
criminal family violence and family homicide, but these are limited to
episodes of family violence that are reported to the police, and only a
small fraction of the instances of violence between marital partners are
ever reported (Federal Bureau of Investigation 1994; Gelles and Straus
1988).

Social surveys are the third source of data. Such surveys are constrained by the low base rates of most forms of abuse and violence in
families and the sensitive and taboo nature of the topic. Some investigators cope with the low base rate problem by employing purposive or non-
representative sampling techniques to identify cases. A second approach
has been to use large available groups of subjects. Investigators of courtship violence have made extensive use of survey research techniques using college students as subjects (Cate et al. 1982; Henton et al. 1983;
Laner 1983; Makepeace 1981, 1983). A third method consists of national
surveys of family violence, most notably those carried out by Straus and
Gelles, in 1976 and 1985. A fourth source of survey data on violence between intimates are the victimization data collected in the National
Crime Victimization Survey (NCVS) conducted semiannually by the U.S.
Bureau of the Census for the U.S. Department of Justice. The Justice Department has published three reports on intimate violence based on the
data collected by the NCVS (Bachman 1994; Gaquin 1977–78; Langan
and Innes 1986).

Each of the major data sources has its own validity problems. Clinical
data are never representative, and few investigators gathering data from
clinical samples employ comparison groups. Official records suffer from
variations in definitions, variable reporting and recording practices, and
biased samples of violent and abusive behaviors and persons (Finkelhor
and Hotaling 1984; Weis 1989; Widom 1988). The biases of social survey
data on intimate violence include inaccurate recall, differential interpretation of questions, and intended and unintended response error (Weis
1989).

This chapter does not draw on data from clinical studies, nor does it
report data from studies using non-representative samples. For the most
part, the discussion of the scope of the problem of family violence draws
on self-report survey data and, where such data are not available or do
not examine a specific facet of family violence, from available official report data.

Because of the various definitions of abuse and neglect, and the differing methodologies used to examine incidence and frequency, there are
inconsistencies in the data on the extent of family violence. Numerous
aspects of research design, including definitions, sampling, measurement, sources of data, and whether the information is collected prospectively or retrospectively, generate varying findings. Even for the most extreme form of violence, homicide, where the data are thought to be the

most reliable and valid (because there is a body that must be attended to), there are inconsistencies depending on the source of the data. The FBI data on homicide are not identical with the National Center for Health Statistics (NCHS) data on murder—some homicides are reported in the FBI data set but not the NCHS data set and vice versa. Thus, where appropriate, this chapter either presents estimates of the range of the problem or provides data from different studies and/or data sources.

Child Maltreatment

Child abuse and neglect, or *child maltreatment,* are general terms that cover a wide range of acts of commission and omission, either carried out by a perpetrator or allowed to happen, which result in injuries ranging from death to serious disabling injury, emotional distress, malnutrition, and illness.

There are six major types of child abuse and neglect (see National Center on Child Abuse and Neglect 1988):

- *Physical abuse.* Acts of commission that result in physical harm, including death, to a child.
- *Sexual abuse.* Acts of commission, including intrusion or penetration, molestation with genital contact, or other forms of sexual acts in which children are used to provide sexual gratification for a perpetrator.
- *Emotional abuse.* Acts of commission that include confinement, verbal or emotional abuse, or other types of abuse such as withholding sleep, food, or shelter.
- *Physical neglect.* Acts of omission that involve refusal to provide health care, delay in providing health care, abandonment, expulsion of a child from a home, inadequate supervision, failure to meet food and clothing needs, and conspicuous failure to protect a child from hazards or danger.
- *Educational neglect.* Acts of omission and commission that include permitting chronic truancy, failure to enroll a child in school, and inattention to specific educational needs.
- *Emotional neglect.* Acts of omission that involve failing to meet the nurturing and affectional needs of a child, exposing a child to chronic or severe spouse abuse, allowing or permitting a child to use alcohol or controlled substances, encouraging the child to engage in maladaptive behavior, refusal to provide psychological care, delays in providing psychological care, and other inattention to the child's developmental needs.

The National Center on Child Abuse and Neglect (NCCAN) has conducted three surveys designed to measure the national incidence of reported and recognized child maltreatment (Burgdorf 1980; NCCAN 1988, 1996). A total of 2.9 million maltreated children were known by the agencies surveyed in 1993.

Table 7.1 presents a summary of the incidence of the six major types of

TABLE 7.1. Estimates of the Total Number of Maltreated Children 1993

Maltreatment Type	Total Number of Cases
Physical abuse	614,100
Sexual abuse	300,200
Emotional abuse	532,200
Neglect	1,961,300
Physical neglect	1,335,100
Emotional neglect	584,100
Educational neglect	397,300
Seriously injured children	565,000

Source: National Center on Child Abuse and Neglect (1996).

Note: Children who experience more than one type of abuse or neglect are reflected in the estimates for each applicable type. As a result, the estimates for the different types of maltreatment sum to more than the total number of maltreated children.

child maltreatment, as well as data on the severity of the impairment caused by the maltreatment. Of the total number of maltreated children, an estimated 614,100 (9.1 per 1,000) were physically abused; 300,200 children (4.5 per 1,000) were sexually abused; 532,200 children (7.9 per 1,000) were emotionally abused; and 1,961,300 children (29.2 per 1,000) were neglected (1,335,100 physical neglect, 584,100 emotional neglect, and 397,300 educational neglect).

A second source of data on the extent of child maltreatment comes from the National Child Abuse and Neglect Data System (NCANDS). NCANDS is a national data collection and analysis project carried out by the National Center on Child Abuse and Neglect (1997).[1] The data are official report data collected from fifty states and the District of Columbia.

In 1995, states received reports representing 2,959,237 individual child victims. Of the 1,112,886 child victims for whom maltreatment was indicated or substantiated and for whom there were data on type of maltreatment,[2] 244,903 experienced physical abuse (3.6 per 1,000); 523,049 experienced neglect (7.6 per 1,000); 29,454 experienced medical neglect (less than 0.1 per 1,000); 126,095 experienced sexual abuse (1.8 per 1,000); 44,648 experienced emotional maltreatment (less than 0.1 per 1,000); 144,489 children were classified as other forms of maltreatment (2.1 per 1,000); and 248 experienced unknown forms of maltreatment.

The National Committee to Prevent Child Abuse also collects data from states on child abuse and neglect reporting (Wang and Daro 1997). The 1997 survey found that an estimated 3.1 million children were reported for child maltreatment in 1996. Of these, 31 percent were substantiated, for an estimate of 969,000 maltreated children in 1996, or a rate of 14.0 per 1,000 children. These data are based on reports from thirty-nine states. Twenty-five percent of the substantiated cases, or 242,250 children, were physically abused; 62 percent, or 600,780, were neglected; 7 percent, or 67,830, were sexually abused; 3 percent, or 29,070, were emotionally abused; and the remaining 4 percent, or 38,760, were classified as "other" maltreatment.

A fourth source of information on violence toward children is self-report data. The National Family Violence Surveys interviewed two nationally representative samples of families—2,146 family members in 1976 and 6,002 family members in 1985 (Straus, Gelles, and Steinmetz 1980; Gelles and Straus 1987, 1988; Straus and Gelles 1986). Violence and abuse were measured by asking respondents to report on their own behavior toward their children in the previous twelve months. Milder forms of violence, violence that most people think of as physical punishment, were the most common. However, even with severe forms of violence, the rates were surprisingly high. Abusive violence was defined as acts that had a high probability of injuring the child. These included kicking, biting, punching, hitting or trying to hit a child with an object, beating up a child, burning or scalding, and threatening or using a gun or a knife. Slightly more than 20 parents in 1,000 (2.3 percent) admitted to engaging in one act of abusive violence during the year prior to the 1985 survey. Seven children in 1,000 were hurt as a result of an act of violence directed at them by a parent in the previous year. Projecting the rate of abusive violence to all children under eighteen years of age who live with one or both parents yeilds an estimate of 1.5 million children who experience acts of abusive physical violence each year and 450,000 children who are injured each year as a result of parental violence.

Sexual Abuse

The official report data cited earlier include the yearly incidence of cases of sexual abuse reported to state child welfare agencies. As with all forms of child maltreatment, reported cases are assumed to be underestimates of the true extent of sexual abuse. Unlike physical violence toward children, there has not yet been a self-report survey that attempts to measure the yearly incidence of sexual abuse, although there have been a number of self-report prevalence studies. Peters, Wyatt, and Finkelhor (1986) estimate prevalence at between 6 and 62 percent for females and 3 and 31 percent for males. A 1985 national survey of 2,626 adult men and women found a life prevalence of sexual abuse reported by 27 percent of the women and 16 percent of the men surveyed (Finkelhor et al. 1990).

Psychological Abuse

Official report data are also assumed to underestimate the true extent of psychological abuse of children. Few self-report surveys attempt to assess the extent of psychological abuse or maltreatment. Using the "psychological aggression" scale from the Conflict Tactics Scales, Vissing and her colleagues (1991) report that 63.4 percent of a national sample of 3,346 parents stated that they used at least one form of psychological aggression at least once in the previous year. This operationalization of psychological aggression is a rather broad definition of psychological maltreatment (items included "insulted or swore at the child" and "did or said something to spite the child").

Child Homicide

The U.S. Advisory Board on Child Abuse and Neglect (1995) estimated that 2,000 children under the age of eighteen are killed by parents or caretakers each year and suggested that this estimate is low. McLain and his colleagues (McLain, Sacks, and Frohlke 1993) report that abuse and neglect kill 5.4 out of every 100,000 children under four years of age, but this estimate is probably low as a result of misclassification of child deaths. A second estimate is that the rate of child death is 11.6 per 100,000 children under four years of age (U.S. Advisory Board on Child Abuse and Neglect 1995).

The National Committee to Prevent Child Abuse and Neglect estimates that 1,046 children were killed by parents or caretakers in 1996, for a rate of 1.56 children per 100,000 (Wang and Daro 1997).

Witnessing Domestic Violence

Children who witness domestic violence have recently been identified as a unique population warranting research and clinical attention (Rosenberg and Rossman 1990). Witnessing is located at the intersection of child abuse and neglect and domestic violence. Researchers and clinicians report that children who witness acts of domestic violence experience negative behavioral and developmental outcomes, independent of any direct abuse or neglect they may also experience from their caretakers (Jaffe, Wolfe, and Wilson 1990; Osofsky 1995; Rosenberg and Rossman 1990).

According to estimates from the two National Family Violence Surveys, between 1.5 and 3.3 million children three to seventeen years of age are exposed to domestic violence each year (Gelles and Straus 1988; Straus, Gelles, and Steinmetz 1980).

Violence in Adult Intimate Relationships

The initial definitions of domestic violence focused on acts of damaging physical violence directed toward women by their spouses or partners (Gelles 1974; Martin 1976). Further research broadened the definition to include sexual abuse, marital rape, and acts of emotional or psychological violence. Feminist scholars conceptualize the problem as one of coercive control of women by their partners (Yllo 1993). The coercion can be physical, emotional, or sexual.

Dating and Courtship Violence

Studies that examine the possibility of violence in dating and courtship find that between 10 and 67 percent of dating relationships involve violence (Sugarman and Hotaling 1989). Researchers have found that the rate of severe violence among dating couples ranged from about 1 percent each year to 27 percent (Arias, Samios, and O'Leary 1987; Lane and Gwartney-Gibbs 1985; Makepeace 1983).

Spouse Abuse

There are as yet no national surveys of reported spouse abuse that collect state data in the same way that child maltreatment report data have been collected and analyzed; thus, most of the data on the extent of violence toward women and between partners come from self-report surveys. One source of self-report survey data is the information collected by the U.S. Department of Justice's National Crime Victimization Survey (NCVS), which obtains data from a representative sample of some 60,000 households twice each year. Violent crimes included in the NCVS include rape, robbery, and assault (but not murder).

According to the NCVS, between 1987 and 1991, intimates committed an annual average of 621,015 rapes, robberies, or assaults (Bureau of Justice Statistics 1994). In 1992, 51 percent of the victims of intimate violence were attacked by boyfriends or girlfriends, 34 percent were attacked by spouses, and 15 percent were attacked by ex-spouses. Most of the violent acts were assaults. Females were ten times more likely to be the victims than were males. The annual rate of intimate violent victimizations was 5 per 1,000 for women and 0.5 per 1,000 for men. The highest rate of intimate victimization was for victims twenty to twenty-four years of age—a rate of 15.5 per 1,000. The lowest rate was for individuals fifty years of age and older (Bachman 1994).

Prior to 1992, the NCVS studies of domestic violence did not specifically ask or cue respondents to the issue of violence between intimates. The Bureau of Justice Statistics redesigned the study and began administering the new survey in 1992. According to data from the redesigned survey, 9 women in 1,000, or 1 million women each year, experience violence at the hands of an intimate (Bachman and Saltzman 1995). The rate of violent victimization at the hands of a stranger was 7.4 per 1,000.

The National Family Violence Surveys have been a second source of self-report data on violence between adult intimates (Gelles and Straus 1988; Straus and Gelles 1986). In 16 percent of the homes surveyed, some kind of violence between spouses had occurred in the year prior to the survey. More than one in four (28 percent) of the couples reported marital violence at some point in their marriages. As with violence toward children, the milder forms of violence were the most common. More than 30 in 1,000 women were victims of abusive violence during the twelve-month period prior to the interview in 1985. Violence against women in intimate relations in most violent households is a pattern, not a single event. On average, a woman who is a victim of abuse is abused three times each year. The rate of intimate violence was highest for those twenty to twenty-four years of age.

There has been much controversy in the field of family violence regarding the extent of male victimization (see, e.g., Wardell, Gillespie and Leffler 1983; Dobash et al. 1992). Data from the earliest studies of spousal violence detected violence by women toward their husbands (see, e.g., Gelles 1974). The two National Family Violence Surveys (Straus, Gelles, and Steinmetz 1980; Straus and Gelles 1986) also found a higher than expected incidence of violence toward men—the rate of violence was the same as or even higher than that reported for male-to-female violence. In addition, women initiated violence about as often as men (Straus 1993). However, the researchers qualified their findings by noting that much of the female violence appeared to be in self-defense and that females, because of their size and strength, appeared to inflict less injury than male attackers. In addition, two national self-report surveys found that women reported victimization by partners or ex-partners ten times more often than men (Bachman 1994; Bureau of Justice Statistics 1994). These differences may be accounted for by the fact that the NCVSs included only victimization serious enough to be considered a crime by the respondents. Studies have found that female partner victimization is more likely to be accompanied by sexual and emotional abuse (Saunders 1988). Female victims of intimate violence also suffer more emotional and psychological consequences than do men (Stets and Straus 1990). A final difference is the quality of male and female violence. Some researchers, such as Wilson and Daly (1992), use anecdotal and qualitative data to make the point that although the actual numbers may appear similar, the quality of female killings differs from male killings. Men, according to Wilson and Daly (1992), often stalk their victims and hunt down and kill spouses who have left them. Men often kill wives after lengthy periods of physical and emotional abuse. Men are much more likely to kill their wives and children in acts of familicide.

Sexual Violence/Marital Rape

A handful of studies have examined sexual violence, or what has been labeled *marital rape*. Finkelhor and Yllo (1985) report that 10 percent of a sample of 323 women said they had been forced to have sex with their husbands. Of the 644 married women interviewed by Russell (1984), 14 percent reported one or more incidents of marital rape. Data from the Second National Family Violence Survey found that 1.2 percent of the 2,934 married women interviewed said they were victims of attempted or completed forced sexual intercourse with their husbands in the previous year (Gelles 1992).

Psychological Abuse

As with child maltreatment, there have been few attempts to assess the extent of psychological abuse among adult intimate partners. One key constraint to obtaining a measure of the extent of psychological abuse is developing an adequate nominal and operational definition of psychological maltreatment. Straus and Sweet (1992), using the "psychological aggression" scale from the Conflict Tactics Scales, found that 74 percent of the men and 75 percent of the women surveyed for the Second National Family Violence Survey reported using at least one form of psychological aggression at least once in the previous year.

Homicide of Intimates

Researchers generally report that intrafamilial homicides account for between 20 and 40 percent of all murders (Curtis 1974). Nearly 700 husbands and boyfriends are killed by their wives and girlfriends each year, whereas more than 1,400 wives and girlfriends are slain by their husbands or boyfriends (Bureau of Justice Statistics 1994).

Elder Abuse

As with child abuse and neglect, the abuse of the elderly includes a range of acts of commission and omission that have harmful consequences for the elderly victim. Elder abuse includes physical abuse, psychological abuse, and material abuse (e.g., financial exploitation), or physical, psychological, or material neglect (Wolf 1995). Some definitions of elder abuse include "self-abuse" or "self-neglect" as a form of elder mistreatment, although some researchers exclude this form of mistreatment and limit elder abuse to acts of omission and commission perpetrated by someone other than the elder victim. The perpetrators of elder abuse can include children, spouses, or others who have a caretaking responsibility for the elder.

Measurement of the extent of elder abuse is even more elusive than the other forms of family violence. Researchers estimate that 5 percent of those sixty-five years or older have been victims of physical abuse, psychological abuse, financial exploitation, and/or neglect in the previous year (Wolf 1995). Pillemer and Finkelhor (1988) interviewed 2,020 community-dwelling (noninstitutionalized) elderly persons in the Boston metropolitan area. Overall, 32 elderly persons per 1,000 reported experiencing physical violence, verbal aggression, or neglect in the past year. The rate of physical violence was 20 per 1,000. Although the conventional view of elder abuse is that of middle-aged children abusing and neglecting their elderly parents, Pillemer and Finkelhor found that spouses were the most frequent abusers of the elderly and that roughly equal numbers of men and women were victims. Women, however, were the victims of the most serious forms of abuse, such as punching, kicking, beating, and choking.

Other Forms of Intimate Violence

Although parent-to-child violence and violence toward women have received the most public attention, physical fights between brothers and sisters are by far the most common form of family violence. Only rarely, however, do parents, physicians, or social workers consider sibling violence as problematic forms of family violence. Violence between siblings often goes far beyond so-called normal violence; for example, at least 109,000 children use guns or knives in fights with siblings each year (Straus, Gelles, and Steinmetz 1980).

Child-to-parent violence is rarely mentioned in public discussions of family violence. Here the reason is less public acceptance for this type of violence and more the shame of the parent-victims who are reluctant to seek help or call attention to their plight for fear of being blamed for the violence. Each year, according to the National Family Violence Survey, between 750,000 and 1 million parents have violent acts committed against them by their teenage children (Cornell and Gelles 1982).

Finally, researchers and clinicians have found significant levels of violence among gay and lesbian couples (Brand and Kidd 1986; Lockhart et al. 1994; Renzetti 1992).

Official and administrative data on the various forms of family violence underestimate the incidence of violence. Even data on the extent of homicide in intimate and family relations are believed to underestimate the true extent of the problem. Although self-report surveys probably also underestimate the extent of family and intimate violence, these studies do yield higher estimates of incidence and prevalence. Generally, self-report studies of violence toward children, toward women, toward parents by adolescents, and toward the elderly conclude that the yearly incidence rates are between 20 and 40 per 1,000. Lifetime prevalence rates range between 200 and 400 per 1,000 (Gelles 1994). Table 7.2 summarizes prevalence rates of different forms of family violence.

Risk and Protective Factors

There has been heated debate about risk and protective factors for family violence. Some argue that violence cuts across all social groups, while others agree that it affects all social groups, but not evenly. Some researchers and practitioners place more emphasis on psychological factors, while others locate the key risk factors among social factors. A third group places the greatest emphasis on cultural factors, for example, patriarchal social organization. In addition, the source of data has an impact not only on measures of incidence and prevalence of family violence but also on what factors and variables are identified as risk and protective

TABLE 7.2. Past Year Prevalence Rates of Family Violence (Per 1,000 Population)

Victimized Population and Study	Yearly Rate	Life Prevalence
Children		
National Center on Child Abuse and Neglect (NIS-3 1996)		
All forms of maltreatment	41.9	
Physical abuse	9.1	
Sexual abuse	4.5	
Emotional abuse	7.9	
Physical neglect	19.9	
Emotional neglect	8.7	
Educational neglect	5.9	
National Center on Child Abuse and Neglect (NCANDS 1997)		
All forms of maltreatment	43.0	
Substantiated or indicated	15.0	
Physical abuse	3.6	
Sexual abuse	1.8	
Neglect	7.6	
Medical neglect	<0.1	
Emotional maltreatment	<0.1	
Other forms	2.1	
National Committee to Prevent Child Abuse (Wang and Daro 1997)		
All forms of maltreatment	47.0	
Substantiated reports	14.0	
Fatal abuse	0.0016	
National Family Violence Survey, 1975 (Straus, Gelles, and Steinmetz 1980)		
All forms of violence	800.0	
Severe violence	530.0	
National Family Violence Survey, 1985 (Straus and Gelles 1988)		
All forms of physical violence	498.0	
Very severe violence	23.0	
Very severe violence that produced an injury	7.0	
Psychological aggression	63.4	
Finkelhor et al. 1990		
Sexual abuse		
Female victims		27%
Male victims		16%
Adult women		
National Family Violence Survey, 1985 (Straus and Gelles (1988)		
Any form of violence	116.0	
Severe violence	34.0	

(continued)

TABLE 7.2. Past Year Prevalence Rates of Family Violence (Per 1,000 Population) (*continued*)

Victimized Population and Study	Yearly Rate	Life Prevalence
Psychological aggression	74.0	
Marital rape	12.0	
National Crime Victimization Survey (Bachman and Saltzman 1995)	9.3	
Adult men		
National Family Violence Survey, 1985 (Straus and Gelles 1988)		
Any form of violence	124.0	
Severe violence	48.0	
Psychological aggression	74.8	
Marital rape	Not asked	
National Crime Victimization Survey (Bachman and Saltzman 1995)	1.4	
The elderly		
Pillemer and Finkelhor (1988)		
All forms of maltreatment	32.0	
Physical violence	20.0	

factors. When basing an analysis on clinical data or official report data, risk and protective factors are confounded with factors such as labeling bias or agency or clinical setting catchment area. Researchers have long noted that certain individuals and families are more likely to be correctly and incorrectly labeled as offenders or victims of family violence; similarly, some individuals and families are insulated from being correctly or incorrectly labeled or identified as offenders or victims (Gelles 1975; Newberger et al. 1977; Hampton and Newberger 1985). Social survey data are not immune to confounding problems either, as social or demographic factors may be related to willingness to participate in a self-report survey and tendencies to providing socially desirable responses.

The definitional issues mentioned earlier also constrain efforts to develop a comprehensive and coherent inventory of risk and protective factors. While this chapter uses a broad definition of *family violence,* many reseachers believe that acts of physical violence are conceptually distinct from and arise from different generative causes than do acts of nonphysical harm. Thus it is nearly impossible in a short discussion to enumerate, by type of violence, each set of risk and protective factors. Some factors will be more strongly related to one form of harm (e.g., injurious physical violence) and may be unrelated to other types of harm (e.g., neglect). Because this chapter examines violence in all types of family and intimate relationships, the task of identifying risk and protective factors becomes even more complex. Some factors are more strongly related to violence in one type of relationship (e.g., parent to child) and are not related to one or more of the other types of family violence (e.g., sibling violence or elder abuse).

The final caveat is that *any* listing of risk and protective factors may unintentionally convey or reinforce a notion of single-factor explanations for family violence. Clearly, no phenomenon as complex as family violence could possibly be explained with a single-factor model. Equally clearly, almost all of the risk and protective factors discussed here and in the literature have relatively modest correlations with family violence. I list risk and protective factors for heuristic purposes, with the full knowledge that multiple factors are related to family violence and that there is often an interaction among risk and protective factors.

With all these caveats in mind, this section reviews the most widely discussed risk and protective factors in the study of family violence and, where appropriate, identifies for which forms of violence and which types of relationships the factors are or are not relevant. By and large, risk and protective factors are discussed if they have been found to be related to family violence in self-report survey research *and* official report data. Because clinical research often does not employ appropriate comparison groups and because clinical research does not typically attempt to isolate risk and protective factors from the factors that brought cases to the specific clinical setting, this section does not review or cite clinical research.

Social and Demographic Risk Factors

The major social and demographic risk factors for family violence appear to be the following.

Age. One of the most consistent risk factors is the age of the offender. As with violence between nonintimates, violence is most likely to be perpetrated by those between eighteen and thirty years of age. Young age is not a risk factor for elder abuse, although the rate of elder abuse is lower than the rate of the other forms of family violence.

Sex. As with nonintimate violence, men are the most likely offenders in acts of intimate violence as well. However, the differences in the rates of offending by men compared with women are much smaller for violence in the family than for violence outside the home. Men and women have somewhat similar rates of child homicide, although women appear more likely to be offenders when the child victim is young (under three years of age) and males are the more likely offenders when the child victim is older.

Income. Although most poor parents and partners do not use violence toward intimates, self-report surveys and official report data find that the rates of all forms of family violence, except sexual abuse, are higher for those whose family incomes are below the poverty line than for those whose income is above the poverty line.

Race. Both official report data and self-report survey data often report that child abuse and violence toward women are overrepresented among minorities. Data from the NCVS indicate that the rate of intimate adult violence is slightly higher for blacks (5.8 per 1,000) than for whites (5.4 per 1,000). The rate of intimate violence for Hispanics is 5.5 per 1,000. The second and third studies of the National Incidence and Prevalence of Child Abuse and Neglect (National Center on Child Abuse and Neglect 1988, 1996) found no significant relationships between the incidence of maltreatment and the child's race or ethnicity. There was no significant relationship for any of the subcategories of maltreatment.

The two National Family Violence Surveys, however, found stronger relationships between race or ethnicity and violence between partners and violence toward children. Although in the first survey the difference in rates between blacks and whites disappeared when income was controlled, an analysis of the larger data set from the Second National Family Violence Survey found that the differences persisted even when income was controlled. The second survey included oversamples of both blacks and Hispanics (Gelles and Straus 1988).

Situational and Environmental Factors

The major situational and environmental factors related to family violence are as follows.

Stress. Unemployment, financial problems, being a single parent, being a teenage mother, and sexual difficulties are all related to violence, as are a host of other stressor events (Gelles and Straus 1988; Gelles 1989; Parke and Collmer 1975; Straus, Gelles, and Steinmetz 1980)

Social Isolation and Social Support. The data on social isolation are somewhat less consistent than the data for the previously listed correlates. First, because so much of the research on family violence is cross-sectional, it is not clear whether social isolation precedes violence or is a consequence of violence in the home. Second, social isolation has been crudely measured, and the purported correlation may be more anecdotal than statistical. Nevertheless, researchers often agree that people who are socially isolated from neighbors and relatives are more likely to be violent in the home. Social support appears to be an important protective factor. A significant source of social support is the availability of friends and family for help, aid, and assistance. The more a family's members are integrated into the community and the more groups and associations they belong to, the less likely they are to be violent (Straus, Gelles, and Steinmetz 1980).

The Intergenerational Transmission of Violence. The notion that abused children grow up to be abusing parents and violent adults has been widely expressed in the child abuse and family violence literature (Gelles 1980). Kaufman and Zigler (1987) reviewed the literature that tested the hypothesis of intergenerational transmission of violence toward children and concluded that the best estimate of the rate of intergenerational transmission appears to be 30 percent (plus or minus 5 percent). Although a rate of 30 percent is substantially less than the majority of abused children, the rate is considerably more than the 2 to 4 percent rate of abuse found in the general population (Straus and Gelles 1986; Widom 1989). Egeland and his colleagues (Egeland, Jacobvitz, and Papatola 1987), who examined continuity and discontinuity of abuse in a longitudinal study of high-risk mothers and their children, found that mothers who had been abused as children were less likely to abuse their own children if they had emotionally supportive parents, partners, or friends. In addition, the abused mothers who did not abuse their children were described as "middle class" and "upwardly mobile," suggesting that they were able to draw on economic resources that may not have been available to the abused mothers who did abuse their children.

Evidence from studies of parental and marital violence indicate that whereas experiencing violence in one's family of origin is often correlated with later violent behavior, such experience is not the sole determining factor. When the intergenerational transmission of violence occurs, it is likely the result of a complex set of social and psychological processes.

Although experiencing and witnessing violence is believed to be an important risk factor, the actual mechanism by which violence is transmitted from generation to generation is not understood.

Gender Inequality. One of the important risk factors for violence against women is gender inequality. Individual, aggregate, and cross-cultural data find that the greater the degree of gender inequality in a relationship, community, and society, the higher the rates of violence toward women (Browne and Williams 1993; Coleman and Straus 1986; Levinson 1989; Morley 1994; Straus 1994b; Straus, Gelles, and Steinmetz 1980).

Presence of Other Violence. A final general finding is that the presence of violence in one family relationship increases the risk that there will be violence in other relationships. Thus children who live in homes where there is domestic violence are more likely to experience violence than are children who grow up in homes where there is no violence between their parents. Moreover, children who witness and experience violence are more likely to use violence toward their parents and siblings than are children who do not experience or see violence in their homes (Straus, Gelles, and Steinmetz 1980).

Research on Victims

Compared with research on offenders, there has been somewhat less research on victims of family violence that focuses on factors that increase or reduce the risk of victimization. Most research on victims examines the consequences of victimization (e.g., depression, psychological distress, suicide attempts, symptoms of post-traumatic stress syndrome) or the effectiveness of various intervention efforts.

Children

The very youngest children appear to be at the greatest risk of being abused, especially for the most dangerous and potentially lethal forms of violence (Fergusson, Fleming, and O'Neil 1972; Gil 1970; Johnson 1974). Not only are young children physically more fragile and thus more susceptible to injury, but their vulnerability makes them more likely to be reported and diagnosed as abused when injured. Older children are underreported as victims of abuse. Adolescent victims may be considered delinquent or ungovernable, and thus thought of as contributing to their own victimization.

Younger boys are more likely to be abused than older boys. The first National Family Violence Survey found that older girls were more likely to be victimized than younger girls (Straus, Gelles, and Steinmetz 1980).

Early research suggested that a number of factors raise the risk of a child being abused. Low-birth-weight babies (Parke and Collmer 1975), premature children (Elmer 1967; Newberger et al. 1977; Parke and Collmer 1975; Steele and Pollack 1974), and handicapped, retarded, or developmentally disabled children (Friedrich and Boriskin 1976; Gil 1970; Steinmetz 1978) were all described as being at greater risk of being abused by their parents or caretakers. However, a review of studies that examine the child's role in abuse calls into question many of these findings (Starr 1988). One key problem is that few investigators used matched comparison groups. Newer studies have failed to find premature or handicapped children being at higher risk for abuse (Egeland and Vaughan 1981; Starr et al. 1984).

Marital Partners

Studies that examine the individual and social attributes of victims of marital violence are difficult to interpret. It is often not clear whether the factors found among victims were present *before* they were battered or are the result of the victimization. Such studies often use small and clinical samples, and fail to include comparison groups.

Battered women have been described as dependent, having low self-esteem, and feeling inadequate and helpless (Ball 1977; Hilberman and Munson 1977; Shainess 1977; Walker 1979). Descriptive and clinical accounts consistently report a high incidence of depression and anxiety among samples of battered women (Hilberman 1980). Sometimes the personality profiles of battered women reported in the literature seem contradictory. While some researchers describe battered women as unassertive, shy, and reserved (Weitzman and Dreen 1982), others present them as aggressive, masculine, frigid, and masochistic (Snell, Rosenwald, and Robey 1964; Ball 1977).

Hotaling and Sugarman (1990) reviewed the wife abuse literature and examined risk markers for abuse. They found few risk markers that identify women at risk of violence in intimate relations. High levels of marital conflict and low socioeconomic status emerged as the primary predictors of increased likelihood of wife assault.

Elder Victims

Research on elder abuse is divided on whether elder victims are more likely to be physically, socially, and emotionally dependent on their caretakers or whether the offender's dependence on the victim increases the risk of elder abuse (see Pillemer 1993; Steinmetz 1993). Conventional wisdom suggests that it is the oldest, sickest, most debilitated and dependent elders who are prone to the full range of mistreatment by their caretakers. However, Pillemer (1993) has found that dependency of the victim is not as powerful a risk factor as is perceived by clinicians, the public, and some researchers.

Theoretical Models of Family Violence

The first people to identify a problem often influence how others will perceive it (Nelson 1984, p. 13). Child abuse and neglect, the first form of family violence to receive scholarly and public attention, was identified by the medical profession in the early 1960s. The initial conceptualizations portrayed abuse and violence between intimates as a rare event, typically caused by the psychopathology of the offender. The perception of the abuser, or violent offender, as suffering from some form of psychopathology has persisted, in part because the first conceptualization of family violence was the guiding framework for the work that followed. The psychopathological or psychiatric conceptualization has also persisted because the tragic picture of a defenseless child, woman, or grandparent subjected to abuse and neglect arouses the strongest emotions in clinicians and others who see or treat the problem of intimate violence. There frequently seems to be no rational explanation for harming a loved one, especially one who appears to be helpless and defenseless.

Family violence has been approached from three general theoretical levels of analysis: the intraindividual level, or the psychiatric model; the social-psychological level; and the sociological or sociocultural level. The *psychiatric model* focuses on the offender's personality characteristics as the chief determinants of violence and abuse of intimates, although some applications focus on the individual personality characteristics of the victims (see, e.g., Snell, Rosenwald and Robey 1964; Shainess 1979). The psychiatric model includes theoretical approaches that link personality disorders, character disorders, mental illness, alcohol and substance abuse, and other intraindividual processes to acts of family violence.

The *social-psychological model* assumes that violence and abuse can best be understood by careful examination of the external environmental factors that affect the family, family organization and structure, and the everyday interactions between intimates that are precursors to acts of violence. Theoretical approaches that examine family structure, learning, stress, the transmission of violence from one generation to the next, and family interaction patterns fit the social-psychological model.

The *sociocultural model* provides a macrolevel analysis. Violence is examined in light of socially structured variables such as inequality, patriarchy, or cultural norms and attitudes about violence and family relations.

Theories

A number of sociological and psychological theories have been developed to explain family violence.

Social Learning Theory. Social learning theory proposes that individuals who experienced violence are more likely to use violence in the home than are those who have experienced little or no violence. The theory's central proposition is that children who either experience violence themselves or witness violence between their parents are more likely to use violence when they grow up. The family is the institution and social group where people learn the roles of husband and wife, parent and child. The home is the prime location where people learn how to deal with various stresses, crises, and frustrations. In many instances, the home is also the site where a person first experiences violence. Not only do people learn violent behavior, but they learn how to justify being violent. For example, hearing a father say "This will hurt me more than it will hurt you," or a mother say "You have been bad, so you deserve to be spanked," contributes to how children learn to justify violent behavior.

Social Situational/Stress and Coping Theory. Social situational/ stress and coping theory explains why violence is used in some situations and not others. The theory proposes that abuse and violence occur because of two main factors. The first is structural stress and the lack of coping resources in a family. For instance, the association between low income and family violence indicates that an important factor in violence is inadequate financial resources. The second factor is the cultural norm concerning the use of force and violence. In contemporary American society, as well as in many other societies, violence in general, and violence toward children in particular, is normative (Straus, Gelles, and Steinmetz 1980; Straus 1994a). Thus individuals learn to use violence both expressively and instrumentally as a means of coping with a pileup of stressor events.

Resource Theory. Resource theory assumes that all social systems (including the family) rest to some degree on force or the threat of force. The more resources—social, personal, and economic—a person can command, the more force he or she can muster. However, the fewer resources a person has, the more he or she will actually use force in an open manner. Thus a husband who wants to be the dominant person in the family but has little education, has a job low in prestige and income, and lacks interpersonal skills may choose to use violence to maintain the dominant position. In addition, family members (including children) may use violence to redress a grievance when they have few alternative resources. Thus, wives who have few social resources or social contacts may use violence toward their husbands in order to protect themselves.

Exchange Theory. Exchange theory proposes that wife abuse and child abuse are governed by the principle of costs and benefits. Abuse is used when the rewards are greater than the costs (Gelles 1983). The private nature of the family, the reluctance of social institutions and agencies to intervene—in spite of mandatory child abuse reporting laws or mandatory arrest laws for spouse abuse—and the low risk of other interventions reduce the costs of abuse and violence. The cultural approval of violence as both expressive and instrumental behavior raises the potential rewards for violence. The most significant reward is social control, or power.

Sociobiological Theory. A sociobiological, or evolutionary, perspective of family violence suggests that violence toward human or nonhuman primate offspring is the result of the reproductive success potential of children and parental investment. The theory's central assumption is that natural selection is the process of differential reproduction and reproductive success (Daly and Wilson 1980). Males can be expected to invest in offspring when there is some degree of parental certainty (how confident the parent is that the child is his or her own genetic offspring), while females are also inclined to invest under conditions of parental certainty. Parents recognize their offspring and avoid squandering valu-

able reproductive effort on someone else's offspring. Children not genetically related to the parent (e.g., stepchildren, adopted children, or foster
children) or children with low reproductive potential (e.g., handicapped
or retarded children) are at the highest risk for infanticide and abuse
(Burgess and Garbarino 1983; Daly and Wilson 1980; Hrdy 1979). Large
families can dilute parental energy and lower attachment to children,
thus increasing the risk of child abuse and neglect (Burgess 1979).

Smuts (1992) applied an evolutionary perspective to male aggression
against females. Smuts (1992), Daly and Wilson (1988), and Burgess and
Draper (1989) argue that male aggression against females often reflects
male reproductive striving. Both human and nonhuman male primates
are postulated to use aggression against females to intimidate females so
that they will not resist future male efforts to mate with them and to reduce the likelihood that females will mate with other males. Thus males
use aggression to control female sexuality to males' reproductive advantage. The frequency of male aggression varies across societies and situations, depending on the strength of female alliances, the support women
can receive from their families, the strength and importance of male alliances, the degree of equality in male-female relationships, and the degree to which males control the economic resources within a society.
Male aggression toward females, both physical violence and rape, is high
when female alliances are weak, when females lack kin support, when
male alliances are strong, when male-female relationships are unbalanced, and when males control societal resources.

Feminist Theory. Feminist theorists (e.g., Dobash and Dobash 1979;
Pagelow 1984; Yllo 1983, 1988) see wife abuse as a unique phenomenon
that has been obscured and overshadowed by what they refer to as a "narrow" focus on domestic violence. The central thesis of this theory is that
economic and social processes operate directly and indirectly to support
a patriarchal (male-dominated) social order and family structure. Patriarchy, which is seen as leading to the subordination of women, causes
the historical pattern of systematic violence directed against wives.

An Ecological Perspective

The *ecological perspective* is an attempt to integrate the three levels of
theoretical analysis (individual, social-psychological, and sociocultural)
into a single theoretical model. James Garbarino (1977) and Jay Belsky
(1980, 1993) have proposed an *ecological model* to explain the complex
nature of child maltreatment. The model rests on three levels of analysis:
the relationship between the organism and the environment, the interacting and overlapping systems in which human development occurs, and
environmental quality. The ecological model proposes that violence and
abuse arise out of a mismatch of parent to child and family to neighborhood and community. The risk of abuse and violence is greatest when the

functioning of the children and parents is limited and constrained by developmental problems. Children with learning disabilities and social or emotional handicaps are at increased risk for abuse. Parents under considerable stress or those who have personality problems are at increased risk for abusing their children. These conditions are worsened when social interaction between the spouses or the parents and children heighten the stress or make the personal problems worse. Finally, if there are few institutions and agencies in the community to support troubled families, the risk of abuse is further raised. Garbarino (1977) identifies two necessary conditions for child maltreatment. First, there must be cultural justification for the use of force against children. Second, the maltreating family is isolated from potent family or community support systems. The ecological model has served as a perspective to examine other forms of family violence. However, the model has mostly served as a heuristic device to organize thinking and research about family violence. There has not yet been an actual empirical test of the integrated model, other than the research conducted by Garbarino in the 1970s.

Summary

One overriding factor that influences the study and consideration of intimate and family violence is the emotional nature of both research and practice. Few other areas of inquiry in the field of criminal justice generate such strong feelings and reactions as do child abuse, child sexual abuse, violence against women, elder abuse, and courtship violence. Even the most grotesque case examples fail adequately to capture the devastating physical and psychological consequences of physical abuse at the hands of a loved one or caretaker. Those in the field of criminal justice not only must face difficult and complex cases but also are often frustrated by the inadequate conceptual and practical resources they can bring to bear on behalf of victims, offenders, and families.

There are no simple answers or "silver bullets." The relative recentness of family and intimate violence as areas of study, and the fact that the first decade of research was dominated by a psychopathology model of causation, resulted in a limited level of theoretical development. Moreover, the emotional nature of family and intimate violence has generated deep and heated controversies over estimates of extent, risk and protective factors, and causal models.

Yet, despite the controversies and limited theoretical development, one conclusion is inescapable. No one factor can explain the presence or absence of family and intimate violence. Characteristics of the child, parent, partners, family, social situation, community, and society are related to which family members are abused and under what conditions. Individual and emotional characteristics, psychological characteristics, and community factors, such as cultural attitudes regarding violence, are moderated and influenced by family structure and family situations. In addition, power and control are common features of nearly all forms of family and intimate violence. Thus, interventions and prevention efforts need to be aimed at the importance of power and control and the functions of the family system if family and intimate violence are to be effectively treated and prevented.

Notes

1. Prior to 1992, state reports of child maltreatment were collected and analyzed by the American Association for Protecting Children (1988, 1989). During 1987, the last year the survey was conducted, 2,178,384 children were reported to state agencies for suspected child abuse and neglect. Of these, it is estimated that 686,000 reports were substantiated by the state Child Protective Service agencies.

2. A *victim* is defined as a child whose case was either substantiated or indicated after an investigation by a Child Protective Services agency. *Substantiated* is defined as a type of investigation disposition that is used when the allegation of maltreatment was supported or founded by state law or state policy. This is considered the highest level of finding by a state agency. *Indicated* is defined as a type of investigation that concludes that maltreatment could not be substantiated under state law or policy, but that there is reason to suspect that the child may have been maltreated or was at risk of maltreatment (National Center on Child Abuse and Neglect 1997).

References

American Association for Protecting Children. 1988. *Highlights of Official Child Neglect and Abuse Reporting, 1986.* Denver, Colo.: American Humane Association.

———. 1989. *Highlights of Official Child Neglect and Abuse Reporting, 1987.* Denver, Colo.: American Humane Association.

Arias, I., M. Samios, and K. D. O'Leary. 1987. "Prevalence and Correlates of Physical Aggression During Courtship." *Journal of Interpersonal Violence* 2:82–90.

Bachman, R. 1994. *Violence Against Women: A National Crime Victimization Survey Report.* Washington, D.C.: U.S. Department of Justice, Bureau of Justice Statistics.

Bachman, R., and L. Saltzman. 1995. *Violence Against Women: Estimates from the Redesigned Survey.* Washington, D.C.: U.S. Department of Justice, Bureau of Justice Statistics.

Ball, M. 1977. "Issues of Violence in Family Casework." *Social Casework* 58:3–12.

Belsky, J. 1980. "Child Maltreatment: An Ecological Integration." *American Psychologist* 35:320–35.

———. 1993. "Etiology of Child Maltreatment: A Developmental-Ecological Approach." *Psychological Bulletin* 114:413–34.

Brand, P. A., and A. H. Kidd. 1986. "Frequency of Physical Aggression in Heterosexual and Female Homosexual Dyads." *Psychological Reports* 59:1307–13.

Browne, A., and K. Williams. 1993. "Gender, Intimacy, and Lethal Violence." *Gender and Society* 7:78–98.

Bureau of Justice Statistics. 1994. *Domestic Violence: Violence Between Intimates.* Washington, D.C.: U.S. Department of Justice, Bureau of Justice Statistics.

Burgdorf, K. 1980. *Recognition and Reporting of Child Maltreatment.* Rockville, Md.: Westat.

Burgess, R. L. 1979. "Family Violence: Some Implications from Evolutionary Biology." Paper presented at the annual meeting of the American Society of Criminology, Philadelphia, November.

Burgess, R. L., and P. Draper. 1989. "The Explanation of Family Violence: The Role of Biological, Behavioral, and Cultural Selection." In *Family Violence,* edited by L. Ohlin and M. Tonry. Chicago: University of Chicago Press.

Burgess, R. L., and J. Garbarino. 1983. "Doing What Comes Naturally? An Evolutionary Perspective on Child Abuse." In *The Dark Side of Families: Current Family Violence Research,* edited by D. Finkelhor, R. Gelles, M. Straus, and G. Hotaling. Beverly Hills, Calif.: Sage.

Cate, R. M., J. M. Henton, F. S. Christopher, and S. Lloyd. 1982. "Premarital Abuse: A Social Psychological Perspective." *Journal of Family Issues* 3:79–90.

Coleman, D. H., and M. A. Straus. 1986. "Marital Power, Conflict, and Violence in a Nationally Representative Sample of American Couples." *Violence and Victims* 1:141–57.

Cornell, C. P., and R. J. Gelles. 1982. "Adolescent to Parent Violence." *Urban Social Change Review* 15:8–14.

Curtis, L. 1974. *Criminal Violence: National Patterns and Behavior.* Lexington, Mass.: Lexington.

Daly, M., and M. Wilson. 1980. "Discriminative Parental Solicitude: A Biological Perspective." *Journal of Marriage and the Family* 42:277–88.

———. *Homicide.* 1988. New York: Aldine DeGruyter.

Dobash, R. E., and R. Dobash. 1979. *Violence Against Wives.* New York: Free Press.

Dobash, R. P., R. E. Dobash, M. I. Wilson, and M. Daly. 1992. "The Myth of Sexual Symmetry in Marital Violence." *Social Problems* 39:71–91.

Egeland, B., D. Jacobvitz, and K. Papatola. 1987. "Intergenerational Continuity of Abuse." In *Child Abuse and Neglect: Biosocial Dimensions,* edited by R. Gelles and J. Lancaster. New York: Aldine de Gruyter.

Egeland, B., and B. Vaughan. 1981. "Failure of 'Bond Formation' as a Cause of Abuse, Neglect, and Maltreatment." *American Journal of Orthopsychiatry* 51:78–84.

Elmer, E. 1967. *Children in Jeopardy: A Study of Abused Minors and Their Families.* Pittsburgh: University of Pittsburgh Press.

Etzioni, A. 1971. "Violence." In *Contemporary Social Problems,* edited by R. K. Merton and R. Nisbet. New York: Harcourt Brace Jovanovich.

Federal Bureau of Investigation. 1994. *Uniform Crime Reports for the United States, 1993.* Washington, D.C.: U.S. Government Printing Office.

Fergusson, D. M., J. Fleming, and D. O'Neil. 1972. *Child Abuse in New Zealand.* Wellington, New Zealand: Research Division, Department of Social Work.

Finkelhor, D., and G. Hotaling. 1984. "Sexual Abuse in the National Incidence Study of Child Abuse and Neglect: An Appraisal." *Child Abuse
and Neglect: The International Journal* 8:23–33.

Finkelhor, D., G. Hotaling, I. A. Lewis, and C. Smith. 1990. "Sexual Abuse in
a National Survey of Adult Men and Women: Prevalence, Characteristics, and Risk Factors." *Child Abuse and Neglect: The International Journal* 14:19–28.

Finkelhor, D., and K. Yllo. 1985. *License to Rape: Sexual Abuse of Wives.*
New York: Holt, Rinehart and Winston.

Friedrich, W. N., and J. A. Boriskin. 1976. "The Role of the Child in Abuse: A
Review of Literature." *American Journal of Orthopsychiatry* 46:580–90.

Gaquin, D. A. 1977–78. "Spouse Abuse: Data from the National Crime Survey." *Victimology: An International Journal* 2:632–42.

Garbarino, J. 1977. "The Human Ecology of Child Maltreatment." *Journal of
Marriage and the Family* 39:721–35.

Gelles, R. J. 1974. *The Violent Home.* Beverly Hills, Calif.: Sage.

———. 1975. "The Social Construction of Child Abuse." *American Journal of
Orthopsychiatry* 45:363–71.

———. 1980. "Violence in the Family: A Review of Research in the Seventies." *Journal of Marriage and the Family* 42:873–85.

———. 1983. "An Exchange/Social Control Theory." In *The Dark Side of
Families: Current Family Violence Research,* edited by D. Finkelhor,
R. Gelles, M. Straus, and G. Hotaling. Beverly Hills, Calif.: Sage.

———. 1989. "Child Abuse and Violence in Single-Parent Families: Parent
Absence and Economic Deprivation." *American Journal of Orthopsychiatry* 59:492–501.

———. 1992. "Marital Rape." Unpublished manuscript.

———. 1993. "Violence Toward Men: Fact or Fiction?" Paper prepared for
the Council on Scientific Affairs, American Medical Association.

———. 1994. "Family Violence, Abuse, and Neglect." In *Families and
Change: Coping with Stressful Events,* edited by P. McKenry and S. Price.
Thousand Oaks, Calif.: Sage.

Gelles, R. J., and M. A. Straus. 1987. "Is Violence Towards Children Increasing? A Comparison of 1975 and 1985 National Survey Rates." *Journal of
Interpersonal Violence* 2:212–22.

———. 1988. *Intimate Violence.* New York: Simon and Schuster.

Gil, D. 1970. *Violence Against Children: Physical Child Abuse in the United
States.* Cambridge, Mass.: Harvard University Press.

Giles-Sims, J. 1983. *Wife-Beating: A Systems Theory Approach.* New York:
Guilford.

Hampton, R. L., and E. H. Newberger. 1985. "Child Abuse Incidence and Reporting by Hospitals: Significance of Severity, Class and Race." *American Journal of Public Health* 75:56–60.

Henton, J., R. Cate, J. Koval, S. Lloyd, and F. S. Christopher. 1983. "Romance
and Violence in Dating Relationships." *Journal of Family Issues* 4:467–
82.

Hilberman, E. 1980. "Overview: 'The Wife-Beater's Wife' Reconsidered."
American Journal of Psychiatry 137:1336–46.

Hilberman, E., and K. Munson. 1977. "Sixty Battered Women." *Victimology*
2:460–70.

Hotaling, G. T., and D. Sugarman. 1990. "A Risk Marker Analysis of Assaulted Wives." *Family Violence* 5:1–13.

Hrdy, S. B. 1979. "Infanticide Among Animals: A Review Classification and Examination of the Implications for Reproductive Strategies of Females." *Ethology and Sociobiology* 1:13–40.

Jaffe, P. G., D. A. Wolfe, and S. K. Wilson. 1990. *Children of Battered Women.* Newbury Park, Calif.: Sage.

Johnson, C. 1974. *Child Abuse in the Southeast: An Analysis of 1172 Reported Cases.* Athens, Ga.: Welfare Research.

Kaufman, J., and E. Zigler. 1987. "Do Abused Children Become Abusive Parents?" *American Journal of Orthopsychiatry* 57:186–92.

Lane, K. E., and P. A. Gwartney-Gibbs. 1985. "Violence in the Context of Dating and Sex." *Journal of Family Issues* 6:45–59.

Laner, M. R. 1983. "Courtship Abuse and Aggression: Contextual Aspects." *Sociological Spectrum* 3:69–83.

Langan, P., and C. A. Innes. 1986. *Preventing Domestic Violence Against Women.* Washington, D.C.: U.S. Department of Justice, Bureau of Justice Statistics.

Levinson, D. 1989. *Family Violence in Cross-Cultural Perspective.* Newbury Park, Calif.: Sage.

Lockhart, L. L., B. W. White, V. Causby, and A. Isaac. 1994. "Letting Out the Secret: Violence in Lesbian Relationships." *Journal of Interpersonal Violence* 9:469–92.

Makepeace, J. M. 1981. "Courtship Violence Among College Students." *Family Relations* 30:97–102.

———. 1983. "Life Events Stress and Courtship Violence." *Family Relations* 32:101–9.

Martin, D. 1976. *Battered Wives.* San Francisco: Glide Publications.

McLain, P., J. Sacks, and R. Frohlke. 1993. "Estimates of Fatal Child Abuse and Neglect, United States, 1979–1988." *Pediatrics* 91:338–43.

Morley, R. 1994. "Wife Beating and Modernization: The Case of Papau New Guinea." *Journal of Comparative Family Studies* 25:25–52.

National Center on Child Abuse and Neglect. 1988. *Study of National Incidence and Prevalence of Child Abuse and Neglect: 1986.* Washington, D.C.: U.S. Department of Health and Human Services.

———. 1996. *Third National Study of the Incidence of Child Abuse and Neglect: 1993.* Washington, D.C.: U.S. Department of Health and Human Services.

———. 1997. *Child Maltreatment 1995: Reports from the States to the National Center on Child Abuse and Neglect.* Washington, D.C.: U.S. Department of Health and Human Services.

Nelson, B. J. 1984. *Making an Issue of Child Abuse: Political Agenda Setting for Social Problems.* Chicago: University of Chicago Press.

Newberger, E., R. Reed, J. H. Daniel, J. Hyde, and M. Kotelchuck. 1977. "Pediatric Social Illness: Toward an Etiologic Classification." *Pediatrics* 60:178–85.

Osofsky, J. 1995. "The Effects of Exposure to Violence on Young Children." *American Psychologist* 50:782–88.

Pagelow, M. 1981. *Woman-Battering: Victims and Their Experiences.* Newbury Park, Calif.: Sage.

————. 1984. *Family Violence*. New York: Praeger.

Parke, R. D., and C. Collmer. 1975. "Child Abuse: An Interdisciplinary Analysis." In *Review of Child Development Research*, vol. 5, edited by M. Hetherington. Chicago: University of Chicago Press.

Peters, S. D., G. E. Wyatt, and D. Finkelhor. 1986. "Prevalence." In *A Sourcebook on Child Sexual Abuse*, edited by D. Finkelhor. Beverly Hills, Calif.: Sage.

Pillemer, K. 1993. "The Abused Offspring Are Dependent: Abuse Is Caused by the Deviance and Dependence of Abusive Caretakers." In *Current Controversies on Family Violence*, edited by R. J. Gelles and D. Loseke. Newbury Park, Calif.: Sage.

Pillemer, K., and D. Finkelhor. 1988. "The Prevalence of Elder Abuse: A Random Sample Survey." *Gerontologist* 28:51–57.

Renzetti, C. 1992. *Intimate Betrayal: Partner Abuse in Lesbian Relationships*. Newbury Park, Calif.: Sage.

Rosenberg, M. S., and B. B. R. Rossman. 1990. "The Child Witness to Marital Violence." In *Treatment of Family Violence*, edited by R. T. Ammerman and M. Hersen. New York: Wiley.

Russell, D. 1984. *Sexual Exploitation: Rape, Child Sexual Abuse, and Workplace Harassment*. Newbury Park, Calif.: Sage.

Saunders, D. G. 1988. "Wife Abuse, Husband Abuse, or Mutual Combat?" In *Feminist Perspectives on Wife Abuse*, edited by K. Yllo and M. Bograd. Newbury Park, Calif.: Sage.

Shainess, N. 1979. "Vulnerability to Violence: Masochism as Process." *American Journal of Psychotherapy* 33:174–89.

Smuts, B. 1992. "Male Aggression Against Women: An Evolutionary Perspective." *Human Nature* 3:1–44.

Snell, J., R. Rosenwald, and A. Robey. 1964. "The Wifebeater's Wife: A Study of Family Interaction." *Archives of General Psychiatry* 11:107–13.

Sommers, C. H. 1994. *Who Stole Feminism? How Women Have Betrayed Women*. New York: Simon and Schuster.

Starr, R. 1988. "Physical Abuse of Children." In *Handbook of Family Violence*, edited by V. B. Van Hasselt, R. L. Morrison, A. S. Bellack, and M. Hersen. New York: Plenum Press.

Starr, R., K. N. Dietrich, J. Fishoff, S. Ceresine, and M. Demorest. 1984. "The Contribution of Handicapping Conditions to Child Abuse." *Topics in Early Childhood Special Education* 4:55–69.

Steele, B., and C. Pollack. 1974. "A Psychiatric Study of Parents Who Abuse Infants and Small Children." In *The Battered Child*, 2nd ed., edited by R. Helfer and C. Kempe. Chicago: University of Chicago Press.

Steinmetz, S. K. 1978. "Violence Between Family Members." *Marriage and Family Review* 1:1–16.

————. 1993. "The Abused Elderly Are Dependent: Abuse Is Caused by the Perception of Stress Associated with Providing Care." In *Current Controversies on Family Violence*, edited by R. J. Gelles and D. Loseke. Newbury Park, Calif.: Sage.

Stets, J. E., and M. A. Straus. 1990. "Gender Differences in Reporting Marital Violence and Its Medical and Psychological Consequences." In *Physical Violence in American Families*, edited by M. A. Straus and R. J. Gelles. New Brunswick, N.J.: Transaction.

Straus, M. A. 1993. "Physical Assaults by Wives: A Major Social Problem." In *Current Controversies on Family Violence*, edited by R. J. Gelles and D. Loseke. Newbury Park, Calif.: Sage.

———. 1994a. *Beating the Devil Out of Them: Corporal Punishment in American Families*. New York: Lexington.

———. 1994b. "State-to-State Differences in Social Inequality and Social Bonds in Relation to Assaults on Wives in the United States." *Journal of Comparative Family Studies* 25:7–24.

Straus, M. A., and R. J. Gelles. 1986. "Societal Change and Change in Family Violence from 1975 to 1985 as Revealed in Two National Surveys." *Journal of Marriage and the Family* 48:465–79.

———. 1988. "Violence in American Families: How Much is There and Why Does It Occur?" In *Troubled Relationships*, edited by E. W. Nunnally and P. M. Cox. Newbury Park, Calif.: Sage.

Straus, M. A., R. J. Gelles, and S. K. Steinmetz. 1980. *Behind Closed Doors: Violence in the American Family*. New York: Doubleday/Anchor.

Straus, M. A., and S. Sweet. 1992. "Verbal Aggression in Couples: Incidence Rates and Relationships to Personal Characteristics." *Journal of Marriage and the Family* 54:346–57.

Sugarman, D. B., and G. T. Hotaling. 1989. "Dating Violence: Prevalence, Context, and Risk Factors." In *Violence in Dating Relationships*, edited by M. A. Pirog-Good and J. E. Stets. New York: Praeger.

U.S. Advisory Board on Child Abuse and Neglect. 1995. *A Nation's Shame: Fatal Child Abuse and Neglect in the United States*. Washington, D.C.: U.S. Department of Health and Human Services.

Vissing, Y. M., M. A. Straus, R. J. Gelles, and J. W. Harrop. 1991. "Verbal Aggression by Parents and Psychosocial Problems of Children." *Child Abuse and Neglect: The International Journal* 15:223–38.

Walker, L. 1979. *The Battered Woman*. New York: Harper and Row.

Wang, C., and D. Daro. 1997. *Current Trends in Child Abuse Reporting and Fatalities: The Results of the 1996 Annual Fifty State Survey*. Chicago: National Committee to Prevent Child Abuse.

Wardell, L., D. L. Gillespie, and A. Leffler. 1983. "Science and Violence Against Women." In *The Dark Side of Families: Current Family Violence Research*, edited by D. Finkelhor, R. Gelles, M. Straus, and G. Hotaling. Beverly Hills, Calif.: Sage.

Weis, J. G. 1989. "Family Violence Research Methodology and Design." In *Family Violence*, edited by L. Ohlin and M. Tonry. Chicago: University of Chicago Press.

Weitzman, J., and K. Dreen. 1982. "Wife-Beating: A View of the Marital Dyad." *Social Casework* 63:259–65.

Widom, C. S. 1988. "Sampling Biases and Implications for Child Abuse Research." *American Journal of Orthopsychiatry* 58:260–70.

———. 1989. "The Cycle of Violence." *Science* 244:160–66.

Wilson, M., and M. Daly. 1992. "Spousal Homicide Risk and Estrangement." *Violence and Victims* 8:3–16.

Wolf, R. S. 1995. "Abuse of the Elderly." In *Families and Violence*, edited by R. J. Gelles. Minneapolis, Minn.: National Council on Family Relations.

Yllo, K. 1983. "Using a Feminist Approach in Quantitative Research." In *The Dark Side of Families: Current Family Violence Research*, edited by

D. Finkelhor, R. Gelles, M. Straus, and G. Hotaling. Beverly Hills, Calif.: Sage.

———. 1988. "Political and Methodological Debates in Wife Abuse Research." In *Feminist Perspectives on Wife Abuse*, edited by K. Yllo and M. Bograd. Newbury Park, Calif.: Sage.

———. 1993. "Through a Feminist Lens: Gender, Power, and Violence." In *Current Controversies on Family Violence,* edited by R. Gelles and D. Loseke. Newbury Park, Calif.: Sage.

8

Drug Control

ROBERT MacCOUN & PETER REUTER

The effort to control illicit drugs seems to have become a permanent element of American social policy in the last third of the twentieth century. A very large fraction of adolescents experiment with illicit drugs, primarily marijuana. Most do no more than experiment, but enough go on to consume them frequently that drug use and selling, as well as drug control itself, have become a major source of harms to the nation. These harms, particularly the ones related to crime, are heavily concentrated in urban minority communities.

The response to drug use and abuse in the United States has been massive punishment aimed particularly at low-level sellers.[1] The other programmatic components of an effort to reduce drug problems, prevention and treatment, have been given short shrift. This contrasts with the policies adopted by a number of Western European nations in which drug use has been seen, and experienced, more as an individual and public health problem. Notwithstanding intrusive, divisive, and expensive policies, the United States has an illicit drug problem that, no matter how measured (number of addicts, crimes, or health damage), is substantially larger than that of any Western European nation. Whether that has anything to do with the drug policies, as opposed to the inequalities, weak governmental sector, and violence that mar American society generally is indeterminable.

Oddly enough, a great deal more is known about the effects of treatment and prevention, which account for no more than 20 percent of this nation's public expenditures on drug control, than about the consequences of enforcement. Even more oddly, that is a consequence of the dedication to punishment; any other program has to justify itself against the suspicion that it is kind to criminals (treatment) or too diffuse (prevention). Since punishment is what drug users and sellers deserve, there is little need (in the eyes of politicians and perhaps the public) for enforcement to demonstrate its effectiveness.

For a review essay, this situation presents a dilemma. There is a large research literature evaluating the effectiveness of drug treatment, and a nascent literature on what constitutes effective drug prevention. However, the systematic studies of drug enforcement are very few indeed. If the review focuses on what we know, it will examine marginal programs, albeit ones that can justify considerable expansion. If, however, the review focuses on the principal control programs, it risks being descriptive and conceptual but lacking in evaluative detail. We have chosen a middle path; prevention and treatment are given more space than their role in U.S. drug policy would justify, but still less than drug enforcement.

We begin with a description of the American drug problem or problems. Before turning to policy description and assessment, we present an analytic framework for thinking about how drug policy affects drug use and related problems, and then what constitutes the elements of drug policy. This is followed by a description of American drug policy and an assessment of the principal programs. A briefer review of the policies of Western European nations serves as a preliminary to a discussion of the future of drug problems and policies in the United States and what might constitute more effective drug policy.

Drug Use and Related Problems

Since the mid-1970s, drug use in the general population has been tracked through two regular surveys, one of the household population (the National Household Survey on Drug Abuse) and the other of high school students (Monitoring the Future). The two surveys tell a consistent story, as illustrated in Figure 8.1.

Patterns of Use

Experimentation with drugs is a common experience among adolescents (Kandel 1993; Shedler and Block 1990). For most birth cohorts since 1960, over half have tried an illicit drug, marijuana being by far the most common. Taking out marijuana, the figure drops dramatically; for example, only 28 percent of high school seniors in 1994 had tried some illicit drug other than marijuana. The birth cohorts coming to maturity in the late 1970s were much more involved with drugs than any others. The figures dropped dramatically in the late 1980s and have started to rise substantially and steadily in the early 1990s (e.g., Johnston, O'Malley, and Bachman 1994).

These surveys have two major limitations: they rely on self-reported illicit conduct, and they are limited in coverage to the general household population. It is generally accepted, nonetheless, that the surveys capture the general trends in occasional drug use. The surveys clearly do much less well in describing trends in dependent use, for at least two reasons: (1) dependent users are more difficult to recruit for an interview because they lead more erratic lives and are more likely to be found among nonhousehold populations (e.g., homeless and incarcerated), and (2) they are less likely to provide truthful responses to survey questions. In apparent recognition of these problems, the federal government did not produce

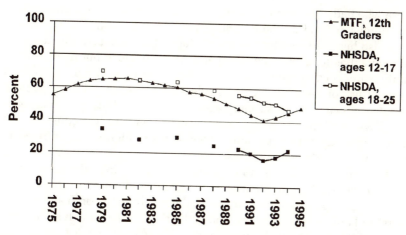

Figure 8.1 Lifetime use of any illicit drug, 1975–1995. *Note:* MTF: Monitoring the Future. NHSDA: National Household Survey on Drug Abuse. *Sources:* Johnston, O'Malley, and Bachman 1994; Substance Abuse and Mental Health Services Administration 1996.

official estimates of the size of the heroin-addicted population for almost twenty years and in doing so recently has relied primarily on other data.

The patterns of drug use across socioeconomic and demographic groups have changed in interesting ways during the last twenty years. The increases in the late 1970s were quite uniform by education and across ethnic groups. The declines in the 1980s were not nearly so uniform. Whereas in 1985 for males there was only a very slight correlation between use of cocaine (as reported in the National Household Survey) and education, by 1990 there was a strong negative correlation, a change that has also been observed (over a longer period) for cigarettes. The educated may be much more sensitive to health (and other) messages about the dangers of drug use.

The best estimates (which are not very good) of the numbers dependent on expensive drugs (principally cocaine and heroin) suggest a very different pattern over time. There was rapid recruitment into heroin use in the late 1960s and early 1970s; by 1975 the number of new heroin initiates had dropped dramatically. However, heroin addiction (at least for those addicted in the United States rather than while with the military in Vietnam) has turned out to be a very long-lived condition; the addicts recruited between 1967 and 1973 were still mostly addicted in 1990, as revealed in a remarkable twenty-four-year follow-up of a California sample (Hser, Anglin, and Powers 1993). It is now estimated that there are about 600,000 heroin addicts, not including those incarcerated, either for drug offenses or for crimes committed to purchase a drug that sells for $1,000 per gram (Rhodes et al. 1995).

Cocaine dependence became prevalent in the 1980s as the pool of those who had experimented with the drug expanded. It is estimated that the number peaked in about 1988 at perhaps 2 million, some of whom were also heroin-dependent. Whether dependence on a stimulant can be maintained as long as narcotic dependence is unclear, but there are certainly many cocaine users who have, over a ten-year period, maintained frequent use of the drug, albeit with less regularity than heroin addicts. Desistance seems to be strongly associated with education; thus those who have continued to be frequent cocaine users are less educated and more criminally active. Cocaine dependence is highly concentrated in inner-city minority communities.

Marijuana dependence is much more prevalent than dependence on either cocaine or heroin. There are a few million who use the drug daily—indeed, frequently each day. However, there is little research about these users, and only a very small fraction of them seek treatment. It seems that, though most of them would like to quit and have been unable to do so, this dependence does not produce great damage to them or to others (Kleiman 1992).

Drugs other than cocaine, heroin, and marijuana are widely used only in certain places or for limited periods. For example, amphetamines are prevalent in Dallas, San Diego, and a few other cities but are almost unheard of in most of the country. The hallucinogen phencyclidine (PCP) was found in the urine of about half of all arrestees in Washington, D.C., in 1987, but the fraction had dropped below 10 percent by 1993. Though such drugs can cause great damage, it is hard to design programs and policies that target such elusive phenomena.

Expenditures on illicit drugs, one metric for the damage they do to society through crime and the generation of criminal incomes, are estimated to be close to $50 billion, roughly 1 percent of personal consumption expenditures (Rhodes et al. 1995). It is likely that no other illicit market has ever generated such a large income to sellers; most of this money goes to those at the bottom of the distribution system, who earn modest incomes; in Washington, D.C., we estimated that the average street dealer working four or five days a week earned about $25,000 per annum (Reuter, MacCoun, and Murphy 1990).

Drug-Related Problems

A respectable research literature supports the proposition that some illicit drugs themselves are no more harmful than alcohol, the most commonly used legal psychoactive. For example, if heroin is provided in pure form under hygienic conditions, heroin addiction involves few more harmful physiological consequences than constipation. Marijuana similarly causes little serious physiological damage. Other drugs, such as PCP, cocaine, and methamphetamines, clearly can cause serious acute problems. However, there is little doubt that all psychoactive drugs, regardless of legal status, adversely affect cognitive development of the young, as well the behavior of adult users as parents, spouses, and members of the community and the labor force.

However, under current conditions, the principal harms associated with drug use are crime and morbidity/mortality that are a consequence of legal status. A large share of those who commit crimes are frequent users of drugs, as revealed by the Drug Use Forecasting (DUF) system; in most cities, over half of users test positive for some drug other than marijuana, usually cocaine. Nor is this simply a reflection of the expenditure preferences of the criminally active. Drug use exacerbates the criminal activity of those who are frequent users of expensive drugs; the same person may commit five times as many offenses when using drugs as when abstinent (e.g., Ball et al. 1982). Moreover, there is a good basis for believing that a large fraction of those now dependent on cocaine and heroin are criminally active. In fact, approximately half of all cocaine and heroin is probably purchased by users who are formally under the control of the criminal justice system—on pretrial release, probation, or parole. Frequent use of marijuana, without involvement with cocaine or heroin, does not seem to be criminogenic in itself, though it may be predictive, inasmuch as it increases the probability of involvement with cocaine and heroin.

The connections between expensive drug use and crime are multiple and complex. Most crimes seem to be the consequence of the extraordinary value of the drugs under a prohibition regime. In the United States a great deal of violence is generated by the markets, both directly and indirectly. For example, a careful study in New York City in 1988 (Goldstein, Brownstein, and Ryan 1992) estimated that 53 percent of homicides were related to drug selling or use; of those, 14 percent were classified as psychopharmacological (68 percent of these involving alcohol), while 74 percent were classified as by-products of drug trafficking (88 percent of these involving crack or powder cocaine).

But the health consequences of illicit drugs are also severe. The share of new AIDS cases that have a primary risk factor of intravenous drug use has now reached about 30 percent (Normand, Vlahov, and Moses 1995). In some areas of the country, particularly around New York City with its large heroin addict population, the HIV rate among intravenous drug users is close to 50 percent. Hepatitis, both B and the more newly discovered C strain, is also rampant among intravenous drug users. Intoxication and the obsessive search for the money to purchase drugs lead to neglect of basic health; tuberculosis is now a major problem among the drug-dependent, who may account for a significant fraction of that disease in the United States. Though the official estimates of deaths from illicit drugs are scarcely 10,000 per annum, representing a rate of less than 0.5 percent per annum for the addict population, cohort studies find rates closer to 1 to 2 percent per annum; the official figures represent only the deaths from acute, as opposed to chronic, effects.

Finally, we note that drug selling has become a common activity among poor minority urban males. For Washington, D.C., we estimate that nearly one-third of African-American males born in the 1960s were charged with drug selling between the ages of eighteen and twenty-four (Saner, MacCoun, and Reuter 1995). This represents a serious problem in many dimensions for the communities in which they live.

Analytic Framework

Discussion of drug problems gives great weight to the role of specific policies targeted at drug use and related problems. Before turning to those policies, it is useful to provide a framework for thinking about the relationship between policy and problems generally, and then between specific programs and parts of the drug problem.

It is tempting to think of drug policies and outcomes in terms of a simple causal chain: *goals → policies → drug use → drug-related harms.* In fact, the situation is considerably more complex, as depicted graphically in Figure 8.2. First, it is widely recognized that many exogenous factors influence both drug policy and drug outcomes, a point we illustrate throughout this chapter. Second, it is likely that goals directly influence not only formal policies but also implementation. In some nations (most notably the Netherlands), implementation more closely reflects national goals than do formal drug laws. Third, formal policies probably directly influence drug outcomes above and beyond their indirect effect via implementation (e.g., drug laws may have a symbolic influence on drug use above and beyond the effects of enforcement on deterrence, incapacita-

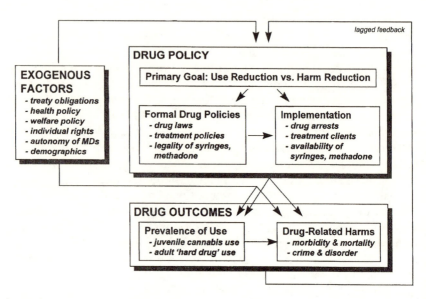

Figure 8.2 Analytic Framework.

tion, price, and availability; MacCoun 1993). Fourth, formal policies and their implementation can each have a direct influence on drug-related harms that may be largely independent of their effect on the prevalence of drug use; indeed, this is the central insight of the European harm reduction movement (see Heather et al. 1993). Finally, prevalence and harms have a lagged feedback effect on drug policy; drug policies have evolved considerably over the past two decades in response to a 1970s heroin epidemic and the 1980s AIDS epidemic.

Measuring the extent of a nation's drug problem requires more than estimating the number of persons using illicit drugs. Drugs differ in the damage they do to their users (e.g., cocaine's acute and chronic harms are greater than those of cannabis) and in the damage their users cause to the rest of society. There may also be differences in how the drugs are used, as summed up in Zinberg's phrase "set and setting" (Zinberg 1984), which would have important consequences for the extent of harms suffered by users of those drugs.

There is no shortcut through this maze of complications—no single indicator will allow for ranking nations in the severity of the damage done by use of illicit psychoactive drugs. A "harm reduction" approach, discussed later, would suggest that we put aside the details of who uses how much of each drug and instead estimate the extent of damages resulting from drug use. Unfortunately, there turns out to be no good basis for estimating those damages at a national level for most nations, and even with a good set of numbers, the final calculation would involve some nasty value judgements (see MacCoun, Reuter, and Schelling 1996).

Effects of Drug Laws on Drug Use

Following MacCoun (1993), we identify seven mechanisms by which drug laws might affect drug use, and summarize the available empirical evidence for each. Three of the mechanisms are suggested by the rational choice model. The first, *fear of legal sanctions,* is at the heart of classical criminology's deterrence theory. In theory, this fear should be a multiplicative function of the perceived certainty and severity of legal sanctions, discounted by their celerity (promptness). A large body of literature suggests that the link between actual and perceived sanction risks is fairly tenuous; that there is a modest but reliable inverse association between perceived sanction certainty and drug offending, and the relationship appears to be causal; that severity of sanctioning has little or no influence on offending, and when increases in severity undermine certainty they are actually counterproductive; and that individuals do not use sanctioning risk information in the manner implied by rational choice models.

Two other rational choice mechanisms are the *availability* of a drug, which should increase the likelihood of use, and the *price* of a drug, which should be inversely related to use. Direct evidence on the impact of these factors is scarce and inconsistent. Analyzing panel data from the annual Monitoring the Future survey of twelfth-grade American students, Bachman, Johnston, and O'Malley (1990) report a negligible correlation between the perceived availability of marijuana and cocaine and the use of those drugs. Reviewing the alcohol literature, where objective availability measures are more feasible and policy variations allow for more refined testing, Single (1988) cites reliable relationships in several studies but no association in others.

With respect to price, the common practice is to note that consumers are less price-sensitive (technically, lower price elasticities of demand) with respect to alcohol and tobacco than with many other commodities. The conventional wisdom is that users of illicit drugs, especially dependent users, should be quite insensitive to price; indeed, some accept this as an economic definition of addiction. But Caulkins and Reuter (1996) review a number of recent studies suggesting that heroin and cocaine users are surprisingly sensitive to price variations (e.g., price elasticities of demand in the −1.0 to −2.0 range). If so, interventions that influence price should yield sizable reductions in drug consumption. Unfortunately, law enforcement has at best modest success in reducing availability or increasing prices of illicit drugs, and the threshold levels of low availability and high price that would make drug use impossible are essentially unattainable.

Rational choice models tend to neglect the important role of moral judgment in legal compliance. For many, the mere fact that a drug is illegal might be sufficient to discourage use, regardless of the risk of getting caught in the act. Theory and research on moral judgment suggest that the strength of this *symbolic threshold effect* is likely to vary across individuals, and within individuals over the life span. But several lines of psychological theory and research suggest the possibility of a countervailing *forbidden fruit effect*, whereby the mere fact that a drug is prohibited may enhance its attractiveness. Presumably, the symbolic threshold and forbidden fruit mechanisms vary inversely within individuals, but little is known about the relative magnitude of these effects, either within individuals or in the population at large.

A sixth mechanism is the *stigmatization* associated with being labeled a drug offender. For noninitiates, stigmatization may be effective in discouraging use. But the labeling theory tradition in psychology and sociology (Braithwaite 1989) suggests that in many circumstances, by enlarging the social and psychological boundaries between the offender and "conventional" society, stigmatization can actually encourage further drug use and other socially deviant activities. A seventh, related mechanism is the influence of drug laws on *informal social controls*, including health-related beliefs, attitudes toward drugs and drug users, and informal norms of situationally appropriate conduct. These informal social controls appear to be at least as important as formal legal controls in shaping drug-using behavior. Unfortunately, we know very little about the interrelationship of formal and informal controls. While it is often asserted that formal controls reinforce informal controls, there is little direct evidence for this proposition, and there are reasons to suspect that formal controls might sometimes undermine, replace, or circumvent informal controls.

Matching Policies to Problems

As should be clear, the drug problem has many elements. Table 8.1 presents a list of eight phenomena that constitute some of the major components of what troubles the nation under the rubric "the drug problem." All contain many elements themselves; for example, the health consequences of drug dependence include an array of problems that affect users and the rest of the community, such as HIV, tuberculosis, and hepatitis C. Crime by users includes both "economic-compulsive crime" and crime induced by the psychoactive properties of the drugs themselves, to use Paul Goldstein's (1985) distinction. The list could be expanded considerably (see MacCoun, Reuter, and Schelling 1996), but we believe each item of a larger list could be associated with one of the four categories of sources used here: initiation, dependence, distribution, and production.

Some of the problems in the list are related not so much to the consequences of drug use itself as to initiation of the young into drug use. The involvement of young people in the subculture surrounding illicit drugs or with the routine violation of law, and their possible progression to drug dependence, are the central concerns here.

Another set of problems is caused by the dependence or abuse of drugs (e.g., spread of AIDS, crimes committed to support expensive illicit drug use) albeit sometimes because of the conditions of use that society has created. Cocaine sells in illegal markets for about twenty times its legal price, which helps explain the high level of property crime associated with dependence on cocaine. Use of dirty needles by heroin addicts is heavily a function of the prohibition on unauthorized possession of hypodermic needles.

Table 8.1. Elements of the Drug Problem

Elements	Source
Adolescents dropping out of school Gateway to other behavioral problems	Initiation
High mortality and morbidity among users and their intimates Crime by users	Drug dependence
Large criminal incomes Violence in competition	Drug distribution
Distortion of source country societies Strains on U.S. foreign policy	Drug production

Other problem elements, such as killings of rival drug dealers, are related not directly to drug use but to the distribution of drugs. Even if drugs did not adversely affect behavior, the struggle for market and contract disputes in an illegal setting would generate (at least in the United States) a great deal of violence. Finally, yet others (e.g., the distortion of social and political institutions in Bolivia, Colombia, and Peru) are a function of the production of the drugs themselves.

If it were possible to eliminate illicit drug use altogether, all of these problems would either vanish or be much ameliorated. But because different elements of the problem have different sources, lowering drug consumption does not necessarily have the desired effect on the other dimensions. Initiation may decline sharply, as suggested previously, even while dependence is worsening. There are also policy trade-offs among these components. For example, we may be able to reduce cocaine use by more stringent enforcement against dealers but suffer, at least in the short run, a worsening of related crime and health problems. Indeed, drug-related homicide appeared to rise in 1990, just as there was mounting evidence of reduced drug consumption (Office of National Drug Control Policy 1990, pp. 117–21).

The traditional classification of programs dealing with drug problems has been enforcement, treatment, and prevention. If we further divide enforcement into the categories of source country control (e.g., crop eradication and refinery destruction) and domestic enforcement (including interdiction of smuggled drugs), we can match program types and the dimensions of the drug problem schematized in Table 8.1. This matching is presented in Table 8.2.

Programs are usually evaluated in terms of the targets suggested by this mapping. Thus primary prevention programs are evaluated mostly in terms of their effect on initiation into drug use; successful prevention efforts will reduce the percentage of nonusers or experimental users who become regular users. Reductions in drug-related violence are neither expected nor measured. Similarly, treatment programs are evaluated in terms of reducing the extent of drug dependence and associated harms.

Of course, programs may affect more than their principal targets; the

Table 8.2. Matching Programs and Problem Elements

Program	→	Targets
Prevention	→	Initiation
Treatment	→	Drug use
Enforcement	→	Distribution
Source country	→	Production controls

effects can even be negative. Increasingly effective treatment may actually worsen initiation problems by removing the most visible and striking negative role models of addicted drug users. That is not a reason for failing to provide funding for drug treatment; it merely points to the difficulty of doing only good.

Other negative interactions, mostly involving enforcement, can be more serious. Consider, for example, the upstream effects of interdiction. If more stringent interdiction works primarily through raising the percentage of shipments intercepted, rather than by raising the labor costs of smuggling through increased incarceration of smugglers, it may actually increase the export demand for the drug. This occurs because interdiction has two effects on export demand. By raising prices in the United States, it decreases the total amount consumed; but it also raises the quantity of exports needed to deliver a ton to the United States. The second effect turns out, under reasonable assumptions about the demand and supply curves of the cocaine industry, to be larger than the first (Reuter, Crawford, and Cave 1988, Appendix A). Thus interdiction may actually increase source country problems by raising the demand for exports of cocaine.

This matching of program types against goals provides a framework for systematic comparative assessment of programs and policies. We must ask of particular policies not simply how they will affect levels of drug use but also what their consequences will be for other dimensions of the drug problem. For example, evaluations of street crackdowns should determine their effect on the crime rate and on recruitment rates. Similarly, in allocating resources between prevention and treatment, we must compare the benefits of reduced initiation now with those of reduced heavy use now; the flow of benefits over time may be very different for the two kinds of programs.

United States' Drug Policy

Drug policy crosses many domains of social policy. Criminal justice, health, and education are all major elements of what is usually described as drug policy. Parsimoniously characterizing policy is difficult. Here we follow the usual pattern of describing only those programs that are specifically aimed at drug use and related problems; we have argued elsewhere that other, more general domains of social policy, related to education, income support, health, and housing, may be just as important, but it is hard to know how to characterize their drug control component. We also say nothing about public rhetoric, which may indeed be an important determinant of drug use.

Enforcement

The amount of punishment levied for drug control purposes has increased massively since 1981, when the concern with cocaine became prominent. Arrests approximately doubled, but this figure conceals a much greater increase in the extent of imprisonment and other penalties; for example, the number of commitments to state and federal prison have risen approximately tenfold over the same period. Table 8.3 presents a series of figures that describe this change.

The number of state and local arrests for drug offenses rose from 581,000 in 1980 to approximately 1,350,000 in 1994 (from 5.5 percent to 9.2 percent of total arrests). But the key to understanding the shift in punishment is to examine the composition of the arrests. In 1980 they were predominantly for marijuana (70 percent); marijuana possession offenses alone accounted for 58 percent of the total. In 1994, heroin and cocaine arrests had come to exceed those for marijuana (47 percent vs. 36 percent), and distribution arrests accounted for a much higher share of the total (27 percent in 1994, compared with 18 percent in 1980).

Imprisonment levels have increased even more dramatically. In 1986, the first year of consistent reporting, there were 40,000 felony convictions for drug trafficking in state courts; six years later, that figure was 86,000, an increase of 115 percent. The percentage of felony drug trafficking convictions resulting in prison sentences has also risen; by 1992 the figure was 55 percent. Felony drug possession convictions and prison commitments were also rising; in 1992, 109,000 persons were convicted of felony possession (which does not include possession with intent to distribute), and 33 percent of these were sentenced to state prison. Federal incarcerations for drug offenses show a similarly rapid increase in the same period as well, from 6,600 in 1986 to 14,800 in 1992; more remarkably, drug commitments now represent about 60 percent of all those sent to federal prison.

Although legislatures, led by Congress, passed statutes in the 1980s and 1990s mandating longer sentences for drug offenders, this apparently has not led to an increase in time served at the state level. Maximum sentences have remained around forty-eight months, of which about one-third of the time is actually served. The principal effect of the statutory

Table 8.3. Trends in Drug Enforcement, 1981–1995

	1980	1985	1990	1994
Drug arrests	581,000	811,000	1,090,000	1,350,000
Heroin and cocaine only	70,000	240,000	590,000	635,000
Distribution only	104,000	192,000	345,000	370,000
Prison inmates				
State	19,000	39,000	149,000	202,000
Federal	4,900	9,500	30,500	51,800

Sources: Federal Bureau of Investigation, various years; Bureau of Justice Statistics, various years.

changes has probably been to ensure that fewer low-level offenders receive sentences of probation, a matter we take up later. Only at the federal level has there been a rise both in the length of sentences (seventy months in 1986 to eighty-seven months in 1992) and in the share of those sentences actually served; by 1992 the fraction was 0.85, reflecting the combined impact of mandatory minimum sentencing statutes, the guidelines of the U.S. Sentencing Commission, and elimination of parole release.

Sentencing figures are of themselves insufficient to show that enforcement has become more stringent; that depends on the ratio of sentences (or years of prison time) to offenses. Estimating the number of offenses (or at least the rate of change in that number) is itself a highly speculative task. We believe that the number of offenses might have risen as rapidly as arrests/sentences/years of prison time between 1980 and 1985, but from 1985 to 1995 it is very likely that the number of offenses and offenders (sales/sellers) was essentially flat and that the stringency of enforcement became greater.

How risky is drug selling or drug possession? The aggregate data suggest that the 1994 risk of being arrested for marijuana possession was about 2 percent per annum; for cocaine the figure was 6 percent per annum. For drug selling, we estimated in a study of the District of Columbia that in 1988 street dealers of drugs faced about a 22 percent probability of imprisonment in the course of a year's selling and that, given expected time served, they spent about one-third of their selling career in prison (Reuter, MacCoun, and Murphy 1990). These figures are consistent with crude calculations at the national level, assuming that each cocaine seller has about ten customers.

Does this make drug selling appropriately risky? One-third of a career in prison seems like a long time. On the other hand, the risk per sale is very small indeed; a seller who works two days a week at this trade may make 1,000 transactions in the course of a year. His imprisonment risk per transaction is only about 1 in 4,500; by that metric it is a great deal less risky than, say, a burglary or robbery. Another way to consider the risk is to look at aggregate figures. It is estimated that American users consume 300 tons of cocaine per annum. If these are sold in 1-gram units, this represents 300 million transactions, which generate fewer than 100,000 prison sentences.

In many ways these figures mirror the realities for property crimes as well. The probability of an individual robbery or burglary resulting in prison is slight, but most individuals who commit these crimes regularly spend a substantial amount of time in prison; they make it up in volume.

It is hard to analyze drug enforcement in contemporary America without reference to race (Tonry 1995). Those arrested for drug selling are predominantly from minority groups, and that disproportion is even higher for prison sentences. In 1992, blacks constituted two-thirds of those admitted to state prison for drug offenses, compared with slightly less than one-half for all nondrug offenses; they constitute 12 percent of the population. Hispanics (10.2 percent of the general population) accounted for 25 percent of commitments for drug offenses, compared with about 15 percent for nondrug offenses.

The disproportion in sentences for crack offenses, for which arrests are overwhelmingly of blacks and Hispanics, has been a major political issue. At the federal level, Congress in 1996 affirmed its views by decisively rejecting a possible downward revision in the 100 to 1 disparity in the amount of drug generating a five-year sentence for crack and for powdered cocaine, despite the recommendation by the Sentencing Commission, a body generally given to great sentencing severity, that the difference be substantially reduced. President Clinton also expressed his disagreement with the Sentencing Commission's recommendation. Though drug problems are disproportionately concentrated in minority urban communities, the sentencing disparities have also been highly divisive.

How Successful Has Enforcement Been?

Evaluating drug enforcement is essentially impossible with current data sets; there are no measures of the number of offenses (comparable to the reports of burglaries in the Uniform Crime Reports or in the National Crime Victimization Survey), so we cannot readily estimate how stringency varies across cities or states for specific drugs. Nor is it clear just what are the right measures of offense levels: the amount sold, the number of users, or the amount of violence and disorder generated by drug use and selling?

Price is the only outcome measure generally available at both the national and metropolitan-area level. Tougher enforcement should, in the short run, raise prices, assuming (as seems reasonable for a mature market) that demand, the relationship between the quantity sought by users and the price charged, remains stable (Reuter and Kleiman 1986). What we observe is that during the period of increasingly tough enforcement, prices for cocaine and heroin have fallen steadily since 1981; by 1995, after adjusting for inflation, they were only about one-third of their 1981 levels. For marijuana, prices rose steadily and substantially from 1981 to 1992 and then fell in the next four years back to their 1981 level. Even more surprising is the observation that crack cocaine, singled out for tough sentencing, both at the national level and in some major states (e.g., California, where possession of small quantities is subject to a mandatory state prison sentence) is no more expensive at the retail level than powder cocaine.

The decline in prices might be explained by a lower demand. It is difficult to assess whether this is an important factor, but certainly consumption is estimated not to have declined substantially. Occasional middle-class use has dropped precipitously; this never constituted a large share of total consumption, but one cannot dismiss the possibility that it was important in determining prices.

If enforcement did not raise prices for drugs, it still might have been successful if it lowered availability. The existing data, mostly from the annual survey of high school seniors, suggests that it has not succeeded in this regard. For example, the percentage of seniors reporting that cocaine was available or readily available was higher in 1989 than in 1980; it began to decline after 1989, probably because the fraction of high school seniors using cocaine had fallen sharply, but it remains well above the 1980 level.

Treatment

Until the late 1960s, treatment for drug dependence was provided almost exclusively in two federal facilities (Lexington and Fort Worth), which had as much penal as therapeutic character. This emphasis reflected the continued legacy of the legal battles around interpretation of the Harrison Act, which ushered in national drug prohibition in 1914; court interpretations of allowable medical practice had discouraged physicians from taking on these patients (Musto 1987).

With the introduction of methadone in the 1970s, specialized programs aimed at those dependent on illicit drugs became widely available. Approximately 700,000 persons now receive treatment each year from programs that receive at least some public funds; this probably represents the vast majority of the total number receiving any kind of treatment. Cocaine (300,000) and heroin (150,000) account for the bulk of treatment episodes, classified according to primary drug of abuse. Estimates of the need for treatment from the National Household Survey suggest that fewer than one-quarter of those in need actually receive treatment in any one year, but these estimates are of questionable value, since most treatment needers in the survey use only marijuana.

The public treatment system is poorly funded, provides inadequate services to its clients, and has a high dropout rate, but nonetheless can justify itself strongly in terms of cost-benefit ratios. Compared with the private treatment system, it has to deal with more severely addicted patients who have a much poorer prognosis; most are unemployed, poorly educated, and without a stable family, three of the predictors of failure in treatment. Compared with the private system, publicly funded programs pay lower wages to their staff, who have less training. The staff-client ratio is higher and the number of contact hours fewer. Yet credible, systematic studies have found benefit-cost ratios for public drug treatment programs that range from $3 to $7 (e.g., Gerstein et al. 1994). Rydell and Everingham (1994) estimate that the United States could reduce cocaine consumption by 1 percent by investing $34 million in additional treatment funds, considerably cheaper than achieving the same outcome with domestic drug law enforcement ($246 million), interdiction ($366 million), or source country controls ($783 million). Notably, this estimate is based on a fairly pessimistic estimate of treatment effectiveness; treatment's cost-effectiveness in their analyses stems largely from the temporary suppression of consumption during treatment, and from treatment's modest costs relative to law enforcement activities.

A major social benefit from treatment comes from reductions in crime, generated by lowered drug use. The classic study of methadone programs (Ball and Ross 1991) showed in-treatment reductions in crime of 70 percent or more. Employment rates and wage rates for clients, during or after treatment, do not show much increase, pointing to the limits of treatment for the drug-dependent population with which these programs now deal. Most of those who enter treatment will relapse into regular drug use within a few months of entry and will have difficulty meeting the behavioral requirements for long-term employment. It is now generally accepted by the treatment community that repeated cycles of treatment and relapse are often necessary before clients make lasting behavioral changes. Many treatment experts believe that the coercive impact of the criminal justice system plays a key role in motivating addicts to seek and complete treatment (Anglin and Hser 1990). The recent growth of "drug courts"— formally or informally organized court procedures designed to divert nonviolent drug offenders to treatment and rehabilitation services—in Miami, Oakland, and other American cities is intended to enhance this justice system function.

Prevention

Illicit drug use, as opposed to dependence, is primarily a youth phenomenon. More than half of those who use illicit drugs are in their late teens or their twenties, and adolescent drug use peaks at an earlier age than that for alcohol, tobacco, or psychoactive prescription drugs (Kandel 1993). Over the past fifteen years, the U.S. federal government has considerably increased funding for programs to prevent adolescent involvement with licit and illicit drugs; in 1995 the figure was about $2 billion. Most of this money is spent by schools, though there is a continuing interest in other institutions, such as churches and recreational facilities, as being more effective at reaching the highest-risk groups.

Early drug prevention programs of the 1970s were largely premised on a rational choice model: if students understand the risks of drug use, they will be more likely to resist initiation. It soon became apparent that there are several problems with this approach. First, perceptions of drug risks are only one factor that influences adolescent drug use; equally or more important are peer influences and pressures (Ellickson 1995). Second, early drug prevention programs provided "risk information" that greatly exaggerated some risks for some drugs (e.g., the addictiveness and neurological consequences of marijuana use); when students' growing samples of observations failed to concur with these messages, the programs were quickly discredited.

While contemporary programs continue to provide risk education, many place much greater emphasis on training students to resist social pressures to use drugs (Ellickson 1995). Ironically, at a time when many youth were ridiculing Nancy Reagan's "Just Say No" campaign, prevention experts were demonstrating that teaching youth how to say no was indeed an effective prevention strategy, at least relative to previous approaches. But the most popular American drug prevention curriculum is Drug Abuse Resistance Education Project (DARE), created by the Los Angeles Police Department in the early 1980s. The DARE program was designed as a largely atheoretical hodgepodge, mixing drug risk education, self-esteem promotion, decision-making skills, and alternatives to drug use; its most distinct feature is that the lessons are given by professional police officers.

In a much-cited analysis of 143 evaluation studies, Tobler (1992) estimated a meta-analytic effect size (ES; the difference between mean outcomes for experimental and control groups, divided by the pooled standard deviation) of .24 on measures of drug use. Programs were notably more effective in influencing drug knowledge (ES = .52) and much less effective at influencing attitudes (ES = .18). Unfortunately, even the more successful programs rarely have effects that persist for more than a few years (e.g., Ellickson, Bell, and McGuigan 1993). This is hardly surprising. Though it pains us, as professors, to admit it, it is of course unrealistic to expect a small sample of classroom experiences to have demonstrable effects on nonclassroom behavior years later. Investing in later booster sessions appears necessary to obtain sustained effects (Botvin et al. 1995).

Tobler found that programs specifically targeting tobacco were most influential (ES = .49); programs focusing on alcohol (ES = .17) or both licit and illicit drugs (ES = .11) had considerably weaker effects. The success of tobacco programs might reflect in part the sheer weight of credible evidence for the dangers of tobacco, especially relative to fairly modest rewards. Moreover, most adolescents have probably met adults who have struggled to quit smoking. On the other hand, alcohol prevention programs face a considerable challenge because alcohol is used so widely (and, frequently, safely) in our society.

More is known about drug prevention's effectiveness than its cost-effectiveness. In theory, prevention efforts could be made more efficient and effective by targeting efforts at those youth at greatest risk; in practice, risk and resilience factors have been identified, but it isn't clear how to single out high-risk students for an intervention without stigmatizing them (possibly undermining any positive effects). Prevention programs are focused almost exclusively on the goal of reducing prevalence. In keeping with this focus, prevention program evaluations (like many treatment evaluations) are preoccupied with establishing program effects on *whether* adolescents use, giving short shrift to the measurement of *amounts* and *styles* of drug use, or the harmful consequences of that use. But the fact is that most adolescent drug users pass through a limited period of experimentation without any lasting effects and acute harms that are fairly modest (e.g., Kandel 1993; Shedler and Block 1990). This raises the question of whether prevention programs shorten the drug-using careers of experimenters or motivate those experimenters to use drugs more cautiously than they might in the absence of exposure to prevention messages. If so, prevention evaluations, by relying so heavily on prevalence indicators, might be underestimating the beneficial effects of the interventions. A more controversial question is whether prevention programs might more effectively reduce aggregate drug harm by actively teaching students to distinguish riskier and less risky *forms* of drug use (i.e., harm reduction). An objection is that harm reduction messages might "send the wrong message," actually encouraging use. If so, such messages might be more effective if targeted exclusively at experienced problem users. Unfortunately, we still know very little about the trade-offs (if any) between prevalence reduction and harm reduction strategies (see MacCoun 1996).

A related issue involves the so-called *gateway* (or stepping-stone) theory: the notion of a causal sequence of drug use, from tobacco and alcohol to marijuana to harder drugs like cocaine or heroin. Recent neurobiological research has shown certain similarities in the brain's responses to marijuana and to heroin, suggesting (weakly) that marijuana may prime the brain for heroin. The sequential pattern is well established in lagged correlational analyses (Ellickson 1995); what is not known is whether the sequence is truly causal and, if so, by what mechanism (MacCoun, Reuter, and Schelling 1996). For example, a gateway effect might occur through the perception that one has safely used marijuana without experiencing addiction, health effects, or legal sanctions, and that one can thus proceed to harder drugs without fear. If so, it might be prudent for prevention programs to explicitly distinguish marijuana from more dangerous drugs, and perhaps to distinguish casual experimentation from the cumulative effects of long-term drug use.

Comparing Policies and Problems Across European Nations

References to the experiences of Britain (medically supervised provision of heroin up to 1965) and the Netherlands (the regulated sale of marijuana by coffee shops) have long been a commonplace of the American drug policy debate. Italy's decriminalization and the Zurich Platzspitz experience have entered that debate more recently. It is clear, however, that descriptions of these policies, let alone the assessments of their effectiveness, fall somewhere between casual and negligent, particularly in the United States.

In fact, Western European nations have indeed adopted a wide variety of formal policies toward controlling illicit drugs. Though all prohibit the consumption and sale of the same drugs that are prohibited in the United States, as required by the various United Nations conventions to which they are signatories, they have gone about implementing those prohibitions in varied ways. For example, Italy criminalized drug possession in 1954, decriminalized in 1975, recriminalized in 1990, and then redecriminalized in a 1993 referendum. Spain imposes no criminal sanctions for possession of small amounts of prohibited substances, while Norway and Sweden aggressively seek out drug users and at least threaten incarceration or mandatory treatment. Some German-speaking cantons of Switzerland, primarily because of concern with the spread of AIDS, have developed programs that allow heroin injectors to consume their drugs under supervision and in government-financed facilities. The Netherlands, while retaining the formal prohibition on cannabis consumption or sale, permits the sale of cannabis by coffee shops.

Nor is the variation only in use of criminal sanctions; it also shows up in prevention and treatment (e.g., Farrell et al. 1996). For example, methadone is the principal modality of treatment for heroin addicts in Great Britain and the Netherlands (where it is liberally available) but is not generally permitted in France or Sweden. Denmark provides extremely easy access to methadone through general practitioners. Some countries that allow methadone (notably Italy) do not permit its use in the maintenance mode that is customary in Britain and the United States. Secondary prevention programs in Britain and Spain target needle users and emphasize "safe use," while Germany and France will allow only abstinence messages.

It is this variation that makes the study of Western European experiences so interesting for those concerned with U.S. drug policy. Decriminalization, needle exchange, the legal availability of "soft drugs"—all staples of the reform agenda—have been tried in Western Europe; ergo, an examination of how these policies have worked in Europe might tell us how they would work in the United States.

Has this variation in policy and rhetoric had any significant consequence for the extent and nature of national drug problems? Alas, we cannot reach a strong judgment on this for a whole array of reasons (MacCoun et al. 1993). First, as seen in Figure 8.2, there is also reverse causation; the nature and extent of a nation's drug problems have an effect on its policy. Second, what is normally thought of as drug policy—drug enforcement, treatment, and prevention—is only part of the relevant policy domain; more general policy decisions with respect to welfare, health, and criminal justice may be equally or more important. And third, it is clear that drug problems are overdetermined, with government policy playing only a partial and perhaps secondary role. Another problem is that relevant data are quite scarce, and the available data are simply not of good quality. Until quite recently, few Western European nations have devoted even modest resources to the systematic collection of data on the problems of illicit drugs.

The Varieties of Drug Policies

Ideally, one might arrange nations along a single policy continuum (e.g., "tolerant vs. punitive"). Figure 8.3, itself an oversimplification, illustrates that countries' policies vary along many dimensions.

Laws.   Though policy as implemented is quite different from the law, nonetheless the law has influence, particularly on enforcement, and important differences exist among the nations we are studying. For example, German criminal law does not allow for police discretion (though it does allow for prosecutorial discretion) when observing an offense. On the other hand, the British police, with their ability to issue cautions for simple possession of cannabis, are able to dispose of numerous offenses without formal adjudication.

Italy and Spain stand out because they do not have criminal sanctions for possession of small amounts of drugs for personal use; this covers not just "soft drugs" but all psychoactive substances. Such possession remains illegal, but the only sanctions available are administrative. These laws have been in place in Spain since 1983 and have been subject to little debate; policy discussion seems to center around the possibility of criminal penalties for use in public settings. For example, in 1989 the mayor of Toledo imposed a 1,500-peseta fine (about fifteen dollars) for

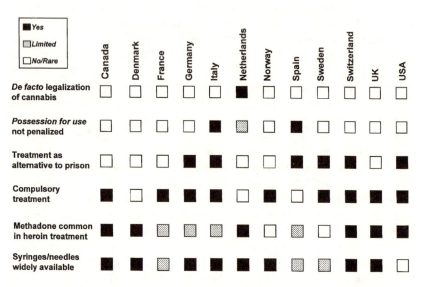

Figure 8.3 Policy indicators (ca. 1990). *Source:* MacCoun et al. 1995.

"consumption of drugs in public thoroughfares . . . discarding or leaving behind syringes or residues that are used or usable for drug consumption" (*Epoca* [Madrid], January 2, 1989, pp. 26–29).

Italy has gone through many changes with respect to criminal sanctions for possession. The initial criminalization of 1954 was reversed in 1975, apparently because of concern about the rising number of heroin-related deaths and a belief that the criminal law was deterring heroin addicts from entering treatment. The deaths continued to rise, leading parliament to recriminalize possession in 1990. Then in 1993 a national referendum led to redecriminalization.

Dutch laws deserve separate discussion because they are so frequently misinterpreted. The Netherlands has adopted a nonprosecution policy approximating de facto legalization for possession and sale of less than thirty grams of cannabis, recently reduced to five grams. Nonetheless, cannabis is formally illicit, and the production and wholesale distribution of cannabis are subject to significant enforcement activities. There is a great deal of ambiguity in the Netherlands cannabis regime, most of it caused by pressures from the international community, particularly from the French, who believe that permissive Dutch policies undermine their own restrictions. Thus coffee shops, which are licensed as outlets for marijuana sales, are subject to intense regulation to mollify other nations; among recent actions contemplated and at least sporadically implemented are restrictions on phone orders and requiring evidence of Dutch residency. Since the drug remains formally illegal, the regulation is all de facto and, as the result of a European court ruling, cannot include specific taxation on marijuana sales. There has been discussion of legalizing the commercial growing of marijuana, but international pressures have deterred the government from formally introducing this proposal in parliament.

Recently a number of significant changes have occurred in other nations, either in law or in the interpretation of existing law. For example, a 1994 German constitutional court ruling has resulted in considerable local variation in the extent to which cannabis possession is criminalized.

Enforcement.   Figure 8.4 presents arrest rates defined as the number of individual offenders per 100,000 population. The most notable feature is the sharp rise in drug arrest rates during the 1980s. This still leaves a major gap with the United States; the U.S. records between 250 and 500 arrests per 100,000 population, and most European nations are under 100 per 100,000.

Data on drug convictions and imprisonments are not available for most European nations. However, compared with the United States, sentences appear to be much shorter for major traffickers, although the differences in time served are probably less substantial. In some countries (e.g., Norway) drug trafficking accounts for a substantial fraction of all sentences of more than five years.

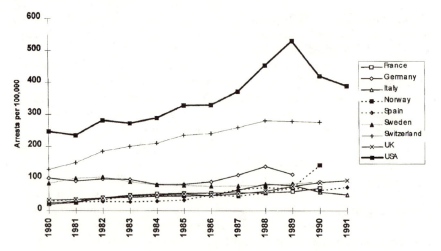

Figure 8.4 Drug arrest rates, 1980–1991. *Source:* MacCoun et al. 1995.

Treatment and Harm Reduction.   The problems of consistency and depth of data on enforcement pale in comparison with those surrounding systematic comparison of treatment provision across nations. However, some broad statements are possible. First, because in many European countries there is more comprehensive government-funded health care provision for the population and little ambivalence about the right of drug addicts to receive health care for their condition, there is little evidence of the chronic shortage of treatment observed in the United States. Second, heroin dominates the treatment populations of Western Europe (except perhaps in Sweden, with its persistently high prevalence of amphetamine addiction). Third, there is great variation in the availability of methadone (see Figure 8.3). Treatment is offered as an alternative to incarceration in most nations. Sweden, a nation that has been perhaps the most consistently opposed to weakening of the criminal sanction against all drug offenses, has also adopted the most aggressive policy toward treatment.

Beyond treatment, a variety of other efforts have been made to reduce the harms of drug abuse in Europe. Most countries have needle exchange programs, aimed at reducing the spread of HIV. Needle exchange has been a highly controversial program in the United States but has been adopted with little debate in Britain, Denmark, the Netherlands, and Switzerland. In Italy and Spain, where possession of syringes is not a criminal offense and they are readily available at low prices from pharmacies, more aggressive distribution of such needles has come about only slowly. Sweden has explicitly and consistently rejected these measures.

Relative Emphasis. Ideally, one might examine comparative budget data as an indicator of relative spending on implementation of various drug policies. For example, Wever (1992) estimates per capita demand reduction expenditures for France (102 ecu), the Netherlands (274 ecu), the United Kingdom (90 ecu), and the United States (610 ecu). Though the United States leads in per capita spending, Wever estimates that it lags behind the others on a per addict basis. It is difficult to assess the validity of such estimates. Nor has anyone attempted to estimate European drug enforcement expenditures.

An alternative approach, though not without problems of its own, is to look at the arrest-to-treatment ratio as a very crude indicator of emphasis (see Figure 8.5). This bypasses the problem of not having sound estimates of the number of users, but given that arrest is only the beginning of the punitive chain, it is by no means definitive.

Though these ratios should not be taken too literally—the ratio of somewhat dubious measures is itself somewhat dubious—the Netherlands is distinctive, as one might expect. What is particularly striking is that, overall, most other nations seem to have struck a close balance between the two policy responses, perhaps in part because so many clients were referred by legal authorities.

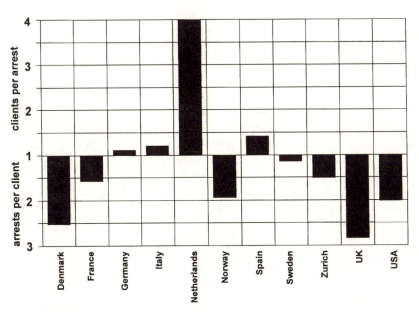

Figure 8.5 Treatment clients per arrest (ca. 1990). *Source:* MacCoun et al. 1995.

One conclusion from this analysis is that rhetoric and formal policies might not accurately reflect the realities of implementation. The statistical measures offered here, admittedly not comprehensive, suggest that there is less variation than meets the eye, with the Netherlands an important exception. The risks of criminal sanctions for drug use do not seem to vary a great deal; the nations with aggressive rhetoric do not in fact arrest large numbers, and those arrests produce minimal sanctions. All nations make a reasonably serious effort to punish traffickers, with severe penalties for those convicted, except for marijuana. Treatment is moderately accessible throughout Europe, though variation in quality may be significant.

The Varieties of Drug Problems

It is difficult to make meaningful cross-national comparisons of the prevalence of drug use in the general population. Few nations conduct regular surveys; indeed, some (e.g., Italy) have conducted none at all, in itself an interesting indication of differences in attitudes toward drug use. Moreover, the surveys often have important differences in their population coverage and the questions asked.

Existing surveys support a few conclusions about prevalence, across nations and over time. First, throughout the 1980s, marijuana has been used by a moderate to high fraction of youth in most Western European nations. Around 1990, lifetime prevalence was generally in the 5 to 20 percent range for those around age fifteen (averaging around 10 percent), and in the 15 to 50 percent range for those around age eighteen (averaging around 40 percent). Bearing in mind that there are large error bands around these estimates, the United States was at the high end of this range, Spain and Sweden were at the low end, and the Netherlands was in the middle of the pack. By 1992, Dutch prevalence had grown sufficiently to match U.S. levels, possibly as a consequence of increased commercial access and promotion of cannabis (see MacCoun and Reuter 1997). Since 1992, prevalence has risen in the United States, Britain, the Netherlands, Canada, Australia, and other nations. This latter trend is not well understood and is not obviously linked to drug policies per se. Second, every Western industrial nation, except perhaps Sweden, suffered at least a moderate heroin epidemic in the last twenty years, and most have 2 to 3 addicts per 100,000 citizens. Third, cocaine has still not had a major impact on Europe, notwithstanding large and growing seizures. Amphetamines are at least as serious a problem as cocaine in most of Europe but are particularly significant in Scandinavia.

A sharp decline in drug use among the general U.S. population did not lead to a decline in the extent of drug dependence and related problems. The same appears to be true of Western Europe. The resolution of this apparent paradox lies simply in the fact that drug dependence is a chronic, lifelong relapsing condition for many current addicts. The drug-dependent population in the early 1990s consists mostly of persons who became dependent in the distant past. The prevalence of drug use among the general population determines the flow of new users into the dependent category, so the decline in that prevalence simply lowered or ended the growth in drug dependence, as best indicated by the increasing age of the heroin-dependent in the United States and Western Europe.

Drug-Related Harms. As already mentioned, drug problems are measured by more than simply the number of drug users. The contribution of needle sharing to the spread of HIV has been a major concern throughout most of Western Europe and has had a profound impact on drug policy in a number of countries. In Italy, Spain, and Switzerland, intravenous drug use has been the primary source of AIDS cases. It has also been a significant factor in France, but this finding turns out to have a heavy regional component; the percentage is high for the south of France but not for Paris, the other major region affected by AIDS. Scandinavia, Britain, and the Netherlands have so far experienced much weaker links between drug use and HIV.

Almost all European nations publish annual figures on drug overdoses; unfortunately, it turns out that definitional differences are so great as to make cross-country comparison almost impossible except for subgroups that have roughly comparable definitions and data collection processes. It has been said, for example, that French authorities will record a death as drug-related only if a needle is still stuck in the arm, while the Germans will include a driving fatality of a onetime client of a drug treatment clinic. Notwithstanding these differences, it is possible to make comparisons over time, since the recording systems seem to have been reasonably stable over the last decade. These data, presented in Figure 8.6, show extremely rapid increases for a number of countries (Denmark, France, Germany, Italy, Spain, and Switzerland) along with reasonably stable figures for others (Britain, Netherlands, Norway, and Sweden).

In all nations, studies indicate high crime rates among drug users, particularly among frequent users of heroin. A few descriptive studies have provided data on the sources of income of those dependent on heroin or cocaine. Variations among nations might reflect differences in sampling and measurement, but the figures are intriguing. In each sample, less than half of addict income comes from licit sources: 48 percent in Amsterdam (33 percent excluding prostitution, which is legal), 18 percent in Liverpool, 7 percent in Oslo, and 20 percent in New York (Bretteville-Jensen and Sutton 1996; Grapendaal, Leuw, and Nelen 1995).

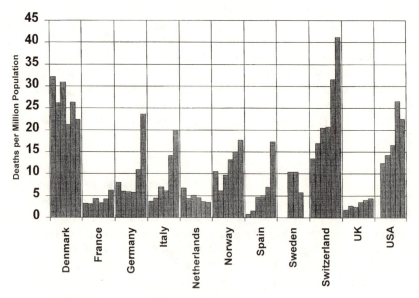

Figure 8.6 Overdose deaths per 1 million population, 1980–1990 (in 2-year intervals). *Source:* MacCoun et al. 1995.

Conclusions

Cross-national comparisons of social policy are fraught with problems. Nonetheless, we draw four lessons. First, European experiences suggest that *depenalization*—the elimination of criminal sanctions for the possession or use of drugs for personal consumption—has little consequence for the extent and severity of drug problems. Depenalization does not clearly increase the demand for drugs, as feared by drug hawks, but, unlike outright legalization, it does little to address the crime and violence associated with drug markets. The severity of the problems we observe arises largely as a result of black markets subject to aggressive enforcement against sellers (MacCoun, Reuter, and Schelling 1996).

Second, the *prevalence* of drug use and the *severity* of drug problems are not related in any simple way; that is, those nations in which a higher fraction of the population has at least experimented with an illicit drug do not necessarily have a more serious drug problem, as measured by the number of those estimated to be drug-dependent or the severity of the aggregate problems resulting from that dependence.

Third, there is considerable variation in the *goals* of drug policy, reflecting differences in the salience of particular aspects of the drug problem; these differences have important consequences for the choice of drug policies. Most notably, several European nations and many European cities have explicitly adopted a *harm reduction* strategy that differs in important ways from the *use reduction* philosophy widely held in the United

States (Heather et al. 1993). If valid, our proposition that prevalence of use and severity of harm are only loosely coupled would suggest the potential benefit of adopting a harm reduction strategy in the United States.

Fourth, we note that many aspects of drug policy are determined not by goals or decisions about the potential efficacy of various drug control strategies but by expectations about, or traditions of, the role of government. National debates about drug control choices are highly constrained, and in each country only certain options are considered. For example, the Swedish population accepts a paternalistic state and will tolerate highly intrusive rules, while in Spain the long experience with the authoritarian Franco regime has created a strong suspicion of any laws that allow the government to regulate private conduct. Drug policies reflect these differences.

Future Trends in U.S. Policy Problems and Research

As currently implemented, U.S. drug policies are unconvincing. They are intrusive, as illustrated by the prevalence of drug testing in the workplace; divisive, because of the disproportionate share of the burdens borne by minority communities; expensive, with an approximate $30 billion annual expenditure on drug control; and yet they leave the nation with a massive drug problem.

There is precious little debate about most aspects of drug policy. Though the 1996 presidential campaign is hardly the gold standard for policy debates, it is quite representative of the quality of the U.S. drug policy debates. The only matters discussed were the extent and credibility of presidential rhetoric and whether there should be more money for interdiction of drugs on their way into the United States. These are at most second-order issues. A wide range of important policies and programs, such as secondary prevention, severity of sentencing for drug offenders, and the growing link between public assistance and drug use, remained undiscussed.

A passionate but largely inconsequential debate has grown up around the proposition that the heart of our problems is prohibition itself. After all, it is argued, most of the crime, death, and disease associated with cocaine, heroin, and marijuana are the result of the drugs being expensive; moreover, there is a consensus that alcohol prohibition failed (Nadelmann 1989). However, though the legalizers get a great deal of media attention and attract sharp attacks from officials at all levels of government, they have not affected the mainstream discussion of drug policy and have achieved no increase in public acceptance. Regrettably, even those who advocate "harm reduction" in the context of prohibition, building on European experiences, have failed to get much of a hearing, in part because of some who see harm reduction (as well as medical marijuana) as a Trojan horse designed to undermine prohibition.

As a consequence, there are reasons to believe that there will be little change in the character of American drug policy in the foreseeable future. It might well continue to be highly punitive, notwithstanding the doubts that any reasonable analysis raises concerning the effectiveness of this emphasis on punishment, particularly the very long federal prison sentences served by low-level drug dealers. High-profile studies showing that treatment, even not very good treatment, is highly cost-effective in terms of crime averted, and that treatment deserves a larger share of the next billion dollars of drug control expenditures than does any kind of enforcement (Rydell and Everingham 1994), have failed to have any policy impact. The drug problem is seen as a component of America's extraordinary crime problem, and thus punishment is viewed as the appropriate response. This manifests itself each time a new drug emerges as a problem; there is a quick call for raising the strictness of criminal penalties for that drug, as happened with amphetamines in 1995. On the other hand, the sizable victories for medical marijuana initiatives in November 1996 in California and Arizona at least suggest the possibility that American views are shifting, perhaps because the baby boom and post-boom cohorts (many of whom inhaled during youthful indiscretions) make up an increasing proportion of the electorate.

Predicting how the drug problem will change is somewhere between difficult and impossible. No one has created any models for projecting patterns of drug use in the general population. The recent upturn, starting in 1992, came as a surprise. David Musto (1987) had long referred to "generational forgetting," the notion that the problems associated with a particular drug would be forgotten after that drug had become less prevalent for a generation, but this is a very general statement with a slender empirical base. Nor are there models projecting what fraction of those who try marijuana will become dependent on some other drug and thus contribute substantially to the nation's crime and health problems.

It is clear, however, that the current population of users dependent on cocaine and heroin is likely to continue in that state for some years to come; Rydell and Everingham (1994) estimated that even if there were no new cocaine users after 1992, it would take ten years before cocaine consumption would fall by half. Heroin consumption has remained fairly stable despite low levels of initiation in the last twenty years. As both drug-using populations become older and suffer from poorer health, the problems they cause society may actually increase.

There are claims of a new heroin epidemic among middle-class young adults. Stories accumulate of heroin deaths on college campuses or other unexpected settings. With heroin prices low and the higher purity allowing snorting rather than injecting of the drug, it is quite plausible that such an upsurge is under way. However, none of the existing indicator systems show this increase. It is particularly surprising that there has been no upturn in the share of young arrestees testing positive for heroin.

What might the sensible reformer aim at as a reasonable target for drug policy in the United States? Though there are some slogans, such as the "public health model," there is a dearth of evidence for more than a few programmatic innovations, such as needle exchange and increased use of treatment options for certain drug-involved offenders. In our view, the Netherlands harm reduction approach, which integrates harm reduction and use reduction strategies within a largely prohibitionist legal regime, seems most promising if the goal is to reduce total drug-related harm. Unfortunately, the preconditions for such a pragmatic policy seem to be lacking in the United States.

A plausible starting point for changing American drug policy is reformulating its goals. The principal (and almost exclusive) goal of drug policy in the United States has been a reduction in the numbers of users—thus the extraordinary attention to the annual estimates of the prevalence of drug use, particularly among adolescents. This preoccupation with prevalence has left the nation ill equipped to cope with the minority of users who consume the majority of drugs and contribute the bulk of the crime and illness associated with drug use; it has diverted attention away from treatment and toward punishment, and led us to forgo opportunities for significantly reducing the rate of HIV transmission (through needle exchange). A more comprehensive set of goals, seeking an appropriate balance between the reduction of harms and the reduction of use, might produce a less divisive and intrusive set of policies.

Acknowledgments   The research reported here was supported by a grant from the Alfred P. Sloan Foundation to RAND's Drug Policy Research Center.

Note

1. We consider here only illicit drugs; in particular, no effort is made to examine policies toward alcohol, though alcohol is responsible for vastly more morbidity and mortality than all the illicit drugs put together (Rice et al. 1990).

References

Anglin, M. Douglas, and Yih-Ing Hser. 1990. "Treatment of Drug Abuse." In *Drugs and Crime,* edited by Michael Tonry and James Q. Wilson. Chicago: University of Chicago Press.

Bachman, Jerald G., Lloyd D. Johnston, and Patrick M. O'Malley. 1990. "Explaining the Recent Decline in Cocaine Use Among Young Adults: Further Evidence That Perceived Risks and Disapproval Lead to Reduced Drug Use." *Journal of Health and Social Behavior* 31:173–84.

Ball, John, Lawrence Rosen, John Flueck, and David N. Narco. 1982. "Lifetime Criminality of Heroin Addicts in the United States." *Journal of Drug Issues* 12:225–39.

Ball, John, and A. Ross. 1991. *The Effectiveness of Methadone Maintenance Treatment: Patients, Programs, Services, and Outcomes.* New York: Springer-Verlag.

Botvin, G. J., E. Baker, L. Dusenbury, E. M. Botvin, and T. Diaz. 1995. "Long-Term Follow-Up Results of a Randomized Drug Abuse Prevention Trial in a White Middle-Class Population." *Journal of the American Medical Association* 273:1106–12.

Braithwaite, John. 1989. *Crime, Shame, and Reintegration.* Cambridge: Cambridge University Press.

Bretteville-Jensen, A. L., and M. Sutton. 1996. "The Income-Generating Behavior of Injecting Drug Users in Oslo." *Addiction* 91:63–80.

Bureau of Justice Statistics. Various years. *Correctional Populations in the United States.* Washington, D.C.: U.S. Department of Justice, Bureau of Justice Statistics.

Caulkins, Jonathan, and Peter Reuter. 1996. "Editorial: The Meaning and Utility of Drug Prices." *Addiction* 91:1261–64.

Ellickson, Phyllis L. 1995. "Schools." In *Handbook on Drug Abuse Prevention,* edited by R. H. Coombs and D. M. Ziedonis. Needham Heights, Mass.: Allyn and Bacon.

Ellickson, Phyllis L., Robert M. Bell, and Kimberly McGuigan. 1993. "Preventing Adolescent Drug Use: Long-Term Results of a Junior High Program." *American Journal of Public Health* 83:856–61.

Farrell, Michael, Jan Neelman, Michael Gossop, Paul Griffiths, Ernst Buning, Emily Finch, and John Strang. 1996. *A Review of the Legislation, Regulation, and Delivery of Methadone in 12 Member States of the European Union: Final Report.* Luxembourg: Office for Official Publications of the European Communities.

Federal Bureau of Investigation. Various years. *Uniform Crime Reports for the United States.* Washington, D.C.: U.S. Government Printing Office.

Gerstein, Dean, Hendrik Harwood, Natalie Suter, and Kathryn Malloy. 1994. *Evaluating Recovery Services: The California Drug and Alcohol Treatment Assessment (CALDATA).* Sacramento: California Department of Alcohol and Drug Programs.

Goldstein, Paul. 1985. "The Drug/Violence Nexus: A Tripartite Concept Framework." *Journal of Drug Issues* 14:493–506.

Goldstein, Paul, Henry Brownstein, and Patrick Ryan. 1992. "Drug-Related Homicide in New York: 1984 and 1988." *Crime and Delinquency* 38:459–76.

Grapendaal, Martin, Ed Leuw, and Hans Nelen. 1995. *A World of Opportunities: Lifestyle and Economic Behavior of Heroin Addicts in Amsterdam.* Albany: State University of New York Press.

Heather, Nicholas, Alex Wodak, Ethan Nadelmann, and Patrick O'Hare, eds. 1993. *Psychoactive Drugs and Harm Reduction: From Faith to Science.* London: Whurr.

Hser, Yih-ing, M. Douglas Anglin, and Keiko Powers. 1993. "A 24-Year Follow-Up of California Narcotics Addicts." *Archives of General Psychiatry* 50:577–84.

Johnston, Lloyd, Patrick O'Malley, and Jerald Bachman. 1994. *National Survey Results on Drug Use from the Monitoring the Future Study, 1975–1994.* Rockville, Md.: National Institute on Drug Abuse.

Kandel, Denise B. 1993. "The Social Demography of Drug Use." *Millbank Quarterly* 69:365–414.

Kleiman, Mark. 1992. *Against Excess: Drug Policy for Results.* New York: Basic Books.

MacCoun, Robert. 1993. "Drugs and the Law: A Psychological Analysis of Drug Prohibition." *Psychological Bulletin* 113:497–512.

———. 1996. "The Psychology of Harm Reduction: Alternative Strategies for Modifying High-Risk Behavior." In *1996 Wellness Lectures.* Oakland, Calif.: California Wellness Foundation and University of California.

MacCoun, Robert, Karyn Model, Heide Phillips-Shockley, and Peter Reuter. 1995. "Comparing Drug Policies in North America and Western Europe." In *Policies and Strategies to Combat Drugs in Europe,* edited by G. Estievehart. Dordrecht: Academic Publishers.

MacCoun, Robert, and Peter Reuter. 1997. "Interpreting Dutch Cannabis Policy: Reasoning by Analogy in the Legalization Debate." *Science* 278: 47–52.

MacCoun, Robert, Peter Reuter, and Thomas Schelling. 1996. "Assessing Alternative Drug Control Regimes." *Journal of Policy Analysis and Management* 15:1–23.

MacCoun, Robert, Aaron Saiger, James Kahan, and Peter Reuter. 1993. "Drug Policies and Problems: The Promise and Pitfalls of Cross-National Comparisons." In *Psychoactive Drugs and Harm Reduction: From Faith to Science,* edited by Nicholas Heather, Alex Wodak, Ethan Nadelmann, and Patrick O'Hare. London: Whurr.

Musto, David. 1987. *The American Disease: Origins of Narcotic Control.* Rev. ed. New York: Oxford University Press.

Nadelmann, Ethan. 1989. "Drug Prohibition in the United States: Costs, Consequences and Alternatives." *Science* 245:739–47.

Normand, Jacques, David Vlahov, and Lincoln E. Moses, eds. 1995. *Preventing HIV Transmission: The Role of Sterile Needles and Bleach.* Washington, D.C.: National Research Council and Institute of Medicine.

Office of National Drug Control Policy. Various years. *National Drug Control Strategy.* Washington, D.C.: U.S. Government Printing Office

Reuter, Peter, G. Crawford, and J. Cave. 1988. *Sealing the Borders: The Effect of Increased Military Participation in Drug Interdiction.* Santa Monica, Calif.: RAND.

Reuter, Peter, and Mark Kleiman. 1986. "Risks and Prices: An Economic Analysis of Drug Enforcement." In *Crime and Justice: An Annual Review of Research,* vol. 7, edited by Michael Tonry and Norval Morris. Chicago: University of Chicago Press.

Reuter, Peter, Robert MacCoun, and Patrick Murphy. 1990. *Money from Crime.* Santa Monica, Calif.: RAND.

Rhodes, William, P. Scheiman, T. Pittayathikhun, L. Collins, and V. Tsarfaty. 1995. *What America's Users Spend on Illegal Drugs, 1988–1993.* Washington, D.C.: Office of National Drug Control Policy.

Rice, Dorothy, Sander Kelman, Leonard Miller, and Sarah Dunmeyer. 1990. *The Economic Costs of Alcohol and Drug Abuse and Mental Illness, 1985.* Rockville, Md.: Alcohol, Drug Abuse and Mental Health Administration.

Rydell, Peter, and Susan Everingham. 1994. *The Costs of Cocaine Control.* Santa Monica, Calif.: RAND.

Saner, Hilary, Robert J. MacCoun, and Peter Reuter. 1995. "On the Ubiquity of Drug Selling Among Youthful Offenders in Washington, D.C., 1985–1991: Age, Period, or Cohort Effect?" *Journal of Quantitative Criminology* 11:337–62.

Shedler, J., and J. Block. 1990. "Adolescent Drug Use and Psychological Health: A Longitudinal Inquiry." *American Psychologist* 45:612–30.

Single, Eric W. 1988. "The Availability of Alcohol: Prior Research and Future Directions." *Drug and Alcohol Review* 7:273–84.

Substance Abuse and Mental Health Services Administration. 1996. *National Household Survey on Drug Abuse: Main Findings, 1994*. Rockville, Md.: U.S. Department of Health and Human Services.

Tobler, Nancy S. 1992. "Drug Prevention Programs Can Work: Research Findings." *Journal of Addictive Diseases* 11:1–28.

Tonry, Michael. 1995. *Malign Neglect*. New York: Oxford University Press.

Wever, Leon. 1992. "Drug Policy Changes in Europe and the USA." *International Journal of Drug Policy* 3:176–81.

Zinberg, Norman. 1984. *Drug, Set and Setting: The Basis for Controlled Intoxicant Use*. New Haven, Conn.: Yale University Press.

Part III

CAUSES OF CRIME

9

Individual Differences and Offending

DAVID P. FARRINGTON

It is plausible to assume that offending, like all other types of behavior, arises from the interaction between the individual and the environment. This chapter focuses on the individual side of the equation. Explanations of the development of criminal persons (i.e., persons with a relatively high likelihood of committing criminal acts in different situations) are not at all incompatible with explanations of the occurrence of criminal acts. On the contrary, a comprehensive theory of crime should aim to explain both.

It is clear that individuals differ in their potential to commit criminal and related types of antisocial acts, given a particular opportunity, situation, or victim. Since "crime" is a socially and legally defined type of behavior, any potential to commit crimes is probably part of a broader potential to commit antisocial acts, but this chapter focuses particularly on crimes. The word *potential* (equivalent to *tendency*) is used in preference to *propensity* or *predisposition* to describe the key theoretical construct underlying regularities in behavior, in order to avoid possible connotations of biological determinism.

An important assumption is that individual differences in criminal potential (or, more precisely, the rank orderings of individuals in terms of criminal potential) are relatively stable over time and in different environments. A great deal of criminal career research (e.g., Farrington 1997a) shows continuity and relative stability in offending over time; even though the absolute level of offending and different types of offending vary with age, the "worst" people at one age tend to be the "worst" at a later age. Similarly, criminal career research shows a great deal of versatility and not much specialization in offending; it is almost as though the most antisocial people commit different types of offenses at random, depending presumably on situational factors and circumstances.

Criminal potential may be disaggregated into many different dimensions, some of which are probably different names for the same underlying construct. Descriptions such as antisocial, aggressive, or hostile seem essentially to refer to people with high criminal potential. Constructs such as low guilt, weak conscience, low self-control, high impulsivity, emotional coldness, callousness, low empathy, fearlessness, egocentricity (self-centeredness), poor conditionability, a poor ability to delay gratification, and a poor ability to manipulate abstract concepts seem more likely to be causes of high criminal potential. Obviously, it is important to establish the key underlying constructs that are linked to individual differences in offending behavior. For ease of exposition, this section focuses on criminal potential.

Long-term *between*-individual differences in criminal potential (intended to explain why some people are more likely to commit offenses in a particular situation than are other people) can be distinguished from short-term *within*-individual variations in criminal potential (intended to explain why people are more likely to commit crimes at some times and in some situations than in other times and situations). Long-term criminal potential is likely to be influenced by biological, individual, family, peer, school, community, and societal factors. Short-term criminal potential is likely to be influenced by situational events such as getting insulted or frustrated, getting drunk, or seeing a tempting criminal opportunity. While both topics are important, the focus in this chapter is on long-term differences in criminal potential.

Criminal potential is likely to depend on energizing, directing, and inhibiting processes (Farrington 1993). Energizing processes are often based on needs: for money, excitement, status with peers, revenge, attention, pleasure, or sexual gratification; to demonstrate toughness; to reduce tension; to escape an unpleasant situation; and so on. Directing processes determine how a person aims to achieve these goals—legally or by criminal or antisocial acts. Any resulting tendency to offend may be opposed by internal inhibitions such as conscience, guilt, or self-control. How the criminal potential becomes the actuality of the criminal act in any situation is likely to depend on cognitive (thinking, decision-making, and problem-solving) processes, as, for example, in the rational choice theory of Clarke and Cornish (1985). There can be individual differences in energizing, directing, inhibiting, and cognitive processes, but in practice most of the relevant research focuses on inhibiting processes.

This chapter aims to summarize knowledge about the most important biological and psychological individual difference factors that are related to offending. It examines genetic, psychophysiological, biochemical, and neuropsychological factors; intelligence, impulsivity, personality, moral reasoning, psychopathy, and sociocognitive factors; and some relevant intervention techniques. Because of space limitations, and in the interests of communicating to a wide and diverse audience, this chapter inevitably oversimplifies some complex issues and is highly selective in reviewing only the most salient studies; for more extensive reviews, see Raine (1993) on biological factors and Blackburn (1993) on psychological factors. The focus here is on explaining the definition and measurement of factors, on describing predictors of offending, and on choosing studies that use self-report and official measures of offending. Most of the research focuses on males.

Biological Influences on Offending

Biological influences can be partitioned into genetic, psychophysiological, neurochemical and hormonal, and neuropsychological factors.

Genetic Factors

There is no doubt that offending tends to run in families: criminal parents tend to have criminal children. For example, in the Cambridge Study in Delinquent Development, which is a long-term study of over 400 London males, 63 percent of men with convicted biological fathers were themselves convicted up to age forty, compared with 30 percent of men with unconvicted biological fathers (Farrington, Barnes, and Lambert 1996). However, the intergenerational transmission of criminality does not necessarily indicate any genetic transmission of criminal potential: this transmission could equally be achieved through environmental influences.

Special behavioral genetic designs are needed to disentangle genetic from environmental influences. The first involves the comparison of identical (monozygotic) and fraternal (dizygotic) same-sex twin pairs. Identical twins share 100 percent of their genes, whereas fraternal twins share about 50 percent of their genes. Arguably, however, the members of both types of twin pairs are exposed to the same shared family environmental influences. According to the rationale of the twin study, if genetic factors are of no importance, identical twins will be no more similar to each other than are fraternal twins. To the extent that genetic factors are important, identical twins should be more similar to each other than are fraternal twins.

The results obtained with twin studies are quite consistent: identical twins are more concordant in their offending than fraternal twins. Raine (1993, p. 56) summarized results from existing studies and found an average concordance rate of 52 percent for identical twins and 21 percent for fraternal twins. However, critics have argued that this is not convincing evidence of a genetic effect because, for example, identical twins are generally treated more similarly (because they look identical) than are fraternal twins. Hence, the greater behavioral similarity of the identical twins could reflect their greater environmental similarity.

The second design involves the study of children who were separated at birth from their biological parents and brought up by adoptive parents. According to the rationale of this design, these adopted children share genetic but not environmental factors with their biological parents, and they share environmental but not genetic factors with their adoptive parents. Hence, the similarity in offending between adopted children and their biological parents should be an indicator of the importance of genetic factors, while the similarity in offending between these children and their adoptive parents should be an indicator of the importance of environmental factors.

Again, the results obtained in adoption studies are quite consistent: generally, the offending of adopted children is significantly related to the offending of their biological parents (Raine 1993, p. 62). However, critics have argued that this is not convincing evidence of a genetic effect, because some children were separated after birth or otherwise may have had some contact with their biological parents, because adoption agencies may have matched characteristics of adoptive and biological parents, or because the link between convicted biological parents and convicted children could have been mediated by some kind of negative labeling effect.

The third, most convincing, design involves comparing the concordance of identical twins reared together and identical twins reared apart. To the extent that environmental factors are important, identical twins reared together will be more similar in their offending than identical twins reared apart. To the extent that genetic factors are important, identical twins reared apart will be just as similar in their offending as identical twins reared together, according to the rationale of this design.

Unfortunately, it is difficult to obtain large samples of identical twins reared in totally different environments from birth. At the present time, there appears to be no adequate study of offending using this method. However, the Minnesota Study of Twins Reared Apart retrospectively assessed the heritability of childhood conduct disorder and adult antisocial personality disorder (measured by the Diagnostic Interview Schedule). The heritability of a trait is the proportion of the total variation in it that is attributable to genetic factors. Grove et al. (1990) found that heritability was 41 percent for childhood conduct disorder and 28 percent for adult antisocial personality disorder. Again, therefore, there are indications of some kind of genetic influence on antisocial behavior, although these heritabilities are lower than those obtained in the largest study of unseparated twins, by Christiansen: 50 percent for violent crimes and 78 percent for property crimes (Cloninger and Gottesman 1987, p. 100).

Raine (1993, pp. 48–54) has attempted to deal with many common arguments concerning genetics and crime. For example, it might be argued that criminality specifically cannot be inherited because crime is socially and legally defined. Nevertheless, genes could influence factors related to criminal potential, such as impulsiveness or aggressiveness, or they could influence biological processes such as neurotransmitters. Another argument is that, to the extent that a trait is genetically influenced, it is fixed at birth and cannot be changed. However, what is fixed at conception is the genetic potential, or "genotype"; the observed behavioral expression of the trait, or "phenotype," depends crucially on environmental factors. For example, height has high heritability, but nutrition in childhood crucially affects the actual height achieved.

Raine (1993) concluded that there was some genetic influence on criminal potential, and that this might be greater for females than for males and greater for adult crime than for juvenile delinquency. He also recommended that there should be more attempts to investigate the ways in which genetic and environmental factors interacted to influence offending. However, little is known about the precise genes that might be involved, or about the precise individual factors related to criminal potential that might be genetically transmitted.

Psychophysiological Factors

Psychophysiology is concerned with the relationship between constructs such as arousal and emotion and physiological measures such as heart rate, skin conductance, and electroencephalographic (EEG) activity. Heart rate can easily be measured by taking the pulse rate. Skin conductance is an indicator of the electrical activity of the skin. It is usually measured from electrodes placed on the hand; increased sweating leads to increased skin conductance. The electroencephalogram measures the electrical activity of the brain (sometimes referred to as "brain waves") and is recorded from electrodes placed on the scalp.

Low arousal and low anxiety are key constructs measured by these psychophysiological variables. As individuals become more aroused and more anxious, their heart rate and skin conductance increase, and the frequency of their alpha waves on the EEG increases. It is hypothesized that people with low arousal and low anxiety are particularly likely to become offenders. Low arousal and boredom lead to sensation seeking and risk taking to increase arousal. Individuals with low anxiety tend to have low internal inhibitions against offending and low guilt.

A related theory focuses on the Behavioral Inhibition System (BIS; Gray 1975), a psychophysiological system whose function is to inhibit behavior in the presence of punishment cues or the threat of punishment. Behavioral inhibition is linked to fearfulness; people with low BIS functioning tend to have low heart rates and low skin conductance, and they tend to be uninhibited, fearless, and antisocial. Some of the relevant research on these theories is concerned with psychophysiological reactivity, but the simplest and most replicable results have been obtained by measuring resting levels of heart rate, skin conductance, and EEG activity.

According to Raine (1993, pp. 166–72), one of the most replicable findings in the literature is that antisocial and criminal people tend to have relatively low heart rates. This was true in the Cambridge Study, where heart rate was measured at age eighteen. More than twice as many of the boys with low heart rates (sixty-five beats per minute or less) were convicted for violence as of the remainder (Farrington 1997b). A low resting heart rate was also significantly associated with self-reported violence and teacher-reported aggression. Furthermore, a low heart rate was significantly related to all three measures of violence independently of all other variables measured in this project. (This was true of only one other variable, namely, poor concentration.)

Raine, Venables, and Williams (1990) measured heart rate, skin conductance, and EEG activity in fifteen-year-old boys, and then measured their convictions up to age twenty-four. The researchers found that low heart rate, low skin conductance, and low-frequency (alpha and theta) brain wave activity all predicted convictions. Other variables (low school achievement, low socioeconomic status, and living in a high-crime area) also predicted convictions but were not related to these psychophysiological measures. Hence, Raine and his colleagues concluded that low cardiovascular, electrodermal, and cortical arousal all predicted offending, independently of academic and social factors.

Neurochemical and Hormonal Factors

Neurotransmitters are chemicals stored in brain cells that carry information between these cells. There are many neurotransmitters, but serotonin has been most replicably related to offending. Low serotonin has been linked to low cortical arousal and low BIS functioning. Unfortunately, the measurement of serotonin levels in the brain requires invasive techniques. The most direct measure involves assessing serotonin metabolites (e.g., 5HIAA) in the cerebrospinal fluid, which requires a lumbar puncture (a needle inserted in the spine). Consequently, most studies have been based on small numbers (typically about thirty) of antisocial or violent patients in hospitals. Nevertheless, these studies reliably show that such patients have low brain serotonin levels (Raine 1993, p. 87).

The largest investigation of the relationship between serotonin and violence was carried out by Moffitt et al. (1997) in the Dunedin Multidisciplinary Health and Development Study in New Zealand. This is a prospective longitudinal survey of over 1,000 children from age three onward. At age twenty-one, 97 percent of the participants who were still alive were interviewed, and 82 percent gave blood samples. Moffitt and her colleagues found that men who were convicted for violence, and those who were high on self-reported violence, tended to have high blood serotonin levels. High blood serotonin levels indicate low brain serotonin levels. These relationships held up after controlling for socioeconomic status, intelligence, smoking, drinking, drug use, and other variables. Interestingly, the relationship between serotonin and violence was stronger for men from disharmonious, noncohesive families. Serotonin was not related to violence among the women.

Hormones, biochemical substances that carry information, are secreted into the bloodstream by endocrine organs located throughout the body. The hormone that has been studied most in relation to offending is testosterone, which is produced by the testes. Testosterone levels are typically measured in blood or saliva samples. Studies of a wide variety of animal species show that when the animals are reproductively active, testosterone facilitates aggression between males, leading to the hypothesis that high testosterone levels in boys from puberty onward might be related to violence.

Most studies of testosterone and aggression have measured verbal aggression rather than physical violence. For example, Olweus (1986, p. 53) found that items such as "When a boy starts fighting with me, I fight back" were significantly correlated with plasma testosterone levels in Stockholm boys aged fifteen to seventeen. However, results of such studies are not always consistent. Comparisons between violent and nonviolent male and female prisoners show significant and replicable associations between high testosterone levels and violence (Archer 1991). Also, testosterone levels were related to adult self-reported violence in a large sample of Vietnam veterans (Windle and Windle 1995).

In the Montreal longitudinal-experimental study, which is a follow-up of Montreal boys from age six, teacher ratings of fighting and bullying were associated with low testosterone levels (in saliva) at age thirteen but with high testosterone levels at age sixteen (Tremblay et al. 1997, p. 281). These results suggest that high testosterone levels after puberty might be related to youth violence.

Neuropsychology and Brain Dysfunction

Neuropsychology is the study of the brain mechanisms that control behavior. To some extent, it is assumed that functions are localized in certain areas of the brain (although there are many exceptions to this). In particular, it is assumed that the "executive functions" of abstract reasoning, anticipation and planning, sustaining attention and concentration, and inhibiting inappropriate behavior are located in the frontal lobes. It follows that damage to the frontal lobes leads to impairment in abstract reasoning and concept formation, lack of foresight and insight, poor concentration, low anxiety, and uninhibited behavior. This "frontal lobe syndrome" is related to offending (Moffitt 1990).

Interest in the frontal lobes began with the famous case of Phineas Gage, a railway worker in the nineteenth century who was the victim of an accident in which an iron rod was blown through his forehead. Amazingly, he survived the accident, but his personality changed dramatically. Before the accident, he was a capable foreman and a reliable worker who was not obviously antisocial. After the accident, he was described as impulsive, irreverent, capricious, frequently swearing, with the intellectual capacity of a child but the animal passions of a strong man (Harlow 1848).

Neuropsychological functioning is usually measured using tests of abstract reasoning, problem solving, sustaining attention and concentration, planning of goal-oriented motor behavior skills, learning of contingency rules, and anticipating of future events in the regulation of behavior. These tests are based on studies of patients with known neurological damage or neurological diseases. Because specific types of patients perform badly on a particular test, a low test score is presumed to indicate a specific (possibly subclinical) neurological dysfunction in the normal population. However, this inference is essentially indirect. In future studies, neurological functioning could be measured more directly using positron emission tomography or magnetic resonance imaging techniques.

Typically, offenders perform badly on neuropsychological tests. For example, in the Dunedin Study, male and female delinquents at age thirteen (defined according to self-reports, teacher reports, parent reports, or police arrests) showed significant impairment on verbal skills, auditory verbal memory, visuospatial analysis, and visual-motor integration (Moffitt 1990, p. 132). Their verbal deficits were more severe than their deficits on nonverbal tests. These results held up after controlling for family adversity measures (parental education, parental income, single-parent status, large family size, poor maternal health, and a disharmonious, noncohesive family). The delinquents who also had attention-deficit disorder were especially poor on measures of executive functioning.

It has also been argued that left-handed people (defined according to the hand used for writing) are more likely to be offenders (Ellis 1990). In right-handers, the left cerebral hemisphere is dominant, and language functions are localized in it. In left-handers, language can be localized in either the left or the right hemisphere, or even in both. Hence, left-handedness is a crude index of decreased brain lateralization for language and therefore may indicate poorer verbal abilities, less behavioral control, and more antisocial behavior, according to the theory. While results are not always consistent, the link between left-handedness and offending is more often supported than disconfirmed. For example, in the Cambridge Study, 55 percent of left-handed men at age eighteen were convicted up to age forty, compared with 39 percent of the remainder.

Interest in the link between neurological functioning and offending has stimulated studies of the relationship between pregnancy and birth complications and later offending. It is assumed that such complications may result in fetal brain damage, which in turn may lead to antisocial and criminal behavior (e.g., because of deficits in executive functioning). However, these studies rarely measure neurological damage or neuropsychological deficits directly, so it is difficult to know what fraction of pregnancy and birth complications actually led to brain damage.

In the Danish perinatal study, Kandel and Mednick (1991) followed up nearly 300 children born in Copenhagen in 1959–1961. They found that birth delivery complications predicted arrests for violence up to age twenty-two; 80 percent of violent offenders scored in the high range of delivery complications, compared with 30 percent of property offenders and 47 percent of nonoffenders. Interestingly, delivery complications especially predicted violence when one or both parents were psychiatrically disturbed. In a later analysis of the same project, Raine et al. (1996) showed that children who had neurological problems in the first week of life (measured by a full neonatal neurological examination conducted by a pediatrician) together with family adversity (early maternal rejection, family conflict, family instability, a criminal parent) were particularly likely to be arrested for violent and nonviolent crimes.

However, the importance of delivery complications was not found by Denno (1990) in the Philadelphia Biosocial Project, a follow-up of nearly 1,000 African-American births in Philadelphia in 1959–1962. Because it was part of the larger Collaborative Perinatal Project, this study included extensive data on pregnancy and delivery complications, but did not predict arrests for violence up to age twenty-two. For males, the only significant biological predictor of arrests in this study was lead intoxication at age seven. Also, pregnancy and delivery complications did not significantly predict official or self-reported offending in the Cambridge Study. It may be that pregnancy and delivery complications predict offending mainly or exclusively when they occur in combination with other family adversities.

Psychological Influences on Offending

An extensive meta-analysis by Lipsey and Derzon (1998) showed that low IQ and psychological factors such as hyperactivity, attention deficit, impulsivity, and risk taking were important predictors of later serious and violent offending.

Intelligence and School Attainment

The idea of objective intelligence testing grew up around the turn of the twentieth century, partly because of the expansion of state education in many countries and because of the perceived need for tests to measure the potential school success of children from different cultural, ethnic, and social class backgrounds. Reflecting the egalitarian spirit of the times, the aim was to develop tests of intellectual capacity that were independent of previous cultural experiences (Wilson and Herrnstein 1985).

The most influential psychologist in the development of intelligence tests was Alfred Binet, who developed tests of abstract reasoning, drawing analogies, and identifying patterns that were appropriate for children of different ages. From the relationship between a child's chronological age and his or her "mental age" (based on the average score of children of a particular age), the IQ was born. For example, if a child of eight achieved a score that was typical of a ten-year-old, that child's IQ would be 125 ($IQ = 100 \times 10/8$). IQ scores were arranged to have a mean of 100 and a standard deviation of about 15, so that about two-thirds of the population scored between 85 and 115. The tests were validated against school performance, so that IQ scores predicted ability to succeed in school. Essentially, IQ tests measure the ability to grasp the essentials of a problem and to respond speedily and accurately.

The use of IQ tests in schools increased greatly until the 1960s. The most widely used tests in the United States were the Wechsler tests (WISC for children and WAIS for adults). Beginning in the 1960s, fierce criticisms were leveled against IQ tests. According to Herrnstein and Murray (1994), this was because of research showing that IQ was highly heritable and that the average IQs of various socioeconomic and ethnic groups were significantly different. Critics argued, for example, that IQ tests were biased and that it was misleading to reduce all aspects of intellectual functioning to one or two numbers. The second of these arguments seems to have more force than the first; numerous attempts to prove bias in testing have not been very successful (Cole 1981).

Despite controversy about the merits of IQ tests, they have been used in numerous criminological studies. Taken together, the results show conclusively that offenders have significantly lower IQ scores than nonoffenders. For example, in the Cambridge Study, one-third of the boys scoring 90 or lower on a nonverbal IQ test (Raven's Progressive Matrices, measuring abstract reasoning) at ages eight to ten were convicted as juveniles—twice as many as among the remainder (Farrington 1992). Low nonverbal IQ was highly correlated with low verbal IQ (measuring vocabulary, word comprehension, and verbal reasoning) and with low school attainment at age eleven; all of these measures predicted juvenile convictions to much the same extent.

Furthermore, low nonverbal IQ predicted self-reported delinquency almost as well as convictions, suggesting that the link between low IQ and delinquency was not caused by the less intelligent boys having a greater probability of being caught. Low nonverbal IQ was about as strong a predictor of juvenile convictions as other important variables (low family income, large family size, poor parental child-rearing behavior, poor parental supervision, and poor concentration), but it was a weaker predictor than having a convicted parent or a daring (risk-taking) personality. Low IQ was a significant predictor of offending in some regression analyses but not in others (depending on the measure of offending).

Low IQ measured very early in life predicts later offending. For example, in a prospective longitudinal survey of Stockholm males, low IQ measured at age three significantly predicted officially recorded offending up to age thirty (Stattin and Klackenberg-Larsson 1993). Frequent offenders (those with four or more offenses) had an average IQ of 88 at age three, whereas nonoffenders had an average IQ of 101. All of these results held up after controlling for social class. Similarly, low IQ at age four predicted arrests up to age twenty-seven in the Perry Preschool Project and court delinquency up to age seventeen in the Collaborative Perinatal Project (Lipsitt, Buka, and Lipsitt 1990; Schweinhart, Barnes, and Weikart 1993).

While the relationship between low IQ and offending is not in doubt, the same cannot be said for the interpretation of it. The two most popular explanations focus on the executive functioning of the brain or on school failure as an intervening variable. When a Wechsler IQ test is used, offenders often perform worse on the verbal subtests than on the nonverbal subtests. This pattern suggests that they find it easier to manipulate concrete objects than abstract concepts, and it is consistent with a deficit in executive functioning. Alternatively, it is argued that IQ tests are designed to measure ability to succeed in school (which may be a different construct from "intelligence"). Hence, low IQ predicts school failure, and there are many criminological theories suggesting that school failure leads to delinquency (e.g., via the intervening construct of status deprivation; Cohen 1955).

Lynam, Moffitt, and Stouthamer-Loeber (1993) completed one of the most important attempts to test these and other possible explanations, using data collected in the Pittsburgh Youth Study, a prospective longitudinal survey of Pittsburgh boys. Unfortunately, their conclusions vary according to the ethnicity of the boys. For African-American boys, low verbal IQ led to school failure and subsequently to self-reported delinquency, but for Caucasian boys the relationship between low verbal IQ and self-reported delinquency held after controlling for all other variables. It may be that poor executive functioning and school failure are plausible explanations of the link between low IQ and offending.

Hyperactivity and Impulsivity

A bewildering number of constructs refer to a poor ability to control behavior. These include hyperactivity, restlessness, clumsiness, impulsiveness, not considering consequences before acting, a poor ability to plan ahead, short time horizons, low self-control, sensation seeking, risk taking, and a poor ability to delay gratification. There are also a number of ways to measure these constructs, including psychomotor tests such as the Porteus Mazes (which measure clumsiness, motor coordination, and the ability to plan ahead); self-report questionnaires (including items such as "I often do and say things without thinking"); ratings by parents, teachers, and peers; and various other psychological tests (e.g., where a child chooses between a small immediate reward and a large delayed one, in order to measure ability to delay gratification). Virtually all these constructs, measured in different ways, are significantly related to measures of offending (Blackburn 1993, pp. 191–96).

Impulsivity is the central construct in two of the most important criminological theories, by Wilson and Herrnstein (1985) and by Gottfredson and Hirschi (1990). Wilson and Herrnstein suggested that whether a person chooses to commit a crime in any situation depends on whether the expected benefits of offending outweigh the expected costs. The benefits of offending, including material gain, peer approval, and sexual gratification, tend to be contemporaneous with the crime. In contrast, many of the costs of offending, such as the risk of being caught and punished, and the possible loss of reputation or employment, are uncertain and long-delayed. Other costs, such as pangs of conscience (or guilt), disapproval by onlookers, and retaliation by the victim are more immediate. As in many other theories, Wilson and Herrnstein emphasize the importance of the conscience as an internal inhibitor of offending, and suggest that it is built up in a conditioning process according to parental reinforcement or punishment of childhood transgressions.

The key individual difference factor in the Wilson-Herrnstein theory is the extent to which people's behavior is influenced by immediate as opposed to delayed consequences. As in other psychological theories, they suggest that individuals vary in their ability to think about or plan for the future, and that this difference is linked to intelligence. The major determinant of offending is a person's impulsivity. More impulsive people are less influenced by the likelihood of future consequences and hence are more likely to commit crimes.

Gottfredson and Hirschi (1990) castigated criminological theorists for ignoring the fact that people differed in underlying criminal propensities and that these differences appeared early in life and remained stable over much of the life course. The key individual difference construct in their theory was low self-control, which referred to the extent to which individuals were vulnerable to the temptations of the moment. People with low self-control were impulsive, took risks, had low cognitive and academic skills, were self-centered, had low empathy, and had short time horizons. Hence, they found it hard to defer gratification, and their decisions to offend were insufficiently influenced by the possible future painful consequences of offending.

Gottfredson and Hirschi argued that crimes were part of a larger category of deviant acts (including substance abuse, heavy smoking, heavy drinking, heavy gambling, sexual promiscuity, truanting, and road accidents), which were all behavioral manifestations of the key underlying theoretical construct of low self-control. They conceded that self-control, as an internal inhibitor, was similar to the conscience; they preferred the term self-control, however, because the idea of the conscience was less applicable to some of the wider category of acts that concerned them (e.g., accidents). They argued that between-individual differences in self-control were present early in life (by ages six to eight), were remarkably stable over time, and were essentially caused by differences in parental child-rearing practices.

In the Cambridge Study, boys nominated by teachers as lacking in concentration or restless, those nominated by parents, peers, or teachers as the most daring, and those who were the most impulsive on psychomotor tests all tended to become offenders. Later self-report questionnaire measures of impulsivity were also related to offending. Daring, poor concentration, and restlessness all predicted both official and self-reported delinquency, and daring was consistently one of the best independent predictors (Farrington 1992).

Most other investigators have reported a link between the constellation of personality factors termed *hyperactivity-impulsivity-attention deficit* (HIA) and offending. For example, in a Swedish longitudinal survey, Klinteberg et al. (1993) found that hyperactivity at age thirteen (rated by teachers) predicted violent offending up to age twenty-six. Some researchers have argued that HIA predicts offending because it essentially measures childhood conduct disorder. However, in the Cambridge Study, HIA at ages eight to ten significantly predicted juvenile convictions independently of conduct problems at the same age (Farrington, Loeber, and Van Kammen 1990).

The most extensive research on different measures of impulsivity was carried out in the Pittsburgh Youth Study by White et al. (1994). The measures that were most strongly related to self-reported delinquency at ages ten and thirteen were teacher-rated impulsivity (e.g., "acts without thinking"), self-reported impulsivity, self-reported undercontrol (e.g., "unable to delay gratification"), motor restlessness (from videotaped observations), and psychomotor impulsivity (on the Trail Making Test). Generally, the verbal behavior rating tests produced stronger relationships with offending than the psychomotor performance tests, suggesting that cognitive impulsivity was more relevant than behavioral impulsivity. Future time perception and delay-of-gratification tests were only weakly related to self-reported delinquency.

To the extent that IQ measures the ability to manipulate abstract concepts, a low IQ should be related to certain types of impulsivity (those involving planning ahead and the consideration of possible future consequences of actions). However, Lynam and Moffitt (1995) concluded that a low IQ and impulsivity were independent risk factors for delinquency.

Temperament and Personality

Personality refers to underlying tendencies to think and behave in particular ways that explain consistencies in behavior over time and in different environments. Personality traits such as sociability or impulsiveness describe broad predispositions to respond in certain ways. Temperament is basically the childhood equivalent of personality. The modern study of child temperament began with Chess and Thomas's (1984) New York Longitudinal Study. Children in their first five years of life were rated on temperamental dimensions by their parents, and these dimensions were combined into three broad categories of easy, difficult, and "slow to warm up" temperament. Having a difficult temperament at ages three to four (frequent irritability, low amenability and adaptability, irregular habits) predicted poor psychiatric adjustment at ages seventeen to twenty-four.

Because it was not very clear exactly what a "difficult" temperament meant in practice, later researchers have used more specific dimensions of temperament. For example, Kagan and his colleagues classified children as inhibited (shy or fearful) or uninhibited at age twenty-one months, and found that children remained significantly stable on this classification up to age seven years. Furthermore, the uninhibited children at age twenty-one months significantly tended to be identified as aggressive at age thirteen years, according to self-reports and parent reports (Schwartz, Snidman, and Kagan 1996).

Temperament even in the first few months of life predicts later behavior. In the Australian Temperament Project, children who were rated by their mothers at ages four to eight months as not amenable, irritable, and showing behavior problems tended to be rated aggressive-hyperactive at ages seven to eight (Sanson et al. 1993). In the Dunedin Study, being undercontrolled (restless, impulsive, with poor attention) at age three predicted aggression, impulsivity, and alienation at age eighteen and antisocial personality disorder and convictions at age twenty-one (Caspi et al. 1996; Caspi and Silva 1995). Hence, the most important study of temperament in relation to offending essentially confirms the diagnostic importance of early impulsivity.

The most popular modern personality theory is probably the Five-Factor Theory, with personality dimensions measured by the Neuroticism, Extraversion, Openness (NEO) Personality Inventory (Digman 1990). However, there is very little research on offending using this questionnaire. Most personality research on offending has used the Minnesota Multiphasic Personality Inventory (MMPI) or the California Psychological Inventory (CPI) (Wilson and Herrnstein 1985, pp. 186–98). Unfortunately, many of the results, for example correlating offending with the MMPI psychopathic deviate scale or the CPI socialization scale, seem essentially tautological. Consequently, the most significant personality research in relation to offending is probably that inspired by the Eysenck theory and the Eysenck Personality Questionnaire (Eysenck 1996).

Eysenck viewed offending as natural and even rational, based on the assumption that human beings were hedonistic, sought pleasure, and avoided pain. He assumed that delinquent acts such as theft, violence, and vandalism were essentially pleasurable or beneficial to the offender. In order to explain why everyone was not a criminal, Eysenck suggested that the hedonistic tendency to commit crimes was opposed by the conscience, which was viewed as a conditioned fear response. The likelihood of people committing crimes depended on the strength of the conscience.

Like Wilson and Herrnstein, Eysenck proposed that the conscience was built up in childhood. Each time a child committed a disapproved act and was punished by a parent, the pain and fear aroused in the child tended to become associated with the act by a process of classical (automatic) conditioning. After children had been punished several times for the same act, they felt fear when they next contemplated it, and this fear tended to stop them from committing it. According to the theory, this conditioned fear response was the conscience, and it would be experienced subjectively as guilt if the child committed a disapproved act.

According to the Eysenck theory, the people who commit offenses are those who have not built up strong consciences, mainly because they have inherently poor conditionability. Poor conditionability is linked to Eysenck's dimensions of personality. People who are high on extraversion (E) build up conditioned responses less well because they have low levels of cortical arousal. People who are high on neuroticism (N) condition less well because their high resting level of anxiety interferes with their conditioning. Also, since neuroticism acts as a drive, reinforcing existing behavioral tendencies, neurotic extraverts should be particularly criminal. Eysenck also predicted that people who are high on psychoticism (P) would tend to be offenders because the traits included in his definition of psychoticism (emotional coldness, low empathy, high hostility, and inhumanity) were typical of criminals. However, the meaning of the P scale is unclear, and it might more accurately be labeled as psychopathy. Zuckerman (1989) suggested that it should be termed "impulsive unsocialized sensation-seeking."

A review of studies relating Eysenck's personality dimensions to official and self-reported offending concluded that high N (but not E) was related to official offending, while high E (but not N) was related to self-reported offending (Farrington, Biron, and LeBlanc 1982). High P was related to both, but this could have been a tautological result, since many of the items on the P scale are connected with antisocial behavior or were selected in light of their ability to discriminate between prisoners and nonprisoners. In the Cambridge Study, those high on both E and N tended to be juvenile self-reported offenders, adult official offenders, and adult self-reported offenders, but not juvenile official offenders. Furthermore, these relationships held independently of other variables such as low family income, low intelligence, and poor parental child-rearing behavior. However, when individual items of the personality questionnaire were studied, it was clear that the significant relationships were caused by the items measuring impulsivity (e.g., doing things quickly without stopping to think). Hence, it is likely that research inspired by the Eysenck theory, like other projects, essentially confirms the link between impulsivity and offending.

More recent studies, based on different personality questionnaires and outstandingly important longitudinal surveys, do not add a great deal of information. For example, Caspi et al. (1994) investigated the relationship between personality and offending in the Dunedin Study in New Zealand and in the Pittsburgh Youth Study. The personality correlates of offending were replicable across different countries, age cohorts, genders, ethnicities, and methods of measuring both personality and delinquency: the delinquents were characterized by high negative emotionality (aggression and alienation) and low constraint (i.e., they were impulsive risk takers).

Morality and Psychopathy

While Eysenck viewed the conscience behavioristically, as a conditioned fear response, other researchers have regarded it as a set of conscious moral principles specifying what is right or wrong. One of the most important cognitive-developmental theories of offending was proposed by Kohlberg (1978). According to this theory, people progress through different stages of moral development as they get older: from the preconventional stage (where they are hedonistic and obey the law only because of fear of punishment) to the conventional stage (where they obey the law because it is the law) to the postconventional stage (where they obey the law if it coincides with higher moral principles such as justice, fairness, and respect for individual rights). The preconventional stage corresponds to rather concrete thinking, whereas abstract thinking is required to progress to the postconventional stage. Clearly, developing moral reasoning is related to developing cognitive abilities.

A key assumption of this theory is that moral behavior depends on moral reasoning. In a modern version of the old idea that delinquents are "morally defective," it is assumed that the likelihood of offending is greatest for people at the lowest (preconventional) stage of moral development. In testing this theory, moral reasoning is usually measured using the Moral Judgment Interview, which has rather subjective scoring. Many of the objections to the cognitive-developmental approach center on its reliance on what people say rather than on what they do. Nevertheless, research generally shows that official delinquents are significantly different from nondelinquents in reasoning more often at the preconventional stage of moral development (Blackburn 1993, pp. 127–33). In other words, according to what they say, offending tends to involve a rather selfish cost-benefit decision for many delinquents, whereas nondelinquent groups are more likely to have internal inhibitions against offending.

One type of offender who is considered to be morally defective is the psychopath. The equivalent psychiatric classification in the *Diagnostic and Statistic Manual of Mental Disorders* (*DSM-IV*) is antisocial personality disorder. The diagnostic criteria for this disorder include repeated offending, repeated lying and conning, impulsivity or failure to plan ahead, irritability and repeated aggressiveness, repeated failure to work, and lack of remorse (American Psychiatric Association 1994, pp. 649–50). This syndrome is based on longitudinal studies by Robins (1979), who consistently demonstrated that a constellation of indicators of childhood antisocial behavior predicted a constellation of indicators of adult antisocial behavior. Similarly, in the Cambridge Study a composite measure of antisocial personality at age ten correlated .38 with the comparable measure at age eighteen, and antisocial personality at age eighteen correlated .55 with the comparable measure at age thirty-two (Farrington 1997a, p. 378).

Hare and his colleagues have consistently criticized the *DSM-IV* criteria for antisocial personality disorder as too behavioral and insufficiently concerned with personality features (Hare, Hart, and Harpur 1991). Hare's Psychopathy Checklist (PCL-R) distinguishes two factor scores. The first is based on personality features such as egocentricity, lying, conning, lack of remorse or guilt, and callousness/lack of empathy, while the second is based on an impulsive, antisocial, and unstable lifestyle. The PCL-R is completed by raters who know the subject (typically a prisoner), on the basis of interview and record data. Although the two factor scores are significantly intercorrelated, the second is more strongly associated with the diagnosis of antisocial personality disorder than the first. Hare and his colleagues argue that the first factor score most closely approximates the classic definition of psychopathic personality. As might perhaps have been expected, psychopathic prisoners tended to have more extensive criminal careers than nonpsychopathic prisoners, although there were some indications of reductions in nonviolent offending after age forty (Hart and Hare 1997, p. 28).

Lynam (1997) developed a childhood version of the PCL-R and completed it in the Pittsburgh Youth Study using mothers' ratings of boys' personality and behavior. Most of the items were significantly related to the boys' serious self-reported delinquency at ages ten to thirteen, especially failure to accept responsibility, lack of empathy, a parasitic lifestyle, glibness, conning, impulsivity, poor planning, and pathological lying. This research agrees with much other work in showing that this constellation of antisocial features is characteristic of the personalities of many offenders, and that it is evident at an early age.

Social Cognitive Skills

Many researchers have argued that offenders use poor techniques of thinking and problem solving in interpersonal situations (Blackburn 1993, pp. 204–9). As already mentioned, offenders are said to be self-centered and callous, with low empathy. They are relatively poor at role taking and perspective taking, and may misinterpret other people's intentions. Their lack of awareness or sensitivity to other people's thoughts and feelings impairs their ability to form relationships and to appreciate the effects of their behavior on other people. They show poor social skills in interpersonal interactions, fidgeting and avoiding eye contact rather than listening and paying attention.

It is further argued that offenders tend to believe that what happens to them depends on fate, chance, or luck rather than on their own actions. Such thinking makes them feel that they are controlled by other people and by circumstances beyond their control. Hence, they often think that there is no point in trying to succeed, so that they lack persistence in aiming to achieve goals. Arguably, offenders often externalize the blame for their acts to other people rather than accept responsibility themselves, and they expect people to believe far-fetched stories. Furthermore, they fail to stop and think before acting, and they fail to learn from experience. These social-cognitive deficits are linked to offenders' concrete as opposed to abstract thinking and their poor ability to manipulate abstract concepts (Ross and Ross 1995). While this constellation of features fits in with many previously cited characteristics of offenders, it has to be said that the evidence in favor of some of them (e.g., the poor social skills of delinquents) is not convincing.

Perhaps the most well-developed theory to explain the development of social-cognitive skills in relation to aggressive behavior is the social information processing model of Dodge (1991). According to this model, children respond to an environmental stimulus by encoding relevant cues, interpreting those cues, retrieving possible behavioral responses from long-term memory, considering the possible consequences of alternative responses, and selecting and performing a behavior. According to Dodge, aggressive children are more likely to interpret cues as hostile, to retrieve aggressive alternative responses, and to evaluate the consequences of aggression as beneficial. Huesmann and Eron (1989) put forward a somewhat similar cognitive script model, in which aggressive behavior depended on stored behavioral repertoires (cognitive scripts) that were learned during early development, and Zaitchik and Mosher (1993) emphasized "macho" scripts and the macho personality constellation.

Implications for Prevention and Treatment

The implications for intervention of many of the biological results is not very clear, largely because of inadequate knowledge of the social and environmental causes of biological variables and of their full causal relationships with offending. For example, consider the correlation between low heart rate and violence. It is known that regular exercise leads to a decrease in the heart rate, but it is not clear that this would lead to any consequential increase in violence. Similarly, smoking leads to an increase in the heart rate, but it is not clear that this would lead to any consequential decrease in violence. Hence, the effect on offending of interventions targeted on the heart rate is uncertain.

Four major types of intervention implications can be drawn from knowledge about biological and psychological influences on offending. First, to the extent that pregnancy and birth complications are important, intensive home visiting in pregnancy and infancy might alleviate these problems. Second, problems arising from low intelligence and attainment, and a poor ability to manipulate abstract concepts, might be reduced by preschool intellectual enrichment programs. Third, antisocial features of the personality (e.g., low empathy, lack of remorse or guilt, egocentricity, poor perspective taking, impulsivity, lack of consideration of possible future consequences of behavior) and poor interpersonal problem-solving skills can be tackled by a variety of cognitive-behavioral skills training programs. Fourth, low-level moral reasoning might be improved by moral development programs; these are often quite similar to the cognitive-behavioral skills programs, but they are discussed separately.

Pregnancy and Infancy Programs

Problems in pregnancy and infancy can be alleviated by home visiting programs designed to help mothers (Farrington 1994). For example, in New York State, Olds and his colleagues randomly allocated 400 mothers to a group that received home visits from nurses during pregnancy, or to a group that received visits both during pregnancy and during the first two years of life, or to a control group that received no visits. Each visit lasted about one and a quarter hours, and the mothers were visited on average every two weeks. The home visitors gave advice about prenatal and postnatal care of the child, about infant development, and about the importance of proper nutrition and avoiding smoking and drinking during pregnancy.

The results of this experiment showed that home visits during pregnancy led to teenage mothers having heavier babies. Also, women who had previously smoked decreased their smoking and had fewer preterm deliveries. In addition, the postnatal home visits caused a decrease in recorded child physical abuse and neglect during the first two years of life, especially by poor, unmarried teenage mothers; 4 percent of visited versus 19 percent of nonvisited mothers of this type were guilty of child abuse or neglect. This last result is important because of the finding that being physically abused or neglected as a child predicts later violent offending. Hence, preventing child physical abuse, apart from its intrinsic benefits, is likely to have long-term benefits in preventing later violent offending.

One of the very few prevention experiments beginning in pregnancy and collecting outcome data on delinquency was the Syracuse (New York) Family Development Research Program (Lally, Mangione, and Honig 1988). The researchers began with a sample of pregnant women and gave them weekly help with child-rearing, health, nutrition, and other problems. In addition, the women's children received free day care, designed to develop their intellectual abilities, up to age five. This was not a randomized experiment, but a matched control group was chosen when the children were three years old. The treated children had significantly higher intelligence than the controls at age three but were not different at age five.

Ten years later, about 120 treated and control children were followed up to about age fifteen. Significantly fewer of the treated children (2 percent as opposed to 17 percent) had been referred to the juvenile court for delinquency offenses, and the treated girls showed better school attendance and school performance. Hence, this prevention experiment agrees with others in showing that early home visits providing advice and support to women in pregnancy and afterward can have later beneficial outcomes, including the reduction of offending.

Preschool Programs

One of the most successful delinquency prevention programs has been the Perry Preschool Project carried out in Michigan by Schweinhart, Barnes, and Weikart (1993). This was essentially a "Head Start" program targeted at disadvantaged African-American children, who were allocated (approximately at random) to experimental and control groups. The experimental children attended a daily preschool program, backed up by weekly home visits, usually lasting two years (covering ages three to four). The aim of the "plan-do-review" program was to provide intellectual stimulation, to increase thinking and reasoning abilities, and to increase later school achievement.

About 120 children in the two groups were followed up to age fifteen, using teacher ratings, parent and youth interviews, and school records. As demonstrated in several other Head Start projects, the experimental group showed gains in intelligence that were rather short-lived. However, they were significantly better in elementary school motivation, school achievement at age fourteen, teacher ratings of classroom behavior at ages six to nine, self-reports of classroom behavior at age fifteen, and self-reports of offending at age fifteen. Furthermore, a later follow-up of this sample showed that, at age nineteen, the experimental group was more likely to be employed, more likely to have graduated from high school, more likely to have received college or vocational training, and less likely to have been arrested.

By age twenty-seven, the experimental group had accumulated only half as many arrests on average as the controls. Also, they had significantly higher earnings and were more likely to be home owners. More of the experimental women were married, and fewer of their children had been born out of wedlock. Hence, this preschool intellectual enrichment program led to decreases in school failure, in offending, and in other undesirable outcomes.

The Perry project is admittedly only one study based on relatively small numbers. However, its results become more compelling when viewed in the context of ten similar American Head Start projects followed up by the Consortium for Longitudinal Studies (1983). With quite impressive consistency, all studies show that preschool intellectual enrichment programs have long-term beneficial effects on school success, especially in increasing the rate of high school graduation and decreasing the rate of special education placements. The Perry project (and its related Curriculum Comparison Study) was the only one to study offending, but the consistency of the school success results in all projects suggests that the effects on offending and antisocial behavior might also be replicable.

Cognitive-Behavioral Skills
Training Programs

Impulsivity and problems of interpersonal interaction can be tackled using cognitive-behavioral skills training techniques. According to the large meta-analyses of Lipsey (1995), these techniques are the most effective in reducing reconviction rates.

As an example, the Ross program aimed to modify the impulsive, egocentric thinking of delinquents, to teach them to stop and think before acting, to consider the consequences of their behavior, to conceptualize alternative ways of solving interpersonal problems, and to consider the impact of their behavior on other people, especially their victims (Ross and Ross 1995). It included social skills training, lateral thinking (to teach creative problem solving), critical thinking (to teach logical reasoning), values education (to teach values and concern for others), assertiveness training (to teach nonaggressive, socially appropriate ways to obtain desired outcomes), negotiation skills training, interpersonal cognitive problem solving (to teach thinking skills for solving interpersonal problems), social perspective training (to teach how to recognize and understand other people's feelings), role-playing, and modeling (demonstration and practice of effective and acceptable interpersonal behavior).

Ross implemented his Reasoning and Rehabilitation Program in Ottawa, Canada, and reported (in a randomized experiment) that it led to a remarkable decrease in reoffending for a small sample in a nine-month follow-up period. His program has been implemented widely in several countries. For example, in Glamorgan, Wales, offenders who completed this program had lower reconviction rates than expected (Knott 1995).

A multimodal intervention program may be more effective than one using a single technique. For example, Tremblay et al. (1995) in Montreal identified about 250 disruptive (aggressive/hyperactive) boys at age six for a prevention experiment. Between ages seven and nine, the experimental group received training, designed to foster social skills and self-control. Coaching, peer modeling, role playing, and reinforcement contingencies were used in small group sessions on such topics as "how to help," "what to do when you are angry," and "how to react to teasing." Also, the boys' parents were trained using the parent management training techniques developed by Patterson (1982). This prevention program proved to be quite successful. At every age from ten to fifteen, the experimental boys had lower self-reported delinquency scores than the control boys.

Moral Development Programs

Kohlberg (1978) argued that increasing the moral reasoning of offenders from the preconventional to the conventional level would lead to a decrease in their antisocial behavior. These ideas were tested by Scharf and

Hickey (1976) in a women's living unit in the correctional facility at Niantic, Connecticut. A democratic regime was introduced in this living unit, with frequent community meetings, and staff conducted Socratic moral discussions of personal dilemmas with inmates. Generally, the inmates viewed the regime as fair and just, their moral reasoning levels increased, and their recidivism rates were lower than those of inmates in control prisons. This evaluation was rather tentative, based on small numbers (twenty-four women), and not well controlled, but the experiment was repeated in Canada with apparently similar effects on the moral reasoning of male prisoners (Duguid 1981).

Similar programs have been implemented with school students. Arbuthnot (1992) randomly allocated forty-eight students nominated by teachers as seriously behavior-disordered (with histories of aggression, impulsivity, disruptiveness, and so forth) either to a moral reasoning program or to a control group. The pretest showed that virtually all were reasoning at the preconventional level. The experimental students discussed moral dilemmas in small groups. The group leaders challenged the students using higher-level reasoning, tried to make them see each dilemma from the viewpoint of all participants (using role-playing exercises), and also taught the students listening and communication skills. The experimental students significantly increased in moral reasoning and in school achievement, and their disciplinary referrals and police and court contacts decreased. Hence, this program seemed to be quite successful.

Conclusions and Future Directions

Many individual difference variables have been shown to be related to offending, including high impulsivity, daring, low self-control, a weak conscience, emotional coldness, low empathy, low guilt, fearlessness or low anxiety, hyperactivity or restlessness, poor attention or concentration, low intelligence, a poor ability to manipulate abstract concepts, self-centeredness, short time horizons, poor perspective taking, and poor moral reasoning. However, more research is needed on how these factors develop over time. Many psychological researchers who begin with very different theories end up with similar conclusions. What is needed is a coordinated program of research to determine how many key theoretical constructs underlie all these variables, what they are, how they are causally related, and how they should best be operationally defined and measured. All of these types of variables need to be measured in the same study. Another problem is how individual difference variables are related to different types of offenders. In particular, to what degree are these negative personality features more characteristic of serious or chronic offenders than of minor or occasional offenders? How psychologically "normal" are minor offenders? How far are many of the results produced by a small minority of multiple problem individuals?

Many biological variables have also been shown to be related to offending, including low heart rate, low skin conductance, low serotonin levels, and high testosterone levels. The most popular underlying constructs that are thought to mediate these relationships are low arousal and fearlessness. More research is needed to go beyond the demonstration of correlations, to test causal hypotheses, and to study the development of biological variables. Because of the perceived need for carefully controlled laboratory or hospital conditions, much past biological research on offending has been based on small, selected samples and has involved largely cross-sectional or retrospective case-control studies. There is a pressing need to measure more biological variables in large-scale community longitudinal surveys, which often have numerous social and psychological measures but few biological ones. These surveys would help to answer causal order problems (e.g., whether biological variables changed social variables or vice versa). More projects like the pioneering Dunedin Study are needed.

A number of "psychological" interventions have proved successful in preventing offending or reoffending, notably early home visiting, preschool intellectual enrichment, cognitive-behavioral skills training, and moral development programs. However, because of small numbers and short follow-up periods, most of these programs provide glimmers of hope rather than convincing evidence that offending can be reduced. Larger-scale, longer-term, randomized experiments on promising intervention techniques are needed to advance knowledge, possibly within the context of longitudinal studies.

It has to be admitted that many of the findings reviewed in this article have not made a strong impression on "mainstream criminology"—largely because many biological and psychological researchers neglect to measure the kinds of social, situational, peer, school, and community variables that are of particular interest to sociological criminologists. All researchers should be encouraged to measure a wide range of variables. Doing so would make it possible to investigate how far different kinds of variables are independently predictive of offending, to establish causal linkages between different kinds of variables, and to determine how far different kinds of variables interact to produce offending. There are already signs in the literature that some biological variables predict offending only when they are combined with some kind of psychosocial disadvantage (Raine et al. 1997). More research is needed on biosocial interactions, possibly leading to more wide-ranging theories of the development of offending. Existing theories typically explain only a small fraction of the many predictors and correlates of offending that have been identified by researchers from different disciplines. Also, more research is needed on females.

It seems clear that multidisciplinary collaboration is needed to advance knowledge about the causes of offending. Ideally, leading biological, psychological, sociological, and criminological researchers should hold a series of meetings to seek agreement on a general causal model, priorities in testing specific theories derivable from it, key variables to be measured, common instrumentation to be used, key design features, and common analytic methods. A coordinated program of research should be planned to test key hypotheses using samples drawn from different places. New longitudinal studies should be mounted to investigate biological and situational influences on offending, as well as the more traditional individual, family, peer, school, and community variables; or additional data collection efforts could be added to existing longitudinal studies. Ideally, the impact of promising interventions should be tested within the new studies. The emphasis in this program would be on multidisciplinary collaboration and on training a new generation of biopsychosocial researchers in criminology. Such a research program should greatly advance knowledge and theories about offending and antisocial behavior, and should provide a firm basis for the implementation of effective intervention techniques.

Acknowledgments I am very grateful to David Cooke and Rolf Loeber for helpful comments on this article.

References

American Psychiatric Association. 1994. *Diagnostic and Statistical Manual of Mental Disorders*. 4th ed. Washington, D.C.: American Psychiatric Association.

Arbuthnot, J. 1992. "Sociomoral Reasoning in Behavior-Disordered Adolescents: Cognitive and Behavioral Change." In *Preventing Antisocial Behavior: Interventions from Birth Through Adolescence,* edited by J. McCord and R. E. Tremblay. New York: Guilford.

Archer, J. 1991. "The Influence of Testosterone on Human Aggression." *British Journal of Psychology* 82:1–28.

Blackburn, R. 1993. *The Psychology of Criminal Conduct*. Chichester, England: Wiley.

Caspi, A., T. E. Moffitt, D. L. Newman, and P. A. Silva. 1996. "Behavioral Observations at Age 3 Years Predict Adult Psychiatric Disorders." *Archives of General Psychiatry* 53:1033–39.

Caspi, A., T. E. Moffitt, P. A. Silva, M. Stouthamer-Loeber, R. F. Krueger, and P. S. Schmutte. 1994. "Are Some People Crime-Prone? Replications of the Personality-Crime Relationship Across Countries, Genders, Races, and Methods." *Criminology* 32:163–95.

Caspi, A., and P. A. Silva. 1995. "Temperamental Qualities at Age 3 Predict Personality Traits in Young Adulthood: Longitudinal Evidence from a Birth Cohort." *Child Development* 66:486–98.

Chess, S., and A. Thomas. 1984. *Origins and Evolution of Behavior Disorders: From Infancy to Early Adult Life*. New York: Brunner/Mazel.

Clarke, R. V., and D. B. Cornish. 1985. "Modelling Offenders' Decisions: A Framework for Research and Policy." In *Crime and Justice: A Review of*

Research, vol. 6, edited by M. Tonry and N. Morris. Chicago: University of Chicago Press.

Cloninger, C. R., and I. I. Gottesman. 1987. "Genetic and Environmental Factors in Antisocial Behavior Disorders." In *The Causes of Crime: New Biological Approaches,* edited by S. A. Mednick, T. E. Moffitt, and S. A. Stack. Cambridge: Cambridge University Press.

Cohen, A. K. 1955. *Delinquent Boys: The Culture of the Gang.* Glencoe, Ill.: Free Press.

Cole, N. S. 1981. "Bias in Testing." *American Psychologist* 36:1067–77.

Consortium for Longitudinal Studies. 1983. *As the Twig is Bent . . . Lasting Effects of Preschool Programs.* Hillsdale, N.J.: Lawrence Erlbaum.

Denno, D. W. 1990. *Biology and Violence: From Birth to Adulthood.* Cambridge: Cambridge University Press.

Digman, J. M. 1990. "Personality Structure: Emergence of the Five-Factor Model." *Annual Review of Psychology* 41:417–40.

Dodge, K. A. 1991. "The Structure and Function of Reactive and Proactive Aggression." In *The Development and Treatment of Childhood Aggression,* edited by D. J. Pepler and K. H. Rubin. Hillsdale, N.J.: Lawrence Erlbaum.

Duguid, S. 1981. "Moral Development, Justice and Democracy in the Prison." *Canadian Journal of Criminology* 23:147–62.

Ellis, L. 1990. "Left- and Mixed-Handedness and Criminality: Explanations for a Probable Relationship." In *Left-Handedness: Behavioral Implications and Anomalies,* edited by S. Coren. Amsterdam: Elsevier.

Eysenck, H. J. 1996. "Personality and Crime: Where Do We Stand?" *Psychology, Crime and Law* 2:143–52.

Farrington, D. P. 1992. "Juvenile Delinquency." In *The School Years,* edited by J. C. Coleman. London: Routledge.

———. 1993. "Motivations for Conduct Disorder and Delinquency." *Development and Psychopathology* 5:225–41.

———. 1994. "Early Developmental Prevention of Juvenile Delinquency." *Criminal Behavior and Mental Health* 4:209–27.

———. 1997a. "Human Development and Criminal Careers." In *The Oxford Handbook of Criminology,* 2nd ed., edited by M. Maguire, R. Morgan, and R. Reiner. Oxford: Clarendon Press.

———. 1997b. "The Relationship Between Low Resting Heart Rate and Violence." In *Biosocial Bases of Violence,* edited by A. Raine, P. A. Brennan, D. P. Farrington, and S. A. Mednick. New York: Plenum.

Farrington, D. P., G. Barnes, and S. Lambert. 1996. "The Concentration of Offending in Families." *Legal and Criminological Psychology* 1:47–63.

Farrington, D. P., L. Biron, and M. LeBlanc. 1982. "Personality and Delinquency in London and Montreal." In *Abnormal Offenders, Delinquency, and the Criminal Justice System,* edited by J. Gunn and D. P. Farrington. Chichester, England: Wiley.

Farrington, D. P., R. Loeber, and W. B. Van Kammen. 1990. "Long-Term Criminal Outcomes of Hyperactivity–Impulsivity–Attention Deficit and Conduct Problems in Childhood." In *Straight and Devious Pathways from Childhood to Adulthood,* edited by L. N. Robins and M. Rutter. Cambridge: Cambridge University Press.

Gottfredson, M., and T. Hirschi. 1990. *A General Theory of Crime.* Stanford, Calif.: Stanford University Press.

Gray, J. A. 1975. *Elements of a Two-Process Theory of Learning.* New York: Academic Press.

Grove, W. M., E. D. Eckert, L. Heston, T. J. Bouchard, N. Segal, and D. T. Lykken. 1990. "Heritability of Substance Use and Antisocial Behavior: A Study of Monozygotic Twins Reared Apart." *Biological Psychiatry* 27:1293–1304.

Hare, R. D., S. D. Hart, and T. J. Harpur. 1991. "Psychopathy and the DSM-IV Criteria for Antisocial Personality Disorder." *Journal of Abnormal Psychology* 100:391–98.

Harlow, J. M. 1848. "Passage of an Iron Rod Through the Head." *Boston Medical and Surgical Journal* 39:389–93.

Hart, S. D., and R. D. Hare. 1997. "Psychopathy: Assessment and Association with Criminal Conduct." In *Handbook of Antisocial Behavior,* edited by D. M. Stoff, J. Breiling, and J. D. Maser. New York: Wiley.

Herrnstein, R. J., and C. Murray. 1994. *The Bell Curve: Intelligence and Class Structure in American Life.* New York: Free Press.

Huesmann, L. R., and L. D. Eron. 1989. "Individual Differences and the Trait of Aggression." *European Journal of Personality* 3:95–106.

Kandel, E., and S. A. Mednick. 1991. "Perinatal Complications Predict Violent Offending." *Criminology* 29:519–29.

Klinteberg, B. A., T. Andersson, D. Magnusson, and H. Stattin. 1993. "Hyperactive Behavior in Childhood as Related to Subsequent Alcohol Problems and Violent Offending: A Longitudinal Study of Male Subjects." *Personality and Individual Differences* 15:381–88.

Knott, C. 1995. "The STOP Program: Reasoning and Rehabilitation in a British Setting." In *What Works: Reducing Reoffending,* edited by J. McGuire. Chichester, England: Wiley.

Kohlberg, L. 1978. "The Cognitive Developmental Approach to Behavior Disorders: A Study of the Development of Moral Reasoning in Delinquents." In *Cognitive Defects in the Development of Mental Illness,* edited by G. Serban. New York: Brunner/Mazel.

Lally, J. R., P. L. Mangione, and A. S. Honig. 1988. "Long-Range Impact of an Early Intervention with Low-Income Children and their Families." In *Parent Education as Early Childhood Intervention,* edited by D. R. Powell. Norwood, N.J.: Ablex.

Lipsey, M. W. 1995. "What Do We Learn from 400 Research Studies on the Effectiveness of Treatment with Juvenile Delinquents?" In *What Works: Reducing Reoffending,* edited by J. McGuire. Chichester, England: Wiley.

Lipsey, M. W., and J. H. Derzon. 1998. "Predictors of Violent or Serious Delinquency in Adolescence and Early Adulthood: A Synthesis of Longitudinal Research." In *Serious and Violent Juvenile Offenders: Risk Factors and Successful Interventions,* edited by R. Loeber and D. P. Farrington. Thousand Oaks, Calif.: Sage.

Lipsitt, P. D., S. L. Buka, and L. P. Lipsitt. 1990. "Early Intelligence Scores and Subsequent Delinquency: A Prospective Study." *American Journal of Family Therapy* 18:197–208.

Lynam, D. R. 1997. "Pursuing the Psychopath: Capturing the Fledgling Psychopath in a Nomological Net." *Journal of Abnormal Psychology* 106: 425–38.

Lynam, D. R., and T. E. Moffitt. 1995. "Delinquency and Impulsivity and IQ: A Reply to Block." *Journal of Abnormal Psychology* 104:399–401.

Lynam, D. R., T. E. Moffitt, and M. Stouthamer-Loeber. 1993. "Explaining the Relation Between IQ and Delinquency: Class, Race, Test Motivation, School Failure or Self-Control?" *Journal of Abnormal Psychology* 102: 187–96.

Moffitt, T. E. 1990. "The Neuropsychology of Juvenile Delinquency: A Critical Review." In *Crime and Justice: A Review of Research,* vol. 12, edited by M. Tonry and N. Morris. Chicago: University of Chicago Press.

Moffitt, T. E., A. Caspi, P. Fawcett, G. L. Brammer, M. Raleigh, A. Yuwiler, and P. Silva. 1997. "Whole Blood Serotonin and Family Background Relate to Male Violence." In *Biosocial Bases of Violence,* edited by A. Raine, P. A. Brennan, D. P. Farrington, and S. A. Mednick. New York: Plenum.

Olweus, D. 1986. "Aggression and Hormones: Behavioral Relationship with Testosterone and Adrenaline." In *Development of Antisocial and Prosocial Behavior: Research, Theories, and Issues,* edited by D. Olweus, J. Block, and M. Radke-Yarrow. Orlando, Fla.: Academic Press.

Patterson, G. R. 1982. *Coercive Family Process.* Eugene, Ore.: Castalia.

Raine, A. 1993. *The Psychopathology of Crime: Criminal Behavior as a Clinical Disorder.* San Diego, Calif.: Academic Press.

Raine, A., P. A. Brennan, D. P. Farrington, and S. A. Mednick, eds. 1997. *Biosocial Bases of Violence.* New York: Plenum.

Raine, A., P. A. Brennan, B. Mednick, and S. A. Mednick. 1996. "High Rates of Violence, Crime, Academic Problems, and Behavioral Problems in Males with Both Early Neuromotor Deficits and Unstable Family Environments." *Archives of General Psychiatry* 53:544–49.

Raine, A., P. H. Venables, and M. Williams. 1990. "Relationships Between Central and Autonomic Measures of Arousal at Age 15 Years and Criminality at Age 24 Years." *Archives of General Psychiatry* 47:1003–7.

Robins, L. N. 1979. "Sturdy Childhood Predictors of Adult Outcomes: Replications from Longitudinal Studies." In *Stress and Mental Disorder,* edited by J. E. Barrett, R. M. Rose, and G. L. Klerman. New York: Raven Press.

Ross, R. R., and R. D. Ross, eds. 1995. *Thinking Straight: The Reasoning and Rehabilitation Program for Delinquency Prevention and Offender Rehabilitation.* Ottawa, Canada: Air Training and Publications.

Sanson, A., D. Smart, M. Prior, and F. Oberklaid. 1993. "Precursors of Hyperactivity and Aggression." *Journal of the American Academy of Child and Adolescent Psychiatry* 32:1207–16.

Scharf, P., and J. Hickey. 1976. "The Prison and the Inmate's Conception of Legal Justice: An Experiment in Democratic Education." *Criminal Justice and Behavior* 3:107–22.

Schwartz, C. E., N. Snidman, and J. Kagan. 1996. "Early Childhood Temperament as a Determinant of Externalizing Behavior in Adolescence." *Development and Psychopathology* 8:527–37.

Schweinhart, L. J., H. V. Barnes, and D. P. Weikart. 1993. *Significant Benefits.* Ypsilanti, Mich.: High/Scope.

Stattin, H., and I. Klackenberg-Larsson. 1993. "Early Language and Intelligence Development and Their Relationship to Future Criminal Behavior." *Journal of Abnormal Psychology* 102:369–78.

Tremblay, R. E., L. Pagani-Kurtz, F. Vitaro, L. C. Masse, and R. D. Pihl. 1995. "A Bimodal Preventive Intervention for Disruptive Kindergarten Boys: Its Impact Through Mid-Adolescence." *Journal of Consulting and Clinical Psychology* 63:560–68.

Tremblay, R. E., B. Schaal, B. Boulerice, L. Arsenault, R. Soussignan, and D. Perousse. 1997. "Male Physical Aggression, Social Dominance, and Testosterone Levels at Puberty." In *Biosocial Bases of Violence,* edited by A. Raine, P. A. Brennan, D. P. Farrington, and S. A. Mednick. New York: Plenum.

White, J. L., T. E. Moffitt, A. Caspi, D. J. Bartusch, D. J. Needles, and M. Stouthamer-Loeber. 1994. "Measuring Impulsivity and Examining Its Relationship to Delinquency." *Journal of Abnormal Psychology* 103: 192–205.

Wilson, J. Q., and R. J. Herrnstein. 1985. *Crime and Human Nature.* New York: Simon and Schuster.

Windle, R. C., and M. Windle. 1995. "Longitudinal Patterns of Physical Aggression: Associations with Adult Social, Psychiatric, and Personality Functioning and Testosterone Levels." *Development and Psychopathology* 7:563–85.

Zaitchik, M. C., and D. L. Mosher. 1993. "Criminal Justice Implications of the Macho Personality Constellation." *Criminal Justice and Behavior* 20:227–39.

Zuckerman, M. 1989. "Personality in the Third Dimension: A Psychobiological Approach." *Personality and Individual Differences* 10:391–418.

10

Communities
and Crime

PER-OLOF H. WIKSTRÖM

The idea that communities (and change) have a strong influence on crime and offending is central within criminology.
It is probably as important as the idea that individual characteristics and
individual development are crucial for understanding offending. However, the links between the two approaches are not well developed. In recent decades there has been increasing awareness that if criminology is
to advance, more attention must be given to integration of individual and
ecological/environmental approaches (e.g., Reiss 1986; Bottoms 1993;
LeBlanc 1993). It boils down to the classical question of how individuals
and environments interact.

In this chapter I consider what aspects of communities are relevant for
understanding and explaining offending and crime. I argue that the social
mechanisms of community influences on offending behavior and the occurrence of crime can best be summarized in terms of community variation and changes in rules, resources, and routines. I begin by reviewing
key research findings on community variation in rates of offenders and
crime and their correlates. Then, building on aspects of contemporary sociological theory, I outline a general framework for understanding relations among communities, individuals, and social action, and show how it
can be applied to crime and offending. I consider the two major theoretical
traditions—social disorganization theory (focusing on the role of community resources and rules) and routine activity theory (focusing on the role
of community routines)—and their potentials for integration.

Community Variation in Offenders, Crimes,
and Their Correlates

Levels of crime vary between nations, between regions within nations,
between urban and rural areas, and between areas within cities. Generally these variations are correlated with variations in other social problems and social and economic characteristics. Area variations in the level
of crime were recognized early in the nineteenth century (see, e.g., Elmer
1933). They were an important background to the development of early
sociologically oriented theories aimed at understanding and explaining

community variations in crime and other social problems (e.g., Durkheim 1952), particularly as they relate to the process of urbanization (e.g., Park, Burgess, and McKenzie 1925; Wirth 1938).

Urban-Rural Differences

Studies in North America and Europe of the relations between measures of urbanization and levels of crime have consistently shown that the crime rate tends to be higher in urban than in rural areas and that crime rates tend to increase with the size of the urban area, although urban areas of the same size may differ significantly in their level of crime. These findings appear to hold for police-recorded crimes (e.g., McClintock and Avison 1968; Wikström 1991c), self-reported delinquency (e.g., Christie, Andenaes, and Skirbekk 1965), and victimization data (e.g., van Dijk and Vivanen 1978; Laub 1983; Sampson 1986). Some studies have shown that some types of crime (i.e., residential burglary and robbery) show a special concentration in big cities (Skogan 1978; Wikström 1991c) and that fear of crime tends to be greater in urban than in rural areas (e.g., Wikström and Dolmén forthcoming). The main national exception to these general patterns appears to be Japan (e.g., Braithwaite 1989).

Theories aiming to explain the relation between urbanization and crime tend to focus on the roles of informal social control and opportunities for crime—assuming, that is, that urbanization goes hand in hand with reduced informal social control and increased opportunities to commit crimes (see Wikström 1991c). This is often seen as a result of a decrease in social integration: more stranger-to-stranger contacts and anonymity, and more diversity in individuals' values and social backgrounds. Increased opportunities for crime are generally understood to result from the concentration of certain types of routine activities, particularly in areas of commerce and public entertainment. Sometimes an interaction between levels of informal social control and opportunities for crime is assumed, meaning that the effects are cumulative (see Wikström and Dolmén forthcoming).

Communities and Offenders

Modern societies, especially larger urban areas, are highly segregated. Economic and other resources, and social groups by socioeconomic status, family type, and ethnic origin are unequally distributed across residential communities (see, e.g., Janson 1980).

Communities vary from homogeneous to highly heterogeneous. The prevalence and mix of different kinds of social activities, including work, family life, and leisure, vary between communities. Some communities are purely residential; others include significant commercial and industrial enterprises. The physical designs of communities vary, with some people living in dense blocks of high-rises and others in areas of single-family homes with spacious gardens. Some communities are stable; others undergo rapid change, including processes of decline or gentrification.

People grow up and live in different communities, and this has important implications for their development and the circumstances of their daily lives. It takes no great imagination to realize that growing up in a poor inner-city area, for example, rather than in a small-town upper-middle-class area has important consequences for an individual's life course. However, our understanding of the social mechanisms of community influences on individual development and behavior is at best rudimentary.

Neighborhood Offender Rates.   Research early in the twentieth century laid the foundation for the ecological study of communities and crime. The prime focus was on variations in community offender rates, particularly male juvenile offender rates, although many other aspects of communities and crime were also studied. An "offender rate" is a measure of the density of offenders per population unit, such as "x arrestees or self-reported offenders per 1,000 residents."

Shaw and McKay's research (1969) in Chicago and other major U.S. cities demonstrated that offender rates varied significantly between communities; that the distribution was highly skewed, with a small number of communities having significantly higher rates; that these community differences tended to persist over time; and that offender rates were correlated with other social and economic aspects of the communities. Communities with high offender rates, generally located in inner-city areas adjacent to the central business district (CBD), tended to be poor communities with high population turnover and large minority populations.

Many studies conducted in North America and Europe have confirmed that offender rates vary significantly between neighborhoods, and that these variations tend to be correlated with social and economic characteristics of the residential population, particularly measures of limited economic resources, family disruption, and other types of social problems, and with variations in residential stability and population heterogeneity (see, e.g., Chilton 1964; Baldwin and Bottoms 1976; Wikström 1991c). However, Shaw and McKay's finding that community offender rate differences show a high degree of stability over time has not been replicated in more recent research (e.g., Schuerman and Kobrin 1986; Taub, Taylor, and Dunham 1984). This has been explained by changes in the "ecological structure" of cities (Bursik and Grasmick 1993, pp. 48–51).

Local Housing Markets.   Research in Sheffield, England (Baldwin and Bottoms 1976; Bottoms, Claytor, and Wiles 1992), and Stockholm (Wikström 1991c) has shown that local housing markets play an important mediating role in residential segregation. Households with meager economic resources are often limited to rented apartments and in some places predominantly to public housing. Area housing patterns fairly well predict population composition (and measures of social instability), which, in turn, fairly well predict area offender rates (Wikström 1991c). However, the same studies also show considerable variation in offender rates between areas characterized by the same type of housing. It has been argued that "the mechanisms of allocation between and within tenure types must be a critical part of any explanation of offender-rate distribution" (Bottoms and Wiles 1986, p. 119) and that "allocation mechanisms can influence not only the differential distribution of social groups within the housing market but also the mix of social groups within an area and the social life they create" (p. 122).

Every housing market produces some less desirable types of housing— slums and public housing projects in the United States (e.g., Sampson 1990), difficult council estates in Britain (e.g., Bottoms and Wiles 1986), and nonprofit housing problem areas in Sweden (e.g., Wikström 1991c)— and these types of areas are of particular importance as producers of high rates of offenders.

The location of areas with high offender rates varies between cities and appears related to the operations of local housing markets. Branting- ham and Brantingham have observed that "in cities with a free housing market, criminal areas tend to be located near the central business dis- trict. In cities with zoning and extensive public housing programs, crimi- nal areas may be located anywhere" (1984, p. 330).

Why Do Offender Rates Vary? There are two (nonexclusive) reasons that explain why area of residence and offending are correlated (Wikström 1990). More crime-prone social groups may be segregated in certain types of neighborhoods. In addition, area contextual characteristics may them- selves influence residents' propensities and motivations to commit crime. The latter influence may be direct or mediated (e.g., through family and school) and divided into situational influences on criminal motivation, such as the presence of temptations and lack of effective informal social controls, and long-term influences, including community influences on conditions for family management and availability in the community of public health services for children.

Community or Individual Effects? A key assumption of many theories aiming to explain neighborhood variation in offender rates is that such variation "can best be understood in terms of variation in the abilities of local communities to regulate and control the behavior of their residents" (Bursik and Grasmick 1993, p. 24), primarily as a result of the influence of community social organization on informal social controls and pat- terns of socialization.

However, some scholars are more skeptical, arguing that communities may have some influence on individuals' offending but that "most of the variation among individuals in criminality can be accounted for by per- sonal traits, family socialization, and (perhaps) school experiences"; furthermore, "high-rate offenders begin offending very early in their lives, well before communal factors—whether peers who are 'rotten apples' or neighborhood social processes that set boundaries, supply targets, or provide surveillance—could play much of a role" (Wilson and Herrnstein 1985, p. 311).

Wilson and Herrnstein's skepticism predominantly concerns the roles of direct situational factors in explaining why individuals become high-rate offenders. Their argument largely ignores the potential importance of long-term community influences on the development of personal traits, family socialization, and school experiences related to risk of future offending. Tonry, Ohlin, and Farrington (1991) have argued that "there are strong theoretical reasons to expect that individual characteristics, family processes, and life transitions interact with community characteristics to explain criminal careers. In particular, trajectories of within-individual longitudinal change may differ between community contexts" (1991, p. 42).

A key methodological problem is whether, or to what degree, community factors' influence on resident's offending behavior can be established empirically. "How do we know that area differences in delinquency rates result from aggregative characteristics of communities rather than the characteristics of individuals selectively aggregated into communities? How do we even know that there are any differences at all in delinquency rates of communities once their differing composition is taken into account?" (Kornhauser 1978, p. 114). This is a tricky problem in light of the great difficulty in specifying all the significant individual and community factors (the theoretical question) and in finding good measures of these factors and methods to separate and weigh their relative importance (the methodological question), especially since these influences are likely to interact and their relative impact to change over an individual's life span.

Few studies have attempted to address this problem empirically, and most of those have been able to study only some limited aspects of it and have faced difficult problems of measurement and methodology that sometimes make it difficult to draw straightforward conclusions.

a. Individual SES, area SES, and offending. One group of studies has compared offending rates by individuals' socioeconomic status (SES) and area or school SES (e.g., Reiss and Rhodes 1961; Braithwaite 1979, pp. 126–57). These studies show that the highest rates are found for lower-SES subjects living in low-SES areas or going to low-SES schools. However, there are some reported exceptions, such as a study carried out in Japan by Matsumoto (see Braithwaite 1979, pp. 123–25).

Wikström (1991a), in a study of housing type (owner-occupied, apartment rented from private landlord or from nonprofit organization), family social class, and family receipt of social welfare benefits, showed that the highest rates of offending were found for juveniles living in nonprofit housing and, when controlling for family SES and social welfare, that the highest rates of offending were found for juvenile, lower-working-class subjects living in nonprofit housing where families were on social welfare.

This body of research indicates that individual social situations interact with broader community characteristics to influence offending behavior. Further evidence comes from a recent study in Pittsburgh.

b. Individual risk factors, neighborhood SES, and juvenile offending. Wikström and Loeber (1997) explored the relations among individual risk factors, neighborhood characteristics, and juvenile offending. The individual risk-factor scale was based on selected individual characteristics believed to measure some key aspects of juveniles' dispositions (lack of guilt and hyperactivity–impulsivity–attention problems) and social situation (poor parental monitoring, poor school motivation, peer delinquency, and positive attitudes toward delinquency) relevant to propensity and motivation to offend. Subjects' neighborhood types were classified by SES on the basis of a factor analysis of Pittsburgh neighborhood census data into high-, medium-, and low-SES areas, with the low-SES group further divided into two groups depending on whether public housing was predominant in the area. Serious offending included car theft, breaking and entering, strong-arming, attack to seriously hurt or kill, forced sex, and selling of drugs. As expected from previous research, the individual risk factors and the risk factor index were correlated with serious offending (Table 10.1).

Comparing the distribution of risk factors by area SES, more subjects in the low- than in the high-SES areas had a lack of guilt, poor parental monitoring, poor school motivation, and delinquent peers; this was not

Table 10.1. Individual Risk Factors Correlated with Serious Delinquency and Area SES.

	Juveniles	
Risk factors	Serious offending Gamma	Area SES Gamma
Dispositions		
Hyperactivity–impulsivity–attention problems	0.38	0.06*
Lack of guilt	0.53	0.23
Social situation		
Poor parental monitoring	0.28	0.27
Poor school motivation	0.50	0.23
Peer delinquency	0.55	0.26
Positive attitude toward delinquency	0.35	−0.08*
RISK FACTOR INDEX	0.57	0.20

All correlations are statistically significant on the 5 percent level or better.

*No clear trend of increase of proportion subjects with risk factor from high to low area SES.

Source: Pittsburgh Youth Study data. Adapted from Wikström and Loeber (1997).

Table 10.2. Percent Boys in Pittsburgh Having Committed Acts of Serious Delinquency by Neighborhood Type and Number of Risk Factors

	Neighborhood SES			
Number of risk factors	HIGH	MEDIUM	LOW (Non–public housing areas)	LOW (Public housing areas)
0	3.4	13.7	13.6	51.3
1–2	32.8	37.5	38.1	53.1
3–6	56.3	60.3	72.9	63.9

Risk defined as belonging to the upper quartile of the distribution of the measure of the risk factor in question. For instance, having a score of 6 on the index of risk factors means that the subject belongs to the upper quartile of all six individual risk measures. Data weighted to correct for oversampling of boys known for antisocial behavior.

Source: Data from the combined middle and oldest sample of the Pittsburgh Youth Study. Adapted from Wikström and Loeber (1997).

true of those scoring high on the hyperactivity–impulsivity–attention problems scale and those having positive attitudes toward delinquency. For the latter groups, the variation by area SES was small, and there was no consistent pattern of highest rates being found in low-SES areas and lowest rates in the high-SES areas (Table 10.2). These findings show that there are clear community variations in most but not all risk factors, and this may also partly explain community variations in offender rates (i.e., some juveniles having more risk factors in some communities compared with others).

One key finding was that serious offending by juveniles with the lowest individual risk factors appeared to be the most affected by community of residence. For subjects with no risk factors, there was a clear community effect on serious offending, while for the other two groups (one to two or three to six), variations in levels of serious offending between neighborhood groups were nonsignificant (see the rows in Table 10.2).

Another key finding was that differences in rates of serious offending were nonsignificant for those living in low-SES public housing areas (see the columns in Table 10.2). This was in clear contrast to those living in the other three neighborhood SES groups, where the number of risk factors made a significant difference in serious offending. This suggests that some aspects of the community environment in low-SES public housing–dominated areas (or, more generally, in areas with a high degree of social and economic deprivation) are of particular importance in influencing male juveniles' involvement in serious offending. There may be threshold effects operating: when certain community factors reach a certain level, they may overshadow the importance of individual risk factors.

The Pittsburgh findings show that most juvenile risk factors vary between communities, and that this may be part of the explanation for community variations in juvenile offender rates. They also show that community of residence is a more important influence on serious offending for juveniles with the lowest risk factors than for others, and that the relation between risk factors and serious offending "breaks down" for those living in the most disadvantaged communities. The Pittsburgh findings differ from other studies of the influence of individual characteristics and community context on juvenile offending in that it indicates a threshold rather than an additive effect of community context.

Other Relevant Studies

Rutter et al. (1974) focused on differences in childhood disorders and antisocial behavior between urban and rural communities, finding that "emotional disorders, conduct disorders and specific reading retardation were all twice as common in ten-year-old children attending schools in an inner London borough as in children of the same age on the Isle of Wight" (p. 532). These differences

> are due in part to the fact that a relatively high proportion of London families experience marital discord and disruption, that many of the parents show mental disorder and antisocial behavior, that families often live in poor social circumstances, and that the schools are more often characterized by a high rate of turnover in staff and pupils. The evidence suggested that these problems stemmed from living in an inner London borough, but further research is required to identify what it is about life in a metropolitan area that predisposes to the development of disorder and deviance. (p. 532)

Kupersmidt et al. (1995) studied childhood aggression in relation to neighborhood (middle or low SES), family context, and peer relations for fifth-grade children in a small southern city in the United States. They found "support for the hypothesis that the neighborhood context is associated with childhood aggression and peer relations over and above the variance accounted for by family characteristics" (p. 368).

Lindström (1996) focused on the relation between neighborhood context, level of family interaction, and serious juvenile offending in eight Stockholm neighborhoods, and showed that the influence of family interaction on serious offending was dependent on neighborhood context (low family interaction was much more strongly related in socially unstable neighborhoods).

The latter two studies suggest that the relations between individual and family characteristics and juvenile offending may be conditional upon the community context. However, they do not identify the potentially significant community factors influencing juvenile offending; instead, they assume that differentiation of neighborhoods by broad social and economic characteristics reflects some important variations in community contexts.

Measuring Community Characteristics' Influence. Another approach is to try to specify and measure the aspects of communities that influence offending and to include them alongside individual characteristics in individual-level models, using multivariate regression-based techniques, to see how well they predict offending. The key community factors in Simcha-Fagan and Schwartz (1986) and Gottfredson, McNeill, and Gottfredson (1991) are community measures of SES and disorganization. The measures of individual characteristics in these studies relate to individual social situation as regards, for example, aspects of the school and peer situations. Lizotte et al. (1994) used measures of community structural characteristics (population poverty, mobility, and heterogeneity) and measures of community organization (e.g., neighborhood integration); they also included measures of (parents') individual integration into the community (e.g., contact with neighbors, membership in organizations, and knowledge of child's peers).

Simcha-Fagan and Schwartz (1986) concluded about the relation between community, family, school, and peer variables and offending measures that "community effects on delinquency are to a large extent mediated by socialization experiences" (p. 695). This conclusion makes sense theoretically, but this was a cross-sectional study and did not directly measure socialization practices.

The amount of variance explained by the community variables in these studies is rather low. Gottfredson, McNeill, and Gottfredson (1991) concluded that "the assumption that community characteristics explain much of the difference among individuals in criminal behavior no longer seems tenable" (p. 221). These results reflect the fact that most juveniles in most communities do not commit serious offenses (or accumulate a large number of offenses), and that some juveniles in all communities commit serious offenses (or accumulate a large number of offenses). Thus, community variables are unlikely to explain any higher proportion of variance at the individual level, although the risk of (serious or high-frequency) offending generally varies by type of neighborhood.

Problems in Estimating Community Effects. The reported findings on community effects may appear devastating for theories about the importance of community influences on offending, but such a conclusion may be premature. First, the studies suggest that the relationship between individual characteristics and offending may be dependent on the context of the community. This is highlighted by Lizotte et al. in their discussion of why their measures of community social disorganization explain so little variance:

> Macro-level variables may provide differing contexts that fundamentally change the way that individual-level factors operate at different

levels of social disorganization. For example, neighborhood integration or parental monitoring may have different effects on individual delinquency in highly disorganized as opposed to highly organized neighborhoods. Another alternative is that for any given individual, the effect of a variable at the individual level may be relative to the level of its structural counterpart. (1994, p. 227)

Second, it may be difficult to disentangle community from individual effects, when individual characteristics refer to aspects of the individual social situation. Some individual characteristics (e.g., sex and race) are clearly unrelated to the context of community residence, although their social consequences may not be unrelated, while others (e.g., peer delinquency and school motivation) may be more or less strongly related. In other words, the individual social situation may be embedded in the community context and difficult to separate out.

Third, these studies do not take into consideration the potential influence of community characteristics on the development of individual characteristics relevant to future offending (for a discussion of how to statistically model individual and community influences, see Raudenbush 1993).

Communities and Criminal Careers. Few studies have addressed influences of community of residence on offending characteristics and the development of individual offending patterns—for example, whether there are community variations in the median age of onset and the duration and escalation of offending over time. Our knowledge of variations in patterns of criminal careers by type of community is limited.

Wikström (1991a), using data from the Project Metropolitan 1953 Stockholm birth cohort, showed that variation in the aggregate level of offending (crimes per 100 juveniles) by area of residence was due to variations in both participation (the percentage having offended) and frequency (the number of crimes per offender). Juveniles living in nonprofit housing had the highest levels of both participation and frequency. This held for all SES groups except those belonging to families of the highest SES, where the difference by type of housing was nonsignificant. Unpublished data also show that the median age of onset in offending was lowest for those living in nonprofit housing and highest for those living in owner-occupied housing.

These findings indicate that aspects of criminal careers vary by communities and may be influenced by community contextual characteristics. Further support for this possibility comes from a study by Loeber and Wikström (1993), which shows the extent to which known juvenile offenders advanced to serious offending varied by community. More juveniles offended in low-SES than in high-SES neighborhoods; of those who did offend, a much higher proportion of juveniles in low-SES neighborhoods developed into serious offenders.

Communities and Crimes

Thus far, this chapter has focused on the relationship between community characteristics and individuals', especially juveniles', offending behavior. Another important research subject is the relationship between community characteristics and occurrence of crimes.

The "environmental criminology" perspective that developed in the 1970s has been defined by Brantingham and Brantingham (1981) as the study of the location of crimes (p. 7). These authors have criticized much earlier research for making the "general assumption that criminal residence locations and crime sites were spatially identical" (p. 24) and have stressed that offenders do not necessarily commit their crimes close to home. By focusing on crimes, this perspective has also brought nonresidential space into focus, since many crimes occur in such settings.

Community Variation in Crime Rates

Community crime rates are not a simple reflection of community offender rates. Some communities have high rates of crime and high rates of offenders, while others have high rates of crime but low rates of offenders. North American and European studies of the distribution of crimes in cities show consistent patterns. First, city-center areas tend to have the highest rates of crime (e.g., Schmid 1960; Pyle 1974; Baldwin and Bottoms 1976; Davidson 1981; Wikström 1991c). Second, among residential areas, the most socially disadvantaged and socially unstable neighborhoods tend to have higher crime rates than others (e.g., Wikström 1985; 1991c) and higher rates of residents victimized locally (e.g., Sampson and Groves 1989; Skogan 1990; Wikström 1991b; Wikström and Dolmén forthcoming).

These patterns become more complicated when one considers specific types of crime, although there appears to be a tendency for some kinds of crime to show similar distributions. For example, Wikström (1991c) factor-analyzed the area variation in Stockholm of eight categories of crime and identified three factors labeled "crimes in private or against the semi-private" (family violence, nonfamily violence in apartments, vandalism in apartments, cellar/attic burglaries, and burglaries of commercial enterprises); "crimes against the private" (residential burglary); and "crimes in public" (violence in public places, vandalism in public places, and thefts of and from cars). Crimes in private or against the semi-private tended to be highest in socially disadvantaged residential areas. Crimes against the private tended to be highest in affluent residential areas. Crimes in public tended to be highest in the city center. However, when the city center was excluded from the analysis, crimes in public tended to be highest in the most socially disadvantaged neighborhoods. These patterns may or may not be specific to Stockholm, but what is clear from other studies is that the distribution of different kinds of crime shows a more or less different pattern of area variation (e.g., Boggs 1965; Pyle 1974; Baldwin and Bottoms 1976).

Hot Spots and Hot Times. Many crimes tend to cluster at specific locations, often referred to as "hot spots" (e.g., Sherman, Gartin, and Buerger 1989; Sherman et al. 1991). Some types of crimes also tend to cluster in time, referred to as "hot times," and these times vary between types of crimes. Against this background, it has been natural to want to learn what factors generate hot spots and hot times (see Eck and Weisburd 1995).

The clustering phenomena highlight community variations in frequency of crimes that are at least in part due to community variations in the prevalence of certain locations within the community. Two prime examples are shopping malls and places with concentrations of bars and other public entertainment establishments.

Offender Residence and Place of Crime Commission. The study of the relation between the distribution of offenders' residences and that of the places of crime commission is generally referred to as the study of "crime and distance" (e.g., Pyle 1974; McIver 1981). European and North American studies of crime and distance reported that there is a "distance-decay" function: the number of crimes committed tends to decrease with the distance from the offender's residence. Violent crimes tend to be committed closer to home than property crimes, a difference that is partly, but not fully, explained by cases of domestic violence. However, many crimes are committed away from the offender's residence, and the distance tends to vary with different offender characteristics. For example, older offenders and those with a longer criminal career tend to offend at greater distances from home than do young and less criminally experienced offenders.

An interesting question is to what degree crimes in different communities are committed by locals or visitors. Wikström (1991c) showed that, in areas in Stockholm where the highest rates of offenders resided (i.e., nonprofit housing areas), a much higher proportion of crimes of violence and vandalism were committed by locals than in other areas (a majority of offenders were locals), and that locals committed more than one-third of theft crimes (p. 224). In sharp contrast, locals accounted for only a tiny proportion of the offenders in the city center. A large proportion of city-center offenders were residents of nonprofit housing areas, suggesting a pattern in which offenders from these areas offend locally or travel to other communities where there are good opportunities for crime. Similarly, juvenile offenders in Stockholm were shown to commit most of their crimes in the city center, at larger shopping malls, at the main public transport network lines, or close to home (Wikström 1994).

The Stockholm findings are consistent with those from U.S. research.

Rengert (1981) showed that the burglars in his Philadelphia study tended to commit their crimes either close to home or in the CBD. Rhodes and Conly showed that areas in the District of Columbia with concentrations of large businesses such as department stores, shopping malls, and large offices, and special land uses such as public services, museums, and libraries "offer good targets and serve as magnets for offenders" (1981, p. 186).

Why Do Communities Vary in the Frequency of Crimes?

Two interacting factors may account for community variation in the frequency of crimes (Wikström 1990). First, communities vary in environmental conditions conducive to crime, including their levels of formal and informal social controls and, partly related to that, their levels of temptations and provocations. Second, communities vary in the presence of individuals (as residents or visitors) with higher propensities to commit crimes.

The Concept of Opportunity.   Areas and places vary in opportunities to commit crime. Different types of crime relate to different kinds of opportunities. The concept of opportunity is more complicated than it may appear at first sight, and its use seems to have caused some confusion (e.g., discussions in Boggs 1965; Rengert 1981; Harries 1981; Wikström 1991c). In some studies it has been used as a control variable (e.g., the denominator in calculating crime rates) and in other studies as an explanatory variable.

It is helpful to distinguish between targets at risk and opportunities. A "target at risk" may be considered any object (or person) that can be the target of the crime (e.g., banks in a study of bank robbery or individuals in a study of assault). One reason for area and place variations in crimes is that areas and places vary in the availability of targets at risk. The concept of "opportunity" sometimes is used to refer to the intersection of individuals and targets and the conditions under which this intersection takes place. According to Rengert, an opportunity "is dependent not only on its specific objective site characteristics, but also on the existence of an individual who can take advantage of these characteristics" (1981, p. 193). Cohen and Felson (1979) have suggested that "the probability that a violation will occur at any specific time and place might be taken as a function of the convergence of likely offenders and suitable targets in the absence of capable guardians" (p. 590). A "capable guardian" is a person (perceived to be) willing and capable to intervene to stop crimes.

Against this background, one would expect that community variation in crimes is a result of community differences in social processes bringing motivated offenders in contact with good environmental conditions to carry out a crime. However, as pointed out by Bursik and Grasmick (1993,

p. 89), this dynamic aspect of the occurrence of crimes has never been fully studied. Moreover, as mentioned out by Felson and Cohen (1980), the role of community characteristics for generating this convergence is "the most underinvestigated question raised by this perspective" (p. 394).

Opportunity in Relation to Predatory and Other Crimes. The concept of opportunity has generally been used in relation to predatory crimes, where there is direct contact between the offender and the target. Application of the opportunity concept to other types of crimes, particularly those that are interactive and expressive, is more complicated. One reason is that it is often difficult to distinguish between "the offender" and "the victim," since these roles sometimes are less than clear. Another reason is that the capable guardian's role in some crimes appears less important (see Wikström 1991c, pp. 187–90; Felson 1993, pp. 116–20).

Wikström (1991c) has suggested that it may often be better to talk about risk meetings and risk relationships than about opportunities, and to try to learn what environmental conditions or relationships tend to generate violence. In expressive types of crimes, it may be more a question of how situations arise that develop into violence or vandalism rather than of an offender taking advantage of an opportunity. There is, for instance, ample evidence that in many cases public entertainment is an environmental condition generative of situations with a high risk of violence (Wikström 1995a). European and North American studies have also shown that street violence tends to occur in areas and places of public entertainment, although there may be great variations depending on their characteristics (e.g., Curtis 1974; McClintock and Wikström 1992; Roncek and Maier 1991; Block and Block 1995).

Felson (1993, p. 109) has suggested use of the term *dispute-related violence,* referring to violence as a result of a perceived wrongdoing causing anger and a wish to punish the other party, and argued that for such crimes to occur "one might expect the following elements to be present: (1) at least one person with a proclivity toward violence; (2) a provocation; (3) supportive third parties" (p. 120).

The Importance of Land Use

It has been claimed that "since illegal activities must feed upon other activities, the spatial and temporal structure of routine legal activities should play an important role in determining the location, type, and quantity of illegal acts occurring in a given society or community" (Cohen and Felson 1979, p. 590). Community variation in legal routine activities is to a large extent a reflection of community variations in land use; therefore, patterns in land use may be regarded as a key to understanding variations in crime (Wikström 1991c).

Large towns and cities are characterized by a social life that is influenced by its heterogeneity and the size and density of the population.

Sites are put to a wide variety of uses, including a multitude of combinations of housing types, industries, shops, and public entertainments, and ranging from purely residential areas to downtown districts with few permanent inhabitants.

Human activities and the related social characteristics and mix of individuals present also vary considerably from one area to another. Since the frequency of different types of activities varies with both the day of the week and the time of day, there is not only a spatial variation in human activities but also a temporal one—variations occur over time in any given area. Together with patterns of residential segregation, the street layout, the structure of the public transport system, and spatial and temporal differences in human activities affect patterns of different social groups' movement throughout the city at different times of the day.

All of this influences community variations in the frequency and types of encounters between people of differing social backgrounds and relationships, the circumstances in which they meet, and the degree to which people of different social backgrounds are exposed to various kinds of material goods under different levels of supervision. This is an important background to area and place variations in the rate and structure of crime, although our understanding of the social mechanisms of these influences is rudimentary.

Few studies have explored relations between land use and crime, but those few have generally shown that there are clear links between the two (see, e.g., Rhodes and Conly 1981; Wikström 1991c; Hirschfield and Bowers 1997).

Communities, Individuals, and Social Action

To understand the relation between the individual and the community, we must understand how purposive social actions are guided and constrained by rules, resources, and routines. Social action is guided and constrained by rules (norms) that either encourage or discourage specific behaviors. Crime is the breaking of rules that are sanctioned by the state (i.e., the law). Rules are learned, interpreted, modified, and changed in social interaction and, particularly, in the process of socialization. Individuals are likely to vary in their moral commitments to follow different kinds of rules and in how they perceive potential consequences of breaking different kinds of rules.

Social action may be regarded as motivated by individuals' desires to achieve gain, security, and respect (Wrong 1994, chap. 4). These goals can be realized by legitimate and illegitimate means. The individual's ability to realize his wants by legal means is facilitated or constrained by his resources. These individual resources can be divided into human capital (e.g., skills) and social capital (e.g., access to supportive, resourceful social networks), with social capital being important for development of human capital (Coleman 1990, chap. 12).

Much social action is an expression of habits or routines that are ordered in time and space (Giddens 1979, 1991). Individual patterns in daily, weekly, and yearly routines can be called *lifestyles.* Individuals vary in lifestyles (see, e.g., Hindelang, Gottfredson, and Garofalo 1978), which are influenced by age (the individual's stage in the life cycle) but also (at any given age) by the individual's rules (e.g., internalized norms) and resources.

Figure 10.1 sets out a tentative general model for describing the relationship between the individual and the community. The basic concept is that the social and built community environment, through the social mechanisms of rules, resources, and routines, influences the individual's social situation, and in the long term, in particular during infancy and childhood, his development of dispositions. Individual acts are purposive and involve decision making that takes place in a community and hence is influenced by (and sometimes also influences) community environment. The model is the starting point for discussing relations among communities, crimes, and offending.

Communities

The concept of "community" is not easily defined, but it generally refers to a common locality. Sometimes it also implies a certain quality of relations among residents in terms of interpersonal ties. But the concept is also used to describe interpersonal ties without reference to a common

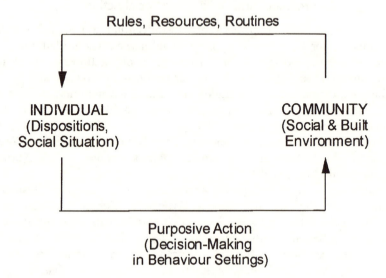

Figure 10.1 A general model for the relationship between the individual and the community.

locality, as in the phrase "academic community" (Wellman and Leighton 1979).

For purposes of this article, a *community* is loosely defined as the social and built environment of a common locality. A *local community* is the area surrounding the individual's place of residence, and the *wider community* is the broader area in which the local community is located. There are no simple criteria for establishing local community boundaries, and a local community will always be embedded in a larger community that will exert influence.

The *environment* is all that is external to the individual (see, e.g., Hawley 1986). The community social environment consists of the patterns of social activities and social relationships in a locality. The *community built environment* is the arrangement of buildings and spaces in a locality.

Individuals

Individuals differ from one another in many ways. They react and respond differently to their environments. At any time, individuals differ in their economic, family, job, or school situations, and in their networks of friends. These may be referred to as differences in *social situation.*

At any time, individuals also vary in skills, temperament, and moral conscience. These differences may be referred to as *dispositions.* Dispositions, once established, tend to be more stable, while social situations, although they can be permanent for long periods, can change from one day to another (e.g., with an outbreak of a civil war or, less dramatically, job loss).

Community Influences on the Individual's Dispositions and Social Situation

Community environments are likely to influence the individual's development of dispositions and his social situation, but also to be an important part of the individual's current social situation. Timms stressed the neighborhood's great importance in socialization: "For much of the first ten or eleven years of life much of the individual's activity is confined to an area within a relatively small radius of his home" (1971, p. 31). Research into individual development suggests that many key characteristics develop early in life and show stability over the life course. It has also been claimed that individual characteristics are most influenced by the environment during the period of most rapid development (e.g., Bloom 1964). The latter two points highlight the fact that community influences on individual dispositions are likely to vary with age and in many cases to be at their peak during the individual's early years (including the prenatal period). The social mechanisms of community influences on the individual can be described in terms of rules, resources, and routines. Key aspects of this influence are summarized in the following.

Communities vary in the degree to which they are able to realize shared rules to guide behavior, to implement effective informal social control and an effective process of socialization.

Communities vary in the economic and social resources of their inhabitants and their social institutions; these may be referred to as variations in community capital. The level of community resources is likely to influence the individual's social capital and the development of his human capital, and thus his potential to realize his desires to achieve gain, security, and respect.

Communities also vary in their patterns of routine activities. Community differences in routine activity patterns mean variation in the prevalence and mix of different kinds of behavioral settings, such as shopping malls and bars, that confront its residents and visitors. The prevalence and mix of behavioral settings in a community also influence the number and kinds of visitors it attracts.

Communities and Social Action

Individuals are purposive agents, and their choices of action involve decision making. Decision making takes place in a behavioral setting. Behavioral settings include supermarkets, homes, classrooms, street corners, and pubs; some of their key characteristics are that they are "naturally occurring units" with "standing patterns of behavior" and "a physical milieu that surrounds or encloses the behavior" (see Moss 1976, pp. 213–47). An important distinction can be made between private and public behavioral settings (see Wikström 1991c).

The behavioral setting, together with the individual's disposition and social situation, guides and constrains the action taken. For instance, it is not unlikely that an impulsive young male school dropout will have different reactions than a somewhat older, cautious academic female to a negative remark about their appearance in a crowded city-center pub on a Saturday night. It is also likely that dispositions and social situation will influence the kind of behavioral settings individuals find themselves in.

Communities vary in the behavioral settings they generate and the frequency with which specific settings occur. Some types of settings are more likely than others to create temptations or provocations that, depending on the dispositions and social situation of individuals, may turn into acts of crime. Although behavioral settings of a certain kind share many general characteristics, it is also important to point out that there may be significant relevant differences that, for example, may influence the level of temptation and provocation (i.e., variations between different supermarkets in systems of protection of goods).

Individuals generally do not have full control over the consequences of their actions. The outcomes of individual action may therefore have intended or unintended consequences for the individual (e.g., his social situation) and the community (e.g., community levels of fear of crime).

Communities, Offenders, and Crime

The individual's propensity to break the rules of law is likely to be a result of his individual disposition and social situation, while the frequency and ways in which he will express his propensity is likely to be influenced by the types of behavioral settings he experiences in his daily life.

An Integrative Theory

Figure 10.2 builds primarily on aspects of contemporary criminological theories such as control theory (Gottfredson and Hirschi 1990), deterrence theory (Andenaes 1974; Cusson 1993), routine activity theory (e.g., Cohen and Felson 1979), and rational choice or decision-making theory (e.g., Clarke and Cornish 1985); it also elaborates on my previous attempts to formulate an integrative theory of factors that influence individual offending behavior (Wikström 1995b, 1996). It is based on the postulates that the individual's capability to resist temptation and provocation (as a function of his dispositions); and that the individual's perceived social costs for breaking the rules of law (as a function of his social situation) are key factors explaining (between-) individual variation

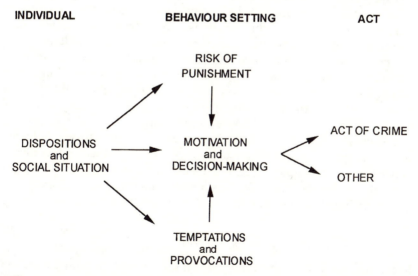

Figure 10.2 A general model of key factors influencing individual offending behavior. *Source:* Modified from Wikström 1996.

in the *propensity* to break the rules of law. Furthermore the presence of a temptation or a provocation (as a function of individual propensity and the characteristics of the behavior setting) and the individual's perceived risk of punishment (as a function of individual propensity and the characteristics of the behavior setting) are key *situational* factors influencing (within-) individual variation in the motivation to break the rules of law and his *decision making* regarding whether to commit a particular criminal act.

One implication of the model is that some behavioral settings may be more "criminogenic" than others, meaning that a less strong propensity to offend is needed before it is turned into action. This is a consequence of high degrees of temptation or provocation, and low risks of punishment, associated with the behavioral setting in question.

Another implication is that some individuals may be thought of as more "crime-prone" than others, meaning that they are less sensitive to the risk of punishment, and that a less strong temptation or provocation is needed to motivate them to break the law than may be needed for others. This is the case because some individuals have a low capacity to resist temptation and provocation (e.g., they are impulsive and short-sighted) and do not view the social costs of breaking legal rules to be high (e.g., they have weak social ties to the community).

A third implication is that the individual's motivation to break the law and his decisions regarding whether to carry out the act result from interaction of the behavioral setting's criminogenic characteristics and his own propensity to break the law.

Community variations in offending and crime are a result of community variations in the prevalence of criminogenic behavioral settings and crime-prone individuals and the rate of their intersection; the latter, in turn, is a consequence of the variations in and dynamics of community resources, rules, and routines. This is to a large extent a result of the social consequences of processes and patterns of land use and residential segregation, which, in turn, have to do with national and local planning policies and "market forces" related to broader societal, political, and economic characteristics, including means of production, division of labor, and distribution of wealth (see Figure 10.3).

It is beyond the scope of this paper to deal fully with this complex issue. In subsequent sections, the focus is restricted to selected theories as they relate to the impact of land use and residential segregation on aspects of community resources, rules, and routines relevant to community variations in offending and crime.

Social Disorganization Theory

Social disorganization theory focuses on the role of community variation in social and economic resources, and the related ability of communities to generate and uphold shared rules for behavior through informal social

NATIONAL POLITICAL-ECONOMICAL CONTEXT
Means of Production (Technology), Division of Labour,
Distribution of Wealth

National and local planning
policies and "market forces"

LAND USE DIFFERENTIATION AND RESIDENTIAL SEGREGATION

Community variations in the
prevalence and mix of social
groups and social activities.

COMMUNITY SOCIAL AND BUILT ENVIRONMENT
Resources, Rules and Routines and Their Dynamics.

Community prevalence in
criminogenic behaviour-settings
and crime prone individuals (as
residents and visitors), and their
intersection.

COMMUNITY RATES
OF CRIME AND OFFENDERS

Figure 10.3 A general model of the flow of influences from national context
to community rates of offending and crime.

controls and socialization. Social disorganization theory basically views
community variation in rules and resources as a result of processes and
patterns of urbanization and residential segregation.

Classic Social Disorganization Theory. The explanation of community
variation in offender rates, particularly male juvenile offender rates, as
developed by Shaw and McKay (1969), focused on the role of residential
segregation (primarily by economic status) in producing community
variation in social organization and its implications for community social controls and the development of a "tradition of crime." Residential
segregation was seen by Shaw and McKay as a consequence of different
social groups' competition over desirable space, the end result being the
creation of "natural areas" with individuals of similar economic and culture status, and often sharing values and norms, tending to be located in
the same community. However, some undesirable areas never became
"natural areas" because of persistent high population mobility and ethnic
heterogeneity. These areas were characterized as "socially disorganized,"
meaning that the community's social organization, in particular its social
institutions, was not apt to fit the varying needs of its constantly changing, ethnically mixed, and low-income population.

Shaw and McKay (1969) consider a high rate of juvenile offending to be a consequence of community social disorganization. Their reasoning: prevalent values and norms concerning crime and deviance are conventional in socially disorganized communities, but it is much more difficult than in other communities to create effective social controls; hence, especially since such areas also are economically disadvantaged, there is a breeding ground for the emergence of crime traditions in which somewhat older males introduce juveniles to crime and deviance (Shaw and McKay 1969, pp. 186–87, 319–20).

Developments in Social Disorganization Theory. Kornhauser's (1978) "social sources of delinquency" may be regarded as the theoretical foundation of contemporary social disorganization theory. Building on Shaw and McKay, she argues for a pure social control model in understanding the link between community characteristics and offending. She dismisses as an important cause the element of culture deviance (a tradition in crime) in Shaw and McKay's theoretical reasoning and argues that there is "in their approach a distinct control model capable of standing alone according to the internal logic of their own theory" (p. 62). She argues that the emergence of a "tradition in crime" (or subculture) is conditional on weak community social controls, but acknowledges that "the tradition," once in place, could enhance the influence of weak social controls on offending behavior (pp. 69–70).

Kornhauser's theoretical interpretation may be summarized. There is residential segregation on economic grounds; communities therefore vary in social and economic resources. At the one extreme there are communities with a wealthy, residentially stable, and homogeneous population; at the other extreme there are communities with a poor, residentially unstable, and heterogeneous population. Social disorganization, defined as lack of "a structure through which common values can be realized and common problems solved" (Kornhauser 1978, p. 63), emerges in poor, residentially unstable, and heterogeneous communities. This is so because it is difficult to realize common values among the residents, due to such factors as poor communication resulting from residents' diverse and changing cultural backgrounds and experiences, but also because the social institutions, due to factors such as lack of money, skills, and personal investments by residents, tend to be inadequate, isolated from each other, and unstable. Poorly functioning social institutions and a lack of common values among community residents result in poor informal social controls and defective socialization, which, in turn, cause high rates of offending by community residents.

Contemporary Social Disorganization Theory: The Systemic Model. Recent authors in the social disorganization tradition (e.g., Sampson 1988; Bursik 1988) generally refer to this approach as the systemic model, emphasizing that interest is focused not only on how community organization influences offending and crime but also on how structural characteristics of society influence community organization. "In the systemic model, community organization is treated as an essential aspect of mass society. It is a structure which has ecological, institutional, and normative dimensions. The local community is viewed as a complex system of friendship and kinship networks and formal and informal associational ties rooted in family life and ongoing socialization processes. At the same time it is fashioned by the large-scale institutions of mass society" (Kasarda and Janowitz 1974, p. 329).

One key feature of contemporary social disorganization theory is its various attempts to further understanding of how social mechanisms of community structure influence juvenile offending behavior. Another feature is the growing interest in the development of dynamic models of change in community organization and the relationship of change to levels of disorder and crime.

a. Communities, families, teenagers, and child rearing. The family, the school, and the peer group are key social institutions in socialization and informal social control. In a number of papers, Robert J. Sampson has highlighted the need for developing a better understanding of the relations among the community context, the community's ability to supervise and control teenage groups, and the conditions for family management and child rearing.

Sampson (1987) has claimed that family disruption is a key structural factor influencing a community's ability to exercise informal social control over juveniles. He has also urged that a community's level of social cohesion—a community's ability to generate moral and social integration among its residents—is another important factor (Sampson 1993a). Sampson has stressed that the community context plays a crucial role for family management and child development, arguing that a key feature of socially disorganized communities is that families in such communities often lack supportive social networks, which has negative consequences for their ability to control and supervise their children.

Sampson makes a strong argument that the community context (economic level, population heterogeneity, residential mobility, and family disruption) has a great impact on community social resources (family social capital, neighborhood social cohesion), which in turn influence informal social controls of juveniles and conditions for socialization, which in turn influence rates of juvenile offending.

b. Ecological socialization. Bronfenbrenner's (1979) model of "ecological socialization" brings an ecological dimension to the study of family socialization and offending behavior. Bronfenbrenner's model highlights the interaction of the family and the neighborhood but also stresses the importance of the neighborhood's embeddedness in the wider community. The model points to the significance of routine activities in socialization and thus has the potential of being integrated with aspects of a routine activity framework. As Martens puts it, Bronfenbrenner is interested in "with whom the child interacts in day-to-day situations, the character of these interactions, and in what way persons outside the family can enhance or inhibit the quality of parent-child interactions" (Martens 1993, p. 124).

c. Communities and the social control of public space. Following Hunter (1985), Bursik and Grasmick (1993) have stressed the importance of different levels of social order in a community: the private (e.g., the family), the parochial (e.g., the neighborhood), and the public (e.g., streets, squares, and public transport), and their links to different agents and mechanisms of social control, such as family members (in the private), neighbors (in the parochial), and the police (in the public). They argue that "perhaps the greatest shortcoming of the basic social disorganization model is its failure to consider the relational networks that pertain to the public sphere of control" (Bursik and Grasmick 1993, p. 37) and advocate "the need to expand the focus of control beyond the internal dynamics of the community" (p. 38).

d. Community disorder and crime. Wesley Skogan has shown the potentially important role that disorder (or incivility) plays for community social organization and serious crime, and against this background has advanced a theory of "disorder and decline." Behaviors counting as disorders include public drinking, street harassment, noisy neighbors, vandalism, and littering. Skogan has shown that disorders are more likely to emerge in socially disorganized communities but that, once having emerged at a certain level, they have an important influence on community organization (i.e., increasing residential instability) and the occurrence of serious crime:

> Disorder not only sparks concern and fear of crime among neighborhood residents; it may actually increase the level of serious crime. Disorder erodes what control neighborhood residents can maintain over local events and conditions. It drives out those for whom stable community life is important, and discourages people with similar values from moving in. It threatens house prices and discourages investment. In short, disorder is an instrument of destabilization and neighborhood decline. (Skogan 1990, p. 3)

Testing Social Disorganization Theory. Sampson and Groves (1989) observe that, although numerous community-level studies show the association between community structural characteristics and crime and delinquency, the social mechanisms of community influences on offending and crime have not been empirically tested. Theirs is probably the first major empirical study to test intervening mechanisms of social disorganization theory.

Using data from the British Crime Survey, Sampson and Groves (1989) created area-level measures for community structural characteristics (i.e., low SES, ethnic heterogeneity, residential mobility, family disruption, and urbanization), intervening variables (i.e., sparse local friendship networks, unsupervised teenage peer groups, low organizational participation), and crime and delinquency. Their findings indicated that the effects of community structural characteristics on victimization and offending were mediated by social disorganization, in particular, the level of unsupervised teenage peer groups.

Empirical support for the relationship between degree of urbanization and community social disorganization, informal social control, disorder, local victimization, and fear of crime has been obtained in a recent series of large household surveys conducted in different regions of Sweden (e.g., Wikström, Torstensson, and Dolmén 1997). Wikström and Dolmén (forthcoming) carried out a path analysis at the neighborhood level. The findings show that the influence of the community level of social disorganization (or social integration) on local personal victimization (and fear of crime) fits empirically to a model where this effect is mediated through community levels of informal social control and disorder.

In probably the first ever cross-national comparative study of community social disorganization and crime, using identical measures of the constructs, Sampson and Wikström (1996) showed that the relation between key constructs based on social disorganization theory and local levels of personal victimization were remarkably invariant in Chicago and Stockholm. The same model explained community variations in the level of local personal victimization in Chicago and Stockholm, although the rates were much higher in Chicago. This is a finding of particular interest given that there are sizable social, political, and economical differences between the United States and Sweden.

Community Routines: Routine Activity Theory

Routine activities are "any recurrent and prevalent activities which provide for basic population and individual needs" (Cohen and Felson 1979, p. 593). Key routine activities relate to family life, work, education, and leisure. The prevalence and mix of different kinds of routine activities vary between communities. Community patterns of routine activities may facilitate or constrain the occurrence of criminogenic behavior settings by influencing community levels of formal and informal social controls and community levels of temptation and provocation. Community patterns of routine activities may also influence the supply of crime-prone individuals by offering a varying degree of attractiveness for non-residents with different propensities to offend.

Key features of routine activity theories were outlined earlier. Here I focus on what such theories can add to the social disorganization perspective in understanding and explaining community variations in crime and offending.

The Roles of the Wider Community. While social disorganization theory tends to focus only on the role of the community of residence on individuals' offending, the routine activity approach broadens the perspective to include the role of the wider community by acknowledging that individuals may, and do, commit crime outside their area of residence. Moreover, it also focuses on visitors' contributions to community crime levels.

Brantingham and Brantingham argue that "crime is an event that occurs when an individual with some criminal readiness level encounters a suitable target in a situation sufficient to activate that readiness potential" (1993, p. 266). Routine activity theory stresses the importance of area differentiations in the prevalence and kinds of routine activities, and the movements between areas they generate, as important background to community variations in crime. Brantingham and Brantingham (1993) describe an individual's "activity space" (i.e., areas and places an individual tends to visit, arguing that this is determined predominantly by the locations of home, work, recreational and entertainment activities, and main lines of transportation) as creating an "awareness space" (i.e., knowledge about areas and places and their characteristics). An individual with some criminal inclination is likely predominantly to look for good targets and to offend within his awareness space. As an individual offender becomes more experienced, he develops more elaborate search behavior, and his awareness space will be influenced by his criminal activities rather than the pattern of legal routine activities.

Social disorganization theory needs to better incorporate the relations between community of residence and the wider community as they relate to understanding of residents' offending behavior.

Community Social Controls by Residents and Others. Social disorganization theory tends to focus on the importance of the social characteristics of community residents but largely ignores the social characteristics of visitors to the area. This may be an important omission, since the population present in some communities (at least at certain times of the day or week) may be dominated by nonresidents who may exercise a significant influence on the community's social life. Social disorganization theory also often ignores the role of formal community social controls (e.g., by police presence) and "techno-prevention."

Felson (1986) differentiated between two key types of agents of informal social control: handlers and guardians. *Handlers* are significant others who influence the individual's motivation to offend. *Guardians* refer to persons willing to intervene to stop an act of crime and thereby influence potential offenders' motivation to offend. People often act as guardians in situations where they are perceived as potential defenders of their own, or their family, friends', or employer's, interests. This puts the emphasis not only on informal social control carried out by residents but also on informal social control carried out by people working in or visiting an area in different capacities. In addition, the guardians of agents of formal social control who have a special obligation to intervene, such as police officers and security guards, should not be overlooked in this context.

Community Social Activities. Social disorganization theory emphasizes the importance of community social institutions (like the family) and related conditions for effective socialization, while largely ignoring the influence of community levels of temptation or provocation generated by the presence and prevalence of commercial and entertainment activities. Integration of potential influences of community social activities outside those exclusively relating to community residents appears to be an important area for development of theories of the influence of community organization on crime and offending behavior.

Future Research

Rates of crime and of offenders vary significantly between communities. These variations are systematically correlated with other community characteristics. Theories have been developed to account for different aspects of these relationships but as yet have not been much tested empirically. This applies, in particular, to the hypothesized social mechanisms of community influences on offending behavior and crime. Thus, "the community-level approach is theoretically strong, yet empirically weak" (Sampson 1993b, p. 428).

I have argued that community influences on crime and offending behavior can be best understood in terms of community variations in rules, resources, and routines. The social disorganization perspective has focused predominantly on community variations in resources and rules, while the routine activity approach, which has not been much applied at the community level, focuses on community variations in routines. The link between community resources, rules, and routines is poorly developed and looks to be an important area for integration.

More specifically, we need to improve our understanding of how community patterns of rules, resources, and routines, in the long term, influence the development of individual dispositions relevant to (future) offending and, in the shorter term, influence aspects of the individual's social situation relevant to his motivation to offend and, the occurrence of criminogenic behavioral settings. A number of subjects are ripe for further research.

Studies of communities and crime have focused largely on the social mechanisms of community influences on individual social situation and its impact (predominantly) on juvenile offending. They have mostly neglected the role of community influences on early individual development of dispositions relevant to future offending propensity. We need a better understanding of whether, or to what degree, community context influences early development of dispositions of relevance to future offending risk.

The role of community factors in shaping criminal careers—for example, as regards age of onset, persistence, escalation in offending, and desistence—has not generated much research. We need studies exploring criminal career features in different types of community contexts and investigating which community aspects influence which variations in criminal career patterns.

Research indicates that the relations at a given time between offending and individual characteristics may be dependent on the community context. We need research exploring the relation between individual characteristics and offending in different types of community contexts. In particular, we need to better understand which community factors account for such differences. In so doing, we need better to understand how the individual social situation is linked to the community context and its relevance for measuring individual and community influences on offending.

The social life of a community is determined not only by its residents, their characteristics, and their social activities but also by the characteristics of the visitors to the area and by what activities are located in the area. The social life of an individual is not lived only in his community of residence but is also influenced by the wider community. We need to develop a better understanding of the interaction between communities of residence and the wider community in its influence on residents' offending behavior. We need to develop a better understanding of the roles of nonresidents, and of social activities not exclusively related to residents, for an area's patterns and rates of crime and offenders.

References

Andenaes, J. 1974. *Punishment and Deterrence.* Ann Arbor, Mich.: University of Michigan Press.

Baldwin, J., and A. E. Bottoms. 1976. *The Urban Criminal.* London: Tavistock.

Block, R., and C. Block. 1995. "Space, Place and Crime. Hot Spots Areas and Hot Spot Places of Liquor-Related Crime." In *Crime and Place,* edited by J. E. Eck and D. Weisburd. Washington, D.C.: Criminal Justice Press.

Bloom, B. S. 1964. *Stability and Change in Human Characteristics.* New York: Wiley.

Bogg, S. L. 1965. "Urban Crime Patterns." *American Sociological Review* 30:899–908.

Bottoms, A. E. 1993. "Recent Criminological and Social Theory: The Problem of Integrating Knowledge About Individual Criminal Acts and Careers and Areal Dimensions of Crime." In *Integrating Individual and Ecological Aspects of Crime,* edited by D. P. Farrington, R. J. Sampson, and P. -O. Wikström. BRÅ Report 1993:1. Stockholm: Allmänna Förlaget.

Bottoms, A. E., A. Claytor, and P. Wiles. 1992. "Housing Markets and Residential Community Crime Careers: A Case Study from Sheffield." In *Crime, Policing, and Place,* edited by D. J. Evans, N. R. Fyfe, and D. T. Herbert. London: Routledge.

Bottoms, A. E., and P. Wiles. 1986. "Housing Tenure and Community Crime Careers in Britain." In *Communities and Crime,* edited by A. J. Reiss and M. Tonry. Chicago: University of Chicago Press.

———. 1995. "Crime and Insecurity in the City." In *Changes in Society,*

Crime and Civil Justice in Europe, vol. 1, edited by C. Fijnaut, J. Goethals, T. Peters, and L. Walgrave. Antwerp: Kluwer Law International.

Braithwaite, J. 1979. *Inequality, Crime and Public Policy.* London: Routledge.

————. 1989. *Crime, Shame and Reintegration.* Cambridge: Cambridge University Press.

Brantingham, P. J., and P. L. Brantingham. 1981. "Introduction: The Dimensions of Crime." In *Environmental Criminology,* edited by P. J. Brantingham and P. L. Brantingham. Beverly Hills, Calif.: Sage.

————. 1984. *Patterns in Crime.* New York: Macmillan.

————. 1993. "Environment, Routine and Situation: Toward a Pattern Theory of Crime." In *Routine Activity and Rational Choice,* edited by R. V. Clarke and M. Felson. New Brunswick, N.J.: Transaction Publications.

Bronfenbrenner, U. 1979. *The Ecology of Human Development.* Cambridge, Mass.: Harvard University Press.

Bursik, R. J. 1988. "Social Disorganization and Theories of Crime and Delinquency: Problems and Prospects." *Criminology* 26:519–51.

Bursik, R. J., and H. G. Grasmick. 1993. *Neighborhoods and Crime.* New York: Lexington.

Chilton, R. J. 1964. "Continuity in Delinquency Area Research: A Comparison of Studies from Baltimore, Detroit, and Indianapolis." *American Sociological Review* 29:71–83.

Christie, N., J. Andenaes, and S. Skirbekk. 1965. "A Study of Self-Reported Crime." *Scandinavian Studies in Criminology* 1:86–116.

Clarke, R. V., and D. Cornish. 1985. "Modeling Offenders' Decisions: A Framework for Research and Policy." In *Crime and Justice: A Review of Research,* vol. 6, edited by Michael Tonry and Norval Morris. Chicago: University of Chicago Press.

Cohen, L. E., and M. Felson. 1979. "Social Change and Crime Rate Trends: A Routine Activity Approach." *American Sociological Review* 44:588–608.

Coleman, J. S. 1990. *Foundations of Social Theory.* Cambridge, Mass.: Belknap Press of Harvard University Press.

Curtis, L. A. 1974. *Criminal Violence.* Lexington, Mass.: Lexington.

Cusson, M. 1993. "Situational Deterrence: Fear During the Criminal Event." *Crime Prevention Studies,* vol. 4, edited by Ronald V. Clarke. Monsey, N.Y.: Criminal Justice Press.

Davidson, R. N. 1981. *Crime and Environment.* London: Croom Helm.

Durkheim, E. 1952. *Suicide.* London: Routledge.

Eck, J. E., and D. Weisburd. 1995. "Crime Places in Crime Theory." In *Crime and Place,* edited by J. E. Eck and D. Weisburd. Washington, D.C.: Criminal Justice Press.

Elmer, M. C. 1933. "Century-Old Ecological Studies in France." *American Journal of Sociology* 39:63–70.

Felson, M. 1986. "Linking Criminal Choices, Routine Activities, Informal Control, and Criminal Outcomes." In *The Reasoning Criminal,* edited by D. B. Cornish and R. V. Clarke. New York: Springer-Verlag.

Felson, M., and L. E. Cohen. 1980. "Human Ecology and Crime: A Routine Activity Approach." *Human Ecology* 8:389–406.

Felson, R. B. 1993. "Predatory and Dispute-Related Violence: A Social Interactionist Approach." In *Routine Activity and Rational Choice,* edited by

R. V. Clarke and M. Felson. New Brunswick, N.J.: Transaction Publications.

Giddens, A. 1979. *Central Problems in Social Theory.* London: Macmillan.

————. 1991. *Modernity and Self-Identity.* Cambridge: Polity Press.

Gottfredson, D. C., R. J. McNeill III, and G. D. Gottfredson. 1991. "Social Area Influences on Delinquency: A Multilevel Analysis." *Journal of Research in Crime and Delinquency* 28:197–226.

Gottfredson, M. R., and T. Hirschi. 1990. *A General Theory of Crime.* Stanford, Calif.: Stanford University Press.

Harries, K. D. 1981. "Alternative Denominators in Conventional Crime Rates." In *Environmental Criminology,* edited by P. J. Brantingham and P. L. Brantingham. Beverly Hills, Calif.: Sage.

Hawley, A. 1986. *Human Ecology: A Theoretical Essay.* Chicago: University of Chicago Press.

Hindelang, M. J., M. R. Gottfredson, and J. Garofalo. 1978. *Victims of Personal Crime: An Empirical Foundation for a Theory of Personal Victimization.* Cambridge, Mass.: Ballinger.

Hirschfield, A., and K. J. Bowers. 1997. "The Effect of Social Cohesion and Levels of Recorded Crime in Disadvantaged Areas." *Urban Studies* 34:1275–95.

Hunter, A. 1985. "Private, Parochial, and Public Orders: The Problem of Crime and Incivility in Urban Communities." In *The Challenge of Social Control,* edited by G. D. Suttles and M. N. Zald. Norwood, N.J.: Ablex.

Janson, C.-G. 1980. "Factorial Social Ecology: An Attempt at Summary and Evaluation." *Annual Review of Sociology* 6:433–56.

Kasarda, J., and M. Janowitz. 1974. "Community Attachment in Mass Society." *American Journal of Sociology* 39:328–39.

Kornhauser, R. R. 1978. *Social Sources of Delinquency.* Chicago: University of Chicago Press.

Kupersmidt, J. B., P. C. Griesler, M. E. DeRosier, C. J. Patterson, and P. W. Davis. 1995. "Childhood Aggression and Peer Relations in the Context of Family and Neighborhood Factors." *Child Development* 66:360–75.

Laub, J. 1983. "Patterns of Offending in Urban and Rural Areas." *Journal of Criminal Justice* 11:120–42.

LeBlanc, M. 1993. "Prevention of Delinquency: An Integrative Multilayered Control Based Perspective." In *Integrating Individual and Ecological Aspects of Crime,* edited by D. P. Farrington, R. J. Sampson, and P.-O. Wikström. BRÅ Report 1993:1. Stockholm: Allmänna Förlaget.

Lindström, P. 1996. "Family Interaction, Neighborhood Context and Deviant Behavior." *Studies in Crime and Crime Prevention* 5:113–19.

Lizotte, A. J., T. P. Thornberry, M. D. Krohn, D. C. Chard-Wierschem, and D. McDowall. 1994. "Neighborhood Context and Delinquency: A Longitudinal Analysis." In *Cross-National Longitudinal Research on Human Development and Criminal Behavior,* edited by E. M. G. Weitekamp and H.-J. Kerner. Dordrecht: Kluwer.

Loeber, R., and P.-O. Wikström. 1993. "Individual Pathways to Crime in Different Types of Neighborhoods." In *Integrating Individual and Ecological Aspects of Crime,* edited by D. P. Farrington, R. J. Sampson, and P.-O. Wikström. BRÅ Report 1993:1. Stockholm: Allmänna Förlaget.

Martens, P. L. 1993. "An Ecological Model of Socialization in Explaining Offending." In *Integrating Individual and Ecological Aspects of Crime,* edited by D. P. Farrington, R. J. Sampson, and P.-O. Wikström. BRÅ Report 1993:1. Stockholm: Allmänna Förlaget.

McClintock, F. H., and N. H. Avison. 1968. *Crime in England and Wales.* London: Macmillan.

McClintock, F. H., and P.-O. Wikström. 1992. "The Comparative Study of Urban Violence: Criminal Violence in Edinburgh and Stockholm." *British Journal of Criminology* 32:505–20.

McIver, P. 1981. "Criminal Mobility." In *Crime Spillover,* edited by S. Hakim and G. F. Rengert. Beverly Hills, Calif.: Sage.

Moss, R. H. 1976. *The Human Context: Environmental Determinants of Behavior.* New York: Wiley.

Park, R. E., E. W. Burgess, and R. D. McKenzie. 1925. *The City.* Chicago: University of Chicago Press.

Peeples, F., and R. Loeber. 1994. "Do Individual Factors and Neighborhood Context Explain Ethnic Differences in Juvenile Delinquency?" *Journal of Quantitative Criminology* 10:141–57.

Pyle, G. F. 1974. *The Spatial Dynamics of Crime.* Research Paper no. 159. Department of Geography, University of Chicago.

Raudenbush, S. W. 1993. "Modeling Individual and Community Effects on Deviance over Time: Multi-Level Statistical Models." In *Integrating Individual and Ecological Aspects of Crime,* edited by D. P. Farrington, R. J. Sampson, and P.-O. Wikström. BRÅ Report 1993:1. Stockholm: Allmänna Förlaget.

Reiss, A. J. 1986. "Why Are Communities Important in Understanding Crime?" In *Communities and Crime,* edited by A. J. Reiss and M. Tonry. Chicago: University of Chicago Press.

Reiss, A. J., and A. L. Rhodes. 1961. "The Distribution of Juvenile Delinquency in the Social Class Structure." *American Sociological Review* 26:720–32.

Rengert, G. 1981. "Burglary in Philadelphia: A Critique of an Opportunity-Structure Model." In *Environmental Criminology,* edited by P. J. Brantingham and P. L. Brantingham. Beverly Hills, Calif.: Sage.

Rhodes, W. M., and C. C. Conly. 1981. "Crime and Mobility: An Empirical Study." In *Environmental Criminology,* edited by P. J. Brantingham and P. L. Brantingham. Beverly Hills, Calif.: Sage.

Roncek, D. W., and P. A. Maier. 1991. "Bars, Blocks, and Crime Revisited: Linking the Theory of Routine Activities to the Empiricism of 'Hot Spots.'" *Criminology* 29:725–53.

Rutter, M., B. Yule, D. Quinton, O. Rowlands, W. Yule, and M. Berger. 1974. "Attainment and Adjustment in Two Geographical Areas III: Some Factors Accounting for Area Differences." *British Journal of Psychiatry* 126:520–33.

Sampson, R. J. 1986. "The Effects of Urbanization and Neighborhood Characteristics on Criminal Victimization." In *Metropolitan Crime Patterns,* edited by R. M. Figlio, S. Hakim, and G. F. Rengert. New York: Criminal Justice Press.

———. 1987. "Urban Black Violence. The Effect of Male Joblessness and Family Disruption." *American Journal of Sociology* 93:348–82.

———. 1988. "Local Friendship Ties and Community Attachment in Mass

Society: A Multilevel Systemic Model." *American Sociological Review* 53:766–79.

———. 1990. "The Impact of Housing Policies on Community Social Disorganization and Crime." *Bulletin of the New York Academy of Medicine* 66:526–33.

———. 1993a. "Family and Community-Level Influences on Crime." In *Integrating Individual and Ecological Aspects of Crime,* edited by D. P. Farrington, R. J. Sampson, and P.-O. Wikström. BRÅ Report 1993:1. Stockholm: Allmänna Förlaget.

———. 1993b. "Linking Time and Place: Dynamic Contextualism and the Future of Criminological Inquiry." *Journal of Research in Crime and Delinquency* 30:426–44.

Sampson, R. J, and W. B. Groves. 1989. "Community Structure and Crime: Testing Social Disorganization Theory." *American Journal of Sociology* 94:774–802.

Sampson, R. J., and P.-O. Wikström. 1996. "Lessons for Policing from Community and Crime Research: A Comparative Look at Chicago and Stockholm Neighborhoods." Paper presented at the International Conference on Problem-Solving Policing as Crime Prevention, Stockholm, September.

Schmid, C. F. 1960. "Urban Crime Areas, Part II." *American Sociological Review* 25:655–78.

Schuerman, L. A., and S. Kobrin. 1986. "Community Careers in Crime." In *Communities and Crime,* edited by A. J. Reiss and M. Tonry. Chicago: University of Chicago Press.

Shaw, C., and H. McKay. 1969. *Juvenile Delinquency and Urban Areas.* Chicago: University of Chicago Press.

Sherman, L. W., P. R. Gartin, and M. E. Buerger. 1989. "Hot Spots of Predatory Crime: Routine Activities and the Criminology of Place." *Criminology* 27:27–55.

Sherman, L. W., R. J. Velke, C. Bridgeforth, and D. Gaines. 1991. "Violent Crimes in Georgetown: Hotspots and Trends." Unpublished manuscript. Washington, D.C.: Crime Control Institute.

Simcha-Fagan, O., and J. E. Schwartz. 1986. "Neighborhood and Delinquency: An Assessment of Contextual Effects." *Criminology* 24:667–703.

Skogan, W. G. 1978. "The Changing Distribution of Big-City Crime." *Urban Affairs Quarterly* 13:33–49.

———. 1990. *Disorder and Decline.* New York: Free Press.

Taub, R. P., D. G. Taylor, and J. D. Dunham. 1984. *Paths of Neighborhood Change: Race and Crime in Urban America.* Chicago: University of Chicago Press.

Timms, D. W. G. 1971. *The Urban Mosaic.* Cambridge: Cambridge University Press.

Tonry, M., L. E. Ohlin, and D. P. Farrington. 1991. *Human Development and Criminal Behavior.* New York: Springer-Verlag.

van Dijk, J. J. M., and A. C. Vivanen. 1978. *Criminal Victimization in the Netherlands.* The Hague: Ministry of Justice.

Wellman, B., and B. Leighton 1979. "Networks, Neighborhoods, and Communities: Approaches to the Study of the Community Question." *Urban Affairs Quarterly* 14:363–90.

Wikström, P.-O. 1985. *Everyday Violence in Contemporary Sweden: Ecological and Situational Aspects.* BRÅ Report 1985:15. Stockholm: Liber Förlag.

———. 1990. "Delinquency and the Urban Structure." In *Crime and Measures Against Crime in the City,* edited by P.-O. Wikström. BRÅ Report 1990:5. Stockholm: Allmänna Förlaget.

———. 1991a. "Housing Tenure, Social Class and Offending." *Criminal Behavior and Mental Health* 1:69–89.

———. 1991b. *Sociala Problem, Brott och Trygghet.* BRÅ Report 1991:5. Stockholm: Allmänna Förlaget.

———. 1991c. *Urban Crime, Criminals and Victims.* New York: Springer-Verlag.

———. 1994. "Ungdomsbrott i Stockholm." Unpublished manuscript. Stockholm: National Police College, Research Unit.

———. 1995a. "Preventing City Centre Crime." In *Building a Safer Society,* edited by M. Tonry and D. Farrington. Chicago: University of Chicago Press.

———. 1995b. "Self-Control, Temptations, Frictions and Punishment: An Integrated Approach to Crime Prevention." In *Integrating Crime Prevention Strategies: Propensity and Opportunity,* edited by P.-O. Wikström, J. McCord, and R. V. Clarke. BRÅ Report 1995:5. Stockholm: Fritzes.

———. 1996. "Causes of Crime and Crime Prevention." In *Preventing Crime and Disorder,* edited by T. Bennett. Cambridge: University of Cambridge, Institute of Criminology.

Wikström, P.-O., and L. Dolmén. Forthcoming. "Urbanization, Social Integration, Informal Social Control, Disorder, Victimization and Fear of Crime." *International Review of Victimology.*

Wikström, P.-O., and R. Loeber. 1997. "The Role of Individual Risk Factors for Serious Juvenile Offending in Different Types of Residential Communities." Paper presented at the Seventh European Conference of Law and Psychology, Stockholm, September.

Wikström, P.-O., M. Torstensson, and L. Dolmén. 1997. *Lokala Problem: Brott och Trygghet I Gävleborgs Län.* Rapport från Problemgruppen 1997:1. Solna: Polishögskolan.

Wilson, J. Q., and R. J. Herrnstein. 1985. *Crime and Human Nature.* New York: Touchstone.

Wirth, L. 1938. "Urbanism as a Way of Life." *American Journal of Sociology* 44:1–24.

Wrong, D. H. 1994. *The Problem of Order: What Unites and Divides Society?* New York: Free Press.

11

Economic Conditions, Work, and Crime

ANNE MORRISON PIEHL

While many citizens, policy makers, politicians, and academics assume that economic conditions drive crime rates, evidence of this relationship has proved elusive. As a result, there is a large disconnect between theory and empirical evidence on this point. For theory building, the notion that crime is a function of economic opportunity has great intuitive appeal. Economic theorists, for example, have long assumed that individuals allocate their time between legal work and crime depending on the relative returns to each activity. Advocates of employment-based solutions to the crime problem also rely on such a causal notion. Nonetheless, there has been surprisingly little convincing evidence to support this belief. This chapter describes both what is currently known and what we can hope to learn about the connection between economics and crime.

Evidence of a connection between the economy and crime has implications for macrolevel policy and for microlevel interventions. If a booming economy yields crime reductions, this is an additional argument for pro-growth macroeconomic policy. If improved earnings potential keeps individuals in the legal sector and out of illegal activity, training programs and subsidized employment are recommended. Furthermore, an understanding of the relationship between economic conditions and criminal behavior may help with our understanding of criminal behavior more generally.

The prima facie time-series evidence—that crime rates have increased since 1960 in the United States while the economy was generally growing—indicates that simple explanations about the relationship between the economy and crime will not be adequate. The picture from cross-sectional evidence poses similar challenges: while it is true that crime rates are higher in poorer communities, and incarceration and arrest rates are higher for people with lower earnings potential, it is also true that most people who commit crime also work in the legal sector and most people with low earnings are not involved in the criminal justice system.

Much of the existing research has been of a very general nature. But in order to use economics to "solve" the crime problem, we need very particular knowledge about how people respond to incentives. Ultimately, this requires a great deal of differentiation among crime types and among different populations (e.g., by age). Furthermore, it is necessary to understand the connection between the economy and crime at three levels: economy-wide, for communities, and for individuals.

The current research reveals that the relationship between economics and crime is not a simple one. It is very hard to discern the true effect of secular economic growth, but we do know that property crime increases in recessions, whereas homicide either falls in recessions or is not responsive to the business cycle. We know that individuals with worse economic prospects are more likely to be involved in crime and in the criminal justice system, and that neighborhoods with fewer working residents have high crime rates. We also know that crime is highly concentrated: certain locations (countries, cities, street corners) have disproportionate levels of crime that cannot be explained by economics alone.

I begin with a discussion of the hypothesized relationship between economics and crime. I go on to present empirical evidence about the relationship between the economy and criminal behavior at the three levels of analysis, covering a variety of data sources and analytic methods. I then consider the possibility that the direction of causality is reversed: running from "crime" to economic conditions. Finally, I present a detailed discussion of the remaining research challenges.

Several recurring issues are important to keep in mind. First, analyses of "crime" sometimes focus on offending, and sometimes on victimization. At the national and community levels, I focus on crime rates because the distinction between victimization and offending is not commonly meaningful. (The distinction can emerge as a result of which data source is used. Also, when various subpopulations are analyzed, the distinction can be very important, e.g., rates of offending among the elderly may be quite different from rates of victimization.) At the individual level, I focus on offending, though there is reason to think there may be a connection between economic status and victimization, which is discussed briefly in the conclusion. Second, there are many different types of crimes: white-collar, property, violent, and drug. This chapter includes evidence about each type of crime. Yet, often, crimes are grouped together into one index, which does not allow understanding of potentially distinct dynamics. When crimes are grouped in this way, property crime constitutes the largest category. Third, it is important to keep in mind that the intensity with which a person is involved in the legal or illegal sector can vary tremendously. Just as a person may be "employed" yet work only a few hours per week, a "criminal" may commit crimes only infrequently. I try to distinguish between "participation" and "intensity" where such distinctions matter to the interpretation of results. Finally, this chapter does not cover poverty per se, welfare state effects, or the connection between economic status and the probability of punishment (e.g., discrimination in law enforcement or the courts).

The Theoretical Relationship

Before thinking about empirical strategies, it is useful to consider the various hypotheses about the links between crime and the economy. This short review is not, by any means, an exhaustive review of the theory of criminal behavior. This section merely reveals that there are many hypotheses about economics and crime which suggest estimation strategies that may be not only different but even competing. Some of these theories emphasize individual behavior, while some operate at a macro (societal) level. Some depend on the level of a causal factor, such as the *level* of unemployment, while others focus on changes in those variables. It will be helpful to bear in mind these theoretical models when thinking about the interpretation of the empirical findings presented in the subsequent section.

Absolute Poverty

The idea that people commit crime out of necessity is a potential explanation for property crime and for violent crimes that are instrumental in some way. If absolute poverty provides the incentive for crime, aggregate crime rates should fall as economies become more developed and incomes rise. In addition, the development of the welfare state should reduce crime. Those programs that provide support to the poorest members of the society should have the largest crime reduction benefits.

Relative Deprivation

Several types of models imply that greater inequality leads to more crime. In time allocation models, individuals decide how to divide their time between the legal and illegal sectors depending on the relative returns in the two sectors. The standard model supposes that the relative returns to time in the illegal sector increase with the earnings and wealth at the top of the income distribution. For those at the bottom of the income distribution, increasing inequality reduces the returns to time working in the legal sector at the same time it increases the returns to criminal activity. As a result, increases in earnings inequality yield increases in criminal activity.

This type of model implies that crime may vary not only with broad trends in the economy but also with cyclical movements in the economy. In particular, relative returns to time may vary with the business cycle. As the economy enters a recession, if legal opportunities dry up faster than illegal ones, again the result will be increased crime. Theories of frustration arising from relative deprivation (which may have more to do with wealth than with earnings) yield the same predictions as models based on income.

Routine Activities

A number of theories about crime emphasize lifestyle choices. Here, crime may "go along with" being unemployed, since a person is in a better position to take advantage of criminal opportunities when his schedule is more flexible. In this case, steady employment is incompatible with intensive criminal activity. Poor economic conditions, then, may shift people from one set of activities to another. This idea is similar to a time allocation model, except here people are "choosing" from a limited number of bundles of activities rather than making choices about much smaller units of time.

Labeling Theory

Labeling theory emphasizes the negative effect on one's prosocial activities of being perceived (rightly or wrongly) as being involved in criminal activity. Thus, it argues that criminal activity and the imposition of sanctions serve to "label" individuals in such a way that, for example, their employment prospects are reduced. This provides for a feedback mechanism: once one becomes involved in crime, employment opportunities fall, and the incentive to commit crime increases. This model has business cycle consequences. When crime increases, the economy suffers. Therefore, if crime rates go up in recessions, the feedback mechanism will deepen or prolong the economic downturn.

Community Health

If vibrant communities provide opportunity, role models, and pride for their residents, a poor economy can lead to disorder and decay. This disorder may, through a variety of mechanisms, get translated into criminal activity. Such hypotheses require that empirical models of crime include community-level variables as well as individual-level indicators.

Social Control

Work can be seen as a means of social control. These hypotheses argue that job stability is an important determinant of criminal involvement, not because of the income but because of the control it exerts over a worker's life.

Criminal Justice "System" Behavior

It is also possible that the enforcement environment varies with economic conditions. For example, during booms, there may be more expenditure by local and state governments and by individuals. This increase

in policing, sentencing, prevention, and private security capacity may reduce the number of crimes from what it would be otherwise.[1] On the
other hand, criminal opportunities may increase with increased legal
economic activity. In an economic boom, not only are there more items
worth stealing, but houses are more likely to be empty because of greater
employment.[2]

While it is obvious that the true relationship between economics and
crime is an empirical question, the variety of theories about the relationship pose challenges to researchers attempting to pin down the quantitative effect. Past attempts to rise to these challenges are outlined in the
next section.

Empirical Approaches to Identifying the Effect of the Economy on Crime

As indicated earlier, analyses of the relationship between economic conditions and crime can take place at several levels. Much of the early work
in this field relied on aggregate data. Particularly during the past fifteen
years, more individual-level data have become available, which has
shifted attention to questions of individual behavior.

Microlevel data often can be aggregated to form community-level
data.[3] While this type of analysis has not provided as many contributions
as individual-level research, this is changing as recent developments in
geographic mapping software make community analyses easier.

This section covers the dominant modes of analysis of crime and criminal behavior. I start with nonexperimental evidence from aggregate analyses, individual-level analyses, and research at the level of the community,
and then turn to experimental evidence bearing on economics and criminal behavior. In each area, I describe the method, the questions it can hope
to answer, and the best estimates of the answers.

Aggregate Analyses

Aggregate analyses draw on time-series data, cross-sectional data, and
"panels" that combine time-series data with cross-sectional data.

Time-Series Data. Early studies of the economy-crime relationship involved the analysis of time-series evidence, in which movements in
crime rates over time are correlated with movements in demographic,
economic, and criminal justice variables. Chiricos (1987) and Freeman
(1983) review the aggregate literature using U.S. data. These studies generally found a modest positive relationship between unemployment and
crime.[4] But if the goal is to explain the long-term trend toward higher
crime rates in the United States since World War II, increases in the rate
of unemployment (or reductions in labor force participation) will not
provide the solution.

These time-series analyses face a fundamental problem: there are few observations, whereas there are, perhaps, many secular trends that must be disentangled. (The same critique applies to cross-national, time-series studies.) Another difficulty is data. The *Uniform Crime Reports* (*UCR*) series is widely felt to have improved substantially over time, due to improvements in reporting practices during the late 1960s, 1970s, and early 1980s. These led to increases in the level of reported crimes. Therefore, use of a time-series empirical approach incorporating *UCR* data means that anything that trended up over this period will look as if it drives crime.

Model specification can be important to the interpretation of the time-series evidence. A number of analysts have tried to do better than simply measure the reduced form of the relationship between the economy and crime. In order to distinguish between theories of absolute deprivation and relative deprivation, one must have separate indicators of poverty and opportunity. One common approach is to argue that one indicator of economic health (e.g., median income) serves as a proxy for opportunity, and another (e.g., unemployment rate) serves as a proxy for motivation. Another approach is to make a similar distinction from the lag structure. Cantor and Land (1985), for example, argue that "opportunity" is captured by the contemporaneous unemployment rate, while "motivation" is captured by the unemployment rate lagged one year. The difficulty with interpreting the results of these stories is that the adequacy of the proxies can never be tested.

In order to abstract from the secular trends, Cook and Zarkin (1985) looked only at the effect of short-term fluctuations. For each of the nine complete business cycles between 1933 and 1981, they calculated the average annual rate of growth in crime from the trough to the subsequent peak, which they compared with the annual rate of growth in crime in the year following the peak (i.e., the first year of the next slump). They found that the effect of the economy varies with crime type: robbery and burglary are countercyclical, auto theft is procyclical, and homicide does not vary with the business cycle. Cook and Zarkin are clear that we cannot extrapolate from an understanding of cyclical movements to an understanding of secular ones.

A more recent study by LaFree and Drass (1996) estimates the effect of income inequality on crime rates, while controlling for economic conditions that were the focus of earlier studies. In contrast to other researchers, they attempt to explain trends in arrests rather than trends in crimes. Since they use *UCR* arrest data rather than crime data, their results may be less subject to the bias described earlier. However, arrests may well be a function of resources allocated to criminal justice enforcement. Changes in the level of policing resources are not well captured in the control variables included in the regressions. LaFree and Drass postulate that it is not general (relative) deprivation but intraracial income inequality that drives crime. They find results consistent with their hypothesis, since intraracial income disparities grew substantially over the past three decades. Nonetheless, it is quite possible that some other factor (or factors) has driven the increases in crime since the 1960s.

Cross-Sectional Data. In comparisons of crime rates across cities at a single time, there occasionally is a positive and marginally statistically significant effect of the unemployment rate on crime (Glaeser and Sacerdote 1996; Butcher and Piehl forthcoming). However, a more salient feature in these comparisons is the stability in crime-rate differentials over time. That is, many cities with currently high crime rates have had consistently high crime rates for some time (e.g., New York, Miami, Los Angeles). Therefore, it may not be that unemployment drives crime, but rather that some other factor causes certain cities to have higher than average crime *and* higher than average unemployment.

Looking for this "third factor," Glaeser and Sacerdote (1996) investigate the relationship between city size (population) and crime. The motivation for this effort is the observation that, in the same way that cities have higher crime rates than suburban and rural areas, larger cities have higher crime rates than small and medium-sized ones. Other researchers are more agnostic about the cause of the stability in city crime rates and turn to explaining changes in crime rates over time. As a result, cross-sectional analyses of the levels of crime are few. Instead, researchers focus on following a panel of cities over time.

Panel Data. When one examines changes in crime rates in comparison with changes in economic conditions at the city or state level, again there is little conclusive evidence of a large role for economic conditions (Butcher and Piehl forthcoming). It may be that there is, in fact, no relationship between changes in crime and changes in economic conditions, or it may be the result of data problems, since crime levels, employment and/or wages, and population must all be measured more accurately when identification of relationships relies on differences in these values and not just their levels.

In a recent study of economic conditions and mortality using state-level data from 1972 to 1991, Ruhm (1996) found that unemployment and homicide are negatively correlated.[5] He does not provide a theory or hypothesis to explain this finding but does mention that alcohol use is also procyclical. Interestingly, he finds that other measures of mortality are also lower when the economy is in recession.

For policy purposes, it would be useful to know the true macro effect of the economy on crime. In the absence of this knowledge, policy makers must use their judgment in deciding how much pro-growth, economic development initiatives are worth. Since there is no convincing methodology for discerning the macro effects of the economy on crime, researchers have more recently concentrated on the individual-level relationships. This effort has been reinforced by the number of hypotheses to explain individual behavior and the increasing availability of micro data and the computational power to analyze it.

Individual-Level Analyses

Individual-level analyses draw primarily on cross-sectional and panel data.

Cross-Sectional Analysis. While it is true that sources of microlevel data are increasingly available, the number of surveys of the general population that include information about criminal activity is small. One source is the National Longitudinal Survey of Youth (NLSY), which has been analyzed by numerous researchers. In 1980, the survey asked the respondents, then between fifteen and twenty-three years old, about particular criminal acts during the previous twelve months. Glaeser and Sacerdote (1996) report no relationship between the local unemployment rate and self-reports of various criminal acts;[6] Butcher and Piehl (forthcoming) use a similar specification and find a positive relationship between local unemployment and a measure summing these various activities for males. Among those in the NLSY who report having committed crimes, Glaeser and Sacerdote (1996) report that higher unemployment is associated with lower probabilities of punishment. The same survey shows that, among males reporting criminal activity, labor force participation is high (95 percent) and equal to that of males not involved in crime (Grogger 1996).

Reuter, MacCoun, and Murphy (1990) found that 75 percent of their sample of young male drug dealers in Washington, D.C., had income from a legitimate job or business.[7] They found that hourly earnings were much higher for drug selling, yet people who sold drugs still worked at legitimate jobs. There are at least two possible explanations for this. Either drug dealing does not offer enough hours at that high wage, and so people supplement their income with other work, or crime and legal work are not substitutes. Legal work may provide important nonpecuniary benefits, such as legitimacy.[8] Also, for white-collar crimes, legal work often creates the entrée for the criminal activity.

In sum, cross-sectional analyses of individuals provide a murky picture.[9] It is certainly true that those in the criminal justice system have worse employment prospects (e.g., lower education, lower employment rates) than the general population. But the peak ages for crime commission are in the middle to late teens, and the usual economic models may not yet apply to such young people. In fact, it is likely that those with worse-looking employment histories (fewer hours, lower wages) in their teen years are in a better position for their lifetime earnings, since they are investing in schooling or are in entry-level jobs that have career prospects. Hence, the appropriate trade-offs for youth may be schooling or other human capital investment, not contemporaneous earnings.

Individual Panel Data.   Most surveys cover either the noninstitutionalized population or the institutionalized population, but not both. In order to get information about time spent incarcerated and time in the community, researchers often study releasees from prison, recording subsequent involvement with the criminal justice system, as well as their employment outcomes. The results from these studies may or may not generalize to the broader population but are a good place to start. If it happens that the criminal activity decisions of ex-prisoners respond to economic incentives, it is reasonable to believe that those of the general population do too.

For seventeen years, Needels (1996) carefully tracked the employment, earnings, and criminal justice system involvement of a group of releasees from Georgia prisons. Those who continued to be involved in the criminal justice system had lower earnings and lower employment rates than those who desisted from crime. Because of concerns that the same factors driving the decision to work may drive the decision to commit crime, Needels estimated crime and earnings simultaneously. She found that those who had better (predicted) labor market opportunities had lower recidivism. Furthermore, controlling for labor market opportunities eliminates the gap between whites and blacks in terms of recidivism; race and education affect earnings but not labor force participation. This paper reports the most convincing evidence that there is a link between earnings and criminal activity among releasees. It is worth investigating whether administrative data, which may be measured with less error than survey data, allowed this relationship to be detected in this study but not in others.

There have been several impressive attempts to collect detailed data about how youth development impacts criminality. Sampson and Laub (1993) reanalyzed the rich data collected by the Gluecks starting in the 1940s. This panel followed 1,000 boys, 500 of whom were delinquent at the time of selection, for eighteen years, collecting information on parents, home life, education, ambitions, and many other factors. Sampson and Laub analyzed both structural and process factors influencing criminal activity, concluding that while structural factors (such as employment opportunities) are important, they are mediated by family processes.

Farrington et al. (1986) analyzed the criminal behavior, school attendance, and employment of about 400 young males in London. The focus of the study was on the ages of eighteen to nineteen, which occurred in 1971–1972. The researchers found that rates of offending were statistically significantly higher when the boys were unemployed than when they were employed. This finding holds even among the sample of youths who had committed offenses when both employed and unemployed. The higher offense rate in periods of unemployment is fully accounted for by offenses for material gain; the "other" offense rate is the same regardless of employment status. Interestingly, the rate of offending while in school was the same as, or lower than, that during periods of employment. While it is not possible to conclude from these results that unemployment drives crime, they do show that, holding a person's inclination toward offending constant, unemployment and criminal acts are correlated events.

Individuals in Communities

Efforts to examine the work-crime relation of individuals in communities draw on both community-level and ethnographic studies.

Neighborhood Effects. Just as individuals with worse labor market prospects are more likely to be involved in crime, poor neighborhoods have higher crime rates. This neighborhood-level relationship (within-city) is much more robust than the relationship between crime and economics at higher levels of aggregation. Many theorists, especially sociologists, attribute this regularity to a structural relationship at the community level rather than merely to the sum of individual experiences (Reiss and Tonry 1986). William Julius Wilson (1996), for example, rests much of the blame on nonemployment: "High rates of joblessness trigger other problems in the neighborhood that adversely affect social organization, including drug trafficking, crime, and gang violence" (Wilson 1996, p. 59).

Structural hypotheses of neighborhood, community, or peer effects require different analytic methods than those presented earlier. Such empirical methods are relatively new, and few empirical studies employ them. In a survey of neighborhood effects on a variety of youth outcomes, Jencks and Mayer write: "Despite the existence of many complex theories about the ways in which neighborhoods affect teenage crime, the evidence for such effects is thin and contradictory" (1990, p. 175).

Case and Katz (1991), who studied neighborhood effects in a survey of inner-city youth in Boston, found that the criminal behavior of adult family members *and* of neighborhood youths influence the likelihood that a given youth will be involved in crime himself. Interestingly, they did not find substantial neighborhood effects "across" outcomes: for example, neighbor criminality does not predict an individual's economic outcomes and vice versa. This suggests that structural relationships may be less important than more direct influences (e.g., role models).

Ethnographic Research. The range of theories in the first section of this chapter, along with the results of the studies by Sampson and Laub (1993), Wilson (1996), and Case and Katz (1991), among others, suggest that the relations between criminal activity and economic conditions are quite complex. Ethnographic research, in which anthropologists spend a great deal of time with individuals in their life contexts, can shed some light on this complexity. Sullivan (1989) studied youths in three New York City neighborhoods. His book describes indirect and complicated relationships among crime and economics. For example, job opportunities and youths' responses to them are mediated by family and neighborhood contexts. Sullivan argues that social factors (such as the "moral noxiousness" of crime) must be taken into account, as well as factors such as the risks of being killed: "[C]riminal economic activity is embedded in the community context to a far greater extent than other kinds of economic activity" (Sullivan 1989, p. 108). Sullivan urges other researchers to pay more attention to the neighborhood context of violence: "Their willingness and ability to employ violence for economic gain, both initially and over time, cannot be understood apart from the context of the non-economic functions of violence in their neighborhoods" (1989, p. 109). Like Sampson and Laub (1993), Sullivan emphasizes that motivation changes with age. Thus, the particular relationship between economic opportunity may be weak at young ages, when crime is a form of recreation. He found that the income motivation for crime became stronger over time. This work recommends a combination of structural and individual explanations for individual criminal behavior.

Experimental Evidence

The experimental evidence on work-crime relationships comes from both social and natural experiments.

Social Experiments.   A final methodological approach is social experimentation. If experiments are well designed and well implemented, they provide the most convincing evidence of causal relationships. The best experiments randomize individuals into "treatment" and "control" groups. Since the two groups start out the same (except for small differences due to randomness), any differences observed later can be attributed to the treatment received. There have been two randomized social experiments focused on crime and employment. Bushway and Reuter (1997) provide a review of experiments targeted toward criminal or "at-risk" populations. Only a few have explicitly included crime as an outcome.

The Transitional Aid Research Project was a randomized experiment in which released inmates were given support similar to unemployment insurance. Needels (1993) reports on a seventeen-year follow-up to the 1976 experiment. The treatment had neither short- nor long-term impact on recidivism. While members of the experimental groups worked substantially fewer weeks than those in the control group in the first year of the program, there were no long-term differences in employment or earnings.

The Job Corps, an intensive residential program for at-risk youths, seems to reduce crime and to have a small positive impact on earnings (Mallar, Lai, and Labovich 1982). It is possible that the increased earnings led to the reduction in crime, or it may be that the social control yields the crime reduction.

While social experiments are potentially very useful for understanding the effects of policies and programs, they often have low completion rates and limited provision of "treatment" (due to poor implementation). These experiments have not yet proved that economic interventions cannot reduce crime. Future experiments should be carefully designed and managed so that, if the null hypothesis is confirmed and no treatment effect is found, we can be sure it is the treatment that failed rather than the experimental design.

In community-level experiments, such as community-level block grants and enterprise zones, crime is not usually the outcome of greatest interest. Often, data on crime rates are not even collected. Bushway and Reuter (1997) provide a discussion of these experiments. The Moving to Opportunity (MTO) experiment operated by the U.S. Department of Housing and Urban Development is currently under way. This program (randomly) moves families from poor neighborhoods to more affluent ones, in which access to jobs is greatly improved. Since crime is an outcome of interest in this study, the results of MTO will help us understand neighborhood effects. However, it will be several years until the long-term results of the program will be known.

Natural Experiments. A final way to get a handle on the relations between economics and crime is to see what happens to crime rates when there is a sudden change in the economic environment. There are not many examples of this type of analysis. Carrington (1996) provides a careful description of the effects of the pipeline boom in Alaska, which provided a large, anticipated, positive shock to the economy. While the focus of his efforts is on quantifying the labor market impacts of the boom, he also reports a large increase in crime (along with increases in other forms of disorder). There are three possible explanations for this finding: first, economic booms cause crime; second, sudden economic booms lead to increasing inequality, which in turn causes crime; and third, sudden economic booms have transitional periods with much chaos, including crime. Under the third explanation, the effects of sudden (or temporary) prosperity will not be the same as the effects of anticipated, sustained economic growth. Without more of these episodes to analyze, it is hard to separate out the various stories; similar analyses of the impact of casinos in depressed areas would be one obvious place to start. Nevertheless, such careful case studies help illuminate the time-series variation so often employed in more aggregate studies.

In sum, it would be helpful to have more "experiments," natural or otherwise, from which to learn. The next section considers the importance of reversing the direction of causality: from criminal involvement to worsening labor market outcomes.

The Effects of Crime on Economic Outcomes

Several researchers have focused on the impact of criminal justice sanctions on employment rather than the impact of economic conditions on criminal justice outcomes. There are two reasons to be concerned about this direction of influence. The first reason is to improve understanding of the other directions of influence. In the studies discussed previously, the role of the economy on crime may be overstated if there is a simultaneous relationship between the crime and the economy. If crime (and any resulting sanctions) leads to worse economic outcomes for individuals or communities, then a cycle is generated. For the most part, the work described earlier treated the economy as exogenous, which means that the positive feedback mechanism was not taken into consideration.

The second reason to be concerned with the effect of the criminal justice system on economic outcomes is that it may bear directly on policy questions. To the extent that criminal justice interventions harm the future productive capacity of individuals, that should be taken into account as a social cost of the sanction.

Freeman (1992) emphasizes this relationship between criminal justice system interventions and subsequent legal work at the individual level. Using the NLSY, which other researchers had used to look at the relationship in the other direction, Freeman found *"massive long-term effects [of having been in jail or on probation] on employment"* (p. 217, emphasis in original). He concludes that those who had served time in jail or on probation worked 10 to 30 percent less than they would have otherwise. These results are not definitive, however, since one can make the same "simultaneity" critique of this specification as of the models I described earlier. The results do raise the importance of simultaneity in the earlier models. Furthermore, they suggest that having a criminal record may be a substantial hindrance to obtaining legal work, which may require rethinking current criminal justice policies or developing additional interventions to help ex-offenders make the transition to legitimate work.

Grogger (1995) considers the effect of arrest on the economic outcomes for young men. Thus, the sample is similar to the one analyzed by Freeman (1992), but the criminal justice sanction is much less intrusive. He concludes that the effects of "arrest are moderate in magnitude and rather short-lived" (p. 51). In an analysis of federal offenders, Waldfogel (1994) found very large effects of conviction on earnings and sizable effects on employment rates. The economic impacts are especially large for those offenders whose offense "involved a breach of trust on the job" (p. 65). Thus, it seems that the impact of criminal justice sanctions on employment outcomes depends heavily on both the severity of the sanction and the type of crime involved.

As the earlier discussion indicates, the literature on economic conditions and crime needs empirical studies that use simultaneous models, so that the causality of crime on economics and that of economics on crime are both incorporated. One study that does this is Needels (1996). In her sample of prison releasees, she found that, for those participating in the legal economy, the length of time incarcerated did not affect earnings while in the community. Of course, there are many other relationships we hope to understand.

This section has emphasized simultaneity at the individual level, but it may be just as important at the community level. Consider a community with a high crime rate. This community is likely to lose in bids to attract economic development into the neighborhood. Also, residents may fare poorly in the labor market if they have difficulty being flexible due to concerns about commuting at night or leaving children unsupervised for short periods of time.

Research Challenges

From the body of empirical research, we know that economic disadvantage, criminal offending, and criminal victimization are concentrated in similar populations. At the same time, however, most of those who are poor do not regularly commit illegal acts. We also know that crime rates increased dramatically during the 1960s and 1970s as absolute economic conditions also were improving. The empirical research reveals some support for the role of economic incentives in crime, but such incentives may not be so relevant for youth or for crimes of violence.

The complex picture that emerges from existing work reveals that many challenges remain if researchers are to understand criminal behavior or to design policy responses. This concluding section lays out just a few of the more pressing questions for those working in this field. They are organized in the reverse order from the discussion of the empirical findings, going from individual-level concerns to those of macroeconomic importance.

Most of the existing work on individuals considers the relations between economics and criminal offending. An important associated concern is the study of victimization. Like offending, victimization is highly concentrated. It would be useful for policy to understand the relationship between economics and victimization. Some evidence on this can be found in Glaeser and Sacerdote (1996), who report no connection between having a job and the likelihood of being a victim. In their results, it is hard to discern effects of family income on the likelihood of victimization, but among those who were victimized, the value of the property taken is positively and significantly related to family income.

Given that much of the research into the role of economics in criminal behavior has been conducted on releasees from incarceration, we must take care in extrapolating the policy implications to other populations. The results indicating the negative effect of incarceration on subsequent work show that incarceration is a very invasive sanction. This suggests that we may need different policies for prevention (for those who have not served time) than for rehabilitation (of those who have), especially since releasees must contend with having a criminal record. More work that systematically compares different segments of the population (general population, arrestees, probationers, releasees from incarceration) appears necessary.

Two areas of particular concern in the economy of the 1990s have not received much attention in the research literature. One is how to combat the draw of drug markets. Freeman (1992) and Reuter, MacCoun, and Murphy (1990) provide some indication of how attractive selling drugs is relative to other economic opportunities available to urban youth. It is not clear whether the best way to encourage teenagers to prepare for legal sector careers requires providing jobs with higher wages, providing jobs with advancement possibilities, improving education, increasing enforcement, or simply providing information so that choices are more informed.

A second central issue in the current economic environment concerns the effect on crime of increased inequality in earnings. Inequality has increased dramatically over the past twenty to thirty years, a development that LaFree and Drass (1996) have shown is correlated with increasing rates of arrest. Freeman (1996) argues that increases in incarceration probabilities were not high enough to offset the improvement in returns from crime relative to legal work over the decade.[10] The extent to which these changes in economic structure place pressure on crime rates is still unresolved. As concern about inequality enters the public debate on labor policy and tax policy, impacts on crime, if known, could be incorporated.

Those concerned about community development have always been concerned with crime. Recently, William Julius Wilson has reinvigorated calls for jobs programs. His argument relies, in part, on predicted crime reductions: "As more people become employed, crime, including violent crime, and drug use will subside" (1996, p. 238). However, the evidence is unclear as to whether a wide-scale jobs program would work. The answers to some of the more fundamental questions raised in this chapter, such as the finding by Case and Katz (1991) that affecting the criminal behavior of peers may have much larger effects, have bearing on the likelihood of such a proposal achieving the desired goals.

Finally, there are two vexing conceptual issues for those concerned with economics and crime. The first involves developing empirical strategies for testing more complex models of crime. The empirical results reported in this essay generally presume linear relationships between the economic variables and the crime measures. However, the need to explain large movements in crime rates over time and large variations over space makes contagion models appear promising. If unemployment affects crime only once it passes a certain threshold, a nonlinear model is required. If the routine activities hypothesis is correct *and* a person's choice of lifestyle depends on the activities of his or her neighbors, then a dynamic contagion model is required. These ideas have received some attention by theorists, but empiricists must incorporate them into their work too.

The last issue is one of macroeconomic policy. How should crime control be figured into calculations about economic growth (e.g., by the Federal Reserve Board)? Since, as was argued earlier, it is impossible to make definitive assessments from time-series evidence, this job requires modeling crime under a variety of assumptions. Given the high costs of fear, victimization, and law enforcement, this exercise is worth undertaking in spite of the inherent imprecision.

Notes

1. See Cook (1986) for an excellent discussion of how the number of crimes results from the interaction between potential offenders and potential victims.

2. There is another literature on the determinants of incarceration as related to the economy. The idea here is that imprisonment is used to regulate the unemployed population. Therefore, in recessions, incarceration rises. To the extent that increased incarceration dampens the crime rate (e.g., through incapacitation or deterrence), crime will be lower in recessions. This literature is not included in this review. Note, however, that to the extent this story is true, the estimates that are presented of a direct effect of the economy on crime rates will be biased toward a negative relationship between unemployment and crime.

3. Linking geographic information to individual data can make identification of individuals easy. Different data sources take different approaches to assuring respondent confidentiality. Some include community-level variables without identifying the location of the community. Others provide geographic information, but only for rather large "communities" (e.g., Standard Metropolitan Statistical Areas). Still others provide community-level aggregates for relatively small units of analysis, obscuring the data where it could be used to identify individuals.

4. Freeman (1983, p. 96) also notes that labor force participation appears to have a closer link than unemployment, and that deterrent variables appear more important than the economic variables. Chiricos (1987) points out that the pattern depends on the type of crime: property crimes appear to be related to the unemployment rate, while violent crimes are not. Several authors have run similar analyses with aggregate data broken down into various demographic groups. Although this provides some additional information, it does not accommodate the basic problems with time-series analysis described in this essay.

5. A 1 percent increase in unemployment is associated with a 1.5 percent decrease in homicide. Interestingly, personal income does not affect homicide when unemployment and basic demographics, including education, are included.

6. The activities included in the survey are relatively minor crimes (mostly theft and larceny) and should not be thought of as *UCR* index crimes.

7. The sample was generated from arrestees for any crime; those who reported drug dealing remained in the sample.

8. Youths in Boston report that having a job provides them with an explanation for the cash they carry. This gives them legitimacy with authority figures, including law enforcement personnel (results of fieldwork associated with a project the author is running in Boston).

9. Strictly speaking, "cross-sectional analysis" as used in this chapter should contain estimates of the effect of an individual's unemployment on his or her criminal activity. Then, works such as Glaeser and Sacerdote (1996) and Butcher and Piehl (forthcoming) would belong in the section on community effects, since they consider the effect of local unemployment rates. However, most analysts would argue that an individual's contemporaneous employment status is endogenous to the decision to commit crime. Therefore, studies that are motivated by individual-level theories include community unemployment rates to break the simultaneity. I reserve the section on community factors for studies that explicitly consider the community context.

10. Freeman further argues that *the propensity of the noninstitutional population to commit crime rose sharply in the 1980s* (Freeman 1995, emphasis in original). To make this point, he calculated the expected reduction in crimes due to the expansion in correctional populations and compared this with the actual U.S. experience. However, Freeman includes drug offenders in his measure of incarceration but does not include drug offenses in the crime measure. When this discrepancy is reconciled, there no longer appears to be a substantial increase in the propensity to commit crime over the 1980s. See Piehl (1995) for a more complete argument on this point.

References

Bushway, Shawn, and Peter Reuter. 1997. "Labor Markets and Crime Risk Factors." In *Preventing Crime: What Works, What Doesn't, What's Promising,* edited by Lawrence Sherman, Denise Gottfredson, Doris MacKenzie, John Eck, Peter Reuter, and Shawn Bushway. A Report to the National Institute of Justice. Department of Criminology and Criminal Justice, University of Maryland.

Butcher, Kristin, and Anne Morrison Piehl. Forthcoming. "Cross-City Evidence on the Relationship Between Immigration and Crime." *Journal of Policy Analysis and Management.*

Cantor, David, and Kenneth Land. 1985. "Unemployment and Crime Rates in the Post–World War II United States: A Theoretical and Empirical Analysis." *American Sociological Review* 50:317–32.

Carrington, William J. 1996. "The Alaskan Labor Market During the Pipeline Era." *Journal of Political Economy* 104:186–218.

Case, Anne C., and Lawrence F. Katz. 1991. "The Company You Keep: The Effects of Family and Neighborhood on Disadvantaged Youths." NBER Working Paper no. 3705. Cambridge, Mass.: National Bureau of Economic Research.

Chiricos, Theodore. 1987. "Rates of Crime and Unemployment: An Analysis of Aggregate Research Evidence." *Social Problems* 34:187–212.

Cook, Philip J. 1986. "The Demand and Supply of Criminal Opportunities." In *Crime and Justice: An Annual Review of Research,* vol. 7, edited by Michael Tonry and Norval Morris. Chicago: University of Chicago Press.

Cook, Philip J., and Gary A. Zarkin. 1985. "Crime and the Business Cycle." *Journal of Legal Studies* 14:115–28.

Farrington, David P., Bernard Gallagher, Lynda Morley, Raymond St. Ledger, and Donald West. 1986. "Unemployment, School Leaving, and Crime." *British Journal of Criminology* 26:335–56.

Freeman, Richard. 1983. "Crime and Unemployment." In *Crime and Public Policy,* edited by James Q. Wilson. San Francisco: ICS Press.

———. 1992. "Crime and the Employment of Disadvantaged Youth." In *Urban Labor Markets and Job Opportunity,* edited by George Peterson and Wayne Vroman. Washington, D.C.: Urban Institute.

———. 1995. "The Labor Market." In *Crime,* edited by James Q. Wilson and Joan Petersilia. San Francisco: ICS Press.

———. 1996. "Why Do So Many Young American Men Commit Crimes and What Might We Do About It?" *Journal of Economic Perspectives* 10:25–42.

Glaeser, Edward, and Bruce Sacerdote. 1996. "Why Is There More Crime in Cities?" NBER Working Paper no. 5430. Cambridge, Mass.: National Bureau of Economic Research.

Grogger, Jeffrey. 1995. "The Effect of Arrests on the Employment and Earnings of Young Men." *Quarterly Journal of Economics* 110:51–71.

———. 1996. "Market Wages and Youth Crime." Unpublished paper. University of California, Santa Barbara.

Jencks, Christopher, and Susan E. Mayer. 1990. "The Social Consequences of Growing Up in a Poor Neighborhood." In *Inner-City Poverty in the United States,* edited by Laurence Lynn Jr. and Michael McGeary. Washington, D.C.: National Academy Press.

LaFree, Gary, and Kriss A. Drass. 1996. "The Effect of Changes in Intraracial Income Inequality and Educational Attainment on Changes in Arrest Rates for African Americans and Whites, 1957 to 1990." *American Sociological Review* 61:614–34.

Mallar, Charles, Kwo-Long Lai, and Gary Labovich. 1982. *Evaluation of the Economic Impact of the Job Corps Program, Third Follow-Up Report.* Princeton, N.J.: Mathematica Policy Research, Inc.

Needels, Karen. 1993. "The Long-Term Effects of TARP." Unpublished paper. Princeton, N.J.: Princeton University.

———. 1996. "Go Directly to Jail and Do Not Collect? A Long-Term Study of Recidivism and Employment Patterns Among Prison Releasees." *Journal of Research in Crime and Delinquency* 33:471–96.

Piehl, Anne Morrison. 1995. "Earnings Inequality and Incarceration over the 1980s." Unpublished paper. Cambridge, Mass.: Harvard University.

Reiss, Albert J., and Michael Tonry, eds. 1986. *Communities and Crime.* Chicago: University of Chicago Press.

Reuter, Peter, Robert MacCoun, and Patrick Murphy. 1990. *Money from Crime.* Santa Monica, Calif.: RAND.

Ruhm, Christopher. 1996. "Are Recessions Good for Youth Health?" NBER Working Paper no. 5570. Cambridge, Mass.: National Bureau of Economic Research.

Sampson, Robert J., and John H. Laub. 1993. *Crime in the Making.* Cambridge, Mass.: Harvard University Press.

Sullivan, Mercer. 1989. *Getting Paid.* Ithaca, N.Y.: Cornell University Press.

Waldfogel, Joel. 1994. "The Effect of Criminal Conviction on Income and the Trust Reposed in the Workmen." *Journal of Human Resources* 29:62–80.

Wilson, William Julius. 1996. *When Work Disappears.* New York: Knopf.

Part IV

CRIME REDUCTION

12

Restorative Justice

JOHN BRAITHWAITE

Restorative justice is a major development in criminological cal thinking, notwithstanding its grounding in traditions of justice from the ancient Arab, Greek, and Roman civilizations that accepted a restorative approach even to homicide (Van Ness 1986, pp. 64–68); from ancient Indian Hindus, for whom "he who atones is forgiven" (Weitekamp 1989); from ancient Buddhist, Taoist, and Confucian traditions that one sees blended today in north Asia (Haley 1996). Taken seriously, restorative justice involves a very different way of thinking about traditional notions such as deterrence, rehabilitation, incapacitation, and crime prevention. It also means transformed foundations of criminal jurisprudence and of our notions of freedom, democracy, and community.

Restorative justice has been the dominant model of criminal justice throughout most of human history for all the world's peoples. A decisive move away from it came with the Norman conquest of much of Europe at the end of the Dark Ages (Van Ness 1986, p. 66; Weitekamp 1989). Transforming crime into a matter of fealty to and felony against the king, instead of a wrong done to another person, was a central part of the monarch's program of domination of his people. Interest in restorative justice was rekindled in the West from the establishment of an experimental victim-offender reconciliation program in 1974 in Kitchener, Ontario (Peachey 1989). Umbreit (1998) reports that there were at least 300 of these programs in North America in the mid-1990s and over 500 in Europe, plus many Southern Hemisphere programs. During the 1980s, there was also considerable restorative justice innovation in the regulation of corporate crime (Rees 1988; Braithwaite 1995).

The 1990s have seen the New Zealand idea of family group conferences spread to many countries, including Australia, Singapore, the United Kingdom, Ireland, South Africa, Palestine, the United States, and Canada, adding a new theoretical vitality to restorative justice thinking. Canadian native peoples' notions of healing circles and sentencing circles (James 1993) also acquired considerable influence, as did the Navajo justice and healing ceremony (Yazzie and Zion 1996). By the 1990s, these various programs came to be conceptualized as restorative justice. Bazemore and Washington (1995) and Van Ness (1993) credit Albert Eglash (1975) with first articulating restorative justice as a restitutive alternative to retributive and rehabilitative justice. As a result of the popularizing work of North American and British activists like Howard Zehr (1985, 1990, 1995), Mark Umbreit (1985, 1990, 1992, 1994a,b, 1998), Kay Pranis (1996), Daniel Van Ness (1986, 1993, 1998), Tony Marshall (1985, 1990, 1992a,b) and Martin Wright (1982, 1992) during the 1980s, and the huge new impetus after 1989 from New Zealanders (Brown 1994; Consedine 1997; Hakaiha 1994; Hassall 1996; Leibrich 1996; Maxwell 1993; Maxwell and Morris 1993, 1996; McElrea 1993; Robertson 1996; Stewart 1993) and Australians (Hyndman, Thorsborne, and Wood 1996; McDonald et al. 1995; Moore and Forsythe 1995; Moore and O'Connell 1994; Mugford and Mugford 1992; O'Connell 1992, 1995; Palk 1995), restorative justice was the emerging social movement for criminal justice reform of the 1990s. Since 1995, two organizations, Ted Watchel's Real Justice in the United States and John MacDonald's Transformative Justice in Australia have offered commercial training in conferencing to thousands of people worldwide. An evaluation research community also emerged in association with the social movement; this community has been much more dominated by Europeans (Blagg 1985; De Haan 1990; Dignan 1992; Marshall 1985, 1990; Marshall and Merry 1990; Messmer 1993; Messmer and Otto 1992a, 1992b; Sessar, Beuerskens, and Boers 1986; Smith, Blagg, and Derricourt 1985; Walgrave 1993, 1994, 1995; Weitekamp 1989) and Canadians (Burford and Pennell 1996; Clairmont 1994; Lajeunesse 1993; LaPrairie 1994, 1995; Ross 1996; Stuart 1996), though Burt Galaway and Joe Hudson (1975) in Minnesota were the early and persistent role models of this research community.

In a longer review essay (Braithwaite 1998), I seek to explain why restorative justice is beginning to take off as a model. Notwithstanding that these beginnings are still modest and marginal, an Immodest Theory is advanced there as to why restorative justice might work, as is a Pessimistic Theory of why it might fail in a number of important respects. The growing body of empirical evidence on the workings of restorative justice is organized around testing these propositions, which are listed in the following. Ironically, this still-limited evidence suggests that the propositions of both theories are plausible. Here I do no more than outline the key propositions that constitute the two theories.

Effects of Restorative Justice Practices

The Immodest Theory	The Pessimistic Theory
• restore and satisfy victims better than existing criminal justice practices	• provide no benefits whatsoever to over 90 percent of victims

- restore and satisfy offenders better than existing criminal justice practices
- restore and satisfy communities better than existing criminal justice practices
- reduce crime more than existing practices because of the claims of reintegrative shaming theory
- reduce crime more than existing criminal justice practices because of the claims of procedural justice theory
- reduce crime more than existing criminal justice practices because of the claims of the theory of bypassed shame
- reduce crime more than existing criminal justice practices because of the claims of defiance theory
- reduce crime more than existing criminal justice practices because of the claims of self-categorization theory
- reduce crime more than existing criminal justice practices because of the claims of crime prevention theory
- deter crime better than practices grounded in deterrence theories
- incapacitate crime better than criminal justice practices grounded in the theory of selective incapacitation
- rehabilitate crime better than criminal justice practices grounded in the welfare model
- are more cost-effective than criminal justice practices grounded in the economic analysis of crime
- secure justice better than criminal justice practices grounded in "justice" or just-deserts theories
- enrich freedom and democracy

- have no significant impact on the crime rate
- can increase victims' fears of revictimization
- can make victims little more than props for attempts to rehabilitate offenders
- can be a "shaming machine" that worsens the stigmatization of offenders
- rely on a kind of community that is culturally inappropriate to industrialized societies
- can oppress offenders with a tyranny of the majority, even a tyranny of the lynch mob
- can widen nets of social control
- fail to redress structural problems inherent in liberalism, such as unemployment and poverty
- can disadvantage women, children, and oppressed racial minorities
- are prone to capture by the dominant group in the restorative process
- can extend unaccountable police power, and can even compromise the separation of powers among legislative, executive, and judicial branches of government
- can trample rights because of impoverished articulation of procedural safeguards

This chapter is limited to more foundational questions about the meaning of restorative justice in order to set up the preceding more detailed review of theory and data. It considers what it is that we should want to be restored by restorative justice and argues for the universality of some of these concerns. Then it explores the need to learn from culturally plural paths to securing these universals by saving and reviving the restorative justice practices that remain in all societies. In this process, what elements of the statist revolution in criminal justice should we also want to save? The conclusion addresses how to put indigenous community justice and liberal state justice in creative tension, with each checking the abuses of the other. Before starting on this journey, when I first delivered this paper as a Dorothy Killam Memorial Lecture at Dalhousie University, I sought to give more concrete meaning to how restorative justice can work with a story of two robbers.

Imagine Two Robbers

A teenager is arrested for a robbery. The police send him to court, where he is sentenced to six months incarceration. As a victim of child abuse, he is both angry with the world and alienated from it. During his period of confinement, he acquires a heroin habit and suffers more violence. He comes out more desperate and alienated than when he went in, sustains his drug habit for the next twenty years by stealing cars, burglarizes dozens of houses, and pushes drugs until he dies in a gutter, a death no one mourns. Probably someone rather like this young man was arrested in your city today, perhaps more than one.

Tomorrow another teenager, Sam, is arrested for a robbery. He is a composite of several Sams I have seen. The police officer refers Sam to a facilitator who convenes a restorative justice conference. When the facilitator asks about his parents, Sam says he is homeless. His parents abused him, and he hates them. Sam refuses to cooperate with a conference if they attend. After talking with the parents, the facilitator agrees that perhaps it is best not to involve them. What about grandparents? No, they are dead. Brothers and sisters? No, he hates his brothers too. Sam's older sister, who was always kind to him, has long since left home, and he has no contact with her. Aunts and uncles? Not keen on them either, because they would always put him down as the black sheep of the family and stand by his parents. Uncle George was the only one he ever had any time for, but he has not seen him for years. Teachers from school? Hates them all. Sam has dropped out. They always treated him like dirt. The facilitator does not give up: "No one ever treated you okay at school?" Well, the hockey coach is the only one Sam can think of ever being fair to him. So the hockey coach, Uncle George, and Sam's older sister are tracked down by the facilitator and invited to the conference, along with the robbery victim and her daughter, who comes along to support the victim through the ordeal.

These six participants sit on chairs in a circle. The facilitator starts by introducing everyone and reminding Sam that although he has admitted to the robbery, he can change his plea at any time during the conference and have the matter heard by a court. Sam is asked to explain what happened in his own words. He mumbles that he needed money to survive, saw the lady, knocked her over, and ran off with her purse. Uncle George is asked what he thinks of this. He says that Sam used to be a good kid, but Sam had gone off the rails. He had let his parents down so badly that they would not even come today. "And now you have done this to this poor lady. I never thought you would stoop to violence," continues Uncle George, building into an angry tirade against the boy. The hockey coach also says he is surprised that Sam could do something as terrible as this. Sam was always a troublemaker at school, but the coach could see a kindly side in Sam that left him shocked about the violence. Sam's sister is invited to comment, but when she seems too emotional to speak, the facilitator moves on to the victim.

The victim explains how much trouble she had to go through to cancel the credit cards in the purse, how she had had no money for the shopping she needed to do the day of the robbery. Her daughter explains that the most important consequence of the crime was that her mother was now afraid to go out on her own. In particular, she is afraid that Sam is stalking her, waiting to rob her again. Sam sneers at this and seems callous throughout. His sister starts to sob. Concerned about how distressed she is, the facilitator calls a brief adjournment so she can comfort her, with help from Uncle George. During the break, the sister reveals that she understands what Sam has been through. She says she was abused by their parents as well. Uncle George has never heard of this, seems shocked, and is not sure that he believes it.

When the conference reconvenes, Sam's sister speaks to him with love and strength. Looking straight into his eyes, the first gaze he could not avoid in the conference, she says that she knows exactly what he has been through with their parents. No details are spoken. But the victim seems to understand what is spoken of by the knowing communication between sister and brother. Tears rush down the old woman's cheeks and over her trembling mouth.

It is his sister's love that penetrates Sam's callous exterior. From then on, he is emotionally engaged with the conference. He says he is sorry about what the victim has lost. He would like to pay it back but has no money or job. He assures the victim he is not stalking her. She readily accepts this now, and when questioned by the facilitator says she thinks she will now feel safe walking out alone. She wants her money back but says it will help her if they can talk about what to do to help Sam find a home and a job. Sam's sister says he can live in her house for a while. The hockey coach says he has some casual work that needs to be done, enough to pay Sam's debt to the victim and a bit more. If Sam does a good job, he will write him a reference for applications for permanent jobs. When the conference breaks up, the victim hugs Sam and tearfully wishes him good luck. He apologizes again. Uncle George quietly slips a hundred dollars to Sam's sister to defray the extra cost of having Sam in the house, and says he will be there for both of them if they need him.

After this incident, Sam has a rocky life punctuated by several periods of unemployment. A year later he has to go through another conference after he steals a bicycle. But he finds work when he can, mostly stays out of trouble, and lives to mourn at the funerals of Uncle George and his sister. The victim gets her money back and enjoys taking long walks alone. Both she and her daughter say that they feel enriched as a result of the conference, that they have a little more grace in their lives.

What Does Restorative Justice Restore?

Sam's conference is an example of restorative justice. Restorative justice means restoring victims, a more victim-centered criminal justice system, as well as restoring offenders and restoring community. First, what does restoring victims mean? It means restoring the property lost or the personal injury, repairing the broken window or the broken teeth (see Table 12.1). It means restoring a sense of security. Even victims of property crimes such as burglary often suffer a loss of security when the private space of their home is violated. When the criminal justice system fails to leave women secure about walking alone at night, half the population is left unfree in a fundamental sense.

Victims suffer when someone violates their bodies or shows them the disrespect of taking things that are precious to them. Sometimes this disrespectful treatment engenders victim shame: "He abused me rather than some other woman because I am trash" or "She stole my dad's car because I was irresponsible and parked it in a risky place." Victim shame often triggers a shame-rage spiral wherein victims reciprocate indignity with indignity through vengeance or by their own criminal acts.

Disempowerment is part of the indignity of being a victim of crime. According to Pettit and Braithwaite's (1990) republican theory of criminal justice, a wrong should not be defined as a crime unless it involves some

Table 12.1 What Does Restoring Victims Mean?

Restore property loss
Restore injury
Restore sense of security
Restore dignity
Restore sense of empowerment
Restore deliberative democracy
Restore harmony based on a feeling that justice has been done
Restore social support

domination of us that reduces our freedom to enjoy life as we choose. It follows that it is important to restore any lost sense of empowerment as a result of crime. This is particularly important where the victim suffers structurally systematic domination. For example, some of the most important restorative justice initiatives in Australia have involved some thousands of Aboriginal victims of consumer fraud by major insurance companies (Fisse and Braithwaite 1993, pp. 218–23). In these cases, victims from remote Aboriginal communities relished the power of being able to demand restoration and corporate reform from "white men in white shirts."

The way that Western legal systems handle crime compounds the disempowerment that victims feel, first at the hands of offenders and then at the hands of a professional, remote justice system that eschews their participation. The lawyers, in the words of Nils Christie (1978) "steal our conflict." The Western criminal justice system has, on balance, been corrosive of deliberative democracy, though the jury is one institution that has preserved a modicum of it. Restorative justice is deliberative justice; it is about people deliberating over the consequences of crimes, and how to deal with them and prevent their recurrence. This contrasts with the professional justice of lawyers deciding which rules apply to a case and then constraining their deliberation within a technical discourse about that rule application. Thus restorative justice restores the deliberative control of justice by citizens.

Restorative justice aims to restore harmony based on a feeling that justice has been done. Restoring harmony alone, while leaving an underlying injustice to fester unaddressed, is not enough. "Restoring balance" is acceptable as a restorative justice ideal only if the "balance" between offender and victim that prevailed before the crime was a morally decent balance. There is no virtue in restoring the balance by having a woman pay for a loaf of bread she has stolen from a rich man to feed her children. Restoring harmony between victim and offender is likely to be possible in such a context only on the basis of a discussion of why the children are hungry and what should be done about the underlying injustice of their hunger.

Restorative justice cannot resolve the deep structural injustices that cause problems like hunger. But we must demand two things of restorative justice. First, it must not make structural injustice worse (in the way, for example, that the Australian criminal justice system does by being an important cause of the unemployment and oppression of Aboriginal people). Indeed, we should hope that restorative justice will provide micro measures that ameliorate macro injustice where this is possible. Second, restorative justice should restore harmony with a remedy grounded in dialogue that takes account of underlying injustices. Restorative justice does not resolve the age-old questions of what should count as unjust outcomes. It is a more modest philosophy than that. It settles for the procedural requirement that the parties talk until they feel that harmony has been restored on the basis of a discussion of all the injustices they see as relevant to the case.

Finally, restorative justice aims to restore social support. Victims of crime need support from their loved ones during the process of requesting restoration. They sometimes need encouragement and support to engage with deliberation toward restoring harmony. Friends sometimes do blame the victim, or more commonly are frightened off by a victim going through an emotional trauma. Restorative justice aims to institutionalize the gathering around of friends during a time of crisis.

Restoring Offenders, Restoring Community

In most cases, a more limited range of types of restoration is relevant to offenders. Offenders have generally not suffered property loss or injury as a result of their own crime, though sometimes loss or injury is a cause of the crime. Dignity, however, is generally in need of repair after the shame associated with arrest. When there is a victim who has been hurt, there is no dignity in denying that there is something to be ashamed about. Dignity is generally best restored by confronting the shame, accepting responsibility for the bad consequences suffered by the victim, and apologizing with sincerity. A task of restorative justice is to institutionalize such restoration of dignity for offenders.

The sense of insecurity and disempowerment of offenders is often an issue in their offending and in discussions about how to prevent further offending. Violence by young men from racial minorities is sometimes connected to their feelings of being victims of racism. For offenders, restoring a sense of security and empowerment is often bound up with employment, the feeling of having a future, or achieving some educational success or sporting success—indeed, any kind of success.

Many patches are needed to sew the quilt of deliberative democracy. Criminal justice deliberation is not as important a patch as deliberation in the parliament, in trade unions, even in universities. But to the extent that restorative justice deliberation does lead ordinary citizens into serious democratic discussion about racism, unemployment, masculinist cultures in local schools, and police accountability, it is not an unimportant element of a deliberatively rich democracy.

The mediation literature shows that satisfaction of complainants with the justice of the mediation is less important than the satisfaction of those who are complained against in achieving mutually beneficial outcomes (Pruitt 1995). Criminal subcultures are memory files that collect injustices (Matza 1964, p. 102). Crime problems will continue to become deeply culturally embedded in Western societies until we reinvent criminal justice as a process that restores a sense of procedural justice to offenders (Tyler 1990).

Finally, Francis Cullen (1994) has suggested that there could be no better organizing concept for criminology than social support, given the

large volume of evidence about the importance of social support for preventing crime. The New Zealand Maori people see our justice system as
barbaric because of the way it requires the defendant to stand alone in
the dock without social support. In Maori thinking, civilized justice requires the offender's loved ones to stand beside him during justice rituals, sharing the shame for what has happened. Hence the shame the offender feels is more the shame of letting his loved ones down than a
Western sense of individual guilt that can eat away at a person. The
shame of letting loved ones down can be readily transcended by simple
acts of forgiveness from those loved ones.

Restoring community is advanced by a proliferation of restorative justice rituals in which social support around specific victims and offenders
is restored. At this micro level, restorative justice is an utterly bottom-up
approach to restoring community. At a middle level, important elements
of a restorative justice package are initiatives to foster community organization in schools, neighborhoods, ethnic communities, and churches,
and through professions and other nongovernmental organizations that
can deploy restorative justice in their self-regulatory practices. At a
macro level, we must design institutions of deliberative democracy
so that concern about issues like unemployment and the effectiveness
of labor market programs have a channel through which they can flow
from discussions about local injustices up into national economic policy-
making debate.

The Universality of Restorative Traditions

I have yet to discover a culture that does not have some deep-seated
restorative traditions. Nor is there a culture without retributive traditions. Retributive traditions once had survival value. Cultures that were
timid in fighting back were often wiped out by more determinedly violent cultures. In the contemporary world, as opposed to the world of our
biological creation, retributive emotions have less survival value. Because risk management is institutionalized in the modern world, retributive emotions are more likely to get us into trouble than out of it, as individuals, groups, and nations.

The message we might communicate to all cultures is that in the world
of the twenty-first century, restorative traditions will be a more valuable
resource than retributive traditions. Yet, sadly, the dominant cultural
forces in the contemporary world communicate just the opposite message.
Hollywood films hammer the message that the way to deal with bad guys
is through violence. Political leaders frequently emphasize the same message. Yet many of our spiritual leaders are helping us to retrieve our
restorative traditions—the Dalai Lama, for example. Archbishop Desmond
Tutu, in a foreword to Jim Consedine's forthcoming new edition of
Restorative Justice, correctly sees a "very ancient yet desperately needed
truth" as underlying restorative justice processes, "rooted as they are in all

indigenous cultures, including those of Africa." He sees his Truth and Reconciliation Commission as an example of restorative justice.

All of the restorative values in Table 12.1 are cultural universals. All cultures value in some way repair of damage to our persons and property, security, dignity, empowerment, deliberative democracy, and harmony based on a sense of justice and social support. These are universals because they are all vital to our emotional survival as human beings and vital to the possibility of surviving without constant fear of violence. The world's great religions recognize that the desire to pursue these restorative justice values is universal, which is why some of our spiritual leaders offer hope against those political leaders who wish to rule through fear and by crushing deliberative democracy. Ultimately, those political leaders will find that they will have to reach an accommodation with the growing social movement for restorative justice, just as they must with the great religious movements they confront. Why? Because the evidence is now strong that ordinary citizens like restorative justice (Morris and Maxwell 1993; Hyndman, Thorsborne, and Wood 1996; Goodes 1995; Moore and Forsythe 1995; Clairmont 1994; Sherman and Barnes 1997).

It is true that the virtues restorative justice restores are viewed differently in different cultures and that opinion about culturally appropriate ways of realizing them differ greatly as well. Hence, restorative justice must be a culturally diverse social movement that accommodates a rich plurality of strategies in pursuit of the truths it holds to be universal. It is about different cultures joining hands as they discover the profound commonalities of their experience of the human condition; it is about cultures learning from each other on the basis of that shared experience; it is about realizing the value of diversity, of preserving restorative traditions that work because they are embedded in a cultural past. Scientific criminology will never discover any universally best way of doing restorative justice. The best path is the path of cultural plurality in pursuit of the culturally shared restorative values in Table 12.1.

A Path to Culturally Plural Justice

A restorative justice research agenda to pursue this path has two elements:

1. Culturally specific investigation of how to save and revive the restorative justice practices that remain in all societies.
2. Culturally specific investigation of how to transform state criminal justice both by making it more restorative and by rendering its abuses of power more vulnerable to restorative justice.

On the first point, I doubt that urban neighborhoods are replete with restorative justice practices that can be retrieved, though there are some. Yet in the more micro context of the nuclear family, the evidence is overwhelming from the metropolitan United States that restorative justice is alive and well, and that families who are more restorative are likely to have less delinquent children than families who are punitive and stigmatizing.

Because families so often slip into stigmatization and brutalization of their difficult members, we need restorative justice institutionalized in a wider context that can engage and restore such families. In most societies, the wider contexts where the ethos and rituals of restorative justice are alive and ready to be piped into the wider streams of the society are schools, churches, and remote indigenous communities. If it is hard to find restorative justice in the disputing practices of our urban neighborhoods, the experience of recent years has been that they are relatively easy to locate in urban schools. This is because of the ethos of care and integration that is part of the Western educational ideal (which, at its best, involves a total rejection of stigmatization) and because the interaction among the members of a school community tends to be more intense than the interaction among urban neighbors. Schools, like families, have actually become more restorative and less retributive than the brutal institutions of the nineteenth century. This is why we have seen very successful restorative conferencing programs in contemporary schools (Hyndman, Thorsborne, and Wood 1996). We have also seen antibullying programs with what I would call a restorative ethos, which have managed in some cases to halve bullying in schools (Olweus 1994; Farrington 1993; Pitts and Smith 1995; Pepler et al. 1993).

More of the momentum for the restorative justice movement has come from the world's churches than from any other quarter. Even in a nation like Indonesia, where the state has such tyrannical power, the political imperative to allow some separation of church and state has left churches as enclaves where restorative traditions could survive. Religions like Islam and Christianity have strong retributive traditions as well, of course, though they have mostly been happy to leave it to the state to do the "dirty work" of temporal retribution.

The second point of the agenda is to explore how to transform state criminal justice. I have said that, in our multicultural cities, we cannot rely on spontaneous ordering of justice in our neighborhoods. There we must be more reliant on state reformers as catalysts of a new urban restorative justice. In our cities, where neighborhood social support is lowest, where the loss from the statist takeover of disputing is most damaging, the gains that can be secured from restorative justice reform are greatest. When a police officer from a tightly knit rural community and with a restorative justice ethos arrests a youth who lives in a loving family, who enjoys social support from a caring school and church, that officer is not likely to do much better or worse by the child than an officer who does not have a restorative justice ethos. Whatever the police do, the child's support network will probably sort the problem out so that serious reoffending does not occur. But when a metropolitan police officer with a restorative justice ethos arrests a homeless child like Sam, who hates the parents who abused him, who has dropped out of school, and is seemingly alone in the world, the restorative police officer can make a difference that will render him more effective in preventing crime than the retributive police officer. At least that is my hypothesis, one we can test empirically.

In the alienated urban context where community is not spontaneously emergent in a satisfactory way, a criminal justice system aimed at restoration can construct a community of care around a specific offender or a specific victim who is in trouble. That is what the story of Sam is about. With the restorative justice conferences being convened in multicultural metropolises like Auckland, Adelaide, Sydney, and Singapore, the selection principle that determines who is invited to the conference is the opposite to that with a criminal trial. We invite to a criminal trial those who can inflict the most damage on the other side. With a conference we invite those who might offer most support to their own side—Sam's sister, uncle, and hockey coach, the victim's daughter.

In terms of the theory of reintegrative shaming, the rationale for who is invited to the conference is that the presence of those on the victim's side builds shame into the conference, while the presence of supporters on the offender's side builds reintegration into the ritual. Conferences can be run in many different ways. Maori people in New Zealand tend to want to open and close their conferences with a prayer. The institutions of restorative justice we build in the city must be culturally plural, quite different from one community to another depending on the culture of the people involved. It is the empowerment principle of restorative justice that makes this possible—empowerment with process control.

From a restorative perspective, the important point is that we have institutions in civil society that confront serious problems like violence rather than sweep them under the carpet, yet do so in a way that is neither retributive nor stigmatizing. Violence will not be effectively controlled by communities unless the shamefulness of violence is communicated. This does not mean that we need criminal justice institutions that set out to maximize shame. On the contrary, if we set out to do that, we risk creating stigmatizing institutions (Retzinger and Scheff 1996). All we need do is nurture micro institutions of deliberative democracy that allow citizens to discuss the consequences of criminal acts, and who is responsible, and who should put them right, and how. Such deliberative processes naturally enable those responsible to confront and deal with the shame arising from what has happened. And if we invite people who enjoy maximum respect and trust on both the offender's and victim's side, we maximize the chances that shame will be dealt with in a reintegrative way.

Decline and Revival in Restorative Traditions

The traditions of restorative justice that can be found in all the world's great cultures have been under attack during the past two centuries.

Everywhere in the world, restorative ideals have suffered serious set-backs because of the globalization of the idea of a centralized state that takes central control of justice and rationalizes it into a punitive regime. Control of punishment strengthened the power and legitimacy of rulers (Foucault 1977). So did control of mercy, the power of royal or presidential pardon. What rulers really wanted was the political power of controlling the police, the prisons, and the courts. Yet at times abuse of that power proved such a threat to their legitimacy that they were forced by political opponents to institutionalize certain principles of fairness and consistency into the state system.

Of course, the new democratic rulers were no more enthusiastic about returning justice to the people than were the tyrants they succeeded; the secret police continued to be important to combating organized threats to the state monopoly of violence, the regular police to disorganized threats. The pretense that the state punished crime in a consistent, politically evenhanded way was part of the legitimation for democratically central-ized justice. Citizens continue to see this as a pretense. They realize that whatever the law says, the reality is one law for the rich, another for the poor; one set of rules for the politically connected, another for the power-less. Philip Pettit and I have sought to show that proportionality in prac-tice is proportional punishment for the poor and impunity for the white-collar criminals (Pettit and Braithwaite 1990, chap. 9). Restorative justice, we contend, has a better chance than just deserts of being made equitably available to both rich and poor.

While it is a myth that centralized state law enabled greater consis-tency and lesser partiality than community-based restorative justice, it is true that abuse of power always was and still is common in community justice, as Carol LaPrairie's work shows for Canada (LaPrairie 1994, 1995). And it is true that state oversight of restorative justice in the com-munity can be a check on abuse of rights in local programs, local political dominations, and those types of unequal treatment in local programs that are flagrantly unacceptable in the wider society. It is equally true that restorative justice can be a check on abuse of rights by the central state. If so, we should expect to find in Canberra that citizens who go through a conference are more likely than citizens who go to court to believe that their rights were respected by the police and the criminal justice system. This is what my colleagues' preliminary results suggest (Sherman and Barnes 1997; Strang and Sherman 1997). We see it in restorative justice conferences in Canberra when a mother asks during the conference that something be done about the police officers who continue to use exces-sive force in their dealings with her son and who continue to victimize her son for things done by others.

The restorative justice ideal could not and should not be the romantic notion of shifting back to a world where state justice is replaced by local justice. Rather, it might aim to use the existence of state traditions of rights, proportionality, and the rule of law as resources to check abuse of power in local justice and to use the revival of restorative traditions to check abuse of state power. In other words, restorative justice constitutionalized by the state can be the stuff of a republic with a richer separation of powers (Braithwaite 1997), with less abuse of power, than could be obtained under either dispute resolution totally controlled by local politics or disputing totally dominated by the state.

Several key elements of North Atlantic criminal justice have been almost totally globalized during the past two centuries: central state control of criminal justice, the idea of crime itself and that criminal law should be codified, the idea that crimes are committed against the state (rather than the older ideas that they were committed against victims or God), the idea of a professionalized police who are granted a monopoly over the use of force in domestic conflicts, the idea of moving away from compensation as the dominant way of dealing with crime by building a state prison system to segregate the good from the bad, and the idea that fundamental human rights should be protected during the criminal process.

Like penal abolitionists (Bianchi and van Swaaningen 1986; Christie 1982), restorative justice theorists see most of these elements of the central state takeover of criminal justice as retrograde. However, unlike the most radical versions of abolitionism, restorative justice sees promise in preserving a state role as a watchdog of rights and concedes that for a tiny fraction of the people in our prisons, it may actually be necessary to protect the community from them by incarceration. While restorative justice means treating many things we now treat as crime simply as problems of living, restorative justice does not mean abolishing the concept of crime. In restorative justice rituals, calling a wrongdoing a crime can be a powerful resource in persuading citizens to take responsibility, to pay compensation, or to apologize, especially with corporate criminals who are not used to thinking of their exploitative conduct in that way (Braithwaite 1995). Restorative justice does not mean abolishing the key elements of the state criminal justice systems that have been globalized this century; it means shifting power from them to civil society, keeping key elements of the statist revolution but shifting power away from central institutions and checking the power that remains by the deliberative democracy from below that restorative justice enables.

Thus I offer an analysis that is unfashionably universal. I believe that restorative justice will come to be a profoundly influential social movement throughout the world during the next century because it appeals to universally shared values and because it responds to the defects of a centralized state criminal justice model that has been totally globalized and has utterly failed in every country where it gained ascendancy. Wherever it has failed, there are criminologists or lawyers within the state itself who are convinced of that failure. And given the global imperatives for states to be competitive by being fiscally frugal, large state expenditures that do not deliver on their objectives are vulnerable to social movements that claim to have an approach that will be cheaper, work better, and be more popular with the people in the long run. Hence we should not be surprised at the irony that some of the most savvy conservative governments in the world, which are most imbued with the imperatives for fiscal frugality, like New Zealand (Maxwell and Morris 1992; Morris and Maxwell 1993) and Singapore (Hsien 1996; Chan 1996), are early movers in embracing the restorative justice movement against the grain of their traditional commitment to state punitiveness. Even here, a United States assistant attorney general has been heard espousing a need to reinvent justice as restorative justice (Robinson 1996).

While I am cautiously optimistic that the empirical evidence will continue to be encouraging about the efficacy and decency of restorative justice compared with retributive justice, there is also evidence that restorative justice often fails. Victims sometimes resent the time involved in deliberation; sometimes they experience heightened fear from meeting offenders; sometimes they are extremely vengeful, though more often I am moved by how forgiving they are when genuinely empowered with process control. In preliminary data from a Canberra study, Strang and Sherman (1997) show that conferences may systematically increase victims' forgiveness and reduce their fear. We need more high-quality research on when and why restorative justice fails, and how to cover the weaknesses of restorative justice with complementary strengths of deterrence and incapacitation (Braithwaite 1993).

Beyond Communitarianism Versus Individualism

Some criminologists in the West are critical of countries like Singapore, Indonesia, and Japan, where crime in the streets is not a major problem, because they think individualism in these societies is crushed by communitarianism or collective obligation. Their prescription is that Asian societies need to shift the balance away from communitarianism and allow greater individualism. I don't find this a very attractive analysis.

Some Asian criminologists are critical of countries like the United States and Australia because they think these societies are excessively individualistic, suffering much crime and incivility as a result. According to this analysis, the West needs to shift the balance away from individualism in favor of communitarianism—away from rights and toward collective responsibilities. I don't find this a very attractive analysis either.

Both sides of this debate can do a better job of learning from each other. We can aspire to a society that is strong on both rights and responsibilities, that nurtures strong communities and strong individuals. Indeed, in the good society, strong communities constitute strong individuals and vice versa. Our objective can be to keep the benefits of the statist revolution at the same time as we rediscover community-based justice. Community justice is often oppressive of rights, often subjects the vulnerable to the domination of local elites, subordinates women, can be procedurally unfair, and tends to neglect structural solutions. Mindful of this, we might rephrase the two challenges posed earlier in the chapter:

1. Helping indigenous community justice learn from the virtues of liberal statism—procedural fairness, rights, and protecting the vulnerable from domination.
2. Helping liberal state justice learn from indigenous community justice—learning restorative community alternatives to individualism.

Together these two challenges ask, How can we save and revive traditional restorative justice practices in a way that helps them become procedurally fairer, that respects fundamental human rights, and that secures protection against domination? The liberal state can be a check on oppressive collectivism, just as bottom-up communitarianism can be a check on oppressive individualism. A healing circle can be a corrective to a justice system that can leave offenders and victims suicidally alone; a Bill of Rights can be a check on a tribal elder who imposes a violent tyranny on young people. The bringing together of these ideals is an old prescription—not just liberty, not just community, but *liberté, égalité, fraternité*. Competitive individualism has badly fractured this republican amalgam. The social movement for restorative justice does practical work to weld an amalgam that is relevant to the creation of contemporary urban multicultural republics. Day to day, the movement is not sustained by romantic ideals in which I happen to believe, like deliberative democracy. Proponents want to do it for Sam and for the old woman Sam pushed over one day. That is what enlists them in the social movement for restorative justice; in the process they are, I submit, enlisted in something of wider political significance.

References

Bazemore, G., and C. Washington. 1995. "Charting the Future of the Juvenile Justice System: Reinventing Mission and Management." *Spectrum: The Journal of State Government* 68:51–66.

Bianchi, H., and R. van Swaaningen, eds. 1986. *Abolitionism: Towards a Non-Repressive Approach to Crime*. Amsterdam: Free University Press.

Blagg, H. 1985. "Reparation and Justice for Juveniles: The Corby Experience." *British Journal of Criminology* 25:267–79.

Braithwaite, John. 1993. "Beyond Positivism: Learning from Contextual Integrated Strategies." *Journal of Research in Crime and Delinquency* 30: 383–99.

———. 1995. "Corporate Crime and Republican Criminological Praxis." In *Corporate Crime: Ethics, Law and State*, edited by F. Pearce and L. Snider. Toronto: University of Toronto Press.

———. 1998. "Restorative Justice: Assessing an Immodest Theory and a Pessimistic Theory." In *Crime and Justice: A Review of Research*, vol. 23, edited by Michael Tonry. Chicago: University of Chicago Press.

———. 1997. "On Speaking Softly and Carrying Sticks: Neglected Dimensions of a Republican Separation of Powers." *University of Toronto Law Journal* 47:305–61.

Brown, M. J. A. 1994. "Empowering the Victim in the New Zealand Youth Justice Process: A Strategy for Healing." Plenary Address to the Eighth International Symposium on Victimology, Adelaide, Australia.

Burford, G., and J. Pennell. 1996. *Family Group Decision Making: New Roles for "Old" Partners in Resolving Family Violence.* Implementation report summary. Newfoundland: Family Group Decision Making Project.

Chan, Wai Yin. 1996. "Family Conferences in the Juvenile Justice Process: Survey on the Impact of Family Conferencing on Juvenile Offenders and Their Families." *Subordinate Courts Statistics and Planning Unit Research Bulletin,* February.

Christie, Nils. 1978. "Conflicts as Property." *British Journal of Criminology* 17:1–15.

———. 1982. *Limits to Pain.* Oxford: Martin Robertson.

Clairmont, Donald. 1994. "Alternative Justice Issues for Aboriginal Justice." Paper prepared for the Aboriginal Justice Directorate. Ottawa: Department of Justice.

Consedine, Jim. 1997. *Restorative Justice: Healing the Effects of Crime.* Christchurch: Ploughshares Publications.

Cullen, Francis T. 1994. "Social Support as an Organizing Concept for Criminology: Presidential Address to the Academy of Criminal Justice Sciences." *Justice Quarterly* 11:527–59.

De Haan, W. 1990. *The Politics of Redress: Crime, Punishment and Penal Abolition.* London: Unwin Hyman.

Dignan, J. 1992. "Repairing the Damage: Can Reparation Work in the Service of Diversion?" *British Journal of Criminology* 32:453–72.

Eglash, Albert. 1975. "Beyond Restitution: Creative Restitution." In *Restitution in Criminal Justice,* edited by Joe Hudson and Burt Galaway. Lexington, Mass.: Lexington.

Farrington, David P. 1993. "Understanding and Preventing Bullying." In *Crime and Justice: A Review of Research,* vol. 17, edited by Michael Tonry. Chicago: University of Chicago Press.

Fisse, Brent, and John Braithwaite. 1993. *Corporations, Crime and Accountability.* Cambridge: Cambridge University Press.

Foucault, Michael. 1977. *Discipline and Punish: The Birth of the Prison.* London: Allen Lane.

Galaway, Burt, and Joe Hudson, eds. 1975. *Considering the Victim.* Springfield, Ill.: Charles C. Thomas.

Goodes, Tim. 1995. "Victims and Family Conferences: Juvenile Justice in South Australia." Unpublished manuscript. Canberra: Australian National University, Research School of Social Sciences, Reintegrative Shaming Experiment (RISE) Library.

Hakaiha, M. 1994. "Youth Justice Teams and the Family Meeting in Western Australia: A Trans-Tasman Analysis." In *Family Conferencing and Juvenile Justice: The Way Forward or Misplaced Optimism?* edited by C. Alder and J. Wunderlitz. Canberra: Australian Institute of Criminology.

Haley, John. 1996. "Crime Prevention Through Restorative Justice: Lessons from Japan." In *Restorative Justice: International Perspectives,* edited by Burt Galaway and Joe Hudson. Monsey, N.Y.: Criminal Justice Press.

Hassall, Ian. 1996. "Origin and Development of Family Group Conferences." In *Family Group Conferences: Perspectives on Policy and Practice,* edited by Joe Hudson, Allison Morris, Gabrielle Maxwell, and Burt Galaway. Sydney: Federation Press and Criminal Justice Press.

Hsien, Lim Li. 1996. "Family Conferencing Good for Young Delinquents: Report." *The Straits Times* (Singapore), March 6. (From IMAGE database.)

Hyndman, Mary, Margaret Thorsborne, and Shirley Wood. 1996. "Community Accountability Conferencing: Trial Report." Queensland: University of Queensland, Department of Education.

James, T. M. 1993. "Circle Sentencing." Yellowknife: Supreme Court of the Northwest Territories.

Lajeunesse, T. 1993. *Community Holistic Circle Healing: Hollow Water First Nation.* Aboriginal Peoples Collection. Ottawa: Supply and Services.

LaPrairie, C. 1994. *Seen But Not Heard: Native People in the Inner City.* Report no. 3: Victimisation and Domestic Violence. Ottawa: Department of Justice.

———. 1995. "Altering Course: New Directions in Criminal Justice and Corrections: Sentencing Circles and Family Group Conferences." *Australian and New Zealand Journal of Criminology* 28:78–99.

Leibrich, J. 1996. "The Role of Shame in Going Straight: A Study of Former Offenders." In *Restorative Justice: International Perspectives,* edited by Burt Galaway and Joe Hudson. Monsey, N.Y.: Criminal Justice Press.

Marshall, T. F. 1985. *Alternatives to Criminal Courts.* Aldershot, England: Gower.

———. 1990. "Results from British Experiments in Restorative Justice." In *Criminal Justice, Restitution and Reconciliation,* edited by Burt Galaway and Joe Hudson. New York: Willow Tree Press.

———. 1992a. "Grassroots Initiatives Towards Restorative Justice: The New Paradigm." Paper presented at the Fulbright Colloquium on Penal Theory and Penal Practice, University of Stirling, Scotland, September.

———. 1992b. "Restorative Justice on Trial in Britain." In *Restorative Justice on Trial: Pitfalls and Potentials of Victim-Offender Mediation—International Research Perspectives,* edited by H. Messmer and H. U. Otto. Dordrecht: Kluwer.

Marshall, T. F., and S. Merry. 1990. *Crime and Accountability: Victim Offender Mediation in Practice.* London: Home Office.

Matza, David. 1964. *Delinquency and Drift.* New York: Wiley.

Maxwell, Gabrielle M. 1993. "Arrangements for Children After Separation? Problems and Possibilities." In *Women's Law Conference Papers: 1993 New Zealand Suffrage Centennial.* Wellington: Victoria University of Wellington.

Maxwell, Gabrielle M., and Allison Morris. 1992. *Family Participation, Cultural Diversity and Victim Involvement in Youth Justice: A New Zealand Experiment.* Wellington: Victoria University of Wellington, Institute of Criminology.

———. 1993. *Family, Victims and Culture: Youth Justice in New Zealand.* Wellington: Victoria University of Wellington, Social Policy Agency and Institute of Criminology.

———. 1996. "Research on Family Group Conferences with Young Offenders in New Zealand." In *Family Group Conferences: Perspectives on*

Policy and Practice, edited by Joe Hudson, Allison Morris, Gabrielle Maxwell, and Burt Galaway. Sydney: Federation Press and Criminal Justice Press.

McDonald, J., D. Moore, T. O'Connell, and M. Thorsborne. 1995. *Real Justice Training Manual: Coordinating Family Group Conferences.* Pipersville, Penn.: Pipers Press.

McElrea, F. W. M. 1993. "The Youth Court in New Zealand: Is This a New Model of Justice?" Paper presented at the University of Cambridge, Institute of Criminology, October 20.

Messmer, H. 1993. "Victim-Offender Mediation in Germany After the Reunification." Paper presented at the Eleventh International Congress on Criminology, Budapest, August 23–27.

Messmer, H., and H. U. Otto, eds. 1992a. *Restorative Justice on Trial: Pitfalls and Potentials of Victim-Offender Mediation—International Research Perspectives.* Dordrecht: Kluwer.

———. 1992b. "Restorative Justice: Steps on the Way Toward a Good Idea." In *Restorative Justice on Trial: Pitfalls and Potentials of Victim-Offender Mediation—International Research Perspectives,* edited by H. Messmer and H. U. Otto. Dordrecht: Kluwer.

Moore, David B., and L. Forsythe. 1995. *A New Approach to Juvenile Justice: An Evaluation of Family Conferencing in Wagga Wagga.* Wagga Wagga, Australia: Charles Sturt University.

Moore, David B., and Terry O'Connell. 1994. "Family Conferencing in Wagga Wagga: A Communitarian Model of Justice." In *Family Conferencing and Juvenile Justice,* edited by Christine Alder and Joy Wundersitz. Canberra: Australian Institute of Criminology.

Morris, Allison, and Gabrielle M. Maxwell. 1993. "Juvenile Justice in New Zealand: A New Paradigm." *Australian and New Zealand Journal of Criminology* 26:72–90.

Mugford, J., and S. Mugford. 1992. "Policing Domestic Violence." In *Policing Australia: Old Issues, New Perspectives,* edited by P. Moir and H. Eijckman. Melbourne: Macmillan.

O'Connell, T. 1992. "Looking at New Initiatives." Paper presented at the Juvenile Justice Seminar, Shellharbour, New South Wales, March 31.

———. 1995. "Integrating Australian Police Conferencing into the Canadian Justice System." Discussion paper prepared for Judge David Arnot, Director General, Aboriginal Justice Directorate, Ottawa, Canada.

Olweus, Dan. 1994. "Annotation: Bullying at School: Basic Facts and Effects of a School-Based Intervention Program." *Journal of Child Psychology and Psychiatry* 35:1171–90.

Palk, G. 1995. "Community Corrections: A Restorative Response to Crime?" Paper presented at the "Conference on Community Corrections in the 21st Century: Challenge, Choice and Change," Griffith University, Centre for Crime Policy and Public Safety, Brisbane, July 3–4.

Peachey, D. E. 1989. "The Kitchener Experiment." In *Mediation and Criminal Justice: Victims, Offenders and Community,* edited by M. Wright and B. Galaway. London: Sage.

Pepler, Debra J., Wendy Craig, Suzanne Ziegler, and Alice Charach. 1993. "A School-Based Antibullying Intervention." In *Understanding and Managing Bullying,* edited by Delwin Tattum. London: Heinemann.

Pettit, Philip, and John Braithwaite. 1990. *Not Just Deserts: A Republican Theory of Criminal Justice.* Oxford: Oxford University Press.

Pitts, John, and Philip Smith. 1995. *Preventing School Bullying.* Police Research Group: Crime Detection and Prevention Series Paper no. 63. London: Home Office.

Pranis, K. 1996. "A State Initiative Toward Restorative Justice: The Minnesota Experience." In *Restorative Justice: International Perspectives,* edited by Burt Galaway and Joe Hudson. Monsey, N.Y.: Criminal Justice Press.

Pruitt, Dean G. 1995. "Research Report: Process and Outcome in Community Mediation." *Negotiation Journal* 77:365–77.

Rees, Joseph V. 1988. *Reforming the Workplace.* Philadelphia: University of Pennsylvania Press.

Retzinger, Suzanne, and Tom Scheff. 1996. "Strategy for Community Conferences: Emotions and Social Bonds." In *Restorative Justice: International Perspectives,* edited by Burt Galaway and Joe Hudson. Monsey, N.Y.: Criminal Justice Press.

Robertson, Jeremy. 1996. "Research on Family Group Conferences in Child Welfare in New Zealand." In *Family Group Conferences: Perspectives on Policy and Practice,* edited by Joe Hudson, Allison Morris, Gabrielle Maxwell, and Burt Galaway. Sydney: Federation Press and Criminal Justice Press.

Robinson, Laurie. 1996. "Linking Community-Based Initiatives and Community Justice: The Office of Justice Programs." *National Institute of Justice Journal,* no. 231 (August):4–7.

Ross, Rupert. 1996. *Returning to the Teachings: Exploring Aboriginal Justice.* London: Penguin Books.

Sessar, K., A. Beuerskens, and K. Boers. 1986. "Wiedergutmachung als Konfliktregelungsparadigma?" *Kriminologisches Journal* 18:86–105.

Sherman, L. W., and G. Barnes. 1997. "Restorative Justice and Offenders' Respect for the Law." Reintegrative Shaming Experiment (RISE) Working Paper no. 3. Canberra: Australian National University, Research School of Social Sciences.

Smith, D., H. Blagg, and N. Derricourt. 1985. "Victim-Offender Mediation Project." Report to the Chief Officers' Group, South Yorkshire Probation Service. Cited in *Crime and Accountability: Victim-Offender Mediation in Practice,* edited by T. Marshall and S. Merry. 1990. London: Home Office.

Stewart, Trish. 1993. "The Youth Justice Co-Ordinator's Role: A Personal Perspective of the New Legislation in Action." In *The Youth Court in New Zealand: A New Model of Justice,* edited by B. J. Brown and F. W. M. McElrea. Auckland: Legal Research Foundation.

Strang, H., and L. W. Sherman. 1997. "The Victim's Perspective." Reintegrative Shaming Experiment (RISE) Working Paper no. 2. Canberra: Australian National University, Research School of Social Sciences.

Stuart, Barry. 1996. "Circle Sentencing: Turning Swords into Ploughshares." In *Restorative Justice: International Perspectives,* edited by Burt Galaway and Joe Hudson. Monsey, N.Y.: Criminal Justice Press.

Tyler, Tom. 1990. *Why People Obey the Law.* New Haven, Conn.: Yale University Press.

Umbreit, Mark. 1985. *Crime and Reconciliation: Creative Options for Victims and Offenders.* Nashville, Tenn.: Abingdon Press.

———. 1990. "The Meaning of Fairness to Burglary Victims." In *Criminal Justice, Restitution and Reconciliation,* edited by Burt Galaway and Joe Hudson. Monsey, N.Y.: Willow Tree Press.

———. 1992. "Mediating Victim-Offender Conflict: From Single-Site to Multi-Site Analysis in the U.S." In *Restorative Justice on Trial: Pitfalls and Potentials of Victim-Offender Mediation—International Research Perspectives,* edited by H. Messmer and H. U. Otto. Dordrecht: Kluwer.

———. 1994a. "Mediating Homicide Cases: A Journey of the Heart Through Dialogue and Mutual Aid." *Victim-Offender Mediation* 5:1–3.

———. 1994b. *Victim Meets Offender: The Impact of Restorative Justice and Mediation.* Monsey, N.Y.: Criminal Justice Press.

———. 1998. "Restorative Justice Through Juvenile Victim-Offender Mediation." In *Restoring Juvenile Justice,* edited by Lode Walgrave and Gordon Bazemore. Monsey, N.Y.: Criminal Justice Press.

Van Ness, Daniel. 1986. *Crime and Its Victims: What We Can Do.* Downers Grove, Ill.: Intervarsity Press.

———. 1993. "New Wine and Old Wineskins: Four Challenges of Restorative Justice." *Criminal Law Forum* 4:251–76.

———. 1998. "Legal Principles and Process." In *Restoring Juvenile Justice,* edited by Lode Walgrave and Gordon Bazemore. Monsey, N.Y.: Criminal Justice Press.

Walgrave, Lode. 1993. "In Search of Limits to the Restorative Justice for Juveniles." Paper presented at the Eleventh International Congress on Criminology, Budapest, August 23–27.

———. 1994. "Beyond Rehabilitation: In Search of a Constructive Alternative in the Judicial Response to Juvenile Crime." *European Journal on Criminal Policy and Research* 2:57–75.

———. 1995. "Restorative Justice for Juveniles: Just a Technique or a Fully Fledged Alternative?" *Howard Journal* 34:228–49.

Weitekamp, E. 1989. "Restitution: A New Paradigm of Criminal Justice or a New Way to Widen the System of Social Control?" Ph.D. diss., University of Pennsylvania.

———. 1998. "The History of Restorative Justice." In *Restoring Juvenile Justice,* edited by Lode Walgrave and Gordon Bazemore. Monsey, N.Y.: Criminal Justice Press.

Wright, M. 1982. *Making Good: Prisons, Punishment and Beyond.* London: Hutchinson.

———. 1992. "Victim-Offender Mediation as a Step Towards a Restorative System of Justice." In *Restorative Justice on Trial: Pitfalls and Potentials of Victim-Offender Mediation—International Research Perspectives,* edited by H. Messmer and H. U. Otto. Dordrecht: Kluwer.

Yazzie, Robert, and James W. Zion. 1996. "Navajo Restorative Justice: The Law of Equality and Justice." In *Restorative Justice: International Perspectives,* edited by Burt Galaway and Joe Hudson. Monsey, N.Y.: Criminal Justice Press.

Zehr, Howard. 1985. *Retributive Justice, Restorative Justice.* Kitchener, Ont.: Canada Victim Offender Ministries Program.

————. 1990. *Changing Lenses: A New Focus for Criminal Justice.* Scottsdale, Pa.: Herald Press.

————. 1995. "Rethinking Criminal Justice: Restorative Justice." Unpublished manuscript. Canberra: Australian National University, Research School of Social Sciences, Reintegrative Shaming Experiment (RISE) Library.

13

Deterrence and Incapacitation

DANIEL S. NAGIN

The criminal justice system dispenses justice by apprehending, prosecuting, and punishing lawbreakers. These activities also prevent crime by two mechanisms, deterrence and incapacitation. Would-be lawbreakers may be deterred from committing crimes by the knowledge that their crime may result in their arrest, prosecution, and sentencing. Thus, deterrence depends on some would-be lawbreakers concluding that the price of crime is prohibitive. The criminal justice system may also avert crime by a nonbehavioral mechanism: the incapacitation of convicted offenders who are incarcerated in jail or prison. During their period of incarceration they are physically restrained from committing crimes against the society at large.

Going back at least to Bentham and Beccaria, scholars have speculated on the deterrent and incapacitative effect of official sanctions, but sustained efforts to empirically verify their effects did not begin until the 1960s. In this chapter I review what is known about deterrence and incapacitation. This review is not intended to be encyclopedic but instead aims to highlight key findings and conclusions. Because evidence up through the early 1980s has been well summarized elsewhere (Blumstein, Cohen, and Nagin 1978; Cook 1980), I focus primarily on research from 1980 onward. Also, this brief review necessarily draws from many sources, including other reviews. Two that deserve special note are my own review of the deterrence literature (Nagin 1998) and Zimring and Hawkins's 1995 review of the evidence on incapacitation. While not always explicitly referenced, the material on incapacitation draws heavily from themes in Zimring and Hawkins.

A Brief Review of Research on Deterrence

Deterrence research has evolved in three distinctive and largely disconnected literatures—interrupted time-series studies, ecological studies, and perceptual studies. Interrupted time-series studies examine the impact of targeted and specific policy interventions such as police crackdowns on open-air drug markets. Here the evidence suggests that such interventions have at least a temporary impact, although decay is commonplace. Ecological studies use natural variations in crime rate and sanctions levels across time and space as the test bed for estimating deterrent effects. These studies search for a negative association between crime rates and sanction levels that can plausibly be interpreted as a deterrent effect (i.e., higher sanction levels lead to lower crime rates). I am convinced that a number of studies have been successful in isolating a deterrent effect. Prior to 1980 these two categories of studies were the mainstay of the deterrence literature. Since that time, another large deterrence literature has emerged that focuses on the links between perceptions of sanction risk and severity and self-reported crime and delinquency. The data for these studies are assembled from surveys. With few exceptions the perceptual studies find that self-reported criminality is lower among people who perceive that sanction risks and costs are higher. Thus, I am persuaded that the collective actions of the criminal justice system exert a substantial deterrent effect.

In this section I outline the methods used in each of the three literatures and highlight the salient findings from each.

Interrupted Time-Series Studies

Interrupted time-series studies examine the impact of targeted policy interventions such as police crackdowns or enactment of statutes changing penalties. The best-designed studies attempt to incorporate important features of a true experiment—a well-defined treatment regime, measurement of response before and after treatment, and a control group. Two classic studies of this genre are Ross's studies of the impact on drunk driving of the British Road Safety Act and of Scandinavian-style drunk driving laws (Ross 1982).

The great proportion of interrupted time-series studies have examined the impact of drunk driving laws or of police crackdowns on drug markets, disorderly behavior, and drunk driving. A less extensive literature has also examined the impact of gun control laws and ordinances. Excellent reviews of these studies are already available from Sherman (1990) and Ross (1982), so I only very briefly summarize their conclusions.

Both Sherman and Ross conclude that interventions are generally successful in generating an initial deterrent effect. In drunk driving interventions this is evidenced by a reduction in fatalities in which the driver is intoxicated, and in drug market crackdowns by reduced dealing. One exception may be interventions that increase sentence severity. If judges or juries believe that the penalties are too harsh, they may respond by refusing to convict guilty defendants, with the result that the policy increases rather than deters the targeted behavior. Indeed, Ross concludes that efforts to deter drunk driving with harsher penalties commonly fail for precisely this reason. Sherman and Ross are also in agreement that the effect is generally only transitory: the initial deterrent effect typically begins decaying even while the intervention is still in effect. However, in some instances the decay is not always complete even following the end of the crackdown.

Perceptual Deterrence Studies

The perceptual deterrence literature examines the relations between perceived sanction risks and either self-reported offending or intentions to offend. This literature was spawned by researchers interested in probing the perceptual underpinnings of the deterrence process. They were motivated by the observation that ultimately deterrence depends on perceptions of the risks (and rewards) of offending and by skepticism that perceived sanction risks are very closely tied to actual risks.

Perceptual deterrence studies have focused on examining the connection of illegal behavior to two categories of sanction variables, the certainty and severity of punishment. The certainty of punishment refers to the probability that a crime will result in apprehension, conviction, or incarceration, whereas severity refers to the seriousness of the ensuing punishment, for example, the length of a prison sentence.

Perceptual deterrence studies have been based on three types of data: cross-sectional survey studies, panel survey studies, and scenario-based studies. In cross-sectional survey studies, individuals are questioned about their perceptions of the certainty and severity of sanctions and about either their prior offending behavior or their future intentions to offend. For example, Grasmick and Bryjak (1980) queried a sample of city residents about their perceptions of the risk of arrest for offenses such as petty theft, drunk driving, or tax cheating, and also whether they thought they would commit each of these acts in the future.

In panel survey studies, the sample is repeatedly surveyed on risk perceptions and criminal behavior. For example, Paternoster et al. (1982) followed a sample of students through their three-year tenure in high school, surveying them on the frequency with which they engaged in various delinquent acts and on their perceptions of the risks and consequences of being caught for each such act.

In scenario-based studies, individuals are questioned about their perceptions of the risks of committing a crime described in a detailed crime vignette and about their own behavior if they found themselves in that situation. Raymond Paternoster and I (Nagin and Paternoster 1993), for instance, constructed a scenario describing the circumstances of a date rape. We then surveyed a sample of college males about their perceptions of the risk of the scenario male being arrested for sexual assault and also about what they themselves would do in the same circumstance.

The cross-sectional and scenario-based studies have consistently found that perceptions of the risk of detection and punishment have negative, deterrent-like associations with self-reported offending or intentions to offend. Such deterrent-like associations with perceived severity are somewhat less consistent, but when individual assessments of the cost of such sanctions are taken into account, statistically significant negative associations again emerge. Only in the panel-based studies have null findings on deterrent-like effects been found.

In panel-based studies, respondents are typically interviewed on an annual cycle. With these data, researchers examine the relationship of behavior between years t and $t + 1$ to risk perceptions at the outset of year t. The goal is to avoid the problem of causal ordering. Is a negative association a reflection of the deterrent impact of risk perceptions on crime or of the impact of criminal involvement on risk perceptions? Generally, these studies have found only weak evidence of deterrent-like associations (Paternoster 1987).

The null findings from the panel-based studies generated a spirited debate on the appropriate time lag between measurements of sanction risk perceptions and criminal involvement. Grasmick and Bursik (1990) and Williams and Hawkins (1986) argued that ideally the measurements should be made contemporaneously because perceptions at the time of the act are what determine behavior.

The argument for temporal proximity is compelling, but the challenge is its practical achievement. People cannot be queried on their risk perceptions on a real-time basis as they encounter criminal opportunities in their everyday lives. The scenario method offers one solution because respondents are not questioned about their actual behavior or intentions but rather are asked about their likely behavior in a hypothetical situation. As already noted, scenario-based research has consistently found deterrent-like relationships in the data. On average, persons who perceived that sanctions were more certain or severe reported smaller probabilities of their engaging in the behavior depicted in the scenario, whether it be tax evasion (Klepper and Nagin 1989), drunk driving (Nagin and Paternoster 1993), sexual assault (Bachman, Paternoster, and Ward 1992), or corporate crime (Paternoster and Simpson 1996). Thus, I believe that a consensus has emerged among perceptual deterrence researchers that the negative association between sanction risk perceptions and offending behavior or intentions is measuring deterrence. This conclusion reframes the question of the deterrent effect of sanctions from the issue of whether people respond to their perceptions of sanction threats to the issue of whether those perceptions are manipulable by policy. This brings us to the issue of the formation of sanction risk perceptions.

The Formation of Sanction Risk Perceptions. The perceptual deterrence literature was motivated by skepticism that perceived and actual sanction threats were tightly linked. Thus, it is curious that perceptual deterrence researchers have given only modest attention to the factors influencing risk perceptions and to the dynamic processes by which they are formed. The source of sanction risk perceptions is important to policy because risk perceptions can be affected by policy only if they are substantially grounded in reality. Perhaps the most important check of the link between perceptions and reality is whether perceptions are updated based on experience with apprehension. A few studies have attempted to test whether offenders update their risk assessments based on experience. Results have been mixed and largely based on student or general population samples rather than on samples of serious offenders. However, one exception is a study by Horney and Marshall (1992) based on a sample of more than 1,000 convicted felons. Within their sample, subjects who had higher arrest ratios (self-reported arrests to self-reported crime) also reported higher risk perceptions. Thus, Horney and Marshall do find evidence that active offenders learn from offending experience.

In my scenario-based research, my coauthors and I have given some attention to the impact of situational factors on risk perceptions (Klepper and Nagin 1989; Nagin and Paternoster 1993). We have done this by experimentally varying scenario conditions (e.g., length of the drive home) and examining the impact of such variation on perceived risk (e.g., the probability of arrest for drunk driving). Results have been mixed. For offenses such as date rape and drunk driving, we find little evidence of risk perceptions being affected by context, but for tax evasion the link was strong. Perceptions of the risk of detection increased with the amount of noncompliance and varied by type of noncompliance (e.g., were higher for deductions than for cash income). For tax compliance, at least, perceptions mirrored the realities of the enforcement process.

Kagan (1989) provides a complementary perspective on the findings for tax evasion. He argues that the visibility of income to the Internal Revenue Service (IRS) exerts an enormously powerful impact on compliance rates. Compliance rates are very high for very visible sources of income such as wages, dividends, and interest for which the IRS receives information reports from payers. Compliance declines substantially for less visible sources of income for which the IRS does not receive information reports but for which there are other practical methods for tracing the income like bank or business records. Examples of this sort of income are proprietorship and partnership income. Finally, compliance rates are negligible for income sources like cash income earned in the informal, underground, and illegal economic sectors, which are virtually untraceable. As Kagan points out, visibility is simply an evocative synonym for detectability. For highly visible sources of income it is easy for the IRS to assemble the accounting information necessary to prove noncompliance; such information is supplied on a computer tape. Thus, the threat of detection is very high. People recognize this, and compliance is correspondingly high. For invisible sources of income it is extremely costly to assemble the required accounting information to prove noncompliance, and here again people seem to respond accordingly by reporting very little of such income.

In summary, the literature on the formation of sanction risk perception is small and narrow in scope. Arguably, measuring the links between sanction policies and sanction risk perceptions is of secondary importance to measuring the links between sanction policy and behavior. Knowing the impact of policy on risk perceptions serves only to clarify the basis for the relationship of policy to behavior but has little value in and of itself. This argument assumes that the linkage between policy and behavior can be firmly established. In fact, evidence on the policy-to-behavior linkage will never be "airtight," even if it is based on data from an experiment. For instance, suppose it was found that a policy of presumptive arrest for spousal assault was associated with a decline in various indicators of spousal abuse in the population at large. One interpretation of such a finding is that it reflects a general deterrent effect. But if there was no evidence that men were generally aware of the policy, the deterrence interpretation would be undercut. Alternatively, if survey evidence showed a general awareness of the policy, the case for the deterrence interpretation would be bolstered.

The dearth of evidence on the policy-to-risk-perceptions connection also leaves unanswered a key criticism of skeptics of the deterrent effects of official sanctions. Even if crime decisions are influenced by sanction risk perceptions, as the perceptual deterrence literature strongly suggests, absent some linkage between policy and perceptions, however imperfect, behavior is immune to policy manipulation. In this sense behavior lacks rationality, not because individuals fail to weigh perceived costs and benefits but because the sanction risk perceptions are not anchored in reality.

Two generic categories of questions about risk perceptions are particularly important. One is whether sanction risk perceptions are well formed at the level of the specific offense (e.g., burglary versus robbery), or do would-be offenders have only a generalized sense of the effectiveness of the enforcement apparatus? For instance, are perceptions of apprehension risk formed principally by broad-based impressions of the police being proactive in suppressing disorder, as suggested by Sampson and Cohen (1988) and Wilson and Boland (1978), or are they more crime-specific and determined by the rate at which police actually solve specific types of crime?

The answer to this question is important for policy. Rational choice models of criminal behavior, such as those posed by economists, predict that escalation of penalties for a specific crime, such as robbery with a firearm, will have the desired effect, namely, fewer gun robberies, but the models also predict an undesirable side effect—an increase in non-gun crime such as robberies with knives and burglary. These predictions require potential offenders to have crime-specific impressions of sanction risks that vary independently of one another, but there is no research on whether this is true. If it is substantially incorrect and impressions of risk for all crime types are closely tied to an overall impression of effectiveness, there may be no substantial crime substitution effects. Indeed, a seemingly targeted sanction policy may have a generalized deterrent effect that extends beyond targeted crimes.

The second category of questions that deserve special attention concerns the dynamics of the risk formation process. How do would-be offenders combine prior experience with the criminal justice system and new information on penalties? How long does it typically take for persons to become aware of new sanctioning regimes? How do they become aware of changes in penalties, and what information sources do they use in updating their impressions? How do novices form impressions of sanction risks? These questions speak to the broader issue of whether sanction risk impressions are easily manipulable.

The Linkage Between Formal and Informal Sanction Processes. In my judgment, the most important contribution of the perceptual deterrence literature does not involve the evidence it has amassed on deterrence effects per se. Rather it is the attention it has focused on the linkage between formal and informal sources of social control. Recognition of this connection antedates the perceptual deterrence literature. For instance, Zimring and Hawkins observe that formal punishment may best deter when it sets off informal sanctions: "Official actions can set off societal reactions that may provide potential offenders with more reason to avoid conviction than the officially imposed unpleasantness of punishment" (1973, p. 174). Andenaes (1974) also makes this argument.

Early perceptual deterrence studies did not consider the connection between formal and informal sanctioning systems, but a review by Williams and Hawkins (1986) prompted a broadening of the agenda to consider this issue. In a nutshell, their position was this: community knowledge of an individual's probable involvement in criminal or delinquent acts is a necessary precondition for the operation of informal sanction processes. Such knowledge can be obtained from two sources: either from the arrest (or conviction or sentencing) of the individual, or from information networks independent of the formal sanction process (e.g., a witness to the crime who does not report such knowledge to the police). Williams and Hawkins observe that deterrent effects may arise from the fear that informal sanctioning processes will be triggered by either of these information sources. They use the term *fear of arrest* to label deterrent effects triggered by the formal sanction process and the term *fear of the act* to label deterrent effects triggered by information networks separate from the formal sanction process. The crux of their argument is that all preventive effects arising from fear of arrest should be included in a full accounting of the deterrent effect of formal sanctions.

I concur, and much of my scenario-based research confirms their argument. This research has consistently found that individuals who report higher stakes in conventionality are more deterred by perceived risk of exposure for lawbreaking. My most salient finding in this regard is related to tax evasion. In the United States, civil enforcement actions by tax authorities are a private matter unless the taxpayer appeals the action. Tax authorities are scrupulous about maintaining this confidentially;

thus, for civil enforcement actions, noncompliers are gambling only with their money, not their reputations. In Klepper and Nagin (1989), a sample of generally middle-class adults was presented with a series of tax non-compliance scenarios. The scenarios laid out the essential features of a tax report—income from different sources, number of exemptions, and various deductions. We then experimentally varied the amount and type of noncompliance (e.g., overstating charitable deductions or understating business income) across tax return line items and found that a majority of respondents reported a nonzero probability of taking advantage of the noncompliance opportunity described in the scenario. Plainly, our re-spondents were generally willing to consider tax noncompliance when only their money was at risk. They also seemed to be calculating; the at-tractiveness of the tax noncompliance gamble was inversely related to the perceived risk of civil enforcement.

The one exception to the rule of confidentiality of enforcement inter-ventions is criminal prosecution. As with all criminal cases, criminal prosecutions for tax evasion are a matter of public record. Here we found evidence of a different decision calculus; seemingly all that was neces-sary to deter evasion was the perception of a nonzero chance of criminal prosecution. Stated differently, if the evasion gamble also involved putting reputation and community standing at risk, our middle-class re-spondents were seemingly unwilling to consider taking the noncompli-ance gamble.

This finding also provides some fresh perspective on the old question of whether the certainty or the severity of punishment is the greater deterrent. If the social and economic costs of punishment are strictly pro-portional to the punishment received—for example, if the cost to the in-dividual of a two-year prison term is twice that of a one-year sentence—certainty and severity will equally affect expected cost. This is because expected cost is simply the multiplicative product of certainty, P, and severity, S. The value of the product, $P \times S$, is equally affected by propor-tional changes in P or S. For example, the impact on expected value of a 50 percent increase in P is the same as a 50 percent increase in S. How-ever, my tax evasion research suggests that people do not perceive that costs are proportional to potential punishment. Instead, they seem to per-ceive that there is a fixed cost associated with merely being convicted or even apprehended if it is public record.

While my tax evasion research does not pin down the specific sources of these costs, other research on the impact of a criminal record on access to legal labor markets suggests a real basis for the fear of stigmatization (Freeman 1995; Waldfogel 1994). Freeman estimates that a record of in-carceration depresses probability of work by 15 to 30 percent, and Wald-fogel estimates that conviction for fraud reduces income by as much as 40 percent.

I emphasize the linkage between formal and informal sanctions be-cause over the long run a policy may erode the foundation of the deterrent effect—fear of stigmatization. For an event to be stigmatizing, it must be relatively uncommon. To illustrate how a policy may cannibalize the basis for its effectiveness, consider the following example. Suppose a policy had the effect of increasing the probability of imprisonment for committing a crime, P(I), by 10 percent and this policy was effective in reducing the number of offenders, N, by 5 percent. *Ceteris paribus,* is it reasonable to assume this reduction in N can be sustained over the long run? I think not. In steady state, the incarcerated population, I, equals $(P(I) \times S) \times (N \times \lambda)$, where S is the average time served in prison and λ is the average rate of offending. The two product terms, $P(I) \times S$ and $N \times \lambda$, respectively, are the average prison term per crime committed and the total number of crimes committed. Thus, their product equals the size of the incarcerated population. Assume for simplicity that the 10 percent increase in P(I) has no impact on λ. Under these circumstances, the 5 percent reduction in N will reduce the crime rate by 5 percent. However, it will also increase the incarcerated population by 5 percent—N declines by 5 percent, but P(I) increases by 10 percent. In turn, the increase in prison population will result in an increase in the proportion of the population with a prison record. Herein lies my reservation about the sustainability of the 5 percent reduction in crime. If in fact fear of stigmatization is a prominent factor in a full accounting of the deterrent effect of formal sanctions, this policy may erode the basis for its effectiveness by making prison records more commonplace.

More generally such erosion in effectiveness seems likely to occur when a policy's preventive effect is not sufficiently powerful to reduce crime by enough to reduce rather than increase the proportion of the population with criminal records. To illustrate, suppose that the 10 percent increase in P(I) reduced N by 15 percent—that is, the elasticity of N with respect to P(I) is -1.5, meaning that each 1 percent increase in P(I) reduces N by 1.5 percent. For an elasticity of -1.5, both crime rate and prison population would decline, the former by 15 percent and the latter by 5 percent. In this case the 15 percent reduction in crime may be sustainable. Indeed, it may even increase over time because the policy decreases rather than increases the population rate of criminal records.

These examples illustrate that the long-term preventive effect of a policy may depend critically upon the magnitude of the response. If the elasticity of the crime rate with respect to the sanction policy variable is great enough to reduce the proportion of the population that is stigmatized, the impact may be sustainable. On the other hand, if the policy increases the proportion stigmatized, the deterrent effect is less likely to be sustainable.

At least with regard to prison sanctions, the evidence suggests that in the United States we are currently in the latter situation. Maurer and Huling (1995) examined recent trends in the proportion of the population under the control of the criminal justice system—incarcerated or on parole or probation. They estimated that these proportions are growing and have reached extraordinarily high levels, particularly for young black men. In 1989, 6.2 percent of white males age twenty to twenty-nine were under the control of the criminal justice system. By 1994 this control percentage had increased to 6.7, or to one in fifteen young adult white males. The statistics for young adult African-American males are even more startling. In 1989 their criminal justice system control rate was 23 percent. By 1994 it had grown to nearly one-third of the population, 30.2 percent, with more than 10 percent of this group incarcerated.

Ecological Studies

Two broad classes of ecological analyses are considered—studies of the deterrent effect of prison and of the police.

The Impact of Prison Population on Crime Rate. Between 1974 and 1994, the number of people incarcerated in state or federal prisons grew from 218,000 to 1,016,000 (Maguire and Pastore 1996). Whether this run-up in prison population has materially affected the crime rate has profound implications for public policy, yet there has been surprisingly little analysis of this question. The few studies that have been done produce a range of conclusions, from that of Zimring and Hawkins (1995), who conclude that the impact has been negligible, to an estimate by Levitt (1996) that each additional prisoner averts about fifteen index crimes.

The paucity of studies is probably attributable to the problem of identification that I wrote about nearly twenty years ago (Nagin 1978; Fisher and Nagin 1978). Figure 13.1 depicts the problem graphically. The figure includes two lines—a crime rate function, $C(p)$, and a prison population function, $P(c)$. The crime rate is depicted as a declining function of the

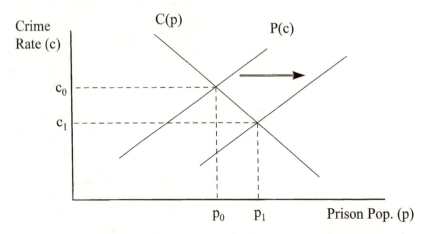

Figure 13.1 The identification problem.

prison population. The downward-sloping crime function reflects the preventive effects of imprisonment through some combination of deterrence and incapacitation. The upward-sloping prison population function captures the impact of crime on the size of the incarcerated population. For any given level of sanction threat—average incarceration time per crime committed—more crime will generate larger prison populations. Studies attempting to measure the impact of prison population on crime rates that do not take into account the mutual interaction of $C(p)$ and $P(c)$ depicted in Figure 13.1 will confound the preventive effect with the effect of crime on prison populations.

To obtain a valid estimate of the preventive effect of imprisonment requires the identification of some factor that affects $P(c)$ but not $C(p)$. An example is a policy that curtails parole boards' powers. Such policies will result in a rightward shift of $P(c)$ that results in an increase in the prison population from p_0 to p_1, which is accompanied by a reduction in the crime rate from c_0 to c_1. In the parlance of econometrics, the exogenously induced shift of $P(c)$ "identifies" $C(p)$ under the assumption that the influence causing the shift in $P(c)$ does not directly impact crime behavior by also shifting $C(p)$.

At least one study has plausibly dealt with the identification problem. Levitt (1996) employs a clever strategy for identifying $C(p)$: shifts in $P(c)$ resulting from court orders to reduce prison overcrowding. The Levitt analysis is based on a panel data set of states for the years 1971 to 1993. For some part of this period the entire prison systems of twelve states were under court order to reduce overcrowding. Levitt found that in the three years prior to the initial filing of overcrowding litigation in these states, their prison population growth rates outpaced the national average by 2.3 percent. In the three years following the initial filing of the overcrowding litigation, their prison population growth lagged behind the national average by 2.5 percent per annum.

Levitt argues that overcrowding litigation affects the crime rate only through its impact on prison population. That is, such litigation shifts $P(c)$ but does not shift $C(p)$. His arguments and supporting evidence are plausible, and more generally the analysis is thorough. Thus, his estimate of the impact of prison population on crime rate, fifteen index crimes averted for each additional man-year of imprisonment, deserves close attention.

Can a study such as that conducted by Levitt provide an all-purpose estimate of the impact of prison population on crime rate? The answer, I believe, is no. Specifically, there is good reason for believing that policies producing equivalent changes in the prison population will not result in the same change in crime rate.

Figure 13.2 is a two-dimensional taxonomy of sanction policies affecting the scale of imprisonment. One dimension, labeled "Type," distinguishes three broad categories: policies regulating certainty of punishment such as laws requiring mandatory imprisonment, policies influenc-

Scope

Type		General	Targeted
	Certainty	Increasing the number of police	Crackdown on drug dealing
	Severity	Broad-based mandatory minimums	"Three-Strikes" laws
	Parole	Parole abolition	No parole for violent offenders

Figure 13.2 Taxonomy of prison sanction policies.

ing sentence length such as determinate sentencing laws, and policies regulating parole powers. The second dimension of the taxonomy, "Scope," distinguishes policies that cast a wide net, such as a general escalation of penalties for broad categories of crime, compared with policies that focus on targeted offenses (e.g., drug dealing) or offenders (e.g., "three-strikes" laws).

The near-500 percent growth in prison population over the last two decades is attributable to a combination of policies belonging to all cells of this matrix. Parole powers have been greatly curtailed, sentence lengths have increased, both in general and for particular crimes (e.g., drug dealing), and judicial discretion to impose nonincarcerative sanctions has been reduced (Tonry 1996). Consequently, any impact on the crime rate of the increase in prison population reflects the effect of an amalgam of potentially interacting policies. By contrast, the impact estimated in the Levitt study measures the preventive effect of reductions in the imprisonment rate induced by the administrative responses to court orders to reduce prison populations. Thus, his estimate would seem only to pertain directly to policies affecting parole powers.

Is this effect generalizable to the whole range of sanction policy options shown in the Figure 13.2 taxonomy? I suspect not. Increased incarceration of individuals convicted of drug offenses has been a major factor contributing to the growth in the prison population in the past decade (Tonry 1995; Zimring and Hawkins 1995). This reflects the impact of statutory changes that require the incarceration of drug offenders (cell 2 of Figure 13.2) and increase the length of that incarceration (cell 3). It is not likely that these drastic increases in penalties for drug dealing have had any material impact on the drug trade (Rydel and Everingham 1994). Indeed, they may have actually increased the rate of other income-generating crime such as robbery, burglary, and larceny by making them comparatively more attractive than dealing. Furthermore, Cohen et al. (forthcoming) find large differences in the nondrug felony offense rates of drug dealers sentenced to prison compared with other types of offenders in prison. Specifically, this study finds that persons convicted of dealing have distinctly lower nondrug felony offending rates than those convicted of robbery and burglary. The implication is that Levitt's work overstates the preventive effects of such "War on Drugs" statutes. More generally, Levitt's estimate is not likely to be informative about policies affecting prison sanctions for specific types of offenses (e.g., longer sentences for armed robbers).

The Impact of Police on Crime Rate.   The largest body of evidence on deterrence in the ecological literature focuses on the police. The earliest generation of studies on the deterrent effect of police examined the linkage of crime rate to measures of police resources (e.g., police per capita) or to measures of apprehension risk (e.g., arrests per crime). These studies were inadequate because they did not credibly deal with the identification problem. If the increased crime rates spur increases in police resources, as seems likely, this impact must be taken into account to obtain a valid estimate of the deterrent effect of those resources.

Wilson and Boland (1978) conducted the first study that in my judgment plausibly identifies the deterrent effect of the arrest ratio. They argued that the level of police resources per se is, at best, only loosely connected to the apprehension threat they pose. Rather, the crucial factor is how the police are mobilized to combat crime; Wilson and Boland argue that only proactive mobilization strategies will have a material deterrent effect. In their words, "By stopping, questioning, and otherwise closely observing citizens, especially suspicious ones, the police are more likely to find fugitives, detect contraband (such as stolen property or concealed weapons), and apprehend persons fleeing from the scene of a crime" (1978, p. 373).

In Wilson and Boland's analysis, identification is achieved by the assumption that proactive and aggressive policing contributes to the determination of apprehension threat, as measured by the arrest ratio, but has no direct effect on the behavior of criminals except through the impact on this ratio. Their identification strategy also depends on the assumption that the choice of policing strategy is independent of the crime rate. In support of this assumption they point out that patrol strategy cannot be predicted by the crime rate. Their cross-sectional analysis of thirty-five cities, in which police aggressiveness is measured by moving violation citations per patrol unit, concluded that the arrest ratio has a substantial deterrent effect on robbery.

The Wilson and Boland study spawned a small flurry of studies; I focus on Sampson and Cohen (1988) because it is notable in two important respects. First, it expands the Wilson and Boland conception of the deterrent effect of policing. Second, it is the only ecological deterrence study I know of that attempts to estimate deterrent effects across subpopulation groups.

The Sampson and Cohen study is based on a 1980 cross section of 171 cities. Their key premise is that "hard" policing of "soft" crime—such as prostitution, drunkenness, and disorderly conduct—deters serious criminality.[1] They explore two alternative mechanisms through which "hard" policing of disorder may deter crime. The first is the Wilson and Boland model: aggressive policing of public disorder deters serious crime indirectly through its impact on the risk of arrest. Alternatively, suppression of "soft" crime may make public spaces more desirable and secure, thereby encouraging law-abiding citizens to reoccupy these public spaces and reassert informal sources of social control, with the result there are fewer attractive crime opportunities.

Sampson and Cohen, like Wilson and Boland, find strong evidence of the risk of arrest deterring robbery. The impact is identified by their expanded measure of police aggressiveness in suppressing incivilities. They also find a negative association between the robbery rate and their measure of aggressiveness. This estimate captures the combined effect of aggressiveness from all source—heightened risk of arrest, changes in the crime opportunity structure due to informal social control, and altered offender perceptions.

A second important innovation by Sampson and Cohen is that they not only estimate a population-wide deterrent effect but also disaggregate this effect across segments of the population—white juveniles, black juveniles, white adults, and black adults. They do this by using arrest rates as surrogate measures of demographic group-specific offense rates. They find a negative deterrent-like association between aggressiveness and arrest rate for all groups, but they also find significant differences by race and age in the magnitude of the effect. For robbery, at least, adults seem to be more deterred by police aggressiveness than do juveniles, with black adults seemingly more deterrable than white adults.

Because the results for specific demographic groups are based on arrest rates, they must be qualified in a number of obvious ways. Even so, the efforts of Sampson and Cohen to disaggregate are laudable and, where feasible, should become standard in deterrence studies. The differences in response across demographic groups identified in this study are a reminder that we would not expect all people or segments of the population to respond in the same way to police aggressiveness. Indeed, there are good reasons for believing the response will vary in the population. For instance, I am not surprised that adults seem to be more deterrable than juveniles because the consequences of apprehension are graver for adults.

Two other noteworthy studies of the impact of police on crime are Levitt (1997) and Marvell and Moody (1996). Both use similar data, a panel data set of large U.S. cities for the period 1970–1992. Using very different statistical methods, both find evidence of a negative (deterrent-like) association between officers per capita and index crimes. Levitt's estimate of the elasticity of the violent crime rate to sworn officers (i.e., the percentage change in the violent crime rate associated with a 1 percent increase in sworn officers) is about −1; for property crime his elasticity estimate is about −0.2. Marvell and Moody elasticities estimates also vary across crime type but average about −0.4.

These studies also provide still another reminder that regression coefficients are only measuring average effects. These elasticities apply to all places and times only under the condition that the impact is invariant over place and time. The studies of Wilson/Boland and Sampson/Cohen and of interrupted time-series analyses of police deployment (Sherman 1990) all point to the not surprising conclusion that the impact of police presence is not constant but is contingent on the way the force is mobilized. Consequently, for any given locale the Levitt and Marvell/Moody deterrent estimates may either greatly overstate or understate the impact of a change in the size of the police force.

Summary Observations on Deterrence

At the outset of this section, I stated that the accumulated evidence on deterrence leads me to conclude that the criminal justice system exerts a substantial deterrent effect. That said, it is also my view that this conclusion is of limited value in formulating policy. Policy options to prevent crime generally involve targeted and incremental changes. Thus, for policy makers the issue is not whether the criminal justice system in its totality prevents crime but whether a specific policy, grafted onto the existing structure, materially adds to the preventive effect. Here I am drawing a distinction between absolute and marginal deterrence.

Figure 13.3 depicts two alternative forms of the response function relating crime rate to sanction levels. Both are downward sloping, which captures the idea that higher sanction levels prevent crime. At the status quo sanction level, S_1, the crime rate, C_1, is the same for both curves. The curves are also drawn so that they predict the same crime rate for a zero sanction level. Thus, the absolute deterrent impact of the status quo sanction level is the same for both curves. But because the two curves have different shapes, they also imply different responses to an incremental increase in sanction level to S_2. The response implied by curve A is small. Accordingly, it would be difficult to detect and likely not sufficient to justify the change as good policy.[2] By comparison, the response depicted in curve B is large and thus more readily detectable, and also more likely to be justifiable as good policy.

While the distinction between absolute and marginal deterrence is useful, it implies an underlying analytical simplicity of the relationship of crime rates to sanction levels that belies the complexity of the phenomenon. Contrary to the implicit suggestion of Figure 13.3, no one curve relates sanction levels to crime rates. The response of crime rates

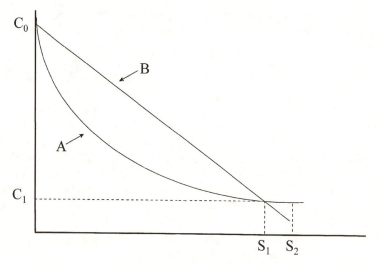

Figure 13.3 Marginal versus absolute deterrent effects.

to a change in sanction policy will depend on the specific form of the policy, the context of its implementation, the process by which people come to learn of it, differences among people in perceptions of the change in risks and rewards that are spawned by the policy, and feedback effects triggered by the policy itself (e.g., a reduction in private security in response to an increase in publicly funded security). Thus, while I am convinced that a number of studies have credibly identified marginal deterrent effects, it is difficult to generalize from the findings of a specific study because knowledge about the factors that affect the efficacy of policy is so limited. Specifically, I see four major impediments to making confident assessments of the effectiveness of policy options for deterring crime.

First, while large amounts of evidence have been amassed on short-term deterrent effects, little is known about long-term effects. Evidence from perceptions-based deterrence studies on the interconnection of formal and informal sources of social control point to a possibly substantial divergence between long- and short-term impacts. Specifically, these studies suggest that the deterrent effect of formal sanctions arises principally from fear of the social stigma that their imposition triggers. Economic studies of the barriers to employment created by a criminal record confirm the reality of this perception. If fear of stigma is a key component of the deterrence mechanism, such fear would seem to depend on the actual meting out of the punishment being a relatively rare event: just as the stigma of Hester Prynne's scarlet *A* depended on adultery being uncommon in Puritan America, a criminal record cannot be socially and economically isolating if it is commonplace. Policies that are effective in the short term may erode the very basis for their effectiveness over the long run if they increase the proportion of the population that is stigmatized. Deterrence research has focused exclusively on measuring the contemporaneous impacts of sanction policies. Long-term consequences have barely been explored.

The second major knowledge gap is that we know little about the connection of risk perceptions to actual sanction policy. The perceptual deterrence literature was spawned by the recognition that deterrence is ultimately a perceptual phenomenon. While great effort has been committed to analyzing the linkage between sanction risk perceptions and behavior, comparatively little attention has been given to examining the origins of risk perceptions and their connection to actual sanction policy.

For several reasons this imbalance should be corrected. One is fundamental: the conclusion that crime decisions are affected by sanction risk perceptions is not a sufficient condition for concluding that policy can deter crime. Unless the perceptions themselves are manipulable by policy, the desired deterrent effect will not be achieved. Beyond this basic point of logic, a better understanding of the policy-to-perceptions link can also greatly aid policy design. For instance, nothing is known about whether the risk perceptions of would-be offenders for specific crimes are formed principally by some overall sense of the effectiveness of the enforcement apparatus or by features of the apparatus that are crime-specific (e.g., the size of the vice squad or the penalty for firearms use). If it is the former, seemingly targeted sanction policies will have a generalized salutary impact across crime types by heightening overall impressions of system effectiveness. If the latter, there will be no such generalized impact. Indeed, would-be offenders may substitute nontargeted offenses for targeted offenses (e.g., committing burglaries in response to increased risk for robbery).

Third, the impact of specific policies—for example, increasing the number of police—will depend on the form of their implementation across population units. Yet estimates of the deterrent effect of such policies from the ecological literature are commonly interpreted as if they apply to all units of the population from which they were estimated. In general this is not the case. Rather, the estimated deterrent effect should be interpreted as the average of the "treatment" effect across population units. For instance, the deterrent impact of more police in any given city will depend on a host of factors, including how the police are deployed. Consequently, the impact in any given city will not be same as the average across all cities; it may be larger, but it could also smaller. Similarly, it is not possible to make an all-purpose estimate of the impact of prison on crime. There are many ways to increase prison population by a given amount, ranging from broad-based policies such as across-the-board increases in sentence length to targeted policies like "three-strikes" statutes. It is likely that the magnitude of the preventive effect will vary materially across these options. The implication is that even though there are credible estimates of average deterrent effects of at least some broad classes of policies, the capacity to translate the average estimates into a prediction for a specific place is limited. This is a major shortcoming in the evidence because crime control is principally the responsibility of state and local government. It is the response of crime to policy in a specific city or state that is relevant to its population, not the average response across all cities and states.

Incapacitation

Compared with deterrence, crime prevention through incapacitation seems simple. The incarceration of active offenders physically isolates them from crime targets in the society at large, whereas crime prevention through deterrence requires that the would-be offender weigh perceived benefits and costs, and that perceived cost be grounded in actual sanction policy. Zimring and Hawkins observe: "The capacity to control rather than influence is the most important reason for the great and persistent popularity of incapacitation as a penal method" (1995, p. 158). In this section I summarize what is known about the size of the preventive effect of incapacitation and explain why the seeming simplicity of crime prevention is more illusion than reality. Cohen (1983) provides an authoritative overview of incapacitation research through the early 1980s.

Estimates of the average number of offenses committed by active offenders, and thereby the number of crimes that might be averted by their incarceration, vary widely. A 1986 report of the National Academy of Sciences, *Criminal Careers and "Career Criminals"* (Blumstein et al. 1986), provides the most complete summary of the evidence on offending rates. One source of evidence is based on the arrest histories of individual offenders. While people are sometimes improperly arrested for a crime they did not commit, the greater problem in inferring offending rates from arrest data is that most crimes do not result in arrest. If apprehension were certain, there would be very few arrests because all but the most impulsive or stupid would be deterred. Statistical correction for this undercounting problem results in estimates of an offense rate ranging from eight to fourteen FBI index crimes per year not incarcerated (free). (The index crimes include murder, rape, robbery, aggravated assault, burglary, larceny, and auto theft.)

The second major source of data on offending rates is self-reports of prison inmates. While self-report data have not been assembled on the full range of index crimes, they have been gathered for two prominent components of the index, robbery and burglary. For these two crimes, estimates of average offending frequency vary enormously from five to seventy-five robberies per year free and from fourteen to fifty burglaries per year free.

While the variability of the average offending rate estimates points to large uncertainties in the magnitude of the preventive effect of incapacitation, even the low-end estimates suggest that incapacitation prevents sizable numbers of crimes. But do they really? For several reasons even the low-end estimates may be overstating the preventive effects of incapacitation.

The distribution of individual offense rates is highly skewed, with a very small percentage of the offending population committing crimes at extraordinary high rates. Figure 13.4 approximates the distribution of self-reported robberies from a sample of California prison inmates reported in an analysis by Visher (1986). Visher found that on average the inmates reported committing 43.4 robberies per year free. However, she also found that about 50 percent of the inmates reported committing fewer than 4 robberies per year free. Why the large discrepancy between the average and the median robbery offense rate? About 5 percent of the sample report committing 180 or more robberies per year free. This small group of very high-rate offenders greatly increases the average offending across all robbers. In recognition of the sensitivity of the mean to these outlying values, Visher computed an adjusted mean in which she truncated self-reported offense rates at 90th percentile value in the sample. With this adjustment the mean rate was reduced by half to 21.8 robberies per year free. Unlike the mean, the median, which is the 50 percent cutoff point in the data, is insensitive to such highly unusual rates of offending. For example, the median of fewer than 4 robberies per year free is unchanged by Visher's adjustment. The large discrepancy between mean and median has important implications for policies intended to capitalize on incapacitation effects. It implies that the vast majority of offenders have offense rates that are far smaller than the average for all offenders. Indeed, Visher's analysis shows that the offense rate of about 90 percent of the sample was less than the mean of the entire sample.

One strategy for finessing the problem of large skew in the distribution of offending is to attempt to take advantage of the skew—identify the

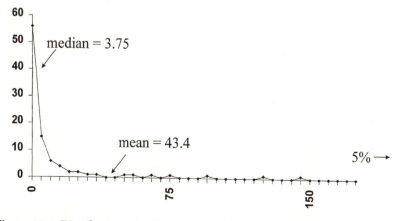

Figure 13.4 Distribution of self-reported robberies among California inmates.

high-rate offenders and sentence this small contingent to lengthy prison terms. Such a strategy of selective incapacitation holds the attraction of economizing on the use of very expensive prison capacity, commonly more than $20,000 to 30,000 per inmate-year, while at the same time averting large numbers of crimes.

For several reasons, selective incapacitation has proved to be a policy chimera. Formidable ethical and legal problems attend the incarceration of persons for what they might do rather that for what they have done. Zimring and Hawkins (1995) provide an excellent summary of this complex philosophical question. But beyond philosophical issues there are practical obstacles. One is the identification of the high-rate offender based on legally permissible factors. Convicts could not be expected honestly to divulge to the court their future crime-committing intentions even if they knew them. Other potential predictors are legally impermissible (e.g., race or sex), highly unreliable in their predictive capacity (e.g., age or employment), or both.

Perhaps the only legally permissible factor with some limited predictive capacity is prior record. Based solely on retributive considerations, offender's records of conviction and sentencing are widely used as sentencing criteria. People with lengthy prior records are widely regarded as more culpable. That said, for several reasons prior record tends to be a highly imperfect predictor of future criminality. First, only a very small percentage of actual crimes committed result in conviction. Thus, prior record provides only a very faint glimmer of actual criminal activity.

Second, a criminal record takes time to accumulate. With time comes age, and age is generally accompanied by a slowing of criminal activity. Perhaps the best-documented empirical regularity in criminology is the age-crime curve. On average, rates of offending rise through adolescence, reach a peak at about age eighteen to twenty, and begin a steady decline thereafter. The central lesson to be learned from this regularity is that for most people rates of offending decline throughout their adult years. Thus, while a long criminal record may be a good signal of very active prior offending, it may also be a signal, due to age, of an individual having entered a period of offending rate decline. Prospectively, such individuals may be poor candidates for incarceration from an incapacitation perspective.

Still another obstacle to a policy of selective incapacitation is that there are probably very few such high-rate offenders at large anyway. Incarceration only requires that an active offender be caught once. Suppose that the probability of apprehension for each crime committed were only one in a hundred. For an offender who on average commits ten crimes per year, the probability of escaping apprehension is 90.4 percent, but for a high-rate offender who commits one hundred crimes per year the probability of escaping apprehension is only 36.6 percent. Thus, the normal enforcement and adjudication processes are likely to capture these high-rate offenders. Blumstein, Cohen, and Canella-Cacho (1993) call this natural screening process for high-rate offenders *stochastic selection.*

Furthermore, this same natural screening process is likely to result in low-rate offenders being screened out from imprisonment more often than higher-rate offenders. Indeed, in Cohen et al. (forthcoming) my colleagues and I found that the average nondrug felony offense rates of convicted but unincarcerated robbers and burglars from Los Angeles County in 1990 were 20 to 40 percent smaller than those of their incarcerated counterparts. The implication is that policies that would increase the incarceration of these previously unincarcerated convicts will have smaller incapacitation benefits than would be expected based on an analysis of the offending histories of the already incarcerated.

Two other factors that add to the chimerical quality of incapacitation as an easy policy solution to the crime control problem are co-offending and offender replacement. Crimes are not always solo affairs. Indeed, criminal acts are commonly committed by groups of offenders. Thus, it is unclear whether the incarceration of one member of a group will avert any crimes at all. Perhaps the group will continue on with one fewer member; alternatively, a new team member may be recruited.

Replacement likely occurs in other settings as well. Incarceration of drug dealers does little to impede the operation of drug markets because the incarcerated dealer is easily replaced. Similarly, the capture of professional auto thieves may have little impact on the overall auto theft rate if chop shops and dealers in stolen cars recruit replacements. Thus, for such crime, incarceration affects only the identity of the person committing the crime, not its volume. More generally, replacement may occur even where the criminal activity does not have a formal organizational structure such as in drug dealing or auto theft rings. The departure of offenders may create market niches for newcomers even without the newcomers being aware that they are filling them. Just as an entrepreneur opening a new store may not realize that the viability of the enterprise depends on the bankruptcy of other stores, a criminal initiate may be unknowingly taking advantage of criminal opportunities left open by the incarceration of a predecessor.

In summary, the crime prevention benefits of incapacitation are highly uncertain. To be sure, there would be a sizable increase in the crime rate from the wholesale release of the incarcerated population. Prisons house large numbers of very dangerous people, but from a policy perspective the issue is not whether to abolish prison but the advisability of the type of incremental adjustment depicted in Figure 13.3. Calibrating the incapacitation impact of incremental changes in prison population remains as precarious as forecasting deterrent impacts.

Conclusion

In this chapter I have reviewed the evidence on the deterrent and incapacitative effect of the threat of arrest, prosecution, and imprisonment. My conclusion is seemingly contradictory. On the one hand, it is my view that the combined deterrent and incapacitation effect generated by the collective actions of the police, courts, and prison system is very large. On the other hand, it is also my view that this same evidence is of limited value in formulating policy. I do not view these as contradictory conclusions because policy is largely incremental—comparatively small changes grafted onto the status quo system of enforcement and penalties. While it is my view that the evidence points to the entire enterprise having a substantial impact, predicting the timing, duration, and magnitude of the impact of incremental adjustments in enforcement and penalties remains largely beyond our reach.

Notes

1. More recently this policing strategy, which involves proactive efforts to suppress disorder by, for example, breaking up congregations of idle young men or making "random" safety checks of vehicles with suspicious drivers, has been credited as a key factor in large reductions in the New York City crime rate (Gladwell 1996).

2. The shape of this response curve is also instructive for making another point: just because the response to an increase in sanctions from S_1 to S_2 is small, it does not follow that response to a reduction in sanction levels from S_1 will be small.

References

Andenaes, Johannes. 1974. *Punishment and Deterrence*. Ann Arbor: University of Michigan Press.

Bachman, Ronet, Raymond Paternoster, and Sally Ward. 1992. "The Rationality of Sexual Offending: Testing a Deterrence/Rational Choice Conception of Sexual Assault." *Law and Society Review* 26:343–72.

Blumstein, Alfred, Jacqueline Cohen, and Jose Canella-Cacho. 1993. "Filtered Sampling from Populations with Heterogenous Event Frequencies." *Management Science* 37:886–98.

Blumstein, Alfred, Jacqueline Cohen, and Daniel Nagin, eds. 1978. *Deterrence and Incapacitation*. Report of the National Academy of Sciences Panel on Research on Deterrent and Incapacitative Effects. Washington, D.C.: National Academy Press.

Blumstein, Alfred, Jacqueline Cohen, Jeffrey Roth, and Christy Visher, eds. 1986. *Criminal Careers and "Career Criminals."* Report of the National Academy of Sciences Panel on Research on Criminal Careers. Washington, D.C.: National Academy Press.

Cohen, Jacqueline. 1983. "Incapacitation as a Strategy for Crime Control: Possibilities and Pitfalls." In *Crime and Justice: An Annual Review of Research*, vol. 5, edited by Michael Tonry and Norval Morris. Chicago: University of Chicago Press.

Cohen, Jacqueline, Daniel Nagin, Garrick Wallstrom, and Larry Wasserman. Forthcoming. "Hierarchical Bayesian Analysis of Arrest Rates." *Journal of the American Statistical Association*.

Cook, Philip. 1980. "Research in Criminal Deterrence: Laying the Groundwork for the Second Decade." In *Crime and Justice: An Annual Review of Research,* vol. 2, edited by Norval Morris and Michael Tonry. Chicago: University of Chicago Press.

Fisher, F. M., and Daniel Nagin. 1978. "On the Feasibility of Identifying the Crime Function in a Simultaneous Model of Crime Rates and Sanction Levels." In *Deterrence and Incapacitation,* edited by Alfred Blumstein, Jacqueline Cohen, and Daniel Nagin. Washington, D.C.: National Academy Press.

Freeman, Richard. 1995. "Why Do So Many Young American Men Commit Crimes and What Might We Do About It?" *Journal of Economic Perspectives* 10(1):25–42.

Gladwell, Malcolm. 1996. "The Tipping Point." *New Yorker,* June 3:32–38.

Grasmick, Harold G., and George J. Bryjak. 1980. "The Deterrent Effect of Perceived Severity of Punishment." *Social Forces* 59:471–91.

Grasmick, Harold G., and Robert J. Bursik Jr. 1990. "Conscience, Significant Others, and Rational Choice: Extending the Deterrence Model." *Law and Society Review* 24:837–61.

Horney, Julie, and Inge H. Marshall. 1992. "Risk Perceptions Among Serious Offenders: The Role of Crime and Punishment." *Criminology* 30:575–93.

Kagan, Robert A. 1989. "On the Visibility of Income Tax Law Violations." In *Taxpayer Compliance,* vol. 2, edited by Jeffrey A. Roth and John Scholz. Philadelphia: University of Pennsylvania Press.

Klepper, Steven, and Daniel Nagin. 1989. "The Deterrent Effect of Perceived Certainty and Severity of Punishment Revisited." *Criminology* 27: 721–46.

Levitt, Steven. 1996. "The Effect of Prison Population Size on Crime Rates: Evidence from Prison Overcrowding Litigation." *Quarterly Journal of Economics* 111:319–52.

———. 1997. "Using Electoral Cycles in Police Hiring to Estimate the Effect of Police on Crime." *American Economic Review* 87:270–90.

Maguire, Kathleen, and Ann L. Pastore, eds. 1996. *Sourcebook of Criminal Justice Statistics, 1995.* Washington, D.C.: U.S. Department of Justice, Bureau of Justice Statistics.

Marvell, Thomas, and Carlisle Moody. 1996. "Specification Problems, Police Levels and Crime Rates." *Criminology* 34:609–46.

Mauer, Marc, and Tracy Huling. 1995. *Young Black Americans and the Criminal Justice System: Five Years Later.* Washington, D.C.: The Sentencing Project.

Nagin, Daniel. 1978. "General Deterrence: A Review of the Empirical Evidence." In *Deterrence and Incapacitation,* edited by Alfred Blumstein, Jacqueline Cohen, and Daniel Nagin. Washington, D.C.: National Academy Press.

———. 1998. "Criminal Deterrence Research: A Review of the Evidence and a Research Agenda for the Outset of the 21st Century." In *Crime and Justice: A Review of Research,* vol. 23, edited by Michael Tonry. Chicago: University of Chicago Press.

Nagin, Daniel, and Raymond Paternoster. 1993. "Enduring Individual Differences and Rational Choice Theories of Crime." *Law and Society Review* 27:467–96.

Paternoster, Raymond. 1987. "The Deterrent Effect of the Perceived Certainty and Severity of Punishment: A Review of the Evidence and Issues." *Justice Quarterly* 4:173–217.

Paternoster, R., L. E. Saltzman, T. G. Chiricos, and G. P. Waldo. 1982. "Perceived Risk and Deterrence: Methodological Artifacts in Perceptual Deterrence Research." *Journal of Criminal Law and Criminology* 73: 1238–58.

Paternoster, Raymond, and Sally Simpson. 1996. "Sanction Threats and Appeals to Morality: Testing a Rational Choice Theory of Corporate Crime." *Law and Society Review* 30:549–84.

Ross, H. Laurence. 1982. *Deterring the Drinking Driver: Legal Policy and Social Control.* Lexington, Mass.: Heath.

Rydel, Peter, and Susan Everingham. 1994. *Controlling Cocaine: Supply Versus Demand Programs.* Santa Monica, Calif.: RAND.

Sampson, Robert J., and Jacqueline Cohen. 1988. "Deterrent Effects of Police on Crime: A Replication and Theoretical Extension." *Law and Society Review* 22:163–89.

Sherman, Lawrence W. 1990. "Police Crackdowns: Initial and Residual Deterrence." In *Crime and Justice: A Review of Research,* vol. 12, edited by Michael Tonry and Norval Morris. Chicago: University of Chicago Press.

Tonry, Michael. 1995. *Malign Neglect: Race, Crime, and Punishment in America.* New York: Oxford University Press.

———. 1996. *Sentencing Matters.* New York: Oxford University Press.

Visher, Christy. 1986. "The RAND Inmate Survey: A Reanalysis." In *Criminal Careers and "Career Criminals,"* edited by Alfred Blumstein, Jacqueline Cohen, Jeffrey Roth, and Christy Visher. Washington, D.C.: National Academy Press.

Waldfolgel, Joel. 1994. "The Effect of Criminal Conviction on Income and the Trust Reposed in the Workmen." *Journal of Human Resources* 29:62–81.

Williams, Kirk R., and Richard Hawkins. 1986. "Perceptual Research on General Deterrence: A Critical Overview." *Law and Society Review* 20:545–72.

Wilson, James Q., and Barbara Boland. 1978. "The Effect of the Police on Crime." *Law and Society Review* 12:367–90.

Zimring, Franklin E., and Gordon J. Hawkins. 1973. *Deterrence: The Legal Threat in Crime Control.* Chicago: University of Chicago Press.

———. 1995. *Incapacitation: Penal Confinement and Restraint of Crime.* New York: Oxford University Press.

14

Crime Prevention

TREVOR BENNETT

During the latter half of the nineteenth century, crime control in many advanced industrial societies was provided primarily by a small number of national institutions. In England and Wales, the new police (first established in London in 1829, with the specific task of preventing crime) were seen as important providers of crime control through the potential deterrent effect of street patrols, their powers relating to public order, and their powers of arrest (Critchley 1978). The use of imprisonment as a national strategy for crime control also grew throughout the nineteenth century as the primary means of punishing, deterring, and reforming convicted offenders (Emsley 1994). During the early part of the twentieth century, the probation service was established with the objective of providing (among other things) various forms of therapeutic regime in order to control criminality by reforming offenders (May 1994). At the time of the inception of each of these national organizations in England and similar institutions in most other Western countries, there was a strong conviction that they would provide an effective means of controlling crime and criminality. However, by the second half of the twentieth century, some of the presumed benefits of these institutions came into question, and by the early 1970s (in part inspired by the findings of criminological research) there was substantial loss of faith in the ability of any of these institutions to control crime (Clarke and Hough 1980; Brody 1976; Lipton, Martinson, and Wilks 1975).

During this same period, there has been an explosion of new ideas and practices, in North America, in Europe, and in many other countries, relating to the provision of crime prevention outside of the formal and national provisions of the criminal justice system. It has been argued that while informal means of controlling crime have always existed, these ideas and practices can be viewed as constituting the beginnings of a new era of crime control, which has been given the name "crime prevention." There are obvious exceptions to this rule, and some programs that are currently thought of as being central to modern thinking about crime prevention (e.g., the Chicago Area Project) occurred substantially before this time. Nevertheless, the spirit of the analysis seems more or less correct.

Over the last three decades there has been a proliferation of crime control activities that were practically unheard of in earlier times. These include growth of personal protection devices, technical control of movement of people and goods, environmental management and design, new forms of private policing, preschool programs, surveillance, defensive community strategies, community improvement programs, opportunity reduction, and privatization of social control through mass private property (Bottoms and Wiles 1996).

The rapid rate of development and change in crime prevention over the last thirty years has to some extent outstripped the ability of researchers and academics to keep pace with it. As we approach the end of the 1990s, there is still no clear or universally accepted definition of what crime prevention is, or what programs or activities should fall under its heading. There is also only partial understanding about which programs work and (when they do) why they work. In this chapter I aim to review some aspects of the current state of knowledge about crime prevention and consider what lessons can be learned about the future from the knowledge gained from the past.

What Is Crime Prevention?

There has never been full agreement on the meaning attached to the concept of crime prevention and the nature of the activities implemented under its name. This situation generates a number of problems when it comes to evaluating past and future developments in crime prevention.

Problems of Definition

The first problem concerns what is meant by the words *crime* and *prevention* in the phrase *crime prevention*. The main problem in relation to the word *crime* lies in its least and most serious forms. At the least serious end of the range, it is problematic whether the concept of crime prevention covers controlling minor offenses, such as traffic violations, and noncrimes, such as some incivilities, nuisances, and social and physical disorder. At the most serious end, it is similarly problematic whether the concept of crime prevention covers insider trading, company fraud, embezzlement, murder, pedophile rings, or sex crimes. To date, the accepted focus of activity for crime prevention has fallen in the middle range. However, the boundaries have never been formally marked. The issue of what the word *prevention* means is also problematic. It could be argued that crime prevention has occurred when at least one offense that would have been committed was not committed. In this sense, crime prevention might not be the same as crime reduction when it occurs at a time when the crime rate is increasing. This position might be resolved by distinguishing between absolute crime prevention (when the crime rate decreases) and relative crime prevention (when the crime rate is lower than some comparative rate). However, issues such as these have not been fully discussed or agreed upon.

Problems of Coverage

Another problem concerns the broad area of activity covered by the concept of crime prevention. There are at least three views on what kinds of activities should be included. The first and broadest definition encompasses any activity that reduces crime. This definition might include the possible deterrent or preventive effects of imprisonment and other activities of the criminal justice system. It might also include other factors that contribute to crime rates but are unrelated to the criminal justice system, such as environmental planning policy or the state of the economy.

A second view is that crime prevention must be something other than what is done by the criminal justice system. Proponents of this view (e.g., van Dijk and de Waard 1991) offer a number of reasons for favoring this definition. One argument is that historically crime prevention has developed as an antidote to the apparent failings of the criminal justice system. Another is that crime prevention is typically "preemptive" to the extent that it occurs before a crime has been committed, unlike reactive actions taken after a crime has been committed (Jeffery 1972).

A third view is that crime prevention should exclude actions directed at offenders. It has been argued that preventing criminals and preventing crimes might not be the same thing because of the possible phenomenon of replacement (new offenders take the place of the prevented offenders; Ekblom and Pease 1995).

Problems of Classification

The problem of classification concerns the way in which the various types of crime prevention activities can be effectively grouped. One of the earliest classification efforts was by Brantingham and Faust (1976), whose typology was based on a public health model relating to the prevention of disease. They divided crime prevention activities into three groups: primary prevention, secondary prevention, and tertiary prevention. Primary crime prevention focused on the physical and social environment and the factors that provided opportunities for crime, such as environmental design and the natural level of security behavior in the population. Secondary crime prevention focused on individuals who were potentially at risk of becoming offenders and aimed to intervene in their lives in such a way that they never committed criminal violations. Tertiary crime prevention focused on individuals who had already committed offenses and aimed to intervene in their lives in a way that would stop them from committing further offenses. There have been many other attempts to classify crime prevention. Van Dijk and de Waard (1991) elaborated Brantingham and Faust's (1976) typology by adding an additional dimension to create a two-dimensional model combining the developmental stage (primary, secondary, or tertiary) with the target group (offenders, situations, or victims). However, there is still no generally accepted system of classification.

Crime Prevention Theories

Ken Pease introduced a paper on crime prevention with the evocative statement that all theories of crime are also theories of crime prevention (Pease 1994). It could easily be rephrased (and reinterpreted) to state that all theories of crime prevention are in fact theories of crime. Taken to its limits, it could be argued that there are no theories of crime prevention but only theories of crime. There is some truth in this, but it also must be acknowledged that, in applying theories of crime to crime prevention, the theories are developed and amended slightly. Hence, it could be argued that there are unique theories of crime prevention, albeit usually linked to one or more of the established theories of crime (or criminality).

In surveying major theories of crime prevention, it is necessary (in order to make the work manageable) to identify them in relation to the main categories of crime prevention. In practice, the most common classifications are based not on the schemes developed by Brantingham and Faust (1976) and van Dijk and de Waard (1991) but on the more intuitive (but basically illogical) classification of (1) situational crime prevention (crime event focused), (2) community crime prevention (community or neighborhood focused), and (3) criminality prevention (offender or potential offender focused).

Situational Theories

Situational crime prevention and related approaches are based on one or more theories of crime or criminality.

Situational Crime Prevention Theory.   Situational prevention is based on opportunity and rational choice theories of the kinds discussed in the following. However, it also combines these theories in a way that perhaps identifies it as a unique theoretical approach. In an early account, Clarke (1980) compared the situational approach with what he thought was the dispositional bias of traditional criminology, which attributed the causes of crime to events that happened in a person's past. In contrast, he argued that situational crime prevention theory is based on the view that the motivation for crime can be generated as a result of (no more than) a combination of immediate situational variables, highly specific features of the individual's history, and factors relating to the person's present life circumstances.

Opportunity Theory.   Situational prevention is primarily based on the concept of opportunity. Mayhew et al. (1976) noted that there were many ways in which opportunities could be conceptualized. They made a distinction between opportunities that attach to people (such as factors relating to their likelihood of victimization) and those that attach to things (such as the physical abundance of the object, the physical security of the object, the levels of surveillance and supervision association with the object, and the object's attractiveness). The concept of opportunities was later developed to include a wide range of factors that affected the effort, the risks, or the rewards of offending (Clarke 1992). Situational prevention is based on the view that (all other things being equal) the greater the opportunities, the greater the number of crimes.

Rational Choice Theory.   Rational choice theory is also integral to situational crime prevention. Clarke (1980), who argued that crime could be conceived as being the outcome of immediate choices and decisions made by potential offenders, noted that research evidence supports the view that people are usually aware of consciously choosing to commit offenses. Clarke (1992) argued that rational choice should be viewed not in terms of mathematical calculations but in terms of decision-making models that give weight to noninstrumental motives and the limited nature of decision making in practice. Cornish (1993) has extended this argument by likening offender decision making to following a "script" in which sections of the action are worked out beforehand. However, particular events that occur in the situation of particular offenses might prompt the offender to abandon or modify the script.

Lifestyle Theory.   Lifestyle theory is different from, but consistent with, situational crime prevention theory. It is most commonly associated with the work of Hindelang, Gottfredson, and Garofalo (1978) and emerged out of a substratum of criminology known as *victimology,* in which the characteristics of victims are compared with the characteristics of non-victims to determine individual crime risks. Within this approach, it is argued that some people lead lives that increase the risk that they, or their property, will come into contact with offenders. In this sense, some lifestyles may create opportunities for crime, which, in turn, affect the likelihood of victimization. Actions taken that reduce the opportunity-generating features of particular lifestyles might lead to reductions in crime risk.

Routine Activity Theory.   Routine activity theory also is different from but consistent with the principles of situational crime prevention. Routine activity theory is most commonly associated with the early research of Cohen and Felson (1979), who argue that in order for a crime to occur there must be three essential conditions: a likely offender, a suitable target, and the absence of capable guardians. While the theory may seem simple, it has considerable power in explaining trends and variations in crime. Cohen and Felson (1979) argued that increases in residential burglary in the United States during the 1960s and 1970s were the result of changes in routine activities, which affected occupancy patterns (guardianship) and the availability of stealable goods (suitable targets). Actions that reduce the occurrence of suitable targets and likely offenders coming together in the absence of capable guardians might reduce opportunities for crime.

Problem-Oriented Policing Theory. Problem-oriented policing and the theoretical assumptions underlying it share many similarities with situational crime prevention. The theory of problem-oriented policing was generated by Goldstein (1990) and elaborated by Eck and Spelman (1987). It is based on the perception that the incidents that police respond to on a daily basis are the symptoms of underlying problems, which, in turn, are the product of underlying causes. Its main approach is based on the view that the underlying causes of problems (including crime) are typically a unique combination of factors relating to the specific situation in which the problem arises. Police officers are encouraged to investigate this unique combination of factors in detail before proposing intervention strategies.

Displacement Theory. Displacement theory might be thought of as one of the rival or countertheories to the various situational theories just discussed. In its simplest form, it is argued that a person prevented from offending will attempt to find some other opportunity to offend. Hence, crimes prevented may simply be displaced to other places or other times. There are a number of types of displacement, including temporal displacement (when the offender commits the offense at a different time); target displacement (when the offender shifts from one type of target to another); geographic displacement (when the offender moves from one area to another); tactical displacement (when the offender changes the way in which the offense is committed); and functional displacement (when the offender shifts from one type of crime to another; Reppetto 1976). The proponents of situational prevention argue that displacement theory need not undermine the principles of the situational approach. The first argument is that displacement is not inevitable, and the proponents of this view typically draw on the empirical evidence which shows that not all crimes prevented are displaced. The second argument is that displacement is not always harmful; proponents of this view argue that displacement can sometimes be benign as well as malign. Benign displacement may occur when the displaced offense is in some way less serious than the prevented offense (Barr and Pease 1990).

Diffusion Theory. Whereas displacement theory might be thought of as a countertheory to situational crime prevention, "diffusion of benefits" theory might be thought of as the countertheory to displacement. The concept of "diffusion of benefits" is based on the idea that crimes prevented in one location, or at one time, might have the effect of reducing crime in another location or at another time. The possible phenomenon of "diffusion of benefits" is also referred to in the literature as the "free rider effect" or the "halo effect." Clarke (1992) provides a number of examples of possible diffusion, including an evaluation of a new system of closed-circuit television (CCTV) on buses, which found that disorder was reduced on the buses fitted with CCTV and also on the remainder of the fleet without CCTV. Clarke (1992) proposes that further research be done to investigate the potential mechanisms involved in diffusion in order to enhance the effectiveness of crime prevention programs.

Community Theories

Community crime prevention programs also are based on a wide range of theories about the causes of crime and criminality at the community or neighborhood level.

Community Disorganization Theory. Community disorganization theory is most closely associated with the work of Shaw and McKay (1942), who argued that delinquency is a product of rapid social change, which causes a breakdown in social control. This occurs as a result of residents losing their ability to socialize and control young people living in the area. Shaw and McKay believed that the most suitable method for dealing with the problem of delinquency in large cities was to develop programs that sought to organize the disorganized areas in order to restore an ability within the community to generate and enforce common norms of behavior.

Community Disorder Theory. Wilson and Kelling (1982) argued in a now famous article that people are fearful not only of crime but also of disorder. Disorder can take the form of disorderly people such as unpredictable groups, beggars, drunks, drug addicts, rowdy teenagers, prostitutes, loiterers, and the mentally disturbed; or of disorderly physical conditions such as abandoned property, abandoned vehicles, broken windows, litter, and dilapidated public areas. They argued that disorder can generate a cycle of decline, which generates both fear and crime. Crime prevention strategies based on this theory would aim to reduce crime by reducing disorder.

Community Empowerment Theory. Community empowerment refers specifically to a number of programs, first implemented in the 1970s, which aimed to involve tenants in the decision making and management of their residential area. The theoretical basis for these programs has been discussed by Hope (1995), who makes a distinction between a "horizontal" dimension of social relations (characterized by levels of social organization and informal social control) and a "vertical" dimension of relations that connect communities to local sources of power and resources. Community empowerment theory is based on the idea that communities will be stronger if they have control of economic and political resources. Programs that have attempted to increase community empowerment have typically attempted to do this through decentralization of housing management and services to the community, and through consultation between the managers of resources and the residents based on the rationale that residents will be more satisfied, which, in turn, will encourage them to stay and take greater interest in, and responsibility for, their area of residence.

Community Regeneration Theory. Taub, Taylor, and Dunham (1984) argued that the overall health of a community is governed by the level of confidence that people have in its economic base. Several important factors in shaping this perception are the level of investment in the community, commercial interest in the area, and the level of maintenance of the housing stock. They also argue that an important motivator in this process is the level of corporate investment. Individual investment decisions made by home owners to maintain and improve their property will to some extent be influenced by the investment decisions of the larger institutions within the community.

Criminality (Potential Offender) Theories

There are many theories of criminality, and the early history of criminology was based almost exclusively on generating and testing theories of criminality. The main task of this section is to comment briefly on the ways in which recent longitudinal research on offender development has contributed to the theoretical debate about criminality prevention.

Risk Factors and Predictors of Delinquency. Research on the predictors of criminality have identified a number of risk factors that differentiate offenders and nonoffenders. Many of these factors have already been identified in well-known psychological or sociological theories of delinquency. Individual factors associated with delinquency include intelligence, hyperactivity, impulsivity, and educational attainment (Farrington 1996). Family and home factors associated with delinquency include poor parental supervision, parental disharmony, parental rejection of the child, and low parental involvement with the child (Farrington 1994). School and educational factors, such as school structure, organization, and function, have been shown to influence school delinquency rates (Rutter et al. 1979). Some of the risk factors identified by this research might provide the basis for an intervention strategy that might reduce the risk of criminality.

Criminal Careers Theory. The criminal careers approach considers the processes by which individuals move into and out of criminal behavior patterns. The key concepts relating to the criminal careers approach are "onset" (the beginnings of the criminal career), "continuation" (the period during the criminal career), and "desistance" (terminating the criminal career). Criminal careers research has also developed concepts relating to "chronic offenders" and the factors that predict high-rate offenders; "duration," which is the length of the criminal career; "specialization," which is the extent to which offenders switch offense types; and "escalation," which concerns the extent to which offenders increase in offense seriousness over time (Farrington 1994). This knowledge can be used as a basis for control strategies, either through the criminal justice system in identifying high-risk offenders or by intervening in the various stages of the criminal career.

Crime Prevention Organizational Strategies

Crime prevention can be thought of in terms of the organizations and mechanisms that deliver crime prevention and the specific projects and schemes that are delivered. In other words, a distinction can be made between organizational strategies (which involve the organizations and mechanisms for delivery) and operational strategies (which are the specific projects and schemes to be delivered). This section concentrates on the former category (organizational strategies), and the following section focuses on the latter category (operational strategies).

Organizational strategies relating to crime prevention can be thought of as operating at various levels including international, national, and local levels.

International Organizational Strategies

A small number of international organizations are either partly or wholly dedicated to devising organizational strategies for crime prevention. These organizations are largely advisory and to date play only a limited role in shaping national and local crime prevention activities. Nevertheless, they are also developing organizations, and it might be expected (taking into account universal trends towards "globalization") that they (or others like them) will become more influential in the future.

One of the newest international organizations is the International Centre for the Prevention of Crime (ICPC), based in Montreal, Canada. It was established in 1994 and has a mission "to harness the world's crime prevention know-how to reduce interpersonal crime, increase community safety, and enhance civic vitality" (ICPC 1995, p. 1). It aims to develop a database of crime prevention information that can be drawn upon by policy makers and practitioners in order to effectively develop crime prevention. It also aims to provide services such as technical assistance and to publish a series of booklets. According to its publicity material, the organization is dedicated to crime prevention focusing on partnerships between agencies and citizens that influence the causes of crime or modify the situations that provide opportunities for victimization (ICPC 1995).

The United Nations also provides crime prevention guidance and advice across nations. This work is currently conducted through the recently created Commission on Crime Prevention and Criminal Justice, based in Vienna, Austria (although the UN has been involved in crime prevention since it was first formed shortly after World War II; UN 1993). The commission, created in 1992 by the Economic and Social Council of the UN, replaced the main preexisting bodies that had worked in the field of crime prevention to that date (namely, the Committee on Crime Prevention and Control, and the Crime Prevention and Criminal Justice Branch). The main aim of this body is to promote multilateral cooperation across member states in relation to crime prevention and to provide information and guidance on crime prevention strategies. The UN is also involved in training and research through a network of institutes, including the United Nations Interregional Crime and Justice Institute in Italy and the European Institute for Crime Prevention and Control in Helsinki (Joutsen 1996).

The third major international organization warranting mention is the Council of Europe. This organization has played a major role in providing information on crime prevention and in guiding crime prevention policy. It is also a key source of international publications on crime prevention across European countries. In 1983, the Committee on Crime Problems created a select committee of "experts" on the "organization of crime prevention," which was tasked with considering general principles of international crime prevention policy that could assist member states (Council of Europe 1988). The committee concluded that crime prevention should be a permanent feature of government programs for controlling crime and recommended that governments support crime prevention agencies at the national and local levels.

National Organizational Strategies

The main substance of crime prevention organizational strategies is determined by national governments. However, there is some variation in the ways in which crime prevention policy is organized at the national level. Some countries (Canada, Sweden, Denmark, and France) have national crime prevention councils, which typically are independent bodies comprising a number of separate agencies. Some countries (the United Kingdom and the Netherlands) have more informal national structures involving a number of government departments or agencies that together shape crime prevention policy. Other countries (Germany, Austria, and Switzerland) make less of a distinction between crime prevention and other aspects of legal and criminal justice policy, and crime prevention is primarily seen as the role of the police and the courts (Graham and Bennett 1995).

One of the newest national councils for crime prevention is the National Crime Prevention Council (NCPC) in Canada. The council was established in June 1994 by the federal minister of justice and the solicitor general of Canada with the view to coordinating activities and sharing information related to crime prevention. The council is split into various committees that address specific aspects of crime prevention, including children and prevention, youth justice, youth consultation, and economic analysis (NCPC 1996). Crime prevention policy in Sweden is organized at the national level by the Swedish National Council for Crime Prevention, which is a governmental agency within the Ministry of Justice. The council has about thirty employees including researchers, public relations officers, and administrators, and its main objective is to reduce crime and increase security (Håkensson 1996). Its main activities involve collecting information about crime and crime prevention in order to provide the government with information and advice and to provide support for local agencies.

Crime prevention in the United Kingdom is organized by a number of government departments and organizations. The key players in crime prevention policy are the Research and Statistics Directorate and the Police Research Group at the Home Office, which conduct original research and advise ministers and the police about crime prevention matters. Other key players include two nongovernmental organizations: the National Association for the Care and Resettlement of Offenders and Crime Concern. The former is a registered charity that was relaunched under this new title in 1966 with the aim (among other things) of involving members of the community in crime prevention and providing support for ex-offenders. The latter is also a registered charity launched by the Home Office in 1988 with the initial remit to coordinate crime prevention activities at the national level.

Crime prevention in the Netherlands is also organized by a number of government departments and by nongovernmental organizations. The focus of crime prevention organizational strategy is through the Directorate of Crime Prevention of the Ministry of Justice in the Hague. The primary crime prevention strategy of the Dutch government is to support crime prevention projects at the local level through government funding. The main emphasis of the Dutch approach to crime prevention is through social prevention and tackling the root causes of crime (van Dijk and Junger-Tas 1988).

Local-Level Strategies

One of the most widespread local-level organizational strategies for delivering crime prevention is the use of multiagency partnerships. In Denmark, the organization of crime prevention at the local level is based around multiagency committees comprising representatives from the schools, the social services sector, and the police (Graham 1990). The main emphasis is on social crime prevention aimed at young people.

France also has a local system of multiagency councils called Communal Crime Prevention Councils, which aim to reduce crime by improving the urban environment, reducing unemployment, improving education, and encouraging social integration (Graham 1990).

The development of multiagency partnerships at the local level has also been an important aspect of crime prevention policy in the United Kingdom. In 1984 the Home Office, in collaboration with other departments, published a circular on crime prevention (Home Office 1984). The main message was that crime prevention was not simply a matter for the police, and that interagency cooperation between the police and other agencies was of great importance in the delivery of successful crime prevention. This circular was followed by a further interdepartmental circular published in 1990, which again promoted the multiagency approach. A further major development was the publication of the Morgan Report, which had the task of monitoring the progress made in the local delivery of crime prevention through the multiagency or partnership approach (Home Office 1991).

One of the largest crime prevention organizational strategies in Britain, which operates at the local level (although originally instigated at the national level), is the Safer Cities Programme (Ekblom 1996). The objectives were to reduce crime, lessen fear of crime, and create safer environments in some of the country's largest urban areas. During phase 1 (1988–1995), central government funds were provided to set up locally based, multiagency partnerships in twenty cities. Local crime prevention activities were designed and implemented by local organizations, which were invited to bid for central government funds. In total, the Safer Cities Programme resulted in the launch of approximately 3,600 crime prevention schemes at the local level (Ekblom 1996).

Crime Prevention Operational Strategies

Crime prevention operational strategies can be divided into the three main categories referred to earlier: (1) situational crime prevention, (2) community crime prevention, and (3) criminality prevention.

Situational Crime Prevention

Situational crime prevention has been defined by Clarke as: "opportunity-reducing measures that are: (1) directed at highly specific forms of crime (2) that involve the management, design or manipulation of the immediate environment in as systematic and permanent way as possible (3) so as to increase the effort and risk of crime and reduce the rewards as perceived by a wide range of offenders" (1992, p. 4). In the same publication, Clarke devised a tabular system of classification that usefully subdivides the main kinds of situational crime prevention activities (see Table 14.1). Clarke's system of classification provided the basis for the system

Table 14.1. Situational Crime Prevention Programs

Increasing the effort of offending	Increasing the risks of offending	Reducing the rewards of offending

Target hardening
  Security upgrading
  Steering column locks
  Antibandit screens
  Publicity campaigns
	Entry/exit screening
	  Automatic ticketing
		Target removal
		  Coin meters

Access control
  Entry phones
  Entry control
  Street closures
	Formal surveillance
	  Police patrols
	  Private security
		Identifying property
		  Property marking

Deflecting offenders
 	
  Street closures
	Surveillance by employees
	  Bus conductors
	  Bus supervisors
	  CCTV
	  Caretakers
		Removing inducements
		
		  Gun control
		  Graffiti control

Controlling facilitators
  Domestic gas toxicity
  Gun control
	Natural surveillance
	  Street lighting
	  Defensible space
		Rule setting
		  Stock control

Adapted from Clarke (1992). All examples can be found in Graham and Bennett (1995).

of classification used in the survey of crime prevention programs in Europe and North America by Graham and Bennett (1995), from which much of the following information has been drawn, and also forms the basis for the system of classification discussed in the following.

Increasing the Effort. One way to reduce criminal opportunities is to increase the effort of offending. This may be done by "target hardening," such as by the use of locks, safes, screens, and reinforced materials. This may be achieved in practice by domestic security surveys and publicity campaigns that encourage potential victims to improve their security levels or behavior. The category of "access control" refers to methods that limit access to whole areas, such as fencing around and within housing estates, road gates, and the routing of roads and footpaths. However, it also has been used to include methods that limit access to specific targets such as entry phone systems and the use of personal identification numbers to gain access to computer systems and bank accounts (Clarke 1992). The category of "deflecting offenders" refers to means by which potential offenders can be channeled away from potential targets or to means by which their motivation to offend can be channeled to more acceptable outlets. "Controlling facilitators" refers to the availability of the means of committing an offense, and includes paint spray cans as facilitators of graffiti and beer glasses as facilitators of violent attacks in bars.

Increasing the Risks. The opportunities for crime can also be reduced if the perceived risks of getting caught are increased. Entry or exit screening involves making access more risky as a result of visual, physical, or electronic checks. Clarke (1992) drew attention to research that has looked at the effectiveness of baggage and passenger screening at international airports, which, he argues, has generated substantial reductions in the number of airplane "skyjackings" since the upgrading of screening procedures. The concept of entry and exit screening can also be extended to include electronic screening of members of the public using transport facilities. The concept of "formal surveillance" is mainly associated with the work of the police in detecting and deterring potential offenders. However, it can also be extended to include the work of private security guards and store detectives who have the explicit function of defending property. Clarke (1992) also includes in the definition of formal surveillance burglar alarms, which he argues can enhance the surveillance role of paid personnel. The category of "surveillance by employees" refers to the surveillance potential of persons employed in occupations whose work does not involve surveillance as a primary function. It has been argued that shop assistants, hotel doormen, park keepers, parking lot attendants, and train conductors can, in addition to their primary functions, prevent or detect crime as a result of their surveillance ability (Clarke 1992). "Natural surveillance" has been defined as the surveillance afforded by people going about their everyday business (Clarke and Mayhew 1980). Oscar Newman's (1972) concept of defensible space draws heavily on the idea of natural surveillance. Similarly, many other environmental design approaches, including Jeffery's concept of "crime prevention through environmental design," also draw on the idea of natural surveillance as a crime prevention mechanism.

Reducing the Rewards. Opportunities for crime can also be reduced if potential offenders believe that the rewards are small or nonexistent. One extreme way of reducing the reward of offending is to remove potential targets completely. An example of "target removal" as a crime prevention strategy is the removal of prepayment gas and electricity coin meters from dwellings. Other examples include various attempts to improve cash handling procedures in stores and other businesses. The category of "identifying property" also includes a wide range of activities. In Britain, property marking frequently involves labeling property (often electrical goods) with a postcode using an ultraviolet pen or labeling bicycles by stamping a postcode on a hidden part of the frame or marking vehicles by etching the car registration number on the windows. In Sweden, householders are sometimes encouraged to mark valuable property using the individual identity number of one of the members of the household (Knutsson 1984). The third category in this section refers to "removing inducements." One of the better-known invitations to vandalism is evidence of deterioration or dilapidation. It was argued by Wilson and

Kelling (1982) that broken windows left unrepaired in a building invite further windows to be broken. The effect of dilapidation in relation to criminal damage against vehicles was studied by Zimbardo (1973), who concluded that, in order for a car to be vandalized, it must first provide some "releaser" stimuli that invite attention. The final category of "rule setting" concerns the effect of rules on governing and controlling behavior. Clarke (1992) gives, as examples of this category, company rules relating to use of telephones or to cash-handling procedures. It is argued that these rules can have a crime prevention effect through regulating and controlling the conduct of both employees and the public.

Community Crime Prevention

There is less agreement found in the literature on the meaning of the concept community crime prevention or the kinds of programs that fall within it. The following system of categorization is based on an amalgam of proposals which is summarized in Table 14.2 and can be found in the literature (see Hope 1995 for an overview).

Community Organization.   The most famous and largest community crime prevention strategy that drew upon these observations was the Chicago Area Project. This project comprised a comprehensive program of community organization and involvement that aimed at preventing the development and continuation of criminality among young people in residential areas (Kobrin 1959). The program started in the early 1930s on an experimental basis in three Chicago neighborhoods that traditionally had high rates of delinquents. Over the next twenty-five years, the number grew to twelve neighborhood organizations. The principal aim was to raise funds to conduct local neighborhood activities directed at the area in general and young people in particular. There have also been more recent attempts to use the principles of community organizing as a means of crime prevention. Skogan (1990) describes a number of more recent experiments in community organizing conducted in Chicago and Minneapolis. The programs were set up by professional community organizers who encouraged local residents to collaborate in community crime prevention activities. The programs focused mainly on the level of crime and criminality prevention rather than on the more general approach to community organization adopted in the Chicago Area Project programs. However, the activities covered by the groups were fairly wide-ranging and included block watch schemes, housing rehabilitation programs, building code enforcement, recreational and job-counseling programs for local youths, workshops on drug abuse, and "phone trees."

Community Defense.   The term *community defense* is used in the literature to refer to a radical change in thinking about community crime prevention that occurred during the early 1970s. The response to crime and

Table 14.2. Community Crime Prevention Programs

			Community Development		
Community Organization	Community Defense	The Built Environment	Community Empowerment	Housing Allocation	Social and Economic Regeneration
Community organizing, Minneapolis	Neighborhood watch, London	Design improvements, England	NACRO estates programs, England	Breda public housing initiative, the Netherlands	Corporate Investment Program, Chicago
Chicago Area Project, Chicago	Disorder enforcement, Newark Citizen patrols, Pecs Projects, Hungary Guardian Angels, USA	Maintenance and repair, Hartford Program, USA	PEP estates programs, England		

All examples can be found in Graham and Bennett (1995).

crime policy during this period moved away from the offender as the focus of intervention (as in the Chicago Area Project) to the victim of crime. One of the most widespread forms of community crime prevention that falls under this heading is neighborhood watch. Another program associated with the community defense approach to crime prevention is disorder control of the kind discussed earlier in relation to the work of Wilson and Kelling (1982). One example of this kind of program was the scheme implemented in Newark, New Jersey, which aimed specifically to tackle social and physical disorder by the use of "clean-up" campaigns and various policing measures (Skogan 1990; Pate et al. 1986). Citizen patrols, the Guardian Angels, and private security patrols are also associated with the community defense approach to community crime prevention. Citizen patrols currently operate in a number of European cities. In Hungary, voluntary patrols have been introduced in combination with other methods in a crime prevention experiment in a residential district of the city of Pecs. The principal aim was to persuade residents to take better security precautions. The patrols also checked property and buildings in the district and reported deficiencies back to the owners and informed the police of any incidents that occurred.

Community Development. A number of different kinds of programs fall under the heading of "community development," including improvements to the built environment, community empowerment, housing allocation policies, and social and economic regeneration. There have been a number of attempts to improve the design and condition of the built environment at the community level as a means of bringing about crime reduction and other general improvements. The Hartford Neighborhood Crime Prevention Program, for example, drew heavily on the ideas of Newman (1972) and Jeffery (1972) in restructuring a residential environment to bring about area-wide reductions in residential crime and fear (Fowler, McCalla, and Mangione 1979). The category of "community empowerment" refers in particular to programs that decentralize housing services and involve tenants in the decision-making process in order to involve them in the direct management of the area (Hope 1995). In Britain, a number of housing management and decentralization strategies were organized during the 1970s by various groups, including the Priority Estates Project run by the Department of the Environment and the Safer Neighborhoods Unit run by the National Association of the Care and Resettlement of Offenders. Another approach to community development is referred to in Table 14.2 as "housing allocation." Research has shown that the social mix of residential areas can be an important factor in determining the crime and criminality profile of the area (Bottoms and Wiles 1988). Housing allocation policy is thus a potential means of affecting these profiles. In the Netherlands, a scheme to redevelop a high-rise public housing estate in the city of Breda involved a series of changes to housing management and housing allocation procedures

(Kalle 1987). The category of "corporate investment" refers to the extent to which economic factors can play a role in the social development of an area. A striking example of the power of corporate investment to change the status of an area and reduce crime is shown in case of the Hyde Park area in Chicago, which included the main site of the University of Chicago. The change in community crime careers in the Hyde Park area was to a large extent the product of the actions of a single corporate body, the University of Chicago, which had an interest in improving the status of the area (Taub, Taylor, and Dunham 1984).

Criminality Prevention

Programs that focus on criminality prevention can be divided into at least three categories based on the level of intervention: family-based strategies, school-based strategies, and youth-based strategies. Table 14.3 presents this classification including illustrative programs.

Family Policy. Research suggests that erratic and inconsistent use of discipline by parents prevents children from learning acceptable behavior (Farrington 1996). Some programs have aimed at educating parents about child-rearing practices and improving parenting skills. One example is the Oregon Social Learning program, for parents of aggressive and delinquent children (see Graham and Bennett 1995, for details of this and other programs referred to in this section). Parents are trained to use positive, noncoercive methods of discipline, to deal consistently and decisively with antisocial behavior, to negotiate acceptable standards of behavior with their children rather than imposing such standards without consulting them, and to develop problem-solving skills and improve communication and interaction within the family. There are also various family support services that assist parents who experience difficult behavioral problems in their children and general family stress. These include financial and material support, child care services, emergency day care, health care, family planning advice, crisis intervention, and counseling. Some family support services provide day nursery facilities, play groups, and after-school clubs, and may target high-risk families and provide advice on a range of activities, including appropriate nutrition, parenting, and home management skills. Some programs are based specifically on preventing homelessness among young people. These include youth centers with emergency shelters and longer-term hostel accommodation and programs that attempt to reunite runaways with their families. Other services include counseling, survival skills training, and assistance with finding employment. One example of this kind of program is the Prejop Project in the Netherlands, which aimed to divert runaways from court and care proceedings. Social workers were based in the vicinity of local police stations so they could provide immediate assistance to young people should they be needed.

Table 14.3. Criminality Prevention Programs

Family Policy	Education Policy	Youth Policy
Parental training Oregon Social Learning Center, USA	Bullying projects Anti-Bullying Project Norway School Safety Project, France	School holiday programs Été-Jeunes Program, France
Family support Tacoma Homebuilders, USA	Preschool education Perry Preschool Program, USA	Youth centers Sosjale Joenits, The Netherlands
Preventing homelessness Prejop Project, The Netherlands	Home-school partnerships LIFT Project, USA	Outreach programs Wincroft Project, England Rotterdam Shopping Centre Project, The Netherlands
	Whole-school projects The Pathe Project, USA	

All examples can be found in Graham and Bennett (1995).

Education Policy. There is some evidence to show that school performance, behavior in school, and perhaps even the general ethos of the school itself may be important factors in the development of criminality. Hence, a number of initiatives have attempted to tackle delinquency at the level of the school. In France, for example, the School Safety Project was set up to reduce bullying and violence in schools. Recruits to the project provided a program of instruction for pupils and helped the teachers in dealing with pupils involved in fighting or bullying. Other programs operate at a much earlier level in the educational process. The Perry Preschool Project was set up in 1962 with the explicit objective of reducing the risk of delinquency. The project randomly allocated 123 black children from low-socioeconomic-level families to a preschool child development program and a control group (58 to the former, 65 to the latter). The preschool program involved the children in the planning of classroom activities as a means of promoting their intellectual and social development. Some other educational programs are based on home-school partnerships. The Linking Interests of Families and Teachers (LIFT) program was set up in Oregon to prevent conduct disorders. The main strategy consists of encouraging prosocial and discouraging antisocial behavior at home and at school through parent training, social skills classes for children, and supervision on the playground. Finally, some educational programs are based on what is sometimes referred to as the "whole school" approach. This includes programs such as the Positive Action Through Holistic Education (PATHE) project, which sought to reduce delinquency by, among other things, strengthening pupil commitment, increasing active participation in school activities, and offering pupils a greater stake in their school.

Youth Policy. Programs that fall under the heading of "youth policy" refer primarily (but not exclusively) to schemes for older children or young adults who have left school. Specifically, they comprise programs which are organized outside of the context of the family or the school. One example is the *Été-Jeunes* Program in France, which ran a range of activities for young people during the summer holidays (including sports, outward-bound activities, discos, and open-air film shows). Special summer activities passports could be purchased, which enabled the program organizers to monitor levels of participation. Other aspects of youth policy concern the use of youth centers, which provide various services. In the Netherlands, a number of youth advisory centers (Sosjale Joenits) spread across the country offer advice and support to young people between eleven and twenty-five on matters relating to housing, employment, education, training, social security, and drug and alcohol problems. They work closely with the police and target runaways, the unemployed, the homeless, and other young people at risk. Their work involves teaching young people how to make decisions about their lives and how to gain self-confidence and self-esteem. The final group of youth programs shown in Table 14.3 are outreach programs. The Wincroft Project in England is an example of this kind of program; it consisted of detached street workers whose main function was to contact and develop relationships with young offenders living in the area. Another program of this kind is the Rotterdam Shopping Centre Project in the Netherlands, which provided specific places in the shopping center where young people could freely congregate.

What Works in Crime Prevention?

The number of evaluations of crime and criminality prevention programs is growing rapidly; there now must be hundreds (if not thousands) of evaluations worldwide that have investigated aspects of situational, community, or criminality prevention programs. One reason the exact number of evaluations is not known is that many of these evaluations are not in the public domain and many more are not circulated widely (e.g., police evaluations and evaluations conducted by single or multiagency groups largely for their own interests). Another reason the exact number of evaluations is not known is that very few metaevaluations of crime prevention programs have attempted to compare the results of a large number of studies in a systematic and controlled way (a research task that is clearly needed).

This situation makes the task of reviewing the evaluation literature in order to determine what works best in crime prevention particularly difficult. The absence of effective meta-analyses and the proliferation of individual studies rule out adopting either as a method of summarizing the literature. The approach adopted here has been to review the results of publications that have summarized evaluation research in any of the three areas of crime and criminality prevention discussed earlier. Hence, the review is based largely on what other reviewers have concluded about program effectiveness.

Evaluations of Operational Strategies

Operational strategies comprise the various projects, schemes, and programs that are delivered with the view of preventing crime (as defined earlier). In the following they have been divided into the three categories discussed earlier. The first section deals with studies that have evaluated crime prevention across these categories.

All Types. In 1987, Poyner conducted a metaevaluation of 122 crime prevention projects spanning situational, community, and criminality prevention programs (Poyner 1993). This is probably the only study to attempt an across-category comparison using the principles of metaevaluation (i.e., including reanalysis of results to generate comparable effect sizes across comparison studies). The selection criteria were based on research that had been published in English, was accessible at the time of the review, and included results on outcome effectiveness. The 122 studies were grouped into six categories: campaigns and publicity, policing and other surveillance, environmental design or improvement, social and community services, security services, and target removal or modification. Each study was given a numerical score depending on whether there was good evidence of a positive effect (coded as +2), some evidence of an effect (+1), no evidence of an effect (0), or evidence that showed that crime actually increased (−1). The results showed that evaluations of campaigns and publicity, policing and other surveillance, environmental design or improvement, and security devices, each showed about the same level of positive effect (averaging a score of +1.30 to +1.35). The highest score (excluding the miscellaneous category) was target removal or modification, which had a score of +1.80. The lowest score was social and community services, which had a score of +0.22. While Poyner is careful to avoid making strong conclusions on the basis of the analysis, it is clear from the results that programs that could be classified under the heading of situational crime prevention showed better results than those that could be classified under the heading of community or criminality prevention.

Situational Crime Prevention.   A small number of publications have summarized the results of situational crime prevention programs. Clarke (1992) presents the findings (and full reprints of the original publications) of what he refers to as twenty-two successful case studies of situational crime prevention programs. The studies span the twelve techniques of prevention discussed earlier and show some evidence of success in preventing crime. Clarke's summary is not intended to be an impartial review of the effectiveness of situational crime prevention, because its intention is to identify evaluations that have shown evidence of success. Nevertheless, the review provides evidence that situational approaches can be effective. A more recent review of the evaluative literature on situational crime prevention programs was conducted by Graham and Bennett (1995) as part of their general survey of crime prevention strategies in North America and Europe. The review selected from a wide range of published evaluations and included both successful and unsuccessful results. Overall, the review confirmed the findings of Clarke (1992) and Poyner (1993) that there are many studies which show that situational crime prevention can be effective in reducing crime. However, there were variations across strategy type in terms of outcome. A number of evaluations showed clear positive results in effectiveness of access control, bus conductors, supervisors, receptionists, target removal, and physical barriers. A number of evaluations also showed unclear or negative results of effectiveness of steering-column locks, security campaigns, security surveys, preventative police patrol, CCTV, street lighting, and property marking.

Community Crime Prevention.   A small number of publications also have summarized the results of community crime prevention programs. Bennett (1996) reviewed the literature on community crime prevention and concluded that there was little evidence that community approaches were effective in reducing crime. The results of research on community organizing approaches have shown that few schemes can be said to have been fully implemented, and (perhaps as a result) there was little evidence of success. The research on neighborhood watch and citizen patrols also has tended to produce generally negative findings. The research on community development and community building is slightly more encouraging, although there are very few studies to draw upon and the results of this research are mixed. Hope (1995) recently reviewed the current state of community crime prevention and concluded that there was little evidence that community crime prevention worked. However, he also noted that there was little evidence that community crime prevention programs had ever been properly or fully implemented. He did not believe that the absence of evidence should be treated as evidence of absence, because there were reasons to believe that community crime prevention should work. He drew attention to what he referred to as a central paradox in criminological research, which, on the one hand, shows that community crime rate is correlated with community-level social and economic factors and, on the other hand, provides little evidence that attempts to change these factors have been effective in changing community crime rates.

Criminality Prevention.   Graham and Utting (1996) reviewed the literature on the impact of family and school-based programs on criminality. They found that evaluations of programs which focus on the family either tended to conclude that there was no effect on delinquency or disruptive behavior or showed effects that were short-lived. Evaluations of programs focused on the school tended to conclude either that there was no effect, or, if there was an effect, that it was small, specific to certain types of behavior (e.g., attendance at school but not behavior in school), or short-lived (occurring only during the period of the intervention or for a short time afterward). Tremblay and Craig (1995) investigated evaluative research studies on the development of antisocial behavior during childhood and provided more positive findings. They concluded that almost all experiments that aimed to prevent disruptive behavior (mostly based on elementary school children) and experiments that aimed to prevent cognitive defects (mostly based on infants and toddlers) showed some positive outcomes. Graham and Bennett (1995) looked at evaluations of a wide range of criminality prevention programs, ranging from projects aimed at preschool children to projects directed at post-school, young adults. They concluded that programs based on the family (parent training, family support, and preventing homelessness) tended to show some positive effects in terms of the well-being of the individual or in terms of the relationships between the child and the family. However, there is little evidence from this research of any lasting behavioral effects. Programs based on the school (bullying projects, preschool education, home-school partnerships, and whole-school projects) tend to generate mixed results. The Perry PreSchool Program showed evidence of both short- and long-term effectiveness in preventing delinquency (although this study has not been fully replicated). Some antibullying programs were also shown to be effective in reducing antisocial behavior in schools and in terms of school crime. However, research into home-school partnerships and whole-school approaches has shown only small or limited effects. Programs based on youths (school holiday programs, youth centers, and outreach programs) have shown some positive findings.

Evaluations of Organizational Strategies

Organizational strategies were described earlier as the organizations and mechanisms for delivering crime prevention, and a distinction was made between strategies at the international, national, and local level. For consistency, this structure has been maintained in the following evaluation. However, there are very few evaluations of international or national organizational strategies to draw upon.

International Programs.   To my knowledge, there are no published evaluations on the effectiveness of international organizations for crime prevention in achieving their objectives. The International Centre for the Prevention of Crime (described earlier) has existed for less than two years and is still in the process of developing. However, it is already achieving some of its objectives to the extent that it has provided useful information for those interested in crime prevention (including a World Wide Web Page). The organizations which were responsible for establishing the Centre (e.g., the European Forum for Urban Safety in France and the Federation of Canadian Municipalities in Canada) had, prior to its inception, successfully organized influential international conferences on crime prevention. The United Nations and the Council of Europe are both very active in organizing conferences, providing training, and disseminating information on crime prevention, and the former has successfully supported associated institutes with responsibilities for crime prevention. However, a fuller evaluation of these organizations' activities would require an investigation into how well these organizations were achieving their objectives and the extent to which information provided by these organizations has shaped crime prevention policy at the national and local level.

National Programs.   There are also few evaluations of national organizations for crime prevention. In England there are two evaluations of crime prevention policy at the national level that have primarily investigated the way in which national policy is generated (Rock 1994; Koch 1996). The latter study by Koch also examined the extent to which national policy influenced policy at the local level and concluded that national policy is adopted at the local level, although there are gaps and time lags in the correspondence between the two.

Local Programs.   The main structure for delivering crime prevention at the local level is the multiagency partnership. A great deal of the early work on multiagency approaches drew attention to the apparent difficulties in bringing different groups of people together to work on a common problem. The work of the Exeter Policing Consultative Group, established in the Devon and Cornwall police force area in England, is perhaps one of the earliest examples of a multiagency partnership in crime prevention. The group included representatives from a number of local agencies, including the police, the local authority, education, churches, the press, trade unions, and transport departments. The evaluation of the program identified a number of problems associated with operating the group (Moore and Brown 1981). Some of the professionals in the group felt that their traditional independence and authority were threatened by involvement with other agencies. Some agency workers believed that the central role of the police encroached on their own professional territories. Another multiagency project evaluated by the Home Office also showed evidence of implementation problems (Hope 1985). The aim was to design effective preventative strategies to reduce school vandalism. Only two of the eleven schools implemented all the recommendations of the group, and three of the schools implemented none. The author noted that many of the projects were dropped by the agencies as a result of pressure of existing organizational priorities.

Despite the fact that the research shows many organizational problems associated with establishing and maintaining multiagency groups, there are many other examples of successful implementation and operational effectiveness of these groups. One of the best-known multiagency partnerships in England is the Kirkholt Burglary Prevention Project, whose aim was to reduce residential burglary on a high-crime, local-authority housing estate (Forrester, Chatterton, and Pease 1988). The published results of the evaluation of the program showed that over the first year burglaries declined by more than 50 percent and multiple victimizations were reduced almost to zero. A similar project conducted in Huddersfield, England, involved collaboration between the police as the lead agency and the local council, victim support, and Huddersfield University (Anderson, Chenery, and Pease 1995a). The aim was to develop and implement a strategy for preventing repeat burglary and motor vehicle crime. The results of the first nine months showed a 24 percent reduction in domestic burglary and a 5 percent decrease in other burglary (Anderson, Chenery, and Pease 1995b). One of the largest programs in England and Wales based on local multiagency partnerships is the Safer Cities program. An evaluation of 300 schemes set up by the summer of 1992 which targeted residential burglary showed evidence of a reduction in burglary risk in the scheme areas (Ekblom 1996).

Crime Prevention Futures

Criminologists have shown that the best predictor of the future is the past. This was originally developed as a truism in relation to predicting the future behavior of individuals from knowledge about past behavior. However, it has also recently been shown to be true in relation to victimization at various levels, including the individual level (victim), the micro level (place), and the macro level (area). Criminologists have also shown that it is hard to predict futures with any accuracy. This is also true at various levels, including predicting which individuals will reoffend and which victimized individuals, places, and areas will be victimized again. The balance of certainty and uncertainty also exists in relation to the future of crime prevention. The best indicators of future trends in crime prevention probably can be found in the developments of past trends and (especially) the most recent developments. However, there is sufficient uncertainty about these predictions to make the exact nature of future developments unknown. Nevertheless, this need not prevent informed speculation.

General Trend Futures

Articles by Bottoms (1990) and Bottoms and Wiles (1996) provide perhaps the most comprehensive prediction of future trends in crime prevention. In the early paper, entitled "Crime Prevention Facing the 1990s," Bottoms identified a link between growing individualism across Western countries and the development of crime prevention based on defensive security. At the time, he expressed a concern that such developments could lead to what he described as a "nightmare" of a society of security hardware protecting homes and businesses, with adult citizens carrying alarms and guns for personal protection. In the later paper, written in collaboration with Paul Wiles, the authors develop the idea of a link between social trends and crime prevention trends in what they refer to as "late modern societies." The authors argue that, in the last twenty to thirty years, in many Western societies, the range of activities that fall under the general heading of crime prevention has expanded dramatically. One aspect of this diversification is a shift away from crime prevention provided by the government and public services (e.g., the police) toward crime prevention provided by private companies and by individuals.

This kind of analysis is immensely useful in identifying the broader framework within which debates about the future of crime prevention can be placed. In particular, their thesis leads to two broad conclusions. The first is that, to some degree, crime prevention is shaped by broad social trends. These developments affect almost all Western societies and, in many senses, may be viewed as beyond our control. The second is that social trends are shaped to some degree by crime prevention. These developments also affect almost all Western societies and need not be viewed as beyond our control. The major warning given by the authors is that, left unchecked, crime prevention will develop naturally in line with market forces. According to most recent trends, such developments may include increased use of electronic surveillance, the generation of "defended locales," the creation of unpoliced "badlands" outside of these defended locales, a move away from traditional community involvement in crime control, a decline in the influence of the state, and an increase in autonomous and privately controlled security (Bottoms and Wiles 1996). Hence, future trends in crime prevention probably depend more than anything else on the amount of influence and control that is asserted at the international, national, and local levels and on the amount of influence and control that is left to market forces.

Organizational Strategies Futures

It might be possible to make a similar connection between future social trends and future organizational strategies. Bottoms and Wiles (1996) drew heavily on the work of social theorists such as Giddens (1990), who argued that there are recognizable characteristics to late modern societies that almost certainly will continue to develop until they are played out. One of these characteristics is the trend toward "globalization" and "localization" mentioned earlier. If this analysis is correct, it would predict that crime prevention would become increasingly organized at the global level (i.e., at the level of international organization) and at the local level (i.e., at the level of multiagency groups and local partnerships). In turn, it would predict a declining role of the state as a result of a general tendency toward a "hollowing out" of the state in most Western societies. Modern social theory would also predict that the role of crime prevention organizational agencies would also continue to change in the direction of providers of information rather than providers of crime prevention activities. Ericson (1992) argued that the police in modern society have taken on the role of "information brokers" in the sense that their role is becoming dominantly one of exchanging information about security between agencies and groups rather than being directly involved in delivering it. The development of information systems, noted by other social theorists as one of the key characteristics of late modern societies, would predict that information systems would become increasingly important in the organization of crime prevention at both the global and the local level.

Operational Strategies Futures

One of the aims of considering the future of operational strategies is to consider what the most promising future might look like. At the moment, there appear to be two major trends in the implementation of crime prevention strategies (which to some extent draw on the global and local approaches discussed earlier). The first, which might be referred to as "targeted crime prevention," is based on the idea that crime prevention can be most effective if a highly specific problem is identified and is tackled with highly specific solutions. It is implicit in problem-oriented policing and situational crime prevention, and is currently a strong part of government policy in Britain (see, generally, Bennett 1996). The second, which might be referred to as "holistic crime prevention," is based on the idea that crime prevention needs to address underlying causes of crime, which in turn are numerous and affect whole communities or whole areas. These ideas are implicit in community development approaches to crime prevention, which aim to improve the general social or economic fabric of a community.

Elements of both specific (targeted) and general (holistic) approaches to crime prevention can be found in other areas of crime prevention theory and practice. Elements of the holistic approach to crime prevention can be found in the work of the Swedish National Crime Prevention Council, which has traditionally taken the view that crime prevention should be based on a thorough understanding of the causes of crime at both the individual and the community level. Elements of a holistic approach can also be found (in a less refined way) in comprehensive programs that aim to implement a large number of strategies in a particular area in the hope that at least some of them will hit the mark. Elements of the targeted approach can be found in particular in problem-oriented policing, which is based on the view that specific problems have highly individualized causes that can be identified by astute police officers who take the trouble to investigate the problem. The choice of intervention strategy may be almost anything that can intervene in the causal cycle. In practice, the solution is likely to be a very specific action relating to the particular location of the problem.

If such developments continue, it might be expected that crime prevention strategies would continue to be based on a wide range of actions operating both at the specific level of the individual target and at the general level of whole communities. This would almost certainly suggest a continued expansion in the number and range of initiatives.

Crime Prevention Theory Futures

It was argued earlier that there may not be such a thing as a crime prevention theory. However, there is evidence of substantial adaptation and development of existing criminological theory to help provide a theoretical orientation to crime prevention activities. The main trend in crime prevention theory is the recent theoretical development toward theoretical integration. In 1994, the Swedish National Council for Crime Prevention hosted a conference with the explicit task of integrating theories relating to individual propensity to commit crime and theories relating to opportunities for crime. The publication resulting from the conference presented evidence of progress in providing a theoretical integration between social and situational approaches (Wikström, Clarke, and McCord 1995). Theoretical integration is also evident in the work of Clarke and Felson, who have attempted to integrate rational choice and routine activities theory and have generated theoretical links between situational crime prevention and problem-oriented policing (Clarke and Felson 1993).

Crime Prevention Research Futures

One of the most important developments of crime prevention research is its link with fundamental research on crime and criminality. There is a growing belief that crime prevention theory and practice cannot develop until more is known about the fundamental nature of crime and criminality. Research on situational crime prevention is currently limited by the fact that very little is known about the mechanisms by which offenders make decisions about offending and the conditions under which they are deterred or not deterred from offending. Very little is known about "deterrence decay," or other kinds of longer-term effects, following successful prevention. Very little is known about "displacement" and "diffusion of benefits" and the conditions under which they occur or do not occur. Research on community crime prevention is especially limited by the current lack of knowledge about the dynamics and mechanisms operating at the community level when there is no intervention strategy present. Research on criminality prevention is also limited by the lack of adequate fundamental research. Research to date has primarily addressed risk factors and criminal careers, and has tended to be quantitative and focused on discrete and measurable factors. Very little is known about the dynamics by which individuals become involved in criminal behavior or about the interaction of individual-, situational-, and community-level factors in this process.

Crime Prevention Evaluation Futures

Methods of evaluating the impact of social interventions have developed enormously over the last twenty years, and successful evaluations have been made of strategies aimed to influence individual development and community development. These changes have been accompanied by substantial improvements in the sophistication of statistical techniques and ease (through the use of computers) of conducting statistical analyses. However, despite these developments, the basic evaluation tools are still fairly crude. The future of crime prevention evaluation needs to include a stronger theoretical and practical basis for deciding whether programs work.

Final Comment

One aim of this article is to provide an overview of the current state of crime prevention and to consider what this might tell us about possible future directions. Substantial activity is currently being conducted under the name of crime prevention, and predictions for the future suggest that this amount of activity is likely to grow. There is also some evidence that the organizational structures to support such activity might also grow. The main problem confronting crime prevention at the moment is not so much doing more (there is plenty of evidence of effort) but of doing something that works (a case for working smarter, not harder).

There is substantial evidence to show that situational crime prevention works at the level of the situation. But there is much less evidence that any of these successes have ever permeated through to the level of the neighborhood, the city, the region, or the country (with certain exceptions relating to protecting or removing whole classes of targets). One important factor that cannot be ignored is that, despite these successes, crime rates at the national level continue to grow in many countries. One possible reason the successes of situational crime prevention do not seem to permeate through to the wider community is that "deterrence decay" and "displacement" together mop up at least part of the successes gained.

There is much less evidence to show that community crime prevention works. Other reviewers have commented on the apparent anomaly that, despite the fact that the research shows that community-level factors are important in determining and explaining crime rates at the neighborhood level, there has been very little success to date in manipulating these factors in a way that could reduce neighborhood crime rate.

There is also only patchy evidence to show that it is possible to intervene in the lives of individuals in order to reduce criminality rates (at least in the longer term). While the research shows evidence of short-term and general behavioral effects, there is less evidence of long-term effects that influence criminality.

The future of crime prevention seems to lie in facing up to these problems and in finding appropriate solutions. The history of crime prevention provides a substantial resource on which to draw in order to devise effective strategies for the future. One of the lessons that can be learned from this resource is that crime prevention needs to be based on accurate information about the nature of crime and criminality and on accurate information about whether or not programs work. Further developments in fundamental research on crime and criminality and in social science methods would certainly help in this respect.

References

Anderson, D., S. Chenery, and K. Pease. 1995a. *Biting Back: Tackling Repeat Burglary and Car Crime.* Crime Detection and Prevention Series Paper no. 58. London: Home Office.

————. 1995b. *Preventing Repeat Victimization: A Report on Progress in Huddersfield*. Police Research Group Briefing Note 4/95. London: Home Office.

Barr, R., and K. Pease. 1990. "Crime Placement, Displacement and Deflection." In *Crime and Justice: A Review of Research*, vol. 12, edited by M. Tonry and N. Morris. Chicago: University of Chicago Press.

Bennett, T. H. 1996. "Community Crime Prevention in Britain." In *Kommunale Kriminalprävention*, edited by T. Trenczek and H. Pfeiffer. Bonn: Forum Verlag Godesberg.

Bottoms, A. E. 1990. "Crime Prevention Facing the 1990s." *Policing and Society* 1:3–22.

Bottoms, A. E., and P. Wiles. 1988. "Crime and Housing Policy: A Framework for Crime Prevention Analysis." In *Communities and Crime Reduction*, edited by T. Hope and M. Shaw. London: HMSO.

————. 1996. "Understanding Crime Prevention in Late Modern Societies." In *Preventing Crime and Disorder: Targeting Strategies and Responsibilities*, edited by T. H. Bennett. Cambridge: Institute of Criminology.

Brantingham, P., and F. Faust. 1976. "A Conceptual Model of Crime Prevention." *Crime and Delinquency* 22:130–46.

Brody, S. 1976. *The Effectiveness of Sentencing*. Home Office Research Study no. 64. London: HMSO.

Clarke, R. V. G. 1980. "Situational Crime Prevention: Theory and Practice." *British Journal of Criminology* 20:136–47.

————. 1992. *Situational Crime Prevention: Successful Case Studies*. New York: Harrow and Heston.

Clarke, R. V. G., and M. Felson. 1993. *Routine Activity and Rational Choice*. Vol. 5 of *Advances in Criminological Theory*. London: Transaction Publishers.

Clarke, R. V. G., and J. M. Hough. 1980. *The Effectiveness of Policing*. Aldershot, England: Gower.

Clarke, R. V. G., and P. Mayhew. 1980. *Designing Our Crime*. London: HMSO.

Cohen, L. E., and M. Felson. 1979. "Social Change and Crime Rate Trends: A Routine Activity Approach." *American Sociological Review* 44:588–608.

Cornish, D. 1993. "Crimes as Scripts." In *Comparative Aspects of Community-Oriented Police Work*, edited by D. Dolling and T. Feltes. Holzkirchen: Felix-Verlag.

Council of Europe. 1988. *Organisation of Crime Prevention*. Strasbourg: Council of Europe, Publications and Documents Division.

Critchley, T. A. 1978. *A History of Police in England and Wales*. London: Constable.

Eck, J. E., and W. Spelman. 1987. *Problem Solving: Problem-Oriented Policing in Newport News*. Washington, D.C.: Police Executive Research Forum.

Ekblom, P. 1996. "Safer Cities and Residential Burglary: A Summary of Evaluation Results." *European Journal on Criminal Policy and Research* 4:22–52.

Ekblom, P., and K. Pease. 1995. "Evaluating Crime Prevention." In *Building a Safer Society: Strategic Approaches to Crime Prevention*, edited by M. Tonry and D. Farrington. Chicago: University of Chicago Press.

Emsley, C. 1994. "The History of Crime and Control Institutions, c. 1770–

c. 1945." In *The Oxford Handbook of Criminology*, edited by M. Maguire, R. Morgan, and R. Reiner. Oxford: Clarendon Press.

Ericson, R. 1992. "Community Policing as Communications Policing." In *Comparative Aspects of Community-Oriented Police Work*, edited by D. Dolling and T. Feltes. Holzkirchen: Felix-Verlag.

Farrington, D. P. 1994. "Human Development and Criminal Careers." In *The Oxford Handbook of Criminology*, edited by M. Maguire, R. Morgan, and R. Reiner. Oxford: Clarendon Press.

———. 1996. *Understanding and Preventing Youth Crime*. York: Joseph Rowntree Foundation.

Forrester, D., M. Chatterton, and K. Pease. 1988. *The Kirkholt Burglary Prevention Project, Rochdale*. Crime Prevention Unit Paper no. 13. London: Home Office.

Fowler, F. J., M. E. McCalla, and T. W. Mangione. 1979. *Reducing Residential Crime and Fear: The Hartford Neighborhood Crime Prevention Program*. Washington, D.C.: U.S. Government Printing Office.

Giddens, A. 1990. *The Consequences of Modernity*. Cambridge, England: Polity Press.

Goldstein, H. 1990. *Problem-Oriented Policing*. London: McGraw-Hill.

Graham, J. 1990. *Crime Prevention Strategies in Europe and North America*. Helsinki: European Institute for Crime Prevention and Control.

Graham, J., and T. H. Bennett. 1995. *Crime Prevention Strategies in Europe and North America*. Helsinki: European Institute of Crime Prevention and Control.

Graham, J., and D. Utting. 1996. "Families, Schools, and Criminality Prevention." In *Preventing Crime and Disorder: Targeting Strategies and Responsibilities*, edited by T. H. Bennett. Cambridge: Institute of Criminology.

Håkensson, M. 1996. "The Swedish National Council for Crime Prevention." *European Journal on Criminal Policy and Research* 4:125–28.

Hindelang, M., M. R. Gottfredson, and J. Garofalo. 1978. *Victims of Personal Crime: An Empirical Foundation for a Theory of Personal Victimization*. Cambridge, Mass.: Ballinger.

Home Office. 1984. *Crime Prevention*. Circular no. 8/84. London: Home Office.

———. 1991. *Safer Communities: The Local Delivery of Crime Prevention Through the Partnership Approach* (Morgan Report). London: Standing Conference on Crime Prevention.

Hope, T. 1985. *Implementing Crime Prevention Measures*. Home Office Research Study no. 86. London: HMSO.

———. 1995. "Community Crime Prevention." In *Building a Safer Society: Strategic Approaches to Crime Prevention*, edited by M. Tonry and D. Farrington. Chicago: University of Chicago Press.

International Centre for the Prevention of Crime. 1995. *Harnessing Crime Prevention Internationally for a Sustainable World*. Montreal: International Centre for the Prevention of Crime.

Jeffery, C. R. 1972. *Crime Prevention Through Enviornmental Design*. London: Sage.

Joutsen, M. 1996. "Crime Prevention on the UN Agenda." In *Seminar on*

Crime Prevention in the European Union, Stockholm, Sweden, May 13–14. Stockholm: Ministry of Justice.

Kalle, E. 1987. "The Prevention of Urban Violence and Insecurity in Post-War Housing: The Case of Geeren-Noord, Breda." In *Urban Violence and Insecurity: The Role of Local Authorities.* Strasbourg: Council of Europe.

Knutsson, J. 1984. *Operation Identification: A Way to Prevent Burglaries?* Report no. 14. Stockholm: National Council for Crime Prevention, Research Division.

Kobrin, S. 1959. "The Chicago Area Project: A 25 Year Assessment." *Annals of the American Academy* 322:19–29.

Koch, B. 1996. "National Crime Prevention Policing in England and Wales, 1979–1995." Ph.D. diss., University of Cambridge.

Lipton, D., R. Martinson, and J. Wilks. 1975. *The Effectiveness of Correctional Treatment: A Survey of Treatment Evaluation Studies.* London: Praeger.

May, T. 1994. "Probation and Community Sanctions." In *The Oxford Handbook of Criminology,* edited by M. Maguire, R. Morgan, and R. Reiner. Oxford: Clarendon Press.

Mayhew, P., R. V. G. Clarke, A. Sturman, and J. M. Hough. 1976. *Crime as Opportunity.* Home Office Research Study no. 34. London: HMSO.

Moore, C., and J. Brown. 1981. *Community Versus Crime.* Dorchester: Bedford Square Press.

National Crime Prevention Council. 1996. *Canada's National Crime Prevention Council Home Page.* URL:http://www.web.apc.org/-ncpc. Canada: National Crime Prevention Council.

Newman, O. 1972. *Defensible Space: Crime Prevention Through Urban Design.* New York: Macmillan.

Pate, A., M. A. Wycoff, W. Skogan, and L. W. Sherman. 1986. *Reducing Fear of Crime in Houston and Newark: A Summary Report.* Washington, D.C.: Police Foundation.

Pease, K. 1994. "Crime Prevention." In *The Oxford Handbook of Criminology,* edited by M. Maguire, R. Morgan, and R. Reiner. Oxford: Clarendon Press.

Poyner, B. 1993. "What Works in Crime Prevention: An Overview of Evaluations." In *Crime Prevention Studies,* vol. 1, edited by R. V. Clarke. New York: Criminal Justice Press.

Reppetto, T. 1976. "Crime Prevention and the Displacement Phenomenon." *Crime and Delinquency* 22:166–77.

Rock, P. 1994. "The Social Organisation of a Home Office Initiative." *European Journal of Crime, Criminal Law and Criminal Justice* 2:141–67.

Rutter, M., B. Maughan, P. Mortimore, and J. Ouston. 1979. *Fifteen Thousand Hours: Secondary Schools and Their Effects on Children.* London: Open Books.

Shaw, C. R., and H. D. McKay. 1942. *Juvenile Delinquency and Urban Areas.* Chicago: University of Chicago Press.

Skogan, W. G. 1990. *Disorder and Decline: Crime and the Spiral of Decay in American Neighborhoods.* New York: Free Press.

Taub, R., D. G. Taylor, and J. D. Dunham. 1984. *Paths of Neighborhood Change.* Chicago: University of Chicago Press.

Tremblay, R. E., and W. M. Craig. 1995. "Developmental Crime Prevention." In *Building a Safer Society: Strategic Approaches to Crime Prevention,* edited by M. Tonry and D. P. Farrington. Chicago: University of Chicago Press.

United Nations. 1993. *Crime Prevention and Criminal Justice Newsletter,* nos. 22/23, July.

van Dijk, J., and J. de Waard. 1991. "A Two-Dimensional Typology of Crime Prevention Projects: With a Bibliography." *Criminal Justice Abstracts* 23:483–503.

van Dijk, J., and J. Junger-Tas. 1988. "Trends in Crime Prevention in The Netherlands." In *Communities and Crime Reduction,* edited by T. Hope and M. Shaw. London: HMSO.

Wikström, P. -O., R. V. Clarke, and J. McCord, eds. 1995. *Integrating Crime Prevention Strategies: Propensity and Opportunity.* Stockholm: National Council for Crime Prevention.

Wilson, J. Q., and G. Kelling. 1982. "Broken Windows: The Police and Neighborhood Safety." *Atlantic Monthly,* March:29–38.

Zimbardo, P. G. 1973. "A Field Experiment in Auto-Shaping." In *Vandalism,* edited by C. Ward. London: Architectural Press.

15

Treatment of Sex Offenders

VERNON L. QUINSEY

The history of the management and treatment of sex offenders has been driven by spectacular incidents of sexual recidivism. Such incidents create strong political pressures on everyone assessing, treating, and making release decisions concerning sex offenders either to become more conservative or to make foolproof decisions. When faced with great uncertainty and strong pressure not to make errors, people are prone to look for certainty in technology or to defer to experts with special knowledge.

Sex offenders are, however, much like other offenders, and the issues of risk pertaining to them are identical. Although there is a technology of assessment and treatment that is specific to sex offenders and a substantial proportion of them are undoubtedly paraphiliacs or sexual deviants, the technology of assessment and treatment that exists specifically for sex offenders is fallible and will not bear the weight of unrealistic expectations. There is no mark of Cain or magic bullet of treatment to eliminate uncertainty.

Community harm in the form of sexual recidivism can, however, be reduced through careful release decisions guided by standardized predictive instruments and phallometric assessments, provision of treatment where appropriate, and programs of community risk management. Nevertheless, even with the best system of assessment, treatment, and management, some sex offenders will inevitably recidivate while under supervision. Thus, recidivism can occur either as the inevitable result of basing decisions on imperfect knowledge or as the result of carelessness or human error. It is important to make a sharp distinction between these two sources of recidivism. The adoption of formal policies for the assessment, treatment, and management of sex offenders should protect decision makers and service providers from being accused of human error when the fault lies in imperfect knowledge.

The goal of the approach recommended in this article is the improvement of the balance between the civil liberties of offenders and public safety by more accurately appraising risk. This risk can then be linked to dispositional decisions, including the provision of interventions designed to reduce it. Of course, dispositional decisions can be made using a variety of criteria, such as just deserts, general and special deterrence, offense seriousness, the number of previous offenses, the degree of recovery from mental illness, and so on. A variety of moral, legal, and historical rationales can be given for the use of particular criteria in making dispositional decisions. Regardless of the rationale for particular dispositional policies, however, tensions between community safety and the civil liberties of offenders are inevitably an issue. The only rational manner in which this issue can be addressed is through accurately appraising the dangerousness of individual sex offenders.

Prediction of Sexual Recidivism

Let us consider the art and science of predicting recidivism among sex offenders. First, it must be decided exactly what negative outcomes of release or relaxation of supervision are at issue. Policy could be concerned about some or all of the following: psychiatric relapse, recidivism of any kind, violent recidivism, and sexual recidivism. The distinction among these is important because their likelihood for any given offender is very different. For example, in a sample of rapists and child molesters assessed at the Oak Ridge maximum security psychiatric facility (Quinsey, Rice, and Harris 1995), 28 percent were later convicted of a new sex offense, 40 percent were arrested or returned for a violent or sexual offense, and 57 percent were arrested or returned to Oak Ridge for any offense. If we were to be concerned with minor offenses or rehospitalization, therefore, we would be much more conservative in our decision making than if we concerned ourselves only with more serious (and rarer) phenomena.

Base Rate Issues

The literature on decision making suggests that the initial step in appraising the dangerousness of an individual is to establish the base rate or the expected likelihood that that person will commit a new violent or sex offense within a specified period of time (e.g., Quinsey and Walker 1992). The initial estimate of the probability that a sex offender will commit a new sexual or violent offense can be made only by examining the results of follow-up studies of similar offenders. The relevant characteristics of the offender in question must be established, and then the frequency of violent and sexual recidivists among offenders with similar characteristics can be used to generate the probability. For clarity, it must be remembered that the focus of such predictive efforts is on the prospective identification of persons who will commit crimes, not on the prediction of the crimes themselves.

Assessors must, therefore, have a reasonable estimate of the base rate before they proceed. The base rate is a function of the rate at which violent crimes are committed and the duration of time that offenders are followed. Clearly, if the interval of time for which the question of dangerousness is relevant is short, it is likely that the base rate will be too low (e.g., Villeneuve and Quinsey 1995).

The initial estimate of the likelihood of recidivism is determined primarily by static or historical variables. Although variables such as offense history cannot change with time, they are vital in anchoring clinical judgment in actuarial reality. One of the reasons this anchoring is so important is that unaided human judgment is remarkably insensitive to dramatic differences in base rate in a prediction context (Cannon and Quinsey 1995). The final appraisal of dangerousness is made by adjusting the initial estimate upward or downward according to dynamic variables such as progress in treatment and type and quality of supervision. The importance of the initial estimate can be seen by considering a hypothetical treatment method that reduces recidivism by half: an offender whose expected likelihood of recidivism is 80 percent will have a likelihood of 40 percent after treatment, whereas one with an initial 10 percent probability will have a posttreatment probability of only 5 percent. (For an extensive discussion of these issues, see Webster et al. 1994.)

The base rate is most important when extreme. For example, if the expected probability of recidivism is very low, say 5 percent, then an appraisal of dangerousness must be 95 percent accurate in order to equal the accuracy of making a decision to release based solely on the base rate (e.g., Quinsey 1980). Predictions of sexual recidivism are worthwhile, therefore, only where its base rate is not extremely low or high. An individual prediction should not be made when the base rate for the population from which the assessed individual comes is too extreme.

Actuarial Assessment

Among sex offenders, a variety of historical factors, such as the number of previous sex offenses, predict the likelihood of sexual and violent recidivism. Among child molesters, the sex of the victim and the relationship of the victim to the offender are also important predictors. Intrafamilial (father-daughter incest) offenders have quite low recidivism rates. Among extrafamilial offenders, those with boy victims have double the recidivism rate of heterosexual offenders (for a review, see Quinsey 1986). A meta-analysis of sexual offender recidivism studies (Hanson and Bussière 1996) has confirmed and extended these findings. Based on sixty-one data sets, sexual deviance, as indexed by phallometrically measured sexual age preferences, prior sex offenses, and versatility of sexual offending, was the strongest predictor. Homosexual child molesters had the highest sexual recidivism rates, and incest offenders the lowest. Unmarried offenders, younger offenders, and those unmotivated for treatment were more likely to reoffend.

In a recent study (Quinsey, Rice, and Harris 1995), 178 sex offenders who had been assessed at a maximum security psychiatric facility were followed for an average of fifty-nine months of opportunity to reoffend. Twenty-eight percent were convicted of a new sex offense, and 40 percent were arrested, convicted, or returned to the psychiatric facility for a violent (including sex) offense. Rapists were more likely to relapse than child molesters. Psychopathy, measures of previous criminal history, and phallometric indices of deviant sexual interests were found to be useful predictors.

A predictor scale was formed by weighting each of the fourteen predictors that was significant in the regression analyses by a number reflecting its univariate correlation with the criterion. The variables, in descending order of the size of their relationship with the criterion, were the Psychopathy Checklist–Revised (Hare 1991), elementary school maladjustment, not having lived with both parents until age sixteen, property offense charges, prior criminal charges against persons, number of previous sexual offenses, history of sexual offenses only against female children (negative), never married or having lived in a common-law relationship, age at index offense (negative), failure on prior conditional release or supervision, initial phallometric assessment indicating deviant sexual age or activity preferences, *DSM-III* criteria for any personality disorder, *DSM-III* criteria for schizophrenia (negative), and alcohol abuse history. Linear relationships ($r = .45$ and .46, respectively) were found between scores on the predictor scale and reconviction for a sexual offense and violent (including sexual) recidivism.

It is of interest that another actuarial instrument, the Violence Risk Appraisal Guide (Harris, Rice, and Quinsey 1993), developed using the same method on a larger sample of offenders (about 10 percent of whom were sex offenders), predicted the sexual and violent recidivism of sex offenders in a cross-validation study more accurately than the instrument described above, which was derived exclusively from a sex offender sample (Rice and Harris 1997). This observation is particularly useful because the general Violence Risk Appraisal Guide does not require phallometric assessment. The twelve predictors in this instrument are, in descending order of their relationship with violent or sexual recidivism: the Psychopathy Checklist–Revised, elementary school maladjustment, not having lived with both parents to age sixteen, adult property offenses, never having been married or lived in a common-law relationship, age at index offense (negative), failure on prior conditional release or supervision, victim injury in index offense (negative), *DSM-III* criteria for any personality disorder, *DSM-III* criteria for schizophrenia (negative), female victim in index offense (negative), and history of alcohol abuse.

In the Rice and Harris (1997) sample of 288 rapists and child molesters, 58 percent committed a new violent or sexual offense, and 35 percent committed a new sexual offense over an average ten-year period of opportunity. The area under the curve in the receiver operator characteristic (ROC) analysis[1] was .76 for violent or sexual reoffending and .60 for sexual reoffending. This level of accuracy is much better than that obtained by relying on clinical intuition (cf. Gardner et al. 1996).

The actuarial instruments developed by my colleagues and myself provide probabilities of violent or sexual recidivism for particular levels of risk score, but these probabilities are accurate only for the population from which they were derived. However, because the predictors of violent recidivism in the actuarial instrument are similar to those that have been successfully used in a variety of contexts and because the derivation offender sample was quite heterogeneous, the instruments can be used to assign persons from different but similar populations to *relative* risk categories with some confidence. In other words, the actuarial instrument can rank the dangerousness of offenders within a different population relative to each other.

Incapacitation

The actuarial models just described are designed to predict violent or sexual recidivism but do not otherwise directly address the seriousness of such recidivism. The anticipated seriousness of a violent offense (should one occur) is important in considering incapacitation, the long-term refusal of community access. In my view, incapacitation should be considered where the actuarially determined risk of violent recidivism is high and when the offender being assessed has committed at least one very serious prior violent offense.

Dynamic Predictors

An actuarial estimate of risk may be adjusted in a very conservative manner based on the idiosyncratic aspects of the particular case. Such adjustment might be indicated by therapeutic outcome, changed opportunities of offending, adequacy of supervision, current compliance with medication or supervision, and so on. It is usually the case with dynamic variables that intuition must be relied upon because of the absence of empirical information. Because of the well-documented unreliability of clinical judgment in general (Dawes, Faust, and Meehl 1989) and of clinical prediction of violent behavior in particular (Quinsey and Ambtman 1979; Quinsey and Maguire 1986), the reliability of clinical appraisals of dangerousness can be markedly increased by averaging the *independently* made judgments of different clinicians (Ashton 1986).

In the best circumstances, the clinicians considering an individual case have a theory that identifies the antecedents of violent or sexual offending for that offender. Such individualized theories are often cast in terms of relapse prevention (Laws 1989). These antecedents are the clinical issues to be considered in adjusting actuarially determined risk.

Both the actuarial model and clinical appraisals rest upon a detailed and corroborated history. Assessments of dangerousness should not be based solely on offender self-reports. This, however, does not imply that more information is necessarily better. Only some potential predictors are in fact related to violent recidivism, and it is these that must be carefully evaluated. The consideration of irrelevant information simply confuses the issue. Even the use of predictors that are known to be individually related to sexual or violent recidivism is problematic in combination with an actuarially derived estimate of risk because the extent to which they are correlated with the actuarial instrument is unknown, as is the weight that should be assigned to them.

E. Phallometric Assessment

As discussed earlier, phallometric data from an initial assessment can be employed as a static predictor in an actuarial model. They can, however, also be employed to identify treatment targets and to monitor changes in sexual interest and, by inference, in the likelihood of committing a new sexual offense. A review of these issues in connection with sexual offenders against children is provided by Quinsey and Lalumiere (1995).

The probative value of phallometric assessments is often unknown because the discriminant and predictive validity of the procedures used in many sexual behavior laboratories have not yet been established. In these cases, it is unknown whether, let alone how well, these assessments can differentiate sex offenders of various kinds from each other or from offenders who have not committed sex crimes, whether these assessments relate to important aspects of a sex offender's history, whether they predict sexual recidivism, or whether changes in phallometric assessment data occasioned by treatment are related to subsequent sexual recidivism. It is insufficient for it to be established that phallometric data collected using *different* procedures and stimuli have these various forms of validity (cf. Quinsey and Laws 1990); the stimuli and procedures that are used in a particular case have themselves to be evaluated.

Because phallometric assessments are not immune from faking (e.g., Quinsey and Chaplin 1988) and the motivation of most inmates is to "pass" them by appearing to have normative sexual interests, test results are more confidently interpreted if evidence of deviant sexual interests is found than if no deviant interests are found. Phallometric assessment reports, therefore, tend to be conservative with respect to risk.

Further, the question of validity of specialized procedures is best thought of as an incremental one. Specifically, what *increase* in predictive efficiency is achieved by a phallometric assessment? This is an important question because a number of instruments have been developed that are less expensive and easier to use and are well known to be related to general recidivism (the Statistical Information about Recidivism Scale [Nuffield 1982]; the Psychopathy Checklist [Hare 1991; Hart, Kropp, and Hare 1988]; the Level of Supervision Inventory [Andrews 1982; Andrews, Kiessling, and Kominos 1983; Andrews 1989; Andrews et al.

1986]) and violent and sexual recidivism (the Psychopathy Checklist [Hare and McPherson 1984]; the Statistical Risk Appraisal Guide described earlier [Harris, Rice, and Quinsey 1993]). A variety of methods of quantifying a person's history of sex offenses are also useful predictors of sexual recidivism.

The issue of the amount of incremental validity that is gained by specialized sex offender assessment is also connected to standardized measures of risk in another way. An offender's history of sex offending is related in a direct way to the probability with which he will show deviant sexual interest in a phallometric assessment. Those with many sex offenses, who have chosen very young victims, and who have selected male children as victims are more likely to show deviant sexual interests in phallometric assessments.

Treatment of Sex Offenders: A Brief Overview

Policies concerning the treatment of sex offenders are necessarily complex because they relate simultaneously to sentencing, probation, and parole policies, the civil liberties of offenders, community safety, and issues of treatment efficacy. Programs of treatment for sex offenders must, therefore, be developed in the context of a variety of policies dealing with offender disposition. In addition, sex offenders are often involved with mental health and social service agencies before, after, or instead of their involvement with the criminal justice system. Clearly, policies pertaining to treatment must be coordinated across a variety of agency and governmental jurisdictions. In view of these considerations, psychological or psychiatric treatments must be viewed as one of a variety of preventive interventions directed at reducing the probability of a sex offender committing a further offense. In the total context of social policies designed to prevent future sexual victimizations, therefore, sex offender treatment programs are most sensibly evaluated in the same manner as incapacitation, special deterrence, community service, parole supervision, and other criminal justice interventions in terms of cost, efficacy, humaneness, and so forth. These various interventions, of course, are not usually incompatible with each other.

Actuarial Assessment and Treatment

The dimensional nature of risk scores can serve to direct the apportionment of treatment and supervisory resources. With respect to reducing the likelihood of recidivism, resources should be concentrated on higher-risk offenders. However, current actuarial models are historical in nature, and the predictors included in them cannot change or are unlikely to change quickly. In particular, they cannot be made to change through active intervention. Although this is an unhappy situation for offenders who are assessed to be of high risk, most offenders are of moderate to low risk. It is likely that the most important consequence of using actuarial models is the identification of offenders who are of low risk and require little, if any, intervention to reduce their risk.

Treatment can be focused on mental health needs, the likelihood of recidivism, or both. Although treatments designed to reduce general recidivism by addressing criminogenic needs among high-risk offenders have been shown to be modestly successful (Andrews et al. 1990; Lipsey 1992), the efficacy of treatments addressing mental health needs and any form of treatment for reducing the likelihood of violent or sexual crimes among serious adult offenders has not yet been demonstrated convincingly because of variability in the outcomes of studies, methodological shortcomings, and limited data (Quinsey et al. 1993).

Before discussing what characteristics sex offender treatment programs should have and how these programs should be coordinated with other societal interventions, it may be helpful to consider in more detail what we do and do not know about the efficacy of treatment programs for sex offenders. Broadly speaking, sex offender treatment programs employ three approaches: *pharmacological,* in which the goal is to reduce sexual arousability and the frequency of deviant sexual fantasies through the use of antiandrogens (e.g., Bradford 1990; Berlin and Meinecke 1981); *psychotherapeutic* or *evocative,* in which the goals include increasing offenders' empathy for the victims of sexual assault together with their sense of responsibility for their sexual crimes (e.g., Frisbie and Dondis 1965); and *cognitive-behavioral,* where the object is to remedy skill deficits, alter cognitions that are believed to be related to sexual offending, and alter deviant patterns of sexual arousal or preference (e.g., Abel 1986; Abel, Becker, and Skinner 1986; Griffiths, Quinsey, and Hingsburger 1989; Marshall et al. 1983; Quinsey et al. 1987). These approaches are not mutually exclusive, and in recent years the trend has been for treatment programs to employ all three approaches to varying degrees. In addition, many programs also employ a cognitive-behavioral relapse-prevention orientation borrowed from the substance abuse area, in which the focus is on eliminating idiosyncratically defined precursors of relapse and teaching the offender more effective ways of coping with these precursors in an extensive period of follow-up supervision (Laws 1989; Pithers 1990; Pithers et al. 1988).

There is a substantial literature on all of these forms of sex offender treatment. Surveys of North American treatment programs can be found in Borzeck and Wormith (1987) and Knopp (1984). A *National Inventory of Treatment Programs for Child Sexual Abuse Offenders* has been prepared by the Canadian Child Welfare Association (1989). Reviews of the literature on the efficacy of treatment can be found in Bradford (1990), Dixen and Jenkins (1981), Kelly (1982), Langevin (1983), Marshall and Barbaree (1990), Quinsey (1973, 1977), Quinsey and Earls (1990), and Quinsey and Marshall (1983).

Relative to the number of sex offenders who are treated each year and the number of articles and books written about sex offender treatment, the evaluative outcome literature is astonishingly small. There may be more authors with published opinions on the effectiveness of sex offender treatment than there are sex offenders in treatment outcome studies. With respect to evaluating the ultimate effect of treatment efforts directed toward reducing the recidivism rates of sexual offenders such as rapists and child molesters, there have been no experimental comparisons of different treatment approaches, almost no comparisons of treated and untreated sex offenders involving random assignment, and very few quasi-experimental studies that compare treated and untreated sex offenders even without random assignment.

Variations in recidivism rates associated with different treatment programs are extremely hazardous to interpret. Differences among recidivism rates across studies are confounded with legal jurisdiction, cohort effects, duration of follow-up, offender characteristics, differential client attrition rates, differences in program integrity and amount of treatment, amount and quality of posttreatment supervision, and a host of other variables. In addition, recidivism measures tend to be noisy and result in comparisons of low statistical power. Even without attempting to attribute variations in recidivism to treatment program characteristics, the variation in recidivism rates in the published literature is truly remarkable (for reviews see Furby, Weinrott, and Blackshaw 1989; Quinsey 1984, 1986).

Although there have been no comparisons of different treatment approaches within the same study using random assignment of offenders to treatment conditions, there have been some recent treatment—no treatment comparisons using matched designs or convenience samples and one comparison of a treatment with a no treatment control using random assignment. Unfortunately, the evidence from these studies is mixed.

Barbaree and Marshall (1988) obtained large differences in recidivism rates, as estimated by official police records and unofficial records of police and child protective agencies, between child molesters given cognitive-behavioral treatment in a community clinic and similar but not randomly assigned clients given no treatment. Recidivism rates over approximately four years were 43 percent and 18 percent, respectively, for untreated and treated extrafamilial heterosexual child molesters; 43 and 13 percent for extrafamilial homosexual child molesters; and 22 and 8 percent for untreated and treated heterosexual incestuous child molesters.

Quite different results were obtained by Rice, Quinsey, and Harris (1991), who determined the recidivism rates over an average 6.3-year follow-up period of 136 extrafamilial child molesters who had received phallometric assessment in a maximum security psychiatric institution from 1972 to 1983. Fifty of these offenders had participated in a behavioral program designed to alter inappropriate sexual age preferences, and some had received social skill and sex education programs as well (Quinsey et al. 1987). Thirty-one percent of the subjects were convicted of a new sexual offense, 43 percent of the total were known to have committed a violent or sexual offense, and 58 percent were arrested for any offense or returned to the maximum security institution. Behavioral laboratory treatment did not affect recidivism. Similar negative results were reported by Hanson, Steffy, and Gauthier (1993) in a retrospective evaluation of a treatment program for incarcerated child molesters involving milieu therapy, counseling, and modification of sexual preferences.

Quinsey, Khanna, and Malcolm (forthcoming) followed 483 inmates who were referred to a sex offender treatment program for an average of forty-four months of opportunity to reoffend: 213 completed the program, 183 were assessed as not requiring it, 52 refused to be assessed, 27 were judged to be unsuitable, and 9 were judged as requiring treatment but did not receive it. Over half of the total sample were rearrested for an offense of any kind, and 38 percent were arrested for a new violent or sexual offense. Treated offenders were the most frequently rearrested for sex offenses. Inmates judged unsuitable for treatment were rearrested least frequently, particularly for sex offenses. Inmates judged as not requiring treatment and those who refused treatment had fewer rearrests for sex offenses than treated subjects, although they had more rearrests for violent offenses. After statistically controlling for the static variables that predicted reoffending, the treatment program was associated with a higher rate of sexual rearrests but had no effect on the composite variable, violent or sexual rearrests. Among treated offenders, clinical assessment of outcome was not significantly associated with recidivism.

The difference in outcomes among the quasi-experimental treatment evaluations reported here illustrates the difficulties in arriving at definitive conclusions concerning treatment efficacy. Among the more important of the myriad of differences between these studies are the locus of the program (maximum security psychiatric facility versus the community), severity of the offense history of the clients/patients treated in the program, differences in amount of client self-selection (including differential attrition), and differences in the amount of treatment received. Any or all of these or other confounded variables could be responsible for the markedly different results. Perhaps the strongest conclusion that one can draw from this literature is that the aspects of treatment, client population, supervision, and setting characteristics related to successful outcome are at present unknown.

Marques et al. (1994) have reported preliminary data from the most ambitious evaluation of sex offender treatment yet undertaken. This prospective follow-up study involves the random assignment of offenders to a cognitive-behavioral treatment program or a nontreatment condition. Specifically, there are three groups in the study matched on age, criminal history, and offense type: 98 treated offenders, 97 men who volunteered but (randomly) were not selected for treatment, 96 men who refused treatment, and 8 men who voluntarily withdrew or were terminated early in treatment.

Subjects were at risk for an average of thirty-four months. During this period 8.2 percent of the treated offenders, 13.4 percent of the untreated volunteers, 12.5 percent of the treatment refusers, and 37.5 percent of the early terminators committed a new sexual offense. These preliminary data indicate that a small treatment effect may be found with more subjects and that noncompliance or withdrawal from treatment is a poor prognostic sign.

The status of the treatment outcome literature explains why treatment variables, such as exposure to a particular treatment or the outcome of a particular treatment, are not yet included in any actuarial model. Clearly, additional treatment program evaluation is the most pressing need in this area. The major implication of this observation is that progress in treatment must be interpreted very cautiously when assessing risk.

Supervision

Dangerousness appears to be inversely related to the quality and intensity of supervision. Some predictors are also relevant to supervision. Criminal versatility, one of the items on the Revised Psychopathy Checklist, refers to the variety of criminal acts that an individual has committed. Criminally versatile offenders are more difficult to supervise than others because there are more potential types of crimes for a supervisor to worry about. The quintessential example of a nonversatile offender is an incestuous child molester who has molested his daughter and committed no other crimes. Supervision for this person ordinarily would be relatively simple because it involves only his access to his daughter.

Dynamic predictors can also be monitored after release to good advantage (Motiuk and Porporino 1989; Quinsey and Walker 1992). Instability of living conditions, noncompliance with medication or supervision, increased drinking, negative affect, and procriminal attitudes are all related to recidivism or relapse. These postrelease predictors can be used to individualize the amount of supervision an offender receives.

Two recent studies, one retrospective and the other using contemporaneous information, have further examined dynamic predictors. In the retrospective study, Zamble and Quinsey (1997) interviewed and gathered file data on 311 newly reincarcerated recidivists defined according to their most serious new offenses: any type of assault against persons (including homicide), robbery and armed robbery, and nonviolent property crimes. Offenses involving rape were included within the violent assault category. In the context of the present study, the comparison of preoffense characteristics of the sixteen rapists and eighty-four nonsexual assaulters is of most interest because it sheds some light on the lifestyle that is associated with rape.

Fewer rapists than nonsexual assaulters were married or in a common-law relationship in the period preceding the offense. Rapists spent only about one-third of the time that the other assaulters did in family activities or in passive activities such as watching television. In compensation, they spent about twice as much time in unstructured socializing with friends and had lower scores on a scale measuring social isolation. Rapists tended to begin drinking sooner after release and used about twice as many types of (nonalcoholic) drugs immediately before the offense. All of the rapists said that they had been worried about the direction of their lives, even more than the strong majority in the comparison set, and almost all felt that their offense was connected to the problems they had been experiencing, as opposed to about half of the others.

For the thirty-day period preceding the offense, rapists reported even higher frequencies of depression and anger than the already high frequencies among the other assaulters. Seven of the sixteen rapists also reported having felt guilt, which was infrequent among the others. At the same time, only four rapists reported sexual frustration, higher than among the other assaulters but lower than one might expect according to theories that emphasize sexual deprivation as a cause of rape. Among measures of emotions in the final forty-eight-hour preoffense period, only sexual frustration remained able to differentiate the subgroups. However, the rate of general frustration rose among the nonsexual subgroup, so that it was significantly higher among the other assaulters than among rapists. Relatively fewer rapists reported a connection between some particular event and the offense. Only five of the sixteen said that they had experienced sexual arousal from anticipatory thoughts of the offense; four of these had masturbated at least once to their offense fantasies, but the other reportedly ignored the thoughts.

Taken together, these results suggest that the rapists had adopted a short-term mating strategy, as opposed to developing more stable, longer-term relationships. From a theoretical viewpoint, the allocation of mating effort to the pursuit of short-term sexual encounters, in combination with the antisocial characteristics of these men, would be likely to result in an insensitive striving for sexual encounters in which the wishes of the recipients of their attention would be likely to be ignored (Quinsey and Lalumiere 1995).

In the second study, Quinsey et al. (1997) compared sixty mentally disordered male offenders who had eloped from the hospital or reoffended while under supervision with fifty-one male offenders who had done neither. Subjects were matched on diagnosis (about half were personality disordered and half psychotic), age, and level of supervision. In addition to an actuarially based estimate of risk of violent or sexual reoffending, proximal dynamic variables were coded from clinical file information recorded either during the month or six-month period before the elopement/reoffense or control date for all subjects, as well as from a control period (usually a year earlier) for the elopers/offenders. Seven dynamic variables statistically differentiated elopers/reoffenders from other patients after controlling for actuarial risk level and also differentiated the period preceding eloping or reoffending from an earlier period among elopers/reoffenders. These robust predictors of eloping/reoffending involved primarily two kinds of items: those involving noncompliance with supervision and antisocial attitudes, and those pertaining to emotional dysphoria and psychiatric symptoms.

The offenses labeled "violent" in this study were three murders, five attempted murders, one wounding, two assaults causing bodily harm, three common assaults, four rapes, and one indecent assault. Violent reoffenders were best differentiated from their controls by a proximal factor labeled "dynamic antisociality." Dynamic antisociality also differentiated the period immediately before the violent offense from a period a year earlier within-subjects. Interestingly, many of the items in the dynamic antisociality factor, such as lack of remorse and empathy, procriminal sentiments, and unrealistic discharge plans, resemble items from the Revised Psychopathy Checklist (Hare 1991).

Developing Programs for Sex Offenders

Programs for sex offenders have to be developed in the context of imperfect but increasing knowledge. More is known about the characteristics of sex offenders than about the efficacy of treatment interventions or the etiology of sex offending. This conclusion has far-reaching implications for the strategy of program development that should be adopted.

The first implication is that there is no identifiable "gold standard" treatment that could be adopted for use without further evaluation. There are interventions that have been shown to produce changes in theoretically relevant measures. However, there is no evidence that improvements in these measures are related to reduced recidivism (cf. Quinsey, Khanna, and Malcolm, forthcoming). In the case of phallometric measurements of sexual preference, for example, it appears that treatment changes the relationship between phallometric measurement and recidivism; pretreatment but not posttreatment phallometric measures of sexual preference predict recidivism (e.g., Rice, Quinsey, and Harris 1991).

To say that treatments have not been convincingly evaluated, however, is neither to say that they do not work nor to assert that different approaches to treatment are of equivalent efficacy. In my view, the best option in these circumstances of relative ignorance is to adopt treatments that fit with what is known about the treatment of offenders in general; have a convincing theoretical rationale in that they are motivated by what we know about the characteristics of sex offenders; have been demonstrated to produce proximal changes in theoretically relevant measures; are feasible in terms of acceptability to offenders and clinicians, cost, and ethical standards; are described in sufficient detail that program integrity can be measured; and can be integrated into existing supervisory procedures.

The second implication of this view is that the treatment of sex offenders has to be viewed not simply as a matter of providing service to offenders and protecting the public but also as a matter of program development. The key to successful program development is to design interventions in such a way that their evaluation tests the theory on which they are based. Such a strategy is called "Program Development Evaluation" (Gottfredson 1984).

Treatment of Offenders

Because sex offenders are by definition criminal offenders, it is reasonable to expect that principles of treatment that apply to offenders in general also apply to sex offenders. The support for a cognitive-behavioral approach to offender treatment in general is based on a much stronger and more extensive literature than for cognitive-behavioral approaches to sex offender treatment. This more general literature, however, indirectly supports the cognitive-behavioral treatment of sex offenders.

The principles of offender treatment have perhaps been best conceptualized by Andrews (1980, 1982), Andrews et al. (1986), and Gendreau and Andrews (1990) in terms of risk, need, and responsivity. Basically, Andrews and his colleagues argue that offender treatment is most effective when targeted at the criminogenic needs of high-risk cases; a similar argument, in the context of managing violent offenders, has been advanced by Quinsey and Walker (1992).

It is equally clear from the general literature on offender treatment that evocative, insight-oriented, nondirective, or milieu approaches have either been ineffective or have raised recidivism rates (Andrews 1982; Gendreau and Andrews 1990). In particular, an evaluation of the Social Therapy Unit milieu therapy program at Oak Ridge found very high postrelease rates of violent recidivism among patients (including a substantial proportion of sex offenders) treated in this confrontational patient-led program. The rate of violent recidivism among psychopathic patients (defined by Hare's Psychopathy Checklist) was higher than that of similarly psychopathic offenders sent to prison (Harris, Rice, and Cormier 1991; Rice, Harris, and Cormier 1992). This program is important because it involved serious offenders and was implemented with great intensity and integrity. These findings raise very serious concerns about programs for psychopathic sex offenders that rely on these techniques.

Programs that foster anticriminal attitudes among inmates through exposure to anticriminal models do appear to be helpful. In speaking of the effectiveness of correctional and parole officers, Andrews (1982) puts it this way: "[A]ttributes of the officer which are relevant to the supervision of offenders include a positive socio-emotional orientation (the relationship principle) in combination with the ability to establish anticriminal contingencies (the contingency principle)." Problem-solving and self-management skill acquisition appears to be helpful to inmates in learning to cope with problems without resorting to (or drifting toward) crime (Zamble and Porporino 1988).

The implications of these conclusions from the literature on offender treatment can be applied to sex offender treatment programs that have not received evaluative attention. In fact, they must be applied because no other relevant information is available to judge the appropriateness of an unevaluated program's rationale and practices.

Based on the correctional treatment literature, characteristics of programs that have some hope of success in reducing recidivism include the following: a skill-based training approach; the modeling of prosocial behaviors and attitudes; a directive but nonpunitive orientation; a focus on modifying antecedents to criminal behavior; a supervised community component in order to assess and teach the offender relevant skills; and a high-risk clientele.

Characteristics of programs that are likely to be ineffective or associated with increased recidivism include these: confrontation without skill building; a nondirective approach; a punitive orientation; a focus on irrelevant (noncriminogenic) factors (e.g., building an offender's self-esteem without modifying his procriminal attitudes; Wormith 1984); and the use of highly sophisticated verbal therapies, such as insight-oriented psychotherapy.

These observations on the characteristics of effective and ineffective programs for offenders in general are relevant to the characteristics of unevaluated types of programs for sex offenders, such as self-help groups. Of course, one cannot say whether these programs will be successful in reducing recidivism because they have not received evaluative attention in the form of comparative follow-up studies.

From the earlier discussion, however, we can make some educated guesses about whether self-help programs are likely to be successful. First, the issue is not limited to who provides the intervention (clinicians or offenders) but includes all of the other program characteristics. The characteristics of successful programs directed by clinicians are likely to be similar to the characteristics of successful programs operated by offenders. There are three exceptions, however. First, offender-led programs cannot effectively use authority. Of course, authority is sometimes clinically indicated and sometimes indicated for reasons of public safety. Second, self-help groups do not contain the technical expertise for certain forms of assessment and treatment. Third, self-help or offender-led groups are much more likely than clinicians to be able to change the climate of institutional opinion in a protherapeutic direction and to provide ongoing support for offenders who are attempting to change.

The success of self-help groups depends on the rationale and organization of the actual program. Self-help groups should not be seen as a substitute for more conventional treatment; indeed, one of the reasons for their development has been the limited availability of other sex offender programs. Self-help groups would benefit from input from clinical staff and should be coordinated with other programs (the worst scenario would be that self-help and staff-led sex offender programs worked at cross-purposes). To speak the obvious, on the other side of this issue, sex offender programs of whatever kind cannot be successful unless they have meaningful input from offender clients.

Theoretical Rationale

The probability and type of recidivism are strongly affected by victim age, sex, and relationship to the offender, the seriousness and nature of the sex offense, and the number of previous sex offenses. Sex offenders are heterogeneous even within categories defined by offense history, and thus a focus of current research is to develop more differentiated taxonomies of sex offenders (Knight and Prentky 1990). Because of this heterogeneity, sex offender treatment programs should be organized so as to take account of these differences.

Perhaps the most important of these differences, and the most relevant for the design of individual treatment programs, is the nature of the offender's sexual preferences. Some offenders have marked paraphilic (sexually deviant) interests in children, sadistic sexual assault, and so on. These sexual preferences can be measured with varying degrees of adequacy by offender self-report, offense history, or phallometric assessment. The measurement of these interests is important because it provides clues to the motivation underlying the offense, an idea as to the nature of possible future acts of sexual aggression, and a focus for treatment intervention. Although phallometric measurement is usually the most accurate method of measuring sexual preferences, it is more useful in a treatment context than in a release decision context. Phallometric assessment data can be faked and are more likely to yield misleading results when offenders are highly motivated to appear to have normal sexual preferences. With respect to phallometric data gathered before and after treatment, therefore, continued evidence of inappropriate sexual preferences is a bad prognostic sign, but a reduction in such interest is not necessarily a good sign.

Other offender characteristics are related to the probability of treatment success and the design of individual programs. Alcohol abuse is a common problem among sex offenders, as it is among offenders more generally. If not effectively addressed, such problems can undermine treatment effectiveness by reducing offender compliance and self-control.

The limitations of current treatment technology also interact with individual differences among offenders. Variations in the seriousness of offense history are among the most important of these. In view of the limitations of current treatment technology, it cannot be expected that very serious sexual offenders, such as serial murderers, will or should be viewed as less of a risk as a result of progress in a treatment program.

This brief description of offender characteristics, although incomplete, suggests an individualized treatment planning process that uses the results of a variety of standardized assessments to formulate a theory of offender motivation and choose a combination of specific interventions designed to prevent recidivism. Thus, for an individual offender, any or all of a variety of interventions, such as treatments designed to reduce sexual arousability, modify inappropriate sexual preferences, control drinking, secure employment, prevent depression, and so forth, might be appropriate. Quinsey and Earls (1990) have explicated this approach in more detail.

This approach is consistent with what is usually described as a behavioral, a cognitive-behavioral, or, more broadly, a social learning–based treatment model. With the exception of antiandrogenic medication or castration, this model currently is the only approach that enjoys *any* evidence of effectiveness in reducing sexual recidivism.

Acceptability to Clinicians

The cognitive-behavioral treatment model is currently the most widely accepted by clinicians working with nonincestuous sex offenders in North America. This wide acceptance has important implications. First, it means that it is easier for additional clinicians to be trained in its use than in other therapies because of the variety of sites where such programs are in operation. Second, these programs have been in existence long enough for several of them to have developed treatment program manuals (e.g., Abel et al. 1984).

Although sex offender treatment programs are common and most clinicians believe that at least some sex offender treatment must occur in the community, there is a reluctance on the part of community residential facilities to accept sex offenders. This reluctance must be dealt with on several levels: by the development of supervisory policies that address safety issues, by educating the public and the people responsible for these facilities, and by arranging financial contingencies.

Acceptability to Offenders

Although sex offenders generally prefer individual treatment or counseling (Langevin, Wright, and Handy 1988), individual treatment is a setting characteristic rather than a specific intervention. Cognitive-behavioral interventions typically employ both group and individual treatments and are acceptable to a substantial proportion of sex offenders. Antiandrogen medication is rejected as a treatment modality by a larger proportion of sex offenders (Hucker, Langevin, and Bain 1988; Langevin, Wright, and Handy 1988; Langevin et al. 1979), although there are certainly enough who comply with this form of treatment to make its use feasible.

Developmentally handicapped sex offenders have been shown to respond well to a cognitive-behavioral approach if it is tailored to their particular needs (Griffiths, Quinsey, and Hingsburger 1989). Programs for these offenders require greater attention to informed consent issues, but these can be overcome, particularly with the help of advocacy organizations.

Of course, sex offenders, as a group, are not distinguished by their enthusiasm for treatment, regardless of the form it takes. Motivating sex offenders to enter and persist in treatment is an important aspect of any treatment program, and, as noted earlier, treatment dropouts appear to have high recidivism rates (Marques et al. 1994). Pretreatment identification of treatable problems in a group context has proved useful in encouraging sex offenders to enter treatment (e.g., Quinsey et al. 1987).

Supervision

The literature suggests, and most practitioners have come to believe, that sex offender treatment programs must involve community follow-up because that is where the offender must learn to control his behavior. Obviously, such community treatment involves ongoing supervision, which might profitably be facilitated, in high-risk cases, through the use of antiandrogenic drugs and electronic surveillance. In any event, community treatment, as a follow-up to institutional programs or as a program in itself, involves teaching sex offenders to avoid high-risk situations and acquire skills for coping with such situations when they occur. A high priority for the continuing development of such community programs is the detailed study of the circumstances surrounding supervisory failure.

Both supervision and treatment must be concentrated on sex offenders who present the greatest danger to the public in terms of the probability of their committing a new offense and its likely seriousness. Such high-risk cases are those best suited for intensive supervision and supervised community living situations. It is vital that these offenders not be released from medium or maximum security institutions directly to the community.

Because of the relatively greater empirical support for the efficacy of the cognitive-behavioral approach to the treatment of sex offenders (particularly in proximal outcome evaluations); the preponderance of treatment programs employing this approach; the existence of detailed treatment manuals; the relatively short-term nature of these interventions; their compatibility with intensive supervision, antiandrogenic medication, and a relapse prevention strategy; and the support for cognitive-behavioral treatments of offenders more generally, cognitive-behavioral treatment strategies for sex offenders have no serious rivals.

There are, however, serious limitations and reservations concerning the cognitive-behavioral treatment of sex offenders. The follow-up literature is extremely weak; reductions in recidivism among more serious offenders have not yet been convincingly demonstrated. Cognitive-behavioral programs vary in the intensity, duration, and many of the details of their treatments. It is simply unknown which, if any, of these differences are associated with greater efficacy, although there is a growing consensus that sex offender programs should be focused on the community adjustment of sex offenders.

Note

1. A plot of the relationship of hits and false alarms over various cutoff points (cf. Rice and Harris 1995). The area under the ROC curve is equivalent to the common language effect size of McGraw and Wong (1992).

References

Abel, G. G. 1986. *The Treatment of Child Molesters.* Rockville, MD: National Institute of Mental Health. "The Treatment of Child Molesters." Unpublished manuscript. (Available from SBC-TM, 722 W. 168th St., Box 17, New York NY 10032.)

Abel, G. G., J. V. Becker, and L. J. Skinner. 1986. "Behavioral Approaches to Treatment of the Violent Sex Offender." In *Clinical Treatment of the Violent Person,* edited by L. H. Roth. New York: Guilford.

Andrews, D. A. 1980. "Some Experimental Investigations of the Principles of Differential Association Through Deliberate Manipulation of the Structure of Service Systems." *American Sociological Review* 45:448–62.

———. 1982. "The Supervision of Offenders: Identifying and Gaining Control over the Factors Which Make a Difference." Report to the Solicitor General of Canada.

———. 1989. "Recidivism Is Predictable and Can Be Influenced: Using Risk Assessments to Reduce Recidivism." *Forum on Corrections Research* 1:11–18.

Andrews, D. A., J. J. Kiessling, and S. Kominos. 1983. *The Level of Supervision Inventory (LSI-6): Interview and Scoring Guide.* Toronto: Ontario Ministry of Correctional Services.

Andrews, D. A., J. J. Kiessling, D. Robinson, and S. Mickus. 1986. "The Risk Principle of Case Classification: An Outcome Evaluation with Young Adult Probationers." *Canadian Journal of Criminology* 28:377–84.

Andrews, D. A., I. Zinger, R. D. Hoge, J. Bonta, P. Gendreau, and F. T. Cullen. 1990. "Does Correctional Treatment Work? A Clinically Relevant and Psychologically Informed Meta-Analysis." *Criminology* 28:369–404.

Ashton, R. H. 1986. "Combining the Judgments of Experts: How Many and Which Ones?" *Organizational Behavior and Human Decision Processes* 38:405–14.

Barbaree, H. E., and W. L. Marshall. 1988. "Deviant Sexual Arousal, Offense History, and Demographic Variables as Predictors of Reoffense Among Child Molesters." *Behavioral Sciences and the Law* 6:267–80.

Berlin, F. S., and C. F. Meinecke. 1981. "Treatment of Sex Offenders with Antiandrogenic Medication: Conceptualization, Review of Treatment Modalities, and Preliminary Findings." *American Journal of Psychiatry* 138:601–7.

Borzeck, M., and J. S. Wormith. 1987. "A Survey of Treatment Programmes for Sex Offenders in North America." *Canadian Psychology* 28:30–44.

Bradford, J. M. W. 1990. "The Antiandrogen and Hormonal Treatment of Sex Offenders." In *Handbook of Sexual Assault: Issues, Theories, and Treatment of the Offender*, edited by W. L. Marshall, D. R. Laws, and H. E. Barbaree. New York: Plenum Press.

Canadian Child Welfare Association. 1989. *National Inventory of Treatment Programs for Child Sexual Abuse Offenders*. Ottawa: National Clearinghouse on Family Violence, Health and Welfare.

Cannon, C. K., and V. L. Quinsey. 1995. "The Likelihood of Violent Behaviour: Predictions, Postdictions, and Hindsight Bias." *Canadian Journal of Behavioural Science* 27:92–106.

Dawes, R. M., D. Faust, and P. E. Meehl. 1989. "Clinical Versus Actuarial Judgment." *Science* 243:1668–74.

Dixen, J., and J. O. Jenkins. 1981. "Incestuous Child Abuse. A Review of Treatment Strategies." *Clinical Psychology Review* 1:211–22.

Frisbie, L. V., and E. H. Dondis. 1965. *Recidivism Among Treated Sex Offenders*. California Mental Health Research Monographs, no. 5. Sacramento: State of California Department of Mental Hygiene.

Furby, L., M. R. Weinrott, and L. Blackshaw. 1989. "Sex Offender Recidivism: A Review." *Psychological Bulletin* 105:3–30.

Gardner, W., C. Lidz, E. P. Mulvey, and E. C. Shaw. 1996. "Clinical Versus Actuarial Predictions of Violence in Patients with Mental Illnesses." *Journal of Consulting and Clinical Psychology* 64:602–9.

Gendreau, P., and D. A. Andrews. 1990. "What the Meta-Analyses of the Offender Treatment Literature Tell Us About 'What Works.'" *Canadian Journal of Criminology* 32:173–84.

Gottfredson, G. D. 1984. "A Theory-Ridden Approach to Program Evaluation: A Method for Stimulating Research-Implementer Collaboration." *American Psychologist* 39:1101–12.

Griffiths, D. M., V. L. Quinsey, and D. Hingsburger. 1989. *Changing Inappropriate Sexual Behavior: A Community-Based Approach for Persons with Developmental Disabilities*. Toronto: Brookes.

Hanson, R. K., and M. T. Brussière. 1996. "Sex Offender Risk Predictors: A Summary of Research Results." *Forum on Corrections Research* 8:10–12.

Hanson, R. K., R. A. Steffy, and R. Gauthier. 1993. "Long-Term Recidivism of Child Molesters." *Journal of Consulting and Clinical Psychology* 61:646–52.

Hare, R. D. 1991. *Manual for the Revised Psychopathy Checklist*. Toronto: Multi-Health Systems.

Hare, R. D., and L. M. McPherson. 1984. "Violent and Aggressive Behavior by Criminal Psychopaths." *International Journal of Law and Psychiatry* 7:35–50.

Harris, G. T., M. E. Rice, and C. A. Cormier. 1991. "Psychopathy and Violent Recidivism." *Law and Human Behavior* 15:625–32.

Harris, G. T., M. E. Rice, and V. L. Quinsey. 1993. "Violent Recidivism of Mentally Disordered Offenders: The Development of a Statistical Prediction Instrument." *Criminal Justice and Behavior* 20:315–35.

Hart, S. D., P. R. Kropp, and R. D. Hare. 1988. "Performance of Male Psychopaths Following Conditional Release from Prison." *Journal of Consulting and Clinical Psychology* 56: 227–32.

Hucker, S., R. Langevin, and J. Bain. 1988. "A Double Blind Trial of Sex Drive Reducing Medication in Pedophiles." *Annals of Sex Research* 1:227–42.

Kelly, R. J. 1982. "Behavioral Reorientation of Pedophiliacs: Can It Be Done?" *Clinical Psychology Review* 2:387–408.

Knight, R. A., and R. A. Prentky. 1990. "Classifying Sexual Offenders: The Development and Corroboration of Taxonomic Models." In *The Handbook of Sexual Assault: Issues, Theories, and Treatment of the Offender*, edited by W. L. Marshall, D. R. Laws, and H. E. Barbaree. New York: Plenum Press.

Knopp, F. H. 1984. *Retraining Adult Sex Offenders: Methods and Models*. Syracuse, N.Y.: Safer Society Press.

Langevin, R. 1983. *Sexual Strands: Understanding and Treating Sexual Anomalies in Men*. Hillsdale, N.J.: Lawrence Erlbaum.

Langevin, R., D. Paitich, S. Hucker, S. Newman, G. Ramsey, S. Pope, G. Geller, and C. Anderson. 1979. "The Effectiveness of Assertiveness Training, Provera and Sex of Therapist in Treatment of Genital Exhibitionism." *Journal of Behavior Therapy and Experimental Psychiatry* 10:275–82.

Langevin, R., P. Wright, and L. Handy. 1988. "What Treatment Do Sex Offenders Want?" *Annals of Sex Research* 1:363–85.

Laws, D. R., ed. 1989. *Relapse Prevention with Sex Offenders*. New York: Guilford Press.

Lipsey, M. W. 1992. "Juvenile Delinquency Treatment: A Meta-Analysis Inquiry into the Variability of Effects." In *Meta-Analysis for Explanation: A Casebook,* edited by H. Cooper, B. S. Cordray, H. Hartmann, L. V. Hedges, R. J. Light, T. A. Louis, and F. Mosteller. New York: Russell Sage Foundation.

Marques, J. K., D. M. Day, C. Nelson, and M. A. West. 1994. "Effects of Cognitive-Behavioral Treatment on Sex Offender Recidivism: Preliminary Results of a Longitudinal Study." *Criminal Justice and Behavior* 21:28–54.

Marshall, W. L., and H. E. Barbaree. 1990. "Outcome of Comprehensive Cognitive-Behavioral Treatment Programs." In *The Handbook of Sexual Assault: Issues, Theories, and Treatment of the Offender*, edited by W. L. Marshall, D. R. Laws, and H. E. Barbaree. New York: Plenum Press.

Marshall, W. L., C. M. Earls, Z. Segal, and J. Darke. 1983. "A Behavioral Program for the Assessment and Treatment of Sexual Aggressors." In *Advances in Clinical Behavior Therapy*, edited by K. D. Craig and R. J. McMahon. New York: Brunner-Mazel.

McGraw, K. O., and S. P. Wong. 1992. "A Common Language Effect Size Statistic." *Psychological Bulletin* 111:361–65.

Motiuk, L. L., and F. J. Porporino. 1989. *Offender Risk/Needs Assessment: A Study of Conditional Releases*. Ottawa: Solicitor General Canada.

Nuffield, J. 1982. *Parole Decision-Making in Canada: Research Towards Decision Guidelines*. Ottawa: Supply and Services Canada.

Pithers, W. D. 1990. "Relapse Prevention with Sexual Aggressors: A Method for Maintaining Therapeutic Gain and Enhancing External Supervision." In *Handbook of Sexual Assault: Issues, Theories, and Treatment of the*

Offender, edited by W. L. Marshall, D. R. Laws, and H. E. Barbaree. New York: Plenum.

Pithers, W. D., K. M. Kashima, G. F. Cumming, L. S. Beal, and M.M. Buell. 1988. "Relapse Prevention of Sexual Aggression." In *Human Sexual Aggression: Current Perspectives,* edited by R. A. Prentky and V. L. Quinsey. New York: Academy of Sciences.

Quinsey, V. L. 1973. "Methodological Issues in Evaluating the Effectiveness of Aversion Therapies for Institutionalized Child Molesters." *Canadian Psychologist* 14:350–61.

———. 1977. "The Assessment and Treatment of Child Molesters: A Review." *Canadian Psychological Review* 18:204–20.

———. 1980. "The Baserate Problem and the Prediction of Dangerousness: A Reappraisal." *Journal of Psychiatry and Law* 8:329–40.

———. 1984. "Sexual Aggression: Studies of Offenders Against Women." In *Law and Mental Health: International Perspectives,* edited by D. Weisstub. New York: Pergamon.

———. 1986. "Men Who Have Sex with Children." In *Law and Mental Health: International Perspectives,* edited by D. Weisstub. New York: Pergamon.

Quinsey, V. L., and R. Ambtman. 1979. "Variables Effecting Psychiatrists' and Teachers' Assessments of the Dangerousness of Mentally Ill Offenders." *Journal of Consulting and Clinical Psychology* 47:353–62.

Quinsey, V. L., and T. C. Chaplin. 1988. "Preventing Faking in the Phallometric Assessments of Sexual Preference." In *Human Sexual Aggression: Current Perspectives,* vol. 528, edited by R. A. Prentky and V. L. Quinsey. New York: New York Academy of Sciences.

Quinsey, V. L., T. C. Chaplin, A. M. Maguire, and D. Upfold. 1987. "The Behavioral Treatment of Rapists and Child Molesters." In *Behavioral Approaches to Crime and Delinquency: Application, Research, and Theory,* edited by E. K. Morris and C. J. Braukmann. New York: Plenum.

Quinsey, V. L., G. Coleman, B. Jones, and I. Altrows. 1997. "Proximal Antecedents of Absconding and Reoffending Among Supervised Mentally Disordered Offenders." *Journal of Interpersonal Violence* 12:794–813.

Quinsey, V. L., and C. M. Earls. 1990. "The Modification of Sexual Preferences." In *The Handbook of Sexual Assault: Issues, Theories, and Treatment of the Offender,* edited by W. L. Marshall, D. R. Laws, and H. E. Barbaree. New York: Plenum, Press.

Quinsey, V. L., A. Khanna, and B. Malcolm. *A Retrospective Evaluation of the Regional Treatment Centre Sex Offender Treatment Program.* Forthcoming.

Quinsey, V. L., and M. Lalumiere. 1995. *The Assessment of Sexual Offenders Against Children.* Newbury Park, Calif.: Sage.

Quinsey, V. L., and D. R. Laws. 1990. "Validity of Physiological Measures of Pedophilic Sexual Arousal in a Sexual Offender Population: A Critique of Hall, Proctor, and Nelson." *Journal of Consulting and Clinical Psychology* 58:886–88.

Quinsey, V. L., and A. M. Maguire. 1986. "Maximum Security Psychiatric Patients: Actuarial and Clinical Prediction of Dangerousness." *Journal of Interpersonal Violence* 1:143–71.

Quinsey, V. L., and W. L. Marshall. 1983. "Procedures for Reducing Inappropriate Sexual Arousal: An Evaluation Review." In *The Sexual Aggressor: Current Perspectives on Treatment*, edited by J. G. Greer and I. R. Stuart. New York: Van Nostrand Reinhold.

Quinsey, V. L., M. E. Rice, and G. T. Harris. 1995. "Actuarial Prediction of Sexual Recidivism." *Journal of Interpersonal Violence* 10:85–105.

Quinsey, V. L., M. E. Rice, G. T. Harris, and M. L. Lalumiere. 1993. "Assessing Treatment Efficacy in Outcome Studies of Sex Offenders." *Journal of Interpersonal Violence* 8:512–23.

Quinsey, V. L., and W. D. Walker. 1992. "Dealing with Dangerousness: Community Risk Management Strategies with Violent Offenders." In *Aggression and Violence Throughout the Lifespan*, edited by R. Peters, K. D. Craig, and V. L. Quinsey. Newbury Park, Calif.: Sage.

Rice, M. E., and G. T. Harris. 1995. "Violent Recidivism: Assessing Predictive Validity." *Journal of Consulting and Clinical Psychology* 63:737–48.

———. 1997. "Cross-Validation and Extension of the Violence Risk Appraisal Guide for Child Molesters and Rapists." *Law and Human Behavior* 21:231–41.

Rice, M. E., G. T. Harris, and C. A. Cormier. 1992. "An Evaluation of a Maximum Security Therapeutic Community for Psychopaths and Other Mentally Disordered Offenders." *Law and Human Behavior* 16:399–412.

Rice, M. E., V. L. Quinsey, and G. T. Harris. 1991. "Sexual Recidivism Among Child Molesters Released from a Maximum Security Psychiatric Institution." *Journal of Consulting and Clinical Psychology* 59:381–86.

Villeneuve, D., and V. L. Quinsey. 1995. "Predictors of General and Violent Recidivism Among Mentally Disordered Prison Inmates." *Criminal Justice and Behavior* 22:397–410.

Webster, C. D., G. T. Harris, M. E. Rice, C. Cormier, and V. L. Quinsey. 1994. *The Violence Prediction Scheme: Assessing Dangerousness in High-Risk Men.* Toronto: University of Toronto, Centre of Criminology.

Wormith, J. S. 1984. "Attitude and Behavior Change of Correctional Clientele: A Three-Year Follow-Up." *Criminology* 22:595–618.

Zamble, E., and F. J. Porporino. 1988. *Coping, Behavior, and Adaptation in Prison Inmates.* New York: Springer-Verlag.

Zamble, E., and V. L. Quinsey. 1997. *The Criminal Recidivism Process.* Cambridge: Cambridge University Press.

Part V

PRECONVICTION PROCESSES AND INSTITUTIONS

16

American Policing

LAWRENCE W. SHERMAN

American policing is a volatile institution. Late-twentieth-century police have generally enjoyed great respect and public trust, yet their conduct has repeatedly ignited explosions of public outrage. Praised for reducing crime and arresting notorious criminals, police have been vilified for their lapses into brutality and corruption. Lavishly supported by more tax dollars than any other agents of criminal justice, they have also had their budgets cut—with thousands of police laid off. Few other institutions, including education and medicine, have received such intense scrutiny, praise, and criticism. No other institution of justice has changed so much in the past half century. None seems more likely to change in the next.

This chapter examines the changing nature of American policing: where policing in America is going, where it is coming from, and why. It considers the big ideas that have shaped police practices since World War II, as well as the dialectic of contradictory public expectations. It examines the major concepts needed to understand the police institution, and to comprehend the divisions within both the police and the public on major issues. It links the development of policing to the evolution of metropolitan areas, social organization, and technology, including the growing influence of social science research. Finally, it forecasts the development of a new vision for policing just appearing on the horizon, victim-centered restorative justice, one that will create new tensions and conflicts in an institution well accustomed to contradictions.

A case study of a management revolution in the New York City Police Department (NYPD) in the past decade introduces the three big ideas in modern police practice: professionalism, community orientation, and results. These popular terms merely skim the surface of a much deeper structure of the police institution, which encompasses four key concepts—legitimacy, information, internal strategy, and external strategy. These concepts help to describe policing as a three-legged stool, in which legitimacy rests on and requires full support from information, internal strategy, and external strategy. The prevailing dialectic of the twentieth century has pitted internal strategy for controlling the police against external strategy for controlling crime, for a battle of procedural versus preventive justice.

Case Study: The NYPD, 7:00 A.M.

On a Friday morning in June 1995, over 100 police officials gather in the cavernous, high-ceiling command and control center of the NYPD. Their 7:00 A.M. meeting is part of a year-old revolution in police management: regularly holding police commanders publicly accountable, in the presence of their peers, for their efforts to reduce crime. Within the next two years, similar management practices will be adopted in Baltimore, New Orleans, Indianapolis, and other large police agencies.

What makes the practice revolutionary is the clear focus on the *results* of police work, and not just its activities. Remarkably, police management has traditionally focused on almost everything but results, from police car leasing to labor union contracts to complaints against police. With a few exceptions such as the Washington, D.C., police in the early 1970s, police managers in the twentieth century were never evaluated on the basis of crime in their communities. Regardless of what policing strategies this revolution produces, the New York–led change in police management is radical surgery. Within eighteen months of its introduction, almost all of the seventy-six precinct commanders in New York will be transferred, demoted, or fired.

Most cities cannot use such big sticks against police commanders. Nor can most cities reward them by promotion to six-figure salaries, as New York can. What they can do is intensify their use of *information* to find more effective crime control strategies without threatening the public perception that police practices are fair and appropriate. A description of a 1995 visit to the NYPD command center for the twice-weekly dawn strategy meetings reveals the most intense use of information in police history.

At the far end of the room is a bank of computers and video projectors, staffed by a group of technicians and the assistant police commissioner for crime statistics. In front of and below them on the main floor is a podium where precinct commanders and their staff will speak to the packed room. On the upper right wall is a banner reading: "We're not just report-takers; we're the police." On the upper left-hand wall is a banner reading:

- Timely, accurate intelligence
- Proactive tactics
- Rapid deployment
- Relentless follow-up

At the back of the room, opposite the podium is the head table, with name cards for the police commissioner, the chief of the department, the first deputy commissioner, and the deputy commissioner for crime control strategy. Other tables flank the room in horseshoe fashion, filled with top patrol and detective managers who supervise the precinct commanders.

At 7:00 A.M. sharp, the chief of the department calls the first precinct commander to the podium. Only four of the seventy-six precinct commands will be discussed that morning. Handouts of several pages for each precinct describe the educational and employment background (with photo) of the precinct commander, with the recent vital statistics of the precinct's numbers of officers, radio calls, reported crimes by offense category, and arrests. As the commander rises to the podium, the video projector beams a computerized pin map showing recent felony crime location patterns in the precinct. The commander begins to discuss a robbery pattern near a subway station in the northern part of the precinct, including its time-of-day and day-of-week concentrations and the descriptions victims gave of the robbers. He then describes a surveillance program the precinct mounted with plainclothes officers who arrested several robbers in the act.

"Did you debrief the robbers on where they got their guns?" shouts out the deputy commissioner for crime control. "Yes, and we got some good leads," the precinct commander replies. The detective supervisor then describes an ongoing attempt to catch a black-market gun dealer operating out of his car near a certain street corner.

"What about your auto thefts?" booms the chief of department. "They are up 30 percent over last year to date. Why?"

The precinct commander turns again to the detective supervisor, who says,"We had a gang of professionals from Jersey hitting us this winter for cars to be shipped overseas in containers. We hit all the local chop shops last year, but these guys had cash orders for certain kinds of cars. So we parked a recent model Mercedes as a decoy and put it under surveillance, making three arrests within two days."

"I see your drug arrests are way up. Are they focused on your disorderly corners or just random?" asks the deputy commissioner for crime control. "We focused on three hot spots," replies the precinct commander. "Each of them had been subjects of repeated community complaints, and had repeated assaults. We had uniformed officers drive up suddenly and check anyone who appeared to be dealing."

More questions, more answers. More maps showing crime patterns, more descriptions of proactive efforts to stop the pattern. More interruptions by top commanders, who periodically ask the technicians to display some citywide graphics. The most impressive is a graph showing narcotics arrests against violent crimes by time of day for the preceding year. Narcotics arrests peaked around 7:00 P.M., then declined to almost nothing as violent crimes rose to a peak around 1:00 A.M. and declined until 4:00 A.M. The top brass say, "We've been making narcotics arrests at the wrong time. Let's get those squads out there later at night when they can do more good." The deputy commissioner for crime control strategy also takes several opportunities to point out the four principles on the wall: "How soon did you spot that pattern? Timely intelligence, principle number one. . . . Did you keep up the pressure on that drug market? Relentless follow-up, principle number four."

The first half hour ends, and the precinct commander is complimented for an excellent performance—in controlling crime, not just talking about it. The next commander takes the podium to face somewhat more critical questioning but overall approval. During the third session, the police commissioner arrives. All rise, and the session is interrupted while he makes some general comments about the overall increase in arrests and extraordinary declines in crime—later hailed in a magazine story entitled "The End of Crime as We Know It." The commissioner compliments top management on their successes to date but then flatly says it's not good enough: crime must be reduced even more. Over the next year, it is.

What happened in New York vividly illustrates the national transition over the period 1955 to 1995 from "professional" policing to "commuity-oriented" policing to "policing for results." In the aftermath of World War II, a generation trained in military bureaucracy imposed far more control on police officers than had ever existed. This increased internal control, widely called the "professional" model, emphasized paperwork and compliance with formal rules. It had different effects in different cities. In western cities dominated by the automobile, the professional idea fostered frequent traffic stops and field interrogations of citizens. In eastern cities with strong traditions of police corruption by gambling and other illicit enterprises, professionalism led to many more constraints on making arrests. A more general effect was frequent transfers of police and support for an impersonal style of interacting with the public—best exemplified by the NYPD's rules against "unnecessary conversation" with members of the public.

After the race riots of the 1960s and again in the 1980s, "community policing" replaced "professionalism" as the big idea. Professionalism was harshly criticized in riot commission reports for its unbending legalism and lack of discretion, its impersonal style and loss of communication with the low-income minority group neighborhoods that had grown to ever larger proportions of the population of our largest cities. Community policing sought to increase the quantity and quality of contacts between police and the public. The specific forms this idea took varied even more than those of professionalism. But the community orientation widely encouraged a "minimalist" approach to law enforcement; minor offenses like drinking on the streets were often overlooked in order to avoid community confrontations, especially in New York, where under-enforcement of the law was a clear policy. By the early 1970s, the average New York patrol officer made about one arrest a year.

By the late 1980s, however, the wisdom of ignoring minor offenses suffered under the onslaught of the crack cocaine epidemic, rising youth homicide, and stray-bullet shootings. At the same time, a third big idea in policing, initially suggested by University of Wisconsin professor

Herman Goldstein in 1979, shifted the focus of police strategy from style to substance, from methods to results. In what was originally called "problem-oriented policing," Goldstein (1979, 1990) suggested that police should pay far more attention to their end product of public safety and less attention to police management as an end in itself. This big idea of policing for results fused with its two predecessors to form the New York approach of 1995, which had elements of all three models: professionally controlled policing of community problems for better results.

Each of these big ideas was adopted in response to volatile public demands on police. Professionalism developed largely in response to scandals over police corruption (Sherman 1978). Community policing developed in response to the growing concentration of poverty in socially isolated inner-city areas, most visibly demonstrated by riots over police brutality. Policing for results was fueled by public concern about a sudden rise in homicide rates among teenagers, who used semiautomatic pistols to make "spray shooting" a new form of homicide in the late 1980s. Each of these specific changes in public expectations followed patterns evident since the founding of police agencies in the mid–nineteenth century. The three big ideas merely rearrange the central elements of those patterns of public expectations and police responses.

Public Expectations

The volatility of policing derives in large part from conflicting public expectations for police conduct. The divided and contradictory nature of these expectations is a "dialectic"—a conflict of opposites through which change takes place, sometimes by resolving the opposites and creating new ones. The dialectic of public expectations for policing is as old as the history of the American police, which is itself a remarkably young institution. A mere fifteen decades ago, American cities first created police agencies amid passionate debates over freedom and public safety, fear of government, and fear of criminals. Creating the agencies intensified those debates, with demands that police do both more and less about certain kinds of crimes and certain kinds of people. These demands have produced many corollary battles over such issues as the recruitment of recent immigrants to serve as police officers, the systems for appointing police chiefs, and the role of public oversight in police discipline. This section reviews those conflicts from the perspective of four key concepts in the structure of policing, outlines the debates in the full sweep of police history, and describes them in greater detail for the past half century.

Four Key Concepts

Four concepts are central to understanding the modern dialectic between public demands to do more and less about crime. *Legitimacy* is the willingness of the public to accept police authority without protest, the public consent to coercion by the agents of all the people. *Information* is the raw material of policing, which police obtain and process in ways that are more or less comprehensive and intrusive in the lives of citizens. *Internal strategy* is the police organization's set of patterns and practices of monitoring and shaping the conduct of police officers, in compliance with organizational rules and law. *External strategy* is the police organization's set of patterns and practices of shaping the conduct of the public, in compliance with community norms and law.

Public support is central to police accomplishing their core mission of preventing crime and achieving justice. Their success in that mission depends heavily on their legitimacy, which German sociologist Max Weber defined as willing public acceptance of the ruler's right to rule (see Gerth and Mills 1946, p. 229). Growing evidence suggests that people generally obey the law not just out of fear of punishment but because they perceive the law and its agents—especially the police—as fair and just (Tyler 1990; Paternoster et al. 1997). Democratic police thus play a crucial role in building a social consensus that we should all obey the law. To the extent that the police themselves symbolize justice and obedience to the law, there may be less crime. To the extent that police symbolize injustice and defiance of the law, the public may imitate the police by breaking the law.

As mentioned earlier, the legitimacy of policing sits on a three-legged stool. Weakness in any of the three legs can threaten police legitimacy and has literally led to some police agencies being abolished. Each of these legs confronts the dilemma of public expectations, the conflict between doing too much and doing too little. One is information: what police know about the conduct of citizens, how police gather the data, and how they process it into information for decision making. The public expects police to gather, store, and process enormous amounts of information. The public is divided over how much and what kinds of information police should collect, and how it should be collected. Introduction of new information technologies, from wiretapping to computers, has generally provoked controversy over privacy rights. So has failure of police to employ these technologies more vigorously in ways that might prevent crime.

Even more controversial is the internal strategy police departments use to monitor and control the conduct of police officers. Among the public, the issue is whether police managers can restrain their colleagues as fairly and objectively as they police the public, given the apparent conflict of interest. Recurrent debates over using civilian agencies to police the police are a prime example. Yet among police managers, the key issue is different: how much information they should seek out at their own initiative, or proactively, versus how much the internal strategy should be reactive to complaints from the public about police misconduct. Installing video cameras to monitor police conduct inside police stations, for example, is a proactive strategy few police agencies had adopted by 1997.

These debates are echoed in the evolution of the external strategy of policing the public, which is the central mission of the organization. Ironically, the effectiveness of organizational practices in fighting crime has historically received low priority from police managers, who pay far more attention to both internal control strategy and information collection. This focus derives in part from successful diversion of public attention from crime prevention to crime retribution. While police were originally created to prevent crime from happening, they quickly found greater success in catching criminals and bringing them to punishment. In the 1970s and 1980s, police leadership was strongly influenced by social scientists who claimed that police cannot control crime but can only respond to crimes once they have happened. Yet by the 1990s, that view was increasingly challenged by the policing-for-results movement, which responded to public demands for more prevention and safer streets. That movement placed the greatest emphasis ever seen on the questions of when, where, and how to deploy police to fight crime.

These three supports for police legitimacy—information, internal strategy, and external strategy—are closely connected. Internal strategy depends on the kinds of information managers have about police officers, as well as on the kinds of work to which police are assigned through external strategy. Computerizing police discipline records has changed internal strategy; so has the growth of undercover (information-gathering and easily corruptible) narcotics units. External strategy also depends on information about where and when crime is concentrated, which was transformed repeatedly in the late twentieth century by information technology. Such innovations as the 911 emergency telephone system transformed public expectations, which further affected external strategies. Police chiefs chose not to adopt certain external crime control strategies, such as field interrogations, because they lacked assurance that their internal controls could limit police tendencies to misconduct. Internal controls also influenced information, ensuring that police properly process crime reports (a major change in the past half century). External strategies shaped discovery of information that citizens try to conceal: knowing who carries guns or drugs, who drives drunk, who abuses their children—these have all depended heavily on whether external control strategies seek out such information.

Public expectations for police require that they gather the right kind of information, keep the threat of crime under control, and restrict misconduct by their officers. The details of how they meet these expectations are the subject of divisions among the public and within the police, and form the outline of police history. They are amply illustrated by the case study of the 1990s police management revolution in New York.

Information. Information is clearly the raw material of the New York management strategy, the resource that makes the 7:00 A.M. discussions possible. One reason police commanders had never before been held accountable for recent crime trends is that no one ever knew what they were—at least not on a timely basis. The crime analyses discussed in the strategy meeting included data from the preceding week and month. Until a major investment in computers in late 1994, the NYPD had always waited months for such analyses, by which time the information could be long out of date. Similarly, in Indianapolis and Prince George's County, Maryland, in mid-1995, nine-month lags for computerized crime data plagued efforts to attack crime. Both of these agencies followed New York's example, cutting that lag to one week within the following year.

Another reason commanders had not been held accountable for crime was that patterns could not be easily visualized in space and time. Advances in computer software allowed rapid production of crime pattern maps, both by the precinct commanders and by the top commanders at headquarters. This information revolution fed the management revolution, allowing top mangers literally to second-guess the precinct commanders on the crime patterns they faced and what should be done about those patterns. Top commanders studying these data the night before the strategy meeting were well prepared to point out gaps in the precinct's strategic plan.

Information about police results was the most limited area of the new approach. Aside from the dramatic citywide drop in crime, the strategy session used no conventional evaluation tools to measure cause and effect. Year-to-date data and prior year-to-date data were analyzed like a corporation's sales figures. No attempt to experiment systematically with different strategies in precincts with similar crime problems was discussed, and no systematic conclusions were drawn about use of different tactics against similar kinds of crime. The cost-effectiveness of investments in police staff hours was not even raised. The implicit premise of the discussion was that policing is an art, not a science, and that crime control objectives can be achieved much like an investigation can lead to an arrest. But much as medicine is an art supported by scientific knowledge, the art of policing in that room could have been enhanced by more scientific testing of hypotheses about police tactics.

Two years later, the NYPD performed such tests on the rival explanations for the citywide drop in crime. Skeptics had suggested that homicides had dropped over 50 percent because of declining numbers of young males, increased incarceration of violent criminals, or reduced drug use. The NYPD's staff analysis of data on these factors over the preceding decade showed that none of them was related to the drop in crime. What remained unexplained was why homicides had dropped in other large cities, like Los Angeles, which had failed to adopt the same changes in strategy as New York. What remained unknown even to the NYPD was the independent effect of each of the many strategies the department had adopted. This information gap became an important part of the misreading of the New York experience by other police agencies.

External Strategy. The information and accountability revolution in New York was widely misrepresented in news media internationally as a "zero-tolerance" full enforcement model. Police as far away as Australia concluded that what worked in New York was arresting everyone observed breaking every law in every place at every time. What they did not know was the highly selective focus of the NYPD enforcement efforts on high-crime places, times, and people. Crime analyses of the estimated 3 percent of addresses that produce over 50 percent of crimes (Sherman, Garten, and Buerger 1989) had a strong influence on the proactive targeting of police resources. Police were directed to specific locations with specific tasks to undertake and were not sent out to roam the streets at random with a general mandate to arrest.

Moreover, a criminological theory underlay the police strategy: Clarke's (1992) concept of crime "facilitators." A large portion of homicides in New York were committed with guns carried illegally in public places, as well as by people who had been drinking. Targeted enforcement of all laws in violent hot spots reduced both gun carrying and intoxication in those places. Removal of these two facilitators is a plausible strategy for reducing homicide in New York City. Doing the same in London or Sydney, however, may have little effect, since few crimes in those cities are committed with guns. The NYPD strategy was arguably appropriate to the crime problems of that city at that time, which may or may not be similar to those in many other U.S. cities—none of which feature the extreme density, size, or pedestrian mobility of New York's population.

The strategic risk the NYPD took was a radical change from a low-arrest to a high-arrest policy for public order offenses such as noise, public urination, jaywalking, and marijuana smoking. From 1993 to 1996, annual misdemeanor arrests rose from 133,000 to 205,000. The previous three decades had seen numerous policies discouraging such arrests, with advance supervisory approval required for gambling arrests (to prevent corruption) and overtime limitations against booking prisoners in a process that could tie up police officers for many hours. In the early 1990s, increased use of videoconferencing with prosecutors drastically reduced the amount of police time required to process an arrest, increasing the potential number of arrests each officer could make. Putting that newly unleashed potential to work, however, would cause a shock to police legitimacy—the public acceptance of police practices as fair and reasonable—that could only be buffered by dramatic success in reducing crime. Once police began locking up middle-class grandmothers for three days for failing to pay a subway fare, the potential for public outrage skyrocketed. But the risk paid off in historic reductions in violent crime, at least in the short run. The question was whether internal strategy for controlling misconduct could keep up with the external strategy for controlling crime.

Internal Strategy.   As the number of arrests in New York rose from 1993 to 1997, so did the number of complaints of police misconduct. The ratio of complaints to arrests remained virtually unchanged, and even declined among misdemeanor arrests where complaints are generally most common. Yet the public perception that police abuses were increasing was strong in many minority communities. By early 1997, another visit to an NYPD strategy session found new watchwords on the walls. Supplementing the four principles of police effectiveness were three symbols of police legitimacy: "CPR means courtesy, professionalism, and respect."

These symbols were backed by a number of supervisory mechanisms. Commanders were grilled by top supervisors not only about robberies of corner grocery stores but also about their recent trends in complaints against police. At that time, there were probably no other police agencies in the United States in which precinct commanders even knew the numbers of complaints filed against their officers in the last month, let alone agencies where commanders had to answer questions about such data. From the standpoint of top management, internal control strategy had taken an almost equal place with external strategy and information, filling out the three-legged stool intended to support public acceptance of the police as legitimate and worthy of public support.

Legitimacy.   But the success of the external strategy may have been too great, creating an imbalance among the stool's three legs. By August 1997, an outrageous incident of police torture threatened the legitimacy of the entire department, feeding a national debate about "zero-tolerance" policing. Whether the NYPD could have been any less vulnerable to the harm done by this incident if it had not publicly claimed so much success in reducing crime is unclear. Perhaps the rapid increase in the odds of New Yorkers being arrested provided too large a target for criticism of police procedures, regardless of what the mayor or police officials claimed about its crime control benefits. But the incident was a prime example of the entire century's dialectic between internal and external strategy, policing for proper procedures versus policing for prevention of crime. The possibility that both goals might be achieved at the same time was rarely mentioned in the ensuing controversy.

Yet the torture incident had no direct causal connection to "policing for results." The incident did not arise from a proactive police attack on a drug market or on a hot spot of gun crime. The incident began reactively with a call for police assistance to break up a fight between two women outside a nightclub. The man who was later tortured simply objected to the manners police used when they arrived at the scene. The officers objected to the man's manners, and one challenged the man to a fistfight by taking off his police gun belt. The incident could just as easily have occurred under the "professional" or "community-oriented" models of police practice. Such eternal contests of manhood among young men help make policing the volatile institution that it is. It is the volatility that has fed the "big ideas" for reinventing the police, more than the other way around. And for all the protest marches over the incident in August, the mayor whose name was allegedly invoked by the accused officer during the torture incident was reelected that November by a very large margin.

Seen in the context of history, the 1990s New York case study appears somewhat less significant. Its dialectic echoes much greater battles over the direction and focus of policing in urban America, as illustrated by some major historical benchmarks in things modern Americans take for granted.

Historical Benchmarks

The initial public expectation for modern police was an extraordinary idea, at least in its time: that police services should be performed free of charge. Prior to the creation of the New York City Police Department in 1845, policing was primarily a fee-for-service business. If your neighbor burglarized your house and you wanted him prosecuted, you would have to pay a fee to the constable to arrest him and to the court to charge him. Charitable organizations supported "public prosecution," or prosecution on behalf of the public. But like the medicine and education of the time, the services were only minimally supported by tax dollars.

Once policing became "socialized" as a "free" public service, police faced a constant struggle for legitimacy. Opponents of the new police system argued against police "spying" by collecting information about the public (Miller 1977). Opponents of the ruling political parties attacked the internal control strategy of having each police officer appointed by the local elected legislator; police were frequently accused of interfering in elections to support the incumbents and keep their jobs (Richardson 1970). Others attacked the police external strategy of making arrests for public order offenses like drunkenness rather than for serious felonies like robbery (Levett 1975)—a debate that has recurred in cycles to the present day.

Police Uniforms.   As police organizations spread to every major city by the end of the nineteenth century, public expectations produced key benchmarks that we also take for granted. Perhaps the most profound— and the most resisted by police themselves—was requiring police to wear uniforms. That innovation was intended to deter both crime and police shirking their duties, both by means of more visible identification of police presence. Yet New York police resisted furiously, and many quit rather than wear "servant's livery."

Police Weapons.   Another innovation resisted by the police was the carrying of firearms. Some of the first constables to take guns on patrol were challenged by their superiors, who called them too cowardly to fight with their fists. The *New York Times* also attacked the first incident of a police officer shooting a criminal, despite a recent incident in which a criminal had fatally shot a policeman. Guns were not required or issued to most big-city police officers until the 1890s.

Police Literacy. Literacy was still another tool resisted by police. Police were not expected to know how to read and write until after World War I. Training was uncommon until the early twentieth century. By that time the automobile had begun to reshape American life, as well as police relations with the middle classes. Traffic enforcement created the first, quite awkward, confrontations between police and large numbers of "respectable" people whose literacy exceeded that of the police.

Radio Cars. One tool police never resisted was police cars dispatched by radio to distant places in response to telephone calls. This technology put an end to foot patrol and created the modern "dial-a-cop" system. The dispersion of police around the low-density city made patrols difficult to supervise and crime difficult to deter. These problems of internal and external control strategy dominated policing for the rest of the twentieth century.

Doing More About Crime

Public demands for police to do more about crime and public conduct have advanced and receded like ocean tides. These demands generally reflect conflict within a community, or "culture wars" over lifestyles or ethnicity. President Theodore Roosevelt, for example, lost a battle to get police to enforce state laws against serving alcohol on Sundays. German immigrants resisted more than Anglo natives insisted. This battle was repeated before, during, and after the total national prohibition of alcohol sales in 1919–1933.

Drunk Driving. Police did little to enforce drunk driving laws until the early 1980s. National interest groups like Mothers Against Drunk Driving (MADD) placed police under enormous pressure to shift from reactive tactics (like accident investigation) to proactive tactics (like roadblock breath tests). From 1974 to 1983, the number of drunk driving arrests rose from 670,000 to almost 1 million, a 50 percent increase (Federal Bureau of Investigation 1994, p. 174). By 1996, about one out of ten arrests in the United States was for drunk driving.

Domestic Violence. Domestic violence was another offense that police widely underenforced until the 1980s. While arrests are hard to measure, since they lack a legal category separate from misdemeanor assaults in general, the latter skyrocketed 260 percent, from around 500,000 in 1983 (Federal Bureau of Investigation 1984, p. 170) to over 1.3 million in 1996

(Federal Bureau of Investigation 1997, p. 214). This increase was the apparent result of intense local lobbying from interest groups even more successful than MADD. These groups focused as much on state legislatures as on police chiefs, winning a wide array of near-permanent legal changes. These new laws first empowered, then required, police to make far more arrests for domestic assault than they ever had before. Perhaps in subtle retaliation against the interest groups, police in more recent years recorded the greatest proportional increase in arrests of women. From 1987 to 1996, there was a 118 percent increase in arrests of women for assault, compared with only a 53 percent increase for males (Federal Bureau of Investigation 1997, p. 219).

Corruption. Police preferences for doing less than major interest groups demand extend to most areas of enforcement. At one extreme, police resist enforcement for reasons of financial gain. Waves of scandal over police bribe taking have periodically rocked most major cities in the twentieth century. Some of these cities have apparently eliminated organized corruption. Others have not. When the issue was enforcement of gambling and liquor laws, the public constituency for police doing more was relatively narrow. That constituency was broadened substantially after the 1970s when some police were revealed to be drug dealers themselves.

Drug Enforcement. The broadened constituency for more policing reflected the rising moral panic over inner-city drug abuse. After the invention of "crack" vastly increased cocaine use, drug arrests nationally more than doubled, from 661,000 in 1983 (Federal Bureau of Investigation 1984, p. 170) to 1,361,000 in 1989 (Federal Bureau of Investigation 1990, p. 172), mostly among young black males. Even then, police were often criticized for not doing more to control publicly visible drug market activity.

Riots. Perhaps the strongest criticism of police for not doing more has been voiced over police response to riots. From the whites-attacking-blacks race riots of the first half of the twentieth century to the blacks-attacking-whites riots of the 1980s and 1990s, police riot control has been called "too little, too late." One public reaction to the race riots of the late 1960s was a substantial increase in police personnel. That was followed by thousands of police being laid off when the economies of big cities collapsed in the mid-1970s, by which time the threat of riots had become (for the moment) a dim memory. But after the Miami riot of 1980, local taxpayers there demanded that police go on a binge of rapid hiring. The net result was that over 10 percent of the police force was criminally indicted within several years. This was a clear trade-off of internal and external control strategy, sacrificing the former for the appearance of the latter.

Doing Less About Crime

Even while some interest groups have demanded that police do more, others demanded less. Police brutality has been the leading underpinning for such demands, often merged with police discourtesy as the most frequent complaint against police. Other issues include police shootings of citizens, high-speed chases, field interrogations, and spying on political groups.

Brutality. For much of the twentieth century, what is now called police brutality was a standard practice in police work. "Third-degree" beatings of suspects accused of serious crimes were commonly used to obtain confessions, which were often admitted as evidence in court. The practice was attacked by such blue-ribbon panels as President Hoover's crime commission, the National Commission on Law Enforcement and Observance (Hopkins 1931), but local police use of such evidence was not ruled unconstitutional by the U.S. Supreme Court until 1936 (*Brown v. Mississippi*, 207 U.S. 278 [1936]). Further restrictions on police coercion of confessions in the 1960s prompted a legitimacy crisis for the Supreme Court itself, including a widely used bumper sticker saying "impeach Earl Warren," who was then the chief justice. The law-and-order politics of "handcuffing the police" at a time of rising crime rates helped to elect President Richard M. Nixon in 1968, and to support police executives like Philadelphia's Frank Rizzo who openly advocated police brutality (Skolnick and Fyfe 1993).

Far more widespread than coerced confessions was summary justice. Rather than bother taking offenders to court, many police dispensed corporal punishment at the point of apprehension. Juvenile shoplifters once got a whack on the rear end before they were returned to their parents, probably for further corporal punishment—but no criminal record. Adults known to the police as repeat offenders, or "goons," were often snatched off the streets by police "goon squads" of four to five officers in a police car. The squads dragged goons into alleys, beat them, took their guns away, and told them to leave town.

Both civil liberties and civil rights groups long opposed these practices in every possible forum: the press, the courts, and the polls. The issue of police brutality was transformed in the 1960s through the claim of race discrimination. This made civil rights groups ultimately the most effective critics of the practices, even though brutality had been used widely against whites as well. White flight to the suburbs and the pattern of predominantly black cities being policed by white officers fed a broad demand for less brutality. By the early 1970s, black mayors and police chiefs began to take over urban police forces, gaining some power to restrain police practices. Lawsuits against police agencies in the 1980s put further pressure on police for less use of force, thanks to yet another Supreme Court decision (*Monell v. Department of Social Services of the*

City of New York, 436 U.S. 658 [1978]). This decision made local police vulnerable to lawsuits in federal court, where multi-million-dollar verdicts against big-city police became common.

By most accounts, there is far less police brutality at the close of the twentieth century than there was for most of it. Yet the ownership of personal video cameras has made proof of continued brutality more graphic. The 1991 beating of Rodney King by the Los Angeles Police Department became a watershed in police history for the sole reason that it was videotaped from afar by an amateur. Rather than George Orwell's *1984* vision of "Big Brother" spying on the public, the century ends with "little brother" spying on the police. These cameras periodically reveal police beatings of suspects who are in handcuffs and under control.

Homicides by Police.   The clearest decline in police use of force has been in police killings of citizens. While most homicides by police have been ruled "justifiable," there was a fifty-year battle over the right to shoot fleeing unarmed felony suspects who had used no deadly force themselves. The major interest group demanding that police do less was a scholarly elite of lawyers, judges, and law professors who formed the American Law Institute, a law reform organization that formulated a Model Penal Code, which it recommended that state legislatures adopt. Many did. The code included a severe restriction on police powers to kill fleeing suspects. But even in 1985, about half the states still allowed police to kill suspects fleeing arrests for crimes that were routinely punished with minimal prison terms, such as burglary.

Police shootings took on a new racial dimension in the 1970s. Repeated protests and riots over police shootings of young black males led many cities to change their shooting policies in the 1970s, which immediately reduced the number of blacks killed in the early 1970s. A National Urban League study estimated that in the 1970s about seven blacks were killed by big-city police for every one white. By the late 1970s, the ratio had dropped to about three blacks for every white (Mendez 1983). Yet the persisting disparity fed the efforts of the Legal Defense Fund of the National Association for the Advancement of Colored People (NAACP) to persuade courts to strike down police powers to shoot unarmed fleeing felons. One of the organization's many lawsuits, *Tennessee v. Garner* (471 U.S. 1 [1985]), reached the Supreme Court in 1985, where the Model Penal Code rule was virtually adopted as the law of the land. Police killings of citizens dropped substantially after *Garner*, even though most big-city police had already changed their policies and had supported the Legal Defense Fund's appeal to the Supreme Court.

High-Speed Chases.   The police may have killed more citizens with their automobiles than with their guns. No reliable national data are available for the number of citizens killed accidentally in the course of high-speed chases, but local estimates are substantial (Alpert and Fridell 1992). Public pressure on police to restrict high-speed chases came from victims of the accidents and their families, who filed increasing numbers of law-suits after 1980. The issue lacked a racial dimension, and hence a broad focused constituency. Nonetheless, many police agencies restricted their policies in the early 1990s, with some prohibiting high-speed chases al-together. These radical restrictions on police powers to catch criminals were given legitimacy by the many deaths resulting from chases on the basis of trivial legal (often traffic) violations. It is hard to justify to many civil juries an accidental killing of an innocent bystander in order to catch suspects wanted solely for running a red light or for failing to stop on police command. With research estimating the risk of death at around 1 percent of all chases (Alpert and Fridell 1992), the risks seemed to many to outweigh the benefits.

Field Interrogations. Far less dangerous, but more racially disparate, is the police practice of field interrogations. Stopping people on the streets to ask for identification is a constitutionally murky and highly debatable practice. The few analyses of police records of such stops suggest that black individuals are far more likely to be stopped than whites. Yet one experiment shows that field interrogations have a deterrent effect on street crime, as many police leaders believe (Boydstun 1975). The trade-off is between using this technique to reduce racial disparity in crime rates versus using it with increases in racial disparity in arrest rates. Cities have resolved this dilemma differently, with northeastern cities like New York using far fewer field interrogations than western cities like Los Angeles. And quite apart from any explicit directives from police ex-ecutives, police officers have often responded to public criticism simply by doing less. After a white Baltimore police officer was suspended for fatally shooting a young black male during a field interrogation in 1996, for example, the number of arrests for carrying concealed weapons dropped by half citywide for three months (Sherman and Koper 1997).

The issue of field interrogations is more qualitative than quantitative. Rather than demanding fewer of them, civil rights and community groups want them to be less oppressive. Polite and friendly discourse between police and citizens is usually called "community policing" rather than "field interrogation," which evokes an image of hostility and coercion. James Baldwin's portrait of the police as an "occupying army" describes the problem police face in gaining legitimacy for use of the technique (1962, pp. 65–67).

Spying on Political Groups. From the earliest days of police agencies in England and the United States, libertarians have feared police spying for political purposes (Miller 1977). While some civilian groups encouraged spying as a means of thwarting political violence, they were limited to a small group of the very rich. Not until the Bolshevik revolution in Russia at the end of World War I did a mass constituency support police spying.

The explosion of a bomb on the doorstep of U.S. Attorney General A. Mitchell Palmer in 1919 led to police raids of labor and socialist groups nationwide, some of which had ideas no more radical than what later became social security. For the next fifty years, big-city police maintained various forms of "red squads" designed to track any group with radical ideas, with all such groups thought to be potentially violent.

The support for red squads waxed and waned with the level of threat from the cold war, Puerto Rican nationalists, and other sources of violence. In a striking example of preventive policing, a New York City undercover operative saved the Statue of Liberty from being bombed by a Puerto Rican nationalist group (Bouza 1976). But as the threat from the Russians declined in the early 1970s, the nation was shocked by the post-Watergate investigation showing how widely federal and local police had committed burglaries, opened and read U.S. mail, planted hidden microphones, and maintained files on both famous and ordinary Americans. Legislative reforms and court orders led to massive destruction of police intelligence files and the abolition of many intelligence units. Local police generally got out of the "radical" business, leaving that controversial area to federal agencies.

Police Responses

Police have responded in several distinct patterns to these pressures to do more or less about crime: resistance and denial, acceptance and change, controlling public image, and controlling police misconduct. Perhaps the least frequent response, although the most intense at century's end, has been controlling crime. Sometimes the response pattern is appropriate to the public demands, reaffirming police legitimacy and allowing police to continue operating with substantial autonomy. When the response is far from what the public demands, police legitimacy is threatened and police operations become micromanaged by external organizations, from the press to interest groups. These outcomes depend heavily on the balance of power among diverse public groups and the extent to which police can forge alliances with some interest groups in their battles against others. But as the century closes, there are signs that how police actually perform their job may become their most important political leverage.

Police responses to public pressure have been led by two key sources of police leadership: executives and union officials. Until recently, the police chiefs (or commissioners, as they are called in some cities) identified strongly with the interests of the rank and file, and have almost always been career officers in the same police agency that they led. Only in the 1980s did national recruitment of chiefs become common, and it remains the exception rather than the rule. These leaders were expected by both police and public to "represent" the police, in every sense. If chiefs lost the support of their "troops," they were usually thought to be incompetent. Keeping rank-and-file support was most easily done by opposing changes in police practices and criticisms of them. Yet as the century draws to a close, few chiefs can afford to represent only the police in its relations with the community; they also are obliged to represent the "community" to the police.

As chiefs became less loyal to police rank-and-file interests in the early 1970s, police unions sprang up like wildfire. Elected presidents of these unions had no doubt about who they served. Police leadership thus became a struggle between union leaders and chiefs, with the latter walking a tightrope between the mayor and voters on one side, and the union president and police officers on the other. As Minneapolis police chief (1980–1989) Anthony Bouza put it, "[A]ny chief who is loved by the officers is not doing the job right" (Bouza 1988). That thought was inconceivable at midcentury but was almost an orthodoxy by century's end.

Resistance and Denial

In the 1950s and 1960s, public demands for changes in policing were often met by resistance and denial. Allegations of brutality were denied. Demands for more minority-group officers were rebuffed on the grounds of "merit" system testing and screening, which often denied police jobs to candidates whose morals were in question—such as fathers of children born out of wedlock. Proposals to increase police accountability were resisted on the grounds that they were unnecessary and dangerous. Having taken police out of the politics of local party "machines," the public would be ill served by any changes that let outsiders control police discipline—or so police leaders told the public. At worst, the police would be "handcuffed," thereby allowing criminals to roam free.

One classic example of such resistance and denial was the Civilian Complaint Review Board referendum of New York City in 1966. Mayor John Lindsay had been elected by a coalition of Republicans and minority-group Democrats critical of the police. As he promised, he established a review board for complaints of police misconduct; the board included civilians not employed by the NYPD. The police union, a newly emergent force in police politics, turned civilian review into a major public issue. Union television commercials showed women walking home at night being pursued by armed robbers. The threat of mayhem from civilian review was clear. So was the response by the voters who bothered to vote in the union-sponsored referendum, which barred the mayor from creating an external civilian review board.

Yet the police union's victory was short-lived. Within four years, two police officers told the *New York Times* of widespread police corruption, leading to creation of a blue-ribbon commission to investigate police corruption. The Knapp Commission's hearings portrayed a police agency run for the benefit of its officers, seriously threatening its legitimacy (Knapp Commission 1973). Only a record number of police officers murdered in the line of duty (ten in one year) kept the department from even greater loss of respect. In the end, the price of resistance and denial was far stronger internal policing than any American police department had ever experienced, backed by the creation of a state prosecutor's office with nothing to do but police the criminal justice system.

A similar case study occurred in Milwaukee, where reformers earlier in the century had given the police chief tenure for life, just like a supreme court justice. Harold Brier served as chief for twenty years under this system (1964–1984), resisting change and denying any need for it throughout the tumultuous 1960s and 1970s. This resistance was almost for its own sake, unrelated to the content of proposed changes. It extended to such technical innovations as development of use of police computers for communications and record keeping. Chief Brier even refused to accept federal funds for law enforcement improvements, on the grounds that federal funding invited federal control. In the end, the state legislature stripped him of his life tenure, and he resigned. His successors have been far less independent and far more affected by the initiatives of the mayor and city council.

The last decade of the century saw the most spectacular case of resistance and denial. Los Angeles police chief Daryl Gates led the agency for over a decade, denying police wrongdoing in a wide range of incidents. He not only resisted change but did so in racially offensive language. He once implied that black people were not "normal." His strong appeal to voters afraid of crime and his permanent civil service tenure protected him from outrage by minority or civil liberties groups. Yet when Rodney King was filmed being beaten by four Los Angeles police officers, the tide of public sentiment turned. When the acquittal of those officers on state charges of assault led to a devastating riot that police did too little to control, both Gates and the law giving him permanent tenure lost credibility. He was replaced by an African-American police executive from Philadelphia who was appointed on a five-year contract. When the successor failed to create enough change to satisfy police critics, he was replaced by another black chief, this time recruited from within the department.

Acceptance and Change

By the 1980s, the pattern of resistance and denial was increasingly replaced by a pattern of acceptance and change. Chief executives like Robert Wadman in Omaha and Benjamin Ward in New York City readily accepted demands that police do more about crime problems like domestic violence and drunk driving. George Hart in Oakland, California, served for over a decade as a white chief in a majority black city by accepting demands for change, acknowledging mistakes, and constantly promoting restraint by officers. Lee Brown in Houston conceded police had lost touch with the community and undertook extensive efforts to rebuild lines of communication. To be sure, much acceptance of change occurred at the end of a lawsuit. The U.S. Civil Rights Act of 1972 barred sex discrimination in employment, opening the door to women serving on police patrol. The few agencies that resisted female applicants were swiftly ordered by federal judges to obey the law. Recruitment and promotion of African-American officers also moved quickly with President Carter's appointees as federal prosecutors and judges. The 1978 Supreme Court decision making police agencies liable to lawsuits by individuals in federal court fed an explosion of litigation against police. A Bureau of Justice Statistics study reported that 314 lawsuits were filed against the Seattle police, 412 against the Los Angeles police, and 565 against the New York City police in 1987 (Bureau of Justice Statistics 1989).

A more important influence than coerced change, however, may have been a new generation of police executives. After a revolution in police educational opportunities in the 1970s, there were literally hundreds of broadly educated police leaders with ambitions for top leadership posts. Many had been sent to Harvard, Berkeley, or other elite institutions under federal or foundation grants. Others put themselves through law school or doctoral programs in criminology, even while working full-time as police officers or managers. All had acquired social contacts and perspectives extending well beyond the police station house. Virtually all had learned the skills and virtues of compromise and negotiation, rather than intransigence on principles of police independence. And most had adopted a totally new posture toward the press, viewing it as the key to survival.

Controlling Public Image

Perhaps no institution has shaped the modern police as much as the modern news media. When Lincoln Steffens first became a police reporter in New York in the 1890s, the police chief quickly informed him that the police would control the news he reported. In exchange, Steffens was guaranteed a steady diet of graphic crime stories to report (Steffens 1931). Such bargains were hard for police to enforce even then, and they had disappeared long before the 1990s. And in cities where only one newspaper dominates the media market, only the growth of television and radio have saved police from serving at the mercy of the press.

By century's end, police leaders saw the news media as the daily taskmaster, the issuers of report cards that could give police honors or flunk them out. The most important task for survival of the police chief—and the legitimacy of the police agency—was to manage the public image of the department. While this once meant suppressing bad news, such as incidents of police wrongdoing, it gradually came to mean looking as fair and objective as possible. While police leaders once issued comments immediately after sensitive incidents, by the 1990s they increasingly said they would have to await the results of a careful investigation before commenting. While police leaders may have once ignored people injured by police, they increasingly went to hospital bedsides and funerals of criminal suspects.

One consequence of this increased sensitivity to public image was the paradox of crime control. The new generation of police leaders had grown up in an era of steadily rising crime. They had also attended college courses in social science, taught by professors who were ideologically opposed to the hypothesis that threats of criminal sanction deter crime. Even academics who saw evidence supporting that hypothesis, such as James Q. Wilson (1968), were read by police leaders as saying that the police had "almost nothing to do with crime, and everything to do with public service" (Behan 1984). In an era with little apparent hope of reducing crime as a means of success, the new generation of police leaders largely disowned the crime problem. As New York City police commissioner at the time of a surge in homicide rates in the late 1980s, Lee Brown managed the police image by frequent reminders that crime was largely determined by factors outside police control.

This was a radical departure from the intransigent position of police leaders in the 1960s. The ability of police to control crime had been a key argument in the attack on the Supreme Court for restricting police investigative powers. The argument was that if police were denied these powers, crime would increase. Similarly, that same earlier generation of police leaders suggested that the more police officers they were allowed to hire, the less crime there would be. And as crime rates and riots accelerated throughout the 1960s, the argument held fast. Any failure to reduce crime was simply a result of insufficient resources or overly restrictive court decisions.

In the mid-1970s, a new factor in police image management helped undermine the argument that police could not affect crime. Social science research, funded by foundations and the federal government, began to test key hypotheses about the effects of police on crime. The Kansas City Patrol Experiment (Kelling et al. 1974) made front-page news around the country by claiming that large increases or reductions in police patrol had no effect on crime. Although this conclusion was subsequently challenged repeatedly by social scientists (Sherman 1986; Sherman and Weisburd 1995), the finding was a convenient tool for mayors struggling with urban bankruptcy in the mid-1970s. Within a year of publication of the Kansas City report, New York's mayor laid off 5,000 police officers to balance the budget. Detroit and other cities did the same by the end of the decade. Only the financial recovery in the 1980s put an end to the cutbacks. Meanwhile, police researchers reported that detectives did little that helped to solve crimes (Greenwood, Chaiken, and Petersilia 1977), and that rapid responses by police to crime reports did not affect the odds of making arrests or preventing injuries (Spelman and Brown 1984).

Faced with this new form of auditing of police claims about their effects against crime, the new generation of police leadership changed strategy. Moving away from crime control as the key source of legitimacy, they sought to strengthen popular support on a personal basis. "Community policing" became a code word for residents getting to know and like their local police officers. Community policing programs were publicly justified as efforts to improve the flow of information to the police, creating a partnership that would help to fight crime. Yet the primary purpose of this new strategy was to manage police image, and deflect public attention from failures to control police misconduct and public crime. The persistence of these failures undermined the image management goals. By century's end, police leaders had little choice but to do everything possible to enhance both internal and external control strategies.

Controlling Misconduct

Public demands for control of police misconduct have focused largely on whether police or civilians do the controlling. Yet empirical evidence suggests that method matters more than structure. Repeated studies have shown virtually no difference in the outcomes of internal investigations conducted by police and civilian oversight agencies. Yet the few examples of changes in misconduct control from reactive to proactive investigations have shown an enormous difference.

Police have long recognized that certain kinds of crimes require proactive methods of law enforcement. Crimes for which there are no complainants, or for which complainants cannot provide adequate evidence to sustain a criminal conviction, are the principal offenses subjected to police-initiated investigations: spying, undercover informants, eavesdropping, surveillance, videotaping, and inspections. These techniques have been used against offenses ranging from drug abuse to drunk driving, from prostitution to carrying weapons. Only rarely, however, have they been used against internal offenses that share the same characteristics: abuses of police authority. Whereas civil libertarians attack the use of these techniques against the public on moral grounds, they favor their use against the police. Whereas police favor the use of these techniques against the public, they attack their use against the police—also on moral grounds.

The key issue in the twenty-first century is likely to be information. Will police agencies routinely recruit some officers to spy on others, as some agencies did intermittently from the 1970s to the 1990s? Will every police station house be monitored by ongoing video recorders, in order to deter or document police brutality (Emery 1997)? Will every police car have a mounted camera, to document both citizen assaults on police and police assaults on citizens? Will police agencies pay informants for evidence leading to arrest and convictions of police officers? These are the questions that will matter far more than who controls the investigation. The answers are likely to be yes to all these questions, at least in the long run. As police successes in crime control fail to allay public fears of police excesses in use of force, there may be little alternative but to treat police crime like any other crime. New York at century's end provides the best example, showing that success at controlling crime offers no insurance against challenges over controls on police. But to the extent that the police image will depend on controlling police crime, the root source of police legitimacy may become overall control of crime.

Controlling Crime

The police approach to crime control has been transformed by two new sources of information. One already discussed is the availability of nearly instant data on crime patterns. The other is social science evaluation results. Initially acting to falsify many long-held theories of crime control, social science in the 1980s and 1990s became a rich source of knowledge about the complex effects of policing. The focus on results increasingly led back to the question of what works, and even the U.S. Congress asked social scientists to take stock of the available knowledge (Sherman et al. 1997). Rather than denying the effects of police on crime, social science has emerged as the only clear measure of those effects.

Resistance to the use of social science information will persist for many years, just as many medical doctors still resist research that contradicts their own experience or instincts. But the institutional collaborations between universities and police agencies have grown steadily over the last three decades of the century. Police have increasingly agreed to test their own theories in controlled experiments that rival medical research in precision and sophistication. They have also agreed to test new theories and hypotheses brought to them by criminologists.

One of these new theories currently being tested is restorative justice: the hypothesis that making offenders repair the harm they cause will increase police legitimacy and reduce repeat offending. This theory may well transform the police agenda in the twenty-first century. But policing will remain a volatile institution. No amount of social science research or success at crime control seems likely to prevent the continuing dialectic between opposing points of view on policing. What *is* likely to change is the focus of that debate: the two opposing points of argument.

The New Police Dialectic

The main criminal justice dialectic of the twentieth century has been the tension between preventive and procedural justice. If the dialectical view of history is correct, however, the poles of the debate will eventually resolve into a synthesis, with a new polar opposite to that synthesis. There is some evidence that such a transformation is occurring. Such practices as police use of computers and cameras in public places, for example, have lost their Orwellian threat, with a synthesis emerging around using more information for both internal and external police strategy. And at the same time that the opposite poles of law versus order moved closer together, widespread recognition of victims' rights has added a new pole to oppose the old ones. Growing attention to crime victims has fostered the emergence of another big idea in policing, one that could easily refocus the police dialectic. That idea is restorative justice.

Since 1992, some Australian police have experimented with a radical alternative to arrest and prosecution for dealing with confessed offenders, tested on all but the most serious offenses—the kinds routinely punished by probation in big American cities—thefts, assaults, burglary, unarmed robbery. This alternative is *restorative* because it tries to repair the harm caused to victims. It is *preventive* because it mobilizes family and friends to help restrain the offender from ever repeating the offense. It is *reintegrative* because it assumes, rather than denies, the obvious fact that the offender will continue to live in the community for all but the most serious offenses (Braithwaite 1989). The method is called (among other names) a *community justice conference* because it assembles a community of people who were affected by the crime: offenders, victims, offenders' families and friends, and victims' families and friends. Led by a trained police officer, the conference format allows the victim to discuss the harm the offense has caused, allows the offender to discuss his views of the offense, and turns to the entire group to set the terms of an agreement the offender must sign as a condition of not being prosecuted. If possible, the process elicits an apology from the offender to the victim, which is often the victim's main concern.

Case Study: Australian Federal Police, 5:00 P.M.

It is a dark winter's evening in Canberra, the capital city of Australia. Police Constable Geoff Knight ushers a young woman into a small, carpeted conference room in a cinder block police station. He asks the woman, who is a bakery sales clerk, to sit down in one of ten chairs arranged in a circle. He picks up some files and looks them over. He then walks out to the lobby of the station to invite a waiting group of people into the conference room. When they are all seated, he introduces everyone around the circle to the entire group: Miss Smith, the bakery sales clerk; Joe, an eighteen-year-old; David, a seventeen-year-old; Joe's father; Joe's mother; David's mother; David's sister; David's sister's husband; Police Constable Henderson; and Police Constable Knight, the conference facilitator.

The facilitator then says,

> We are here because of what happened with Joe and David last month at the Manuka shopping center. I invited Miss Smith to be here as a community representative to talk about the effect of people fighting like Joe and David did in front of her bakery on the weekends, because it happens far too often. As you know, Joe and David have agreed to attend this diversionary conference instead of being prosecuted in court for their offense, which could result in their acquiring a criminal

record. Joe and David, you have the right to stop this proceeding at any time, and to request a court hearing instead. The purpose of this conference is to discuss what should be done about what happened, and to reach an agreement on how Joe and David should repair the harm they have caused.

Constable Knight then asks Joe and David to describe what happened on the night in question. They both tell how they had gone out that night to a dance club, where they were drinking with friends. They had never met each other before. After leaving the club, David was standing at a bus stop when Joe punched him. It turned out later that Joe had mistaken David for someone else who had insulted him in the dance club. The two had fallen to the ground, fighting for some time before Constable Henderson and several other officers arrived. Henderson separated the fighters and charged them both with misdemeanor assault. David's mother had to come take him home from the police station because he was a juvenile. Joe had simply walked out and gone home.

Constable Knight then asks each of the family members present to describe how they heard about what happened and their feelings about it. Joe's parents say the first they knew about it was the next day when Joe's neck began hurting; a visit to the doctor revealed that his collarbone had been broken in the fight. This meant that Joe would be unable to enter the army as scheduled for basic training. That was very upsetting to his parents. David's sister talks a lot about how David should grow up, or risk throwing his life away.

Constable Knight then asks Miss Smith to describe her feelings about the many fights that happen near the bakery where she works. She describes how fights make her afraid to work there. Fights also upset the customers, who say they are reluctant to come back after they see one. Constable Henderson elaborates on the problems of young men getting drunk and causing trouble at the shops, and how difficult it is for him to break up the fights.

Facilitator Knight then asks the group, one person at a time, to suggest what Joe and David should do to make up for the harm they have caused. David's sister suggests that he go to the Salvation Army to donate $10 every week for a year, the equivalent of the $500 fine he might have paid if he had gone to court and been sentenced. She makes a point of requiring the weekly visits, rather than mailing in the money, in order to keep reminding David of the harm he has caused. Joe agrees to a similar plan with a different charity. The family members agree to accept responsibility for ensuring that the agreement is carried out. Everyone signs the form Sergeant Brown prepares to put the agreement in writing.

Knight then leaves the room to make copies of the agreement. While he is out, Joe and David talk about how friendly they had become in the police van after they realized that mistaken identity had led to the fight. Knight returns with the copies. He reminds Joe and David that if they fail to carry out the terms of the agreement, their cases can still be referred to court for prosecution. He thanks them for coming and bids them good night.

Since July 1, 1995, the Canberra Reintegrative Shaming Experiments have made substantial progress toward providing a very strong scientific test of the theory and practice of restorative community justice conferences. Preliminary analyses of the first 156 cases of juvenile property offenses involving almost 200 offenders compared cases sent at random either to court or to community conferences: conferences last almost six times as long as court adjudication (seventy minutes vs. twelve minutes); conferences involve almost three times as many friends and relatives of the offenders present in the room and participating in the process as court; court cases begin treatment more quickly after arrest than conferences, but court requires more appearances to finalize the outcome; penalties were similar in court and conference cases, with more community service in conference cases.

Victims appear to benefit more from disposition of cases at conferences than from disposition in court. Not one case assigned to court had a victim present at court, whereas victims attended 82 percent of conference cases involving personal victims. Victims almost never receive compensation or an apology from the court process; almost all conferences attended by victims produced an apology, compensation, or both. Conferences make victims less fearful of the offender and crime than does court.

Offenders appear to benefit more from the conferencing approach than from formal prosecution. Offenders feel more ashamed of themselves and their crimes after conferences than court. Conferences make offenders feel more obligation to repay society for their crime. Conferences increase offenders' respect for police and the legal system more than court. Conferences make offenders feel closer to more of their friends and family than court. Conferences give offenders no less fear of formal punishment than court. Conferences give offenders more concern about family reactions if they reoffend. Offenders are more likely to say they will not reoffend after conference than after court.

Whether these results will show that conferences prevent more future crime than court remains to be seen. But what seems clear so far is that victims find the conferences far more restorative, and offenders find them more procedurally just. As long as court prosecution stands for retribution, community conferences will pose a dialectic with restoration. Repairing past harm will stand opposed to inflicting more harm. Treating offenders as a resource for helping victims will stand opposed to ignoring victims entirely. Treating offenders inconsistently on a conference-by-conference basis will stand opposed to the retributive fairness principle of standard sentences. Whatever the results of the method for repeat offending rates, the idea of restorative community policing could reshape policing solely on the basis of its moral principles. In the next century as in the last, conflict between moral tensions will continue to make policing a volatile institution.

References

Alpert, Geoffrey, and Lorie Fridell. 1992. *Police Vehicles and Firearms: Instruments of Deadly Force.* Prospect Heights, Ill.: Waveland.
Behan, Cornelius. 1984. Lecture to the undergraduate course on police administration, University of Maryland Institute of Criminal Justice and Criminology, October 25, 1984.
Bouza, Anthony. 1976. *Police Intelligence.* New York: AMS Press.
———. 1988. Personal communication to author.
Boydstun, John. 1975. *The San Diego Field Interrogation Experiment.* Washington, D.C.: Police Foundation.
Braithwaite, John 1989. *Crime, Shame and Reintegration.* Cambridge: Cambridge University Press.
Bureau of Justice Statistics. 1989. *National Survey of Law Enforcement Agencies, 1987.* Washington, D.C.: U.S. Department of Justice, Bureau of Justice Statistics.
Clarke, Ronald V. 1992. *Situational Crime Prevention.* Guilderland, N.Y.: Harrow and Heston.
Emery, Richard D. 1997. "Four Ways to Clean Up the Police." *New York Times,* August 26, p. A23, Washington edition.
Federal Bureau of Investigations. Various years. *Crime in the United States,* [*various years*]. Washington, D.C.: U.S. Government Printing Office.
Gerth, Hans H., and C. Wright Mills. 1946. *From Max Weber.* New York: Oxford University Press.
Goldstein, Herman. 1979. "Improving Policing: A Problem-Oriented Approach." *Crime and Delinquency* 25:236–58.
———. 1990. *Problem-Oriented Policing.* New York: McGraw-Hill.
Greenwood, Peter, Jan Chaiken, and Joan Petersilia. 1977. *The Criminal Investigation Process.* Lexington, Mass.: Lexington.
Hopkins, Ernest Jerome. 1931. *Our Lawless Police.* New York: Viking.
Kelling, George, Tony Pate, Duane Dieckman, and Charles Brown. 1974. *The Kansas City Preventive Patrol Experiment: Summary Report.* Washington, D.C.: Police Foundation.
Knapp Commission. 1973. *The Knapp Commission Report on Police Corruption.* New York: George Braziller.
Levett, Allan E. 1975. "Centralization of City Police in the Nineteenth Century United States." Ph.D. diss., University of Michigan, Department of Sociology.
Mendez, Gary. 1983. "The Role of Race and Ethnicity in the Incidence of Police Use of Deadly Force." Report to the National Institute of Justice. New York: National Urban League.
Miller, Wilbur. 1977. *Cops and Bobbies.* Chicago: University of Chicago Press.
Paternoster, Ray, Robert Brame, Ronet Bachman, and Lawrence W. Sherman. 1997. "Do Fair Procedures Matter? Procedural Justice in the Milwaukee Domestic Violence Experiment." *Law and Society Review* 31:163–204.

Richardson, James F. 1970. *The New York Police: Colonial Times to 1901.* New York: Oxford University Press.

Sherman, Lawrence. 1978. *Scandal and Reform: Controlling Police Corruption.* Berkeley: University of California Press.

————. 1986. "Policing Communities: What Works?" In *Communities and Crime,* edited by Albert J. Reiss Jr. and Michael Tonry. Chicago: University of Chicago Press.

Sherman, Lawrence W., Patrick R. Gartin, and Michael E. Buerger. 1989. "Hot Spots of Predatory Crime: Routine Activities and the Criminology of Place." *Criminology* 27: 27–55.

Sherman, Lawrence W., Denise Gottfredson, Doris MacKenzie, Peter Reuter, John Eck, and Shawn D. Bushway. 1997. *Preventing Crime: What Works? What Doesn't? What's Promising?* Washington, D.C.: United States Department of Justice.

Sherman, Lawrence W., and Christopher S. Koper. 1997. "Effects of Police Gun Seizures on Criminal Shooting Injuries." Unpublished manuscript. University of Maryland, Department of Criminology and Criminal Justice.

Sherman, Lawrence W., and David Weisburd. 1995. "General Deterrent Effects of Police Patrol in Crime 'Hot Spots': A Randomized, Controlled Trial." *Justice Quarterly* 12:625–48.

Skolnick, Jerome, and James Fyfe. 1993. *Above the Law: Police and the Excessive Use of Force.* New York: Free Press.

Spelman, William, and Dale Brown. 1984. *Calling the Police: Citizen Reporting of Serious Crime.* Washington, D.C.: National Institute of Justice.

Steffens, Lincoln. 1931. *Autobiography.* New York: Harcourt, Brace.

Tyler, Tom R. 1990. *Why People Obey the Law.* New Haven, Conn.: Yale University Press.

Wilson, James Q. 1968. *Varieties of Police Behavior.* Cambridge, Mass.: Harvard University Press.

17

Prosecution

CANDACE McCOY

Threprosecutor is the government's representative and advocate in all phases of criminal adjudication. Except for the daily operations of public police, prosecution is the most powerful component of the criminal justice process because of the number of offenders and victims it affects and because it dominates decision making about the legal course of every case. In the United States, the prosecutor reviews the cases of all defendants arrested by the police, exercises independent investigatory powers, determines the factual and legal sufficiency of each case and whether to dismiss or pursue it, officially files the charges, negotiates the conditions of guilty pleas, and serves as the trial attorney whose client is the state.

Prosecution includes all these tasks, but individual prosecutors may engage in many other activities. It is often said that the prosecutor is both a law enforcement official and an officer of the court, a statement that alludes to the variety of relationships prosecutors maintain with other officials throughout the justice system. In the United States, prosecutors work with the police to develop and evaluate evidence and are expected to advise the police on compliance with constitutional standards. They maintain a friendly rivalry with defense attorneys in assessing the facts in each case and making agreements to revise the charges or to make sentencing recommendations to the judge in return for defendants' guilty pleas. They are expected to demonstrate concern for the plight of victims and witnesses, although in trials their client is the state—loosely, "the public interest"—and not individual victims of crime. Their relationship to judges, although perhaps not widely acknowledged as such, is characterized by rough parity in the degree of influence on the eventual sentence a convicted offender will serve (Jacoby 1980; McDonald 1979). Finally, in the United States at least, prosecutors are almost always elected public officials or are appointed by local elected officials, so they are important players in political life.

The Organization of Prosecution

The prosecution function in the United States is radically decentralized. Each county in each state usually elects a local prosecutor, although two

457

states elect a state attorney general who then appoints local prosecutors. One estimate is that there are approximately "twenty-eight hundred local offices of prosecution within the states" (Holten and Jones 1982, p. 182). Historically, there are two reasons for this decentralization: the American colonists resisted assertions of authority by attorneys general appointed by the English king, and when they designed their own justice systems did not permit authority to be centralized. Moreover, believing in equal access to justice for all citizens, they rejected the English system of private prosecution in which prosecutions were initiated only by victims who had the money to do so. Colonial Americans embraced the concept of *public* prosecution, and with it the idea that a local attorney would be paid from public funds to handle local law enforcement matters (Friedman 1993, pp. 29–30). Although incidents of private prosecutors being paid by victims of crime are discernible throughout American history, the reasons victims or their families would pay a private attorney to prosecute along with the government's attorney are that public prosecutors were notoriously underpaid and incompetent, or that the victims desired more vengeance than the public prosecutor was likely to provide (Ireland 1995).

Today, counties with small populations still adhere to the pattern of using public funds to contract with a private attorney who will prosecute all accused people. In larger jurisdictions, however, case volume makes prosecution a full-time job. Each county prosecutor hires a staff of mostly young attorneys and their support personnel, who shoulder the work of the office guided by whatever operating procedures and policies the chief prosecutor enforces. Most chief prosecutors have complete control over their own policies and practices, constrained only by the broad outlines of the criminal law and court procedure as eventually enforced by the judiciary.

The federal system, by contrast, involves an attorney general appointed by the president who appoints a chief prosecutor for each federal district, of which there are ninety-four in the states and territories. Although in principle this more hierarchical arrangement might be expected to maintain consistent prosecution practices as delineated in Department of Justice directives, in practice there is considerable room for variation between districts, especially considering that the U.S. attorneys in each district are drawn from the ranks of party faithful with close ties to local political constituencies (Eisenstein 1978).

Political ties usually exert only indirect influence on prosecutorial decisions. Prosecutors are accountable to the voters and thus almost always maintain a tough "law-and-order" image in public appearances. Their most important rhetoric, however, is directed to juries in the roughly 10 percent of felony cases that end in jury trials. There, they must demonstrate a nuanced knowledge of community attitudes and local political climate regarding particular types of crime and criminals. Some communities favor stringent victimless crime enforcement, for instance, while others do not. Partisan political considerations, moreover, occasionally directly influence prosecutorial decisions, either in expecting favoritism for influential citizens in corrupt jurisdictions or in expecting enthusiastic participation by local prosecutors in anticrime or prosocial initiatives in political vogue at the time. Ambitious chief prosecutors often support their political party's stances because the job of local prosecutor is usually regarded, and often serves, as a springboard to higher political office or to a judgeship.

In managing their organizations, chief prosecutors in larger jurisdictions determine their deputies' specializations and assignments. Chief prosecutors can organize their offices however they like, often assigning some deputies to "task forces" that pay particular attention to particular types of crime or offenders—white-collar crime, for example, or repeat offenders. How these cases are processed is also a matter of office policy. Some prosecutors prefer "vertical prosecution," for example, in which one deputy handles a case from initial charging all the way through trial if necessary. Others prefer "horizontal prosecution," in which each deputy specializes in a particular task such as charging, plea bargaining, trial presentation, or sentencing advocacy, so a case is passed along by specialists who successively apply their particular expertise to it.

Any professional, of course, works toward a primary goal. The mission of prosecutors is to convict the guilty and to advocate for legally appropriate sentences. The reverse side of this is that prosecutors must refrain from pursuing the innocent—at least, the legally if not the factually innocent. This is both an administrative and an ethical constraint. Considering the great number of cases that prosecutors must handle daily, few advocates will wish to spend time and money on cases that have little hope of ending in conviction should the prosecution's burden of proof of guilt beyond a reasonable doubt not be met.

Uncertainty as to whether the evidence of guilt will be sufficient to convict permeates the prosecutorial enterprise from start to finish. To start, the police bring the cases of all arrestees to the prosecutor for a decision on whether to continue by filing formal charges or to decline to prosecute. The organizational conditions and policies surrounding this decision provide an excellent illustration of the dynamics of discretion in American prosecutors' offices (Katzman 1991).

In the United States, when the police arrest an adult felony defendant, all state laws require that the case be quickly "booked" (i.e., a record of the facts of the alleged crime, a preliminary statement of the law that was broken, and the personal identifiers of the defendant will be prepared). In a short time—usually within forty-eight hours—a prosecutor must review the police reports, decide whether the evidence is strong enough to warrant further action, and decide exactly what violations of which statutes will be formally charged. Almost all serious cases proceed to arraignment (at which the defendant is formally informed of the charges and asked to enter a plea); few prosecutors believe the police would arrest for no reason.

At this point, however, nonserious cases (primarily misdemeanors and felony property offenses) are often declined. Prosecutors may exercise discretion not to prosecute for a great variety of reasons. While serious felony declination is mostly due to shaky evidence, prosecutors might decline to pursue lower-level criminal allegations because they do not perceive the potential punishment to be worth the trouble or because they believe the offender does not deserve a jail term.

State laws regarding disposition of these nonserious cases, including juvenile prosecutions, vary. Most often, a prosecutor will demand that the accused admit guilt and agree to participate in a "diversion program," often involving drug or alcohol treatment. In return, the prosecutor will not make formal charges or will drop any charges already made. The result is that the offender will have no criminal record and the prosecutor will have assured a measure of social control and, optimistically, rehabilitation. A thoughtful prosecutor has thus worked to prevent a juvenile or petty criminal from being stigmatized with a criminal conviction—an important consideration for juveniles whose lives may change for the worse by being labeled "delinquent." A pretrial diversion program may involve restitution to the victim, voluntary public service, or other conditions. If a person accomplishes the requirements of such a program, formal charges—if made— are dismissed, leaving no criminal record. But if the person does not fulfill the program requirements, the prosecutor may then pursue the original charges.

The point is that the prosecutor has complete power to decide who will receive the benefits of diversion, the conditions necessary to avoid criminal charges, and whether to restart prosecution due to noncompliance. As a matter of policy, the prosecutor has determined who might be capable of rehabilitation or, indeed, whether a person is guilty of the crime or not. And the prosecutor has arguably "widened the net" of state control over the lives of people accused of crime, because defendants assigned to diversion programs probably would not have received such extensive conditions of compliance if they had proceeded through regular adjudication into court and been sentenced by a judge. This is simply one example of the great discretionary power the prosecutor can wield over the lives of a great number of people—and all before their cases ever get near a courtroom.

If the prosecutor brings formal charges against the defendant, procedures vary among the various states, but all have some device for determining whether there is probable cause to proceed. In some states, prosecutors generally take the case to a grand jury, which will probably indict the defendant on whatever charges the prosecutor presents. (A famous claim by Robert Morganthau, district attorney for the Borough of Manhattan in New York, is that a prosecutor can get a grand jury to "indict a ham sandwich.") In most states, though, the court holds a preliminary hearing before a judge or magistrate in which the prosecutor presents the alleged facts and may call witnesses, and in which the defense may offer its own version of the alleged facts or challenge the legality of government actions. The judge at the preliminary hearing decides whether there is probable cause to believe that a crime was committed and that the defendant committed it. If so, the defendant is "bound over" to the felony court for further prosecution.

Changing Decisions

How does the prosecutor decide which charges to affix to the case at these early stages? Prosecutorial policies about what charges to make, and whether and when to dismiss or reduce those charges, generally follow either a "legal sufficiency" or a "trial sufficiency" policy. "Thus, if one knows the [charging] policy of the prosecutor, one should be able to predict an expected dispositional pattern" (Jacoby 1979, p. 79).

The difference between a legal sufficiency model and a trial sufficiency model is demonstrated by imagining the job of the deputy prosecutor who first sees the police reports on people arrested. Unlike the requirement of mandatory felony prosecution in some European countries (Langbein 1977; Herrmann 1976; but cf. Stemmler 1994), American law is silent on what a district attorney should do with the cases the police bring to court. By default, then, prosecutors have the power and discretion to dismiss cases by declining to seek formal charges. What considerations guide this decision? The policy in some prosecutors' offices is to evaluate each case in terms of the prediction of whether it will produce a conviction at trial. Thus, the deputy will not set serious charges on a case in which, legal prediction indicates, the defendant could not be proved guilty beyond a reasonable doubt. Such a case would not proceed to arraignment and instead would be dismissed. This is the trial sufficiency model.

Other prosecutors follow a legal sufficiency model—the evidence in each case must meet the legal standard specific to each stage of the prosecution. Since the highest degree of proof is the trial standard of "beyond a reasonable doubt," with earlier stages such as arraignment requiring only a showing of probable cause, cases are rarely dismissed quickly under a legal sufficiency approach. Of course, a greater volume of these cases will be dismissed, or prosecuted on lower charges, once they reach the trial stage, because the stricter standard of proof will not be met for trial. Proponents of the legal sufficiency model maintain that it allows evidence of guilt to develop as the prosecution proceeds, so that by the time the case gets to trial there is enough to prove guilt beyond a reasonable doubt even though proof might have been ambiguous at the charging stage. They argue that this assures that the benefits of law enforcement are not inadvertently squandered when cases are dismissed too soon.

Proponents of the trial sufficiency model, however, claim that it treats people accused of crime more ethically and represents a wiser use of prosecutorial resources. From a civil liberties perspective, it is said to be wrong to detain or interfere with the freedom of people who have done nothing wrong—or, at least, against whom wrongdoing cannot be proved. From an administrative perspective, it is inefficient and expensive to perform work that will probably have no advantageous result. Jacoby (1979) also describes "system efficiency" and "defendant rehabilitation" models for characterizing prosecution policies.

That identical debates have arisen in other countries demonstrates that disagreements over policies on evidentiary sufficiency and rights of the accused are not idiosyncratic to the United States. In Britain, a prosecution service independent of the police was instituted only a decade ago, partly in response to findings of the Royal Commission on Criminal Procedure that police-controlled prosecution was tremendously inefficient in quickly filtering out cases for lack of evidence (Royal Commission on Criminal Procedure 1981, which led to the Prosecution of Offences Act 1985). The commission found that 43 percent of charges against felony defendants acquitted at trial should have been dismissed at earlier stages because of failure even to make a prima facie case (Crisp and Moxon 1994).

Thus, the prosecutor's office shapes its caseload primarily through policies about how stringent the requirements of proof will be at the earliest stages of prosecution. What will happen to the case farther down the road to court? A classic study of felony prosecutions in New York City in 1977 found that prosecutors (operating under the trial sufficiency model of "identifying evidentiary and other problems early in the process") declined to prosecute—or judges declined to indict at preliminary hearing—40 percent of the cases brought to them by the police (Vera Institute of Justice 1981, p. 144). In return for the defendants' guilty pleas, prosecutors later agreed to lower charges in another 41 percent. The major reason prosecutors gave for this case deterioration—or, one might say, "purification"—was that conviction probably could not be obtained at trial. In turn, the major explanation for why conviction was unlikely was that the victim had a relationship with the defendant—as a spouse, friend, relative, or coworker—and the victim's testimony was likely to be unavailable, ambivalent, or compromised.

Of course, deciding how well the testimony or other evidence will hold up "down the road to court" requires considerable discernment and experience. Generally, these are the qualities on which prosecutors rely in making decisions to decline prosecution, dismiss prosecutions already begun, or agree to convictions on charges less serious than those in the indictment. In the United States, except for courts' interpretations of defendants' rights under the federal and state constitutions, there is no central legal authority that gives any guidance in making these prosecutorial decisions. In general, prosecutors have complete discretion whether to charge a suspect with a crime and, if so, what crimes to include in the charges, how many counts of the crime or crimes to charge, whether later to dismiss the charges altogether or reduce the degree of severity of the charge or the number of counts as part of an agreement with defense counsel, and whether to recommend a particular sentence to the judge as part of a guilty plea agreement (Newman 1966). Prosecutors also have complete control over how the government's case will be presented if the case goes to trial.

Exercising Discretion

Prosecutors' immense powers raise the most important issues concerning prosecution in the scholarly and policy-oriented literature: What is prosecutorial discretion, what function does it serve, and how much should it be controlled? Kenneth Culp Davis's classic definitional statement is that a legal officer "has discretion whenever the effective limits on his power leave him free to make a choice among possible courses of action or inaction" (Davis 1969, p. 4).

The "effective limits" on the American prosecutor's choices are exceedingly loose. External controls include only the other institutions of the criminal justice system; grand juries (rarely) might refuse to indict, or judges (rarely, but more often) might refuse to accept a negotiated guilty plea. The law itself permits review of the propriety of prosecutorial actions only in the most egregious circumstances. "It says something about the wide berth the judiciary has given prosecutorial power that the leading case invalidating an exercise of prosecutorial discretion is the century-old decision in *Yick Wo v. Hopkins*" (Vorenberg 1981, p. 1539, citing 118 U.S. 356 [1886], which held that racial discrimination was an impermissible motive for bringing criminal charges).

Short of engaging in illegal behavior themselves, then, prosecutors have virtually unlimited legal authority to decide which actions they will take in accomplishing any of the tasks listed earlier (Vorenberg 1981, p. 1540, note 71, listing "an unbroken line of [Supreme Court] cases upholding prosecutors' powers to decide who and how to charge"). In making discretionary decisions, they may rely on community sentiment, personal values, and their own experience and training. Moreover, their actions are constrained by professional ethics and, realistically, by the fact that county officials rarely grant the prosecutor's office a large chunk of the law enforcement budget. In 1990, for example, local jurisdictions nationwide spent nearly 65 billion dollars on justice system operations, including police, courts, prosecution, public defenders and corrections. Police protection took 58.4 percent of that budget, while prosecution accounted for 6.8 percent and public defense 2 percent (Bureau of Justice Statistics 1994).

There are many advantages in wielding such broad discretion. Prosecutors can manage the work of their offices efficiently, weeding out weak cases, putting other routine ones on the "assembly line" (Packer 1968) to guilty pleas, and preparing fully for trial those high-stake cases in which defendants refuse to plead guilty. They can expend more resources on cases that will have important consequences in the community by convicting repeat offenders, for example, or by "getting to Mr. Big" in drug cases or white-collar offenses, thereby (they hope) deterring future crime. They can work with great flexibility, unencumbered by rigid oversight from any official other than the yearly budget review by legislative agencies and periodic disagreements with judges over the proper disposition of particular types of cases. They can uphold the law as they want and as their community wants, unconstrained either by strict laws or by intransigent bureaucrats at other levels of government.

But the disadvantages of broad discretion are also many. Simple incompetence may go unreviewed and uncorrected. Personal whim or prejudice could influence decision making. Or racial, gender, or class bias might infect the prosecutorial process. Oversight of such unprincipled actions is very sketchy, basically amounting to personal supervision by superiors in the prosecutor's office, who may themselves be biased or not attuned to problems with their subordinates' thought processes and decisions.

Capital Punishment

Considering that prosecutors have power over defendants' lives that can extend even to the decision to seek the death penalty, these are not trivial concerns. For instance, empirical research on the racially biased application of capital punishment indicates that changes in the law over the past three decades have significantly constrained judicial discretion and with it the biased imposition of the death penalty by judges (*Furman v. Georgia*, 408 U.S. 238 [1972], which struck down the death penalty as "freakishly imposed"; a voluminous legal literature chronicles subsequent state statutory changes limiting judges' discretion in capital sentencing: the eventual result was a smaller but arguably fairer capital punishment system). But empirical research also indicates that prosecutors are often racially prejudiced in deciding whether to indict a defendant on capital charges, and that this bias manifests itself in how the prosecutor interprets the facts of the case under investigation (Paternoster 1984; Paternoster and Kazyaka 1988). Racial discrimination by judges and juries is not at issue here, since they decide only the cases brought to them; if the prosecutor does not decide that the case is eligible for the death penalty, a decision whether to inflict capital punishment is not before them.

Few prosecutors would be so crude as to indict a black man for a capital offense while indicting a white in identical circumstances only on noncapital charges. But research has discerned a nationwide pattern of frequent capital indictments for black men who have killed white victims, while the deaths of black victims—whether killed by white or black offenders—much less often prompt prosecutors to regard the cases as important enough for "death specification" (Gross and Mauro 1984). Similarly, some prosecutors regard "felony murders," cases in which death occurs in connection with a rape, robbery, kidnapping, or other serious felony, in which blacks disproportionately participate, to be especially deserving of capital indictments, while gang-related killings and other potentially capital crimes by whites are not regarded as sufficiently depraved for the prosecutor to seek the death penalty.

Summarizing their comprehensive and methodologically sophisticated study of post-*Furman* capital punishment in South Carolina, Paternoster and Kazyaka found:

> Prosecutors' decisions to seek the death penalty are, in part, based upon the egregiousness of the offense and the criminal history of the defendant. When these facts are controlled, however, prosecutors' decisions to seek a death sentence are significantly influenced by the race of both the victim and the offender. Further, this racial effect varies from urban to rural jurisdictions. The data reveal that for similarly aggravated cases prosecutors are more likely to seek death in a white-victim than in a black-victim homicide, unless it is especially heinous. (1988, p. 405)

Of course, prosecutors who apply the law more stringently against minorities, or those who are careful *not* to do so, are perhaps only responsive to the wishes of community residents and leaders who vote.

Geographic Disparity

But this raises another thorny dilemma of unbounded prosecutorial discretion: geographic disparity. Prosecutors in different—sometimes adjacent—jurisdictions often decide to implement very different policies about legal factors that should make a difference in decisions about how vigorously to prosecute. The result is predictable: widely divergent disposition patterns. Although it seems intuitively unfair that a defendant in one county may be prosecuted and convicted of a particular crime while another factually identical defendant in the next county will be convicted of a lesser crime or even diverted from prosecution altogether, in order to remedy this situation it would be necessary to place all locally elected prosecutors under central authority—and even then, geographic unanimity would not be assured, if the federal experience is any indication.

Controls on Discretion

Certainly, it is easier to describe and understand the sources of unwise or arbitrary prosecutorial decisions than to do something about them. Given the difficulties previously described, what is the remedy? "Bounding" discretion—that is, placing limits on the ambit of choices the prosecutor has at each decision point—is the usual response. But even this approach has great difficulties in implementation. Various attempts to change the law to remove or limit prosecutorial discretion have been notorious failures. More promising are programs in which prosecutors themselves design and implement internal controls.

One of the earliest mandatory sentencing statutes involving external limits on both judicial and prosecutorial discretion was New York's "Rockefeller drug law," which prescribed severe mandatory prison sentences for narcotics offenses and included a prohibition on plea bargaining. An evaluation demonstrated that arrests, indictment rates, and conviction rates all declined after the effective date of the law, imprisonment rates remained stable, trials in drug cases tripled, and case processing times doubled (Joint Committee on New York Drug Law Evaluation 1978). Offenders facing mandatory sentences decided they had nothing to lose by going to trial, thus forcing the system to meet a more exacting standard of proof. However, the smaller pool of offenders who were indeed convicted and sentenced to imprisonment received harsher sentences than before.

The implementation of New York's mandatory minimum statute stands as an example of what is likely to happen if all components of the criminal justice system conscientiously follow legislatures' admonition to exercise no discretion at all. But the experience in Michigan was different, because prosecutors found ways to exercise discretion even though the face of the law forbade it. The Michigan Felony Firearms Statute created a new offense of "possession of a firearm while engaged in a felony," specifying a two-year mandatory prison term that could not be shortened by parole and had to be served consecutively after the sentence imposed for the underlying felony. Prosecutors applied the law so as to strive for "business as usual." Only 62 percent of the eligible offenders were charged with the "mandatory" firearms violations. Charging practices varied wildly among local prosecutors' offices throughout the state, however: in some courts 100 percent of the cases requiring firearms charges were filed, while in others none of the eligibles received the firearms charge (Bynum 1982, Table 4.1). Heumann and Loftin observed a similar tendency in prosecutorial decisions. Felonious assaults were often reduced to misdemeanor offenses to avoid the mandatory sentencing requirements. Once the charge bargain was complete, judges would sentence offenders to misdemeanor offenses instead of crimes requiring the imposition of the two-year mandatory sentence (Heumann and Loftin 1979).

Tonry summarizes this research and points to the exercise of prosecutorial discretion—despite a law forbidding its exercise—as one reason that mandatory minimum sentencing does not work as planned: "The severity of penalties . . . has led in many instances to reluctance on the part of prosecutors to prosecute some violations, where penalties seem to be out of line with the seriousness of the offense" (1992, pp. 245–46). He also notes that judges will strive to circumvent the worst excesses of mandatory minima if prosecutors do not, also as a mechanism to avoid the harsh penalties that seem disproportionate to the severity of the offense or the character of the offender. Nevertheless, although discretion so applied in individual cases might mitigate a sentence's severity, the length of prison terms imposed on the group of convicted offenders taken as a whole is likely to rise. Tonry later chronicled the use of mandatory sentencing for drug offenders in the federal system. He concluded that prosecutors often declined to charge the crimes that would carry mandatory sentences or would convince the judge to disregard or circumvent the mandatory sentence because of the defendant's "substantial assistance" to the government. Nevertheless, in the great volume of cases that *were* charged and eligible for five-year mandatory prison terms, sentences were so uniformly harsh as to pack the federal prisons overfull with drug dealers, runners, and users. Troubling questions of disparity arose again because the drug offenders who ended up in prison were disproportionately black—suggesting that prosecutors might offer the benefits of discretionary "substantial assistance" motions mostly to whites. Another cause of disparities is that the U.S. Congress enacted harsher mandatory minimum sentences for drug offenses involving crack cocaine likely to be committed by blacks, compared with lighter penalties for offenses involving powder cocaine, for which many more whites are prosecuted (Tonry 1995).

The lesson of mandatory minimum sentencing, then, is that it ratchets sentencing severity upward in general, but that prosecutors and judges often use their discretion to prevent many defendants from feeling its full force. That legal officials would use their authority to circumvent the law might seem strange, at least if one interprets these statutes to mean what they say on their face: that severe penalties are mandatory, thus prohibiting discretionary choices. Proponents of mandatory sentencing statutes say they will *eliminate* discretion, not control or "bound" it. Prosecutors and judges have resisted such statutes—even to the point of acting illegally—because discretion serves essential purposes. Whether that discretion could be recognized and regulated rather than eliminated is another matter.

Plea Bargaining

One essential purpose of using discretion is to individualize decisions. Prosecutorial and judicial discretion has always mitigated the harshest aspects of the American criminal justice system, most particularly through the operation of the guilty plea process. To European observers accustomed to controlling discretion tightly, this is nevertheless not surprising when the fact that the American penal code is much severer than those in other Western countries is also taken into account. Since criminal penalties in the United States are easily the harshest among the democratic nations, it is predictable that prosecutors and judges strain to soften the hardest blows and to bring the average sentences for "normal crimes" (Sudnow 1965) down to a civilized level. But to a public terrified and fed up with crime, any sentence not as harsh as the law would allow smacks of leniency. Politicians pander to these sentiments, promising harsher and harsher sentencing as a way to get votes. Under such circumstances, it is proof of the prosecutor's remarkable resilience and power within the wider criminal justice system that plea bargaining continues to operate at all.

Yet the practice of pleading guilty in return for an easier sentence than would be expected after a trial—or, at least, what the defendant *thinks* is an easier sentence, or *expects* after trial—exists in virtually all American criminal courts (Schulhofer 1984). Because the practice rests on the assumption that a defendant has no incentive to admit guilt, preferring to have a trial in which guilt or innocence would be determined after a full evidentiary hearing, most people believe that prosecutors accept the defendants' guilty pleas in order to save the time and expense of trials—but at the cost of giving criminals more of a "break" than they deserve. Most prosecutors and judges also offer this explanation for the persistence of plea bargaining, stating that without it the courts would break down under the burden of trying every case. Such an explanation is easily understood by a public that is well aware of the time and money spent in highly publicized jury trials, but it does not erase their displeasure with the idea of "dealing" with criminals.

In their candid moments, however, prosecutors admit that administrative efficiency is only one reason that they exercise their unconstrained discretion to accept guilty pleas in return for promises to dismiss or reduce charges or to recommend particular punishments to the sentencing judge. In virtually all misdemeanor cases, for instance, they know that "the process is the punishment"—that defendants will plead guilty without any sentencing concessions, so as to avoid spending more time and money in court than the sentence would cost them (Feeley 1979).

In felony cases in which evidence of guilt is ambiguous or some key element might not be provable, prosecutors plea-bargain because a guilty plea masks weaknesses in the case. Many organizational policies permit the prosecutor to accept a guilty plea to lesser charges and thus avoid having to prove the case at trial. The outcome is roughly equivalent to what would happen if the top charges could not be proved at trial, the reasoning goes, and if the defendant pleads guilty voluntarily a plea bargain is not lenient—it is exactly what the evidence would bear. But advocates of due process argue that if there are evidentiary weaknesses in the prosecutor's case, a defendant should be allowed to challenge them and be sentenced on the facts that can actually be proved rather than negotiated. Finally, in serious felony cases in which the evidence is unassailable—prosecutors call them "dead bang" or "slam dunk" guilty cases—defendants know they might as well plead guilty and get on with the business of serving their sentences rather than waiting for the inevitable trial conviction. (This is especially true for those defendants held in jail without bail, awaiting trial.)

Only in the serious felonies in which the defendant will surely spend a long time in prison whether convicted either by guilty plea or by trial is the defendant likely to demand a trial. The punishment will be harsh either way. In this circumstance, the prosecutor will attempt to secure a guilty plea—thus avoiding lengthy and expensive proof and the uncertainty of a freak acquittal—and will offer a lower sentence in return for the guilty plea (Mather 1979; on uncertainty, see Albonetti 1986). That sentence will be achieved either by dropping some charges, thus lowering the defendant's sentencing "exposure," or by presenting the arrangement to the court and asking that the judge sentence in accord with the prosecutor's recommendation. Few judges balk. Since the defendant will in any case stay in prison for a considerable time under the plea bargain, but less (perhaps) than would have been determined after trial, prosecutors regard this negotiated outcome as "win-win" for all parties concerned.

But some people—victims, the general public, and due process advocates—criticize the system. Their criticisms derive from very different concerns and interpretations of how plea bargaining works. Many members of the public, convinced that criminals get undeserved leniency, regard plea bargaining as nefarious backroom dealing in which wily defense lawyers mask their clients' faults and obtain wrist slaps for them in exchange for allowing lazy prosecutors to avoid trials. Moreover, many victims criticize the plea-bargaining system as disrespectful of their suffering, treating them as mere pieces of evidence expected to testify but not to be informed of developments in the case. Over the past two decades, most prosecutors have taken this criticism to heart and instituted a variety of victim/witness programs, often as a branch of the prosecutor's office, which provide emotional support and court-related information to victims at all stages of the proceedings. Often motivated by political ideology or agendas, other victims and their supporters demand abolition of plea bargaining and a host of other reforms of criminal procedure as "victims' rights" (McCoy 1993).

By contrast, due process critics argue that plea bargaining is essentially coercive. Because prosecutors promise a lesser sentence in return for a guilty plea, but threaten a harsher sentence should the defendant be convicted at trial, the difference in sentence—the "trial penalty" or "confession reward"—could be regarded as a way to force a defendant to give up the right to trial. Defendants who truly have viable defenses to the charges will sometimes plead guilty despite the possibility of acquittal, so as to avoid even harsher punishment in the event of conviction. These critics also charge that prosecutors bluff about how severely the court will treat the charges and evidence should the case go to trial, thus coercing guilty pleas and high punishments from defendants who would not be treated so severely were the case aired publicly (Alschuler 1968, 1981).

To be effective, it seems, any reform of plea bargaining would have to take all these disparate criticisms into account, which might not be as difficult as it seems. With the exception of the politically motivated "leniency" critics, all the critics might agree on the remedy, though for different reasons. The remedy would be to provide more public evidentiary airing, whether in the form of full-blown jury trials, bench trials, or preliminary hearings. Concerned members of the public, victims, and defendants alike would thereby see the effect of the evidence actually produced, rather than have it discussed only in private in plea negotiations (McCoy 1993). If guilty pleas follow a preliminary hearing, they are likely to be more fully informed on the part of both the defendant and the victim. More ardent reformers would also find ways to constrain the prosecutor's discretion to use the trial penalty, perhaps requiring that the sentencing "offer" in return for a guilty plea be made part of the record following the preliminary hearing, and that the sentence following trial would be no more severe than that offer unless new evidence were later found unexpectedly.

Bounding the prosecutor's discretion in plea bargaining in this way, skeptics respond, would prompt all defendants to demand trials, thus causing the system to grind to a halt. This has not been the experience in those few jurisdictions that have forbidden prosecutors to drop charges or offer lower sentences in return for guilty pleas. In the most extensive of such reforms, the attorney general of the state of Alaska in 1975 ordered all local prosecutors to refrain from making plea bargains (Rubinstein, Clarke, and White 1980). If a defendant was willing to plead guilty, he or she had to do so without any promises from the prosecutor. (Alaska is one of the few states in which local prosecutors are under the supervision of the state attorney general, thus avoiding the problems of widely disparate policies and personalities in decentralized local jurisdictions.)

Defendants continued pleading guilty at roughly the same rates. Nevertheless, although they did not always demand trials, a significant minority of them did. The guilty plea rate dropped from 90 percent to 80 percent, approximately. This means the trial rate doubled, from 10 percent to 20 percent. While this is not the wholesale system breakdown skeptics would predict, nevertheless it is a significant new demand for court time. Critics of plea bargaining were delighted, because the 10 percent of defendants who chose to go to trial were apparently the type of defendants whose cases were indeed defensible and thus should not have been pleading guilty in return for ephemeral benefits.

Other jurisdictions limit plea bargaining by assuring prosecutors and defenders that trials will not be long and expensive, thus undercutting the administrative efficiency rationale for guilty pleas. In Philadelphia courts observed by Schulhofer (1984) in the early 1980s, the majority of felony cases went through trials; they were not jury trials, however, but quick evidentiary hearings before a judge—bench trials. In Los Angeles in the 1960s, an equivalent was the "slow plea of guilty," in which a transcript of the preliminary hearing was forwarded to the trial judge, who reviewed it and held a bench trial to probe any ambiguities. Organizational structures like these provide the public airing of evidence necessary to demonstrate to the defendant, the victim, and the public that the punishment fits the crime and not the plea bargain. But they also undercut the leniency critique because critics can see exactly the points of factual ambiguities in a case and understand how that affects the sentence.

Conclusion

Reforming plea bargaining is a prime example of what it would take to bound prosecutorial discretion. Not surprisingly, few local prosecutors feel the need to do so, and if any such controls were to be instituted, they would probably come from the appellate courts. Prosecutors are more likely to embrace programs that increase the power and visibility of the office, preferably also serving real community needs and addressing the very real problem of crime in its many manifestations. The most recent innovative program that fits this description is community prosecution. Modeled on the example of community policing, which seeks to prevent crime by working with neighborhood residents and coordinating local government response to community problems likely to breed crime, "community prosecutors" target quality-of-life offenses:

> In general, Neighborhood District Attorneys work with citizens and police to help come up with ways to control the types of street behavior and low-level disorder that threaten neighborhood safety. An important part of the NDAs' role is to provide answers, feedback, and explanations—especially explanations of legal constraints that prohibit the police from doing what citizens think they ought to do to deal with certain conditions. The NDAs' core activity, however, is devising alternative responses. (Boland 1996, p. 37)

"Devising alternative responses," of course, means that the prosecutor might work to organize a variety of new programs designed to divert the criminally accused from the normal stream of prosecution and adjudication. These programs can be regarded as humane and rehabilitative or as simply another example of strong political power exerting itself to achieve the goals its supporters want. Prosecutors have always had immense power, and they have used it for good and ill. That is unlikely to change soon; it is only the forms in which the power is wielded that are recast.

References

Albonetti, Celesta A. 1986. "Criminality, Prosecutorial Screening, and Uncertainty: Toward a Theory of Discretionary Decision Making in Felony Case Processings." *Criminology* 24:623–44.

Alschuler, Albert W. 1968. "The Prosecutor's Role in Plea Bargaining." *University of Chicago Law Review* 36:50–112.

———. 1981. "The Changing Plea Bargaining Debate." *California Law Review* 69:652–730.

Boland, Barbara. 1996. "What Is Community Prosecution?" *National Institute of Justice Journal,* no. 231:2–4.

Bureau of Justice Statistics. 1994. *Justice Expenditure and Employment, 1990.* Washington, D.C.: U.S. Department of Justice, Bureau of Justice Statistics.

Bynum, Timothy S. 1992. "Prosecutorial Discretion and the Implementation of a Legislative Mandate." In *Implementing Criminal Justice Policies,* edited by Merry Morash. Beverly Hills, Calif.: Sage.

Crisp, Debbie, and David Moxon. 1994. *Case Screening by the Crown Prosecution Service: How and Why Cases Are Terminated.* Home Office Research Study no. 137. London: HMSO.

Davis, Kenneth Culp. 1969. *Discretionary Justice: A Preliminary Inquiry.* Baton Rouge: Louisiana State University Press.

Eisenstein, James. 1978. *Counsel for the United States: U.S. Attorneys in the Political and Legal Systems.* Baltimore, Md.: Johns Hopkins University Press.

Feeley, Malcolm. 1979. *The Process Is the Punishment.* New York: Russell Sage.

Friedman, Lawrence M. 1993. *Crime and Punishment in American History.* New York: Basic Books.

Gross, Stanley, and R. Mauro. 1984. "Patterns of Death: An Analysis of Racial Disparities in Capital Sentencing." *Stanford Law Review* 37:27–153.

Herrmann, Joachim. 1976. "The German Prosecutor." In *Discretionary Justice in Europe and America,* edited by Kenneth Culp Davis. Urbana: University of Illinois Press.

Heumann, Milton, and Colin Loftin. 1979. "Mandatory Sentencing and the Abolition of Plea Bargaining: The Michigan Felony Firearms Statute." *Law and Society Review* 13:393–430.

Holten, N. Gary, and Melvin E. Jones. 1982. *The System of Criminal Justice.* 2nd ed. Boston: Little, Brown.

Ireland, Robert M. 1995. "Privately Funded Prosecution of Crime in the Nineteenth-Century United States." *American Journal of Legal History* 34:43–58.

Jacoby, Joan E. 1979. "The Charging Policies of Prosecutors." In *The Prosecutor,* edited by William F. McDonald. Beverly Hills, Calif.: Sage.

———. 1980. *The American Prosecutor: A Search for Identity.* Lexington, Mass.: Lexington.

Joint Committee on New York Drug Law Evaluation. 1978. *The Nation's Toughest Drug Law: Evaluating the New York Experience.* A Project of the Association of the Bar of the City of New York and the Drug Abuse Council, Inc. Washington, D.C.: U.S. Government Printing Office.

Katzman, Gary. 1991. *Inside the Criminal Process.* New York: Norton.

Langbein, J. H. 1977. *Comparative Criminal Procedure: Germany.* St. Paul, Minn.: West Publishing.

Mather, Lynn. 1979. *Plea Bargaining or Trial?* Lexington, Mass.: Lexington.

McCoy, Candace. 1993. *Politics and Plea Bargaining: Victims' Rights in California.* Philadelphia: University of Pennsylvania Press.

McDonald, William F. 1979. "The Prosecutor's Domain." In *The Prosecutor,* edited by William F. McDonald. Beverly Hills, Calif.: Sage.

Nagel, Ilene H., and Stephen J. Schulhofer. 1992. "A Tale of Three Cities: An Empirical Study of Charging and Bargaining Practices Under the Federal Sentencing Guidelines." *Southern California Law Review* 66:501–66.

Newman, Donald J. 1966. *Conviction: The Determination of Guilt or Innocence Without Trial.* Report of the American Bar Foundation's Survey of the Administration of Criminal Justice in the United States, edited by Frank Remington. Boston: Little, Brown.

Packer, Herbert. 1968. *The Limits of the Criminal Sanction.* Palo Alto, Calif.: Stanford University Press.

Paternoster, Raymond. 1984. "Prosecutorial Discretion in Requesting the Death Penalty: A Case of Victim-Based Racial Discrimination." *Law and Society Review* 18:437–78.

Paternoster, Raymond, and Ann Marie Kazyaka. 1988. "The Administration of the Death Penalty in South Carolina: Experiences over the First Few Years." *South Carolina Law Review* 39:245–414.

Royal Commission on Criminal Procedure. 1981. *Report Presented to Parliament by Command of Her Majesty January 1981.* Cmnd. 8092. London: HMSO.

Rubinstein, Michael, Stevens H. Clarke, and Teresa J. White. 1980. *Alaska Bans Plea Bargaining.* Washington, D.C.: U.S. Government Printing Office.

Schulhofer, Steven. 1984. "Is Plea Bargaining Inevitable?" *Harvard Law Review* 97:1037–107.

Stemmler, Susanne. 1994. "Incentive Structures and Organizational Equivalents of Plea Bargaining in German Criminal Courts." Ph.D. diss., Pennsylvania State University.

Sudnow, David. 1965. "Normal Crimes: Sociological Features of the Penal Code in the Public Defender's Office." *Social Problems* 12:255–76.

Tonry, Michael. 1992. "Mandatory Penalties." In *Crime and Justice: A Review of Research,* vol. 16, edited by Michael Tonry. Chicago: University of Chicago Press.

———. 1995. *Malign Neglect: Race, Crime, and Punishment in America.* New York: Oxford University Press.

Vera Institute of Justice. 1981. *Felony Arrests: Their Prosecution and Disposition in New York City's Courts.* Rev. ed. New York: Longman.

Vorenberg, James. 1981. "Decent Restraint of Prosecutorial Power." *Harvard Law Review* 94:1521–73.

18

Jails

RICHARD S. FRASE

Hans Mattick once described American jails as "an unknown and neglected area of justice" (1974, p. 777). This
statement remains true, although much has been learned in the past
twenty-five years about the nation's jails and jail inmates. The available
data suggest that most jails are better today than they were in the past—
newer, more fully staffed, better equipped, and safer. Yet serious problems remain, reflecting persistent patterns of jail organization and function that have existed for centuries: too many jails today are still locally
run institutions that are uneconomically small, poorly financed, overwhelmed by the diversity and transience of their inmate populations,
and insufficiently attuned to the correctional and personal needs of these
inmates.

Jails lie at the center of the criminal justice system. They are inti-
mately related to every stage of pretrial and posttrial procedure, and are
the detention facility that affects the community most directly and most
frequently. Despite many changes in recent years, jails remain one of the
most resistant of all criminal justice institutions to fundamental reform.
Many of the essential problems of jails identified in the 1920s remain today, and probably will for the foreseeable future.

The problems of jails are the result of their disparate functions; their
highly transient and fluctuating inmate populations; their uneconomic
scale of operations; their typical staffing and administrative control; and
their sheer diversity. Although some jails hold only one gender, or only
sentenced inmates, most jails must accommodate a wide variety of custodial functions, including pretrial detention, service of short sentences,
and miscellaneous temporary detentions of convicted or unconvicted
adults and juveniles, both male and female. Jails are the custodial dumping ground of last resort, when no other appropriate holding facility is
available.

Since most jail inmates are released or transferred within a few days,
processing costs are high, and treatment possibilities are limited. In any
case, most jails are too small to provide efficiently all of the services required to meet diverse inmate needs. Most jails, especially smaller ones,
also experience wide day-to-day fluctuations in the size and makeup of

their inmate populations, producing unused capacity and/or overcrowding in some or all units. Jails are typically controlled and staffed by local sheriffs and police departments, whose primary concern is law enforcement, not jail administration or corrections. Jails are also deeply enmeshed in local politics; sheriffs are elected, and most police chiefs are appointed by local officials.

Finally, jails are essentially *atypical*; their diversity of function, size (very small to very large), location (urban, suburban, rural county seats), administrative control (local, multicounty, state, or federal), and personnel (law enforcement or civilian) defies any simplistic theory, management program, or reform strategy. This diversity also severely limits our ability to collect and meaningfully interpret data on jail inmates and operations. Inadequate data limit our understanding of what jails do, how their functions have changed over time, and how jails and jail functions can be improved. Even when we think we know what needs to be done, the close connection between jails and local politics limits our ability to make major changes in jail organization or operations. It is clear, however, that both jail measurement and jail reform must be based on a broad, "systemic" approach, taking into account all of the elements, both within and outside of the criminal process, that determine the nature and size of current and future jail populations.

Prior to the inauguration of federal jail censuses and surveys in 1970, most of what was known about jails was anecdotal. The federal jail studies have vastly expanded our knowledge about jails and their inmates, but some of the most important aspects of jailing are still documented very poorly, or not at all. Nevertheless, the available data provide a basis for taking stock of the current jail situation and designing future data collection, policy analysis, and reform efforts.[1]

Contemporary Jails and Jail Inmates

Until the federal government began surveying local jails in 1970, it was not even possible to say how *many* jails there are, let alone describe the nature of their facilities, operations, and inmate populations. The data collected since then are a great improvement but have several major limitations. The federal definition of a *jail* is underinclusive and has been changed at least once; moreover, the variables reported, as well as their definitions and categorizations, have changed over time. These limitations should be kept in mind when reading the following description of "contemporary" jails and jail inmates; for some key variables, the only available data are from the earliest surveys.

Jail Buildings and Operations

The basic definition used in all federal jail statistics since 1970 is any locally operated facility intended primarily for general adult, postarraignment detention and/or short-term sentencing. This definition excludes a large number of local facilities that serve much the same function as, and hold many of the same persons, before, after, or intermittently with, the institutions meeting the preceding definition, for example: drunk tanks, police and court lockups, treatment facilities, halfway houses, and prison prerelease centers.

The exclusion of all lockups is especially problematic; there are at least as many police and sheriff's lockups as there are "jails," and both types of institution handle large numbers of very short-term commitments. In 1993, about 3,200 police departments operated one or more "lockups," which had an average capacity of ten inmates and an average maximum holding authority of twenty-two hours (Bureau of Justice Statistics 1996a [number of departments times percent with lockups]). About 185 sheriff departments had lockups, with an average capacity of forty-nine inmates and an average holding authority of twelve hours (Bureau of Justice Statistics 1996c). In 1988, two-fifths of persons released from "jails" had been detained for one day or less (Bureau of Justice Statistics 1990a, p. 5).

The jail definition above also excludes all jails in the states that have exclusively state-run jails (Connecticut, Delaware, Hawaii, Rhode Island, and Vermont); state-run jails in states that also have some locally run jails (e.g., Alaska and West Virginia); and all federally run jails (as of 1993 there were seven; about two-thirds of the 18,000 federal jail inmates were boarded in local jails).

The 1970 Jail Census identified 4,037 locally run jails with authority to hold adults for more that forty-eight hours. Subsequent jail censuses were conducted in 1972, 1978, 1983, 1988, and 1993; however, only limited information has been published from the 1993 census. Surveys of jail inmates, usually also including some information on the jails themselves (e.g., rated capacity and occupancy rates), were conducted in 1972, 1982, and in every noncensus year after 1983 (namely, in 1984 through 1987, 1989 through 1992, and 1994 through 1996).

By 1972, the number of "over-forty-eight-hour-authority" jails had fallen by 3 percent, to 3,921. In 1978, the definition was modified to exclude facilities not authorized to hold inmates after they are arraigned in court. At the time of the definition change, such arraignment was assumed to ordinarily occur within forty-eight hours of arrest (Bureau of Justice Statistics 1980, p. 49); more recently, this assumed time frame has been extended to seventy-two hours (Bureau of Justice Statistics 1995b, p. 14). The 1978 Jail Census produced a total count of 3,493 jails. Subsequent censuses showed further slight declines in the number of jails: to 3,338 in 1983; 3,316 in 1988 (including eight privately operated jails under contract to local governments); and 3,304 in 1993 (including seventeen that were privately operated). Thus, the total number of jails surveyed fell 18 percent between 1970 and 1993; however, the decline after the adoption of the current definition in 1978 was only 5 percent. The most recent American Correctional Association Jail Directory reports only 2,994 jails (1996, p. xiv), or 9 percent less than the 1993 jail census figure.

Structural Factors: Jail Age, Size, and Design.   As of 1988, about one-quarter of U.S. jails (holding 18 percent of all inmates) were at least fifty years old; on the other hand, 11 percent were less than five years old, and 12 percent were five to ten years old.

More than half of all jails hold fewer than 50 inmates on a typical day (and account for less than 10 percent of all jail inmates). At the other extreme, about 13 percent of jails hold 250 or more prisoners (and account for over two-thirds of all inmates). In 1993, there were seventy-six jails holding 1,000 or more inmates.

Most inmates are held in multibed units. In 1988, "general-housing" units (which held 88 percent of all jail inmates) were holding an average of 2.3 inmates per unit, with about fifty square feet of occupied cell space per inmate.

Jails differ not only in age, size, and cell space but also in the design of the residential units. Traditionally, jail and prison architecture has reflected a linear design, which provides intermittent supervision of inmates by staff who remain in a central, secure area, except when patrolling the corridors containing inmate cells (Nelson 1988; Zupan and Menke 1991). Such jails are also sometimes referred to as "first-generation" jails (Cornelius 1996, p. 7). More recently, some "second-generation" jails have incorporated a design that permits remote audiovisual supervision of large numbers of cells from a secure central control room; cell doors are electronically activated from the control room, communication with inmates is by intercom, and officers have very little direct contact with inmates.

Both intermittent- and remote-supervision jails presuppose a high risk of destructive inmate behavior, which thus requires major investments in high-security hardware and vandal-resistant fixtures; despite such investments, serious violence and vandalism problems persist in these jails. The cost of remote-supervision jails is further increased by their reliance on sophisticated locking and communications technology.

Beginning in the 1970s, some new or remodeled jails have been based on a "direct-supervision" concept (these are sometimes also referred to as "new-generation," "third-generation," or "podular" jails). Direct-supervision design seeks to improve security and inmate-staff interaction, and to reduce construction and maintenance costs (as well as stress-producing noise levels associated with high-security design materials; Zupan and Menke 1991) by placing correctional officers *inside* the residential unit. As of 1988, about a dozen jails were using this approach, with perhaps a hundred more under design or construction; preliminary results from such jails indicate substantial cost savings for construction and operation, as well as improved security, cleanliness, and staff morale (Nelson 1988). However, these jails place additional demands on correctional officers, which may require improvements in staff training or selection (Kerle 1991, p. xv; Cornelius 1996, p. 52).

Overcrowding and Court Intervention. Jail censuses since 1983 have reported data on the "rated capacity" and occupancy rates of jails, by size of the jail. In 1996, 92 percent of the nation's jail capacity was occupied. Occupancy rates were higher in larger jails: 96 percent occupancy in jails with 1,000 or more inmates, but only 71 percent in jails with fewer than 50 inmates. All of these data must be interpreted very cautiously, however. "Rated capacity" is supposedly determined by state and local "rating officials," but these jail-reported figures are not subject to independent evaluation according to recommended cell space or other standards (Mattick 1974, p. 801). Moreover, one-day occupancy rates for groups of same-size jails do not reveal how many jails were overcrowded at some point (or even repeatedly) during the year. Finally, overall occupancy data can be very misleading; a jail with 90 percent occupancy may be seriously overcrowded in certain cell areas (e.g., those used for adult males) and almost empty in other areas (e.g., those reserved for females and juveniles; Bureau of Justice Statistics 1971, p. 4).

Recent jail censuses have also reported data on the number of jails under court order or consent decree to reduce crowding or address other inadequate conditions of confinement. The 1988 census reported that 404 jails had been ordered to limit the number of inmates held, and 412 jails were under court order or consent decree for specific conditions (including crowded living units and/or inadequate recreation facilities, medical services, staffing, visiting, library, inmate classification, food service, disciplinary or grievance policies, and fire safety). A total of 320 jails were subject to both types of court intervention; the net total of 496 jails, subject to one or both types of intervention, represented 15 percent of the 3,316 jails surveyed. A 1992 survey of the 503 largest jail jurisdictions (those with an average daily population of at least 100 inmates in 1988) found that over 30 percent were subject to court intervention.

Jail Functions. Most local jails serve a wide variety of functions and may detain adult males and females, as well as some juveniles, in some or all of the following categories: persons awaiting arraignment, trial, or sentencing; juveniles awaiting transfer to juvenile authorities or facilities; adults awaiting transfer to another county or state, or to federal or military authorities; persons facing mental health commitment hearings; persons held as material witnesses, in protective custody, or for contempt of court; convicts sentenced to a jail term (usually for one year or less, but sometimes for longer terms); convicts facing revocation of parole or probation; convicts awaiting transfer to prison (including those serving lengthy periods in jail because of prison overcrowding); and prison inmates temporarily held in jail for court appearances (on new charges, as witnesses, or as parties in civil litigation).

Although most jails serve *all* of these functions listed, at least from time to time, some more specialized jails hold inmates only in certain legal status or demographic categories. There are at least 18 jails nationwide that hold only female inmates, and over 500 that hold only males (Bureau of Justice Statistics 1992b, p. 2). Some jails are used only for pretrial detention; others (often called "workhouses," "houses of correction," "work-release centers," etc.) receive only sentenced inmates. In 1988, 96 percent of jails reported that they had authority to accept convicted male misdemeanants, and 68 percent said they could receive convicted male felons; for females, the proportions were 75 and 57 percent. Twenty-nine percent of the jails reported that they were authorized to detain juveniles at least temporarily. Of these, forty jails (1.2 percent of the total) did not maintain either sight or sound separation of juveniles from adults. (Such separation is generally required in order for states to receive federal grants under the 1974 Juvenile Justice and Delinquency Prevention Act and subsequent federal legislation; see Schwartz 1991, p. 220.)

Considerable variation exists from state to state in the types of sentences that may be served in jail. Thus, although most states limit jail terms to one year, some states (e.g., Pennsylvania)[2] regularly use local jails for longer sentences. Also, some states (*not* necessarily the same as above) make very heavy use of jail for felony sentencing, and consequently have comparatively large jail populations relative to their state prison populations. For example, about two-thirds of convicted felons in Minnesota receive a jail sentence (compared with a national average of about 25 percent); largely for this reason, Minnesota's jail population has been roughly equal to its prison population over most of the past twenty years, whereas the total U.S. prison population remained about two times higher than the U.S. jail population during this period (Frase 1993, p. 331; see also Figure 18.2).

Jail Control and Location. Although state jail inspection programs are common (see later discussion), the actual administration and operation of jails continue to be almost exclusively the domain of local law enforcement officials. As of 1993, sheriffs appeared to control almost 80 percent of local jails, with police chiefs running most of the other 20 percent.[3] A few jails are operated by non–law enforcement officials, for example, Kentucky's elected "county jailors" (Kentucky Constitution, § 99); the New York City commissioner of corrections (N.Y. Corrections Law, § 600-a); and the New Hampshire county departments of corrections (New Hampshire Statutes § 28.12). There are also at least two dozen regional or multijurisdiction jails (Bureau of Justice Statistics 1996b, p. 13), most of which are probably run by law enforcement officials.

The 1972 census was the only one to report information on jail location: about three-fifths of jails were in a sheriff's office, police station, or courthouse, one-third occupied a separate building, and the rest had other accommodations. Larger jails were more likely to be in a separate structure. Whether in a combined or separate structure, jails have traditionally been located close to centers of population, whereas state prisons are often built in more remote locations.

Personnel. Jail staffing has been reported in all five jail censuses. However, there are no consistent or recent data on the numbers and types of part-time and nonpayroll workers, on whom jails have traditionally relied heavily, especially for teachers and treatment staff. The following figures generally include part-time as well as full-time workers, and all nonpayroll employees who actually worked at the jail during the twenty-four-hour period preceding the survey date (Bureau of Justice Statistics 1990a, p. 8).

Correctional officers made up 71 percent of all jail employees in 1993; the remaining staff consisted of administrators (6 percent), clerical and maintenance workers (13 percent), "educational" staff (1 percent), "professional and technical staff"[4] (7 percent), and "other" (1 percent). There were 2.8 inmates per employee, and 3.9 inmates per correctional officer (guard). However, since jails operate twenty-four hours a day, 365 days a year (Mattick 1974, p. 805), the national inmate-to-guard ratio *per work shift* is four or five times higher. The largest jails (1,000 or more inmates) and those that are most overcrowded (more than 110 percent occupancy) have inmate-to-staff ratios about twice as high as the smallest (fewer than 50 inmates) and least crowded (less than 75 percent occupancy).

In 1993, 70 percent of total payroll staff, and 76 percent of payroll correctional officers, were male. About 70 percent of both total payroll staff and payroll correctional officers were non-Hispanic whites, about 23 percent were non-Hispanic blacks, and about 7 percent were Hispanic. As indicated in later discussion, the jail inmate population is about 90 percent male but only about 40 percent non-Hispanic white.

Costs. Total estimated jail expenditures in 1993 were $9.6 billion; about 70 percent of the total was spent on operations, and the remaining 30 percent was for capital expenses. It is not known whether inmate-paid fees (e.g., in work-release programs) were deducted from the reported operating costs, or whether capital expenses include bond interest and other long-term financing costs. In 1993, the average cost of operations per inmate per year was $14,667.

Programs. Two-thirds of the 3,316 jails surveyed in 1988 lacked "medical facilities" of any kind. Among those with some kind of facilities, 404 jails had health units or infirmaries with beds, 568 had health units or infirmaries without beds, 291 had detoxification facilities, and 179 jails reported having psychiatric or other facilities. At the time of the 1988 Jail Census, about half of jails did some testing for HIV infection, but less than 3 percent tested all inmates.

In the 1983 Jail Census, 85 percent of jails reported that they provided assessments or screening for physical health, mental health, suicide potential, alcohol intoxication, drug use, and/or other health problems; 17 percent gave physical exams to all inmates. But only 15 percent had a nurse available in the jail on a daily basis, and only about 5 percent reported daily availability of a doctor, paramedics, or mental health personnel; 60 percent *never* had a nurse available (even "on call"); 40 percent never had a doctor available, 45 percent never had mental health personnel, and 58 percent never had paramedics.

Inmate death rates provide an indirect measure of jail medical and psychiatric care (although they also reflect staffing and security levels, celling arrangements, and the nature of inmate populations). In 1993, there were 149 inmate deaths per 100,000 inmates. Over a third of the deaths were suicides; 10 percent were a result of AIDS; and 45 percent were caused by other illnesses. Homicides accounted for only 3 percent.

Fifty-four percent of jails offered work-release programs in 1988, and the proportion was much higher in the largest jail jurisdictions. About 6 percent of all jail inmates participated in such programs. Seventy-three percent of jails offered weekend sentence programs, which involved about 13 percent of inmates serving a jail sentence. The 1992 Jail Inmate Survey reported work-release programs in 71 percent of the 503 largest jail population jurisdictions; in addition, 36 percent of these jurisdictions were offering an alternative-to-incarceration program such as electronic monitoring (23 percent) or day reporting (8 percent).

Scattered information on other jail programs and facilities has also been reported from time to time. In 1972, the following proportions of jails offered the services indicated: group counseling (17 percent); vocational assessment (9 percent); vocational training (14 percent); prevocational training (7 percent); remedial education (11 percent); job placement (13 percent); alcoholic treatment (35 percent); drug treatment (26 percent); and religious services (59 percent). The majority of programs were run by organizations or officials from outside the jail. In addition, 62 percent of jails claimed to offer "recreational facilities," mostly radio and/or television; only the largest jails were likely to have sports equipment or an exercise yard. In 1983, 68 percent of jails claimed to provide exercise activities outside the cell for at least one hour per day.

The 1972 Jail Census also reported on the separation of inmate categories; whereas most jails housed juveniles and mental patients separately, and many also separated drunk driving and work release inmates, the vast majority of jails did not separate pretrial from sentenced inmates, or first offenders from repeaters.

Jail Inmates

Although state and federal prison populations have been measured annually since 1925, the first systematic, nationwide jail population statistics were not collected until 1970.[5] One-day inmate counts were taken on March 15, 1970, and again on June 30, 1972, and February 15, 1978. Beginning in 1982, annual surveys and censuses have counted or estimated jail populations at midyear, and have also reported average daily population figures for the previous twelve-month period. In most years since 1982, data have also been reported on the number of inmates admitted to or released from jails.

Inmate Counts (Population "Stocks"). On June 28, 1996, U.S. jails held an estimated total of 518,492 inmates, which was less than half the number of inmates held in state and federal prisons (1,112,448) on that date. The estimated average daily jail population for the previous twelve-month period was 515,432. Unfortunately, there are no data on the range and variance in daily jail populations, which would indicate the extent and location of major under- and overutilization problems. State jail studies have sometimes found a number of jails standing *empty* on the survey date (Mattick 1974, pp. 800–801); on the other hand, occasional population "spikes" can severely overload jail facilities and staff.

Jail Inmate Turnover (Population "Flows"). The one-day and daily average inmate "stock" data summarized earlier provide one useful measure of the size of jail operations. But from the point of view of jail administration and programming, an equally important measure is the volume, over time, of inmate admissions and discharges (Mattick 1974, p. 794). High inmate turnover imposes major administrative costs, and the resultant short average duration of jail commitments limits the information that can be obtained about each inmate's needs, as well as the quality and variety of programs it is feasible for jails to provide.

Beginning in 1982, the federal jail surveys and censuses began to collect data on annual jail "flows" as well as "stocks." In 1993 (the most recent year for which such data are available), there were estimated to have been 13,245,000 jail admissions, of which 9,796,000 were "new" bookings (excluding transfers from other facilities and returns from escape, weekday or work release, medical appointments, or court appearances). By comparison, there were only 518,562 admissions (including 341,722 new court commitments) to state and federal prisons in 1993 (Maguire and Pastore 1995, p. 544, Table 6.23).

Jail "stock" and "flow" data can also be used to compute rough estimates of the average duration of each jail commitment.[6] The average daily jail population in 1993 was 466,155; when divided by the total annual jail admissions figure, this yields an estimated average (i.e., mean) duration of thirteen days per jail commitment. However, the distribution of these durations is highly skewed, with a large number of very short durations at the low end and a long "tail" at the high end composed of a relatively small number of very long durations. The 1988 Jail Census provides the only detailed national data on the duration of jail commitments. For all persons released during the seven days preceding the census, the *median* time served in jail was three days (compared with an estimated 1988 *mean* duration of twelve days, using the method previously described). Thirty-nine percent of released inmates had spent one day or less in jail, and about two-thirds had spent a week or less. On the other hand, 3 percent had spent at least six months in jail, and 1 percent had spent more than one year. Data based on surveys of jail inmate "stocks" produce much longer durations. In 1989, the mean and median times that unconvicted inmates had already spent in jail were 3.4 and 1.5 months; for inmates sentenced to jail, the mean and median times already served were 5 and 2.4 months.

Demographic and Other Inmate Characteristics. As of June 30, 1996, 1.6 percent of jail inmates were less than eighteen years old and would thus be classified as juveniles in many states. Over two-thirds of these 8,100 inmates had been convicted or were awaiting trial as adults. Age data for adult inmates were last reported for 1989. In that year, about one-third of inmates were eighteen to twenty-four years old, 43 percent were twenty-five to thirty-four, and 23 percent were thirty-five or older. The remainder of this discussion of jail inmates focuses on adult inmates, except where the available statistics do not exclude juveniles.

In recent years, about 90 percent of adult jail inmates have been male. Female inmates are much more likely to be charged with or convicted of a drug offense than are male inmates, and are much less likely to be in jail for a violent crime (Bureau of Justice Statistics 1991d). Females are also much more likely to be first offenders.

The only consistently reported data on the legal status of jail inmates are on the number of "unconvicted" and "convicted" inmates. In 1996, convicted inmates constituted 49 percent of adult jail inmates. This group includes inmates serving a misdemeanor or felony jail sentence, as well as those awaiting sentencing, appeal, transfer to prison, or other proceedings; however, no recent data are available on the relative numbers within each of these subcategories. The 1970 Jail Census reported that the 48 percent of convicted inmates included 5 percent "awaiting further legal action," 36 percent serving a sentence of one year or less, and 7 percent serving a longer sentence. The 1983 Jail Census reported that 5 percent of inmates were awaiting sentencing, 42 percent were serving a sentence, and about 2 percent were "technical violators" (presumably awaiting parole or probation revocation).

The majority of jail inmates belong to racial or ethnic minorities. In 1996, 42 percent of inmates (including juveniles) were white non-Hispanic; 41 percent were black non-Hispanic, 16 percent were Hispanic (of all races), and 2 percent were of other races. There were 111 white non-Hispanic jail inmates per 100,000 white non-Hispanic U.S. residents. For black non-Hispanics the rate was 666 per 100,000 residents.

The incarceration rates for Hispanics and for other races were 290 and 80 per 100,000, respectively.

Over one-half of jail inmates surveyed in 1989 reported that they had never been married; only about one-fifth were currently married. In the 1978 survey, 43 percent of inmates claimed to have supported one or more dependents before being incarcerated, with a median of 2.5 dependents each. More than two-thirds of the women in jail in 1989 had children under the age of sixteen (Bureau of Justice Statistics 1992b).

Sixty-four percent of jail inmates in 1989 reported being employed prior to their incarceration, 53 percent full-time and 11 percent part-time. Forty-six percent reported that they were high school graduates; however, as many as one-half of jail inmates are estimated to be functionally illiterate (Cornelius 1996, p. 32).

Almost a quarter of the jail inmates surveyed in 1989 had been charged with a drug offense. Another 23 percent were charged with violent offenses, and 30 percent with property offenses. Less than 2 percent of inmates were charged with drunkenness or other "morals" crimes (including disorderly conduct, unlawful assembly, vagrancy, and commercialized vice). Among unconvicted jail inmates, the most common offense types were violent and property crimes; for convicted inmates, property and public-order offenses (especially drunk driving: 14 percent) were the most common.

More than three-quarters of jail inmates surveyed in 1989 had a prior juvenile and/or adult sentence of probation or incarceration, and more than half had two or more prior sentences. Fifty-seven percent had previously been incarcerated as a juvenile and/or adult. Forty-six percent were on probation, parole, pretrial release, or other release when they were arrested on their current offense.

In the 1989 survey, 78 percent of jail inmates reported having used illegal drugs at some point in their lives. Seventy-one percent had used marijuana, and 50 percent had used cocaine or crack; the proportions reporting using heroin, amphetamines, barbiturates, or LSD varied between 17 and 22 percent. The following additional information was obtained for convicted inmates: 21 percent reported that they were or had been an alcoholic; 44 percent had used drugs in the month before their current offense; and 57 percent reported having been under the influence of drugs and/or alcohol at the time of the offense.

Eight percent of jail inmates surveyed in 1989 reported having previously been sent by a court to a mental hospital or mental health treatment program. Thirteen percent reported having taken medication prescribed by a doctor for an emotional or mental problem.

Major Recent Changes and Their Likely Causes

The first nationwide sample survey of American jails, conducted by the National Council on Crime and Delinquency in 1966, concluded that

"[i]n the vast majority of city and county jails and local short-term institutions, no significant progress has been made in the past fifty years"
(1967, p. 162). Thirty years later, it is possible to give a somewhat less
pessimistic report: *some* progress appears to have been made in a number
of areas. However, detailed comparisons over time are hampered by the
limitations in the national data, noted earlier (changing definitions and
variables reported).

Changes in Jail Facilities and Operations

There are fewer "jails" now than when federal jail surveys began in 1970,
especially fewer very small jails; on the other hand, there are now more
very large jails (over 250 inmates). As a result, the "average" jail now
holds almost four times as many inmates as it did in 1970: there were 40
inmates per jail in 1970, and 157 in 1996 (assuming no further decline in
the number of jails since the 1993 Census). The increase in very large
jails is probably the combined result of rising arrest rates in cities and ur-
banized suburbs, and the closing of some smaller jails in these areas. The
reduction in very small jails may be due to a combination of economic,
legal, and political factors. Since small jails are much more costly to operate, they eventually impose unacceptable fiscal burdens on local property taxpayers—especially those in small towns and rural counties with
declining economies or populations. The filing or threat of legal challenges to inadequate jail facilities or operations may have further tended
to weed out the smallest, least efficient jails. Finally, some of these
smaller jurisdictions may have also consolidated their trial courts and/or
law enforcement agencies into countywide or multicounty systems, thus
further reducing the need to maintain or replace some small jails.

Jail "capacity" has been greatly expanded in recent years. When capacity was first measured in 1978, jails reported a total of 247,342
"beds"; "rated capacity" (as determined by state or local "rating officials") was first estimated in 1982 at 250,000. By June of 1996, rated capacity had risen to 562,020. It is not known how consistent these measures are over time, or how they compare with recommended standards
for inmate cell space, classification, or jail facilities and programs.

Despite the capacity increases noted previously, jail overcrowding became a serious problem in the 1980s. In 1970, only about 5 percent of
jails reported total inmate populations greater than their "design capacity"; overall jail capacity or occupancy rates were not reported. In
1978, 64 percent of reported "jail beds" were occupied. By 1982, national
jail populations occupied 84 percent of total "rated capacity." The national jail occupancy rate rose steadily in the subsequent years, reaching
a high of 108 percent in 1989; since then, the rate has declined steadily,
and was 92 percent in 1996.

Jails have also changed internally. It appears that inmates are now less
likely to be single-celled, and that the average jail cell is newer (because

of the substantial expansion of jail capacity noted earlier); to a lesser extent, it seems likely that the average jail structure or residential unit is also newer, although much of the expanded capacity probably involved simply adding beds to existing units. Some newer jails use the "direct-supervision" concept (placing guards *inside* the residential unit rather than in a separate, secure area outside), which seems to reduce costs and improve security and morale (see earlier discussion).

Jail staffing has been reported in all five jail censuses, but the reported variables and their definitions have frequently changed. The current definitions were adopted in 1983, and most of the data reported since then combine all full-time, part-time, and nonpayroll employees (see earlier discussion).

Since 1983, jail staffing appears to have increased more than inmate populations, causing a decline in inmate-to-staff ratios. In 1983, there were 3.5 inmates per jail employee; in 1993, 2.8. For correctional officers, the 1983 and 1993 figures were 5.0 and 3.9. Yet, paradoxically, jail operating costs (most of which are for personnel) fell by 11 percent on a per-inmate, inflation-adjusted basis between 1983 and 1993 (Bureau of Justice Statistics 1995b, p. 10). This is a rather ominous finding because it suggests that jail personnel are even more underpaid than they were previously (salaries were already very low in 1983; Thompson and Mays 1991, p. 242). There are not nearly enough "new-generation" jails to yield substantial, nationwide cost savings, nor do such savings seem attributable to the greater efficiency of larger jails. The simplest explanation—that staffing and/or cost data are seriously defective—is hardly more reassuring.

Perhaps as a result of increased average jail size and/or the threat of litigation, more jails now have medical facilities. In 1972, 86 percent of jails lacked any such facility (even an infirmary); by 1988, this figure was "only" 67 percent. Improved medical care might be one reason that jail inmate death rates have been declining (from 232 deaths per 100,000 inmates in 1983 to 149 in 1993). But most of the mortality decline is the result of a drop in jail suicides, which probably reflects the changes in jail staffing and celling noted earlier.

In recent years, there may have been some increase in the use of jail-release and jail-alternative programs, perhaps in response to the pressure of jail crowding and inmate legal challenges. In 1972, 43 percent of jails had work-release programs, and 46 percent had weekend sentence programs. By 1988, the proportions were 54 and 73 percent, respectively, with about 38,000 inmates participating in one of these programs.

In addition to the two programs already described, many jail inmates and potential inmates are now being supervised in other community-based programs, but precise data are not available. Beginning in 1995, annual jail surveys have separately reported the number of "inmates" who were subject to the "jurisdiction" of local jail authorities but who were not actually being held in the jail (in prior years, such persons were simply counted as "inmates" and were included in all jail inmate counts and population averages). In 1996, 12 percent of jail "jurisdiction" inmates (72,977) were reported to be subject to some form of "community supervision," with two-thirds in community service, weekender (detention), or other work-release or work-crew programs. Most of the remainder was subject to home detention or treatment programs. These figures provide an indication of the variety of jail-alternative programs now being used, but they tell us nothing about the total number of persons participating. The figures presumably exclude some participating inmates who *were* housed in the jail as of the survey date. It also seems likely that jails did not identify and report all of the community supervision "inmates" under their jurisdiction (especially those who were released full-time). And, of course, many more offenders in "intermediate sanctions" programs are supervised by probation, parole, and other authorities (Morris and Tonry 1990), and thus are neither in jail nor under jail "jurisdiction."

Since 1970 there appears to have been a slight shift away from local, law enforcement control of jails. There are now a few privately run or multijurisdiction jails, and two more states (Hawaii and Vermont) have taken complete control over jailing. By and large, however, the traditional organizational structure remains securely intact.

Changes in Jail Inmate Populations

As shown in Figure 18.1, total jail inmate populations have increased substantially since 1970: the average daily jail population in 1996 (515,432) was more than three times larger than the inmate count taken in February of 1970 (160,863).[7] Jail populations remained fairly constant between 1970 and 1978 but began to increase at some point between the 1978 and 1982 jail surveys; the average annual growth rate during this four-year period was 7.6 percent.[8] Between 1982 and 1989, average daily populations increased by an average of 9.1 percent per year; the largest increases were in 1985 (14.9 percent), 1988 (15.7 percent), and 1989 (15.1 percent). Since 1989, average daily populations have increased by an average of 4.2 percent per year.

What explains these increases in jail populations and the varying rates of growth from year to year? The ability to predict, or at least understand, inmate population changes is important not only in jail planning but also in evaluating the actual and potential role of jails in the criminal process. One obvious point of comparison is contemporaneous variations in the numbers of prison inmates. As shown in Figure 18.2, state and federal prison "custody" populations (excluding inmates held in local jails because of prison crowding, or otherwise within the "jurisdiction" but not actual custody of prison authorities; Bureau of Justice Statistics 1982) have also increased dramatically since 1970, and indeed increased even more than jail populations; the year-end U.S. prison population was over five times larger in 1995 than it was in 1970.[9]

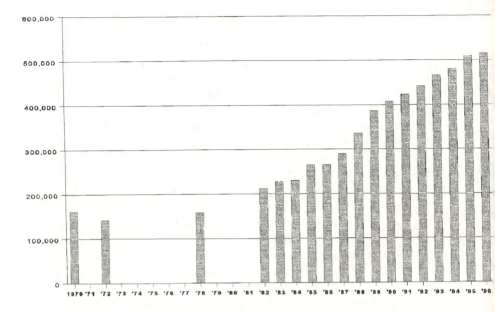

Figure 18.1 Jail inmates, 1970–1996. Average Daily Populations, including juveniles. *Note:* Figures for 1970, 1972, and 1978 are one-day counts; 1982 and later figures are July–June averages. *Sources:* Bureau of Justice Statistics 1971, 1974, 1981, 1983, 1984, 1986, 1987a, 1987b, 1989b, 1990a, 1990b, 1991c, 1992a, 1993, 1995b, 1996b, and 1997.

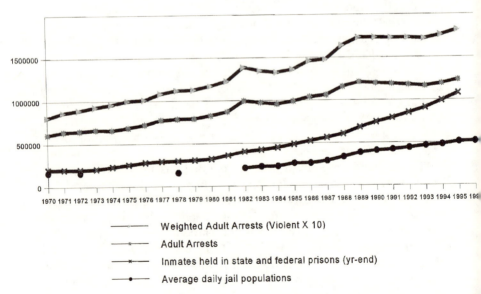

Figure 18.2 Jail inmates, 1970–1996. Compared to prison populations, adult arrest rate and weighted adult arrest rate. *Note:* Arrest data scaled down (divided by 10). *Sources:* Jail populations. see Figure 18.1; Prison populations. Bureau of Statistics 1984–1992, 1996b, 1997; arrests: Federal Bureau of Investigation 1972–1996.

Both the jail and prison population increases appear to be due in part to major increases in adult criminal caseloads. Although some juveniles are held in jail, juveniles represent a small and decreasing percentage of jail inmates—5 percent in 1970, decreasing to a low of .6 percent in 1992 and rising slightly to .9 percent in 1993.[10] (More recent figures are somewhat higher (1.6 percent in 1996) but are not directly comparable: since 1994, jails have been asked to report the number of inmates under eighteen, rather than the number of juveniles.)

Since nationwide data on prosecution and conviction rates are not available for all offenses, arrest statistics provide the best measure of adult criminal caseloads. As shown in Figure 18.2, adult arrests doubled between 1970 and 1995. However, average jail populations increased even faster, more than tripling during this period. Some of the greater increase in jail (and prison) populations is due to increases in adult arrests for serious violent crimes (murder, rape, robbery, and aggravated assault). However, even when these violent crimes are heavily weighted (i.e., multiplied by ten)[11] in the adult arrest measure, average jail populations still increased faster than weighted adult arrest rates (the latter increased by only about 125 percent between 1970 and 1995).

As shown in Figure 18.2, jail populations remained fairly constant in the 1970s, while adult arrests and prison populations rose by 30 percent or more. Adult jail populations did increase, but only slightly (up 2.4 percent from 1970 to 1978). What explains this marked discrepancy in "expected" adult jail populations, and what lessons does this period hold for future efforts to control jail population increases? Limited jail capacity seems an unlikely explanation; state and local authorities have, in recent decades, seemingly shown little reluctance to operate overcrowded penal institutions. Moreover, jails were *less* crowded in the 1970s than in the 1980s.

One plausible explanation for slower growth in pretrial populations might be the continued spread of release on recognizance and other bail reforms. Although these reforms began in the 1960s and had been widely adopted by the early 1970s (Zimring and Frase 1980, pp. 296–349), their spread may have continued into the later years of that decade. In 1988 through 1992, about one-third of felons were not released prior to disposition of their charges (Bureau of Justice Statistics 1995b, p. 13) This rate is about the same as that reported for 1971 by Wayne Thomas (Zimring and Frase 1980, p. 325). It is possible, however, that release rates in misdemeanor cases increased during this period. Bail reform might also have indirectly affected postconviction jail populations (which also remained unchanged during the 1970s). Inmates who spend little or no time in pretrial detention are less likely to be convicted and receive a jail sentence (and vice versa; Zimring and Frase 1980, pp. 311–12; Frase and Weigend 1995, p. 356).

Other possible explanations for static jail populations in the 1970s include reduced arrest rates for high-jail-use crimes such as public drunkenness and violent crimes; increases in the speed or rate of prosecutor screening (dismissal) of arrests; and "speedy trial" reforms (which directly reduce pretrial custody and, as suggested earlier, might indirectly affect jail-sentenced populations). These various hypotheses, alone or in combination, provide fertile ground for research into the causes and prevention of jail population increases.

As for the period after 1978, why did jail populations increase so much faster than arrests? Jail populations more than tripled between February 1978 and June 1996, whereas adult arrests and weighted adult arrests (violent times ten) increased by only 60 and 68 percent, respectively, from 1977 to through the end of 1995. The "drug war" that was launched in the late 1980s appears to have caused a noticeable acceleration in arrest and detention rates in 1988 (Figure 18.2). Yet total and weighted adult arrests leveled off between 1990 and 1993, while jail and prison populations continued to rise. The proportions of convicted and unconvicted inmates remained constant throughout most of the 1980s and early 1990s, suggesting a general increase in punitiveness. Further research will be needed to identify all of the sources of this increase; it is probable, however, that police, prosecution, and sentencing decisions all played important roles.

Changes in Inmate Population Characteristics

Unconvicted inmates have constituted between 50 and 52 percent of adult inmates in every year these data were reported, except for 1982 (57 percent), 1986 (53 percent), and 1995 (56 percent). Assuming the data are accurate, at least at the national level,[12] what explains these occasional variations? The atypically high proportions of unconvicted inmates in each of these three years seem to have reflected, in part, sharp increases in adult arrests in the immediately preceding years (which would initially have a greater impact on pretrial populations). The high proportion of unconvicted inmates in 1995 was also the result of a sudden leveling off in the number of convicted jail inmates between 1993 and 1995. (No conviction status data were reported for 1994.) One contributing factor was a substantial decrease from 1994 to 1995 in the number of inmates held in local jails because of prison overcrowding: the number of such "prison backlog" inmates increased from 6,470 in 1983 to 45,618 in 1994 but then fell to 32,739 in 1995 (Bureau of Justice Statistics 1995b, p. 14; Bureau of Justice Statistics 1996b, pp. 6–7). Another possible factor may have been the increased use of alternative, noncustodial sentencing options such as community service and electronically monitored home detention, in place of jail sentencing. However, many of these options are also used in lieu of pretrial jail custody, and it is not clear why they would differentially affect unconvicted and convicted jail inmate populations.

Although jail populations are overwhelmingly male, the proportion of females has increased steadily: from 5 percent of adult inmates in 1970, to 7 percent in 1983, and 11 percent in 1996. Jail populations are also increasingly composed of black and/or Hispanic inmates. The proportion of black non-Hispanic inmates rose from 37.5 percent in 1983 (Bureau of Justice Statistics 1991d, p. 3) to 44.2 percent in 1993, before falling somewhat to 41.1 percent in 1996. The proportion of Hispanic inmates increased from 14.3 to 15.6 in this thirteen-year period. Jail incarceration rates (per 100,000 residents) for blacks (including Hispanic blacks) increased sharply in 1988 and 1989 (Bureau of Justice Statistics 1995b, p. 2).

These gender and racial shifts are due in part to the differential impacts of the "war on drugs" (Bureau of Justice Statistics 1991b, p. 2). The proportion of jail inmates charged or convicted of a drug offense increased from 9 percent in 1983 to 23 percent in 1989. Over the same period, the proportion of violent offenders decreased from 31 to 23 percent, while the proportion of property offenders fell from 39 to 30 percent. The proportion of inmates charged with drunkenness, disorderly conduct, and vagrancy has fallen steadily, reflecting declines in arrests for these crimes.[13] Although precise data are lacking, the proportion of jail inmates with mental health problems has probably increased since the early seventies as a result of the sharp reductions in state mental hospital populations and tightening of requirements for involuntary commitment (Kalinich, Embert, and Senese 1991, pp. 80–81).

It seems likely that an increasing proportion of sentenced jail inmates are felons rather than misdemeanants. Between 1986 and 1992, the proportion of felons receiving a jail sentence increased from 21 to 26 percent (Bureau of Justice Statistics 1995b, p. 13). There was no increase in the average duration of such sentences (seven months). In addition, throughout the 1980s, more and more felons remained in jail waiting for space to become available in overcrowded state prisons. Since the overall proportion of convicted jail inmates did not increase during this period, fewer sentenced misdemeanants must have been held.

To summarize: changes in recent years have improved jail conditions and economic efficiency, and have removed some especially problematic inmates (juveniles and drunks). However, other problematic categories (women with children, the mentally ill, drug addicts, HIV-positive individuals, and felons) have been added, and most jails remain locally controlled and uneconomically small. Ironically, it is quite likely that the substantial expansions of jail facilities and staffing, achieved in recent decades, have strongly reinforced traditional approaches to jailing and have made it even harder to effect the necessary fundamental changes.

Problems and Policy Issues Confronting Jails

The previous descriptions of jails and jail inmates have suggested a number of practical and policy issues, some of them new but most of them long-standing. The following discussion begins by identifying the special management problems faced by jail administrators and staff, and then examines the major policy and research issues in jailing—what can and should be done today, and in the years ahead, to address the remaining shortcomings in our jails and help them better define and achieve their purposes.

Special Management Problems of Jails

Although jails have many features in common with other custodial institutions, especially state and federal prisons, jails face unique problems—some of them inherent in the functions jails serve and others resulting from the traditional manner in which jails have been operated.

Multiple Jail Functions, with Uncertain Missions. Because most jails provide general detention as well as correctional custody, they must accommodate a wide range of functions and categories of inmates. These diverse missions complicate jail administration and aggravate the economic problems of jailing discussed below.

Jails also confront several critical ambiguities as to their most basic missions. For example, is it appropriate to "treat" unconvicted inmates, if they are presumed innocent (Mattick 1974, p. 832)? The Supreme Court has held that such inmates may not be "punished" (*Bell v. Wolfish*, 441 U.S. 520 [1979]) but has upheld pretrial detention conditions that serve a legitimate custodial or "regulatory" purpose (including the prevention of further crime) (idem; *U.S. v. Salerno*, 481 U.S. 739 [1987]). In the case of noncustodial programs, it appears that formal conviction status is less and less important; pretrial release and diversion programs frequently include probation-like requirements (e.g., periodic reporting; drug testing; treatment, education or employment). However, such requirements may be justified by the "consent" of defendants (in return for release); it is unclear whether any of these requirements can be imposed on detainees.

After conviction, uncertainty remains as to what "correctional" measures should be applied to jail inmates. May those who are awaiting sentencing, appeal, transfer to other correctional facilities, or disposition of parole or probation revocation proceedings be required to accept "treatment"? For those actually serving a jail term, what purposes is such a sentence expected to serve? Court orders imposing jail sentences rarely specify any purposes. In light of these uncertainties, as well as budget and staffing limitations, jail administrators probably settle on the minimum definition of their role: provision of secure custody (i.e., no escapes and no serious injuries or illness to inmates or staff) and compliance with any legally required standards for facilities and handling of prisoners.

Inmate Transience. The short duration and high turnover of jail inmates imposes high administrative costs, and limits the ability of staff to get to know inmates—or even identify those in need of special treatment or precautions (e.g., monitoring of suicide risks; segregation of especially vulnerable or dangerous inmates). Short jail durations also prevent the application of correctional or ameliorative treatments that require some time to be effective.

Inefficiencies Due to Small, Highly Varying Populations. The smaller size of jails, in comparison to prisons, prevents economies of scale, thus increasing per-inmate costs and discouraging the hiring of specialized staff. Jails are also inherently likely to be underused or overcrowded, or to suffer both of these problems in alternation, because of the large variations in daily inmate populations that occur in a small institution and the need to separate juveniles, females, and other groups (Mattick 1974, p. 809; Bureau of Justice Statistics 1990a, p. 6). A small or medium-sized jail whose maximum capacity equals its largest daily population will tend to be inefficiently underused most of the time. Yet any lesser design capacity ensures periodic or chronic overcrowding—especially on weekends, when jails must accommodate both higher arrest rates and "weekender" sentences. Overcrowding, in turn, overloads already strained jail resources and aggravates every other problem of jail administration. Compared with prisons, jails are also less insulated from sudden increases in crime and/or arrest rates, which can overwhelm the jail long before additional capacity can be added. In contrast, prison inmates arrive months or years after their arrest; during this period, many decisions occur which can delay, reduce, or avoid the need for prison custody.

Particular Inmate Problems and Needs. Certain groups of jail inmates pose exceptional management problems, particularly in the period immediately following arrest and admission to jail (Cornelius 1996, pp. 29–42). Since jailing, unlike prison commitment, marks the *start* of custody for most inmates, very little is yet known about each inmate's problems, especially those that are hidden or difficult to diagnose; in any case, jails generally lack the time and specialized staff needed for proper diagnosis. Moreover, some physical and psychological conditions are likely to be seriously aggravated by the onset of incarceration. This is especially the case for the interrelated problems of chemical dependency, anxiety, and depression; many jail inmates arrive with an elevated risk of suicide, which increases in the first hours of custody (Winfree and Wooldredge 1991, p. 64).

As soon as they arrive in jail, drunks and drug-impaired inmates require a separate and secure area in which to sober up; addicts may suffer severe withdrawal symptoms (yet may not be visibly impaired at the time of jail admission); other inmates may have serious injuries or communicable or life-threatening illnesses (including HIV inflection, hepatitis, and pneumonia). Juveniles and females require separate housing from adult males. The aged, disabled, mentally deficient, protected witnesses, and other vulnerable adults also require separate housing or close supervision; in many cases, the only practical way to protect such inmates is to place them in isolation cells, although this increases the risk of medical complications or suicide. Other adults (and, increasingly, some juveniles) require separate handling because of their particular degree of dangerousness and/or gang affiliation or involvement in personal disputes (all of which are difficult to assess at the time of admission).

Most of these groups also require special services throughout their commitment: schooling for juveniles; medical and/or counseling treatment for alcoholics, drug users, pregnant women, and inmates with mental or physical illnesses; emergency dental care; and provision of special visiting or other accommodations to the needs of inmates, usually female, who have sole custody of minor children. Medical and dental problems are very common, since most jail inmates (especially heavy drug and alcohol users) have previously neglected their health (Cornelius 1996, p. 38).

Jail Politics and Staffing. All of the preceding problems are inherent in the operation of a small facility serving traditional jail functions or receiving the problematic inmate groups just described. But these problems are compounded by certain other jail characteristics that, although not inherent, are long-standing and peculiarly resistant to change. First, the fact that almost all jails are locally run means that they are subject to the vagaries of local politics and the limitations of local budgets; politics and tight budgets also affect prisons, but these pressures may be attenuated by the influence of a larger state correctional bureaucracy, more sources of revenue, and/or less dominance by particular political or economic interests. Second, most jails are staffed by law enforcement personnel whose interests, training, and abilities do not necessarily qualify them highly for jail work (see later discussion).

Current Policy and Research Issues

What can and should be done to improve the conditions in jails and in jails' effectiveness in improving their inmates—or at least not making them worse? The following discussion addresses, first, the problem of defining the proper functions of jails, which in turn defines the size and nature of jail facilities and programs that are needed today and in the future. A second set of policy and research issues relates to the fundamental issues of jail organization and control that remain even if jail functions are properly defined: where should jails be located, and who should control them? Although these considerations may suggest the need for radical restructuring of most jails, past history indicates that this is unlikely to occur in most states. Hence the need to turn to a third set of issues: How can existing jails be improved? The discussion ends with a final, cautionary note: whether the issue is jail definition, reorganization, or amelioration, researchers and policy makers must understand the serious limits that the available data, and the inherently diverse and complex nature of jails and jail needs, place on any attempt at rational jail planning.

Defining Essential Jail Functions and Needs. Many of the problems of jail management are the result of overcrowding, understaffing, or other jail resource inadequacies. Thus, the most fundamental challenge is to decide which kinds of persons actually need to be held in short-term custody. If significant numbers of inmates can be kept out of jail entirely, or if their terms of incarceration can be shortened, current per-inmate jail resources, and thus the quality of jail operations, can be improved, and court intervention may be avoided. Careful definition of jail functions and needs is even more important when planning future jail facilities and operations; underbuilt jails will be inadequate to the demands placed on them, while overbuilt jails are either inefficient (as a result of high per-inmate costs) or overused (simply because cell space is available) relative to the actual need for jail custody.

Jail researchers have long recognized the importance of maximizing various forms of jail "diversion" (Mattick 1974, pp. 822–30; Thompson and Mays 1991, p. 246; Cornelius 1996, pp. 55–58). Reducing the large number of very short commitments would be especially valuable, given the administrative burdens of high inmate turnover and the impossibility of providing much in the way of programming to such inmates.

Opportunities for diversion exist at each stage of the criminal process, beginning with the definition of crime. For example, the legislative and judicial decriminalization of public drunkenness and vagrancy appears to have substantially reduced the number and proportion of jail inmates charged with these and related offenses since the early 1970s. Most juveniles have also been diverted from jail.

Other forms of diversion that operate to reduce the number and/or duration of jail commitments include greater use of police citation or prosecutor summons, in lieu of arrest or extended custody; bail reform measures that encourage release on recognizance or easier-to-meet financial conditions; availability of judges for bail hearings during high-arrest evening and weekend hours; more frequent and/or earlier prosecutor screening and dismissal of weak or inappropriate charges; pretrial diversion, drug courts, and other alternatives to formal conviction; and "speedy trial" measures and reduced delays in sentencing and appeals (Zimring and Frase 1980, pp. 471–92).

Of course, pretrial "reforms" can also *increase* jail populations (e.g., the enactment of preventive detention laws, which permit pretrial detention based on explicit predictions of offender dangerousness, not just risk of nonappearance in court). Mandatory-arrest policies (e.g., for domestic assault) can have a similar effect, as can police decisions to more aggresively enforce certain offenses, such as drugs, drunk driving, or miscellaneous-minor or "public order" offenses subject to a "zero tolerance" policing strategy.

"Diversion" can also operate at the postconviction stage, through broader use of community-based sentencing options that eliminate jail custody or reduce its average duration (see Tonry and Lynch 1996). Indeed, jail inmates provide an ideal group for alternative sentencing; their shorter sentences—measured in months rather than years—are comparable in duration to the typical custody terms imposed in those foreign countries that often substitute intermediate sanctions for custody (Frase 1990, pp. 648–51). Sentenced jail inmate populations can also be reduced by increasing good time credits or early release on parole; by lowering the frequency and/or duration of commitments based on alleged probation or parole violations;[14] and by reducing the number of inmates held in jail because of prison overcrowding.

Again, some sentencing reforms may *increase* local inmate populations, such as greater use of jails for prison prerelease programming, or substitution of jail terms (with or without other community-based conditions) for the prison terms currently being given to many nonviolent felons. Any long-term assessment of the need for sentenced-inmate jail capacity must consider whether these kinds of changes are desirable, or at least probable. The desirability of such changes in felony sentencing policy depends on assumptions about the benefits of community-based corrections (discussed below), and on assessments of the likelihood that reduced costs due to shorter custody terms will outweigh the increased per-inmate costs and/or lower the overall quality of custodial care, which may result from the use of local (and usually smaller) facilities. Ultimately, the need for sentenced-inmate jail capacity, whether for felons or misdemeanants, depends on the following question: Are short custodial terms *ever* necessary, given the variety of punitive, noncustodial sentencing options?

Of course, jail diversion has its limits and its own costs. Thus, although some researchers believe that pretrial detention is still being overused (Jackson 1991, p. 38, a view that finds considerable support in the lower arrest-based detention rates in several foreign countries; see Frase 1990; Frase and Weigend 1995), it cannot be denied that current nonappearance and rearrest rates among released defendants are quite high: one-quarter of released felons fail to appear at least once, and 14 percent are rearrested before trial (10 percent for a felony; Bureau of Justice Statistics 1994). Rearrest rates may also be high for sentenced offenders who receive nonjail sanctions. Whether most of these problems can be managed by more careful supervision or other measures short of full-time incarceration is a major issue for future research and law reform.

Evaluating the Need for Major Jail Reorganization. Even after the need for short-term custody has been carefully defined, important issues remain as to where jails should be located and who should control them. The inherent problems of inefficiency and local control have led virtually all jail experts, at least as far back as 1920, to recommend some sort of regionalization, state takeover, or other radical reorganization of some or all jail functions (Mattick 1974, pp. 833–35; Goldfarb 1975, p. 450; Mays and Thompson 1991, p. 16).

Despite these repeated proposals, relatively few state-run or multi-jurisdiction jails appear to exist (although informal cooperation, especially the "boarding" of inmates in another jurisdiction's jail, is quite common). In 1995, federal jail surveys identified twenty-three jails that were being operated jointly by formal agreement between two or more jurisdictions. In that year, there were only five states with completely state-run jails. In addition, a few state-run jails, jail farms, or camps are found in a handful of other states.

Aside from the natural reluctance of local officials to give up the patronage or other powers provided by jail control, there are several legitimate arguments against regionalization. In the case of pretrial inmates, jails need to remain close to the trial courts they serve in order to minimize transportation costs and delays, and permit convenient access of attorneys to their clients. It is no accident that the states with exclusively state-run jails are geographically very small and/or have small state populations, resulting in state takeover of other local government functions (Mays and Thompson 1991, pp. 12–13). Most states continue to operate courts at the city and/or county level.

As for sentenced inmates, there are fewer problems of maintaining access to courts and attorneys. However, some sentenced inmates are still pursuing appeals or are facing new charges or required court appearances. In any case, sentenced inmates—as well as those in pretrial detention—may benefit from being housed closer to their home communities in order to preserve their ties to family, existing employment, and other sources of support, and to encourage the use of mediation and other victim-centered restorative justice programs.

The siting of regional jail facilities is problematic even apart from the need to preserve community ties. Most urban residents do not want a large penal institution next door. But if regional jails are located in less populated areas, to lessen community resistance and to equalize travel times to and from participating communities, these jails will have difficulty operating community-based programs. Work-, education-, and treatment-release options, as well as many in-jail programs, rely heavily on public and private community resources, and require that the jail not be located too far from the population centers where these resources are concentrated.

Thus, a decision to shift inmates to regional institutions may represent a preference in favor of state-enforced standards and economies of scale over the benefits of convenient court access and community-based corrections, described earlier. But very little is currently known about these trade-offs. Much more research is needed on the experiences of existing regional jails and the actual effects of different jail locations.

Another reform option would be to keep some or all jails local but to change the authorities charged with their supervision and operation. Jails in some jurisdictions are already being run by non–law enforcement officials (see earlier discussion). With or without civilian jail control, some jail guards and other staff are permanent jail employees rather than sworn law enforcement officers temporarily assigned to the jail.

There are a number of disadvantages to using police or sheriff's department personnel to staff and manage jails (Mattick 1974, pp. 804–5, 810; Mays and Thompson 1991, p. 5). Such personnel rarely have any special training for jail work and are likely to view such work—especially its correctional functions—as less important than other law enforcement work. As Hans Mattick put it long ago, police personnel are mainly interested in putting offenders *in* jail, whereas the goal of a correctional worker should be to prepare inmates to get *out* of jail and live as productive and law-abiding citizens (Mattick 1974, p. 804). Moreover, there is some evidence that sheriff's deputies assigned to jail duty earn less than other department employees, or may be assigned to the jail because of injury, probationary status, or poor job performance elsewhere (Thompson and Mays 1991, p. 242). In smaller jails, sworn law enforcement personnel are also more likely to work part-time rather than full-time at the jail; as a result, they are less familiar with and committed to jail operations and inmates.

On the other hand, there may be some advantages to law enforcement control and staffing of jails. In comparison to nonsworn guards and jailers, law enforcement officers may be more likely to have civil service or union status, which can produce higher qualifications and higher pay (Mattick 1974, p. 804). There may also be some value in giving the officials who have power to *fill* the jail (by making arrests) a stake in safely managing the institution.

Despite these possible advantages, past experience suggests that the best long-term goal would be to incorporate jails into comprehensive community corrections or court services agencies, subject to state standards, supervision, and financial assistance. Such agencies could better implement and coordinate the wide variety of pretrial and sentencing programs operating out of, or parallel with, the jail (see previous discussions of diversion and jail-run, community-based programs).

Another option is privatization of some or all jail operations (Cornelius 1996, pp. 49–50). Contracting for food service, medical care, and some other jail functions has long existed, but totally private-run jails are still very rare. There are enough of them, however, to justify further research into whether their supposed advantages (greater flexibility and lower costs) outweigh the objections some have raised to turning important matters of public justice over to private entrepreneurs (Cox and Osterhoff 1991, pp. 227–39).

Improving Existing Jail Operations. Assuming that most jails will continue, for the foreseeable future, to be locally sited, and controlled and staffed by local law enforcement personnel, how can the operations of these institutions be improved? In particular, what ameliorative strategies are available to well-intentioned states, local governments, jailers, jail researchers and reformers, and jail inmates themselves?

At the state level, more could be done to define and enforce minimum standards for local jails (American Correctional Association 1981). Meaningful enforcement requires a regular inspection program; legal power to obtain jail closure or limitations on use; and the political and judicial will to impose these sanctions. A recent survey of the forty-four states with primarily locally run jails found that only six states lacked any kind of state jail standards. However, only twenty-nine states had statutorily required jail inspection programs, and only seven had jail standards enforceable in the courts (Mays and Thompson 1991, pp. 19–21). Even where state standards exist, along with the means and will to enforce them, it is unlikely that much will be achieved in the absence of state aid or subsidy programs, tied to standards compliance (Mattick 1974, p. 831; Mays and Thompson 1991, pp. 14–15). The extent of current noncompliance is reflected in the fact that only a quarter of the nation's jails have chosen to seek "accreditation" under the American Correctional Association's jail standards; of these, only 10 percent (seventy-nine jails) have obtained this distinction (Cornelius 1996, p. 61).

At the local level, jail reformers and government officials need to adopt better research, planning, and policy-making procedures (Mattick 1974, p. 842; Thompson and Mays 1991, p. 245; Cornelius 1996,pp. 57–58). One idea—which would benefit all aspects of local criminal justice, not just jails—would be to create a multiagency planning group similar to the statewide sentencing guidelines commissions now operating in many states. Such a body, composed of representatives of the courts, local corrections, police, prosecution, defense, and the general public, could take a comprehensive, long-term view of local criminal justice problems, options, and resources, and avoid narrow or crisis-driven decision making.

In recent years, jail inmates have also been an important source of improvement in jail conditions—by means of lawsuits to enforce constitutionally required humane treatment and civil rights, as well as certain statutorily based rights (especially rights of the disabled and rights of free exercise of religion; see Mattick 1974, pp. 835–41; Champion 1991, pp. 197–215; Cornelius 1996, pp. 21–28). About one-fifth of all jails are, or have been, involved in litigation (Mays and Thompson 1991, p. 10).

The most common procedural vehicle for inmate lawsuits is the federal Civil Rights Act (42 U.S. Code § 1983). As of this writing, however, it is unclear whether inmate litigation, and especially the Civil Rights Act (CRA), will continue to play such an important role. The Prison Litigation Reform Act of 1995 (18 U.S. Code § 3626 et seq.; 28 U.S. Code § 1915; 42 U.S. Code § 1977e) attempts to sharply limit CRA suits by requiring court orders and consent decrees to be narrowly drawn, extending no further than necessary to prevent the violations of rights of the particular inmate or inmates bringing the suit (not potential inmate victims represented in a "class action"), and giving substantial weight to public safety and the operation of the criminal justice system. The act also allows courts to reopen and modify existing orders and consent decrees (including inmate population caps) that do not meet such standards; limits the award of attorneys' fees in CRA cases; increases inmate filing fees and costs; and requires inmates to first exhaust all available administrative remedies within the correctional system. The act will have a particularly strong impact on jail litigation, which has relied heavily on class action suits because individual inmate claims are quickly rendered moot by the inmate's release (Mattick 1974, p. 841). It remains possible that portions of the act will be held unconstitutional.

Jail supervisors seeking to improve their operations should welcome all of the ameliorative strategies described here, since they provide jailers with needed guidance in defining optimum jail functions, and valuable political and legal leverage to ensure that essential jail needs compete successfully for limited local and state funds. Jailers seeking to implement politically unpopular policies of diversion and improved jail standards need all the help they can get. Jailers also need to give more attention to public relations and media coverage. News stories can actually be helpful, informing the public about jail problems that would otherwise remain out of sight and receive low priority (Mays and Thompson 1991, p. 11). Jailers should also understand that public opinion is not implacably punitive or resistant to siting of local facilities, at least when the public is presented with accurate data on jail problems, needs, and options (Welsh et al. 1991, pp. 138–47).

Jail researchers can assist all of these efforts. First it is necessary, however, to recognize the serious limitations of existing jail data and take steps to improve that data. In the past, jail studies have not attracted sustained, academic research interest. The occasional local or state government jail reports are limited and inconsistent in their coverage, and they generally do not address long-term trends, systemic factors determining jail needs, or major reform possibilities.

The national jail data are better but have some serious limitations. The federal definition of a jail has changed over the years and has always been underinclusive; it excludes all short-term lockups, even though these facilities are at least as numerous as jails, are sometimes quite large, and may hold inmates for as long as or longer than the median duration of jail commitments (see earlier discussion).

There are also a number of problems with the jail data themselves. Different variables have been reported from year to year, and definitions or categorization of key variables (e.g., staffing, celling, age of cells and facility) have changed several times. The published federal reports do not follow a uniform format in either order or content; some "Inmates" reports also contain data on jail facilities, and vice versa. Some crucial data items are of uncertain reliability. For example, it seems unlikely that inflation-adjusted operating costs per inmate declined in the 1980s, if inmate-to-staff ratios were also falling substantially. "Overcrowding" data are not based on any independent or consistent definition of "capacity." And inmate conviction-status definitions may also lack consistency over time and across jurisdictions.

The aggregate quality of most of the published federal data also limits its usefulness for jail research and planning. Jails are extremely diverse in their size, functions, staffing, and programs, and the special problems of these many jail subtypes cannot be understood from nationwide figures or even from data broken down by region, state, or jail size. Rural, multifunction jails face different problems than urban, single-purpose facilities. What is needed is a better typology or modeling of jails (Klopfas 1991), based on distinct jail types. We also need separate data and in-depth research on nontraditional jails—single-sex, single-function, multijurisdictional, or state-run facilities; jails controlled, supervised, or staffed by non–law enforcement personnel. Of course, even aggregate data for a single jail or jail type can be highly misleading; for example, one-day or average occupancy rates tell us nothing about the extent of fluctuations up (or down) from day to day, or within the different demographic or legal status inmate groups that require separate celling.

Finally, we lack any national or consistent state or local data on some very important issues. For example, all of the national data on persons held in jail is based on inmate "stocks" and is heavily biased in favor of long-term jail commitments. Annual inmate "flow" populations are at least twenty times greater and probably include a far higher proportion of minor and first offenders. In addition, we have almost no information on the proportions of convicted jail inmates who are awaiting sentencing or appeal; serving a misdemeanor versus a felony sentence; or sentenced directly to jail versus committed as a result of a probation or parole violation, post–prison release programming, or temporary transfer (e.g., for hearings on new charges). Among both pretrial and convicted inmates, those held under work release and other intermittent confinement are not separated out. More detailed inmate data (along with better data on misdemeanor and felony probation conditions for persons not subject to jail jurisdiction) would be very useful in determining the extent to which jails, or certain jails, have successfully made use of the diversion strategies previously discussed.

Even with much-improved data, however, rational jail planning will always be difficult, given the multitude of factors that determine jail needs in any particular locality and the unpredictable nature of many of these factors. Jail populations are determined not only by crime rates but also by every aspect of criminal justice functioning, including legislative, police, prosecutorial, judicial, and correctional decisions. Jail needs are also affected by major changes in the juvenile justice system, chemical dependency and mental health care, and even levels of welfare coverage. All of these factors are subject to sudden, unpredictable shifts (often dictated by political, media, or philosophical fads), and the changes that occur can interact in unpredictable ways that may have a large—and immediate—impact on the nature and size of average and peak inmate populations.

For jail planners and administrators, perhaps the best defense against the inherent unpredictability of jail capacity needs is to design custody systems and alternatives that can be quickly and cheaply expanded and contracted.[15] Since noncustody alternatives cost less and involve little or no construction, jurisdictions with well-developed community-based programs will be better prepared to accommodate caseload fluctuations.

Acknowledgments This article is dedicated to the memory of Hans W. Mattick, who first introduced me to the subject of jails and taught me the importance of studying criminal justice issues from a systemic, empirically based perspective.

Notes

1. In order to avoid cluttering the remainder of this chapter with a barrage of footnotes, the federal data are generally reported by year but without further citation to specific reports (all of which are contained in the list of references). Citations are provided when there are several jail reports for one year, or when data from one year appear in a report for a different year.

2. Any term of less than two years must ordinarily be served in a county jail; sentences of two to five years may be served in either a state or a county facility (42 Pa. Consol. Statutes §9762).

3. Federal jail surveys have not examined this key issue, except to indicate that about 80 percent of jails are county-operated (Bureau of Justice Statistics 1983, p. 2). Law enforcement reports indicate that in 1993, about 620 local police departments and 2,435 local sheriffs had "primary responsibility" for running jail operations (Bureau of Justice Statistics 1996c, p. 12; Bureau of Justice Statistics 1996c, p. 13). The estimated total, 3,055 jails, is less than the 3,304 jails identified in the 1993 Jail Census; however, many agencies operate more than one jail.

4. This category must include counseling and medical staff, and perhaps also systems analysts, dispatchers, and cooks. Medical staff are discussed later in the chapter.

5. Decennial census data on jail inmates have been reported since 1880 (Cornelius 1996, p. 4) but may not be comparable (the 1970 Census reported far fewer jail inmates than were covered in the separate federal jail census conducted in that year).

6. The formula relating inmate population stocks (P), flow (F: the number of admissions per year), and time (T: the average duration per admission, in years) is: $P = F \times T$ (Zimring and Frase 1980, p. 490). T then equals $P \div F$.

7. Average daily populations figures were not computed until 1982, so comparisons to prior years are only approximate. Also, as noted earlier,

pre-1995 jail population counts include an unknown number of inmates under community supervision. It is unclear how many of these cases are included in the average daily population figures for each year before and after 1995.

8. The estimated average annual growth over N years is computed by taking the Nth root of the fraction: ending (higher) population divided by beginning (lower) population. The total increase from 1978 to 1982 was 34.2 percent, which averages out to 8.6 percent per year, including the effects of growth "compounding." Annual growth rates computed in this way are not comparable over differing lengths of time because growth over longer periods reflects greater effects of compounding.

9. The actual ratio, 5.66, overstates the true increase; prison population data for 1970 and earlier years are limited to "felons," and the 1971–1973 data are limited to inmates with a maximum sentence greater than one year. Since 1974, data have been reported on all persons held in state or federal prisons, regardless of legal status (Bureau of Justice Statistics 1982).

10. The number of jails authorized to receive juveniles also fell: in 1970, about 69 percent of jails had authority to hold juveniles at least temporarily; by 1988, this figure had fallen to 29 percent (Bureau of Justice Statistics 1991a, p. xiii).

11. For an explanation of the use of different weightings, to control for variations in caseload severity across jurisdictions, see Frase 1990, p. 657.

12. Data on the conviction status of inmate "stocks" must be used with extreme caution. In addition to the problem of differing definitions of "conviction" (e.g., some inmates awaiting sentencing or appeal may not be included; Bureau of Justice Statistics 1990a, p. 9), it must be remembered that many inmates serve part or all of their jail or prison "sentence" prior to trial or entry of a guilty plea. Such persons thus appear briefly, or not at all, in the status of a "convicted" inmate (Frase 1990, p. 658), and this phenomenon is not necessarily constant in different times and places. Thus, cross-jurisdictional and time-series analyses should, whenever possible, utilize court-based data on pretrial detention and sentencing decisions; such data are now available for felony cases but not for misdemeanors.

13. In 1972, 10 percent of jail inmates were charged as drunks or vagrants, and another 17 percent were charged with "other" crimes (probably including disorderly conduct). In 1983, only 3 percent of inmates were charged with drunkenness, vagrancy, disorderly conduct, or various "morals" crimes; in 1989, the proportion was less than 2 percent (Bureau of Justice Statistics 1991d, p. 4).

14. In recent years, however, it seems more likely that such commitments have increased; changes in technology (e.g., drug testing; electronic monitoring; and computerized warrant and conviction records) have made it easier to detect violations of release conditions.

15. In the past, local authorities have all too often relied on makeshift jails, jail barges, and similar inadequate custodial facilities (Welch 1991).

References

American Correctional Association. 1981. *Standards for Adult Local Detention Facilities.* 2nd ed. College Park, Md.: American Correctional Association.

————. 1996. *National Jail and Adult Detention Directory 1996–1998*. 7th ed. Lanham, Md.: American Correctional Association.

Bureau of Justice Statistics. 1971. *National Jail Census, 1970*. Washington, D.C.: U.S. Department of Justice, Bureau of Justice Statistics.

————. 1974. *Survey of Inmates of Local Jails, 1972*. Washington, D.C.: U.S. Department of Justice, Bureau of Justice Statistics.

————. 1975. *The Nation's Jails: A Report of the Census of Jails from the 1972 Survey of Inmates of Local Jails*. Washington, D.C.: U.S. Department of Justice, Bureau of Justice Statistics.

————. 1980. *Profile of Jail Inmates: Sociodemographic Findings from the 1978 Survey of Inmates of Local Jails*. Washington, D.C.: U.S. Department of Justice, Bureau of Justice Statistics.

————. 1981. *Census of Jails, 1978*. Vol. 1. Washington, D.C.: U.S. Department of Justice, Bureau of Justice Statistics.

————. 1982. *Prisoners, 1925–81*. Washington, D.C.: U.S. Department of Justice, Bureau of Justice Statistics.

————. 1983. *Jail Inmates, 1982*. Washington, D.C.: U.S. Department of Justice, Bureau of Justice Statistics.

————. 1984. *The 1983 Jail Census*. Washington, D.C.: U.S. Department of Justice, Bureau of Justice Statistics.

————. 1984–1992. *Prisoners in State and Federal Institutions on December 31, [1982–1989]*. Washington, D.C.: U.S. Department of Justice, Bureau of Justice Statistics.

————. 1986. *Jail Inmates, 1984*. Washington, D.C.: U.S. Department of Justice, Bureau of Justice Statistics.

————. 1987a. *Jail Inmates, 1985*. Washington, D.C.: U.S. Department of Justice, Bureau of Justice Statistics.

————. 1987b. *Jail Inmates, 1986*. Washington, D.C.: U.S. Department of Justice, Bureau of Justice Statistics.

————. 1988a. *Census of Local Jails, 1983*. Vol. 5, *Selected Findings, Methodology, and Summary Tables*. Washington, D.C.: U.S. Department of Justice, Bureau of Justice Statistics.

————. 1988b. *Jail Inmates, 1987*. Washington, D.C.: U.S. Department of Justice, Bureau of Justice Statistics.

————. 1990a. *Census of Local Jails, 1988*. Washington, D.C.: U.S. Department of Justice, Bureau of Justice Statistics.

————. 1990b. *Jail Inmates, 1989*. Washington, D.C.: U.S. Department of Justice, Bureau of Justice Statistics.

————. 1991a. *Census of Local Jails, 1988*. Vol. 1, *Selected Findings, Methodology and Summary Tables*. Washington, D.C.: U.S. Department of Justice, Bureau of Justice Statistics.

————. 1991b. *Drugs and Jail Inmates, 1989*. Washington, D.C.: U.S. Department of Justice, Bureau of Justice Statistics.

————. 1991c. *Jail Inmates, 1990*. Washington, D.C.: U.S. Department of Justice, Bureau of Justice Statistics.

————. 1991d. *Profile of Jail Inmates, 1989*. Washington, D.C.: U.S. Department of Justice, Bureau of Justice Statistics.

————. 1992a. *Jail Inmates, 1991*. Washington, D.C.: U.S. Department of Justice, Bureau of Justice Statistics.

————. 1992b. *Women in Jail, 1989.* Washington, D.C.: U.S. Department of Justice, Bureau of Justice Statistics.

————. 1993. *Jail Inmates, 1992.* Washington, D.C.: U.S. Department of Justice, Bureau of Justice Statistics.

————. 1994. *Pretrial Release of Felony Defendants, 1992.* Washington, D.C.: U.S. Department of Justice, Bureau of Justice Statistics.

————, 1995a. *Felony Sentencing in State Courts, 1992.* Washington, D.C.: U.S. Department of Justice, Bureau of Justice Statistics.

————. 1995b. *Jails and Jail Inmates, 1993–94.* Washington, D.C.: U.S. Department of Justice, Bureau of Justice Statistics.

————. 1996a. *Local Police Departments, 1993.* Washington, D.C.: U.S. Department of Justice, Bureau of Justice Statistics.

————. 1996b. *Prison and Jail Inmates, 1995.* Washington, D.C.: U.S. Department of Justice, Bureau of Justice Statistics.

————. 1996c. *Sheriff's Departments, 1993.* Washington, D.C.: U.S. Department of Justice, Bureau of Justice Statistics.

————. 1997. *Prison and Jail Inmates at Midyear 1996.* Washington, D.C.: U.S. Department of Justice, Bureau of Justice Statistics.

Champion, D. 1991. "Jail Inmate Litigation in the 1990s." In *American Jails: Public Policy Issues*, edited by J. Thompson and G. Mays. Chicago: Nelson-Hall.

Cornelius, G. 1996. *Jails in America.* 2nd ed. Lanham, Md.: American Correctional Association.

Cox, N., and W. Osterhoff. 1991. "Managing the Crisis in Local Corrections: A Public-Private Partnership Approach." In *American Jails: Public Policy Issues*, edited by J. Thompson and G. Mays. Chicago: Nelson-Hall.

Federal Bureau of Investigation. 1972–1996. *Uniform Crime Reports for the United States, [1971–1995].* Washington, D.C.: U.S. Government Printing Office.

Frase, R. 1990. "Comparative Criminal Justice as a Guide to American Law Reform: How Do the French Do It? How Can We Find Out? And Why Should We Care?" *California Law Review* 78:539–683.

————. 1993. "Implementing Commission-Based Sentencing Guidelines: The Lessons of the First Ten Years in Minnesota." *Cornell Journal of Law and Public Policy* 2:279–337.

Frase, R., and T. Weigend. 1995. "German Criminal Justice as a Guide to American Law Reform: Similar Problems, Better Solutions?" *Boston College International and Comparative Law Review* 18:317–60.

Goldfarb, R. 1975. *Jails: The Ultimate Ghetto.* Garden City, N.Y.: Anchor Press/Doubleday.

Jackson, P. 1991. "Competing Ideologies in Jail Confinement." In *American Jails: Public Policy Issues*, edited by J. Thompson and G. Mays. Chicago: Nelson-Hall.

Kalinich, D., P. Embert, and J. Senese. 1991. "Mental Health Services for Jail Inmates: Imprecise Standards, Traditional Philosophies, and the Need for Change." In *American Jails: Public Policy Issues*, edited by J. Thompson and G. Mays. Chicago: Nelson-Hall.

Kerle, K. 1991. "Introduction." In *American Jails: Public Policy Issues*, edited by J. Thompson and G. Mays. Chicago: Nelson-Hall.

Klopfas, J. 1991. "Disaggregating Jail Use: Variety and Change in Local Corrections over a Ten-Year Period." In *American Jails: Public Policy Issues*, edited by J. Thompson and G. Mays. Chicago: Nelson-Hall.

Maguire, K., and A. Pastore, eds. 1995. *Sourcebook of Criminal Justice Statistics, 1994.* Washington, D.C.: U.S. Department of Justice, Bureau of Justice Statistics.

Mattick, H. 1974. "The Contemporary Jails of the United States: An Unknown and Neglected Area of Justice." In *Handbook of Criminology*, edited by Daniel Glazer. Chicago: Rand McNally.

Mays, G., and J. Thompson. 1991. "The Political and Organizational Context of American Jails." In *American Jails: Public Policy Issues*, edited by J. Thompson and G. Mays. Chicago: Nelson-Hall.

Morris, N., and M. Tonry. 1990. *Between Prison and Probation: Intermediate Punishments in a Rational Sentencing System.* New York: Oxford University Press.

National Council on Crime and Delinquency. 1967. "Corrections in the United States." Reprinted in President's Commission on Law Enforcement and Administration of Justice, *Task Force Report: Corrections.* Washington, D.C.: U.S. Government Printing Office.

Nelson, W. 1988. *Cost Savings in New Generation Jails.* Washington, D.C.: U.S. Department of Justice.

Schwartz, I. 1991. "Removing Juveniles from Adult Jails: The Unfinished Agenda." In *American Jails: Public Policy Issues*, edited by J. Thompson and G. Mays. Chicago: Nelson-Hall.

Thompson, J., and G. Mays. 1991. "Paying the Piper but Changing the Tune: Policy Changes and Initiatives for the American Jail." In *American Jails: Public Policy Issues*, edited by J. Thompson and G. Mays. Chicago: Nelson-Hall.

Tonry, M., and M. Lynch. 1996. "Intermediate Sanctions." In *Crime and Justice: A Review of Research,* vol. 20, edited by Michael Tonry. Chicago: University of Chicago Press.

Welch, M. 1991. "The Expansion of Jail Capacity: Makeshift Jails and Public Policy." In *American Jails: Public Policy Issues*, edited by J. Thompson and G. Mays. Chicago: Nelson-Hall.

Welsh, M., M. Leone, P. Kinkade, and H. Pontell. 1991. "The Politics of Jail Overcrowding: Public Attitudes and Official Policies." In *American Jails: Public Policy Issues*, edited by J. Thompson and G. Mays. Chicago: Nelson-Hall.

Winfree, L. T., and J. Wooldredge. 1991. "Exploring Suicides and Deaths by Natural Causes in America's Jails: A Panel Study of Institutional Change, 1978 and 1983." In *American Jails: Public Policy Issues*, edited by J. Thompson and G. Mays. Chicago: Nelson-Hall.

Zimring, F., and R. Frase. 1980. *The Criminal Justice System: Materials on the Administration and Reform of the Criminal Law.* Boston: Little, Brown.

Zupan, L., and B. Menke. 1991. "The New Generation Jail: An Overview." In American Jails: Public Policy Issues, edited by J. Thompson and G. Mays. Chicago: Nelson-Hall.

Part VI

POSTCONVICTION PROCESSES AND INSTITUTIONS

19

The Juvenile Court

BARRY C. FELD

Ideological changes in the cultural conceptions of children
and in strategies of social control during the nineteenth
century led to the creation of the first juvenile court in Cook County, Illinois, in 1899. Culminating a century-long process of differentiating
youths from adult offenders, Progressive Era reformers combined new
theories of social control with new ideas about childhood and created the
juvenile court as a social welfare alternative to criminal courts to respond
to criminal and noncriminal misconduct by youths (Fox 1970; Platt
1977).

The Supreme Court's decision *In re Gault*, 387 U.S. 1 (1967), began
to transform the juvenile court into a very different institution than the
Progressives contemplated. Progressives envisioned an informal court
that intervened in the child's "best interests." In *Gault*, the Supreme
Court engrafted formal procedures at trial onto the juvenile court's individualized treatment sentencing schema. Although the Court did not intend to alter the juvenile court's therapeutic mission, in subsequent
decades, judicial and legislative responses to *Gault* have modified juvenile courts' jurisdiction, purposes, and procedure. As a result, juvenile
courts now converge procedurally and substantively with adult criminal courts.

Since the 1970s, three types of judicial, administrative, and legal
changes have accelerated the convergence between juvenile and criminal
courts. These changes constitute a form of criminological "triage" as
states remove noncriminal youths from juvenile courts' jurisdiction,
transfer increasing numbers of persistent and serious young offenders to
criminal courts for prosecution as adults, and impose punitive sentences
on those "ordinary" delinquents who remain within the jurisdiction of
the juvenile courts. Progressive reformers regarded noncriminal misconduct by juveniles that would not be a crime if committed by an adult,
such as truancy or incorrigibility, as an important part of the juvenile
court's "child-saving" mission. However, recent reforms at the "soft end"
of the court's clientele limit the dispositions that judges may impose on
noncriminal offenders and even remove status offenses from juvenile
court jurisdiction. Simultaneously, as a result of rising public and politi-

cal concern about youth crime and violence at the "hard end" of the court's clientele, states use a variety of legislative strategies to transfer increasing numbers of youths from juvenile courts to criminal courts in order to punish them as adults. As the juvenile court's jurisdiction contracts at both the "soft" and "hard" ends, states also modify its exclusive commitment to rehabilitating offenders. The sentences that judges impose on "ordinary" delinquents charged with crimes increasingly reflect criminal courts' goals of punishment rather than focus exclusively on youths' welfare and "real needs." Judges base proportionate and determinate sentences on the present offense and prior record. As criminal social control increasingly supersedes social welfare as a primary purpose of juvenile court sentences, *Gault*'s concerns about the quality of procedural justice acquire greater salience. Although in theory juvenile courts' procedural safeguards closely resemble those of criminal courts, in reality juveniles receive fewer protections than the minimum insisted upon for adult offenders.

The recent substantive and procedural convergence between juvenile and criminal courts eliminates many of the conceptual and operational differences in strategies of social control for youths and adults. With the juvenile court's transformation from an informal rehabilitative agency into a scaled-down second-class criminal court for young offenders, some question the need to maintain a separate youth justice system.

Origins of the Juvenile Court

Prior to the creation of juvenile courts, the common law's infancy defense provided the only special legal protections for young offenders charged with crimes. The common law conclusively presumed that children less than seven years old lacked criminal capacity, while those fourteen years of age and older possessed full criminal responsibility. The law rebuttably presumed that young offenders between the ages of seven and fourteen years lacked criminal capacity. If found to be criminally responsible, youths as young as twelve could be, and were, executed by the state (Streib 1987).

Because applying the criminal law to young offenders often presented the unpalatable prospect of criminal conviction and punishment as an adult, jury or judicial nullification to avoid excessive punishment excluded many youths from control, especially those charged with minor offenses (Bernard 1992). To avoid the equally undesirable consequences of undeservedly harsh punishment or inappropriately lenient sanctions, special institutions, Houses of Refuge, and reformatories for youths proliferated in the early to mid–nineteenth century, and, by the turn of the century, juvenile courts formally separated young offenders from adults (Platt 1977; Ryerson 1978).

The Progressive Juvenile Court

Economic modernization at the end of the nineteenth century transformed America from a rural agrarian society into an urban industrial one. Immigrants from southern and eastern Europe and rural Americans flooded into the burgeoning cities to take advantage of new economic opportunities. Assimilating and acculturating peoples whose cultural traditions, religions, and languages differed from those of the dominant Anglo-Protestant Europeans who had arrived a few generations earlier posed a significant nation-building challenge.

The economic transformation also affected family structure and functions, reduced the number and spacing of children, shifted economic functions from the home to other work environments, modernized and privatized family life, and substantially modified the social roles of women and children. The idea of childhood is socially constructed. During this period, the upper and middle classes rejected an earlier vision of young people as miniature adults, small versions of their parents, and instead promoted a newer view of children as vulnerable, corruptible innocents who required special attention, instruction, and preparation for life (Kett 1977).

Modernization and industrialization sparked the Progressive movement, which addressed a host of social problems (Hofstadter 1955; Wiebe 1967). Progressives believed that professionals and experts could develop rational and scientific solutions, and that benevolent governmental intervention could control the process of social change (Allen 1964, 1981). Progressives attempted to "Americanize" immigrants and the poor through a variety of agencies of assimilation and acculturation to become sober, virtuous, middle-class Americans like themselves (Rothman 1980). Significantly, Progressive reformers coupled their trust of state power with the changing cultural conception of children and entered the realm of "child-saving" (Platt 1977). Child-centered Progressive reforms, such as the juvenile court, child labor and welfare laws, and compulsory school attendance laws, both reflected and advanced the changing imagery of childhood (Kett 1977).

Ideological changes in theories of crime causation led Progressives to formulate new criminal justice and social control policies (Allen 1981). Positive criminology rejected "free will," asserted a scientific determinism of deviance, and sought to identify the causes of crime and delinquency (Rothman 1980). The assumption that antecedent factors caused behavior reduced actors' moral responsibility for their criminal conduct and justified efforts to reform offenders rather than punish them. Applying medical analogies to the treatment of offenders, a growing class of social science professionals fostered the "Rehabilitative Ideal," which assumed a degree of malleability of human behavior and general agreement about the appropriate directions of human change (Allen 1964). The "Rehabilitative Ideal" permeated Progressive criminal justice reforms such as probation and parole, indeterminate sentences, and the juvenile court, and fostered informal, highly flexible and discretionary policies and practices.

Progressive "child-savers" described juvenile courts as benign, non-punitive, and therapeutic, although modern writers question whether the movement should be seen as a humanitarian attempt to save poor and immigrant children, or as an effort to expand state social control over them (Fox 1970). The legal doctrine of *parens patriae*, the state as parent, legitimated intervention and supported the view that juvenile courts conducted civil rather than criminal proceedings. Characterizing juvenile court proceedings as civil and nonpunitive achieved reformers' desire to remove children from the adult criminal system and allowed them greater flexibility to supervise and treat children. The juvenile courts' noncriminal status jurisdiction reflected the social construction of childhood and adolescence that emerged during the nineteenth century, and allowed them to enforce their normative conception of childhood dependency. Predelinquency intervention allowed "child-savers" to respond to noncriminal misbehavior such as smoking, sexual activity, truancy, immorality, or living a wayward, idle, and dissolute life, and thereby forestall premature adult autonomy (Schlossman 1977).

The juvenile court's "Rehabilitative Ideal" envisioned a specialized judge trained in social sciences and child development whose empathic qualities and insight would aid in making individualized dispositions. Social service personnel, clinicians, and probation officers would help the judge decide and pursue the "best interests" of the child. Progressives assumed that a rational, scientific analysis of the social circumstances would reveal the proper diagnosis and prescribe the cure. Because the reformers acted benevolently, individualized their solicitude, and intervened scientifically, they saw no reason to circumscribe narrowly the power of the state. Rather, they maximized discretion to diagnose and treat, and focused on the child's character and lifestyle rather than on the crime (Ryerson 1978; Rothman 1980).

By separating children from adults and providing a rehabilitative alternative to punishment, juvenile courts rejected both the criminal law's jurisprudence and its procedural safeguards such as juries and lawyers. Court personnel used informal procedures and a euphemistic vocabulary to eliminate stigma and any implication of a criminal proceeding. They conducted confidential, private hearings, limited access to court records, and adjudicated youths to be "delinquents" rather than criminals. In theory, a child's "best interests," background, and welfare guided dispositions. Court personnel accorded only minor significance to a youth's offense because it provided, at most, only a "symptom" of his or her "real" needs. Because each child's circumstances differed, judges imposed indeterminate, nonproportional sentences that potentially continued for the duration of minority (Mack 1909).

The Constitutional Domestication of the Juvenile Court

By the 1960s, several forces combined to erode the rehabilitative premises of the Progressive juvenile court, undermine support for coercive socialization in juvenile courts, and produce a series of Supreme Court constitutional decisions that affected civil rights, criminal procedures, and juvenile justice administration. As a result of the migration of African Americans from the rural South to the urban North and West during the 1930s, 1940s, and 1950s, racial equality and social justice emerged as a national rather than a regional legal issue by the 1960s (Massey and Denton 1993). Thus, the U.S. Supreme Court's due process revolution in criminal and juvenile justice was part of the broader civil rights agenda that began with its 1954 decision in *Brown v. Board of Education* to end school segregation.

The Progressives who created the juvenile court believed that the new social sciences provided effective tools with which to change people, and that it was proper to socialize and acculturate the children of the poor and immigrants so that they could become middle-class Americans. By the time *Gault* was decided, the Progressives' consensus about state benevolence, the legitimacy of imposing certain values on others, and the efficacy of rehabilitation all had become matters of intense dispute (Allen 1981). During the turbulent 1960s, rising rates of youth crime and urban racial disorders focused political and judicial attention on criminal justice administration. Left-wing critics characterized government rehabilitation programs as coercive instruments of social control. Liberals questioned treatment personnel's exercise of clinical discretion that often resulted in unequal and disparate treatment of similarly situated offenders. Conservatives advocated a "war on crime" to repress rather than rehabilitate offenders and decried juvenile courts that "coddled" young criminals. In the 1960s, the justice systems' treatment of racial minorities provided the crucial link between distrust of governmental benevolence, concern about social service personnel's discretionary decision making, the crisis of "law and order," and the Supreme Court's due process jurisprudence. The Warren Court's due process revolution reflected a judicial effort to expand civil rights, protect minorities from state officials, infuse government services with greater equality, and impose procedural restraints on official discretion.

The Supreme Court's juvenile court decisions in *Gault* and several later cases mandated procedural safeguards in delinquency proceedings and focused judicial attention initially on whether the child committed an offense as a prerequisite to sentencing. In shifting the formal focus of juvenile courts from "real needs" to legal guilt, *Gault* identified two crucial disjunctions between juvenile justice rhetoric and reality: the theory versus the practice of rehabilitation, and the differences between the procedural safeguards afforded adults and those available to juveniles. *Gault* ruled that youths charged with crimes who faced institutional confinement required basic procedural safeguards such as advance notice of charges, a fair and impartial hearing, assistance of counsel, an opportunity to confront and cross-examine witnesses, and the privilege against self-incrimination (Feld 1984).

In *In re Winship*, 397 U.S. 358 (1970), the Court concluded that the risks of erroneous convictions and the need to protect against government power required the state to prove a youth's delinquency by the criminal law's standard of proof "beyond a reasonable doubt" rather than by lower civil standards of proof. In *Breed v. Jones*, 421 U.S. 519 (1975), the Court posited a functional equivalence between criminal trials and delinquency proceedings, and held that the ban on double jeopardy precluded criminal reprosecution following a delinquency conviction.

In *McKeiver v. Pennsylvania*, 403 U.S. 528 (1971), however, the Court denied to juveniles the constitutional right to jury trials and halted the extension of full procedural parity with adult criminal prosecutions. *McKeiver* reasoned that "due process" and "fundamental fairness" in delinquency proceedings required only "accurate fact-finding," a requirement that a judge could satisfy as well as a jury. Unlike its earlier analyses in *Gault* and *Winship,* which recognized that procedural safeguards also protected against governmental oppression, the Court in *McKeiver* denied that juveniles require such protection and instead invoked the stereotype of a sympathetic, paternalistic juvenile court judge. Unfortunately, *McKeiver* did not analyze or elaborate upon the differences between treatment as a juvenile and punishment as an adult that justified the procedural differences between the two systems.

Together, *Gault, Winship*, and *McKeiver* precipitated a procedural and substantive revolution in the juvenile court system that unintentionally but inevitably transformed its original Progressive conception and fostered its convergence with criminal courts. By emphasizing criminal procedural regularity in the determination of legal guilt, the Supreme Court shifted the initial focus of juvenile courts' delinquency proceedings from paternalistic assessments of a youth's "real needs" to proof he or she committed a crime. By formalizing the connection between criminal conduct and coercive intervention, the Court made explicit a relationship that previously was implicit and unacknowledged, and thereby reinforced punitive rather than rehabilitative impulses. Greater procedural formality and "criminalization" provided an organizational impetus to deal with noncriminal status offenders outside of the traditional juvenile justice process. And, although *McKeiver* emphasized juvenile courts' benevolent dispositions, *Gault*'s procedural reforms legitimated more punitive sanctions for young offenders charged with criminal offenses.

Although the constitutional cases provide a general framework, each state's juvenile code defines how its juvenile courts will process young offenders. In most states, juvenile court jurisdiction encompasses criminal and noncriminal misconduct by all persons under eighteen years of age, although in some states adult criminal court jurisdiction begins at sixteen or seventeen years of age. In addition, even where juvenile court jurisdiction extends until eighteen years of age, some states exclude younger youths charged with serious offenses and place them automatically in adult criminal court. In a few states, juvenile and criminal courts exercise concurrent jurisdiction over young offenders, and the prosecutor's decision to charge a youth as a juvenile or as an adult determines the forum in which the case will be heard. Consequently, juvenile courts in different jurisdictions may confront and respond to widely different clientele (Snyder and Sickmund 1995).

Early proponents of the traditional juvenile court painted an idealized portrait of procedural informality as a means to its rehabilitative ambitions (Mack 1909). Judicial discretion and informality fostered organizational diversity rather than legal uniformity (Rothman 1980). With *Gault's* imposition of formal procedures and the more recent emergence of punitive as well as therapeutic goals, states' juvenile courts no longer conform with the traditional rehabilitative model, or even with one another. Juvenile courts vary on a number of structural, philosophical, and procedural dimensions, and may be arrayed along a continuum from informal to formal procedures with corresponding substantive differences (Stapleton, Aday, and Ito 1982). "Traditional" courts may continue to intervene in a child's "best interests" on an informal, discretionary basis. More formal and legalistic "due process" courts may emphasize rule-oriented decision making and greater recognition of juveniles' legal rights. While juvenile courts vary substantially among the states, they also vary considerably within a single state. Although the same laws— statutes, court opinions, and rules of procedure—typically apply to all juvenile courts within a state, structural and geographic variations substantially affect juvenile justice administration. Differences in social structure affect juvenile crime rates and juvenile justice administration, the presence of counsel, pretrial detention, and sentencing practices (Sampson and Laub 1993; Feld 1991, 1993).

Procedural Justice in Juvenile Courts

Procedure and substance intertwine inextricably in juvenile courts. The Progressives' *parens patriae* ideology coupled substantive decisions in the child's "best interests" with informal discretionary procedures. The Supreme Court in *Gault* emphasized the disjunctions between rehabilitative rhetoric and punitive reality, and insisted on greater procedural protections for delinquents. Since *Gault*, the increased emphasis on procedural formality corresponds with an increased emphasis on punishment in juvenile courts both in legal theory and in administrative practice. Beginning in the middle to late 1970s, states began to adopt "designated felony," "serious offender," mandatory minimum, and determinate sentencing laws to impose more consequential sanctions on some young offenders. During this period, some legislatures revised their juvenile codes' purpose clauses to eliminate rhetorical support for rehabilitation, and several state court decisions endorsed punishment as a legitimate component of juvenile court sentences. These changes repudiate many of the fundamental original assumptions that juvenile courts should treat youths differently than adults, that juvenile courts operate in a youth's "best interest," and that "rehabilitation" requires an indeterminate period that cannot be limited by fixed-time punishment. These changes contradict *McKeiver*'s premise that delinquents require fewer procedural safeguards than do adult criminal defendants because juvenile courts treat youths rather than punish them.

The formal procedures of juvenile and criminal courts have converged under *Gault*'s impetus. There remains, however, a substantial gulf between theory and reality, between the "law on the books" and the "law in action." Theoretically, states' laws entitle delinquents to formal trials and the assistance of counsel. In actuality, the quality of procedural justice remains far different. More than three decades ago, the Supreme Court decried that "the child receives the worst of both worlds: he gets neither the protections accorded to adults nor the solicitous care and regenerative treatment postulated for children" (*Kent v. United States*, 383 U.S. 541, 556 [1966]). Despite the criminalizing of juvenile courts, most states provide neither special procedures to protect juveniles from their own immaturity nor the full panoply of adult procedural safeguards. Instead, states treat juveniles just like adult criminal defendants when equality redounds to their disadvantage and use less adequate juvenile court safeguards when those deficient procedures provide an advantage to the state (Feld 1984). Based on depictions of courtroom dramas and publicized criminal trials, young people have a cultural expectation of what a "real" trial should be. The contrast between the ideal process prescribed for an adult defendant, a jury trial and a vigorous defense lawyer, and the "actualized caricature" of a juvenile bench trial fosters a sense of injustice that may delegitimate the legal process (Ainsworth 1991).

Jury Trials in Juvenile Court

Although the right to a jury trial constitutes a critical procedural safeguard for youths charged with crimes, less than a dozen states grant juveniles any right to a jury trial, and the vast majority uncritically follow the Supreme Court's lead in *McKeiver v. Pennsylvania*. Without citing any empirical evidence, the *McKeiver* Court posited virtual parity between the factual accuracy of juvenile and adult trials to rationalize denying youths a jury trial. But juries provide special protections to assure factual accuracy, use a higher evidentiary threshold when they apply *Winship*'s "proof beyond a reasonable doubt" standard, and acquit more readily than do judges (Feld 1984). Analyses of comparable juvenile and criminal cases conclude that prosecutors find it easier to obtain convictions in delinquency than in criminal proceedings.

Juvenile court judges convict youths more readily than would juries for several reasons. Judge and jury fact-finding differs because the former may preside over hundreds of cases every year, while the latter decide only one or two matters. As a result of hearing many cases routinely, judges become less meticulous in considering evidence, evaluate facts more casually, and apply the concepts of reasonable doubt and presumption of innocence less stringently than do jurors. Although judges' personal characteristics differ from those of jurors, the legal process prevents defendants from determining how those factors might affect their decisions. Through voir dire, litigants may question jurors about their attitudes, beliefs, and experiences in order to assess how those factors may influence how they will decide the case. No comparable opportunity exists to explore a judge's background to determine the presence of judicial biases. In addition to the novelty of deciding cases, juries and judges evaluate testimony differently. Juvenile court judges hear testimony from the same police and probation officers on a regular basis and develop settled opinions about their credibility. Similarly, as a result of hearing earlier charges against a juvenile, or presiding over a detention hearing or pretrial motion to suppress evidence, a judge already may have a predetermined view about a youth's credibility, background, and character. Fact-finding by a judge differs from that by a jury because an individual fact finder does not have to discuss the evidence with a group before reaching a conclusion. Although judges instruct jurors explicitly about the law they will apply to a case, when judges preside at a bench trial, it becomes more difficult to determine whether they have correctly understood and applied the law (Feld 1984; Ainsworth 1991).

Moreover, *McKeiver* ignored the fact that constitutional procedures also prevent governmental oppression. In *Duncan v. Louisiana*, 391 U.S. 145 (1968), the Supreme Court held that the Constitution guaranteed adult criminal defendants the right to a jury both to assure factual accuracy *and* to protect against governmental oppression. *Duncan* emphasized that juries guard against a weak or biased judge, inject the community's values into law, and increase the visibility and accountability of justice administration. Youths, especially, require these protective safeguards because juvenile court judges often labor behind closed doors, immune from public scrutiny. Appellate courts acknowledge that juvenile court cases exhibit far more procedural errors than do adult criminal cases, and suggest that secrecy and confidentiality may foster a judicial casualness toward the law that visibility might restrain (Feld 1988b).

Juries have symbolic significance for juvenile courts out of all proportion to their practical impact. In practice, juveniles in the few states that theoretically provide them with a right to a jury trial seldom exercise the right. Surveys report that juveniles receive a jury trial in perhaps 1 to 3 percent of delinquency cases, a rate substantially lower than that of adult criminal defendants (Feld 1995). As a symbol, granting juveniles the right to a jury requires honesty about punishment imposed in the name of treatment and the need to protect against even benevolent governmental coercion. Perhaps ironically, even as states "get tough" on delinquents and adopt harsher sentencing laws, some jurisdictions that previously afforded juveniles the right to a jury trial have repealed those safeguards in order to foster greater administrative efficiency to repress youth crime (e.g., *Wis. Stat. Ann.* § 48.02.02(2) [1996]). Legislators apparently experience no dissonance between "cracking down" to punish or deter youthful criminal misconduct and using procedures under which none of them would consent to be tried.

The Right to Counsel in Juvenile Court

Procedural justice hinges on access to and the assistance of counsel. When the Supreme Court decided *Gault*, attorneys appeared in about 5 percent of delinquency proceedings (Feld 1993). Despite *Gault's* formal legal changes, however, the actual delivery of legal services to juveniles lagged behind. In the immediate aftermath of *Gault*, observers in two metropolitan juvenile courts systematically monitored institutional compliance with the decision and reported that juvenile court judges neither adequately advised juveniles of their right to counsel nor appointed counsel for them (Stapleton and Teitelbaum 1972). Others reported that even when lawyers appeared in delinquency cases, they seldom participated in any meaningful way.

In the decades since *Gault*, the promise of an attorney remains unrealized; in many states, half or less of all juveniles receive the assistance of counsel to which the Constitution entitles them (Feld 1993). Evaluations of legal representation in 1978 found that lawyers represented only 22.3 percent of juveniles in Winston-Salem, North Carolina, and only 45.8 percent in Charlotte, North Carolina (Clarke and Koch 1980). A study in a southeastern jurisdiction reported rates of representation of 26.2 and 38.7 percent, and another in a large midwestern county reported attorneys represented 41.8 percent of juveniles (Bortner 1982). Extensive research in Minnesota reported that the majority of youths appeared in juvenile courts without counsel, and that juvenile court judges removed a substantial minority of unrepresented youths from their homes (30.7 percent) or confined them in state juvenile correctional institutions (26.5 percent) (Feld 1989). The rates of representation varied enormously from county to county; attorneys represented nearly 100 percent of youths in some counties and fewer than 5 percent of youths in several other counties (Feld 1993). The only study that reports statewide data or makes interstate comparisons of presence of counsel found that in three of the six states surveyed, lawyers represented only 37.5 percent, 47.7 percent, and 52.7 percent of juveniles charged with delinquency or status offenses (Feld 1988a).

Several factors explain why so many youths appear without legal assistance in juvenile courts. Affluent parents may be reluctant to retain an attorney. Public-defender legal services may be inadequate or nonexistent in nonurban areas. Juvenile court judges may encourage and readily find waivers of the right to counsel in order to ease their administrative burdens. Judges may give cursory and misleading advice that inadequately conveys the importance of the right to counsel and suggests that waiver is simply a formal technicality. More traditional, treatment-oriented judges may resent legal advocacy that attempts to limit their discretion. Judges may also predetermine the likely disposition they will impose on a juvenile, and decline to appoint counsel when they anticipate a probationary sentence. In many instances, juveniles may plead guilty and judges dispose of their case at the same hearing without benefit of counsel. Whatever the reason, many juveniles who face potentially coercive state action never see a lawyer, waive their right to counsel without consulting an attorney, and do not appreciate the legal consequences of their decision (Feld 1989).

Waiver of counsel is the most common explanation for why so many juveniles appear without legal assistance. Most state courts use the adult legal standard—"knowing, intelligent, and voluntary" waiver under the "totality of the circumstances"—to assess the validity of juveniles' waivers of constitutional rights (*Fare v. Michael C.*, 442 U.S. 707 [1979]). Whether a child can "knowingly, intelligently, and voluntarily" waive his or her rights if he or she does so alone and without consulting with an attorney remains the crucial question. Closed, confidential juvenile court proceedings exacerbate the problems if judges encourage youths to waive counsel, create the impression that the waiver colloquy is a meaningless technicality, and then decide whether a juvenile asserts or relinquishes his or her rights.

Many commentators criticize the "totality" approach to juveniles' waivers of rights as an example of treating juveniles just like adults when formal equality puts them at a practical disadvantage (Rosenberg 1980; Melton 1989). Juveniles simply do not possess the capacity of adults to waive their constitutional rights in a knowing and intelligent manner (Grisso 1981). The host of legal restrictions that states protectively impose on children to limit their ability, for example, to enter contracts, convey property, marry, drink, drive, vote, or even donate blood recognize that children have different competencies than adults. Whereas states recognize these developmental differences for other purposes, most states allow juveniles to waive constitutional rights such as *Miranda* and the right to counsel without restriction and confront the power of the state alone and unaided.

Even when attorneys represent juveniles, they may not perform effectively for their clients. Institutional pressures to maintain stable, cooperative working relations with other personnel in the system may conflict with effective adversarial advocacy. Organizational pressures to cooperate in a closed system, judicial hostility toward adversarial litigants, role ambiguity created by the dual goals of rehabilitation and punishment, reluctance to help juveniles "beat a case," or an internalization of a court's treatment philosophy may compromise the role of counsel in juvenile court.

Several studies indicate that juveniles represented by lawyers receive more severe sentences than do similarly situated youths who appear in court without an attorney (Clarke and Koch 1980; Feld 1993). While complex relationships exist among the factors that influence the appointment of counsel and those that produce more severe dispositions, the presence of counsel consistently appears to be an aggravating factor in sentencing. Juvenile court judges remove juveniles from their homes and incarcerate larger proportions of juveniles represented by lawyers than they do those who appear without counsel, even after controlling for the effect of other legal variables such as the present offense, prior record, or previous dispositions (Feld 1993).

Several possible explanations exist for the apparent relationship between procedural formality, as evidenced by the presence of counsel, and more severe sentences. The lawyers who appear in juvenile court simply may be incompetent and prejudice their clients' cases. Although we lack systematic qualitative evaluations of the actual performance of counsel in juvenile courts, the available evidence strongly suggests that even in jurisdictions where juvenile court judges routinely appoint counsel, the lawyers may be neither competent nor effective (Knitzer and Sobie 1984; American Bar Association 1995). Or, juvenile court judges' familiarity with a case early in a proceeding may alert them to the eventual disposition that they will impose following a conviction, and they may appoint counsel when they anticipate more severe consequences. In most jurisdictions, the same judge who presides at a youth's arraignment and detention hearing later will decide the case on the merits and then pronounce a sentence. Perhaps judges base their initial decisions to appoint counsel on evidence obtained in these preliminary stages, which also influences their subsequent sentencing decisions (Ainsworth 1991). If so, the court's extensive familiarity with a case prior to the fact-finding hearing raises basic questions about the fairness and objectivity of the adjudicative process. Finally, judges simply may feel free to impose more severe sentences on juveniles who appear with counsel. Adherence to the formalities of due process insulates judges' sentences from appellate reversal. In short, the price for the use of formal procedures in juvenile courts may be similar to that experienced by adult criminal defendants who insist on a jury trial rather than pleading guilty. Although judges may not explicitly punish juveniles just because they appear with counsel, they may sentence more leniently those youths who appear without legal assistance and contritely "throw themselves on the mercy of the court."

Jurisdiction over Noncriminal Status Offenders

Critics have questioned extensively the definition and administration of status jurisdiction in the post-*Gault* decades (Teitelbaum and Gough 1977). Beginning with the President's Commission on Law Enforcement and Administration of Justice (1967), which recommended narrowing the range of misconduct for which juvenile courts could intervene, many professional organizations have advocated reform or elimination of the juvenile court's status jurisdiction. Critics focused on its adverse impact on children, its disabling effects on families, schools, and other agencies that refer status offenders, and the legal and administrative issues status offenses raise for juvenile courts (Andrews and Cohn 1974; Rosenberg 1983).

Until the 1970s, most states treated status offenses as a category of delinquency, and detained and incarcerated status delinquents in the same institutions with criminal delinquents even though they had committed no crimes. Parental referrals overloaded juvenile courts with intractable family disputes, diverted scarce judicial resources from other tasks, and exacerbated rather than ameliorated family conflict (Andrews and Cohn 1974). Social service agencies and schools used the court as a "dumping ground" to impose solutions rather than to address the underlying sources of conflict. Defining and processing status offenses raised legal issues of "void for vagueness," equal protection, and procedural justice for juvenile courts (Rubin 1985). Status jurisdiction allowed judges to exercise broad discretion to intervene and prevent unruliness or immorality from ripening into criminality. Judges' exercise of standardless discretion often reflected individual values or personal prejudices, and disproportionately affected poor, minority, and female juveniles (Chesney-Lind 1988).

Three post-*Gault* trends—diversion, deinstitutionalization, and decriminalization—represent judicial and legislative responses to these criticisms of juvenile courts' treatment of noncriminal youths. The Federal Juvenile Justice and Delinquency Prevention Act of 1974 (42 U.S. Code §§ 5601 et seq. [1983]) required states to begin a process of removing noncriminal offenders from secure detention and correctional facilities. Federal and state restrictions on commingling status and delinquent offenders in institutions provided the impetus to divert some status offenders from juvenile courts and decarcerate those who remained in the system.

Diversion

Because *Gault* increased juvenile courts' procedural formality, it provided an administrative impetus to deal with or deliver services to youths on an informal basis through diversion programs. Just as the original juvenile court diverted youths from adult criminal courts, diversion programs shift away from juvenile court youths who are eligible to enter that system. Several analysts question whether police or juvenile courts have implemented diversion programs coherently or successfully (Klein 1979; Polk 1984). Law enforcement interests in social control and a juvenile justice ideology of early identification and treatment both expand inherently, lend themselves to overreaching, and subtly co-opt reforms intended to reduce justice system involvements. Klein (1979), for example, contends that diversion programs do not limit themselves to youths who would otherwise enter the juvenile justice system but also encompass youths whom police previously would counsel and release if they dealt with them at all. As a result, rather than reducing courts' client population, diversion may have had the opposite effect of "widening the net" of social control and subjecting youths to other forms of intervention. Moreover, diversion provides a rationale to shift discretion from the juvenile court itself, where *Gault* subjects decisions to some procedural regularity, to police or intake "gatekeepers" on the periphery of the system who continue to operate on an informal pre-*Gault* basis with no accountability.

Deinstitutionalization

Federal and state bans on secure confinement of noncriminal youths provided an impetus to deinstitutionalize them. Although the numbers of status offenders in secure detention facilities and institutions declined by the mid-1980s, judges sent only a small proportion of status offenders to secure institutions; most remain eligible for commitment to group homes or other places of nonsecure confinement (Sutton 1988). Amendments to the Federal Juvenile Justice Act in 1980 weakened even the restrictions on placement in secure facilities. Probation officers may charge status offenders who run away from nonsecure placements or violate court orders with contempt of court, a delinquent act, and judges may then order them incarcerated (Schwartz 1989a). Bishop and Frazier (1992) report that judges' power to find youths who violate a court order in contempt allows them to "bootstrap" status offenders into delinquents and constitutes an important continuing source of gender bias in juvenile justice administration.

Decriminalization

Juvenile courts originally classified status offenses as a form of generic delinquency. In recent decades, however, most states have "decriminalized" conduct proscribed only for children—incorrigibility, runaway, truancy—and created new nondelinquency labels such as persons or children in need of supervision (PINS or CHINS) (Rubin 1985). Other state legislatures relabel these "juvenile nuisances" as dependent or neglected or as children in need of protection and services (Rosenberg 1983; Bishop and Frazier 1992). Label changes simply shift youths from one jurisdictional category to another without significantly limiting courts' dispositional authority. By manipulating classifications, states and juvenile justice personnel may relabel former status offenders downward as dependent or neglected youths, upward as delinquent offenders, or laterally into private-sector treatment facilities (Handler and Zatz 1982; Weithorn 1988).

Many youths whom juvenile courts previously could have handled as status offenders, especially those who are middle-class and female, increasingly enter the private mental health or chemical dependency treatment systems via diversion, court referral, or voluntary parental commitment (Schwartz 1989b). The Supreme Court in *Parham v. J.R.*, 442 U.S. 609 (1979), ruled that when parents "voluntarily" commit their children to secure treatment facilities, a physician's determination that confinement constitutes medically appropriate "treatment" provides the appropriate "due process" framework. Most states' civil commitment laws do not provide juveniles with the same procedural safeguards as they do adults. While some children's psychological dysfunction or substance abuse requires medical attention, many youths' commitments result from status-like social or behavioral conflicts, self-serving parental motives, or medical entrepreneurs coping with underutilized hospitals (Weithorn 1988). The "hidden system" of psychiatric and chemical dependency "treatment" facilities provides a readily available and easily accessible institutional system for troublemaking youth funded by third-party insurance payments. The increased rate of juvenile psychiatric commitments coincided directly with the deinstitutionalization of status offenders (Schwartz, Jackson-Beeck, and Anderson 1984). The combination of psychiatric hospitals seeking profits, health maintenance organizations with funds to reinvest in other care modalities, insurance and Medicaid coverage for inpatient mental health care, and the malleability of diagnostic categories permits service providers to "medicalize" deviance and incarcerate troublesome children without meaningful judicial supervision (Weithorn 1988; Schwartz 1989b).

Historically, the child welfare, juvenile justice, and mental health systems dealt with relatively interchangeable youth populations and shifted them from one system to another depending on social attitudes, available funds, and imprecise legal definitions. The transfer of some noncriminal juveniles from publicly funded facilities to private mental health and chemical dependency facilities may constitute the institutional successor to the juvenile justice system for the care and control of problematic youths. Whether parents or the state confines youths for their "best interests," for "waywardness" and "disobedience," for "adjustment reactions" symptomatic of adolescence, or for "chemical dependency," these trends revive the imagery of diagnosis and treatment on a discretionary basis without regard to formal procedures.

Waiver of Jurisdiction over Serious Juvenile Offenders

Public concerns about and political responses to serious youth crime and violence fuel a desire to "get tough" and "crack down" on young offenders. This punitive response represents the most recent swing in the pendulum-like "cycle of juvenile justice" (Bernard 1992). Frustration with the intractability of crime in general, the recent rise in youth violence, gun crimes, and homicide in particular, and the racial characteristics of violent young perpetrators provide the political impetus to transfer increasing numbers of youths to criminal courts for prosecution as adults and to expand the sanctioning powers of juvenile courts. Legislative changes to "get tough" simplify the process to transfer larger numbers of young offenders to adult court, or to require juvenile court judges to impose determinate or mandatory minimum sentences based on the seriousness of a youth's present offense or prior record.

Young people commit a disproportionate amount of serious crime. The Federal Bureau of Investigation (FBI) reported that the overall rate of serious crimes committed by juveniles and adults peaked around 1980, declined in the mid-1980s, and then rebounded by the early 1990s (Federal Bureau of Investigation 1992; Snyder and Sickmund 1995). The bulk of all FBI serious crime arrests consist of property offenses rather than violent crimes; during the 1980s, the rate of property crimes remained relatively stable or increased slowly (Snyder and Sickmund 1995). By contrast, although violent crimes constitute a much smaller component of the overall serious crime index, the rates of juvenile violence, especially homicide and gun-related violence, surged dramatically from the mid-1980s, to 1993 (Snyder and Sickmund 1995). The dramatic escalation in homicide rates accompanied the proliferation of guns among black youths involved in the "crack" cocaine drug distribution industry (Blumstein 1995). Moreover, police arrest minority youths five times more often than white youths for crimes of violence, and seven and a half times more often for homicide (Federal Bureau of Investigation 1992). Thus, recent changes in juvenile court waiver and sentencing statutes that provide more severe sanctions for violent offenses, although neutral on their face, will have a disparately severe impact on minority youths because of racial differences in patterns of offending.

Whether states should try to punish persistent or violent young offenders in adult criminal court or attempt to rehabilitate them in juvenile court poses difficult theoretical and practical problems. Waiver decisions implicate both juvenile court sentencing policies and the relationship between juvenile and criminal court sentencing philosophies and practices. Virtually every state has adopted one or more statutory strategies to prosecute some juveniles as adults (Snyder and Sickmund 1995). The alternative methods include judicial waiver of juvenile court jurisdiction, legislative exclusion of some offenses from juvenile court jurisdiction, and prosecutorial choice of forum between concurrent jurisdictions. Each of these statutory strategies allocates to a different branch of government—judicial, legislative, and executive—the decision whether to sentence a youth as a criminal or a delinquent. Each statutory strategy emphasizes a different balance of sentencing policy values, relies on different organizational actors, uses a different administrative process, and elicits different information to determine whether a particular young offender should be tried and sentenced as an adult or a child.

Judicial waiver represents the most prevalent transfer policy in virtually all jurisdictions (Snyder and Sickmund 1995). A juvenile court judge can waive juvenile court jurisdiction on a discretionary basis after conducting a hearing to determine whether a youth is "amenable to treatment" or poses a threat to public safety. Judicial case-by-case clinical assessment of a youth's potential for rehabilitation and dangerousness reflects the individualized sentencing discretion characteristic of traditional juvenile courts.

Legislative waiver or offense exclusion constitutes another common transfer mechanism, one that frequently supplements judicial waiver provisions. This strategy emphasizes the seriousness of the offense and reflects the retributive values of the criminal law. Because legislatures create juvenile courts, they possess considerable latitude to define the court's jurisdiction and to exclude youths from juvenile court based on their age and the seriousness of their offenses, for example, youths sixteen or older and charged with murder. Indeed, legislative line drawing that sets the maximum age of juvenile court jurisdiction at fifteen or sixteen, below the general eighteen-year-old-age of majority, results in the adult criminal prosecution of the largest numbers of chronological juveniles (Snyder and Sickmund 1995).

Prosecutorial waiver, or giving both juvenile and criminal courts concurrent jurisdiction over some crimes, represents a third method several states use to remove some young offenders from the juvenile justice system. With prosecutorial waiver, both juvenile and criminal courts share concurrent jurisdiction over certain ages and offenses, typically older youths and serious crimes, and a prosecutor's decision to charge a youth as a juvenile or adult determines the judicial forum (McCarthy 1994; Snyder and Sickmund 1995). To the extent that a prosecutor's decision to charge the case in criminal courts divests the juvenile court of jurisdiction, prosecutorial waiver constitutes a form of offense-based decision making like legislative offense exclusion.

Each method to decide whether to prosecute a youth as a criminal or a delinquent has supporters and critics. Proponents of judicial waiver emphasize its consistency with juvenile courts' rehabilitative sentencing philosophy and contend that individualized judgments provide an appropriate balance of flexibility and severity (Zimring 1991). Critics object that juvenile court judges lack valid or reliable clinical tools with which to assess a youth's amenability to treatment or to predict dangerousness, and argue that judges' exercise of standardless discretion results in abuses and inequalities (Feld 1987, 1990; Fagan and Deschenes 1990).

Proponents of legislative waiver endorse "just desserts" retributive sentencing policies; advocate sanctions based on relatively objective characteristics such as the seriousness of the offense, culpability, and criminal history; and assert that offense exclusion fosters greater consistency, uniformity, and equality among similarly situated offenders (Feld 1995). Critics question whether legislators can exclude offenses and remove discretion without making the process excessively rigid, and whether politicians can resist their own demagogic impulses to "get tough" and adopt expansive lists of excluded offenses, thereby substantially increasing the number of youths whom they transfer inappropriately to criminal court (Zimring 1981, 1991).

Proponents of concurrent jurisdiction prosecutorial waiver claim that prosecutors can function as more neutral, balanced, and objective gatekeepers than either "soft" juvenile court judges or "get-tough" legislators (McCarthy 1994). Critics of prosecutorial waiver strategies contend that prosecutors, as locally elected officials, succumb to the same political pressures to appear "tough" and posture on crime, often lack the breadth of experience or maturity that judges possess, and exercise their discretion subjectively and idiosyncratically, thus introducing even greater variability into juvenile justice administration (Bishop and Frazier 1991).

Judicial Waiver

In *Kent v. United States*, 383 U.S. 541 (1966), the Supreme Court required juvenile courts to provide youths with some procedural protections when they made jurisdictional transfer decisions. Later, in *Breed v. Jones*, 421 U.S. 519 (1975), the Court required states to make the jurisdictional decision whether or not to transfer a youth before proceeding on the merits of the charge. Although *Kent* and *Breed* provide the formal procedural framework within which judges make waiver decisions, the substantive bases of the waiver decision pose the principal difficulties. Most jurisdictions provide for discretionary waiver based on a juvenile court judge's assessment of a youth's "amenability to treatment" or "dangerousness." In practice, judges emphasize a youth's age, prior exposure to correctional treatment and clinical "prognosis," and current offense and prior record (Fagan and Deschenes 1990; Podkopacz and Feld 1996). Some states provide neither offense nor minimum-age restrictions, while others limit judicial waiver to felony offenses or older juveniles (Snyder and Sickmund 1995).

Asking a judge to assess a youth's "amenability to treatment" assumes that effective treatment programs exist for some serious or persistent juvenile offenders and that valid and reliable diagnostic tools enable clinicians or juvenile court judges to differentiate the potential treatment responsiveness of various youths. Similarly, asking a judge to decide whether a youth poses a threat to public safety requires judges to predict future dangerousness even though clinicians lack the technical capacity reliably to predict low base-rate serious criminal behavior (Monahan 1981). Without uniform or objective criteria to guide transfer decisions, judges apply these discretionary statutes inconsistently within a state, and racial and geographic disparities frequently ensue (Fagan, Forst, and Vivona 1987; Fagan and Deschenes 1990; Podkopacz and Feld 1996).

While judicial waiver decisions implicate the tensions between individualized sentencing, discretion, and the rule of law, they also involve the relationship between juvenile and criminal court sentencing practices. Juvenile and adult courts often pursue inconsistent sentencing goals when youths make the transition to criminal courts. Despite public and legislative concern about youth violence, judges in most states judicially transfer more juveniles who chronically commit property crimes like burglary than those who commit violent crimes against the person (Snyder and Sickmund 1995). When these youths appear in criminal courts as adult first offenders, judges typically fine the majority of these judicially waived young property offenders or place them on probation, and even those confined receive jail or prison sentences comparable in length to those that juvenile court judges could impose on juveniles with prior records convicted as delinquents (Podkopacz and Feld 1996; Snyder and Sickmund 1995). The lack of congruence between judicial waiver and criminal sentencing decisions occurs because judges frequently waive older chronic offenders who have "outworn their welcome" in juvenile court, even though they may not appear as the most serious offenders in the adult "stream of cases." A lack of integration of juvenile and adult criminal records further frustrates rational social control when youths make the transition from the juvenile to the adult justice system. Although a record of persistent offending, whether as a juvenile or as an adult, provides the "best evidence" of career criminality, the traditional rule of confidentiality in juvenile court proceedings to avoid stigmatizing delinquents often hinders criminal courts' access to juvenile conviction records (Blumstein et al. 1986). The failure to include the juvenile component of an adult offender's criminal history stems from the confidential nature of juvenile court records, the functional and physical separation of the respective court services staffs, and the difficulty of compiling and maintaining criminal histories through several different bureaucracies (Feld 1995). As a result, adult criminal courts often traditionally relied primarily on the seriousness of the present offense and the prior adult criminal history in making sentencing decisions. More recently, however, criminal courts increasingly use juvenile convictions to sentence adult offenders (Feld 1995). The expansion and integration of juvenile records in adult sentencing decisions subordinates the traditional rehabilitative goals of avoiding stigma to the public safety interests of reliably identifying career criminals and provide another indicator of convergence between the two systems.

Legislative Exclusion of Offenses, Offense Criteria, and Waiver Decisions

Legislative waiver statutes simply exclude certain offenses from juvenile court jurisdiction. Some jurisdictions exclude only capital crimes or murder, while others place youths charged with rape, armed robbery, and other offenses in adult criminal court. While most states prescribe some minimum age for "automatic adulthood," typically sixteen years, others prosecute as adults youths as young as thirteen charged with murder (Snyder and Sickmund 1995). Excluded offense statutes constitute a legislative normative judgment that certain crimes are so serious that those who commit them *deserve* to be tried and sentenced as adults. Excluding only the most serious crimes integrates juvenile waiver and adult sentencing practices and enables criminal courts to sentence violent or chronic young offenders more consistently (Feld 1995).

Within the past two decades, states' laws increasingly use offense criteria rather than clinical assessments of offenders' "amenability to treatment" as the bases for waiver decision (Feld 1987, 1995). About half the states have amended their judicial waiver statutes to reduce their inconsistency and to improve the fit between waiver decisions and criminal sentencing practices (Feld 1987; Snyder and Sickmund 1995). Legislatures use offense criteria to structure judicial discretion, to restrict waiver only to certain serious offenses, or to require special procedures, shift the burden of proof, or create a presumption for waiver for youths charged with a serious present offense or those with an extensive prior record. Using serious offense criteria and specifying special waiver procedures limits judicial discretion and increases the likelihood that criminal courts will impose significant sanctions on those youths whom juvenile courts judges waive (Feld 1995; Podkopacz and Feld 1996).

About half of the states now exclude at least some youths from juvenile court jurisdiction based on offenses and age, and the list of excluded offenses continues to grow. Violent crimes and those committed while using a firearm receive special legislative attention. Legislation that targets very serious or violent crimes also increases the likelihood that criminal courts will impose significant adult sentences on these serious young offenders.

Statutes that use offense criteria either as sentencing guidelines to control judicial waiver discretion or to exclude certain offenses from juvenile court jurisdiction provide one indicator of a policy shift from an offender-oriented treatment sentencing philosophy to a more retributive one. Laws that structure or eliminate judicial discretion repudiate rehabilitation at least with respect to "hard-core" offenders, narrow juvenile court jurisdiction, marginally reduce its clientele, and deny juvenile courts the opportunity to treat certain youths without even inquiring into their personal characteristics. Because minority youths commit a disproportionate amount of gun-related and violent crimes, the legislative efforts to impose more severe sentences on violent offenders disproportionately affect black youths.

The increased emphasis on punishing younger offenders as adults and targeting violent or capital crimes exposes at least some youths to the possibility of execution for the crimes they committed as juveniles. In *Thompson v. Oklahoma*, 487 U.S. 815 (1988), a plurality of the Supreme Court ruled that executing an offender for a crime committed at fifteen years of age violated the Eighth Amendment prohibition on "cruel and unusual punishment." However, in *Stanford v. Kentucky*, 492 U.S. 361 (1989), the Court concluded that a state would not violate the Constitution if it executed a youth for a crime committed at sixteen or seventeen years of age. Moreover, state courts routinely uphold sentences of "life without possibility of parole" for youths as young as thirteen convicted and sentenced as adults, and they do not require any proportionality analyses or special consideration of youthfulness as a mitigating factor. Both the erosion of juvenile court jurisdiction over serious offenders and the conclusion that they are as criminally responsible as adults undermine the rationale that younger offenders differ qualitatively from adults or need a juvenile court separate from the adult criminal justice system.

Punishment in Juvenile Courts: Sentencing Delinquent Offenders

Punishment is premised on the notions that responsible actors make blameworthy choices and deserve to suffer prescribed consequences. Courts typically impose determinate and proportionate sentences for past behavior, and sanction on the basis of relatively objective legal factors such as seriousness of offense, culpability, or criminal history (von Hirsch 1976). Treatment, by contrast, focuses on the mental health, status, and future welfare of the individual rather than on the commission of prohibited acts (Allen 1964, 1981). Treatment assumes that antecedent factors caused the undesirable behavior, and that intervention can improve the offender's future well-being. Because individualized justice deems all personal and social characteristics as relevant and does not assign controlling significance to any one factor, courts typically exercise wide discretion to impose nonproportionate and indeterminate sentences.

These presumed differences between juvenile treatment and criminal punishment underlay the Supreme Court's decision in *McKeiver v. Pennsylvania* to deny jury trials in delinquency proceedings. As states increasingly "get tough," however, the ever-tenuous distinctions between treatment and punishment blur even further. Legislative purpose clauses and court opinions, juvenile court sentencing statutes and actual sentencing practices, conditions of institutional confinement, and evaluations of programs' effectiveness consistently indicate that treating juveniles closely resembles punishing adult criminals.

Legislative Purposes of Juvenile Courts

A statement of legislative purpose provides one indicator of whether coercive intervention constitutes punishment or an "alternative purpose" of treatment (*Allen v. Illinois*, 478 U.S. 364 [1986]; Gardner 1982). Most states' juvenile court statutes contain a purposes clause that declares the underlying legislative rationale as an aid to courts in interpreting the law (Feld 1988b). In the decades since *Gault* and *McKeiver*, more than one-quarter of the states have redefined their juvenile codes' statements of legislative purpose to de-emphasize rehabilitation and the child's "best interest," and to assert the importance of protecting public safety, imposing sanctions consistent with the seriousness of the offense, and ensuring individual responsibility and system accountability (Walkover 1984). Many courts recognize that these changes in purpose clauses signal a basic philosophical reorientation in juvenile justice, and yet endorse the role of sanctions commensurate with age, offense seriousness, and prior history (Feld 1988b).

Juvenile Courts' Sentencing Legislation and Practices

Sentencing statutes and judicial practices provide another indicator that juvenile courts punish rather than treat delinquents. Originally, juvenile courts imposed indeterminate and nonproportionate sentences to achieve the child's "best interests." More recently, however, many states' juvenile court sentencing laws increasingly emphasize punishment. Again, these changes reflect sentencing decisions by the various arms of government: determinate sentencing statutes to control judicial discretion; mandatory minimum statutes that reflect legislative sentencing priorities; and correctional parole release guidelines to regularize sentencing decisions by the executive branch. Despite the juvenile court's history of indeterminate sentencing, about one-third of the states now use the present offense, prior record, or both to regulate at least some juvenile court sentencing decisions through determinate or mandatory minimum sentencing statutes or correctional administrative guidelines (Feld 1988b).

The clearest departure from traditional juvenile court sentencing practices occurred in 1977 when Washington State enacted just desserts legislation that established presumptive sentences with a standard range proportionate to the offender's age, the seriousness of the present offense, and the length of the prior record (Feld 1988b). Other states also use offense, criminal history, and statutory "aggravating and mitigating" factors to impose determinate and proportionate sentences and "graduated sanctions" on juveniles.

A number of states impose mandatory minimum sentences on youths convicted of certain "designated felonies." Legislators typically "prescribe" these mandatory sentencing laws for "violent and repeat offenders," "aggravated juvenile offenders," "serious juvenile offenders," or "designated felons." Terms of mandatory confinement range from twelve to eighteen months, to age twenty-one, or to the adult limit for the same offense. Mandatory minimum sentences based on the offense preclude any consideration of the offender's "real needs."

Several states' departments of corrections adopted administrative release guidelines that use offense criteria to specify mandatory minimum and proportionate "length of stay" terms of confinement. These determinate guidelines reflect decisions by the executive branch, typically departments of corrections, juvenile justice agencies, or youth service agencies, to regularize release decisions based on the present offense and other "risk" factors, such as prior record, probation, or parole status.

Although statutory mandates influence juvenile court judges' sentencing decisions, practical bureaucratic considerations and paternalistic assumptions about children also influence their discretionary decisions. Moreover, the exercise of broad discretion in the pursuit of individualized justice raises concerns about its discriminatory impact (McCarthy and Smith 1986; Fagan, Slaughter, and Hartstone 1987). Poor and minority youths are disproportionately overrepresented in juvenile correctional institutions relative to white youths (Kempf-Leonard, Pope, and Feyerherm 1995). Several studies analyze the extent to which legal offense factors, sociodemographic variables, or system processing variables influence juvenile court judges' sentencing decisions.

Evaluations of juvenile court sentencing practices yield two general findings (McCarthy and Smith 1986; Fagan, Slaughter, and Hartstone 1987). First, judges focus primarily on the seriousness of the present offense and prior record when they sentence delinquents. In multivariate studies, these legal and offense variables typically explain about 25 to 30 percent of the variance in sentencing (Clarke and Koch 1980; McCarthy and Smith 1986; Feld 1989). Practical bureaucratic considerations, such as avoiding scandals and unfavorable political and media attention, constrain juvenile court judges to impose more formal and restrictive sentences on more serious offenders (Bortner 1982). Complex organizations develop bureaucratic strategies to simplify individualized assessments, and the present offenses and prior records provide a routine basis to rationalize decisions.

Second, after controlling for offense variables, the "individualized justice" of juvenile courts results in racial disparities in sentencing juveniles. The prevalence of racial disparities in states' juvenile courts and institutions prompted Congress to amend the Juvenile Justice and Delinquency Prevention Act to require states applying for federal funds to review and evaluate the sources of minority overrepresentation (42 U.S. Code § 5633(a)(16) 1988 & Supp. V 1993). Virtually every state that has examined racial bias in juvenile courts confirms its presence at pretrial detention and sentencing. Juvenile justice decision making is a multi-stage process; screening and processing decisions cumulate and amplify racial disparities as minority youths proceed through sequential stages of the system (Kempf-Leonard, Pope, and Feyerherm 1995; Feld 1995; Bishop and Frazier 1996).

Juvenile courts, as extensions of criminal courts, give primacy to offense factors when they sentence youths. To the extent that *parens patriae* ideology legitimates individualization and differential processing, it exposes "disadvantaged" youths to the prospects of more extensive state intervention. The recent changes in juvenile court sentencing laws and practices question the underlying premises of individualized justice and the unequal and idiosyncratic exercises of discretion, and emphasize the seriousness of the offense rather than the offenders' "needs" in a desire to "get tough." In turn, the legislative emphases on offense seriousness interact with racial differences in patterns of offending and discretionary juvenile court screening and processing decisions to amplify the disproportionate overrepresentation of minority youths in correctional institutions.

Conditions of Juvenile Confinement

Examining the correctional facilities to which judges send young offenders and evaluating their effectiveness provides another indicator of whether juvenile courts punish or treat. *Gault* belatedly recognized the long-standing contradictions between rehabilitative rhetoric and punitive reality of juvenile corrections. Several historical studies of the early Progressive training schools provide a dismal account of institutions that failed to rehabilitate and could scarcely be distinguished from adult penal facilities (Rothman 1980; Schlossman 1977). Contemporary evaluations of juvenile institutions reveal a continuing gap between rehabilitative rhetoric and punitive reality (Bartollas, Miller, and Dinitz 1976; Feld 1977; Lerner 1986). This research describes overcrowded institutions with inadequate treatment programs in which staff physically abused inmates, imposed degrading make-work, and failed to prevent inmate violence and predation. Youths filed lawsuits in which they challenged their conditions of confinement in juvenile detention facilities and correctional institutions, and courts found that staff physically beat, brutalized, and abused inmates, injected them with psychotropic drugs for social control purposes, deprived them of minimally adequate care and individualized treatment, locked them in solitary confinement for prolonged periods, required repetitive and degrading make-work such as scrubbing floors with a toothbrush, provided minimal clinical services, and sometimes detained youths under conditions worse than those imposed on adults (Feld 1988b). Although juvenile correctional institutions are not as uniformly deplorable as those of most adult prison systems, rehabilitative euphemisms such as "providing a structured environment" should not disguise the punitive reality of juvenile confinement (Forst, Fagan, and Vivona 1989).

The recent "get tough" changes in juvenile court sentencing laws exacerbate institutional overcrowding. Such laws confine serious and chronic offenders to mandatory minimum or longer terms in overcrowded facilities that suffer from limited physical mobility and inadequate program resources and staff, and foster intense interaction among the most problematic youths in the system (Bartollas, Miller, and Dinitz 1976; Feld 1977, 1981). These juvenile correctional "warehouses" can exhibit most of the negative features of adult prisons. Although a few states have experimented successfully with small, community-based juvenile treatment facilities, the correctional pendulum is currently swinging toward incarcerating more delinquents for longer periods in training schools and youth prisons.

The juvenile court "treatment model" assumes that social or psychological factors cause delinquent behavior, that judges should individualize sentences based on treatment needs, that release should be based on when the juvenile improves, and that successful treatment will reduce recidivism. Unfortunately, evaluations of juvenile rehabilitation programs provide scant support that confinement in institutions effectively treats youths rather than punishes them, or reduces their recidivism rates (Lab and Whitehead 1988, 1990). The National Academy of Science's panel on "Research on Rehabilitation Techniques" concluded: "The current research literature provides no basis for positive recommendations about techniques to rehabilitate criminal offenders. The literature does afford occasional hints of intervention that may have promise, but to recommend widespread implementation of those measures would be irresponsible. Many of them would probably be wasteful, and some would do more harm than good in the long run" (Sechrest, White, and Brown 1979, p. 102). Although several researchers offer literature reviews, meta-analyses, or program descriptions that stress that some types of intervention may have positive effects on selected clients under certain conditions (Melton 1989; Greenwood and Zimring 1985; Garrett 1985; Andrews et al. 1990), most positive findings are "suggestive," have not been replicated, or do not produce substantial reductions in recidivism when applied to larger samples of young offenders.

For a variety of reasons, the juvenile courts' claim of rehabilitation remains "unproven." Many evaluations of treatment effectiveness lack methodological rigor or use insufficiently sensitive outcome measures (Sechrest, White, and Brown 1979). Many treatment programs lack a theoretical rationale or consistent intervention strategies based on that rationale. Many studies fail to assess whether the program staff implemented the treatment with integrity (Gendreau and Ross 1987). Thus, the inability to measure treatment effectiveness may reflect methodological flaws, poorly implemented programs, or, in fact, the absence of effective methods of treatment.

Conclusion

For more than three decades since *Gault*, juvenile courts have deflected, co-opted, ignored, or accommodated constitutional and legislative reforms with minimal institutional change. States have transformed the juvenile court from its original model as a social service agency into a deficient criminal court that provides young people with neither positive treatment nor criminal justice. It effectively punishes young offenders but uses procedures under which no adult would consent to be tried. Moreover, public and political concerns about youth crime, drugs, gangs, and violence support policies to repress rather than rehabilitate young offenders. Fiscal constraints, budget deficits, and competition from other interest groups suggest little basis for optimism that states soon will expand treatment services for delinquents.

The emergence of punitive juvenile justice policies coincides with social indicators that reveal a broader decline in the welfare of children in general and minority youths in particular (National Commission on Children 1991; National Research Council 1993; Lindsey 1994). Beginning in the 1970s and accelerating in the 1980s, a number of economic, family, and structural changes adversely affected the social circumstances and futures of many young people (National Research Council 1993). Structural unemployment, out-of-wedlock childbirth, racial isolation, the feminization of poverty, and the dependency of children cause poverty and the "risk" of criminality to fall disproportionately heavily on minority children (Massey and Denton 1993).

The original juvenile court attempted to combine social welfare and social control in one institution. The Progressives envisioned a social service agency in a judicial setting and attempted to fuse the juvenile court's welfare mission with the power of state coercion. The juvenile court's inability to achieve its welfare mission does not result simply from inadequate implementation. Rather, the juvenile court's primary flaw lies in the *idea* that we can successfully combine social welfare and penal social control in one agency. Providing for child welfare is a societal responsibility rather than a judicial one. Juvenile courts lack control over the resources necessary to meet child welfare needs. Indeed, they lack resources exactly because of the gender, class, and racial characteristics of their clients. Moreover, many young people who desperately need social services do not commit crimes, and many youths who commit crimes do not require or will not respond to social services. Because states do not provide adequate social services to meet the needs of all young people, the juvenile court's welfare ideology legitimates the exercise of judicial coercion of some.

The juvenile court inevitably subordinates social welfare to criminal social control because of its inherent penal focus. States define juvenile courts' jurisdiction on the basis of a youth's committing an offense, and this premise detracts from any subsequent compassionate response. The juvenile court welfare *idea* chooses among the characteristics of certain children—*not* their lack of decent education, which is *not their fault*, nor their unmet health needs, which are *not their fault*, nor their dysfunctional family or adverse social circumstances, which are *not their fault*, but an instance of conduct in which they violated the criminal law and which *is their fault*. Unlike their social conditions, criminal behavior is the one characteristic for which adolescents are at least partly responsible. As long as the juvenile court welfare idea highlights that aspect of youths that rationally elicits the least sympathy and ignores environmental conditions that evoke a desire to help, the juvenile court simply reinforces the public's antipathy to young law violators.

Nearly a century ago, Progressive reformers had to choose between initiating structural social reforms that would ameliorate criminogenic forces or ministering to the individuals damaged by those adverse social conditions. Driven by class and ethnic antagonisms, they ignored the social-structural implications of their own theories of delinquency and chose instead to "save children" and, incidentally, to preserve their own power and privilege (Platt 1977; Rothman 1980). "Child-saving" satisfied humanitarian impulses without engendering more fundamental social change. As a result, the juvenile court welfare idea espoused deterministic causes of delinquent behavior and then individualized its sanctions (Ryerson 1978). On the one hand, to punish people for behavior that society "caused" may lead to charges of hypocrisy. On the other hand, to subscribe to deterministic explanations of behavior undermines individual responsibility and erodes the expressive, condemnatory function of criminal law.

A century later, we face the same choice between "rehabilitating" damaged individuals and initiating fundamental social-structural change. In making this choice, the juvenile court welfare idea constitutes an obstacle to child welfare reform. The *existence* of the juvenile court provides an alibi to avoid fundamental improvement. Conservatives can deprecate it as a welfare system, albeit one that "coddles" criminals, while liberals can bemoan its lack of resources and inadequate options. But either stance is akin to sticking fingers in the dike while the flood of adverse social indicators of youth pour over the top in a torrent. A society that cares for the welfare of its children does so directly by supporting families, communities, schools, and social institutions that nurture all young people, not by incarcerating its most disadvantaged children and pretending that doing so is "for their own good." Providing for child welfare is ultimately a societal responsibility. It is unrealistic to expect juvenile courts or any other legal institutions to ameliorate the social ills that afflict young people or to significantly reduce youth crime.

Uncoupling policies of social welfare from penal social control is central to considering alternatives to the juvenile court welfare idea. Once we frame child welfare policy reforms in terms of child welfare rather than crime control, the possibilities for positive intervention for young people expand. For example, a public health approach to youth crime that identifies the social, environmental, and ecological correlates of violence such as poverty, the proliferation of handguns, and the commercialization of violence suggests wholly different intervention strategies than simply incarcerating minority youths. Youth violence is part of an ecological structure; high rates of crime occur in areas of concentrated poverty, high teenage pregnancy, and dependency on Aid to Families with Dependent Children (Massey and Denton 1993). Using these social indicators to identify census tracts or even zip codes for community organizing, economic development, and preventive and remedial intervention provides more promise than continuing a failed policy of incarceration.

Three aspects of youth crime and violence suggest future social welfare and public policy directions. First, it is imperative to provide a *hopeful future for young people.* As a result of economic changes since the 1980s, the ability of families to raise children, to prepare them for the transition to adulthood, and to provide them with a more promising future has declined (National Commission on Children 1991; National Research Council 1993). Most social indicators of the status of young people (e.g., poverty, disease, teenage pregnancy, suicide, and crime) are negative, and these adverse trends are accelerating. Without realistic hope for their future, young people fall into despair, nihilism, and violence (Lindsey 1994).

Second, it is imperative that public policy pursue *racial and social justice.* A generation ago, the Kerner Commission warned that the United States was "moving toward two societies, one black, one white—separate and unequal" (National Advisory Commission on Civil Disorders 1968, p. 1). The Kerner Commission predicted that to continue present policies was "to make permanent the division of our country into two societies; one, largely Negro and poor, located in the central cities; the other, predominantly white and affluent, located in the suburbs" (p. 1). Many of the problems of youth violence that the juvenile court confronts today are the bitter harvest of racial segregation, concentrated poverty, and urban social disintegration.

Third, youth violence is becoming increasingly lethal as the *proliferation of handguns* transforms altercations into homicidal encounters (Blumstein 1995). Young people in 1992 committed three-quarters of homicides with firearms; only a policy of disarmament will begin to stem the tide. The National Rifle Association's alternative proposal that states authorize all citizens to carry concealed weapons simply assures an escalation of the carnage.

While politicians may be unwilling to invest scarce social resources in young "criminals," particularly those of other colors or cultures, a demographic shift and an aging population give all of us a stake in young people and encourage us to invest in their human capital for our own future well-being and to maintain an intergenerational compact. One generation ago, the elderly constituted the largest segment of the population in poverty, and public policies such as Social Security, Supplementary Security Income, and Medicare dramatically improved their material conditions. Today, children constitute the largest segment of the population in poverty, and the youngest, minorities, and those living in single-parent families experience the greatest penury. Social Security–like public policies to provide for child health and welfare, lift young people out of poverty, and ease the transition from adolescence to productive adulthood can prevent future crime for considerably less than the costs of expanding juvenile and criminal justice expenditures after the fact.

References

Ainsworth, Janet E. 1991. "Re-imagining Childhood and Reconstructing the Legal Order: The Case for Abolishing the Juvenile Court." *North Carolina Law Review* 69:1083–133.

Allen, Francis A. 1964. *The Borderland of the Criminal Law: Essays in Law and Criminology.* Chicago: University of Chicago Press.

———. 1981. *The Decline of the Rehabilitative Ideal: Penal Policy and Social Purpose.* New Haven, Conn.: Yale University Press.

American Bar Association. 1995. *A Call for Justice: An Assessment of Access to Counsel and Quality of Legal Representation in Delinquency Proceedings.* Washington, D.C.: ABA Juvenile Justice Center.

Andrews, D. A., Ivan Zinger, Robert D. Hoge, James Bonta, Paul Gendreau, and Francis T. Cullen. 1990. "Does Correctional Treatment Work? A Clinically Relevant and Psychologically Informed Meta-Analysis." *Criminology* 28:369–404.

Andrews, R. Hale, and Andrew H. Cohn. 1974. "Ungovernability: The Unjustifiable Jurisdiction." *Yale Law Journal* 83:1383–409.

Bartollas, Clemens, Stuart J. Miller, and Simon Dinitz. 1976. *Juvenile Victimization.* New York: Wiley.

Bernard, Thomas J. 1992. *The Cycle of Juvenile Justice.* New York: Oxford University Press.

Bishop, Donna M., and Charles S. Frazier. 1988. "The Influence of Race in Juvenile Justice Processing." *Journal of Research in Crime and Delinquency* 25:242–63.

———. 1991. "Transfer of Juveniles to Criminal Court: A Case Study and Analysis of Prosecutorial Waiver." *Notre Dame Journal of Law, Ethics and Public Policy* 5:281–302.

———. 1992. "Gender Bias in Juvenile Justice Processing: Implications of the JJDP Act." *Journal of Criminal Law and Criminology* 82:1162–86.

———. 1996. "Race Effects in Juvenile Justice Decision-Making: Findings of a Statewide Analysis." *Journal of Criminal Law and Criminology* 86:392–414.

Blumstein, Alfred. 1995. "Youth Violence, Guns, and the Illicit-Drug Industry." *Journal of Criminal Law and Criminology* 86:10–36.

Blumstein, Alfred, Jacqueline Cohen, Jeffrey A. Roth, and Christy A. Visher, eds. 1986. *Criminal Careers and "Career Criminals."* Washington, D.C.: National Academy Press.

Bortner, M. A. 1982. *Inside a Juvenile Court*. New York: New York University Press.

Chesney-Lind, Meda. 1988. "Girls and Status Offenses: Is Juvenile Justice Still Sexist?" *Criminal Justice Abstracts* 20:144–65.

Clarke, Stevens H., and Gary G. Koch. 1980. "Juvenile Court: Therapy or Crime Control, and Do Lawyers Make a Difference?" *Law and Society Review* 14:263–308.

Fagan, Jeffrey, and Elizabeth Piper Deschenes. 1990. "Determinates of Judicial Waiver Decisions for Violent Juvenile Offenders." *Journal of Criminal Law and Criminology* 81:314–47.

Fagan, Jeffrey, Martin Forst, and Scott Vivona. 1987. "Racial Determinants of the Judicial Transfer Decision: Prosecuting Violent Youth in Criminal Court." *Crime and Delinquency* 33:259–86.

Fagan, Jeffrey, Ellen Slaughter, and Eliot Hartstone. 1987. "Blind Justice? The Impact of Race on the Juvenile Justice Process." *Crime and Delinquency* 33:224–58.

Federal Bureau of Investigation. 1992. *Uniform Crime Reports for the United States, 1991*. Washington, D.C.: U.S. Government Printing Office.

Feld, Barry C. 1977. *Neutralizing Inmate Violence: Juvenile Offenders in Institutions*. Cambridge, Mass.: Ballinger.

———. 1981. "A Comparative Analysis of Organizational Structure and Inmate Subcultures in Institutions for Juvenile Offenders." *Crime and Delinquency* 27:336–63.

———. 1984. "Criminalizing Juvenile Justice: Rules of Procedure for Juvenile Court." *Minnesota Law Review* 69:141–276.

———. 1987. "Juvenile Court Meets the Principle of Offense: Legislative Changes in Juvenile Waiver Statutes." *Journal of Criminal Law and Criminology* 78:471–533.

———. 1988a. "*In re Gault* Revisited: A Cross-State Comparison of the Right to Counsel in Juvenile Court." *Crime and Delinquency* 34:393–424.

———. 1988b. "Juvenile Court Meets the Principle of Offense: Punishment, Treatment, and the Difference It Makes." *Boston University Law Review* 68:821–915.

———. 1989. "The Right to Counsel in Juvenile Court: An Empirical Study of When Lawyers Appear and the Difference They Make." *Journal of Criminal Law and Criminology* 79:1185–346.

———. 1990. "Bad Law Makes Hard Cases: Reflections on Teen-Aged Axe-Murderers, Judicial Activism, and Legislative Default." *Journal of Law and Inequality* 8:1–101.

———. 1991. "Justice by Geography: Urban, Suburban, and Rural Variations in Juvenile Justice Administration." *Journal of Criminal Law and Criminology* 82:156–210.

———. 1993. *Justice for Children: The Right to Counsel and Juvenile Courts*. Boston, Mass.: Northeastern University Press.

———. 1995. "Violent Youth and Public Policy: A Case-Study of Juvenile Justice Law Reform." *Minnesota Law Review* 79:965–1128.

Forst, Martin, Jeffrey Fagan, and T. Scott Vivona. 1989. "Youth in Prisons and Training Schools: Perceptions and Consequences of the Treatment-Custody Dichotomy." *Juvenile and Family Court Journal* 40:1–14.

Fox, Sanford J. 1970. "Juvenile Justice Reform: An Historical Perspective." *Stanford Law Review* 22:1187–239.

Gardner, Martin. 1982. "Punishment and Juvenile Justice: A Conceptual Framework for Assessing Constitutional Rights of Youthful Offenders." *Vanderbilt Law Review* 35:791–847.

Garrett, Carol J. 1985. "Effects of Residential Treatment on Adjudicated Delinquents: A Meta-Analysis." *Journal of Research in Crime and Delinquency* 22:287–308.

Gendreau, Paul, and Bob Ross. 1987. "Revivification of Rehabilitation: Evidence from the 1980s." *Justice Quarterly* 4:349–407.

Greenwood, Peter, and Franklin Zimring. 1985. *One More Chance: The Pursuit of Promising Intervention Strategies for Chronic Juvenile Offenders.* Santa Monica, Calif.: RAND.

Grisso, Thomas. 1981. *Juveniles' Waiver of Rights.* New York: Plenum Press.

Handler, Joel F., and Julie Zatz, eds. 1982. *Neither Angels nor Thieves: Studies in Deinstitutionalization of Status Offenders.* Washington, D.C.: National Academy Press.

Hofstadter, Richard. 1955. *The Age of Reform: From Bryan to F.D.R.* New York: Knopf.

Kempf-Leonard, Kimberly, Carl Pope, and William Feyerherm. 1995. *Minorities in Juvenile Justice.* Thousand Oaks, Calif.: Sage.

Kett, Joseph F. 1977. *Rites of Passage: Adolescence in America 1790 to the Present.* New York: Basic Books.

Klein, Malcolm W. 1979. "Deinstitutionalization and Diversion of Juvenile Offenders: A Litany of Impediments." In *Crime and Justice: An Annual Review of Research*, vol. 1, edited by Norval Morris and Michael Tonry. Chicago: University of Chicago Press.

Knitzer, Jane, and Merle Sobie. 1984. *Law Guardians in New York State: A Study of the Legal Representation of Children.* Albany, N.Y.: New York State Bar Association.

Lab, Steven P., and John T. Whitehead. 1988. "An Analysis of Juvenile Correctional Treatment." *Crime and Delinquency* 34:60–83.

———. 1990. "From 'Nothing Works' to 'The Appropriate Works': The Latest Stop on the Search for the Secular Holy Grail." *Criminology* 28:405–17.

Lerner, Steven. 1986. *Bodily Harm.* Bolinas, Calif.: Common Knowledge Press.

Lindsey, Duncan. 1994. *The Welfare of Children.* New York: Oxford University Press.

Mack, Julian W. 1909. "The Juvenile Court." *Harvard Law Review* 23:104–22.

Massey, Douglas S., and Nancy Denton. 1993. *American Apartheid: Segregation and the Making of the Underclass.* Cambridge, Mass.: Harvard University Press.

McCarthy, Belinda, and Brent L. Smith. 1986. "The Conceptualization of Discrimination in the Juvenile Justice Process: The Impact of Administrative Factors and Screening Decisions on Juvenile Court Dispositions." *Criminology* 24:41–64.

McCarthy, Francis Barry. 1994. "The Serious Offender and Juvenile Court Reform: The Case for Prosecutorial Waiver of Juvenile Court Jurisdiction." *St. Louis University Law Journal* 38:629–71.

Melton, Gary B. 1989. "Taking *Gault* Seriously: Toward a New Juvenile Court." *Nebraska Law Review* 68:146–81.

Monahan, John. 1981. *The Clinical Prediction of Violent Behavior.* Rockville, Md.: U.S. Department of Health and Human Services.

National Advisory Commission on Civil Disorders. 1968. *Report of the National Advisory Commission on Civil Disorders.* Washington, D.C.: U.S. Government Printing Office.

National Commission on Children. 1991. *Beyond Rhetoric: A New American Agenda for Children and Families.* Washington, D.C.: U.S. Government Printing Office.

National Research Council. 1993. *Losing Generations: Adolescents in High-Risk Settings* Washington, D.C.: National Academy Press.

Platt, Anthony. 1977. *The Child Savers.* 2nd ed. Chicago: University of Chicago Press.

Podkopacz, Marcy Rasmussen, and Barry C. Feld. 1996. "The End of the Line: An Empirical Study of Judicial Waiver." *Journal of Criminal Law and Criminology* 86:449–92.

Polk, Kenneth. 1984. "Juvenile Diversion: A Look at the Record." *Crime and Delinquency* 30:648–59.

President's Commission on Law Enforcement and Administration of Justice. 1967. *The Challenge of Crime in a Free Society.* Washington, D.C.: U.S. Government Printing Office.

Rosenberg, Irene M. 1980. "The Constitutional Rights of Children Charged with Crime: Proposal for a Return to the Not So Distant Past." *University of California Los Angeles Law Review* 27:656–721.

———. 1983. "Juvenile Status Offender Statutes: New Perspectives on an Old Problem." *University California Davis Law Review* 16:283–323.

Rothman, David J. 1980. *Conscience and Convenience.* Boston: Little, Brown.

Rubin, H. Ted. 1985. *Juvenile Justice: Policy, Practice, and Law.* 2nd ed. New York: Random House.

Ryerson, Ellen. 1978. *The Best-Laid Plans: America's Juvenile Court Experiment.* New York: Hill and Wang.

Sampson, Robert J., and John H. Laub. 1993. "Structural Variations in Juvenile Court Processing: Inequality, the Underclass, and Social Control." *Law and Society Review* 27:285–311.

Schlossman, Steven. 1977. *Love and the American Delinquent.* Chicago: University of Chicago Press.

Schwartz, Ira M. 1989a. (*In*)*Justice for Juveniles: Rethinking the Best Interests of the Child.* Lexington, Mass.: Lexington.

———. 1989b. "Hospitalization of Adolescents for Psychiatric and Substance Abuse Treatment." *Journal of Adolescent Health Care* 10:1–6.

Schwartz, Ira M., Marilyn Jackson-Beeck, and Roger Anderson. 1984. "The Hidden System of Juvenile Control." *Crime and Delinquency* 30:371–85.

Sechrest, Lee B., Susan O. White, and Elizabeth D. Brown, eds. 1979. *The Rehabilitation of Criminal Offenders.* Washington, D.C.: National Academy Press.

Snyder, Howard N., and Melissa Sickmund. 1995. *Juvenile Offenders and Victims: A National Report.* Washington, D.C.: U.S. Department of Justice, Office of Juvenile Justice and Delinquency Prevention.

Stapleton, W. Vaughan, David P. Aday Jr., and Jeanne A. Ito. 1982. "An Empirical Typology of American Metropolitan Juvenile Courts." *American Journal of Sociology* 88:549–64.

Stapleton, W. Vaughan, and Lee E. Teitelbaum. 1972. *In Defense of Youth: A Study of the Role of Counsel in American Juvenile Courts.* New York: Russell Sage.

Streib, Victor L. 1987. *Death Penalty for Juveniles.* Bloomington: Indiana University Press.

Sutton, John R. 1988. *Stubborn Children: Controlling Delinquency in the United States.* Berkeley: University of California Press.

Teitelbaum, Lee E., and Aidan R. Gough. 1977. *Beyond Control: Status Offenders in the Juvenile Court.* Cambridge, Mass.: Ballinger.

von Hirsch, Andrew. 1976. *Doing Justice.* New York: Hill and Wang.

Walkover, Andrew. 1984. "The Infancy Defense in the New Juvenile Court." *University of California Los Angeles Law Review* 31:503–62.

Weithorn, Lois A. 1988. "Mental Hospitalization of Troublesome Youth: An Analysis of Skyrocketing Admission Rates." *Stanford Law Review* 40:773–838.

Wiebe, Robert H. 1967. *In Search for Order 1877–1920.* New York: Hill and Wang.

Zimring, Franklin. 1981. "Notes Toward a Jurisprudence of Waiver." In *Readings in Public Policy,* edited by John C. Hall, Donna Martin Hamparian, John M. Pettibone, and Joseph L. White. Columbus, Ohio: Academy for Contemporary Problems.

———. 1991. "The Treatment of Hard Cases in American Juvenile Justice: In Defense of Discretionary Waiver." *Notre Dame Journal of Law, Ethics and Public Policy* 5:267–280.

20

Sentencing

KEVIN R. REITZ

In the past twenty-five years the landscape of American sentencing has undergone vast changes. These include explosions in the number of sentenced offenders, as well as structural reorderings of the laws that govern sentencing. Putting these two trends together, we are in the midst of a period of ferment unprecedented in the history of U.S. criminal punishment.

One window into the scope of change since 1970 is supplied by raw statistics. In 1970, on any given day, the nation's prisons housed a reported 196,429 offenders. Jail populations added approximately 129,189 inmates, so that the U.S. confinement total included about 325,618 persons (American Bar Association 1994, p. xxxv; Cahalan 1986, p. 76). In the next quarter century, American prisons more than *quintupled* in size, reaching a one-day population of 1,182,169 by the end of 1996 (Bureau of Justice Statistics 1997b). As of June 30, 1996, jails across the country grew to hold an estimated 518,492 persons. At midyear 1996, the total adult incarcerated population was 1,630,940 inmates (Bureau of Justice Statistics 1997a). Taking the nation's population growth into account, the U.S. incarceration rate had risen by a factor of 3.75, from 160 inmates per 100,000 general population in 1970 to 600 per 100,000 in 1995 (see U.S. Department of Commerce 1995, p. 15).

This expansion was not planned in advance, and, even with the benefit of hindsight, its causes are not well understood (Zimring and Hawkins 1991). Deliberate or not, explicable or not, the upswing in the use of confinement appears to be ongoing. American prisons and jails were growing at a rate of 189 new inmates per day between mid-1995 and mid-1996 (Bureau of Justice Statistics 1997a). While theories of pendulum swings might foretell an eventual reversal of the incarceration explosion, so far there is little evidence of such a shift in the national statistics.

Alongside the trend of escalation of confinement, there has been widespread experimentation across the country with new institutions and systems for the apportionment of criminal punishment. Rehabilitation, once the guiding theoretical light of American sentencing structures, has fallen by the wayside in the past two and a half decades, leaving policy makers scrambling for an alternative blueprint. Further, as criminal punishment has grown into an ever-more-sizable enterprise, governments have become increasingly interested in managerial tools for controlling systemic throughputs and outputs. Many jurisdictions have created sentencing commissions, some have abolished parole boards, all have enacted mandatory penalty statutes for selected crimes, and a growing number have adopted sentencing guidelines. Such fluctuations in policy and legal architecture are the chief subject of the discussion that follows.

A Brief History of American Sentencing Policy Since 1970

In 1970, all American sentencing systems were built on the ideas that most criminal offenders could be rehabilitated, and that this goal could best be accomplished through a system of individualized decisions about punishment. The approach, which dated back to the late nineteenth century, was called *indeterminate sentencing* because of the unpredictability of the sentences it produced. Sentencing judges had discretion to choose sanctions from a wide range of options and were expected to tailor their sentences to the particular "correctional" needs of each offender. Unsurprisingly, the penalties imposed tended to reflect the idiosyncrasies of the judge assigned to the case. No fixed rules governed courts' judgments (except that maximum statutory penalties could not be exceeded), there was no requirement that judges give reasons for their decisions, and no meaningful review of sentencing orders was available to the government or defendant (see, generally, Frankel 1973). In cases of imprisonment, a parole board held further case-by-case authority to determine actual lengths of confinement. According to the theory of the day, the parole board was called upon to watch and discern when each prisoner had successfully been rehabilitated and could be returned to society. As with the initial sentence imposed by judges, parole release decisions were essentially unguided by rule or principle, went unexplained, and were not appealable (see Frankel 1973; Morris 1974).

To say that indeterminate sentencing systems were designed on a rehabilitative model is not to say that rehabilitation was pursued seriously or accomplished with frequency. Despite the good intentions of many people in the corrections field, this was seldom the case. For one thing, most plausible programs to counsel or educate criminals are expensive, and U.S. legislatures have never had great enthusiasm for major spending in the area. For another, few existing programs ever succeeded in producing demonstrable rehabilitation in offender populations. Such operational difficulties led to a fundamental irony: the large building blocks of the high-discretion sentencing system were ostensibly in service of a treatment agenda, but no one could say with confidence how to perform the miracle on the ground level.

As the general justificatory aim of the sentencing structure, rehabilitation came crashing down in the 1970s. For some liberal analysts, the treatment program had produced cruel excesses in punishment, avowedly "for the offender's own good" (see Allen 1964, 1981). The principal change in perception, however, was a growing sense of futility. An influential empirical survey by Robert Martinson, with the provocative title "What Works?" (1974), contributed to a new conventional belief that "nothing works" where the rehabilitation of criminals is concerned. This sound-bite capsulation was a brusque simplification of Martinson's findings, which were discouraging on the whole, but which also found that a handful of programs had achieved modest improvements in the behavior of their clientele (see Lipton, Martinson, and Wilks 1975). Still, the message "heard" in the public and policy communities can be more significant than the message "delivered" in the academic literature.

For a number of reasons, the time was probably ripe for the idea that "nothing works." Going into the 1970s, a number of societal currents had worn down patience with the rehabilitative experiment and were signaling widespread receptivity to alternative approaches. Reported crime rates, including homicide rates, had jumped sharply during the 1960s; these alarming changes had coincided with a decade of slightly diminishing incarceration rates. With only a bit of imagination, one could link one trend with the other (e.g., Wilson 1975). In the same period, controversial defense-oriented rulings by the Supreme Court under Earl Warren had produced sentiment in some quarters that the legal system was "coddling criminals," and spawned an enduring public reaction against "lenient judges." Support for the death penalty, which had sputtered at submajority levels in the 1960s, soared to supermajority status during the next decade. For the first time in the nation's history, law and order became a national political issue in the presidential campaigns of the mid-1960s and early 1970s (see Feeley and Sarat 1980.)

Even for sophisticated policy makers, who understood that rehabilitation "occasionally works," the intellectual and political climate of the 1970s made it difficult to maintain that rehabilitation theory should continue to dictate the framework of *entire* sentencing systems. Instead, reformist objectives were demoted to a second order of priority, as in the following formulations: such programs should be attempted, but only in conjunction with punishments imposed for other purposes (Packer 1968). They should be limited to convicts who volunteer to participate (Morris 1974). They should be pursued only for discrete subclasses of offenders who could be shown amenable to treatment (Frankel 1973). The crash in prominence of the treatment model had been stunning. As Albert Alschuler wrote in 1978, "[T]hat I and many other academics adhered in large part to this reformative viewpoint only a decade or so ago seems almost incredible to most of us today" (p. 552).

The fall of the rehabilitative ideal (see Allen 1981) has had a powerful effect on American sentencing law and practice. On one level, it created a policy vacuum that has yet to be filled. The last twenty-five years can be characterized as a period in which no single policy viewpoint has stood squarely behind the operation of U.S. sentencing structures—unless it has been the view that rehabilitation was *not* the way to go. To be sure, competing formulations have been offered. For example, observers have argued that incapacitation-oriented policy has rushed into the vacuum left by reformative theory (Zimring and Hawkins 1995) or that some version of retribution theory has become the new guiding light of American punishment practices (von Hirsch 1993). There is only a modicum of truth to such categorical claims, however. Since the 1970s, throughout the many provinces of criminal justice, there has been spasmodic and overlapping interest in policies of incapacitation, retribution, and deterrence. It requires a degree of recklessness (or wishfulness) to state that any of these ideas has become the dominant engine of sentencing law—in even a single U.S. jurisdiction.

What remains clear is that the compassionate and optimistic attitudes of rehabilitation theory have dropped far from their pre-1970s position. The public, and public officials, are now less likely to view criminals as disadvantaged, ill-treated members of society who can be changed for the better. This has had an interactive effect on viewpoints about other extant sentencing policies. Once the softening tendency of rehabilitation theory is removed, the other mainstream goals of punishment can be pressed toward visions of increased severity. If it seems that criminals cannot be changed, and have only themselves to blame for their behavior, then the most pivotal compunctions against harsh dispositions have been swept aside. There is no compelling argument against incapacitating as many offenders as the system can accommodate, for as long as possible (see Zimring and Hawkins 1995); there is less to say in opposition to severe and even mandatory punishments in pursuit of increased marginal deterrence; and there are weaker moral claims to be marshaled against those whose retributive sense, driven by outrage at criminal behaviors, tells them that extremely harsh sentences are morally required (see Cullen and Gilbert 1982).

In summary, it might be said that widespread disillusionment with the treatment model has done two things: it has thrown criminal law into an ongoing crisis of justification, and, by default, it has helped fuel the upward spiral of American prison sentences. No one can quantify such effects with precision. The alchemy of belief structures is hard enough to map in individuals, let alone whole legal and political communities. Less speculation is needed, however, to comment on the impact of rehabilitation's demise on the structural architecture of U.S. sentencing systems. It is to that subject that we now turn.

The Shift Toward Determinate Sentencing Structures

The macrocomponents of indeterminate sentencing structures (if not their micromanifestations on a day-to-day basis) were built on the idea that rehabilitation could be accomplished in large numbers of cases. Once that belief had lost force, all the virtues of indeterminacy could be recast as vices: Why should legislatures have so little to say about criminal punishment if sensitive, individualized judgments were not really at issue? Why should judges possess nearly unconstrained sentencing authority, and how could it be defended against charges of gross arbitrariness, if no one believed in the efficacy of offender-based sanctioning? Why should parole boards, also vulnerable to sharp claims of caprice, be empowered to attempt the impossible—the detection of the mythical moment when rehabilitation had occurred? Why should the public, increasingly cynical about the criminal justice system, have to endure the disingenuousness of sentences that *sounded* impressive when pronounced, only to learn through repeated experience that "time served" was another matter?

For a combination of such reasons, and with a variety of results, indeterminate sentencing systems in many U.S. jurisdictions have given way since 1970 to an array of "determinate" sentencing reforms. All such reforms possess a common feature: they seek to cabin, or even eliminate, the former reservoirs of case-by-case sentencing discretion held by judges and parole officials. In the place of such individualized sentencing authority, all determinate systems emphasize decision making on a systemwide basis. In some instances this "attack on case-specific discretion" has been performed by statutory enactment; more often, in recent years, it has been advanced through sentencing guidelines created by a sentencing commission. The following sections outline the main structural innovations that have been attempted, and will assess the status of the ongoing national shift toward determinacy in sentencing structures.

Statutory Determinacy

Beginning in the mid-1970s, a handful of states, including Arizona, California, Colorado, Illinois, Indiana, and North Carolina, modified their prior practices of indeterminate sentencing to provide for greater specificity in authorized punishments as a matter of statutory command (see Tonry 1996, p. 28). California, for example, adopted—and still follows—a "multiple-choice" approach under which each offense carries three potential punishments. For example, the current provision concerning first-degree burglary specifies that the sentence options for the offense are "imprisonment in the state prison for two, four, or six years" (California Penal Code, Title 13, 461, 1996). In the normal case, the trial judge is directed to impose the middle, or "presumptive," sentence laid out for each crime. As alternatives, the judge can select the "mitigated" or "aggravated" term, provided adequate reasons are cited on the record. Once the court pronounces sentence in the California scheme, the stated judgment bears reasonable relation to the sentence actually served by the offender. Although prison terms are subject to discounts such as "good time," the determinate reform legislation abolished the parole board's authority to decide release dates.

Other statutory determinate sentencing reforms of the 1970s, such as those in Arizona, Colorado, Illinois, Indiana, and (for a few years) North Carolina, followed a somewhat different scheme. Their criminal codes were amended to set forth "ranges" of potential punishment for each offense, as opposed to the fixed integers in California law. Still, the overall plan was similar: typically, these statutes provided a "presumptive" range for ordinary cases, with the bookends of "aggravated" and "mitigated" ranges available for unusual circumstances. Thus the judge was limited in punishment options (slightly or sharply, depending on the width of the ranges contained in the applicable statutes). A few states, such as Arizona, Illinois, and Indiana, joined California in the elimination of parole release (Bureau of Justice Assistance 1996, pp. 26–27).

The defining strength and weakness of statutory determinate reforms resulted from their reliance on legislatures to choose specific penalties (or narrowed ranges) for specific crimes. Jurisdiction-wide uniformity in sentencing can be promoted in this way, but state legislatures do not usually have the time or expertise to ponder exact punishments with care. Nor do legislatures have the attention span needed to monitor the sentencing system in operation, and make periodic adjustments in the matrix of presumptive sentences. Indeed, the experience in jurisdictions that enacted statutory determinate laws was that their legislators tended to pass crazy-quilt amendments over time. Contrary to hopes and expectations, the prison populations in states like California, Colorado, and North Carolina grew even more quickly than before sentencing reforms were instituted. In part these problems were attributable to changes in the political climates of individual states, but they led many to conclude that legislative determinacy was too blunt an instrument for the finely tuned decisions necessary for running a sentencing system (see Tonry 1996, p. 28).

Sentencing Commissions and Guidelines

In the late 1970s and early 1980s, several U.S. jurisdictions began to experiment with determinate reform based on the creation of a new administrative agency for sentencing policy: the sentencing commission. The earliest commissions appeared in Minnesota, Pennsylvania, Florida, and Washington. By 1996, more than twenty U.S. jurisdictions, including the federal system, had chartered such entities. It is fair to say that the commission-based approach has become the most popular vehicle of sentencing reform in the last decade of the twentieth century. Since 1990 alone, new commissions have been constituted in Arkansas, Kansas, Louisiana, Maryland, Massachusetts, Michigan, Missouri, Montana, North Carolina, Ohio, Oklahoma, South Carolina, and Virginia (see Frase 1995). In contrast, no jurisdiction has adopted a statutorily based determinate structure since 1980 (Tonry 1996).

The sentencing commission was first proposed by Judge Marvin Frankel (1973) as a means to bring legal principles to bear on sentencing decisions in a uniform, rather than haphazard, way. Frankel's central concern was that discretionary actors such as judges and parole officials followed no rhyme or reason beyond their own personal instincts. He argued that no one would tolerate such "lawlessness" in litigation concerning a contract dispute or the repossession of a refrigerator. Punishment decisions, more important than much of the other routine business of the courts, were deserving of at least a comparable degree of care. Frankel therefore suggested that uniform standards for sentencing decisions should be promulgated by a sentencing commission for application by courts throughout whole jurisdictions. (Later, *sentencing guidelines* became the term of art for such rules.) As with other areas of the law, Frankel argued that sentencing judges should be required to explain their sentencing decisions on the record, subject to thoughtful appellate review.

For some people, Frankel's "rule-of-law" argument was sufficient by itself to support his suggestion of a sentencing commission and a positive law of sentencing. In the decades following the early 1970s, however, other motivations (not all of them friendly to Frankel's original vision) have added to the trend toward proliferating commissions and guidelines. Speaking generally, these have sprung from the discovery that sentencing commissions can pursue systemic objectives, such as the control of prison populations, that formerly slipped through planners' fingers when judges and parole officials made policy decisions one case at a time.

Sentencing commissions have proven able, if so instructed, to restrain prison growth through the creation and monitoring of sentencing guidelines, assisted by computer projection models. Alternatively, they can predict and manage the contours of a pro-growth policy, if that is what is wanted (Tonry 1993). Although not a central feature of Frankel's scheme, sentencing commissions have attracted interest in part because they add a "resource management" capability to correctional planning. In the 1990s, states that have chartered commissions have frequently cited overcrowding and budgetary stress as primary factors in their decision to do so (Knapp 1993).

The constraint of prison growth has not been the sole motivation of commission-based reforms across the country. In some jurisdictions an agency of systemic competency was sought by policy makers who believed their judges were being too *lenient* when imposing sentences. Thus, in Pennsylvania, Virginia, and the federal system, commissions began their work with the resolution to increase aggregate sentence severity (although targeting some offenses more than others). In other places, such as Minnesota and Washington, commissions operated for a period of years to restrain prison size, only to turn to a pro-growth course when asked to do so by their legislatures. In short, commissions have shown that they can be effective instruments of policy implementation, whether the prevailing impetus is one of lenity or severity.

This is not to say that the introduction of sentencing commissions has had no effect on the policy-making *process*. Commissions have added elements of predictability and manipulability to legislative decision making about criminal punishments—and these new elements of the deliberative process have sometimes changed outcomes. For example, commissions are regularly asked to forecast the prison impact of proposals to amend guidelines or enact new sentencing legislation such as mandatory penalties or three-strikes laws. On occasion, sobering cost projections have dissuaded state legislatures from passing measures they might otherwise have enacted. Alternatively, the commissions' ability to calibrate sentences throughout the guidelines grid has created opportunities for legislative compromises combining the *increase* of sentences for some offenses that the legislature most cares about (such as violent crimes) with *decreases* in sentences for other offense types (such as property and drug crimes). Legislatures have sometimes been grateful to be able to take dramatic action with respect to crimes that generate the highest public concern, and to do so without incurring the obligation of new prison construction. Without the commissions' ability to manipulate sentencing patterns line by line through offense categories, however, such trade-offs could not be engineered (see American Bar Association 1994, pp. 23–27).

For the reasons canvased here, the idea of the sentencing commission has won favor with diverse constituencies, including those who promote law-and-order policies, those who think incarceration expansion has spun out of control, and those who simply want greater thoughtfulness and intentionality to guide the operation of sentencing systems on a macro level. Heading into the twenty-first century, the "resource management" capability of sentencing commissions is likely to be a major selling point for jurisdictions that have not yet incorporated such entities, as well as a sustaining feature of existing commissions.

Mandatory Penalties

Since 1970, the "attack on case-specific discretion" has not always taken the form of a reworking of the sentencing structure as applied across the criminal code. It is much simpler, as a legislative matter, to create determinate sentencing laws that attach to one offense at a time. For example, some states have laws specifying that the penalty for aggravated murder must be a life term in prison without the possibility of parole. Such a provision is highly determinate in two senses: first, it removes the case-specific discretion of the trial judge to impose any sentence other than the mandatory penalty; second, after the sentence is pronounced, the law removes any case-specific discretion on the part of the parole board to release the prisoner during his natural life.

A variation on this theme is the mandatory *minimum* penalty, which statutorily cuts off discretion to choose a sentence below, but not above, the stated minimum. For instance, a law might provide that, for a certain drug offense, the judge must impose a prison term of at least ten years. If the maximum authorized sentence under the statute is twenty years, the judge retains discretion to select a term between one decade and two but may not go lower than ten years. If the provision also restricts parole eligibility during the mandatory minimum prison term (which is a common device in such statutes), the legislature has extinguished the parole board's release discretion for that duration as well.

Since the 1970s, federal and state legislatures have enacted large numbers of mandatory penalty provisions, and the public popularity of such measures seems to remain high. Such "mandatories" commonly apply to crimes involving serious violence, drugs, or firearms. Another species is keyed to criminal record: "habitual offender" laws have long been used to require heavier-than-normal sentences for criminals with substantial prior convictions. In the 1990s a potent variant of the habitual-offender approach emerged in the form of "three strikes you're out" laws. Congress and many states have now adopted three-strikes laws, which operate on a similar plan: upon conviction for a third "serious" felony (these are defined differently from place to place), the judge must sentence the offender to a life term of imprisonment without parole.

Mandatory sentencing statutes have been adopted in jurisdictions that otherwise use indeterminate sentencing schemes, in jurisdictions that have taken a statutory determinacy approach, and in sentencing commission jurisdictions. In other words, legislatures have regarded mandatory penalties as a permissible and desirable means to produce zones of "hyperdeterminacy" within every available structural environment. From a legislator's point of view, there is no more forceful way to express a policy judgment about what the sanction should be for a designated fact pattern. The motivating rationale is that every scenario of that type should result in an identical sentence, with perfect uniformity across offenders and zero discretion exercised by government officials (such as judges and parole boards) at the case level.

From the perspective of nonlegislative actors in the sentencing system, the wisdom and effectiveness of mandatory penalties are frequently challenged. In jurisdictions with sentencing commissions and guidelines, commissions often observe that mandatories tend to be out of kilter with the scaling of offenses and punishments attempted by the guidelines. Moreover, since mandatory penalties cannot be altered short of legislative amendment, they are exempt from the commissions' ongoing processes of setting priorities and manipulating sentences to accommodate the realities of finite resources. For example, a jurisdiction that incarcerates large numbers of drug offenders for mandatory terms will have reduced flexibility to free up prison bed space for violent offenders. To the extent that a sentencing commission is powerless to tilt the balance between drugs and violence in incarcerated populations, the jurisdiction has deprived itself of one advantage of having a commission in the first place.

On the ground level of individual sentences, trial judges are probably the most vocal critics of mandatory sentencing laws. Legislatures, when drafting such statutes, tend naturally to have unsympathetic offenders in mind—those criminals the public most fears and wants taken off the streets. On the case-specific level, in contrast, judges encounter offenders across a spectrum of blameworthiness and apparent dangerousness. Over a period of time, many judges have accumulated experiences in which the mandatory penalty was far removed from their sense of justice in a given case (e.g., Forer 1994). Usually on such occasions the judge follows the law against personal instincts, although some courts have found creative dodges to circumvent the statutes.[1]

The preceding complaints would carry less weight if mandatory penalty provisions actually achieved their objective of hyperdeterminacy. There is overwhelming evidence, both recent and historical, that this does not occur. A recent survey by Michael Tonry (1996, chap. 5) charted the operation of such laws dating back to England's Black Act in the eighteenth century and forward to a recent study by the U.S. Sentencing Commission (1991) during the Bush administration. Time and again, Tonry documented the tendencies of mandatories to exacerbate rather than eliminate sentencing disparities, to create unintended bulges of discretion in prosecutors, to prompt nullification and avoidance strategies in courts and juries, to produce administrative bottlenecks (such as occur when large numbers of defendants refuse to plead guilty), and to fail in their goal of increasing the average severity of sentences.

One lesson of mandatory penalties may be that it is impossible to iron out all discretion at the case-specific level. Judges and parole officials may be taken out of the discretionary loop, but this still leaves prosecutors with unchecked power to file charges under the mandatory provision, to decline to do so, or to bargain down to less formidable charges. The U.S. Sentencing Commission study (1991) concluded that federal prosecutors have been selective in their use of mandatory laws and have brought charges in only a fraction of the cases in which such laws apply. Further, once such prosecutorial discretion is exercised, no remaining governmental decision maker has authority to second-guess the decision (see Alschuler 1978). Thus the legislative vision of hyperdeterminacy can be disrupted by the eddies and currents of individual case processing.

Mandatory penalties have proliferated in all jurisdictions since 1970 despite the objections on grounds of policy and justice that have been leveled against them. In the absence of a change in the politics of law and order, widespread repeal or dilution of such statutes is unlikely. It is probable that mandatories will continue to exist as attempted pockets of hyperdeterminacy within all varieties of sentencing structures, indeterminate and determinate. Sentencing commissions can expect to enter recurring debates about the wisdom and expense of new mandatory provisions, and must anticipate that policy decisions and prison population controls will have to "work around" the firm edifices of such statutes.

The Staying Power of Indeterminacy

Although there have been impressive shifts in sentencing structure across the country in the last quarter century, a plurality of American jurisdictions continue to plow ahead with the high-discretion model of indeterminate sentencing. Some of these states have chartered temporary sentencing commissions only to decide, ultimately, that they were not wanted on a permanent basis. Other states have not taken even such exploratory steps toward determinate reform. Jurisdictions that retain the traditional approach, and that have no active commission to pursue structural reform, include Alabama, Connecticut, the District of Columbia, Georgia, Hawaii, Idaho, Iowa, Kentucky, Mississippi, Nebraska, Nevada, New Hampshire, New Jersey, New Mexico, New York, North Dakota, Rhode Island, South Dakota, Texas, Vermont, West Virginia, and Wyoming (Bureau of Justice Assistance 1996, pp. 26–27). Given the permutations among "determinate" sentencing systems, it is fair to say that the traditional indeterminate structure remains the most prevalent model of U.S. sentencing practice.

As under determinate regimes, indeterminacy can produce a wide range of sentencing patterns. In 1995, Texas, the state with the highest per capita incarceration rate in the country, built its prison populations out of indeterminate sentences. So did North Dakota, the state with the lowest incarceration rate (Bureau of Justice Statistics 1996, p. 3). Indeterminate states, compared with one another, have markedly different sentencing patterns for violent crime, drug crime, and property crime (see Zimring and Hawkins 1991, chap. 6). Other observable outcomes, such as the racial composition of state prisons, are similarly divergent: indeterminate states achieve both high and comparatively low rates of racial disparity in sentenced populations (Blumstein 1993, p. 755, Table 3). There is, in short, no obvious correlation between the overarching structure that a jurisdiction chooses to erect for sentencing decisions and such details as the harshness, lenity, or distribution of punishments.

Still, large differences exist between traditional and "reformed" sentencing structures. Indeterminate systems produce their results without the benefit of generally applied legal principles, uniformity in sentences imposed, planning, predictability, and systemic oversight. Deliberate manipulations in sentencing patterns are quite difficult to engineer. For states that retain parole boards, release dates can be advanced to lessen crowding pressures, but often this is not politically feasible. In indeterminate jurisdictions, there is no statewide mechanism to structure judicial sentences to meet conditions of prison crowding, or to emphasize the incarceration of violent over nonviolent offenders. Likewise, the policy judgments that underlie individual punishment decisions are unspecified. Sentencing judges need not concur with one another on whether the wealth of defendants (or any other aspect of the cases they hear) is an aggravating, mitigating, or impermissible factor in calculating appropriate penalties. Sentencing policy, writ small, is fashioned one judge at a time and one parole board at a time (see Frankel 1973).

This state of affairs may have seemed appropriate in the heyday of rehabilitation theory, when the "diagnosis" and "treatment" of criminals were at issue. It is more difficult to explain the persistence of indeterminate structures in the postrehabilitative era. What, one might ask, are the reasons that have supported such systems in the wake of Marvin Frankel's scathing—and unanswered—indictment of the indeterminate program? Two main explanations might be proffered for the staying power of indeterminacy: (1) the entrenchment of existing legal structures and their component bureaucracies; and (2) the absence of a unified theory to replace the rehabilitative model as the foundation of system design.

Simple inertia favors the continuation of existing frameworks for sentencing in most jurisdictions. The switch from indeterminacy to determinacy requires both study and effort. More important, it involves the relocation of sentencing authority in favor of some entities (such as the sentencing commission) and away from others (such as the parole board; see Knapp 1993). Such changes are at least unfamiliar and, for agencies whose turf is threatened, can be highly unwelcome. As with any large reform project, an overhaul of the sentencing system is vulnerable to the expressed fear that "we will be worse off than before." In some jurisdictions, judges and prosecutors have opposed proposals for sentencing guidelines—and vehement opposition from either constituency has proven the death knell of start-up commissions. In other states, influential judges and prosecutors have stood behind the idea of sentencing reform, and the credibility of such individuals has contributed much to the ambitious undertaking of ground-up reform. Key proponents in their respective states have included Chief Justice Douglas Amdahl of the Minnesota Supreme Court, King County (Seattle) District Attorney Norman Maleng, Multnomah County (Portland, Oregon) District Attorney Michael Schrunk, and North Carolina Superior Court Judge Thomas Ross.

An additional retarding factor in the current sentencing reform era, at least through the 1980s, has been the inaction of national law reform organizations with credibility and influence in state legislatures. The American Law Institute, whose prestigious Model Penal Code prompted a revolution in criminal code reform after its adoption in 1962, has never revisited its endorsement of indeterminate sentencing formulated in the 1950s (American Law Institute 1985b, p. 10). Eighty percent of U.S. states have borrowed heavily from the Model Penal Code, including its sentencing provisions (see American Law Institute 1985a, p. xi). No comparably authoritative law reform model has been designed for the emerging era of sentencing commissions and guidelines.

Other organizations, such as the American Bar Association, the National Conference of Commissioners on Uniform State Laws, and the National Council on Crime and Delinquency, issued aspirational reports on the structure of sentencing law in the 1970s—before any American jurisdiction had adopted guidelines—and then fell silent through the 1980s (see Reitz and Reitz 1995). Indeed, the project of sentencing reform has proceeded largely at the state-by-state level, without the coordinating efforts of such national organizations. In 1993, the American Bar Association finally reentered the field with newly revised Criminal Justice Standards for Sentencing, which rejected the model of indeterminacy and endorsed the state sentencing commission approach of jurisdictions such as Minnesota, Washington, and Oregon (American Bar Association 1994, p. xxi). Other organizations of stature, meanwhile, have remained dormant.

It would be unfair to attribute the residual vitality of indeterminate sentencing entirely to inertia or inattention. Many people continue to believe that the traditional approach is superior to newer reforms. And in a world that is lacking a vision of sentencing theory powerful and coherent enough to replace the eroded foundations of rehabilitation, there are understandable attractions to a process that is both indistinct on a systemic level and highly particularized to the individual case.

An undoubted benefit of a nonregularized, high-discretionary system of sentencing is that it is capacious enough to include any and all theories of punishment. If one is uncertain about the best course to follow among contending theories of desert, incapacitation, deterrence, and, once in a while, rehabilitation, it may seem wise to keep all options open (see Packer 1968). Indeed, historian David Rothman (1980) has argued that this was part of the original allure of rehabilitation theory. Lacking any positive plan for crime reduction, the designers of indeterminate systems believed that unlimited inquiry into the facts of each case would yield productive conclusions. As Yogi Berra similarly believed, "You can observe a lot just by watching."

A faith in induction, and in the wisdom of judges, lends continuing support to the institution of high-discretion sentencing. Even among those who perceive the downsides of indeterminacy, there are some who take the view that the "cure" of sentencing guidelines is worse than the "disease" (e.g., Uelman 1992). The perceived excesses of some determinate laws, such as mandatory penalties and the labyrinthine provisions of the federal sentencing guidelines, are often cited as evidence that we are better off with the defects of discretion (Alschuler 1991; Forer 1994). There is force to the claim that a horrific determinate scheme, enforceable across an entire jurisdiction, is worse than an indeterminate scheme, which inevitably results in a patchwork of good, bad, and indifferent outcomes.

For reasons of momentum, attachment, and ambivalence about alternatives, indeterminate sentencing is not likely to disappear any time soon. Its continued vitality will turn in large degree on the future successes or failures of the guideline reforms, as they approach and enter their third decade of existence. The following pages speculate, optimistically, on some of the prospects for advancement in that quarter.

Future Issues in American Sentencing

No one should pretend to know what lies ahead for U.S. sentencing laws, policies, practices, and structures. The history of criminal punishment is littered with "reforms" that, at one time, were touted as the wave of progress, only to be jettisoned as anachronisms or even abominations by later generations who, once again, thought of themselves as "reformers" (see Rothman 1980). Indeed, one universal truth of Anglo-American punishment systems might be the following: all approaches that have so far been tried for the sanctioning of criminals have, sooner or later, come to appear moribund. The inherent frustrations of the enterprise—the fact that no one knows how to engineer large changes in the incidence of crime, and that no punishment can ever compensate for the loss inflicted by a serious crime—contribute to a recurring cycle of innovation and disillusionment.

For the present, multiple dissatisfactions with traditional indeterminate sentencing systems have been driving American jurisdictions toward determinate alternatives. The new commission-based structures address some of the evils of prior law, but, even assuming they yield a net policy gain over their indeterminate precursors, it is unlikely that the latest reforms will pull U.S. crime rates down to levels of public acceptability, or will satisfy popular appetites for sanctions in egregious cases. Thus, after a grace period of uncertain duration, the cycle of disappointment may well churn forward to envelop the spanking new sentencing commissions of the 1980s and 1990s.

With this possibility in mind, the following outlines three areas of policy development that the criminal justice community might pursue with profit in the coming decade. Allowing for an environment of change, all three suggestions have a great deal to do with the improvement of mechanisms for deliberative lawmaking and coordinated administration, and have less to do with the specific content of punishment decisions. Substantively, a high priority should be placed on the articulation of *realistic* goals for sentencing systems, while recognizing that these can shift with the passage of time. Procedurally, punishment structures should aspire to build institutions that can facilitate the implementation of such realistic policy initiatives and adapt to changes in underlying approach.

Getting Realistic Policy into Sentencing Decisions

In general, although there have been signs of progress in the last several years, the new determinate sentencing jurisdictions have not done enough to incorporate sophisticated punishment policy into systemic decision making. For instance, theories of selective incapacitation have been debated in the criminological literature throughout the current era of sentencing commissions and guidelines (see Zimring and Hawkins 1995). It was not until 1995, however, that the first sentencing commission (in the state of Virginia) made extensive use of this knowledge base to draft incapacitation-oriented guidelines targeted at high-rate recidivists (see Kern 1995). Similarly, Norval Morris's theory of "limiting retributivism" has been in prominent circulation for many years (see Morris 1974), but only recently has anyone argued that sentencing guidelines, such as those in force in Minnesota, should be conceived to operate along Morrisonian lines (see Frase 1997). No commission to date has *explicitly* adopted a limiting retributive approach (cf. American Bar Association 1994, pp. 13–14, recommending such an experiment).

Because of their capacity for systemwide coordination, determinate sentencing jurisdictions can implement innovations such as those noted earlier, as well as others. We do not know yet what the outcomes will be, but the search for a replacement for the cornerstone theory of rehabilitation is likely to demand experimentation along numerous dimensions. We should be glad that Virginia is "trying on" incapacitation theory for size; we should encourage Minnesota to ratify and refine its Morrisonian machinery; and we should further watch the Pennsylvania guidelines with interest, since they incorporate yet another approach to sentencing policy, prescribing different substantive goals for different layers of the state guidelines grid (see next section). The mid-1990s may contain the seeds of an important trend in the evolution of sentencing structures: the proliferation of efforts to mold punishment decisions to explicit goal-oriented criteria.

Along the way, it will be crucial for sentencing commissions (or whoever holds systemwide authority over sentencing policy) to inject a healthy dose of reality into the engineering of sentencing structures. Rehabilitation failed not because it could never be achieved in practice but because the theory fell so far short of the overbroad claims that had been made for it. Similarly, deterrent and incapacitative programs, according to our best research, yield only small (albeit real) reductions in crime in the community (see Blumstein et al. 1986). It is a recipe for poor systemic design, and for public and political dissatisfaction, to oversell the prospective utilitarian payoffs that will accompany changes in sentencing laws. Without deliberate efforts to inculcate an informed debate of punishment policy—that is, one that appreciates that the criminal justice system operates at the margin of human behavior—even the best-designed sentencing system in the world will perennially be vulnerable to the claim that "more needs to be done."

Further Development of Intermediate Punishments

One of the great unsolved puzzles of the 1980s and 1990s is how to write sentencing guidelines for nonprison sanctions. Although there has been widespread agreement among policy makers and academics that creative exploitation of "intermediate punishments" (defined as those sanctions in between the harshness of prison and the laxity of regular probation) would be a good idea in principle, and might be the only realistic way to stem the tide of prison growth, no American jurisdiction has yet implemented a systemwide program of intermediate punishments that has meaningfully diverted offender populations away from incarcerative sanctions (see Morris and Tonry 1990; Tonry 1996, chap. 4).

A large part of the problem, in the view of experienced sentencing reformers like Michael Tonry (1996) and Kay Knapp (1993), is that the machinery of sentencing guidelines has not yet become fine-tuned enough to give structure to trial court decisions about intermediate sanctions. The guidelines now in operation have proven useful for specifying the "in-out line" (i.e., the line between those offenders who should be confined and those who should not) and durations of confinement. It is a far more subtle undertaking, however, to prescribe the type and intensity of nonprison sanctions that include such things as intensive probation, community service, drug treatment, victim restitution, day fines, home confinement, forfeitures, and various forms of community treatment (see American Bar Association 1994, pp. 85–94).

Interesting experiments, still in their early stages, are under way in North Carolina and Pennsylvania, and may provide guidance for other jurisdictions in the years to come. The North Carolina sentencing commission devised a new "structured sentencing" grid in 1994 that layers intermediate punishments according to their level of intrusiveness. In a few of the grid's cells (those that govern large numbers of the state's less serious cases), intermediate sanctions are the only option available to the judge. Since its effective date in 1994, the new law has pushed down North Carolina's confinement rate, following felony convictions, from 48 percent in 1993 to 28 percent in 1995 (Lubitz 1996). However, because of offsetting increases in the penalties for violent offenders, the state's prison system has seen rapid growth in the same period. From 1994 to 1995, in fact, North Carolina led the nation in percentage of prison growth—with a whopping 24 percent upswing in prison population in a single year (Bureau of Justice Statistics 1996, p. 5, Table 4). Clearly, the state's new system will bear watching, to see what its long-term impacts will be, but it is too early to say that North Carolina has solved the puzzle of intermediate punishments.

A similar experiment in Pennsylvania is a favorite of mine because, in concept, it tries to provide necessary links between sentencing theory and the choice of intermediate punishments. The state's guideline matrix, as designed in 1994, is divided into four zones. For the most serious cases, incarceration is the only sentencing option. As one descends through the other guideline layers, however, "restrictive intermediate punishments" become available and, descending further, "restorative sanctions" are increasingly numerous among recommended sentences. Also (and here is what is especially attractive about the Pennsylvania system), each of the four zones of the guidelines grid is accompanied with narrative explanatory statements that set forth a changing hierarchy of sentencing purposes. At level 4 (the most serious cases), retribution and incapacitation are dominant concerns. Moving downward to other levels, priorities of victim restitution, community service, and offender treatment become more prominent (see Kramer and Kempinen 1995). The Pennsylvania guidelines might be considered "three-dimensional." They begin with a flat representation of the punishment menu on a familiar two-axis grid. This is then supplemented with narrative guidance that enriches the scant information contained in each guideline box. Ultimately, some combination like this will be needed to create a textured decision-making process for the full menu of sanctioning choices.

The North Carolina and Pennsylvania guidelines may not prove to be ideal models for other jurisdictions in every respect. Still, they stand as serious efforts, fashioned by people who have watched others try and fail, to address one of the highest-priority items on the current agenda of sentencing reform. In the coming years, it will be incumbent upon policy makers to remain aware of, and learn from, such ongoing experiments.

Better Understanding of Systems-Building Issues

Sentencing systems, when examined as a whole, are one of the most complex and multilayered of all governmental bureaucracies (see Zimring 1976). Instead of relying on two or three relevant decision makers, with power to influence the outcome of individual cases, the final sentence for any single offender might be determined through the collective input of legislators, sentencing commission members, police officers, prosecutors, probation officers, trial judges, appellate judges, correctional officials, and parole boards. It would not be unusual, in fact, in the "life history" of a single case of criminal punishment, for this entire cast of characters to be mobilized. Indeed, the list of relevant players only lengthens if we include nongovernmental input into sentencing decisions: the defendant himself, the defense attorney, and the victim all have potentially significant roles to play in the decision-making process.

Because sentencing guideline systems have not existed for very long, we are still in the rudimentary stages of understanding how the parts of such systems relate to the whole. Accordingly, deliberate changes in the workings of guideline systems are sometimes difficult to engineer. Maneuvers in darkness tend to be imprecise. As sentencing commissions and guideline structures have increased in numbers and in time of operation, however, our knowledge base about them has steadily grown. Using the lens of comparative study of multiple systems, the store of *supportable* observations about guideline sentencing is now considerably greater than it was, say, ten years ago. And given the pace of reform at the state level, we can expect the coming decade to produce an even stronger current of new experience.

Comparative systemic study will be an increasingly powerful and important policy tool. It will assist in grappling with questions such as (1) What is the most desirable allocation of sentencing discretion as between sentencing commissions and trial courts, and how is it achieved? (2) Why do some guideline systems appear to shift power to prosecutors more so than other systems? How can a jurisdiction deliberately encourage one result or the other? (3) Which systems have proven particularly effective at managing prison population growth, and how did they do it? (4) What is the desired role for the appellate judiciary in guideline structures, and how should the statutes and rules be arranged to encourage such appellate activity?

Projects directed to "design" questions of this kind have been undertaken in small numbers in the 1980s and 1990s, and will gain importance in coming years. New sentencing commissions, such as those in Massachusetts and Maryland, have benefited from extensive cross-jurisdictional surveys during their start-up phases, before making recommendations about systemic design to their legislatures. The Pennsylvania commission, before reworking its guidelines in 1994, undertook a national study of other guideline states to discover ways in which Pennsylvania, one of the first guideline jurisdictions, may have fallen "behind the times" (see Kramer and Kempinen 1995). In 1996, the Bureau of Justice Assistance issued the *National Assessment of Structured Sentencing,* which was one of the first attempts to compile comparative information about the sentencing systems of all fifty states. And the American Bar Association, working from 1989 to 1994, issued the new edition of its *Standards for Sentencing,* based heavily on a study of the structural models of up-and-running state systems (American Bar Association 1994).

Comparative analyses will be important to advocates of the new determinate reform structures, as well as their skeptics and critics. For better or worse, we have no choice but to carry on a continuous series of natural experiments in criminal punishment. Discontinuation, even temporarily, is not an option. One benefit of the present reform era has been the generation of a number of alternative legal structures for sentencing. As Justice Brandeis famously hoped, the states are functioning well as "laboratories" for innovation (see Reitz 1996). The hard-won value of such experimentation, however, can only be harvested through watchful interjurisdictional study.

It is possible that the next twenty-five years will witness changes in criminal sentencing that rival those of the previous quarter century. Indeed, in light of the heaves and lurches that U.S. punishment systems have been (and still are) experiencing, the only "sure bet" for the future is that things will not remain as they are today. It is possible that the experimental character of the last twenty-five years will continue, yielding still-greater diversity in the structures of state and federal sentencing systems. At the extreme, there could be fifty-one materially different American approaches by the year 2025. Alternatively, and more likely, the coming decades may produce a consensus that, at least for the time being, the Frankelian sentencing commission—or some close relative of it—is the best option available to us. This was the position recently adopted by the American Bar Association (1994). Such provisional judgments cannot rest on claims of timeless truth (history teaches us to beware of such arrogance) but can be founded only on the most informed judgments about policy and process we are able to make. It is therefore to be hoped that rational inquiry can play an expanding role in the grim but necessary business of criminal punishment.

Note

1. For example, the California Supreme Court held that trial judges have statutory authority to dismiss charges brought under the state's three-strikes law; see *People v. Superior Court of San Diego County*, 917 P. 2d 628 (Cal. 1996).

References

Allen, F. A. 1964. *The Borderland of Criminal Justice: Essays in Law and Criminology.* Chicago: University of Chicago Press.

———. 1981. *The Decline of the Rehabilitative Ideal: Penal Policy and Social Purpose.* New Haven, Conn.: Yale University Press.

Alschuler, A. 1978. "Sentencing Reform and Prosecutorial Power: A Critique of Recent Proposals for 'Fixed' and 'Presumptive' Sentencing." *University of Pennsylvania Law Review* 126:550–77.

———. 1991. "The Failure of Sentencing Guidelines: A Plea for Less Aggregation." *University of Chicago Law Review* 58:901–51.

American Bar Association. 1994. *Standards for Criminal Justice, Sentencing.* 3rd ed. Washington, D.C.: ABA Press.

American Law Institute. 1985a. *Model Penal Code and Commentaries.* Part I, *General Provisions, §§ 1.01 to 2.13.* Philadelphia: American Law Institute.

———. 1985b. *Model Penal Code and Commentaries.* Part I, *General Provisions, §§ 6.01. to 7.09.* Philadelphia: American Law Institute.

Blumstein, A. 1993. "Racial Disproportionality of U.S. Prison Populations Revisited." *University of Colorado Law Review* 64:743–60.

Blumstein, A., J. Cohen, J. A. Roth, and C. A. Visher, eds. 1986. *Criminal Careers and "Career Criminals."* Washington, D.C.: National Academy Press.

Bureau of Justice Assistance. 1996. *National Assessment of Structured Sentencing.* Washington, D.C.: U.S. Department of Justice, Bureau of Justice Assistance.

Bureau of Justice Statistics. 1996. *Prison and Jail Inmates, 1995.* Washington, D.C.: U.S. Department of Justice, Bureau of Justice Statistics.

———. 1997a. *Prison and Jail Inmates at Midyear 1996.* Washington, D.C.: U.S. Department of Justice, Bureau of Justice Statistics.

————. 1997b. *Prisoners in 1996.* Washington, D.C.: U.S. Department of Justice, Bureau of Justice Statistics.

Cahalan, M. W. 1986. *Historical Corrections Statistics in the United States, 1850–1984.* Washington, D.C.: U.S. Government Printing Office.

Cullen, F. T., and K. E. Gilbert. 1982. *Reaffirming Rehabilitation.* Cincinnati, Ohio: Anderson.

Feeley, M. M., and A. D. Sarat. 1980. *The Policy Dilemma: Federal Crime Policy and the Law Enforcement Assistance Administration, 1968–1978.* Minneapolis: University of Minnesota Press.

Forer, L. G. 1994. *A Rage to Punish: The Unintended Consequences of Mandatory Sentencing.* New York: Norton.

Frankel, M. E. 1973. *Criminal Sentences: Law Without Order.* New York: Hill and Wang.

Frase, R. S. 1995. "State Sentencing Guidelines: Still Going Strong." *Judicature* 78:173–79.

————. 1997. "Sentencing Principles in Theory and Practice." In *Crime and Justice: A Review of Research,* vol. 22, edited by Michael Tonry. Chicago: University of Chicago Press.

Kern, R. 1995. "Sentence Reform in Virginia." *Federal Sentencing Reporter* 8:84–88.

Knapp, K. A. 1993. "Allocation of Discretion and Accountability Within Sentencing Structures." *University of Colorado Law Review* 64:679–705.

Kramer, J., and C. Kempinen. 1995. "The Reassessment and Remaking of Pennsylvania's Sentencing Guidelines." *Federal Sentencing Reporter* 8:74–79.

Lipton, D., R. Martinson, and J. Wilks. 1975. *Effectiveness of Correctional Treatment.* Springfield, Mass.: Praeger.

Lubitz, R. L. 1996. Letter to author from executive director of North Carolina Sentencing and Policy Advisory Commission, October 3.

Martinson, R. 1974. "What Works? Questions and Answers About Prison Reform." *Public Interest* 35:22–54.

Morris, N. 1974. *The Future of Imprisonment.* Chicago: University of Chicago Press.

Morris, N., and M. Tonry. 1990. *Between Prison and Probation: Intermediate Punishments in a Rational Sentencing System.* New York: Oxford University Press.

Packer, H. L. 1968. *The Limits of the Criminal Sanction.* Stanford, Calif.: Stanford University Press.

Reitz, K. R. 1996. "The Federal Role in Sentencing Law and Policy." *Annals of the American Academy of Political and Social Science* 543:116–29.

Reitz, K. R., and C. R. Reitz. 1995. "Building a Sentencing Reform Agenda: The ABA's New Sentencing Standards." *Judicature* 78:189–95.

Rothman, D. J. 1980. *Conscience and Convenience: The Asylum and Its Alternatives in Progressive America.* Boston: Little, Brown.

Tonry, M. 1993. "The Success of Judge Frankel's Sentencing Commission." *University of Colorado Law Review* 64:713–22.

————. 1996. *Sentencing Matters.* New York: Oxford University Press.

Uelman, G. F. 1992. "Federal Sentencing Guidelines: A Cure Worse Than the Disease." *American Criminal Law Review* 29:899–905.

U.S. Department of Commerce. 1995. *Statistical Abstract of the United States, 1995.* Washington, D.C.: U.S. Government Printing Office.

U.S. Sentencing Commission. 1991. *Special Report to the Congress: Mandatory Minimum Penalties in the Federal Criminal Justice System.* Washington, D.C.: U.S. Sentencing Commission.

von Hirsch, A. 1993. *Censure and Sanctions.* Oxford: Clarendon Press.

Wilson, J. Q. 1975. *Thinking About Crime.* New York: Basic Books.

Zimring, F. E. 1976. "A Consumer's Guide to Sentencing Reform: Making the Punishment Fit the Crime." *Hastings Center Report* 6:13–17.

Zimring, F. E., and G. Hawkins. 1991. *The Scale of Imprisonment.* Chicago: University of Chicago Press.

———. 1995. *Incapacitation: Penal Confinement and the Restraint of Crime.* New York: Oxford University Press.

21

Probation and Parole

JOAN PETERSILIA

*P*robation is a sentence served under supervision in the community, while *parole* is the supervised early release of inmates from correctional institutions. Although the terms are often used interchangeably, there are three important differences:

1. Probation is a dispositional *alternative* to prison, whereas parole implies that the offender has already served a portion of his or her sentence incarcerated.
2. Probation is a sentencing option available to local judges, who determine the form probation will take. Parole results from an administrative decision made by a legally designated paroling authority. Under parole, the power to determine when an offender may be released and the power to fix supervision conditions pass from the hands of the court to an agency within the executive branch of the state.
3. Probation can be a state or local activity, administered by one of more than 2,000 separate agencies in the United States. Parole is always a state function and is administered by a single agency.

In other major respects, probation and parole are similar. In both, information about an offender is gathered and presented to a decision-making authority. That authority has the power to release the offender under specific conditions, and a new crime or technical violation of these conditions may lead to enhanced restrictions or incarceration. Most important, probation and parole—the core of the system known as *community corrections*—have a common mission. Both are designed around the concept of offender reintegration, a key element of which is dealing with the offender's problems in his or her social and community context. It also means avoiding as much as possible the isolating and labeling effects of incarceration.

The Bureau of Justice Statistics (BJS) reports that at the end of 1995, 3.8 *million* adult men and women were on state or federal probation or parole in the United States (see Figure 21.1)—or nearly 2 percent of all U.S. adult citizens. And, 70 percent of *all* adults under "correctional control" are being supervised on probation and parole, so that there are three times as many offenders serving criminal sentences in the community as

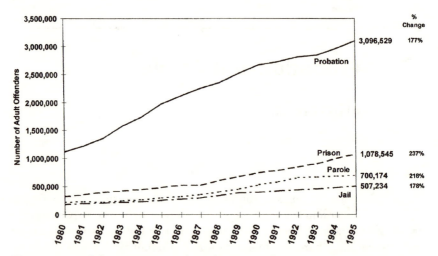

Figure 21.1 Adults in prison, jail, probation, and parole, 1985–1995. *Source:* Bureau of Justice Statistics, 1997, *Correctional Populations In the United States, 1995.*

there are prisoners (Bureau of Justice Statistics 1996b). In addition, more than 520,000 juveniles were placed on probation in 1993—80 percent of all juveniles formally adjudicated by the courts (Butts 1996).

Despite their wide usage and importance, probation and parole agencies have always been poorly staffed, variously administered, and woefully underfunded. Nationally, community corrections receives less than 10 percent of state and local government expenditures for corrections, even though these agencies supervise nearly three-fourths of correctional clients (Petersilia 1995a). And, despite the fact that community corrections populations have grown at a rate similar to that of prisons and jails, funding for only prisons and jails has increased; spending for probation and parole remains unchanged from what it was in 1977 (Langan 1994).

Community corrections has been unable to compete effectively for public funds because it suffers from a "soft on crime" image and, as a result, maintains little public support. Citizens perceive that granting an offender probation is "letting him off" without punishment, and releasing offenders early to parole means that they do less time in custody— and both amount to undue leniency.

Offenders, by contrast, consistently judge intensive supervision—and the related fines, restitution, drug tests, and home confinement—as *more* onerous than incarceration (Petersilia and Deschenes 1994). Further, the evidence indicates that the use of parole does *not* lead to a lessening of the amount of time prisoners actually serve. In fact, the opposite has been shown to be true: offenders under a nonparole system may actually serve *less* time than those under a parole system. After parole was abolished in Connecticut, the average time served by offenders in its prisons plummeted to 13 percent of the sentence. Now that parole has been reinstated, serious offenders are serving at least 50 percent of their sentences, with violent offenders serving longer. As Burke wrote:

> The rhetoric implies that parole is somehow soft on crime. Nothing can be further from the truth. Parole means that criminals must *earn* their way out of prison, demonstrate that they are no longer a risk, and agree to cooperate with stringent requirements if they are to be released. The absence of parole means that offenders simply walk out the door of the prison at the end of a pre-determined period of time, no questions asked. The choice is between parole, which means *earned* release, and no parole, which means *automatic* release. (Burke 1995, p. 11)

Yet, probation and parole are frequently depicted as permissive, uncaring about crime victims, and blindly advocating a rehabilitative ideal while ignoring the reality of violent criminals. The attacks have intensified in recent years, as both probation and parole have come to symbolize a wide variety of complaints with the justice system, and citizens have demanded that offenders be held more accountable for their crimes.

Unfortunately, the public does not really understand the multifaceted nature of probation and parole, nor their importance to justice system decision making and public safety. Community corrections is not merely the "workhorse" of the U.S. justice system; its services are humanitarian to offenders, an important human point of contact for crime victims, and a vital means of public protection. Moreover, when properly funded, community-based corrections provides one of the most best means for delivering effective offender rehabilitation programs, particularly substance abuse treatment.

The History and Philosophy of Probation and Parole

Probation and parole were both founded in the United States in the mid-1800s by humanitarian reformers who had two goals in mind: the reformation of offenders and the reduction of institutional crowding. After the Civil War, the focus shifted to dealing with individual offenders, rather than focusing on the crime that had been committed. As Allen et al. (1985, p. 42) note, this recognition of the importance of individualization of treatment and punishment eventually led to the question: Do *all* offenders need to be imprisoned in order for them to stop their criminal behavior? Gradually, each state and eventually the federal government answered this question with a qualified no, and began identifying categories of offenders who were suitable for probation and early release on parole (Rothman 1980).

Probation

Probation in the United States began in 1841 with the innovative work of John Augustus, a Boston boot maker who was the first to post bail for a man charged with being a common drunk under the authority of the Boston Police Court. When the man appeared before the judge for sentencing, Mr. Augustus made a report to the court on the details of the offense and the offender, and argued that a release to the community was justified. Augustus asked the judge to defer sentencing for three weeks and release the man into Augustus's custody. At the end of this brief probationary period, the offender convinced the judge of his reform and received a nominal fine. The concept of the "presentence investigation" and "probation supervision" had been born.

During the following years, until his death in 1859, Augustus bailed out over 1,800 persons in the Boston courts. Of the first 1,100 offenders he discussed in his autobiography, he claimed only 1 had forfeited bond, and asserted that, with help, most eventually led upright lives. Augustus also wrote that he was motivated by the belief that "the object of the law is to reform criminals and to prevent crime and not to punish maliciously or from a spirit of revenge" (Augustus 1939, p. 17).

From the beginning, the "helping" role of Augustus met with scorn from law enforcement officials. But Augustus persisted, and the Massachusetts court gradually accepted the notion of probation, first for juveniles and later for adults. An experiment in providing services for children (resembling probation) was inaugurated in 1869. In 1878, Massachusetts was the first state to formally adopt a probation law for juveniles. By 1927, all states except Wyoming had adopted juvenile probation laws. Public support for adult probation was more difficult to come by, but by 1956 all states had adopted adult probation laws (Petersilia 1997).

As Rothman (1980) observed some years later, probation developed in the United States very haphazardly, and with no real thought. Missions were unclear and often contradictory, and from the start there was tension between the law enforcement and rehabilitation purposes of probation. Today, probation departments are responsible for dozens of activities, including court-related civil functions (e.g., stepparent adoption investigations, minority-age marriage investigations).

Between 1950 and 1970, U.S. probation evolved in relative obscurity, although from the start it was the "growth industry" of corrections. A number of reports issued in the 1970s brought national attention to the inadequacy of probation services and their organization. The National Advisory Commission on Criminal Justice Standards and Goals observed that probation was the "brightest hope for corrections" but was "failing to provide services and supervision" (1973, p. 112). In 1974, a widely publicized review of rehabilitation programs purportedly showed probation's ineffectiveness (Martinson 1974). Two years later, the U.S. Comptroller General's Office released a report concluding that probation as currently practiced was a "failure," and that U.S. probation systems were "in crisis" (1976, p. 3). The report urged, "Since most offenders are sentenced to probation, probation systems must receive adequate resources. But something more fundamental is needed. The priority given to probation in the criminal justice system must be reevaluated" (p. 74).

Unfortunately, these reports were published at about the time the U.S. prison boom began. With prisons becoming overcrowded, all policy attention was directed toward institutional corrections, and the serious "reexamination" of probation never took place. In 1996, another national commission on crime called for "reinventing" and "reinvesting" in probation and parole (Bell and Bennett 1996, p. 49).

Parole

Parole, like the prison and probation, is primarily an American invention. Judges in the second half of the nineteenth century sentenced criminals largely to flat terms, a practice that often forced governors to issue mass pardons or prison wardens to release prisoners randomly to relieve crowding. Parole grew largely as a necessary relief value for that failed system.

Parole was conceived by Zebulon Brockway, a Michigan penologist who proposed a two-pronged strategy for managing prison populations and preparing inmates for reentry into the community: indeterminate sentencing coupled with parole release. He was given a chance to put his proposal into practice in 1876 when he was appointed superintendent at a new youth reformatory, the Elmira Reformatory in New York. He instituted a system of indeterminacy and parole release, and is commonly credited as the father of both in the United States. His ideas reflected the tenor of the times—a belief that criminals could be reformed, and that every prisoner's treatment should be individualized.

On being admitted to Elmira, each inmate (males between the ages of sixteen and thirty) was placed in the second grade of classification. Six months of good conduct meant promotion to the first grade; misbehavior could result in being placed in the third grade, from which the inmate would have to work his way back up. Continued good behavior in the first grade resulted in release.

Paroled inmates remained under the jurisdiction of authorities for an additional six months, during which the parolee was required to report on the first day of every month to his appointed volunteer guardian (from which parole officers evolved) and provide an account of his situation and conduct (Abadinsky 1997). Indeterminate sentences and parole spread rapidly through the United States. New York was the first state formally to adopt all the components of a parole system: indeterminate sentences, a system for granting release, postrelease supervision, and specific criteria for parole revocation. By 1927, only three states—Florida, Mississippi, and Virginia—were without a parole system, and by 1942 all states had such systems. The percentage of prisoners released on parole grew from its inception; it rose from 44 percent in 1940 to a high of 72 percent in 1977, after which release on parole began to decline (Maguire and Pastore 1995). But, like probation, the tremendous growth in parole as a concept did not imply uniform development or quality practices. As Bottomley wrote, "[I]t is doubtful whether parole ever really operated consistently in the United States either in principle or practice" (1990, p. 323).

Parole boards operate under different sentencing schemes and have a great deal of discretion; states vary markedly in the proportion and kinds of inmates who are released on parole, and the kinds of supervision offenders receive; and, like probation, parole has struggled for adequate funding and never been able to show that its services reduce offender recidivism. The 1967 President's Commission on Law Enforcement and Administration of Justice observed that "there are wide discrepancies between . . . what parole purports to be and the actual situation in most jurisdictions" (1967, p. 64). As with probation, numerous task forces and studies over the years have endorsed the concept and legitimacy of parole but have found fault with the system's actual workings.

In the early 1970s, both the indeterminate sentence and parole came under serious attack. Crime control advocates denounced parole supervision as being largely nominal and ineffective; social welfare advocates decried the lack of meaningful and useful rehabilitation programs. Discontent with treatment effectiveness (Martinson 1974; Palmer 1992) was accompanied by the presentation of David Fogel's (1975) "justice model" and Andrew von Hirsch's (1976) "just deserts" model, both of which explicitly excluded any concern about crime control as a goal of sentencing and called for the elimination of indeterminate sentencing and discretionary parole release.

These two thrusts had both popular and political support. In 1976, Maine became the first state to eliminate parole. The following year, California and Indiana joined Maine in establishing determinate sentencing legislation and abolishing discretionary parole release. By 1996, eleven states had abolished discretionary parole release (Washington, Oregon, California, New Mexico, Minnesota, Illinois, Indiana, Virginia, North Carolina, Delaware, and Maine). Interestingly, in Colorado, Connecticut, and Florida, earlier decisions to eliminate parole have been reversed. In Florida, for example, a new Controlled Release Authority was established in 1990 to carry out essentially the same responsibilities that had been removed from the parole board in 1983.

The percentage of prisoners released on parole has steadily declined, and the latest figures show that just 36 percent of prison releasees are paroled (see Figure 21.2). Thirty-seven percent of prisoners released in 1994 were "mandatory releases," meaning that the inmate has served his required maximum sentence and release was required by law. For the first time since statistics have been compiled on this issue, the BJS re-

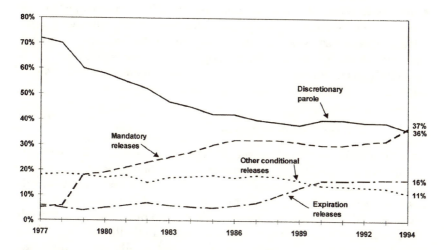

Figure 21.2 Percent of state prisoners released by various methods. *Source:* Bureau of Justice Statistics, 1996a, *Correctional Populations in the United States, 1994.*

ported that in 1994 mandatory releasees surpassed parole releasees (and if one adds the "expiration releasees," which can be considered a type of mandatory release, there is an even bigger imbalance between parole and mandatory release).

Unfortunately, the attacks on probation and parole will continue unless the public comes to better understand and appreciate community corrections. But understanding probation and parole is difficult. The terms are ambiguous, implying a legal status, an alternative to incarceration, a service-delivery mechanism, and an organizational entity. As David Fogel observed of probation: "[P]robation lacks a forceful imagery that other occupations in criminal justice can claim: police catch criminals, prosecutors try and get them locked up, judges put them in prison, wardens keep them there, but what do probation officers *do?*" (1984, p. 164). The truth is that probation and parole officers *do* plenty, and they do much more than just supervise offenders.

Probation and Parole in Modern Sentencing Practice

Probation and parole have always performed dual functions: assisting the decisional process (the "investigation" function" for probation, and the "release" function for parole), and "supervision" for those offenders judged suitable for community release.

The vast majority of crimes are not punished with a prison sentence. Of every 100 felony arrests by the police, 54 result in convictions, which, in turn, produce 22 probation sentences, 18 jail sentences, and 14 prison sentences (Boland, Mahanna, and Stones 1992). The criminal justice system operates as a large offender-selection bureaucracy, removing some clients at each stage while passing others on to the next decision point. The critical players are community corrections officials, whose chief responsibility is to assess risk and release to the community offenders who have the lowest probability of further crime.

The Granting of Probation

Anyone who is convicted, as well as many of those arrested, comes into contact with the probation department, and probation officials, operating with a great deal of discretion, dramatically affect most subsequent processing decisions. Their input not only affects the subsequent liberties offenders will enjoy, but also has an influence on public safety, since they recommend (within certain legal restraints) which offenders will be released back to their communities, and judges usually accept their sentence recommendations.

Probation officials are involved in decision making long before sentencing, often beginning from the point of a crime being noted by the police. They usually perform the personal investigation to determine whether a defendant will be released on his own recognizance or bail. Probation reports are the primary source of information the court uses to determine which cases will be deferred from formal prosecution. If the case is deferred, probation officers will also supervise the diverted offender; their recommendation will be primary in establishing whether the offender has successfully complied with the diversionary sentence, and hence that no formal prosecution will occur.

For persons who violate court-ordered conditions, probation officers are responsible for deciding which violations will be brought back to the court's attention, and what subsequent sanctions to recommend. When the court grants probation, probation staff have great discretion over which court-ordered conditions to enforce and monitor. And when an offender goes to prison, the offender's initial security classification (and eligibility for parole) will be based on information contained in the presentence investigation. Finally, when the offender is released from jail or prison, probation staff often provide his or her community supervision.

No other justice agency is involved with the offender and his case as comprehensively as the probation department. Every other agency completes its work and then hands the case over to the next decision maker. The police arrest offenders and hand them over to the prosecutor who files charges; the prosecuter hands them to the judge who sentences; the judge finally hands them to the warden who confines. But the probation department interacts with all of these agencies, provides the data that influence each of their processing decisions, and takes charge of the offender's supervision at any point when the system decides to return the offender to the community (of course, for parolees, parole officers usually assume this function).

From the point of arrest, information about the offenders' crime and criminal background is accumulated and eventually presented to the court if the case proceeds through prosecution and sentencing. This document is known as the *presentence investigation* (PSI) or *presentence report* (PSR).

The PSI is a critically important document, since over 90 percent of all felony cases are eventually resolved through a negotiated plea, and the major decision of the court is whether imprisonment will be imposed. Research has repeatedly shown that the judge's knowledge of the defendant is usually limited to the information contained in the PSI. As a result, there is a high correlation between the recommendation of the PO and the judge's sentence. Research has found that recommendations for probation are adopted by the sentencing judge between 65 and 95 percent of the time.

The PSI typically includes information on the seriousness of the crime, the defendant's risk, the defendant's circumstance, a summary of the legally permissible sentencing options, and a recommendation for or against prison. If recommending prison, the PSI recommends sentence length; if recommending probation, the PSI recommends sentence length and the conditions to be imposed.

The BJS reports that U.S. judges sentence to probation or probation with jail 80 percent of all adults convicted of misdemeanors and about 60 percent of all adults convicted of felonies (crimes punishable by more than one year in prison)—or fully two-thirds of all persons convicted of a crime (Bureau of Justice Statistics 1996). But for felony convictions, only 30 percent of offenders are sentenced to straight probation requiring no jail sentence (see Table 21.1). For those sentenced to jail for a felony conviction, the average jail term is seven months, while the average length of felony probation is forty-seven months (Bureau of Justice Statistics 1995).

Researchers have attempted to identify factors that predict the prison versus probation decision, when both defendants have been convicted of the same offense. Petersilia and Turner (1986) analyzed the criminal records and case files of approximately 16,500 males, each of whom had been convicted of selected felony crimes in one of seventeen California counties in 1980. They found that a person was more likely to receive a prison sentence if he:

- had two or more conviction counts (i.e., convicted of multiple charges)
- had two or more prior criminal convictions
- was on probation or parole at the time of the arrest
- was a drug addict
- used a weapon during the commission of the offense or seriously injured the victims

Table 21.1. Felony Sentences Imposed by State and Federal courts, by Offense, United States, 1990

Most serious conviction offense	Total (%)	Incarceration Total (%)	Prison (%)	Jail (%)	Straight probation
All offenses	100	70	44	26	30
Violent offenses					
Murder/manslaughter	100	95	91	4	5
Rape	100	86	67	19	14
Robbery	100	90	74	16	10
Aggravated assault	100	72	45	27	26
Other violent	100	67	42	25	33
Property offenses					
Burglary	100	75	54	21	25
Larceny	100	64	39	25	36
Motor vehicle theft	100	75	46	29	25
Other theft	100	62	38	24	38
Fraud/forgery	100	52	32	20	48
Fraud	100	46	25	21	54
Forgery	100	59	40	19	41
Drug offenses					
Possession	100	64	35	29	36
Trafficking	100	77	51	26	23

Source: Bureau of Justice Statistics, 1994b, *Felony Sentences in the United States, 1990.*

Note: For persons receiving a combination of sentences, the sentence designation came from the most severe penalty imposed—prison being the most severe, followed by jail, then probation.

For all offenses except assault, offenders having three or more of these characteristics had an 80 percent or greater probability of going to prison in California, regardless of the type of crime of which they were currently convicted (Petersilia and Turner 1986).

For offenders granted probation, the court decides how the probation sentence will be imposed. The most common method of imposing a probation sentence is for the judge to formulate a prison sentence and then suspend the prison sentence in favor of probation. In this way, the jail or prison term has been legally imposed but held in abeyance to be reinstated if the offender fails to abide by the probation conditions. Offenders are presumed to be more motivated to comply with probation by knowing what awaits should they fail to do so. About 50 percent of all probation sentences are imposed in this "suspended sentence" manner (Latessa and Allen 1997).

It is the judge's responsibility to enumerate the conditions the probationer must abide by. The conditions are usually recommended by probation officers and contained in the PSI. But they may also be designed by the judge, and judges are generally free to construct any terms of probation they deem necessary. Judges also often authorize the setting of "such other conditions as the probation officer may deem proper to impose" or leave the mode of implementation of a condition to the discretion of the probation officer.

The required conditions usually fall into one of three realms:

- Standard conditions imposed on all probationers include such requirements as reporting to the probation office, notifying the agency of any change of address, remaining gainfully employed, and not leaving the jurisdiction without permission.
- Punitive conditions, which are usually established to reflect the seriousness of the offense, increase the intrusiveness and painfulness of probation. Examples are fines, community service, victim restitution, house arrest, and drug testing.
- Treatment conditions are imposed to force probationers to deal with significant problems or needs, such as substance abuse, family counseling, or vocational training.

Over the years, the number of offenders subject to punitive and treatment conditions has increased. The most common include residential placement, alcohol- or drug-abuse treatment and testing, and mental health counseling. Almost half of all felony probationers are given one or more special conditions, the most common being drug testing, which is imposed upon more than a third of all felony probationers (Langan and Cunniff 1992).

More stringent conditions also increase the chances of failure. According to the BJS, a lower percentage of offenders is successfully completing their probation terms. In 1986, 74 percent of those who exited probation successfully completed their terms; in 1992, the figure was 67 percent, and by 1994, it had dropped to 60 percent (Langan 1996).

In legal terms, the probation conditions form a contract between the offender and the court (Klein 1997). The contract states the conditions, at least theoretically, the offender must abide by to remain in the community. The court requires that the probation officer provide the defendant with a written statement setting forth all the conditions to which the sentence is subject. The offender signs the contract, and the probation officer is the "enforcer" of the contract, responsible for notifying the court when it is not being fulfilled. Probation may be revoked if probationers fail to comply with these conditions and obey the reasonable requests of the probation staff to meet their treatment obligations.

Even though many court-ordered conditions are not actively enforced, the probation population is so large that revoking even a small percentage of them or revoking all those who are rearrested can have a dramatic impact on prison admissions. Current estimates indicate that between 30 and 50 percent of all new prison admissions are probation and parole failures. Texas, for example, reported that in 1993 approximately two-thirds of all prison admissions were either probation or parole violators. In Oregon, the figure was over 80 percent, and in California, over 60 percent (Parent et al. 1994). A recent analysis by Petersilia (1995b) found that "true" technical violators (those returned for rule infractions rather than a new crime), however, made up only 4 percent of the total prison admissions in 1991.

Because of the scarcity of prison beds, policy makers have begun to wonder whether revoking probationers and parolees for technical violations (i.e., infractions of the conditions of supervision, rather than for a new crime) makes sense. Several states are now structuring the court's responses to technical violations. Missouri has opened up the Kansas City Recycling Center, a forty-one-bed facility operated by a private contractor to deal exclusively with technical violators who have been recommended for revocation. Mississippi and Georgia use ninety-day boot camp programs, housed in separate wings of the state prisons, for probation violators. Although empirical evidence is scant regarding the effects of these programs, system officials believe that they serve to increase the certainty of punishment, while reserving scarce prison space for the truly violent.

Release on Parole

Parole boards determine how much time offenders must spend in confinement and whether parole should be revoked if the offender fails to comply with the release conditions. Parole boards—usually composed of no more than ten individuals—also have the authority to rescind an established parole date, issue warrants and subpoenas, set conditions of supervision, restore offenders' civil rights, and grant final discharges. They may also order the payment of restitution or supervision fees as a condition of parole release.

The decision to grant parole is usually made by a governor-appointed parole board. These men and women review case files, interview inmates, and determine whether eligible offenders should be released. Parole eligibility is determined by statutory requirements and usually occurs upon the completion of the minimum sentence less any good-time credits.

Parole is a way of completing a prison sentence in the community. Legally speaking, parolees are still "prisoners" who can be recalled to serve the remainder of their sentence in prison if the parole board deems their adjustment to the community inadequate, because they either have failed to obey the conditions of their release or have committed another crime while on parole.

In recent years, external factors have increasingly influenced parole decision making. These include prison crowding, the availability of community resources should the offender be released, and the presence of a parole plan verifying future residence and employment. A recent survey by the American Paroling Authorities (APA) found that parole boards judge the availability of community resources and the presence of a parole plan as much more important than prison crowding (Runda, Rhine, and Wetter 1994). Thirty-three (of fifty-five) jurisdictions reported that prison crowding was not important or not considered in parole release decisions; the remaining jurisdictions viewed it as important or of some importance.

What factors *do* parole boards consider important? The APA survey showed that only nine items were ranked as "important." The single most important factor was the nature of the offender's current offense. This was followed closely by "any history of prior violence" and "prior felony convictions." "Possession of a firearm" ranked fourth. The remaining five items were previous incarceration, prior parole adjustment, prison disciplinary record, psychological reports, and victim input. Victim input was the only type of individual input that was ranked among the most critical factors that boards considered (Runda, Rhine, and Wetter 1994).

The results of this survey suggest that most paroling authorities embrace incapacitation and a modified "just deserts" philosophy when making release decisions. The nature of the current offense and the use of a firearm address the type of crime committed. The focus on a prior record of violence, prior felony convictions, and previous incarcerations emphasizes the past in relation to the issue of incapacitation and how much time an offender should serve prior to parole eligibility. None of the items judged most important emphasized offender rehabilitation or program participation as salient.

In recent years, an attempt has been made to make the paroling process more accountable and less discretionary. The parole release decision was traditionally arrived at by the case study method, also referred to as "clinical judgments." In this process, the board member, caseworker, or parole agency collects as much information as possible, combines it in unique way, mulls over the results, and reaches a decision.

The problem with this method is that it often results in idiosyncratic or discriminatory policies. More important, clinical judgments are often not predictive of subsequent criminal behavior, and assessing recidivism risk is the major component affecting the release decisions. Researchers have shown that statistical predictions of recidivism are superior to clinical judgments, and they urge parole boards to use actuarial devices, now commonly referred to as "risk assessment" or prediction instruments. The earliest and most well developed of these systems is the U.S. Parole Commission's Salient Factor Score (SFS). The SFS is calculated by summarizing the points assessed for various background factors. This total is then combined with an offense severity scale to form a matrix or grid. Those inmates who are sentenced for the least serious crimes and are least likely to reoffend (statistically) would be the first to be released on parole. By 1994, half of all paroling agencies reported they had adopted some form of parole guidelines and used formal risk assessment instruments (Runda, Rhine, and Wetter 1994).

Unfortunately, while the objective classification systems predict recidivism better than clinical judgments, they are far from perfect. Klein and Caggiano (1986) applied six well-known risk assessment models to parole outcome data from Texas, California, and Michigan. A variety of recidivism measures were used. The best overall recidivism predictive items were prior criminality, young age, drug abuse, and poor employment history. They concluded, however, that "when all the variables were used together, they [the six models] did not predict more than 10 percent of the variance on any of the measures of recidivism" (Klein and Caggiano 1986, p. 31). Petersilia and Turner (1986) came to similar conclusions for a sample of felony probationers.

There is also a trend toward more openness in parole agency operations. Most boards now notify the prosecuting attorney, the sentencing judge, and law enforcement of scheduled parole hearings. Victims are also included more frequently, and the public and the media are permitted to attend parole hearings in one-half of U.S. jurisdictions. Likewise, the votes of individual board members are now a matter of record in most jurisdictions (Runda, Rhine, and Wetter 1994).

Recent sentencing changes have dramatically affected the use of parole. Between 1975 and 1995, the U.S. sentencing system went from one where sentencing codes of every state had some form of indeterminacy to one where every state had revised, replaced, or seriously considered determinate sentencing.

As of November 1995, thirty-five states retained some form of discretionary release of inmates, but nineteen of these were limited to certain kinds of offenses. In New York, for example, the board's discretion over second-term violent felons was curtailed (National Institute of Corrections 1995). Sixteen other states have paroling authorities who continue hearing only cases committed before indeterminate sentences were abolished in their state. Although parole was abolished in eleven states, several are among the largest (California, Illinois, plus the U.S. Parole Commission). This, combined with increasing restrictions placed on numerous other parole boards, caused the dramatic decline in the percentage of offenders released by way of parole (shown in Figure 21.2).

At release, the parole board specifies the conditions under which the parolee must abide in order to remain in the community. This process is identical to that for probationers—and, in fact, in some jurisdictions, probation officers are responsible for supervising both parolees and probationers. Here, too, it has been shown that conditions are increasing, parole agents have difficulty monitoring all of them, and the revocation of parole failures contributes significantly to prison crowding.

In 1991, Rhine and his colleagues discovered that the average number of standard conditions of parole was fifteen—the most common condition, of course, was to "obey all laws." Seventy-eight percent required "gainful employment" as a standard condition; 61 percent, "no association with persons of criminal records"; 53 percent, to "pay all fines and restitution"; and 47 percent, to "support family and all dependents." As

Holt concludes: "None of these can be consistently met. Thus, we design systems so that almost all parolees are likely to fail at some point. . . . Unfortunately parole conditions serve as much to comfort agencies and parole boards, and help the release decision withstand public scrutiny, than to establish realistic expectations for the parolee" (1998, p. 10).

Parole agents are responsible for recommending to parole boards whether to return parolees to prison for violating their conditions of release. The Supreme Court in *Morrissey v. Brewer,* 408 U.S. 471 (1972), set out the due process guarantees applicable in parole revocation proceedings. The process must include a preliminary hearing before an impartial decision maker to assess whether there is probable cause to believe that a violation occurred. If probable cause is found, a full revocation hearing must be held that provides the parolee with written notice of the charges, disclosure of the evidence, and an opportunity to cross-examine witnesses. A year later, *Gagnon v. Scarpelli*, 411 U.S. 778 (1973), held that legal counsel should be extended, on a case-by-case basis, to probationers or parolees facing possible revocation.

Once these procedures have been followed, the decision to revoke parole rests entirely with the parole board. In some ways, parole boards are under public pressure to revoke when a violation has been brought to their attention—after all, the offender has already been given one chance, and his continued disregard for the law strikes many as further demeaning the process. Recent data show that 49 percent of offenders granted parole are successfully discharged, and 48 percent are returned to prison at some point in their parole period (Bureau of Justice Statistics 1994c).

The Risks Posed by Current Probationers and Parolees

The process of "granting probation" and "parole release" results in a population of offenders serving criminal sentences in the community. Some assume that the population of offenders under community supervision consists of nonserious offenders. This misperception of the seriousness of the risk posed by offenders in the community is part of the reason probation and parole agencies have difficulty competing with prisons and jails for funding (Petersilia 1995b). The public may perceive that the population is nonserious, and, hence, that there is little need to provide more funding for their supervision and services. Available data suggest, however, that probation and parole populations have grown in numbers, and that their characteristics have become more serious. For example, the percentage of probationers convicted of felonies in New York State during the first half of the twentieth century rarely exceeded 10 percent of the probationer population (Rothman 1980, p. 108). Today, half of all offenders on probation have been convicted of a felony.

Surveys of probation and parole officials consistently show that they believe their current caseloads are becoming more difficult to manage because more of their populations are drug users, are mentally ill, or have been diagnosed with medical problems such as AIDS or tuberculosis. A national survey conducted in 1988 showed that three-fourths of proba- tion and parole agency directors felt that offenders' needs were greater than in the past and that their offenders were more difficult to manage (Guynes 1988).

Probation and parole officers are increasingly worried about their per- sonal safety. Lindner and Bonn (1996) found there was a great concern among officers regarding their personal safety, and most officers sup- ported the carrying of weapons. Of course, the carrying of firearms has serious implications, and the subject is controversial among community corrections professionals. As one officer put it in the Linder and Bonn survey: "Probation officers may not want to carry guns as it may interfere with the social service/rehabilitative role." But another wrote in: "Many staff carry guns without agency authorization because of fear." Lindner and Bonn concluded, "In recent years attitudes have turned around 100 percent and most probation officers would prefer to carry weapons" (1996, p. 21).

Note how far from John Augustus's vision we have moved. In his auto- biography Augustus wrote that "probation officers just need to have a good heart." Today, it appears they believe they need much more. Two- thirds of parole and probation agencies now permit officers to carry weapons all the time, and most permit them to carry them for specific purposes (e.g., while making arrests or transporting offenders; Camp and Camp 1995).

Probation and Parole Supervision

Once released to the community, the offender comes under the control of a probation or parole officer, who enforces the rules, helps the offender gain employment, and meets regularly with the offender. This *supervi- sion* function is widely regarded as the most significant responsibility of probation and parole agencies, and at this stage probation and parole agencies operate similarly. In about thirty states and in the federal sys- tem, supervision officers have combined caseloads of probation and pa- role clients.

The goals of probation and parole supervision are identical: to protect the community and help rehabilitate offenders. These dual functions are referred to as the "law enforcement" function, which emphasizes surveil- lance of the offender and close control on behavior, and the "social work" function, which attempts to provide supportive services to meet offenders' needs. Both have always been part of community corrections, and debating which should be of higher priority has always caused strain. As David Fogel wrote, "[A] parole officer can be seen going off to his/her appointed rounds with Freud in one hand and a .38 Smith and Wesson in the other hand" (1992, p. xiv). Currently, the social work function has given way to the law enforcement function, and probation and parole officers are less interested today in treating clients than in controlling their behavior (Harris, Clear, and Baird 1989).

The first decision to be made about an offender's supervision is his or her assignment to an officer's caseload. Over the years, probation caseloads have grown from what was thought to be an ideal size of 30 to 1 in the mid-1970s to today, when the average adult regular supervision caseload is reported to be 117 to 1. Parole caseloads average 84:1—smaller than probation caseloads, but former inmates require more extensive services. In both probation and parole, nearly 90 percent of offenders are supervised on regular caseloads (as opposed to intensive or specialized); the cost of regular supervision for probation is estimated to be about $200 per year, per offender, and the average cost for parole is estimated at about $975 per year, per offender (Camp and Camp 1995).

Unfortunately, reducing caseload size alone has never been shown to reduce recidivism. If services are not provided and matched to offenders' needs, and surveillance is simply increased, it is likely that reducing caseload size merely increases the chance for detection of violations and subsequent revocation (Petersilia and Turner 1993).

Some agencies assign offenders randomly to officers (but this is not common), others assign offenders based on geography or special needs (e.g., sex offenders, drug offenders, domestic abusers, individuals with AIDS), and yet others base assignments on the use of recidivism prediction instruments. These "risk and needs" instruments score offenders based on their "risk" to the community (using factors such as prior criminal record) and their "need" for services (e.g., alcohol, drug, psychological). Their score then places them in different levels of supervision (minimum, medium, and intensive).

Once an offender is assigned to a caseload, supervision usually centers around the "casework model" or the "brokerage model." In the past, community corrections workers had primary responsibility for supervision and treatment—a "hands-on" approach. But as caseloads have grown, officers are increasingly being forced to refer inmates to existing community social service programs or to contract directly for services.

There is wide variation among jurisdictions regarding the extent and quality of services provided to probationers and parolees. Some jurisdictions have more resources and a historical commitment to providing rehabilitation, whereas others are struggling under huge caseloads with little to spare for either delivering or contracting for special services. In those jurisdictions, officers can do little but monitor court-ordered conditions and, if violations are uncovered, bring the offender back to the court's or parole board's attention. It is safe to say, however, that overall the services are woefully inadequate to meet the needs of today's community corrections clients. The "average" *felony* probationer sees a probation officer about once a month, the "average" parolee, about twice a month (Langan 1994; Camp and Camp 1995).

Assessing Probation's and Parole's Effectiveness

The most commonly asked question about community corrections is, Does it work? By "work," most mean whether the person on probation or parole refrained from further crime, and whether the services provided by community corrections agencies made a difference in the outcome. Recidivism is currently the primary outcome measure for probation and parole, as it is for all corrections programs. Unfortunately, current data do not allow us to answer this question with certainty.

To provide an answer, system officials would need to randomly assign offenders to different levels of supervision, and then track them for a sufficient follow-up period to systematically record rearrests and other recidivism measures. If recidivism rates were different, we could attribute the differences to probation or parole services because we would have isolated the independent effects of other crime and offender characteristics known to be associated with recidivism (e.g., prior record, age). Very few randomized experiments have been conducted in community corrections, although in recent years they have become more common.

What we do know, nationally speaking, are the recidivism rates of specific populations that have been tracked for research purposes. The BJS, the statistical data-gathering agency of the U.S. Department of Justice, has conducted the largest of these studies.

For the probation population as a whole, we do not know the percentage who get rearrested while on probation because half of all adult probationers have been convicted of misdemeanors and have not been the subject of recidivism research. For *felony* adult probationers, the best recidivism data come from the BJS study by Langan and Cunniff (1992). They found that within three years of sentencing, while still on probation, 43 percent of felons were rearrested for a crime within the state. Half of the arrests were for a violent crime (murder, rape, robbery, or aggravated assault) or a drug offense (drug trafficking or drug possession). The authors estimated that recidivism would have been higher had out-of-state arrests been included.

For parolees, the BJS-estimated recidivism rates are even higher. Beck and Shipley (1989) identified 108,580 men and women released in eleven states in 1983 and tracked them for three years. They found that 62 percent had been rearrested for a felony or serious misdemeanor, and 41 percent had been sent back to prison. In sum, the BJS estimates that about 43 percent of felony probationers are rearrested within three years, compared with 62 percent of parolees. For both probationers and parolees, the risk of recidivism is highest in the first year after sentencing or release on parole.

Studies have also consistently shown that a number of factors are associated with recidivism. The best predictors of probation recidivism were summarized by Morgan (1993); they are conviction crime (property offenders have higher rates); prior criminal record (the more convictions, the higher the recidivism), employment (unemployment is associated with higher recidivism), age (younger offenders have higher rates), family composition (persons living with spouse or children have lower rates), and drug use (heroin addicts have highest recidivism rates). Similar factors have been found to predict parole outcomes (Petersilia and Turner 1986).

Another way to examine probation and parole effectiveness is to look at the proportion of the overall crime problem attributable to parolees and probationers. The best measure comes from various data sources compiled by the BJS, which are summarized in Figure 21.3. The figure indicates that of all persons arrested for felony crimes in 1990, 17 percent were on probation and 8 percent were on parole at the time of their current arrest. When viewed this way, about a quarter of all serious crime arrests made in the United States were attributable to persons who were on probation or parole at the time of the offense, and 44 percent of persons in prison were on probation or parole at the time of the offense that landed them in prison.

Such high recidivism rates have led to the common perception that "nothing works." Of course, it is important to remember that 90 percent of probationers and parolees are on caseloads where they are seen less than once a month, and the funds available to support their supervision and services are generally less than $1,000 per offender—when effective treatment programs are estimated to cost $12,000 to $15,000 per year, per client (Institute of Medicine 1990). It is no wonder that recidivism rates are so high. In a sense, we get what we pay for, and, as yet, we have never

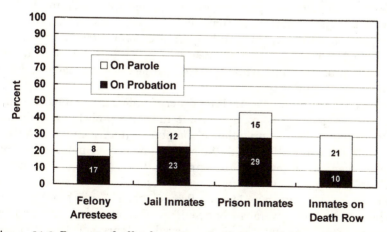

Figure 21.3 Percent of offenders on probation or parole at time of offense. Sources: Bureau of Justice Statistics, 1993a, *Felony Defendants in Large Urban Counties, 1990;* Bureau of Justice Statistics, 1993b, *Jail Inmates, 1992;* Bureau of Justice Statistics, 1993c, *Survey of State Prison Inmates, 1992;* and Bureau of Justice Statistics, 1994a, *Capital Punishment, 1993.*

chosen to invest sufficiently in community-based programs. Nevertheless, this criticism of community corrections has led to a call for new programs that would be tougher and more intensive than regular probation and parole.

The Emergence of Intermediate Sanctions

Since the early 1980s, jurisdictions have struggled to find criminal sanctions that fall between routine probation or parole and incarceration; hence, the emergence of "intermediate" or "middle-range" penalties. Intermediate sanctions were initially developed in the mid-1970s in the southern United States (primarily Georgia), the region with the highest rate of incarceration and the earliest prison crowding problems. But as prison crowding became commonplace across the nation, so did the search for alternatives, and during the past decade every state has implemented a variety of intermediate sanction programs ("ISP").

In and of themselves, ISPs don't imply any particular type of program. Rather, ISP is a generic term, and programs take a variety of forms. The most popular are intensive probation or parole, house arrest, electronic monitoring, boot camps, drug courts, day reporting centers, community service, and specialized (mostly drug-related or sex offender) probation and parole caseloads.

Figure 21.4 shows how an ideal model of a graduated or intermediate sanctions system would be structured. It shows a variety of sanctions—differing in costs and punitiveness—that would be available to judges in sentencing offenders. Officials would choose the sanction that best matched the offender's conviction crime and risk of recidivism. If violations occurred in one ISP program, offenders might be moved to a higher-severity sanction, rather than immediately being incarcerated, thereby saving additional dollars in handling the less serious recidivists. Establishing such a system of intermediate sanctions has been the major development in probation and parole agencies during the last decade, and it is still very much a priority.

The activities conducted in ISPs differ significantly among jurisdictions and programs. For example, some intensive probation/parole ISP programs have a heavy surveillance component (increasing drug testing and contacts), while others with the same name may be more treatment-focused (mandating treatment participation). Still other intensive probation/parole programs may combine heavy doses of both surveillance and treatment (for a complete review, see Petersilia and Turner 1993).

There have been several recent reviews of research on intermediate sanctions. The interested reader is referred to Tonry and Lynch (1996) and Clear and Braga (1995) for a more detailed discussion. ISP evaluations, regardless of the particular program, have produced rather consistent findings. The most important are the following:

1. Most ISPs have been probation-*enhancement* programs rather than

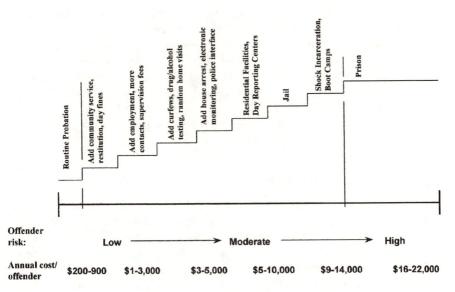

Figure 21.4 An ideal model of intermediate sanctions.

prison or jail *diversion* programs. They seek a "tougher" probation to re-place traditional methods, and they target the "toughest" probation cases. This approach can reduce crowding and related costs only by substantial reductions in failure rates compared with traditional probation. But the stringent conditions and strict enforcement associated with most ISP pro-grams mean they produce a *higher* failure rate of technical violations. As a result, most ISPs implemented to date have not saved money, since the intermediate sanction is usually more expensive than the routine proba-tion programs they supplant.

2. Well-implemented ISPs *do* restore credibility to the justice system and provide a much-needed spectrum of punishments to match the spec-trum of risk posed by criminals. Policy makers, judges, corrections prac-titioners, and the public strongly support intermediate sanctions for non-violent offenders. Offenders judge certain ISP programs as more punitive than short incarceration terms. This is particularly true in ISPs that in-clude mandatory work and drug testing requirements.

3. For offenders who do not present unacceptable risks of violence, well-managed intermediate sanctions offer a cost-effective way to keep them in the community at less cost than imprisonment and with no worse prospect for criminality (Tonry and Lynch 1996, p. 137).

4. Intermediate sanctions may offer promise as a way to get and keep offenders in drug and other treatment programs. With drug treatment programs, at least, there is evidence that coerced treatment programs can reduce both later drug use and later crimes, and there is evidence in the ISP and boot camp literatures that these programs can increase treatment participation (Tonry and Lynch 1996, p. 137).

5. The most important finding from the intermediate sanctions literature is that programs must deliver high "doses" of *both* treatment and
surveillance to assure public safety and reduce recidivism. "Treatment"
alone is not enough, nor is "surveillance" by itself adequate. Programs
that can increase offender-to-officer contacts *and* provide treatment
have reduced recidivism. Petersilia and Turner (1993) found that offenders who received drug counseling, held jobs, paid restitution, and
did community service were arrested 10 to 20 percent less often than
others.

Future Considerations

Although no one can predict the future, it is likely to be characterized by
a greater number of probationers and parolees who have increasingly serious social and personal problems. Taxes are unlikely to increase, resulting in fewer social services being available to community corrections
clients. A greater number of arrests and prosecutions will require that a
growing share of probation budgets be devoted to preparing presentence
investigations, with a concomitant decrease in the funds allocated to offender supervision. All of this means that offenders will receive fewer
services to help them deal with their underlying problems, assuring that
recidivism rates will remain high—and public support for community
corrections will remain low.

At the same time, some glimmers of hope are emerging. However, it is
again the practical, rather than the humanistic or reintegrative, appeal of
community corrections that is likely to be important. Today, less than
half of felony convictions result in a prison term, and the average prison
term served is less than two years. Yet states, which are struggling financially to keep up with the demands of imposing that level of imprisonment, are being forced to make some hard choices regarding spending
priorities. Many states must either continue to make cuts in vital social
programs (especially higher education) to pay for expanded prisons, or
take a hard look at who is currently in prison and decide whether some
could be punished in tough but less expensive community-based programs. For example, RAND analysts estimate that when the California
three-strikes law is fully implemented, it will consume 18 percent of the
state budget, leaving scarcely 1 percent of state funds available for higher
education in the twenty-first century (Greenwood et al. 1994).

Such dire predictions have forced the California legislature, for the
first time in over two decades, to acknowledge the limitations of incarceration as punishment. In 1995, the state provided $2 million dollars in
seed money to encourage local probation departments to develop intermediate sanctions for nonviolent offenders, expressly for the purpose of
reducing commitments to state prisons. Other states (Minnesota, North
Carolina, Pennsylvania) are also trying a number of methods to realign
community corrections, intermediate sanctions, and prison policy—in-

cluding structured sentencing guidelines, Community Corrections Acts (mechanisms by which state funds are granted to local governments to foster local sanctions to be used in lieu of prison), and financial incentives to counties to handle prison-bound offenders locally.

So, probation and parole agencies find themselves in a unique position: they are being blamed for the "revolving door" justice problem and high levels of crime, and yet they also are being asked to solve the problem they are seen as causing. They *can* be an important part of the solution if they are given adequate resources to do the job. Research has now identified the key aspects of successful community-based interventions (Palmer 1996), the target groups programs are most effective with (Gendreau 1996), and how best to implement successful community-based programs (Harris and Smith 1996). The next step must be to test these interventions scientifically—providing service *and* surveillance.

With this evidence in hand, we might finally deliver community corrections programs that live up to their early promises—protecting citizens while fostering offender rehabilitation. And when policy makers stare at the million-plus U.S. prison population and ask, Do all these offenders *really* need to be locked up? the answer will be "no" because we have proven unequivocally that we can implement more cost-effective, humane, and crime-reducing programs in the community.

Acknowledgments I would like to thank Barry Nidorf, Tim Matthews, Ronald Corbett, Greg Markley, and Don Stiles, and all the members of the American Probation and Parole Association (APPA) for their constant assistance over the past decade in helping me better understand the practice and promise of community corrections.

References

Abadinksy, Howard. 1997. *Probation and Parole: Theory and Practice.* Upper Saddle River, N.J.: Prentice Hall.

Allen, Harry, Chris W. Eskridge, Edward J. Latessa, and Gennaro Vito. 1985. *Probation and Parole in America.* New York: Free Press.

Augustus, John. [1852] 1939. "A Report of the Labors of John Augustus, for the Last Ten Years, in Aid of the Unfortunate." Boston: Wright and Hasty. Reprinted as John Augustus, *The First Probation Officer.* New York: The National Probation Association.

Beck, Allen, and Bernard Shipley. 1989. *Recidivism of Prisoners Released in 1983.* Washington, D.C.: U.S. Department of Justice, Bureau of Justice Statistics.

Bell, Griffin B., and William J. Bennett. 1996. *The State of Violent Crime in America.* Washington, D.C.: U.S. Department of Justice, Bureau of Justice Statistics.

Boland, Barbara, Paul Mahanna, and Ronald Stones. 1992. *The Prosecution of Felony Arrests, 1988.* Washington, D.C.: U.S. Department of Justice, Bureau of Justice Statistics.

Bottomley, Keith A. 1990. "Parole in Transition: A Comparative Study of Origins, Developments, and Prospects for the 1990s." In *Crime and Justice: A Review of Research*, vol. 12, edited by Michael Tonry and Norval Morris. Chicago: University of Chicago Press.

Bureau of Justice Statistics. *Census of Probation and Parole, 1991*. Unpublished. Washington, D.C.: U.S. Department of Justice, Bureau of Justice Statistics.

———. 1993a. *Felony Defendants in Large Urban Counties, 1990*. Washington, D.C.: U.S. Department of Justice, Bureau of Justice Statistics.

———. 1993b. *Jail Inmates, 1992*. Washington, D.C.: U.S. Department of Justice, Bureau of Justice Statistics.

———. 1993c. *Survey of State Prison Inmates, 1991*. Washington, D.C.: U.S. Department of Justice, Bureau of Justice Statistics.

———. 1994a. *Capital Punishment, 1993*. Washington, D.C.: U.S. Department of Justice, Bureau of Justice Statistics.

———. 1994b. *Felony Sentences in the United States, 1990*. Washington, D.C.: U.S. Department of Justice, Bureau of Justice Statistics.

———. 1994c. *National Corrections Reporting Program, 1992*. Washington, D.C.: U.S. Department of Justice, Bureau of Justice Statistics.

———. 1995. *Correctional Populations in the United States, 1993*. Washington, D.C.: U.S. Department of Justice, Bureau of Justice Statistics.

———. 1996a. *Correctional Populations in the United States, 1994*. Washington, D.C.: U.S. Department of Justice, Bureau of Justice Statistics.

———. 1996b. "Probation and Parole Population Reaches Almost 3.8 Million." U.S. Department of Justice, Bureau of Justice Statistics Press Release, June 30, 1996.

———. 1997. *Correctional Populations in the United States, 1995*. Washington, D.C.: U.S. Department of Justice, Bureau of Justice Statistics.

Burke, Peggy. 1995. *Abolishing Parole: Why the Emperor Has No Clothes*. Lexington, Ky.: American Probation and Parole Association.

Butts, Jeffrey A. 1996. *Offenders in Juvenile Court, 1993*. Washington, D.C.: U.S. Department of Justice, Juvenile Justice and Delinquency Prevention.

Camp, George M., and Camille Camp. 1995. *The Corrections Yearbook 1995: Probation and Parole*. South Salem, N.Y.: Criminal Justice Institute.

Clear, Todd, and Anthony A. Braga. 1995. "Community Corrections." In *Crime*, edited by James Q. Wilson and Joan Petersilia. San Francisco: Institute for Contemporary Studies.

Comptroller General of the United States. 1976. *State and County Probation: Systems in Crisis, Report to the Congress of the United States*. Washington, D.C.: U.S. Government Printing Office.

Fogel, David. 1975. *We Are the Living Proof . . . : The Justice Model for Corrections*. Cincinnati, Ohio: Anderson.

———. 1984. "The Emergence of Probation as a Profession in the Service of Public Safety: The Next Ten Years." In *Probation and Justice: Reconsideration of Mission*, edited by Patrick D. McAnany, Doug Thomson, and David Fogel. Cambridge, Mass.: Oelgeschlager, Gunn and Hain.

———. 1992. "Foreword." In *Dangerous Men: The Sociology of Parole*, edited by Richard McCleary. New York: Harrow and Heston.

Gendreau, Paul. 1996. "The Principles of Effective Intervention with Offenders." In *Choosing Correctional Options That Work: Defining the Demand*

and Evaluating the Supply, edited by Alan Harland. Thousand Oaks, Calif.: Sage.

Greenwood, Peter, C. Peter Rydell, Allan Abrahamse, and Jonathan Caulkins. 1994. *Three Strikes and You're Out: Estimating the Benefits and Costs of California's New Mandatory-Sentencing Law.* Santa Monica, Calif.: RAND.

Guynes, Robert. 1988. *Difficult Clients, Large Caseloads Plague Probation, Parole Agencies.* Washington, D.C.: National Institute of Justice.

Harris, Patricia, Todd Clear, and Christopher Baird. 1989. "Have Community Supervision Officers Changed Their Attitudes Toward Their Work?" *Justice Quarterly* 6:233–46.

Harris, Philip, and Stephen Smith. 1996. "Developing Community Corrections: An Implementation Perspective." In *Choosing Correctional Options That Work: Defining the Demand and Evaluating the Supply,* edited by Alan Harland. Thousand Oaks, Calif.: Sage.

Holt, Norm. 1998. "Parole in America." In *Community Corrections: Probation, Parole, and Intermediate Sanctions,* edited by Joan Petersilia. New York: Oxford University Press.

Institute of Medicine, Committee for the Substance Abuse Coverage Study. 1990. "A Study of the Evolution, Effectiveness, and Financing of Public and Private Drug Treatment Systems." In *Treating Drug Problems,* vol. 1, edited by D. R. Gerstein and H. J. Harwood. Washington, D.C.: National Academy Press.

Klein, Andrew R. 1997. *Alternative Sentencing, Intermediate Sanctions, and Probation.* Cincinnati, Ohio: Anderson.

Klein, Stephen, and Michael Caggiano. 1986. *The Prevalence, Predictability, and Policy Implications of Recidivism.* Santa Monica, Calif.: RAND.

Langan, Patrick. 1994. "Between Prison and Probation: Intermediate Sanctions." *Science* 264:791–93.

———. 1996. *Personal Communication.* Washington, D.C.: U.S. Department of Justice, Bureau of Justice Statistics.

Langan, Patrick, and Mark A. Cunniff. 1992. *Recidivism of Felons on Probation, 1986–89.* Washington, D.C.: U.S. Department of Justice, Bureau of Justice Statistics.

Latessa, Edward J., and Harry E. Allen. 1997. *Corrections in the Community.* Cincinnati, Ohio: Anderson.

Lindner, Charles, and Robert Bonn. 1996. "Probation Officer Victimization and Fieldwork Practices: Results of a National Study." *Federal Probation* 60(2):16–23.

Maguire, Kathleen, and Ann L. Pastore, eds. 1995. *Sourcebook of Criminal Justice Statistics, 1994.* Washington, D.C.: U.S. Department of Justice, Bureau of Justice Statistics.

Martinson, Robert. 1974. "What Works? Questions and Answers About Prison Reform." *Public Interest* 35:22–54.

McGarry, Peggy. 1988. *Handbook for the New Parole Board Member.* 2nd ed. Philadelphia: Center for Effective Public Policy.

Morgan, Kathryn. 1993. "Factors Influencing Probation Outcome:A Review of the Literature." *Federal Probation* 57(2):23–29.

National Advisory Commission on Criminal Justice Standards and Goals. 1973. *Corrections.* Washington, D.C.: U.S. Government Printing Office.

National Institute of Corrections. 1995. *Status Report on Parole, 1995: Results of an NIC Survey.* Longmont, Colo.: National Institute of Corrections.

Palmer, Ted. 1992. *The Re-Emergence of Correctional Intervention.* Newbury Park, Calif.: Sage.

———. 1996. "Programmatic and Nonprogrammatic Aspects of Successful Intervention." In *Choosing Correctional Options that Work,* edited by Allen Harland. Thousand Oaks, Calif.: Sage.

Parent, Dale, Dan Wentwork, Peggy Burke, and Becky Ney. 1994. *Responding to Probation and Parole Violations.* Washington, D.C.: National Institute of Justice.

Petersilia, Joan. 1995a. "A Crime Control Rationale for Reinvesting in Community Corrections." *Prison Journal* 75:479–96.

———. 1995b. "How California Could Divert Nonviolent Prisoners to Intermediate Sanctions." *Overcrowded Times* 6(3):4–8.

———. 1997. "Probation in the United States." In *Crime and Justice: A Review of Research,* vol. 22, edited by Michael Tonry. Chicago: University of Chicago Press.

Petersilia, Joan, and Elizabeth Piper Deschenes. 1994. "Perceptions of Punishment: Inmates and Staff Rank the Severity of Prison Versus Intermediate Sanctions." *Prison Journal* 74:306–28.

Petersilia, Joan, and Susan Turner. 1986. *Prison Versus Probation in California: Implications for Crime and Offender Recidivism.* Santa Monica, Calif.: RAND.

———. 1993. "Intensive Probation and Parole." In *Crime and Justice: A Review of Research,* vol. 17, edited by Michael Tonry. Chicago: University of Chicago Press.

President's Commission on Law Enforcement and Administration of Justice. 1967. *Task Force Report: Corrections.* Washington, D.C.: U.S. Government Printing Office.

Rothman, David J. 1980. *Conscience and Convenience: The Asylum and Its Alternatives in Progressive America.* Boston: Little, Brown.

Runda, John, Edward Rhine, and Robert Wetter. 1994. *The Practice of Parole Boards.* Lexington, Ky.: Association of Paroling Authorities.

Tonry, Michael, and Mary Lynch. 1996. "Intermediate Sanctions." In *Crime and Justice: A Review of Research,* vol. 20, edited by Michael Tonry. Chicago: University of Chicago Press.

von Hirsch, Andrew. 1976. *Doing Justice: The Choice of Punishments.* New York: Hill and Wang.

22

Prisons

ROY D. KING

The Growth of Imprisonment

The massive growth in the use of imprisonment during the last two decades has not been confined to the United States, although some of the most remarkable features of this phenomenon can be observed there, or happened there first. I try to convey the extent of the changes in the United States through periodic snapshots, for two reasons. First, as an intermittent visitor from the United Kingdom, this is very much how I have seen things develop. Second, as the steady drip of daily "news" in any country turns imperceptibly into its "history" without much sense of any particular moment as being "historic," there may be some advantage in looking at the state of things at some of those moments—even ones that have been arbitrarily determined by the exigent rules of study leave by wandering scholars.

I first visited the United States for the calendar year 1973 to undertake a study of parole systems. In some ways it was a signal year for prisons because it marked the beginning of the upturn in prison population after a decade in which the American use of imprisonment had substantially declined. But it did not then seem as though Americans were on the threshold of a sea change in penal politics. Indeed, it was the year in which Blumstein, reviewing the gently oscillating imprisonment rates of the United States, Canada, and Norway over substantial time spans, first published his homeostatic hypothesis expounding the inherent tendency toward stability of punishment (Blumstein and Cohen 1973). With the publication of *Kind and Usual Punishment,* Jessica Mitford (1973) cut through prison rhetorics, shattering any remaining illusions following a century of prison reform, in a way that seemed to do for *The American Prison Business* (as the book was subsequently renamed for the British market) what her *American Way of Death* had done for the funeral parlor. By then, as if anticipating her judgment, the experts on the National Advisory Commission on Criminal Justice Standards and Goals had produced its report on corrections, which concluded:

> The pervasive overemphasis on custody that remains in corrections creates more problems than it solves. Our institutions are so large that

their . . . very scale . . . dehumanizes, denies privacy, encourages violence, and defies decent control. A moratorium should be placed on the construction of any large correctional institution. We already have too many prisons. If there is any need at all for more institutions, it is for small, community-related facilities in or near the communities they serve. (National Advisory Committee 1973, p. 12)

The intention of the commission was to formulate, for the first time, national criminal justice standards and goals for crime reduction and prevention at the state and local levels. In many ways it was a prosaic report, but in its emphasis on the setting of achievable standards as the yardstick for measuring correctional performance, it held out the possibility at least that political hyperbole, both liberal and conservative, might one day be subordinated to the rational appreciation of the evidence in driving criminal justice policy. Theirs was far from an abolitionist agenda. The commission recognized that there remained confirmed and dangerous offenders who required protracted confinement during the course of which, at least, they would represent no danger to the community at large; the problem was that far too many offenders were classified as dangerous and incarcerated as such. Like the 1967 report of the President's Commission on Law Enforcement and Administration of Justice, it looked forward to an increased emphasis on corrections in the community.

Nor were these just the aspirations of professionals. In 1970, Norval Morris and Gordon Hawkins published *The Honest Politician's Guide to Crime Control*, in which they assumed dictatorial powers and offered their "cure for crime." Although none of their ukases directly addressed the use of imprisonment, they were carefully agnostic about the claims for its effects, and in their program to reduce the problem of crime it is clear that imprisonment would have played a smaller and more selective part. The following year, David Rothman concluded his influential study, *The Discovery of the Asylum,* with the belief that America had "been gradually escaping from institutional responses, and one can foresee the period when incarceration will be used still more rarely than it is today" (1971, p. 295).

Although, in retrospect, 1973 was indeed something of a watershed for American corrections, Rothman's perception of the rarity of imprisonment distanced him somewhat from the position of the National Advisory Commission. It also betrayed an insularity that occasionally afflicts American scholarship as well as American politics, for his assertion about the sparing use of imprisonment only makes sense if virtually all the rest of what was then called the free world is ignored. Thus, the total number of adults in custody in 1972 (337,692 in federal, state and local institutions) produced an incarceration rate for the United States of around 162 per 100,000 citizens, which was probably about as low as it had been at any time since the creation of the Federal Bureau of Prisons forty years earlier. It had fallen from 357,293 or 175.3 per 100,000 in the year before Rothman's book was published, a drop of over 5 percent.[1] But by world standards—outside the gulags of the Eastern bloc, China, and South Africa under apartheid—this was, arguably, still an extraordinarily high use of custody: twice as much as in England and Wales, where the comparable rate was 80; four times as much as Japan (47); and nine times as much as the Netherlands, where it was just 19 per 100,000.[2] Even then, in the land of the free, a remarkable number of people were behind bars. Although one can only hazard speculative guesses as to the upper and lower limits of imprisonment in Brezhnev's Soviet Union, the imprisonment rate in South Africa, at 446 per 100,000, was more than two and a half times that of the United States.

Nevertheless, it did seem as though the prison would have a smaller part to play in the future of American corrections. And a growing body of evidence, soon to be reviewed by Lipton, Martinson, and Wilks (1975), suggested that in corrections nothing worked much better than anything else (not, as was so often reported, that "nothing works"). If the expensive use of prisons neither deterred nor rehabilitated those who experienced their frighteningly impoverished regimes, the scene was apparently set for a major shift toward community corrections with the emphasis on more open programs of supervision rather than custodial sanctions. At least such measures would be cheaper.

But it did not happen. In 1973 the prison population in the United States had already begun to rise, and it quite quickly grew on a steeper curve than had been seen at any time since before the Second World War, producing widespread crowding and serious deterioration in prison conditions.

When I next visited the United States for the academic year 1983–1984, this time to carry out research in the "new-generation" prison at Oak Park Heights in Minnesota and to examine policies in relation to dangerous prisoners in federal penitentiaries, the climate in relation to penal politics had changed. Over a thousand prisoners were back on death row, and after a moratorium lasting ten years, executions were once again taking place, some thirty-seven states having death penalty legislation in place that had been revised since the *Furman* ruling. In October 1983, two guards were killed in the Control Unit at Marion, the federal penitentiary that, in effect, had come to replace Alcatraz, and the controversial long-standing lockdown there began. The guards' fellow officers, not surprisingly, were still shell-shocked when I interviewed them just weeks after the murders, and they wanted the death penalty introduced for killings on federal territory.

Many prison systems had become grossly crowded, and conditions in them had deteriorated sharply. This was not surprising. After all, the intervening decade had seen a virtual doubling of the adult population in prisons and jails, from 337,692 at year-end 1972 to a new high of 621,582 at year-end 1982. By 1983–1984, the prison population had grown to 736,000, with an incarceration rate of 318 per 100,000. This was now three and a half times the rate in England and Wales, where the incarceration rate had increased by a more modest 10 percent and then stabilized at about 83 per 100,000. In Japan, the use of imprisonment had continued to fall and had become only about an eighth of the U.S. rate. In the Netherlands, incarceration rates had increased almost as rapidly as in the United States but from a much lower base: at 31 per 100,000, it was still less than a tenth the American rate. Although South Africa incarcerated 480 per 100,000, this was now only 50 percent greater than the American rate. According to Zimring and Hawkins (1991), new prison capacity had not remotely kept pace with the increase in imprisonment. Overspill populations were dispersed from state prisons to local jails either as an emergency measure or, as in Alabama, Louisiana, Mississippi, and New Jersey, routinely. By 1983, the courts had declared the entire prison systems of Alabama, Florida, Mississippi, Oklahoma, Rhode Island, Tennessee, and Texas, as well as all male prisons in Michigan, to be in breach of Eighth Amendment protections against cruel and unusual punishment; in a further twenty-one states, some facilities were operating under court orders or consent decrees as a result of crowding or conditions of confinement; another seven states were involved in litigation about crowding or conditions of release.

But there were also signs that this was an America in which the courts were growing tired of class actions against prison administrations; in any case, it was by no means self-evident that success in the courts led to real change in the prisons. Wise prison administrations had quickly learned how to use the courts for their own benefit—for example, by using suits on prison conditions to gain support for additional funds—but most prison administrations learned to live with litigation, often employing specialists to deal with these matters not just at headquarters but also in the prisons themselves. The American Correctional Association had established a set of prison standards and a voluntary system of accreditation that was designed, though it was not always successful in this regard, to protect accredited institutions from pursuit through the courts, and the Federal Bureau of Prisons had signed up to the process, submitting its own institutions for accreditation. But there was a growing confidence that prison administrations could cope with the worst problems that the courts might throw at them.

In the mid-1970s an unholy alliance had been formed between liberals and conservatives, both of whom attacked the injustices of a criminal justice system that, in pursuit of the rehabilitative ideal, had relied on judicial discretion to tailor sentences to the individual culpability and circumstances of offenders, and on executive discretion to link release dates to prisoners' behavior and the programs they had signed up for in prison. Both camps sought mandatory sentencing, or the more extensive use of sentencing guidelines, but for different reasons. Andrew von Hirsch (1976), in the definitive modern statement of "just deserts theory," was concerned about justice in an unjust world. Together with other left-of-center liberals, he wanted accountability and an end to discrepancies that too often served to discriminate against blacks and other disadvantaged groups, whereas conservatives such as James Q. Wilson (1975) wanted an end to what they saw as namby-pamby sentencing and a criminal justice process so full of holes that it allowed too many perpetrators to escape the full rigor of the criminal law. By 1983, ten states had abolished their parole boards entirely, and several others had established administrative guidelines for parole release; forty-nine states had enacted laws requiring minimum sentences of incarceration for specified crimes, and many had begun to experiment with new forms of sentencing guidelines designed by the judiciary or by appointed sentencing commissions. And although some states were grappling with the implications such sentencing reforms would have for prison populations—for example, by introducing prison building programs, particularly in some southern states, or by drawing up guidelines that attempted to keep population and prison capacity in balance, as in Minnesota, or by triggering emergency powers when prisons reached their capacity, as in Michigan—this debate was beginning to be resolved in favor of conservatives who wanted little more than locking up offenders and throwing away the keys. In a few states, new laws were introduced providing for life sentences without parole.

Prison managers were more at ease with what they were doing than had been the case ten years earlier: then they had lost confidence in the whole rehabilitative task of prisons, whereas now they felt they had at least minimal public support for their ability to keep large numbers of criminals off the streets. Certainly there was an acceptance of the role of prisons: at best, to hold prisoners in humane conditions and where possible to provide facilities for offenders willing and able to make use of them; at worst, simply to protect the public through the incapacitation of offenders for the duration of their sentence.

My most recent visits to the United States took place in 1994 and 1995, when I undertook an inquiry into conditions on death row at the Oklahoma State Prison at McAlester on behalf of Amnesty International (1994), and then to attend the subsequent accreditation hearing. At that time, there were 2,890 prisoners on death row, nearly three times as many as a decade earlier. In the intervening years the prison population of the United States had grown in quite breathtaking ways—indeed, it had more than doubled again. Some of the biggest increases had been in the federal system. At the end of 1995 there were 100,250 federal prisoners, more than three times as many as there had been during my research in 1983–1984, and 1,026,882 state prisoners—a total of 1,127,132 (409 per 100,000). To these had to be added the 507,044 persons who were in local jails according to the midyear survey, producing a total adult population in custody of nearly 1.6 million and an adult incarceration rate of 600 per 100,000 population (Bureau of Justice Statistics 1996).

In 1984, the Sentencing Reform Act had introduced "truth in sentencing" to the federal justice system, creating a commission to establish sentencing guidelines that took effect in 1987. Under the guidelines, persons convicted of federal offenses became more likely than previously to be imprisoned and are required to serve 85 percent of the actual sentence. The Comprehensive Crime Control Act of 1984 and the Anti-Drug Abuse Act of 1986 greatly enhanced the proactive role of the federal government in Reagan's escalation of the "war on drugs," and mandatory prison sentences for many drug offenses proliferated. After 1988, when the tragic consequences of Willie Horton's tenth furlough release were used as a "wedge" issue in the Bush campaign against Dukakis, it became virtually impossible for politicians to take reasoned positions on criminal justice issues for fear of being branded "soft on crime." Willie Horton, in prison for murder, had completed nine furloughs without incident as part of his rehabilitation; he failed to return from the tenth, and nine months later he raped a woman and stabbed her companion. The end point of such political dishonesty was Clinton's 1994 embrace of proposals for federal mandatory life sentences for third-time violent offenders, first pioneered in Washington State in 1993 and quickly mimicked in thirteen other states. (Some three-strikes laws preserve an element of judicial discretion, and even in California—where they did not—the California Supreme Court has held that judicial discretion is not precluded.)

In terms of the international comparisons I made earlier, the United States had overtaken South Africa, by now emerging from apartheid, and left it far behind, incarcerating proportionately 40 percent more of its citizens in 1992 (519 compared with 368 per 100,000). Compared with other Western countries, of course, the differences had become astronomical: five and a half times as many as in England and Wales (93 per 100,000), where the prison population had continued to rise until 1987 but then stabilized before falling back somewhat; ten times as many as the Netherlands (49) in spite of a major and continuing increase in the use of custody there; and 14 times as many as Japan (36), whose incarceration rate had continued to fall until it crossed over with that of the Netherlands.

It is important to remember that total figures for imprisonment in the United States as a whole conceal huge variations between states. At the end of 1994, the District of Columbia, a wholly urban jurisdiction with a very high proportion of black residents, as well as large numbers of transients attracted to the nation's capital, incarcerated an astonishing 1,583 per 100,000. Elsewhere incarceration rates for adults sentenced to more than one year (i.e., normally excluding jail populations, although several states—Alaska, Connecticut, Delaware, Hawaii, Rhode Island, Vermont, and the District of Columbia—have integrated prison and jail systems) varied from a high of 636 per 100,000 in Texas to a low of 78 in North Dakota. In general, the southern states had by far the highest incarceration rates, averaging 451 per 100,000, followed by the West with an average of 333, the Midwest at 297, and the Northeast with 285. Apart from

North Dakota, only Maine (118), Minnesota (100), and West Virginia (at 106 widely divergent from other southern states) had incarceration rates remotely resembling those to be found in Western Europe, although a further ten states had rates of between 150 and 200. At the other extreme, another ten states in addition to Texas had incarceration rates in excess of 400 per 100,000. With the highest incarceration rate, and the highest rate of growth in prison population in 1993–1994 of 28.5 percent, Texas is probably set to replace California as the state with the highest prison population. We know a good deal about what has happened in California thanks to the case study by Zimring and Hawkins (1994). The prison population in that state quadrupled during the eleven-year period from 1980 to 1990. To get some sense of what this level of increase means consider the following: the Californian prison population (excluding jails) in 1980 was less than half the size of the West German prison and jail population, then the largest in Europe; by 1990, it was larger than the combined prison and jail populations of West Germany and the United Kingdom (England and Wales, Scotland, and Northern Ireland), which by then had taken over as the largest European system. Perhaps more awesomely, half of all the adults in custody in England and Wales in 1990 could have been fitted neatly, though presumably with considerable discomfort, into the dozen or so jail facilities of a single local jurisdiction—Los Angeles County.

Zimring and Hawkins claimed that never had "a prison system grown by so much in so short a time" (1994, p. 83) as it had in California during the 1980s. However, there have certainly been other extraordinary periods of growth elsewhere, some admittedly more recent, but which nevertheless need to be taken into account because they demonstrate clearly that prison growth is not just an American phenomenon. Over approximately the same period reviewed by Zimring and Hawkins, the prison population in Spain tripled from just over 10,000 in 1979 to more than 31,000 in 1989. In Italy, traditionally one of the more sparing users of imprisonment in Europe, Pavarini (1994) reported that the prison population reached 50,000 at the beginning of 1993 and that it had doubled during the preceding two years. In the comparisons already cited, it will have been noted that the prison population and incarceration rate in the Netherlands has risen steeply—from 19 per 100,000 in 1972, it declined further to 17 in 1975, then rose to 24 in 1978, 31 in 1984, and 49 in 1992. In September 1994, the prison population in the Netherlands rose to 8,535, producing an incarceration rate of 55 per 100,000, and the Dutch have planned for a prison capacity of 13,000 by the end of 1996, which will bring their incarceration rate to 78 per 100,000. This pattern was effectively the mirror image of what had happened over the previous quarter of a century, when the Dutch prison population fell from 6,730 in 1950 to 2,356 in 1975. Nils Christie sadly observed that "the Netherlands had tripled its prison population since 1975, and that Europe had thereby lost its most spectacular case of tolerance."

It is true that in all these cases the scale of *imprisonment*, proportionate to the total population, pales almost to insignificance compared with the American experiment with mass incarceration: nevertheless, when viewed historically and strictly from within national boundaries, the scale and nature of the *change* has, in some cases, been somewhat comparable.

When one turns to the countries of the former Soviet Union, Eastern Europe, and the Baltic States, however, it is possible to make comparisons with the United States in terms of both the scale of imprisonment and, potentially, the scale of the change. As shown in Table 22.1, the pattern in many of these countries has been remarkably similar.

Since 1980, these countries had seen escalating prison populations, reaching recent peaks between 1985 and 1987 shortly before the break-up of the Soviet empire, although far higher populations have been estimated for earlier periods); in the euphoric days after gaining independence, or the assumption of democratic status, the prison populations fell rapidly, reaching troughs between 1989 and 1991. Since then, however, these countries have experienced dramatically rising populations. Thus in Romania and Belarus a two-and-a-half-fold increase in the prison population has been experienced in five years and three years, respectively. In Russia the rate of increase has been proportionately less spectacular, but it has taken off from such a large base that the average annual increase in population has been equivalent to the addition of virtually the entire prison population of England and Wales every year since 1990 (although most of that increase has occurred since 1993). Indeed, all the evidence points to Russia having overtaken the United States in terms of its incarceration rates in 1992–1993, with 558 as against 519 per 100,000 of its citizens in custody (Mauer 1995). It is still necessary to be cautious about such comparisons, however; it is possible that the Russian statistics included juveniles in custody, whereas the American statistics did not (see Christie 1994, p. 191).

Table 22.1. Numbers Held in Penal Institutions and Rates per 100,000 General Population for Selected Countries

	1985–1987 Peak		1989–1991 Trough		Mid–late 1994	
	Total	Rate	Total	Rate	Total	Rate
USSR*	1,525,600					
Russia			698,000	470	885,000	590
Ukraine			120,000	230	180,000	345
Belarus**	31,204	310	14,235	140	35,720	345
Lithuania	14,888	415	8,586	230	12,782	340
Poland	110,182	295	40,321	105	62,719	165
Romania	60,269	265	16,429	70	43,990	195

*Data from USSR taken from Detkov (1992). All other statistics in this table taken from Walmsley (1996), Appendix A.

**Data for Belarus relates to sentenced adults only.

Accounting for Prison Growth

How can these astonishing differences between countries and the trans-formations in their prison populations over time be explained? The first thing to say is that, in spite of the dramatic changes that occur *within* national or state boundaries, the differences *between* jurisdictions tend to be so great and so persistent that they seem to be related to deep-seated social-structural or cultural features of those societies. Western European states, by and large, have enduringly lower rates of imprisonment than those in Eastern Europe or the United States. Within the United States, the South and West have persistently higher rates than the Midwest or the Northeast. Changes in the relative positions of different societies do, of course, occur—the Netherlands and Japan, for example—but are comparatively rare and themselves require special explanation.

The idea that crime and punishment are linked to the social structure of societies derives from the criticisms of what Beccaria's (1764) version of classical social contract theory did not account for. Durkheim ([1893] 1964; [1895] 1938), for example, raised issues about both crime and punishment as indicators of social health, which threw light on deviations from the spontaneous and meritocratic division of labor in society that, for him, was a desirable feature, if not a necessary condition of order in society. The similarities between Durkheim's analysis of the forced, rather than spontaneous, division of labor in society and Marx's account of the exploitative relationship between economic classes has, perhaps, been insufficiently recognized, although both conceived of at least some criminal activity as social protest in response to social conditions (see Taylor, Walton, and Young 1973). But whereas for Durkheim punishment was the expression of outrage to the collective social conscience, for Marx it was just an instrument of class domination. Zimring and Hawkins (1991) criticized Blumstein's "homeostatic hypothesis" not so much because of the subsequent, manifestly nonhomeostatic, developments in American imprisonment but because of its mistaken claim to Durk-heimian ancestry and because it failed to note, and therefore did not attempt to explain, the extraordinary differences between the scale of imprisonment in the United States, Norway, and Canada. However, Zimring and Hawkins (1991) argue that although Rusche and Kirkheimer (1939), who have been claimed by others to be the true inheritors of the Marx-Engels legacy, failed to explain the growth of imprisonment in terms of the demands of the labor market, they were right to insist that penal systems had to be understood as an integral part of the whole social system.

Nils Christie personal communication argues that the numbers of its citizens that a society is prepared to put behind bars reveals something very important about the nature of that society, even when the statistics are taken crudely at their face value. A conventional sociological view, taking elements from both Durkheim and Marx, might hold that a society with very low rates of imprisonment per 100,000 population is a society at ease with itself, and that this, in turn, might suggest that the social, economic, and cultural divisions in that society are either quite small or else are well justified and accepted. On the face of it, the reverse proposition seems equally tenable: that a society with high rates of imprisonment is likely to be a society divided against itself, and that this reflects either the extent of social divisions or the lack of legitimacy accorded to such divisions (although the United States and Russia appear to feel quite comfortable with very high rates of imprisonment indeed). But Christie is suggesting something deeper than these formulations convey, something to do with the characteristic ways in which a country, or rather its people, approaches social problems. At bottom, Christie believes that high incarceration rates reflect a society's choice to define the problems of inner cities, such as "wife-abuse, selling sex, selling crack, killings, crime" as "targets for war rather than targets for drastic social reform" (Christie 1994, p. 198). This is a view he shares with Louk Hulsman (1974), who has also recently argued (at the Twenty-fifth Annual Conference of the European Group for the Study of Deviance and Social Control held at the University of Wales, Bangor, September 1996) that many "troubles" that are currently defined as crimes can be given alternative meanings that are better addressed outside the criminal justice system. I shall return to this later.

However, Pease (1994) has warned that statistics on comparative rates of incarceration per 100,000 population in the form of international league tables should not be used as a measure of the relative punitiveness of those societies, at least not without a great deal of other information. Such statistics are often used superficially, indeed tendentiously, whereby the descriptive "more than elsewhere" tends to slide into the moral "too many." Pease notes that "more than elsewhere" could still be too few depending on the value position one takes, just as "less than elsewhere" could still be too many. He points out that incarceration rates conflate differences in crime with differences in the responses to crime, and really show the effects of some (unknown) combination of national differences in crime rates, clear-up rates, the identification and processing of offenders, and the choice of final sanctions. With the size of the prison population, or numbers admitted to custody as the numerator, Pease argues, it would make sense to use the general population as the denominator for incarceration rates only if people were imprisoned randomly. No alternative numerators and denominators are without their difficulties, and Pease suggests that it would be prudent to use a variety of measures to make sense of international differences in prison use. Prison admissions compared with convictions would, he argues, give the most persuasive measure of sentencing punitiveness, whereas prison population compared with convictions would provide a better measure of punitiveness, which would take account of both sentencing and discretionary release.

Pease (1994) questions the conventional wisdom that, with comparative incarceration rates as the measure, places the United Kingdom among the most punitive countries in Europe. He draws attention to the effect of "bark and bite" sentencing and, if pressed to a conclusion, on the basis of imperfect data, suggests that sentences pronounced in British courts may be marginally more severe than elsewhere in Europe; after taking account of discretionary release, however, the severity of sentencing in Britain is probably somewhat lower than international practice generally for all offenses except homicide. But above all what Pease's work has shown is the extreme complexity of making meaningful international comparisons on imprisonment. A full analysis would need to take account of definitions of crime, crime rates for specific offenses, arrests, pretrial diversion and alternative institutional arrangements for offenders, prosecutions, remands on bail or in custody, convictions, sentencing, and discretionary release. A great deal remains to be done, both in terms of the clarification and analysis of available international statistics and in the development of meaningful cross-national research. Meanwhile, we are dependent on imperfect proxies.

Clearly, one of the most important variables at stake in any accounting for the growth of imprisonment is the level of crime, and, not surprisingly, several writers have addressed this topic. Rutherford (1985) has argued that the use of imprisonment was not simply an automatic response to crime but a policy choice to respond to whatever level of crime in a particular way. Thus, in the period 1908 to 1938, the prison population in England and Wales was halved to one of the lowest rates in Europe, even though over the same period the level of recorded crime nearly tripled. Rutherford attributes the change to policy choices made initially by Winston Churchill on the basis of a deep skepticism about the value of imprisonment, especially in regard to a stage army of petty offenders who constantly moved through the revolving door of imprisonment on very short sentences. On the basis of cross-national data, moreover, Rutherford shows dramatically different responses to crime during the period 1950 to 1978. In England and Wales, for example, the use of imprisonment nearly doubled, but this was a far slower rate of increase than the four-and-a-half-fold increase in recorded crime rates. In Japan, there was a reduction of about 27 percent in the crime rate, but the imprisonment rate fell by 65 percent, more than twice as much. Both these examples show crime rates and imprisonment rates moving in the same direction, albeit at different speeds. Much more remarkable was the case of the Netherlands, where during this period the crime rate quadrupled while the imprisonment rate fell by nearly two-thirds.

The generally accepted explanation for the Netherlands being able to reduce its incarceration rates in spite of rapidly rising crime has been offered by Downes (1988). It involves a generalized "culture of tolerance" operating within the context of an unusually generous welfare state and a "politics of accommodation" that enabled political and administrative elites to carry through their policies without incurring fierce opposition or public hostility. Those policies were based, initially, on an early acceptance of the rehabilitative ideal, and although that ideal did not survive, the critique of the deleterious effects of prison which it ushered in did. Thus the psychiatric and existential ideas of scholars, particularly from the University of Utrecht, continued to exercise an influence on policy, partly through the training of prosecutors and judges. Since then, of course, the incarceration rate in the Netherlands has risen dramatically—which shows, argues Christie (1994), the vulnerability of tolerance from above. It was not a particularly democratic system, but it worked as long as the elites were prepared to resist the pressures of modernity. In the Netherlands today, argues Christie, the security of the welfare state has been undermined by the withdrawal of benefits; influential scholars have retired, and their chairs of criminology have been left unfilled; senior officials of the old school have been replaced by managerialists; and, as Dutch criminal justice policy has come under sustained international pressure to toughen its stance on drugs, the old certainties of the "joint moral community" have crumbled. (Although Christie talks of the virtues of the Netherlands in the past tense, all things are relative. To this outsider, at least, the Netherlands remains a more tolerant and humane society than most.) The public, the politicians, and the media have become increasingly vocal, driving the criminal justice system toward more custodial solutions. Downes (1997) provides the best analysis of recent changes in the Dutch prison population. He shows that increases in imprisonment have partly reflected real increases in crime and in the fear of crime, particularly in the context of a European community without borders and with perceived problems about integrating minorities. Rutherford (1996) has recently discussed the new managerialism in the Netherlands.

Relating imprisonment to crime rates in cross-national studies means that the problems Pease identified for incarceration rates are further compounded by the difficulties of getting reliable crime statistics. In 1992–1993, while conducting research in Russian prisons, I made some "back of the envelope" calculations to demonstrate the extraordinary differences in the rate of imprisonment between England and Wales and the new Russian Federation. Thus in 1992, in very rounded figures, there were 5.5 million recorded crimes, or 10,900 for every 100,000 citizens, in England and Wales but only 2.7 million recorded crimes, or 1,800 for every 100,000 Russian citizens—six times fewer. Yet Russia then had a total prison population of 760,000, or 506 per 100,000, compared with 46,500, or 93 per 100,000, in England and Wales—proportionately five times as many. On the face of it, Russia's imprisonment rate, relative to its officially recorded crime rate, was thirty times as great as that for England and Wales (King 1994). Such a difference is so huge that substantial parts of it are likely to remain even after more sophisticated analysis (which cannot yet be done for lack of Russian data), but it is clear that it takes no account of differences in reporting and recording of crime and gives no weight to possible differences in the seriousness of crimes.

An alternative way of comparing crime rates in different countries is through the use of direct victimization surveys. Three International Crime Surveys, coordinated by the Dutch Ministry of Justice, have been carried out in 1989, 1992, and 1996. All told, twenty countries have taken part in the first two surveys, involving a total of some 55,000 interviews, usually by telephone, inquiring about experience of crime during the preceding year. (Eight countries participated in both the 1989 and 1992 surveys, plus a further seven in the first and five in the second.) The methodological difficulties of conducting such research, and interpreting its results, are considerable: sample sizes in each country were small and response rates comparatively low; calculations of risk relate only to certain kinds of crime and take no account of the frequency or seriousness of victimizations; furthermore, the technique depends on the accurate recall of respondents and leaves the definition of criminal events largely in their hands. Nevertheless, for all their limitations, such studies provide a valuable supplement to official crime data and a useful addition to our understanding of international comparisons on crime and imprisonment.

Results from the International Crime Survey (van Dijk and Mayhew 1992) confirm that Japan, with low official crime rates and low imprisonment rates, also has the lowest victimization rate. Poland, whose prison population has been increasing rapidly since 1991, has a victimization rate much higher than is indicated by its police statistics, and somewhat higher than those recorded for England and Wales, Italy, and Spain. Most intriguingly, the conventional wisdom that crime rates in the United States greatly exceed those of other countries is undermined. Although the United States, along with New Zealand, the Netherlands, Canada, and Australia, is in the highest category for overall victimization rates (between 27.5 and 30 percent reporting incidents in the last year), in none of the categories for particular crimes was the United States the most victimized: five countries reported more thefts of cars, three countries more thefts from cars and more burglaries, six countries more robberies, and two countries more assaults and sexual incidents. It is true that a significant part of the crime problem in the Netherlands is attributable to bicycle theft, but the fact that it shares the same overall victimization rate as the United States suggests that we should look elsewhere than to crime rates for an explanation of the phenomenal growth in imprisonment in the United States compared with other countries, and more toward the relative levels of fear of crime.

It is tempting to argue that when seriousness of crime is taken into account, particularly the amount of violent crime, the United States is justified in its high imprisonment rates compared with other countries. Even if that were true—and it is worth noting that Russian officials proffer the same reason for their own high incarceration rates—it is not a satisfactory explanation of the recent growth in American imprisonment. The report of the National Criminal Justice Commission (Donziger 1996) has pointed out that the murder rate in the United States, as measured officially and reasonably reliably by *Uniform Crime Reports* (*UCR*), dropped by 9 percent from 1980 to 1992, and in 1994 was virtually the same as in 1970, and lower than it had been in 1930s when the incarceration rate was one-fifth of current levels. For other crimes, *UCR* rates are less reliable because they reflect changes in reporting to the police and recording by the police as well as changes in criminal activity. Here the picture shown by the National Crime Victimization Survey, which covers rape, robbery, and assault, as well as personal theft, household theft, burglary, and motor vehicle theft, is one of relative stability since 1973, in contrast with the more volatile but generally more steeply rising tide of crime represented in official statistics.

Zimring and Hawkins (1991, 1994) have reviewed the relationship between index crime rates and imprisonment for the United States as a whole and for California in particular. They show that, since 1950, there are major discontinuities between the two rates for the United States, with the steepest increase in index crime occurring during the 1960s when rates of imprisonment were decreasing, and a sharp downturn in index crime rates during the 1980s when rates of imprisonment were increasing. If anything, over the period there was a small negative correlation between the two rates: the same pattern was revealed when trends in the most serious violent crimes were plotted against imprisonment. Of course, the technical methodological problems associated with a clear demonstration of cause and effect here are immense, not least because of the need to allow for time lags. In a sense the jury is still out on that: as Zimring and Hawkins (1994) note, to have performed such a radical experiment as California has without assessing the impact of so much extra imprisonment on crime rates would be unforgivable. Meanwhile, they point out that the thesis that increased imprisonment caused a decline in crime suffered a setback in the late 1980s when crime rates edged back up toward 1980 levels while imprisonment continued to increase at unprecedented rates.

Rutherford (1985) sought to explain the decline in use of imprisonment at various times in the United Kingdom, and in the Netherlands, in terms of deliberately adopted reductionist policies. He has also argued that, at other times, the United Kingdom and the United States have pursued deliberately expansionist policies.[3] In 1976, when the Crime Control Act was carried into law, it contained a provision that the National Institute of Law Enforcement and Criminal Justice should survey existing and future needs in correctional facilities and determine the effect of anticipated sentencing reforms such as mandatory minimum sentences. A year later the National Institute of Law Enforcement and Criminal Justice (1977) presented a preliminary report to Congress. The report concluded that there was little evidence of any explicit policy regarding an "appropriate" level for the prison population, and that the increase in prison populations to date owed more to a surge in intake, driven by local factors, rather than the length of time served. Using dynamic modeling techniques, however, it also concluded that prison populations would be highly sensitive to policy decisions. In a subsequent report the National Institute of Justice (1981) found that prison populations increased in the years following prison construction in ways that closely approximated the change in capacity, giving credence to the so-called build and fill hypothesis.

In the preceding years, prison capacity and prison conditions had been at the heart of the debate on corrections: James Q. Wilson (1977) memorably argued that existing facilities were too lacking in amenity to enable many judges in good conscience to send offenders there, while Milton Rector (1977), the director of the National Council on Crime and Delinquency, feared that judges would send throngs of inmates to sparkling new prisons. In an echo of that debate in the English context, King and Morgan (1981) argued for the more even sharing of misery between the grossly crowded local prisons (analogous to American jails) and the uncrowded training prisons in an (unsuccessful) attempt to offset a major new prison building program. The moral issues in such debates are by no means as clear-cut as the protagonists often proclaim.

But the direct links between policies and sentencing reforms are hard to pin down. Zimring and Hawkins (1991) have provided a comprehensive review of possible explanations for the increase in American imprisonment—from the changing demography in terms of the sex, age, and race of the criminogenic population, through build and fill, cost-benefit analysis of various crime control options, including incapacitative sentencing, to the displacement of indeterminate sentencing by mandatory sentencing and the emergence of sentencing commissions—and find them wanting in various ways. They describe a broad pattern of prison growth across the United States, but without a single, clear-cut policy precursor. Zimring and Hawkins concede that the increased use of imprisonment in the longer term may have derived indirectly from the switch to determinate sentencing through greater exposure of the use of imprisonment to the political process, especially where it involved reallocating sentencing powers from the courts to legislatures rather than to sentencing commissions. But they rightly conclude that aggregate analysis is unlikely to get us much further: the issues are so complex that detailed case studies at local levels are likely to be more fruitful.

On sentencing commissions, Tonry (1987a) has shown that differences in the local culture and environments within which they work make it impossible to generalize: in some, such as Minnesota, prison capacity was taken to be a constraint on sentencing; in others it was not. Tonry has also been scathing in his criticisms of the U.S. Sentencing Commission, particularly about the way in which possibilities of departures from the guidelines have been closed off. And on mandatory sentences Tonry

(1987b) suggests that the impact is less great than is commonly believed, because in many cases they are redundant and in others they can be circumvented. In their later case study of California, Zimring and Hawkins (1994) argue that the dramatic increase in the prison population there was a revolution of practice rather than of theory or legislative policy. In particular, the celebrated shift to "just deserts" sentencing in 1977 was not the mechanical cause of the huge increase that occurred four years later: indeed, initially it produced a decline in prison numbers as many sentences were leveled downward.

The National Criminal Justice Commission (Donziger 1996) attributes the huge growth in imprisonment in the United States to the heightened political sensitivity of criminal justice issues in which politicians have either capitalized on, or been constrained by, a national fear of and obsession with crime. The result has been a national hoax in which politicians have talked tough, and public debate has been reduced to sound-bite slogans in which the real risks to the public, and the actual operation of the criminal justice system, are never exposed to proper analysis. Meanwhile, the true causes of crime, and the underlying social problems associated with it, are ignored, and resources are diverted from education and welfare programs into an ineffective, and even counterproductive, war on crime. In such a climate "truth in sentencing" has taken root in the public mind as ensuring that criminals get what observers think the courts intended, even though all those directly concerned with the criminal justice system always understood full well that early release was important both to maintaining order in prison and to regulating supervision after release and was fully taken into account by judges when they fixed sentences. Truth-in-sentencing laws will increase time served without commensurate improvements in public safety, argues the commission, while mandatory minimum sentences have served both to increase the likelihood and the length of prison sentences, particularly in relation to drug offenders in the so-called war on drugs. Tonry (1995), too, has written of the political mendacity which has implied, on the one hand, that welfare benefit levels will allow a modest but decent living standard and, on the other, that harsh penalties and escalating prison populations will make Americans safe. Neither premise is well founded, and together they have conspired to produce a state of "malign neglect" that needs to be reversed.

The National Criminal Justice Commission highlights the role of special interest groups in the expansion of imprisonment in the United States, citing the campaigns of the National Rifle Association in support of increased congressional expenditure on prison construction and the early initiatives on "three strikes." Christie (1994) has described the push of private enterprise, both in terms of building and managing prisons and in the supply of technological hardware, as one of the driving forces in the huge expansion of the American crime control industry. While the capacity of private prisons in the United States now exceeds the size of several Western European prison systems, they accommodate only a small fraction—less than 2 percent—of the total American prison population. It seems more likely that they are a response to, rather than a cause of, the increased demand for imprisonment, although they now create a pressure for at least the maintenance of the system as it is (though few state employees have sought to argue themselves out of their jobs either). Whether public or private, what cannot now be overlooked is that prisons provide an important source of employment in many communities that have suffered industrial decline.

Where, then, does this leave us in accounting for these transformations in prison populations? Zimring and Hawkins (1991) dismiss the notion that the broad pattern they describe somehow reflects a public mood as unhelpful: but it is hard to resist the idea that political rhetorics have indeed manipulated public fears and created a climate in which the public feels comfortable with the increased use of imprisonment so far and has come to expect further increases as more or less inevitable. Zimring and Hawkins give too little credence to the impact that low-frequency but horrific crimes, and high-profile escapes, have on public opinion and politicians—even the most liberal of whom have to temper their views if they wish to be elected. Although legislative and other changes may be difficult to relate to increases in imprisonment, Zimring and Hawkins (1991, 1994) themselves have shown how federal and state planners project increases in imprisonment, predicated on expected demographic and policy changes, and then act on them, producing a self-fulfilling prophecy. Moreover, in myriad ways, it seems as though the climate that is thus created influences thousands of individual sentencing decisions that are thought to be congruent with what the public demands or expects.

An example of the process at work is to be found in the recent "talking up" of the prison population in England and Wales. For a remarkable period, lasting nearly a decade, a succession of Conservative home secretaries, on the advice of senior officials, had sought to bring prison population and prison capacity into balance through policies that emphasized crime prevention and what came to be called "principled sentencing," culminating in the Criminal Justice Act of 1991. The report into the riot at Strangeways Prison by Lord Justice Woolf (Home Office 1991) nurtured a consensus about prison reform, which was embraced by the then home secretary, Kenneth Baker. Though he fell short of giving an undertaking to prevent prisons exceeding their stated capacities, by December 1992 the prison population had dropped to 40,722. Suddenly, perhaps fearing that the Labour Party might steal its clothes as the party of law and order, the Conservatives decided to renew the war on crime with policies that were to become more extreme. The provisions of the 1991 act were reversed by the new home secretary, Kenneth Clarke, immediately after the election; when Clarke moved to the Treasury, his successor, Michael Howard, announced to the party conference in October 1993 that "prison works" and that the success of the system would no longer be judged by how well it keeps numbers down. After that, in a climate influenced by the killing of the infant James Bulger by two schoolchildren, and the mass slaughter of children and their teacher at Dunblane, Howard began to embrace more and more American policies—mandatory sentencing, honesty in sentencing (as it is known in Britain), the abolition of parole, and three, or rather two, strikes and you're out. Some of these proposals were vigorously attacked at the time, especially by former Home Secretaries no longer burdened by office and by senior judges. Following the general election of May 1997, the law and order rhetoric has cooled, but it remains to be seen whether the new Labour government will try to reverse current trends. Meanwhile, the prison population rose continuously until it stood at 62,040 in December 1997, an increase of 52.3% in six years. It is currently projected to rise to 92,000 by the year 2005.

That such rhetorics are transferable across state boundaries is evidenced not just by the example of what is now happening in England and Wales, or what has recently happened in the Netherlands, but also by the extraordinary similarity in the discourse on crime and punishment that has been emerging in the former Soviet Union and the countries of Eastern Europe. Turning back the clock in the United States, or arresting these developments in England and Wales or the Netherlands may not be easy, but ways back toward principled sentencing and the rational assessment of the consequences of criminal justice policy will have to be found. In the process, alternative and more compassionate ways of dealing with troubles along the lines suggested by Christie, Hulsman, Tonry, and others must have a larger place. Meanwhile, it would also be instructive to look in detail at the success in resisting or reversing the trends that has been achieved in Germany and in Finland. The situation in the newly emergent and fledgling democracies in Russia and Eastern Europe is altogether more daunting. What may well now be in the cards, once crime rates really do take off in tandem with economic and commercial exploitation, is an explosion of imprisonment that could return to the levels that were once seen under Brezhnev. The need for systematic research that demonstrates the social and economic consequences of increased imprisonment, including its impact on the crime problem, has never been greater.

Who Goes to Prison, Why, and for How Long: Prison Admissions and Populations

It would not be surprising if the public thought that the greater use of imprisonment resulted in more violent and dangerous offenders being put, and kept, behind bars. After all, this is what the rhetoric has been about. But a moment's reflection would surely give one pause. Doesn't this require one to assume that the criminal justice system has perversely pursued a path in which it conspired to incarcerate the small fry and leave the big fish swimming free? And, if so, doesn't it further require the belief that somehow or other the new legislation has reversed that process and provided a mechanism to catch, lock up, and throw away the key on the real sharks? Well, yes: that is what, in effect, some politicians ask us to believe. A somewhat more criminologically sophisticated observer might suppose otherwise, however. Wouldn't a more reasonable assumption be that our imperfect criminal justice systems do an imperfect job but catch within their nets a reasonable sample of the fish available to be caught? More intensive fishing and narrowing the mesh will catch some more big fish but many more minnows at the margins of criminality. But in that case, sentencing more of *them* to imprisonment is likely to produce a dilution rather than a concentration of the dangerousness of the prison population. What has actually happened to the composition of our prison populations?

It is important to note here the difference between prison population and prison admissions—or what, in an unfortunate echo of economic warehousing, is sometimes referred to as *stock and flow*. The size and nature of the prison population at any one time are products of who is sentenced to imprisonment in the first place and the length of time they actually serve. Somewhat surprisingly, so far, there does not appear to have been any major increase in the amount of time served in U.S. prisons—despite truth-in-sentencing provisions—and at the point of admission to custody, maximum sentence lengths have actually declined. Thus, although the mean time served by prisoners whose first release was in 1992 was twenty-two months compared with twenty months for those released in 1985, an increase of 10 percent, the median showed a reduction from fourteen months to thirteen months. For new court commitments the mean maximum sentence length fell from seventy-eight months in 1985 to sixty-seven months in 1992. It seems, therefore, that the growth in American prison populations has been driven more by the numbers of new admissions, partly as a result of mandatory sentencing, than by length of sentence (although this is likely to change with the widespread passage of "three-strikes" laws in the mid-1990s).

This is different from the position in Europe, by and large, where increasing populations, at least until recently, have been driven upward by increases in time served rather than by new receptions: thus in England and Wales the proportion of new receptions sentenced to four years or over more than doubled, from 3 percent in 1981 to 8 percent in 1991, and the proportions serving such sentences in the prison population increased from 21 to 42 percent over the same period. There is reason to suppose that this will change in the future in both cases. In the United States it is still not possible to determine the outcome of provisions affecting time served because many prisoners subject to truth-in-sentencing provisions have yet to be released; and although the proportion of new court commitments receiving sentences of ten years or more has fallen from 19.7 percent in 1985 to 17.7 percent in 1992, since the absolute number of such commitments has gone up dramatically, there is a growing number of long-term prisoners in the population. To some extent this is showing up in release data: the proportion of prisoners, released in 1985, who had served longer than ten years was 0.6 percent, but by 1992 it had risen to 1.4 percent, and that trend will presumably continue. Headline cases have suggested that some prisoners as yet barely out of school may be candidates for pensions or geriatric medicine by the time they are released, though their numbers are probably quite small. In Europe, and the United Kingdom in particular, the talking up of imprisonment has already increased admissions, as well as time served.

Using the estimated numbers of prisoners in custody in state correctional institutions over the period 1980 to 1993 (Bureau of Justice Statistics 1995), it is at first apparent that the biggest single increase in prison population is indeed accounted for by violent offenders—an additional 221,200 of them, or 42 percent of the total prison growth. But this tells only part of the story. The remaining three, nonviolent, major offense categories accounted for 57 percent of the prison growth between them—drug offenders for 31 percent, property offenders for 19 percent, and public order offenders for 7 percent. Looked at another way, the proportion of those then in custody who are serving sentences for violence has declined from 58.5 percent in 1980 to 47.6 percent in 1993. And although the total numbers serving sentences for violent offenses increased every year, and by 127.6 percent over the period in question, this was a substantially smaller increase than for the prison population as a whole—180 percent. Moreover, the increases in violent offenders were most marked for the lesser offenses of violence: for example, numbers of prisoners serving sentences for "other sexual assaults" (not, of course, to be discounted but still less serious) increased by 568.5 percent compared with those for the much more serious category of "rape," which increased by 146.9 percent; and numbers serving sentences for (again, not of no account, but less serious) assaults increased by 214.2 percent compared with 58.8 percent for the more serious robbery. It is possible that a higher proportion of those convicted of less serious offenses may have originally been charged with more serious crimes than was formerly the case, since plea bargains may be more readily embraced in the context of mandatory sentencing. However, as they stand, these data do not support a public image of ever greater violence. Of course, by far the most noticeable thing about the changing prison population in the United States has been the phenomenal growth in the numbers in custody for drug offenses: up from 19,000 in 1980 to 186,000 in 1993—an increase of 878.9 percent that, for the rest of the world if not for middle Americans, beggars belief—so that one in every four or five prisoners was doing time for drugs compared with one in every fifteen or sixteen in 1980. The explosion in drug offenders is so dramatic that it inevitably distorts the rest of the picture, but even if drug offenders are excluded from the calculations the proportion of the remainder in for violence has still fallen slightly—from 63 percent to 61 percent—with property offenders also falling from 32 percent to 30 percent, while public order offenders have increased from 4 percent to 8 percent.

In federal facilities these tendencies were even more marked. Of the 81,206 offenders in federal prisons in 1993, only 13 percent were sentenced for violent offenses, and 10.4 percent were serving sentences for property crimes. A massive 59.8 percent were sentenced for drug offenses, and a further 15.7 percent for public order offenses. In 1980, 33.8 percent of the 19,471 federal prisoners had been sentenced for violence, with 23.9 percent for property crimes, 25.2 percent for drug offenses, and 10.5 percent for public order offenses. Once again, after removing drug offenders from the equation, there has still been a fall in the proportion of federal prisoners serving time for violent offenses from 45 percent to 33 percent.

These shifts in the proportions of the prison population sentenced for different kinds of offenses are staggering in their scale, and together with the length of sentence and time served data, they give much more support to the idea that the dangerous character of the prison population has been diluted rather than concentrated. This is so in spite of the fact that the use of prison population data provides the most stringent test of the hypothesis. The citizen could properly, and reasonably, expect that the worst kind of violent offenders get the longest sentences: as a result, they inevitably stack up in prison systems, appearing in the statistics year after year, and this has the effect of accentuating the apparent violence that the criminal justice system is dealing with. If one looks at *admissions* to the prison system in the course of a year rather than the number of people in prison at any one time, a rather different picture emerges of the levels of violence being processed. In 1985, violent offenders accounted for 35.1 percent of state prison admissions, but by 1992 this had fallen to 28.6 percent; for federal prisons, violent offenders accounted for 12.9 percent of admissions in 1980 but only 7.8 percent in 1992.

Apologists who have sought to justify the enormous growth in prison populations have sometimes cultivated a view of the dangerous character of the prison population in deceitful ways. Tonry (1995), among others, has exposed the way in which this is done. Thus he quotes Steven Dillingham, then director of the Bureau of Justice Statistics, whose task it is to provide nonpartisan commentary on such matters, as saying at the attorney general's 1991 crime summit that "95 percent of state prisoners have been convicted of violent crimes, or are recidivists." The trick here, of course, is in the use of the word *or* and the implication, by lumping them together, that "recidivists" are the same as violent offenders. The truth is very different. Only 45 percent of those incarcerated in state and federal prisons combined are violent offenders—some of whom will have committed one-shot offenses without much likelihood of offending again. Moreover, about two-fifths of those in prison had never previously been sentenced to prison, and of those who had been in custody before, most had previously been convicted of nonviolent offenses. John DiIulio, who, as Tonry notes "ought to know better," has also claimed that "more than 95 percent of state prisoners are violent criminals, repeat criminals (with two or more felony convictions), or violent repeat criminals." Such claims simply cannot be sustained by any reading of the published statistics, and it is incumbent on scholars to point out that the implied equivalencies of dangerousness simply do not obtain in reality. At least James Q. Wilson, who more than any other writer has argued for the greater use of imprisonment, makes no bones about his preparedness to condone the use of imprisonment for *non*dangerous offenders. In an interview published in *Criminal Justice Matters,* he is unrepentant and criticizes both Labour and Conservative politicians in the United Kingdom for making a fundamental mistake in the 1970s: "They wanted to keep prison for those who had committed the most heinous crimes" (Wilson 1996, p. 4).

The extraordinary way in which nearly a quarter of the capacity of the American prison system has been given over to drug offenders reflects, of course, the escalating impact of the continuing "war on drugs," although the real upsurge in the prison population as a result of imprisonment for drugs took place in 1988–1989 with an increase of 50 percent in a single year. James Q. Wilson (1996) has suggested that the arrival of crack cocaine on urban streets in 1985 led to a sharp upturn in violent juvenile crime involving gang killings which subsided after 1993 as crack cocaine ceased to be the drug of choice. No doubt the very high profile given to such activities in the mid-1980s contributed to the war mentality: but given strong evidence from the national household surveys conducted for the National Institute on Drug Abuse that use of most illicit drugs declined through the 1980s, and that the largest growth in drug arrests—a forty-seven-fold increase—had occurred between 1959 and 1973, it might be thought that the war on drugs was belated and unnecessary. And that mandatory terms of imprisonment are an unduly stringent weapon against a form of behavior that, more than most, lends itself to alternative social or medical meanings—in terms of different lifestyles, for example, or as a problem of addiction. In any event, what is certain is that the operation of the "war on drugs" has hugely exacerbated the racial disproportion that is to be found in U.S. prisons.

In 1980, some 46.3 percent of the 303,643 sentenced men and 51.1 percent of sentenced women prisoners under state or federal jurisdiction were African Americans (46.5 percent of the 315,974 total); in 1993, these proportions had risen to 50.7 percent of the vastly increased number of 878,298 men and 51.7 percent of the 59,968 women serving sentences of a year or more (50.8 percent of the 932,266 total). The proportion of African Americans in jails, whether convicted or unconvicted, was somewhat lower, although it had increased more quickly than was the case for prisons—from 40.5 percent in 1988 to 44.2 percent in 1993. Taking prisons and jails, and both sexes together, in 1993 blacks accounted for 49 percent of those in custody, even though they constituted only 12 percent of the resident population of the United States. Moreover, 46 percent of the new recruits to death row and nearly 37 percent of those executed during 1993 were black, as were almost 41 percent of the prisoners still on death row at year-end. (Data in this paragraph are from Maguire and Pastore 1996, sect. 6, and Maguire and Pastore 1997, sect. 6.)

Although blacks were represented four times as frequently in prison and jail populations as in the general population, Tonry (1994) has pointed out that this understates the level of racial disproportion in American prisons, since it takes no account of the underrepresentation of whites. In 1993, white Americans also accounted for 49 percent of the prison and jail population but constituted 85 percent of resident Americans. This is seen more clearly if one looks at racially disaggregated incarceration rates for men and women in state and federal prisons: for blacks, the incarceration rate was 1,471 per 100,000, seven times higher than for whites, who had incarceration rate of 207 per 100,000. To these must be added 653 per 100,000 resident black Americans and 113 per 100,000 resident white Americans in local jails, producing total incarceration rates for 1993 of 2,124 for blacks and 320 for whites.

Demographically speaking, however, the fastest-growing minority group in state and federal prisons is Hispanic prisoners. Since Hispanics may be of any race, they have generally been included (as above) in black and white counts, although some tables identify them separately. Even when they are separately identified, there is more uncertainty about the figures than usual because of differences in recording procedures; however, the Bureau of Justice Statistics reports that they rose from 7.7 percent of state and federal prisoners in 1980 to 14.3 percent in 1993, during which time the incarceration rate per 100,000 Hispanic residents tripled from 163 to 529. In 1993, Hispanics also accounted for 15.1 percent of the jail population, with a jail incarceration rate of 290 per 100,000 Hispanic residents. In some states there are also significant groups of other minorities, for example, Native Americans, most notably in Alaska, and Asians, especially in California, who are overrepresented in the custodial populations.

All told, about two-thirds of the 1993 state and federal prison population and three-quarters of new prison admissions were accounted for by blacks, Hispanics, Asians, and Native Americans; about three-fifths of the jail population in 1993 was also drawn from these minority groups. There are, of course, considerable variations between states in terms of race-specific incarceration rates, but these sometimes produce counterintuitive results: thus, in 1988, the ratio of black to white incarceration rates reached a high of 19 to 1 in the generally progressive state of Minnesota, with its geographic and culturally affinitive neighbor Wisconsin only eight places higher up the league table with a ratio of almost 12 to 1. South Carolina and Mississippi had ratios of just under and just over 4 to

1 respectively, while California was just below and Florida a little above the national average of around 6 to 1. Tonry (1994) explains these differences in terms of the relative size of minority groups, their geographic location in urban or rural areas, and the visibility of their crimes in the context of the overall incarceration rates for those states.

Tonry reviews the available evidence that has a bearing on the worsening of racial disproportion in American prisons and jails, and concludes that it "is the result of deliberate policy choices of federal and state officials to 'toughen' sentencing, in an era of falling and stable crime rates, and to launch a 'War on Drugs' during a period when all general population surveys showed declining levels of drug use" (1994, p. 110). A single example will have to suffice here: thus Clarke (1992) showed that white admissions to North Carolina prisons remained steady from 1970 through 1990, while black admissions doubled from 1980 to 1990. In 1984, about twice as many whites (10,269) in North Carolina were arrested for drug offenses as blacks (5,021); five years later, that difference was wiped out as drug arrests for blacks had increased by 183 percent to 14,192 whereas white arrest rates increased by only 36 percent to 14,007.

In the same article, Tonry argues that much, though not all, of the overrepresentation of blacks in American prisons over the past twenty years is associated with their disproportionate participation in "imprisonable crimes" like homicide, robbery, aggravated assault, and rape. This echoes the conclusions drawn earlier by Blumstein (1982) for the United States and by Hood (1992) for some English jurisdictions. However, the national policy decision to launch a "war on drugs" and local police decisions to focus on street trafficking foreseeably increased black arrests, prosecutions, convictions, and incarcerations. According to the Sentencing Project, drug policies constituted the single most important factor in determining why, in 1989, one in every four black men aged twenty to twenty-nine was in jail, in prison, or on probation or parole; and why, five years later, the proportion had risen to one in every three (Mauer 1990, 1995). Having fought for, and gained, the vote in the 1960s, it seems that a substantial portion of the black population of the United States has been disenfranchised again.

Shocking though these statistics are, Tonry (1994) has shown that, when one compares racially disaggregated incarceration rates, the United States is not as far out of line with at least some other English-speaking countries as is commonly believed. Thus in England and Wales during 1990, and combining remand and sentenced prisoners (equivalent to American jail and prison populations), whites were incarcerated seven times less frequently, at a rate of 77 per 100,000, than blacks (primarily Caribbean), whose rate was 547 per 100,000. This disparity receives so little publicity, argues Tonry, because of the small proportion of blacks in the total population of England and Wales. Tonry ingeniously argues that if blacks and whites in England and Wales (1.8 percent and 94.1 percent) were found in the same proportion as blacks and whites in the United

States (12 percent and 80 percent), and each group was still incarcerated at its current rate, then in 1990 there would have been more blacks (32,748) than whites (30,732) in the prison population of England and Wales, and the overall incarceration rate would have been 140 instead of 89 per 100,000 total population. He goes on to describe similar patterns in Australia and Canada (in spite of a ban on the collection and dissemination of racially disaggregated statistics there), suggesting that many countries handle their most prominent and visible minority groups no less differentially than does the United States. If this is so, it seems unlikely that such a phenomenon would be restricted to the English-speaking world. Reliably comparable data are hard to come by, but Pavarini (1994) has demonstrated that during those two years of astonishing growth in the Italian prison population, 1991–1992, the proportion confined for drug offenses rose from 20 percent to 60 percent, and the proportion of black immigrants incarcerated rose from 5 percent to 20 percent. There is clearly a need here for further cross-national research.

A final word needs to be said about the numbers and proportions of women in custody. Since 1980, the number of sentenced females in state and federal prisons has been increasing at one and a half times the rate for male prisoners—by an average of 12 percent per annum, compared with 8.5 percent—producing a total increase of 386 percent between 1980 and 1994 compared with 214 percent for males. It seems likely that, in part, this is a result of mandatory sentencing: the federal sentencing guidelines, for example, now prevent judges from considering factors such as the subordinate part women play in many crimes, their lower likelihood of reoffending, or their family responsibilities, which they would previously have taken into account (Donziger 1996). Although female prisoners still account for only 6 percent of the American prison population, this is noticeably higher than 1980, when they accounted for less than 4 percent. Not surprisingly, given the other trends already discussed, the rate of increase for black women—who in 1993 had an incarceration rate of 165 per 100,000 resident black women—has been faster than for white women, whose incarceration rate was 23 per 100,000. According to the National Criminal Justice Commission, American female prisoners are even more likely than men to be in custody for drug offenses, and more than half (51 percent) have either no convictions or only one prior conviction, compared with 39 percent of male prisoners (although this difference is partly reflected in shorter sentences for women). More than three-quarters of the women in state prisons have children (Donziger 1996). Furthermore, women make up almost 10 percent of the jail population, so that all told there are over 100,000 American women behind bars.

There is some reason to believe that this, too, is a trend that is not confined to the United States. Thus, of the Council of Europe countries providing data in both 1984 and 1993, only Greece, Turkey, and Ireland reported a declining proportion of women prisoners, whereas fourteen countries reported increases. In some cases these were substantial: in Spain the proportion of women prisoners tripled, from 3.3 percent to 9.4 percent; in Denmark, Portugal, and Sweden the proportion doubled; and in the Netherlands it increased by about 50 percent. In England and Wales the increase was much more modest, about 15 percent, but was still sufficient to give rise to renewed concern both about the consequences of such a sentencing policy in relation to women and about the capacity of the prison system to provide appropriate facilities for them. I am acutely aware that selecting time periods on the basis of the availability of international data presents an arbitrary picture. Between 1990 and 1996, the number of women in prison in England and Wales rose by 56 percent to 2,500. No doubt the situation has changed elsewhere since the Council of Europe figures were published.

Behind the Walls

It would be surprising indeed if these changes in the size and shape of prison populations had not been accompanied by profound changes to the quality of life behind bars, but the fact is it is hard to know. For a variety of reasons, not least the difficulty of mostly white academics conducting research in increasingly black prisons, there seems to have been rather less research on prison conditions and prison subcultures than there once was. In any case, with scores of federal prisons, hundreds of state prisons, and thousands of local jails, all in situations subject to rapid change, the likelihood is that there will be considerable variation both within and between jurisdictions. Not only will it be hard to generalize from the findings of localized research studies to the wider scene, but those very findings may be out-of-date by the time they are published. In this section, therefore, I seek to draw attention to some major themes, which, as it were, must have had an impact, but it may be taken as read that in each case there is a pressing need for substantial, and preferably comparative, research.

Perhaps the obvious place to start is with crowding. If all systems worked to a common standard of capacity measured in square feet or meters per prisoner, it would be possible to get a clearer picture of the level of crowding in institutions. Most countries have space standards to which they aspire and which are expressed in the designs of new facilities. But all prison systems have to use accommodations inherited from a past in which standards usually, though by no means always, were lower, and they may try to take account of this by linking space standards to length of time spent in cells. The standards vary widely. The American Correctional Association's Commission for Accreditation on Corrections, for example, sets a standard of at least 80 square feet of total floor space per occupant for general inmate housing when confinement exceeds ten hours a day but only 50 square feet per prisoner in dormitories; prisons in England and Wales have operating standards for existing, but refurbished, cells of 5.5 square meters (about 60 square feet) for single occupancy but only about 40 square feet per prisoner for cells in double occupancy, and also have a current target (so far achieved for about a third of the prison population) that specifies prisoners will spend twelve hours a day out of cells; the Russian Federation has an aspirational norm of 2.5 square meters (about 27 square feet) for remand prisoners, even though they would not spend any time out of cells except for daily exercise and weekly showers; the European Rules simply establish the single-occupancy cell as the preferred norm without reference to size or time spent in cells, and some countries such as the Netherlands have tried to stand firmly behind that principle.

In practice, aspirational standards may mean little, and prison systems tend to rate and rerate the capacity of their institutions depending on the circumstances they face. Most systems probably operate with a notion of the minimum or "normal" capacity, which allows them some flexibility over the classification and allocation of prisoners, and a maximum capacity with which they can respond to the current pressures from the courts. Often the best that can be done in assessing overcrowding is to compare actual population with such rated capacities—although one can be fairly certain that this will considerably understate the "true" level of crowding in each jurisdiction and offer no serious basis for comparison between jurisdictions. With that in mind, the federal system was estimated to be operating at 25 percent over capacity at the end of 1994, and eight states—Montana (198 percent), Hawaii (197 percent), California (184 percent), Ohio (171 percent), Oklahoma (170 percent), Maryland (169 percent), Iowa (167 percent), and Illinois (161 percent)—as well as the District of Columbia (151 percent) were occupied between 50 and 100 percent above rated capacity. The average occupancy rate for state prisons in 1994 was 129 percent. The latest (September 1994) Council of Europe occupancy rates for those member, and would-be-member, states that reported data show enormous, and probably not very meaningful, variations, from a low of 54 percent in Turkey to a high of 168 percent in Greece. In the Netherlands, the occupancy rate of 102.8 percent has meant the breaking of the single-cell philosophy, whereas the apparently better occupancy rate for England and Wales of 100.6 percent has to be judged in relation to a rated capacity that includes both double celling and dormitory accommodation. Moreover, since then the prison population has shot up in England and Wales, so that the occupancy rate in September 1996 was 107 percent. Seventeen of the twenty-three European states reported that their systems were operating below capacity, but such reports can conceal more than they reveal.

To get a better idea of the extent and significance of overcrowding, it is sometimes necessary to rely on more anecdotal materials, which are more graphic. Thus, according to the National Criminal Justice Commission, the real meaning of occupancy statistics in the United States is that three out of four inmates are housed in facilities where the living space for two people is the size of a walk-in closet (Donziger 1996).

Russia reports 85 percent occupancy to the Council of Europe, but this includes huge amounts of accommodation in the corrective labor colonies inherited from the Soviet past. Many have been closed, although several hundred remain. These may not be as "crowded" as they once were, but large numbers of prisoners sleep in cramped dormitories, often in inhospitable climates and in situations where the work that once helped sustain the old system is no longer available in the new market economy. But conditions in the colonies generally compare favorably, as far as crowding is concerned, with those that obtain in the urban remand prisons. Thus, when I was conducting research in Butyrka remand prison in Moscow in 1992, I visited several large, so-called general cells, which originally provided about thirty square feet per prisoner for twenty-five prisoners but now held sixty or seventy prisoners for twenty-three hours a day. Three years later the United Nations special rapporteur, Nigel Rodley, described the conditions as "infernal . . . the senses of smell, touch, taste and sight are repulsively assailed. The conditions are cruel, inhuman and degrading: they are torturous" (United Nations 1995, p. 22). By the time of his visit, these cells contained more than eighty prisoners, and there was "insufficient room for everyone to lie down, sit down or even stand up at the same time." In Kresty Remand prison in Saint Petersburg I talked to prisoners in a cell that would probably have just met the American Correctional Association standard of eighty square feet had it contained one prisoner. Use of similar-sized cells for three prisoners in England and Wales had been described as inhuman and degrading by the Council of Europe Committee for the Prevention of Torture (Council of Europe 1991). But there were ten, not three, prisoners in this cell, and I was told that sometimes it held as many as sixteen prisoners, who occasionally lost consciousness because the ventilation was so poor that it was difficult to breathe. I did not know whether to believe this at the time, but in a similar facility in Ekaterinburg in 1995, several prisoners died in just such circumstances from lack of oxygen. Nor is this apparently a unique occurrence. General Kalinin, the then head of the Russian Department of Penitentiaries, was quoted as saying at a Parliamentary hearing on October 24, 1995: "I have to confess that sometimes official reports on prisoners' deaths do not convey the real facts. In reality prisoners die from overcrowding, lack of oxygen, and poor prison conditions. Cases of death from lack of oxygen took place in almost all large pre-trial detention centers in Russia" (Moscow Centre for Prison Reform 1996, pp. xv).

The remand prisons in Europe are more properly to be compared with jail facilities in the United States. The capacity of American jails is determined by ratings made by state or local officials as to the maximum number of beds or inmates who can be allocated to the facilities—and nearly a quarter of a million beds were added to the system between 1983 and 1993. Without an enforceable standard of square feet per prisoner it is impossible to say whether these additional beds improved conditions or simply made existing conditions more cramped, and it would probably require a massive research effort to find out. The reported 96.8 percent occupancy rate for American jails as a whole in 1993 is perhaps not very meaningful as a measure of crowding, nor is the fact that only eight states—Virginia, South Carolina, New Jersey, Texas, California, Massachusetts, Washington, and Pennsylvania—together with the District of Columbia reported jail populations above stated capacities. Given the huge variations in size of jails—from fewer than fifty beds to more than a thousand—and the fact that the twenty-five largest jurisdictions accommodated 30 percent of all jail inmates, it is likely that a few key states set the tone. If so, the auguries are not good. Maricopa County, Arizona, is one of the twenty-five largest jail jurisdictions, and though it is insignificant compared with Los Angeles or New York, it still accounted for over 5,000 inmates in its seven facilities in 1994. In 1993, 1,600 new beds were provided as a response to overcrowding in Phoenix's main jails, but in this case at least they constituted a "tent city" accommodating both men and women under canvas. In a recent interview with the British newspaper *Mail on Sunday* (November 24, 1996), the sheriff appeared to glory in the impoverished regime: offenders against jail discipline have "the opportunity to work themselves back to those sweltering tents by joining the chain gang cleaning up the trash and debris in the middle of Phoenix."

This hardening of attitude toward imprisoned offenders, exemplified by the reported remarks of the sheriff of Maricopa County, who boasted that he was the first corrections official in the world to put women on a chain gang and that it was possible to find his tent city by using one's sense of smell, should not be taken as typical. The majority of prison staff are probably perfectly decent individual citizens trying to perform the difficult roles that societies too unthinkingly assign to them, in circumstances that would stretch the patience of saints. But it is nevertheless disturbing and more than just a straw in the wind. It is perhaps a natural extension of that discourse on crime castigated by Nils Christie and others. If one uses the vocabulary of war to deal with matters that are defined as criminal, it is but a short step to defining the perpetrators as "enemies" and ascribing to them attributes that make them initially less deserving of the most basic amenities and civilities, and ultimately less than human. The end of that road is, of course, the extermination camp.

Such attitudes may not be unrelated to changes in the staff profiles of those charged with the care of prisoners. As the prison population has expanded in the United States, so has the number of correctional staff employed to guard and supervise their detention. According to Donziger (1996), the number of correctional officers has doubled in recent years in most states and has tripled in some. Numbers of jail staff have grown even more quickly than numbers of inmates over the period 1983–1993, so that nationally the number of inmates to each frontline correctional officer fell from 5.0 in 1983 to 3.9 in 1993. There were, however, considerable regional variations, so that there were twice as many inmates per correctional officer in western states (5.3) as there were in northeastern states (2.5). The same pattern of staff growth has been found in England and Wales: between 1971 and 1986, three new members of staff, two of them frontline uniformed officers, were added to the system for every two additional prisoners. Indeed, British prisons have proportionately almost twice as many staff as American prisons, with the number of prisoners for each member of uniformed staff falling from 3.48 in 1971 to 2.47 in 1986 and to 2.0 in 1992. In some European jurisdictions, such as the Netherlands, the staff-prisoner ratio approaches 1 to 1 and there has long been a tradition of training staff so that they recognize the need for programs that will assist the rehabilitation of prisoners who will one day be returned to the communities whence they came. It seems probable, however, that the fast recruitment that has taken place in Britain and the United States will have brought into correctional services many new staff who share unsympathetic public perceptions about predatory criminals, "welfare scroungers," and so on. It is likely, also, that incoming staff will have much more instrumental attitudes toward the prison as a workplace, and it is doubtful whether staff training programs will have been sufficiently maintained to establish a more professional approach. Certainly Donziger (1996) argues that the increased prison staff has immensely increased the political clout of the unions that represent prison guards, although there have been intriguing differences between the recent histories of Britain and the United States in this regard.

When I visited the United States in 1983, the power of the Prison Officers' Association (POA) in Britain was at its height and was in marked contrast to the localized and largely ineffective guards unions with which state administrations negotiated terms and conditions. The POA was the last of the trade unions able to withstand the onslaught of the Thatcher government's antiunion legislation, precisely because government industrial relations policies, as well as its stance on law and order, were inconsistent with any kind of confrontation with either the police or prison officers. Even as late as 1986, the POA came out of negotiations intended to create a "fresh start," but with a thinly disguised government agenda of undercutting the union's capacity to hold the system to ransom, with a package of pay and conditions that exceeded those to which most university graduates would aspire. Since then, however, the government has successfully used both the threat and the actuality of privatization—which has grown more quickly to take a proportionately much larger role in the prison system of England and Wales than it has in the United States—to break the power of the union. Union influence has further declined as staff numbers have been progressively reduced since 1996 in the search for efficiency savings, in spite of the increase in prison population. However, the spectacular growth in imprisonment across the United States has hugely increased the power of guards unions. The California Correctional Peace Officers Association, which grew from 4,000 to 23,000 members, has, like the POA, achieved salary levels for its members that far exceeded those for Californian schoolteachers or associate professors at the university. And prison guards in Illinois were able to push through legislation that prevented the privatization of prisons.

Many of the prisoners at Ekaterinburg and many of the inmates for whom the sheriff of Maricopa County is responsible are awaiting trial and not yet found guilty of any offense, but it has long been one of the ironies of prison systems that such remand prisoners often suffer the worst conditions. However, it seems likely that the hardening of attitudes toward offenders has been driven by a perception on the part of the public and correctional officials alike that prison systems increasingly have to deal with a hard core of extremely ruthless and dangerous criminals. As we saw earlier, prison populations have grown largely through the recruitment of many more marginal offenders, and this has actually had the effect of diluting the level of dangerousness in the system as a whole. Nevertheless, there has also been a buildup of difficult and dangerous offenders whose very long sentences mean that they accumulate in the system year upon year. Such prisoners, or at least the way in that they are perceived and the policies that are developed toward them, can have a profound effect on the nature of the prison system and the attitudes of staff who work in it, and there is good reason to suppose that the control of such prisoners has loomed large in American corrections over the last fifteen years.

Although any analysis of the prison literature reveals that there are major areas of comparability in the experiences of staff and prisoners in different countries, it also seems probable that important differences are to be found between cultures, on the one hand, and between different levels of security, on the other. Moczydlowski (1992), for example, has provided an account of the particular forms of corruption that flowed from the economic and social organization in Polish prisons under the old regime. Downes (1988) has reflected on the differences in what he called the "depth" of imprisonment in the Netherlands and in England, as reported by Dutch and British subjects. King and McDermott (1995) preferred to characterize what Downes called the "depth" of imprisonment as the "weight" of imprisonment; they argued that this varied, in English prisons at least, according to how deeply prisoners became embroiled in the security and control procedures of the system. Prisoners in high-security prisons and in units intended for problem prisoners reported a much heavier burden of imprisonment than those in lower-security institutions. In what remains the only empirical cross-cultural study of "deep end" maximum-security confinement, King (1991) was able to show that prisoners and staff felt safer in the "new-generation" high-security prison at Oak Park Heights in Minnesota than in Gartree Prison, which exercised a similar function within the prison system of England and Wales. Moreover, this level of safety was achieved without cost to the prison regime because prisoners in Oak Park Heights spent more time out of their cells and had more programs at their disposal than their British counterparts.

Oak Park Heights, however, has almost certainly always been an exceptional prison; it has long been a showplace, with the correctional world beating a path to its door. Few would suggest otherwise than that, generally speaking, American prisons are more violent institutions than British prisons, and that this not so much *reflects* a more violent society outside but *magnifies* that violent society, not least because of the racial disproportions in custody already discussed. Whatever the reasons for the violence in American prisons, there can be little doubt that the response to it by correctional authorities has been to cut programs and to lock prisoners down. The precise ways in which these matters interact are still poorly understood and underresearched, but the circumstances that led to the lockdown at the federal Marion Control Unit in Illinois in 1983 have already been noted. Once a lockdown has begun, it may be very difficult indeed to end it, and British and European practices have been mostly predicated on having sufficient staff operating in nonconfrontational ways so that the necessity for such lockdowns has been avoided. In the United States, however, there has been an increasing resort to developing specialist institutions or euphemistically described special housing units (SHUs) within institutions, which are in more or less permanent lockdown status and operate with no, or minimal, programs. Such institutions or units, often referred to as "super-max," are run more or less explicitly with a view to general and individual deterrence, but holding open the possibility that after a period of good behavior prisoners might be returned to general population units or institutions. Some thirty-four jurisdictions appear to have developed super-max facilities of one kind or another to deal with those prisoners whom they characterize as the "worst of the worst." Even before the invention of such facilities, about half of all prisoners in the United States were held in what were then defined as maximum-security institutions—a problem of overclassification in security terms that the Federal Bureau sought to change, with some success, by the introduction of more objective systems of classification in the early 1980s.

The danger in such closed super-max facilities, in a climate where the attitudes of the public and some officials offer little sympathy to offenders, is that prison staff may grossly exceed their powers. Even where atrocities do not happen, the "normal" regime offers little or nothing but the most basic essentials for life: thus death row prisoners routinely spent twenty-three hours a day in shared cells in McAlester in Oklahoma, which, despite its newness, fell below American Correctional Association standards for space and international standards for natural light and ventilation. Prisoners routinely left their cells only to exercise in small yards with high walls and no facilities, or to bathe, and then only with their cell mate, from whose company there was no relief. On the rare occasions they had legal or other visits they were in handcuffs, leg irons, and waist chains and were accompanied by three officers. The further danger of such facilities, however, is that they come to set the standard for the systems of which they are a part, feeding back into ever-hardening attitudes of staff: if the conditions for these prisoners have to be so austere, it becomes more and more difficult to justify the provision of educational and rehabilitative programs for others. That such problems are not confined to super-max institutions is evidenced by the fact that in one of Maricopa County's jails it is alleged that officers used an electrical stun gun on the testicles of an offender and pushed his head so far down onto his chest while he was strapped into a restraint chair that he died of "positional asphyxia."

A U.S. Department of Justice report on events in Maricopa County notes that "the use of excessive force is facilitated by inadequate staffing levels" and by the "youthfulness and inexperience of staff." It might be added that the fact that such incidents can occur betrays the lack of care and supervision that can run right to the top of correctional departments. In a federal court judgment on Pelican Bay, it was held that the California Department of Corrections had "failed to provide inmates . . . with constitutionally adequate medical and mental health care, and have permitted and condoned a pattern of using excessive force, all in conscious disregard of the serious harm that these practices inflict. . . . [The] defendants have subjected plaintiffs to 'unnecessary and wanton infliction of pain' in violation of the Eighth Amendment of the United States Constitution." Moreover, it was clear that the Court did not trust the department to mend its ways: "[W]e glean no serious or genuine commitment to significantly improving the delivery of health care services, correcting the pattern of excessive force, or otherwise remedying the constitutional violations found herein which have caused, and continue to cause, significant harm to the plaintiffs. . . . Nor are we confident that defendants will promptly rectify constitutional deficiencies absent intervention by this Court" (*Madrid v. Gomez,* F. Supp. 3rd 1995). The Court therefore appointed a special master, experienced in prison administration, to oversee the drawing up and implementation of solutions to the problems identified by the case.

Prison litigation in state and federal courts has, at times, provided both a powerful remedy for past abuses and a potential curb on future abuses; it has to be regarded as one of the most important developments that has influenced life behind the walls. If nothing else, it has offered a glimmer of hope to those in otherwise hopeless situations. That it is not a wholly effective remedy is all too evident. In appointing a special master for Pelican Bay, the U.S. District Court cited numerous instances of previous failures on the part of correctional administrations to conform with court decrees and recommendations. The National Prison Project's status report on state prisons and the courts for 1995 listed nine states whose entire prison systems were under court order or consent decrees, thirty-three jurisdictions in which major institutions were under court order or consent decrees, with eleven jurisdictions in which litigation was pending. Seven jurisdictions had formerly been under such orders but had been released from active supervision. All told, some twenty-four jurisdictions past and present had received the attention of court—appointed special masters, monitors, or mediators—and eight jurisdictions, past and present, had been cited for contempt in respect of the orders against them. Only three jurisdictions—Minnesota, New Jersey, and North Dakota—have not been involved in overcrowding or conditions litigation.

In 1995, a bill was introduced in the U.S. Congress to restrict the power of the federal courts to monitor prison conditions. The recently retired cofounder and director of the NPP, Al Bronstein, was quoted in an interview with the *Philadelphia Inquirer* (March 2, 1995) as saying that "the progress we've made in bringing our prisons into the 20th century is being eroded." But it is the twenty-first century, of course, that beckons, and even if there were no curbs on the courts, their willingness and capacity to intervene would be unlikely to match the scale of the problems that face and will continue to face those in prison in the United States. It is hard to see how prison conditions in the United States will improve without a major reorientation not just of law-and-order policies but of education and welfare programs. Such a reorientation will require either the reeducation of the general public and politicians on a massive scale or at least the capacity to learn lessons from experience. If, and when, prison populations are cut to a point that brings them more in line with what a prison system might realistically hope to achieve as part of the repertoire available to the criminal justice system, it will be necessary to redevelop programs of staff training. But the fact that it is possible for prisoners to bring meaningful court actions against prison administrations at all remains at least a demonstration of democracy at work. As Dostoyevsky (1860) noted, "[T]he standards of a nation's civilization can be judged by opening the doors of its prisons," and who, after all, speaks for the prisoners who died in Ekaterinburg?

Notes

1. All comparative statistics have to be treated with caution and should not be imbued with a spurious precision. It is difficult to get a run of historic data that have been collected on a comparable basis year on year. In a complex system composed of scores of federal, hundreds of state, and thousands of local facilities, the margins for error become greater the farther back one goes. My figure is taken from Zimring and Hawkins (1991), who in turn rely on Cahalan (1979). Jail figures are particularly likely to be subject to error.

2. In making international comparisons, the statistics should be treated with even greater caution. It is not always clear that one is comparing like with like. The comparative incarceration rates quoted here are abstracted from Rutherford (1985). The incarceration rate for the United States in 1972

cited by Rutherford differs marginally from the one quoted earlier by Zimring and Hawkins (1991).

3. By concentrating on the comparable *rate of increase* in the prison populations of England and Wales and the United States between 1950 and 1985, however, Rutherford sometimes seems to ignore the differences in the relative *scale of imprisonment* between the two countries, which were of a quite different order at the beginning and continued to diverge right up until 1994.

References

Amnesty International. 1994. *United States of America, Conditions for Death Row Prisoners in H-Unit, Oklahoma State Penitentiary.* London: International Secretariat.

Beccaria, Cesare. 1764. *An Essay on Crimes and Punishments.* New York: Bobbs-Merrill.

Blumstein, Alfred. 1982. "On the Racial Disproportionality of United States Prison Populations." *Journal of Criminal Law and Criminology* 73:1259–81.

Blumstein, Alfred, and Jacqueline Cohen. 1973. "A Theory of the Stability of Punishment." *Journal of Criminal Law and Criminology* 64:198–207.

Bureau of Justice Statistics. 1995. *Correctional Populations in the United States, 1993.* Washington, D.C.: U.S. Department of Justice, Bureau of Justice Statistics.

———. 1996. *Prison and Jail Inmates, 1995.* Washington, D.C.: U.S. Department of Justice, Bureau of Justice Statistics.

Cahalan, Margaret. 1979. "Trends in Incarceration in the United States Since 1880." *Crime and Delinquency* 25:9–41.

Christie, Nils. 1994. *Crime Control as Industry: Towards Gulags, Western Style.* 2nd ed. London: Routledge.

Clarke, Stevens H. 1992. "North Carolina Prisons Growing." *Overcrowded Times* 3(4):1, 11–13.

Council of Europe. 1991. *Report to the United Kingdom Government on the Visit to the United Kingdom Carried Out by the European Committee for the Prevention of Torture and Inhuman or Degrading Treatment or Punishment on Its Visit to the United Kingdom from 29 July to 10 August 1990.* Strasbourg: Council of Europe.

Detkov, M. G. 1992. *The Content of the Penal Policy of the Soviet State and Its Implementation Through Punishments Involving Deprivation of Liberty in the 1930s, 1940s and 1950s.* Domodyedovo: Ministry of the Interior of the Russian Federation.

Donziger, Stephen, ed. 1996. *The Real War on Crime.* New York: Harper-Collins.

Dostoyevsky, Fyodor. 1860. *The House of the Dead.* London: Heinemann.

Downes, David. 1988. *Contrasts in Tolerance: Post-War Penal Policy in the Netherlands and England and Wales.* Oxford: Clarendon.

———. 1997. "The Buckling of the Shields: Dutch Penal Policy 1985–1995." In *International Prison Systems*, edited by Nigel South and Robert Weiss. London: Gordon and Breach.

Durkheim, Émile. [1893] 1964. *The Division of Labour in Society.* New York: Free Press.

———. [1895] 1938. *The Rules of Sociological Method.* Chicago: University of Chicago Press.

Home Office. 1991. *Prison Disturbances April 1990.* Report of an Inquiry by the Rt. Hon. Lord Justice Woolf (Parts I and II) and His Honour Judge Stephen Tumim (Part II), Cm. 1456, February 1991. London: HMSO.

Hood, Roger. 1992. *Race and Sentencing.* Oxford: Oxford University Press.

Hulsman, Louk. 1974. "Criminal Justice in the Netherlands." *Delta: A Review of Arts, Life and Thoughts in the Netherlands* 16:7–19.

King, Roy D. 1991. "Maximum-Security Custody in Britain and the USA: A Study of Gartree and Oak Park Heights." *British Journal of Criminology* 31(2):126–52.

———. 1994. "Russian Prisons After *Perestroika:* End of the Gulag?" *British Journal of Criminology* 34(special issue):62–82.

King, Roy D., and Kathleen McDermott. 1995. *The State of Our Prisons.* Oxford: Clarendon Press.

King, Roy D., and Rod Morgan. 1981. *The Future of the Prison System.* Farnborough, England: Gower.

Lipton, Douglas, Robert Martinson, and Judith Wilks. 1975. *The Effectiveness of Correctional Treatment: A Survey of Correctional Treatment Studies.* New York: Praeger.

Maguire, Kathleen, and Ann L. Partore, eds. 1996. *Sourcebook of Criminal Justice Statistics—1995.* Washington, D.C.: U.S. Government Printing Office.

———. 1997. *Sourcebook of Criminal Justice Statistics—1996.* Washington, D.C.: U.S. Government Printing Office.

Mauer, Marc. 1990. *Young Black Men and the Criminal Justice System: A Growing National Problem.* Washington, D.C.: The Sentencing Project.

———. 1995. "The International Use of Incarceration." *Prison Journal* 75(1): 113–23.

Mitford, Jessica. 1973. *Kind and Usual Punishment: The Prison Business.* New York: Knopf.

Moczydlowski, Pawel. 1992. *The Hidden Life of Polish Prisons.* Bloomington: Indiana University Press.

Morris, Norval, and Gordon Hawkins. 1970. *The Honest Politician's Guide to Crime Control.* Chicago: University of Chicago Press.

Moscow Centre for Prison Reform. 1996. *In Search of a Solution: Crime, Criminal Policy and Prison Facilities in the Former Soviet Union.* Moscow: Human Rights Publishers.

National Advisory Commission on Criminal Justice Standards and Goals. 1973. *Corrections.* Washington, D.C.: U.S. Government Printing Office.

National Institute of Justice. 1981. *American Prisons and Jails,* vols. 1–5. Washington, D.C.: U.S. Government Printing Office.

National Institute of Law Enforcement and Criminal Justice. 1977. *Prison Population and Policy Choices.* Washington, D.C.: U.S. Government Printing Office.

New York State Special Commission. 1972. *Attica: The Official Report of the New York State Special Commission on Attica.* New York: Bantam Books.

Pavarini, Massimo. 1994. "The New Penology and Politics in Crisis: The Italian Case." *British Journal of Criminology* 34(special issue):49–61.

Pease, Ken. 1994. "Cross-National Imprisonment Rates: Limitations of Method and Possible Conclusions." *British Journal of Criminology* 34(special issue):116–30.

President's Commission on Law Enforcement and Administration of Justice. 1967. *The Challenge of Crime in a Free Society.* Washington, D.C.: U.S. Government Printing Office.

Rector, Milton. 1977. "Are More Prisons Needed Now?" In *Should We Build More Prisons?* edited by Matthew Matlin. Hackensack, N.J.: National Council on Crime and Delinquency.

Rothman, David. 1971. *The Discovery of the Asylum: Social Order and Disorder in the New Republic.* Boston: Little, Brown.

Rusche, Georg, and Otto Kirkheimer. 1939. *Punishment and Social Structure.* New York: Columbia University Press.

Rutherford, Andrew. 1985. *Prisons and the Process of Justice.* Oxford: Oxford University Press.

———. 1996. *Transforming Criminal Policy.* Winchester, England: Waterside Press.

Taylor, Ian, Paul Walton, and Jock Young. 1973. *The New Criminology.* London: Routledge and Kegan Paul.

Tonry, Michael. 1987a. "Sentencing Guidelines and Their Effects." In *The Sentencing Commission and Its Guidelines,* edited by Andrew von Hirsch, Kay Knapp, and Michael Tonry. Boston: Northeastern University Press.

———. 1987b. *Sentencing Reform Impacts.* Washington, D.C.: National Institute of Justice.

———. 1994. "Racial Disproportion in U.S. Prisons." *British Journal of Criminology* 34(special issue):97–115.

———. 1995. *Malign Neglect: Race, Crime, and Punishment in America.* New York: Oxford University Press.

United Nations. 1995. *Report of the Special Rapporteur, Mr. Nigel S. Rodley, Submitted Pursuant to Commission on Human Rights Resolution 1994/ 37: Visit by the Special Rapporteur to the Russian Federation,* E/CN. 4/1995/34/Add.1, 16 November 1994. New York: United Nations, Economic and Social Council.

van Dijk, Jan J. M., and Pat Mayhew. 1992. *Criminal Victimisation in the Industrialised World.* The Hague: Dutch Ministry of Justice.

von Hirsch, Andrew. 1976. *Doing Justice.* New York: Hill and Wang.

Walmsley, Roy. 1996. *Prison Systems in Central and Eastern Europe: Progress, Problems and the International Standards.* Helsinki: European Institute for Crime Prevention and Control.

Wilson, James Q. 1975. *Thinking About Crime.* New York: Basic Books.

———. 1977. "The Political Feasibility of Punishment." In *Justice and Punishment,* edited by J. B. Cederblom and William L. Blizen. Cambridge, Mass.: Ballinger.

———. 1996. "Crimes and Misdemeanours: Interview with Roger Matthews and Tim Newburn." *Criminal Justice Matters* 25(Autumn):4–5.

Zimring, Franklin E., and Gordon Hawkins. 1991. *The Scale of Imprisonment.* Chicago: University of Chicago Press.

———. 1994. "The Growth of Imprisonment in California." *British Journal of Criminology* 34(special issue):83–96.

23

Private Prisons

RICHARD W. HARDING

Bankrupt, the states of the old Confederacy had all, within a decade or so of the end of the Civil War, adopted some variant of the system of leasing out inmate labor. Control of the state's inmates, prisons, and equipment would be sold to the highest bidder. The successful entrepreneur's profit lay in selling inmate labor or its fruits and in charging prisoners themselves or their families for subsistence and accommodation (Etheridge and Marquart 1993).

This system, whose earliest American origins had emerged in Kentucky in 1825, was corrupt and brutal. Prisoners' rights were nonexistent, conditions inhumane, and any notion of rehabilitation or improvement inconsequential. However, in the post–Civil War context, it was in a perverse sense "successful." "The southern states were able [affordably] to accommodate the increased number of criminal offenders that resulted from the shattered economy and the abolition of slavery. And widespread reliance on the criminal sanction and convict labor served as a means to control the black population" (Feeley 1991, p. 5). Similarly, privatization was "an efficient solution for the rapidly growing western states," particularly Nebraska, Kansas, Oklahoma, Oregon and California (p. 5).

This foray into prison privatization lasted in some states for half a century or more. Carried out in this way, it had raised profound questions about the state's authority over and responsibility for prisoners. Understandably, this history has colored the ideological objections of some critics to the second, and current, phase of prison privatization, which commenced in the mid-1980s. Yet, in truth, the contemporary model is quite different in its structure.

Donahue has cogently identified ambiguity in the very terminology of *privatization:* the first use "involves removing certain responsibilities, activities or assets from the collective realm . . . [while] the second meaning [is] retaining collective financing but delegating delivery to the private sector" (1989, p. 215). Nineteenth-century prison privatization fell into the first category—the state completely divesting not just a function but also responsibility for it, just as in modern times the worldwide mania for privatization has resulted in divesting responsibility for railroads or water supplies or postal services to entrepreneurs. This kind of privatization is all too often marked by erosion of public accountability and sacrifice of the public interest in the supposed quest for greater efficiency—a notion that invariably is equated with greater profits. As with early prison privatization, social costs never seem to figure in the bottom line.

However, modern prison privatization is quite different. It refers to a process whereby the state continues to fund the full agreed costs of incarceration, while the private sector, for the agreed payment, provides management services, both "hotel" (including custodial) and programmatic. The type and standard of these services are specified by the state. Invariably, these are no less than those applicable to the public prison sector. Compliance procedures are negotiated and put in place. Of course, the state hopes and intends that the agreed costs of these services can and will be lower than those at which it can deliver them directly itself. For all that, the arrangement is a classic example of Donahue's second category—delegation of service delivery, rather than sale of an economic resource. The prisoner remains the state's prisoner and ultimately its responsibility.

Another difference from the early experience of prison privatization is that such arrangements are almost invariably made institution by institution, rather than systemwide. The opportunity for profit thus lies simply in the entrepreneur's ability to deliver the agreed services to a particular institution at a cost below the negotiated sum, rather than in his untrammeled discretion as to how to dispose most profitably of the resources of a total system or of that particular institution.

Perceived this way, it is apparent that the crucial questions about private prisons will revolve around the following sorts of issues: first and foremost, how public accountability is to be maintained in relation to this core state function; related to this, whether a strict dichotomy is maintained between the allocation of punishment (by its nature public) and its administration (an aspect of delegable service delivery); what services and standards are contracted; how procurement contracts are let; whether bidders are suitably vetted as to probity; how contract compliance is to be achieved; whether the overall deal constitutes value for money; whether the public component of the total prison system is congruent with the private component and vice versa; and, generally, whether the whole system is enhanced or diminished by privatization.

These are all pragmatic questions, albeit ones identified against the sociopolitical backdrop that the state must remain accountable for the carrying out of what remains a core state function. Like most such questions, they are susceptible to some degree of empirical observation and measurement, as will be seen later.

The Sociopolitical Context of Prison Privatization in the United States

McDonald has reminded us that, long before the mid-1980s, "private firms had been contracting without much controversy with federal and state governments to provide a variety of discrete services to correctional facilities, such as health care, prison industry programs, counseling, vocational training, education, maintenance and food services" (1992, pp. 361–62). More than that, there was already widespread implementation of the practice of for-profit private, as well as not-for-profit voluntary sector, operation of entire correctional facilities. However, "little controversy was provoked because these facilities were typically found at the 'soft' end of the correctional continuum: halfway houses, residential treatment programs, detention centers for illegal immigrants, work release facilities, group homes for juveniles, and penal farms" (p. 362).

As a result of a variety of factors, the pressure for private sector participation at the "hard" end of the correctional continuum—adult imprisonment—gradually built up from the mid-1970s, until finally, a decade later, it became irresistible. These factors included exponential increases in prison populations; consequential overcrowding of facilities; deterioration of prison conditions to the point where particular prisons or even total state systems were subjected to federal court supervision; political or constitutional inhibitions against state (or local) governments expending taxpayers' funds on new prisons; and a dawning realization that some of these problems could be finessed, at least temporarily, by involving the private sector. As these factors coalesced, so commenced the emergence of a vibrant and self-confident private sector ready and willing to turn a profit from this activity.

Increases in Prison Populations

In the fifteen-year period 1960–1975, U.S. imprisonment rates were fairly consistent at 105 to 115 per 100,000 (Thomas and Logan 1993, p. 215). Physical plant reflected the expectation that these levels of imprisonment would continue to be the norm; construction programs were modest, focusing as much on replacement or refurbishment of existing facilities as on accommodation increase. However, from 1975 onward there began a period of unprecedented growth in both prison and the jail populations, to the point where by late 1996 the overall incarceration rate was about 600 per 100,000 and the total number of prisoners about 1.7 million.

Overcrowding and Federal Court Supervision

In this context, the existing plant became stretched to the uttermost. With overcrowding came deteriorating prisoner health, increased custodial death rates including suicide, and repressive conditions inimical to prisoner correction (Paulus 1988). The civil rights movement had already started to put an intense spotlight on prison conditions. Consequently, as the effects of overcrowding became more acute and more apparent, "cruel and unusual punishment" challenges under the Eighth Amendment, as well as privacy protection suits, became increasingly frequent.

At one time, no fewer than thirty-seven of the fifty states were subject to federal court supervisory orders or consent decrees (National Prison Project 1989), some such as Rhode Island and Texas for periods in excess of a decade.

Inhibitions on Expenditure

From the mid-1970s onward, the temper of the times was that governments must do more for less. The public was demanding that, while essential services should be supplied at a higher quality, this must be done by "downsized" public sector workforces and with reduced capital outlays. "Obvious illustrations of this somewhat paradoxical set of pressures and its consequences were soon to be provided by the referendum on Proposition 13 in California, . . . on Proposition 2½ in Massachusetts, and the tax reductions produced by [President Reagan's] Economic Recovery Act of 1981" (Thomas and Logan 1993, p. 218). In the criminal justice field, these general pressures against "big-spending big-government" were exacerbated by growing public disillusionment with the notion of rehabilitation, increasing fear of crime, resultant demands for tougher sentencing policies, and the developing attitude that convicted criminals should serve their sentences in sparse conditions.

Yet the costs of keeping up with the explosion in prisoner numbers were potentially horrendous. Apart from running costs, there were the capital outlays. Taking 1988 as a base year, Thomas and Logan (1993, p. 216) estimated that the notional cost of the construction program required to house just the extra prisoners coming into the population would be of the order of $5.98 billion annually. To attempt to raise such funds from taxpayers would be political suicide at the best of times. Few governments—state or local—would dare recklessly to swim against such a strong tide.

Finessing the Political and Legal Constraints

Yet something had to be done. The political or legal hazards of bond raising for prison construction could perhaps be evaded if the private sector were persuaded to raise the capital as part of a leaseback and management contract. Drawing on a financing device known as issuing "certificates of participation"—first used by Ohio, a state that had consistently resisted privatization but faced the common governmental problem of how to raise money for public works without contravening legal barriers or risking electoral wrath—various funding models were developed. Naturally their details differed (McDonald 1992, pp. 385–94; Harding 1997, pp. 12–13), but all had one thing in common: from the outset they enabled the standard U.S. private prison contract to be one to *design, construct, finance, and manage* (DCFM) an institution.

This feature should be emphasized, for it was not initially the case in

Australia and the United Kingdom, the two countries that first followed the United States down the privatization track. These countries were not so constrained by law nor yet inhibited by the prevailing sociopolitical culture from drawing upon the public purse. What drove them much more was the need to break the power of uniformed officers and their unions, power that often had led not only to significant featherbedding and cost escalation but also to stifling control over programs and penal regimes (Harding 1997, pp. 134–36). This objective could perfectly well be achieved by *management-only* contracts (i.e., of an institution designed, constructed, financed, and owned by the government itself), and initially these were the standard arrangements. Subsequently, however, as comparable criminal justice and general political pressures began to bite, these countries have shifted to the American DCFM contractual approach.

The drawback of DCFM contracts is that, because the leaseback period is normally rather long (up to forty years in some cases) so as to enable the state to amortize the capital costs relatively painlessly, the expectation is that the linked management component of the arrangement will likewise normally be quite long. Nominally, of course, contracts are terminable or may not be renewed at the end of the initial period. However, there are real practical and financial constraints upon the state's adopting such a course when it is tied in with a private operator through debt. This tends to erode the ability of the state to make the contractor fully accountable for the regime standards. It is not, of course, literally impossible to achieve this, but it is structurally more difficult than with management-only contracts.

The financing hurdle having been circumvented, there was one further legal issue to be addressed—whether the imprisonment function could constitutionally be delegated or subcontracted to the private sector. A 1989 report of the American Bar Association, picking up on earlier criticisms made by privatization's most prominent early critic, Ira Robbins, argued that "there can be no doubt that an attempt to delegate total operational responsibility for a prison or jail would raise grave questions of constitutionality under both the federal Constitution and the constitutions of the fifty states" (Robbins 1988, p. 39). McDonald, citing the Supreme Court decision in *Carter v. Carter Coal Company*, 298 U.S. 238 (1936), comments that this opinion is trying to inject "life into an issue that has been dead for some time, at least at the federal level" (1990, p. 181). Thomas likewise observes that despite opportunities to do so, "no court has invalidated a contract award on constitutional grounds at any point during the history of correctional privatization" (1996, p. 15).

Nevertheless, all the main states where the private sector currently operates—including Texas, Florida, Tennessee, Arizona, Louisiana, Kentucky, New Mexico, and Virginia—have chosen to authorize privatization by specific enabling legislation. This prudent approach has also permitted them to create suitable procurement mechanisms, as well as mandatory standards and mechanisms to be included in the contract. Only three of the eighteen U.S. jurisdictions where, as of December 31, 1996, private prisons were operative have relied simply on inherent executive or implied statutory power to privatize.

The Emergence of Private Sector Entrepreneurs

In the mid-1980s, then, a new industry was waiting to emerge. Thomas and Logan (1993, pp. 219–21) suggest that

> the true beginnings of the correctional privatization movement . . . [lay in the formation] of the Nashville-based Corrections Corporation of America ("CCA") in 1983. . . . CCA joined the embryonic private corrections industry with multiple advantages no other firm enjoyed. It had been able . . . to obtain substantial working capital, to persuade a number of experienced and highly regarded correctional administrators to move from the public to the private sector [and] to establish a division of labor within its corporate structure which called for senior business and senior corrections executives to exercise decision-making powers in their respective areas of expertise. (1993, pp. 219–21)

CCA at once started to pick up DCFM contracts in several states in relation to local jails. Drawing on this experience, it was thus positioned to become one of the two beneficiaries (the other was the Wackenhut Corrections Corporation) of the 1988 decision of the Texas Department of Criminal Justice to contract out four 500-bed facilities to the private sector. By demonstrating the acceptability of the private sector as operators of major *state*-level prisons, this decision marked the transition of the private prisons industry from the status of an "interesting experiment" to "maturity" (Thomas 1994, p. 5; 1996, pp. 18–19).

The Spread of Private Prisons

The contemporary significance of private prisons can best be gauged by the extent to which they have become integral to the total prison system. Could that system cope without them? Has their role de facto become irreversible?

Numerous factors must be regarded when attempting to answer these questions. They include the number of operational private prisons; their rated capacity; the number and rated capacity of private prisons that have been procured but are not yet operational; the percentage of the total prison population held or to be held in private prisons; the security levels of those prisons; the number of separate states that have adopted privatization; and the number and commercial viability of companies involved in the industry.

As of December 31, 1988—the year in which according to Thomas (1996, pp. 18–19) maturity was attained—there was a handful of operational private prisons in the United States, and the rated capacity of those, plus the newly commissioned Texas prisons, was still a mere 5,000. This represented less than 1 percent of the total number of prisoners then incarcerated in the United States. However, in the ensuing eight years, there have been exponential increases. As of December 31, 1996, there were 118 operational or commissioned facilities in the United States, the rated capacity of which was about 78,000. This represented about 5 percent of the total prison and jail population.

Table 23.1 shows the numbers and capacities of private prisons in the United States between 1973 and 1996. As is evident from Table 23.1, there was a surge (from 92 to 118) in the industry between the end of 1995 and the end of 1996. New projects are now coming onstream faster than others are being completed. One also can infer, since the 7 prisons that became newly operational during 1995 added 9,000 beds to the rated capacity, that privatized facilities are tending to get larger. Although this trend was not so marked in 1996 (9 new prisons and 6,800 extra prisoners), nevertheless, the rated capacity of 26 of the 118 private prisons listed as of December 31, 1996, was 1,000 or more, and the bulk of such contracts were recent (Thomas, Bollinger, and Badalamenti 1997). Indeed, CCA will open a 2,000-bed prison in Texas in 1998, while in mid-1996 the New Mexico government awarded to Wackenhut Corrections Corporation a DCFM contract in relation to a 2,200-bed prison (Prison Reform Trust 1996a, p. 3). These two facilities will be by far the largest private prisons in the world to date.

However, the percentage of prisoners held or to be held in such prisons in the United States is still, at just under 5 percent, quite small. An equally cogent perspective is that the raw numbers involved are substantial, being equivalent to the combined prison populations of, say, Japan and Malaysia or, alternatively, South Korea and Australia. The idea of looking for additional inmate accommodation equivalent to the populations of two whole national prison systems indicates how integral privatization has become to the viability of American imprisonment.

Of course, percentages vary between states, with, for example, about one-quarter of Texas prisoners and about 10 percent of Florida prisoners being held in the private sector. Obviously, private prisons are more integral to penal administration in such states than in those that have barely dipped their toes in the water. The latter could perhaps still reverse direction if they so desired. Surprisingly, California—the imprisonment capital of the free world—still falls into this category. The map indicates levels of apparent commitment as of mid-1996.

As for security ratings, these also indicate how integral the private sector has become to American imprisonment. An early criticism of privatization was that the private sector only took on responsibility for "cream puffs"—that is, minimum-security prisoners at the soft end of the incarceration spectrum and posing no unusual behavioral or custodial problems. There was some justice to this observation. But it was the govern-

Table 23.1. Private Prisons in the United States, March 31, 1993 to December 31, 1996

Date	March 31, 1993	June 30, 1994	December 31, 1994	December 31, 1995	December 31, 1996
Number of private prisons					
Operational	54	60	68	75	84
Procured	18	18	20	17	34
Total	72	78	88	92	118
Rated capacity					
Operational	19,667	23,226	30,821	39,665	46,442
Procured	8,727	18,692	18,334	17,994	31,173
Total	28,394	41,918	49,155	57,659	77,615

Source: Calculated from Thomas 1994; Thomas 1995b; Thomas and Bollinger 1996; and Thomas, Bollinger, and Badalamenti 1997.

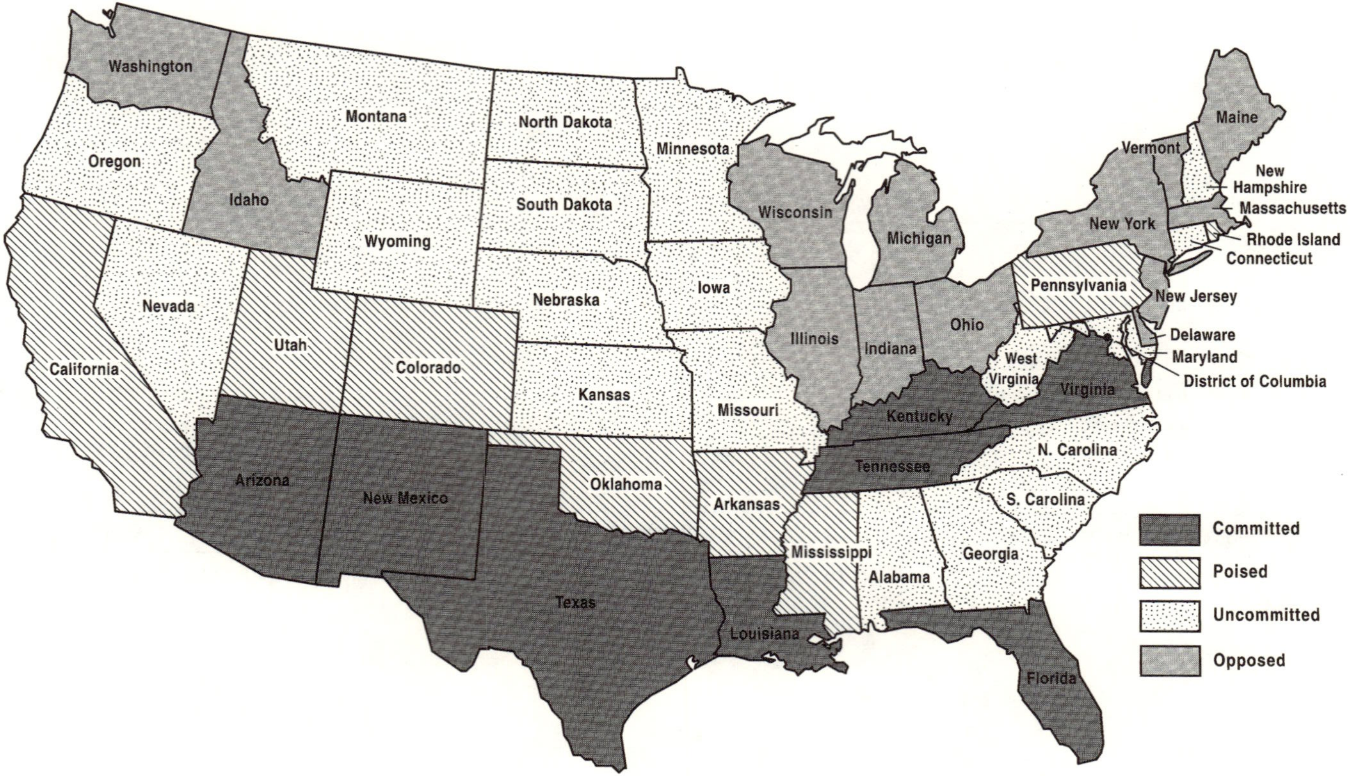
Washington
Oregon
California
Idaho
Nevada
Montana
Wyoming
Utah
Arizona
Colorado
New Mexico
North Dakota
South Dakota
Nebraska
Kansas
Oklahoma
Texas
Minnesota
Iowa
Missouri
Arkansas
Louisiana
Wisconsin
Illinois
Michigan
Indiana
Kentucky
Tennessee
Mississippi
Alabama
Ohio
West Virginia
Virginia
N. Carolina
S. Carolina
Georgia
Florida
Pennsylvania
New York
Vermont
Maine
New Hampshire
Massachusetts
Rhode Island
Connecticut
New Jersey
Delaware
Maryland
District of Columbia
Committed
Poised
Uncommitted
Opposed

Figure 32.1 Commitment to prison privatization, by state, March 31, 1993. Not pictured: Alaska

ment authorities, not private entrepreneurs, who made decisions about what kind of prison, with what level of security regime, and what class of inmate would be privatized, and their initial caution was understandable and proper. The first opportunity the private sector was given to compete for the operation of a maximum-security prison arose in 1990, when the U.S. Marshals Service called for bids relating to the Leavenworth Detention Center in Kansas. Bidding was keen, with CCA being successful; the facility opened in 1992.

Since then, maximum-security private prisons have started to come onstream at regular intervals. As of December 31, 1996, the security ratings were thirty-seven minimum, fifty-eight minimum/medium, sixteen catering for all security levels, and seven maximum security prisons (Thomas, Bollinger, and Badalamenti 1997). The profile of the private sector component of the total prison system is now broadly comparable with that of the public sector component.

As for locations, as of December 31, 1996, private prisons were found or commissioned in twenty-five states, the District of Columbia, and Puerto Rico (though as yet operational in only eighteen states). Five states (Kansas, New Jersey, Ohio, Rhode Island, and Washington) appear on this list only because privatized federal facilities happen to be located within their boundaries, so there is not necessarily local support for privatization. (Interestingly, twelve states—seven of which do not have privatized facilities within their own boundaries—have "outsourced" parts of their prison populations to private prisons in other states.) Moreover, two other states have so far made only tiny commitments. But the remaining eighteen, representing one U.S. state in three, accommodate state and/or local prisoners, mostly the former, under arrangements authorized by state law and look set to expand. Thomas now goes as far as to anticipate the possibility that there may be 276,000 beds in operational or commissioned private prisons by the end of the year 2001 (Thomas, Bollinger, and Badalamenti 1997, pp. x–xii)—exponential growth indeed.

With regard to operators, on December 31, 1996, no less than fifteen were active within the United States. However, CCA and Wackenhut between them dominate market share, and no more than four other companies would seem to have a viable future. Takeovers and amalgamations of the sort characterized by the 1995 takeover of Corrections Partners Inc. by CCA seem certain to occur before long (Thomas and Bollinger 1996, p. v; Harding 1997, pp. 79–80). This is another indicator of an industry that is maturing commercially.

Weighing up the foregoing factors, it is evident that private prisons in the United States are here to stay. A critical mass has been reached in terms of prison and inmate numbers and percentages, custodial responsibilities as manifested by security ratings, participating states, and commercial maturity. In addition, the financing arrangements tie governments into private sector participation in ways that would be difficult and expensive to unscramble.

Privatization in Australia and the United Kingdom

Although commencing a little later than in the United States, the privatization movement has also taken hold in Australia and the United Kingdom. One can likewise say with confidence that private prisons are there to stay.

In Australia the first private prison—at Borallon, in the state of Queensland—was commissioned in 1988 and became operational in 1990. Since then, five more private prisons have been opened in Queensland itself and in three other states, and two more procurement contracts have been let. As of late 1996, about 2,500 prisoners were held in private prisons; this was about 15.0 percent of the national prison population. When, by the end of 1999, the next two prisons are operational, the number will be 3,600 and the percentage an estimated 20.3 (Harding 1997, p. 6). By U.S. standards the numbers are trivial but the percentage enormous.

Australia, like the United States, is a federal state. Four of the eight main jurisdictions have so far permitted privatization, and a fifth is now actively considering doing so. By the end of 1998, one state—Victoria—will hold almost half (about 1,350) of its prisoners in private prisons. Queensland already has one-third (about 1,050) of its population in such facilities. The full range of security ratings is covered in these states, as in Australia generally. Activity so far has been dominated by three companies—one associated with CCA, another associated with Wackenhut, and the third with Group 4, a British-Swedish consortium, which is the market leader in the United Kingdom.

In the United Kingdom the two dominant American companies also head consortia that are prominent players. Each has so far had to take a back seat to Group 4, while a fourth company, Securicor, is just starting to make its mark. The American companies regard overseas activities as being strategically important. CCA, whose 1994 annual report to stockholders stated that "[t]here are powerful market forces driving our industry, and its potential has barely been touched" (p. 7), has recently done a stock deal relating to 20 percent of its issued capital with Sedexho S.A., a French company that is a major provider of both "hotel" and programmatic services to prisons in France and also a general services supplier in more than sixty other countries. Wackenhut, likewise in its 1994 annual report has spoken of "preparing for the third millennium and *the globalization of privatized corrections*" (p. 2, emphasis added), in anticipation of which it has established "a central corporate infrastructure capable of sustaining global operations."

By way of brief excursus, it must be said that it is this archetypally American quest for new markets that has concerned many of the critics of privatization, both within the United States and overseas (Feeley 1991; Nellis 1991; Lilly and Knepper 1992; Christie 1993; Moyle 1993; Baldry 1994; Sparks 1994). Their fear is that penal policy itself will come to be driven simply by the companies' commercial need for a global increase in the use of imprisonment. The justification for this claim is assessed later.

To revert to the main point, the first private prison to become operational in the United Kingdom opened in 1992. Three more have subsequently come onstream. Taking account of operational prisons, firm contracts, and requests for proposals, by the end of the century about 6,800 prisoners will be held in private prisons in the United Kingdom. This would constitute about one-ninth of the present prisoner population. There will be eleven such prisons, which means that their average rated capacity would be in the top half of what is normal in the United Kingdom. As with Australia, the full range of security ratings will be covered.

It would seem, then, that private prisons are integral to penal administration in the United Kingdom also. There was, however, one wild card—that the Labour Party having won the 1997 British election, would change course. The relevant Labour spokesman had been repeatedly on the record as saying that not only would there be no further privatization but also that the existing program would be cut back. It always seemed likely that this purist braggadocio would give way to political realism (Harding 1997, pp. 7–9), for to carry out such a program would cost many hundreds of millions of pounds, an outlay that would expend the prison construction budget for years to come without adding a single bed to already stretched prison capacity. Social democratic governments have to cope with fiscal constraints these days in exactly the same way as economic rationalist governments do, and in the event the incoming Labour government within three weeks of being elected backed away from these postures. It will be a case of business as usual, as far as the private sector is concerned (Prison Reform Trust 1996b, p. 1). Subsequently, while reiterating that "responsibility for the incarceration of offenders must remain with the state," the Home Secretary (prisons minister) not only endorsed the previous government's privatization plans but also renewed an existing contract on the basis that, both operationally and financially, this was the only way that the problems created by an ever-increasing prison population could be managed (Prison Reform Trust 1997, p. 2).

The Fundamental Principle of Accountability

With modern privatization, the prisoner remains the state's prisoner and responsibility, confinement standards and practices are specified at a level no less than that applicable to public sector prisons, and compliance procedures are put in place. In other words, the private entrepreneur remains *accountable* to the state, for he is a delegate, not an independent agent. This, at any rate, is the theory. But how does accountability work in practice?

Accountability in matters of public administration generally is subject to the problem of *capture* or *co-optation*. This terminology has been used to describe situations where "regulators come to be more concerned to serve the interests of the industry with which they are in regular contact than the more remote and abstract public interest" (Grabosky and Braithwaite 1986, p. 198). Predisposing factors include situations where the regulator and the regulatee are drawn from the same sort of professional background and tend to share common subcultural values; gross disparity between the sheer size of the industry and the resources of the regulator, so that the scale of the job to be done means that shortcuts must be taken and discretion exercised; working in a culture where there is little or no organizational support for a firm approach toward the process of regulation, for example, because the regulator is also assigned the role of promoting or facilitating the successful development of the business; and too close a relational distance between regulator and regulatee, leading to a reduced propensity to invoke formal sanctions to enforce compliance (Black 1976).

Conforming with these criteria, capture has thus emerged as a prominent problem in areas such as occupational health and safety (most frequently in the mining industries), environmental protection, banking and financial services, and civil aviation. There are tangible early signs that regulatory regimes governing private prisons are also vulnerable, principally because the regulators and the regulatees are part of the same professional subculture and because the relational distance is so close.

There is an additional structural reason that capture may occur—that the public sector prison authorities, as the regulators of private prison standards and performance, may well overidentify with the problems and needs of the private sector operators. For, in a sense, the public sector *needs* the private sector to succeed, and cannot afford to reveal its failures too starkly. This is because the entrepreneur has become in reality the public sector's agent for the attainment of its formal goals and the discharge of its statutory responsibilities (Sherman 1980). It has thus been posited, on the basis of detailed analysis of the regulation of private prisons: "Whenever the principal operator in a public service industry is empowered to contract out or to delegate to others some part of its own operational responsibilities, and in so doing it takes on the role of regulatory agency in relation to the activities of those delegates, there is a high risk that some degree of capture or co-optation will occur" (Harding 1997, p. 48).

For this reason, the preferred model of privatization is one where responsibility for the allocation and supervision of private prison contracts does not lie with the public prison authority itself but with some other independent body (Harding 1997, pp. 158–65). Unfortunately, the archetypal American model is precisely the one identified as being potentially most flawed—the public authority selecting and then supposedly supervising the private sector operator. Commenting on such a situation, the

Tennessee Select Oversight Committee—a subcommittee of the state legislature, supplemented by experts—observed:

> The Tennessee Department of Corrections ("TDOC") central office was placed in an awkward role by being contract and compliance monitor, while trying to assist CCA [the prison operator] in the understanding of policy, TDOC system issues, compliance requirements, etc. . . . The state should establish an independent monitoring and operational compliance capability for corrections contracts. . . . The potential conflicts and the complexities require a separate contract monitor. (Tennessee Select Oversight Committee on Corrections 1995, p. 64)

Comparable role conflicts, with consequential lapses in accountability, have been identified in the British and Australian systems (Harding 1997, pp. 42–47). It is important to emphasize that this is not necessarily an adverse reflection on the personnel involved; lapses are a structural inevitability.

That being so, the optimal American model is that found in Florida. The first phase of privatization in that state was marked by a reluctance, tantamount to refusal, of the Department of Corrections to use its statutory power so as to involve the private sector. Accordingly, in 1993 the legislature set up a new body, the Florida Correctional Privatization Commission, to perform this function (Thomas 1995b). Statutes require that each private prison contract provide for the appointment of a monitor:

> [The contract] shall require the selection and appointment of a full-time contract monitor. The contract monitor shall be appointed and supervised by the commission. The contractor is required to reimburse the commission for the salary and expenses of the contract monitor. It is the obligation of the contractor to provide suitable office space for the contract monitor at the correctional facility. The contract monitor shall have unlimited access to the correctional facility. (Florida Statutes 1993, ch. 957.04(1)(g))

Thus, the monitor works to a different line of command, one that is not responsible for the public sector prisons in the state and is indeed in some sense a competitor of the public sector.

However, even this model has its limitations. Foremost among them is that of resources. A single monitor—with virtually no administrative support and no provision made for backup—is simply not adequate to oversee standards and contract compliance in a large prison. (One of the existing Florida private prisons holds 1,318 prisoners.) To do the job, that person is likely to have to cut corners, to depend on guidance from the contractors, to reduce on-site inspection time, and so on. The bones of the model are strong, but it needs much more flesh.

The other American privatization states to a greater or lesser extent leave the public sector authorities in something of a role conflict when it comes to making the private operator fully accountable for contract compliance. A stronger model is found, however, in the United Kingdom. There, the monitoring system is resource-rich (at least two senior officials, plus administrative support, for each private prison), though with a somewhat confused reporting line. However, there is extra structural strength at a key point—that the external (contract compliance) monitors are also responsible for inmate disciplinary processes. Officers employed by the private operators can file disciplinary charges, but adjudication is carried out by the monitors in the name and on behalf of the public authority. This is an immensely important symbol that prisoners, whether held in public or private prisons, remain the state's prisoners and that the state must continue to take ultimate responsibility for their control and welfare.

In the United States the conventional position is that discipline is the sole responsibility of the contractor—a frontline management tool for running a prison effectively. The main exception to this is, once more, Florida. In that state, while disciplinary hearings are initially conducted by the contractor's staff, the latter may not directly impose punishments. Instead, they must make recommendations to a classification officer, who is an official of the state Department of Corrections. That person, in turn, will either accept the recommendations or prepare a written statement explaining the basis for rejection or modification. Subject to a further appeal process, the classification officer's amended recommendation becomes the applicable punishment. This is a somewhat more confused symbol of the state's continuing ultimate responsibility for the control and welfare of prisoners than that found in the United Kingdom. But for all that, a symbol it is, standing in stark contrast to the normal American position.

Accountability Processes in the Public and Private Systems

One must be careful in referring to accountability deficits not to speak as if the public system were some sort of paragon. Quite the contrary. Despite the burgeoning of class actions as to conditions—a line of litigation now progressively being constricted by the Supreme Court and by federal legislation—much of the prison regime remains beyond the reach of external supervision (Bronstein and Gainsborough 1996). However, in two respects accountability is stronger—or at any rate less weak—with regard to private prisons.

The first relates to American Correctional Association (ACA) accreditation. The American accreditation system is voluntary, and to this point only 80 percent of public system prisons have sought or obtained accreditation. Yet private prison contracts invariably require that the company obtain such accreditation within a specified period—an obligation that public correctional authorities have been somewhat reluctant to impose on themselves. To be sure, this is not the most demanding test, and in some regards even leaves U.S. prisons short of compliance with the

United Nations Standard Minimum Rules for the Treatment of Prisoners (1957). But it is a lot better than nothing.

The second concerns litigation for deprivation of civil rights under 42 U.S.C. §1983. Thomas (1991) argues that the private sector's nominal vulnerability to litigation under this provision exceeds that of the public sector because private corporations derive no protection from the Eleventh Amendment. The precise impact of this difference has yet to be seen, though to date, as far as is known, there are very few cases in the pipeline.

In Australia and the United Kingdom, the overall picture is that the private sector is subject to all of the same accountability processes as the public sector—the ombudsman or prisons ombudsman, boards of visitors, the chief inspector of prisons in the United Kingdom, parliamentary scrutiny, and so on—and that in practice these processes seem so far to have been applied a little more vigorously than in relation to the public sector itself. In addition, private prisons have on-site monitoring systems not found in public prisons (Harding 1997, pp. 51–66).

So it can be said that the formal mechanisms of accountability are somewhat more far-reaching in relation to the private than the public sector. To say this is not to contradict the already identified danger and occasional reality of capture or co-optation. It is simply to emphasize that, whatever defects of accountability there are in the private sector, they do not arise because it is somehow a shabby version of a shining public sector.

Essential Elements of Accountability

Several of the key elements of effective accountability are implicit in the foregoing discussion. It is useful to make these and the other elements explicit, so that they may be kept before one in assessing the place that private prisons may have in the penal regimes of the future. These elements are as follows (Harding 1997, pp. 27–31):

1. The distinction between the allocation and the administration of punishment must be rigorously maintained, with the private sector's role being confined to its administration;
2. There must be safeguards to ensure that penal policy cannot be driven by those who stand to make a profit out of it;
3. The private sector's activities and its relationship with governments must be open and publicly visible;
4. What is expected of the private sector must be clearly specified in statutes, contracts, and other relevant documentation;
5. A dual system must not be permitted to evolve, one in which there is a run-down and demoralized public sector and a renovated and vibrant private sector;
6. Independent research and evaluation, with untrammeled publication rights, must be built into private sector arrangements;

7. Custodial regimes, programs, and personnel must be equitable and culturally appropriate;
8. The probity of contractors must be checked and monitored;
9. Financial accountability must be effective; and
10. The state must in the last resort be able to reclaim the management of private sector prisons.

Naturally, compliance with such all-encompassing standards varies, both within the United States and in the other privatization countries. But it is possible to make some generalizations about the American position, as follows.

First, the allocation-administration dichotomy has been inadequately understood and applied. Potentially, it is a raw point in the development of privatization, one that, if mishandled, could bring American privatization under intense scrutiny.

Second, despite their gung-ho rhetoric of expansion, the companies have so far not been driving penal policy. The commencement of contemporary privatization lagged far behind those exponential increases in prison population that brought on the crises of overcrowding and court supervision and that highlighted the inability of the public sector to finance the required new accommodation. Indeed, there is an immense and still increasing amount of slack to take up. Even if prison populations magically began to decrease tomorrow, there is a long lag in new accommodation, as well as a huge backlog of substandard accommodation awaiting private sector participation, in the context of public sector financial constraints.

Third, the procurement process is no less open to public scrutiny for prison contracts than for anything else; and though this aspect of American public administration can be corrupt, there is to date no evidence to suggest that this has been the case with private prison contracts. The alleged problems revolve more around alleged "lowballing," to get a contract and then jack up the price upon renewal, than around corruption. Contracts are publicly accessible, and there is growing sophistication and skill in the manner in which contracting agencies specify what it is they require for their money. Also, there is already a strong research tradition to support outsider evaluation of the actual prison operations, not merely of the abstract documentation.

It is a tough business, however, not one for the commercially fainthearted; and there is certainly a widespread belief among critics (Lilly and Knepper 1992; Baldry 1994) that the probity and ethics of some of the operators leave something to be desired. In some respects, procedures for investigating such concerns are deficient. The probity in doubt is more attitudinal (antidemocratic, indifferent to prisoner welfare, racist, and so on) than financial. As to the latter, the way contracts are structured leaves very little room for even the most imaginative forms of embezzlement, so the accountability with which we are concerned is mainly that of ensuring that the services contracted for at the agreed price are actually delivered—contract compliance. As mentioned, there can be a problem of regulatory capture here.

As for reclaiming the private prison, all states adequately cater to this, in either the enabling statute or the contract or both. Indeed, there is one example of this already having occurred: the 1995 termination by the federal Immigration and Naturalization Service (INS) of the contract of Esmor (now reincorporated as Correctional Services Corporation) to manage a facility in Elizabeth, New Jersey (Thomas 1996, p. 39; Harding 1997, pp. 77–78). This was done following major disturbances at the prison and clear evidence of malpractice toward inmates. However, as mentioned previously, some inhibitions naturally arise out of the fact that the typical DCFM contract contemplates a long-term relationship between the parties as being the norm; contract cancellation is the last resort, to be used only in extreme cases.

The Achievements and Benefits of Prison Privatization

However, rather than dwelling on accountability solely from the point of view of breaches of desirable standards, it is instructive to try to assess what privatization has achieved. Areas of failure and deficiency, and how these may be remedied, should emerge as the counterpoint to such a discussion.

Confinement Quality

The quality of confinement in the public prison system of the United States has been below acceptable standards for decades, as evidenced by the fact that so many systems or parts of systems—still thirty-six as at mid-1996 (National Prison Project 1996)—were operating or have operated under court order or consent decree. In crime prevention terms, the standard of confinement actually matters. The prison experience is notorious for causing further deterioration in the chronic offender's ability to cope in the outside world. Public hostility to humanitarian issues and philosophical disillusionment with rehabilitation (Martinson 1974) should not distract one from this fundamental point. A penal objective, minimalist enough to suit the temper of the times, would be to ensure that the prisoner does not undergo further social or character deformation while incarcerated (Cross 1971). In this context, in a seminal article, Logan has developed a "confinement quality index" that provides a viable way of evaluating and comparing prison performance: "The criteria proposed here for comparative evaluation of prisons are normative, rather than consequentialist or utilitarian. They are based on a belief that individual prisons ought to be judged primarily according to the propriety and quality of what goes on inside their walls—factors over which prison officials may have considerable control" (1992, p. 579).

Logan goes on to identify eight distinct dimensions of prison regime quality: security, safety, order, care, activity, justice, conditions, and management. These notions are further specified by identification of subthemes. A confinement quality index can then be formulated, drawing on formal documentation and protocols, staff perceptions, and prisoner attitudes. Comparative ratings can be made using statistical methods.

Numerous evaluations have already been made, not exactly in terms of Logan's index but certainly in ways that are congruent with it. The findings of these studies need not be set out here; comprehensive metareviews are available (Thomas and Logan 1993; Shichor 1995; Bottomley et al. 1996; Thomas 1996). Suffice it to say that, to date, the private sector generally measures up better than the public. While this is not surprising—given its newness, the relief of prisoners at getting away from the overcrowding and the stultifying rituals of the public system, the comparative youth of its staff, and the enthusiasm of the wardens, most of whom are frustrated refugees from the red tape and demoralization of the public sector—it is nevertheless indicative that alternative means of service delivery may indeed raise the performance of the system.

The other main point is that it is now apparent that measuring tools can be found, and that the very occurrence of privatization has stimulated their development. The tradition of public prison systems had been wholly input-directed; and although such an approach is not literally the antithesis of evaluation, nevertheless the two notions sit uneasily together. By contrast, the output-oriented ambience of privatized prisons—an ambience that is now moving into the public prison system—is more susceptible to measuring aspects of performance (Donahue 1989, pp. 79–82).

Contract Compliance

There are other ways of getting a handle on confinement quality and its close cousin, contract compliance. They include accreditation, prisoner litigation, and contract renewals.

It is an invariable condition of contracts, often mandated by statute, that the private American operators obtain American Correctional Association accreditation for the prisons within a defined time limit after commencing operations. This requirement is imposed even by those states that have not imposed the same obligation on their own state agencies in relation to the public prisons (Keve 1996, p. 132; Harding 1997, pp. 138–39). These standards focus on regime quality, due process, staff training, and the whole range of matters that are directed at making incarceration a tolerable experience. There is no known example to date of a private prison failing to reach this threshold level (Thomas 1996, p. 42).

Thomas also points out that "a recent and reasonably careful review . . . fails to reveal a single [privatized] facility that is operating under a consent decree or court order as a consequence of suits brought against it by prisoner plaintiffs" (1996, p. 40). This is in marked contrast to the public sector. While it is early, and litigation may still be in the pipeline, this is nevertheless some indication that the standards contracted are adequate and that there is broad compliance with them.

As for contract renewals, there are two examples of nonrenewal (in addition to the contract termination of the INS facility at Elizabeth, New Jersey, mentioned earlier). Thomas (1996, p. 39) tellingly points out that the operators concerned are no longer in the business—a contrast indeed with disgraced public agencies, such as those responsible for the mayhem at Attica or Santa Fe.

Prisoners' Rights and the Prison Regime

Another way of gauging the performance of the private sector is to focus on those aspects of incarceration that can cause so much difficulty in the public system, namely, overcrowding, disturbances and riots, inmate drug use, escapes, suicide and self-harm, intimidation, gangs and bullying, health, including AIDS, racism, and the treatment of vulnerable and protection prisoners. Obviously, such matters are key aspects of Logan's confinement quality index. Each is of such importance that it can justifiably stand on its own as a performance indicator.

Yet none of those factors has yet been subjected to the kinds of rigorous evaluation that are now found in relation to the public system (e.g., Jacobs 1977—the prison regime; Paulus 1988—health; Genders and Player 1989—race relations; Adams 1994—riots). Again, this is not surprising, reflecting the recency of private prisons as an identifiable sector of penal administration. A brief overview of the situation to date (Harding 1997, pp. 123–27, 129–30) has identified some early problems with riot control and suicide prevention in private prisons, though more tangibly in the United Kingdom and Australia than in the United States. Clearly, these areas should be kept under review as privatization continues to spread.

Costs

The catalysts for contemporary privatization were cost shifting of capital outlays and cost control of recurrent expenditures. The first objective has been achieved through the DCFM contract and the funding device of certificates of participation. An additional benefit has been the reduction of construction costs, for, when contracting directly for construction projects, government agencies have been notoriously soft targets for both companies and workers. Furthermore, it has now become common practice for the state to require the bidder to identify a suitable location, arrange for its purchase, and obtain all the necessary planning permits; this is another area where considerable savings are starting to be made.

As for operating costs, there are many evaluations available that seem to establish the superior efficiency of the private over the public sector

(Thomas 1996, pp. 22–38). Of course, one must be careful to compare like with like; if cost reduction were simply a function of inferior conditions, a whole different set of ethical and political considerations would come into play. Nevertheless, taking account of such factors, it has been said that "so much experience and so much evidence about correctional privatization supports the hypothesis that privatization is capable of yielding meaningful cost savings" (p. 37).

It should be said, however, that a U.S. government agency has recently expressed, albeit rather lamely, a contrary opinion. Reviewing five post-1991 cost and quality evaluations, the General Accounting Office stated that "we could not conclude . . . that privatization of correctional facilities will not save money. However, these studies do not offer substantial evidence that savings have occurred" (General Accounting Office 1996, p. 3). In many ways the report is inadequate: for example, it ignores several other key studies and partially misconstrues those it does examine. Generally, its greatest deficiency is that it appears to have been carried out by an agency that understands very little about the social, structural, and human dynamics of prisons—a weakness characterized by the fact that the authors seem to expect laboratory-like, experimental stability as a basis for comparative evaluations and thus would deny any validity to studies that fail to meet these unattainable criteria. Thomas's conclusion is certainly to be preferred, and has subsequently been fortified by a detailed study of the Louisiana system (Archambeault and Deis 1996).

In this context it is important to note that no American state mandates acceptance of the cheapest bid; a qualitative element is retained in the procurement criteria, but only after a threshold cost criterion has been met. In several states, this threshold is expressed in terms of a percentage saving on what it would notionally cost the public sector to do the same job: for example, 7 percent in Florida and 10 percent in Texas and Kentucky. In other states, the formula is more flexible: for example, in Tennessee if "the contractor is providing at least the same quality of services as the state at a lower cost or if the contractor is providing services superior to those provided by the state at essentially the same cost" (Tennessee Statutes, 41-24-105(d)).

Once the applicable criterion has been met, costs are assigned a significant but not a determinative role. Once more, the exact protocols differ. For example, Florida is highly formulaic, mandating precise scores in numerous subareas according to clearly defined criteria. But at the other end of the spectrum, Virginia provides that, after interviewing and negotiating with offerors who have reached the final short list, "the Department shall select the offeror which, in its opinion, has made the best proposal and shall award the contract to that offeror" (a formula derived from Virginia Statutes 53.1-262, 1–5). Clearly, it is possible in principle for a contract to be awarded to a company that is not the lowest bidder. Information is not available on whether this has actually happened in any state. However, the hazards of accepting a "lowball" bid are evident enough.

In Australia, procurement documents usually specify that the contract will not necessarily be awarded to the lowest bidder—though to date the lowest bidder has always been successful. In the United Kingdom, the notion of "deliverability" is built into the evaluation of bids, likewise with the intent of retaining the possibility of permitting lawful acceptance of a bid that may not be the cheapest but seems to be the best. In fact, this has actually happened; the very first contract of all, relating to the Wolds, was awarded to a bidder that came in as only the second lowest (Harding 1997, pp. 100–101).

Enhancing the Prison System as a Whole

It is all too easy to slip into speaking of "private prisons" as if they were a discrete entity. However, to do so is to risk obscuring the fact that the prison system of each state is an integrated one, albeit with public and private components or sectors. This perception accords with the fundamental view that the prisoner remains the state's prisoner, for whose custody, safety, and welfare the state ultimately remains responsible. It also accords with practical realities such as prisoner transfers between institutions, statewide applicability of special needs programs, parole, and so on.

Cross-Fertilization Between the Private and Public Sectors

In the long run, the most robust justification for privatization may lie in its impact on the performance of the public prison sector, with consequential improvement of the system as a whole. This does not merely relate to costs—though, as already mentioned, the evidence is now stacking up unambiguously that the private sector can deliver comparable services more cheaply.

No less significant is the question of program quality and regime standards. The early research evidence, now starting to accumulate, suggests that experienced inmates (a highly relevant data source but one habitually ignored in public sector corrections), staff, and managers each regards private prisons as by and large doing a better job than public systems (Harding 1997, pp. 115–19). The experience of the Tennessee Select Oversight Committee lends support to such impressions. In that state, the private contractor must provide either the same quality of services as the state at a lower cost or superior services at essentially the same cost. As contract renewal time approached with regard to the South Central Correctional Facility, run by Correctional Corporation of America, the Select Oversight Committee commenced a series of intensive reviews, lining up South Central against two comparable state-managed prisons. In the year that passed between the first and the second such reviews, both the private and the state prisons raised their standards by between 8 and 15 percent—not merely in terms of cost control but also by measurable qualitative standards (akin to Logan's confinement quality index). Evidently, competitive oversight by an independent monitor was a mechanism for bringing about mutual improvement (Tennessee Select Oversight Committee on Corrections 1995).

Again, there is emerging evidence to indicate that this is not an isolated case. For example, states such as Louisiana that require ACA accreditation of private prisons and previously had not imposed a comparable requirement on themselves are now starting to do so. There is even clearer evidence in the United Kingdom experience of standards being lifted through the example of the private sector (Harding 1997, pp. 139–43).

Public prison systems have been allowed to run down for decades. Privatization, because it must be purposeful and its objectives specified if prison services are to be contracted out at all, paradoxically provides a circuit breaker for the public system to assess where it is going and how it is going to get there. Those highly motivated personnel who still enter the public system, despite demoralizing decades of governmental neglect and public indifference, now have a tool they can use to bring about change. The signs are that they are starting to use this tool effectively.

Market Testing

This last assertion is borne out by the experience with "market testing." In a broad sense this means no more than that the public authority seeks to ascertain a "true price" at which its own agents can deliver given services, so that this may be compared with the price offered by the private sector. This may simply be so as to have a benchmark against which to see whether the private sector bids are realistic (the British and Australian way), or it may be to ascertain in a tightly focused way whether value is being offered for money (the U.S. model).

However, there is a British and Australian variant to this, one that permits the public sector to bid against the private sector *in a genuine contest*. The decision as to whether a new prison is to be allocated to the public or the private sector will thus be made only *after the bids are received*. Clearly, the public sector must not be judge in its own cause, so quite elaborate "Chinese wall" arrangements have to be made to handle bids (or, better still, the whole system constructed so that contracts are awarded by a body that is not itself operationally involved in the running of prisons). As long as these procedural mechanisms can be sorted out, this kind of market testing is at the cutting edge of the privatization debate.

For its explicit premise is that the public sector, goaded or liberated by the presence of the private sector, can and will improve its performance. This means formulating its outputs more carefully, rethinking its staffing inputs, meeting applicable regime standards, being monitored in the same way as the private sector, putting a price on the package, sticking to that price in the reassuring knowledge that the contracting authority must also keep its side of the bargain, devolving control, and so on. In principle, this kind of market testing—both the winning of a contract and then satisfactory performance—is the acid test of the efficacy of privatization. If the public sector can outperform the private sector, cross-fertilization must surely have occurred.

In the United States, there is no precise equivalent to this kind of market testing, though there does not seem any reason of principle why such procedures should not be allowed to develop. The nearest approach to date seems to be competition between two levels of government within any given state entity (e.g., the state and the county over running a county jail) and competition between two states as to whether one can accommodate the other's prisoners more cheaply than it can house them itself. But these are distorted models of competition from which one can learn very little.

By contrast, in both the United Kingdom and Australia, there have been examples of market testing in which the public sector has outbid the private sector. In the United Kingdom this occurred in relation to Manchester-Strangeways prison. This 1,100-bed prison had been torched and ransacked in 1990, was being rebuilt at public expense, and was due to be reopened in 1994. The Home Office called for management contract bids. Three were received from the private sector and one from the Prison Service agency itself. The quasi-independent Contracts and Competition Group within the Home Office eventually awarded the contract to the Prison Service.

This decision was received with a great deal of cynicism, with critics suggesting that the public sector had always had the inside running in relation to such an important British prison in an area where trade unionism was so strong. However, other information suggests that the contest had been genuine and the outcome reached on the merits. Unfortunately, the Home Office soon played into the hands of the cynics. Having in effect contracted to pay fixed amounts in return for specified inputs and outputs for a period of five years, it almost immediately "breached" the contract with its own agency by subjecting Manchester to the same level of funding cuts and centralized directives as were imposed on the remainder of public sector prisons. An official inquiry commented: "If market testing of the management of existing prisons is to establish credibility within and outside the Prison Service, . . . the prison [must be] treated as closely as possible to a privately-run establishment" (Tumim 1996, p. 114).

In Australia the market-testing exercise in which the public sector beat the private sector was of a more radical kind, being a DCFM contract. This necessarily involved the public sector agency—the Queensland Corrective Services Commission—entering into consortium arrangements with private sector entrepreneurs, in particular a construction company. Yet so well had the commission learned from the experience of seeing two earlier contracts bid and awarded to the private sector that it was now able successfully to beat them at their own game. The prison was scheduled to receive its first intake of prisoners in the second half of 1997.

The private sector, however, was not convinced that the procedure met probity standards, believing that the commission had in effect pre-judged its own cause in its own favor—the same concern as had risen in the United Kingdom with regard to Manchester-Strangeways. An official inquiry (Legislative Assembly of Queenland 1996) ruled that the procedure had been proper and the outcome justified, but nevertheless that henceforth the commission as a purchaser of prison services should be differentiated from the commission as a provider. Accordingly, a separate public sector provider—QCorr—was set up and incorporated. This will certainly strengthen the bidding system for future prison contracts. Meanwhile, the construction and commissioning of Woodford went ahead, the initial intake of prisoners being received in March 1997.

Market testing of this kind, then, is still at a fledgling stage. But it is at the cutting edge of privatization and should become part of the American approach if the full benefits of privatization are to be realized.

The Future of Privatization: Expansion

The likelihood is that the three established markets—the United States, Australia, and the United Kingdom—will continue to expand. The United States is by far the most important of these markets because of its enormous prisoner population (the highest rate of peacetime civilian incarceration in the history of the world). Even if Thomas's estimate of 276,000 is not met, it would be surprising if under 150,000, or about 9 percent of the nation's inmates, were held in private prisons by the year 2001. The United Kingdom is a little more problematic, but Australia seems certain to continue further down the privatization path. Of course, only small numbers are involved there—at most 7,500 inmates in the United Kingdom and 5,000 in Australia by 2001.

The most probable areas for expansion into new markets are developed, Westernized, anglophone countries such as New Zealand (already committed to the request for proposals stage for one prison) and Canada (just dipping its toe into the water). It should be noted that it is often said that France already has adopted privatization. But in the relevant sense this is not in fact the case, for the model adopted in that country is that the state retains total custodial control of facilities while contracting out only program services and some of the "hotel" services—a completely different model of privatization, known appropriately enough as *prisons semi-privees*.

The main companies are also actively looking for other areas: Africa, South America, parts of Asia, Europe, even Israel. They may well make some progress—perhaps in South Africa, the Philippines, Thailand,

Panama, Venezuela, or Papua New Guinea. However, they will generally encounter strong cultural and political resistance so that expansion into new markets is likely to be slow and fragmented (Harding 1997, pp. 150–15).

Accountability

Although there are strong economic forces driving privatization, they will ultimately be negated if the quality of the services deteriorates below an acceptable standard. Effective accountability is crucial not only in the public interest but also to secure the survival of private sector corrections. So far, background factors—expanding prison populations, fiscal constraints, the demoralization of public system corrections—have combined to give privatization a dream run. However, repetitive or systemwide failures by the private sector, of the sort found at Attica or Santa Fe, would cause the debate about private prisons to be relocated.

The kind of accountability requirements identified in this chapter must be safeguarded. Contracts must be written clearly; they must encapsulate prisoners' rights and regime standards; contract compliance and on-site monitoring must be provided for; information about the whole gamut of prison operations must be publicly accessible; and, above all, the regulators must avoid capture or co-optation. Effective accountability also is crucial if the positive impact of privatization is to spill over into the public sector component of the total prison system.

Research

The actual working of accountability mechanisms must be a prime item in the research agenda. Research of this kind should habitually be carried out at both the micro level (particular facilities) and the macro level (systemwide), and the authorities and the companies must be prepared to cooperate with this. In the past there has been some ambivalence in this regard, with the authorities in the United Kingdom and the operating companies in Australia sometimes being less than cooperative. To date, however, there does not seem to have been the same problem in the United States.

Another key area for research is the quality of confinement. The ideas developed by Logan (1992) are tangible and measurable, and should form part of the ongoing research agenda of both the private and the public sectors. The most sensitive areas of confinement should receive particular attention: deaths and self-injury in custody; prisoner health and safety generally, including AIDS and communicable diseases; drug use in prisons; and racism. A comparative private-public perspective will usually enhance such research, which should provide crucial performance indicators.

Above all, perhaps, if we are talking about value for money, the efficacy and impact of various kinds of program should be regularly evaluated. While there are so many independent variables in recidivism research that it would be well-nigh impossible to attribute better or worse recidivism scores to the impact of confinement in and programs at a private sector rather than a public sector prison, nevertheless intermediate outcomes can be evaluated. These include successful completion of trade or educational diplomas, employment upon release, maintenance of supportive family situations while incarcerated, and other matters that are well understood to be associated with desistance from or delayed resumption of criminal careers. Once more, a comparative element is essential.

In summary, the advent of private prisons provides an opportunity to build a research/modification/evaluation loop more firmly into prison operations, to the overall benefit of inmates, operators, and the public interest.

Conclusions

In corrections, fashions come and fashions go; nothing is permanent. Private prisons came back into fashion in the mid-1980s in a format that was fundamentally more acceptable than the model of a century earlier. Undoubtedly, privatization possesses the potential to bring about improvement across the whole system. But by the same token, serious slippage in accountability mechanisms and quality control could have a deleterious effect on prison regimes. This might occur, for example, if whole systems were contracted out (raised as a possibility for Tennessee in 1997) or if the right to use prison labor went with the contract (hinted at in Georgia in 1996).

As private prisons are here to stay for the foreseeable future, it is incumbent on everyone involved—governments, legislatures, private operators, public prison authorities, prisoners' rights lawyers, activist groups, researchers, the media, and citizens generally—to try to ensure that they are effectively regulated and properly accountable. If that is done, future questions regarding the true value of private prisons in penal administration will be able to be identified more sharply and answered more definitively.

References

Adams, R. 1994. *Prison Riots in Britain and the USA.* London: Macmillan.

American Bar Association. 1989. *Report to the House of Delegates, February 13, 1989.* Washington, D.C.: American Bar Association, Criminal Justice Section.

Archambeault, W., and D. Deis. 1996. *Cost Effectiveness Comparisons of Private Versus Public Prisons in Louisiana: A Comprehensive Analysis of*

Allen, Avoyelles and Winn Correctional Centres. Baton Rouge: Louisiana State University.

Baldry, E. 1994. "U.S.A. Prison Privateers: Neo-Colonialists in a Southern Land." In *Private Prisons and Police: Recent Australian Trends,* edited by P. Moyle. Sydney: Pluto Press.

Black, D. 1976. *The Behavior of Law.* New York: Academic Press.

Bottomley, K., A. James, E. Clare, and A. Liebling. 1996. "Evaluating Private Prisons: The Criminological Challenge." Paper presented at the annual conference of the Australian and New Zealand Society of Criminology, Wellington, New Zealand, January/February.

Bronstein, A., and J. Gainsborough. 1996. "Prison Litigation: Past, Present and Future." *Overcrowded Times* 7(3):1, 15–20.

Christie, N. 1993. *Crime Control as Industry: Towards GULAGS, Western Style?* London: Routledge.

Cross, R. 1971. *Punishment, Prison and the Public: An Assessment of Penal Reform in the Twentieth Century by an Armchair Penologist.* London: Stevens and Sons.

Donahue, J. 1989. *The Privatization Decision: Public Ends, Private Means.* New York: Basic Books.

Etheridge, P., and J. Marquart. 1993. "Private Prisons in Texas: The New Penology for Profit." *Justice Quarterly* 10:29–48.

Feeley, M. 1991. "The Privatization of Prisons in Historical Perspective." *Criminal Justice Research Bulletin* 6(2):1–10.

Genders, E., and E. Player. 1989. *Race Relations in Prisons.* Oxford: Clarendon Press.

General Accounting Office. 1996. *Private and Public Prisons: Studies Comparing Operational Costs and/or Quality of Service.* Washington, D.C.: General Accounting Office.

Grabosky, P., and J. Braithwaite. 1986. *Of Manners Gentle: Enforcement Strategies of Australian Business Regulatory Agencies.* Melbourne: Oxford University Press.

Harding, R. 1997. *Private Prisons and Public Accountability.* New Brunswick, N.J.: Transaction.

Jacobs, J. 1977. *Stateville: The Penitentiary in Mass Society.* Chicago: University of Chicago Press.

Keve, P. 1996. *Measuring Excellence: The History of Corrections Standards and Accreditation.* Washington, D.C.: American Correctional Association.

Legislative Assembly of Queensland. 1996. *Construction of the New Woodford Correctional Centre.* Report No. 34. Brisbane: Government of Queensland.

Lilly, J., and P. Knepper. 1992. "An International Perspective on the Privatization of Corrections." *Howard Journal* 31:174–91.

Logan, C. 1992. "Well Kept: Comparing Quality of Confinement in Private and Public Prisons." *Journal of Criminal Law and Criminology* 83:577–613.

Martinson, R. 1974. "What Works? Questions and Answers About Prison Reform." *Public Interest* 35:22–54.

McDonald, D. 1990. "When Government Fails: Going Private as a Last Resort." In *Private Prisons and the Public Interest,* edited by D. McDonald. Brunswick, N.J.: Rutgers University Press.

———. 1992. "Private Penal Institutions." In *Crime and Justice: A Review of Research,* vol. 16, edited by Michael Tonry. Chicago: University of Chicago Press.

Moyle, P. 1993. "Privatisation of Prisons in New South Wales and Queensland: A Review of Some Key Developments in Australia." *Howard Journal* 32:231–50.

National Prison Project. 1989. *Status Report: The Courts and the Prisons.* Washington, D.C.: National Prison Project.

———. 1996. *The Annual Status Report on the States and the Courts.* Washington, D.C.: National Prison Project.

Nellis, M. 1991. "Electronic Monitoring of Offenders in England and Wales: Recent Developments and Future Prospects." *British Journal of Criminology* 31:165–88.

Paulus, P. 1988. *Prison Crowding: A Psychological Perspective.* New York: Springer-Verlag.

Prison Reform Trust. 1996a. *Prison Privatisation Report International,* no. 3. London: Prison Reform Trust.

———. 1996b. *Prison Privatisation Report International,* no. 10. London: Prison Reform Trust.

———. 1997. *Prison Privatisatism Report International, no. 12.* London: Prison Reform Trust.

Robbins, I. 1988. *The Legal Dimensions of Private Incarceration.* Washington, D.C.: American Bar Association.

Sherman, L. 1980. "Three Models of Organizational Corruption in Agencies of Social Control." *Social Problems* 27:478–91.

Shichor, D. 1995. *Punishment for Profit: Private Prisons, Public Concerns.* Newbury Park, Calif.: Sage.

Sparks, R. 1994. "Can Prisons Be Legitimate? Penal Politics, Privatization, and the Timeliness of an Old Idea." In *Prisons in Context,* edited by R. King and M. Maguire. Oxford: Clarendon Press.

Tennessee Select Oversight Committee on Corrections. 1995. *Comparative Evaluation of Privately-Managed CCA Prison and State-Managed Prototypical Prisons.* Nashville, Tenn.: Tennessee Legislature.

Thomas, C. 1991. "Prisoners' Rights and Correctional Privatization." *Business and Professional Ethics Journal* 10:3–46.

———. 1994. *Private Adult Correctional Facility Census.* 7th ed. Gainesville: University of Florida, Center for Studies in Criminology and Law.

———. 1995a. *Planning for the Future of the Florida Correctional Privatization Commission.* Gainesville: University of Florida, Center for Studies in Criminology and Law.

———. 1995b. *Private Adult Correctional Facility Census.* 8th ed. Gainesville: University of Florida, Center for Studies in Criminology and Law.

———. 1996. "Correctional Privatization: The Issues and the Evidence." Paper presented at the Privatization of Correctional Services Conference, Toronto, Canada, July.

Thomas, C., and D. Bollinger. 1996. *Private Adult Correctional Facility Census.* 9th ed. Gainesville: University of Florida, Center for Studies in Criminology and Law.

Thomas, C., D. Bollinger, and J. Badalamenti. 1997. *Private Adult Correc-*

tional Facility Census. 10th ed. Gainesville: University of Florida, Center for Studies in Criminology and Law.

Thomas, C., and C. Logan. 1993. "The Development, Present Status, and Future Potential of Correctional Privatization in America." In *Privatizing Correctional Institutions,* edited by G. Bowman, S. Hakim, and P. Seidenstat. Brunswick, N.J.: Transaction.

Tumim, S. 1996. *H.M. Prison Manchester: Report of a Full Inspection by H.M. Chief Inspector of Prisons.* London: Home Office.

Part VII

PUNISHMENT

24

Penal Theories

ANDREW VON HIRSCH

Undertaking a survey of recent penal philosophy requires, initially, identifying the main questions to be addressed. One long-debated question is whether and why the institution of the penal sanction should exist at all. A second question is how much punishment should be imposed on those who are found to offend. Although this second "how much?" question has received somewhat less philosophical attention than the first, it is more directly relevant to the practical concerns of penologists—hence it is the topic of this article.

The distinction between "why?" and "how much?" is important because the answers to the two questions can differ significantly. It is possible to assert that the criminal sanction exists (at least in part) to prevent crime, and still insist (on fairness grounds) that the quanta of punishments be determined chiefly on desert-based grounds of the seriousness of the offense.[1]

The distinction is also important because it affects the themes a survey such as this should choose for emphasis. Consequentialist general justifications—ones that treat the criminal sanction's existence as being warranted chiefly by its crime-preventive effects—have generated an extensive corpus of philosophical literature. Retributive or desert-based justifications have done so also; and there exist a wide variety of retributive accounts, ranging from talionic notions of requiting evil for evil, through "moral paternalist" theories, to theories emphasizing the communicative character of punishment (for a valuable and excellent summary, see Duff 1996).[2]

A survey addressing the quanta of punishments calls for a somewhat different emphasis, however, because the discussion has been patterned differently. While consequentialist accounts (which would base "how much?" decisions on the anticipated crime-preventive effects) have been vigorously debated, they have tended to be couched in rather general terms. Of the various retributive theories, most have not addressed scaling issues at all; however, one version of desert theory (a censure-based one) has generated a considerable body of theory on the "how much?" question—including discussion of a variety of subissues concerning penal criteria. The rather extended discussion herein of this version reflects this: whether contemporary desert theorists ultimately are correct or mistaken, they have had more to say on the particulars of how much to punish. Had such a survey been written in Bentham's time, the emphasis would have been reversed, for utilitarians then offered more on the specifics of penal policy.

A discussion of how much to punish assumes that the criminal sanction is the appropriate response to the behaviors the state now defines as criminal. That assumption has been challenged by recent "restorative justice" perspectives emphasizing, in various forms, notions of remedying the harm done by criminal behavior to victims, communities, or both. Because such arguments are still being developed, a definitive account cannot readily be offered today; the present discussion will, rather, just sketch some salient themes and issues.

Finally, and with some trepidation on my part, this survey addresses "law-and-order" perspectives manifested in the plethora of drastic penal responses being enacted in the United States (and some other countries) today. These approaches do not comport well either with penal consequentialism or with desert-based notions of proportionality. The measures involved, and the manner of their enactment, appear to be designed to express or reflect strong sentiments of resentment of crime and of criminals. The question to be discussed is whether any conceptual basis can be articulated, what it would be, and what its problems are.

Penal Consequentialism

During the opening decades of the twentieth century, American penal theorists developed a strongly consequentialist sentencing ideology—one that remained influential through end of the sixties. This ideology stressed two themes: rehabilitation and incapacitation. The judge was supposed to fashion the disposition to promote the offender's resocialization. The penalty also was supposed to reflect the likelihood of the offender's reoffending: if his prognosis was favorable, he was to be given a sentence in the community; if unfavorable, he was to be imprisoned—and thereby separated from the community as long as he remained a risk (Rothman 1980; Allen 1981).

According to this ideology, the degree of gravity of the offender's conduct was deemed relatively unimportant. Someone convicted of a serious crime could be given a mild sentence if the likelihood of his returning to crime seemed slight, or if such a response would promote his reintegration into society. Conversely, someone convicted of a lesser offense could be given a long prison sentence if his criminal record or social background indicated a significant risk of recidivism. Proportionality—the notion of punishments reflecting the gravity of the offense—was deemed no ideal. Such "retributive" thinking was seen as unprogressive and impractical because it meant that some offenders would continue to be punished after they had successfully been rehabilitated, whereas others would have to be released (having completed their "deserved" sentences) even though they remained a danger to society. The gravity of the offense had only a residual role, in providing the basis for statutory maximum sentences; those maxima, however, were set high—so that their only effect was to bar draconian terms of confinement for lesser crimes (Rothman 1980).

Linked with these ideas was the notion of sweeping discretion for deciding the quantum of sentence. Within the (high) statutory maxima, the judge normally had the choice of *any* sentence, including a fine, probation, or a prison sentence. Parole boards likewise had broad discretion to decide what portion of a prison sentence an offender should serve. There were no explicit standards or guidelines governing sentencing judges' and parole boards' decisions, and those decisions ordinarily were not reviewable. This wide discretion purportedly was justified by the prevailing ideology because it would permit officials familiar with the particular case to choose the disposition tailored to the offender's need for treatment and his or her likelihood of returning to crime.

Practice was often at variance with the theory. The system's wide discretion permitted judges to rely on other considerations in their sentences (e.g., the seriousness of the offense, or the need to deter others), without having to explain why. But this flexibility also helped preserve the ideology because it left freedom in practice for judges to use these other ideas, without needing to challenge the dominant notions. And dominant these notions were: when one reads influential sources of the time—for example, the American Law Institute's Model Penal Code of 1962—the emphasis on treatment, prediction, and discretion is apparent (American Law Institute 1962).

The Decline of the Traditional Model

Beginning in the early 1970s, the foundations of the traditional model began to erode. One important development was disappointment with treatment efforts. After decades of rhetoric about rehabilitation, criminologists began to test treatment methods systematically. The results of such studies came slowly, but by the 1970s several surveys of treatment studies had been published. The results were not encouraging: although many offenders did not return to crime, this tended to occur as often (or nearly as often) among untreated as among treated individuals: the treatment itself had little perceptible influence (Sechrest, White, and Brown 1979).

Some researchers suggested at the time that *no* treatments worked (Martinson 1974), but that surely was an exaggeration. A select minority of treatment programs did seem to succeed, when applied to certain offender subpopulations whose characteristics had been carefully matched to program type. Experimentation continues today with such "targeted" treatment programs, with some reported successes (Palmer 1992). But it has not been possible to show that rehabilitation can *routinely* be made to work for the bulk of offenders coming before the courts.

The other key element of the traditional model—restraint of those predicted to be higher risks—also faced critical scrutiny. The forecasting of criminal behavior had interested American criminologists since the 1920s, with a modicum of success achieved in the next decades (Gottfredson 1967). However, the criterion for success was one-sided, addressing only the ability of prediction techniques to identify those who did subsequently offend. The obverse side—the problem of *false-positives*—was seldom considered: what proportion of those identified as potential recidivists would *not* be found to offend again, when permitted to remain at large.

When researchers began to turn their attention to this problem of overprediction, its formidable dimensions became apparent. Although prediction methods were able to identify certain groups of offenders having a higher-than-average statistical probability of recidivism, these methods showed a disturbing incidence of false-positives: for violent crimes, at least two false-positives for every true positive (Monahan 1981). Such mistaken forecasts could be gravely damaging to the individuals involved, for they could lead to their prolonged incarceration (see, e.g., von Hirsch 1972).

The wide discretion permitted by the traditional model also came under attack for allowing discrepant decisions (Frankel 1972). Research showed that most sentencing courts, acting with wide discretion, did tend to develop "going rates" for various classes of crime and criminals. But these tariffs were just averages, so that individual sentencers remained free to deviate from them (if aware of them at all) whenever they chose. That departure from the norm could be made without giving adequate (or any) reasons; and the statistical norm itself was not the result of careful deliberation about what the sentencing policy ought to be.

By the mid-1970s, it became apparent that the traditional model was in need of revision. Three points, in particular, began to emerge. First, rehabilitation should not be used as the basis for sentence choice—or, in any event, should be given this role sparingly. While experimentation with treatment programs should continue, and amenable offenders be offered treatment during their sentences, a defendant ordinarily should not be incarcerated *in order* to receive treatment (Morris 1974), as the Model Penal Code had proposed (Model Penal Code 1962, sect. 7.01(1)(b)).

Second, prediction-based judgments concerning whether and how long to imprison should be restrained by appropriate limits (Morris 1974). How constraining those limits should be and what their conceptual basis should be have remained a matter of debate. But schemes permitting virtually unrestricted resort to prediction should be abolished—such as Maryland's Defective Delinquent Law (von Hirsch 1972), which permitted indeterminate and possibly even lifetime confinement (albeit with treatment) on the basis of forecasts about the offender's propensity to re-offend.

Third, sentencing decisions should be made subject to the rule of law. Standards should set forth what factors should primarily be relied upon in deciding the sentence—and possibly also what sentences (or ranges of sentence) are normally recommended (Frankel 1972). This interest in standards for sentencing, in turn, stimulated thought about penal ratio-nales. The drafters of standards needed to address whether the sentence should depend chiefly on the gravity of the crime of conviction, or on the previous criminal history, or on other factors. To deal with such ques-tions, theory helped—because the different theories pointed toward dif-ferent criteria.

Bounded Consequentialism

In the last two decades, some former adherents of the traditional model have tried to amend and refurbish that doctrine. Although the emphasis on crime prevention remained, limits would be imposed to correct the manifest injustices. This approach has been associated with Norval Mor-ris (Morris 1982, chap. 5) and, in considerable part, has been suscribed to in the American Bar Association's most recent draft sentencing standards (American Bar Association 1993). The model involves the following two main elements.

First, minimum norms of proportionality should be observed: persons convicted of lesser or intermediate-level offenses should not face the pos-sibility of lengthy imprisonment, even if their estimated likelihood of recidivism is high. Proportionality, however, should serve only as (in Morris's words) a "limiting principle," rather than constituting the main determinant of the sentence (Morris 1982, chap. 5). Offense seriousness should, in other words, set only certain outer bounds, beyond which the penalty would plainly infringe norms of justice.

Second, within these outer bounds, the sentence would continue to be determined on consequentialist grounds—for example, on the basis of the defendant's probability of recidivism (Morris and Miller 1985). Con-victs with significant risks of committing further serious offenses could thus be confined (within applicable desert limits), while the (more nu-merous) remainder of offenders should be given sentences in the commu-nity. Such community punishments—including middle-level sanctions designed to have more "bite" than ordinary probation—should be allo-cated according to guidelines relying on both offense-related and offender-related factors (Morris and Tonry 1990).

Concurrently with the development of these ideas, efforts were made to improve prediction methods. Whereas traditional prediction indices aimed at forecasting whether the offender would commit any further crime, new forecasting techniques sought to identify the potential high-rate serious offenders. Estimates of the net crime-preventive effects of employing these techniques also were devised. In a well-known study, RAND Corporation researcher Peter Greenwood estimated that a policy of "selective incapacitation"—involving long prison terms for high-risk convicted robbers and reduced prison terms for medium- and low-risk robbers—could reduce the robbery rate by as much as 15 or 20 percent, without causing prison populations to rise (Greenwood 1982; Wilson 1983, chaps. 8, 10). When criminologists began scrutinizing this "selective incapacitation" research, however, these optimistic claims began eroding: the large projected crime-prevention effects could shrink considerably when prediction scales were derived from more representative samples of the possible offender population, and when estimates of offenders' residual criminal careers were scaled down to more realistic levels (Blumstein et al. 1986). Interest in selective incapacitation thus has waned since the end of the 1980s—and, indeed, not much research has been conducted in this area during the 1990s (Zimring and Hawkins 1995).

Besides these concerns about predictive effectiveness, ethical queries were raised concerning the peripheral role that selective-incapacitation schemes assign to the gravity of the offense. The RAND model, for example, calls for *much* longer prison terms for high-risk robbers (about eight years) than for low- and medium-risk ones (only one year). Such large differentials in the punishment of offenders convicted of similar crimes seem morally problematic—even for the adherents of bounded consequentialism, for whom offense gravity should provide some significant limits. Smaller sentence differentials might alleviate this problem of disproportionality but would shrink the projected crime-prevention payoffs of the strategy considerably.

Notwithstanding selective-incapacitation's difficulties, bounded consequentialism has the continuing attraction of seeming to synthesize both proportionality and consequentialist concerns. However, the theory's details remain undeveloped. One unresolved issue is that of delineating the proportionality limits: how broad or narrow should these be? The theory's advocates have yet to resolve, for example, whether the gravity of the offense furnishes only upper limits on the sentence or lower limits as well. Michael Tonry, for example, suggests that desert should supply only upper limits (Tonry 1994). Without lower limits, however, sentences fall to zero—unless sustainable on other grounds. This, in turn, raises the question of what those other grounds should be. Tonry urges that "parsimony" in punishing should be borne strongly in mind in setting the sanction below the applicable upper desert limit, but it remains to be explicated how this notion can provide much guidance (see von Hirsch 1993, epilogue).

What also needs to be clarified is the grounds for such proportionality constraints. One suggestion has been that the limits should rest on common understandings of what penalty levels would seem manifestly excessive (Morris 1974; Monahan 1982; Morris and Miller 1985). That, however, would mean that the constraints would be no stronger than those which popular morality would insist upon (see Zimring and Hawkins 1995, chap. 4). Alternatively, the limits could be rationalized on substantive fairness grounds; it might be argued, for example, that punishments (as a censure-conveying measures) should bear some reasonable relationship to the degree of blameworthiness of the offenses involved.[3] Such a censure-based argument, however, raises the question why the limits should be mere outer constraints and not determine rankings of punishments more closely (see later discussion and also von Hirsch 1988).

Improving the Utilitarian Formula

The end of the 1970s also witnessed efforts to revive Benthamite utilitarian calculations by interpreting "utility" in economic terms. Sentences would thus be determined through a cost-benefit analysis, weighing the estimated costs of punishment against penalties' crime-preventive benefits. The sentence for each type of crime would be determined by the optimum balance of such benefits against costs (Posner 1977, chap. 7).

The manifest practical difficulty of such an approach has been that of gauging the crime-preventive yield: unless it is possible to estimate how much more crime is prevented by adding a given quantum to the sentence, the formula yields indeterminate results. Too little is known, however, about punishment's marginal deterrent effects to make such estimates possible (Blumstein, Cohen, and Nagin 1978). Problems of justice also arise: for example, the formula supports seemingly disproportionate sentences when the net preventive benefits are large enough (see von Hirsch 1976, chap. 7).

Could the utilitarian principle be improved upon? Two Australian authors, John Braithwaite and Phillip Pettit (1990), have put forward a suggested reformulation in which the measure of "utility" would no longer be satisfaction or cost-reduction *simpliciter* but the promotion of personal autonomy. A harsh system of punishment, they argue, might conceivably be efficient in preventing crime but would not facilitate choice: fear-provoking sanctions would diminish, not enhance, citizens' sense of control over their own lives. These authors also provide suggestions on sentencing criteria. They urge a "decremental" strategy, according to which penalties would progressively be reduced until crime (or fear thereof) begins to rise. Incapacitative terms of confinement, however, would be retained for high-risk offenders.

To what extent does the Braithwaite-Pettit reformulation help? In certain contexts, it seems to: vicarious criminal liability, for example, would be ruled out on grounds of its choice-threatening character because that would expose citizens to penal consequences that they could not avoid through their own choice not to offend. But would the theory provide comparable safeguards with respect to punishing the convicted? It does not seem clear, for example, that the theory would bar the use of harsh sentences for certain lesser or intermediate crimes. If protecting choice in the aggregate is the aim, such measures could arguably be defensible on the grounds that they would make only a few convicted offenders suffer, whereas the many (by being protected better against crime) would have their own choices better protected (for fuller discussion, see von Hirsch and Ashworth 1992; von Hirsch 1993, chap. 3).

Proportionality and Desert

Criminologists' interest in desert dates from the mid-1970s, with the publication of a number of works arguing that this notion, far from being arcane or reactionary, is the central requirement of justice in punishing (Kleinig 1973; von Hirsch 1976; Singer 1979). Once broached, the idea of desert quickly became influential. A number of U.S. states' sentencing-guidelines systems have explicitly relied on it; some European sentencing-reform efforts (particularly those of Sweden and, more recently, England) have done likewise, although these schemes make use of statutory statements of guiding principle rather than specific, numerical guidelines.

The groundwork for this revival of interest in desert had been laid already in the postwar literature of analytical moral philosophy. These writings supplied a principled critique of aggregate cost-benefit thinking about social and penal issues—suggesting how such reckonings were capable of sacrificing individual rights to serve majority interests (Rawls 1971; Williams 1973). The philosophical literature also began exploring the conception of desert, suggesting how it constitutes an integral part of everyday moral judgments (Morris 1968; Strawson 1974; Kleinig 1973).

Basic Ideas: Proportionality and Censure

Desert theory purports to be about *just* outcomes: the emphasis is on what the offender fairly merits for his crime. The central organizing principle for deciding the quanta of punishments is the principle of proportionality or "commensurate deserts"—requiring that the severity of the penalty be proportionate to the gravity of the conduct of which the defendant has been convicted. The criterion for deciding the quantum of punishment thus is retrospective rather than consequentialist: the seriousness of the violation the defendant has committed (von Hirsch 1985; Ashworth 1989).

The theory addresses two objections that traditionally have been made to the idea of retributive punishment. One has been that deserved punishment is somehow incomprehensible, that it rests on "metaphysical" notions of requital of evil for evil. Contemporary desert theorists provide a simpler explanation, however—one emphasizing the idea of penal censure. Punishment, they point out, is a blaming institution. The difference between a criminal and a civil sanction lies, generally, in the fact that the former involves censure of the actor. Fairness thus requires that penalties be allocated consistently with their blaming implications: the severity of the punishments (and thereby the degree of blame visited on the actor) should thus be ordered consistently with the degree of blameworthiness (i.e., the seriousness) of the defendant's criminal conduct (von Hirsch 1985; Duff 1986; Ashworth 1989). Disproportionate or disparate punishments are unjust because they treat offenders as more or less worthy of blame than the reprehensibleness of their conduct has warranted.

The other objection has been to the seeming harshness of retributive punishment, to its supposed exaction of an eye for an eye. Once the paying back of evil for evil is no longer seen as the underlying idea, however, penal desert no longer demands visitation of suffering equal to the harm done. What is required instead is punishment that is *proportionate* to the seriousness of the criminal conduct. Proportionate punishments—even if not involving harm-for-harm equivalence—could suffice to convey blame for various crimes according to their degree of reprehensibleness. Indeed, many desert theorists have advocated substantial reductions of penalty levels (von Hirsch 1976; Singer 1979; Duff 1986; Ashworth 1989).

This emphasis on punishment's censuring features has coincided with a larger change in criminological thinking. The blaming aspects of punishment were formerly regarded as highly problematic. According to then-influential labeling theories, penal stigma not only created objective social impediments to the reintegration of the offender but also generated "secondary deviance"—that is, induced the offender to identify himself as deviant, and hence to be more prone to continue offending (see, e.g., Lemert 1967).

The influence of labeling theories has been waning, however, and positive uses of penal censure are being noted. John Braithwaite (operating within a strongly consequentialist theory) suggests that "shaming" can play an important reintegrative role (Braithwaite 1989). David Garland points to the symbolic role of punishment, conveyed through penal censure, as having considerably greater social importance than sanctions' immediate crime-preventive effects (Garland 1990).

Desert theorists, especially in the last decade, have emphasized the ethical role of penal censure. Blaming, it has been pointed out, is a form of communication suited only to beings capable of moral agency: one can blame a person for wrongdoing, but not a beast for harmful behavior. Responding to criminal wrongdoing through blame gives the individual the opportunity to respond in ways that are typically those of an agent capable of moral deliberation: to recognize the wrongfulness of the action; to feel remorse; to make efforts to desist in the future—or to try to give reasons that the conduct was not actually wrong (Duff 1986; von Hirsch 1993; Narayan 1993). By contrast, a purely deterrent sanction takes the form of desist-or-else: the individual must simply comply or face the consequences, and no moral judgment of any sort is solicited from him.

Desert as "Determining" or "Limiting"?

If the principle of proportionality is so important, is it a "determining" or merely a "limiting" principle? While our sense of justice tells us that criminals should be punished as they deserve, there do not seem to be definite quanta of severity associated with our desert-based judgments. Armed robbers have committed a serious offense, deserving of substantial punishment, but it is not self-evident whether that should consist of two years of confinement, three years, or some shorter or longer period.

One response to this problem has been Norval Morris's: to say that desert is merely a limiting principle. It tells us, he asserts, not how much robbers deserve but only some broad outer limits beyond which their punishments would be *un*deserved (Morris 1982, chap. 5). Within such limits, the sentence can be decided on other (e.g., predictive) grounds. This view, however, could mean that persons who commit similar crimes can receive very different amounts of punishment. If punishment embodies blame as a central characteristic, it would seem problematic to visit such different degrees of severity, and hence of implicit blame, on comparably blameworthy transgressions (von Hirsch 1985, chap. 4).

A conceivable opposite response, but scarcely a plausible one, would be the heroic intuitionist view: that if we only ponder hard enough we will perceive deserved quanta of punishments, that robbers ordinarily deserve so-and-so many months or years of confinement, and so forth. Our intuitions, however, are not so helpful.

Desert theorists' way out of this apparent dilemma has been to point to a crucial distinction between the comparative ranking of punishments and the anchoring of the penalty scale. With respect to comparative rankings, *ordinal* proportionality provides considerable guidance: persons convicted of similar crimes should receive punishments of comparable severity (save in special aggravating or mitigating circumstances altering the harm or culpability of the conduct); and persons convicted of crimes of differing gravity should suffer punishments correspondingly graded in onerousness. These ordinal-proportionality requirements are no mere limits, and they are infringed when equally reprehensible conduct is punished markedly unequally in the manner that Morris proposes (von Hirsch 1985, chaps. 4, 12).

Desert can provide less constraint, however, on the penalty scale's overall dimensions and anchoring points. This is because the censure expressed through penal deprivations is, to a degree, a convention. When a penalty scale reflects the comparative gravity of crimes, altering its magnitude and anchoring points (and thus making pro rata decreases or increases in the prescribed sanctions) constitutes a change in that convention.

This distinction helps resolve the dilemma just mentioned. The leeway that desert allows in fixing the anchoring points explains why we cannot perceive a single right or fitting penalty for a crime. Whether x months, y months, or somewhere in between is the appropriate penalty for robbery depends on how the scale has been anchored and what punishments are prescribed for other crimes. Once those anchoring points are decided, however, the more restrictive requirements of ordinal proportionality apply. This accounts for desert theorists' objection to giving short prison terms to some robbers and long ones to other robbers, on the basis, say, of predictive factors not reflecting the degree of seriousness of the conduct. But does not this purported solution still leave the anchoring of the scale too wide open? Could it not permit a quite severe penalty scale, as long it is not *so* harsh as to impose drastic penalties on manifestly trivial crimes? A recent attempted answer is that high overall severity levels are inconsistent with the moral functions of penal censure. Through punishments' censuring features, as mentioned earlier, the criminal sanction offers a normative reason for desistence that can be offered human beings seen as moral agents: that doing certain acts is wrong and hence should be refrained from. Punishment's material deprivations can then be viewed as providing a supplemental disincentive—as providing humans (given human fallibility and the temptations of offending) an additional prudential reason for complying with the law (von Hirsch 1993, chap. 2; Narayan 1993). The higher penalty levels rise, however, the less the normative reasons for desistence supplied by penal censure will matter, and the more the system becomes in effect a bare system of threats (in Hegel's apt words, a stick that might be raised to a dog). To the extent this argument is accepted, it points toward keeping penalties at moderate levels (see, more fully, von Hirsch 1993, chap. 5)

Gauging Crimes' Seriousness and Punishments' Severity

The rank-ordering requirement of proportionality presupposes a capacity to grade crimes according to their seriousness. As a practical matter, ranking crimes' gravity has been a manageable task: a number of American state sentencing commissions have been able to fashion systematic rankings of crime seriousness for their guidelines, with relatively little controversy (see, e.g., Parent 1988). However, these commissions assigned these rankings on the basis of their members' intuitive sense of various crimes' gravity. To what extent can theory supplement intuition?

The seriousness of crime has two main elements: the degree of harmfulness (or risk of harm) of the conduct, and the extent of the actor's culpability. With respect to culpability, the substantive criminal law can help—because its theories of fault have analogues for sentencing. The substantive criminal law already distinguishes intentional (i.e., purposive, knowing, or reckless) conduct from negligent conduct. Sentencing law could make fuller use of distinctions such as these (although these implications have yet to be spelled out in much detail).

With harm, the problem has been to compare the injuriousness of criminal acts that invade different interests—to compare takings of property with, say, invasions of privacy. Here, a broad notion of quality of life can be helpful: invasions of different interests can be compared according to the extent to which they typically affect a person's *standard of living*—understood in the broad sense of that term, including noneconomic as well as economic well-being. (This conception of the living standard is taken from Sen 1987.) Such an analysis facilitates comparisons: burglary and assault may affect different interests, but they nevertheless may be compared in their impacts on a standard person's quality of life (von Hirsch and Jareborg 1991; von Hirsch 1993, chap. 4; Ashworth 1995, chap.4).

The living-standard idea can also be helpful in comparing the severity of various penalties. Severity can be gauged not in terms of individual offenders' varying sensitivities but rather in terms of how different penalties *typically* would affect the quality of a person's life (von Hirsch 1993, chap. 4).

Role of the Prior Criminal Record

Another issue is the role of an offender's prior criminal convictions. Most penal systems do adjust the severity of the sanction to reflect the defendant's criminal history, but it has been a matter of controversy how much weight the criminal record should have, and why. A predictive rationale for sentencing would give principal emphasis to prior arrests and convictions because those factors are most correlated with future offending. A desert theory, by contrast, accords principal weight to the gravity of the current offense; that is, indeed, a salient operational difference between prediction-based and desert-based schemes (see von Hirsch 1985, chap. 11). But the question remains whether the record should be given *any* weight.

Some desert theorists have argued for a modest adjustment for the prior record—in the form of a penalty discount for first offenders or for those with few prior convictions (Wasik 1987; Ashworth 1995, chap. 6). This can be explained as a way of recognizing human fallibility in the criteria for punishment. The first offender who is given a somewhat scaled-down punishment is censured for his act but nevertheless accorded some moral respect for the fact that his inhibitions against wrongdoing appear to have functioned on prior occasions, and some sympathy or tolerance for the all-too-human frailty that can lead to such a lapse (von Hirsch 1985, chap. 7; von Hirsch 1991). With repetition, however, this extenuation diminishes and eventually is lost. While this view permits a limited differentiation to be made on the basis of prior convictions, the primary emphasis would remain on the gravity of the current offense.

Inclusion of Crime Control Aims?

Desert theory sets priorities among sentencing aims: it assumes that it is more important to have proportionately ordered sanctions than to seek other objectives—say, incapacitating those deemed higher risks. This understandably evokes discomfort: why cannot one seek proportionality *and* pursue other desired ends, whether they be treatment, incapacitation, or something else?

To a degree, a desert model permits consideration of other aims, namely, to the extent this is consistent with the proportionate ordering of penalties. Thus, when there is a choice between two noncustodial sanctions of approximately equivalent severity (say, a day fine of so many days' earnings and intensive probation for a specified duration), proportionality constraints are not offended when one of these is chosen over the other on, say, treatment grounds. Desert theorists thus have come forward with schemes for using intermediate, noncustodial penalties—according to which these would be ranked in severity according to the gravity of the crime, but penalties of roughly equivalent onerousness could be substituted for one another when treatment or feasibility concerns so indicate (von Hirsch, Wasik, and Greene 1989).[4]

Nevertheless, a pure desert model remains a constraining one: ulterior aims may be relied on only where these do not substantially alter the comparative severity of penalties. Giving substantial extra prison time to persons deemed high risks would thus breach the model's requirements. Why not, then, relax the model's constraints to allow greater scope to such other aspirations? If the aim of relaxing these constraints is crime-preventive, however, it should be borne in mind that a penalty scale that observes proportionality requirements would itself have collateral crime-preventive effects—in such deterrence as is achieved by the scale generally, and such incapacitation as its prescribed use of imprisonment might yield. Proposed departures would thus be shown capable of yielding *more* prevention than a straightforward proportionality-oriented scheme could provide.

A possibility—sometimes referred to as a "modified" desert model—would be to relax the constraints to a limited degree. Proportionality would ordinarily determine comparative punishment levels, but deviations would be permitted in case of extraordinarily grave risks (Robinson 1987; Bottoms and Brownsword 1983). Or else, deviations would ordinarily be permitted, but these would be restricted ones: say, a deviation of no more than 10 or 15 percent (von Hirsch 1993, chap. 6). These mixed approaches still make desert the primary determinant for the ordering of penalties, but they give some extra scope for ulterior purposes. Even such schemes remain constraining, however: especially dangerous offenders might be given extra prison time, but not the ordinary potential recidivist; some extra leeway might be granted to suit a noncustodial penalty to the offender's apparent treatment needs, but not a great deal.

Could still more scope be given to nondesert considerations? In a hybrid rationale, either desert will predominate or something else will. If—in the ordinary case—the seriousness of the crime is the penalty's primary determinant, the system remains desert-dominated. If other (say, crime-preventive) aims are given the greater emphasis, however, that creates a system dominated by those aims and reintroduces the problems spoken of earlier—for example, those relating to equity among offenders, and those of insufficient systematic knowledge of preventive effects.

Other Issues: Severity and Social Deprivation

Does desert lead to harsher penalties? Since the theory emerged and became influential at a time when penalty levels rose in many jurisdictions, critics have argued that the theory must in part be responsible for such increases (see, e.g., Hudson 1987). However, desert theory itself does not call for harsher penalties—indeed, as noted earlier, it permits (indeed, arguably points toward) considerable penalty reductions. Moreover, the sentence reform schemes that rely explicitly on notions of desert tend not to be severe ones: the Minnesota and Oregon sentencing guidelines, for example, call for relatively modest penalties by U.S. standards (see Tonry 1993).[5] Measures that most clearly call for tougher sanctions tend to use criteria inconsistent with proportionality: mandatory sentences, for example, select particular offense categories for harsh treatment, without regard to the gravity of the offense involved or the penalties imposed for other offenses. (Such measures appear to be influenced by rather different "law-and-order" perspectives, discussed later in this chapter). Severity levels vary considerably among jurisdictions—and seem to be influenced in large part by local traditions and by political trends.

Another key issue concerns the relations between just punishment and social deprivation. Many offenders live in grim social environments that restrict their opportunities for living satisfactory, law-abiding lives. Should such persons be punished differently? It has been pointed out that desert theory at least does not *add* to the punishment imposed on deprived persons, whereas penal consequentialism would, to the extent that social deprivation is a sign, say, of greater dangerousness (see von Hirsch 1976, chap. 17). But the question remains whether such persons deserve *reduced* punishments. Arguably, reductions could be warranted on grounds of reduced culpability—in view of the greater obstacles such persons face in leading law-abiding lives (Gardner 1976; Hudson 1995). Granting such mitigation would, however, create a host of practical and political difficulties—so that the perplexity remains (cf. Tonry 1994 with von Hirsch 1993, epilogue).

Restorative Justice

During the last decade or so, "restorative" conceptions have been emerging, aimed at repairing the personal and social damage done by the criminal act. Such views have generated a wide variety of programmatic responses, some quite ambitious: New Zealand, for example, has replaced its juvenile justice system with a scheme of offender-victim negotiation. This chapter does not attempt a survey of such schemes; its concern, rather, is with the theoretical basis for restorative justice approaches.

An important threshold question is whether notions of victim or community restoration should be seen as grounds for punishing, or for replacing punishment with something else. Some conceptions adhere to a punitive paradigm but use restoration as part of the rationale for punishing; working within a desert-oriented framework, for example, the philosopher R. A. Duff argues that sentences should (within reasonable proportionality limits) be designed to elicit an understanding on the part of the offender of his wrongdoing and to try to achieve a renewal of trust between him and the community (Duff 1986, chap. 9; 1996). Alternatively, restorative approaches can be used within a limited ambit: various schemes have been put forward, for example, according to which victim compensation or mediation would be used for certain types of offenses (often, of lesser or intermediate gravity), leaving the penal system to cope with the remainder (including the graver crimes). As the present boundaries between criminal and tort law have been historically conditioned, it may well be possible to shift these somewhat in favor of compensatory approaches.

Discussions of restorative justice, however, often put forward the more ambitious aim of replacing punishment. It is suggested that the whole penal paradigm is mistaken; and that justice, properly understood, should not be punitive at all but should aim instead at restoring victim interests and social ties. It is this more ambitious conception that will be discussed here.

Varieties of Restorative Aims

What is the purpose of restorative justice? Different versions of restorativism seem to have differing aims, either singly or in combination (for a thoughtful survey and analysis, see Zedner 1994).

Victim Restitution. Requiring a wrongdoer to compensate his victim is a familiar idea that underpins existing tort law. Someone who has been criminally victimized ordinarily also has a tort claim against the perpetrator; and criminal courts long have had powers to order the perpetrator to pay compensation, along with any punishment imposed—although these powers are used sparingly in practice.

A version of restorative justice aims chiefly at making offenders provide restitution: the focus is on the nature and extent of victims' injuries, material and psychological; and on determining how offenders can contribute to the alleviation of those injuries. This involves compensating the victim for material loss and perhaps for psychic injuries as well (Barnett 1977).

Conflict Resolution. Another approach emphasizes reconciliation. Crime is seen as a form of conflict, and the appropriate response that which helps resolve the conflict. Mediation between offender and victim thus is emphasized, seeking dispositions that help the parties understand one another and remove sources of further conflict (Christie 1978). The approach thus stresses reconciliation and healing, with informal negotiation preferred over formal dispositions.

Community Restoration. Yet another strand of thinking emphasizes the community. Crime is seen as an assault on community interests—both in its challenge to norms of peaceable coexistence and in the fear that it engenders among the citizenry. The response to crime, then, should be one designed to reaffirm the norms that have been infringed and to repair frayed communal bonds (Cragg 1992; Pettit 1993). It should also aim at alleviating communal insecurity by reducing the likelihood of further offending and alleviating fears (Pettit 1993).

These differing aims carry differing implications. The first version, victim compensation, is concerned with making the victim whole, so that the severity of the response depends on the extent of the victim's injuries and the ability of the offender to pay. Censure of the conduct would not necessarily be involved, and crime prevention is given little emphasis (see Barnett 1977). The second version, conflict resolution, may involve compensation, but the focus is on achieving an understanding between victim and offender; if only partial compensation would suffice to satisfy the parties, so be it. Consistency also would have little importance—similar offenses may give rise to different settlements among the different parties involved. Community restoration would have still different implications: tougher interventions would be possible, to the extent these might reaffirm community norms or reduce public insecurity.

How Much Guidance on "How Much"?

If restorativism is to be useful as a theoretical framework, it needs to be capable of providing a modicum of guidance on how much intervention would be permissible, and of what kind. To what extent can it do so?

The idea of victim restitution does provide a metric—one that looks to the extent of the victim's injuries. Conceptual models for gauging injury can be drawn from the jurisprudence of tort law. Conflict resolution is already more elusive because of the problem of applying the conflict analogy to crimes. Typical conflicts are those in which there is a matter in contention (say, a disputed property boundary), concerning which each party has a colorable claim. Mediating such disputes is fairly well understood, and involves seeking a settlement so as to accord a modicum of satisfaction to both parties. The mediator thus tends to avoid declaring who is right and instead tries to find ways of reducing tensions. With crime, no such disputed claims may be involved: the robber takes something that is admittedly the victim's. The parties may be strangers having little expectation of future dealings and hence little practical interest in reconciliation. The focus thus may shift to questions of compensating the victim and expressing some form of censure or quasi censure of the victimizing act.

With community restoration, matters become still more elusive. Restorativists speak of restoring the harm done by victimizing offenses to communal standards or communal bonds. However, no clear principles have been suggested or come readily to mind on how such communal injury can be assessed (see Ashworth 1993; Zedner 1994). That impact, moreover, depends not only on the character of the criminal conduct but also on how robust the community's social or moral bonds were in the first place.

Community restoration is sometimes said also to involve reducing insecurity, that is, reassuring citizens of their continued safety. To the extent this involves reducing crime, it is simply penal consequentialism in a new guise—and faces the familiar problems, spoken of earlier, of how crime prevention may effectively and fairly be achieved. Devising a metric for alleviating fear of crime would seem still more difficult; little is known about how sanctions can influence levels of fear, and those levels depend so much on media, social, and political factors, as well as actual crime rates.

What of Limits?

A still more important issue, perhaps, is that of the limits on permissible intervention: when, and to what extent, if ever, should the offender's interests in his liberty take precedence over the various victim and communal interests involved? Without carefully delineated and soundly based limits, restorative sanctioning (especially in its community-oriented variety) could become a frightening prospect.

Limits are not readily derivable from the aims of restorativism themselves. Victim compensation depends on the victim's injuries or foreseeable injuries—so that even when the actor's culpability is relatively slight, large compensation may be due if warranted by the extent of injury (see Ashworth 1993). Conflict resolution as an aim likewise offers no clear limits—especially when no interest remains in dispute, and when the remedy is an uncertain mixture of compensation and censure. Communal restoration provides still more meager grounds for limits: almost any communal interest can be said to be set back by a criminal act, and prevention of crime or fear of crime could warrant quite drastic interventions.

To the extent restorativists address this critical issue of limits at all, they assert that it can be dealt with by imposing outer proportionality constraints (Van Ness 1993; Cavadino and Dignan 1993). The analogy they invoke is that of bounded consequentialism, discussed previously, in which a penalty scheme's crime-preventive aim would be limited by bounds (perhaps, only upper limits) relating to the gravity of the offense. Two kinds of difficulties remain, however. One, noted earlier, is that bounded consequentialism itself seems to offer rather little guidance in locating the proportionality bounds, or specifying how constraining they should be.

The other, still more troublesome, problem is that of supplying a rationale. With bounded consequentialism, a rationale could be formulated: for example, that since *punishment* (with its censuring features) is involved, sanctions should not be grossly out of keeping with the degree of blameworthiness of the offense. However, restorativism (at least in its more ambitious versions) purports to jettison the punishment paradigm and replace it with a new remedial one giving censure a less central, defining role. With censure less clearly in the picture, this kind of argument for proportionality weakens or fails, and it is not clear what other arguments remain.

What the foregoing queries are meant to point to is the need for a clearer conceptual framework. The literature of restorativism needs not yet greater enthusiasm but more reflection. The aims need to be specified more carefully, as should be the grounds for deciding the extent and kind of intervention. Most important, there must be better grounding for the limits on restorative interventions which a free society should insist upon.

"Law-and-Order" Perspectives

Recent years have witnessed a proliferation of law-and-order responses to crime, especially in the United States. These are introduced with strident rhetoric about crime and criminals, and they often involve drastic sanctions. Paradigmatic of this approach is California's "three-strikes" law, calling for terms of twenty-five years to life after two convictions of intermediate-level felonies such as burglary, followed by a third conviction of any crime classified as a felony (including various routine thefts). Other states have likewise adopted harsh mandatory sentences (see Tonry 1992)—albeit seldom quite as draconian as the California measure.

What is notable about such measures is that they scarcely purport to be justifiable in traditional criminal justice policy terms. True, the rhetoric sometimes speaks in terms of prevention ("getting repeat offenders off the streets") or desert (giving such individuals "their due"). But it is doubtful that these are seriously conceived as the aims. First, the measures often infringe on even rudimentary notions of proportionality. How could a third-time burglar deserve near-life imprisonment, especially when those convicted of more serious, violent offenses ordinarily receive so much less? Second, the measures likewise often have little plausibility as crime prevention measures. Three strikes seems plainly deficient as an incapacitant strategy because offenders usually would receive their third conviction late in their expected criminal careers, and would continue to be confined long after such careers' likely termination. Projections of probable preventive effect—such as those that accompanied the "selective incapacitation" proposals of the mid-1980s—are seldom supplied.[6]

If the aim appears to be neither desert nor prevention, what is it? To a considerable extent, these measures involve appeals to popular resentment: they are expressive of fear and loathing of crime and of criminals. As such, they have much in common with other recent measures targeting unpopular groups—such as California's Proposition 187 (passed by popular initiative at the same time as three strikes) barring education and nonemergency medical care to children of illegal immigrants. Such appeals to resentment can have political benefits, and reflect an ideology of purging "undesirables" from the body politic.

But does law and order *merely* involve such appeals to resentment, or can it be given intellectual content? Of what kind? One (quite critical) writer talks about "symbolic" punishments (Tonry 1992, pp. 265–67)—but symbolic of *what*? As mentioned earlier, the communicative character of punishment is receiving increasing attention. Could not law and order be seen as a communication, albeit one of a special kind?

On one version of the communicative view, it could be. Punishment, on this version, is primarily a denunciatory institution: its function is to convey, in dramatic fashion, disapproval of certain kinds of persons or conduct. That disapproval aims not so much at increasing levels of compliance as at reflecting and expressing the social norms and attitudes themselves. Repeat burglars are to be given decades-long prison sentences as a way of giving public expression of condemnation of such persons. On this view, it would not be necessary (as preventionists hold) to try to make the penalty optimally effective; nor (as desert theorists wish) to make the penalty commensurate in its severity with the gravity of the crime. The focus would be on the public: on giving voice to condemnatory attitudes. If imprisonment (or imprisonment for long terms) does this expressive job best, so be it.[7]

In a censure-based theory of desert, the censure is visited upon the offender, perceived as a person capable of moral agency. Certain conduct is deemed harmful and blameworthy; a sanction is imposed that conveys a certain measure of blame for the conduct. However, how much the actor is blamed should comport with the degree of reprehensibleness of his conduct. And since the blame is being conveyed through the medium of penal deprivation, the severity of that treatment should reflect the gravity of his criminal conduct and not more: hence the requirements of proportionality.

On the law-and-order version of the denunciatory account, however, the convicted offender is excluded from the moral universe of discourse, instead serving merely as the object of and conduit for public messages of denunciation. If tougher sanctions express that message best, they would be deemed preferable—and the offender is allowed no standing to claim that that sanction overstates the blame due him.

Such a theory is ethically problematic because it treats the offender as little more than an object. It also provides no principled grounds for limitation. If the aim is to devise sanctions that register disapproval of the conduct in as visible and dramatic a form as possible, there is no reason for rejecting sanctions (however harsh) that seem to provide the best drama.

It is not only in theory but in practice that this lack of limitation obtains. On a desert view, the limits of proportionality apply; on preventive conceptions, the preventive effects need empirically to be estimated—which may be no easy matter, as the debate over selective indication suggests. But if public drama is the criterion, it could never be evident when a measure has overstepped.

Acknowledgments The author is grateful to Andrew Ashworth, Antony Duff, Judith Greene, Nils Jareborg, Michael Tonry, and Lucia Zedner for their comments on earlier versions of this chapter.

Notes

1. For such a view, see von Hirsch 1993, chap. 2; Narayan 1993; and discussion in the second part of this chapter. For the distinction between "why punish?" and "how much?" generally, see Hart 1968, chap. 1.

2. Among the versions of retributivism that have been discussed recently by philosophers are views that punishment (1) serves to remove the "unfair advantage" the offender obtains through benefiting by others' self-restraint, while not restraining himself, (2) justifiably expresses certain "punitive emotions," or (3) provides a moral benefit to the wrongdoer. For a critical analysis of these, see Duff 1996. The version of retributivism that emphasizes the censuring character of punishment is discussed more fully later in this chapter.

3. Tonry (1994) maintains that his suggested upper limits on permissible penalties should be based on a proportionality analysis of the kind summarized in the second part of this chapter—and this analysis is based on such notions of blameworthiness.

4. For a comparison of the treatment of noncustodial sanctions under desert and bounded-consequentialist perspectives, respectively, see von Hirsch 1993, chap. 7.

5. The Oregon sentencing commission's effort to keep penalties at such modest levels has been complicated, however, by the recent voter approval of a popular initiative mandating high mandatory minima for certain more serious offenses. The federal sentencing guidelines, which tend to prescribe severe sanctions, are not primarily desert-based (see von Hirsch 1993, chap. 10).

6. The selective-incapacitation proposals were put forward with elaborate projections of their crime-preventive impact and were debated explicitly in those terms—see discussion in second part of this chapter. By contrast, mandatory minima usually are put forward with little or no evidence offered

of the likely preventive benefits; the available evidence tends to suggest those impacts are small (see Tonry 1992); and the occasional assertions made of dramatic preventive benefits can turn out to be derisory on more careful analysis (see Zimring and Hawkins 1991, chap. 4).

7. This view differs from Durkheimian conceptions of punishment as promoting social solidarity in that it purports not merely to describe a societal function of the criminal sanction but to provide the normative basis for penal policy. Dan M. Kahan (1996) develops such a denunciatory conception: the emphasis on punishment as public drama is present in his account, as is the rejection of desert constraints. He does state a preference for "shameful" community punishments because he believes these could be made to have sufficient dramatic content; he also seems to view such rituals as having possible long-run deterrent effects. But it would require no great shift to move from his view to the one spoken of here: it would simply be assumed that his suggested alternatives in fact provide insufficient drama, compared with the expressiveness of tough prison sentences.

References

Allen, Francis A. 1981. *The Decline of the Rehabilitative Ideal.* New Haven, Conn.: Yale University Press.

American Bar Association. 1993. *Criminal Justice Standards for Sentencing Alternatives and Procedures*, reprinted in *Criminal Law Reporter* 52:53–70.

American Law Institute. 1962. *Model Penal Code.* Philadelphia: American Law Institute.

Ashworth, Andrew. 1989. "Criminal Justice and Deserved Sentences." *Criminal Law Review* 1989:340–55.

———. 1993. "Some Doubts About Restorative Justice." *Criminal Law Forum* 4:277–99.

———. 1995. *Sentencing and Criminal Justice.* 2nd ed. London: Butterworths.

Barnett, Randy. 1977. "Restitution: A New Paradigm of Criminal Justice." *Ethics* 87:279–301.

Blumstein, Alfred, Jacqueline Cohen, and Daniel Nagin, eds. 1978. *Deterrence and Incapacitation.* Report of the National Academy of Sciences Panel on Research on Deterrent and Incapacitative Effects. Washington, D.C.: National Academy Press.

Blumstein, Alfred, Jacqueline Cohen, Jeffrey Roth, and Christy Visher, eds. 1986. *Criminal Careers and "Career Criminals."* Report of the National Academy of Sciences Panel on Research on Criminal Careers. Washington, D.C.: National Academy Press.

Bottoms, A. E., and Roger Brownsword. 1983. "Dangerousness and Rights." In *Dangerousness: Problems of Assessment and Prediction*, edited by J. W. Hinton. London: Allen and Unwin.

Braithwaite, John. 1989. *Crime, Shame and Reintegration.* Cambridge: Cambridge University Press.

Braithwaite, John, and Phillip Pettit. 1990. *Not Just Deserts: A Republican Theory of Justice.* Oxford: Oxford University Press.

Cavadino, Michael, and James Dignan. 1993. *Reparation, Retribution and*

Rights. Sheffield: Centre for Criminological and Legal Research, University of Sheffield.

Christie, Nils. 1978. "Conflicts as Property." *British Journal of Criminology* 17:1–15.

Cragg, Wesley. 1992. *The Practice of Punishment: Toward a Theory of Restorative Justice*. London: Routledge.

Duff, R. A. 1986. *Trials and Punishments*. Cambridge: Cambridge University Press.

———. 1996. "Penal Communications: Recent Work in the Philosophy of Punishment." In *Crime and Justice: A Review of Research,* vol. 20, edited by Michael Tonry. Chicago: University of Chicago Press.

Frankel, Marvin. 1972. *Criminal Sentences: Law Without Order*. New York: Hill and Wang.

Gardner, Martin. 1976. "The Renaissance of Retribution: An Examination of 'Doing Justice.'" *Wisconsin Law Review* 1976:781–815.

Garland, David. 1990. *Punishment and Modern Society*. Chicago: University of Chicago Press.

Gottfredson, Don M. 1967. "Assessment and Prediction Methods in Crime and Delinquency." In *Task Force Report: Juvenile Delinquency and Youth Crime*. President's Commission on Law Enforcement and Administration of Justice. Washington, D.C.: U.S. Government Printing Office.

Greenwood, Peter W. 1982. *Selective Incapacitation*. Santa Monica, Calif.: RAND.

Hart, H. L. A. 1968. *Punishment and Responsibility*. Oxford: Oxford University Press.

Hudson, Barbara A. 1987. *Justice Through Punishment: A Critique of the "Justice" Model of Corrections*. Basingstoke, England: Macmillan.

———. 1995. "Beyond Proportionate Punishment: Difficult Cases and the 1991 Criminal Justice Act." *Crime, Law and Social Change* 22:59–78.

Kahan, Dan M. 1966. "What Do Alternative Sanctions Mean?" *University of Chicago Law Review* 63:591–653.

Kleinig, John. 1973. *Punishment and Desert*. The Hague: Martinus Nijhoff.

Lemert, E. M. 1967. *Human Deviance, Social Problems, and Social Controls*. Englewood Cliffs, N.J.: Prentice-Hall.

Martinson, Robert. 1974. "What Works: Questions and Answers About Prison Reform." *Public Interest* 35:22–54.

Monahan, John. 1981. *Predicting Violent Behavior: An Assessment of Clinical Techniques*. Beverly Hills, Calif.: Sage.

———. 1982. "The Case for Prediction in the Modified Desert Model for Criminal Sentencing." *International Journal of Law and Psychology* 5:103–13.

Morris, Herbert. 1968. "Persons and Punishment." *Monist* 52:475–501.

Morris, Norval. 1974. *The Future of Imprisonment*. Chicago: University of Chicago Press.

———. 1982. *Madness and the Criminal Law*. Chicago: University of Chicago Press.

Morris, Norval, and Marc Miller. 1985. "Predictions of Dangerousness." In *Crime and Justice: An Annual Review of Research*, vol. 6, edited by Michael Tonry and Norval Morris. Chicago: University of Chicago Press.

Morris, Norval, and Michael Tonry. 1990. *Between Prison and Probation.* New York: Oxford University Press.

Narayan, Uma. 1993. "Appropriate Responses and Preventive Benefits: Justifying Censure and Hard Treatment in Legal Punishment." *Oxford Journal of Legal Studies* 13:167–82.

Palmer, Ted. 1992. *The Re-Emergence of Correctional Intervention.* Newbury Park, Calif.: Sage.

Parent, Dale. 1988. *Structuring Sentencing Discretion: The Evolution of Minnesota's Sentencing Guidelines.* Stoneham, Mass.: Butterworth.

Pettit, Phillip. 1993. "Not Just Deserts, Even in Sentencing." *Current Issues in Criminal Justice* 4:225–37.

Posner, Richard A. 1977. *Economic Analysis of Law.* Boston: Little, Brown.

Rawls, John. 1971. *A Theory of Justice.* Cambridge, Mass.: Harvard University Press.

Robinson, Paul. 1987. "Hybrid Principles for the Distribution of Criminal Sanctions." *Northwestern Law Review* 82:19–42.

Rothman, David J. 1980. *Conscience and Convenience.* Boston: Little, Brown.

Sechrest, Lee, Susan White, and Elisabeth Brown, eds. 1979. *The Rehabilitation of Criminal Offenders.* Washington, D.C.: National Academy of Sciences.

Sen, Amartya. 1987. *The Standard of Living.* Cambridge, Mass.: Harvard University Press.

Singer, Richard G. 1979. *Just Deserts: Sentencing Based on Equality and Desert.* Cambridge, Mass.: Ballinger.

Strawson, Peter F. 1974. "Freedom and Resentment." In *Freedom and Resentment and Other Essays,* edited by Peter F. Strawson. London: Methuen.

Tonry, Michael. 1992. "Mandatory Penalties." In *Crime and Justice: A Review of Research,* vol. 16, edited by Michael Tonry. Chicago: University of Chicago Press.

———. 1993. "Sentencing Commissions and Their Guidelines." In *Crime and Justice: A Review of Research*, vol. 17, edited by Michael Tonry. Chicago: University of Chicago Press.

———. 1994. "Proportionality, Parsimony, and Interchangeability of Punishments." In *Penal Theory and Penal Practice,* edited by R. A. Duff, S. Marshall, R. Dobash, and R. Dobash. Manchester, England: Manchester University Press.

Van Ness, Daniel W. 1993. "New Wine and Old Wineskins: Four Challenges of Restorative Justice." *Criminal Law Forum* 4:251–78.

von Hirsch, Andrew. 1972. "Prediction of Criminal Conduct and Preventive Confinement of Convicted Persons." *Buffalo Law Review* 21:717–58.

———. 1976. *Doing Justice.* New York: Hill and Wang.

———. 1985. *Past or Future Crimes.* New Brunswick, N.J.: Rutgers University Press.

———. 1988. "Selective Incapacitation Reexamined." *Criminal Justice Ethics* 7(1):19–35.

———. 1991. "Criminal Record Rides Again." *Criminal Justice Ethics* 10(2):2, 55–57.

———. 1993. *Censure and Sanctions.* Oxford: Oxford University Press.

von Hirsch, Andrew, and Andrew Ashworth. 1992. "Not Not Just Deserts: A

Response to Braithwate and Pettit." *Oxford Journal of Legal Studies* 12:83–98.

von Hirsch, Andrew, and Nils Jareborg. 1991. "Gauging Criminal Harm: A Living-Standard Analysis." *Oxford Journal of Legal Studies* 11:1–38.

von Hirsch, Andrew, Martin Wasik, and Judith Greene. 1989. "Punishments in the Community and the Principles of Desert." *Rutgers Law Journal* 20:595–618.

Wasik, Martin. 1987. "Guidance, Guidelines, and Criminal Record." In *Sentencing Reform: Guidance or Guidelines*, edited by Martin Wasik and Ken Pease. Manchester, England: Manchester University Press.

Williams, Bernard. 1973. "A Critique of Utilitarianism." In *Utilitarianism: For and Against,* edited by J. J. C. Smart and Bernard Williams. Cambridge: Cambridge University Press.

Wilson, James Q. 1983. *Thinking About Crime.* Rev. ed. New York: Basic Books.

Zedner, Lucia. 1994. "Reparation and Retribution: Are They Reconcilable?" *Modern Law Review* 57:228–50.

Zimring, Franklin E., and Gordon Hawkins. 1991. *The Scale of Imprisonment.* Chicago: University of Chicago Press.

———. 1995. *Incapacitation.* New York: Oxford University Press.

25

Intermediate Sanctions

MICHAEL TONRY

Since 1980, three major trends led to widespread development of intermediate sanctions, punishments that fall between prison and probation in their severity and intrusiveness. First, rehabilitative considerations lost credibility as rationales for sentencing
(Allen 1964; Lipton, Martinson, and Wilks 1975; Sechrest, White, and
Brown 1979). Second, "just deserts" became seen as the primary rationale for sentencing, bringing with it a logic of punishments proportioned
to the seriousness of crimes committed and a movement to narrow officials' discretion (e.g., Morris 1974; von Hirsch 1976). Third, crime control policy has become a staple political issue, and proponents of "law
and order" have persistently called for harsher penalties. With this came
a widespread belief that most sentences to ordinary probation are insufficiently punitive and substantial political pressure for increases in the
severity of punishments.

These developments resulted in a sextupling in the number of state
and federal prisoners between 1972 (196,092) and 1997 (1,280,000) and
in substantial overcrowding of American prisons. At year-end 1996,
the federal prison system was operating at 125 percent of rated capacity,
and state systems were operating on average at 116 percent of capacity.
Thirty-seven state systems and the District of Columbia were operating
above rated capacity (Bureau of Justice Statistics 1998).

During the mid-1980s, intermediate sanctions such as intensive supervision, house arrest, and electronic monitoring were oversold as being
able simultaneously to divert offenders from incarceration, reduce recidivism rates, and save money while providing credible punishments that
could be calibrated to the severity of offenders' crimes. Like most propositions that seem too good to be true, that one was not true.

During the past decade's experimentation, we have learned that some
well-run programs can achieve some of their goals, that some conventional goals are incompatible with each other, and that the availability of
new sanctions presents almost irresistible temptations to judges and corrections officials to use them for offenders other than those for whom the
program was created.

The goals of diverting offenders from prison and providing tough, rigorously enforced sanctions in the community have proven largely incompatible. A major problem is that close surveillance of offenders reveals higher levels of technical violations than are discovered in less intensive sanctions, even though there is little reason to suppose that offenders in new programs commit technical violations at higher rates. But if they do breach a curfew, stop performing community service, get drunk, or violate a no-drug-use condition, closer monitoring makes the chances of discovery high. Once the discovery is made, punitive actions—typically revocation and confinement—often follow (e.g., Ryan 1997, p. 108).

A second major problem is that elected officials and practitioners often prefer to use intermediate sanctions for less serious offenders than programs were designed for. Many evaluations of intensive supervision programs and boot camps, for example, have shown that any realistic prospects of saving money or prison beds require that they be used mostly for offenders who otherwise would have served prison terms.

Yet many elected officials resist assigning prison-bound offenders to intermediate sanctions because they are risk-averse. Even in the best-run programs, offenders sometimes commit serious new crimes, and officials are understandably concerned that they will be held responsible for supporting the program. As a result, many elected officials support new intermediate sanctions but then take pains to limit eligibility to low-risk offenders.

Practitioners, particularly prosecutors and judges, also often resist using intermediate sanctions for the offenders for whom they were designed. Partly this is because they, too, are reluctant to be seen as responsible for crimes committed by participants. This is why judges are often unwilling to cooperate in projects in which—as part of experimental evaluations—target categories of offenders are to be randomly assigned to a community penalty or incarceration (e.g., Petersilia and Turner 1993).

Partly judges' "misuse" of intermediate sanctions, sometimes called "net widening," occurs because they believe new community penalties are more appropriate for some offenders than either prison or probation. Forced by limited program options to choose between confinement and probation (e.g., Kempinen 1997), they will often choose probation because confinement is seen as too severe or too disruptive of the offender's and his family's lives, albeit with misgivings because they believe ordinary probation too slight a sanction. Once house arrest or intensive supervision becomes available, those penalties may appear more appropriate than either probation or confinement.

This chapter surveys research on the most widely used intermediate sanctions—boot camps, intensive supervision probation (ISP), house arrest and electronic monitoring, community service, fines, and day-reporting centers. Probably the most important lesson learned from recent experience with intermediate sanctions is that they are seldom likely to achieve their goals unless means can be found to set and enforce policies governing their use. Otherwise, the combination of officials' risk aversion and practitioners' preferences to be guided solely by their personal views about appropriate penalties in individual cases is likely to undermine program goals. This is why most new and proposed sentencing guidelines systems—such as those in Ohio (Rauschenberg 1997), Massachusetts (H. Tonry 1996), and North Carolina (Wright 1997)—and Pennsylvania's revised guidelines (Kempinen 1997) explicitly incorporate intermediate sanctions into their guidelines systems.

General Impediments to Effective Intermediate Sanctions

In retrospect, it was naive (albeit from good intention) for promoters of new intermediate sanctions to assure skeptics that recidivism rates would fall, costs be reduced, and pressure on prison beds diminish if new programs were established. The considerable pressures for net widening and the formidable management problems involved in implementing new ideas interact in complex ways to frustrate new programs. Although these challenges are now well understood, that knowledge has been hard-won.

Recidivism

Consider first recidivism rates. From influential evaluations of community service (McDonald 1986), intensive supervision (Petersilia and Turner 1993), and boot camps (MacKenzie and Souryal 1994), to mention only a few, comes a robust finding that recidivism rates (for new crimes) of offenders sentenced to well-managed intermediate sanctions do not differ significantly from those of comparable offenders receiving other sentences. Equally robust findings from many evaluations also show, however, that rates for violation of technical conditions, and ensuing revocation rates, are generally higher.

The evaluation findings on recidivism and revocation rates elicit different reactions from different people and in light of different conceptions of how the corrections system ought to work. From one perspective, the higher rates are good: the programs are intended to be punitive, and high revocation rates show that they are. From another perspective they are bad: they result in increased costs for case processing and imprisonment, and all because of noncriminal actions. However they are viewed, high failure rates illuminate a major impediment to aspirations to reduce prison use by use of intermediate sanctions.

Prison Beds

The combination of net widening and elevated rates of technical violations and revocations makes prison bed savings difficult to achieve. For programs to which judges directly sentence offenders, a 50 percent rate of prison diversion is commonly counted a success. Consider how the numbers work out. The 50 percent diverted from prison save prison beds. The 50 percent diverted from probation are a different story. They would not otherwise have occupied prison beds, and if half suffer revocation and imprisonment, they represent new demand for beds, and a much higher demand than would otherwise exist because many more of their technical violations will be discovered and acted upon. In addition, many of those who were diverted from prison will commit new crimes or technical violations and suffer revocation.

Whether a particular program will save or require net prison beds depends on why offenders' participation is revoked and in what percentage of cases, and whether they are sent to prison and for how long. Glib assumptions that new "diversion" programs will reduce prison use will often, maybe even usually, be wrong.

Cost Savings

The third often-claimed goal of intermediate sanctions is to save money. Interactions among all the preceding difficulties make dollar savings unlikely except in the best of cases. If a majority of program participants are diverted from probation rather than from prison, and if technical violation and revocation rates are higher in the intermediate sanction than in the ordinary probation and parole programs to which offenders would otherwise be assigned, the chances of net cost savings are slight. For boot camps, for example, assuming typical levels of participant noncompletion and typical levels of postprogram revocation, Dale Parent has calculated that "the probability of imprisonment has to be around 80 percent just to reach a break-even point—that is, to have a net impact of zero on prison bed-space" (Parent 1995a, p. 141).

No one who has worked with the criminal justice system should be surprised by the observation that the system is complex, and that economic and policy ramifications ripple through it when changes are made in any one of its parts. Sometimes that truism has been overlooked, to the detriment of programs on behalf of which oversimplified claims were made. Georgia, for example, operated a pioneering ISP that at one time was claimed to have achieved remarkably low recidivism rates (for new crimes) and to have saved Georgia the cost of building two prisons (Erwin and Bennett 1987). It was later realized that many or most of those sentenced to ISP were low-risk offenders convicted of minor crimes who otherwise would have received probation. From serving initially as an exemplar of successful ISP programs that save money and reduce recidivism rates, Georgia's ISP program now serves as an exemplar of net-widening programs that increase system costs and produce higher rates of revocation for violation of technical conditions (Clear and Byrne 1992, p. 321).

Experience with Intermediate Sanctions

Writing about experience with intermediate sanctions bears some resemblance to shooting at a moving target. Although it typically takes at least three years from the time an evaluation is conceived until results are published, the programs themselves keep changing. Thus Doris MacKenzie (1995), describing the results of an assessment of boot camps in eight states, took pains to explain that some of them changed significantly during and after the assessment. For example, the South Carolina program, initially a sentencing option to which offenders were sentenced directly by judges (and thus highly vulnerable to net widening) was reorganized as a corrections program in which participants were selected by corrections officials from among offenders sentenced to prison. Similarly, programs in some states that had focused primarily on discipline and physical labor were reorganized to include a much larger component of drug treatment and educational opportunities.

Still, an evaluation literature has continued to accumulate, and lessons learned in some states a few years ago can be useful to policy makers in other states that are designing new programs or redesigning old ones. In order, the following subsections discuss research on boot camps, ISP, house arrest and electronic monitoring, day-reporting centers, community service, and day fines.

A prefatory note is required. For the most part, the evaluation literature raises doubts about the effectiveness of intermediate sanctions at achieving the goals their promoters commonly announce. This does not mean that there are no effective programs. Only a handful have been carefully evaluated, and many of those have in the aftermath been altered. Many sophisticated and experienced practitioners believe that their programs are effective, and some no doubt are. The evaluation literature does not "prove" that programs cannot succeed but that many have not and that managers can learn from that past experience. Sometimes that learning may be expressed as program adaptations intended to make achievement of existing goals more likely. Sometimes it may lead to a reconceptualization of goals.

The available literature consists of a handful of fairly sophisticated evaluations funded by the U.S. Departmment of Justice, a larger number of small, typically less sophisticated studies of local projects, and a large number of uncritical descriptions of innovative programs. There have been a number of efforts to synthesize the evaluation literature on intermediate sanctions, sometimes in edited collections (McCarthy 1987; Byrne, Lurigio, and Petersilia 1992; Tonry and Hamilton 1995), sometimes in books by one or two authors (Morris and Tonry 1990; Anderson 1998), and sometimes in article-length literature reviews (Clear and Braga 1995; Tonry and Lynch 1996).

This chapter devotes only a few pages to each intermediate sanction and emphasizes the more substantial evaluations and literature reviews. In some cases, for example, concerning ISP (Petersilia and Turner 1993) and boot camps (MacKenzie 1995; MacKenzie and Piquero 1994), relatively recent and detailed literature reviews are available for readers who want more information. In other cases, for example, concerning fines (Hillsman 1990) and community service (Pease 1985), the best literature reviews are more dated; there has been relatively little American research on these latter subjects in recent years, however, and these articles, despite their early dates, cover most of the important research. In still other cases, notably including day-reporting centers, most of the available literature is descriptive and no literature reviews are available.

Boot Camps

The emerging consensus from assessments of boot camps must be discouraging to their founders and supporters. Although promoted as a means to reduce recidivism rates, corrections costs, and prison crowding, most boot camps have no discernible effect on subsequent offending and tend to increase costs and crowding (Parent 1995a; MacKenzie 1995). Most have been diversion programs that have drawn many of their participants from among offenders who otherwise would not have been sent to prison. In many, one-third to one-half of participants fail to complete the program and are sent to prison as a result. In most, close surveillance of offenders after completion and release produces rates of violations of technical conditions and of revocations that are higher than for comparable offenders in less intensive programs.

The news is not all bad. Programs to which imprisoned offenders are transferred by corrections officials for service of a 90- or 180-day boot camp sentence in lieu of a longer conventional sentence do save money and prison space, although they, too, often experience high failure rates and higher-than-normal technical violation and revocation rates.

Boot camp prisons have spread rapidly since the first two were established in Georgia and Oklahoma in 1983. By April 1993, according to a National Institute of Justice report (MacKenzie 1993), thirty states and the U.S. Bureau of Prisons were operating boot camps. According to the results of a survey of local jurisdictions in May 1992, ten jail boot camps were then in operation and thirteen other jurisdictions were planning to open jail boot camps in 1992 or 1993 (Austin, Jones, and Bolyard 1993). The earliest were opened in 1986 in New Orleans and in 1988 in Travis County, Texas.

Boot camps vary widely in their details (MacKenzie and Parent 1992; MacKenzie and Piquero 1994). Some last 90 days, some 180. Admission in some states is controlled by judges, in others by corrections officials. Some primarily emphasize discipline and self-control; others incorporate extensive drug and other rehabilitation elements. Some eject one-third to one-half of participants, others less than 10 percent. Most admit only males, usually under age twenty-five, and often subject to crime of conviction and criminal history limits, though there are exceptions to each of these generalizations.

The reasons for boot camps' popularity are self-evident. Many Americans have experienced life in military boot camps and remember the experience as not particularly pleasant but as an effective way to learn self-discipline and how to work as part of a team. A series of studies by the Public Agenda Foundation and Doble Associates in Alabama, Delaware, North Carolina, Oregon, and Pennsylvania, for example, found that the public is more supportive of intermediate sanctions than is widely known, but also found that they want such penalties to be burdensome and for that reason were especially in favor of boot camps (Higgins and Snyder 1996; Begasse 1997; Doble 1997; Doble and Immerwahr 1997; Farkas 1997).

Most of what we know about the effects of boot camps on participants comes from a series of studies by Doris MacKenzie and colleagues at the University of Maryland (e.g., MacKenzie and Shaw 1990, 1993; MacKenzie 1993, 1995; MacKenzie and Souryal 1994), from a General Accounting Office survey of research and experience (U.S. General Accounting Office 1993), and from an early descriptive overview of boot camps commissioned by the National Institute of Justice (Parent 1989).

Doris MacKenzie and her colleagues looked closely in Louisiana at effects on prisoners' self-esteem (MacKenzie and Shaw 1990). One early hypothesis concerning boot camps was that successful completion would increase participants' self-esteem, which in turn would lead to more effective participation in the free community and reduced recidivism. The first half of the hypothesis was found to be correct; using psychometric measures, MacKenzie and Shaw found that successful participants' self-esteem was enhanced compared with that of comparable prisoners in conventional prisons. Unfortunately, later assessments of successful participants after release found that their enhanced self-esteem soon disappeared (a plausible explanation for why the second half of the hypothesis concerning recidivism was not confirmed).

One tentative finding concerning possible positive effects of rehabilitative programs on recidivism merits emphasis. Although MacKenzie and her colleagues concluded overall that boot camps do not by themselves result in reduced recidivism rates, they found evidence in Illinois, New York, and Louisiana of lower rates of recidivism on some measures that they associated with strong rehabilitative emphases in those states' boot camps (MacKenzie and Souryal 1994; MacKenzie 1995, p. 155). An earlier article describes a "somewhat more positive" finding that graduates under intensive supervision after release "appear to be involved in more positive social activities (e.g., work, attending drug treatment) than similar offenders on parole or probation" (MacKenzie and Shaw 1993, p. 465).

If a primary goal is to reduce prison use, the policy implications of research on boot camps are straightforward. Parent sees at least three: "First, boot camps should recruit offenders who have a very high probability of imprisonment" (1995a, p. 143). This means that participants should be selected by corrections officials from among prisoners rather than by judges from among sentenced offenders. Second, boot camps should minimize failure rates by reducing in-program and postrelease failures. This means that misconduct within the boot camp should be punished within the boot camp whenever possible rather than by transfer to a regular prison, and that misconduct after release should be dealt with within the supervision program whenever possible rather than by revocation and reincarceration. Third, participants in boot camps should be selected from among prisoners who otherwise would serve a substantial term of imprisonment. Transfer of prisoners serving nine-month terms to a 180-day boot camp is unlikely to reduce costs and system crowding. Transfer of prisoners serving two- or three-year mandatory minimum terms is likely to reduce both.

Intensive Supervision

Intensive supervision for probationers and parolees (ISP) was initially the most popular intermediate sanction, has the longest history, and has been the most extensively and ambitiously evaluated. Contemporary programs, with caseloads ranging from two officers for twenty-five probationers to one officer for forty probationers, are typically based on surveillance, cost, and punishment rationales. ISP has been the subject of the only multisite experimental evaluation involving random allocation of eligible offenders to ISP and to whatever the otherwise appropriate sentence would have been (Petersilia and Turner 1993). Two exhaustive syntheses of the American ISP literature have been published (U.S. General Accounting Office 1990; Petersilia and Turner 1993) and do not differ significantly in their conclusions from those offered here.

Evaluation findings parallel those for boot camps. Diversion programs in which judges control placement tend to draw more heavily from offenders who would otherwise receive less restrictive sentences than from offenders who would otherwise have gone to prison or jail. A multisite ISP evaluation by the RAND Corporation, in which jurisdictions agreed in advance to cooperate with a random assignment system for allocating offenders to sanctions, was unable to evaluate ISP programs for which judges controlled entry when judges refused to accept the outcomes of the randomization system (Petersilia and Turner 1993).

Like the boot camp evaluations, the ISP evaluations have concluded that offenders sentenced to ISP do not have lower recidivism rates for new crimes than do comparable offenders receiving different sentences, but that, because of closer surveillance, they typically experience higher rates of violation of technical conditions and higher rates of revocation. Also like boot camps, early proponents argued that ISP, while reducing recidivism rates and rehabilitating offenders, also would save money and prison resources (Petersilia, Lurigio, and Byrne 1992, pp. ix–x); evaluations suggest that the combination of net widening, high revocation rates, and related case-processing costs makes the cost savings claims improbable for most programs.

One tantalizing positive finding from the ISP evaluation literature parallels a boot camp finding (MacKenzie and Shaw 1993): in some sites, ISP did succeed in increasing participants' involvement in counseling and other treatment programs (Petersilia and Turner 1993). The drug treatment literature demonstrates that participation, whether voluntary or coerced, can reduce both drug use and crime by drug-using offenders (Anglin and Hser 1990). Because Drug Use Forecasting data (e.g., National Institute of Justice 1994) indicate that half to three-fourths of arrested felons in many cities test positive for drug abuse, ISP may hold promise as a device for getting addicted offenders into treatment and keeping them there (Gendreau, Cullen, and Bonta 1994).

Few corrections programs are new in the sense that they haven't been tried before. From the 1950s through the early 1970s, probation departments experimented with caseload size in order to learn whether smaller caseloads permitting more contact between officers and probationers would enable officers to provide better services and thereby enhance probation's rehabilitative effectiveness. The best-known project, in California, featured caseloads ranging from "intensive" (20 offenders) to "ideal" (50), "normal" (70 to 130), and "minimum" (several hundred). Lower caseloads produced more technical violations but indistinguishable crime rates (Carter, Robinson, and Wilkins 1967).

A survey of forty-six intensive supervision programs established in the 1970s found that they either had no effect on recidivism rates or increased them, and that they diverted few offenders from prison but instead mostly recruited from people who otherwise would have received probation (Banks et al. 1977). Not surprisingly, ISP based on rehabilitative rationales withered away.

Notwithstanding the discouraging evaluation findings, ISP was adopted in most states in the 1980s and 1990s. Often this was more attributable to institutional and professional goals of probation agencies and personnel than to the putative goals of the new programs (Tonry 1990). A General Accounting Office survey in 1989 identified programs in forty states and the District of Columbia (U.S. General Accounting Office 1990; Byrne and Pattavina 1992). ISP programs probably now exist in every state.

Although ad hoc intensive supervision in individual cases presumably occurs in every probation system, no other country has adopted widespread programs of intensive probation. Small-scale pilot projects were started in the Netherlands in 1993 (Tak 1994, 1995). In England, as in the United States, variable caseload projects to test treatment effectiveness hypotheses were conducted in the 1960s and early 1970s, with the same discouraging results (Folkard, Smith, and Smith 1974, 1976), and were soon abandoned. A series of pilot projects in eight sites, linked with Home Office evaluations, appear to have diverted offenders from prison and to have met with approval from judges and probation officers, but in many sites they have encountered substantial implementation problems (Mair 1994; Mair et al. 1994).

Here, too, the policy implications are straightforward. Because recidivism rates for new crimes are no higher for ISP participants than for comparable imprisoned offenders, ISP is a cost-effective prison alternative for offenders who do not present unacceptable risks of violence. ISP may offer a promising tool for facilitating treatment for drug-using offenders and, both by itself and linked with other sanctions, can provide credible midlevel punishments as part of a continuum of sanctions.

The challenges are to devise ways to assure that programs are used for the kinds of offenders for whom they are designed, and to reduce rates of revocation for technical violations. Sentencing guidelines systems may hold promise for reducing the extent of net widening by judges (Tonry 1997, 1998). The technical violation problem can be addressed, as Lurigio and Petersilia (1992, p. 14) note, by imposing only conditions that relate to a particular offender's circumstances rather than imposing long lists of general standard conditions.

House Arrest and Electronic Monitoring

The lines that distinguish community penalties begin to blur after ISP. House arrest, often called home confinement, has as a precursor the curfew condition traditionally attached to many probation sentences; it may be ordered as a sanction in its own right or as a condition of ISP (Ball, Huff, and Lilly 1988). Most affected offenders, however, do not remain in their homes but instead are authorized to work or participate in treatment, education, or training programs. Finally, house arrest is sometimes, but not necessarily, backed up by electronic monitoring; Renzema (1992), for example, reports that 10,549 people were on house arrest in Florida in August 1990, of whom 873 were on electronic monitoring.

House arrest comes in several versions. In an early Oklahoma program (Meachum 1986), for example, prison inmates were released early subject to participation in a home confinement program. In Florida, which operates the largest and most diverse home confinement programs, most are programs to which judges sentence "otherwise prison-bound offenders." In some states, especially in connection with electronic monitoring, house arrest is used in place of pretrial detention (Maxfield and Baumer 1990).

House arrest programs expanded rapidly beginning in the mid-1980s. The earliest programs were typically small (from thirty to fifty offenders) and often were used mostly for driving-while-intoxicated and minor property offenders (this was also true of most of the early electronic monitoring programs; Morris and Tonry 1990, chap. 7). Since then, programs have grown and proliferated. The largest program is in Florida, where more than 13,000 offenders were on house arrest in 1993 (Blomberg, Bales, and Reed 1993). Programs coupled with electronic monitoring, a subset, existed nowhere in 1982, in seven states in 1986, and in all fifty states in October 1990 (Renzema 1992, p. 46).

Considered by itself, the use of electronic monitoring has grown even more from its beginnings in 1983 in the Mexico courtroom of Judge Michael Goss and the Florida courtroom of Judge J. Allison DeFoor II (Ford and Schmidt 1985). In 1986, only 95 offenders were subject to monitoring (Renzema 1992, p. 41), a number that rose to 12,000 in 1990 (Baumer and Mendelsohn 1992, p. 54) and to a daily count of 50,000 to 70,000 in 1992 and 1993 (Lilly 1995, p. 113).

Manufacturers of electronic monitoring equipment no doubt expect eventually to sell their products worldwide. Within the English-speaking countries, the United States is at present the major market. In early 1993, the Northern Territory of Australia was the only state operating front-end house arrest programs; Western Australia, South Australia, and Queensland operated prison-release programs. Altogether, these programs contained 330 to 400 offenders, of whom approximately half were subject to electronic monitoring (Biles 1993).

English policy makers toyed with electronic monitoring in the late 1980s and established a pilot project in three sites in 1989–1990. Judges and police were skeptical about the use of electronically monitored house arrest as a custody alternative, and rates of offender noncompliance were high (Mair and Nee 1990; Mair 1995b). The evaluators characterized their findings as inconclusive. Although the Criminal Justice Act 1991 authorized use of electronic monitoring in conjunction with curfew orders, no monitoring equipment was in use in England and Wales late in 1997, though another series of pilot projects had been conducted.

No American evaluations of house arrest programs of the scale or sophistication of the best on boot camps or ISP have been published. One analysis of agency data for Florida's prison-diversion house arrest program concluded that it drew more offenders from among the prison-bound than from the probation-bound (Baird and Wagner 1990), but that conclusion was based on dubious analyses (for a detailed discussion, see M. Tonry 1996, chap. 4).

A case study of the development, implementation, and evolution of an early-prison-release program in Arizona cautions that house arrest programs are likely to share the prospects and problems of intermediate sanctions generally. Originally conceived as a money-saving system for early release of low-risk offenders, the program—which combined house arrest with electronic monitoring—wound up costing money. One problem was that, in addition to satisfying stringent statutory criteria (no violent or sex crimes, no prior felony convictions), inmates had to be approved for release by the parole board, which proved highly risk-averse and released very few eligible inmates. When the program became operational, the rate of revocation for technical violations (34 percent of participants) was twice that for ordinary parolees. Finally, many probation officers subverted the program by operating it not as an early-release system for low-risk offenders but as a mechanism for establishing tighter controls and closer surveillance than would otherwise be possible (Palumbo, Clifford, and Snyder-Joy 1992).

There are no other large-scale evaluations. House arrest coupled with electronic monitoring has been the subject of many small studies and a linked set of three studies in Indianapolis (Baumer, Maxfield, and Mendelsohn 1993). Both of two recent literature reviews stress the scantiness of the research evidence on prison diversion, recidivism, and cost-effectiveness. On recidivism, Renzema notes that most of the "research is uninterpretable because of shoddy or weak research designs" (1992, p. 49). The most comprehensive review observes that "we know very little about either home confinement or electronic monitoring" (Baumer and Mendelsohn 1992, p. 66). Baumer and Mendelsohn, who stress that "the incapacitative and public safety potential of this sanction have probably been considerably overstated" (1992, pp. 64–65), predict that house arrest will continue to be used primarily for low-risk offenders and will play little role as a custody alternative. There is little reason to believe that house arrest is any less vulnerable to net widening than is ISP or likely to achieve different findings on recidivism.

Day-Reporting Centers

Day-reporting centers, like the remaining two sanctions to be discussed (community service and day fines), differ from those already discussed in that they were developed earlier and much more extensively outside the United States than in. The earliest American day-reporting centers— places where offenders spend their days under surveillance and participating in treatment and training programs while sleeping elsewhere— date from the mid-1980s. The English precursors, originally called day centers and now probation centers, began operation in the early 1970s. Most of our knowledge of American day-reporting centers comes from descriptive writing; no published literature as yet provides credible findings on the important empirical questions.

The English programs date from creation of four "day-training centres" established under the Criminal Justice Act of 1972, charged to provide intensive training programs for persistent petty offenders whose criminality was believed rooted in general social inadequacy, and from creation of ad hoc day centers for serious offenders that were set up by a number of local probation agencies. For a number of reasons, the training centers were adjudged unsuccessful and were soon closed.

The probation-run day centers, however, thrived after enabling legislation was enacted in 1982, numbering at least eighty by 1985, and serving thousands of offenders by the late 1980s (Mair 1995a, p. 133). Programs vary, with some emphasizing control and surveillance more than others, some operating as a therapeutic community, and most offering a wide range of (mostly compulsory) activities. The maximum term of involvement is sixty days, and some programs have set thirty-day or forty-five-day limits.

A major Home Office study concluded that "most centres unequivocally saw their aim as diversion from custody" (Mair 1994, p. 5), that more than half of the participating offenders had previously been imprisoned, and that 47 percent had six or more prior convictions (Mair 1995a, p. 135). A later reconviction study (Mair and Nee 1992) found a two-year reconviction rate of 63 percent. However, George Mair writes, though "on the face of it this may look high . . . the offenders targeted by centres represent a very high-risk group in terms of probability of reconviction" (Mair 1995a, p. 137). In addition, the reconviction data did not distinguish between those who completed the program and those who failed. The results were seen as so promising that the Criminal Justice Act of 1991 envisioned a substantial expansion in the use of day-reporting centers.

A 1989 survey for the National Institute of Justice identified twenty-two day-reporting centers in eight states (Parent 1990), though many others have since opened. Most American centers opened after 1985. The best-known (at least the best-documented) centers were established in Massachusetts—in Springfield (Hampton County Sheriff's Department) and in Boston (the Metropolitan Day Reporting Center)—and both were based in part on the model provided by the English day centers (Larivee 1995; McDevitt and Miliano 1992).

As with the English centers, American programs vary widely. Many are corrections-run programs into which offenders are released early from jail or prison. Some, however, are sentencing options to which offenders are sentenced by judges, and some are used as alternatives to pretrial detention (Parent 1995b). Programs range in duration from forty days to nine months and program content varies widely (Parent 1995b). Most require development of hour-by-hour schedules of each participant's activities; some are highly intensive, with ten or more supervision contacts per day; and a few include twenty-four-hour-per-day electronic monitoring (McDevitt and Miliano 1992). Unfortunately, no substantial evaluations have been published (a number of small in-house evaluations are cited in Larivee 1995 and in McDevitt and Miliano 1992).

Community Service

Community service is the most underused intermediate sanction in the United States. Used in many countries as a midlevel penalty to replace short prison terms for moderately severe crimes, in the United States community service is used primarily as a probation condition or as a penalty for trifling crimes like motor vehicle offenses. This is a pity because community service is a burdensome penalty that meets with widespread public approval (e.g., Higgins and Snyder 1996; Doble 1997), is inexpensive to administer, produces public value, and can to a degree be scaled to the seriousness of crimes.

Doing work to benefit the community as a substitute for other punishments for crime has a history that dates at least from imperial Rome. Modern use, however, is conventionally dated from a 1960s effort by judges in Alameda County, California, to avoid having to impose fines for traffic violations on low-income women, when they knew that many would be unable to pay and would be in danger of being sent to jail as a result (Morris and Tonry 1990, chap. 6).

The California program attracted widespread interest and influenced the establishment of community service programs in the United States and elsewhere. The English pilot projects in the early 1970s (Young 1979), followed by Scottish pilots in the late 1970s (McIvor 1992), discussed later, both led to programs that have been fully institutionalized as a penalty that lies between probation and imprisonment in those countries' sentencing tariffs. In the United States, many millions of dollars were spent in the 1970s by the Law Enforcement Assistance Administration, for programs for adults, and by the Office for Juvenile Justice and Delinquency Prevention, for programs for children, but with little lasting effect (McDonald 1992).

Community service has not come into widespread use as a prison alternative in the United States (Pease 1985 and McDonald 1986 provide detailed accounts with many references). Largely as a result, there has been little substantial research on the effectiveness of community service as an intermediate punishment.

With the exception of one major American study (McDonald 1986), the most ambitious evaluation research has been carried out elsewhere. In England and Wales, Scotland, and the Netherlands, community service orders (CSOs) were statutorily authorized with the express aim that they serve as an alternative to short-term incarceration. In each of these countries, research was undertaken to discover whether CSOs were being used as replacements for short-term prison sentences (generally, yes, in about half of cases) and whether their use had any effect on recidivism rates for new crimes (generally, no). The American study, of a pilot community service program in New York City intended to substitute for jail terms up to six months, reached similar conclusions (McDonald 1986).

In law and in practice, CSOs in England are regarded as more intrusive and punitive than probation and as an appropriate substitute for imprisonment (Lloyd 1991). CSOs can involve between 40 and 240 hours of work supervised by a community service officer; failure to participate or cooperate can result in revocation. It is generally estimated that half of those sentenced to community service would otherwise be sentenced to prison, and half would receive less severe penalties (Pease 1985). Reoffending rates are believed and generally found to be neither higher nor lower than those of comparable offenders sent to prison (Pease 1985).

The Scottish experience trails several years behind the English but closely resembles it. An experimental program was established in 1977, permanent enabling legislation was enacted in 1978, and CSOs were implemented nationwide in the early 1980s. Offenders are sentenced to 40 to 240 hours of work, to be completed within one year. A five-year-long evaluation concluded that half of offenders sentenced to CSOs would otherwise have been confined, that both judges and offenders thought community service an appropriate penalty, and that reconviction rates after three years (63 percent) compared favorably with reconviction rates following incarceration (McIvor 1992, 1995).

The story in the Netherlands, where 10 percent of convicted offenders were sentenced to community service in 1992 and where government policy called for successive annual 10 percent increases in the number of CSOs ordered, is similar. Pilot projects began in 1981 with the express aim of establishing a penalty that would be used in place of short terms of imprisonment. The British pattern of a maximum sentence of 240 hours to be performed within one year was followed. Evaluations reached the by-now-expected conclusion that recidivism rates were no worse but that judges were using CSOs both for otherwise prison-bound and otherwise suspended sentence–bound offenders (with the balance as yet unknown; van Kalmthout and Tak 1992; Tak 1994, 1995). In 1989, the Penal Code was amended to institutionalize CSOs as authorized sanctions.

The only well-documented American community service project, operated by the Vera Institute of Justice, was established in 1979 in the Bronx, one of the boroughs of New York, and eventually spread to Manhattan, Brooklyn, and Queens. The program was designed as a credible penalty for repetitive property offenders who had previously been sentenced to probation or jail and who faced a six-month or longer jail term for the current conviction. Offenders were sentenced to seventy hours of community service under the supervision of Vera foremen. Participants were told that attendance would be closely monitored and that nonattendance and noncooperation would be punished. A sophisticated evaluation concluded that recidivism rates were unaffected by the program, that prison diversion goals were met, and that the program saved taxpayers' money (McDonald 1986, 1992).

Both American and European research and experience show that community service can serve as a meaningful, cost-effective sanction for offenders who would otherwise have been imprisoned. The policy implications are clear. For offenders who do not present unacceptable risks of future violent (including sexual) crimes, a punitive sanction that costs much less than prison to implement, that promises no higher reoffending rates, and that creates negligible risks of violence by those who would otherwise be confined has much to commend it.

Monetary Penalties

Monetary penalties for nontrivial crimes have yet to catch on in the United States. That is not to deny that millions of fines are imposed every year. Fines are nearly the sole penalty for traffic offenses and in many courts are often imposed for misdemeanors (Hillsman, Sichel, and Mahoney 1984; Cole et al. 1987). And in many courts, most fines are collected. Although ambiguous lines of authority and absence of institutional self-interest sometimes result in haphazard and ineffective collection, courts that wish to do so can be effective collectors (Cole 1992).

Nor is it to deny that convicted offenders in some jurisdictions are routinely ordered to pay restitution and in most jurisdictions are routinely ordered to pay growing lists of fees for probation supervision, for urinalyses, and for use of electronic monitoring equipment. A survey of monetary exactions from offenders carried out in the late 1980s identified more than thirty separate charges, penalties, and fees that were imposed by courts, administrative agencies, and legislatures (Mullaney 1988). These commonly included court costs, fines, restitution, and payments to victim compensation funds, and often included a variety of supervision and monitoring fees.

The problem is neither that monetary penalties are not imposed nor that they cannot be collected, but that, as George Cole and his colleagues reported when summarizing the results of a national survey of judges' attitudes about fines, "At present, judges do not regard the fine alone as a meaningful alternative to incarceration or probation" (Cole et al. 1987, p. 5).

This American inability to see fines as serious penalties stands in marked contrast to the legal systems of other countries. In the Netherlands, the fine is legally presumed to be the preferred penalty for every crime, and Section 359(6) of the Code of Criminal Procedure requires judges to provide a statement of reasons in every case in which a fine is not imposed. In Germany in 1986, for another example, 81 percent of all sentenced adult criminals were ordered to pay a fine, including 73 percent of those convicted of crimes of violence (Hillsman and Greene 1992, p. 125). In Sweden in 1979, fines constituted 91 percent of all sentences (Casale 1981). In England in 1980, fines were imposed in 47 percent of convictions for indictable offenses (roughly equivalent to American felonies); these included 45 percent of convicted sex offenders, 24 percent of burglars, and half of those convicted of assault (Morris and Tonry 1990, chap. 4).

European monetary penalties often take the form of "day fines," in use in the Scandinavian countries since the turn of the century and in Germany since the 1970s. Day fines scale amounts both to the defendant's ability to pay (some measure of daily income) and to the seriousness of the crime (expressed as the number of daily income units assessed; Grebing 1982).

There have been a number of experimental efforts to introduce day fines to the United States. The initial pilot project was conducted in Staten Island, New York, in 1988–1989, again under the auspices of the Vera Institute of Justice. Judges, prosecutors, and other court personnel were included in the planning, and implementation was remarkably successful. Most judges cooperated with the new voluntary scheme, the distribution of fines imposed changed in ways that showed that judges were following the system, the average fine imposed increased by 25 percent, the total amount ordered on all defendants increased by 14 percent, and 70 percent of defendants paid their fines in full (Hillsman and Greene 1992).

The Staten Island findings, while not unpromising, are subject to two important caveats. First, the participating court had limited jurisdiction and handled only misdemeanors; the use of day fines for felonies thus remains untested. Second, applicable statutes limited total fines for any charge to $250, $500, or $1,000, depending on the misdemeanor class, and thus artificially capped fines at those levels and precluded meaningful implementation of the scheme in relation to other than the lowest-income defendants.

A second modest pilot project was conducted for twelve weeks in 1989 in Milwaukee (McDonald, Greene, and Worzella 1992), and four projects funded by the Bureau of Justice Assistance of the U.S. Department of Justice were established in the early 1990s in Maricopa County (Phoenix), Arizona; Bridgeport, Connecticut; Polk County, Iowa; and Coos, Josephine, Malheur, and Marion Counties in Oregon (Turner 1995). The Milwaukee project applied only to noncriminal violations, resulted in reduced total collections, and was abandoned. The Phoenix project, known as FARE (for Financial Assessments Related to Employability), was conceived as a sanction between unsupervised and supervised probation. The Iowa pilot included only misdemeanants, and the Oregon projects included misdemeanants and probationable felonies (excluding Marion County, the largest, which covered only misdemeanants). Only in Connecticut did the pilot cover a range of felonies and misdemeanors. In mid-1997, the Phoenix project remained in operation; the others had ceased operation. The Bureau of Justice Assistance (1996) published a manual on organization of day-fine projects that reprints key forms and protocols from the four pilot projects.

A RAND Corporation evaluation of the Arizona, Connecticut, Iowa, and Oregon projects was funded by the National Institute of Justice; except in Phoenix, the findings were disappointing (Turner and Petersilia 1996). Given the limited reach of the projects, however, even more positive results would not have demonstrated that day fines show promise of becoming an intermediate sanction capable—as in Europe—of diverting large numbers of felony offenders from prison. The Bureau of Justice Assistance manual (1996) is conspicuously uninformative about the evaluation findings but hints at the pilots' limited success: "It is clear from the experiences to date that much careful thought must be given to making day fines an option in specific jurisdictions" (Bureau of Justice Assistance 1996, p. 5).

A further cautionary note comes from England and Wales, which tried, unsuccessfully, to launch a day-fine system (because calculations were based on weekly rather than daily income, it was called a "unit-fines" system). Pilot projects were established in four magistrates' courts and evaluated by the Home Office Research Unit. The findings were positive: magistrates and other court personnel were pleased with the new system, anticipated problems about determining defendants' incomes proved soluble, low-income defendants received smaller fines, and more fines were fully paid, and earlier, than previously (Moxon, Sutton, and Hedderman 1990; Moxon 1995b). As a result, the Criminal Justice Act of 1991, which effected a substantial overhaul of English sentencing laws, established a national system of unit fines to take effect in October 1992.

The unit-fines system was abandoned seven months later for reasons that remain unclear. The immediate precipitant was a series of media stories of preposterous sentences that discredited the entire system. In one case, a defendant was fined £1200 (late in 1997, $2,040) for throwing a potato chip bag on the ground. In another much-publicized case, a defendant was fined £500 for illegal parking after his car, worth £250, broke down on a road where parking was prohibited (Moxon 1995a).

Why these (and many comparable) cases were sentenced as they were, and why the government so quickly repudiated its own innovation, are unclear. The specific problems that deprived the scheme of its credibility and led to its repeal were soluble. Some observers speculated that many magistrates disapproved in principle of what were in effect sentencing guidelines for fines and consequently used overly literal enforcement to undermine them. Some blamed the developers for not anticipating foreseeable problems in implementation and application. Whatever the real explanation, the system is no longer, and developers of day-fine systems in the United States will ignore the English experience at their peril.

Is There a Future for Intermediate Sanctions?

Despite the seemingly disheartening evaluation findings that suggest that most intermediate sanctions do not reduce recidivism, corrections costs, and prison crowding while simultaneously enhancing public safety, there is a future for intermediate sanctions. There is a need to develop credible, enforceable sanctions between prison and probation that can provide appropriate deserved penalties for offenders convicted of midlevel crimes, and numerous studies document the capacity of well-managed corrections departments to implement such programs. There is a need to help offenders establish conventional, law-abiding patterns of living, and the evaluation literature suggests ways that can be facilitated. There is a need to develop intermediate sanctions that can serve as cost-effective substitutes for confinement, and the evaluation literature suggests how this can be done. Finally, there is a need to devise ways to assure that intermediate sanctions are used for the kinds of offenders for whom particular programs were created, and experience with parole and sentencing guidelines shows how that can be done.

Three major obstacles stand in the way. The first, and the most difficult, is the modern American preoccupation with absolute severity of punishment and the related widespread view that only imprisonment counts. The average lengths of prison sentences are much greater in the United States than in other Western countries (Tonry 1995, Table 7-1). The ten-, twenty-, and thirty-year minimum sentences that are in vogue for drug and violent crimes are unimaginable in most countries, as is the proliferation in the 1990s of "three-strikes" laws requiring very long or life sentences for third-time offenders.

This absolute severity frustrates efforts to devise intermediate sanctions for the psychological (not to mention political) reason that few other sanctions seem commensurable with a multiyear prison sentence. By contrast, half or more of offenders convicted of violent crimes in Sweden, Germany, and England are sentenced to fines (abandonment of unit fines in England did not result in a reduction in the use of fines, which continued to be imposed on a "tariff" fixed-amount basis).

In those countries, the prison sentences thereby avoided would have involved months or at most a year or two, making a burdensome financial penalty an imaginable alternative. By contrast, most of the American day-fine pilot projects used day fines as punishments for misdemeanors or noncriminal ordinance violations or as a punishment between supervised and unsupervised probation. Likewise, with the rare exception of New York's community service project started by the Vera Institute, except for the most venial offenses, CSOs are generally ordered as probation conditions and not as sentences in their own right.

Successful efforts have been made in Europe to replace prison sentences of six or fewer months (moderately severe penalties in those countries) with day fines in Germany (Weigend 1995) and with CSOs in the Netherlands (Tak 1994). In Sweden, however, less than a quarter of prison sentences are for terms of six months or longer (Jareborg 1994), and in the Netherlands less than 15 percent are for a year or longer. Equivalent crimes in the United States would be punished by terms measured in years; in 1991, 57 percent of state prison inmates were sentenced to terms longer than five years (Beck et al. 1993).

The second, not unrelated, obstacle to fuller development of intermediate sanctions is widespread commitment to "just deserts" rationales for punishment and the collateral idea that the severity of punishment should vary directly with the seriousness of the crime. This has been translated in the federal and most state sentencing guidelines systems into policies that tie punishments to the offender's crime and criminal history and little else.

Such policies and their commitment to "proportionality in punishment" constitute a gross oversimplification of the cases that come before criminal courts. Crimes that share a label can be very different; robberies range from schoolyard takings of basketballs to gangland assaults on banks. Offenders committing the same crime can be very different; a thief may have been motivated by a sudden impulse, by the need to feed a hungry child, by a craving to buy drugs, or by a conscious choice to make a living as a thief.

Punishments likewise vary. Despite a common label, two years' imprisonment can be served in a maximum-security prison of fear and violence, in a minimum-security camp, at home under house arrest, or in some combination of these and other regimes. Even a single punishment may be differently experienced; three years' imprisonment may be a rite of passage for a young gang member, a death sentence for a frail seventy-year-old, or the ruin of the lives of an employed forty-year-old man and his dependent spouse and children.

Nonetheless, commitment to ideas of proportionality is widespread, and it circumscribes the roles that intermediate sanctions can play. Although few people would disagree with the empirical observations in the preceding two paragraphs, sentencing policies based on ideas of proportionality somehow reify the sentencing categories into something meaningful. If guidelines specify a twenty-four-month prison term for offense X with criminal history Y, it seems unfair to sentence one offender to community service or house arrest when another like-situated offender (in the narrow terms of the guidelines) is sentenced to twenty-four months. It seems more unfair to sentence one offender subject to a twenty-four-month guidelines sentence to house arrest when an offender convicted of a less serious crime receives an eighteen-month prison sentence.

Commitment to proportionality interacts with the modern penchant for severe penalties. If crimes punished by months of incarceration in other countries are punished by years in the United States, comparisons between offenders are more stark. If in Sweden, two offenses are ordinarily punished by thirty- and sixty-day prison terms, imposition of a day-fine order on the more serious offender, out of consideration for the effects of a prison term on his family and employment, produces a contrast between a thirty-day sentence and a sixty-unit day-fine. Convert the example to American presumptive sentences of two and four years, and the contrast is jarring between an intermediate sanction in lieu of a four-year sentence and two years in prison for someone convicted of a less serious crime.

Net widening is the third obstacle to further development of intermediate sanctions. There are two solutions. The first is to shift control over program placements from judges to corrections officials wherever possible. For some programs such as boot camps and some forms of ISP and house arrest, this is relatively easy and would make it likelier that such programs would achieve their goals of saving money and prison space without increasing recidivism rates.

Transfers of authority to corrections officials can, however, at best be a partial solution. No one wants all sentencing authority shifted into bureaucratic hands. Judges, after all, are concerned with questions of liberty and justice, and most people would probably rest easier having judges making threshold decisions about confinement.

The alternative is to structure judges' decisions about intermediate sanctions by use of sentencing guidelines. A substantial body of evaluation and other research demonstrates that well-conceived and implemented guidelines systems can change sentencing patterns in a jurisdiction and achieve high levels of judicial compliance (M. Tonry 1996, chaps. 2, 3).

Most state guidelines systems, however, establish presumptions for who is sent to state prisons and for how long, but they do not set presumptions concerning nonprison sentences or choices between prison and other sanctions. Two broad approaches for setting guidelines for nonprison sentences have been tried (Tonry 1997, chaps. 3, 4). The first, which seems to have been a dead end, is to establish "punishment units" in which all sanctions can be expressed. Thus, a year's confinement might equal ten units, a month of house arrest three units, and a month's community service two units. A twenty-unit sentence could be satisfied by any sanction or combination of sanctions equaling twenty. This idea was taken furthest in Oregon, where sentencing guidelines, in addition to setting presumptive ranges for jail and prison sentences, specified a number of punishment units for various crime/criminal history combinations. Oregon, however, never set policies governing unit values, sometimes metaphorically described as exchange rates, and neither there nor anywhere else has the idea been taken further.

The overwhelming problem lies in the idea of proportionality mentioned earlier, as can be illustrated by Washington State's more modest effort at exchange rates. Partial confinement and community service were authorized as substitutes for presumptive prison terms on the bases of one day's partial confinement or three day's community service for one day of confinement. The partial confinement/confinement exchange is probably workable (for short sentences; house arrest, assuming that to count as partial confinement, is seldom imposed for more than a few months), but the community service exchange is not.

Starting with the idea that imprisonment is more unpleasant than community service, the Washington sentencing commission decided that the exchange must be governed by an idea of comparable intrusion in the offender's life; hence, three, 8-hour days' community service per day in prison. The difficulty is that CSOs, to be credible, must be enforced, and experience in this country and elsewhere instructs that they must be short. That is why the New York program provided 70 hours' obligation and the Dutch, English, and Scottish programs establish an upper limit of 240 hours. Under Washington's policy, that range would permit community service in place of three to ten days' confinement.

When punitive literalism governs, the range for substitutions between prison and community penalties is tiny. A system like New York's community service program, 70 hours' work in place of six months' jail, can be justified (the idea was to give repetitive property offenders some meaningful enforced penalty rather than impose a jail term that no one expected would have deterrent effects), but it requires a loosening of proportionality constraints that no sentencing commission has yet been prepared to endorse.

The other approach is to establish different areas of a sentencing guidelines grid in which different presumptions about choice of sentence govern. Both North Carolina (Wright 1997) and Pennsylvania (Kramer and Kempinen 1997; Kempinen 1997) adopted such systems in 1994. One set of crime/criminal history combinations is presumed appropriate only for prison sentences; a second is presumed subject to a judicial choice between prison sentences or intensive community sanctions (including split sentences with elements of both); a third is presumed subject to a choice between intensive or nonintensive community sanctions (or some of both); and a fourth is presumed subject only to nonintensive community sanctions. The Pennsylvania and North Carolina systems took effect in the fall of 1994, both in conjunction with programs of state funding for development of local intermediate sanctions programs; early indications are that they have achieved partial success as a means to increase judicial use of intermediate sanctions and to make their use more consistent (Lubitz 1997; Kempinen 1997).

Conclusion

Experience to date supports a number of generalizations about intermediate sanctions. First, for offenders who do not present unacceptable risks of violence, well-managed intermediate sanctions offer a cost-effective way to keep them in the community at less cost than imprisonment and with no worse later prospect for criminality. Second, intermediate sanctions are highly vulnerable to net widening when entry is controlled by judges; sentencing guidelines may be able to diminish this problem by setting standards for judges' decisions. Third, intermediate sanctions may offer promise as a way to get and keep offenders in drug and other treatment programs. Fourth, community service and monetary penalties remain woefully underdeveloped in the United States, and much could be learned from the experiences of European countries. Fifth, intermediate sanctions are unlikely to come into widespread use as prison alternatives unless sentencing theories and policies become more expansive and move away from oversimplified ideas about proportionality in punishment.

References

Allen, Francis A. 1964. *The Borderland of Criminal Justice*. Chicago: University of Chicago Press.

Anderson, David C. 1998. *Sensible Justice: Alternatives to Prison*. New York: The New Press.

Anglin, Douglas, and Yih-Ing Hser. 1990. "Treatment of Drug Abuse." In *Drugs and Crime*, edited by Michael Tonry and James Q. Wilson. Chicago: University of Chicago Press.

Austin, James, Michael Jones, and Melissa Bolyard. 1993. *The Growing Use of Jail Boot Camps: The Current State of the Art*. Research in Brief. Washington, D.C.: National Institute of Justice.

Baird, S. C., and D. Wagner. 1990. "Measuring Diversion: The Florida Community Control Program." *Crime and Delinquency* 36:112–25.

Ball, R. A., C. R. Huff, and J. R. Lilly. 1988. *House Arrest and Correctional Policy*. Newbury Park, Calif.: Sage.

Banks, J., A. L. Porter, R. L. Rardin, T. R. Silver, and V. E. Unger. 1977. *Phase I Evaluation of Intensive Special Probation Projects*. Washington, D.C.: Law Enforcement Assistance Administration, National Institute of Law Enforcement and Criminal Justice.

Baumer, Terry L., M. G. Maxfield, and R. I. Mendelsohn. 1993. "A Comparative Analysis of Three Electronically Monitored Home Detention Programs." *Justice Quarterly* 10:121–42.

Baumer, Terry L., and Robert I. Mendelsohn. 1992. "Electronically Monitored Home Confinement: Does It Work?" In *Smart Sentencing: The Emergence of Intermediate Sanctions*, edited by James M. Byrne, Arthur J. Lurigio, and Joan Petersilia. Newbury Park, Calif.: Sage.

Beck, Allen, Darrell Gilliord, Lawrence Greenfeld, Caroline Harlow, Thomas Heste, Louis Jankowski, Tracy Snell, James Stephan, and Daniele Morton. 1993. *Survey of State Prison Inmates, 1991*. Washington, D.C.: Bureau of Justice Statistics.

Begasse, Jen Kiko. 1997. "Oregonians Support Alternatives for Nonviolent Offenders." In *Sentencing Reform in Overcrowded Times: A Comparative Perspective*, edited by Michael Tonry and Kathleen Hatlestad. New York: Oxford University Press.

Biles, David. 1993. "Noncustodial Penalties in Australia." *Overcrowded Times* 4(1):7–9.

Blomberg, Thomas G., William Bales, and Karen Reed. 1993. "Intermediate Punishment: Redistributing or Extending Social Control?" *Crime, Law, and Social Change* 19:187–201.

Bureau of Justice Assistance. 1996. *How to Use Structured Fines (Day Fines) as an Intermediate Sanction*. Washington, D.C.: U.S. Department of Justice, Bureau of Justice Assistance.

Bureau of Justice Statistics. 1998. *Prison and Jail Inmates at Midyear 1997*. Washington, D.C.: U.S. Department of Justice, Bureau of Justice Statistics.

Byrne, James M., Arthur J. Lurigio, and Joan Petersilia, eds. 1992. *Smart Sentencing: The Emergence of Intermediate Sanctions*. Newbury Park, Calif.: Sage.

Byrne, James M., and April Pattavina. 1992. "The Effectiveness Issue: Assessing What Works in the Adult Community Corrections System." In *Smart*

Sentencing: The Emergence of Intermediate Sanctions, edited by James M. Byrne, Arthur J. Lurigio, and Joan Petersilia. Newbury Park, Calif.: Sage.

Carter, R. M., J. Robinson, and L. T. Wilkins. 1967. *The San Francisco Project: A Study of Federal Probation and Parole*. Berkeley: University of California Press.

Casale, Silvia G. 1981. *Fines in Europe*. Fines in Sentencing Working Paper no. 10. New York: Vera Institute of Justice.

Clear, Todd R., and Anthony A. Braga. 1995. "Community Corrections." In *Crime*, edited by James Q. Wilson and Joan Petersilia. San Francisco: ICS Press.

Clear, Todd R., and James M. Byrne. 1992. "The Future of Intermediate Sanctions: Questions to Consider." In *Smart Sentencing: The Emergence of Intermediate Sanctions*, edited by James M. Byrne, Arthur J. Lurigio, and Joan Petersilia. Newbury Park, Calif.: Sage.

Cole, George F. 1992. "Monetary Sanctions: The Problem of Compliance." In *Smart Sentencing: The Emergence of Intermediate Sanctions*, edited by James M. Byrne, Arthur J. Lurigio, and Joan Petersilia. Newbury Park, Calif.: Sage.

Cole, George F., Barry Mahoney, Marlene Thornton, and Roger A. Hanson. 1987. *The Practices and Attitudes of Trial Court Judges Regarding Fines as a Criminal Sanction*. Washington, D.C.: National Institute of Justice.

Doble, John. 1997. "Survey Shows Alabamians Support Alternatives. In *Sentencing Reform in Overcrowded Times: A Comparative Perspective*, edited by Michael Tonry and Kathleen Hatlestad. New York: Oxford University Press.

Doble, John, and Stephen Immerwahr. 1997. "Delawareans Favor Prison Alternatives." In *Sentencing Reform in Overcrowded Times: A Comparative Perspective*, edited by Michael Tonry and Kathleen Hatlestad. New York: Oxford University Press.

Erwin, Billie, and Lawrence Bennett. 1987. *New Dimensions in Probation: Georgia's Experience with Intensive Probation Supervision*. Research in Brief. Washington, D.C.: National Institute of Justice.

Farkas, Steve. 1997. "Pennsylvanians Prefer Alternatives to Prison." In *Sentencing Reform in Overcrowded Times: A Comparative Perspective*, edited by Michael Tonry and Kathleen Hatlestad. New York: Oxford University Press.

Folkard, M. S., D. E. Smith, and D. D. Smith. 1974. *IMPACT*. Vol. 1, *The Design of the Probation Experiment and an Interim Evaluation*. London: HMSO.

———. 1976. *IMPACT*. Vol. 2, *The Results of the Experiment*. London: HMSO.

Ford, Daniel, and Annesley K. Schmidt. 1985. *Electronically Monitored Home Confinement*. Research in Action. Washington, D.C.: National Institute of Justice.

Gendreau, Paul, Francis T. Cullen, and James Bonta. 1994. "Intensive Rehabilitation Supervision: The Next Generation in Community Corrections?" *Federal Probation* 58:72–78.

Grebing, Gerhardt. 1982. *The Fine in Comparative Law: A Survey of 21 Countries*. Occasional paper no. 9. Cambridge: University of Cambridge, Institute of Criminology.

Higgins, Damon, and R. Claire Snyder. 1996. "North Carolinians Want Alternative Sentences for Nonviolent Offenders." *Overcrowded Times* 7(4):1, 12–15.

Hillsman, Sally. 1990. "Fines and Day Fines." In *Crime and Justice: A Review of Research*, vol. 12, edited by Michael Tonry and Norval Morris. Chicago: University of Chicago Press.

Hillsman, Sally, and Judith A. Greene. 1992. "The Use of Fines as an Intermediate Sanction." In *Smart Sentencing: The Emergence of Intermediate Sanctions*, edited by James M. Byrne, Arthur J. Lurigio, and Joan Petersilia. Newbury Park, Calif.: Sage.

Hillsman, Sally, Joyce Sichel, and Barry Mahoney. 1984. *Fines in Sentencing: A Study of the Use of the Fine as a Criminal Sanction*. Washington, D.C.: National Institute of Justice.

Jareborg, Nils. 1994. "The Swedish Sentencing Reform." In *The Politics of Sentencing Reform*, edited by Chris Clarkson and Rod Morgan. Oxford: Oxford University Press.

Kempinen, Cynthia. 1997. "Pennsylvania Revises Sentencing Guidelines." *Overcrowded Times* 8(4):1, 14–18.

Kramer, John, and Cynthia Kempinen. 1997. "Pennsylvania's Sentencing Guidelines: The Process of Assessment and Revision." In *Sentencing Reform in Overcrowded Times: A Comparative Perspective*, edited by Michael Tonry and Kathleen Hatlestad. New York: Oxford University Press.

Larivee, John J. 1995. "Day Reporting in Massachusetts." In *Intermediate Sanctions in Overcrowded Times*, edited by Michael Tonry and Kate Hamilton. Boston: Northeastern University Press.

Lilly, Robert J. 1995. "Electronic Monitoring in the U.S." In *Intermediate Sanctions in Overcrowded Times*, edited by Michael Tonry and Kate Hamilton. Boston: Northeastern University Press.

Lipton, Douglas, Robert Martinson, and Judith Wilks. 1975. *The Effectiveness of Correctional Treatment: A Survey of Correctional Treatment Evaluations*. New York: Praeger.

Lloyd, C. 1991. *National Standards for Community Service Orders: The First Two Years of Operation*. London: Home Office Research and Planning Unit.

Lubitz, Robin. 1997. "North Carolina Legislature Considers Sentencing Change." In *Sentencing Reform in Overcrowded Times: A Comparative Perspective*, edited by Michael Tonry and Kathleen Hatlestad. New York: Oxford University Press.

Lurigio, Arthur J., and Joan Petersilia. 1992. "The Emergence of Intensive Probation Supervision Programs in the United States." In *Smart Sentencing: The Emergence of Intermediate Sanctions*, edited by James M. Byrne, Arthur J. Lurigio, and Joan Petersilia. Newbury Park, Calif.: Sage.

MacKenzie, Doris Layton. 1993. "Boot Camp Prisons 1993." *National Institute of Justice Journal* 227:21–28.

———. 1995. "Boot Camps: A National Assessment." In *Intermediate Sanctions in Overcrowded Times*, edited by Michael Tonry and Kate Hamilton. Boston: Northeastern University Press.

MacKenzie, Doris Layton, and Dale Parent. 1992. "Boot Camp Prisons for Young Offenders." In *Smart Sentencing: The Emergence of Intermediate*

Sanctions, edited by James M. Byrne, Arthur J. Lurigio, and Joan Petersilia. Newbury Park, Calif.: Sage.

MacKenzie, Doris Layton, and A. Piquero. 1994. "The Impact of Shock Incarceration Programs on Prison Crowding." *Crime and Delinquency* 40:222–49.

MacKenzie, Doris Layton, and J. W. Shaw. 1990. "Inmate Adjustment and Change During Shock Incarceration: The Impact of Correctional Boot Camp Programs." *Justice Quarterly* 7:125–50.

———. 1993. "The Impact of Shock Incarceration on Technical Violations and New Criminal Activities." *Justice Quarterly* 10:463–87.

MacKenzie, Doris Layton, and C. Souryal. 1994. *Multi-Site Evaluation of Shock Incarceration*. Report to the National Institute of Justice. College Park: University of Maryland, Department of Criminology and Criminal Justice.

Mair, George. 1988. *Probation Day Centres*. London: HMSO.

———. 1994. "Intensive Probation in England and Wales." *Overcrowded Times* 5(4):4–6.

———. 1995a. "Day Centres in England and Wales." In *Intermediate Sanctions in Overcrowded Times*, edited by Michael Tonry and Kate Hamilton. Boston: Northeastern University Press.

———. 1995b. "Electronic Monitoring in England and Wales." In *Intermediate Sanctions in Overcrowded Times*, edited by Michael Tonry and Kate Hamilton. Boston: Northeastern University Press.

Mair, George, and Claire Nee. 1990. *Electronic Monitoring: The Trials and Their Results*. London: HMSO.

———. 1992. "Day Centre Reconviction Rates." *British Journal of Criminology* 32:329–39.

Mair, George, Charles Lloyd, Claire Nee, and Rae Subbett. 1994. *Intensive Probation in England and Wales: An Evaluation*. London: HMSO.

Maxfield, M., and T. Baumer. 1990. "Home Detention with Electronic Monitoring: Comparing Pretrial and Postconviction Programs." *Crime and Delinquency* 36:521–36.

McCarthy, Belinda, ed. 1987. *Intermediate Punishments: Intensive Supervision, Home Confinement, and Electronic Surveillance*. Monsey, N.Y.: Criminal Justice Press.

McDevitt, Jack, and Robyn Miliano. 1992. "Day Reporting Centers: An Innovative Concept in Intermediate Sanctions." In *Smart Sentencing: The Emergence of Intermediate Sanctions*, edited by James M. Byrne, Arthur J. Lurigio, and Joan Petersilia. Newbury Park, Calif.: Sage.

McDonald, Douglas. 1986. *Punishment Without Walls: Community Service Sentences in New York City*. New Brunswick, N.J.: Rutgers University Press.

———. 1992. "Punishing Labor: Unpaid Community Service as a Criminal Sentence." In *Smart Sentencing: The Emergence of Intermediate Sanctions*, edited by James M. Byrne, Arthur J. Lurigio, and Joan Petersilia. Newbury Park, Calif.: Sage.

McDonald, Douglas, Judith Greene, and Charles Worzella. 1992. *Day Fines in American Courts: The Staten Island and Milwaukee Experiments*. Issues and Practices. Washington, D.C.: National Institute of Justice.

McIvor, Gill. 1992. *Sentenced to Serve: The Operation and Impact of Community Service by Offenders*. Aldershot, England: Avebury.

———. 1995. "CSOs Succeed in Scotland." In *Intermediate Sanctions in Overcrowded Times*, edited by Michael Tonry and Kate Hamilton. Boston: Northeastern University Press.

Meachum, Larry R. 1986. "House Arrest: Oklahoma Experience." *Corrections Today* 48(6):102–10.

Morris, Norval. 1974. *The Future of Imprisonment*. Chicago: University of Chicago Press.

Morris, Norval, and Michael Tonry. 1990. *Between Prison and Probation: Intermediate Punishments in a Rational Sentencing System*. New York: Oxford University Press.

Moxon, David. 1995a. "England Abandons Day Fines." In *Intermediate Sanctions in Overcrowded Times*, edited by Michael Tonry and Kate Hamilton. Boston: Northeastern University Press.

———. 1995b. "England Adopts Day Fines." In *Intermediate Sanctions in Overcrowded Times*, edited by Michael Tonry and Kate Hamilton. Boston: Northeastern University Press.

Moxon, David, Mike Sutton, and Carol Hedderman. 1990. *Unit Fines: Experiments in Four Courts*. London: HMSO.

Mullaney, Fahy G. 1988. *Economic Sanctions in Community Corrections*. Washington, D.C.: National Institute of Corrections.

National Institute of Justice. 1994. *Drug Use Forecasting (DUF): 1993 Annual Report*. Washington, D.C.: National Institute of Justice.

Palumbo, Dennis J., Mary Clifford, and Zoann K. Snyder-Joy. 1992. "From Net-Widening to Intermediate Sanctions: The Transformation of Alternatives to Incarceration from Benevolence to Malevolence." In *Smart Sentencing: The Emergence of Intermediate Sanctions*, edited by James M. Byrne, Arthur J. Lurigio, and Joan Petersilia. Newbury Park, Calif.: Sage.

Parent, Dale. 1989. *Shock Incarceration: An Overview of Existing Programs*. Washington, D.C.: National Institute of Justice.

———. 1990. *Day Reporting Centers for Criminal Offenders: A Descriptive Analysis of Existing Programs*. Washington, D.C.: National Institute of Justice.

———. 1995a. "Boot Camps Failing to Achieve Goals." In *Intermediate Sanctions in Overcrowded Times*, edited by Michael Tonry and Kate Hamilton. Boston: Northeastern University Press.

———. 1995b. "Day Reporting Centers." In *Intermediate Sanctions in Overcrowded Times*, edited by Michael Tonry and Kate Hamilton. Boston: Northeastern University Press.

Pease, Ken. 1985. "Community Service Orders." In *Crime and Justice: An Annual Review of Research*, vol. 6, edited by Michael Tonry and Norval Morris. Chicago: University of Chicago Press.

Petersilia, Joan, Arthur J. Lurigio, and James M. Byrne. 1992. "Introduction: The Emergence of Intermediate Sanctions." In *Smart Sentencing: The Emergence of Intermediate Sanctions*, edited by James M. Byrne, Arthur J. Lurigio, and Joan Petersilia. Newbury Park, Calif.: Sage.

Petersilia, Joan, and Susan Turner. 1993. "Intensive Probation and Parole." In

Crime and Justice: A Review of Research, vol. 17, edited by Michael Tonry. Chicago: University of Chicago Press.

Rauschenberg, Fritz. 1997. "Ohio Guidelines Take Effect." *Overcrowded Times* 8(4):1, 10–11.

Renzema, Marc. 1992. "Home Confinement Programs: Development, Implementation, and Impact." In *Smart Sentencing: The Emergence of Intermediate Sanctions*, edited by James M. Byrne, Arthur J. Lurigio, and Joan Petersilia. Newbury Park, Calif.: Sage.

Ryan, James E. 1997. "Who Gets Revoked? A Comparison of Intensive Supervision Successes and Failures in Vermont." *Crime and Delinquency* 43:104–18.

Sechrest, Lee B., Susan O. White, and Elizabeth D. Brown, eds. 1979. *The Rehabilitation of Criminal Offenders: Problems and Prospects.* Washington, D.C.: National Academy Press.

Tak, Peter J. P. 1994. "Sentencing in the Netherlands." *Acta Criminologica* 7:7–17.

———. 1995. "Sentencing and Punishment in the Netherlands." In *Sentencing Reform in Overcrowded Times: A Comparative Perspective*, edited by Michael Tonry and Kathleen Hatlestad. New York: Oxford University Press.

Tonry, Hunter. 1996. "Commission Proposes Massachusetts Guidelines." *Overcrowded Times* 7(4):1, 7–8.

Tonry, Michael. 1990. "Overt and Latent Functions of Intensive Supervision Probation." *Crime and Delinquency* 36:174–91.

———. 1995. *Malign Neglect: Race, Crime, and Punishment in America.* New York: Oxford University Press.

———. 1996. *Sentencing Matters.* New York: Oxford University Press.

———. 1997. *Intermediate Sanctions in Sentencing Guidelines.* National Institute of Justice Issues and Practices. Washington, D.C.: U.S. Department of Justice, National Institute of Justice.

———. 1998. "Intermediate Sanctions in Sentencing Guidelines." In *Crime and Justice: A Review of Research*, vol. 23, edited by Michael Tonry. Chicago: University of Chicago Press.

Tonry, Michael, and Kate Hamilton, eds. 1995. *Intermediate Sanctions in Overcrowded Times.* Boston: Northeastern University Press.

Tonry, Michael, and Kathleen Hatlestad, eds. 1997. *Sentencing Reform in Overcrowded Times: A Comparative Perspective.* New York: Oxford University Press.

Tonry, Michael, and Mary Lynch. 1996. "Intermediate Sanctions." In *Crime and Justice: A Review of Research*, vol. 20, edited by Michael Tonry. Chicago: University of Chicago Press.

Turner, Susan. 1995. "Day-Fine Projects Launched in Four Jurisdictions." In *Intermediate Sanctions in Overcrowded Times*, edited by Michael Tonry and Kate Hamilton. Boston: Northeastern University Press.

Turner, Susan, and Joan Petersilia. 1996. *Day Fines in Four U.S. Jurisdictions.* RAND no. 1153-NIJ. Santa Monica, Calif.: RAND.

U.S. General Accounting Office. 1990. *Intermediate Sanctions: Their Impacts on Prison Crowding, Costs, and Recidivism Are Still Unclear.* Gaithersburg, Md.: General Accounting Office.

———. 1993. *Prison Boot Camps: Short-Term Prison Costs Reduced, but*

Long-Term Impact Uncertain. Washington, D.C.: U.S. General Accounting Office.

van Kalmthout, Anton M., and Peter J. P. Tak. 1992. *Sanctions-Systems in the Member-States of the Council of Europe: Deprivation of Liberty, Community Service, and Other Substitutes.* Boston: Kluwer.

von Hirsch, Andrew. 1976. *Doing Justice: The Choice of Punishments.* New York: Hill and Wang.

Weigend, Thomas. 1995. "Fines Reduce Use of Prison Sentences in Germany." In *Intermediate Sanctions in Overcrowded Times,* edited by Michael Tonry and Kate Hamilton. Boston: Northeastern University Press.

Wright, Ronald F. 1997. "North Carolina Avoids Early Trouble with Guidelines." In *Sentencing Reform in Overcrowded Times: A Comparative Perspective,* edited by Michael Tonry and Kathleen Hatlestad. New York: Oxford University Press.

Young, Warren, 1979. *Community Service Orders.* London: Heinemann.

26

Correctional Treatment

GERALD G. GAES

Proponents of rehabilitation are encouraged by the results of recent meta-analyses of the correctional treatment literature. This is because they believe that meta-analysis provides sufficient insight to enable the design of programs that maximize treatment effectiveness. To what extent is this renewed optimism warranted?

There are promising signals that some interventions reduce recidivism. Yet there is much more research to be done to justify confidence in the effects of correctional interventions, and to understand the conditions under which these interventions work most effectively. The "nothing works" conclusion is unwarranted. However, the "some things work for some people" principle can be construed as trivial unless social scientists can demonstrate that "some things" refers to a well-defined set of interventions and "some people" refers to sizable and definable percentages of the treatment population.

Since most of the intervention literature has been targeted at juveniles and most of the recent discussions of meta-analyses cover primarily juvenile treatments, in this chapter I review juvenile and adult treatments together. The theoretical and methodological paradigms[1] for understanding and evaluating correctional interventions have changed over time. However, a common thread is woven through the modern history of intervention. As many social scientists have concluded, it is extremely difficult to conceptualize, design, implement, and analyze correctional programs.

This chapter reviews the history of rehabilitation research to introduce the paradigms of the past. To analyze the paradigms of the present, the following topics are discussed: the principles of effective correctional treatment; process evaluations; the technique of meta-analysis; the recommendations of the National Academy of Sciences (NAS) Panel on Research on Rehabilitative Techniques (NAS Panel; see Sechrest, White, and Brown 1979); and an analysis of a subdomain of intervention research regarding the effects of intensive drug treatment in prison on postrelease outcomes. This last topic is used as a kind of case study to show what happens when a small correctional treatment subdomain is put under a methodological microscope. The following topics concerning the future are considered: system-level and cost-benefit models, strong inference designs, and the integration of correctional treatment theory with other current criminological theoretical paradigms.

The NAS Panel defined *rehabilitation* in a quite satisfactory way: "Rehabilitation is the result of any planned intervention that reduces an offender's further criminal activity. . . . The effects of maturation and the effects associated with 'fear' or 'intimidation' are excluded" (Sechrest, White, and Brown 1979, pp. 4–5). With this definition in hand, I begin by reviewing the theoretical paradigms of the early history of American corrections, when rehabilitation was called reformation, and the prison was viewed as an institution for the transformation of the criminal.

Past

The concept of American prisoner reformation originated in the Jacksonian era. Reformers of that period wanted to make the prison "an institution that would teach inmates the lessons of order and discipline" (Rothman 1995, p. 117). Early intervention models called for "isolation, obedience, and a steady routine of labor" (p. 117). Reformers conceptualized criminality as a failure of the socializing institutions such as family, church, or school. Therefore, it was the task of the prison to restore the inmate's sense of obedience and morality. Reformers hoped the early penitentiary system would produce rehabilitation through silence and harsh punishment.

By 1867, Wines and Dwight reported, the penitentiary system was fundamentally flawed because reformation required self-discipline rather than penitence and isolation (Rotman 1995). The Progressive Era saw the ascendancy of social workers, psychiatrists, and psychologists. The medical model emerged at the turn of the twentieth century. It was based on the belief that social interventions analogous to the successful medical interventions that had been developed in the diagnosis and treatment of such diseases as tuberculosis and rabies could be developed to change human behavior. Thus, successful human interventions required correct diagnosis or classification followed by appropriate treatment. In the early 1950s, as a result of a series of riots, a reexamination of the prison system led to a rejuvenation of the rehabilitative ideal. The new therapeutic model was intended to counteract what Goffman characterized as the depersonalizing influence of the "total institution" (Rotman 1995).

From the mid-1970s to the present, belief in the possibility of reformation has encountered both skeptics and supporters. Martinson's article on rehabilitation, "What Works? Questions and Answers About Prison Reform," published in the *Public Interest* in 1974, was a watershed event. In many ways, it ended a 150-year-old era of optimism about the possibilities of reforming the offender. Although many social scientists oversimplified the conclusion of this article into the peremptory conclusion that "nothing works," Martinson made very specific criticisms. He seriously questioned the designs and methodologies of many of the treatment studies. He cautioned that treatment might indeed be working, but that the research was so flawed that it was unable to detect any true effects. He suggested that we needed better theory construction, and that some studies that found effects failed to rule out competing explanations. In Martinson's summary, however, his pessimism about the effects of rehabilitation was apparent. He considered, and rejected, the possibility that society should decarcerate low-risk offenders and incapacitate high-risk offenders, rather than pursue a strategy of rehabilitation. He rejected this strategy because he considered it unjust. His concluding proposals were that we study the possibility that punishment has deterrence as its central purpose and that there may be more effective forms of social control than imprisonment.

In 1979, Martinson recanted his earlier position on rehabilitation but was still cautious in his conclusions. He decided that treatment programs could be beneficial (reduce recidivism), neutral (no effect on recidivism), or harmful (increase recidivism), depending on the conditions under which they were delivered, and that no treatment at that time was "inherently either substantially helpful or harmful" (Martinson 1979, p. 254). Thus, treatment effectiveness depended on the capabilities of staff and the resources devoted to implementing and maintaining an intervention.

Martinson's *Public Interest* article drew from but slightly preceded Lipton, Martinson, and Wilks's (1975) more exhaustive survey of correctional treatment evaluations. The criticisms of the rehabilitation literature represented in both of these publications were largely supported by the NAS Panel (Sechrest, White, and Brown 1979). However, continued efforts by other social scientists have awakened a renewed interest in the possibilities of correctional intervention.

The Martinson critique was a lightning rod for a convergence of political ideologies calling for determinate sentences and de-emphasis of prisoner reformation. Wilson (1975) argued that the main purpose of prison was to incapacitate and punish offenders, rather than to rehabilitate them. Other critics argued that the treatment rationales for sentencing and corrections policies gave too much discretion to treatment providers to control the timing of an offender's release and, accordingly, to determine the amount of punishment a prisoner experienced (von Hirsch 1976).

The Present

A number of social scientists have consistently rejected the "nothing works" proposition. Instead, they have argued that there are empirically established conditions under which treatment can work for some kinds of offenders (Andrews et al. 1990; Gendreau and Ross 1987; Lipsey 1989, 1992; Palmer 1975, 1992). Most of this research is based on interventions with juveniles, often in noncustodial settings. More important, there has been a renewed sense of optimism about rehabilitation because of the results of several reviews that use meta-analysis to study the rehabilitation studies.

The Principles of Correctional Treatment

Over the two and a half decades since Martinson's 1974 article, the occasional early rebuttals of his conclusions by treatment advocates have grown into a chorus. The arguments of rehabilitation proponents have been bolstered by methodological developments in the synthesis of research literatures. As a result of meta-analyses of the treatment literature and some critical thinking about the nature of interventions, a corpus of treatment principles has been delineated. Although there remains some disagreement among researchers on the theoretical and empirical bases for these principles, these "rules" form a set of testable hypotheses that can be used to develop the next generation of treatment research. I have abstracted these principles from articles or books written by Andrews (1995); Gendreau and Andrews (1991); Lipsey (1992, 1995); Loesel (1995); McGuire and Priestly (1995); and Palmer (1992). It is no accident that these principles are couched in the language of psychological intervention. The rejuvenation of a treatment paradigm has been led by psychologists, some of whom have argued for a new "psychology of criminal conduct" (see especially Andrews and Bonta 1994).

Criminogenic Needs. Treat *only* those human deficits that are directly related to the propensity to commit crime. These needs include procriminal attitudes, procriminal associates, impulsivity, weak socialization, below average verbal intelligence, a taste for risk, weak problem-solving/self-control skills, the early onset of antisocial behavior, poor parental practices, and deficits in educational, vocational, and employment skills (Andrews 1995). Static characteristics such as age, race, and sex may be important in understanding why interventions work; however, from the perspective of intervention, research must focus on mutable (dynamic) characteristics that can be demonstrated to be related to the propensity to commit crime.

Multimodal Programs. Treat *all* of the deficits simultaneously. If an individual has multiple deficits that, in combination, increase the propensity toward crime, all deficits must be addressed.

Responsivity. Match client learning styles with staff teaching styles. Programs must be tailored to the specific needs and learning styles of the clients.

Risk Classification. Use the highest level of treatment intensity for those clients who are predicted to be most likely to recidivate. Either do not treat low-risk clients or use low treatment intensity for them. There may be a small proportion of the most risky clients who are not treatable. The effect of the risk principle may be modest (Lipsey 1995). Although client characteristics do moderate treatment outcomes, variability in treatment is more important than variability in the background characteristics of clients.

Skills-Oriented and Cognitive-Behavioral Treatments. Use programs that teach clients skills that allow them to understand and resist antisocial behavior. Use effective social learning principles to model and shape prosocial behavior.

Program Implementation. Treat offenders in well-supported programs. The best intervention will fail if there are insufficient funds or a lack of commitment from treatment staff, administrators, or support staff. This can be particularly problematic if a program is conducted within an institutional setting primarily designed for custody purposes. Community settings may be more appropriate.

Dosage and Researcher Involvement. Use treatment that involves researchers in both the design and evaluation of the intervention. Use high doses of intervention, since they are associated with lower recidivism rates. Lipsey (1995) suggested that researcher involvement could be interpreted as experimenter bias, such that a researcher's participation in both the design and evaluation of a treatment could result in a stronger effect than the "true," unbiased outcome. However, he also argued that since smaller research studies yield larger effects, the overarching principle is one of treatment integrity (e.g., Weisburd 1993). Small-scale studies with tight monitoring of program implementation by researchers ensure the optimum level of treatment. It may well be the case that both principles operate. Unfortunately, while both determinants produce a greater treatment effect, only treatment integrity yields an unbiased result. Disentangling these influences is an important research question for the future.

Although there are many points of agreement among advocates of rehabilitation effectiveness, there are also points of disagreement. Palmer may be the most consistent, yet cautious, advocate of rehabilitation. In his 1992 book, *The Re-Emergence of Correctional Intervention*, Palmer synthesized nine meta-analyses, fifteen multitopic literature reviews, and eight special-topic reviews. To give a sense of his cautious optimism, I paraphrase two of his treatment caveats:

> If we do not categorize interventions into different classes, then, taken as a whole, there are many instances in which interventions have not consistently demonstrated effectiveness. If programs are broken out into classes, even the best-performing classes of interventions have often failed to demonstrate a treatment effect.

The most successful programs can be categorized as behavioral, cognitive-behavioral, skill oriented, multimodal, or family intervention. Even among these programs, there is some inconsistency across the meta-analyses and research reviews.

Palmer has argued that if rehabilitation is to succeed, a number of goals should be met. These include better-designed studies, replications of "successful" programs, systematic variation in the studies, frequent analyses of client subgroups, and studies of process—how interventions work. This last point is consistent with the complaints of a great many researchers who have tried to understand and summarize this large body of studies.

Process Evaluations

Many social scientists who have tried to summarize the treatment literature have been frustrated by the absence of specific program descriptions in most evaluation reports. Lipsey (1992), Palmer (1992), and Antonowicz and Ross (1994), among others, have all protested that it is rare for social scientists carefully to document the programs under evaluation. However, documentation of the program is not the real issue. More important is the extent to which a program has been successfully implemented; this is difficult to know unless the evaluation report sets out the program's goals and the methods by which they are to be achieved, and then carefully describes whether the program was implemented as planned. To document this, of course, would require a description of the program itself. Every program evaluation ought to include a carefully constructed synopsis of program procedures that can be used to characterize the nature and scope of the interventions.

Sechrest and Rosenblatt (1987) have summarized what should be included in a process evaluation report: a discussion of the plausibility of the theory supporting the intervention, program staff qualifications, treatment intensity, treatment length, descriptions of the degree to which the intervention is focused, the clarity and precision of a treatment protocol, and the extent to which the treatment plan accounts for differences in the abilities, learning styles, and amenability of the clients of proposed interventions. The evaluator should also document staff commitment, the degree to which there is a supervisory plan, and the degree to which the program provides structured feedback to staff on how well they are delivering treatment (Sechrest and Rosenblatt 1987). It is clear that many of the components of a sound process evaluation tap into the theoretical dimensions and principles of effective treatment delivery. Unfortunately, it is rare for even the most fundamental program descriptions to be found in treatment evaluations.

Perhaps funding agencies should require that program evaluations include treatment process reports. While it may be understandable that scholarly journals are reluctant to publish these seemingly mundane aspects of the evaluation, perhaps editors could require that process evaluation appendixes be submitted when articles are submitted and, if the article is accepted for publication, that the authors agree to provide copies of the appendixes to those who request them. As trivial as this requirement may seem, the unavailability of information on program processes may be holding back the advance of the social science of intervention.

The Meta-Analysis Paradigm

Meta-analysis is a set of methodological and statistical tools that allows the scientist or social scientist to summarize a particular research domain (see especially Cooper and Hedges 1994). Meta-analysis, also called *research synthesis,* has permeated the fields of medicine, public health, education, and psychology, among others. A common metric, called an *effect size,* is used to compare results from different studies. Any modern discussion of effective treatment must include the results of meta-analyses of the treatment literature.

This discussion of meta-analysis includes four sections. First, I review Mark Lipsey's work, the best meta-analyses that have been conducted on correctional treatment (Lipsey 1989, 1992, 1995). I then review Loesel's (1995) paper, which summarized all of the meta-analyses conducted on the correctional treatment literature, and a 1993 paper by Lipsey and Wilson, which summarized 290 meta-analyses conducted in the fields of health/mental health, work settings, and education. Next, I examine some of the problems with meta-analysis that have been noted by prominent methodologists and statisticians in this field. Finally, I discuss the use of research registers, now primarily employed in the field of medicine, to record studies at their inception. The correctional evaluation research field could benefit from a similar set of procedures that are used to record studies from their inception.

Lipsey's Meta-Analytic Assessment of Juvenile Delinquency Treatment. Mark Lipsey's analysis of over 400 studies representing juvenile delinquency interventions is by far the most comprehensive published assessment of treatment evaluations.[2] Lipsey's initial analysis and report assessed the effect of treatment on delinquent behavior (Lipsey 1989, 1992).

To be included in this meta-analysis, a study had to meet certain conditions. There had to be at least one contrast between a treatment and a comparison (control) condition. The study had either to employ random assignment of subjects or to include pretreatment and posttreatment measures on the outcome—plus either a procedure that allowed matching of treatment and comparison subjects or an assessment of the variables that permitted evaluation of similarities and dissimilarities in the treatment and comparison groups.

A doctoral student in psychology was trained to code each of the studies that met these criteria on 154 items. These 154 items can be analytically grouped as method variables (e.g., equivalence of groups, study design, attrition), study context (e.g., year of publication, affiliation of the researcher, discipline of the researcher), nature of treatment (e.g., treatment type, duration, intensity), and nature of subjects (e.g., race, sex, age, prior rate of delinquency).

Lipsey chose Cohen's d (Cohen 1988) as the common metric for measuring effect size. Cohen's d is the difference between the mean scores for treatment and comparison groups divided by the pooled standard deviations of these groups. The effect size was positive if treatment outcomes were better than comparison outcomes and negative if the opposite occurred. Thus, effect size was the number of standard deviation units by which the treatment group outperformed the comparison group. Where means were not reported, an attempt was made to change reported results to Cohen's d. In addition, Lipsey weighted each effect size by a coefficient based on the sample sizes of the treatment and comparison groups. These coefficients "penalized" studies with small samples by reducing the effect size proportionally.

Using Lipsey's selection criteria, 397 studies contained enough information to compute an effect size, forming a distribution of effect sizes. After weighting each effect size by its variance, the average effect size was .103. Looking at only the 293 studies that used random assignment, the same weighting produced an average effect size of .110. By selecting only those studies that used random assignment and did not experience appreciable attrition, the process resulted in 78 studies with a weighted average effect size of .140. At least at a crude level, it appears that more methodologically sound studies showed larger average effect sizes.

To provide an intuitive sense of the substantive meaning of effect size, Rosenthal and Rubin (1982) have shown how to transform this measure into a statistic that is more substantively meaningful. An effect size of .10 standard deviation units is equivalent to a 10 percent reduction from a baseline of 50 percent recidivating, resulting in a recidivism level of 45 percent. Lipsey reasoned that since recidivism is such an unreliably measured criterion, the average effect size should be corrected for attenuation due to unreliability. After correcting for attenuation, the effect size became .20, which represents a 20 percent reduction from a baseline of 50 percent recidivating, resulting in a recidivism level of 40 percent.

Lipsey's coders rated every study on 154 dimensions. To examine the relations between these dimensions and effect size, Lipsey used multiple regression. The regression analysis showed that 47 percent of the variability in weighted effect sizes was attributable to the coded variables. Method variables, which were entered first, explained 25 percent of the variability in effect size. Treatment variables accounted for an additional 22 percent of the variability in effect size. By far the largest single cluster of variables that contributed to the variability in effect size pertained to treatment modality. In situations where the researcher provided the treatment or was influential in the treatment, there were larger effect sizes than when other researchers evaluated the intervention. Treatment in public facilities, custodial institutions, and the juvenile justice system was associated with smaller effect sizes than treatment in community settings. Treatment that was behavioral, skill-oriented, or multimodal was associated with larger effect sizes than treatment that was based on deterrence, family counseling, group counseling, or individual counseling. Because the treatment modality effect depended on whether the treatment was delivered in a juvenile justice or community setting, these conclusions have to be qualified accordingly. For example, employment training had the highest average effect size when it was delivered in the juvenile justice setting. When it was delivered in non–juvenile justice settings, it actually had a negative effect size, indicating that the intervention increased delinquency.

Lipsey was able to show that skill-oriented, multimodal, behavioral treatments reduced recidivism from a baseline of 50 percent by 20 to 40 percent, resulting in a recidivism level as low as 30 percent. Lipsey noted that these are the treatment types that corresponded to those defined as "clinically relevant" in a meta-analysis conducted by Andrews et al. (1990).

In a follow-up paper, Lipsey (1995) reported the average effect sizes for this same body of studies for outcomes other than delinquent recidivism. According to the results of these meta-analyses, treatment improved outcomes defined as psychological assessments, interpersonal adjustment, school participation, academic performance, and vocational accomplishment. By correlating these outcomes with delinquency, he found that neither academic performance nor psychological measures were significantly correlated with delinquency; however, interpersonal adjustment, school participation, and vocational accomplishment were correlated. Lipsey noted that the assumption that psychological change is a necessary condition of delinquency reduction was not supported by the results of his analysis. However, he also noted that the measures of psychological change covered a wide range of measurements and that more specific subcategories of psychological change may be needed before any mediating effect can be found.

At face value, Lipsey's results are very encouraging, especially for juvenile justice interventions. However, despite the strengths of meta-analysis, it has some limitations.

Other Correctional Treatment Meta-Analyses. Loesel (1995) has published a review of meta-analyses of correctional treatment. He identified thirteen. The smallest included only 8 studies, and the largest 443 studies; however, there is considerable overlap in their coverage. Most meta-analyses have synthesized juvenile interventions exclusively. Only Andrews et al. (1990), Antonowicz and Ross (1994), Loesel and Koeferl (1989), and Redondo (1994) examined adult interventions. According to

Loesel, about 20 percent of the primary studies have been evaluations of adult interventions. For example, the analysis by Andrews utilized eighty studies involving only thirteen adult interventions. Among the meta-analyses reviewed by Loesel, the most comprehensive by far was Lipsey's (1992) analysis that included only juvenile interventions. As more primary studies of adult correctional treatment interventions become available, juvenile and adult treatments should be evaluated separately, since successful interventions for these two subpopulations may be very different.

Although these meta-analyses adopted different coding conventions, all measured effect sizes for recidivism, even if other outcomes were analyzed. Effect sizes varied from the .05–.08 range to as high as .36. Loesel has observed that Lipsey's study, which was the most comprehensive and the least likely to suffer from a biased selection of studies, probably sets the lower limit for treatment effect sizes at about .10. Citing Lipsey and Wilson (1993), Loesel noted that this average effect size is modest, especially compared with those found in evaluations of various psychological, social, and educational interventions in other fields. Loesel pointed out that there are many possible explanations for this relatively weak average effect size, ranging from the intractable nature of the problems addressed by correctional treatments to the methodological problems inherent in measuring interventions in applied settings. For most meta-analyses, the more rigorous the design, the smaller the effect size. Although this is not what Lipsey found, his analysis began with the most methodologically rigorous of the juvenile delinquency treatment studies.

Across all of these studies, when mode of treatment was measured, behavioral, skill-oriented, and multimodal interventions had the highest effect sizes. There are, however, exceptions to this general rule. Not all studies measured the same treatment modalities, and not all studies found the same effects. Perhaps coding conventions varied across these studies, or perhaps coding reliability was not very high. Most of these meta-analyses did not report coder reliability. There are more specific differences and contradictions as well. For example, Andrews et al. found strong support for the "risk principle," which specifies that the highest-risk offenders need the most intensive treatment, while Antonowicz and Ross (1994) found no support, and Lipsey (1995) found weak support.

There was a great deal of diversity among these studies in the type of variables that were coded and analyzed as moderators of effect size. A moderator variable is one that determines the level of the effect size. It may have methodological or substantive importance. Methodological moderators are important in establishing the internal and external validity of the results of a meta-analysis. Substantive moderator variables aid in theory development, and ultimately reveal the best strategies in developing an intervention. Moderator variables can measure characteristics of the treatment setting such as the community versus an institution, or specific characteristics of the population, such as adult versus juvenile. Moderator variables that reflect characteristics and the composition of the treated and untreated populations have largely been ignored by the meta-analysts. According to Loesel, "[T]hese include the offender's history of prior adjustment problems and antisocial behavior, the duration of residence, the age of inmates, the activation of coping mechanisms, offender personality, objective and subjective crowding, the stability of group relations, the extent of control and repression, features of the subculture, the degree of isolation from external reality, the ecological design, and so forth" (1995, p. 96).

A sense of the level of effect size can be obtained by comparing one domain of research with another. The level of an effect size should not be confused with its substantive significance. Both Loesel and Lipsey have cogently argued that the practical significance of an effect size depends on a broader understanding of the costs associated with interventions relative to the costs of *not* intervening. Later in this chapter, I present an extremely simple model to show how treatment effect size can be incorporated into a systems-level model that allows us to begin to understand the practical significance of interventions.

The Relative Level of Correctional Treatment Effect Sizes Compared with Effect Sizes in Other Research Domains. Meta-analysis has become a growth industry. In 1993, Lipsey and Wilson collected 290 studies involving 302 meta-analyses covering a large variety of interventions. These studies were grouped into three intervention domains: work-setting or organizational programs, mental health or health interventions, and educational programs. Correctional treatment was classified as a subdomain of mental health or health interventions. It is difficult to draw substantive conclusions from this literature, since, as Lipsey and Wilson noted, the quality and comprehensiveness of meta-analyses vary remarkably.

Lipsey and Wilson's data provide a very crude idea of the relationship between correctional treatment interventions and other domains. Among the 302 meta-analyses, over 90 percent had mean effect sizes of .10 or larger, and 85 percent had mean effect sizes of .20 or larger. This implies that nearly every mental health/health, education, and work-setting treatment has positive effects. At the time of this review, Lipsey and Wilson found 10 meta-analyses of treatment programs for offenders, and the range of effect sizes varied from a low of .17 to a high of .77.[3] This yielded an unweighted average effect size for correctional interventions of about .36, while across all three domains among the 302 meta-analyses, the unweighted average effect size was .50.

Unlike meta-analyses of the medical literature, Lipsey and Wilson (1993) found that studies with random-assignment designs had higher effect sizes than did studies using other research designs. The picture seemed even more confusing when Lipsey and Wilson reported the differences in effect size in studies that compared meta-analyses of both random and nonrandom designs. Lipsey and Wilson computed the difference in effect sizes by subtracting the nonrandom effect size from the effect size for random design studies. The range was −1.0 to 1.6, with an average of .05. Thus, in some meta-analyses, nonrandom designs overestimated effect size relative to random designs, while in many other studies, such designs underestimated the effect size.

Since we have no theoretical or methodological reason for understanding why such large discrepancies exist, these data present a very uncertain picture. Consistent with the medical literature, Lipsey and Wilson (1993) found a publication bias in effect size. Published studies had an average effect size of .53, while unpublished studies had an average effect size of .39.

When Lipsey and Wilson limited the meta-analyses to studies that met certain conditions of rigor, they were able to cull from the original 302 analyses a more refined set of 156 studies. The average effect size for these studies was .47. If we accept Lipsey and Wilson's conclusions at face value, psychological interventions appear to have dramatic effects. Whether these conclusions hold up when meta-analysis becomes a more mature methodology remains to be seen. But it is clear, on average, that correctional interventions appear to be less effective than psychological, health, and training interventions. This does not necessarily diminish the importance of treatment, since small effect sizes can be extremely important.

It is troubling that even within a research subdomain such as correctional treatment, there appears to be wide variability in the average effect sizes found by different meta-analysts. Lipsey (1992) has argued that this variability can be attributed to the incompleteness of most of the meta-analyses. Thus, the effect sizes have depended on which sample of the entire pool of treatment literature a particular meta-analyst has chosen to synthesize. In addition to variability in average effect sizes among the different studies, there may be considerable variability in the coding conventions adopted by researchers that have been used to analyze substantive and methodological variables. The differences in the coding of these variables could result from problems in interrater reliability among the coders, problems in the coding conventions adopted by the evaluators, and limited information in the original studies that introduces a great deal of error. This may be especially true when a coder is trying to catalog a study according to some theoretically derived set of categories (Loesel 1995).

Problems with Meta-Analyses. Although meta-analysis has gained wide appeal and is used extensively in medicine, education, and the social sciences, certain precautions are necessary that are not unlike those that apply to primary research studies (Hall et al. 1994). The analysis of effect sizes, by either regression or analysis of variance techniques, requires certain statistical adjustments (Hedges 1994); however, it is equally important to design secondary analyses of moderator variables so that one is not on a "fishing expedition." Just as primary research should be guided by theory and previous knowledge, research syntheses must satisfy these same criteria.

Analogous to the problem of subject selection bias in an individual evaluation study is the possibility of bias in the selection of studies included in a meta-analysis. Publication bias can take several forms. There can be reporting bias resulting from the failure by authors to report statistically nonsignificant results. There can also be retrieval bias. When the researcher collects studies to synthesize, it is much more difficult to gather unpublished studies or discarded studies that represent statistically nonsignificant results. Begg (1994) has examined this issue in some detail. Citing other studies of publication bias, Begg reported evidence that the odds of having a study published were as much as 3.4 times higher for studies that demonstrate statistical significance than for those that demonstrate nonsignificance. The lowest odds he found were 1.8 in favor of studies finding statistical significance for an effect.

Although not completely satisfactory, certain techniques can be used to infer whether there is publication bias. These should be used and reported. Even though the researcher may indicate that his or her search of the "fugitive" literature has been exhaustive, it would be more compelling if some assessment of the bias were also included in the reported analysis of the data. Begg considers publication bias to be "the greatest methodological threat to validity of a meta-analysis" (1994, p. 407). He further asserts that "results of the meta-analysis should be very compelling before we regard them as definitive" (p. 408). One way to begin to address the problem of publication bias is to establish research registers.

A research register is a compilation of all initiated research projects in a particular domain (Dickersin 1994). It can be a database of planned, ongoing, or completed studies. Dickersin has compiled a list of research registers and has characterized them as concentrating "to a large extent, on 'prospective' registration at the time a project is initiated" (1994, p. 72). All twenty-six registers Dickersin compiled were organized around medical studies—most of them clinical trials. Dickersin admitted that her compilation was not systematic. However, one of the reasons that research registers are primarily medical is because many are established to notify potential clients of the availability of clinical trials and treatments, and to recruit patients into medical studies. According to Dickersin, research registers are also used for record keeping. They serve to inform oversight agencies, and those trying to assess the state of the art in a particular medical domain.

Dickersin's field is medical research, and her inquiries and analyses seem to be confined to that research domain. Her insights, however, may be equally (or more) relevant to the social sciences in general, and to program and treatment evaluations in particular. Registers are a way to overcome publication bias; Dickersin argued that most research syntheses were based on published studies and estimated that only 50 to 80 percent of all studies had been published. She also cited five studies that she claimed demonstrated "consistent and persuasive evidence for the existence of publication bias" (1994, p. 75), whether the designs were observational or experimental.

Dickersin acknowledged that the social sciences have moved ahead of the medical sciences in the use of sophisticated methods for synthesizing research, but she also claimed that some areas of medicine may be better situated for meta-analyses because of the existence of clinical research registers. As an example, she cited the Oxford Database of Perinatal Trials (ODPT; Chalmers et al. 1986). The ODPT was originally developed to record published studies, but there has been a recent effort to identify unpublished studies as well. It is a composite of "all known randomized trials both completed and ongoing conducted during the perinatal period" (1994, p. 77). Dickersin noted that the ODPT has been used to produce 400 meta-analyses. An electronic version is updated every six months, including the meta-analyses.

Research registers have been used to study potential publication bias in several medical domains. Dickersin summarized some of these studies in which three of the four registers that have been studied showed evidence of publication bias. Published studies in these registers apparently showed larger effect sizes than did the unpublished studies.

Research registers should be developed in the social sciences. Although the existence of such registers may not completely solve the problem of publication bias, if we make registers a common practice in social science research in general and program evaluation research in particular, we can begin to have greater confidence in our coverage of all studies initiated, ongoing, and completed in a particular research domain.

In the chronological history of rehabilitation, the report of the Panel on Research on Rehabilitative Techniques (Sechrest, White, and Brown 1979) was an important milestone. Many of the problems recorded by the panel, and many of its recommendations, are as relevant today as they were in 1979. The report followed, and essentially confirmed, the conclusions reached by Martinson (1974) and by Lipton, Martinson, and Wilks (1975). Yet, the essential recommendations of the NAS Panel have not been followed. The policy recommendations were clear and concise:

> [T]he research on offender rehabilitation should be pursued more vigorously, more systematically, more imaginatively, and more rigorously. Specifically, treatments should be based upon strong theoretical rationales, perhaps involving total programs rather than weak or piecemeal treatments. In addition, the strength and integrity of all treatments should be monitored and fully documented, along with documentation of the costs of the operation of treatment. To implement this recommendation it is essential that researchers become more involved in developing appropriate methodologies for evaluations of interventions and that appropriate funding agencies support research on criminal rehabilita-

tion while making the criteria for funding more rigorous with respect to experimental design, theoretical rationale, and monitoring of integrity and strength of treatment. (Sechrest, White, and Brown 1979, p. 10)

Many of the mistakes in theory, implementation, and methodology made in the past continue to be made today. There are still too few instances of studies in which researchers draw clear implications from a theoretical paradigm, design instruments directly to assess their constructs, assess the extent to which an intervention has actually taken place, and exercise sufficient rigor to ensure that their research has both internal and external validity.

Instead, meta-analysis has become the preferred tool when, individually, poorly designed studies offer little or no insight into program interventions. Unfortunately, although meta-analysis may give us some insight into the best treatment practices, the foundation of studies on which the research synthesis is based is rather fragile. Even if meta-analysis can be used to separate the wheat from the chaff, ultimately, meta-analysis should suggest a definitive set of studies. Those studies must still be conducted to confirm or disconfirm the implications of the meta-analysis. If, through meta-analysis, we learn that interventions must be multimodal, behaviorally oriented, and tailored to the client, then to test these assumptions we should design and implement a series of studies using different staff, different treatment sites, and different evaluators in the most rigorous designs possible, having sufficient power and sufficient internal and external validity to justify drawing conclusions from the findings. Meta-analysis should not be an end unto itself.

The methodological criticisms outlined in the NAS Panel's report need to be reread and studied. The panel emphasized the desirability of the use of experimentation and, wherever possible, random assignment of subjects to treatment and control groups. Although statistical methods have been developed to address some of the problems encountered in observational studies, where possible randomized designs can serve as a foundation against which to judge the efficacy of quasi-experimental and other designs. Choosing randomized designs does not mean we discount ethical concerns. However, as the panel argued, if we have no scientific foundation for making judgments about effective treatment, it is probably more unethical to deliver treatment in this knowledge vacuum.

If randomization cannot be accomplished, the panel concluded, "The retreat from randomization should be as limited as possible" (Sechrest, White, and Brown 1979, p. 66). Thus, in the absence of a randomized design, there should at least be a comparison group. When using quasi-experimental designs, a great deal of thought should go into understanding the nature of the possible differences between the treatment and comparison groups, and the nature of any processes that may contaminate group differences. Those processes can mute or exaggerate a potential effect.

The panel also discussed issues concerning the power of any given study, problems inherent in measuring recidivism, the need for more development in methodology when randomization is not feasible, an understanding of cost-benefit analysis in the context of treatment programs, and the possibility that the effect of rehabilitation can be measured by changes in crime rates.

Rezmovic's (1979) paper on methodology, commissioned by the NAS Panel, reviews all of the relevant problems inherent in evaluation research design. His overall conclusion was that the evaluation research conducted up to that time was, in general, woefully inadequate. Fienberg and Grambsch (1979) give a qualitative sense of the methodological problems with evaluation studies. They selected two 10 percent samples from the original set of studies collected by Lipton, Martinson, and Wilks (1975). Problems noted included poor definitions; poor interrater reliability; noncomparability of treatment and control groups; methodological shortcomings of studies considered to be sound by Lipton, Martinson, and Wilks; uncritical acceptance of statistical analysis by coders; ex post facto designs; failure to test or control for differences between experimental and control groups; differences in posttreatment supervision levels resulting in noncomparability in recidivism risk; lack of blind assessment of intervening variables; misinterpretation of statistical results; lack of multivariate statistical controls; confounding of important variables strongly related to risk of recidivism; no comparison group at all; and selection bias in the assignment of clients to treatment.

Lipsey's (1992) meta-analysis gives a quantitative sense of the level of methodological sophistication of many of these studies. Lipsey also carefully selected evaluation studies based on their rigor. These studies overlap a great deal with the Lipton, Martinson, and Wilks (1975) sample, but Lipsey's set of studies also cover the period up to 1986. Although Lipsey's graduate student coders were probably not as methodologically sophisticated as Fienberg and Grambsch, nevertheless, they identified quite a few "holes" in the methodologies of the "better" studies.

The studies were rated on a number of methodological criteria. Here I list some of those criteria—for example, high level of statistical power—and indicate the extent to which Lipsey's coders indicated that the studies met a certain level of methodological rigor. Then I indicate the percentage of studies that met each criterion. The criteria were as follows:

- High level of representativeness of sampling, 31.2 percent
- High level of statistical power, 23.3 percent
- High or very high level of confidence/explicitness of assignment procedure, 88 percent
- High level of treatment/control group comparability, 34.5 percent
- No difference pre to post in the attrition of the treatment group, 54.4 percent
- No difference pre to post in the attrition of the control group, 55.5 percent

- Direction of treatment/control group differences favoring neither group, 1.6 percent
- Missing data in the direction of treatment/control group differences favoring neither group, 72 percent
- Yes, to the validity of primary delinquency measure demonstrated, 3.6 percent
- High level of blind collection of outcome data, 12.4 percent
- High or very high level of confidence/explicitness of treatment amount, 50.1 percent
- High or very high level of confidence/explicitness of treatment amount/intensity, 40 percent
- High level of integrity of treatment implementation, 9.6 percent.

Of the approximately 400 studies in Lipsey's meta-analysis, 13.8 percent used random assignment after matching subjects, and 30.2 percent used random assignment without matching. The remaining studies used regression discontinuity (0.9 percent), waiting list control (2.7 percent), nonrandom assignment matched on pretest (3.2 percent), nonrandom assignment matched on individual features (8.4 percent), nonrandom assignment matched on demographics (16.0 percent), groupwise matching (5.0 percent), random assignment with serious degradation (6.1 percent), individual selection (7.2 percent), and a convenience comparison group (6.3 percent).

How can the apparent problems in the methodology of these studies be reconciled with the effects purported to be found by the meta-analysts? Are treatment effects so robust that, despite the errors, treatment can make a difference? Are there biases and artifacts that, in the aggregate, compose a kind of noisy background through which treatment results still can be detected? Is there still the possibility that, despite the assiduous efforts by Lipsey and other research synthesists, the meta-analyses in the correctional treatment literature represent subtle publication biases? If the meta-analyses are valid, then it is time to conduct a study or series of studies based on the collective wisdom of the research synthesis findings using greater methodological rigor.

An Analysis of the Effect of Intensive Drug Treatment in Prison on Postrelease Outcomes

This section briefly reviews the effects of intensive drug treatment in prison on postrelease outcomes. This subdomain of the treatment literature was selected because it contains a relatively small set of studies, yet it is a particularly important area because of the strong connection between drug use and crime rates of individuals who are both criminals and drug abusers (Nurco et al. 1988).

As part of a recent evaluation of a correctional drug treatment program for adults, I reviewed the prior research (Gaes 1997) on this topic. All of the studies in this domain concluded that in-prison drug treatment conducted in therapeutic communities can have dramatic effects in reducing postrelease recidivism and drug relapse. My reading of these studies suggests a more cautious set of conclusions. Although the levels of methodological sophistication varied a great deal, all these studies had the same fundamental flaw. A combination of selection and attrition in the program treatment groups meant that there were probably significant differences in the treatment and comparison groups that could account for the research findings. In Gaes (1997), I presented a theoretical model of selection effects to show how these studies could easily be contaminated by processes that could favor finding a treatment effect or mitigate against such an effect.

The model of selection effects is represented in Figure 26.1. By definition, selection processes can result in a biased selection of clients into treatment, or in a biased selection of clients out of treatment. This latter effect is usually called *attrition;* however, it is also logical to view attrition as a theoretical extension of selection bias. Recognizing the possibility of selection bias is only the first step in a quasi-experimental design. Although a great deal of attention has been given to the problem of statistical adjustments for selection bias (see especially Wainer 1986), the methods are mathematically sophisticated, not readily accessible, and still somewhat controversial. In the absence of randomization, or a relatively strong quasi-experimental design, such as a regression discontinuity design (Trochim 1984), researchers should be extremely careful to understand and describe the kinds of pressures that exist in an adult correctional institution where assignment to institutions and programs often depends on a systematic process that favors some inmates over others. Recording and understanding these processes will lead to a better understanding not only of subject selection and attrition but also of the efficacy of treatment.

The Future

Although the discussion in previous sections suggests some future directions for the correctional treatment paradigm, this last section emphasizes the advantages of system and cost-benefit models, strong inference designs, and better theory on the nature of correctional interventions.

System and Cost-Benefit Models of Treatment Programs

One of the recommendations of the NAS Panel (Sechrest, White, and Brown 1979) was to call for cost-benefit analyses of treatment programs. While this may still be premature, given the state of the evaluation research literature, it is probably useful to think of program interventions from the point of view of a systems-level model. Such models have the advantage of allowing social scientists to understand the broader context

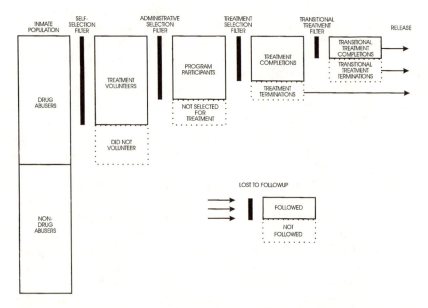

Figure 26.1 Theoretical model of selection effects in drug treatment programs.

of an intervention and to begin to make explicit some of the public policy issues that often get debated with very little theoretical or empirical insight. A recent analysis by Caulkins et al. (1997) examined the effects of alternative drug policies on the price and consumption of cocaine. By examining the plausibility of their models and assumptions, one can accept or challenge their conclusion that community drug treatment is far more effective than federal mandatory minimum sentencing or federal law enforcement practices in reducing the consumption of cocaine. Analogously, one can begin to define system-level models for alternative strategies to treat juvenile or adult offenders.

Figure 26.2 shows a simple systems-level model for the treatment of individuals who are held in custody. We assume that for every 1,000 individuals, 200 treatment beds are available (an assumption that may or may not be warranted in any specific system). Other assumptions are noted in the branching probabilities of the model. For example, I assume that 80 percent of all inmates who receive treatment also complete treatment, and that the effect size of treatment is .10, which reduces recidivism from a baseline of 50 percent to 45 percent. I also assume that for those who drop out of treatment, the probability of recidivating is higher than the 50 percent baseline. I have arbitrarily chosen these branching ratios to make several points.

If we compare this hypothetical systems-level model to one in which no treatment was offered, we get a clear idea of the systems-level impact.

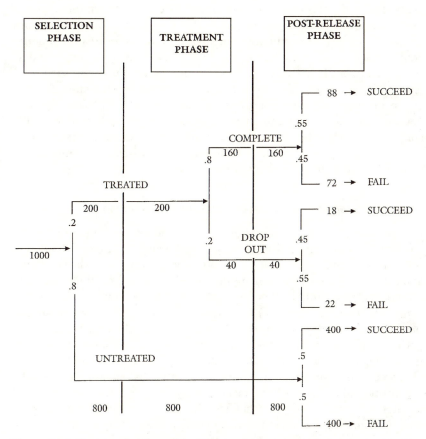

Figure 26.2 Systems-level model of treatment programs' impact.

For every 1,000 inmates who passed through a system that delivered treatment, 506 would succeed. For every 1,000 inmates who passed through a system with no treatment, 500 would succeed. This is a marginal increase in success of 6 inmates. If the effect size were .20, holding constant the other assumptions, then out of every 1,000 inmates, 517 would succeed relative to a baseline of 500, a marginal increase of 17 inmates. Finally, if all other assumptions were held constant and the effect size increased to .40, the marginal effect would be an additional 30 inmates succeeding. Although these are simple models, one can begin to envision how the different system components interact and affect the final outcome. Even with this simple model, it is apparent that in a system with a limited number of treatment beds, the marginal decrease in recidivism will be relatively small unless dramatic effect sizes can be produced through treatment.

After we specify the system probabilities, we have to define the costs. These include the costs of treatment, the costs of supervision, and the costs of custody. With the help of economists we can determine opportunity costs, appropriate discounts, and other important economic assumptions. We can begin to compare systems-level models for treatment delivered in custody or under criminal justice supervision against models where treatment is delivered in the community. Although the social science of correctional evaluation research may not be mature enough to begin to develop precise parameters for these models, it does serve as a heuristic device in thinking about the total system. Each branch of this simple model must be subject to scientific inquiry and analysis. Alternative models can be constructed for different classes of clients, or for simulations of different treatment modalities.

Strong Inference Designs and Moderator Variables

One of the failings of the correctional evaluation research literature is that few studies use what Platt (1964) called "strong inference." Platt was trained as a biophysicist, but his tenets equally apply to both the "hard" and the "soft" sciences. A strong inference design requires the scientist to articulate clearly both the theoretical reasons and under what conditions a behavioral change (outcome) is expected to occur. The scientist should propose alternative hypotheses or mechanisms of change. A crucial experiment or test should then be conducted. A crucial test includes measurement of the theoretical mechanism that hypothetically causes a change in outcome, development of procedures that ensure the scientific reliability and validity of the measurement of these intervening causal mechanisms, and proof that changes in these mechanisms are associated with changes in outcomes. Even when a design employs random assignment of clients to conditions, strong inference is bolstered by measurement of the mechanism that mediates change. When the design is quasi-experimental, measuring the mechanism of change is even more important.

In order to give these concepts substance, suppose that a social scientist is interested in the effect of cognitive skills training on postrelease recidivism. Even when random assignment is used, the researcher should articulate what cognitive skills are and propose a method to measure those skills. Assuming the measurement device meets sufficient levels of reliability and validity, clients' cognitive skills could be measured prior to and after training. If the experimental group receiving cognitive skills training demonstrates lower recidivism levels relative to the control group that had no such training, one could conclude that cognitive skills are an important dimension in reducing recidivism. However, a stronger inference can be made if it is demonstrated that the level of cognitive skills increases after training, and that the measured level of cognitive skills after training is also correlated to the level of recidivism. In a quasi-experimental design, this procedure is even more important, since it allows competing explanations or competing causes to be ruled out.

Many of the social scientists who have reviewed the rehabilitation literature have also called for a better understanding of "moderator" variables. These are variables that mitigate the influence of a treatment. If cognitive skills training works only for certain subclasses of clients and not for others, moderator variables can be used to distinguish these subclasses. Furthermore, moderator variables can be used to inform our theoretical understanding of the mechanisms of rehabilitative change. If cognitive skills training works only on males who are over twenty years old, who have minimal coping skills, and who have moderate to high levels of intellectual functioning, this not only indicates some of the possible practical limitations of the training but also may lead to a different theoretical orientation about the nature of cognitive skills acquisition.

Theory Development

By saving the discussion of theory development until the end of this chapter, I do not intend to diminish its importance. If, as social scientists, we make the claim that we know how to reduce criminality, we should be arguing that our knowledge is based on an understanding of the theoretical causes of delinquency and adult criminality. Andrews and Bonta (1994) have concluded that a "psychology of criminal conduct" forms the theoretical basis for understanding and treating criminal behavior. Their efforts are devoted to understanding individual differences in the conduct of human behavior and modifying cognitions and behavior that are antisocial. By its very nature, treatment must have the individual as its focus. Theorists such as Andrews and Bonta are beginning to merge the psychological and sociological orientations toward understanding criminality into a set of principles that can be applied as intervention strategies. This does not mean, of course, that there are not also structural explanations for criminality implying broader, sweeping, societal interventions. Clearly, theory development must proceed at both levels of abstraction.

A psychology of criminal conduct is predicated on the principles of effective correctional treatment listed at the beginning of this chapter. These principles require further theoretical explication if our understanding and knowledge base about correctional treatment are to improve. For example, the responsivity principle asserts that client styles must be matched with the styles of treatment providers. But what is meant by styles? Why is matching important? To get beyond intuition and tautology, the theoretical importance of this principle needs fleshing out. This is also true of the risk principle. One argument made in favor of the risk principle is that the highest-risk offenders need the greatest level of intervention. But if offenders are at such high risk, would intervention efforts be wasted? Better understanding of the theoretical components of risk should provide clearer understanding of how to attack the problem and with what likely success. Thus, if adult risk were predicated on age, criminal history, marital status, and level of human capital (education, job skills), then hypotheses could be tested concerning which risk factors could be ameliorated and which were resistant to change. Clearly, there is a theoretical nexus between risk and criminogenic needs. This relationship deserves much more attention.

Recent theorists have argued that a certain momentum and continuity to criminality are established at a very young age and persist throughout the life course (Wilson and Herrnstein 1985; Gottfredson and Hirschi 1990; Moffit 1993). Other theorists such as Sampson and Laub (1993) postulate that, despite the correlation of illegal behavior over time, large changes in observed behavior can be accounted for by variations in social control. By studying social institutions such as family and job stability over time and by examining separate cohorts of delinquents and non-delinquents, Sampson and Laub were able to demonstrate how adult institutions of informal social control can modify criminal behavior. The challenge to theoreticians who advocate prison treatment interventions is to discover how prison programs can change a persistent disposition toward illegal behaviors or to show how training and treatment assist the individual in embedding himself or herself in social institutions that inhibit the propensity toward a criminal lifestyle.

Horney, Osgood, and Marshall (1995) used a retrospective design to assess the relationship between criminal activity and "local life circumstances." One advantage to their study was that they were measuring "local life circumstances" that could change often in a relatively short period of time, and they captured associated changes in self-reported offending, if such changes occurred. Horney and her colleagues found that informal institutions such as school, living with a wife, work, heavy drinking, and illegal drug use were associated with changes in criminal activity. Both attending school and living with a wife decreased the odds of offending. Work, living with a girlfriend, heavy drinking, and illegal drug use increased the odds of offending. Changes in the formal mechanisms of social control, probation, and parole had no impact on the odds of reoffending. They also showed that the informal social control mechanism had effects whether an individual was offending at a high, intermediate, or low rate. I mention the Sampson and Laub (1993) and Horney, Osgood, and Marshall (1995) studies to make the point that we must consider both dispositional and situational factors in our correctional treatment theory development. Better theory will allow us to more clearly articulate the intervention strategies.

Conclusion

I have purposely avoided the question of whether we ought to treat offenders. Prior reviews, including one I coauthored (Logan and Gaes 1993), often raise this question. This has the effect of confusing and distorting the essential research problem. Whether we ought to treat, train, or counsel offenders is a public policy question that depends on ideology, resources, and a thorough understanding of the implications of our programs. Social science can contribute only to the last of these. Unless it can be demonstrated that treatment has negative consequences on prison or postrelease behavior, there are as many reasons to justify the continued use of treatment in the absence of demonstrated effectiveness as there are reasons to oppose programs in the presence of proven effectiveness.

If treatment were proven ineffective, one could still justify its use because it gives inmates hope (Conrad 1981), it symbolizes society's larger goals of civility and the Protestant ethic of hard work and self-discipline, and it creates a work environment that attracts correctional workers and treatment-oriented staff who serve as role models and promote a humane environment (Cullen and Gilbert 1982). If programs were proven effective, one could justify discontinuing treatment because it is inherently unfair to provide training to violators of the law when law-abiding citizens may not have access to the same programs; because prison should serve to punish, not to "correct"; and because punishment has a symbolic, expressive role (Garland 1990), and providing treatment may diminish the force of that expression for society's larger purposes. Of course, these issues touch on essential belief systems, philosophies of punishment, and the purposes and roles of the prison in modern society.

Many reviews of the correctional treatment literature end with an exhortation to do more or to do less. This has the effect of producing a cacophony of voices, those who want to be heard in favor of program interventions and those who want to go on record in opposition. It is time to turn down the volume. Our energies should be devoted to more precise conceptualization, proper design, sound measurement, thorough analysis, and well-reasoned conclusions rather than to the sarcastic, ad hominem attacks too often evident in this literature.

Notes

The opinions expressed in this paper are solely those of the author and are not intended to represent the policies or practices of the Federal Bureau of Prisons or the U.S. Department of Justice.

1. I use the word *paradigm* in its most general sense—to suggest various theoretical and methodological approaches that have been used, or could be used, to deduce whether offenders can be rehabilitated.

2. The National Institute on Drug Abuse–funded CDATE analysis of treatment interventions (Lipton and Pearson 1996) will be an important addition to the literatures. Intended as the most comprehensive set of intervention studies ever collected, it is supposed to be a compilation and meta-analysis of all of the treatment studies conducted from 1968 to 1994.

3. It appears that Lipsey and Wilson (1993) recorded average effect sizes for all variables analyzed in the meta-analyses. Thus, for the correctional treatment literature, rather than represent the average effect size for only the delinquency outcome, they represented the other outcomes as well. Even if

this were the convention, I am still not sure why the smallest effect was not .10 as in Lipsey (1992).

References

Andrews, D. A. 1995. "The Psychology of Criminal Conduct and Effective Treatment." In *What Works: Reducing Reoffending*, edited by J. McGuire. New York: Wiley.

Andrews, D. A., and J. Bonta. 1994. *The Psychology of Criminal Conduct.* Cincinnati, Ohio: Anderson.

Andrews, D. A., I. Zinger, R. D. Hoge, J. Bonta, P. Gendreau, and F.T. Cullen. 1990. "Does Correctional Treatment Work? A Psychologically Informed Meta-Analysis." *Criminology* 28:369–404.

Antonowicz, D., and R. R. Ross. 1994. "Essential Components of Successful Rehabilitation Programs for Offenders." *International Journal of Offender Therapy and Comparative Criminology* 38:97–104.

Begg, C. B. 1994. "Publication Bias." In *The Handbook of Research Synthesis,* edited by H. Cooper and L. Hedges. New York: Russell Sage Foundation.

Caulkins, J. P., C. P. Rydell, W. L. Schwabe, and J. Chiesa. 1997. *Mandatory Minimum Drug Sentences: Throwing Away the Key or the Taxpayer's Money?* Santa Monica, Calif.: RAND.

Chalmers, I., J. Hetherington, M. Newdick, L. Mutch, A. Grant, M. Enkin, A. Enkin, and K. Dickersin. 1986. "The Oxford Database of Perinatal Trials: Developing a Register of Published Reports of Controlled Trials." *Controlled Clinical Trials* 7:306–24.

Cohen, J. 1988. *Statistical Power Analysis for the Behavioral Sciences.* Hillsdale, N.J.: Lawrence Erlbaum.

Conrad, J. P. 1981. "A Lost Ideal, a New Hope: The Way Toward Effective Correctional Treatment." *Journal of Criminal Law and Criminology* 72:1699–734.

Cooper, H., and L. V. Hedges. 1994. *The Handbook of Research Synthesis.* New York: Russell Sage Foundation.

Cullen, F. T., and K. Gilbert. 1982. *Reaffirming Rehabilitation.* Cincinnati, Ohio: Anderson.

Dickersin, K. 1994. "Research Registers." In *The Handbook of Research Synthesis,* edited by H. Cooper and L. V. Hedges. New York: Russell Sage Foundation.

Fienberg, S., and P. Grambsch. 1979. "An Assessment of the Accuracy of the Effectiveness of Correctional Treatment." In *The Rehabilitation of Criminal Offenders: Problems and Prospects,* edited by L. Sechrest, S. O. White, and E. D. Brown. Washington, D.C.: National Academy of Sciences.

Gaes, G. G. 1997. "A Review of Recent Studies of High-Intensity Adult Correctional Drug Treatment Programs: The Problem of Selection Bias and Possible Solutions." Unpublished manuscript. Washington, D.C.: Federal Bureau of Prisons.

Garland, D. 1990. *Punishment and Modern Society: A Study in Social Theory.* Chicago: University of Chicago Press.

Gendreau, P., and D. Andrews. 1991. "Tertiary Prevention: What the Meta-Analyses of the Offender Treatment Literature Tells Us About 'What

Works.'" *Canadian Journal of Criminology* 32:173–84.

Gendreau, P., and R. R. Ross. 1987. "Revivification of Rehabilitation: Evidence from the 1980's." *Justice Quarterly* 4:349–407.

Gottfredson, M. R., and T. Hirschi. 1990. *A General Theory of Crime.* Stanford, Calif.: Stanford University Press.

Hall, J. A., L. Tickle-Degnen, R. Rosenthal, and F. Mosteller. 1994. "Hypotheses and Problems in Research Synthesis." In *The Handbook of Research Synthesis,* edited by H. Cooper and L. Hedges. New York: Russell Sage Foundation.

Hedges, L. V. 1994. "Statistical Considerations." In *The Handbook of Research Synthesis,* edited by H. Cooper and L. Hedges. New York: Russell Sage Foundation.

Horney, J., D. W. Osgood, and I. H. Marshall. 1995. "Criminal Careers in the Short Term: Intra-Individual Variability in Crime and Its Relation to Local Life Circumstances." *American Sociological Review* 60:655–73.

Lipsey, M. W. 1989. "The Efficacy of Intervention for Juvenile Delinquency: Results from 400 Studies." Paper presented at the 41st annual meeting of the American Society of Criminology, Reno, Nevada, November.

———. 1992. "Juvenile Delinquency Treatment: A Meta-Analytic Inquiry into the Variability of Effects." In *Meta-Analysis for Explanation: A Casebook,* edited by T. D. Cook, H. Cooper, D. S. Cordray, H. Hartmann, L. V. Hedges, R. J. Light, T. A. Louis, and F. Mosteller. New York: Russell Sage Foundation.

———. 1995. "What Do We Learn from 400 Research Studies on the Effectiveness of Treatment with Juvenile Delinquents?" In *What Works: Reducing Reoffending,* edited by J. McGuire. New York: Wiley.

Lipsey, M. W., and D. B. Wilson. 1993. "The Efficacy of Psychological, Educational, and Behavioral Treatment." *American Psychologist* 48:1181–209.

Lipton, D., R. Martinson, and J. Wilks. 1975. *The Effectiveness of Correctional Treatment.* New York: Praeger.

Lipton, D. S., and F. S. Pearson. 1996. "What Works in Correctional Intervention? The CDATE Project." Unpublished manuscript. New York: National Development and Research Institutes.

Loesel, F. 1995. "The Efficacy of Correctional Treatment: A Review and Synthesis of Meta-Evaluations." In *What Works: Reducing Reoffending,* edited by J. McGuire. New York: Wiley.

Loesel, F., and P. Koeferl. 1989. "Evaluation Research on Correctional Treatment in West Germany: A Meta-Analysis." In *Criminal Behavior and the Justice System: Psychological Perspectives,* edited by H. Wegener, F. Loesel, and J. Haisch. New York: Springer-Verlag.

Logan, C. H., and G. G. Gaes. 1993. "Meta-Analysis and the Rehabilitation of Punishment." *Justice Quarterly* 10:245–63.

Martinson, R. 1974. "What Works? Questions and Answers About Prison Reform." *The Public Interest* 35:22–45.

———. 1979. "Symposium on Sentencing, Part II: New Findings, New Views: A Note of Caution Regarding Sentencing Reform." *Hofstra Law Review* 7:243–58.

McGuire, J., and P. Priestly. 1995. "Reviewing 'What Works': Past, Present, and Future." In *What Works: Reducing Reoffending,* edited by J. McGuire. New York: Wiley.

Moffit, T. E. 1993. "Adolescence-Limited and Life-Course-Persistent Anti-social Behavior: A Developmental Taxonomy." *Psychological Review* 100:674–701.

Nurco, D., T. Hanlon, T. Kinlock, and K. Duszynski. 1988. "Differential Patterns of Narcotics Addicts over an Addiction Career." *Criminology* 26:407–23.

Palmer, T. 1975. "Martinson Revisited." *Journal of Research in Crime and Delinquency* 12:133–52.

———. 1992. *The Re-Emergence of Correctional Intervention.* Newbury Park, Calif.: Sage.

Platt, J. R. 1964. "Strong Inference." *Science* 146:1314–19.

Redondo, S. 1994. "El Tratamiento de la Delinquencia en Europa: Un Estudio Meta-Analitico." Ph.D. diss., University of Barcelona.

Rezmovic, E. L. 1979. "Methodological Considerations in Evaluating Correctional Effectiveness: Issues and Chronic Problems." In *The Rehabilitation of Criminal Offenders: Problems and Prospects,* edited by L. Sechrest, S. O. White, and E. D. Brown. Washington, D.C.: National Academy of Sciences.

Rosenthal, R., and D. B. Rubin. 1982. "A Simple, General-Purpose Display of Magnitude of Experimental Effect." *Journal of Educational Psychology* 74:166–69.

Rothman, D. J. 1995. "Perfecting the Prison: United States, 1789–1865." In *The Oxford History of the Prison: The Practice of Punishment in Western Society,* edited by N. Morris and D. J. Rothman. New York: Oxford University Press.

Rotman, E. 1995. "The Failure of Reform: United States, 1865–1965." In *The Oxford History of the Prison: The Practice of Punishment in Western Society,* edited by N. Morris and D. J. Rothman. New York: Oxford University Press.

Sampson, R. J., and Laub, J. H. 1993. *Crime in the Making: Pathways and Turning Points Through Life.* Cambridge, Mass: Harvard University Press.

Sechrest, L., and A. Rosenblatt. 1987. "Research Methods." In *Handbook of Juvenile Delinquency,* edited by H. C. Quay. New York: Pergamon Press.

Sechrest, L., S. O. White, and E. D. Brown, eds. 1979. *The Rehabilitation of Criminal Offenders: Problems and Prospects.* Washington, D.C.: National Academy of Sciences.

Trochim, W. M. K. 1984. *Research Design for Program Evaluation: The Regression Discontinuity Approach.* Beverly Hills, Calif.: Sage.

von Hirsch, A. 1976. *Doing Justice: The Choice of Punishments.* New York: Hill and Wang.

Wainer, H. 1986. *Drawing Inferences from Self-Selected Samples.* New York: Springer-Verlag.

Weisburd, D., with A. Petersino and Gail Mason. 1993. "Design Sensitivity in Criminal Justice Experiments." In *Crime and Justice: A Review of Research,* vol. 17, edited by M. Tonry. Chicago: University of Chicago Press.

Wilson, J. Q. 1975. *Thinking About Crime.* New York: Basic Books.

Wilson, J. Q., and R. Herrnestein. 1985. *Crime and Human Nature.* New York: Simon and Schuster.

27

Capital Punishment

ROGER HOOD

When Cesare Beccaria published his celebrated essay *On Crimes and Punishments* in 1764, he raised both moral and utilitarian objections to capital punishment. It not only was an unacceptably cruel weapon for an enlightened state to employ but also was less effective than imprisonment as a deterrent, and counterproductive in the moral message it conveyed, for it legitimized the very behavior—killing—which the law sought to repress (Bowers 1984, pp. 6–7). Those who have continued to support the use of capital punishment for murder have taken the opposite view, namely, that it expresses and reinforces the moral indignation that citizens rightly feel when another citizen is killed, that those who have killed have forfeited their own right to life, and that no other penalty can have such a strong deterrent effect.[1]

Moral and utilitarian arguments remain at the center of the debate on the legitimacy of capital punishment. Those who believe that it is justly deserved for the taking of a life and those who are opposed to it because they regard it as a violation of the offender's right to life and of his claim to humane treatment will not be affected by evidence, one way or another, as to the unique power of the death penalty to deter murder or other serious crime. Similarly, those utilitarians who base their support for the death penalty on a belief that it saves innocent lives through its general deterrent effects will not necessarily be greatly influenced by claims that it is inhumane per se. But the argument is rarely as simple as this because the case for or against capital punishment often rests on a balancing of both moral and utilitarian considerations.

Thus, those who favor capital punishment because they believe it has a stronger deterrent effect than any length of imprisonment might not be swayed by evidence to the contrary if they also believe that it is warranted on grounds of desert.[2] But they might if it could be shown that deterrence demanded such a high rate of executions that those who had committed murders not deserving of death, such as some domestic homicides, had to be executed in order to achieve an overall deterrent effect. In other words, pursuing deterrence would reap injustice. They might also be swayed against capital punishment by evidence that the death penalty cannot in practice be applied without an unacceptable degree of unfairness, arbitrariness, or discrimination; that it too frequently produces error or other unwarranted practices, such as the execution of persons who cannot be held fully responsible; or that it cannot be enforced without undue cruelty. In essence the case for the death penalty rests on showing *both* that it is useful *and* that it can be applied fairly, without a degree of arbitrariness and cruelty unacceptable to contemporary social values. It is necessary, therefore, to approach the question of capital punishment from both normative and utilitarian points of view, and always in relation to how it is applied in practice.

Within this framework, this chapter discusses the following:

- International trends in the use of the death penalty
- The extent to which capital punishment has been proscribed by norms established in international human rights law, and the American response to such developments
- The use of capital punishment in the United States, including a brief review of the historical pattern of death sentences and executions; regional variations in executions; the numbers on "death row"; and some characteristics of those sentenced to death and executed
- The extent to which the administration of capital punishment in the United States conforms to international standards for humane treatment of persons threatened with the death penalty or under sentence of death—including the question of wrongful convictions and executions
- The attempt in the United States to devise statutes that protect capital punishment from constitutional challenge and the extent to which they have been successful in securing a more equitable infliction of capital punishment
- The evidence with regard to capital punishment's effectiveness as a general deterrent to murder
- And, finally, some reflections on the reasons that capital punishment persists in the United States of America

The Death Penalty in Its International Context

The modern movement to abolish the death penalty has its roots deeply entrenched in the liberal ideas that spawned the Enlightenment in Europe and fed humanitarian and democratic values in Western societies. Inspired by Beccaria, the death penalty for murder was abolished by the rulers of Tuscany and Austria in 1786 and 1787 and, under the empresses Elizabeth and Catherine II, also came close to being abandoned in Russia. Although these first attempts were later reversed, the abolition, or at least the restriction, of capital punishment became a hallmark of enlightened law reform. Thus, in 1786, Pennsylvania abolished the death penalty for all crime save first-degree murder, followed by Virginia in 1796, Ohio in 1815, and later in the century by most other states (Bowers 1984, p. 8). And it was an American state, Michigan, closely followed by Rhode Island and Wisconsin, that led the way in totally abolishing capital punishment for murder in 1846, nearly twenty years before Portugal (1864) became the first European state to do so. Italy, Holland, Romania, Sweden, Finland, Norway, Denmark, Austria, Prussia, and Switzerland had all abandoned capital punishment by the early years of the twentieth century, as had many South American states once they gained their independence (Radzinowicz and Hood 1986, p. 672). In the modern period there has been an even closer link between the triumph of progressive liberal humanitarian ideals and the abolition of capital punishment, especially after the demise of authoritarian regimes: witness Germany and Italy after the Second World War; Romania after the fall of Ceauşescu; Hungary and the Czech and Slovak Republics after the fall of communism; and, most dramatic of all, South Africa after the collapse of apartheid.

However, abolition of capital punishment has not always been permanent. In the 1930s, it was reintroduced and widened in its scope by authoritarian governments in Spain, Italy, and Austria, and was given a horrifying new dimension in Nazi Germany. Sometimes it was abolished and reinstated several times, as in the Soviet Union in 1920–1921 and 1947–1950, and in more recent times in Argentina as military governments came and went.

Looked at on a worldwide scale, the pace of change toward abolition of capital punishment as an international norm has been remarkable. The number of countries that had abandoned the death penalty had swollen from 23 in 1965 to 73 in 1996, with 58 of them having no capital punishment for any offenses, civil or military, in peacetime or war. In addition, another 30 had not executed any person for ten years or more (so-called abolitionist de facto countries). In other words, more than half the member states of the United Nations (UN) had abolished capital punishment either in law or in practice. According to Amnesty International, executions were reported in 1996 from only 39 of 194 countries, and 3,500 of the 4,272 recorded, or 82 percent, had taken place in one country: China.

Although the death penalty still exists in many Asian countries and throughout the Islamic nations of North Africa and the Middle East, only one Western European nation now has capital punishment on its statute book for murder (Turkey, where no one has been executed since 1984 and the government has recently announced that it plans to abolish capital punishment). All the rest (with the exception of Britain, Cyprus, and Malta) have abolished it completely, as have Australia and New Zealand. Furthermore, the abolitionist movement has spread into the countries formerly dominated by the Soviet Union in Eastern Europe. Both Russia and the Ukraine made a commitment to get rid of the death penalty when they acceded to the Council of Europe, and Russia did so by presidential decree in April 1997. Even though a few nations have recently reinstated the death penalty (the Philippines, Papua New Guinea, and Gambia, after a military coup), international practice is moving resolutely in the other direction.

American states have been through several cycles of abolition and re-

instatement of the death penalty since the nineteenth century, such that
only two of ten states that abolished capital punishment between 1897
and 1917 do not now have the death penalty on their statute books (Bowers 1984).[3] In 1972, following a moratorium on executions in 1967
brought about by a sustained legal challenge to the constitutionality of
capital punishment, the Supreme Court ruled in *Furman v. Georgia,* 408
U.S. 238 (1972), that the death penalty was being applied in an arbitrary,
capricious, and discriminatory manner contrary to the Eighth and Fourteenth Amendments of the Constitution of the United States. Many of
those who had fought so hard for abolition hoped that capital punishment had thereby been eliminated in the United States (Meltsner 1973).
However, all but a few of the previously retentionist states quickly re-
drafted their statutes, which within four years were held to meet constitutional standards in *Gregg v. Georgia,* 428 U.S. 153 (1976); *Profitt v.
Florida,* 428 U.S. 242 (1976); and *Jurek v. Texas,* 428 U.S. 262 (1976).
And as recently as 1996, Kansas and New York (following the defeat
of Governor Mario Cuomo) brought back the death penalty—thirty-two
years after the last person had been executed in New York. There have
also been attempts to reinstate the death penalty in at least half the abolitionist states, including Michigan and Rhode Island which abolished
capital punishment well over a hundred years ago. Furthermore, many
bills—over 180 in thirty-eight states in 1994 alone—were introduced in
retentionist states to expand the range of aggravating circumstances and
to streamline processes of appeals so as to hasten executions (National
Coalition to Abolish the Death Penalty 1994). Most of these bills failed,
but they signify the mood in America on this subject. Of particular significance in this respect was the Violent Crime Control Act of 1994,
which expanded the compass of the death penalty under U.S. federal
law. Capital punishment became the discretionary penalty for more than
fifty additional offenses, including some in which it was not necessary
for death to have ensued from the act.[4] Thus, despite the enthusiasm of
many American states for abolition in earlier years, there are now forty
retentionist jurisdictions in the United States: thirty-eight states, the federal government, and the U.S. military. Only twelve states and the District of Columbia have remained abolitionist.

The Human Rights Movement and
the Death Penalty

Although Article 3 of the Universal Declaration of Human Rights of 1948
stated that "[e]veryone has the right to life, liberty and security of the person," this did not proscribe the use of the death penalty for crimes for
which it was appointed by law. However, the language of "right to life"
was to become a powerful vehicle for opposition to the death penalty in
the postwar years. Following its initiative in commissioning surveys of
the use of capital punishment and its effects on the rate of criminality

(United Nations 1962, 1967), the General Assembly of the UN adopted a resolution in 1977 calling for "the progressive restriction of the number of offenses for which the death penalty may be imposed with a view to the desirability of abolishing the punishment" (Hood 1996, p. 4). The European Convention on Human Rights (ECHR) was the first international instrument to embrace abolition as a policy objective when, in 1982, the Committee of Ministers of the Council of Europe adopted Protocol No. 6 to the convention, Article 1 of which provides for the abolition of the death penalty in peacetime. Seven years later, in December 1989, the UN General Assembly adopted the Second Optional Protocol to the International Covenant on Civil and Political Rights (ICCPR), Article 1 of which states that "[n]o one within the jurisdiction of a State party to the present Optional Protocol shall be executed."[5] In June 1990, the General Assembly of the Organization of American States adopted the Protocol to the American Convention on Human Rights to Abolish the Death Penalty (ACHR). Article 1 calls upon countries to abstain from the use of the death penalty, but it does not impose an obligation on them to erase it from the statute book, thus making it possible for de facto abolitionist countries also to ratify the protocol (Schabas 1993a, pp. 162–77, 228–48, 279–83). None of these instruments went so far as to ban the use of the death penalty in wartime, but a significant move was made in this direction when, in 1994, the Parliamentary Assembly of the Council of Europe recommended that a further protocol to the ECHR should be established to provide for the complete abolition of the death penalty, with no possibility of reservations being entered for its retention in any special circumstances. Indeed, most European states have already abolished the death penalty for all crimes on grounds of human rights. As the Spanish reply to a recent UN survey declared: "[W]hat more degrading or afflictive punishment can be imagined than to deprive a person of his life" (Hood 1996, p. 4). And in conformity with such sentiments, the UN Commission on Human Rights in April 1997 adopted a resolution calling on all countries which retained capital punishment to consider suspending executions with a view to completely abolishing the death penalty.

The United States of America has not accepted that an appeal to universal human rights can limit its sovereign power to impose capital punishment within its territories. Unlike any other Western nation, it voted against the adoption of the Second Optional Protocol to the International Covenant.[6] And when, in June 1992, it ratified the ICCPR, the United States entered reservations both with respect to the prohibition on executing persons who committed the crime when below the age of eighteen and to Article 7, which proscribes cruel and unusual treatment or punishment. The United States declared that it would only be bound by this article to the extent that 'cruel, inhuman or degrading treatment or punishment' means the cruel and unusual treatment or punishment prohibited by the Fifth, Eighth or Fourteenth Amendments to the Constitution of the United States. The UN Human Rights Committee has ruled that these reservations are incompatible with the object and purpose of the Covenant and are therefore invalid. These episodes vividly illustrate the reluctance of the United States to change its practices of capital punishment in response to normative claims that it is a violation of human rights: an unacceptably inhuman and degrading punishment per se (Schabas 1995, pp. 278–82; 1996, pp. 13–56). Indeed, when the new death penalty statutes were ruled not to be unconstitutional in *Gregg v. Georgia* in 1972, the Supreme Court, by a seven-to-two majority, stated that they could not be regarded as beyond "evolving standards of decency," because elected representatives in thirty-five states had shown that capital punishment enjoyed widespread public support (Haines 1996, pp. 52–54).

Death Sentences and Executions in the United States

In 1995, over 20,000 culpable homicides (referred to as murders in the *Uniform Crime Reports*) were recorded by the police in the United States, equivalent to 9.5 per 100,000 population—a rate nearly ten times that in England and Wales. Most of these murders were intraracial, rather than interracial. Eighty-three percent of white victims were killed by white offenders, and 93 percent of black victims were killed by black offenders. Three-quarters of the victims were male, and roughly half were white and half black, although African-Americans account for only 12 percent of the U.S. population.

Excluding lynchings, it has been calculated that more than 14,000 Americans have been judicially executed since 1608, or an average of about 35 a year (Haines 1996, p. 7). In the present century executions reached a peak in the 1930s, averaging 175 a year in the five years 1935–1939. After the Second World War, executions began to decline. They averaged 82 a year in the quinquennium 1950–1954, but between 1965 and 1969 only 10 people were executed: the last two in 1967, the year the Supreme Court imposed a national moratorium on executions.

Of the 3,859 persons executed between 1930 and 1967 (33 under federal and 3,826 under state law), 45 percent were white, 54 percent black, and 1 percent of other ethnic origin. Only 32 (0.8 percent) were women, the majority of whom were white. Altogether, 87 percent were executed for murder, 12 percent for rape, and 2 percent for other offenses, mainly robbery and kidnapping. Yet whereas 95 percent of whites were executed for murder and less than 3 percent for rape, as many as a fifth of the African Americans were executed for rape. Indeed, of all those executed for rape, nine out of ten were black. The last executions for rape took place in 1964 (Bowers 1984, p. 74).

Between the first post-*Gregg* execution (of Gary Gilmore by the State of Utah in January 1977) and the end of 1996, 358 persons were executed. The number of offenders received into prison under sentence of death was at first low: only 218 in the five years 1978–1982, an average of 43 a year. However, in the two years 1993 and 1994, the number received rose to 286, a yearly average of 143. Yet, considering that about 5,000 murders a year were potentially "death-eligible" under the new statutes, the probability of being sentenced to death remained quite remote (Pierce and Radelet 1990–1991, p. 713). The probability of being executed was even lower. In the quinquennium 1978–1982, only five executions took place, and while the number in 1996 was fifty-six, this was still roughly equivalent to one in a hundred of those eligible.

In the post-*Gregg* period the majority (58 percent) of those executed were whites who had killed whites, but a substantial minority were blacks who had killed whites (22 percent). Altogether 83 percent of executions were for murders where the victims were white. Black defendants who killed black victims accounted for 11 percent of executions, but only seven persons (just over 1 percent) have been executed for murders involving a white defendant and black victim since 1977. It is not surprising, therefore, that much research has been carried out to see whether these differential ratios are the product of racial discrimination in the use capital punishment.

The number of death sentences and executions has always varied considerably between states and between counties within states, such that some commentators have pointed out that "the most powerful predictor of differential imposition of the death penalty is . . . not substantive law, but . . . geographical region." Even so, executions have been largely concentrated in a few states. In the mid-1980s, Zimring and Hawkins noted that executions in the post-*Gregg* period had been restricted to the same—southern—states that had formerly made the most use of this penalty (excluding New York, which had not at that time reintroduced the death penalty). Furthermore, they predicted that if states with large death row populations that at that time had not recommenced executions were to do so—most notably California and Illinois—there would inevitably be a large surge in the number put to death each year (Zimring and Hawkins 1986, p. 89; Bienen et al. 1990, pp. 780–81). What has happened?

Ten years more experience has shown that the number of states that have "broken through the barrier" to recommence executions has greatly increased. By 1985, 70 percent of the executions had taken place in four southern states: Texas, Florida, Louisiana, and Georgia. The only nonsouthern states to have resumed executions were Utah and Nevada. Eleven years later, by mid-1996, the proportion of executions that were in the southern states had fallen to 57 percent, and Illinois, Delaware, Oklahoma, Arizona, California, Washington, Pennsylvania, Idaho, Maryland, Nebraska, Montana, and Wyoming had all "broken the barrier."

By 1988, twenty-five of the thirty-six states with capital punishment had not yet executed a prisoner, but by the end of 1997, only ten out of thirty-eight (including New York and Kansas) had not done so. It is too early to say whether these ten states will resume executions, for the American experience has proven to be disconcerting to those who have normally assumed that states that do not execute anyone for a period of ten years may be safely regarded as abolitionist de facto. Since 1990, Arizona, California, Oregon, Kentucky, Washington, and Wyoming have resumed executions after more than a quarter of a century.

Thus, Zimring and Hawkins's conclusion—which was endorsed by Zimring in a study a few years later (Zimring 1990–1991)—that the quickening pace of executions has not been accompanied by a parallel increase in the number of executing states now needs to be revised in the light of experience. They also concluded that "the concentration of executions in the South has *increased* rather than diminished as we have moved into the 1980s. . . . Fifty-six of the past fifty-eight executions have taken place in the South." In 1995, however, forty-three of the fifty-six executions were in the South. On the other hand, although executions have resumed in what Zimring and Hawkins called the "bellwether states" (California, Illinois, and Pennsylvania), they have done so, at least until now, without having the "momentous effects" predicted.[7] Executions rose from sixteen in 1989 to fifty-six in 1995. Although the number fell to forty-five in 1996, this was largely due to stays of execution in Texas awaiting the outcome of a constitutional challenge to new procedures for accelerating the appeal process: a challenge that was denied by the Texas Court of Criminal Appeals at the end of 1996. In 1997, seventy-one were executed. When seen in the light of the large number of prisoners—nearly 3,400—under sentence of death, at least 300 a year would have to be executed over the next decade, in addition to new cases, to clear the "backlog."

Human Rights and the Administration of Capital Punishment

In respect of countries that have retained the death penalty, the UN has adopted Standards and Safeguards Guaranteeing the Rights of Those Facing the Death Penalty. Of particular relevance to the situation in the United States are those safeguards aimed to ensure that capital punishment is implemented only for the most serious intentional crimes with lethal or other extremely grave consequences; to exempt those under the age of eighteen at the time of the commission of the crime, as well as fixing an upper age limit beyond which no death sentences are imposed or executions carried out; to exempt those who are or have become insane or are suffering from mental retardation or extremely limited mental competence; to ensure that the death penalty is applied only where there is no possibility of wrongful conviction, and after a fair trial with legal assistance and adequate time and facilities to prepare a defense; to provide for mandatory appeal and mandatory review for clemency in all cases, and to ensure that no executions are carried out until all procedures have been completed; and to carry out executions so as to inflict the minimum possible suffering.[8]

Nearly all these safeguards have been breached in recent years in the United States (Hood 1997). As regards limiting the death penalty to crimes with lethal consequences, it should be noted that until the Supreme Court ruled it a constitutional violation in *Coker v. Georgia*, 433 U.S. 584 (1977), rape was punishable by death in nineteen states. And, as mentioned earlier, in 1994 Congress introduced capital punishment for a number of offenses under the federal Criminal Code which do not necessarily involve loss of life.

The United States does not abide by the safeguard that bans the death penalty for those who commit the offense before their eighteenth birthday. Indeed, the Supreme Court, in the cases of *Stanford v. Kentucky*, 492 U.S. 361 (1989), and *Wilkins v. Missouri*, 492 U.S. 937 (1990), held that it was not unacceptable to the values of contemporary American society to impose the death penalty on those aged sixteen and seventeen. Only thirteen of the thirty-eight states have set the minimum age at eighteen, and it remains at age sixteen in twenty-one states despite the fact that most of the juveniles who have been sentenced to death were heavily impaired by mental disorder and severe abuse, and that these factors had not, in many cases, been effectively brought forward in mitigation at either their trials or their appeals (Robinson and Stephens 1992). Indeed, between 1990 and 1995, thirty-six young men were sentenced to death for crimes they had committed before their eighteenth birthday and, including those sentenced in earlier years, forty-seven such offenders were still on death row at the end of 1996 in fifteen different states (Streib 1995; Amnesty International 1997). Six of the nine executions known to have been inflicted throughout the world between 1990 and 1994 on "juvenile-convictees" occurred in the United States, and one each occurred in Saudi Arabia, Pakistan, and Yemen (Amnesty International 1995).

Only a few countries, such as Russia and the Ukraine, have laws that prohibit the execution of the aged (usually over the age of sixty-five or seventy). The United States is not one of them. In 1995, the oldest person awaiting execution in America was seventy-six, having been sentenced to death when he was sixty-five.

In spite of the decision of the Supreme Court in *Ford v. Wainwright*, 477 U.S. 399 (1986), that the mentally incompetent shall not be executed, this ruling does not bar the execution of those who subsequently recover from mental illness (Miller and Radelet 1993). Thus psychiatrists have been faced with an ethical dilemma: Should they treat a mentally ill patient so that he becomes competent to be executed? (Harding 1994; Radelet 1996). It has been alleged that some prisoners who have shown distinct signs of mental illness have been executed in recent years in the United States. The case of Ricky Ray Rector, executed in Arkansas in 1992, is often cited as an example, and in several states death sentences have been upheld on mentally ill defendants (Ledewitz 1991, pp. 657–61).

In *Penry v. Lynaugh,* 492 U.S. 302 (1989), the Supreme Court decided that mentally disordered offenders were not "categorically" exempt from capital punishment and that the defendant, who was mentally retarded, with an IQ of 50 to 65, who had organic brain damage and a history of considerable physical and emotional abuse as a child, should not be spared the death penalty—because, although mental disorder diminished his blameworthiness, it was also held to increase the probability of dangerous behavior in the future (Schabas 1994b).[9] Nevertheless in 1988, in the wake of public outrage at the execution of a man with an IQ of 65, Georgia became the first state to exempt such persons from capital punishment. So far, only nine other states have followed suit.[10] Thus, twenty-eight states have no bar on the execution of the mentally incompetent.

The quality of legal advice is crucial in capital cases at all stages of the process. A decision to go to trial, rather than plead guilty, for instance, appears greatly to increase the odds of receiving a death sentence. Although it was laid down over a decade ago in *Strickland v. Washington,* 46 U.S. 668 (1984), that defendants in capital cases had a right to *effective* counsel, the reality in many cases is very different. In the southern states, "three-quarters of those convicted of capital murder and sentenced to death had been represented by court-appointed attorneys, and by contrast only one third of those represented by the private Bar received the death penalty" (quoted in Hodgkinson et al. 1996, p. 21). In both Florida and Georgia, defendants who had been represented by a court-appointed rather than a private attorney, when all other relevant factors had been accounted for, were much more likely to be sentenced to death: the odds were 2.6 times higher in Georgia (Bowers 1983, pp. 1078–83; Baldus, Woodworth, and Pulaski 1989, p. 158). Court-appointed lawyers are comparatively poorly paid and therefore less likely to spend as much time dealing with the case, and far too many are inexperienced: as many as half have been found to be dealing with their first capital case. According to Stephen Bright, the director of the Southern Center for Human Rights, the most a court appointed attorney in 1991 could be paid in the South was fifty dollars an hour, more usually a rate of thirty dollars for time spent in court and twenty for out-of-court work (Bright 1994). Writing in 1994, Justice Brennan concluded "notwithstanding the heroic efforts of Resource Centers and appellate projects throughout the country, the meager hourly rates and expenditure caps that many states impose on appointed counsel in capital cases do not suggest that a solution to this crisis is imminent" (Brennan 1994, p. 3). Once on death row, indigent prisoners (nearly everyone) are not entitled to a state-appointed attorney beyond their first appeal. Despite heroic efforts by the Legal Aid and Defense Fund of the National Association for the Advancement of Colored People (NAACP) and the various Resource Centers, the funds are entirely insufficient to provide the assistance required. The sixteen attorneys at the Texas Death Penalty Resource Center were so overwhelmed by cases that there were seventy-five death row inmates in Texas in 1993 with no representation, many of whom were scheduled for execution within five weeks (Death Penalty Information Center 1994, p. 19). And now that the Resource Centers (recently re-named Post-Conviction Defender Organizations) have lost their federal funding, the situation is set to get worse, not better.

The existence of capital punishment requires that jurors should be "death-qualified" (i.e., not be adamantly opposed to the death penalty). This has been shown to bias capital juries in certain ways: in social and ethnic composition, in their willingness to bring in guilty verdicts, and in lessening their concern for defendants' rights (Hood 1996, pp. 112–14). This may be one reason, although of course not the only one, that wrongful convictions can occur. There is ample evidence that mistakes have been made in the United States, as in other countries. Hugo Bedau and Michael Radelet's exhaustive study showed that at least twenty-three clearly innocent persons have been executed in the United States during this century, and a congressional report in 1993 noted that, since 1973, at least forty-eight persons had been released from death row with significant evidence of their innocence, some of them having been convicted on the basis of perjured testimony or because the prosecution improperly withheld exculpatory evidence (Radelet, Bedau, and Putnam 1992; U.S. Senate, Committee on the Judiciary 1993, pp. 2, 8). It takes an extreme utilitarian to claim, as do Stephen Markman and Paul Cassell in the *Stanford Law Review* (1988), that the execution of a few innocent persons is justified if it helps to control murder by deterring others (see Bedau and Radelet 1988).

The proportion of cases heard on appeal before federal courts in which a constitutional error in the imposition of a capital conviction and/or sentence has been found has been remarkably high—at least 45 percent, despite the fact that appeals had been rejected in state courts (Liebman 1990–1991, p. 541 n. 15; Brennan 1994, pp. 3–4).[11] But because the complex system of state and federal review has allowed many years (at great cost) to pass before executions can proceed, there have been attempts to curtail the right to make habeas corpus petitions. In 1989 the Supreme Court had ruled in *Teague v. Lane,* 489 U.S. 288 (1989), that, in general, federal habeas corpus petitioners would not be allowed to benefit from any rules pertaining to the application of the death penalty unless they had been introduced prior to the defendant's conviction becoming final (White 1994, pp. 19–23). Two years later, in *McCleskey v. Zant,* 499 U.S. 467 (1991), the court ruled that prisoners would be obliged to set forward all their legal arguments at first appeal or, if not, to show good cause why they had not been filed earlier: a stiff test, to say the least, when appeals have to be filed within a short period after conviction. Thus in *Herrera v. Collins,* 506 U.S. 390 (1993), where the family had come forward with fresh evidence eight years after conviction, the court upheld a Texas statute forbidding the appellate courts from considering newly discovered evidence supporting a claim of innocence in capital cases, unless the evidence had been filed within thirty days of the conclusion of the trial. Furthermore, the Supreme Court has required federal courts to reject all claims if the proper procedures had not been followed in state courts. This may not sound unreasonable, but to make it fair would require the kind of expert legal assistance that is so rarely available to poor defendants. For instance, Roger Coleman filed his appeal three days late in Virginia. Although this was his attorney's error, a federal court decided in *Coleman v. Thompson,* 111 S. Ct. 2546 (1991), that he had thereby procedurally defaulted, and it refused to hear his constitutional claim before he was executed. Furthermore, the Anti-Terrorism and Effective Death Penalty Act, which became law in April 1996, is aimed to limit both the number of habeas corpus appeals to federal courts allowed to prisoners and to ensure that they are all made within six months from the denial of state appeals (provided that a state has "opted in" by ensuring adequate legal assistance to those sentenced to death, a condition no state has yet complied with). Such restrictions on habeas corpus led Justice Blackmun, a former supporter of capital punishment, to conclude that the death penalty can never be imposed fairly (Bedau 1987, pp. 242–43).

Although most states include, as part of mandatory appellate review of a death sentence, a "proportionality review" to assess "whether the death sentence is excessive or disproportionate to the penalty imposed in similar cases, considering both the crime and the defendant," there is no constitutional obligation to do so.[12] Furthermore, the Supreme Court has held, in *Maggio v. Williams,* 464 U.S. 46 (1983), that such a review (in a state where it was mandatory) was sufficient if the appeal court compared the death sentence with cases from the same narrow judicial district rather than making the comparison with cases drawn from right across the state (van Duizend 1984, p. 11). In any case, this safeguard appears to have had little impact. In a study of Supreme Court proportionality reviews in five states, it was found that the death penalty had been considered to be comparatively excessive in only one case (Dix 1979; Wallace and Sorensen 1994, p. 286). Similarly, the detailed study by Baldus, Woodworth, and Pulaski of proportionality reviews by the Georgia Supreme Court showed that only in very rare instances were sentences vacated because they were deemed to be "excessive and disproportionate" (1989, pp. 404, 408–19; Gross and Mauro 1984, pp. 83–92). Thus, the evidence suggests that there is reason to be very skeptical about whether proportionality review can ever eliminate an element of arbitrariness and capriciousness in the choice of the very few who are eventually put to death.

Although all states in America provide for an automatic consideration for pardon or clemency by the state executive, this has become largely a nugatory process. Of the 4,800 death sentences imposed since 1976 (leaving aside some pardons granted as a result of court decisions), a mere thirty-six clemency applications have been granted (U.S. Senate, Committee on the Judiciary 1993). This is a much smaller proportion than in the past, when one in five prisoners might have expected to have his sentence commuted to life imprisonment (Bedau 1991; Radelet and Zsembik 1993). In part, this must be due to the growth in the number of successful appeals granted by the courts, and some may argue that this has meant that the cases that are left for clemency consideration are of so little merit and so egregious that it is not surprising the granting of clemencies has declined so markedly. This has, no doubt, had an influence, but clemency has been refused to defendants who by no stretch of the imagination could be called the worst offenders. To take but two examples: Warren McCleskey was executed even though the prosecutor had offered to reduce the charge to noncapital murder in exchange for a guilty plea; and John Spinkellink, the first person to be executed in Florida when capital punishment was resumed, was said by the assistant attorney general to be "the least obnoxious person on death row in terms of the crime he committed" (quoted in Greenberg 1982, pp. 926–27; also Kaplan 1984, pp. 186–87). It seems that clemency has become so influenced by political consequences that few state governors or their appointees are prepared to exercise their discretion in the defendant's favor.

The last of the international standards refers to carrying out the punishment so as to inflict the minimum of suffering. Electrocution, first introduced in New York in 1888 as a supposedly more humane form of execution than hanging, is still used by twelve states; the gas chamber, which was regarded by some as an even more speedy, modern system when introduced in 1924, remains the method employed by eight states. The majority, however, have moved to the supposedly even more humane and cleaner method of lethal injection, despite objections from physicians (American College of Physicians 1994; American Medical Association 1993; Radelet 1996). Introduced by Oklahoma in 1977, lethal injection was first used in Texas in 1982 and within a few years had been adopted by the majority of states (Zimring and Hawkins 1986, pp. 243–60). By 1996 lethal injection was the method used by twenty-seven states.[13]

Although there have been reports that some persons have suffered greatly during execution in the electric chair, its use has not been ruled unconstitutional (Denno 1994a), nor has it been held to be in breach of the ICCPR by the UN Human Rights Committee. But the Human Rights Committee did hold Canada to be in breach of the covenant for extraditing another prisoner to California to face execution in the gas chamber, a method that has subsequently been ruled unconstitutional by a federal judge, *Fierro v. Gomez*, 865 F. Supp. 1387 (N.D. Cal. 1994; Schabas 1993b, 1994c, pp. 916–17).

Of far greater concern than the method of execution has been the length of time, and the conditions of confinement, under which American prisoners are kept on "death row," awaiting the decision whether to execute them. It is known that the reactions of prisoners on death row are similar to those of terminally ill hospital patients, exacerbated by the physical conditions of confinement for up to twenty-two hours a day. Such conditions have been described in one of the best studies as "an austere world in which condemned prisoners are treated as bodies kept alive to be killed" (Johnson and Carroll 1985, pp. 8–15), as reflected in the evocative title of Helen Prejean's book *Dead Man Walking* (1993). This and other evidence suggests that whatever case may be made for capital punishment, it is in practice impossible to administer in the United States without involving unacceptable cruelty and suffering. By the end of 1997, nearly 3,400 prisoners were under sentence of death, 47 percent of them white, 41 percent black, and 8 percent Hispanic. Nearly all of them (98.5 percent) were male. Among states with the death penalty (not counting Kansas and New York, which have only recently reintroduced it), only New Hampshire and Wyoming had no prisoners on death row in mid-1996. At that time, ten states had fewer than fifteen prisoners,[14] but eleven had more than a hundred.[15] Many of these states have large numbers of prisoners on death row because they have rarely executed anyone (California, Pennsylvania, and Illinois), but several are states with high rates of executions (Florida, Texas, Georgia, and Missouri). On the other hand, Virginia and Louisiana, which occupy third and fourth rank among states that execute, have relatively modest death row populations. Thus, there is no simple correlation between the number of death sentences imposed and the willingness of the state to execute.

Before the campaign to abolish capital punishment began in the 1960s, the average time a condemned prisoner spent on death row was about sixteen months: the last person to be executed before the moratorium in 1967 had been convicted in 1965. Under the operation of the revised death penalty statutes, the period has lengthened enormously. Those executed in 1995 had spent an average of eleven years under sentence of death, double the average time for those executed in 1985. To take but one example, in Utah a prisoner was executed in 1992 after spending eighteen years in confinement on death row for a crime committed when he was nineteen.

The opinion of international courts on the cruelty of keeping persons for such lengthy periods under sentences of death contrasts with the silence of the U.S. Supreme Court on this subject. In 1989, the European Court of Human Rights ruled that it would be a breach of the provisions of the ECHR for the United Kingdom to extradite a prisoner named Soering to Virginia (*Soering v. UK*, 161 Eur. CT. H. R, ser. A 34 [1989]), because his inevitably long wait on death row would amount to inhuman and degrading treatment.[16] In a similar vein, the Judicial Committee of the Privy Council in London, which hears appeals from various small Commonwealth countries, in reviewing the cases of men held in appalling conditions for up to eleven years under sentence of death in Jamaica and other Caribbean countries, decided that no prisoner should wait more than five years under sentence of death, and it hinted that three years should probably be the maximum (*Pratt v. Attorney General of Jamaica* [1993] 4 All E.R. 763 and 783 P.C.; Schabas 1994a). The practice in the United States is again out of line with these international standards.

In summary, all the evidence reviewed here indicates that, although the new death penalty statutes in the United States were crafted so as to control the arbitrary and inhumane imposition of capital punishment, they have not been put into effect in a way that avoids the breach of several safeguards designed to protect the rights and ensure fair and humane treatment for those under sentence of death. Indeed, opponents of capital punishment argue that no death penalty statute can be tailored so as to meet the constitutional standards that ought to be the hallmark of a state committed to the protection of human rights.

Trying to Restrict the Death Penalty and Make It Less Arbitrary

In the 1960s, the death penalty was mandatory for first-degree murder in twenty-two of the forty-two states of the United States. After the *Furman* decision in 1972 ruled that all extant death penalty statutes were unconstitutional because execution had become so freakish an event that it was "cruel and unusual in the same sense that being struck by lightning is cruel and unusual," several states again enacted statutes that made death mandatory, but now for specifically defined categories of murder, such as the killing of a law enforcement officer or killing while carrying out a robbery. In a series of cases, beginning with *Woodson v. North Carolina,* 428 U.S. 280 (1976), and *Roberts v. Louisiana,* 428 U.S. 325 (1976), the Supreme Court struck down mandatory statutes of this kind, regarding them as still too broad and too rigid. By not allowing the introduction of any mitigating circumstances, they were liable both to invite juries to acquit, thereby reintroducing an undesirable element of arbitrariness, and, where imposed, to be in some cases disproportionate to the circumstances of the case (Stein 1985).

In approving new state statutes, the Supreme Court, in *Gregg v. Georgia,* 428 U.S. 153 (1976) and other cases,[17] was obviously convinced that the definitions of capital murder were sufficiently narrow to avoid arbitrariness and discrimination while at the same time broad enough to allow judges and juries[18] the discretion necessary to treat each case on its specific merits. These statutes, although differing quite substantially in both their objectives and their form (Acker and Walsh 1989, p. 1362; Acker and Lanier 1994a, 1994b, 1995), therefore listed a number of specific aggravating circumstances, such as murder carried out during a contemporaneous felony (especially rape or armed robbery), murder of law enforcement personnel, or those that are "heinous, atrocious or cruel." Some states, such as Florida, listed legally relevant mitigating circumstances in the statute, but others did not. Trials were to be bifurcated, with a separate hearing before a jury to determine sentence.

It is beyond contention that the U.S. Supreme Court, over the last fifteen years, has interpreted these statutes in ways that have loosened rather than tightened the constraints on the discretion of judges and juries: a process that has been aptly called "deregulating death" (Weisberg 1984, p. 321; Hood 1996, pp. 150–58).[19] Indeed, the Supreme Court has declared that it is "unwilling to say that there is any one right way for a state to set up its capital sentencing scheme" (*Spaziano v. Florida,* 468 U.S. 447 [1984]; Gillers 1985).

In some jurisdictions the statute is in effect mandatory if the sentencer finds that aggravating circumstances outweigh mitigating factors, or if it is found that one or more aggravating factors exist, but no mitigating features have been established.[20] In most jurisdictions, however, the sentencer "weighs" the aggravating against the mitigating factors in deciding whether a death sentence should be imposed. Under both formulas there is much room for different perceptions, subjective judgments, and theories of crime causation to influence the interpretation of events on which a life or death decision rests (Denno 1994b). This is particularly so where the sentencer is required to consider as an aggravating factor whether the murder was "heinous, atrocious or cruel" or some similar test (Acker and Lanier 1994b, pp. 124–30).

Legal scholars in America have thus come to the conclusion that it is impossible concurrently to maximize both flexibility and nonarbitrariness, or to encapsulate in legal rules decisions that ultimately rest on the subjective moral evaluations of prosecutors, juries, and judges (Nathanson 1985). This conclusion echoes that reached by the Royal Commission on Capital Punishment of 1953 in Britain: "[I]t is impracticable to frame a statutory definition of murder which would effectively limit the scope of capital punishment and would not have over-riding disadvantages in other respects" (United Kingdom 1953, p. 278).[21]

This, of course, is because such statutes leave room for the exercise of discretion at all stages of the process. A number of studies in Illinois, Colorado, Georgia, South Carolina, New Jersey, and North Carolina have charted what has happened to those cases that appeared on the facts, to be legally eligible for the death sentence (e.g., Murphy 1984; Baldus, Woodworth, and Pulaski 1989; Bienen et al. 1988, p. 287; 1990, p. 744). Typically they show that in half to two-thirds of cases that might "on paper" have been eligible for a death sentence, the defendant was not charged with capital murder. Of the minority who were charged, around a third were likely to be convicted of capital murder, of whom a minority were sentenced to death, and only a very few of these actually executed. To take some examples: in North Carolina, only 1 of 319 defendants originally indicted for first-degree murder was eventually executed (Nakell and Hardy 1987, pp. 108–9); and in New Jersey a county prosecutor decided not to proceed with a capital charge in half the felony-murders with at least one statutory aggravating factor (the most likely group to receive a death sentence). At the end of the process, only 41 of 134 death-eligible cases in New Jersey were actually convicted of capital murder, and only 15 of these (just over a third) were sentenced to death. In other words, only 11 percent of those originally indicted with a death-eligible murder received the death penalty. On a national scale, Baldus and his colleagues have estimated that, from a pool of between 2,000 and 4,000 "death-eligible" cases processed annually in the United States, only 250 to 300 death sentences result: a rate of 6 to 15 percent (Baldus, Woodworth, and Pulaski 1986, pp. 145–56; see also Stein 1985, p. 1806). The chances of being executed were, of course, even lower.

It may be objected that all this evidence shows is that the statutes do indeed work well in sifting out, from the mass of cases, the truly "death-worthy." To what extent is this the case? Are like cases being treated alike and only the most egregious sentenced to death? To demonstrate whether or not this is the case requires a methodology that will be able to "match" cases in relation to legally relevant variables so that "like are compared with like." In an attempt to do this, Baldus, Woodworth, and Pulaski (1989) embarked on a massive study of the imposition of the death penalty in Georgia, comparing its use under the pre-*Furman* statute with its use under the constitutionally approved current statute. They developed a regression analysis, based on the 20 to 30 most statistically significant and legally legitimate variables (out of 150 used in the initial analysis) in order to produce a "culpability index." Six groups of cases were identified, within each of which the cases had a similar rate of death sentences, ranging from a group among whom less than one in ten was predicted to get the death sentence to a group in which all were predicted to be sentenced to death. The cases in each group were therefore not necessarily factually similar but were similarly "culpable" in the sense that a particular combination of aggravating and mitigating circumstances produced a similar probability—either low, medium, or high—of their being sentenced to death. On this basis it was possible to assess the extent to which the new legislation has reduced the incidence of arbitrary and discriminatory death sentences among cases of similar culpability. Baldus, Woodworth, and Pulaski made the judgment that, among the relatively small proportion of eligible murder cases in Georgia sentenced to death, the penalty would be presumptively "excessive" if not more than 35 percent of like cases received it, and that it would only be "presumptively even-handed" for those cases in which the death-sentencing rate among similar cases was 80 percent and over. This, like many other issues concerning the death penalty, is ultimately a matter for moral and political judgment.

Five conclusions can be drawn from this study, conclusions that are in line with those emanating from several other inquiries (e.g., Barnett 1985; Gross and Mauro 1984, 1989).

First, as might be expected from the preceding discussion, the new capital statutes have drawn the bounds of eligibility to include a far greater number of cases than prosecutors, judges, or juries are willing to see sentenced to death.

Second, that the application of the new statutes had been successful in ensuring that more of those sentenced to death were among the most culpable—that there was less overlap between those sentenced to death and those who received life imprisonment than was the case under the pre-*Furman* statutes.

Third, that the new capital statutes had led to greater "evenhandedness," in the sense that there were fewer instances where the less serious types of cases were sentenced to death. While prior to *Furman* four out of every ten death sentences were judged to be presumptively "excessive" (in the sense that fewer than 35 percent in that category were sentenced to death), after *Furman* only 13 percent were "excessive." And while before *Furman* only 23 percent were "even handed" (at least 80 percent in that category being sentenced to death), after *Furman* the proportion was 51 percent. The researchers therefore concluded that the reform of the capital statutes had created a more selective and less arbitrary system. Nevertheless, a third of the death sentence cases had characteristics that put them in a category where a wide range—varying between 35 and 70 percent—of "like" offenders were sentenced to death (Baldus, Woodworth, and Pulaski 1989, p. 92). The case of Warren McCleskey, an African-American man sentenced to death for shooting a white policeman during a robbery (whose case, according to Baldus, was in a "culpability" band where the probability of a death sentence was 31 percent), was compared with sixteen other cases of police killings in the same county in Georgia. None of the defendants in these cases had been sentenced to death, and only one had even advanced to a death penalty trial.

The fourth finding was that there was no longer a significant discrimination against black defendants—although this remains a contentious issue. The fact that black defendants were overrepresented among those convicted of capital murders, especially among those who killed whites, was explained by differences in the types of murders that are intraracial and those committed against persons of a different race. It was found that a considerably higher proportion of black defendant/white victim cases were committed in circumstances, such as murders in the course of committing a felony, that made them death-eligible (75 percent) than white defendant/black victim cases (30 percent). In comparison, white/white and black/black cases were capital murders in only 20 and 9 percent of instances, respectively (see Paternoster 1984, p. 767). When this and other factors were taken into account, Baldus, Woodworth, and Pulaski found in the post-*Furman* sample no race of defendant discrimination, and this has been confirmed by several other studies (Gross and Mauro 1984, pp. 71–72, 82; Radelet 1981; Paternoster 1984, Nakell and Hardy 1987, pp. 143–46).

Fifth, like many other inquiries, Baldus, Woodworth, and Pulaski found a "race of victim effect." Those who killed white persons were considerably more likely to be sentenced to death than those who killed blacks, regardless of the race of the defendant (see Zeisel 1981, p. 465; Radelet and Vandiver 1986, p. 105). Indeed, 84 percent of the prisoners executed in the United States since 1977 were convicted of killing a white victim, even though white victims made up only about half of homicide victims (Amnesty International 1995, p. 4). Nevertheless, the gap had narrowed between the death sentence rate of white defendants/white victims and black defendants/white victims. Before *Furman* it had been, in Georgia, 23 percentage points (8 percent vs. 31 percent). After *Furman* it had narrowed to 13 percentage points (22 percent vs. 35 percent), but that, of course, is equivalent to a rate that was still 56 percent higher when a black defendant was involved. The disparity in the treatment of cases involving white and black victims was greatest in the cases of medium gravity, where the general probability of being sentenced to death was around fifty-fifty. Here, the difference was as high as 20 to 36 percentage points, the odds of a death sentence in white victim cases being 61 percent and in black victim cases only 25 percent.[22] Baldus and his colleagues calculated that a third of all the death sentences for killing a white victim may result from this strong tendency to treat white victim cases so much more seriously (Baldus, Woodworth, and Pulaski 1989, pp. 155, 160).

A review of twenty-eight studies by the U.S. General Accounting Office concluded that "in 82 percent of the studies, race of victim [white] was found to influence the likelihood of being charged with capital murder or receiving the death penalty. . . . This finding was remarkably consistent across data sets, states, data collection methods, and analytical techniques. . . . [However,] . . . the race of offender influence is not so clear cut" (U.S. General Accounting Office 1990, p. 6). The race of victim effect, therefore, can be correctly characterized as "a real and robust phenomenon" (Gross 1985, p. 1279).

Capital Punishment and General Deterrence

To many laymen the threat of death is self-evidently a more effective deterrent than life imprisonment. As the Victorian English judge, James Fitzjames Stephen, put it: "[T]he plain truth is that statistics are no guide at all. . . . the question as to the effect of capital punishment on crime must always be referred, not to statistics, but to the general principles of human nature" (quoted in Radzinowicz and Hood 1986, p. 674).

But although it is highly probable that there are instances where someone has refrained from murder for fear of execution, this in itself is an insufficient basis on which to conclude that the existence of the death penalty on the statute book, plus the threat of execution, will lead to a lower rate of murder per head of population than would be the case without this ultimate penalty. In other words, the issue is not whether the death penalty deters some people but whether, when all the circumstances surrounding the use of capital punishment are taken into account, it is associated with a marginally lower rate of the kind of murders for which capital punishment is appointed. The reason one must take account of and weigh the influence of all its effects is that capital punishment has several drawbacks that might counteract any deterrent effect it could have. It must be recognized that it is very difficult to find empirical data relating to deterrence that would utterly convince either a committed proponent of the death penalty or an opponent. What can be done, however, is to weigh all the evidence carefully and attempt to reach a balanced conclusion, always remembering, of course, that general deterrence is only one of the justifications that might be considered for or against the death penalty. Issues of humanity, of respect for human rights, of discrimination, and of the danger of wrongful conviction must all be weighed against any claims for deterrence.

Deterrence will naturally depend on the communication of a threat that the penalty of death will be inflicted on the person who commits murder. Yet democratic societies do not threaten all who commit culpable homicides—even those that retain it as the mandatory penalty for certain types of murder—and the threat of execution is therefore both uncertain and usually quite remote. In the United States, despite the increase in the number of executions in recent years and the strong support for the death penalty voiced by prominent politicians, the probability of being executed if charged with a culpable homicide remains very low—around 1 in 1,000. Even restricting the calculation to those murders that are statutorily "death-eligible," the probability of being sentenced to death in the United States is only about 1 in 10 and of being executed between 0.6 and 1.25 per hundred. Any rational actor would see this as a very remote risk, and probably much lower than the risks of being killed by the police or the victim. In any case, for any rational calculation of these probabilities to affect an offender's decision whether to commit the offense he or she must know, first, whether the act is likely to be classed as a capital offense and, second, whether the prosecutor will place it in that limited class that is likely to attract a high risk of execution. Murders that are described as "especially heinous, atrocious, or cruel" are likely to be carried out by psychopathic personalities or persons who have lost control of their normal inhibitions.

The inevitable arbitrariness and discrimination—usually against the poorest and least powerful persons in society—in the infliction of capital punishment, along with outcries against the execution of the wrongfully convicted and the equally inevitable cruelties associated with the administration of capital punishment, may all combine to lessen respect for law and the legitimacy of the authority of the criminal justice system. It is not surprising, therefore, to find that opponents of the death penalty speak of its degrading, brutalizing, and even murder-stimulating effects, rather than its moralizing impact on society (Bowers 1984, pp. 271–335; 1988).

For all these reasons, the intuitive arguments in favor of the deterrent impact of the death penalty are not as self-evident as they first appear. What is the empirical evidence?

If the death penalty has a capacity to deter murder more than any other penalty, one would expect to find (1) a rise in murder associated with the abolition of the death penalty (2) lower rates of murder in states with the death penalty than in similar states without it; and (3) an inverse (negative) correlation between the rate of executions and the rate of murder. But before making the assumption that such statistical associations—if found—are evidence of deterrence, it is necessary to ensure that all other factors that might explain changes in the incidence of murder have been taken into account and controlled for. This is exceptionally hard to do.

It is particularly difficult to compare rates of capital murder with the incidence of executions because they usually interact with each other. If capital punishment is vigorously enforced, it may be much more difficult to obtain a conviction for capital murder, and therefore one would naturally expect a lower conviction rate for murder to be associated with a higher rate of executions.[23] Furthermore, because statistics of the number of capital murders can be obtained only after convictions have been recorded, many studies that correlate the number of executions with the number of culpable homicides include, in the dependent variable, offenses that would not be subject to capital punishment at all, making any correlations a spurious test of the deterrence hypothesis. It is also obvious that any change in the use of the death penalty may itself be associated with social and penal changes that may affect the rate of murder, and that unless these are taken into account, no definite conclusions can be drawn about the impact of the death penalty alone. Put simply, correlations are not in themselves proof of causation.

One of the simplest tests of the preventive or deterrent effect of capital punishment is to see whether, following abolition, there is a change in the incidence of homicide, and more specifically of those murders that were formerly capital. Although a rise in homicide might not necessarily be caused by the removal of the deterrent—there might be other concomitant causes—one would not expect there to be a fall in homicides if it were true that capital punishment is a major restraint on murder.

All the evidence points in the same direction—to refute the claims that the death penalty is a major restraining factor. To take some examples: in Australia, where the last executions occurred in the mid-1960s, the reported homicide rate per 100,000 of the population has fallen, and the murder rate has changed very little. In 1993, seventeen years after the abolition of the death penalty, the homicide rate in Canada was 27 percent lower than it had been in 1975, the year before abolition. On the other hand, if there are social factors creating an increase in violence as a whole in society, one would expect the rate of murder to rise. And, if the abolition of capital punishment lessened the deterrent effect, one would expect murder to rise at a rate equivalent to serious violent crime in general (Bowers 1984, pp. 113–14). However, nowhere to my knowledge has that happened. For example, in England and Wales, since the abolition of the death penalty, the increase in violent crimes as a whole has far outstripped the rise in the number of murders.

Several studies have been conducted to see whether highly publicized executions are followed by a lower rate of homicides. Some studies have found such an effect, but several have found the opposite and have regarded the increase in murders as proof of the "brutalization" hypothesis. The causal links derived from such data are especially hard to interpret. The most that can be concluded from this evidence is that highly publicized executions may in some instances "defer" homicides, but they do not, over the longer term, reduce them. A recent sophisticated time-series analysis in the United States of the relationship between publicized executions between 1940 and 1986 and the incidence of homicide in the following year concluded that the overall effect of executions on homicide rates was "essentially zero" (Bailey and Peterson 1989, p. 739).

It has been claimed that the death penalty is a proven deterrent because in some states of the United States the homicide rate fell when executions were resumed. But the danger of drawing this inference can be illustrated by comparing trends in states that do and do not have the death penalty. For example, a fall in the homicide rates of Florida and Georgia of 21 and 23 percent, respectively, between 1980 and 1985 was attributed to the resumption of executions in those states. Yet during the same period homicides had also fallen by 26 percent in New York State, where no death penalty existed.

The well-known comparative studies in the United States by Thorsten Sellin of groups of contiguous states with similar socioeconomic characteristics, some of which had the death penalty and some of which did not, showed that the average annual rate of homicide in these states for the years 1940–1955 bore no relationship to whether or not death was the maximum penalty for murder (Sellin 1959, pp. 22–28; 1977, pp. 41–52). In addition, Sellin's studies found no evidence that the police or prison staff were better protected in states that had, and used, capital punishment. Not only have more recent reviews of such comparative studies failed to find a consistent relationship between the number of executions in a state and the number of homicides (abolitionist states in the majority of cases having fewer homicides); states that abolished the death penalty have generally tended to have a smaller increase in homicides than their retentionist neighboring states (Bowers 1984, pp. 103–14, 279–80; Lempert 1983, pp. 100–101). The general conclusion is that "[t]he homicide rates in those states which have carried out executions since 1977 are higher than in those states which have the death penalty but have not executed anyone, which in turn are higher than in those states that do not have the death penalty. The figures for 1993, expressed as homicide rates per one-hundred-thousand population, are 9.35, 5.72 and 5.22 respectively" (Hodgkinson et al. 1996, p. 4).

Despite the fact that comparative analyses have methodological shortcomings because they cannot control for the effects of all variables on the murder rate, it is remarkable that the findings have all pointed in the same direction. Not a single such study has provided support for the view that the availability of capital punishment, whether in law or practice, has a superior deterrent effect.

In order to try to remedy the problem that murder rates and execution rates may both be affected by other variables, a number of studies during the 1970s and 1980s applied multiple regression techniques to an econometric analysis of the data, controlling for demographic, social, and economic factors that might affect the incidence of homicide, so as to isolate the impact of the execution rate. They either analyzed fluctuations over considerable periods of time in the rates of executions and homicides in the United States as a whole, controlling for the effect of such variables, or analyzed the variations between states in executions and homicides over various time periods. Some of these studies—the most highly publicized ones—found evidence consistent with the deterrent hypothesis, but others by reputable researchers found no support whatsoever for a deterrent effect.

Two economists, Isaac Ehrlich and Stephen Layson, claimed to show very substantial negative correlations between the probability of execution and the rate of homicide. One of Ehrlich's studies led him to estimate that an additional execution was associated with between 7 and 8 fewer murders, while in another he suggested that the payoff might be as high as 20 to 24 fewer murders per execution (Ehrlich 1975, 1977). Layson reached a similar conclusion, estimating that each execution had produced between 8.5 and 28 fewer homicides (Layson 1985, 1986). The very wide variation in the magnitude of these effects immediately raises problems of interpretation and validity.

Several replications of these studies have suggested that this supposed deterrent effect is a spurious finding because the researchers had included in their time series a period during the 1960s and 1970s when the death penalty was practically in abeyance and during which all serious crimes, including homicide, rose markedly (Bowers and Pierce 1975; Bowers 1984, pp. 320–22). This appears to give support to the view that the increased homicide rate was caused by the decline in executions, whereas when this period was excluded from the time series there was no negative association over a long period between the rate of executions and homicides, indicating no support for the deterrent hypothesis. Consistent with these results is the finding that states with capital punishment that placed a moratorium on executions during the 1960s experienced no greater increase in their murder rate than did those that had never used capital punishment (Forst 1977). There is good evidence to suggest, therefore, that an upsurge in the rate of homicide during this period was coincidental with the moratorium on capital punishment and not caused by it.

Furthermore, the use of a statistical model drawn from economics has been attacked on a number of grounds as inappropriate for the study of the complex issue of murder and capital punishment. The first objection is that such a model rests on the theory of rational choices, of "utility maximization," whereas it is well known that the circumstances and situations in which many murders take place, let alone the mental characteristics and passions of those who commit such offenses, do not conform in the majority of cases to this model of rationality. The second objection is that these studies have used, as their dependent variable, the aggregate of all homicides and nonnegligent manslaughters, whether they were subject to the death penalty or not. Aggregating all homicides will confound and distort the effects of executions on the rate of capital murder because there may be different motivations for capital and noncapital murders, or there may be differences in the ratio of capital to noncapital murders between states or over time. The third problem is that the "execution rate" in these studies was computed as a proportion of the homicide rate, or the arrest or conviction rate for homicide. In other words, the numerator and denominator were not independent of each other and, because executions are relatively rare in comparison with the number of homicides, even a small error in these rates may have produced what one expert critique has called "unusually strong spurious appearances of a deterrent effect" (Klein, Forst, and Filatov 1978). Fourth, the aggregation of all data from different states in the time-series analyses makes the assumption that an execution in an executing state will affect the rate of homicides in the following year (the usual time lag specified by these studies), whether they occur in the executing state or not. Clearly, this is an unsatisfactory test of the deterrent hypothesis. Fifth, there have been strong criticisms of the mathematical formulations used, which many critics regard as inappropriate for the type of data studied. Finally, such studies have been criticized for not including certain variables that are known to have a strong impact on the homicide rate, such as gun ownership and possession of firearms. There are, of course, many factors that might affect the incidence of crimes in general and homicide over a period of time, irrespective of the existence of capital punishment. No study can take all of them into account at once (Fox and Radelet 1989; Hood 1996, pp. 203–10).

In short, the absence of sufficient controls, when taken in conjunction with the other problems already mentioned, should lead any dispassionate analyst to conclude that econometric analyses have not provided evidence from which it would be prudent to infer that capital punishment has any marginally greater deterrent effect than alternative penalties. It therefore seems right to echo the conclusions of the panel set up by the American National Academy of Sciences published twenty years ago: "Any policy use of scientific evidence on capital punishment will require extremely severe standards of proof. The non-experimental research to which the study of the deterrent effects of capital punishment is necessarily limited will almost certainly be unable to meet those standards of proof" (Klein, Forst, and Filatov 1978).

The evidence in support of or against the deterrence argument may not be sufficiently clear-cut to lead anyone with a prior position favorable or opposed to capital punishment to change his or her mind on these grounds alone. However, those who wish to argue that the death penalty is justified because it reduces the rate of murder and saves the lives of potential victims should consider whether the evidence is sufficiently conclusive, and the effects sufficiently large, to override the other strong objections based on human rights, arbitrariness, discrimination, brutalizing effects, and error. Looked at this way, the balance of the evidence definitely favors the abolitionist position, whatever intuitive beliefs people may hold about the deterrent effects of executions.

If capital punishment were to be used to try to obtain a strong deterrent effect, it would have to be enforced mandatorily and without exceptions on a large scale across all categories of homicide. That is not an option for democratic states bound by the rule of law and concern for humanity and respect for human rights. It is futile, therefore, for such states to retain the death penalty for very few murders, somewhat arbitrarily imposed, on the grounds that it is justified as a deterrent measure of unique effectiveness.

The Politics of Abolition

Several hypotheses have been advanced as to why capital punishment has remained so strongly entrenched in the United States when it has disappeared from the penal armory of almost all the countries that share with the United States a common political heritage and culture. Some commentators have suggested that the nature of American federalism, under which capital punishment is in practice mostly a matter of state law and for state politics, has meant that the issue has been more isolated from international pressures; others have emphasized the populist nature of American politics and the influence of public opinion on its political institutions, particularly when public opinion is roused by reports of heinous murders; others have pointed to the failure to organize an effective nationwide political campaign in the United States; and yet others have argued that the wrong strategy has been followed, namely, an attempt to abolish the death penalty through the courts rather than the political processes. Probably all these factors have interacted to make the campaign against capital punishment less effective than it has been in other Western countries.

Why, for example, has there been so little concern about miscarriages of justice in America? In Britain it was undoubtedly a potent influence in bringing about abolition. Indeed, it has become even more potent as a restraint on Parliament reinstating the death penalty since it has been proven, after hard-fought and long campaigns, that a substantial number of persons who formerly would have been executed had been wrongfully convicted. The list is long and includes not only those wrongly convicted of terrorist offenses. The former Conservative Party home secretary, Michael Howard, a staunch supporter of tough penal policies, changed his mind about capital punishment, recognizing that mistakes are inevitable in any system of human justice and that the putting to death of some innocent persons is a logical but unacceptable consequence of capital punishment (see, generally, Dando 1996, pp. 13–16).

In a recent review of the campaign against the death penalty in America, Herbert Haines has suggested that the question of miscarriages of justice has not had an influential impact on the debate because there has not been sufficient uncontroversial evidence that innocent people have been executed (Haines 1996, pp. 87–92). The fact that, in America, there is a complex and lengthy process of appeals under which many death sentences are overturned may have convinced most people that only the truly guilty are executed. And yet serious doubts continue to be raised. One is left, therefore, with a need to explain why they have had such a small political impact. In part this may be due to the fact that concern about a possible wrongful conviction in one state has little effect on others. But more likely it is due to the failure to mount effective campaigns with widespread media support, for opinion polls suggest that even if the chances of wrongful conviction were 1 in 1,000, some 30 percent of those who favor the death penalty would withdraw their support. This would bring overall support for capital punishment down to little over half among the population as a whole and would create an entirely different political atmosphere (Maguire and Pastore 1996, Table 2.74).

Haines characterizes the organization of political opposition to capital punishment as having "too few members, too little money . . . and too little broad appeal in the messages the movement has tried to deliver." But perhaps of more importance is the fact that so many public offices in America, from police chief, to prosecutor, to judges and state governors, are held on the basis of the popular vote (Haines 1996, pp. 4–5). Whereas in Britain it has been possible for members of Parliament to vote on the death penalty as a matter of "individual conscience" without fear of losing their seats because of their opinion on this issue, this has apparently not been perceived to be the case in the United States, especially in recent years. Indeed, one of the leading members of the anti–capital punishment movement, Hugo Bedau, has stated, "It is now widely assumed that no political candidate in the United States can hope to run for president, governor, or other high elective office if he or she can successfully be targeted as 'soft on crime'; the candidate's position on the death penalty has become the litmus test" (Bedau 1996, p. 50). But there is another side to this coin. Pierce and Radelet (1991) suggest that, far from simply being driven by public opinion, many politicians in the United

States have supported the death penalty and manipulated the evidence purely for their own political gain (see also Death Penalty Information Center 1996). Popular democracy may well have a stronger influence in America, but it is worth noting that the movement to the right in British politics in the 1980s did not produce a Parliamentary majority for capital punishment, even though Prime Minister Thatcher was in favor of it and there has been a sharp rise in violent crime accompanied by more repressive penal measures (Hood 1996, pp. 15–16).

The prime strategy against the death penalty in the United States was forged by civil rights lawyers in the 1960s and appeared, at first, to have been a resounding success. When, in 1972, the Supreme Court in *Furman v. Georgia* declared the capital punishment statutes of all the states to be unconstitutional, many believed that the backlog of cases would be so immense, and the period since the last execution so long, that in practice no state would start the process up again. Of course, they were proven wrong. The main reason, as is well known, is that only two members of the seven-man *Furman* Court ruled that capital punishment was unconstitutional per se: in other words, that it was cruel and unusual punishment however it might be administered (Haines 1996, pp. 14–16). The Court in *Gregg* and other cases in 1976 argued that the fact that democratically elected state legislatures had passed new capital statutes was proof that capital punishment was not out of step with "evolving standards of decency," or, to put it in another language, capital punishment did not violate contemporary notions of human rights. This seems to imply that human rights are defined by majority legislative opinion rather than by some external criteria: a notion that would be foreign to the conception of human rights under European Community law.

Public opinion has been frequently cited as a major factor in the decision whether to abolish, retain, or reinstate the death penalty. But public opinion has been shown to be a very slippery concept as far as the death penalty is concerned. As all other research on attitudes shows, there is a large gap between the sort of "off the top of the head opinion," which is tapped by opinion polls conducted on the telephone or in the street, and the complex weighing up of considerations of the kind that juries have to undertake. Even though polls may give the impression that a large majority of persons support capital punishment under aggravated circumstances of the kind found in the statutes of most American states, the behavior of prosecutors and jurors suggests that only in the most egregious cases is there some degree of consensus about who should be sentenced to death. Nevertheless, it cannot be denied that public opinion has shifted back toward greater support for the death penalty. Whereas in 1953 six out of ten citizens supported its use, by 1965 only four out of ten did so. But, by 1991, seven out of ten were again in favor (Maguire, Pastore, and Flanagan 1993, Table 2.54).

Yet in other Western democracies—Britain, France, and Canada, for instance—the death penalty has been abolished despite continuing strong support for it. This is because these countries' democratic traditions emphasize the importance of elected representatives exercising their own judgment on issues relating to law and human rights rather than allowing popular sentiment to be the determining factor in penal policy. By contrast, in several states of the United States, the question has been decided by popular vote. For example, the electorate of Oregon abolished the death penalty in 1964 but voted to reinstate it in 1978 and (after that law had been found unconstitutional) again in 1984. Similarly, California reinstated capital punishment after a plebiscite (Bedau 1987, pp. 153–63).

Yet public opinion in the United States is not intractable on the subject of capital punishment. It will vary according to the conditions under which the death penalty is applied and the confidence in available alternatives. Thus, there is evidence to suggest that the public does not favor capital punishment when its use is regarded as cruel. For example, a national opinion poll in the wake of the decision in *Penry v. Lynaugh*, 492 U.S. 302 (1989), showed that 71 percent of those responding believed that the Supreme Court had been wrong in upholding the death sentence of mentally retarded persons (Marshall 1991, p. 324). It has also been shown that when respondents are presented with an alternative to the death penalty (admittedly a severe one), their support for capital punishment declines. A series of studies in the United States, begun by William Bowers, have asked members of the public whether they would support the death penalty if the alternative were life imprisonment without possibility of parole and with restitution to the victim. These surveys have shown, over seven states, that no more than 43 percent, and often no more than a quarter, of respondents would favor the death penalty if this alternative were available (Bowers 1993; Death Penalty Information Center 1993). It has also been shown that when supporters of the death penalty were provided with information about the lack of proof of its deterrent effect, a relatively small but still significant proportion said that they would change their opinion. Gallup Poll data in the United States suggest that if supporters were convinced that abolition of the death penalty would not increase the homicide rate, the proportion in favor would drop from 70 to 55 percent (Zeisel and Gallup 1989; Ellsworth and Gross 1994). In other words, public opinion is influenced by utilitarian considerations and is not a mere expression of retributive sentiment.

Looking at the subject from an international perspective, one sees no clear connection between support for the death penalty and the incidence of homicide. The percentage of the public in favor of capital punishment is much higher in the United Kingdom and Japan, which have comparatively low homicide rates, than in the Scandinavian countries and the Netherlands, where the homicide rate is much higher. And among countries with relatively low homicide rates, some are abolitionist, like Spain, Austria, and the United Kingdom, while others retain the death penalty, such as Japan and the People's Republic of China.

Why has America remained so unimpressed by the human rights arguments that have led so many other countries, including South Africa and several former communist states of Eastern Europe, to abolish capital punishment? It has been suggested that this difference probably reflects the fact that in recent years executions have been a matter entirely affecting state, not federal, government (Hoffmann 1996), where there is likely to be much lower interest in international conventions. Indeed, a mission to the United States by the International Commission of Jurists in 1996 was dismayed to find "a general lack of awareness amongst state officials, and even amongst judges, lawyers, and teachers, of the obligations under the international instruments that the country has ratified." Even so, it has to be recognized that the U.S. federal government has supported a "hands-off" policy through its defensive response to the attempts to get international agreement on abolition through the Second Optional Protocol to the ICCPR.

It is true that the Supreme Court has remained deeply divided on the legitimacy of capital punishment, and has by only a narrow majority of five to four rejected systemic challenges to the constitutionality of death penalty statutes (White 1994, pp. 11–14).[24] But the issues raised have related to the administration of the death penalty rather than the fundamental question of whether it is constitutional per se. The issue in *McKleskey v. Kemp*, for example, was about whether the death penalty was being applied in a systematically discriminatory manner. The Court held that it was not, but the legislative remedy proposed was not to abolish capital punishment but to introduce into Congress the Racial Justice Bill, which would—had it been passed—have allowed courts "to consider evidence showing a consistent pattern of racially discriminatory death sentences in the sentencing jurisdiction, taking into account the nature of the cases being compared, the prior records of the offenders, and other statutorily appropriate non-racial characteristics." The appellant would have had to show statistically that the disparity was significant and that his particular case fitted the pattern of racially discriminatory sentencing, and the prosecution would have been given the opportunity to rebut the evidence and the inferences drawn from it (Tabak 1990–1991). This would have been a tough test for defendants to respond to. Nevertheless, the threat it was believed to pose to the operation of the death penalty was such that this title was thrown out of the 1994 Violent Crime Control Act as it passed through the Senate. It remains debatable whether any legislative formula or judicial practice can be devised that can satisfactorily eliminate the objectionable features of discrimination or other forms of arbitrariness from the enforcement of capital punishment without undermining the whole institution of the death penalty (Baldus, Woodworth, and Pulaski 1994; Berk, Boger, and Weiss 1993; Paternoster 1993).

In the view of some commentators, these legalistic attempts to abolish the death penalty not only failed but also have reinforced capital punishment by forcing the states to redefine capital murder more narrowly, so that, in theory at least, it is enforced only in relation to the most shocking cases of murders for whom there is little public sympathy. Bedau's view is that

> each of these reforms tended to entrench yet deeper what remained of the death penalty. The result is that tearing out the root has become more and more difficult, not least because abolition efforts in a given jurisdiction often have had little or no effect on a neighboring jurisdiction. . . . As the century comes to a close the prospects for complete abolition are not encouraging; the death penalty has become part of partisan political campaigning in a manner impossible to have predicted a generation ago. (1996, p. 62)

Indeed it has been suggested that, by concentrating on the litigation strategy, the death penalty in the United States was largely ignored at the level of public policy (Rutherford 1996, p. 269). That may be true, but throughout Europe and in other parts of the world where the death penalty has been abolished, the political initiative has largely derived its force from the belief that capital punishment is indeed a barbaric penalty out of step with contemporary values of humanity. Thus, the changes brought about through decisions of constitutional courts or embodied in the constitutions of emerging free nations, as in Hungary, South Africa, and the Czech and Slovak Republics, have all been possible because of support from the government and its legal officers. In other words, the political argument cannot succeed without a conception that the death penalty is, in principle and in practice, an unacceptable infringement on human rights.

In the United States, capital punishment remains as a painful penal symbol: rarely enforced, applied in an unacceptably arbitrary way, often in flagrant violation of international standards for the protection of prisoners, and for no gain in the diminution of murder. Only when politicians in state and federal government reject populism as a basis for deciding this issue and accept that there is a moral objection to capital punishment will America join those nations that have declared the death penalty incompatible with a political culture that values human rights.

Notes

1. Such views were held, for example, by John Stuart Mill; see Radzinowicz and Hood (1986, pp. 685–86) and, for the pros and cons of the debate, van den Haag and Conrad (1989).

2. Most utilitarians would not, of course, hold such a view. Bentham, for example, held that if a lesser punishment can be as effective as capital punishment in restraining people from murder, then any punishment beyond what is effective would be unjustifiable cruelty. A similar view was expressed by Justice White when giving the Supreme Court's judgment in *Coker v. Georgia*, 433 U.S. 587 (1977), that if capital punishment is not a deterrent it is "nothing more than the purposeless and needless imposition of pain and suffering" (97 S. Ct. 2861 [1977] at 2866).

3. These were Colorado, Kansas, Minnesota, Washington State, Oregon,

North Dakota, South Dakota, Tennessee, Arizona, and Missouri. Only Minnesota and North Dakota remain abolitionist.

4. Namely, the attempted assassination of the president, and for large-scale drug offenses "as part of a continuing criminal enterprise." However, there have been no executions under federal law since 1965.

5. Article 2, like the Sixth Protocol to the ECHR, allows a reservation to be made "which provides for the application of the death penalty in time of war pursuant to a conviction for a most serious crime of a military nature committed during wartime." The reservation can be made only at the time of ratification or accession.

6. The other countries that voted against adoption of the Second Optional Protocol were Afghanistan, Bahrain, Bangladesh, Cameroon, China, Djibouti, Egypt, Indonesia, Iran, Iraq, Jordan, Kuwait, Maldives, Morocco, Nigeria, Oman, Pakistan, Qatar, Saudi Arabia, Sierra Leone, Somalia, Syrian Arab Republic, Tanzania, and Yemen. Malaysia and Sudan later advised the secretariat that they had also intended to vote against. See Schabas (1993a, p. 170).

7. California (3), Illinois (7), Pennsylvania (2). Ohio is the only "bellwether state" not to have resumed executions (Zimring and Hawkins 1986, pp. 130, 143, 128, 135).

8. See Hood (1996), Appendix 3, for a full list of these safeguards.

9. See Hood (1996, pp. 94–95) for a discussion of and references to the large literature on the problems of predicting future violent behavior.

10. The states are Arkansas, Colorado, Indiana, Georgia, Maryland, Kansas, Kentucky, New Mexico, Tennessee, and Washington.

11. Forty-two (12.5 percent) of those executed between January 1, 1973, and July 31, 1996, had given up their appeals.

12. *Pulley v. Harris,* 465 U.S. 37 (1984), held that there was no constitutional requirement for the appeal court to compare the sentence of death with sentences imposed in similar cases: it was an additional safeguard but not a critical one.

13. Three states have retained hanging, and two execute by firing squad. In several states the defendant has a choice, usually between lethal injection and the former method, depending on the date of their conviction.

14. Federal, Federal Military, Colorado, Connecticut, Delaware, Montana, Nebraska, New Jersey, New Mexico, South Dakota, Utah, Washington. Other states with relatively low death row populations were Idaho (19), Maryland (17), and Oregon (22).

15. California (444); Texas (394); Florida (351); Pennsylvania (200); Illinois (164); North Carolina (154); Ohio (150); Alabama (144); Oklahoma (119); Georgia (108); Texas (102). Missouri was next with 92.

16. However, the ruling of the Canadian Supreme Court in relation to the extradition of *Kindler* to Pennsylvania, *Kindler v. Canada* (*Ministry of Justice*), Criminal Reports 8 C.R. (4th) 1–67 (1991), shows that there is still no international consensus on this issue.

17. *Profitt v. Florida,* 428 U.S. 242 (1976), and *Jurek v. Texas,* 428 U.S. 262 (1976).

18. The responsibility for imposing a death sentence lies in some states with the judge, in some with the jury, and in some the judge can override the decision of the jury if he considers it to have been too lenient or too severe.

19. For example, the Court held in *Lockett v. Ohio* (1978) that all mitigat-

ing factors should be considered and weighed in the balance, even if they are not among those specifically listed in the statute. In *Zant v. Stephens* (1983), the Court held that all aggravating circumstances could be considered regardless of whether they related to the aggravating circumstance which had brought the defendant within the scope of the death penalty provisions of the statute. The statutory aggravating factor merely acted to narrow the class of persons eligible for the death sentence, and that once such narrowing had taken place, all factors of aggravation and mitigation should be considered. See Wallace and Sorensen 1994, p. 284 n. 13.

20. In *Blystone v. Pennsylvania,* 494 U.S. 299 (1990), the U.S. Supreme Court ruled that this did not violate the ruling against a mandatory death penalty so long as the jury were allowed to review all the mitigating factors.

21. Similarly, Justice Harlan in the case of *McGautha v. California,* 402 U.S. 183 (1971), declared: "To identify before the fact those characteristics of criminal homicides and their perpetrators which call for the death penalty, and to express these characteristics in language which can be fairly understood and applied by the sentencing authority appear to be tasks which are at present beyond human ability" (p. 204).

22. Baldus et al. (1989, p. 154, Table 32). See also Gross and Mauro (1989, pp. 74–75).

23. For example, since the abolition of the death penalty in England and Wales in 1965, it has been easier to convict persons charged with homicide of murder rather than the lesser offense of manslaughter: the proportion convicted of murder among all those convicted of a homicide has increased from 28 to 41 percent.

24. *McCleskey v. Kemp,* 481 U.S. 279 (1987), and *Blystone v. Pennsylvania,* 494 U.S. 299 (1990).

References

Acker, J. A., and E. R. Walsh. 1989. "Challenging the Death Penalty Under State Constitutions." *Vanderbilt Law Review* 42:1299–363.

Acker, J. R., and C. S. Lanier. 1994a. "In Fairness and Mercy: Statutory Mitigating Factors in Capital Punishment Law." *Criminal Law Bulletin* 30:299–345.

———. 1994b. "Parsing This Lexicon of Death: Aggravating Factors in Capital Sentencing Statutes." *Criminal Law Bulletin* 30:107–52.

———. 1995. "Matters of Life and Death: The Sentencing Provisions of the Capital Punishment Statutes." *Criminal Law Bulletin* 31:19–60.

American College of Physicians, Human Rights Watch, the National Council toAbolish the Death Penalty, and Physicians for Human Rights. 1994. *Breach of Trust: Physician Participation in Executions in the United States.* Philadelphia: American College of Physicians.

American Medical Association. 1993. "Council on Ethical and Judicial Affairs. American Medical Association: Physician Participation in Capital Punishment." *Journal of the American Medical Association* 270: 365–68.

Amnesty International. 1995. *Juveniles and the Death Penalty: Executions Worldwide Since 1985.* London: Amnesty International Publications.

———. 1997. *United States of America: Death Penalty Developments in 1996.* London: Amnesty International Publications.

Bailey, W. C., and R. D. Peterson. 1989. "Murder and Capital Punishment: A Monthly Time-Series Analysis of Execution Publicity." *American Sociological Review* 54:722–43.

Baldus, D. C., G. Woodworth, and C. A. Pulaski Jr. 1986. "Arbitariness and Discrimination in the Administration of the Death Penalty: A Challenge to State Supreme Courts." *Stetson Law Review* 15:133–261.

———. 1989. *Equal Justice and the Death Penalty: A Legal and Empirical Analysis.* Boston: Northeastern University Press.

———. 1994. "Reflections on the 'Inevitability' of Racial Discrimination in Capital Sentencing and the 'Impossibility' of Its Prevention, Detection and Correction." *Washington and Lee Law Review* 51:359–419.

Barnett, A. 1985. "Some Distribution Patterns for the Georgia Death Sentence." *University of California, Davis, Law Review* 18:1327–63.

Beccaria, Cesare. [1764] 1963. *On Crimes and Punishments.* Englewood Cliffs, N.J.: Prentice-Hall.

Bedau, H. A. 1987. *Death Is Different.* Boston: Northeastern University Press.

———. 1991. "The Decline of Executive Clemency in Capital Cases." *New York University Review of Law and Social Change* 18:255–72.

———. 1996. "The United States." In *Capital Punishment: Global Issues,* edited by P. Hodgkinson and A. Rutherford. Winchester, England: Waterside Press.

Bedau H. A., and M. L. Radelet. 1988. "The Myth of Infallibility: A Reply to Markham and Cassell." *Stanford Law Review* 41:161–70.

Berk, R. A., J. Boger, and R. Weiss. 1993. "Research on the Death Penalty: Chance and the Death Penalty." *Law and Society Review* 27:89–110, 125–27.

Bienen, L. B., N. A. Weiner, P. D. Allison, and D. L. Mills. 1990. "The Reimposition of Capital Punishment in New Jersey: Felony Murder Cases." *Albany Law Review* 54:709–817.

Bienen, L. B., N. A. Weiner, D. W. Denno, P. A. Allison, and D. L. Mills. 1988. "The Reimposition of Capital Punishment in New Jersey: The Role of Prosecutorial Discretion." *Rutgers Law Review* 41:27–372.

Bowers, W. J. 1983. "The Pervasiveness of Arbitrariness and Discrimination under Post-*Furman* Capital Statutes." *Journal of Criminal Law and Criminology* 74:1067–100.

———. 1984. *Legal Homicide: Death as Punishment in America, 1864–1982.* Boston: Northeastern University Press.

———. 1988. "The Effect of Executions is Brutalization, not Deterrence." In *Challenging Capital Punishment,* edited by K. C. Haas and J. A. Inciardi. Newbury Park, Calif.: Sage.

———. 1993. "Capital Punishment and Contemporary Values: People's Misgivings and the Court's Misperceptions." *Law and Society Review* 27:157–75.

———, ed. 1997. *The Death Penalty in America: Current Controversies.* New York: Oxford University Press.

Bowers, W. J., and G. L. Pierce. 1975. "The Illusion of Deterrence in Isaac Ehrlich's Research on Capital Punishment." *Yale Law Journal* 85:187–208.

Brennan, Justice William A., Jr. 1994. "Neither Victims nor Executioners." *Notre Dame Journal of Law, Ethics and Public Policy: Symposium on Capital Punishment* 8:1–9.

Bright, Stephen B. 1994. "Counsel for the Poor: The Death Sentence Not for the Worst Crime, But the Worst Lawyer." *Yale Law Journal* 103:1835–83.

Dando, Shigemitsu. 1996. "Towards the Abolition of the Death Penalty." *Indiana Law Journal* 72:6–19.

Death Penalty Information Center. 1993. *Sentencing for Life: Americans Embrace Alternatives to the Death Penalty.* Washington, D.C.: Death Penalty Information Center.

———. 1994. *The Future of the Death Penalty in the US: A Texas-Sized Crisis.* Washington, D.C.: Death Penalty Information Center.

———. 1996. *Killing for Votes: Politicizing the Death Penalty Process.* Washington, D.C.: Death Penalty Information Center.

Denno, Deborah W. 1994a. "Is Electrocution an Unconstitutional Method of Execution? The Engineering of Death over a Century." *William and Mary Law Review* 35:551–692.

———. 1994b. "Testing *Penry* and Its Progeny." *American Journal of Criminal Law* 22:1–75.

Dix, George E. 1979. "Appellate Review of the Decision to Impose Death." *Georgetown Law Journal* 68:97–161.

Ehrlich, Isaac. 1975. "The Deterrent Effect of Capital Punishment: A Question of Life and Death." *American Economic Review* 65:397–417.

———. 1977. "Capital Punishment and Deterrence: Some Further Thoughts and Additional Evidence." *Journal of Political Economy* 85:74–88.

Ellsworth, P. C., and S. R. Gross. 1994. "Hardening of the Attitudes: American's Views on the Death Penalty." *Journal of Social Issues* 50:19–25.

Forst, B. E. 1977. "The Deterrent Effect of Capital Punishment: Cross-Sectional Analysis of the 1960s." *Minnesota Law Review* 61:743–67.

Fox, J. A., and M. L. Radelet. 1989. "Persistent Flaws in Econometric Studies of the Deterrent Effect of the Death Penalty." *Loyola of Los Angeles Law Review* 23:29–44.

Gillers, S. 1985. "The Quality of Mercy: Constitutional Accuracy at the Selection Stage of Capital Sentencing." *University of California, Davis, Law Review* 18:1037–111.

Greenberg, J. 1982. "Capital Punishment as a System." *Yale Law Journal* 91:908–36.

Gross, S. R. 1985. "Race and Death: The Judicial Evaluation of Evidence of Discrimination in Capital Sentencing." *University of California, Davis, Law Review* 18:1275–325.

Gross S. R., and R. Mauro. 1984. "Patterns of Death: An Analysis of Racial Disparities in Capital Sentencing and Homicide Victimization." *Stanford Law Review* 37:27–153.

———. 1989. *Death and Discrimination: Racial Disparities in Capital Sentencing.* Boston: Northeastern University Press.

Haines, Herbert H. 1996. *Against Capital Punishment: The Anti–Death Penalty Movement in America 1972–1994.* New York: Oxford University Press.

Harding, Roberta M. 1994. "'Endgame': Competency and the Execution of Condemned Inmates." *St. Louis University Public Law Review* 14:105–52.

———. 1996. "The Gallows and the Gurney: Analyzing the (Un)Constitutionality of the Methods of Execution." *Boston University Public Interest Law Journal* 6:153–78.

Hodgkinson, Peter, H. A. Bedau, M. L. Radelet, G. Dummall, and K. Massey. 1996. *Capital Punishment in the United States of America: A Review of the Issues.* London: Parliamentary Human Rights Group.

Hoffmann, J. L. 1996. "Justice Dando and the 'Conservative' Argument for Abolition." *Indiana Law Review* 72:21–24.

Hood, Roger. 1996. *The Death Penalty: A World-Wide Perspective.* 2nd ed. Oxford: Clarendon Press.

———. 1997. "The Death Penalty: The USA in World Perspective." *Florida State University Journal of Transnational Law and Policy* 6:517–41.

International Commission of Jurists. 1996. *Administration of the Death Penalty in the United States.* Geneva: International Commission of Jurists.

Johnson, Robert, and John L. Carroll. 1985. "Litigating Death Row Conditions: The Case for Reform." In *Prisoners and the Law*, edited by Ira P. Robbins. New York: Clark Boardman.

Kaplan, J. 1984. "Administering Capital Punishment." *University of Florida Law Review* 36:177–92.

Klein, L. R., B. Forst, and V. Filatov. 1978. "The Deterrent Effect of Capital Punishment: An Assessment of the Evidence." In *Deterrence and Incapacitation*, edited by A. Blumstein, J. Cohen and D. Nagin. Washington, D.C.: National Academy Press.

Layson, S. A. 1985. "Homicides and Deterrence: A Re-Examination of the United States Time Series Evidence." *Southern Economic Journal* 52:68–88.

———. 1986. "United States Time-Series Homicide Regressions with Adaptive Expectations." *Bulletin of the New York Academy of Medicine* 62:589–600.

Ledewitz, Bruce. 1991. "Sources of Injustice in Death Penalty Practice: The Pennsylvania Experience." *Dickinson Law Review* 95:651–90.

Lempert, R. 1983. "The Effect of Executions on Homicides: A New Look in an Old Light." *Crime and Delinquency* 29:88–115.

Liebman, James S. 1990–1991. "More Than 'Slightly Retro': The Rehnquist Court's Rout of Habeas Corpus Jurisdiction in *Teague v. Lane.*" *New York University Review of Law and Social Change* 18:537–635.

Maguire, Kathleen, and Ann L. Pastore, eds. 1996. *Sourcebook of Criminal Justice Statistics, 1995.* Washington, D.C.: U.S. Department of Justice, Bureau of Justice Statistics.

Maguire, Kathleen, Ann L. Pastore, and Timothy J. Flanagan, eds. 1993. *Sourcebook of Criminal Justice Statistics, 1992.* Washington, D.C.: U.S. Department of Justice, Bureau of Justice Statistics.

Markman, S. J., and P. G. Cassell. 1988. "Protecting the Innocent: A Response to the Bedau-Radelet Study." *Stanford Law Review* 41:121–60.

Marshall, T. R. 1991. "Public Opinion and the Rehnquist Court." *Judicature* 74:322–29.

Meltsner, Michael. 1973. *Cruel and Unusual: The Supreme Court and Capital Punishment.* New York: Random House.

Miller, Kent S., and Michael L. Radelet. 1993. *Executing the Mentally Ill: The Criminal Justice System and the Case of Alvin Ford.* London: Sage.

Murphy, E. L. 1984. "Application of the Death Penalty in Cook County." *Illinois Bar Journal* 73:90–95.

Nakell, Barry, and Kenneth A. Hardy. 1987. *The Arbitrariness of the Death Penalty.* Philadelphia: Temple University Press.

Nathanson, S. 1985. "Does It Matter If the Death Penalty Is Arbitrarily Administered?" *Philosophy and Public Affairs* 14:149–64.

National Coalition to Abolish the Death Penalty. 1994. *1994 Survey of State Legislation.* Washington, D.C.: National Coalition to Abolish the Death Penalty.

Paternoster, R. 1984. "Prosecutorial Discretion in Requesting the Death Penalty: A Case of Victim-Based Racial Discrimination." *Law and Society Review* 18:737–78.

———. 1993. "Assessing Capriciousness in Capital Cases." *Law and Society Review* 27:111–23.

Pierce, G. L., and M. L. Radelet. 1990–1991. "The Role and Consequences of the Death Penalty in American Politics." *New York University Review of Law and Social Change* 18:711–28.

Prejean, Helen. 1993. *Dead Man Walking: An Eyewitness Account of the Death Penalty in the United States.* New York: Random House.

Radelet, Michael L. 1981. "Racial Characteristics and the Imposition of the Death Penalty." *American Sociological Review* 46:918–27.

———. 1996. "Physician Participation." In *Capital Punishment: Global Issues and Prospects,* edited by P. Hodgkinson and A. Rutherford. Winchester, England: Waterside Press.

Radelet, Michael L., H. A. Bedau, and C. Putnam. 1992. *In Spite of Innocence: Erroneous Convictions in Capital Cases.* Boston: Northeastern University Press.

Radelet, M., and M. Vandiver. 1986. "Race and Capital Punishment: An Overview of the Issue." *Crime and Social Justice* 25:94–113.

Radelet, Michael L., and Barbara A. Zsembik. 1993. "Executive Clemency in Post-*Furman* Capital Cases." *University of Richmond Law Review* 27:289–314.

Radzinowicz, Leon, and Roger Hood. 1986. *A History of English Criminal Law, Volume 5: The Emergence of Penal Policy.* London: Stevens.

Robinson D. A., and O. H. Stephens. 1992. "Patterns of Mitigating Factors in Juvenile Death Penalty Cases." *Criminal Law Bulletin* 28:246–75.

Rutherford, Andrew. 1996. "Abolition: A Tale of Two Struggles." In *Capital Punishment: Global Issues and Prospects,* edited by P. Hodgkinson and A. Rutherford. Winchester, England: Waterside Press.

Schabas, W. A. 1993a. *The Abolition of the Death Penalty in International Law.* Cambridge: Grotius Publications.

———. 1993b. "Note on *Kindler v. Canada* (*Minister of Justice*)." *American Journal of International Law* 87:128–33.

———. 1994a. "Execution Delayed, Execution Denied." *Criminal Law Forum* 5:180–93.

————. 1994b. "International Norms on Execution of the Insane and Mentally Retarded." *Criminal Law Forum* 4:95–117.

————. 1994c. "Soering's Legacy: The Human Rights Committee and the Judicial Committee of the Privy Council Take a Walk Down Death Row." *International and Comparative Law Quarterly* 43:913–23.

————. 1995. "Invalid Reservations to the International Covenant of Civil and Political Rights: Is the United States Still a Party?" *Brooklyn Journal of International Law* 21:277–325.

————. 1996. *The Death Penalty as Cruel Treatment and Torture: Capital Punishment Challenged in the World's Courts.* Boston: Northeastern University Press.

Sellin, T., ed. 1959. *The Death Penalty.* Philadelphia: American Law Institute.

————. 1977. Contribution to *The Death Penalty: Retribution or Deterrence?* UNAFEI Resource Material Series no. 13. New York: United Nations.

Stein, G. M. 1985. "Distinguishing Among Murders When Assessing the Proportionality of the Death Sentence." *Columbia Law Review* 85:1786–807.

Streib, Victor. 1995. *The Juvenile Death Penalty Today: Present Death Row Inmates Under Juvenile Death Sentences and Death Sentences and Executions for Juvenile Crimes, January 1, 1973 to September 15, 1994.* Cleveland, Ohio: Cleveland State University.

Tabak, R. J. 1990–1991. "Is Racism Irrelevant? Or Should the Fairness in Death Sentencing Act Be Enacted to Substantially Diminish Racial Discrimination in Capital Sentencing?" *New York University Review of Law and Social Change* 18:777–806.

United Kingdom. 1953. *Report of the Royal Commission on Capital Punishment 1949–1953.* London: HMSO.

United Nations. 1962. *Capital Punishment.* Report by Marc Ancel. New York: United Nations.

————. 1967. *Capital Punishment: Developments 1961 to 1965.* Report by Norval Morris. New York: United Nations.

U.S. General Accounting Office. 1990. *Death Penalty Sentencing: Research Indicates Pattern of Racial Disparities.* Washington, D.C.: U.S. Government Printing Office.

U.S. Senate, Committee on the Judiciary. 1993. *Innocence and the Death Penalty: Assessing the Danger of Mistaken Executions.* Report of the Subcommittee on Civil and Constitutional Rights. 103rd Cong., 1st sess. Washington, D.C.: U.S. Government Printing Office.

van den Haag, Ernest, and John Conrad. 1989. *The Death Penalty: A Debate.* New York: Plenum Press.

van Duizend, Richard. 1984. "Comparative Proportionality Review in Death Sentence Cases." *State Court Journal* 8:9–13, 21–23.

Wallace, D. W., and J. R. Sorensen. 1994. "Missouri Proportionality Review: An Assessment of a State Supreme Court's Procedures in Capital Cases." *Notre Dame Journal of Law, Ethics, and Public Policy* 8:281–315.

Weisberg, Robert. 1984. "Deregulating Death." In *1983 Supreme Court Review,* edited by P. B. Kurland, G. Cooper, and D. J. Hutchinson. Chicago: University of Chicago Press.

White, Welsch S. 1994. *The Death Penalty in the Nineties: An Examination of the Modern System of Capital Punishment.* Ann Arbor: University of Michigan Press.

Zeisel, Hans. 1981 "Race Bias in the Administration of the Death Penalty: The Florida Experience." *Harvard Law Review* 95:456–68.

Zeisel, H., and A. M. Gallup. 1989. "Death Penalty Sentiment in the United States." *Journal of Quantitative Criminology* 5:285–96.

Zimring, F. L. 1990–1991. "Ambivalence in State Capital Punishment Policy." *New York University Review of Law and Social Change* 18:729–42.

Zimring, F. L., and G. Hawkins. 1986. *Capital Punishment and the American Agenda.* Cambridge: Cambridge University Press.

Index